Business Law 60

Drake University

Richard A Mann | Barry S. Roberts

CENGAGE
Learning·

Australia • Brazil • Japan • Korea • Mexico • Singapore • Spain • United Kingdom • United States

Business Law 60: Drake University

Richard A Mann | Barry S. Roberts

Senior Project Development Manager:
Linda deStefano

Market Development Manager:
Heather Kramer

Senior Production/Manufacturing Manager:
Donna M. Brown

Production Editorial Manager:
Kim Fry

Sr. Rights Acquisition Account Manager:
Todd Osborne

Business Law and the Regulation of Business,
Eleventh Edition
Richard A. Mann | Barry S. Roberts
© 2014 and 2011 Cengage Learning. All rights reserved.

For product information and technology assistance, contact us at
Cengage Learning Customer & Sales Support, 1-800-354-9706

For permission to use material from this text or product,
submit all requests online at **cengage.com/permissions**
Further permissions questions can be emailed to
permissionrequest@cengage.com

This book contains select works from existing Cengage Learning resources and was produced by Cengage Learning Custom Solutions for collegiate use. As such, those adopting and/or contributing to this work are responsible for editorial content accuracy, continuity and completeness.

Compilation © 2013 Cengage Learning

ISBN-13: 978-1-285-91829-7

ISBN-10: 1-285-91829-0

Cengage Learning
5191 Natorp Boulevard
Mason, Ohio 45040
USA
Cengage Learning is a leading provider of customized learning solutions with office locations around the globe, including Singapore, the United Kingdom, Australia, Mexico, Brazil, and Japan. Locate your local office at:
international.cengage.com/region.

Cengage Learning products are represented in Canada by Nelson Education, Ltd.
For your lifelong learning solutions, visit **www.cengage.com/custom.**
Visit our corporate website at **www.cengage.com.**

Printed in the United States of America

Brief Contents

Chapter 2   **Business Ethics**.. 15

Chapter 7   **Intentional Torts** 129

Chapter 8   **Negligence and Strict Liability** 150

Chapter 9   **Introduction to Contracts** 178

Chapter 10   **Mutual Assent**.. 194

Chapter 11   **Conduct Invalidating Assent**................................ 216

Chapter 12   **Consideration** 236

Chapter 13   **Illegal Bargains**.. 256

Chapter 14   **Contractual Capacity** 275

Chapter 15   **Contracts in Writing** 291

Chapter 16   **Third Parties to Contracts** 317

Chapter 17   **Performance, Breach, and Discharge** 336

Chapter 18   **Contract Remedies**..................................... 354

Chapter 19   **Introduction to Sales and Leases**.......................... 376

Chapter 20   **Performance** 397

Chapter 21   **Transfer of Title and Risk of Loss** 418

Chapter 22   **Product Liability: Warranties and Strict Liability** 435

Appendix B   **Uniform Commercial Code** B-1

Appendix F   **Dictionary of Legal Terms** F-1

Chapter 2

BUSINESS ETHICS

Our characters are the result of our conduct.

ARISTOTLE, IN NICOMACHEAN ETHICS (C. 335 BCE)

CHAPTER OUTCOMES

After reading and studying this chapter, you should be able to:

1. Describe the difference between law and ethics.

2. Compare the various ethical theories.

3. Describe cost-benefit analysis and explain when it should be used and when it should be avoided.

4. Explain Kohlberg's stages of moral development.

5. Explain the ethical responsibilities of business.

Business ethics is a subset of ethics: no special set of ethical principles applies only to the world of business. Immoral acts are immoral, whether or not a businessperson has committed them. In the past few years, countless business wrongs, such as insider trading, fraudulent earnings statements and other accounting misconduct, price-fixing, concealment of dangerous defects in products, and bribery, have been reported almost daily. Companies such as Enron, World-Com, Adelphia, Parmalat, Arthur Anderson, and Global Crossing have all violated the law, and some of these firms no longer exist as a result of these ethical lapses. In 2004, Martha Stewart was convicted of obstructing justice and lying to investigators about a stock sale. More recently, Bernie Madoff perpetrated the largest Ponzi scheme in history with an estimated loss of $20 billion in principal and approximately $65 billion in paper losses. In May 2011, Galleon Group (a hedge fund) billionaire, Raj Rajaratnam, was found guilty of fourteen counts of conspiracy and securities fraud.

Ethics can be defined broadly as the study of what is right or good for human beings. It attempts to determine what people ought to do, or what goals they should pursue. **Business ethics**, as a branch of applied ethics, is the study and determination of what is right and good in business settings. Business ethics seeks to understand the moral issues that arise from business practices, institutions, and decision making, and their relationship to generalized human values. Unlike legal analyses, analyses of ethics have no central authority, such as courts or legislatures, upon which to rely; nor do they follow clear-cut universal standards. Nonetheless, despite these inherent limitations, it still may be possible to make meaningful ethical judgments. To improve ethical decision making, it is important to understand how others have approached the task.

Some examples of the many business ethics questions may clarify the definition of business ethics. In the employment relationship, countless ethical issues arise regarding the safety and compensation of workers, their civil rights (such as equal treatment, privacy, and freedom from sexual harassment), and the legitimacy of whistle-blowing. In the relationship between business and its customers, ethical issues permeate marketing techniques, product safety, and consumer protection. The relationship between business and its owners bristles with ethical questions involving corporate governance, shareholder voting, and management's duties to the shareholders. The relationship among competing businesses involves numerous ethical matters, including fair competition and the effects of collusion. The interaction between business and society at large presents additional ethical dimensions: pollution of the physical environment, commitment to the community's economic and social infrastructure, and depletion of natural resources. Not only do all of these issues recur at the international level, but also additional ones present themselves, such as bribery of foreign officials, exploitation of developing countries, and conflicts among differing cultures and value systems.

In resolving the ethical issues raised by business conduct, it is helpful to use a seeing-knowing-doing model. First, the decision maker should *see* (identify) the ethical issues involved in the proposed conduct, including the ethical implications of the various available options. Second, the decision maker should *know* (resolve) what to do by choosing the best option. Finally, the decision maker should *do* (implement) the chosen option by developing and implementing strategies.

This chapter first surveys the most prominent ethical theories (the knowing part of the decision, on which the great majority of philosophers and ethicists have focused). The chapter then examines ethical standards in business and the ethical responsibilities of business. It concludes with five ethical business cases, which give the student the opportunity to apply the seeing-knowing-doing model. The student (1) identifies the ethical issues presented in these cases; (2) resolves these issues by using one of the ethical theories described in the chapter, some other ethical theory, or a combination of the theories; and (3) develops strategies for implementing the ethical resolution.

Law versus Ethics

As discussed in Chapter 1, moral concepts strongly affect the law, but law and morality are not the same. Although it is tempting to say that "if it's legal, it's moral," such a proposition is generally too simplistic. For example, it would seem gravely immoral to stand by silently while a blind man walks off a cliff if one could prevent the fall by shouting a warning, even though one would not be legally obligated to do so. Similarly, moral questions arise concerning "legal" business practices, such as failing to fulfill a promise that is not legally binding, exporting products banned in the United States to developing countries where they are not prohibited, or slaughtering baby seals for fur coats. The mere fact that these practices are legal does not prevent them from being challenged on moral grounds.

Just as it is possible for legal acts to be immoral, it is equally possible for illegal acts to seem morally preferable to following the law. For example, it is the moral conviction of the great majority of people that those who sheltered Jews in violation of Nazi edicts during World War II and those who committed acts of civil disobedience in the 1950s and 1960s to challenge segregation laws in the United States were acting properly and that the laws themselves were immoral.

Ethical Theories

Philosophers have sought for centuries to develop dependable and universal methods for making ethical judgments. In earlier times, some thinkers analogized the discovery of ethical principles with the derivation of mathematical proofs. They asserted that people could discover fundamental ethical rules by applying careful reasoning *a priori*. (*A priori* reasoning is based on theory rather than experimentation and deductively draws conclusions from cause to effect and from generalizations to particular instances.) In more recent times, many philosophers have concluded that although careful reasoning and deep thought assist substantially in moral reasoning, experience reveals that the complexities of the world defeat most attempts to fashion precise, *a priori* guidelines. Nevertheless, a review of the most significant ethical theories can aid the analysis of business ethics issues.

ETHICAL FUNDAMENTALISM

Under **ethical fundamentalism**, or absolutism, individuals look to a central authority or set of rules to guide them in ethical decision making. Some look to the Bible; others look to the Koran or to the writings of Karl Marx or to any number of living or deceased prophets. The essential characteristic of this approach is a reliance on a central repository of wisdom. In some cases, such reliance is total. In others, followers of a religion or a spiritual leader may believe that all members of the group are obligated to assess moral dilemmas independently, according to each person's understanding of the dictates of the fundamental principles.

ETHICAL RELATIVISM

Ethical relativism is a doctrine asserting that actions must be judged by what individuals feel is right or wrong for themselves. It holds that when any two individuals or cultures differ regarding the morality of a particular issue or action, they are both correct because morality is relative. However, although ethical relativism promotes open-mindedness and tolerance, it has limitations. If each person's actions are always correct for that person, then his behavior is, by definition, moral and therefore exempt from criticism. Once a person concludes that criticizing or punishing behavior in some cases is appropriate, he abandons ethical relativism and faces the task of developing a broader ethical methodology.

Although bearing a surface resemblance to ethical relativism, situational ethics actually differs substantially. **Situational ethics** holds that developing precise guidelines for effectively navigating ethical dilemmas is difficult because real-life decision making is so complex. To judge the morality of someone's behavior, the person judging must actually put herself in the other person's shoes to understand what motivated the other to choose a particular course of action. Situational ethics, however, does not cede the ultimate judgment of the propriety of an action to the actor; rather, it insists that, prior to evaluation, a person's decision or act be viewed from the actor's perspective.

UTILITARIANISM

Utilitarianism is a doctrine that assesses good and evil in terms of the consequences of actions. Those actions that produce the greatest net pleasure compared with net pain are better in a moral sense than those that produce less net pleasure. As Jeremy Bentham, one of the most influential proponents of utilitarianism, proclaimed, a good or moral act is one that results in "the greatest happiness for the greatest number."

The two major forms of utilitarianism are act utilitarianism and rule utilitarianism. **Act utilitarianism** assesses each separate act according to whether it maximizes pleasure over pain. For example, if telling a lie in a particular situation produces more overall pleasure than pain, then an act utilitarian would support lying as the moral thing to do. Rule utilitarians, disturbed by the unpredictability of act utilitarianism and its potential for abuse, follow a different approach. **Rule utilitarianism** holds that general rules must be established and followed even though, in some instances, following rules may produce less overall pleasure than not following them. It applies utilitarian principles in developing rules; thus, it supports rules that on balance produce the greatest satisfaction. Determining whether telling a lie in a given instance would produce greater pleasure than telling the truth is less important to the rule utilitarian than deciding whether a general practice of lying would maximize society's pleasure. If lying would not maximize pleasure generally, then one should follow a rule of not lying even though on occasion telling a lie would produce greater pleasure than would telling the truth.

Utilitarian notions underlie cost-benefit analysis, an analytical tool used by many business and government managers today. **Cost-benefit analysis** first quantifies in monetary terms and then compares the direct and indirect costs and benefits of program alternatives for meeting a specified objective. Cost-benefit analysis seeks the greatest economic efficiency according to the underlying notion that, given two potential acts, the act achieving the greatest output at the least cost promotes the greatest marginal happiness over the less-efficient act, other things being equal.

The chief criticism of utilitarianism is that in some important instances it ignores justice. A number of situations would maximize the pleasure of the majority at great social cost to a minority. Another major criticism of utilitarianism is that measuring pleasure and pain in the fashion its supporters advocate is extremely difficult, if not impossible.

DEONTOLOGY

Deontological theories (from the Greek word *deon*, meaning duty or obligation) address the practical problems of utilitarianism by holding that certain underlying principles are right or wrong regardless of any pleasure or pain calculations. Believing that actions cannot be measured simply by their results but must be judged by means and motives as well, deontologists judge the morality of acts not so much by their consequences but by the motives that lead to them. A person not only must achieve just results but also must employ the proper means.

The best-known deontological theory was proffered by the eighteenth-century philosopher Immanuel Kant. Under Kant's *categorical imperative*, for an action to be moral it (1) must potentially be a universal law that could be applied consistently and (2) must respect the autonomy and rationality of all human beings and not treat them as an expedient. That is, one should not do anything that he or she would not have everyone do in a similar situation. For example, you should not lie to colleagues unless you support the right of all colleagues to lie to one another. Similarly, you should not cheat others unless you advocate everyone's right to cheat. We apply Kantian reasoning when we challenge someone's behavior by asking: what if everybody acted that way?

Under Kant's approach, it would be improper to assert a principle to which one claimed personal exception, such as insisting that it was acceptable for you to cheat but not for anyone else to do so. This principle could not be universalized because everyone would then insist on similar rules from which only they were exempt.

Kant's philosophy also rejects notions of the end justifying the means. To Kant, every person is an end in himself or herself. Each person deserves respect simply because of his or her humanity. Thus, any sacrifice of a person for the greater good of society would be unacceptable to Kant.

In many respects, Kant's categorical imperative is a variation of the Golden Rule; and, like the Golden Rule, the categorical imperative appeals to the individual's self-centeredness.

As does every theory, Kantian ethics has its critics. Just as deontologists criticize utilitarians for excessive pragmatism and flexible moral guidelines, utilitarians and others criticize deontologists for rigidity and excessive formalism. For example, if one inflexibly adopts as a rule to tell the truth, one ignores situations in which lying might well be justified. A person hiding a terrified wife from her angry, abusive husband would seem to be acting morally by falsely denying that the wife is at the person's house. Yet a deontologist, feeling bound to tell the truth, might ignore the consequences of truthfulness, tell the husband where his wife is, and create the possibility of a terrible tragedy. Another criticism of deontological theories is that the proper course may be difficult to determine when values or assumptions conflict.

SOCIAL ETHICS THEORIES

Social ethics theories assert that special obligations arise from the social nature of human beings. Such theories focus not only on each person's obligations to other members of society but also on the individual's rights and obligations within the society. For example, **social egalitarians** believe that society should provide each person with equal amounts of goods and services regardless of the contribution each makes to increase society's wealth.

Two other ethics theories have received widespread attention in recent years. One is the theory of **distributive justice** proposed by Harvard philosopher John Rawls, which seeks to analyze the type of society that people in a "natural state" would establish if they could not determine in advance whether they would be talented, rich, healthy, or ambitious, relative to other members of society. According to distributive justice, the society contemplated through this "veil of ignorance" is the one that should be developed because it considers the needs and rights of all its members. Rawls did not argue that such a society would be strictly egalitarian and that it would unfairly penalize those who turned out to be the most talented and ambitious. Instead, Rawls suggested that such a society would stress equality of opportunity, not of results. On the other hand, Rawls stressed that society would pay heed to the least advantaged to ensure that they did not suffer unduly and that they enjoyed society's benefits. To Rawls, society must be premised on justice. Everyone is entitled to his or her fair share in society, a fairness all must work to guarantee.

In contrast to Rawls, another Harvard philosopher, Robert Nozick, stressed liberty, not justice, as the most important obligation that society owes its members. **Libertarians** stress market outcomes as the basis for distributing society's rewards. Only to the extent that one meets market demands does one deserve society's benefits. Libertarians oppose social interference in the lives of those who do not violate the rules of the marketplace; that is, in the lives of those who do not cheat others and who disclose honestly the nature of their transactions with others. The fact that some end up with fortunes while others accumulate little simply proves that some can play in the market effectively while others cannot. To libertarians, this is not unjust. What is unjust to them is any attempt by society to take wealth earned by citizens and distribute it to those who did not earn it.

These theories and others (e.g., Marxism) judge society in moral terms by its organization and by the way in which it distributes goods and services. They demonstrate the difficulty of ethical decision making in the context of a social organization: behavior that is consistently ethical from individual to individual may not necessarily produce a just society.

OTHER THEORIES

The preceding theories do not exhaust the possible approaches to evaluating ethical behavior; several other theories also deserve mention. **Intuitionism** holds that a rational person possesses inherent powers to assess the correctness of actions. Though an individual may refine and strengthen these powers, they are just as basic to humanity as our instincts for survival and self-defense. Just as some people are better artists or musicians, some people have more insight into ethical behavior than others. Consistent with intuitionism is the **good person philosophy**, which declares that if individuals wish to act morally, they should seek out and emulate those who always seem to know the right choice in any given situation and who always seem to do the right thing. One variation of these ethical approaches is the *Television Test,* which directs us to imagine that every ethical decision we make is being broadcast on nationwide television. An appropriate decision is one we would be comfortable broadcasting on national television for all to witness.

Ethical Standards in Business

In this section, we explore the application of the theories of ethical behavior to the world of business.

CHOOSING AN ETHICAL SYSTEM

In their efforts to resolve the moral dilemmas facing humankind, philosophers and other thinkers have struggled for years to refine the various systems previously discussed. All of the systems are limited, however, in terms of applicability and tend to produce unacceptable prescriptions for action in some circumstances. But to say that each system has limits is not to say it is useless. On the contrary, a number of these systems provide insight into ethical decision making and help us formulate issues and resolve moral dilemmas. Furthermore, concluding that moral standards are difficult to articulate and that moral boundaries are imprecise is not the same as concluding that moral standards are unnecessary or nonexistent.

Research by the noted psychologist Lawrence Kohlberg provides some insight into ethical decision making and lends credibility to the notion that moral growth, like physical growth, is part of the human condition. **Kohlberg** observed that people progress through sequential **stages of moral development** according to two major variables: age and reasoning. During the first level—the *preconventional level*—a child's conduct is a reaction to the fear of punishment and, later, to the pleasure of reward. Although people who operate at this level may behave in a moral manner, they do so without understanding why their behavior is moral. The rules are imposed upon them. During adolescence—Kohlberg's *conventional level*—people conform their behavior to meet the expectations of groups, such as family, peers, and eventually society. The motivation for conformity is loyalty, affection, and trust. Most adults operate at this level. According to Kohlberg, some reach the third level—the *postconventional level*—at which they accept

and conform to moral principles because they understand *why* the principles are right and binding. At this level, moral principles are voluntarily internalized, not externally imposed. Moreover, individuals at this stage develop their own universal ethical principles and may even question the laws and values that society and others have adopted (see Figure 2-1 for Kohlberg's stages of moral development).

Kohlberg believed that not all people reach the third, or even the second, stage. He therefore argued that essential to the study of ethics was the exploration of ways to help people achieve the advanced stage of post-conventional thought. Other psychologists assert that individuals do not pass sequentially from stage to stage but rather function in all three stages simultaneously.

Whatever the source of our ethical approach, we cannot avoid facing moral dilemmas that challenge us to recognize and do the right thing. Moreover, for those who plan business careers, such dilemmas necessarily will have implications for many others—employees, shareholders, suppliers, customers, and society at large.

CORPORATIONS AS MORAL AGENTS

Because corporations are not persons but rather artificial entities created by the state, whether they can or should be held morally accountable is difficult to determine. Though, clearly, individuals within corporations can be held morally responsible, the corporate entity presents unique problems.

Commentators are divided on the issue. Some insist that only people can engage in behavior that can be judged in moral terms. Opponents of this view concede that corporations are not persons in any literal sense but insist that the attributes of responsibility inherent in corporations are sufficient to justify judging corporate behavior from a moral perspective.

Ethical Responsibilities of Business

Many people assert that the only responsibility of business is to maximize profit and that this obligation overrides any ethical or social responsibility. Although our economic system of modified capitalism is based on the pursuit of self-interest, it also contains components to

Figure 2-1
Kohlberg's Stages of Moral Development

Levels	Perspective	Justification
Preconventional (Childhood)	Self	Punishment/Reward
Conventional (Adolescent)	Group	Group Norms
Postconventional (Adult)	Universal	Moral Principles

check this motivation of greed. Our system has always recognized the need for some form of regulation, whether it be by the "invisible hand" of competition, the self-regulation of business, or government regulation.

REGULATION OF BUSINESS

As explained and justified by Adam Smith in *The Wealth of Nations* (1776), the capitalistic system is composed of six "institutions": economic motivation, private productive property, free enterprise, free markets, competition, and limited government. As long as all these constituent institutions continue to exist and operate in balance, the factors of production—land, capital, and labor—combine to produce an efficient allocation of resources for individual consumers and for the economy as a whole. To achieve this outcome, however, Smith's model requires that a number of conditions be satisfied: "standardized products, numerous firms in markets, each firm with a small share and unable by its actions alone to exert significant influence over price, no barriers to entry, and output carried to the point where each seller's marginal cost equals the going market price." E. Singer, *Antitrust Economics and Legal Analysis*.

History has demonstrated that the actual operation of the economy has satisfied almost none of these assumptions. More specifically, the actual competitive process falls considerably short of the assumptions of the classic economic model of perfect competition:

> Competitive industries are never perfectly competitive in this sense. Many of the resources they employ cannot be shifted to other employments without substantial cost and delay. The allocation of those resources, as between industries or as to relative proportions within a single industry, is unlikely to have been made in a way that affords the best possible expenditure of economic effort. Information is incomplete, motivation confused, and decision therefore ill informed and often unwise. Variations in efficiency are not directly reflected in variations of profit. Success is derived in large part from competitive selling efforts, which in the aggregate may be wasteful, and from differentiation of products, which may be undertaken partly by methods designed to impair the opportunity of the buyer to compare quality and price.
>
> C. Edwards, *Maintaining Competition*

In addition to capitalism's failure to allocate resources efficiently, it cannot be relied on to achieve all of the social and public policy objectives a pluralistic democracy requires. For example, the free enterprise model simply does not address equitable distribution of wealth, national defense, conservation of natural resources, full employment, stability in economic cycles, protection against economic dislocations, health and safety, social

security, and other important social and economic goals. Increased **regulation of business** has occurred not only to preserve the competitive process in our economic system but also to achieve social goals extrinsic to the efficient allocation of resources, the "invisible hand" and self-regulation by business having failed to bring about these desired results. Such intervention attempts (1) to regulate both "legal" monopolies, such as those conferred by law through copyrights, patents, and trade symbols, and "natural" monopolies, such as utilities, transportation, and communications; (2) to preserve competition by correcting imperfections in the market system; (3) to protect specific groups, especially labor and agriculture, from marketplace failures; and (4) to promote other social goals. Successful government regulation involves a delicate balance between regulations that attempt to preserve competition and those that attempt to advance other social objectives. The latter should not undermine the basic competitive processes that provide an efficient allocation of economic resources.

CORPORATE GOVERNANCE

In addition to the broad demands of maintaining a competitive and fair marketplace, another factor demanding the ethical and social responsibility of business is the sheer size and power of individual corporations. The five thousand largest U.S. firms currently produce more than half of the nation's gross national product.

In a classic study published in 1932, Adolf Berle and Gardner Means concluded that great amounts of economic power had been concentrated in a relatively few large corporations, that the ownership of these corporations had become widely dispersed, and that the shareholders had become far removed from active participation in management. Since their original study, these trends have continued steadily. The five hundred to one thousand large publicly held corporations own the great bulk of the industrial wealth of the United States. Moreover, these corporations are controlled by a small group of corporate officers.

Historically, the boards of many publicly held corporations consisted mainly or entirely of inside directors (corporate officers who also serve on the board of directors). During the past two decades, however, as a result of regulations by the U.S. Securities and Exchange Commission and the stock exchanges, the number and influence of outside directors has increased substantially. Now the boards of the great majority of publicly held corporations consist primarily of outside directors, and these corporations have audit committees consisting entirely of outside directors. Nevertheless, a number of instances of corporate misconduct have been revealed in the first years of this century. In response to these business scandals—involving companies such as Enron, WorldCom, Global Crossing, Adelphia, and Arthur Andersen—in 2002 Congress passed the Sarbanes-Oxley Act. This legislation seeks to prevent these types of scandals by increasing corporate responsibility through the imposition of additional corporate governance requirements on publicly held corporations. (This statute is discussed further in Chapters 6, 35, 39, and 43.)

These developments raise a large number of social, policy, and ethical issues about the governance of large, publicly owned corporations. Many observers insist that companies playing such an important economic role should have a responsibility to undertake projects that benefit society in ways that go beyond mere financial efficiency in producing goods and services. In some instances, the idea of corporate obligations comes from industrialists themselves.

Arguments against Social Responsibility

A number of arguments oppose business involvement in socially responsible activities: profitability, unfairness, accountability, and expertise.

Profitability   As Milton Friedman and others have argued, businesses are artificial entities established to permit people to engage in profit-making, not social, activities. Without profits, they assert, there is little reason for a corporation to exist and no real way to measure the effectiveness of corporate activities. Businesses are not organized to engage in social activities; they are structured to produce goods and services for which they receive money. Their social obligation is to return as much of this money as possible to their direct stakeholders. In a free market with significant competition, the selfish pursuits of corporations will lead to maximizing output, minimizing costs, and establishing fair prices. All other concerns distract companies and interfere with achieving these goals.

Unfairness   Whenever companies stray from their designated role of profit-maker, they take unfair advantage of company employees and shareholders. For example, a company may support the arts or education or spend excess funds on health and safety; however, these funds rightfully belong to the shareholders or employees. The company's decision to disburse these funds to others who may well be less deserving than the shareholders and employees is unfair. Furthermore, consumers can express their desires through the marketplace, and shareholders and employees can decide privately whether they wish to make charitable contributions. In most cases, senior management consults the board of directors about supporting social concerns but does not seek the approval of the company's major stakeholders, thereby effectively disenfranchising these shareholders from actions that reduce their benefits from the corporation.

Accountability   Corporations, as previously noted, are private institutions that are subject to a lower standard of accountability than are public bodies. Accordingly, a company may decide to support a wide range of social causes and yet submit to little public scrutiny. But a substantial potential for abuse exists in such cases. For one thing, a company could provide funding for a variety of causes its employees or shareholders did not support. It also could provide money "with strings attached," thereby controlling the recipients' agendas for less than socially beneficial purposes. For example, a drug company that contributes to a consumer group might implicitly or explicitly condition its assistance on the group's agreement never to criticize the company or the drug industry.

This lack of accountability warrants particular concern because of the enormous power corporations wield in modern society. Many large companies, like Walmart, Toyota, or ExxonMobil, generate and spend more money in a year than all but a handful of the world's countries. If these companies suddenly began to vigorously pursue their own social agendas, their influence might well rival, and perhaps undermine, that of their national government. In a country like the United States, founded on the principles of limited government and the balance of powers, too much corporate involvement in social affairs might well present substantial problems. Without clear guidelines and accountability, companies pursuing their private visions of socially responsible behavior might well distort the entire process of governance.

There is a clear alternative to corporations engaging in socially responsible action. If society wishes to increase the resources devoted to needy causes, it has the power to do so. Let the corporations seek profits without the burden of a social agenda, let the consumers vote in the marketplace for the products and services they desire, and let the government tax a portion of corporate profits for socially beneficial causes.

Expertise   Even though a corporation has an expertise in producing and selling its product, it may not possess a talent for recognizing or managing socially useful activities. Corporations become successful in the market because they can identify and meet the needs of their customers. Nothing suggests that this talent spills over into nonbusiness arenas. In fact, critics of corporate participation in social activities worry that corporations will prove unable to distinguish the true needs of society from their own narrow self-interests.

ARGUMENTS IN FAVOR OF SOCIAL RESPONSIBILITY

First, it should be recognized that even the critics of business acknowledge that the prime responsibility of business is to make a reasonable return on its investment by producing a quality product at a reasonable price. They do not suggest that business entities be charitable institutions. They do assert, however, that business has certain obligations beyond making a profit or not harming society. Such critics contend that business must help to resolve societal problems, and they offer a number of arguments in support of their position.

THE SOCIAL CONTRACT

Society creates corporations and gives them a special social status, including the granting of limited liability, which insulates owners from liability for debts their organizations incur. Supporters of social roles for corporations assert that limited liability and other rights granted to companies carry a responsibility: corporations, just like other members of society, must contribute to its betterment. Therefore, companies owe a moral debt to society to contribute to its overall well-being. Society needs a host of improvements, such as pollution control, safe products, a free marketplace, quality education, cures for illness, and freedom from crime. Corporations can help in each of these areas. Granted, deciding which social needs deserve corporate attention is difficult; however, this challenge does not lessen a company's obligation to choose a cause. Corporate America cannot ignore the multitude of pressing needs that remain, despite the efforts of government and private charities.

A derivative of the social contract theory is the **stakeholder model** for the societal role of the business corporation. Under the stakeholder model, a corporation has fiduciary responsibilities—duty of utmost loyalty and good faith—to all of its stakeholders, not just its stockholders. Historically, the stockholder model for the role of business has been the norm. Under this theory, a corporation is viewed as private property owned by and for the benefit of its owners—the stockholders of the corporation. (For a full discussion of this legal model, see Chapter 35.) The stakeholder model, on the other hand, holds that corporations are responsible to society at large and more directly to all those constituencies on which they depend for their survival. Thus, it is argued that a corporation should be managed for the benefit of all of its stakeholders—stockholders, employees, customers, suppliers, and managers, as well as the local communities in which it operates. (See Figure 2-2 for the stakeholder model of corporate responsibility; compare it with Figure 35-1.)

Less Government Regulation According to another argument in favor of corporate social responsibility, the more responsibly companies act, the less the government must regulate them. This idea, if accurate, would likely appeal to those corporations that typically view regulation with distaste, perceiving it as a crude and expensive way of achieving social goals. To them, regulation often imposes inappropriate, overly broad rules that hamper productivity and require extensive recordkeeping procedures to document compliance. If companies can use more flexible, voluntary methods of meeting a social norm, such as pollution control, then government will be less tempted to legislate norms.

Figure 2-2
The Stakeholder Model

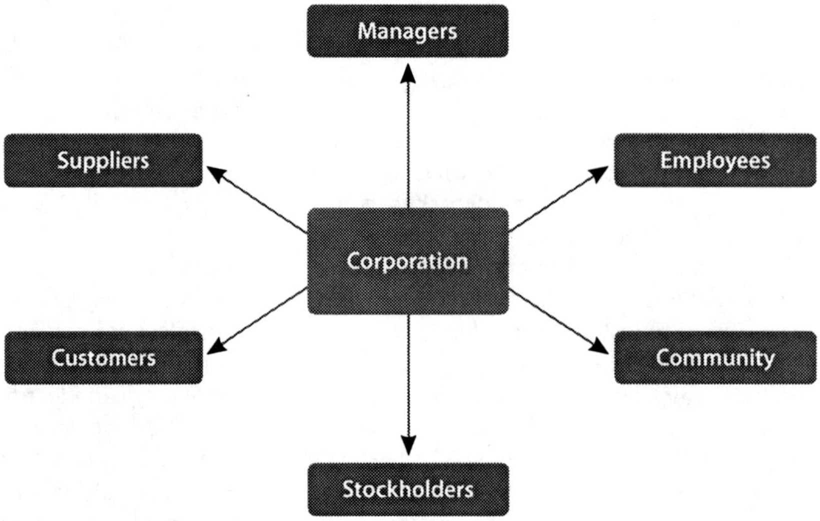

© Cengage Learning 2014

The argument can be taken further. Not only does anticipatory corporate action lessen the likelihood of government regulation, but also social involvement by companies creates a climate of trust and respect that reduces the overall inclination of government to interfere in company business. For example, a government agency is much more likely to show some leniency toward a socially responsible company than toward one that ignores social plights.

Long-Run Profits Perhaps the most persuasive argument in favor of corporate involvement in social causes is that such involvement actually makes good business sense. Consumers often support good corporate images and avoid bad ones. For example, consumers generally prefer to patronize stores with "easy return" policies. Even though such policies are not required by law, companies institute them because they create goodwill—an intangible though indispensable asset for ensuring repeat customers. In the long run, enhanced goodwill often rebounds to stronger profits. Moreover, corporate actions to improve the well-being of their communities make these communities more attractive to citizens and more profitable for business.

CHAPTER SUMMARY

Definitions

Ethics study of what is right or good for human beings

Business Ethics study of what is right and good in a business setting

Ethical Theories

Ethical Fundamentalism individuals look to a central authority or set of rules to guide them in ethical decision making

Ethical Relativism asserts that actions must be judged by what individuals subjectively feel is right or wrong for themselves

Situational Ethics one must judge a person's actions by first putting oneself in the actor's situation

Utilitarianism moral actions are those that produce the greatest net pleasure compared with net pain
* *Act Utilitarianism* assesses each separate act according to whether it maximizes pleasure over pain
* *Rule Utilitarianism* supports rules that on balance produce the greatest pleasure for society
* *Cost-Benefit Analysis* quantifies the benefits and costs of alternatives

Deontology holds that actions must be judged by their motives and means as well as their results

Social Ethics Theories focus on a person's obligations to other members in society and on the individual's rights and obligations within society
* *Social Egalitarians* believe that society should provide all its members with equal amounts of goods and services regardless of their relative contributions
* *Distributive Justice* stresses equality of opportunity rather than results
* *Libertarians* stress market outcomes as the basis for distributing society's rewards

Other Theories
* *Intuitionism* a rational person possesses inherent power to assess the correctness of actions
* *Good Person* individuals should seek out and emulate good role models

Ethical Standards in Business

Choosing an Ethical System Kohlberg's stages of moral development is a widely accepted model (see Figure 2-1)

Corporations as Moral Agents because a corporation is a statutorily created entity, it is not clear whether it should be held morally responsible

Ethical Responsibilities of Business

Regulation of Business government regulation has been necessary because all the conditions for perfect competition have not been satisfied and free competition cannot by itself achieve other societal objectives

Corporate Governance vast amounts of wealth and power have become concentrated in a small number of corporations, which in turn are controlled by a small group of corporate officers

Arguments against Social Responsibility

* *Profitability* because corporations are artificial entities established for profit-making activities, their only social obligation should be to return as much money as possible to shareholders
* *Unfairness* whenever corporations engage in social activities, such as supporting the arts or education, they divert funds rightfully belonging to shareholders and/or employees to unrelated third parties
* *Accountability* a corporation is subject to less public accountability than public bodies are
* *Expertise* although a corporation may have a high level of expertise in selling its goods and services, there is absolutely no guarantee that any promotion of social activities will be carried on with the same degree of competence

Arguments in Favor of Social Responsibility

* *The Social Contract* because society allows for the creation of corporations and gives them special rights, including a grant of limited liability, corporations owe a responsibility to society
* *Less Government Regulation* by taking a more proactive role in addressing society's problems, corporations create a climate of trust and respect that has the effect of reducing government regulation
* *Long-Run Profits* corporate involvement in social causes creates goodwill, which simply makes good business sense

QUESTIONS

1. You have an employee who has a chemical imbalance in the brain that causes him to be severely unstable. The medication that is available to deal with this schizophrenic condition is extremely powerful and decreases the taker's life span by one to two years for every year that the user takes it. You know that his doctors and family believe that it is in his best interest to take the medication. What course of action should you follow?

2. You have a very shy employee who is from another country. After a time, you notice that the quality of her performance is deteriorating rapidly. You find an appropriate time to speak with her and determine that she is extremely distraught. She tells you that her family has arranged a marriage for her and that she refuses to obey their contract. She further states to you that she is thinking about committing suicide. Two weeks later, after her poor performance continues, you determine that she is on the verge of a nervous breakdown; and once again she informs you that she is going to commit suicide. What should you do? Consider further that you can petition a court to have her involuntarily committed to a mental hospital. You know, however, that her family would consider such a commitment an extreme insult and that they might seek retribution. Does this prospect alter your decision?

3. You receive a telephone call from a company you never do business with requesting a reference on one of your employees, Mary Sunshine. You believe Mary performs in a generally incompetent manner, and you would be delighted to see her take another job. You give her a glowing reference. Is this right? Explain.

4. You have just received a report suggesting that a chemical your company uses in its manufacturing process is very dangerous. You have not read the report, but you are generally aware of its contents. You believe that the chemical can be replaced fairly easily, but that if word gets out, panic may set in among employees and community members. A reporter asks if you have seen the report, and you say no. Is your behavior right or wrong? Explain.

5. You and Joe Jones, your neighbor and friend, bought lottery tickets at the corner drugstore. While watching the lottery drawing on television with you that night, Joe leaped from the couch, waved his lottery ticket, and shouted, "I've got the winning number!" Suddenly, he clutched his chest, keeled over, and died on the spot. You are the only living person who knows that Joe, not you, bought the winning ticket. If you substitute his ticket for yours, no one will know of the switch and you will be $10 million richer. Joe's

only living relative is a rich aunt whom he despised. Will you switch his ticket for yours? Explain.

6. Omega, Inc., a publicly held corporation, has assets of $100 million and annual earnings in the range of $13 to $15 million. Omega owns three aluminum plants, which are profitable, and one plastics plant, which is losing $4 million a year. Because of its very high operating costs, the plastics plant shows no sign of ever becoming profitable, and there is no evidence that the plant and the underlying real estate will increase in value. Omega decides to sell the plastics plant. The only bidder for the plant is Gold, who intends to use the plant for a new purpose: to introduce automation, and to replace all existing employees. Would it be ethical for Omega to turn down Gold's bid and keep the plastics plant operating indefinitely, for the purpose of preserving the employees' jobs? Explain.

7. You are the sales manager of a two-year-old electronics firm. At times, the firm has seemed on the brink of failure, but recently it has begun to be profitable. In large part, the profitability is due to the aggressive and talented sales force you have recruited. Two months ago, you hired Alice North, an honors graduate from the State University, who decided that she was tired of the Research Department and wanted to try sales.

Almost immediately after you sent Alice out for training with Brad West, your best salesperson, he began reporting to you an unexpected turn of events. According to Brad, "Alice is terrific: she's confident, smooth, and persistent. Unfortunately, a lot of our buyers are good old boys who just aren't comfortable around young, bright women. Just last week, Hiram Jones, one of our biggest customers, told me that he simply won't continue to do business with 'young chicks' who think they invented the world. It's not that Alice is a know-it-all. She's not. It's just that these guys like to booze it up a bit, tell some off-color jokes, and then get down to business. Alice doesn't drink, and, although she never objects to the jokes, it's clear she thinks they're offensive." Brad felt that several potential deals had fallen through "because the mood just wasn't right with Alice there." Brad added, "I don't like a lot of these guys' styles myself, but I go along to make the sales. I just do not think Alice is going to make it."

When you call Alice in to discuss the situation, she concedes the accuracy of Brad's report but indicates that she's not to blame and insists that she be kept on the job. You feel committed to equal opportunity but don't want to jeopardize your company's ability to survive. What should you do?

8. Major Company subcontracted the development of part of a large technology system to Start-up Company, a small corporation specializing in custom computer systems. The contract, which was a major breakthrough for Start-up Company and crucial to its future, provided for an initial development fee and subsequent progress payments, as well as a final date for completion.

Start-up Company provided Major Company with periodic reports indicating that everything was on schedule. After several months, however, the status reports stopped coming, and the company missed delivery of the schematics, the second major milestone. As an in-house technical consultant for Major Company, you visited Start-up Company and found not only that it was far behind schedule but also that it had lied about its previous progress. Moreover, you determined that this slippage put the schedule for the entire project in severe jeopardy. The cause of Start-up's slippage was the removal of personnel from your project to work on short-term contracts to obtain money to meet the weekly payroll.

Your company decided that you should stay at Start-up Company to monitor its work and to assist in the design of the project. After six weeks and some progress, Start-up is still way behind its delivery dates. Nonetheless, you are now familiar enough with the project to complete it in-house with Major's personnel.

Start-up is still experiencing severe cash flow problems and repeatedly requests payment from Major. But your CEO, furious with Start-up's lies and deceptions, wishes to "bury" Start-up and finish the project using Major Company's internal resources. She knows that withholding payment to Startup will put it out of business. What do you do? Explain.

9. A customer requested certain sophisticated tests on equipment he purchased from your factory. Such tests are very expensive and must be performed by a third party. The equipment was tested as requested and met all of the industry standards, but showed anomalies which could not be explained. Though the problem appeared to be very minor, you decided to inspect the unit to try to understand the test data—a very expensive and time-consuming process. You informed the customer of this decision. A problem was found, but it was minor and was highly unlikely ever to cause the unit to fail. Rebuilding the equipment would be very expensive and time-consuming; moreover, notifying the customer that you were planning to rebuild the unit would also put your overall manufacturing procedures in question. Should you fix the problem, ship the equipment as is, or inform the customer?

10. You are a project manager for a company making a major proposal to a Middle Eastern country. Your major competition is from Japan.

  a. Your local agent, who is closely tied to a very influential sheikh, would receive a 5 percent commission if the proposal were accepted. Near the date for the decision, the agent asks you for $150,000 to grease the skids so that your proposal is accepted. What do you do?

  b. What do you do if, after you say no, the agent goes to your vice president, who provides the money?

  c. Your overseas operation learns that most other foreign companies in this Middle Eastern location bolster their business by exchanging currency on the gray market. You discover that your division is twice as profitable as budgeted due to the amount of domestic currency you have received on the gray market. What do you do?

BUSINESS ETHICS CASES

The business ethics cases that follow are based on the kinds of situations that companies regularly face when conducting business. You should first read each case carefully and in its entirety before attempting to analyze it. Second, you should identify the most important ethical issues arising from the situation. Often it is helpful to prioritize these issues. Third, you should identify the viable options for addressing these issues and the ethical implications of the identified options. This might include examining the options from the perspectives of the various ethical theories as well as the affected stakeholders. Fourth, you should reach a definite resolution of the ethical issues by choosing what you think is the best option. You should have a well-articulated rationale for your resolution. Finally, develop a strategy for implementing your resolution.

Pharmakon Drug Company

BACKGROUND

William Wilson, senior vice president of research, development, and medical (RD&M) at Pharmakon Drug Company, received both his Ph.D. in biochemistry and his M.D. from the University of Oklahoma. Upon completion of his residency, Dr. Wilson joined the faculty at Harvard Medical School. He left Harvard after five years to join the research group at Merck & Co. Three years later, he went to Burroughs-Wellcome as director of RD&M, and, after eight years, Dr. Wilson joined Pharmakon in his current position.

William Wilson has always been highly respected as a scientist, a manager, and an individual. He has also been an outstanding leader in the scientific community, particularly in the effort to attract more minorities into the field.

Pharmakon concentrates its research efforts in the areas of antivirals (with a focus on HIV), cardiovascular, respiratory, muscle relaxants, gastrointestinal, the central nervous system, and consumer health care (i.e., nonprescription or over-the-counter [OTC] medicines). Dr. Wilson is on the board of directors of Pharmakon and the company's executive committee. He reports directly to the chairman of the board and CEO, Mr. Jarred Swenstrum.

DECLINING GROWTH

During the previous eight years, Pharmakon experienced tremendous growth: 253 percent overall with yearly growth ranging from 12 percent to 25 percent. During this period, Pharmakon's RD&M budget grew from $79 million to $403 million, and the number of employees rose from 1,192 to 3,273 (see Figure 2-3). During the previous two years, however, growth in revenue and earnings had slowed considerably. Moreover, in the current year, Pharmakon's revenues of $3.55 billion and earnings before taxes of $1.12 billion were up only 2 percent from the previous year. Furthermore, both revenues and earnings are projected to be flat or declining for the next five years.

The cessation of this period's tremendous growth and the likelihood of future decline have been brought about principally by two causes. First, a number of Pharmakon's most important patents have expired and competition from generics has begun and could continue to erode its products' market shares. Second, as new types of health-care delivery organizations evolve, pharmaceutical companies' revenues and earnings will in all likelihood be adversely affected.

PROBLEM AND PROPOSED SOLUTIONS

In response, the board of directors has decided that the company must emphasize two conflicting goals: increase the number of new drugs brought to market and cut back on the workforce in anticipation of rising labor

Figure 2-3 *Pharmakon Employment*

Attribute/Years Ago	1	2	3	4	5	6	7	8
Total Employment	3,273	3,079	2,765	2,372	1,927	1,619	1,306	1,192
Minority Employment	272 (8.35%)	238 (7.7%)	196 (7.15%)	143 (6.0%)	109 (5.7%)	75 (4.6%)	53 (4.1%)	32 (2.7%)
Revenue ($ million)	3,481	3,087	2,702	2,184	1,750	1,479	1,214	986
Profit ($ million)	1,106	1,021	996	869	724	634	520	340
RD&M Budget ($ million)	403	381	357	274	195	126	96	79

Figure 2-4
Pharmakon
Affirmative Action
Program

Pharmakon Drug Company
Equal Employment Opportunity Affirmative Action Program

POLICY

It is the policy of Pharmakon Drug Co. to provide equal employment opportunities without regard to race, color, religion, sex, national origin, sexual orientation, disability, and veteran status. The Company will also take affirmative action to employ and advance individual applicants from all segments of our society. This policy relates to all phases of employment, including, but not limited to, recruiting, hiring, placement, promotion, demotion, layoff, recall, termination, compensation, and training. In communities where Pharmakon has facilities, it is our policy to be a leader in providing equal employment for all of its citizens.

RESPONSIBILITY FOR IMPLEMENTATION

The head of each division is ultimately responsible for initiating, administering, and controlling activities within all areas of responsibility necessary to ensure full implementation of this policy.

The managers of each location or area are responsible for the implementation of this policy.

All other members of management are responsible for conducting day-to-day activities in a manner to ensure compliance with this policy.

and marketing costs and declining revenues. Accordingly, Dr. Wilson has been instructed to cut costs significantly and to reduce his workforce by 15 percent over the next six months.

Dr. Wilson called a meeting with his management team to discuss the workforce reduction. One of his managers, Leashia Harmon, argued that the layoffs should be made "so that recent gains in minority hiring are not wiped out." The percentage of minority employees had increased from 2.7 percent eight years ago to 8.3 percent in the previous year (see Figure 2-3). The minority population in communities in which Pharmakon has major facilities has remained over the years at approximately 23 percent. About 20 percent of the RD&M workforce have a Ph.D. in a physical science or in pharmacology, and another 3 percent have an M.D.

Dr. Harmon, a Ph.D. in pharmacology and head of clinical studies, is the only minority on Dr. Wilson's seven-member management team. Dr. Harmon argued that RD&M has worked long and hard to increase minority employment and has been a leader in promoting Pharmakon's affirmative action plan (see Figure 2-4). Therefore, she asserted, all layoffs should reflect this commitment, even if it meant disproportionate layoffs of nonminorities.

Dr. Anson Peake, another member of Dr. Wilson's management team and director of new products, argued that Pharmakon's RD&M division has never discharged a worker except for cause and should adhere as closely as possible to that policy by terminating individuals solely based on merit. Dr. Rachel Waugh, director of product development, pointed out that the enormous growth in employment over the last eight years—almost

a trebling of the workforce—had made the company's employee performance evaluation system less than reliable. Consequently, she contended that because laying off 15 percent of her group would be extremely difficult and subjective, she preferred to follow a system of seniority.

Dr. Wilson immediately recognized that any system of reducing the workforce would be difficult to implement. Moreover, he was concerned about fairness to employees and maintaining the best-qualified group to carry out the area's mission. He was very troubled by a merit or seniority system if it could not maintain the minority gains. In fact, he had even thought about the possibility of using this difficult situation to increase the percentage of minorities to bring it more in line with the minority percentage of the communities in which Pharmakon had major facilities.

Mykon's Dilemma

Jack Spratt, the newly appointed CEO of Mykon Pharmaceuticals, Inc., sat at his desk and scratched his head for the thousandth time that night. His friends never tired of telling him that unless he stopped this habit he would remove what little hair he had left. Nevertheless, he had good reason to be perplexed—the decisions he made would determine the future of the company and, literally, the life or death of thousands of people.

As a young, ambitious scientist, Spratt had gained international fame and considerable fortune while rising quickly through the ranks of the scientists at Mykon. After receiving a degree from the Executive MBA program at the Kenan-Flagler Business School, University of North Carolina at Chapel Hill, he assumed, in rapid succession, a number of administrative positions at the company, culminating in his appointment as CEO. But no one had told him that finding cures for previously incurable diseases would be fraught with moral dilemmas. Although it was 3:00 A.M., Spratt remained at his desk, unable to stop thinking about his difficult choices. His preoccupation was made worse by the knowledge that pressure from governments and consumers would only increase each day he failed to reach a decision. This pressure had mounted relentlessly since the fateful day he announced that Mykon had discovered the cure for AIDS. But the cure brought with it a curse: there was not enough to go around.

BACKGROUND

Mykon, a major international research-based pharmaceutical group, engages in the research, development, manufacture, and marketing of human health-care products for sale in both the prescription and over-the-counter (OTC) markets. The company's principal prescription medicines include a range of products in the following areas: antiviral, neuromuscular blocking, cardiovascular, anti-inflammatory, immunosuppressive, systemic antibacterial, and central nervous system. Mykon also manufactures other products such as muscle relaxants, antidepressants, anticonvulsants, and respiratory stimulants. In addition, the company markets drugs for the treatment of congestive heart failure and the prevention of organ rejection following transplant.

Mykon's OTC business primarily consists of cough and cold preparations and several topical antibiotics. The company seeks to expand its OTC business in various ways, including the reclassification of some of its prescription drugs to OTC status. Mykon's OTC sales represented 14 percent of the company's sales during last year.

Mykon has a long tradition of excellence in research and development (R&D). The company's expenditures on R&D for the last three financial years constituted 15 percent of its sales.

Mykon focuses its R&D on the following selected therapeutic areas, listed in descending order of expenditure amount: antivirals and other antibiotics, cardiovascular, central nervous system, anticancer, anti-inflammatory, respiratory, and neuromuscular.

Mykon sells its products internationally in more than 120 countries and has a significant presence in two of the largest pharmaceutical markets—the United States and Europe—and a growing presence in Japan. It generated approximately 43 percent and 35 percent of the company's sales from the previous year in the United States and Europe, respectively. The company sells essentially the same range of products throughout the world.

PRODUCTION

Mykon carries out most of its production in Rotterdam in the Netherlands and in Research Triangle Park, North Carolina, in the United States. The latter is the company's world headquarters. The company's manufacturing processes typically consist of three stages: the manufacture of active chemicals, the incorporation of these chemicals into products designed for use by the consumer, and packaging. The firm has an ongoing program of capital expenditure to provide up-to-date production facilities and relies on advanced technology, automation, and computerization of its manufacturing capability to help maintain its competitive position.

Production facilities are also located in ten other countries to meet the needs of local markets and to overcome legal restrictions on the importation of finished products. These facilities principally engage in product formulation and packaging, although plants in certain countries manufacture active chemicals. Last year, Mykon had more than seventeen thousand employees, 27 percent of whom were in the United States. Approximately 21 percent of Mykon's employees were engaged in R&D, largely in the Netherlands and the United States. Although unions represent a number of the firm's employees, the firm has not experienced any significant labor disputes in recent years, and it considers its employee relations to be good.

RESEARCH AND DEVELOPMENT

In the pharmaceutical industry, R&D is both expensive and prolonged, entailing considerable uncertainty. The process of producing a commercial drug typically takes between eight and twelve years as it proceeds from discovery through development to regulatory approval and finally to the product launch. No assurance exists that new compounds will survive the development process or obtain the requisite regulatory approvals. In addition, research conducted by other pharmaceutical companies may lead at any time to the introduction of competing or improved treatments.

Last year Mykon incurred approximately 95 percent of its R&D expenditures in the Netherlands and the United States. Figure 2-5 sets out the firm's annual

Figure 2-5
Mykon R&D
Expenditures

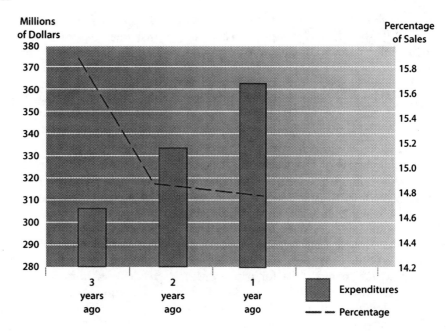

expenditure on R&D in dollars and as a percentage of sales for each of the last three financial years.

JACK SPRATT

> Every society, every institution, every company, and most important, every individual should follow those precepts that society holds most dear. The pursuit of profits must be consistent with and subordinate to these ideals, the most important of which is the Golden Rule. To work for the betterment of humanity is the reason I became a scientist in the first place. As a child, Banting and Best were my heroes. I could think of no vocation that held greater promise to help mankind. Now that I am CEO I intend to have these beliefs included in our company's mission statement.

These sentiments, expressed by Jack Spratt in a newsmagazine interview, capture the intensity and drive that animate the man. None who knew him was surprised when he set out years ago—fueled by his prodigious energy, guided by his brilliant mind, and financed by Mykon—for the inner reaches of the Amazon Basin to find naturally occurring medicines. Spratt considered it to be his manifest destiny to discover the cure for some dread disease.

His search was not totally blind. Some years earlier, Frans Berger, a well-known but eccentric scientist, had written extensively about the variety of plant life and fungi that flourished in the jungles of the Bobonaza River region deep in the Amazon watershed. Although he spent twenty years there and discovered nothing of

medical significance, the vast number and intriguing uniqueness of his specimens convinced Spratt that it was just a matter of time before a major breakthrough would occur.

Spratt also had some scientific evidence. While working in Mykon's laboratory to finance his graduate education in biology and genetics, Spratt and his supervisors had noticed that several fungi could not only restore damaged skin but, when combined with synthetic polymers, had significant effects on internal cells. Several more years of scientific expeditions and investigations proved promising enough for Mykon to send Spratt and a twenty-person exploration team to the Amazon Basin for two years. Two years became five, and the enormous quantity of specimens sent back eventually took over an entire wing of the company's sizable laboratories in Research Triangle Park, North Carolina.

Upon Spratt's return, he headed up a group of Mykon scientists who examined the Amazonian fungi for pharmacological activity. After several years of promising beginnings and disappointing endings, they discovered that one fungus destroyed the recently identified virus HIV. Years later, the company managed to produce enough of the drug (code named Sprattalin) derived from the fungus to inform the Food and Drug Administration (FDA) that it was testing what appeared to be a cure for HIV. It was the happiest moment of Jack Spratt's life. The years of determined effort, not to mention the $800 million Mykon had invested, would now be more than fully rewarded.

Spratt's joy was short-lived, though. Public awareness of the drug quickly spread, and groups pressured the FDA to shorten or eliminate its normal approval process, which ordinarily takes more than seven years. People dying from the virus's effects demanded immediate access to the drug.

THE DRUG

Mirroring the insidiousness of HIV itself, the structure of Sprattalin is extraordinarily complex. Consequently, it takes four to seven months to produce a small quantity, only 25 percent of which is usable. It is expensive; each unit of Sprattalin costs Mykon $20,000 to produce. The projected dosage ranges from ten units for asymptomatic HIV-positive patients who have normal white blood cell counts to fifty units for patients with low white blood cell counts and full-blown AIDS. The drug appears to eliminate the virus from all patients regardless of their stage of the disease. However, it does not have any restorative effect on patients' compromised immune systems. Accordingly, it is expected that asymptomatic HIV-positive patients will revert to their normal life expectancies. It is not clear what the life expectancy will be of patients with fullblown AIDS, although it is almost certain that their life expectancy would be curtailed.

Supply of Sprattalin The company has estimated that the first two years of production would yield enough Sprattalin to cure 6 percent of all asymptomatic HIV-positive patients. Alternatively, the supply would be sufficient to treat 4 percent of all patients with full-blown AIDS. Children constitute 10 percent of all people living with HIV/AIDS. See Figures 2-6 and 2-7 for statistics on the HIV/AIDS epidemic.

Interested parties have argued that the solution to production problems is clear: build larger facilities. However, even with production levels as low as they are, the bottleneck in supply occurs elsewhere. The fungus on which the whole process depends is incredibly rare, growing only in two small regions near Jatun Molino, Ecuador, along the Bobonaza River. At current harvesting rates, scientists predict that all known deposits will be depleted in three years, and many of them insist that production should be scaled back to allow the fungus to regenerate itself.

Presently there are no known methods of cultivating the fungus in the laboratory. Apparently, the delicate ecology that allows it to exist in only one region of the earth is somehow distressed enough by either transport or lab conditions to render it unable to grow and produce the drug's precursor. Scientists are feverishly trying to discover those factors that will support successful culture. However, with limited quantities of the starting

Figure 2-6
UNAIDS/WHO

Global Summary of the HIV/AIDS Epidemic, December 2010

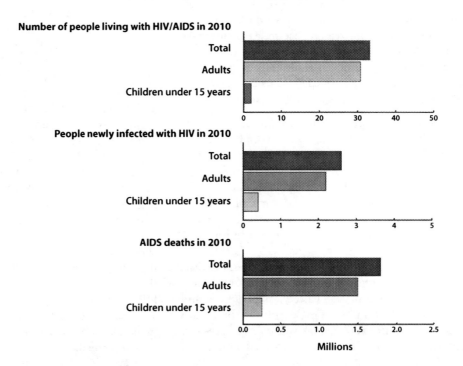

Figure 2-7
Regional Statistics for HIV and AIDS End of 2010

Region	Adults & Children Living with HIV/AIDS	Adults & Children Newly Infected	Adult Prevalence	AIDS-related Deaths in Adults & Children
Sub-Saharan Africa	22.9 million	1.9 million	5.0%	1.2 million
North Africa & Middle East	470,000	59,000	0.2%	35,000
South and South-East Asia	4 million	270,000	0.3%	250,000
East Asia	790,000	88,000	0.1%	56,000
Oceania	54,000	3,300	0.3%	1,600
Latin America	1.5 million	100,000	0.4%	67,000
Caribbean	200,000	12,000	0.9%	9,000
Eastern Europe & Central Asia	1.5 million	160,000	0.9%	90,000
North America	1.3 million	58,000	0.6%	20,000
Western & Central Europe	840,000	30,000	0.2%	9,900
Global Total	**34 million**	**2.7 million**	**0.8%**	**1.8 million**

© Cengage Learning 2014

material and most of that pressured into production, the company has enjoyed no success in this endeavor. Because of Sprattalin's complexity, attempts to synthesize the drug have failed completely, mainly because it is not known how the drug works; thus, Sprattalin's effectiveness remains shrouded in mystery.

Allocation of Sprattalin   In response to the insufficient supply, a number of powerful consumer groups have made public their suggestions regarding the allocation of Sprattalin. One proposition advanced would use medical records to establish a waiting list of possible recipients based on the length of time they have been in treatment for the virus. The argument is that those people who have waited the longest and are most in danger of dying should be the first to find relief.

Other groups propose an opposite approach, arguing that because supply is so drastically short, Mykon should make Sprattalin available only to asymptomatic HIV patients. They require the least concentrations of the drug to become well, thus extending the drug's supply. They also have the greatest likelihood of returning to full life expectancies. Under this proposal, people who have full-blown AIDS would be ineligible for treatment. Such patients have previously come to terms with their impending mortality, have fewer psychological adjustments to make, and represent, on a dosage basis, five healthier patients. In meting the drug out in this manner, proponents argue, the drug can more readily meet the highest public health objectives to eradicate the virus and prevent further transmission.

Others propose that only patients who contracted the virus through no fault of their own should have priority. This approach would first make Sprattalin available to children who were born with the virus, hemophiliacs and others who got the virus from blood transfusions, rape victims, and health-care workers.

One member of Sprattalin's executive committee has suggested a free market approach: the drug should go to the highest bidder.

Pricing of Sprattalin   In addition to supply problems, Mykon has come under considerable criticism for its proposed pricing structure. Because of extraordinarily high development and production costs, the company has tentatively priced the drug at levels unattainable for most people afflicted with HIV. Perhaps never before in the history of medicine has the ability to pay been so starkly presented as those who can pay will live, while those who cannot will die.

Even at these prices, though, demand far exceeds supply. Jack Spratt and the rest of the Mykon executives predict that the company could easily sell available supplies at twice the proposed price.

A growing number of Mykon executives disagree with the passive stance the company has taken in pricing the product. In their view, a 20 percent markup represents a meager return for the prolonged risk and high levels of spending that the company incurred to develop the drug. Moreover, it leaves little surplus for future investment. Furthermore, eight years is too long to amortize the R&D expenses because Sprattalin, though the first, is unlikely to be the last anti-HIV drug, now that Mykon has blazed a path. Other, more heavily capitalized companies are racing to reverse engineer the drug, and the availability of competing drugs remains only a matter of time. Accordingly, the company cannot realistically count on an eight-year window of opportunity.

Foreign markets further exacerbate the pricing perplexity. Other countries, with less privatized health care, have already promised their citizens access to Sprattalin at any price. Some industrial countries, for instance, are willing to pay up to $2 million per patient. They do not, however, wish to subsidize the drug for the United States. At the same time, some voices in the United States insist that supplies should go first to U.S. citizens.

On the other hand, countries with the most severe concentration of the HIV infection cannot afford to pay even Mykon's actual costs. Jack Spratt feels a very real moral obligation to help at least some of these people, whether they can pay or not.

MAKING THE DECISION

In the past few months, Jack Spratt had seen many aspects of the most important project in his life become not only public knowledge but also public domain. Because of the enormous social and political consequences of the discovery, it is unlikely that the government will allow Mykon to control the destiny of either Sprattalin or ultimately the company.

Addressing the public's concern over access to the drug while ensuring future prosperity of his company had become like walking a tightrope with strangers holding each end of the rope. He knew of no way to satisfy everyone. As Jack Spratt sat at his desk, sleep remained an eon away.

Oliver Winery, Inc.

BACKGROUND

Paul Oliver, Sr., immigrated to the United States in 1930 from Greece. After working for several wineries, he started Oliver Winery, Inc., which eventually found a market niche in nonvarietal jug wines. Through mass-marketing techniques, the company established a substantial presence in this segment of the market. Ten years ago, Paul, Jr., joined the firm after receiving a degree in enology (the study of wine making). He convinced his father of the desirability of entering a different segment of the wine market: premium varietals. To do this, the company needed a large infusion of capital to purchase appropriate vineyards. Reluctantly, Paul, Sr., agreed to take the company public. The initial public offering succeeded, and 40 percent of the company's stock went into outsiders' hands. Also, for the first time, outsiders served on the board of directors. Although Paul, Jr., wanted to use a new name for the premium varietal to appeal to a more upscale market, his father insisted on using the name Oliver.

BOARD MEETING

The board of directors met, along with Janet Stabler, the director of marketing of Oliver Winery, Inc. The following directors were in attendance:

Paul Oliver, Sr.,
      chairman of the board, founder of the company
Paul Oliver, Jr., CEO,
      has an advanced degree in enology
Cyrus Abbott, CFO,
      has an MBA
Arlene Dale, comptroller,
      has a CPA with a master's degree in accounting
Raj Ray, COO,
      has a master's degree in industrial engineering
LaTasha Lane, VP Legal,
      has a J.D. degree
Elisabeth Constable, union representative to the board,
      has a GED degree
Rev. John W. Calvin, outside director,
      has a Doctor of Divinity degree
Carlos Menendez, outside director,
      has an MFA degree

Oliver, Sr.: The next item on the agenda is a proposal to develop a new line of wines. Janet Stabler will briefly present the proposal.

Stabler: Thank you. The proposal is to enter the fortified wine market. It's the only type of wine in which unit sales are increasing. We'll make the wines cheaply and package them in pint bottles with screw-on caps. Our chief competitors are Canandaigua with Richard's Wild Irish Rose, Gallo with Thunderbird and Night Train Express, and Mogen David with MD 20/20. We'll market the wine with little or no media advertising by strategically sampling the product to targeted consumers. That's it in a nutshell.

Oliver, Sr.: Any questions before we vote?

Menendez: Who'll buy this wine?

Calvin: From what I know about the consumers of your competitors, it appears to me that it's bought by homeless winos.

Stabler: Not entirely. For example, pensioners on a fixed income would find the price of the wine appealing. Thunderbird has been recently introduced into England and has become very popular with the yuppie crowd.

Calvin: Then why put it in pint bottles?

Stabler: For the convenience of consumers.

Menendez: Why would pensioners want a small bottle?

Calvin: Homeless people want it in pints so they can fit it in their hip pockets. They obviously don't have a wine cellar to lay away their favorite bottles of Mad Dog.

Stabler: The pint size also keeps the price as low as possible.

Calvin: Translation: The homeless don't have to panhandle as long before they can make a purchase. Also, why would you increase the alcoholic content to 18 percent and make it so sweet if it weren't for the wino market?

Stabler: Many people like sweet dessert wines and 18 percent is not that much more than other types of wines that have 12 percent alcohol.

Menendez: Is it legal?

Lane: Sure. We sell to the retailers. It may be against the law to sell to intoxicated persons, but that's the retailers' business. We cannot control what they do.

Calvin: Isn't this product intended for a perpetually intoxicated audience that many people consider to be ill? Wouldn't we be taking advantage of their illness by selling highly sugared alcohol that suppresses their appetite? I've spoken to drinkers who claim to live on a gallon of this type of product a day.

Oliver, Jr.: What will this do to our image? We're still trying to get our premium wines accepted.

Stabler: Of course we won't use the Oliver name on these wines. We will use another name.

Menendez: Is it okay to do that?

Stabler: Why not? Canandaigua, Gallo, and Mogen David all do the same thing. None of them put their corporate name on this low-end product.

Abbott: We're getting away from the crux of the matter. Profit margins would be at least 10 percent higher on this line than our others. Moreover, unit sales might increase over time. Our other lines are stagnant or decreasing. The public shareholders are grousing.

Dale: Not to mention that our stock options have become almost worthless. I'm only a few years from retirement. We need to increase the profitability of the company.

Ray: Operationally, this proposal is a great fit. We can use the grapes we reject from the premium line. It will also insulate us from bad grape years because any grape will do for this wine. We can fill a lot of our unused capacity.

Constable: And hire back some of the workers who were laid off!

Stabler: It's a marketing dream. Just give out some samples to "bell cows."

Menendez: What are bell cows?

Stabler: Opinion leaders who will induce other consumers to switch to our brand.

Calvin: You mean wino gurus?

Oliver, Sr.: Look, if we don't do it, others will. In fact, they already have.

Abbott: And they'll get richer and we'll get poorer.

Lane: Gallo pulled out of several of these skid-row markets as did Canandaigua. Little good it did. The alcoholics just switched to malt liquor, vodka, or anything they could get their hands on.

Dale: I think our concern is misplaced. These people are the dregs of society. They contribute nothing.

Calvin: They're human beings who need help. We're profiting off their misfortune and misery.

Oliver, Sr.: We can take that up when we decide on what charities to support. Anyone opposed to the proposal?

Calvin: Is this a done deal? I believe we should contribute half of our profits from this product to support homeless shelters and other programs that benefit indigent and homeless people. If not, I must resign from this board.

Sources

Carrie Dolan, "Gallo Conducts Test to Placate Critics of Its Cheap Wine," *The Wall Street Journal*, June 16, 1989, p. B3.

Alix M. Freedman, "Winos and Thunderbird Are a Subject Gallo Doesn't Like to Discuss," *The Wall Street Journal*, February 25, 1988, p. 1.

Frank J. Prial, "Experiments by a Wine Maker Fails to Thwart Street Drunks," *The New York Times*, February 11, 1990, p. A29.

JLM, Inc.

BACKGROUND

Sitting in her office, Ellen Fulbright, director of human resources (HR) for JLM, Inc., thought over the decisions confronting her. To help her decide, she mentally reviewed how they had arisen.

After receiving her MBA and J.D. degrees from a highly regarded university, she joined a prestigious New York law firm where she specialized in employment law. After seven years at the law firm, she was hired by one of the firm's clients as general counsel. When that company was acquired by JLM, she joined its legal staff and within a few years had been promoted to her current position.

Fulbright's rapid advancement resulted from her having made a positive impression on Rasheed Raven, JLM's CEO. Raven is a hard-driving, bottom-line-oriented pragmatist in his early forties. Raven, a graduate of Howard University, had begun his business career on Wall Street, which he astounded with his aggressive but successful takeover strategies. After acquiring fifteen unrelated manufacturing companies, he decided to try his hand at the turnaround business. He organized JLM as an umbrella for his acquired companies. Soon he earned the reputation as the best in the business by transforming JLM into the leader in the industry.

JLM is a highly successful turnaround company. Typically, JLM purchases companies that are in serious financial trouble and manages them until they become successful companies. At that time, JLM either retains them in its own portfolio of companies or sells them off to other enterprises.

REFERENCE LETTER POLICY

About a year after Fulbright had become HR director, Raven called her into his office and showed her a newspaper article. It reported, in somewhat sensational fashion, that several defamation suits had resulted in multimillion-dollar judgments against companies that had written negative letters of references about former employees. Raven told her that he was concerned about this and that he wanted her to develop an HR policy covering letters of reference.

In researching the issue, she discovered several articles in which the authors decried the recent spate of companies that had decided to stop writing letters of reference. According to their data, they believed that these companies had overreacted to the actual risk posed by defamation suits. Based on these articles and her own inclination toward full disclosure, she proposed that the company continue to permit letters of reference but that all letters with negative comments must be reviewed by her.

Raven did not receive her proposal favorably and sought a second opinion from her old law firm. His analysis of the firm's advice was: "We get nothing but brownie points for writing reference letters, but we face the possibility of incurring the cost of a legal defense or, worse yet, a court judgment. This is a 'no-brainer.' We have no upside and all downside." Raven ordered that, henceforth, company employees would no longer write letters of reference but would simply verify dates of employment.

Although Fulbright was personally and professionally miffed by his decision, she drew up the policy statement as directed. Fulbright believed that because JLM frequently took over companies that needed immediate downsizing, this policy would be unfair and extremely detrimental to longtime employees of newly purchased companies.

TAKEOVER OF DIVERSIFIED MANUFACTURING, INC.

After a number of years of steady growth, Diversified Manufacturing began experiencing huge financial losses and its immediate survival was in serious doubt. After careful consideration, Raven decided that Diversified was an ideal takeover target in that its core businesses were extremely strong and presented great long-term economic viability.

Upon acquiring Diversified, JLM quickly decided that it had to rid Diversified of some of its poorly performing companies and that it had to reduce the size of Diversified's home office staff by 25 percent. Raven relentlessly orchestrated the reduction in force, but at Fulbright's urging he provided the discharged executives with above-average severance packages, including excellent outplacement services.

THE PROBLEM

The reduction in force was disruptive and demoralizing in all the usual ways. But for Fulbright there was a further complication: the "no reference letter" policy. She was extremely troubled by its application to three discharged Diversified employees and to one discharged JLM employee.

The Salacious Sales Manager　Soon after taking over Diversified, Fulbright became all too aware of the story of Ken Byrd, Diversified's then national sales manager. Ken is an affable man of fifty who had been an unusually effective sales manager. Throughout his career, his sales figures had always doubled those of his peers. He achieved rapid advancement despite a fatal flaw: he is an inveterate and indiscreet womanizer. He could not control his hands, which slapped backs so well, nor his tongue, which persuaded so eloquently. He had two approaches to women. With a woman of equal or superior rank in the company, he would politely, but inexorably, attempt to sweep her off her feet. With these women, he would be extremely charming and attentive, taking great care to avoid being offensive or harassing. In contrast, with a woman of subordinate rank, he would physically harass her. Less openly, but much too often, he would come up behind a woman, reach around her, and grab her. He invariably found this amusing—his victims, however, did not.

Fulbright could not believe that such a manager had stayed employed at Diversified so long, let alone been continually promoted to positions of greater responsibility and power. As Fulbright investigated the situation, she discovered that numerous sexual harassment complaints had been filed with Diversified concerning Byrd's behavior. To protect Byrd, Diversified dealt with these complaints by providing money and undeserved promotions to the complainants to smooth over their anger. Thus, Diversified successfully kept the complaints in-house and away from the courts and the Equal Employment Opportunity Commission.

After JLM's takeover of Diversified, Fulbright quickly discharged Byrd. Her satisfaction in getting rid of him was short-lived, however. His golden tongue and stellar sales record had landed him several job offers. Her dilemma was that she was uncomfortable about unleashing this deviant on an unsuspecting new employer. But JLM's policy forbade her from writing any letters or answering questions from prospective employers.

The Fruitless Juice   Melissa Cuthbertson had been a vice president in procurement for Diversified's Birch-Wood division with direct responsibility over the ordering of supplies and raw materials. Birch-Wood manufactured a full line of baby food products, including fruit juices that were labeled "100% fruit juice." To cut costs, Stanley Aker, the division's president, had arranged for an unscrupulous supplier to provide high-fructose corn syrup labeled as juice concentrate. Because standard testing in the industry was unable to detect the substitution, the company did not get caught. Emboldened, Aker gradually increased the proportion of corn syrup until there were only trace amounts of fruit juice left in the "juice." A company employee discovered the practice and after the takeover brought the matter to Fulbright's attention through JLM's internal whistle-blowing channel, which Fulbright had established. She referred the matter to Raven, who called in Aker and Cuthbertson and confronted them with the accusation. They admitted it all, explaining that nutritionally the corn syrup was equivalent to the fruit juice. But at 60 percent of the cost of fruit juice, the corn syrup made a big difference to the bottom line. Raven told them that such conduct was not permitted and that they must properly dispose of the adulterated juice.

That night Aker and Cuthbertson had the juice moved from Birch-Wood's New York warehouse and shipped to its Puerto Rico warehouse. Over the course of the next few days, the "juice" was sold in Latin America as "apple juice." Aker reported to Raven that the juice had been properly disposed of and that Birch-Wood had sustained only a small loss during that quarter. When Raven discovered the truth, he immediately discharged Aker and Cuthbertson, telling them "that if he had anything to do with it, neither of them would ever work again." Fulbright was to meet soon with Raven to discuss what should be done about Aker and Cuthbertson.

The Compassionate CFO   Jackson Cobb, JLM's former chief financial officer, is a brilliant analyst. Through hard work, he had earned an excellent education that honed his innate mathematical gifts. His natural curiosity led him to read widely, and this enabled him to bring disparate facts and concepts to bear on his often novel analyses of financial matters. But he had no interest in implementing his insights, for his only enjoyment was the process of discovering connections. Fortune—or fate—had brought him together with Raven, who is twenty years younger than Cobb. Theirs was definitely a case of opposites attracting. Raven cared little about ideas; he cared primarily about money. Cobb cared little about money; he cared primarily about ideas. Raven took Cobb's insights and translated them into action with spectacular success. Their relationship brought new meaning to the concept of synergy. When Raven formed JLM, he brought Cobb on as CFO and installed him in an adjoining office.

Their relationship continued to flourish, as did JLM's bottom line, until Cobb's wife became terminally ill. During the eighteen months she languished, Cobb spent as much time as he could taking care of her. After forty years of marriage, he was unwilling to leave her welfare to the "kindness of strangers." At his own expense, he installed a state-of-the-art communication center in his home. By virtue of computers, modems, video cameras, faxes, copiers, mobile telephones, and the like, he had available to him the same data and information as he had at his office. He could be reached by telephone at all times. But he was not in the office next to Raven; he was not present at Raven's daily breakfast meetings; he was not on the corporate jet en route to business meetings. After their many years of working together, Raven was enraged at the loss of immediate access to Cobb. He felt that Cobb had betrayed him and demanded that Cobb resume his old working hours. Cobb refused, and Raven fired him. Because of his age, Cobb was experiencing difficulty in finding new employment, and Fulbright wanted to write a letter on his behalf.

Sword Technology, Inc.

BACKGROUND

Sitting in his office, Stephen Hag, CEO of Sword Technology, Inc., contemplated the problems that had been perplexing him for some time. They had begun when he took his company international, and they kept coming. But today he was no more successful in devising a solution than he had been previously. Slowly, his thoughts drifted to those early days years ago when he and his sister Marian started the company.

The company's first product was an investment newsletter stressing technical analysis in securities investing. A few years later, he developed what became a "killer app": a computer program that defines an entirely new market and through customer loyalty substantially dominates that market. His software program enabled investors to track their investments in stocks, bonds, and futures. By combining powerful analytical tools with an accessible graphical interface, it appealed to both professional and amateur investors. Moreover, it required users to download information from the company's database. With one of the most extensive databases and the cheapest downloading rates in the industry, the company soon controlled the U.S. market. Sword then went public through a highly successful IPO (an initial public offering of the company's common stock), and its stock is traded on the NASDAQ Stock Market. The company is required to file periodic reports with the Securities and Exchange Commission.

The company used cash from sales of software, online charges, and the IPO to try to enter the hardware side of the computer industry. It began manufacturing modems and other computer peripherals. A nagging problem, however, plagued the company's manufacturing efforts. Although Sword's modem could convert data more quickly and efficiently than most of its competitors, because of high labor costs it was unable to market its modem successfully. To reduce manufacturing costs, especially labor costs, the company decided to move its manufacturing facilities overseas. And that's when the trouble began.

Stephen's thoughts returned to the present. He reopened the folder labeled "Confidential: International Issues" and began perusing its contents.

TRANSFER PRICING

The first item he saw was an opinion letter from the company's tax attorney. It dealt with Excalibur Technology, the first overseas company Sword established. Excalibur, a wholly owned subsidiary of Sword, is incorporated in Tolemac, an emerging country with a rapidly growing economy. To encourage foreign investment, Tolemac taxes corporate profits at a significantly lower rate than the United States and other industrial nations. Excalibur manufactures modems for Sword pursuant to a licensing agreement under which Excalibur pays Sword a royalty equal to a specified percentage of the modems' gross sales. Excalibur sells all of its output at a fair market price to Sword, which then markets the modems in the United States. Stephen had been closely involved in structuring this arrangement and had insisted on keeping the royalty rate low to minimize taxable income for Sword. Stephen reread the opinion letter:

> Section 482 of the Internal Revenue Code authorizes the Internal Revenue Service to allocate gross income, deductions,

credits, and other common allowances among two or more organizations, trades, or businesses under common ownership or control whenever it determines that this action is necessary "in order to prevent evasion of taxes or clearly to reflect the income of any such organizations, trades, or businesses." IRS Regulation 1.482-2(e) governing the sale or trade of intangibles between related persons mandates an appropriate allocation to reflect the price that an unrelated party under the same circumstances would have paid, which normally includes profit to the seller. The Regulations provide four methods for determining an arm's-length price. In our opinion, under the only method applicable to the circumstances of Sword Technology, Inc., and Excalibur Technology, the royalty rate should be at least three times the current one. If the IRS were to reach the same conclusion, then the company would be liable for the taxes it underpaid because of the understatement of income. Moreover, the company would be liable for a penalty of either 20 percent or 40 percent of the tax deficiency, unless the company can show that it had reasonable cause and acted in good faith.

Stephen had spoken to the tax attorney at length and learned that the probability of an audit was about 10 percent and that many multinational companies play similar "games" with their transfer pricing. The attorney also told him that he believed that if the company were audited, there was at least a 90 percent probability that the IRS would agree with his conclusion and at least a 70 percent probability that it would impose a penalty. Because the dollar amount of the contingent tax liability was not an insignificant amount, Stephen had been concerned about it for the six weeks since he had received the letter.

CUSTOMS AND CUSTOMS

Soon after Excalibur had manufactured the first shipment of modems, a new problem arose: getting them out of Tolemac. It took far too long to clear customs, thus undermining their carefully planned just-in-time manufacturing schedules. Stephen hired a local export broker, who distributed cash gifts to customs officials. Miraculously, the clearance time shortened and manufacturing schedules were maintained. The export broker billed the company for his services and the amount of the cash gifts. Although the broker assured Stephen that such gifts were entirely customary, Stephen was not entirely comfortable with the practice.

THE THORN IN HIS SIDE

Tolemac was not Stephen's only problem. Six months after commencing operations in Tolemac, Sword began serious negotiations to enter the Liarg market. Liarg is a developing country with a large population and a larger national debt. Previously, Sword had encountered great difficulties in exporting products to Liarg. Stephen's sister, Marian, COO of Sword, took on the challenge of establishing a Liarg presence.

They decided that setting up a manufacturing facility in Liarg would achieve two objectives: greater access to the Liarg marketplace and lower-cost modems. At first, the Liarg government insisted that Sword enter into a joint venture, with the government having a 51 percent interest. Sword was unwilling to invest in such an arrangement, countering with a proposal for a wholly owned subsidiary. Marian conducted extensive negotiations with the government, assisted by a Liarg consulting firm that specialized in lobbying governmental officials. As part of these negotiations, Sword made contributions to the reelection campaigns of key Liarg legislators who were opposed to wholly owned subsidiaries of foreign corporations. After the legislators' reelection, the negotiations quickly reached a successful conclusion. On closing the contract, Sword flew several Liarg officials and their wives to Lake Tahoe for a lavish three-day celebration. All of these expenses were reported in the company's financial statements as payments for legal and consulting fees.

Marian then hired an international engineering firm to help design the manufacturing plant. Two weeks later, they submitted plans for the plant and its operations that fully complied with Liarg regulations regarding worker health and safety as well as environmental protection. But, as Marian had explained to Stephen, the plant's design fell far short of complying with U.S. requirements. Marian noted that, under the proposed design, the workers would face exposure to moderately high levels of toxic chemicals and hazardous materials. The design also would degrade the water supply of nearby towns. However, the design would generate significant savings in capital and operational costs as compared with the design used in their U.S. facility. Marian assured Stephen that all quality control systems were in place so the modems produced in this plant would be indistinguishable from their U.S. counterparts. Stephen and Marian have had long discussions about what to do about the plant.

Stephen then took from the folder an article that had appeared in a number of U.S. newspapers.

CHILDREN AND CHIPS

A twelve-year-old Liarg child recently spoke at an international conference in New York denouncing the exploitation of children in the Liarg computer chip industry. The child informed the outraged audience that he had worked in such a plant from age four to age ten. He asserted that he was just one of many children who were so employed. He described the deplorable working conditions: poor ventilation, long hours, inadequate food, and substandard housing. The pay was low. But, because their families could not afford to keep them at home, the children were hired out to the factory owners, who especially wanted young children because their small fingers made them adept at many assembly processes.

Stephen had read the article countless times, thinking about his own children. He knew that if they set up a plant in Liarg, they would have to buy chip components from Liarg suppliers. He also knew that there would be no way for Sword to ensure that the chips had not been made with child labor.

Another labor issue also troubled Stephen. Marian told him that she had met considerable resistance from the Liarg executives they had hired when she suggested that women should be hired at the supervisory level. They maintained that it was not done and would make it impossible to hire and control a satisfactory workforce at the plant. Moreover, they insisted on hiring their relatives as supervisors. When Marian protested this nepotism, they assured her that it was customary and asserted that they could not trust anyone not related to them.

TO OUTSOURCE OR NOT TO OUTSOURCE

Once again Stephen glanced over the cost data. Sword's labor costs for supporting its database services and hardware were eviscerating the company's profits. After racking his brain endlessly, he had concluded that wherever it made financial and strategic sense Sword should utilize business process outsourcing (BPO); that is, long-term contracting out of non-core business processes to an outside provider in order to lower costs and thereby increase shareholder value.

Stephen had examined a number of potential countries on the basis of many factors, including time zone, communications infrastructure, technical training, English language skills of the workforce, and—most critically—costs. Liarg had emerged as the optimal choice. He anticipated reducing labor and associated overhead costs by 45 to 50 percent.

He planned to start by offshoring half of the call center operations, soon to be followed by a third of the low-end software development such as maintenance and coding. Assuming all went as he envisioned, he expected to move offshore back-office operations and higher-level software development. As his imagination soared, he saw the potential to amplify the company's operations with round-the-clock development.

Stephen realized that embarking on this course would result in reducing the staffing at the company's U.S. call centers. He expected he could achieve some reductions through attrition and reassignment, but considerable layoffs would be necessary. He hoped that outsourcing the low-end software development would enable the company to redeploy its software developers to higher-level and more profitable assignments. Moreover, the recent rollback in the number of visas had resulted in difficulty in hiring sufficient numbers of software developers with the necessary skills. If Sword were to offshore back-office operations, Stephen expected an impact on current employees comparable to offshoring the call centers.

On top of all these concerns had come a letter from the company's outside legal counsel regarding payments made to foreign officials.

MEMORANDUM OF LAW

The Foreign Corrupt Practices Act makes it unlawful for any domestic company or any of its officers, directors, employees, or agents or its stockholders acting on its behalf to offer or give anything of value directly or indirectly to any foreign official, political party, or political official for the purpose of

1. influencing any act or decision of that person or party in his or its official capacity,

2. inducing an act or omission in violation of his or its lawful duty, or

3. inducing such person or party to use its influence to affect a decision of a foreign government in order to assist the domestic concern in obtaining or retaining business.

An offer or promise to make a prohibited payment is a violation even if the offer is not accepted or the promise is not performed. The 1988 amendments explicitly excluded facilitating or expediting payments made to expedite or secure the performance of routine governmental actions by a foreign official, political party, or party official. Routine governmental action does not include any decision by a foreign official regarding the award of new business or the continuation of old business. The amendments also added an affirmative defense for payments that are lawful under the written laws or regulations of the foreign official's country. Violations are punishable by fines of up to $2 million for companies; individuals may be fined a maximum of $100,000 or imprisoned up to five years, or both. Fines imposed upon individuals may not be paid directly or indirectly by the domestic company on whose behalf they acted. In addition, the courts may impose civil penalties of up to $16,000.

The statute also imposes internal control requirements on all reporting companies. Such companies must

1. make and keep books, records, and accounts, that in reasonable detail, accurately and fairly reflect the transactions and dispositions of the assets of the company; and

2. devise and maintain a system of internal controls that ensure that transactions are executed as authorized and recorded in conformity with generally accepted accounting principles, thereby establishing accountability with regard to assets and ensuring that access to those assets is permitted only with management's authorization.

Any person who knowingly circumvents or knowingly fails to implement a system of internal accounting controls or knowingly falsifies any book, record, or account is subject to criminal liability.

Vulcan, Inc.

THE COMPANY

Vulcan, Inc. is a multinational Fortune 200 company engaging principally in the exploration for and extraction of minerals. It is listed on the New York Stock Exchange and has more than 615 million shares outstanding.

THE MEETING (MARCH 7)

On March 5, Stewart Myer, the company's CEO, personally telephoned Martha Bordeaux, the vice president for finance; Lamont Johnson, the chief geologist; and Natasha Bylinski, the vice president for acquisitions, to arrange a March 7 meeting at the Atlanta airport. He emphasized to each of them the need for the utmost secrecy, directing them to arrange their travel to Atlanta as a connection to other and different destinations. When they all arrived at the meeting room, Myer reemphasized the need for complete secrecy. He then asked Johnson to present his report.

THE REPORT

Johnson read his report:

> Over the past few years we have conducted extensive aerial geophysical surveys of the areas west of the Great Plains. These revealed numerous anomalies or extreme variations in the conductivity of rocks. One appeared particularly encouraging, so late last year we began a ground geophysical survey of the southwest portion of the Z segment in Montana. This survey confirmed the presence of anomalies.

Accordingly, on January 14 we drilled some core samples and sent them to our lab. The results were so extraordinarily promising that on February 10 we obtained more core samples and had them chemically assayed. On February 25, we received the assay, which revealed an average mineral content of 1.17 percent copper and 8.6 percent zinc over 600 feet of the sample's 650-foot length.

Johnson then commented, "In my forty years in the business I have never seen such remarkable test results. On a scale of one to ten, this is an eleven."

THE REACTION

Bordeaux exclaimed, "Our stock price will go through the roof!" Bylinski retorted, "So will land prices!"

THE STRATEGY

Myer interrupted, "Look, we're not here to celebrate. There are a lot of better places to do that. We can't keep a lid on this for very long so we have to strike soon. We need to line up the right agents to acquire the land. We must fragment the acquisitions to keep the sellers in the dark. Most critical is maintaining absolute secrecy. No one else in the company must know this. I will decide who needs to know and I will tell them. It is your duty to the company to keep totally quiet. Now, let's discuss the acquisition plan."

When asked how he had managed to obtain core samples without tipping off the owners of the land, Johnson explained, "We pretended to be a motion picture company looking for locations to remake the movie *High Noon*. We drilled the samples in isolated areas and quickly filled the holes. To further cover our tracks we drilled some barren core samples from land we owned and hid the cores on our land."

THE PLAN

Bylinski outlined the plan to acquire the land. "We only own about 20 percent of the land we want and we have options on another 15 percent. However, we currently own none of the principal portion. So we have a lot of work to do. We will employ several agents to negotiate the purchases. We will instruct them not to disclose that they are acting for us. In fact, we will order them not to disclose they are acting for anyone. We need to acquire approximately twenty square miles of additional land."

Bordeaux asked, "What if the locals start getting curious?"

Myer replied, "I'll deal with that later if it arises."

STOCK OPTIONS

On March 15, Vulcan issued stock options at $23.50 per share to thirty of its executives, including Myer, Bordeaux, Johnson, and Bylinski. At this time neither the stock option committee nor the board of directors had been informed of the strike or the pending land acquisition program.

THE RUMORS

While the land acquisition plan was nearing completion, rumors about a major strike by Vulcan began circulating throughout the business community. On the morning of March 20, Bordeaux read an account in a national newspaper reporting that ore samples had been sent out of Montana and inferring from that fact that Vulcan had made a rich strike. Bordeaux called Myer and told him about the article.

THE PRESS RELEASE

Myer prepared the following press release, which appeared in morning newspapers of general circulation on March 21:

> During the past few days the press has reported drilling activities by Vulcan and rumors of a substantial copper discovery. These reports greatly exaggerate. Vulcan has engaged in normal geophysical explorations throughout the West. We routinely send core samples to verify our visual examinations. Most of the areas drilled have been barren or marginal. When we have additional information we will issue a statement to shareholders and the public.

LAND ACQUIRED

On April 6, Vulcan completed its land acquisition program. It had employed seven different agents. In total, it had acquired thirty-seven parcels from twenty-two different sellers at prices ranging from $300 to $600 per acre. The land cost a total of approximately $6 million.

OFFICIAL ANNOUNCEMENT

At 10:00 A.M. on April 11, Myer released on behalf of Vulcan an official announcement of a strike in Montana containing at least 30 million tons of high-grade copper and zinc ore. The release appeared on the wire services at 10:30 A.M. The price of Vulcan stock shot up eleven points to $38 by the close of business that day and continued to rise, reaching a price of $56 on May 16. (Figures 2-8 and 2-9 show the price and volume of Vulcan stock.)

Figure 2-8
Stock Price of
Vulcan, Inc. (note
irregular intervals on
time axis)

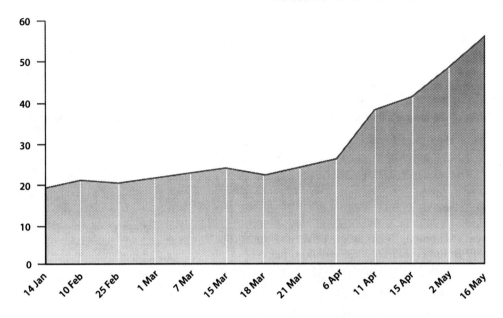

Loose Lips

Prior to the April 11 official announcement, a number of people purchased Vulcan stock with knowledge of the mineral discovery. Some people also purchased land adjacent to Vulcan's holdings in Montana. These purchasers included the following:

The Vulcan Executives   Myer, Bordeaux, Johnson, and Bylinski each purchased shares or calls on several occasions during this time period. See Figure 2-10 for a listing of their purchases.

The Eager Eavesdropper   After leaving the March 7 meeting, Bordeaux and Bylinski went to the airport lounge to wait for their flights. They excitedly—and loudly—discussed what they had learned at the meeting. Several people overheard their remarks, and one of them, Rae Bodie, immediately called her broker and bought fifteen hundred shares of Vulcan stock. Ms. Bodie also purchased a large tract of land next to Vulcan's site in Montana for approximately $600 per acre.

The Crestfallen Security Guard   On March 9, Johnson went into the home office very early to finish up

Figure 2-9
Average Daily
Volume of Vulcan,
Inc., Stock for Week
(in 1,000s)

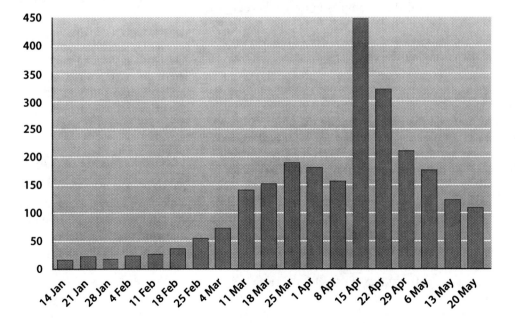

Figure 2-10
Purchases of Vulcan Stock by Selected Executives

Purchaser	Date	Shares	Price	Calls	Price
Myer	Jan. 20	10,000	18.00		
	Feb. 25	10,000	20.00		
	March 2	15,000	21.25		
	March 7			5,000	22.25
	March 15			5,000	23.75
Bordeaux	March 7	10,000	22.00		
	March 15			7,500	23.75
	March 18	5,000	24.00		
Johnson	Jan. 20	5,000	18.00		
	Feb. 25	8,000	20.00		
	March 1	12,000	21.00		
	March 7	6,000	22.00		
	March 15	4,000	23.50		
Bylinski	March 7	5,000	22.00		
	March 15	3,000	23.50		
	March 18			4,000	24.25

the exploratory work on the new find. At the elevator he encountered Celia Tidey, one of the company's security guards. Johnson knew her fairly well since they both had worked for Vulcan for more than fifteen years. Noting her despondent visage, Johnson asked her what was wrong. She related to him her tale of woe: her husband had become disabled and lost his job while her son needed an expensive medical procedure and their health insurance did not cover it. Johnson felt great empathy for her plight. He told her that big doings were afoot at Vulcan and that if she bought Vulcan stock soon she would make a lot of money in a month or so. She took her savings and bought two hundred shares of Vulcan stock, which were as many shares as she could buy.

The Avaricious Agent William Baggio, one of the agents hired to acquire the land, inferred that whatever was up had to be good for Vulcan. Accordingly, on March 21, he purchased twenty-five hundred shares of Vulcan and five thousand acres of land adjacent to the Vulcan property.

The Trusted Tippee On March 8, Myer called Theodore Griffey, his oldest and dearest friend. After

getting Griffey to swear absolute confidentiality, Myer told him all the details of the strike. After hanging up the telephone, Griffey immediately purchased fifteen thousand shares of Vulcan stock. Griffey then told his father and sister about the land; both of them bought fifteen thousand shares.

The Scampering Stockbroker Morris Lynch, Myer's stockbroker, was intrigued by Myer's purchases of an unusually large volume of Vulcan shares. During the last two weeks of March, he put a number of his other clients into Vulcan, telling them, "I've looked at this stock and it's good for you." About a dozen of his clients purchased a total of eight thousand shares.

The Land Grab After the official announcement on April 11, several of Vulcan's competitors began exploring the area and purchased large tracks of land, bidding up the price of land to $2,250 per acre. Both Bodie and Baggio sold their newly acquired land to Vulcan competitors at this higher price.

Chapter 7

INTENTIONAL TORTS

Torts are infinitely various, not limited or confined, for there is nothing in nature but may be an instrument for mischief.

CHARLES PRATT (QUOTED IN *THE GUIDE TO AMERICAN LAW*, VOL. 10)

CHAPTER OUTCOMES

After reading and studying this chapter, you should be able to:

1. Identify and describe the torts that protect against intentional harm to personal rights.

2. Explain the application of the various privileges to defamation suits and how they are affected by whether the plaintiff is (a) a public figure, (b) a public official, or (c) a private person.

3. Describe and distinguish the four torts comprising invasion of privacy.

4. Identify and describe the torts that protect against harm to property.

5. Distinguish among interference with contractual relations, disparagement, and fraudulent misrepresentation.

All forms of civil liability are either (1) voluntarily assumed, as by contract, or (2) involuntarily assumed, as imposed by law. **Tort** liability is of the second type. Tort law gives persons relief from civil wrongs or injuries to their persons, property, and economic interests. Examples include assault and battery, automobile accidents, professional malpractice, and products liability. This law has three principal objectives: (1) to compensate persons who sustain harm or loss resulting from another's conduct, (2) to place the cost of that compensation only on those parties who should bear it, and (3) to prevent future harms and losses. Thus, the law of torts reallocates losses caused by human misconduct. In general, a tort is committed when (1) a duty owed by one person to another (2) is breached, (3) proximately

causing (4) injury or damage to the owner of a legally protected interest.

Each person is legally responsible for the damages proximately caused by his tortious conduct. Moreover, as we will discuss in Chapter 29, businesses that conduct their business activities through employees are also liable for the torts their employees commit in the course of employment. The tort liability of employers makes the study of tort law essential to business managers.

Injuries may be inflicted intentionally, negligently, or without fault (strict liability). We will discuss intentional torts in this chapter and cover negligence and strict liability in Chapter 8.

The same conduct may, and often does, constitute both a crime and a tort. For example, let us assume that Johnson has committed an assault and battery against West. For the commission of this crime, the state may take appropriate action against Johnson. In addition, Johnson has violated West's right to be secure in his person, and so has committed a tort against West. Regardless of the criminal action brought by the state against Johnson, West may bring a civil tort action against Johnson for damages. But an act may be criminal without being tortious; by the same token, an act may be a tort but not a crime.

In a tort action, the injured party sues to recover compensation for the injury sustained as a result of the defendant's wrongful conduct. The purpose of tort law, unlike criminal law, is to compensate the injured party, not to punish the wrongdoer. In certain cases, however, courts may award exemplary or **punitive damages**, which are damages over and above the amount necessary to compensate the plaintiff. In cases in which the defendant's tortious conduct has been intentional—or in some states, reckless—and outrageous, showing malice or a fraudulent or evil motive, most courts permit a jury to award punitive damages. The allowance of punitive damages is designed to punish and make an example of the defendant and thus deter others from similar conduct.

PRACTICAL ADVICE

When bringing a lawsuit for an intentional tort, consider whether it is appropriate to ask for punitive damages.

PHILIP MORRIS USA v. WILLIAMS

SUPREME COURT OF THE UNITED STATES, 2007
549 U.S. 346, 127 S.CT. 1057, 166 L.ED.2D 940

http://scholar.google.com/scholar_case?case=3002949669360902078&q=549+U.S.+346&hl=en&as_sdt=2,34

FACTS This lawsuit arises out of the death of Jesse Williams, a heavy cigarette smoker. Williams' widow represents his estate in this state lawsuit for negligence and deceit against Philip Morris, the manufacturer of Marlboro, the brand that Williams smoked. A jury found that Williams' death was caused by smoking; that Williams smoked in significant part because he thought it was safe to do so; and that Philip Morris knowingly and falsely led him to believe that this was so. The jury found that both Philip Morris and Williams were negligent and that Philip Morris had engaged in deceit. In respect to deceit, it awarded compensatory damages of about $821,000 along with $79.5 million in punitive damages.

The trial judge subsequently found the $79.5 million punitive damages award "excessive" and reduced it to $32 million. Both sides appealed. The Oregon Court of Appeals rejected Philip Morris' arguments and restored the $79.5 million jury award. Subsequently, the Oregon Supreme Court rejected Philip Morris' arguments that the trial court should have instructed the jury that it could not punish Philip Morris for injury to persons not before the court and that the roughly 100:1 ratio of the $79.5 million punitive damages award to the compensatory damages amount was "grossly excessive."

The U.S. Supreme Court granted Philip Morris *certiorari* on its claims that (1) Oregon had unconstitutionally permitted it to be punished for harming nonparty victims; and (2) Oregon had in effect disregarded "the constitutional requirement that punitive damages be reasonably related to the plaintiff's harm."

DECISION The Oregon Supreme Court's judgment is vacated, and the case is remanded.

OPINION Breyer J. This Court has long made clear that "punitive damages may properly be imposed to further a State's legitimate interests in punishing unlawful conduct and deterring its repetition." [Citations.] At the same time, we have emphasized the need to avoid an arbitrary determination of an award's amount. Unless a State insists upon proper standards that will cabin the jury's discretionary authority, its punitive damages system may deprive a defendant of "fair notice ... of the severity of the penalty that a State may impose," [citation]; it may threaten "arbitrary punishments," *i.e.*, punishments that reflect not an "application of law" but "a decisionmaker's caprice," [citation]; and, where the amounts are sufficiently large, it may impose one State's (or one jury's) "policy choice," say as to the conditions under which (or even whether) certain products can be sold, upon "neighboring States" with different public policies, [citation].

For these and similar reasons, this Court has found that the Constitution imposes certain limits, in respect both to procedures for awarding punitive damages and to amounts forbidden as "grossly excessive." [Citation] (requiring judicial review of the size of punitive awards); [citation] (review must be *de novo*); [citation] (excessiveness decision depends upon the reprehensibility of the defendant's conduct, whether the award bears a reasonable relationship to the actual and potential harm caused by the defendant to the plaintiff, and the difference between the award and sanctions "authorized or imposed in comparable cases"); [citation] (excessiveness more likely where ratio exceeds single digits). Because we shall not decide whether the award here at issue is "grossly excessive," we need now only consider the Constitution's procedural limitations.

In our view, the Constitution's Due Process Clause forbids a State to use a punitive damages award to punish a defendant for injury that it inflicts upon nonparties or those whom they directly represent, i.e., injury that it inflicts upon those who are, essentially, strangers to the litigation.

* * *

* * * [W]e can find no authority supporting the use of punitive damages awards for the purpose of punishing a defendant for harming others. We have said that it may be appropriate to consider the reasonableness of a punitive damages award in light of the *potential* harm the defendant's conduct could have caused. But we have made clear that the potential harm at issue was harm potentially caused *the plaintiff.* [Citation] ("We have been reluctant to identify concrete constitutional limits on the ratio between harm, or potential harm, *to the plaintiff* and the punitive damages award") * * *

* * * Evidence of actual harm to nonparties can help to show that the conduct that harmed the plaintiff also posed a substantial risk of harm to the general public, and so was particularly reprehensible—although counsel may argue in a particular case that conduct resulting in no harm to others nonetheless posed a grave risk to the public, or the converse. Yet for the reasons given above, a jury may not go further than this and use a punitive damages verdict to punish a defendant directly on account of harms it is alleged to have visited on nonparties.

* * * We therefore conclude that the Due Process Clause requires States to provide assurance that juries are not asking the wrong question, i.e., seeking, not simply to determine reprehensibility, but also to punish for harm caused strangers.

* * *

The instruction that Philip Morris said the trial court should have given distinguishes between using harm to others as part of the "reasonable relationship" equation (which it would allow) and using it directly as a basis for punishment. The instruction asked the trial court to tell the jury that "you *may* consider the extent of harm suffered by others *in determining what [the] reasonable relationship is*" between Philip Morris' punishable misconduct and harm caused to Jesse Williams, "*[but] you are not to punish the defendant for the impact of its alleged misconduct on other persons, who may bring lawsuits of their own* in which other juries can resolve their claims...." [Citation.] And as the Oregon Supreme Court explicitly recognized, Philip Morris argued that the Constitution "prohibits the state, acting through a civil jury, from using punitive damages to punish a defendant for harm to nonparties." [Citation.]

* * *

As the preceding discussion makes clear, we believe that the Oregon Supreme Court applied the wrong constitutional standard when considering Philip Morris' appeal. We remand this case so that the Oregon Supreme Court can apply the standard we have set forth. Because the application of this standard may lead to the need for a new trial, or a change in the level of the punitive damages award, we shall not consider whether the award is constitutionally "grossly excessive."

INTERPRETATION In most states, a jury may award punitive damages if a defendant's tortious conduct is intentional and outrageous, but the amount of damages must not be grossly excessive and may not punish the defendant for harm caused to parties other than the plaintiff.

ETHICAL QUESTION Is it ethical to impose punishment in a civil case without the protections provided to defendants in a criminal proceeding? Explain.

CRITICAL THINKING QUESTION Can juries be adequately instructed to make the distinction required by the U.S. Supreme Court? Explain.

Tort law is primarily common law, and, as we mentioned in Chapter 1, the Restatements, prepared by the American Law Institute (ALI), present many important areas of the common law, including torts. You will recall that although they are not law in themselves, the Restatements are highly persuasive in the courts. Since then, the Restatement has served as a vital force in shaping the law of torts. Between 1965 and 1978, the institute adopted and promulgated a second edition of the Restatement of Torts, which revised and

superseded the First Restatement. This text will refer to the second Restatement simply as the Restatement.

In 1996, the ALI approved the development of a new Restatement, called Restatement Third, Torts: Liability for Physical and Emotional Harm, which addresses the general or basic elements of the tort action for liability for accidental personal injury, property damage, and emotional harm but does not cover liability for economic loss. This work replaces comparable provisions in the Restatement Second, Torts. The final work is published in two volumes. Volume 1 was published in 2009 and covers liability for negligence causing physical harm, duty, strict liability, factual cause, and scope of liability (traditionally called proximate cause). Volume 2 covers affirmative duties, emotional harm, landowner liability, and liability of actors who retain independent contractors. Volume 2 was approved and published in 2011.

Because this new Restatement applies to nonintentional torts, it will be covered extensively in the next chapter, and it will be cited as the "Third Restatement." A few of its provisions, however, do apply to intentional torts and will be included in this chapter. Comment c to Section 5 of the Third Restatement provides that the Second Restatement remains largely authoritative in explaining the details of specific intentional torts and their related defenses.

The Institute's Restatement Third, Torts: Economic Torts and Related Wrongs will update coverage on torts that involve economic loss or pecuniary harm *not* resulting from physical harm or physical contact to a person or property. The project will update coverage of economic torts in Restatement Second, Torts and address some topics not covered in prior Restatements. The Institute began this project in 2004 and after several years of inactivity the project was resumed in 2010. In 2012, a portion of Chapter 1 of the Tentative Draft was approved.

Intent, as used in tort law, does not require a hostile or evil motive. Rather, it means that the actor desires to cause the consequences of his act or that he believes the consequences are substantially (almost) certain to result from it. (See Figure 7-1, which illustrates intent.) The Third Restatement provides that "[a] person acts with the intent to produce a consequence if: (a) the person acts with the purpose of producing that consequence; or (b) the person acts knowing that the consequence is substantially certain to result."

The following examples illustrate the definition of intent: (1) If Mark fires a gun in the middle of the Mojave Desert, he intends to fire the gun; but when the bullet hits Steven, who is in the desert without Mark's knowledge, Mark does not intend that result. (2) Mark throws a bomb into Steven's office in order to kill Steven. Mark knows that Carol is in Steven's office and that the bomb is substantially certain to injure Carol, although Mark has no desire to harm her. Mark is, nonetheless, liable to Carol for any injury caused Carol. Mark's intent to injure Steven is *transferred* to Carol.

Infants (persons who have not reached the age of majority, which is eighteen years in almost all states) are held liable for their intentional torts. The infant's age and knowledge, however, are critical in determining whether the infant had sufficient intelligence to form the required intent. Incompetents, like infants, are generally held liable for their intentional torts.

Even though the defendant has intentionally invaded the interests of the plaintiff, the defendant will not be liable if such conduct was privileged. A defendant's conduct is ***privileged*** if it furthers an interest of such social importance that the law grants immunity from tort liability for damage to others. Examples of privilege include self-defense, defense of property, and defense of others. In addition, the plaintiff's consent to the defendant's conduct is a defense to intentional torts.

Figure 7-1
Intent

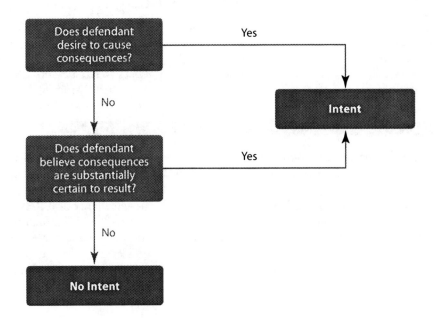

Harm to the Person

The law provides protection against harm to the person. Generally, intentional torts to the person entitle the injured party to recover damages for bodily harm, emotional distress, loss or impairment of earning capacity, reasonable medical expenses, and harm the tortious conduct caused to property or business.

BATTERY

Battery is an intentional infliction of harmful or offensive bodily contact. It may consist of contact causing serious injury, such as a gunshot wound or a blow on the head with a club. Or it may involve contact causing little or no physical injury, such as knocking a hat off of a person's head or flicking a glove in another's face. Bodily contact is offensive if it would offend a reasonable person's sense of dignity. Such contact may be accomplished through the use of objects, such as Gustav's throwing a rock at Hester with the intention of hitting her. If the rock hits Hester or any other person, Gustav has committed a battery.

ASSAULT

Assault is intentional conduct by one person directed at another that places the other in apprehension of imminent (immediate) bodily harm or offensive contact. It is usually committed immediately before a battery, but if the intended battery fails, the assault remains. Assault is essentially a mental rather than a physical intrusion. Accordingly, damages for it may include compensation for fright and humiliation. The person in danger of immediate bodily harm must have *knowledge* of the danger and be apprehensive of its imminent threat to his safety.

FALSE IMPRISONMENT

The tort of **false imprisonment** or *false arrest* is the act of intentionally confining a person against her will within fixed boundaries if the person is conscious of the confinement or harmed by it. Such restraint may be brought about by physical force, the threat of physical force, or by force directed against a person's property. Damages for false imprisonment may include compensation for loss of time, physical discomfort, inconvenience, physical illness, and mental suffering. Merely obstructing a person's freedom of movement is not false imprisonment so long as a reasonable alternative exit is available.

Merchants occasionally encounter potential liability for false imprisonment when they seek to question a suspected shoplifter. A merchant who detains an innocent person may face a lawsuit for false imprisonment. However, most states have statutes protecting the merchant, provided she detains the suspect with probable cause, in a reasonable manner, and for not more than a reasonable time.

> ### PRACTICAL ADVICE
> When detaining a suspected shoplifter, be careful to conform to the limitations of your state's statutory privilege.

INFLICTION OF EMOTIONAL DISTRESS

Under the Second and Third Restatements, a person is liable for **infliction of emotional distress** when that person by extreme and outrageous conduct intentionally or recklessly causes severe emotional distress to another. The person is liable for that emotional distress and, if the emotional distress causes bodily harm, also for the resulting bodily harm. **Recklessness** is conduct that evidences a conscious disregard of or an indifference to the consequences of the act committed. With respect to infliction of emotional distress, the Third Restatement explains that an

> actor acts recklessly when the actor knows of the risk of severe emotional disturbance (or knows facts that make the risk obvious) and fails to take a precaution that would eliminate or reduce the risk even though the burden is slight relative to the magnitude of the risk, thereby demonstrating the actor's indifference.

Damages may be recovered for severe emotional distress even in the absence of any physical injury. Liability for infliction of emotional distress, however, arises only when the person seeking recovery has suffered *severe* emotional disturbance and when a reasonable person in the same circumstances would suffer severe disturbance. Thus, the Third Restatement is imposing an objective—not a subjective—test. Accordingly, there is no liability for mental harm suffered by an unusually vulnerable plaintiff, unless the defendant knew of the plaintiff's special vulnerability. Under the "extreme and outrageous" requirement, a person is liable only if the conduct goes beyond the bounds of human decency and would be regarded as intolerable in a civilized community. Ordinary insults and indignities are not enough for liability to be imposed, even if the person desires to cause emotional disturbance. Examples of this tort include sexual harassment on the job and outrageous and prolonged bullying tactics employed by creditors or collection agencies attempting to collect a debt, or by insurance adjusters trying to force a settlement of an insurance claim.

FERRELL V. MIKULA

COURT OF APPEALS OF GEORGIA, 2008, RECONSIDERATION DENIED, 2008
627 S.E.2D 7

http://scholar.google.com/scholar_case?case=12901711244406213270&q=FERRELL+v.+MIKULA&hl=en&as_sdt=2,34

FACTS On Friday night, August 6, 2006, eighteen-year-old Racquel Ferrell and thirteen-year-old Kristie Ferrell went to Ruby Tuesday. After they ate and paid their bill, the girls left the restaurant, got into their car, and drove out of the parking lot. As they entered the highway, Racquel noticed a black truck following her very closely with its headlights on high. A marked police car by the side of the road pulled onto the highway between the girls' car and the following truck and pulled the car over. The officer pulled Racquel out of the car, placed her in handcuffs, and put her in the back seat of his patrol car. Another officer removed Kristie from the car, placed her in handcuffs, and put her in the back of another patrol car.

All of the police officers gathered to talk to the driver of the truck that had been following the Ferrells, who turned out to be a uniformed off-duty police officer working as a security guard for Ruby Tuesday. The officer who arrested Racquel returned to the patrol car where she was being held and told her if she had not paid her Ruby Tuesday bill, she was going to jail. She protested, and the officer conferred again with the other officers, then returned to the car and said, "It was a mistake." He explained that the manager at the restaurant had sent the off-duty officer after them because he said the girls had not paid their bill, but they did not fit the description of the two people who had walked out without paying. The officers removed the handcuffs from Racquel and Kristie and returned them to their car. After asking for Racquel's driver's license and obtaining information about both girls, the officer told them they were free to go.

Christian Mikula had been an assistant manager for about a month, and was the only manager at Ruby Tuesday that night. One of the servers, Robert, reported that his customers at Table 24 had a complaint, so Mikula talked to the couple and told them he would take care of the food item in question. The customers were a man and a woman in their late twenties to early thirties. Mikula left the table to discuss the matter with Robert, after which server Aaron told Mikula that the patrons at Table 24 had left without paying. Mikula looked at the table, confirmed they had not left any money for the bill, and went out the main entrance. He saw a car pulling out of the parking lot, and said to the off-duty officer, "Hey, I think they just left without paying." The officer said, "Who, them?" Mikula said, "I think so," and the officer got up and went to his vehicle.

Mikula knew the officer was going to follow the people in the car and would stop them, but did not ask the officer if he had seen who got into the car. He did not give the officer a description of the people at Table 24, and did not know the race, age, gender, or number of people in the car being followed. He did not know if there were people in any of the other cars in the parking lot. He did not ask any other people in the restaurant if they had seen the people at Table 24 leave the building, which had two exits. He did not know how long the people had been gone before Aaron told him they left, or whether another customer had picked up money from Table 24. He could have tried to obtain more information to determine whether the people in the car he pointed out were the people who had been sitting at Table 24, but did not do so.

Racquel Ferrell and the parents of Kristie Ferrell sued Ruby Tuesday, Inc. and its manager, Christian Mikula, for false imprisonment and intentional infliction of emotional distress. The trial court granted the defendants' motion for summary judgment on all counts. The Ferrells appealed.

DECISION Summary judgment on the claim for intentional infliction of emotional distress is affirmed; summary judgment on the claim for false imprisonment is reversed.

OPINION Barnes, C. J. In this case, the Ferrells were detained without a warrant, and thus have a claim for false imprisonment ***. [Citation.] "False imprisonment is the unlawful detention of the person of another, for any length of time, whereby such person is deprived of his personal liberty." [Citation.] "The only essential elements of the action being the detention and its unlawfulness, malice and the want of probable cause need not be shown." [Citations.]

The evidence in this case clearly establishes that the Ferrells were detained. Although "'imprisonment' was originally intended to have meant stone walls and iron bars, ... under modern tort law an individual may be imprisoned when his movements are restrained in the open street, or in a traveling automobile." [Citation.] Ruby Tuesday does not argue otherwise, but instead argues that the evidence established sufficient probable cause and the plaintiffs failed to establish that Mikula acted with malice. But malice is not an element of false imprisonment, ***. Further, *** the mere existence of probable cause standing alone has no real defensive bearing on the issue of liability [for false imprisonment]. [Citation.]

* * *

Arresting or procuring the arrest of a person without a warrant constitutes a tort, "unless he can justify under some of the exceptions in which arrest and imprisonment without a warrant are permitted by law, [citations]". Generally, one "who causes or directs the arrest of another by an officer without a warrant may be held liable for false imprisonment, in the absence of justification, and the burden of proving that such imprisonment lies within an exception rests upon the person ... causing the imprisonment." [Citations.] * * *

Accordingly, as the Ferrells have established an unlawful detention, the next issue to consider is whether Mikula "caused" the arrest. Whether a party is potentially liable for false imprisonment by "directly or indirectly urg[ing] a law enforcement official to begin criminal proceedings" or is not liable because he "merely relates facts to an official who then makes an independent decision to arrest" is a factual question for the jury. [Citation.] The party need not expressly request an arrest, but may be liable if his conduct and acts "procured and directed the arrest." [Citation.]

* * *

Here, Mikula told the officer that the car leaving the parking lot contained people who left without paying for their food, although he did not know or try to ascertain who was in the car. He also knew the officer was going to detain the people in the car and could have tried to stop him, but made no attempt to do so. Accordingly, the trial court erred in granting summary judgment to the defendants on the plaintiffs' false imprisonment claim.

* * *

The Ferrells also contend that the trial court erred in granting summary judgment to the defendants on their claim for intentional infliction of emotional distress. The elements of a cause of action for intentional infliction of emotional distress are: (1) intentional or reckless conduct; (2) that is extreme and outrageous; (3) a causal connection between the wrongful conduct and the emotional distress; and (4) severe emotional distress. [Citation.] Further,

> [l]iability for this tort has been found only where the conduct has been so outrageous in character, and so extreme in degree, as to go beyond all possible bounds of decency, and to be regarded as atrocious, and utterly intolerable in a civilized community. Generally, the case is one in which the recitation of the facts to an average member of the community would arouse his resentment against the actor, and lead him to exclaim, "Outrageous!"

[Citation.]

In this case, the action upon which the Ferrells base their emotional distress claim is being stopped by the police, placed in handcuffs, and held in a patrol car for a short period of time before being released. While this incident was unfortunate, the question raised by the evidence was whether the restaurant manager's actions were negligent, not whether he acted maliciously or his conduct was extreme, atrocious, or utterly intolerable. Accordingly, the trial court did not err in granting the defendants' motion for summary judgment on the Ferrells' claim for intentional infliction of emotional distress.

INTERPRETATION False imprisonment is the unlawful detention of the person of another, for any length of time, whereby such person is deprived of his personal liberty unless there is a legally recognized justification. Liability is imposed under the tort of infliction of emotional distress for intentional or reckless conduct that is extreme and outrageous and that causes severe emotional distress.

CRITICAL THINKING QUESTION Do you agree that the manager's conduct was negligent at most and thus not reckless?

Harm to the Right of Dignity

The law also protects a person against intentional interference with, or harm to, his right of dignity. This protection covers a person's reputation, privacy, and right to freedom from unjustifiable litigation.

DEFAMATION

As we discussed in Chapter 4, the tort of **defamation** is a false communication that injures a person's reputation by disgracing him and diminishing the respect in which he is held. An example would be the publication of a false statement that a person had committed a crime or had a loathsome disease.

Elements of Defamation The elements of a defamation action are (1) a false and defamatory statement concerning another; (2) an unprivileged publication (communication) to a third party; (3) depending on the status of the defendant, negligence or recklessness on her part in knowing or failing to ascertain the falsity of the statement; and (4) in some cases, proof of special harm caused by the publication. The burden of proof is on the plaintiff to prove the falsity of the defamatory statement.

If the defamatory communication is handwritten, typewritten, printed, pictorial, or in any other medium with similar communicative power, such as a television or radio broadcast, it is designated as **libel**. If it is spoken or oral, it is designated as **slander**. In either case, it must be communicated to a person or persons other than the one who is defamed, a process referred to as its *publication*. Thus, if Maurice writes a defamatory letter about Pierre's character that he hands or mails to Pierre, this is not a publication because it is intended only for Pierre. The publication must have been intentional or the result of the defendant's negligence.

Any living person, as well as corporations, partnerships, and unincorporated associations, may be defamed. Unless a statute provides otherwise, no action may be brought for defamation of a deceased person.

A significant trend affecting business has been the bringing of defamation suits against former employers by discharged employees. It has been reported that such suits account for approximately one-third of all defamation lawsuits. The following case demonstrates the consequences of failing to be careful in discharging an employee.

> ### PRACTICAL ADVICE
>
> Consider whether you should provide employment references for current and former employees, and if you decide to do so, take care in what you say. See the "Business Law in Action" feature on the next page.

FRANK B. HALL & CO., INC. v. BUCK

COURT OF APPEALS OF TEXAS, FOURTEENTH DISTRICT, 1984
678 S.W.2D 612, *CERT. DENIED*, 472 U.S. 1009, 105 S.CT. 2704, 86 L.ED.2D 720 (1985)
http://scholar.google.com/scholar_case?case=17495651340574040653&q=678+S.W.2d+612&hl=en&as_sdt=2,34

FACTS On June 1, 1976, Larry W. Buck, an established salesman in the insurance business, began working for Frank B. Hall & Co. In the course of the ensuing months, Buck brought several major accounts to Hall and produced substantial commission income for the firm. In October 1976, Mendel Kaliff, then president of Frank B. Hall & Co. of Texas, informed Buck that his salary and benefits were being reduced because of his failure to generate sufficient income for the firm. On March 31, 1977, Kaliff and Lester Eckert, Hall's office manager, fired Buck. Buck was unable to procure subsequent employment with another insurance firm. He hired an investigator, Lloyd Barber, to discover the true reasons for his dismissal and for his inability to find other employment.

Barber contacted Kaliff, Eckert, and Virginia Hilley, a Hall employee, and told them he was an investigator and was seeking information about Buck's employment with the firm. Barber conducted tape-recorded interviews with the three in September and October of 1977. Kaliff accused Buck of being disruptive, untrustworthy, paranoid, hostile, untruthful, and of padding his expense account. Eckert referred to Buck as "a zero" and a "classical sociopath" who was ruthless, irrational, and disliked by other employees. Hilley stated that Buck could have been charged with theft for certain materials he brought with him from his former employer to Hall. Buck sued Hall for damages for defamation and was awarded over $1.9 million by a jury—$605,000 for actual damages and $1,300,000 for punitive damages. Hall then brought this appeal.

DECISION Judgment for Buck affirmed.

OPINION Junell, J. Any act wherein the defamatory matter is intentionally or negligently communicated to a third person is a publication. In the case of slander, the act is usually the speaking of the words. Restatement (Second) Torts § 577 comment a (1977). There is ample support in the record to show that these individuals intentionally communicated disparaging remarks to a third person. The jury was instructed that "Publication means to communicate defamatory words to some third person in such a way that he understands the words to be defamatory A statement is not published if it was unauthorized, invited or procured by Buck and if Buck knew in advance the contents of the invited communication." In response to special issues, the jury found that the slanderous statements were made and published to Barber.

***

A defamer cannot escape liability by showing that, although he desired to defame the plaintiff, he did not desire to defame him to the person to whom he in fact intentionally published the defamatory communication. The publication is complete although the publisher is mistaken as to the identity of the person to whom the publication is made. Restatement (Second) of Torts § 577 comment l (1977). Likewise, communication to an agent of the person defamed is a publication, unless the communication is invited by the person defamed or his agent. Restatement § 577 comment e. We have already determined that the evidence is sufficient to show that Buck did not know what Kaliff, Eckert or Hilley would say and that he did not procure the defamatory statements to create a lawsuit. Thus, the fact that Barber may have been acting at Buck's request is not fatal to Buck's cause of action. There is absolutely no proof that Barber induced Kaliff, Eckert or Hilley to make any of the defamatory comments.

* * *

When an ambiguity exists, a fact issue is presented. The court, by submission of proper fact issues, should let the jury render its verdict on whether the statements were fairly susceptible to the construction placed thereon by the plaintiff. [Citation.] Here, the jury found (1) Eckert made a statement calculated to convey that Buck had been terminated because of serious misconduct; (2) the statement was slanderous or libelous; (3) the statement was made with malice; (4) the statement was published; and (5) damage directly resulted from the statement. The jury also found the statements were not substantially true. The jury thus determined that these statements, which were capable of a defamatory meaning, were understood as such by Barber.

* * *

We hold that the evidence supports the award of actual damages and the amount awarded is not manifestly unjust. Furthermore, in responding to the issue on exemplary damages, the jury was instructed that exemplary damages must be based on a finding that Hall "acted with ill will, bad intent, malice or gross disregard to the rights of Buck." Although there is no fixed ratio between exemplary and actual damages, exemplary damages must be reasonably apportioned to the actual damages sustained. [Citation.] Because of the actual damages [$605,000] and the abundant evidence of malice, we hold that the award of punitive damages [$1,300,000] was not unreasonable. * * *

INTERPRETATION The key elements of defamation are that the statements made are false, injure the plaintiff's reputation, and are published.

ETHICAL QUESTION Did Hall's employees act ethically? Did Buck act ethically in hiring an investigator to obtain the information? Explain.

CRITICAL THINKING QUESTION How should a company respond to inquiries for information about former or current employees? Explain.

Business Law in Action

If you own or manage a business, you can expect employees to leave for a variety of reasons. When your present or former employees apply for work elsewhere, their potential new employers may well call you to verify their employment history and ask your opinion of them as employees. Should you give that information?

Many employers have stopped giving meaningful references for former employees. Some employers verify only employment dates and job titles of former employees. Others give no information at all. The reason? Fear of liability for defamation and of incurring large legal expenses to defend a lawsuit.

Are those fears justified? Does the benefit of minimizing risk outweigh the cost of shutting down a legitimate and valuable information system? Consider the following points:

* A number of the states have enacted statutes that provide varying degrees of protection against liability for defamation to companies that give job references for current or former employees.
* An employer is liable for a false statement only if she was negligent in attempting to establish its truth.
* Employment references enjoy qualified privilege, unless the employer communicates the statements to people with no need to know their contents or publishes them out of spite.
* Employment references are valuable. Employers who expect to get useful information about job applicants should also be willing to give it.

You can reduce the risk of liability when giving employment references if you . . .

* Endeavor to ensure that all statements you publish about an employee are true. Your effort can be used as a defense against negligence.
* Make sure you publish statements only to people with a legitimate need to know (i.e., potential employers).
* Regulate the giving of references in your company. Make sure people who work for you understand who may give references and who may not. And make sure they know that no one is ever to publish statements maliciously.
* Ask your existing employees to give you written consent to provide references for them.

Source: Ramona L. Paetzold and Steven L. Wilborn, "Employer (Ir)rationality and the Demise of Employment References," *American Business Law Journal*, May 1992, 123–42.

Defenses to Defamation Privilege is immunity from tort liability granted when the defendant's conduct furthers a societal interest of greater importance than the injury inflicted upon the plaintiff. Three kinds of privileges apply to defamation: absolute, conditional, and constitutional.

Absolute privilege, which protects the defendant regardless of his motive or intent, has been confined to those few situations in which public policy clearly favors complete freedom of speech. Such privilege includes (1) statements made by participants in a judicial proceeding regarding that proceeding; (2) statements made by members of Congress on the floor of Congress and by members of state and local legislative bodies; (3) statements made by certain executive branch officers while performing their governmental duties; and (4) statements regarding a third party made between spouses when they are alone.

Qualified or *conditional privilege* depends on proper use of the privilege. A person has a conditional privilege to publish defamatory matter to protect her own legitimate interests or, in some cases, the interests of another. Conditional privilege also extends to many communications in which the publisher and the recipient have a common interest, such as letters of reference. Conditional privilege, however, is forfeited by a publisher who acts in an excessive manner, without probable cause, or for an improper purpose.

The First Amendment to the U.S. Constitution guarantees freedom of speech and freedom of the press. The U.S. Supreme Court has applied these rights to the law of defamation by extending a form of *constitutional privilege* to defamatory and false statements about public officials or public figures so long as it is done without malice. For these purposes, *malice* is not ill will but clear and convincing proof of the publisher's knowledge of falsity or reckless disregard of the truth. Thus, under constitutional privilege, the public official or public figure must prove that the defendant published the defamatory and false comment with knowledge or in reckless disregard of the comment's falsity and its defamatory character. However, in a defamation suit brought by a private person (one who is neither a public official nor a public figure), the plaintiff must prove that the defendant published the defamatory and false comment with malice *or* negligence.

Congress enacted Section 230 of the *Communications Decency Act of 1996 (CDA)* granting immunity to Internet service providers (ISPs) from liability for defamation when publishing information originating from a third party. A court has interpreted this provision of the CDA as immunizing an ISP that refused to remove or retract an allegedly defamatory posting made on its bulletin board. The immunity granted by the CDA to ISPs has spawned a number of lawsuits urging ISPs to reveal the identities of subscribers who have posted allegedly defamatory statements. To date, ISPs have complied, generating additional litigation by angry ISP patrons attempting to keep their identities protected by asserting that their right to free speech is being compromised.

Because Section 230 of the CDA grants immunity only to ISPs, there is the possibility that employers will be held liable for some online defamatory statements made by an employee. Section 577(2) of the Restatement of Torts provides that a person who intentionally and unreasonably fails to remove defamatory matter that she knows is exhibited on property in her possession or under her control is liable for its continued publication. Therefore, employers in control of e-forums, such as electronic bulletin boards and chat rooms, should act quickly to remove any defamatory statement brought to their attention.

INVASION OF PRIVACY

The invasion of a person's right to privacy actually consists of four distinct torts: (1) appropriation of a person's name or likeness; (2) unreasonable intrusion on the seclusion of another; (3) unreasonable public disclosure of private facts; or (4) unreasonable publicity that places another in a false light in the public eye.

It is entirely possible and not uncommon for a person's right of privacy to be invaded in a manner entailing two or more of these related torts. For example, Bart forces his way into Cindy's hospital room, takes a photograph of Cindy, and publishes it to promote his cure for Cindy's illness along with false statements about Cindy that would be highly objectionable to a reasonable person. Cindy would be entitled to recover on any or all of the four torts comprising invasion of privacy.

Appropriation Appropriation is the unauthorized use of another person's name or likeness for one's own benefit, as, for example, in promoting or advertising a product or service. The tort of appropriation, which seeks to protect the individual's right to the exclusive use of his identity, is also known as the "right of publicity." In the example above, Bart's use of Cindy's photograph to promote Bart's business constitutes the tort of appropriation. The following case involving Vanna White is also an example of appropriation.

> ### PRACTICAL ADVICE
> When using another person's identity for your own purposes, be sure to obtain that person's written consent.

WHITE V. SAMSUNG ELECTRONICS

UNITED STATES COURT OF APPEALS, NINTH CIRCUIT, 1992
971 F.2D 1395, *CERT. DENIED,* 508 U.S. 951, 113 S.CT. 2443, 124 L.ED.2D 660 (1993)
http://scholar.google.com/scholar_case?case=15763501998860364615&q=971+F.2d+1395&hl=en&as_sdt=2,34

FACTS Plaintiff, Vanna White, is the hostess of *Wheel of Fortune,* one of the most popular game shows in television history. Samsung Electronics and David Deutsch Associates ran an advertisement for videocassette recorders that depicted a robot dressed in a wig, gown, and jewelry chosen to resemble White's hair and dress. The robot was posed in a stance, for which White is famous, next to a game board, which is instantly recognizable as the *Wheel of Fortune* game show set. The caption of the ad read: "Longest-running game show. 2012 AD." Defendants referred to the ad as the "Vanna White" ad. White neither consented to the ads, nor was she paid for them. White sued Samsung and Deutsch under the California common law right of publicity. The district court granted summary judgment against White on this claim.

DECISION Judgment reversed.

OPINION Goodwin, J. White argues that the district court erred in granting summary judgment to defendants on White's common law right of publicity claim. In *Eastwood v. Superior Court,* [citation], the California court of appeal stated that the common law right of publicity cause of action "may be pleaded by alleging (1) the defendant's use of the plaintiff's identity; (2) the appropriation of plaintiff's name or likeness to defendant's advantage, commercially or otherwise; (3) lack of consent, and (4) resulting injury." [Citation.] The district court dismissed White's claim for failure to satisfy *Eastwood's* second prong, reasoning that defendants had not appropriated White's "name or likeness" with their robot ad. We agree that the robot ad did not make use of White's name or likeness. However, the common law right of publicity is not so confined.

The *Eastwood* court did not hold that the right of publicity cause of action could be pleaded only by alleging an appropriation of name or likeness. *Eastwood* involved an unauthorized use of photographs of Clint Eastwood and of his name. Accordingly, the *Eastwood* court had no occasion to consider the extent beyond the use of name or likeness to which the right of publicity reaches. That court held only that the right of publicity cause of action "may be" pleaded by alleging, *inter alia,* appropriation of name or likeness, not that the action may be pleaded only in those terms.

The "name or likeness" formulation referred to in *Eastwood* originated not as an element of the right of publicity cause of action, but as a description of the types of cases in which the cause of action had been recognized. The source of this formulation is Prosser, *Privacy,* 48 Cal.L.Rev. 383, 401–07 (1960), one of the earliest and most enduring articulations of the common law right of publicity cause of action. In looking at the case law to that point, Prosser recognized that right of publicity cases involved one of two basic factual scenarios: name appropriation, and picture or other likeness appropriation. [Citation.]

Even though Prosser focused on appropriations of name or likeness in discussing the right of publicity, he noted that "[i]t is not impossible that there might be appropriation of the plaintiff's identity, as by impersonation, without use of either his name of his likeness, and that this would be an invasion of his right of privacy." [Citation.] At the time Prosser wrote, he noted however, that "[n]o such case appears to have arisen." [Citation.]

Since Prosser's early formulation, the case law has borne out his insight that the right of publicity is not limited to the appropriation of name or likeness. In *Motschenbacher v. R.J. Reynolds Tobacco Co.,* [citation], the defendant had used a photograph of the plaintiff's race car in a television commercial. Although the plaintiff appeared driving the car in the photograph, his features were not visible. Even though the defendant had not appropriated the plaintiff's name or likeness, this court held that plaintiff's California right of publicity claim should reach the jury.

In *Midler,* this court held that, even though the defendants had not used Midler's name or likeness, Midler had stated a claim for violation of her California common law right of publicity because "the defendants *** for their own profit in selling their product did appropriate part of her identity" by using a Midler sound-alike. [Citation.]

In *Carson v. Here's Johnny Portable Toilets, Inc.,* [citation], the defendant had marketed portable toilets under the brand name "Here's Johnny"—Johnny Carson's signature "Tonight Show" introduction—without Carson's permission. The district court had dismissed Carson's Michigan common law right of publicity claim because the defendants had not used Carson's "name or likeness." [Citation.] In reversing the district court, the sixth circuit found "the district court's conception of the right of publicity *** too narrow" and held that the right was implicated because the defendant had appropriated Carson's identity by using, *inter alia,* the phrase "Here's Johnny." [Citation.]

These cases teach not only that the common law right of publicity reaches means of appropriation other than name or likeness, but that the specific means of appropriation are relevant only for determining whether the defendant has in fact appropriated the plaintiff's identity. The right of publicity does not require that appropriations of identity be accomplished through particular means to be actionable. It is noteworthy that the Midler and Carson defendants not only avoided using the plaintiff's name or likeness, but they also avoided appropriating the celebrity's voice, signature, and photograph. The photograph in Motschenbacher did include the plaintiff, but because the plaintiff was not visible the driver could have been an actor or dummy and the analysis in the case would have been the same.

Although the defendants in these cases avoided the most obvious means of appropriating the plaintiffs' identities, each of their actions directly implicated the commercial interests which the right of publicity is designed to protect. As the Carson court explained:

> [t]he right of publicity has developed to protect the commercial interest of celebrities in their identities. The theory of the right is that a celebrity's identity can be valuable in the promotion of products, and the celebrity has an interest that may be protected from the unauthorized commercial exploitation of that identity *** If the celebrity's identity is commercially exploited, there has been an invasion of his right whether or not his "name or likeness" is used.

[Citation.] It is not important how the defendant has appropriated the plaintiff's identity, but whether the defendant has done so. *Motschenbacher, Midler,* and *Carson* teach the impossibility of treating the right of publicity as guarding only against a laundry list of specific means of appropriating identity. A rule which says that the right of publicity can be infringed only through the use of nine different methods of appropriating identity merely challenges the clever advertising strategist to come up with the tenth.

Indeed, if we treated the means of appropriation as dispositive in our analysis of the right of publicity, we would not only weaken the right but effectively eviscerate it. The right would fail to protect those plaintiffs most in need of its protection. Advertisers use celebrities to promote their products. The more popular the celebrity, the greater the number of people who recognize her, and the greater the visibility for the product. The identities of the most popular celebrities are not only the most attractive for advertisers, but also the easiest to evoke without resorting to obvious means such as name, likeness, or voice.

Consider a hypothetical advertisement which depicts a mechanical robot with male features, an African-American complexion, and a bald head. The robot is wearing black high-top Air Jordan basketball sneakers, and a red basketball uniform with black trim, baggy shorts, and the number 23 (though not revealing "Bulls" or "Jordan" lettering). The ad depicts the robot dunking a basketball one-handed, stiff-armed, legs extended like open scissors, and tongue hanging out. Now envision that this ad is run on television during professional basketball games. Considered individually, the robot's physical attributes, its dress, and its stance tells us little. Taken together, they lead to the only conclusion that any sports viewer who has registered a discernible pulse in the past five years would reach: the ad is about Michael Jordan.

Viewed separately, the individual aspects of the advertisement in the present case say little. Viewed together, they leave little doubt about the celebrity the ad is meant to depict. The female shaped robot is wearing a long gown, blond wig, and large jewelry. Vanna White dresses exactly like this at times, but so do many other women. The robot is in the process of turning a block letter on a game-board. Vanna White dresses like this while turning letters on a game-board but perhaps similarly attired Scrabble-playing women do this as well. The robot is standing on what looks to be the *Wheel of Fortune* game show set. Vanna White dresses like this, turns letters, and does this on the *Wheel of Fortune* game show. She is the only one. Indeed, defendants themselves referred to their ad as the "Vanna White" ad. We are not surprised.

Television and other media create marketable celebrity identity value. Considerable energy and ingenuity are expended by those who have achieved celebrity value to exploit it for profit. The law protects the celebrity's sole right to exploit this value whether the celebrity has achieved her fame out of rare ability, dumb luck, or a combination thereof. We decline Samsung and Deutsch's invitation to permit the evisceration of the common law right of publicity through means as facile as those in this case. Because White has alleged facts showing that Samsung and Deutsch had appropriated her identity, the district court erred by rejecting, on summary judgment, White's common law right of publicity claim.

INTERPRETATION The tort of appropriation protects a person's exclusive right to exploit the value of her identity.

CRITICAL THINKING QUESTION What are the interests protected by this tort?

Intrusion Intrusion is the unreasonable and highly offensive interference with the solitude or seclusion of another. Such unreasonable interference includes improper entry into another's dwelling, unauthorized eavesdropping on another's private conversations, and unauthorized examination of another's private papers and records. The intrusion must be highly offensive or objectionable to a reasonable person and must involve private matters. Thus, there is no liability if the defendant examines public records or observes the plaintiff in a public place. This form of invasion of privacy is committed once the intrusion occurs—publicity is not required.

Public Disclosure of Private Facts   Under the tort of **public disclosure of private facts**, liability is imposed for publicity given to private information about another, if the matter made public would be highly offensive and objectionable to a reasonable person. Like intrusion, this tort applies only to private, not public, information about an individual; unlike intrusion, it requires publicity. Under the Restatement, the publicity required differs in degree from "publication" as used in the law of defamation. This tort requires that private facts be communicated to the public at large or that they become public knowledge, whereas publication of a defamatory statement need be made only to a single third party. Thus Kathy, a creditor of Gary, will not invade Gary's privacy by writing a letter to Gary's employer informing the employer of Gary's failure to pay the debt, but Kathy would be liable if she posted in the window of her store a statement that Gary will not pay a debt owed to her. Some courts, however, have allowed recovery where the disclosure was made to only one person. Also, unlike defamation, this tort applies to truthful private information if the matter published would be offensive and objectionable to a reasonable person of ordinary sensibilities.

False Light   The tort of **false light** imposes liability for highly offensive publicity placing another in a false light if the defendant knew that the matter publicized was false or acted in reckless disregard of the truth. For example, Edgar includes Jason's name and photograph in a public "rogues' gallery" of convicted criminals. Because Jason has never been convicted of any crime, Edgar is liable to Jason for placing him in a false light.

As with defamation, the matter must be untrue; unlike defamation, it must be "publicized," not merely "published." Although the matter must be objectionable to a reasonable person, it need not be defamatory. In many instances, the same facts will give rise to actions both for defamation and for false light.

Defenses   The defenses of absolute, conditional, and constitutional privilege apply to publication of any matter that is an invasion of privacy to the same extent that such defenses apply to defamation.

MISUSE OF LEGAL PROCEDURE

Three torts comprise the **misuse of legal procedure**: malicious prosecution, wrongful civil proceedings, and abuse of process. Each protects an individual from being subjected to unjustifiable litigation. *Malicious prosecution* and *wrongful civil proceedings* impose liability for damages caused by improperly brought proceedings, including harm to reputation, credit, or standing; emotional distress; and the expenses incurred in defending against the wrongfully brought lawsuit. *Abuse of process* consists of using a legal proceeding (criminal or civil) to accomplish a purpose for which the proceeding is not designed. This misuse of procedure applies even when there is probable cause or when the plaintiff or prosecution succeeds in the litigation.

Harm to Property

The law also provides protection against invasions of a person's interests in property. Intentional harm to property includes the torts of (1) trespass to real property, (2) nuisance, (3) trespass to personal property, and (4) conversion.

REAL PROPERTY

Real property is land and anything attached to it, such as buildings, trees, and minerals. The law protects the possessor's rights to the exclusive use and quiet enjoyment of the land. Accordingly, damages for harm to land include compensation for the resulting diminution in the

CONCEPT REVIEW 7-1

Privacy

	Appropriation	Intrusion	Public Disclosure	False Light
Publicity	Yes	No	Yes	Yes
Private Facts	No	Yes	Yes	No
Offensiveness	No	Yes	Yes	Yes
Falsity	No	No	No	Yes

value of the land, the loss of use of the land, and the discomfort caused to the possessor of the land.

Trespass A person is liable for **trespass to real property** if he intentionally (1) enters or remains on land in the possession of another, (2) causes a thing or a third person to so enter or remain, or (3) fails to remove from the land a thing that he is under a duty to remove. Liability exists even though no actual damage is done to the land.

It is no defense that the intruder acted under the mistaken belief of law or fact that he was not trespassing. If the intruder intended to be on the particular property, his reasonable belief that he owned the land or had permission to enter on it is irrelevant. However, an intruder is not liable if his presence on the land of another is not caused by his own actions. For example, if Shirley is thrown onto Roy's land by Jimmy, Shirley is not liable to Roy for trespass, although Jimmy is.

A trespass may be committed on, beneath, or above the surface of the land, although the law regards the upper air, above a prescribed minimum altitude for flight, as a public highway. No aerial trespass occurs unless the aircraft enters into the lower reaches of the airspace and substantially interferes with the landowner's use and enjoyment.

Nuisance A nuisance is a nontrespassory invasion of another's interest in the private use and enjoyment of land. In contrast to trespass, nuisance does not require interference with another's right to exclusive possession of land but imposes liability for significant and unreasonable harm to another's use or enjoyment of land. Examples of nuisances include the emission of unpleasant odors, smoke, dust, or gas, as well as the pollution of a stream, pond, or underground water supply.

> **PRACTICAL ADVICE**
>
> In using, manufacturing, and disposing of dangerous, noxious, or toxic materials take care not to create a nuisance.

PERSONAL PROPERTY

Personal property is any type of property other than an interest in land. The law protects a number of interests in the possession of personal property, including an interest in the property's physical condition and usability, an interest in the retention of possession, and an interest in the property's availability for future use.

Trespass Trespass to personal property consists of the intentional dispossession or unauthorized use of the personal property of another. Although the interference

with the right to exclusive use and possession may be direct or indirect, liability is limited to instances in which the trespasser (1) dispossesses the other of the property; (2) substantially impairs the condition, quality, or value of the property; or (3) deprives the possessor of use of the property for a substantial time. For example, Albert parks his car in front of his house. Later, Ronald pushes Albert's car around the corner. Albert subsequently looks for his car but cannot find it for several hours. Ronald is liable to Albert for trespass.

Conversion Conversion is an intentional exercise of dominion or control over another's personal property that so seriously interferes with the other's right of control as justly to require the payment of full value for the property. Thus, all conversions are trespasses, but not all trespasses are conversions. Conversion may consist of the intentional destruction of the personal property or the use of the property in an unauthorized manner. For example, Barbara entrusts an automobile to Ken, a dealer, for sale. After he drives the car eight thousand miles on his own business, Ken is liable to Barbara for conversion. On the other hand, in the example in which Ronald pushed Albert's car around the corner, Ronald would not be liable to Albert for conversion.

Harm to Economic Interests

Economic interests comprise a fourth set of interests the law protects against intentional interference. Economic or pecuniary interests include a person's existing and prospective contractual relations, a person's business reputation, a person's name and likeness (previously discussed under appropriation), and a person's freedom from deception. In this section, we will discuss business torts—those torts that protect a person's economic interests.

INTERFERENCE WITH CONTRACTUAL RELATIONS

Interference with contractual relations involves interfering intentionally and improperly with the performance of a contract by inducing one of the parties not to perform it. (Contracts are discussed extensively in Part III of this text.) The injured party may recover the economic loss resulting from the breach of the contract. The law imposes similar liability for intentional and improper interference with another's prospective contractual relation, such as a lease renewal or financing for construction.

In either case, the rule requires that a person act with the purpose or motive of interfering with another's contract or with the knowledge that such interference is substantially certain to occur as a natural consequence of her actions. The interference may occur by prevention through the use of physical force or by threats. Frequently, the interference is accomplished by inducement, such as the offer of a better contract. For instance, Calvin may offer Becky, an employee of Fran under a contract that has two years left, a yearly salary of $5,000 per year more than the contractual arrangement between Becky and Fran. If Calvin is aware of the contract between Becky and Fran and of the fact that his offer to

Becky will interfere with that contract, then Calvin is liable to Fran for intentional interference with contractual relations.

PRACTICAL ADVICE

Recognize that inducing another person's employees to breach a valid agreement not to compete or not to disclose confidential information may be improper interference with contractual relations.

TEXACO, INC. v. PENNZOIL, CO.

COURT OF APPEALS OF TEXAS, FIRST DISTRICT, 1987
729 S.W.2D 768, *CERT. DENIED*, 485 U.S. 994, 108 S.CT. 1305, 99 L.ED.2D 686 (1988)

http://scholar.google.com/scholar_case?case=11763000609638124594&q=729+S.W.2d+768&hl=en&as_sdt=2,34

FACTS Pennzoil negotiated with Gordon Getty and the J. Paul Getty Museum over the purchase by Pennzoil of all the Getty Oil stock held by each. Gordon Getty, who was also a director of Getty Oil, held about 40.2 percent of the outstanding shares of Getty Oil. The Museum held 11.8 percent. On January 2, a Memorandum of Agreement was drafted, setting forth the terms reached by Pennzoil, Gordon Getty, and the Museum. After increasing the offering price to $110 per share plus a $5 "stub" or bonus, the board of directors of Getty Oil voted on January 3 to accept the Pennzoil deal. Accordingly, on January 4 both Getty Oil and Pennzoil issued press releases, announcing an agreement in principle on the terms of the Memorandum of Agreement but at the higher price.

Having learned of the impending sale of Getty Oil stock to Pennzoil, Texaco hurriedly called several in-house meetings, and hired an investment banker as well, to determine a feasible price range for acquiring Getty Oil. On January 5, Texaco decided on $125 per share and authorized its officers to take any steps necessary to conclude a deal. Texaco met first with a lawyer for the Museum, then with Gordon Getty. Texaco stressed to Getty that if he hesitated in selling his shares, he might be "locked out" in a minority position. On January 6, the Getty Oil board of directors voted to withdraw from the Pennzoil deal and unanimously voted to accept the $125-per-share Texaco offer. Pennzoil sued and won an award of $7.53 billion in compensatory damages and $3 billion in punitive damages based on tortious interference with a contract. Texaco appealed.

DECISION Judgment of trial court affirmed.

OPINION Warren, J. New York law requires knowledge by a defendant of the existence of contractual rights as an element of the tort of inducing a breach of that

contract. [Citation.] However, the defendant need not have full knowledge of all the detailed terms of the contract. [Citations.]

The element of knowledge by the defendant is a question of fact, and proof may be predicated on circumstantial evidence. [Citation.] Since there was no direct evidence of Texaco's knowledge of a contract in this case, the question is whether there was legally and factually sufficient circumstantial evidence from which the trier of fact reasonably could have inferred knowledge.

* * *

We find that an inference could arise that Texaco had some knowledge of Pennzoil's agreement with the Getty entities, given the evidence of Texaco's detailed studies of the Pennzoil plan, its knowledge that some members of the Getty board were not happy with Pennzoil's price, and its subsequent formulation of strategy to "stop the [Pennzoil] train" * * *

* * *

A necessary element of the plaintiff's cause of action is a showing that the defendant took an active part in persuading a party to a contract to breach it. [Citation.] Merely entering into a contract with a party with the knowledge of that party's contractual obligations to someone else is not the same as inducing a breach. [Citation.] It is necessary that there be some act of interference or of persuading a party to breach, for example by offering better terms or other incentives, for tort liability to arise. [Citations.] The issue of whether a defendant affirmatively took steps to induce the breach of an existing contract is a question of fact for the jury. [Citation.]

* * *

The evidence discussed above on Texaco's calculated formulation and implementation of its ideal strategy to acquire Getty is also inconsistent with its contention that it was merely the passive target of Getty's solicitation campaign and did nothing more than to accept terms that Getty Oil and the Museum had proposed. The evidence showed that Texaco knew it had to act quickly, and that it had "24 hours" to "stop the train." Texaco's strategy was to approach the Museum first, through its "key person" Lipton, to obtain the Museum's shares, and then to "talk to Gordon." It knew that the Trust instrument permitted Gordon Getty to sell the Trust shares only to avoid a loss, and it knew of the trustee's fear of being left in a powerless minority ownership position at Getty Oil. Texaco notes indicated a deliberate strategy to "create concern that he will take a loss;" "if there's a tender offer and Gordon doesn't tender, then he could wind up with paper"; and "pressure." This evidence contradicts

the contention that Texaco passively accepted a deal proposed by the other parties.

INTERPRETATION The tort of interference with contractual relations protects a party to a contract from a third party who intentionally and improperly induces the other contracting party not to perform the contract.

ETHICAL QUESTION Did Getty or Texaco act unethically? Explain.

CRITICAL THINKING QUESTION Does the protection afforded by this tort conflict with society's interest in free competition? Explain.

DISPARAGEMENT

The tort of **disparagement** or injurious falsehood imposes liability upon one who publishes a false statement that results in harm to another's monetary interests

if the publisher knows that the statement is false or acts in reckless disregard of its truth or falsity. This tort most commonly involves intentionally false statements that cast doubt on another's right of ownership in or on the quality of another's property or products. Thus Simon,

CONCEPT REVIEW 7-2
Intentional Torts

Interest Protected	Tort
Person	
Freedom from contact	Battery
Freedom from apprehension	Assault
Freedom of movement	False imprisonment
Freedom from distress	Infliction of emotional distress
Dignity	
Reputation	Defamation
Privacy	Appropriation
	Intrusion
	Public disclosure of private facts
	False light
Freedom from wrongful legal actions	Misuse of legal procedure
Property	
Real	Trespass
	Nuisance
Personal	Trespass
	Conversion
Economic	
Contracts	Interference with contractual rights
Goodwill	Disparagement
Freedom from deception	Fraudulent misrepresentation

while contemplating the purchase of a stock of merchandise that belongs to Marie, reads an advertisement in a newspaper in which Ernst falsely asserts he owns the merchandise. Ernst has disparaged Marie's property in the goods.

Absolute, conditional, and constitutional privileges apply to the same extent to the tort of disparagement as they do to defamation. In addition, a competitor has conditional privilege to compare her products favorably with those of a rival, even though she does not believe that her products are superior. No privilege applies, however, if the comparison contains false assertions of specific unfavorable facts about the competitor's property.

PRACTICAL ADVICE

When commenting on the products or services offered by a competitor, take care not to make any false statements.

The pecuniary loss an injured person may recover is that which directly and immediately results from impairment of the marketability of the property disparaged. Damages also may be recovered for expenses necessary to counteract the false publication, including litigation expenses, the cost of notifying customers, and the cost of publishing denials.

FRAUDULENT MISREPRESENTATION

Fraudulent misrepresentation imposes liability for the monetary loss caused by a justifiable reliance on a misrepresentation of fact intentionally made for the purpose of inducing the relying party to act. For example, Smith misrepresents to Jones that a tract of land in Texas is located in an area where oil drilling has recently commenced. Smith makes this statement knowing it is not true. In reliance upon the statement, Jones purchases the land from Smith. Smith is liable to Jones for intentional

---

Ethical Dilemma

What May One Do to Attract Clients from a Previous Employer?

FACTS Carl Adle and Louise Bart formed a law firm as partners, and Anne Lily, Marvin Thomas, and Tim Jones joined the newly formed firm of Adle & Bart as associates (nonpartner employees). After about five years, Lily, Thomas, and Jones became disenchanted with the law firm and decided to form their own, to be called Lily, Thomas & Jones.

Lily and Thomas suggested to Jones that they contact approximately five hundred of Adle & Bart's current clients. Lily and Thomas had prepared a model letter to inform clients about the new law firm (Lily, Thomas & Jones) and to encourage them to leave Adle & Bart and to become clients of the new firm. The letter also indicated that Lily, Thomas & Jones would offer legal services far better than those of Adle & Bart: billing rates would be more reasonable, service more prompt, and legal representation more effective and successful. The reference to success was aimed, in part, at three large clients who recently lost lawsuits under Adle & Bart representation. Although the losses had not resulted from malpractice or mishandling by Adle & Bart, Lily and Thomas knew that significant amounts of money had been at issue and that the clients were sensitive about the results of the lengthy litigation.

The letter included two postage-paid form letters for the prospective client to sign and mail. One form letter was addressed to Adle & Bart, informing them of the client's desire to discontinue the client-attorney relationship and requesting the firm to forward all files to Lily, Thomas &

Jones. The other form letter, addressed to Lily, Thomas & Jones, requested representation.

Jones is reluctant about the proposed mailing. Lily and Thomas, in turn, argue that their new firm is not doing as well as they expected. They essentially give Jones an ultimatum: join in the letter or leave the firm. Jones, who has thoroughly alienated Adle & Bart, does not believe he has any immediate alternative job opportunities.

Social, Policy, and Ethical Considerations

1. Should Jones agree to the proposed mailing? Is it ethical for those forming the new firm to use a client list of their former employer when seeking clients?

2. What practical steps could Jones take to assist him in his decision?

3. What are the competing social interests at stake in this controversy?

4. How would your answers differ, if at all, if the firms were accounting firms rather than law firms?

5. In what manner, if at all, should the law protect existing businesses from competition? Under what circumstances might competition become unfair, and how should laws be tailored to deter unfair practices?

6. Should Jones be concerned about the comparisons the letter makes between the new firm and Adle & Bart?

or fraudulent misrepresentation. Although fraudulent misrepresentation is a tort action, it is closely connected with contractual negotiations; we will discuss its relationship to contracts in Chapter 11.

> **PRACTICAL ADVICE**
> When describing your products or services, take care not to make any false statements.

CHAPTER SUMMARY

Harm to the Person

Battery intentional infliction of harmful or offensive bodily contact

Assault intentional infliction of apprehension of immediate bodily harm or offensive contact

False Imprisonment intentional confining of a person against her will

Infliction of Emotional Distress extreme and outrageous conduct intentionally or recklessly causing severe emotional distress

Harm to the Right of Dignity

Defamation false communication that injures a person's reputation
- *Libel* written or electronically transmitted defamation
- *Slander* spoken defamation

Invasion of Privacy
- *Appropriation* unauthorized use of a person's identity
- *Intrusion* unreasonable and highly offensive interference with the seclusion of another
- *Public Disclosure of Private Facts* highly offensive publicity of private information
- *False Light* highly offensive and false publicity about another

Misuse of Legal Procedure torts of malicious prosecution, wrongful civil proceeding, and abuse of process that protect an individual from unjustifiable litigation

Harm to Property

Real Property land and anything attached to it
- *Trespass to Real Property* wrongfully entering on land of another
- *Nuisance* a nontrespassory interference with another's use and enjoyment of land

Personal Property any property other than land
- *Trespass to Personal Property* an intentional taking or use of another's personal property
- *Conversion* intentional exercise of control over another's personal property

Harm to Economic Interests

Interference with Contractual Relations intentionally causing one of the parties to a contract not to perform

Disparagement publication of false statements about another's property or products

Fraudulent Misrepresentation a false statement, made with knowledge of its falsity, intended to induce another to act

QUESTIONS

1. The Penguin intentionally hits Batman with his umbrella. Batman, stunned by the blow, falls backward, knocking Robin down. Robin's leg is broken in the fall, and he cries out, "Holy broken bat bones! My leg is broken!" Who, if anyone, has liability to Robin? Why?

2. CEO was convinced by his employee, M. Ploy, that a coworker, A. Cused, had been stealing money from the company. At lunch that day in the company cafeteria, CEO discharged Cused from her employment, accused her of stealing from the company, searched through her purse over her objections, and finally forcibly escorted her to his office to await the arrival of the police, whom he had his secretary summon. Cused is indicted for embezzlement but subsequently is acquitted upon establishing her innocence. What rights, if any, does Cused have against CEO?

3. Ralph kisses Edith while she is asleep but does not waken or harm her. Edith sues Ralph for battery. Has a battery been committed?

4. Claude, a creditor seeking to collect a debt, calls on Dianne and demands payment in a rude and insolent manner. When Dianne says that she cannot pay, Claude calls Dianne a dead-beat and says that he will never trust Dianne again. Is Claude liable to Dianne? If so, for what tort?

5. Lana, a ten-year-old child, is run over by a car negligently driven by Mitchell. Lana, at the time of the accident, was acting reasonably and without negligence. Clark, a newspaper reporter, photographs Lana while she is lying in the street in great pain. Two years later, Perry, the publisher of a newspaper, prints Clark's picture of Lana in his newspaper as a lead to an article concerning the negligence of children. The caption under the picture reads: "They ask to be killed." Lana, who has recovered from the accident, brings suit against Clark and Perry. What is the result?

6. The *Saturday Evening Post* featured an article entitled "The Story of a College Football Fix," characterized in the subtitle as "A Shocking Report of How Wally Butts and Bear Bryant Rigged a Game Last Fall." Butts was athletic director of the University of Georgia, and Bryant was head coach of the University of Alabama. The article was based on a claim by one George Burnett that he had accidentally overheard a long-distance telephone conversation between Butts and Bryant in the course of which Butts divulged information on plays Georgia would use in the upcoming game against Alabama. The writer assigned to the story by the *Post* was not a football expert, did not interview either Butts or Bryant, and did not personally see the notes Burnett had made of the telephone conversation. Butts admitted that he had a long-distance telephone conversation with Bryant but denied that any advance information on prospective football plays was given. Has Butts been defamed by the *Post*?

7. A patient confined in a hospital, Joan, has a rare disease that is of great interest to the public. Carol, a television reporter, requests Joan to consent to an interview. Joan refuses, but Carol, nonetheless, enters Joan's room over her objection and photographs her. Joan brings a suit against Carol. Is Carol liable? If so, for what tort?

8. Owner has a place on his land where he piles trash. The pile has been there for three months. John, a neighbor of Owner, without Owner's consent or knowledge, throws trash onto the trash pile. Owner learns that John has done this and sues him. What tort, if any, has John committed?

9. Chris leaves her car parked in front of a store. There are no signs that say Chris cannot park there. The storeowner, however, needs the car moved to enable a delivery truck to unload. He releases the brake and pushes Chris's car three or four feet, doing no harm to the car. Chris returns and sees that her car has been moved and is very angry. She threatens to sue the storeowner for trespass to her personal property. Can she recover?

10. Carr borrowed John's brand-new Ford for the purpose of going to the store. He told John he would be right back. Carr then decided, however, to go to the beach while he had the car. Can John recover from Carr the value of the automobile? If so, for what tort?

CASE PROBLEMS

11. Marcia Samms claimed that David Eccles had repeatedly and persistently called her at various hours, including late at night, from May to December, soliciting her to have illicit sexual relations with him. She also claimed that on one occasion Eccles came over to her residence to again solicit sex and indecently exposed himself to her. Mrs. Samms had never encouraged Eccles but had continuously repulsed his "insulting, indecent, and obscene" proposals. She brought suit against Eccles, claiming she suffered great anxiety and fear for her personal safety and severe emotional distress, demanding actual and punitive damages. Can she recover? If so, for what tort?

12. National Bond and Investment Company sent two of its employees to repossess Whithorn's car after he failed to complete the payments. The two repossessors located Whithorn while he was driving his car. They followed him and hailed him down in order to make the repossession. Whithorn refused to abandon his car and demanded evidence of their authority. The two repossessors became impatient and called a wrecker. They ordered the driver of the wrecker to hook Whithorn's car and move it down the street while Whithorn was still inside the vehicle. Whithorn started the car and tried to escape, but the wrecker lifted the car off the road and progressed seventy-five to one hundred feet until Whithorn managed to stall the wrecker. Has National Bond committed the tort of false imprisonment?

13. William Proxmire, a U.S. senator from Wisconsin, initiated the "Golden Fleece of the Month Award" to publicize

what he believed to be wasteful government spending. The second of these awards was given to the federal agencies that had for seven years funded Dr. Hutchinson's research on stress levels in animals. The award was made in a speech Proxmire gave in the Senate; the text was also incorporated into an advance press release that was sent to 275 members of the national news media. Proxmire also referred to the research again in two subsequent newsletters sent to one hundred thousand constituents and during a television interview. Hutchinson then brought this action alleging defamation resulting in personal and economic injury. Assuming that Hutchinson proved that the statements were false and defamatory, would he prevail?

14. Capune was attempting a trip from New York to Florida on an eighteen-foot-long paddleboard. The trip was being covered by various media to gain publicity for Capune and certain products he endorsed. Capune approached a pier by water. The pier was owned by Robbins, who had posted signs prohibiting surfing and swimming around the pier. Capune was unaware of these notices and attempted to continue his journey by passing under the pier. Robbins ran up yelling and threw two bottles at Capune. Capune was frightened and tried to maneuver his paddleboard to go around the pier. Robbins then threw a third bottle that hit Capune on the head. Capune had to be helped out of the water and taken to the hospital. He suffered a physical wound that required twenty-four sutures and, as a result, had to discontinue his trip. Capune brought suit in tort against Robbins. Is Robbins liable? If so, for which tort or torts?

15. Ralph Nader, who has been a critic of General Motors Corp. for many years, claims that when General Motors learned that Nader was about to publish a book entitled *Unsafe at Any Speed*, criticizing one of its automobiles, the company decided to conduct a campaign of intimidation against him. Specifically, Nader claims that GMC (a) conducted a series of interviews with Nader's acquaintances, questioning them about his political, social, racial, and religious views; (b) kept him under surveillance in public places for an unreasonable length of time including close observation of him in a bank; (c) caused him to be accosted by women for the purpose of entrapping him into illicit relationships; (d) made threatening, harassing, and obnoxious telephone calls to him; (e) tapped his telephone and eavesdropped by means of mechanical and electronic equipment on his private conversations with others; and (f) conducted a "continuing" and harassing investigation of him. Nader brought suit against GMC for invasion of privacy. Which, if any, of the alleged actions would constitute invasion of privacy?

16. Bill Kinsey was charged with murdering his wife while working for the Peace Corps in Tanzania. After waiting six months in jail, he was acquitted at a trial that attracted wide publicity. Five years later, while a graduate student at Stanford University, Kinsey had a brief affair with Mary Macur. He abruptly ended the affair by telling Macur he

would no longer be seeing her because another woman, Sally Allen, was coming from England to live with him. A few months later, Kinsey and Allen moved to Africa and were subsequently married. Soon after Bill ended their affair, Macur began a letter-writing campaign designed to expose Bill and his mistreatment of her. Macur sent several letters to both Bill and Sally Kinsey, their parents, their neighbors, their parents' neighbors, members of Bill's dissertation committee, other faculty, and the president of Stanford University. The letters contained statements accusing Bill of murdering his first wife, spending six months in jail for the crime, being a rapist, and other questionable behavior. The Kinseys brought an action for invasion of privacy, seeking damages and a permanent injunction. Will the Kinseys prevail? If so, for what tort?

17. Plaintiff, John W. Carson, was the host and star of *The Tonight Show*, a well-known television program broadcast by the National Broadcasting Company. Carson also appeared as an entertainer in nightclubs and theaters around the country. From the time he began hosting *The Tonight Show*, he had been introduced on the show each night with the phrase "Here's Johnny." The phrase "Here's Johnny" is still generally associated with Carson by a substantial segment of the television viewing public. To earn additional income, Carson began authorizing use of this phrase by outside business ventures.

Defendant, Here's Johnny Portable Toilets, Inc., is a Michigan corporation engaged in the business of renting and selling "Here's Johnny" portable toilets. Defendant's founder was aware at the time he formed the corporation that "Here's Johnny" was the introductory slogan for Carson on *The Tonight Show*. He indicated that he coupled the phrase with a second one, "The World's Foremost Commodian," to make "a good play on a phrase." Carson brought suit for invasion of privacy. Should Carson recover? If so, for which tort?

18. Lemmie L. Ruffin, Jr., was an Alabama licensed agent for Pacific Mutual Life Insurance and for Union Fidelity Life Insurance Company. Union wrote group health insurance policies for municipalities, while Pacific did not. Plaintiffs Cleopatra Haslip, Cynthia Craig, Alma M. Calhoun, and Eddie Hargrove were employees of Roosevelt City, Alabama. Ruffin gave the city a single proposal for health and life insurance for its employees, which the city approved. Both companies provided the coverage; however, Union provided the health insurance and Pacific provided the life insurance. This packaging of coverage by two different and unrelated insurers was not unusual. Union would send its billings for health premiums to Ruffin at Pacific Mutual's office. The city clerk each month issued a check for those premiums and sent it to Ruffin. Ruffin, however, did not remit to Union the premium payments he received from the city; instead, he misappropriated most of them. When Union did not receive payment from the city, it sent notices of lapsed health coverage to the plaintiffs, who did not know that their health policies had been canceled.

Plaintiff Haslip was subsequently hospitalized and because the hospital could not confirm her health coverage, it required her to make a partial payment on her bill. Her physician, when he was not paid, placed her account with a collection agency, which obtained against Haslip a judgment that damaged her credit. Plaintiffs sued Pacific Mutual and Ruffin for fraud. The case was submitted to a jury, which was instructed that if it found liability for fraud, it could award punitive damages. The jury returned verdicts for the plaintiffs and awarded Haslip $1,040,000, of which at least $840,000 was punitive damages. The Supreme Court of Alabama affirmed the trial court's judgment. Pacific Mutual appealed. Decision?

19. Susan Jungclaus Peterson was a twenty-one-year-old student at Moorhead State University who had lived most of her life on her family farm in Minnesota. Though Susan was a dean's list student her first year, her academic performance declined after she became deeply involved in an international religious cult organization known locally as The Way of Minnesota, Inc. The cult demanded an enormous psychological and monetary commitment from Susan. Near the end of her junior year, her parents became alarmed by the changes in Susan's physical and mental well-being and concluded that she had been "reduced to a condition of psychological bondage by The Way." They sought help from Kathy Mills, a self-styled "deprogrammer" of minds brainwashed by cults.

On May 24, Norman Jungclaus, Susan's father, picked up Susan at Moorhead State. Instead of returning home, they went to the residence of Veronica Morgel, where Kathy Mills attempted to deprogram Susan. For the first few days of her stay, Susan was unwilling to discuss her involvement. She lay curled in a fetal position in her bedroom, plugging her ears and hysterically screaming and crying while her father pleaded with her to listen. By the third day, however, Susan's demeanor changed completely. She became friendly and vivacious and communicated with her father. Susan also went roller skating and played softball at a nearby park over the following weekend. She spent the next week in Columbus, Ohio, with a former cult member who had shared her experiences of the previous week. While in Columbus, she spoke daily by telephone with her fiancé, a member of The Way, who begged her to return to the cult. Susan expressed the desire to get her fiancé out of the organization, but a meeting between them could not be arranged outside the presence of other members of The Way. Her parents attempted to persuade Susan to sign an agreement releasing them from liability for their actions, but Susan refused. After nearly sixteen days of "deprogramming" Susan left the Morgel residence and returned to her fiancé and The Way. Upon the direction of The Way ministry, she brought an action against her parents for false imprisonment. Will Susan prevail? Explain.

20. Debra Agis was a waitress in a restaurant owned by the Howard Johnson Company. On May 23, Roger Dionne, manager of the restaurant, called a meeting of all waitresses at which he informed them "there was some stealing going on." Dionne also stated that the identity of the party or parties responsible was not known and that he would begin firing all waitresses in alphabetical order until the guilty party or parties were detected. He then fired Debra Agis, who allegedly "became greatly upset, began to cry, sustained emotional distress, mental anguish, and loss of wages and earnings." Mrs. Agis brought this complaint against the Howard Johnson Company and Roger Dionne, alleging that the defendants acted recklessly and outrageously, intending to cause emotional distress and anguish. The defendants argued that damages for emotional distress are not recoverable unless physical injury occurs as a result of the distress. Will Agis be successful on her complaint?

TAKING SIDES

Edith Mitchell, accompanied by her thirteen-year-old daughter, went through the checkout at Walmart and purchased several items. As they exited, the Mitchells passed through an electronic antitheft device, which sounded an alarm. Robert Canady, employed by Walmart as a "people greeter" and security guard, forcibly stopped Edith Mitchell at the exit, grabbed her bag, and told her to step back inside. The security guard never touched Edith or her daughter and never threatened to touch either of them. Nevertheless, Edith Mitchell described the security guard's actions in her affidavit as "gruff, loud, rude behavior." The security guard removed every item Mitchell had just purchased and ran it through the security gate. One of the items still had a security code unit on it, which an employee admitted could have been overlooked by the cashier. When the security guard finished examining the contents of Mitchell's bag, he put it on the checkout counter. This examination of her bag took ten or fifteen minutes. Once her bag had been checked, no employee of Walmart ever told Mitchell she could not leave. Mitchell was never threatened with arrest. Mitchell brought a tort action against Walmart.

a. Explain on which torts should Mitchell base her claim against Walmart?

b. What arguments would support Walmart denial of liability for these torts?

c. Which party should prevail? Explain.

Chapter 8

NEGLIGENCE AND STRICT LIABILITY

Nothing is so easy as to be wise after the event.

B. BRANWELL (1859)

CHAPTER OUTCOMES

After reading and studying this chapter, you should be able to:

1. List and describe the three required elements of an action for negligence.

2. Explain the duty of care that is imposed on (a) adults, (b) children, (c) persons with a physical disability, (d) persons with a mental deficiency, (e) persons with superior knowledge, and (f) persons acting in an emergency.

3. Differentiate among the duties that possessors of land owe to trespassers, licensees, and invitees.

4. Identify the defenses that are available to a tort action in negligence and those that are available to a tort action in strict liability.

5. Identify and describe those activities giving rise to a tort action in strict liability.

Whereas intentional torts deal with conduct that has a substantial certainty of causing harm, negligence involves conduct that creates an unreasonable risk of harm. The basis of liability for negligence is the failure to exercise reasonable care under the circumstances for the safety of another person or his property, which failure proximately causes injury to such person or damage to his property, or both. Thus, if the driver of an automobile intentionally runs down a person, she has committed the intentional tort of battery. If, on the other hand, the driver hits and injures a person while driving with no reasonable regard for the safety of others, she is negligent.

Strict liability is not based on the negligence or intent of the defendant but rather on the nature of the activity in which he is engaging. Under this doctrine, defendants who engage in certain activities, such as keeping animals or carrying on abnormally dangerous conditions, are held liable for injuries they cause, even if they have exercised the utmost care. The law imposes this liability to bring about a just reallocation of loss, given that the defendant engaged in the activity for his own benefit and probably is better prepared than the plaintiff is to manage the risk inherent in the activity through insurance or otherwise.

As mentioned in Chapter 7, the American Law Institute (ALI) has published the Restatement Third, Torts: Liability for Physical and Emotional Harm (the "Third Restatement"). This new Restatement addresses the general or basic elements of the tort action for liability for accidental personal injury, property damage, and emotional harm, but does not cover liability for economic loss. "Physical harm" is defined as bodily harm (physical injury, illness, disease, and death) or property damage (physical impairment of real property or tangible personal property). The Third Restatement replaces comparable provisions in the Restatement Second, Torts. However, the Third Restatement does not cover the following matters, which remain governed by the Second Restatement: protection of reputation or privacy, economic loss, or domestic relations; determination of the recoverable damages and their amount; and the standards for liability of professionals for malpractice. Otherwise, this chapter reflects the Third Restatement's provisions.

The ALI's Restatement Third, Torts: Economic Torts and Related Wrongs will update coverage on torts that involve economic loss or pecuniary harm *not* resulting from physical harm or physical contact to a person or property. This project will update coverage of economic torts in Restatement Second, Torts and address some topics not covered in prior Restatements. The ALI began this project in 2004, and after several years of inactivity, the project was resumed in 2010. In 2012, a portion of Chapter 1 of the Tentative Draft was approved.

Negligence

A person acts negligently if the person does not exercise reasonable care under all the circumstances. Moreover, the general rule is that a person is under a duty to all others at all times to exercise reasonable care for the safety of other persons and their property.

As the comments to the Third Restatement explain, an action for **negligence** consists of five elements, each of which the plaintiff must prove:

1. **Duty of care:** that a legal duty required the defendant to conform to the standard of conduct established for the protection of others;

2. **Breach of duty:** that the defendant failed to exercise reasonable care;

3. **Factual cause:** that the defendant's failure to exercise reasonable care in fact caused the harm the plaintiff sustained;

4. **Harm:** that the harm sustained is of a type protected against negligent conduct; and

5. **Scope of liability:** that the harm sustained is within the "scope of liability," which historically has been referred to as "proximate cause."

We will discuss the first two elements in the next section, "Breach of Duty of Care"; we will cover the last three elements in subsequent sections.

Breach of Duty of Care

Negligence consists of conduct that creates an unreasonable risk of harm. In determining whether a given risk of harm was unreasonable, the following factors are considered: (1) the foreseeable probability that the person's conduct will result in harm, (2) the foreseeable gravity or severity of any harm that may follow, and (3) the burden of taking precautions to eliminate or reduce the risk of harm. Thus, the standard of conduct, which is the basis for the law of negligence, is usually determined by a cost-benefit or risk-benefit analysis.

Reasonable Person Standard

The duty of care imposed by law is measured by the degree of carefulness that a reasonable person would exercise in a given situation. The **reasonable person** is a fictitious individual who is always careful and prudent and never negligent. What the judge or jury determines a reasonable person would have done in light of the facts revealed by the evidence in a particular case sets the standard of conduct for that case. The reasonable person standard is thus *external* and *objective*.

Children   A child is a person below the age of majority, which in almost all states has been lowered from twenty-one to eighteen. The standard of conduct to which a child must conform to avoid being negligent is that of a reasonably careful person of the same age, intelligence, and experience under all the circumstances. The law applies a test that acknowledges these three factors, because children do not have the judgment, intelligence, knowledge, and experience of adults. Moreover, children as a general rule do not engage in activities entailing high risk to others, and their conduct normally does not involve a potential for harm as great as that of adult conduct. A child who engages in a dangerous activity that is characteristically undertaken by adults, however, such as flying an airplane or driving a boat or car, is held in almost all states to the standard of care applicable to adults.

Physical Disability If a person is ill or otherwise physically disabled, the standard of conduct to which he or she must conform to avoid being negligent is that of a reasonably careful person with the same disability. Thus, a blind person must act as a reasonable person who is blind. However, the conduct of a person during a period of sudden incapacitation or loss of consciousness resulting from physical illness is negligent only if the sudden incapacitation or loss of consciousness was reasonably foreseeable to the actor. Examples of sudden incapacitation include heart attack, stroke, epileptic seizure, and diabetes.

Mental Disability A person's mental or emotional disability is not considered in determining whether conduct is negligent unless the person is a child. The defendant is held to the standard of conduct of a reasonable person who is not mentally or emotionally disabled, even though the defendant is, in fact, incapable of conforming to the standard. When a person's intoxication is voluntary, it is not considered as an excuse for conduct that is otherwise lacking in reasonable care.

Superior Skill or Knowledge If a person has skills or knowledge beyond those possessed by most others, these skills or knowledge are circumstances to be taken into account in determining whether the person has acted with reasonable care. Thus, persons who are qualified and who practice a profession or trade that requires special skill and expertise are required to use the same care and skill that members of their profession or trade normally possess. This standard applies to such professionals as physicians, dentists, attorneys, pharmacists, architects, accountants, and engineers and to those who perform a skilled trade such as an airline pilot, electrician, carpenter, and plumber. If a member of a profession or skilled trade possesses greater skill than that common to the profession or trade, she is required to exercise that greater degree of skill.

Emergencies An **emergency** is a sudden and unexpected event that calls for immediate action and permits no time for deliberation. In determining whether a defendant's conduct was reasonable, the fact that he was at the time confronted with a sudden and unexpected emergency is taken into consideration. The standard is still that of a reasonable person under the circumstances—the emergency is simply part of the circumstances. If, however, the defendant's own negligent or tortious conduct created the emergency, he is liable for the consequences of this conduct even if he acted reasonably in the resulting emergency situation. Moreover, failure to anticipate an emergency may itself constitute negligence.

Violation of Statute The reasonable person standard of conduct may be established by legislation or administrative regulation. Some statutes do so by expressly imposing civil liability on violators. In cases in which a statute does not expressly provide for civil liability, courts may adopt the requirements of the statute as the standard of conduct if the statute is designed to protect against the type of accident the defendant's conduct causes and the accident victim is within the class of persons the statute is designed to protect.

If the statute is found to apply, the great majority of the courts hold that an unexcused violation is **negligence** *per se*; that is, the violation conclusively shows negligent conduct (breach of duty of care). In a minority of states, the violation is considered merely to be evidence of negligence. In either event, the plaintiff must also prove legal causation and injury.

For example, a statute enacted to protect employees from injuries requires that all factory elevators be equipped with specified safety devices. Arthur, an employee in Leonard's factory, and Marian, a business visitor to the factory, are injured when the elevator fails because the safety devices have not been installed. The court may adopt the statute as a standard of conduct as to Arthur, and hold Leonard negligent *per se* as to Arthur, but not as to Marian, because Arthur, not Marian, is within the class of persons the statute is intended to protect. Marian would have to establish that a reasonable person in the position of Leonard under the circumstances would have installed the safety device. (See Figure 8-1 illustrating negligence and negligence *per se*.)

On the other hand, compliance with a legislative enactment or administrative regulation does not prevent a finding of negligence if a reasonable person would have taken additional precautions. For instance, driving at the speed limit may not constitute due care when traffic or road conditions require a lower speed. Legislative or administrative rules normally establish *minimum* standards.

PRACTICAL ADVICE
Assess the potential liability for negligence arising from your activities and obtain adequate liability insurance to cover your exposure.

Figure 8-1
*Negligence and
Negligence* per se

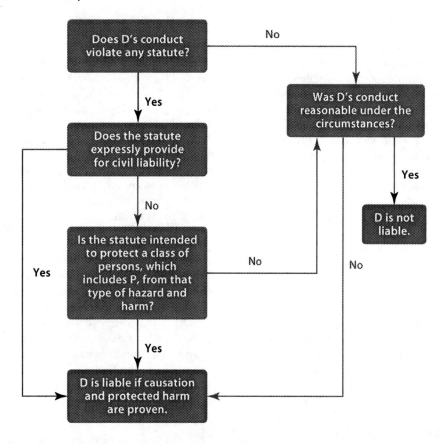

© Cengage Learning 2014

RYAN V. FRIESENHAHN

COURT OF APPEALS OF TEXAS, 1995
911 S.W.2D 113, AFF'D, 41 TEX. SUP. J. 261, 960 S.W.2D 656 (1998)
http://scholar.google.com/scholar_case?case=5075518384525866053&q=911+S.W.2d+113&hl=en&as_sdt=2,34

FACTS Todd Friesenhahn, son of Nancy and Frederick Friesenhahn, held an "open invitation" party at his parents' home that encouraged guests to "bring your own bottle." Sabrina Ryan attended the party, became intoxicated, and was involved in a fatal accident after she left the party. Sandra and Stephen Ryan, Sabrina's parents, sued the Friesenhahns for negligence, alleging that the Friesenhahns were aware of the underage drinking at the party and of Sabrina's condition when she left the party. The trial court granted summary judgment for the Friesenhahns.

DECISION Judgment reversed.

OPINION Rickhoff, J.

NEGLIGENCE *PER SE*
Accepting the petition's allegations as true, the Friesenhahns were aware that minors possessed and consumed alcohol on their property and specifically allowed Sabrina to become intoxicated. The Texas Alcoholic Beverage Code provides

that one commits an offense if, with criminal negligence, he "makes available an alcoholic beverage to a minor." [Citation.] The exception for serving alcohol to a minor applies only to the minor's adult parent. [Citation.]

An unexcused violation of a statute constitutes negligence *per se* if the injured party is a member of the class protected by the statute. [Citation.] The Alcoholic Beverage Code was designed to protect the general public and minors in particular and must be liberally construed. [Citation.] We conclude that Sabrina is a member of the class protected by the Code.

In viewing the Ryans' allegations in the light most favorable to them, we find that they stated a cause of action against the Friesenhahns for the violation of the Alcoholic Beverage Code.

COMMON LAW NEGLIGENCE
The elements of negligence include (1) a legal duty owed by one person to another; (2) breach of that duty; and

(3) damages proximately caused by the breach. [Citation.] To determine whether a common law duty exists, we must consider several factors, including risk, foreseeability, and likelihood of injury weighed against the social utility of the defendant's conduct, the magnitude of the burden of guarding against the injury and consequences of placing that burden on the defendant. [Citation.] We may also consider whether one party has superior knowledge of the risk, and whether one party has the right to control the actor whose conduct precipitated the harm. [Citation.]

As the Supreme Court in [citation] explained, there are two practical reasons for not imposing a third-party duty on social hosts who provide alcohol to adult guests: first, the host cannot reasonably know the extent of his guests' alcohol consumption level; second, the host cannot reasonably be expected to control his guests' conduct. [Citation.] The Tyler court in [citation] relied on these principles in holding that a minor "had no common law duty to avoid making alcohol available to an intoxicated guest [another minor] who he knew would be driving." [Citation.]

We disagree with the Tyler court because the rationale expressed [by the Supreme Court] in [citation] does not apply to the relationship between minors, or adults and minors. The adult social host need not estimate the extent of a minor's alcohol consumption because serving minors any amount of alcohol is a criminal offense. [Citation.] * * *

* * *

* * * [S]erving minors alcohol creates a risk of injury or death. Under the pled facts, a jury could find that the Friesenhahns, as the adult social hosts, allowed open invitations to a beer bust at their house and they could foresee, or reasonably should have foreseen, that the only means of arriving at their property would be by privately operated vehicles; once there, the most likely means of departure would be by the same means. That adults have superior knowledge of the risk of drinking should be apparent from the legislature's decision to allow persons to become adults on their eighteenth birthday for all purposes but the consumption of alcohol. [Citations.]

While one adult has no general duty to control the behavior of another adult, one would hope that adults would exercise special diligence in supervising minors—even during a simple swimming pool party involving potentially dangerous but legal activities. We may have no special duty to watch one adult to be sure he can swim, but it would be ill-advised to turn loose young children without insuring they can swim. When the "party" is for the purpose of engaging in dangerous and illicit activity, the consumption of alcohol by minors, adults certainly have a greater duty of care. [Citation.]

* * * In view of the legislature's determination that minors are not competent to understand the effects of alcohol, we find sufficient legislative intent to support our holding that, taken from the pleadings before us, a duty exists between the adult social host and the minor guest. Accordingly, we find that the Ryans' petition stated a common-law cause of action.

INTERPRETATION A violation of a statute constitutes negligence *per se* if the injured party is a member of the class protected by the statute.

ETHICAL QUESTION When should a parent be held liable for her child's negligence? Explain.

CRITICAL THINKING QUESTION Should a court extend social host liability for providing alcohol to an adult guest? Explain?

Duty to Act

As stated earlier, the general rule is that a person is under a duty to all others at all times to exercise reasonable care for the safety of the others' person and property. On the other hand, subject to several exceptions, a duty of care does not exist when the other's person or property is at risk for reasons other than the conduct of the person. This rule applies even though the person may be in a position to help another in peril. For example, Adolf, an adult standing at the edge of a steep cliff, observes a baby carriage with a crying infant in it slowly heading toward the edge and certain doom. Adolf could easily prevent the baby's fall at no risk to his own safety. Nonetheless, Adolf does nothing, and the baby falls to its death. Adolf is under no legal duty to act and therefore incurs no liability for failing to do so.

Nonetheless, special relations between the parties may impose an affirmative duty of reasonable care on the defendant to aid or protect the other with respect to risks that arise within the scope of the relationship. Thus, in the previous example, if Adolf were the baby's parent or babysitter, Adolf would be under a duty to act and therefore would be liable for not taking action. The special relations giving rise to an affirmative duty to aid or protect another include (1) a common carrier with its passengers, (2) an innkeeper with its guest, (3) an employer with its employees, (4) a school with its students, (5) a landlord with its tenants with respect to common areas under the landlord's control, (6) a business open to the public with its customers, and (7) custodian with those in its custody including parents with their children. The Third Restatement leaves it to the courts whether to recognize additional relationships as sufficient to impose an affirmative duty. Furthermore, state and federal statutes and administrative regulations as well as local ordinances may impose an affirmative duty to act for the protection of another.

In addition, when a person's prior conduct, even though not tortious, creates a continuing risk of physical harm, the person has a duty to exercise reasonable care to prevent or minimize the harm. For example, Alice innocently drives her car into Frank, rendering him unconscious. Alice leaves Frank lying in the middle of the road, where he is run over by a second car driven by Rebecca. Alice is liable to Frank for the additional injuries inflicted by Rebecca. Moreover, a person who begins a rescue by taking charge of another who is imperiled and unable to protect himself incurs a duty to exercise reasonable care under the circumstances. Furthermore, a person who discontinues aid or protection is under a duty of reasonable care not to leave the other in a worse position. For example, Ann finds Ben drunk and stumbling along a dark sidewalk. Ann leads Ben halfway up a steep and unguarded stairway, where she then abandons him. Ben attempts to climb the stairs but trips and falls, suffering serious injury. Ann is liable to Ben for having left him in a worse position. Most states have enacted Good Samaritan statutes to encourage voluntary emergency care. These statutes vary considerably, but they typically limit or disallow liability for some rescuers under specified circumstances.

There are special relationships in which one person has some degree of control over another person, including (1) a parent with dependent children, and (2) an employer with employees when the employment facilitates the employee's causing harm to third parties. The parent and the employer each owe a duty of reasonable care under the circumstances to third persons with regard to foreseeable risks that arise within the scope of the relationship. Depending on the circumstances, reasonable care may require controlling the activities of the other person or merely providing a warning. Generally, the duty of parents is limited to dependent children; thus when children reach majority or are no longer dependent, parents no longer have control and the duty of reasonable care ceases. The duty of employers includes the duty to exercise reasonable care in the hiring, training, supervision, and retention of employees. This duty of employers is independent of the vicarious liability of an employer for an employee's tortious conduct during the course of employment, and extends to conduct by the employee that occurs both inside and outside the scope of employment so long as the employment facilitates the employee causing harm to third parties. The Third Restatement provides the following example of an employer's duty:

> Don is employed by Welch Repair Service, which knows that Don had several episodes of assault in his previous employment. Don goes to Traci's residence, where he had previously been dispatched by Welch, and misrepresents to Traci that he is there on Welch business to check repairs that had previously been made in Traci's home. After Traci admits Don, he assaults Traci. Welch is subject to a duty under this subsection with regard to Don's assault on Traci.

SOLDANO V. O'DANIELS

CALIFORNIA COURT OF APPEALS, FIFTH DISTRICT, 1983
141 CAL.APP.3D 443, 190 CAL.RPTR. 310
http://scholar.google.com/scholar_case?case=6364984666656533477&q=190+Cal.Rptr.+310&hl=en&as_sdt=2,34

FACTS On August 9, the plaintiff's father, Darrell Soldano, was shot and killed at the Happy Jack Saloon. The defendant owns and operates the Circle Inn, an eating establishment across the street from the Happy Jack Saloon. On the night of the shooting, a patron of the Happy Jack Saloon came into the Circle Inn and informed the Circle Inn bartender that a man had been threatened at Happy Jack's. The patron requested that the Circle Inn bartender either call the police or allow the patron to use the Circle Inn phone to call the police. The bartender refused either to make the call or to allow the Happy Jack patron to use the phone. The plaintiff alleges that the actions of the Circle Inn employee were a breach of the legal duty that the Circle Inn owed to the decedent. The defendant maintains that there was no legal obligation to take any action, and therefore there was no duty owed to the decedent. The trial court dismissed the case on the defendant's motion for summary judgment.

DECISION The appellate court reversed and remanded the case for trial.

OPINION Andreen, J. There is a distinction, well rooted in the common law, between action and nonaction. [Citation.] It has found its way into the prestigious Restatement Second of Torts (hereafter cited as "Restatement"), which provides in section 314: "The fact that the actor realizes or should realize that action on his part is necessary for another's aid or protection does nor of itself impose upon him a duty to take such action." * * *

***

As noted in [citation], the courts have increased the instances in which affirmative duties are imposed not by direct rejection of the common law rule, but by expanding the list of special relationships which will justify departure from that rule.

***

Section 314A of the Restatement lists other special relationships which create a duty to render aid, such as that of a common carrier to its passengers, an innkeeper to his guest, possessors of land who hold it open to the public, or one who has a custodial relationship to another. A duty may be created by an undertaking to give assistance. [Citation.]

Here there was no special relationship between the defendant and the deceased. It would be stretching the concept beyond recognition to assert there was a relationship between the defendant and the patron from Happy Jack's Saloon who wished to summon aid. But this does not end the matter.

It is time to re-examine the common law rule of nonliability for nonfeasance in the special circumstances of the instant case.

***

We turn now to the concept of duty in a tort case. The [California] Supreme Court has identified certain factors to be considered in determining whether a duty is owed to third persons. These factors include:

the foreseeability of harm to the plaintiff, the degree of certainty that the plaintiff suffered injury, the closeness of the connection between the defendant's conduct and the injury suffered, the moral blame attached to the defendant's conduct, the policy of preventing future harm, the extent of the burden to the defendant and consequences to the community of imposing a duty to exercise care with resulting liability for breach, and the availability, cost, and prevalence of insurance for the risk involved. [Citation.]

We examine those factors in reference to this case. (1) The harm to the decedent was abundantly foreseeable; it was imminent. The employee was expressly told that a man had been threatened. The employee was a bartender. As such he knew it is foreseeable that some people who drink alcohol in the milieu of a bar setting are prone to violence. (2) The certainty of decedent's injury is undisputed. (3) There is arguably a close connection between the employee's conduct and the injury: the patron wanted to use the phone to summon the police to intervene. The employee's refusal to allow the use of the phone prevented this anticipated intervention. If permitted to go to trial, the plaintiff may be able to show that the probable response time of the police would have been shorter than the time between the prohibited telephone call and the fatal shot. (4) The employee's conduct displayed a disregard for human life that can be characterized as morally wrong: he was callously indifferent to the possibility that Darrell Soldano would die as the result of his refusal to allow a person to use the telephone. Under the circumstances before us the bartender's burden was minimal and exposed him to no risk: all he had to do was allow the use of the telephone. It would have cost him or his employer nothing. It could have saved a life. (5) Finding a duty in these circumstances would promote a policy of preventing future harm. A citizen would not be required to summon the police but would be required, in circumstances such as those before us, not to impede another who has chosen to summon aid. (6) We have no information on the question of the availability, cost, and prevalence of insurance for the risk, but note that the liability which is sought to be imposed here is that of employee negligence, which is covered by many insurance policies. (7) The extent of the burden on the defendant was minimal, as noted.

***

We acknowledge that defendant contracted for the use of his telephone, and its use is a species of property. But if it exists in a public place as defined above, there is no privacy or ownership interest in it such that the owner should be permitted to interfere with a good faith attempt to use it by a third person to come to the aid of another.

***

We conclude that the bartender owed a duty to the plaintiff's decedent to permit the patron from Happy Jack's to place a call to the police or to place the call himself.

It bears emphasizing that the duty in this case does not require that one must go to the aid of another. That is not the issue here. The employee was not the good samaritan intent on aiding another. The patron was.

INTERPRETATION Although a person may not have a duty to help another, in a case such as this, a person has a duty not to hinder others who are trying to help.

CRITICAL THINKING QUESTION Should the courts go beyond the rule of this case and impose an affirmative duty to go to the aid of another person who is in peril if it can be done without endangerment? Explain.

DUTIES OF POSSESSORS OF LAND

The right of possessors of land to use that land for their own benefit and enjoyment is limited by their duty to do so in a reasonable manner. By the use of their land, possessors of land cannot cause unreasonable risks of harm to others. Liability for breach of this obligation may arise from conduct in any of the three areas of torts discussed in this and the preceding chapter: intentional harm, negligence, or strict liability. Most of these cases fall within the classification of negligence.

In conducting activities on her land, the possessor of land is required to exercise reasonable care to protect others who are not on her property. For example, a property owner who constructs a factory on her premises must take reasonable care that it is not unreasonably dangerous to people off the site. Moreover, a business or other possessor of land that holds its premises open to the public owes those who are lawfully on the premises a duty of reasonable care with regard to risks that arise within the scope of the relationship.

In most states and under the Second Restatement, the duty of a possessor of land to persons who come on the land usually depends on whether those persons are trespassers, licensees, or invitees. In about fifteen states, however, licensees and invitees are owed the same duty. In addition, at least nine states have abandoned these distinctions and simply apply ordinary negligence principles of foreseeable risk and reasonable care to all entrants on the land including trespassers. The Third Restatement has adopted this last—the unitary—approach.

Second Restatement In accordance with the historical—and still majority—approach to the duties of possessors of land, the Second Restatement provides for varying duties depending on the status of the entrant on the land.

A **trespasser** is a person who enters or remains on the land of another without the possessor's consent or a legal privilege to do so. The possessor of the land is *not* liable to adult trespassers for his failure to maintain the land in a reasonably safe condition. Nonetheless, the possessor is not free to inflict intentional injury on a trespasser. Moreover, most courts hold that upon discovery of the presence of trespassers on the land, the lawful possessor is required to exercise reasonable care for their safety in carrying on her activities and to warn the trespassers of potentially dangerous conditions that the trespassers are not likely to discover.

A **licensee** is a person who is privileged to enter or remain on land only by virtue of the lawful possessor's consent. Licensees include members of the possessor's household, social guests, and salespersons calling at private homes. A licensee will become a trespasser, however, if he enters a portion of the land to which he is not invited or remains on the land after his invitation has expired. The possessor owes a higher duty of care to licensees than to trespassers. The possessor must warn the licensee of dangerous activities and conditions (1) of which the possessor has knowledge or reason to know and (2) the licensee does not and is not likely to discover.

If he is not warned, the licensee may recover if the activity or dangerous condition resulted from the possessor's failure to exercise reasonable care to protect him from the danger. To illustrate: Henry invites a friend, Anne, to his place in the country at 8:00 P.M. on a winter evening. Henry knows that a bridge in his driveway is in a dangerous condition that is not noticeable in the dark. Henry does not inform Anne of this fact. The bridge gives way under Anne's car, causing serious harm to Anne. Henry is liable to Anne.

An **invitee** is a person invited upon land as a member of the public or for a business purpose. A *public invitee* is a person who is invited to enter or remain on land as a member of the public for a purpose for which the land is held open to the public. Such invitees include those who use public parks, beaches, or swimming pools, as well as those who use government facilities, such as a post office or an office of the recorder of deeds, where business with the public is transacted openly. A *business visitor* is a person invited to enter or remain on premises for a purpose directly or indirectly concerning business dealings with the possessor of the land, such as one who enters a store or a worker who enters a residence to make repairs. With respect to the condition of the premises, the possessor of land is under a duty to exercise reasonable care to protect invitees against dangerous conditions they are unlikely to discover. This liability extends not only to those conditions of which the possessor actually knows but also to those of which she would discover by the exercise of reasonable care. For example, David's store has a large glass front door that is well lighted and plainly visible. Maxine, a customer, mistakes the glass for an open doorway and walks into the glass, injuring herself. David is not liable to Maxine. If, on the other hand, the glass was difficult to see and a person foreseeably might have mistaken the glass for an open doorway, then David would be liable to Maxine if Maxine crashed into the glass while exercising reasonable care.

Third Restatement The status-based duty rules just discussed have been rejected by the Third Restatement, which adopts a unitary duty of reasonable care to entrants on the land.

[Except for "flagrant trespassers,"] a land possessor owes a duty of reasonable care to entrants on the land with regard to:

1. conduct by the land possessor that creates risks to entrants on the land;

2. artificial conditions on the land that pose risks to entrants on the land;

3. natural conditions on the land that pose risks to entrants on the land; …

This rule is similar to the duty land possessors owed to invitees under the Second Restatement except that it extends the duty to all who enter the land, including trespassers, with the exception of "flagrant trespassers." This rule requires a land possessor to use reasonable care to investigate and discover dangerous conditions and to use reasonable care to eliminate or improve those dangerous conditions that are known or should have been discovered by the exercise of reasonable care. However, some risks cannot reasonably be discovered, and the land possessor is not subject to liability for those risks. In addition, a land possessor is not liable to an ordinary trespasser whose unforeseeable presence results in an unforeseeable risk.

A different rule applies to "flagrant trespassers." The Third Restatement requires that a land possessor only (1) refrain from intentional, willful, or wanton conduct that harms a flagrant trespasser and (2) exercise reasonable care on behalf of flagrant trespassers who are imperiled and helpless. The Third Restatement does not define "flagrant trespassers" but instead leaves it to each jurisdiction to determine at what point an ordinary trespasser becomes a "flagrant trespasser." The comments to the Third Restatement explain:

The idea behind distinguishing particularly egregious trespassers for different treatment is that their presence on another's land is so antithetical to the rights of the land possessor to exclusive use and possession of the land that the land possessor should not be subject to liability for failing to exercise the ordinary duty of reasonable care otherwise owed to them as entrants on the land. It stems from the idea that when a trespass is sufficiently offensive to the property rights of the land possessor it is unfair to subject the possessor to liability for mere negligence.

The Third Restatement provides an illustration of a flagrant trespasser: "Herman engaged in a late-night burglary of the Jacob liquor store after it had closed. While leaving the store after taking cash from the store's register, Herman slipped on a slick spot on the floor, fell, and broke his arm. Herman is a flagrant trespasser...."

PRACTICAL ADVICE

Take care to inspect your premises regularly to detect any dangerous conditions and either remedy the danger or post prominent warnings of any dangerous conditions you discover.

LOVE V. HARDEE'S FOOD SYSTEMS, INC.

COURT OF APPEALS OF MISSOURI, EASTERN DISTRICT, DIVISION TWO, 2000
16 S.W.3D 739
http://scholar.google.com/scholar_case?case=12304910341505965816&hl=en&as_sdt=2&as_=1&oi=scholarr

FACTS At about 3:15 P.M. on November 15, 1995, plaintiff, Jason Love, and his mother, Billye Ann Love, went to the Hardee's Restaurant in Arnold, Missouri, owned by defendant, Hardee's Food Systems, Inc. There were no other customers in the restaurant between 3:00 P.M. and 4:00 P.M., but two or three workmen were in the back doing construction. The workmen reported that they did not use the restroom and did not see anyone use the restroom. When Jason went to use the restroom, he slipped on water on the restroom floor. He fell backwards, hit his head, and felt a shooting pain down his right leg. He found himself lying in an area of dirty water, which soaked his clothes. There were no barricades, warning cones, or anything else that would either restrict access to the bathroom or warn of the danger.

Jason stated after the fall that his back and leg were "hurting pretty bad." His mother reported the fall. The supervisor filled out an accident report form, which reported that the accident occurred at 3:50 P.M. The supervisor testified that the water appeared to have come from someone shaking his hands after washing them. The

supervisor could not recall the last time the restroom had been checked. Jason was taken to a hospital emergency room. As a result of his injuries, he underwent two back surgeries, missed substantial time from work, and suffered from continuing pain and limitations on his physical activities.

Hardee's had a policy requiring that the restroom be checked and cleaned every hour by a maintenance person, who was scheduled to work until 3:00 P.M., but normally left at 1:00 P.M. The supervisor could not recall whether the maintenance person left at 1:00 P.M. or 3:00 P.M. on November 15, and the defendant was unable to produce the time clock report for that day.

It was also a store policy that whenever employees cleaned the tables, they would check the restroom. If an employee had to use the restroom, then that employee was also supposed to check the restroom. The restaurant supervisor did not ask if any employees had been in the restroom, or if they had checked it in the hour prior to the accident, and did not know if the restroom was actually inspected or cleaned at 3:00 P.M. The restaurant had shift inspection checklists on which the manager would report on the cleanliness of the restrooms and whether the floors were clean and dry. However, the checklists for November 15 were thrown away.

Jason Love filed a lawsuit against Hardee's Food Systems, Inc. to recover damages for negligence. The jury returned a verdict in the plaintiff's favor in the amount of $125,000.

DECISION The judgment of the trial court is affirmed.

OPINION Crane, J. In order to have made a submissible case, plaintiff had to show that defendant knew or, by using ordinary care, could have known of the dangerous condition and failed to use ordinary care to remove it, barricade it, or warn of it, and plaintiff sustained damage as a direct result of such failure. [Citation.]

"In order to establish constructive notice, the condition must have existed for a sufficient length of time or the facts must be such that the defendant should have reasonably known of its presence." [Citation.] [Prior] cases *** placed great emphasis on the length of time the dangerous condition had been present and held that times of 20 or 30 minutes, absent proof of other circumstances, were insufficient to establish constructive notice as a matter of law. [Citations.]

                              ***

Defendant's liability is predicated on the foreseeability of the risk and the reasonableness of the care taken, which is a question of fact to be determined by the totality of the circumstances, including the nature of the restaurant's business and the method of its operation. [Citations.]

In this case the accident took place in the restaurant's restroom which is provided for the use of employees and customers. The cause of the accident was water, which is provided in the restroom. The restaurant owner could reasonably foresee that anyone using the restroom, customers or employees, would use the tap water provided in the restroom and could spill, drop, or splash water on the floor. Accordingly, the restaurant owner was under a duty to use due care to guard against danger from water on the floor.

There was substantial evidence to support submissibility. *** [The water] was on the floor of the restroom and the supervisor testified it appeared that someone had shaken water from his hands on the floor.

Next, there was evidence from which the jury could infer that, if the water was caused by a non-employee, the water was on the floor for at least 50 minutes, or longer, because there was evidence that no other customers were in the store to use the restroom after 3:00 P.M. and the workmen on the site advised that they had not used the restroom.

In addition, plaintiff adduced evidence from which the jury could have found that defendants' employees had the opportunity to observe the hazard. The restroom was to be used by the employees and was supposed to be checked by them when they used it; employees cleaning tables were supposed to check the restroom when they cleaned the tables; and a maintenance man was supposed to check and clean the restroom every hour.

There was evidence from which the jury could have inferred that the maintenance man charged with cleaning the restroom every hour did not clean the restroom at 3:00 P.M. as scheduled on the day of the accident. There was testimony that the maintenance man usually left at 1:00 P.M. *** This could have created a span of 2 hours and 50 minutes during which there was no employee working at the restaurant whose primary responsibility was to clean the restroom. [Citation.]

There was also evidence from which the jury could have inferred that the restroom was not inspected by any employee who had the responsibility to inspect it during that same time period. The supervisor testified that he could not recall the last time the restroom had been checked and did not ask any employees if they had been in the restroom or had checked it in the hour before the accident. ***

INTERPRETATION The owner or possessor of property is liable to an invitee if the owner knew or, by using ordinary care, could have known of the dangerous condition and failed to use ordinary care to remove it, barricade it, or warn of it, and the invitee sustained damage as a direct result of such failure.

CRITICAL THINKING QUESTION Should customers be required to look for dangers?

RES IPSA LOQUITUR

A rule of circumstantial evidence has developed that permits the jury to infer both negligent conduct and causation from the mere occurrence of certain types of events. This rule, called *res ipsa loquitur*, meaning "the thing speaks for itself," applies when the accident causing the plaintiff's physical harm is a type of accident that ordinarily happens as a result of the negligence of a class of actors of which the defendant is the relevant member. For example, Camille rents a room in Leo's motel. During the night, a large piece of plaster falls from the ceiling and injures Camille. In the absence of other evidence, the jury may infer that the harm resulted from Leo's negligence in permitting the plaster to become defective. Leo is permitted, however, to introduce evidence to contradict the inference of negligence.

Factual Cause

Liability for the negligent conduct of a defendant requires that the conduct in fact caused harm to the plaintiff. The Third Restatement states: "Tortious conduct must be a factual cause of physical harm for liability to be imposed." A widely applied test for causation in fact is the **but-for test:** A person's conduct is a cause of an event if the event would not have occurred but for the person's negligent conduct. That is, conduct is a factual cause of harm when the harm would not have occurred absent the conduct. For instance, Arnold fails to erect a barrier around an excavation. Doyle is driving a truck when its accelerator becomes stuck. Arnold's negligence is not a cause in fact of Doyle's death if the runaway truck would have crashed through the barrier even if it had been erected. Similarly, failure to install a proper fire escape to a hotel is not the cause in fact of the death of a person who is suffocated by the smoke while sleeping in bed during a hotel fire.

If the tortious conduct of Adam is *insufficient* by itself to cause Paula's harm, but when Adam's conduct is combined with the tortious conduct of Barry, the combined conduct is sufficient to cause Paula's harm, then Adam and Barry are each considered a factual cause of Paula's harm.

The but-for test, however, is not satisfied when there are two or more causes, each of which is *sufficient* to bring about the harm in question and each of which is active at the time harm occurs. For example, Wilson and Hart negligently set fires that combine to destroy Kennedy's property. Either fire would have destroyed the property. Under the but-for test, either Wilson or Hart, or both, could argue that the fire caused by the other would have destroyed the property and that he, therefore, is not liable. The Third Restatement addresses this problem of multiple *sufficient* causes by providing, "If multiple acts exist, each of which alone would have been a factual cause under [the but-for test] of the physical harm at the same time, each act is regarded as a factual cause of the harm." Under this rule the conduct of both Wilson and Hart would be found to be a factual cause of the destruction of Kennedy's property.

Scope of Liability (Proximate Cause)

As a matter of social policy, legal responsibility has not followed all the consequences of a negligent act. Tort law does not impose liability on a defendant for all harm factually caused by the defendant's negligent conduct. Liability has been limited—to a greater extent than with intentional torts—to those harms that result from the risks that made the defendant's conduct tortious. This "risk standard" limitation on liability also applies to strict liability cases. The Third Restatement provides the following example: Richard, a hunter, finishes his day in the field and stops at a friend's house while walking home. His friend's nine-year-old daughter, Kim, greets Richard, who hands his loaded shotgun to her as he enters the house. Kim drops the shotgun, which lands on her toe, breaking it. Although Richard was negligent for giving Kim his shotgun, the risk that made Richard negligent was that Kim might shoot someone with the gun, not that she would drop it and hurt herself (the gun was neither especially heavy nor unwieldy). Kim's broken toe is outside the scope of Richard's liability, even though Richard's tortious conduct was a factual cause of Kim's harm.

FORESEEABILITY

Determining the liability of a negligent defendant for unforeseeable consequences has proved to be troublesome and controversial. The Restatement and many courts have adopted the following position:

1. If the actor's conduct is a substantial factor in bringing about harm to another, the fact that the actor neither foresaw nor should have foreseen the extent of the harm or the manner in which it occurred does **not** prevent him from being liable.

2. The actor's conduct may be held not to be a legal cause of harm to another where, after the event and looking back from the harm to the actor's negligent conduct, it appears to the court highly extraordinary that it should have brought about the harm.

A comment to the Third Restatement explains that

the foreseeability test for proximate cause is essentially consistent with the standard set forth in this [Restatement]. Properly understood, both the risk standard and a foreseeability test exclude liability for harms that were sufficiently unforeseeable at the time of the actor's tortious conduct that they were not among the risks—potential harms—that made the actor negligent. Negligence limits the requirement of reasonable care to those risks that are foreseeable.

For example, Steven, while negligently driving an automobile, collides with a car carrying dynamite. Steven is unaware of the contents of the other car and has no reason to know about them. The collision causes the dynamite to explode, shattering glass in a building a block away. The shattered glass injures Doria, who is inside the building. The explosion also injures Walter, who is walking on the sidewalk near the collision. Steven would be liable to Walter because Steven should have realized that his negligent driving might result in a collision that would endanger pedestrians nearby. Doria's harm, however, was beyond the risks posed by Steven's negligent driving and he, accordingly, is not liable to Doria.

PALSGRAF V. LONG ISLAND RAILROAD CO.

COURT OF APPEALS OF NEW YORK, 1928
248 N.Y. 339, 162 N.E. 99

FACTS Palsgraf was on the railroad station platform buying a ticket when a train stopped at the station. As it began to depart, two men ran to catch it. After the first was safely aboard, the second jumped onto the moving car. When he started to fall, a guard on the train reached to grab him and another guard on the platform pushed the man from behind. They helped the man to regain his balance, but in the process they knocked a small package out of his arm. The package, which contained fireworks, fell onto the rails and exploded. The shock from the explosion knocked over a scale resting on the other end of the platform, and it landed on Mrs. Palsgraf. She then brought an action against the Long Island Railroad Company to recover for the injuries she sustained. The railroad appealed from the trial and appellate courts' decisions in favor of Palsgraf.

DECISION Judgment for Palsgraf reversed.

OPINION Cardozo, C. J. The conduct of the defendant's guard, if a wrong in its relation to the holder of the package, was not a wrong in its relation to the plaintiff, standing far away. Relatively to her it was not negligence at all. Nothing in the situation gave notice that the falling package had in it the potency of peril to persons thus removed. Negligence is not actionable unless it involves the invasion of a legally protected interest, the violation of a right. "Proof of negligence in the air, so to speak, will not do." [Citations.] "Negligence is the absence of care, according to the circumstances." [Citations.]

* * *

If no hazard was apparent to the eye of ordinary vigilance, an act innocent and harmless, at least to outward seeming, with reference to her, did not take to itself the quality of a tort because it happened to be wrong, though apparently not one involving the risk of bodily insecurity, with reference to some one else. "In every instance, before negligence can be predicated of a given act, back of the act must be sought and found a duty to the individual complaining, the observance of which would have averted or avoided the injury." [Citations.]

* * *

A different conclusion will involve us, and swiftly too, in a maze of contradictions. A guard stumbles over a package which has been left upon a platform. It seems to be a bundle of newspapers. It turns out to be a can of dynamite. To the eye of ordinary vigilance, the bundle is abandoned waste, which may be kicked or trod on with impunity. Is a passenger at the other end of the platform protected by the law against the unsuspected hazard concealed beneath the waste? If not, is the result to be any different, so far as the distant passenger is concerned, when the guard stumbles over a valise which a truckman or a porter has left upon the walk? The passenger far away, if the victim of a wrong at all, has a cause of action, not derivative, but original and primary. His claim to be protected against invasion of his bodily security is neither greater nor less because the act resulting in the invasion is a wrong to another far removed. In this case, the rights that are said to have been violated, the interests said to have been invaded, are not even of the same order. The man was not injured in his person nor even put in danger. The purpose of the act, as well as its effect, was to make his person safe. If there was wrong to him at all, which may very well be doubted, it was wrong to a property interest only, the safety of his package. Out of this wrong to property, which threatened injury to nothing else, there has passed, we are told, to the plaintiff by derivation or succession a right of action for the invasion of an interest of another order, the right to bodily security. The diversity of interests emphasizes the futility of the effort to build the plaintiff's right upon the basis of a wrong to some one else. * * * One who jostles one's neighbor in a crowd does not invade the rights of others standing at the outer fringe when the unintended contact casts a bomb upon the ground. The wrongdoer as to them is the man who carries the bomb, not the one who explodes it without suspicion of the danger.

INTERPRETATION Even if the defendant's negligent conduct in fact caused harm to the plaintiff, the defendant is not liable if the defendant could not have foreseen injuring the plaintiff or a class of persons to which the plaintiff belonged.

CRITICAL THINKING QUESTION Should a person be held liable for all injuries that her negligence in fact causes? Explain.

SUPERSEDING CAUSE

An intervening cause is an event or act that occurs after the defendant's negligent conduct and with that negligence causes the plaintiff's harm. If the intervening cause is deemed a **superseding cause**, it relieves the defendant of liability for that harm.

For example, Carol negligently leaves in a public sidewalk a substantial excavation without a fence or warning lights, into which Gary falls at night. Darkness is an intervening, but not a superseding, cause of harm to Gary because it is a normal consequence of the situation caused by Carol's negligence. Therefore, Carol is liable to Gary. In contrast, if Carol negligently leaves an excavation in a public sidewalk into which Barbara intentionally shoves Gary, under the Second Restatement as a matter of law Carol is not liable to Gary because Barbara's conduct is a superseding cause that relieves Carol of liability. The Third Restatement rejects this exception to liability, stating,

Whether Gary's harm is within the scope of Carol's liability for her negligence is an issue for the factfinder. The factfinder will have to determine whether the appropriate characterization of the harm to Gary is falling into an unguarded excavation site or being deliberately pushed into an unguarded excavation site and, if the latter, whether it is among the risks that made Carol negligent.

An intervening cause that is a foreseeable or normal consequence of the defendant's negligence is not a superseding cause. Thus, a person who negligently places another person or his property in imminent danger is liable for the injury sustained by a third-party rescuer who attempts to aid the imperiled person or his property. The same is true of attempts by the endangered person to escape the peril, as, for example, when a person swerves off the road to avoid a head-on collision with an automobile driven negligently on the wrong side of the road. It is commonly held that a negligent defendant is liable for the results of necessary medical treatment of the injured party, even if the treatment itself is negligent.

PETITION OF KINSMAN TRANSIT CO.

UNITED STATES COURT OF APPEALS, SECOND CIRCUIT, 1964
338 F.2D 708

http://scholar.google.com/scholar_case?case=7870539560920231106&q=338+F.2d+708&hl=en&as_sdt=2,34

FACTS The *MacGilvray Shiras* was a ship owned by the Kinsman Transit Company. During the winter months when Lake Erie was frozen, the ship and others moored at docks on the Buffalo River. As oftentimes happened, one night an ice jam disintegrated upstream, sending large chunks of ice downstream. Chunks of ice began to pile up against the *Shiras*, which at that time was without power and manned only by a shipman. The ship broke loose when a negligently constructed "deadman" to which one mooring cable was attached pulled out of the ground. The "deadman" was operated by Continental Grain Company. The ship began moving down the S-shaped river stern first and struck another ship, the *Tewksbury*. The *Tewksbury* also broke loose from its mooring, and the two ships floated down the river together. Although the crew manning the Michigan Avenue

Bridge downstream had been notified of the runaway ships, they failed to raise the bridge in time to avoid a collision because of a mix-up in the shift changeover. As a result, both ships crashed into the bridge and were wedged against the bank of the river. The two vessels substantially dammed the flow of the river, causing ice and water to back up and flood installations as far as three miles upstream. The injured parties brought this action for damages against Kinsman, Continental, and the city of Buffalo. The trial court found the three defendants liable, and they appealed from that decree.

DECISION Decree of trial court affirmed as to liability.

OPINION Friendly, J. The very statement of the case suggests the need for considering *Palsgraf v. Long Island*

RR., [citation], and the closely related problem of liability for unforeseeable consequences.

* * *

We see little similarity between the *Palsgraf* case and the situation before us. The point of *Palsgraf* was that the appearance of the newspaper-wrapped package gave no notice that its dislodgement could do any harm save to itself and those nearby, and this impact, perhaps with consequent breakage, and not by explosion. In contrast, a ship insecurely moored in a fast flowing river is a known danger not only to herself but to the owners of all other ships and structures down river, and to persons upon them. No one would dream of saying that a shipowner who "knowingly and wilfully" failed to secure his ship at a pier on such a river "would not have threatened" persons and owners of property down-stream in some manner. The shipowner and the wharfinger in this case having thus owed a duty of care to all within the reach of the ship's known destructive power, the impossibility of advance identification of the particular person who would be hurt is without legal consequence. [Citations.] Similarly the foreseeable consequences of the City's failure to raise the bridge were not limited to the *Shiras* and the *Tewksbury*. Collision plainly created a danger that the bridge towers might fall onto adjoining property, and the crash of two uncontrolled lake vessels, one 425 feet and the other 525 feet long, into a bridge over a swift ice-ridden stream, with a channel only 177 feet wide, could well result in a partial damming that would flood property upstream.

* * *

All the claimants here met the *Palsgraf* requirement of being persons to whom the actors owed a "duty of care," * * *. But this does not dispose of the alternative argument that the manner in which several of the claimants were harmed, particularly by flood damage, was unforeseeable

and that recovery for this may not be had—whether the argument is put in the forthright form that unforeseeable damages are not recoverable or is concealed under a formula of lack of "proximate cause."

* * *

Foreseeability of danger is necessary to render conduct negligent; where as here the damage was caused by just those forces whose existence required the exercise of greater care than what was taken—the current, the ice, and the physical mass of the *Shiras*, the incurring of consequences other and greater than foreseen does not make the conduct less culpable or provide a reasoned basis for insulation. [Citation.] The oft encountered argument that failure to limit liability to foreseeable consequences may subject the defendant to a loss wholly out of proportion to his fault seems scarcely consistent with the universally accepted rule that the defendant takes the plaintiff as he finds him and will be responsible for the full extent of the injury even though a latent susceptibility of the plaintiff renders this far more serious than could reasonably have been anticipated. [Citation.]

The weight of authority in this country rejects the limitation of damages to consequences foreseeable at the time of the negligent conduct when the consequences are "direct," and the damage, although other and greater than expectable, is of the same general sort that was risked.

INTERPRETATION The unforeseeability of the exact manner and extent of a loss will not limit liability where the persons injured and the general nature of the damage were foreseeable.

CRITICAL THINKING QUESTION Compare this decision with that in the *Palsgraf* case and attempt to reconcile the two decisions.

Harm

The plaintiff must *prove* that the defendant's negligent conduct proximately caused **harm to a legally protected interest.** Certain interests receive little or no protection against such conduct, while others receive full protection. The courts determine the extent of protection for a particular interest as a matter of law on the basis of social policy and expediency. For example, negligent conduct that is the proximate cause of harmful contact with the person of another is actionable. Thus, if Bob while driving his car negligently runs into Julie, a pedestrian, who is carefully crossing the street,

Bob is liable for physical injuries Julie sustains as a result of the collision. On the other hand, if Bob's careless driving causes the car's side view mirror to brush Julie's coat but results in no physical injuries to her or damage to the coat, thus causing only offensive contact with Julie's person, Bob is not liable because Julie did not sustain harm to a legally protected interest.

The courts traditionally have been reluctant to allow recovery for negligently inflicted emotional distress. This view has gradually changed, and the majority of courts now hold a person liable for negligently causing emotional distress if bodily harm—such as a heart attack—results from the distress. And though, in the majority of states, a defendant is not liable for conduct resulting solely in emotional disturbance, some courts have recently allowed recovery of damages for negligently inflicted emotional distress even in the absence of physical harm when a person's negligent conduct places another in immediate danger of bodily harm. The Third Restatement follows the minority approach: a person whose negligent conduct places another in immediate danger of bodily harm is subject to liability to the other for serious emotional disturbance caused by reaction to the danger even though the negligent conduct did not cause any impact or bodily harm to the other. Furthermore, in a majority of states and under the Third Restatement liability for negligently inflicted emotional distress arises in the following situation: A negligently causes serious bodily injury to B. If C is a close family member of B and witnesses the injury to B, then A is liable to C for serious emotional disturbance C suffers from witnessing the event.

Defenses to Negligence

Although a plaintiff has established by a preponderance of the evidence all the required elements of a negligence action, he may nevertheless fail to recover damages if the defendant proves a valid defense. As a general rule, any defense to an intentional tort is also available in an action in negligence. In addition, certain defenses are available in negligence cases that are not defenses to intentional torts. These are contributory negligence, comparative negligence, and assumption of risk. (See Figure 8-2 illustrating the defenses to a negligence action.)

Figure 8-2
Defenses to a Negligence Action

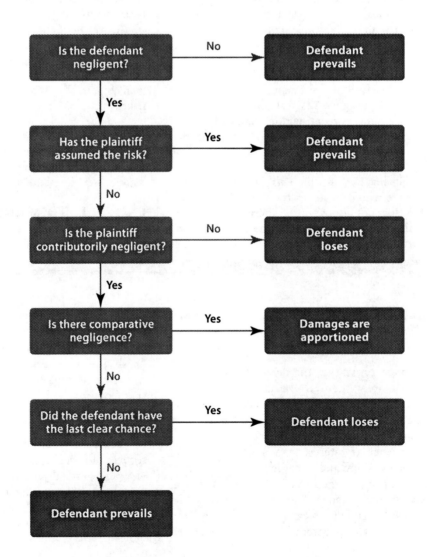

CONTRIBUTORY NEGLIGENCE

Contributory negligence is defined as conduct on the part of the plaintiff that falls below the standard to which he should conform for his own protection and that is a legal cause of the plaintiff's harm. The Third Restatement's definition of negligence as the failure of a person to exercise reasonable care under all the circumstances applies to the contributory negligence of the plaintiff. In those few jurisdictions that have not adopted comparative negligence (Alabama, Maryland, North Carolina, Virginia, and Washington, D.C.), the contributory negligence of the plaintiff, whether slight or extensive, prevents him from recovering *any* damages from the defendant.

Notwithstanding the contributory negligence of the plaintiff, if the defendant had a **last clear chance** to avoid injury to the plaintiff but did not avail himself of such a chance, the contributory negligence of the plaintiff does not bar his recovery of damages.

COMPARATIVE NEGLIGENCE

The harshness of the contributory negligence doctrine has caused all but a few states to reject its all-or-nothing rule and to substitute the doctrine of **comparative negligence**, which is also called comparative fault or comparative responsibility. (In states adopting comparative negligence, the doctrine of last clear chance has been abandoned.)

Approximately a dozen states have judicially or legislatively adopted "pure" comparative negligence systems. (The Third Restatement of Torts: Apportionment of Liability advocates this form of comparative negligence.) Under *pure comparative negligence* damages are divided between the parties in proportion to the degree of fault or negligence found against them. For instance, Matthew negligently drives his automobile into Nancy, who is crossing against the light. Nancy sustains damages in the amount of $10,000 and sues Matthew. If the trier of fact (the jury or judge, depending on the case) determines that Matthew's negligence contributed 70 percent to Nancy's injury and that Nancy's contributory negligence contributed 30 percent to her injury, then Nancy would recover $7,000.

Most states have adopted the doctrine of "modified" comparative negligence. Under *modified comparative negligence* the plaintiff recovers as in pure comparative negligence unless her contributory negligence was equal to or greater than that of the defendant, in which case the plaintiff recovers nothing. Thus, in the example above, if the trier of fact determined that Matthew's negligence and Nancy's contributory negligence contributed 40 percent and 60 percent, respectively, to her injury, then Nancy would not recover anything from Matthew.

MOORE v. KITSMILLER

COURT OF APPEALS OF TEXAS, TWELFTH DISTRICT, TYLER, 2006
201 S.W.3D 147, *REVIEW DENIED*

http://scholar.google.com/scholar_case?q=201+S.W.3D+147&hl=en&as_sdt=2,34&case=5663712118613187322&scilh=0

FACTS In the spring of 2001, Kitsmiller purchased a house in Van Zandt County to use as rental property. In mid-June, he hired B & H Shaw Company, Inc. (B & H) to install a replacement septic tank in the back yard. The septic tank was located about two or three feet from a concrete stoop at the back door of the garage. B & H mounded dirt over the septic tank and the lateral lines going out from it upon completion. Sometime after B & H installed the septic tank, Kitsmiller smoothed out the mounds of dirt over the septic tank and lateral lines. Kitsmiller then leased the property to Moore and his wife on July 27. Kitsmiller testified that he viewed the back yard about a week or ten days prior to leasing the property to the Moores and stated that the dirt around the septic system looked firm.

On August 7, the Moores moved in. On August 11, Moore and his wife went into the back yard for the first time, and as he stepped off the stoop, he was unable to see the ground and could only see his wife and the bag of trash in his left arm. His wife testified that the ground looked flat. Moore testified that he had only taken a few steps off the stoop when his left leg sank into a hole, causing him to fall forward into his wife. As he tried to steady himself with his right foot, it hung and then sank, causing him to fall backward on his head and back. Moore testified that the injury to his back required surgery and affected his ability to earn a living.

Moore filed suit against Kitsmiller and B & H. He sought damages for past and future pain and suffering, past and future mental anguish, past and future physical impairment, and past and future loss of earning capacity. In their answers to Moore's suit, both Kitsmiller and B & H pleaded the affirmative defense of contributory negligence.

During the jury trial, Moore testified Kitsmiller should have notified him where the septic tank and lateral lines were located and that the dirt should have remained mounded over the tank and lines. Martin, an on-site septic tank complaint investigator for both the Texas

Commission on Environmental Quality and Van Zandt County, testified that dirt should have been mounded over the septic tank and lateral lines, so that when the dirt settled, there would be no holes in the ground around the septic tank or lateral lines.

The jury determined that (1) both Kitsmiller and Moore were negligent, but B & H was not; (2) Kitsmiller was 51 percent negligent and Moore was 49 percent negligent; and (3) Moore was entitled to $210,000 in damages. On September 29, 2004, the trial court entered a judgment in favor of Moore and against Kitsmiller in the amount of $210,000 plus interest and costs. Applying comparative negligence, the trial court entered a modified final judgment on November 1, 2004, awarding Moore $107,100 plus interest and costs based upon Moore's contributory negligence. Moore appealed all issues involving his contributory negligence.

DECISION The judgment of the trial court is affirmed.

OPINION Worthen, C. J. Moore argues that his wife and Kitsmiller testified that the back yard was flat at the time of the occurrence. He contends that no one could have anticipated any danger from walking into the yard. Therefore, Moore argues that there is no evidence in the record to support the jury's determination that he was contributorily negligent.

Contributory negligence contemplates an injured person's failure to use ordinary care regarding his or her own safety. [Citation.] This affirmative defense requires proof that the plaintiff was negligent and that the plaintiff's negligence proximately caused his or her injuries. [Citation.] Negligence requires proof of proximate cause. [Citation.] Proximate cause requires proof of both cause in fact and foreseeability. [Citation.] The test for cause in fact is whether the negligent act or omission was a substantial factor in bringing about an injury without which the harm would not have occurred. [Citation.] Foreseeability requires that a person of ordinary intelligence should have anticipated the danger created by a negligent act or omission. [Citation.]

Because comparative responsibility involves measuring the party's comparative fault in causing the plaintiff's injuries, it necessitates a preliminary finding that the plaintiff was in fact contributorily negligent. [Citation.] The standards and tests for determining contributory negligence ordinarily are the same as those for determining negligence, and the rules of law applicable to the former are applicable to the latter. [Citation.] The burden of proof on the whole case is on the plaintiff. [Citation.] However, on special issues tendered by the defendant presenting an affirmative defense such as contributory negligence, the burden of proof is on the defendant to prove the defense by a preponderance of the evidence. [Citation.]

When attacking the legal sufficiency of an adverse finding on an issue on which the party did not have the burden of proof, that party must demonstrate there is no evidence to support the adverse finding. [Citation.] To evaluate the legal sufficiency of the evidence to support a finding, we must determine whether the proffered evidence as a whole rises to a level that would enable reasonable and fair minded people to differ in their conclusions. [Citation.] We sustain a no evidence issue only if there is no more than a scintilla of evidence proving the elements of the claim. [Citation.] In making this determination, we must view the evidence in the light most favorable to the verdict, crediting favorable evidence if reasonable jurors could and disregarding contrary evidence unless reasonable jurors could not. [Citation.] The trier of fact may draw reasonable and logical inferences from the evidence. [Citation.] It is within the province of the jury to draw one reasonable inference from the evidence although another inference could have been made. [Citation.]

* * *

Moore testified that when he stepped off the stoop into the back yard for the first time on August 11, 2001, he could only see his wife and the plastic bag of trash he was carrying in his left hand. The jury was allowed to draw an inference from this evidence that Moore was not watching where he was walking. An individual must keep a proper lookout where he is walking, and a jury is allowed to make a reasonable inference that failure to do so was the proximate cause of his injuries. [Citation.] It was reasonable for the jury to make an inference from Moore's testimony that his failure to keep a proper lookout where he was walking contributed to the occurrence.

Moore contends that the only reasonable inference the jury could have made was that, even if he had been watching where he was walking, he would not have been able to avoid stepping in the holes because they were not visible to the naked eye. The jury could have made that inference, but chose not to do so. Shaw's testimony that Martin's photographs showed the depressions could have been present at the time of the occurrence could have led the jury to believe that Moore's contention was not a reasonable inference. We conclude that the jury made a reasonable inference from the evidence in finding Moore contributorily negligent.

INTERPRETATION In cases in which both the plaintiff and defendant are negligent, under comparative negligence the law apportions damages between the parties in proportion to the degree of fault or negligence found against them.

CRITICAL THINKING QUESTION Is it fair that the plaintiff recovers damages despite being contributorily negligent? Explain.

ASSUMPTION OF RISK

A plaintiff who has voluntarily and knowingly assumed the risk of harm arising from the negligent or reckless conduct of the defendant cannot recover for such harm. In **express assumption of the risk**, the plaintiff expressly agrees to assume the risk of harm from the defendant's conduct. Usually, but not always, such an agreement is by contract. Courts usually construe these exculpatory contracts strictly and will hold that the plaintiff has assumed the risk only if the terms of the agreement are clear and unequivocal. Moreover, some contracts for assumption of risk are considered unenforceable as a matter of public policy. See Chapter 13.

In *implied assumption of the risk*, the plaintiff voluntarily proceeds to encounter a known danger. Thus, a spectator entering a baseball park may be regarded as consenting that the players may proceed with the game without taking precautions to protect him from being hit by the ball. Most states have abolished or modified the defense of implied assumption of risk. Some have abandoned it entirely while others have merged implied assumption of risk into their comparative negligence systems.

Reflecting this general trend the Third Restatement of Torts: Apportionment of Liability has abandoned the doctrine of implied voluntary assumption of risk: it is no longer a defense that the plaintiff was aware of a risk and voluntarily confronted it. But if a plaintiff's conduct in the face of a known risk is unreasonable, it might constitute contributory negligence, thereby reducing the plaintiff's recovery under comparative negligence. This new Restatement limits the defense of assumption of risk to express assumption of risk, which consists of a contract between the plaintiff and another person to absolve the other person from liability for future harm. Contractual assumption of risk may occur by written agreement, express oral agreement, or conduct that creates an implied-in-fact contract, as determined by the applicable rules of contract law. Some contractual assumptions of risk, however, are not enforceable under other areas of substantive law or as against public policy.

> ### PRACTICAL ADVICE
> Consider having customers and clients sign waivers of liability and assumption of risk forms, but realize that many courts limit their effectiveness.

STRICT LIABILITY

In some instances a person may be held liable for injuries he has caused even though he has not acted intentionally or negligently. Such liability is called **strict liability**, absolute liability, or liability without fault. The courts have determined that certain types of otherwise socially desirable activities pose sufficiently high risks of harm regardless of how carefully they are conducted, and that therefore those who carry on these activities should bear the cost of any harm that such activities cause. The doctrine of strict liability is not based on any particular fault of the defendant but on the nature of the activity in which he is engaging.

Activities Giving Rise to Strict Liability

We will discuss in this section the following activities that give rise to strict liability: (1) performing abnormally dangerous activities and (2) keeping animals. In addition, strict liability is imposed upon other activities. For example, nearly all states have imposed a limited form of strict product liability upon manufacturers and merchants who sell goods in a *defective condition* unreasonably dangerous to the user or consumer. This topic is covered in Chapter 22.

ABNORMALLY DANGEROUS ACTIVITIES

A person who carries on an abnormally dangerous activity is subject to strict liability for physical harm resulting from the activity. The Third Restatement provides that "An **activity is abnormally dangerous** if: (1) the activity creates a foreseeable and highly significant risk of physical harm even when reasonable care is exercised by all actors; and (2) the activity is not one of common usage." The court determines whether an activity is abnormally dangerous by applying these factors. Activities to which the rule has been applied include collecting water or sewage in such quantity and location as to make it dangerous; storing explosives or flammable liquids in large quantities; blasting or pile driving; crop dusting; drilling for or refining oil in populated areas; and emitting noxious gases or fumes into a settled community. On the other hand, courts have refused to apply the rule where the activity is a "natural" use of the land, such as drilling for oil in the oil fields of Texas or transmitting gas through a gas pipe or electricity through electric wiring.

PRACTICAL ADVICE

Determine if any of your activities involve abnormally dangerous activities for which strict liability is imposed and be sure to obtain adequate insurance.

KLEIN V. PYRODYNE CORPORATION

SUPREME COURT OF WASHINGTON, 1991
117 WASH.2D 1, 810 P.2D 917

http://scholar.google.com/scholar_case?case=7983277736024137446&q=810+P.2d+917&hl=en&as_sdt=2,34

FACTS Pyrodyne Corporation contracted to display the fireworks at the Western Washington State Fairgrounds in Puyallup, Washington, on July 4, 1987. During the fireworks display, one of the five-inch mortars was knocked into a horizontal position. A shell inside ignited and discharged, flying five hundred feet parallel to the earth and exploding near the crowd of onlookers. Danny and Marion Klein were injured by the explosion. Mr. Klein suffered facial burns and serious injuries to his eyes. The parties provided conflicting explanations for the improper discharge, and because all the evidence had exploded, there was no means of proving the cause of the misfire. The Kleins brought suit against Pyrodyne under the theory of strict liability for participating in an abnormally dangerous activity.

DECISION Judgment for the Kleins.

OPINION Guy, J. The modern doctrine of strict liability for abnormally dangerous activities derives from *Fletcher v. Rylands*, [citation], in which the defendant's reservoir flooded mine shafts on the plaintiff's adjoining land. *Rylands v. Fletcher* has come to stand for the rule that "the defendant will be liable when he damages another by a thing or activity unduly dangerous and inappropriate to the place where it is maintained, in the light of the character of that place and its surroundings." [Citation.]

The basic principle of *Rylands v. Fletcher* has been accepted by the Restatement (Second) of Torts (1977). [Citation.] Section 519 of the Restatement provides that any party carrying on an "abnormally dangerous activity" is strictly liable for ensuing damages. The test for what constitutes such an activity is stated in section 520 of the Restatement. Both Restatement sections have been adopted by this court, and determination of whether an activity is an "abnormally dangerous activity" is a question of law. [Citations.]

Section 520 of the Restatement lists six factors that are to be considered in determining whether an activity is "abnormally dangerous." The factors are as follows:

(a) existence of a high degree of risk of some harm to the person, land or chattels of others; (b) likelihood that the harm that results from it will be great; (c) inability to eliminate the risk by the exercise of reasonable care; (d) extent to which the activity is not a matter of common usage; (e) inappropriateness of the activity to the place where it is carried on; and (f) extent to which its value to the community is outweighed by its dangerous attributes. Restatement (Second) of Torts § 520 (1977). As we previously recognized in [citation], the comments to section 520 explain how these factors should be evaluated: Any one of them is not necessarily sufficient of itself in a particular case, and ordinarily several of them will be required for strict liability. On the other hand, it is not necessary that each of them be present, especially if others weigh heavily. Because of the interplay of these various factors, it is not possible to reduce abnormally dangerous activities to any definition. The essential question is whether the risk created is so unusual, either because of its magnitude or because of the circumstances surrounding it, as to justify the imposition of strict liability for the harm that results from it, even though it is carried on with all reasonable care. Restatement (Second) of Torts § 520, comment f (1977). Examination of these factors persuades us that fireworks displays are abnormally dangerous activities justifying the imposition of strict liability.

We find that the factors stated in clauses (a), (b), and (c) are all present in the case of fireworks displays. Any time a person ignites aerial shells or rockets with the intention of sending them aloft to explode in the presence of large crowds of people, a high risk of serious personal injury or property damage is created. That risk arises because of the possibility that a shell or rocket will malfunction or be misdirected. Furthermore, no matter how much care pyrotechnicians exercise, they cannot entirely eliminate the high risk inherent in setting off powerful explosives such as fireworks near crowds.

* * *

The factor expressed in clause (d) concerns the extent to which the activity is not a matter "of common usage."

The Restatement explains that "[a]n activity is a matter of common usage if it is customarily carried on by the great mass of mankind or by many people in the community." Restatement (Second) of Torts § 520, comment i (1977). As examples of activities that are not matters of common usage, the Restatement comments offer driving a tank, blasting, the manufacture, storage, transportation, and use of high explosives, and drilling for oil. The deciding characteristic is that few persons engage in these activities. Likewise, relatively few persons conduct public fireworks displays. Therefore, presenting public fireworks displays is not a matter of common usage.

***

The factor stated in clause (e) requires analysis of the appropriateness of the activity to the place where it was carried on. In this case, the fireworks display was conducted at the Puyallup Fairgrounds. Although some locations—such as over water—may be safer, the Puyallup Fairgrounds is an appropriate place for a fireworks show because the audience can be seated at a reasonable distance from the display. Therefore, the clause (e) factor is not present in this case.

The factor stated in clause (f) requires analysis of the extent to which the value of fireworks to the community outweighs its dangerous attributes. We do not find that this factor is present here. This country has a longstanding tradition of fireworks on the 4th of July. That tradition suggests that we as a society have decided that the value of fireworks on the day celebrating our national independence and unity outweighs the risks of injuries and damage.

In sum, we find that setting off public fireworks displays satisfies four of the six conditions under the Restatement test; that is, it is an activity that is not "of common usage" and that presents an ineliminably high risk of serious bodily injury or property damage. We therefore hold that conducting public fireworks displays is an abnormally dangerous activity justifying the imposition of strict liability.

INTERPRETATION The courts impose strict liability for harm resulting from an abnormally dangerous activity, as determined in light of the place, time, and manner in which the activity was conducted.

CRITICAL THINKING QUESTION If an activity is abnormally dangerous, should the law abolish it? Explain.

KEEPING OF ANIMALS

Strict liability for harm caused by animals existed at common law and continues today with some modification. As a general rule, those who possess animals for their own purposes do so at their peril and must protect against harm those animals may cause to people and property.

Trespassing Animals Owners and possessors of animals, except for dogs and cats, are subject to strict liability for any physical harm their animals cause by trespassing on the property of another. There are two exceptions to this rule: (1) keepers of animals are not strictly liable for animals incidentally straying upon land immediately adjacent to a highway on which they are being lawfully driven, although the owner may be liable for negligence if he fails to control them properly and (2) in some western states, keepers of farm animals, typically cattle, are not strictly liable for harm caused by their trespassing animals that are allowed to graze freely.

Nontrespassing Animals Owners and possessors of wild animals are subject to strict liability for physical harm caused by such animals, whether or not they are trespassing. Accordingly the owner or possessor is liable even if she has exercised reasonable care in attempting to restrain the wild animal. *Wild animals* are defined as those that, in the particular region in which they are kept, are known to be likely to inflict serious damage and that cannot be considered safe, no matter how domesticated they are. The Third Restatement has a similar definition: "A wild animal is an animal that belongs to a category of animals that have not been generally domesticated and that are likely, unless restrained, to cause personal injury." The court determines whether a category of animals is wild. Animals included in this category are bears, lions, elephants, monkeys, tigers, deer, and raccoons. On the other hand, iguanas, pigeons, and manatees are not considered wild animals because they do not pose a risk of causing substantial personal injury.

Domestic animals are those animals that are traditionally devoted to the service of humankind and that as a class are considered safe. Examples of domestic animals are dogs, cats, horses, cattle, and sheep. Owners and possessors of domestic animals are subject to strict liability if they knew, or had reason to know, of an animal's dangerous tendencies abnormal for the animal's category. The animal's dangerous propensity must be the cause of the harm. For example, a keeper is not liable for a dog that bites a human merely because he knows that the dog has a propensity to fight with other dogs. On the other hand, a person whose 150-pound Old

English sheepdog has a propensity to jump enthusiastically on visitors would be liable for any damage caused by the dog's playfulness. About half of the states statutorily impose strict liability in dog cases even where the owner or possessor does not know, and did not have reason to know, of the dog's dangerous tendencies.

PALUMBO V. NIKIRK

SUPREME COURT, APPELLATE DIVISION, SECOND DEPARTMENT, NEW YORK, 2009
59 A.D.3D 691, 874 N.Y.S.2D 222, 2009 N.Y. SLIP OP. 01454
http://scholar.google.com/scholar_case?case=7266290354304468850&q=2009+NY+Slip+Op+1454&hl=en&as_sdt=2,34

FACTS The plaintiff, a mail carrier, sustained injuries when he allegedly was bitten and attacked by a dog on the front steps of the defendants' house as he attempted to deliver the mail. The plaintiff, who crossed over the defendants' lawn and driveway from the house next door, and whose view of the dog was obstructed by a bush, did not see the dog or hear it bark until he opened the lid of the mailbox and was bitten. The plaintiff brought an action to recover damages for personal injuries. The Supreme Court, Nassau County, granted the defendants' motion for summary judgment dismissing the complaint. The plaintiff appealed.

DECISION Summary judgment is affirmed.

OPINION *Per curiam.* To recover upon a theory of strict liability in tort for a dog bite or attack, a plaintiff must prove that the dog had vicious propensities and that the owner of the dog, or person in control of the premises where the dog was, knew or should have known of such propensities [citations]. "Vicious propensities include the 'propensity to do any act that might endanger the safety of the persons and property of others in a given situation'" [citations].

Here, the defendants established their prima facie entitlement to judgment as a matter of law by presenting evidence that the dog had never bitten, jumped, or growled at anyone prior to the incident in question, nor had the dog exhibited any other aggressive or vicious behavior [citations]. In opposition, the plaintiff failed to come forward with any proof in evidentiary form that the dog had ever previously bitten anyone or exhibited any vicious propensities. Furthermore, the presence of a "Beware of Dog" sign on the premises, the breed of the dog, and the owner's testimony that the dog was always on a leash were insufficient to raise a triable issue of fact as to the dog's vicious propensities in the absence of any evidence that prior to this incident the dog exhibited any fierce or hostile tendencies [citations].

INTERPRETATION Owners and possessors of domestic animals are subject to strict liability if they knew, or had reason to know, of the animal's vicious propensities.

CRITICAL THINKING QUESTION Is the burden on the plaintiff to establish the animal's prior vicious propensities too difficult to sustain?

Defenses to Strict Liability

Because the strict liability of one who carries on an abnormally dangerous activity or keeps animals is not based on his negligence, the ordinary **contributory negligence** of the plaintiff is *not* a defense to such liability. The law in imposing strict liability places the full responsibility for preventing harm on the defendant. Nevertheless, some states apply the doctrine of **comparative negligence** to some types of strict liability. The Third Restatement provides that if the plaintiff has been contributorily negligent in failing to take reasonable precautions, the plaintiff's recovery in a strict-liability claim for physical harm caused by abnormally dangerous activities or keeping of animals is reduced in accordance with the share of comparative responsibility assigned to the plaintiff.

Under the Second Restatement of Torts voluntary **assumption of risk** is a defense to an action based on strict liability. If the owner of an automobile knowingly and voluntarily parks the vehicle in a blasting zone, he may not recover for harm to his automobile. The assumption of risk, however, must be voluntary. Where blasting operations are established, for example, the possessor of nearby land is not required to move away and may recover for harm suffered.

The more recent Third Restatement of Torts: Apportionment of Liability has abandoned the doctrine of implied voluntary assumption of risk in tort actions

Ethical Dilemma

What Are the Obligations of a Bartender to His Patrons?

FACTS John Campbell, age twenty-two, was recently hired as a management trainee for the Stanton Hotel. The Stanton features a health club, swimming pool, ski slopes, and boating facilities. The management trainee program is an eighteen-month program during which the trainees rotate jobs to gain exposure to all phases of hotel operations. There is no formal orientation, and each trainee is randomly assigned to jobs.

John's first assignment was at the restaurant/bar working with Mr. Arnold, a bartender who was fifty years old and quite experienced. Mr. Arnold commented to John that John was lucky to be working the bar during the skiing season. Mr. Arnold explained that skiers frequently come in from the slopes to warm up. He told John that all tips are shared equally and that the more it snows and the colder it gets, the better the bar business.

One day, John observed that Mr. Arnold was serving drinks to two young men who appeared to be about twenty-two or twenty-three. John overheard the men planning to ski an hour or so more and then drive over to meet friends at a neighboring hotel. One of the men appeared self-contained and unaffected by the drinks. His friend, however, was gradually getting louder, although he was not making a disturbance.

John noticed that Mr. Arnold had already served three rounds of bourbon to the men. When Mr. Arnold was preparing the fourth round, John said to him, "Don't you think they've had enough? They're going back on the slopes." Mr. Arnold replied, "Kid, you've got a lot to learn."

Social, Policy, and Ethical Considerations

1. What action, if any, should John take?
2. What are the potential risks to the two men who are drinking? Are public safety issues involved?
3. What management policies should the hotel institute with regard to its liquor policies and athletic operations?
4. Do the drinking companions bear an ethical responsibility for each other's drinking?
5. How should society balance the interests of freedom of business and individual conduct (i.e., drinking) with the competing interests of protecting public safety?

generally: it is no longer a defense that the plaintiff was aware of a risk and voluntarily confronted it. This Restatement limits the defense of assumption of risk to express assumption of risk, which consists of a contract between the plaintiff and another person to absolve the other person from liability for future harm.

The Third Restatement: Liability for Physical and Emotional Harm recognizes a limitation on strict liability for abnormally dangerous activities and keeping of animals when the victim suffers harm as a result of exposure to the animal or activity resulting from the victim's securing some benefit from that exposure. The Third Restatement gives the following example: "if the plaintiff is a veterinarian or a groomer who accepts an animal such as a dog from the defendant, the plaintiff is deriving financial benefits from the acceptance of the animal, and is beyond the scope of strict liability, even if the dog can be deemed abnormally dangerous."

CHAPTER SUMMARY
NEGLIGENCE

Breach of Duty of Care

Definition of Negligence conduct that falls below the standard established by law for the protection of others against unreasonable risk of harm

Reasonable Person Standard degree of care that a reasonable person would exercise under all the circumstances
* *Children* must conform to conduct of a reasonable person of the same age, intelligence, and experience under all the circumstances
* *Physical Disability* a disabled person's conduct must conform to that of a reasonable person under the same disability

- *Mental Disability* a mentally disabled person is held to the reasonable person standard of a reasonable person who is not mentally deficient
- *Superior Skill or Knowledge* if a person has skills or knowledge beyond those possessed by most others, these skills or knowledge are circumstances to be taken into account in determining whether the person has acted with reasonable care
- *Emergencies* the reasonable person standard applies, but an unexpected emergency is considered part of the circumstances
- *Violation of Statute* if the statute applies, the violation is negligence *per se* in most states

Duty to Act a person is under a duty to all others at all times to exercise reasonable care for the safety of the others' person and property; however, except in special circumstances, no one is required to aid another in peril

Duties of Possessors of Land
- *Second Restatement* a land possessor owes the following duties: (1) not to injure intentionally *trespassers*; (2) to warn *licensees* of known dangerous conditions licensees are unlikely to discover for themselves; and (3) to exercise reasonable care to protect *invitees* against dangerous conditions land possessor should know of but invitees are unlikely to discover
- *Third Restatement* adopts a unitary duty of reasonable care to all entrants on the land except for flagrant trespassers: a land possessor must use reasonable care to investigate and discover dangerous conditions and must use reasonable care to eliminate or improve those dangerous conditions that are known or should have been discovered by the exercise of reasonable care

Res Ipsa Loquitur permits the jury to infer both negligent conduct and causation

Factual Cause and Scope of Liability

Factual Cause the defendant's conduct is a factual cause of the harm when the harm would not have occurred absent the conduct

Scope of Liability (Proximate Cause) Liability is limited to those harms that result from the risks that made the defendant's conduct tortious
- *Foreseeability* excludes liability for harms that were sufficiently unforeseeable at the time of the defendant's tortious conduct that they were not among the risks that made the defendant negligent
- *Superseding Cause* an intervening act that relieves the defendant of liability

Harm

Burden of Proof plaintiff must prove that defendant's negligent conduct caused harm to a legally protected interest

Harm to Legally Protected Interest courts determine which interests are protected from negligent interference

Defenses to Negligence

Contributory Negligence failure of a plaintiff to exercise reasonable care for his own protection, which in a few states prevents the plaintiff from recovering anything

Comparative Negligence damages are divided between the parties in proportion to their degree of negligence; applies in almost all states

Assumption of Risk plaintiff's express consent to encounter a known danger; some states still apply implied assumption of the risk

STRICT LIABILITY

Activities Giving Rise to Strict Liability

Definition of Strict Liability liability for nonintentional and nonnegligent conduct

Abnormally Dangerous Activity strict liability is imposed for any activity that (1) creates a foreseeable and highly significant risk of harm and (2) is not one of common usage

Keeping of Animals strict liability is imposed for wild animals and usually for trespassing domestic animals

Defenses to Strict Liability

Contributory Negligence is not a defense to strict liability

Comparative Negligence some states apply this doctrine to some strict liability cases

Assumption of Risk express assumption of risk is a defense to an action based upon strict liability; some states apply implied assumption of risk to strict liability cases

---

QUESTIONS

1. A statute that requires railroads to fence their tracks is construed as intended solely to prevent injuries to animals straying onto the right-of-way. B & A Railroad Company fails to fence its tracks. Two of Calvin's cows wander onto the track. Nellie is hit by a train. Elsie is poisoned by weeds growing beside the track. For which cow(s), if any, is B & A Railroad Company liable to Calvin? Why?

2. Martha invites John to come to lunch. Martha knows that her private road is dangerous to travel, having been heavily eroded by recent rains. She doesn't warn John of the condition, reasonably believing that he will notice the deep ruts and exercise sufficient care. John's attention, while driving over, is diverted from the road by the screaming of his child, who has been stung by a bee. He fails to notice the condition of the road, hits a rut, and skids into a tree. If John is not contributorily negligent, is Martha liable to John?

3. Nathan is run over by a car and left lying in the street. Sam, seeing Nathan's helpless state, places him in his car for the purpose of taking him to the hospital. Sam drives negligently into a ditch, causing additional injury to Nathan. Is Sam liable to Nathan?

4. Vance was served liquor while he was an intoxicated patron of the Clear Air Force Station Noncommissioned Officers' Club. He later injured himself as a result of his intoxication. An Alaska state statute makes it a crime to give or to sell liquor to intoxicated persons. Vance has brought an action seeking damages for the injuries he suffered. Could Vance successfully argue that the United States was negligent *per se* by its employee's violation of the statute?

5. A statute requires all vessels traveling on the Great Lakes to provide lifeboats. One of Winston Steamship Company's boats is sent out of port without a lifeboat. Perry, a sailor, falls overboard in a storm so heavy that had there been a lifeboat it could not have been launched. Perry drowns. Is Winston liable to Perry's estate?

6. Lionel is negligently driving an automobile at excessive speed. Reginald's negligently driven car crosses the center line of the highway and scrapes the side of Lionel's car, damaging its fenders. As a result, Lionel loses control of his car, which goes into the ditch, wrecking the car and causing personal injuries to Lionel. What can Lionel recover?

7. Ellen, the owner of a baseball park, is under a duty to the entering public to provide a reasonably sufficient number of screened seats to protect those who desire such protection against the risk of being hit by batted balls. Ellen fails to do so.

    a. Frank, a customer entering the park, is unable to find a screened seat and, although fully aware of the risk, sits in an unscreened seat. Frank is struck and injured by a batted ball. Is Ellen liable?

    b. Gretchen, Frank's wife, has just arrived from Germany and is viewing baseball for the first time. Without asking any questions, she follows Frank to a seat. After the batted ball hits Frank, it caroms into Gretchen, injuring her. Is Ellen liable to Gretchen?

8. CC Railroad is negligent in failing to give warning of the approach of its train to a crossing and thereby endangers Larry, a blind man who is about to cross. Mildred, a bystander, in a reasonable effort to save Larry, rushes onto the track to push Larry out of danger. Although Mildred acts as carefully as possible, she is struck and injured by the train.

a. Can Mildred recover from Larry?

b. Can Mildred recover from CC Railroad?

9. Two thugs in an alley in Manhattan held up an unidentified man. When the thieves departed with his possessions, the man quickly gave chase. He had almost caught one when the thief managed to force his way into an empty taxicab stopped at a traffic light. The Peerless Transport Company owned the cab. The thief pointed his gun at the driver's head and ordered him to drive on. The driver started to follow the directions while closely pursued by a posse of good citizens, but then suddenly jammed on the brakes and jumped out of the car to safety. The thief also jumped out, but the car traveled on, injuring Mrs. Cordas and her two children. The Cordases then brought an action for damages, claiming that the cab driver was negligent in jumping to safety and leaving the moving vehicle uncontrolled. Was the cab driver negligent? Explain.

10. Timothy keeps a pet chimpanzee that is thoroughly tamed and accustomed to playing with its owner's children. The chimpanzee escapes, despite every precaution to keep it on the owner's premises. It approaches a group of children. Wanda, the mother of one of the children, erroneously thinking the chimpanzee is about to attack the children, rushes to her child's assistance. In her hurry and excitement, she stumbles and falls, breaking her leg. Can Wanda recover from Timothy for her personal injuries?

CASE PROBLEMS

11. Hawkins slipped and fell on a puddle of water just inside the automatic door to the H. E. Butt Grocery Company's store. The water had been tracked into the store by customers and blown through the door by a strong wind. The store manager was aware of the puddle and had mopped it up several times earlier in the day. Still, no signs had been placed to warn store patrons of the danger. Hawkins brought an action to recover damages for injuries sustained in the fall. Was the store negligent in its conduct?

12. Escola, a waitress, was injured when a bottle of soda exploded in her hand while she was putting it into the restaurant's cooler. The bottle came from a shipment that had remained under the counter for thirty-six hours after being delivered by the bottling company. The bottler had subjected the bottle to the method of testing for defects commonly used in the industry, and there is no evidence that Escola or anyone else did anything to damage the bottle between its delivery and the explosion. Escola brought an action against the bottler for damages. Because she is unable to show any specific acts of negligence on its part, she seeks to rely on the doctrine of *res ipsa loquitur*. Should she be able to recover on this theory? Explain.

13. Hunn injured herself when she slipped and fell on a loose plank while walking down some steps. The night before, while entering the hotel, she had noticed that the steps were dangerous, and although she knew from her earlier stays at the hotel that another exit was available, she chose that morning to leave via the dangerous steps. The hotel was aware of the hazard, as one of three other guests who had fallen that night had reported his accident to the desk clerk then on duty. Still, the hotel did not place cautionary signs on the steps to warn of the danger, and the steps were not roped off or otherwise excluded from use. Hunn brought an action against the hotel for injuries she sustained as a result of her fall. Should she recover? Explain.

14. Fredericks, a hotel owner, had a dog named Sport that he had trained as a watchdog. When Vincent Zarek, a guest at the hotel, leaned over to pet the dog, it bit him. Although Sport had never bitten anyone before, Fredericks was aware of the dog's violent tendencies and, therefore, did not allow it to roam around the hotel alone. Vincent brought an action for injuries sustained when the dog bit him. Is Fredericks liable for the actions of his dog? Explain.

15. Led Foot drives his car carelessly into another car. The second car contains dynamite, a fact which Led had no way of knowing. The collision causes an explosion that shatters a window of a building half a block away on another street. The flying glass inflicts serious cuts on Sally, who is working at a desk near the window. The explosion also harms Vic, who is walking on the sidewalk near the point of the collision. Toward whom is Led Foot negligent?

16. A foul ball struck Marie Uzdavines on the head while she was watching the Metropolitan Baseball Club (The Mets) play the Philadelphia Phillies at the Mets' home stadium in New York. The ball came through a hole in a screen designed to protect spectators sitting behind home plate. The screen contained several holes that had been repaired with baling wire, a lighter weight wire than that used in the original screen. Although the manager of the stadium makes no formal inspections of the screen, his employees do try to repair the holes as they find them. Weather conditions, rust deterioration, and baseballs hitting the screen are the chief causes of these holes. The owner of the stadium, the city of New York, leases the stadium to the Mets and replaces the entire screen every two years. Uzdavines sued the Mets for negligence under the doctrine of *res ipsa loquitur*. Is this an appropriate case for *res ipsa loquitur*? Explain.

17. Two-year-old David Allen was bitten by Joseph White-head's dog while he was playing on the porch at the Allen residence. Allen suffered facial cuts, a severed muscle in his left eye, a hole in his left ear, and scarring over his fore-head. Through his father, David sued Whitehead, claiming that, as owner, Whitehead is responsible for his dog's actions. Whitehead admitted that (a) the dog was large, mean-looking, and frequently barked at neighbors; (b) the dog was allowed to roam wild; and (c) the dog frequently chased and barked at cars. He stated, however, that (a) the dog was friendly and often played with his and neigh-bors' children; (b) he had not received previous complaints about the dog; (c) the dog was neither aggressive nor threatening; and (d) the dog had never bitten anyone before this incident. Is Whitehead liable?

18. Larry VanEgdom, in an intoxicated state, bought alcoholic beverages from the Hudson Municipal Liquor Store in Hudson, South Dakota. An hour later, VanEgdom, while driving a car, struck and killed Guy William Ludwig, who was stopped on his motorcycle at a stop sign. Lela Walz, as special administrator of Ludwig's estate, brought an action against the city of Hudson, which operated the liquor store, for the wrongful death of Ludwig. Walz alleged that the store employee was negligent in selling intoxicating beverages to VanEgdom when he knew or could have observed that VanEgdom was drunk. Decision?

19. Carolyn Falgout accompanied William Wardlaw as a social guest to Wardlaw's brother's camp. After both parties had consumed intoxicating beverages, Falgout walked onto a pier that was then only partially completed. Wardlaw had requested that she not go on the pier. Falgout said, "Don't tell me what to do," and proceeded to walk on the pier. Wardlaw then asked her not to walk past the completed portion of the pier. She ignored his warnings and walked to the pier's end. When returning to the shore, Falgout got her shoe caught between the boards. She fell, hanging by her foot, with her head and arms in the water. Wardlaw rescued Falgout, who had seriously injured her knee and leg. She sued Wardlaw for negligence. Decision?

20. Joseph Yania, a coal strip-mine operator, and Boyd Ross visited a coal strip-mining operation owned by John Bigan to discuss a business matter with Bigan. On Bigan's property there were several cuts and trenches he had dug to remove the coal underneath. While there, Bigan asked the two men to help him pump water from one of these cuts in the earth. This particular cut contained water eight to ten feet in depth with sidewalls or embankments sixteen to eighteen feet in height. The two men agreed, and the process began with Ross and Bigan entering the cut and stand-ing at the point where the pump was located. Yania stood at the top of one of the cut's sidewalls. Apparently, Bigan taunted Yania into jumping into the water from the top of the sidewall—a height of sixteen to eighteen feet. As a result, Yania drowned. His widow brought a negligence action against Bigan. She claims that Bigan was negligent "(1) by urging, enticing, taunting, and inveigling Yania to jump into the water; (2) by failing to warn Yania of a dan-gerous condition on the land; and (3) by failing to go to Yania's rescue after he jumped into the water." Was Bigan negligent?

TAKING SIDES

Rebecca S. Dukat arrived at Mockingbird Lanes, a bowling alley in Omaha, Nebraska, at approximately 6:00 P.M. to bowl in her league game. The bowling alley's parking lot and adjacent sidewalk were covered with snow and ice. Dukat proceeded to walk into the bowling alley on the only sidewalk provided in and out of the building. She testified that she noticed the sidewalk was icy. After bowling three games and drinking three beers, Dukat left the bowling alley at approximately 9:00 P.M. She retraced her steps on the same sidewalk, which was still covered with ice and in a condition that, according to Frank Jameson, general manager of Mockingbird Lanes, was "unacceptable" if the bowling alley were open to customers. As Dukat proceeded along the sidewalk to her car,

she slipped, attempted to catch herself by reaching toward a car, and fell. She suffered a fracture of both bones in her left ankle as well as a ruptured ligament. Dukat sued Mockingbird Lanes, seeking damages for her for personal injuries. Mockingbird denied liability for Dukat's personal injuries.

a. What arguments would support Dukat's claim for her personal injuries?

b. What arguments would support Mockingbird's denial of liability for Dukat's personal injuries?

c. Which side should prevail? Explain.

PART III
CONTRACTS

Chapter 9   Introduction to Contracts

Chapter 10   Mutual Assent

Chapter 11   Conduct Invalidating Assent

Chapter 12   Consideration

Chapter 13   Illegal Bargains

Chapter 14   Contractual Capacity

Chapter 15   Contracts in Writing

Chapter 16   Third Parties to Contract

Chapter 17   Performance, Breach, and Discharge

Chapter 18   Contract Remedies

Chapter 9

INTRODUCTION TO CONTRACTS

A promise is a debt, and I certainly wish to keep all my promises to the letter; I can give no better advice.

THE MAN OF LAW IN THE *CANTERBURY TALES*, GEOFFREY CHAUCER (FOURTEENTH CENTURY)

CHAPTER OUTCOMES

After reading and studying this chapter, you should be able to:

1. Distinguish between contracts that are covered by the Uniform Commercial Code and those covered by the common law.

2. List the essential elements of a contract.

3. Distinguish among (a) express and implied contracts; (b) unilateral and bilateral contracts; (c) valid, void, voidable, and unenforceable agreements; and (d) executed and executory contracts.

4. Explain the doctrine of promissory estoppel.

5. Identify the three elements of enforceable quasi contract and explain how it differs from a contract.

Every business enterprise, whether large or small, must enter into contracts with its employees, its suppliers of goods and services, and its customers in order to conduct its business operations. Thus, contract law is an important subject for the business manager. Contract law is also basic to fields of law treated in other parts of this book, such as agency, partnerships, corporations, sales of personal property, negotiable instruments, and secured transactions.

Even the most common transaction may involve many contracts. For example, in a typical contract for the sale of land, the seller promises to transfer title, or right of ownership, to the land; and the buyer promises to pay an agreed-upon purchase price. In addition, the seller may promise to pay certain taxes, and the buyer may promise to assume a mortgage on the property or to pay the purchase price to a creditor of the seller. If the parties have lawyers, they very likely have contracts with

these lawyers. If the seller deposits the proceeds of the sale in a bank, he enters into a contract with the bank. If the buyer rents the property, he enters into a contract with the tenant. When one of the parties leaves his car in a parking lot to attend to any of these matters, he assumes a contractual relationship with the owner of the lot. In short, nearly every business transaction is based on contract and the expectations the agreed-upon promises create. It is, therefore, essential that you know the legal requirements for making binding contracts.

Development of the Law of Contracts

Contract law, like the law as a whole, is not static. It has undergone—and is still undergoing—enormous changes.

In the nineteenth century, almost total freedom in forming contracts was the rule. However, contract formation also involved many technicalities, and the courts imposed contract liability only when the parties complied strictly with the required formalities.

During the twentieth century, many of the formalities of contract formation were relaxed, and as a result, contractual obligations usually are recognized whenever the parties clearly intend to be bound. In addition, an increasing number of promises are now enforced in certain circumstances, even though such promises do not comply strictly with the basic requirements of a contract. In brief, the twentieth century left its mark on contract law by limiting the absolute freedom of contract and, at the same time, by relaxing the requirements of contract formation. Accordingly, we can say that it is considerably easier now both to get into a contract and to get out of one.

Common Law

Contracts are primarily governed by state common law. An orderly presentation of this law is found in the Restatements of the Law of Contracts, a valuable authoritative reference work extensively relied on and quoted in reported judicial opinions.

The Uniform Commercial Code

The sale of personal property is a large part of commercial activity. Article 2 of the **Uniform Commercial Code** (the Code, or UCC) governs such sales in all states except Louisiana. A **sale** consists of the passing of title to goods from seller to buyer for a price. A contract for sale includes both a present sale of goods and a contract to sell goods at a future time. The Code essentially defines **goods** as tangible personal property. **Personal property** is any property other than an interest in real property (land). For example, the purchase of a television set, an automobile, or a textbook is a sale of goods. All such transactions are governed by Article 2 of the Code, but in cases in which the Code has not specifically modified general contract law, the common law of contracts continues to apply. In other words, the law of sales is a specialized part of the general law of contracts, and the law of contracts governs unless specifically displaced by the Code. See *Pittsley v. Houser* in Chapter 19.

Amendments to Article 2 were promulgated in 2003 to accommodate electronic commerce and to reflect development of business practices, changes in other law, and other practical issues. To date no states have adopted them. However, at least forty of the states have adopted the 2001 Revisions to Article 1, which applies to all of the articles of the Code.

Types of Contracts Outside the Code

General contract law (**common law**) governs all contracts outside the scope of the Code. Such contracts play a significant role in commercial activities. For example, the Code does *not* apply to employment contracts, service contracts, insurance contracts, contracts involving **real property** (land and anything attached to it, including buildings, as well as any right, privilege, or power in the real property, including leases, mortgages, options, and easements), and contracts for the sale of intangibles such as patents and copyrights. These transactions continue to be governed by general contract law. Figure 9-1 summarizes the types of law governing contracts.

See *Fox v. Mountain West Electric, Inc.,* later in this chapter.

Figure 9-1
*Law Governing
Contracts*

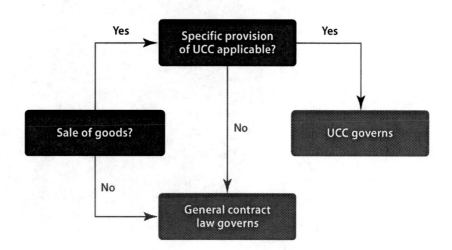

Definition of Contract

Put simply, a **contract** is a binding agreement that the courts will enforce. The Restatement Second, Contracts more precisely defines a contract as "a promise or a set of promises for the breach of which the law gives a remedy, or the performance of which the law in some way recognizes a duty." A *promise* manifests or demonstrates the intention to act or to refrain from acting in a specified manner.

Those promises that meet *all* of the essential requirements of a binding contract are contractual and will be enforced. All other promises are *not* contractual, and usually no legal remedy is available for a **breach** of, or a failure to properly perform, these promises. (The remedies provided for breach of contract, which include compensatory damages, equitable remedies, reliance damages, and restitution, are discussed in Chapter 18.) Thus, a promise may be contractual (and therefore binding) or noncontractual. In other words, all contracts are promises, but not all promises are contracts, as illustrated by Figure 9-2.

Requirements of a Contract

The four basic requirements of a contract are as follows:

1. **Mutual assent.** The parties to a contract must manifest by words or conduct that they have agreed to enter into a contract. The usual method of showing mutual assent is by offer and acceptance.

2. **Consideration.** Each party to a contract must intentionally exchange a legal benefit or incur a legal detriment as an inducement to the other party to make a return exchange.

3. **Legality of object.** The purpose of a contract must not be criminal, tortious, or otherwise against public policy.

4. **Capacity.** The parties to a contract must have contractual capacity. Certain persons, such as adjudicated incompetents, have no legal capacity to contract, whereas others, such as minors, incompetent persons, and intoxicated persons, have limited capacity to contract. All others have full contractual capacity.

In addition, though in a limited number of instances a contract must be evidenced by a writing to be enforceable, in most cases an oral contract is binding and enforceable. Moreover, there must be an *absence* of invalidating conduct, such as duress, undue influence, misrepresentation, or mistake. (See Figure 9-3.) As the *Steinberg v. Chicago Medical School* case shows, a promise meeting all of these requirements is contractual and legally binding. However, if any requirement is unmet, the promise is noncontractual. We will consider these requirements separately in succeeding chapters.

Figure 9-2
Contractual and Noncontractual Promises

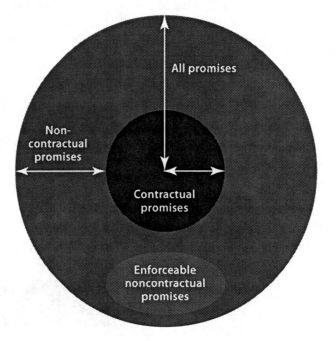

Figure 9-3
Validity of Agreements

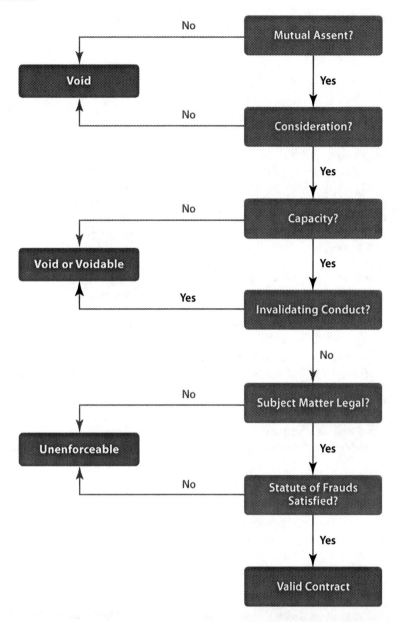

STEINBERG V. CHICAGO MEDICAL SCHOOL

ILLINOIS COURT OF APPEALS, 1976
41 ILL.APP.3D 804, 354 N.E.2D 586

http://scholar.google.com/scholar_case?case=13765816040578352414&q=354+N.E.2d+586&hl=en&as_sdt=2,34

FACTS Robert Steinberg applied for admission to the Chicago Medical School as a first-year student and paid an application fee of $15. The school, a private educational institution, rejected his application. Steinberg brought an action against the school, claiming that it did not evaluate his and other applications according to the academic entrance criteria printed in the school's bulletin.

Instead, he argues, the school based its decisions primarily on nonacademic considerations, such as family connections between the applicant and the school's faculty and members of its board of trustees and the ability of the applicant or his family to donate large sums of money to the school. Steinberg asserts that by evaluating his application according to these unpublished criteria, the school breached the contract it had created when it accepted his application fee. The trial court granted the defendant's motion to dismiss, and Steinberg appealed.

DECISION Trial court's dismissal reversed and case remanded.

OPINION Dempsey, J. A contract is an agreement between competent parties, based upon a consideration sufficient in law, to do or not do a particular thing. It is a promise or a set of promises for the breach of which the law gives a remedy, or the performance of which the law in some way recognizes as a duty. [Citation.] A contract's essential requirements are: competent parties, valid subject matter, legal consideration, mutuality of obligation and mutuality of agreement. Generally, parties may contract in any situation where there is no legal prohibition, since the law acts by restraint and not by conferring rights. [Citation.] However, it is basic contract law that in order for a contract to be binding the terms of the contract must be reasonably certain and definite. [Citation.]

A contract, in order to be legally binding, must be based on consideration. [Citation.] Consideration has been defined to consist of some right, interest, profit or benefit accruing to one party or some forbearance, disadvantage, detriment, loss or responsibility given, suffered, or undertaken by the other. [Citation.] Money is a valuable consideration and its transfer or payment or promises to pay it or the benefit from the right to its use, will support a contract.

In forming a contract, it is required that both parties assent to the same thing in the same sense [citation] and that their minds meet on the essential terms and conditions. [Citation.] Furthermore, the mutual consent essential to the formation of a contract must be gathered from the language employed by the parties or manifested by their words or acts. The intention of the parties gives character to the transaction, and if either party contracts in good faith he is entitled to the benefit of his contract no matter what may have been the secret purpose or intention of the other party. [Citation.]

Steinberg contends that the Chicago Medical School's informational brochure constituted an invitation to make an offer; that his subsequent application and the submission of his $15 fee to the school amounted to an offer; that the school's voluntary reception of his fee constituted an acceptance and because of these events a contract was created between the school and himself. He contends that the school was duty bound under the terms of the contract to evaluate his application according to its stated standards and that the deviation from these standards not only breached the contract, but amounted to an arbitrary selection which constituted a violation of due process and equal protection. He concludes that such a breach did in fact take place each and every time during the past ten years that the school evaluated applicants according to their relationship to the school's faculty members or members of its board of trustees, or in accordance with their ability to make or pledge large sums of money to the school. Finally, he asserts that he is a member and a proper representative of the class that has been damaged by the school's practice.

The school counters that no contract came into being because informational brochures, such as its bulletin, do not constitute offers, but are construed by the courts to be general proposals to consider, examine and negotiate. The school points out that this doctrine has been specifically applied in Illinois to university informational publications.

* * *

We agree with Steinberg's position. We believe that he and the school entered into an enforceable contract; that the school's obligation under the contract was stated in the school's bulletin in a definitive manner and that by accepting his application fee—a valuable consideration— the school bound itself to fulfill its promises. Steinberg accepted the school's promises in good faith and he was entitled to have his application judged according to the school's stated criteria.

INTERPRETATION An agreement meeting all of the requirements of a contract is binding and legally enforceable.

ETHICAL QUESTION Is it ethical for a school to consider any factors other than an applicant's merit? Explain.

CRITICAL THINKING QUESTION Should the courts resolve this type of dispute on the basis of contract law? Explain.

Classification of Contracts

Contracts can be classified according to various characteristics, such as method of formation, content, and legal effect. The standard classifications are (1) express or implied contracts; (2) bilateral or unilateral contracts; (3) valid, void, voidable, or unenforceable contracts; and (4) executed or executory contracts. These classifications are not mutually exclusive. For example, a contract may be express, bilateral, valid, and executory.

EXPRESS AND IMPLIED CONTRACTS

Parties to a contract may indicate their assent either in words or by conduct implying such willingness. For instance, a regular customer known to have an account at a drugstore might pick up an item at the drugstore, show it to the clerk, and walk out. This is a perfectly valid contract. The clerk knows from the customer's conduct that she is buying the item at the specified price and wants it charged to her account. Her actions speak as effectively as words. Such a contract, formed by conduct, is an implied or, more precisely, an **implied in fact** contract; in contrast, a contract in which the parties manifest assent in words is an **express contract**. Both are contracts, equally enforceable. The difference between them is merely the manner in which the parties manifest their assent.

PRACTICAL ADVICE

Whenever possible, try to use written express contracts that specify all of the important terms rather than using implied in fact contracts.

FOX V. MOUNTAIN WEST ELECTRIC, INC.

SUPREME COURT OF IDAHO, 2002
137 IDAHO 703, 52 P.3D 848; REHEARING DENIED, 2002

http://scholar.google.com/scholar_case?q=52+P.3D+848&hl=en&as_sdt=2,34&case=12020421688825080366&scilh=0

FACTS Lockheed Martin Idaho Technical Company (LMITCO) requested bids for a comprehensive fire alarm system in its twelve buildings located in Idaho Falls. Mountain West Electric (MWE) was in the business of installing electrical wiring, conduit and related hookups, and attachments. Fox provided services in designing, drafting, testing, and assisting in the installation of fire alarm systems. The parties decided that it would be better for them to work together with MWE taking the lead on the project. The parties prepared a document defining each of their roles and jointly prepared a bid. MWE was awarded the LMITCO fixed-price contract. In May 1996, Fox began performing various services at the direction of MWE's manager.

During the course of the project, many changes and modifications to the LMITCO contract were made. MWE and Fox disagreed on the procedure for the compensation of the change orders. MWE proposed a flow-down procedure, whereby Fox would receive whatever compensation LMITCO decided to pay MWE. Fox found this unacceptable and suggested a bidding procedure to which MWE objected. Fox and MWE could not reach an agreement upon a compensation arrangement with respect to change orders. Fox left the project on December 9, 1996, after delivering the remaining equipment and materials to MWE. MWE contracted with Life Safety Systems to complete the LMITCO project.

Fox filed a complaint in July 1998 seeking money owed for materials and services provided to MWE by Fox. MWE answered and counterclaimed seeking monetary damages resulting from the alleged breach of the parties' agreement by Fox. The district court found in favor of MWE holding that an implied in fact contract existed. Fox appealed.

DECISION The decision of the district court is affirmed.

OPINION Walters, J.

IMPLIED-IN-FACT CONTRACT

This Court has recognized three types of contractual relationships:

> First is the express contract wherein the parties expressly agree regarding a transaction. Secondly, there is the implied in fact contract wherein there is no express agreement, but the conduct of the parties implies an agreement from which an obligation in contract exists. The third category is called an implied in law contract, or quasi contract. However, a contract implied in law is not a contract at all, but an obligation imposed by law for the purpose of bringing about justice and equity without reference to the intent or the agreement of the parties and, in some cases, in spite of an agreement between the parties. It is a non-contractual obligation that is to be treated procedurally as if it were a contract, and is often refered (sic) to as quasi contract, unjust enrichment, implied in law contract or restitution.

[Citation.]

"An implied in fact contract is defined as one where the terms and existence of the contract are manifested by the conduct of the parties with the request of one party and the performance by the other often being inferred from the circumstances attending the performance." [Citation.] The implied-in-fact contract is grounded in the parties' agreement and tacit understanding. [Citation.] ***

[UCC §] 1-205(1) defines "course of dealing" as "a sequence of previous conduct between the parties to a particular transaction which is fairly to be regarded as establishing a common basis of understanding for interpreting their expressions and other conduct."

***

Although the procedure was the same for each change order, in that MWE would request a pricing from Fox for the work, which was then presented to LMITCO, each party treated the pricings submitted by Fox for the change orders in a different manner. This treatment is not sufficient to establish a meeting of the minds or to establish a course of dealing when there was no "common basis of understanding for interpreting [the parties'] expressions" under [UCC §] 1-205(1).

*** After a review of the record, it appears that the district court's findings are supported by substantial and competent, albeit conflicting, evidence. ***

Using the district court's finding that pricings submitted by Fox were used by MWE as estimates for the change orders, the conclusion made by the district court that an implied-in-fact contract allowed for the reasonable compensation of Fox logically follows and is grounded in the law in Idaho. [Citation.]

This Court holds that the district court did not err in finding that there was an implied-in-fact contract using the industry standard's flow-down method of compensation for the change orders rather than a series of fixed price contracts between MWE and Fox.

UNIFORM COMMERCIAL CODE

Fox contends that the district court erred by failing to consider previous drafts of the proposed contract between the parties to determine the terms of the parties' agreement. Fox argues the predominant factor of this transaction was the fire alarm system, not the methodology of how the system was installed, which would focus on the sale of goods and, therefore, the Uniform Commercial Code ("UCC") should govern. Fox argues that in using the UCC various terms were agreed upon by the parties in the prior agreement drafts, including terms for the timing of payments, payments to Fox's suppliers and prerequisites to termination.

MWE contends that the UCC should not be used, despite the fact that goods comprised one-half of the contract price, because the predominant factor at issue is services and not the sale of goods. MWE points out that the primary issue is the value of Fox's services under the change orders and the cost of obtaining replacement services after Fox left the job. MWE further argues that the disagreement between the parties over material terms should prevent the court from using UCC gap fillers. Rather, MWE contends the intent and relationship of the parties should be used to resolve the conflict.

This Court in [citation], pointed out "in determining whether the UCC applies in such cases, a majority of courts look at the entire transaction to determine which aspect, the sale of goods or the sale of services, predominates." [Citation.] It is clear that if the underlying transaction to the contract involved the sale of goods, the UCC would apply. [Citation.] However, if the contract only involved services, the UCC would not apply. [Citation.] This Court has not directly articulated the standard to be used in mixed sales of goods and services, otherwise known as hybrid transactions.

The Court of Appeals in *Pittsley v. Houser*, [citation], focused on the applicability of the UCC to hybrid transactions. The court held that the trial court must look at the predominant factor of the transaction to determine if the UCC applies. [Citation.]

The test for inclusion or exclusion is not whether they are mixed, but, granting that they are mixed, whether their predominant factor, their thrust, their purpose, reasonably stated, is the rendition of service, with goods incidentally involved (e.g., contract with artist for painting) or is a transaction of sale, with labor incidentally involved (e.g., installation of a water heater in a bathroom). This test essentially involves consideration of the contract in its entirety, applying the UCC to the entire contract or not at all.

[Citation.] This Court agrees with the Court of Appeals' analysis and holds that the predominant factor test should be used to determine whether the UCC applies to transactions involving the sale of both goods and services.

One aspect that the Court of Appeals noted in its opinion in *Pittsley*, in its determination that the predominant factor in that case was the sale of goods, was that the purchaser was more concerned with the goods and less concerned with the installation, either who would provide it or the nature of the work. MWE and Fox decided to work on this project together because of their differing expertise. MWE was in the business of installing electrical wiring, while Fox designed, tested and assisted in the installation of fire alarm systems, in addition to ordering specialty equipment for fire alarm projects.

The district court found that the contract at issue in this case contained both goods and services; however, the predominant factor was Fox's services. The district court found that the goods provided by Fox were merely incidental to the services he provided, and the UCC would provide no assistance in interpreting the parties' agreement.

This Court holds that the district court did not err in finding that the predominant factor of the underlying transaction was services and that the UCC did not apply.

INTERPRETATION An implied in fact contract is formed by the conduct of the parties; in cases in which a contract provides for both goods and services, the common law applies if the predominant factor of the contract is the provision of services.

CRITICAL THINKING QUESTION Why should the legal rights of contracting parties depend on whether a contract is or is not for the sale of goods?

BILATERAL AND UNILATERAL CONTRACTS

In the typical contractual transaction, each party makes at least one promise. For example, if Adelle says to Byron, "If you promise to mow my lawn, I will pay you $10," and Byron agrees to mow Adelle's lawn, Adelle and Byron have made mutual promises, each agreeing to do something in exchange for the promise of the other. When a contract is formed by the exchange of promises, each party is under a duty to the other. This kind of contract is called a **bilateral contract**, because each party is both a **promisor** (a person making a promise) and a **promisee** (the person to whom a promise is made).

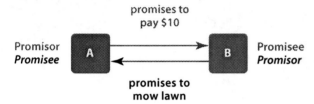

But suppose that only one of the parties makes a promise. Adelle says to Byron, "If you will mow my lawn, I will pay you $10." A contract will be formed when Byron has finished mowing the lawn and not before. At that time, Adelle becomes contractually obligated to pay $10 to Byron. Adelle's offer was in exchange for Byron's act of mowing the lawn, not for his promise to mow it. Because Byron never made a promise to mow the lawn, he was under no duty to mow it. This is a **unilateral contract** because only one of the parties has made a promise.

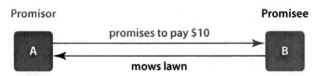

Thus, whereas a bilateral contract results from the exchange of a promise for a return promise, a unilateral contract results from the exchange of a promise either for performing an act or for refraining from doing an act. In cases in which it is not clear whether a unilateral or bilateral contract has been formed, the courts presume that the parties intended a bilateral contract. Thus, if Adelle says to Byron, "If you will mow my lawn, I will pay you $10," and Byron replies, "Okay, I will mow your lawn," a bilateral contract is formed.

PRACTICAL ADVICE

Because it is uncertain whether the offeree in a unilateral contract will choose to perform, use bilateral contracts wherever possible.

VALID, VOID, VOIDABLE, AND UNENFORCEABLE CONTRACTS

By definition a **valid contract** is one that meets all of the requirements of a binding contract. It is an enforceable promise or agreement.

A **void contract** is an agreement that does not meet all of the requirements of a binding contract. Thus, it is no contract at all; it is merely a promise or an agreement that has no legal effect. An example of a void agreement is an agreement entered into by a person whom the courts have declared incompetent.

A **voidable contract**, on the other hand, though defective, is not wholly lacking in legal effect. A voidable contract is a contract; however, because of the manner in which the contract was formed or a lack of capacity of a party to it, the law permits one or more of the parties to avoid the legal duties the contract creates. If the contract is voided, both of the parties are relieved of their legal duties under the agreement. For instance, through intentional misrepresentation of a material fact (fraud), Thomas induces Regina to enter into a contract. Regina may, upon discovery of the fraud, notify Thomas that by reason of the misrepresentation, she will not perform her promise, and the law will support Regina. Although the contract induced by fraud is not void, it is voidable at the election of Regina, the defrauded party. Thomas, the fraudulent party, may make no such election. If Regina elects to avoid the contract, Thomas will be released from his promise under the agreement, although he may be liable for damages under tort law for fraud.

A contract that is neither void nor voidable may nonetheless be unenforceable. An **unenforceable contract** is one for the breach of which the law provides no remedy. For example, a contract may be unenforceable because of a failure to satisfy the requirements of the statute of frauds, which requires certain kinds of contracts to be evidenced by a writing to be enforceable. Also, the statute of limitations imposes restrictions on the time during which a party has the right to bring a lawsuit for breach of contract. After the statutory time period has passed, a contract is referred to as unenforceable, rather than void or voidable. Figure 9-3 lists the requirements of a binding contract and the consequences of failing to satisfy each requirement.

PRACTICAL ADVICE

Be careful to avoid entering into void, voidable, and unenforceable contracts.

EXECUTED AND EXECUTORY CONTRACTS

A contract that has been fully carried out by all of the parties to it is an **executed contract**. Strictly speaking, an executed contract is no longer a contract, because all of the duties under it have been performed; but having a term for such a completed contract is useful. By comparison, the term **executory contract** applies to contracts that are still partially or entirely unperformed by one or more of the parties.

Promissory Estoppel

As a general rule, promises are not enforceable if they do not meet all the requirements of a contract. Nevertheless, in certain circumstances, the courts enforce noncontractual promises under the doctrine of **promissory estoppel** to avoid injustice. A noncontractual promise is enforceable when it is made under circumstances that should lead the promisor reasonably to expect that the promisee, in reliance on the promise, would be induced by it to take definite and substantial action or to forbear, and the promisee does take such action or does forbear (see Figure 9-2). For example, Gordon promises Constance not to foreclose for a period of six months on a mortgage Gordon owns on Constance's land. Constance then expends $100,000 to construct a building on the land. His promise not to foreclose is binding on Gordon under the doctrine of promissory estoppel.

PRACTICAL ADVICE

Take care not to make promises on which others may detrimentally rely.

SKEBBA V. KASCH

COURT OF APPEALS OF WISCONSIN, 2006
2006 WI APP 232, 724 N.W.2D 408; REVIEW DENIED, 2007 WI 59

www.wicourts.gov/ca/opinion/DisplayDocument.html?content=html&seqNo=26899

FACTS Kasch and his brother owned M.W. Kasch Co. Kasch hired Skebba as a sales representative, and over the years promoted him first to account manager, then to customer service manager, field sales manager, vice president of sales, senior vice president of sales and purchasing, and finally to vice president of sales. When M.W. Kasch Co. experienced serious financial problems in 1993, Skebba was approached by another company to leave Kasch and work for them. When Skebba told Kasch he was accepting the new opportunity, Kasch asked what it would take to get him to stay. Skebba told Kasch that he needed security for his retirement and family and would stay if Kasch agreed to pay Skebba $250,000 if one of these three conditions occurred: (1) the company was sold; (2) Skebba was lawfully terminated; or (3) Skebba retired. Kasch agreed to this proposal and promised to have the agreement drawn up. Skebba turned down the job opportunity and stayed with Kasch from December 1993 through 1999 when the company assets were sold.

Over the years, Skebba repeatedly but unsuccessfully asked Kasch for a written summary of this agreement. Eventually, Kasch sold the business receiving $5.1 million dollars for his 51 percent share of the business. Upon the sale of the business, Skebba asked Kasch for the $250,000 Kasch had previously promised to him. Kasch refused and denied ever having made such an agreement. Instead, Kasch gave Skebba a severance agreement, which had been drafted by Kasch's lawyers in 1993. This agreement promised two years of salary continuation on the sale of the company, but only if Skebba was not hired by the successor company. The severance agreement also required a set-off against the salary continuation of any sums Skebba earned from any activity during the two years of the severance agreement. Skebba sued, alleging breach of contract and promissory estoppel.

The jury found there was no contract, but that Kasch had made a promise upon which Skebba relied to his detriment, that the reliance was foreseeable, and that Skebba was damaged in the amount of $250,000. The trial court concluded that, based on its reading of applicable case law, it could not specifically enforce the promise the jury found Kasch made to Skebba because there were other ways to measure damages. The trial court held that since Skebba could not establish what he had lost by relying on Kasch's promise he had not proved his damages.

DECISION Order of trial court reversed and case remanded.

OPINION Kessler, J. Kasch did *not* promise to pay Skebba more than Skebba would have earned at the job Skebba turned down. Kasch did *not* promise that total income to Skebba would be greater than in the turned-down job, no matter how long he remained with Kasch. Kasch *only* promised that if Skebba stayed, Kasch would pay Skebba $ 250,000 (the sum Skebba wanted for his retirement), at the earliest of (1) Kasch selling the business, (2) Skebba retiring, or (3) Skebba being lawfully terminated. Skebba stayed. Kasch sold the business while Skebba was still employed by Kasch. Kasch refused to pay as promised.

The purpose of promissory estoppel is to enforce promises where the failure to do so is unjust. *U.S. Oil Co., Inc. v. Midwest Auto Care Servs.*, [citation]. In this case, the trial court specifically relied on parts of [the] *Hoffman* [case] in determining that specific performance of the promise could not be awarded and in concluding that Skebba had not properly established damages. *Hoffman* was the first case in Wisconsin to adopt promissory estoppel. * * * [T]he *Hoffman* court explained its adoption of a cause of action based on promissory estoppel as grounded in section 90 of the Restatement of Contracts which:

> does not impose the requirement that the promise giving rise to the cause of action must be so comprehensive in scope as to meet the requirements of an offer that would ripen into a contract if accepted by the promisee. Rather the conditions imposed are:
>
> 1. Was the promise one which the promisor should reasonably expect to induce action or forbearance of a definite and substantial character on the part of the promisee?
>
> 2. Did the promise induce such action or forbearance?
>
> 3. Can injustice be avoided only by enforcement of the promise?

[Citation.]

The *Hoffman* court explains that the first two of these requirements are facts to be found by a jury or other fact-finder, while the third is a policy decision to be made by the court. [Citations.] In making this policy decision, a court must consider a number of factors in determining whether injustice can only be avoided by enforcement of the promise. *U.S. Oil*, [citation]. The court in *U.S. Oil* adopted those considerations set forth in the Restatement (Second) of Contracts § 139(2), (1981):

a. the availability and adequacy of other remedies, particularly cancellation and restitution;

b. the definite and substantial character of the action or forbearance in relation to the remedy sought;

c. the extent to which the action or forbearance corroborates evidence of the making and terms of the promise, or the making and terms are otherwise established by clear and convincing evidence;

d. the reasonableness of the action or forbearance; [and]

e. the extent to which the action or forbearance was foreseeable by the promisor.

[Citation.]

The record does not indicate that the trial court here applied the considerations our supreme court announced in *U.S. Oil*. Instead, the trial court apparently relied on the *Hoffman* court's discussion of various damage theories that the court explained might be appropriate once the determination had been made to enforce the promise by application of promissory estoppel. * * *

* * *

A court, in fashioning a remedy, can consider any equitable *or* legal remedy which will "prevent injustice." * * *

As later commentators have noted, Wisconsin, with its landmark *Hoffman* decision, is one of a small group of states which recognizes that to fulfill the purpose of promissory estoppel—*i.e.*, prevent injustice—a court must be able to fashion a remedy that restores the promisee to where he or she would be if the promisor had fulfilled the promise. [Citation.] In this case, Skebba performed—he remained at M.W. Kasch—in reliance on Kasch's promise to pay $250,000 to him if one of three conditions occurred. Kasch enjoyed the fruits of Skebba's reliance—he kept on a top salesperson to help the company through tough financial times and he avoided the damage that he believed Skebba's leaving could have had on M.W. Kasch's reputation in the industry. Accordingly, to prevent injustice, the equitable remedy for Skebba to receive is Kasch's specific performance promised-payment of the $250,000.

The record in this case, considered in light of the *U.S. Oil* tests and the jury's findings, compels specific performance of the promise because otherwise Kasch will enjoy all of the benefits of induced reliance while Skebba will be deprived of that which he was promised, with no other available remedy to substitute fairly for the promised reward. * * * [In short, every factor this court requires to be considered supports enforcement of the promise through promissory estoppel. The trial court submitted the promissory estoppel cause of action to the jury. The jury concluded that the promise had been made, that Skebba relied on the promise to his detriment, and that such reliance was foreseeable by Kasch. The jury also found that Skebba's damages were the amount Skebba testified Kasch promised to pay Skebba if he was still employed when the company was sold, that is, $250,000. * * *

* * * In this case, specific performance *is* the *necessary* enforcement mechanism to prevent injustice for Skebba's reliance on the promise the jury found Kasch had made to him.

INTERPRETATION The courts will enforce a promise that the promisor should reasonably expect to induce detrimental reliance by the promisee if the promisee takes such action and justice requires enforcement.

ETHICAL QUESTION Did Kasch act ethically? Explain.

CRITICAL THINKING QUESTION What could Skebba have done to better protect his interests? Explain.

Quasi Contracts

In addition to express and implied in fact contracts, there are implied in law or quasi contracts, which were not included in the previous classification of contracts for the reason that a quasi (meaning "as if") contract is not a contract at all but based in restitution. The term *quasi contract* is used because the remedy granted for quasi contract is similar to one of the remedies available for breach of contract.

A quasi contract is not a contract because it is based neither on an express nor on an implied promise. Rather, a *contract implied in law* or **quasi contract** is an obligation imposed by law to avoid injustice. For example, Willard by mistake delivers to Roy a plain, unaddressed envelope containing $100 intended for Lucia. Roy is under no contractual obligation to return it, but Willard is permitted to recover the $100 from Roy. The law imposes a quasi-contractual obligation on Roy to prevent his unjust enrichment at the expense of Willard. Such a recovery requires three essential elements: (1) a benefit conferred upon the defendant (Roy) by the plaintiff (Willard); (2) the defendant's (Roy's) appreciation or knowledge of the benefit; and (3) acceptance or retention of the benefit by the defendant (Roy) under circumstances making it inequitable for him to retain the benefit without compensating the plaintiff for its value.

Not infrequently, quasi contracts are used to provide a remedy when the parties enter into a void contract, an unenforceable contract, or a voidable contract that is avoided. In such a case, the law of quasi contracts will determine what recovery is permitted for any performance rendered by the parties under the invalid, unenforceable, or invalidated agreement.

JASDIP PROPERTIES SC, LLC v. ESTATE OF RICHARDSON

COURT OF APPEALS OF SOUTH CAROLINA, 2011

395 S.C. 633, 720 S.E.2D 4

http://scholar.google.com/scholar_case?case=3098899484583065486&q=
JASDIP+PROPERTIES+SC,+LLC+v.+ESTATE+OF+RICHARDSON&hl=en&as_sdt=4,232

FACTS On May 5, 2006, Stewart Richardson (Seller) and JASDIP Properties SC, LLC (Buyer) entered into an agreement for the purchase of certain property in Georgetown, South Carolina. The purchase price for the property was to be $537,000. The buyer paid an initial earnest money deposit of $10,000. The balance was due at the closing on or before July 28, 2006. Thereafter the seller granted the buyer extensions to the closing date in return for additional payments of $175,000 and $25,000, each to be applied to the purchase price. The buyer was unable to close in a timely fashion, and the seller rescinded the contract.

Thereafter, the buyer brought suit against the seller (1) contending that the seller would be unjustly enriched if allowed to keep the money paid despite the rescission of the agreement and (2) requesting $210,000. The $210,000 consisted of the $10,000 earnest money deposit and $200,000 in subsequent payments. The buyer later filed an amended complaint requesting $205,000, stating that the agreement permitted the seller to retain half of the $10,000 earnest money deposit.

A jury determined that neither party had breached the contract and awarded no damages on that basis. The buyer then requested a ruling by the trial court on its action for unjust enrichment. The trial court denied the buyer's claim for unjust enrichment. The buyer appealed arguing that all the evidence presented at trial, as well as the jury's verdict, supports a finding that the agreement was rescinded or abandoned and that this requires restitution of $205,000 to the buyer.

DECISION Judgment of the trial court is reversed, and the case is remanded.

OPINION Konduros, J. "Restitution is a remedy designed to prevent unjust enrichment." [Citation.]

("Unjust enrichment is an equitable doctrine, akin to restitution, which permits the recovery of that amount the defendant has been unjustly enriched at the expense of the plaintiff."). "The terms 'restitution' and 'unjust enrichment' are modern designations for the older doctrine of quasi-contract." [Citation.] "[Q]uantum meruit, quasi-contract, and implied by law contract are equivalent terms for an equitable remedy." [Citation.]

"Implied in law or quasi-contract are not considered contracts at all, but are akin to restitution which permits recovery of that amount the defendant has been benefitted at the expense of the plaintiff in order to preclude unjust enrichment." [Citation.] ***

"To recover on a theory of restitution, the plaintiff must show (1) that he conferred a non-gratuitous benefit on the defendant; (2) that the defendant realized some value from the benefit; and (3) that it would be inequitable for the defendant to retain the benefit without paying the plaintiff for its value." [Citation.] "Unjust enrichment is usually a prerequisite for enforcement of the doctrine of restitution; if there is no basis for unjust enrichment, there is no basis for restitution." [Citation.]

Buyer seeks the $175,000 and $25,000 payments as well as the $10,000 in earnest money *** Additionally, in its amended complaint, Buyer states that under the Agreement, Seller can only keep half of the $10,000 in earnest money and only requests a total of $205,000. An issue conceded in the trial court cannot be argued on appeal. [Citation.] Therefore, Buyer is bound by that concession and entitled to $5,000 of the earnest money at most.

The $175,000 and $25,000 payments both explicitly stated that they were towards the purchase price. Additionally, Buyer paid $10,000 in an earnest money deposit. The unappealed finding of the jury was that neither party breached the Agreement. An unchallenged ruling, right or wrong, is the law of the case. [Citation.] Based on the jury's finding that Buyer did not breach, we find Buyer is entitled to the money paid towards the purchase price as well as half of the earnest money under the theory of restitution. Buyer met the requirements to recover under the theory of restitution: (1) Buyer paid Seller $205,000 towards the purchase price and the sale did not go through despite the fact that neither party breached; (2) Seller kept the $205,000 although he also retained the Property; and (3) Seller keeping the $205,000 is inequitable because the Seller still has the Property, the jury found neither party breached, and the evidence supports that Buyer intended to go forward with the purchase. Therefore, the trial court erred in failing to find for Buyer for its claim of unjust enrichment. Accordingly, we reverse the trial court's determination that Buyer was not entitled to restitution and award Buyer $205,000.

INTERPRETATION Implied in law or quasi contracts are not considered contracts at all, but are akin to restitution which permits recovery of that amount the defendant has been benefited at the expense of the plaintiff in order to prevent unjust enrichment.

CRITICAL THINKING QUESTION Why does the law allow a recovery in quasi contract?

CONCEPT REVIEW 9-1

Contracts, Promissory Estoppel, and Quasi Contracts

	Contract	Promissory Estoppel	Quasi Contract
Type of Promise	Contractual	Noncontractual	None Void Unenforceable Invalidated
Requirements	All of the essential elements of a contract	Detrimental and justifiable reliance	Benefit conferred and knowingly accepted
Remedies	Equitable Compensatory Reliance Restitution	Promise enforced to the extent necessary to avoid injustice	Reasonable value of benefit conferred

Business Law in Action

Armed with a hastily scribbled work order, Jonas, an employee of Triton Painting Service, heads to 109 Millard Road. He works for two full days power cleaning, priming, and painting the exterior of the house. Satisfied with his work, Jonas moves on to his next job. When the homeowners, the Prestons, return from their vacation several days later, they are shocked to see their formerly "Palatial Peach" home painted "Santa Fe Sand." They are even more surprised when they receive a call from Triton demanding payment for the paint job.

Errors such as this sometimes occur in business. It was the homeowners at 104 Millard Road who had contracted to pay Triton $1,200 for an exterior paint job using Santa Fe Sand. But Jonas felt sure enough he had the correct house number, and no one stopped him from doing the work. And even though the Prestons had not chosen the color, they now have a freshly painted house because of Triton's error. Should the Prestons have to pay? If so, how much? What does the law say about this?

To begin with, there was no contract between Triton and the Prestons. Therefore Triton cannot sue the Prestons for breach of contract. A suit in quasi contract is Triton's best bet, but to prevail, Triton must prove unjust enrichment. One factor affecting Triton's success is whether the Prestons, in good faith, dislike the new color. However, even if they do not dislike Santa Fe Sand, another factor is whether the house needed repainting. It would be unfair to require the Prestons to pay for an unnecessary service. Moreover, because the Prestons were out of town they could not have stopped Jonas from doing the work. Finally, because they received services rather than goods, they cannot now give back the service. Under these circumstances, it is hardly equitable to make the Prestons pay for what was clearly Triton's mistake.

CHAPTER SUMMARY

Development of the Law of Contracts

Common Law most contracts are primarily governed by state common law, including contracts involving employment, services, insurance, real property (land and anything attached to it), patents, and copyrights

The Uniform Commercial Code (UCC) Article 2 of the UCC governs the sales of goods
- *Sale* the transfer of title from seller to buyer
- *Goods* tangible personal property (personal property is all property other than an interest in land)

Definition of a Contract

Contract binding agreement that the courts will enforce

Breach failure to properly perform a contractual obligation

Requirements of a Contract

Mutual Assent the parties to a contract must manifest by words or conduct that they have agreed to enter into a contract

Consideration each party to a contract must intentionally exchange a legal benefit or incur a legal detriment as an inducement to the other party to make a return exchange

Legality of Object the purpose of a contract must not be criminal, tortious, or otherwise against public policy

Capacity the parties to a contract must have contractual capacity

Classification of Contracts

Express and Implied Contracts
* *Implied in Fact Contract* contract in which the agreement of the parties is inferred from their conduct
* *Express Contract* an agreement that is stated in words either orally or in writing

Bilateral and Unilateral Contracts
* *Bilateral Contract* contract in which both parties exchange promises
* *Unilateral Contract* contract in which only one party makes a promise

Valid, Void, Voidable, and Unenforceable Contracts
* *Valid Contract* one that meets all of the requirements of a binding contract
* *Void Contract* no contract at all; without legal effect
* *Voidable Contract* contract capable of being made void
* *Unenforceable Contract* contract for the breach of which the law provides no remedy

Executed and Executory Contracts
* *Executed Contract* contract that has been fully performed by all of the parties
* *Executory Contract* contract that has yet to be fully performed

Promissory Estoppel

Definition a doctrine enforcing some noncontractual promises

Requirements a promise made under circumstances that should lead the promisor reasonably to expect that the promise would induce the promisee to take definite and substantial action, and the promisee does take such action

Remedy a court will enforce the promise to the extent necessary to avoid injustice

Quasi Contract

Definition an obligation not based upon contract that is imposed by law to avoid injustice; also called an implied in law contract

Requirements a court will impose a quasi contract when (1) the plaintiff confers a benefit upon the defendant, (2) the defendant knows or appreciates the benefit, and (3) the defendant's retention of the benefit is inequitable

Remedy the plaintiff recovers the reasonable value of the benefit she conferred upon the defendant

QUESTIONS

1. Owen telephones an order to Hillary's store for certain goods, which Hillary delivers to Owen. Nothing is said by either party about price or payment terms. What are the legal obligations of Owen and Hillary?

2. Minth is the owner of the Hiawatha Supper Club, which he leased for two years to Piekarski. During the period of the lease, Piekarski contracted with Puttkammer for the resurfacing of the access and service areas of the supper club. Puttkammer performed the work satisfactorily. Minth knew about the contract and the performance of the work. The work, including labor and materials, had a reasonable value of $2,540, but Puttkammer was never paid because Piekarski went bankrupt. Puttkammer brought an action against Minth to recover the amount owed to him by Piekarski. Will Puttkammer prevail? Explain.

3. Jonathan writes to Willa, stating, "I'll pay you $150 if you reseed my lawn." Willa reseeds Jonathan's lawn as requested. Has a contract been formed? If so, what kind?

4. Calvin uses fraud to induce Maria to promise to pay money in return for goods he has delivered to her. Has a contract been formed? If so, what kind? What are the rights of Calvin and Maria?

5. Anna is about to buy a house on a hill. Prior to the purchase, she obtains a promise from Betty, the owner of the adjacent property, that Betty will not build any structure that would block Anna's view. In reliance on this promise, Anna buys the house. Is Betty's promise binding? Why or why not?

CASE PROBLEMS

6. Mary Dobos was admitted to Boca Raton Community Hospital in serious condition with an abdominal aneurysm. The hospital called upon Nursing Care Services, Inc., to provide around-the-clock nursing services for Mrs. Dobos. She received two weeks of in-hospital care, forty-eight hours of postrelease care, and two weeks of at-home care. The total bill was $3,723.90. Mrs. Dobos refused to pay, and Nursing Care Services, Inc., brought an action to recover. Mrs. Dobos maintained that she was not obligated to render payment in that she never signed a written contract, nor did she orally agree to be liable for the services. The necessity for the services, reasonableness of the fee, and competency of the nurses were undisputed. After Mrs. Dobos admitted that she or her daughter authorized the forty-eight hours of postrelease care, the trial court ordered compensation of $248 for that period. It did not allow payment of the balance, and Nursing Care Services, Inc., appealed. Decision?

7. St. Charles Drilling Co. contracted with Osterholt to install a well and water system that would produce a specified quantity of water. The water system failed to meet its warranted capacity, and Osterholt sued for breach of contract. Does the Uniform Commercial Code apply to this contract?

8. Helvey brought suit against the Wabash County REMC (REMC) for breach of implied and express warranties. He alleged that REMC furnished electricity in excess of 135 volts to Helvey's home, damaging his 110-volt household appliances. This incident occurred more than four years before Helvey brought this suit. In defense, REMC pleads that the Uniform Commercial Code's (UCC's) Article 2 statute of limitations of four years has passed, thereby barring Helvey's suit. Helvey argues that providing electrical energy is not a transaction in goods under the UCC but rather a furnishing of services that would make applicable the general contract six-year statute of limitations. Is the contract governed by the UCC? Why?

9. Jack Duran, president of Colorado Carpet Installation, Inc., began negotiations with Fred and Zuma Palermo for the sale and installation of carpeting, carpet padding, tile, and vinyl floor covering in their home. Duran drew up a written proposal that referred to Colorado Carpet as "the seller" and to the Palermos as the "customer." The proposal listed the quantity, unit cost, and total price of each item to be installed. The total price of the job was $4,777.75. Although labor was expressly included in this figure, Duran estimated the total labor cost at $926. Mrs. Palermo in writing accepted Duran's written proposal soon after he submitted it to her. After Colorado Carpet delivered the tile to the Palermo home, however, Mrs. Palermo had a disagreement with Colorado Carpet's tile man and arranged for another contractor to perform the job. Colorado Carpet brought an action against the Palermos for breach of contract. Does the Uniform Commercial Code apply to this contract?

10. On November 1, the Kansas City Post Office Employees Credit Union merged into the Kansas City Telephone Credit Union to form the Communications Credit Union (Credit Union). Systems Design and Management Information (SDMI) develops computer software programs for credit unions, using Burroughs (now Unisys) hardware. SDMI and Burroughs together offered to sell to Credit Union both a software package, called the Generic System, and Burroughs hardware. Later in November, a demonstration of the software was held at SDMI's offices, and the Credit Union agreed to purchase the Generic System software. This agreement was oral. After Credit Union was converted to the SDMI Generic System, major problems with the system immediately became apparent, so SDMI filed suit against Credit Union to recover the outstanding contract price for the software. Credit Union counterclaimed for damages based upon breach of contract and negligent and fraudulent misrepresentation. Does the Uniform Commercial Code apply to this contract?

11. Insul-Mark is the marketing arm of Kor-It Sales, Inc. Kor-It manufactures roofing fasteners and Insul-Mark distributes them nationwide. In late 1985, Kor-It contracted with Modern Materials, Inc., to have large volumes of screws coated with a rust-proofing agent. The contract specified that the coated screws must pass a standard industry test and that Kor-It would pay according to the pound and length of the screws coated. Kor-It had received numerous complaints from customers that the coated screws were rusting, and Modern Materials unsuccessfully attempted to remedy the problem. Kor-It terminated its relationship with Modern Materials and brought suit for the deficient coating. Modern Materials counterclaimed for the labor and materials it had furnished to Kor-It. The trial court held that the contract (a) was for performance of a service, (b) not governed by the Uniform Commercial Code, (c) governed by the common law of contracts, and (d) therefore, barred by a two-year statute of limitations. Insul-Mark appealed. Decision?

12. Max E. Pass, Jr., and his wife, Martha N. Pass, departed in an aircraft owned and operated by Mr. Pass from Plant City, Florida, bound for Clarksville, Tennessee. Somewhere over Alabama the couple encountered turbulence, and Mr. Pass lost control of the aircraft. The plane crashed, killing both Mr. and Mrs. Pass. Approximately four and a half months prior to the flight in which he was killed, Mr. Pass had taken his airplane to Shelby Aviation, an aircraft service company, for inspection and service. In servicing the aircraft, Shelby Aviation replaced both rear wing attach point brackets on the plane. Three and one

half years after the crash, Max E. Pass, Sr., father of Mr. Pass and administrator of his estate, and Shirley Williams, mother of Mrs. Pass and administratrix of her estate, filed suit against Shelby Aviation. The lawsuit alleged that the rear wing attach point brackets sold and installed by Shelby Aviation were defective because they lacked the bolts necessary to secure them properly to the airplane. The plaintiffs asserted claims against the defendant for breach of express and implied warranties under Article 2 of the Uniform Commercial Code (UCC), which governs the sale of goods. Shelby Aviation contended that the transaction with Mr. Pass had been primarily for the sale of services, rather than of goods, and that consequently Article 2 of the UCC did not cover the transaction. Does the UCC apply to this transaction? Explain.

13. In March, William Tackaberry, a real estate agent for Weichert Co. Realtors, informed Thomas Ryan, a local developer, that he knew of property Ryan might be interested in purchasing. Ryan indicated he was interested in knowing more about the property. Tackaberry disclosed the property's identity and the seller's proposed price. Tackaberry also stated that the purchaser would have to pay Weichert a 10 percent commission. Tackaberry met with the property owner and gathered information concerning the property's current leases, income, expenses, and development plans. Tackaberry also collected tax and zoning documents relevant to the property. In a face-to-face meeting on April 4, Tackaberry gave Ryan the data he had gathered and presented Ryan with a letter calling for a 10 percent finder's fee to be paid to Weichert by Ryan upon "successfully completing and closing of title." Ryan refused to agree to the 10 percent figure during this meeting. Tackaberry arranged a meeting, held three days later, where Ryan contracted with the owner to buy the land. Ryan refused, however, to pay the 10 percent finder's fee to Weichert. What, if anything, is Weichert entitled to recover from Ryan? Explain.

TAKING SIDES

Richardson hired J. C. Flood Company, a plumbing contractor, to correct a stoppage in the sewer line of her house. The plumbing company's "snake" device, used to clear the line leading to the main sewer, became caught in the underground line. To release it, the company excavated a portion of the sewer line in Richardson's backyard. In the process, the company discovered numerous leaks in a rusty, defective water pipe that ran parallel with the sewer line. To meet public regulations, the water pipe, of a type no longer approved for such service, had to be replaced either then or later, when the yard would have to be excavated again. The plumbing company proceeded to repair the water pipe. Though Richardson inspected the company's work daily and did not express any objection to the extra work involved in replacing the water pipe, she refused to pay any part of the total bill after the company completed the entire operation. J. C. Flood Company then sued Richardson for the costs of labor and material it had furnished.

a. What arguments would support J. C. Flood's claim for the costs of labor and material it had furnished?

b. What arguments would support Richardson's refusal to pay the bill?

c. For what, if anything, should Richardson be liable? Explain.

Chapter 10

MUTUAL ASSENT

It is elementary that for a contract to exist there must be an offer and acceptance.

ZELLER V. FIRST NATIONAL BANK & TRUST, TALES, 79 ILL. APP. 3D 170, 34 ILL. DEC. 473, 398 N.E.2D 148 (1979)

CHAPTER OUTCOMES

After reading and studying this chapter, you should be able to:

1. Identify the three essentials of an offer and explain briefly the requirements associated with each.

2. State the seven ways by which an offer may be terminated other than by acceptance.

3. Compare the traditional and modern theories of definiteness of acceptance of an offer, as shown by the common law "mirror image" rule and by the rule of the Uniform Commercial Code.

4. Describe the five situations limiting an offeror's right to revoke her offer.

5. Explain the various rules that determine when an acceptance takes effect.

Though each of the requirements for forming a contract is essential to its existence, mutual assent is so basic that frequently a contract is referred to as an agreement between the parties. Enforcing the contract means enforcing the agreement; indeed, the agreement between the parties is the very core of the contract. As we discussed in Chapter 9, a contractual agreement always involves either a promise exchanged for a promise (*bilateral contract*) or a promise exchanged for a completed act or forbearance to act (*unilateral contract*).

The way in which parties usually show mutual assent is by offer and acceptance. One party makes a proposal (offer) by words or conduct to the other party, who agrees by words or conduct to the proposal (acceptance).

A contract may be formed by conduct. Thus, though there may be no definite offer and acceptance, or definite acceptance of an offer, a contract exists if both parties' actions manifest (indicate) a recognition by each of them of the existence of a contract. To form a contract, the agreement must be objectively manifested. The important thing is what the parties indicate to one another by spoken or written words or by conduct. The law, therefore, applies an *objective* standard and is concerned only with the assent, agreement, or intention of a party as it reasonably appears from his words or actions. The law of contracts is not concerned with what a party may have actually thought or the meaning that he intended to convey even if his subjective understanding or intention differed from the meaning he objectively indicated by word or conduct. For example, if Joanne seemingly offers to sell to Bruce her Chevrolet automobile but intended to offer and believes that she is offering her Ford automobile, and Bruce accepts the offer, reasonably believing it was for the Chevrolet, a contract has been formed for the sale of the Chevrolet. Subjectively, Joanne and Bruce are not in agreement as to the subject matter. Objectively, however, there is agreement, and the objective manifestation is binding.

The Uniform Commercial Code's (UCC's or Code's) treatment of mutual assent is covered in greater detail in Chapter 19.

OFFER

An **offer** is a definite undertaking or proposal made by one person to another indicating a willingness to enter into a contract. The person making the proposal is the **offeror**. The person to whom it is made is the **offeree**. When it is received, the offer confers on the offeree the power to create a contract by acceptance, which is an expression of the offeree's willingness to comply with the terms of the offer. Until the offeree exercises this power, the outstanding offer creates neither rights nor liabilities.

Essentials of an Offer

An offer need not take any particular form to have legal effect. To be effective, however, it must (1) be communicated to the offeree; (2) manifest an intent to enter into a contract; and (3) be sufficiently definite and certain. If these essentials are present and the offer has not terminated, the offer gives the offeree the power to form a contract by accepting the offer.

COMMUNICATION

To provide his part of the mutual assent required to form a contract, the offeree must know about the offer; he cannot agree to something about which he has no knowledge. Accordingly, the offeror must communicate the offer in an intended manner. For example, Oscar signs a letter containing an offer to Ellen and leaves it on top of the desk in his office. Later that day, Ellen, without prearrangement, goes to Oscar's office, discovers that he is away, notices the letter on his desk, reads it, and then writes on it an acceptance that she dates and signs. No contract is formed because the offer never became effective: Ellen became aware of the offer by chance, not by Oscar's intentional communication of it.

Not only must the offer be communicated to the offeree, but the communication must also be made or authorized by the offeror. If Jones tells Black that she plans to offer White $600 for a piano, and Black promptly informs White of Jones's intention, no offer has been made. There was no authorized communication of any offer by Jones to White. By the same token, if David should offer to sell to Lou his diamond ring, an acceptance of this offer by Tia would not be effective, as David made no offer to Tia.

An offer need not be stated or communicated by words. Conduct from which a reasonable person may infer a proposal in return for either an act or a promise amounts to an offer.

An offer may be made to the general public. No person can accept such an offer, however, until and unless he knows that the offer exists. For example, if a person, without knowing of an advertised reward for information leading to the return of a lost watch, gives information leading to the return of the watch, he is not entitled to the reward. His act was not an acceptance of the offer because he could not accept something of which he had no knowledge.

INTENT

To have legal effect, an offer must manifest an intent to enter into a contract. The **intent** of an offer is determined objectively from the words or conduct of the parties. The meaning of either party's manifestation is based on what a reasonable person in the other party's position would have believed.

Occasionally, a person exercises her sense of humor by speaking or writing words that—taken literally and without regard to context or surrounding circumstances—could be construed as an offer. The promise is intended as a joke, however, and the promisee as a reasonable person should understand it to be such. Therefore, it is not an offer. Because the person to whom it is made realizes or should realize that it is not made in earnest, it should not create a reasonable expectation in his mind. No contractual intent exists on the part of the promisor, and the promisee is or reasonably ought to be aware of that fact. If, however, the intended joke is so real that the promisee as a reasonable person under all the circumstances believes that the joke is in fact an offer, and so believing accepts, the objective standard applies and the parties have entered into a contract.

A promise made under obvious excitement or emotional strain is likewise not an offer. For example, Charlotte, after having her month-old Cadillac break down for the third time in two days, screams in disgust, "I will sell this car to anyone for $10!" Lisa hears Charlotte and hands her a $10 bill. Under the circumstances, Charlotte's statement was not an offer if a reasonable person in Lisa's position would have recognized it merely as an excited, nonbinding utterance.

It is important to distinguish language that constitutes an offer from that which merely solicits or invites offers. Such proposals, although made in earnest, lack the intent to enter into a contract and are therefore not deemed offers. As a result, a purported acceptance does not bring

about a contract but operates only as an offer. Proposals that invite offers include preliminary negotiations, advertisements, and auctions.

> ### Practical Advice
> Make sure that you indicate by words or conduct what agreement you wish to enter.

Catamount Slate Products, Inc. v. Sheldon

Supreme Court of Vermont, 2004
2003 VT 112, 845 A.2D 324

http://scholar.google.com/scholar_case?case=12161607133389120155&q=2003+VT+112&hl=en&as_sdt=2,22

FACTS The Reed Family owns and operates Catamount Slate Products, Inc. (Catamount), a slate quarry and mill, on 122 acres in Fair Haven, Vermont. The Sheldons own neighboring property. Since 1997, the parties have been litigating the Reeds' right to operate their slate business and to use the access road leading to the quarry. In 2000, the parties agreed to try to resolve their disputes in a state-funded mediation with retired Judge Arthur O'Dea serving as mediator. Prior to the mediation, Judge O'Dea sent each party a Mediation Agreement outlining the rules governing the mediation. Paragraph nine of the Mediation Agreement stated that—

> i. all statements, admissions, confessions, acts, or exchanges … are acknowledged by the parties to be offers in negotiation of settlement and compromise, and as such inadmissible in evidence, and not binding upon either party unless reduced to a final agreement of settlement. Any final agreement of settlement must be in writing and signed by every party sought to be charged.

The mediation was held on September 5, 2000. Judge O'Dea began the session by reaffirming the statements made in the Mediation Agreement. After ten hours, the parties purportedly reached an agreement on all major issues. Judge O'Dea then orally summarized the terms of the resolution with the parties and counsel present. The attorneys took notes on the terms of the agreement with the understanding that they would prepare the necessary documents for signature in the coming days.

The resolution required the Reeds to pay the Sheldons $250 a month for the right to use the access road, with payments to commence on October 1, 2000. The parties also agreed to a series of terms governing the operation of the slate quarry. These terms were to be memorialized in two distinct documents, a Lease Agreement and a Settlement Agreement.

On September 7, 2000, two days after the mediation, the Sheldons' attorney, Emily Joselson, drafted a letter outlining the terms of the settlement and sent copies to James Leary, the Reeds' attorney, and Judge O'Dea. Within a week, Leary responded by letter concurring in some respects and outlining the issues on which the Reeds disagreed with Joselson's characterization of the settlement.

On October 1, 2000, the Reeds began paying the $250 monthly lease payments, but, since the settlement agreement was not final, the parties agreed that the money would go into an escrow account maintained by the Sheldons' counsel. The check was delivered to the Sheldons' attorney with a cover memo stating, "This check is forwarded to you with the understanding that the funds will be disbursed to your clients only after settlement agreement becomes final. Of course, if the settlement agreement does not come to fruition, then the funds must be returned to my clients." The parties continued to exchange letters actively negotiating the remaining details of the Lease and Settlement Agreements for the better part of the next five months.

In February 2001, while drafts were still being exchanged, Christine Stannard, the Reeds' daughter, saw a deed and map in the Fair Haven Town Clerk's Office which led her to believe that the disputed road was not owned by the Sheldons, but was a town highway. The Reeds then refused to proceed any further with negotiating the settlement agreement. A written settlement agreement was never signed by either party.

The Sheldons then filed a motion to enforce the settlement agreement. The trial court granted the option, finding that the attorneys' notes taken at the end of the mediation and the unsigned drafts of the Lease and Settlement Agreements sufficiently memorialized the agreement between the parties and thus constituted an enforceable settlement agreement.

DECISION Judgment of the trial is reversed and remanded.

OPINION Skoglund, J. The question before us is whether the oral agreement reached at mediation, when combined with the unexecuted documents drafted subsequently, constituted a binding, enforceable settlement agreement. Parties are free to enter into a binding contract without memorializing their agreement in a fully executed document. [Citation.] In such an instance, the mere intention or discussion to commit their agreement to writing will not prevent the formation of a contract prior to the document's execution. [Citations.]

"On the other hand, if either party communicates an intent not to be bound until he achieves a fully executed document, no amount of negotiation or oral agreement to specific terms will result in the formation of a binding contract." [Citation.] The freedom to determine the exact moment in which an agreement becomes binding encourages the parties to negotiate as candidly as possible, secure in the knowledge that they will not be bound until the execution of what both parties consider to be a final, binding agreement.

We look to the intent of the parties to determine the moment of contract formation. [Citation.] Intent to be bound is a question of fact. [Citation.] "To discern that intent a court must look to the words and deeds [of the parties] which constitute objective signs in a given set of circumstances." [Citation.] In [citation], the Second Circuit articulated four factors to aid in determining whether the parties intended to be bound in the absence of a fully executed document. [Citation.] The court suggested that we

> consider (1) whether there has been an express reservation of the right not to be bound in the absence of a writing; (2) whether there has been partial performance of the contract; (3) whether all of the terms of the alleged contract have been agreed upon; and (4) whether the agreement at issue is the type of contract that is usually committed to writing. [Citations.]

The language of the parties' correspondence and other documentary evidence presented reveals an intent by the mediation participants not to be bound prior to the execution of a final document. First, the Mediation Agreement Judge O'Dea sent to the parties prior to the mediation clearly contemplates that any settlement agreement emanating from the mediation would be binding only after being put in writing and signed. Paragraph nine of the Agreement expressly stated that statements made during mediation would not be "binding upon either party unless reduced to a final agreement of settlement" and that "any final agreement of settlement [would] be in writing and signed by every party sought to be charged." Further, Judge O'Dea reminded the parties of these ground rules at the outset of the mediation.

* * *

Even more compelling evidence of the Reeds' lack of intent to be bound in the absence of a writing is the statement in the cover letter accompanying the Reeds' $250 payments to the Sheldons' attorney saying, "This check is forwarded to you with the understanding that the funds will be disbursed to your clients only after settlement agreement becomes final. Of course, if the settlement agreement does not come to fruition, then the funds must be returned to my clients." This factor weighs in favor of finding that the Reeds expressed their right not to be bound until their agreement was reduced to a final writing and executed.

Because there was no evidence presented of partial performance of the settlement agreement, we next consider the third factor, whether there was anything left to negotiate. * * *

As stated by the Second Circuit in [citation], "the actual drafting of a written instrument will frequently reveal points of disagreement, ambiguity, or omission which must be worked out prior to execution. Details that are unnoticed or passed by in oral discussion will be pinned down when the understanding is reduced to writing" (internal quotations and citations omitted). [Citation.] This case is no exception. A review of the lengthy correspondence in this case makes clear that several points of disagreement and ambiguity arose during the drafting process. Beyond the location of seismic measurements and the definition of "overblast," correspondence indicates that the parties still had not reached agreement on the term and width of the lease, acceptable decibel levels and notice provisions for blasts, the definition of "truck trips," and whether all claims would be dismissed without prejudice after the execution of the agreement. Resolution of these issues was clearly important enough to forestall final execution until the language of the documents could be agreed upon. In such a case, where the parties intend to be bound only upon execution of a final document, for the court to determine that, despite continuing disagreement on substantive terms, the parties reached a binding, enforceable settlement agreement undermines their right to enter into the specific settlement agreement for which they contracted.

The fourth and final factor, whether the agreement at issue is the type of contract usually put into writing, also weighs in the Reeds' favor. Being a contract for an interest in land, the Lease Agreement is subject to the Statute of Frauds and thus generally must be in writing. * * *

* * *

In conclusion, three of the four factors indicate that the parties here did not intend to be bound until the execution of a final written document, and therefore we hold that the parties never entered into a binding settlement agreement.

INTERPRETATION The intent of the parties to be bound to a contract is determined by an objective standard of what a reasonable person would have believed based on the words and conduct of the parties.

CRITICAL THINKING QUESTION Does the decision rendered by the court establish a policy that is best for society? Explain.

Preliminary Negotiations If a communication creates in the mind of a reasonable person in the position of the offeree an expectation that his acceptance will conclude a contract, then the communication is an offer. If it does not, then the communication is a preliminary negotiation. Initial communications between potential parties to a contract often take the form of preliminary negotiations, through which the parties either request or supply the terms of an offer that may or may not be made. A statement that may indicate a willingness to make an offer is not in itself an offer. For instance, if Brown writes to Young, "Will you buy my automobile for $3,000?" and Young replies, "Yes," there is no contract. Brown has not made an offer to sell her automobile to Young for $3,000. The offeror must demonstrate an intent to enter into a contract, not merely a willingness to enter into a negotiation.

Advertisements Merchants desire to sell their merchandise and thus are interested in informing potential customers about the goods, terms of sale, and price. But if they make widespread promises to sell to each person on their mailing list, the number of acceptances and resulting contracts might conceivably exceed their ability to perform. Consequently, a merchant might refrain from making offers by merely announcing that he has goods for sale, describing the goods, and quoting prices. He is simply inviting his customers and, in the case of published advertisements, the public, to make offers to him to buy his goods. His advertisements, circulars, quotation sheets, and displays of merchandise are *not* offers because (1) they do not contain a promise and (2) they leave unexpressed many terms that would be necessary to the making of a contract. Accordingly, his customers' responses are not acceptances because no offer to sell has been made.

Nonetheless, a seller is not free to advertise goods at one price and then raise the price once demand has been stimulated. Although as far as contract law is concerned, the seller has made no offer, such conduct is prohibited by the Federal Trade Commission as well as by legislation in most states. Moreover, in some circumstances a public announcement or advertisement may constitute an offer if the advertisement or announcement contains a definite promise of something in exchange for something else and confers a power of acceptance on a specified person or class of persons. The typical offer of a reward is an example of a definite offer, as is the situation presented in the landmark *Lefkowitz v. Great Minneapolis Surplus Store, Inc.* case, which follows.

LEFKOWITZ V. GREAT MINNEAPOLIS SURPLUS STORE, INC.

SUPREME COURT OF MINNESOTA, 1957
251 MINN. 188, 86 N.W.2D 689

http://scholar.google.com/scholar_case?case=13653982577998135778&q=251+Minn.+188&hl=en&as_sdt=2,22

FACTS On April 6, 1956, Great Minneapolis Surplus Store published an advertisement in a Minneapolis newspaper reporting that "Saturday, 9:00 A.M. sharp; 3 brand new fur coats worth up to $100; first come, first served, $1 each." Lefkowitz was the first to arrive at the store, but the store refused to sell him the fur coats because the "house rule" was that the offers were intended for women only and sales would not be made to men. The following week, Great Minneapolis published a similar advertisement for the sale of two mink scarves and a black lapin stole. Again Lefkowitz was the first to arrive at the store on Saturday morning, and once again the store refused to sell to him, this time because Lefkowitz knew of the house rule. This appeal was from a judgment awarding the plaintiff the sum of $138.50 as damages for breach of contract.

DECISION Judgment for Lefkowitz affirmed.

OPINION Murphy, J. The defendant * * * relies upon authorities which hold that, where an advertiser publishes in a newspaper that he has a certain quantity or quality of goods which he wants to dispose of at certain prices and on certain terms, such advertisements are not offers which become contracts as soon as any person to whose notice they may come signifies his acceptance by notifying the other that he will take a certain quantity of them. Such advertisements have been construed as an invitation for an offer of sale on the terms stated, which offer, when received, may be accepted or rejected and which, therefore does not become a contract of sale until accepted by the seller; and until a contract has been so made, the seller may modify or revoke such prices or terms. [Citations.] ***

On the facts before us we are concerned with whether the advertisement constituted an offer.

***

The test of whether a binding obligation may originate in advertisements addressed to the general public is "whether the facts show that some performance was promised in positive terms in return for something requested."

***

Whether in any individual instance a newspaper advertisement is an offer rather than an invitation to make an offer depends on the legal intention of the parties and the surrounding circumstances. [Citations.] We are of the view on the facts before us that the offer by the defendant of the sale *** was clear, definite, and explicit, and left nothing open for negotiation. The plaintiff having successfully managed to be the first one to appear at the seller's place of business to be served, as requested by the advertisement, and having offered the stated purchase price of the article, he was entitled to performance on the part of the defendant. We think the trial court was correct in holding that there was in the conduct of the parties a sufficient mutuality of obligation to constitute a contract of sale.

INTERPRETATION Although advertisements generally do not constitute offers, under some circumstances they do.

ETHICAL QUESTION Should Lefkowitz be entitled to damages? Why?

CRITICAL THINKING QUESTION Should an advertisement generally be construed as *not* constituting an offer? Explain.

Auction Sales The auctioneer at an auction sale does not make offers to sell the property being auctioned but invites offers to buy. The classic statement by the auctioneer is, "How much am I offered?" The persons attending the auction may make progressively higher bids for the property, and each bid or statement of a price or a figure is an offer to buy at that figure. If the bid is accepted, customarily indicated by the fall of the hammer in the auctioneer's hand, a contract results. A bidder is free to withdraw his bid at any time prior to its acceptance. The auctioneer is likewise free to withdraw the goods from sale *unless* the sale is advertised or announced to be without reserve.

If the auction sale is advertised or announced in explicit terms to be **without reserve**, the auctioneer may not withdraw an article or lot put up for sale unless no bid is made within a reasonable time. Unless so advertised or announced, the sale is with reserve. A bidder at either type of sale may retract his bid at any time prior to its acceptance by the auctioneer; such retraction, however, does not revive any previous bid.

DEFINITENESS

The terms of a contract, all of which are usually contained in the offer, must be clear enough to provide a court with a reasonable basis for determining the existence of a breach and for giving an appropriate remedy.

It is a fundamental policy that contracts should be made by the parties, not by the courts; accordingly, remedies for a breach must in turn have their basis in the parties' contract. Where the parties have intended to form a contract, the courts will attempt to find a basis for granting a remedy. Missing terms may be supplied by course of dealing, usage of trade, or inference. Thus, uncertainty as to incidental matters seldom will be fatal so long as the parties intended to form a contract. Nevertheless, the more terms the parties leave open, the less likely it is that they have intended to form a contract. Moreover, given the great variety of contracts, stating the terms that are essential to all contracts is impossible. In most cases, however, material terms would include the parties, subject matter, price, quantity, quality, and time of performance.

See *DiLorenzo v. Valve and Primer Corporation* in Chapter 12.

Open Terms With respect to agreements for the sale of goods, the UCC provides standards by which the courts may determine omitted terms, provided the parties intended to enter into a binding contract. The Code provides missing terms in a number of instances, where, for example, the contract fails to specify the price, the time or place of delivery, or payment terms. The Restatement has adopted an approach similar to the Code's in supplying terms omitted from the parties' contract.

Under the Code, an offer for the purchase or sale of goods may leave open particulars of performance to be specified by one of the parties. Any such specification must be made in good faith and within limits set by commercial reasonableness. **Good faith** is defined as honesty in fact in the conduct or transaction concerned. Under the 2001 Revised UCC Article 1, good faith means honesty in fact and the observance of reasonable commercial standards of fair dealing. **Commercial reasonableness** is a standard determined in terms of the business judgment of reasonable persons familiar with the practices customary in the type of transaction involved and in terms of the facts and circumstances of the case.

See *DiLorenzo v. Valve and Primer Corporation* in Chapter 12.

PRACTICAL ADVICE

To make an offer that will result in an enforceable contract, make sure you include all the necessary terms.

Output and Requirements Contracts An **output contract** is an agreement of a buyer to purchase a seller's entire output for a stated period. In comparison, a **requirements contract** is an agreement of a seller to supply a buyer with all his requirements for certain goods. Even though the exact quantity of goods is not specified and the seller may have some degree of control over his output and the buyer over his requirements, under the Code and the Restatement, such agreements are enforceable by the application of an objective standard based on the good faith of both parties. Thus, a seller who operated a factory only eight hours a day before the agreement was made cannot operate the factory twenty-four hours a day and insist that the buyer take all of the output. Nor can the buyer expand his business abnormally and insist that the seller still supply all of his requirements.

Duration of Offers

An offer confers upon the offeree a power of acceptance, which continues until the offer terminates. The ways in which an offer may be terminated, other than by acceptance, are through (1) lapse of time, (2) revocation, (3) rejection, (4) counteroffer, (5) death or incompetency of the offeror or offeree, (6) destruction of the subject matter to which the offer relates, and (7) subsequent illegality of the type of contract the offer proposes.

LAPSE OF TIME

The offeror may specify the time within which the offer is to be accepted, just as he may specify any other term or condition in the offer. Unless otherwise terminated, the offer remains open for the *specified* time. Upon the expiration of that time, the offer no longer exists and cannot be accepted. Any purported acceptance of an expired offer will serve only as a new offer.

If the offer does not state the time within which the offeree may accept, the offer will terminate after a *reasonable* time. Determining a "reasonable" time is a question of fact, depending on the nature of the contract proposed, the usages of business, and other circumstances of the case (including whether the offer was communicated by electronic means). For instance, an offer to sell a perishable good would be open for a far shorter period of time than an offer to sell undeveloped real estate.

PRACTICAL ADVICE

Because of the uncertainty as to what is a "reasonable time," it is advisable to specify clearly the duration of offers you make.

SHERROD v. KIDD

COURT OF APPEALS OF WASHINGTON, DIVISION 3, 2007
155 P.3D 976

http://scholar.google.com/scholar_case?case=7607426217314840344&q=155+P.3d+976&hl=en&as_sdt=2,22

FACTS David and Elizabeth Kidd's dog bit Mikaila Sherrod. Mikaila through her guardian ad litem (GAL) made a claim for damages against the Kidds (defendants). On June 14, 2005, the Kidds offered to settle the claim for $31,837. On July 12, Mikaila through her GAL sued the Kidds. On July 20, the Kidds raised their settlement offer to $32,843. The suit was subject to mandatory arbitration. The parties proceeded to arbitration on April 28, 2006. On May 5, the arbitrator awarded Mikaila $25,069.47. On May 9, the GAL wrote to the Kidds and purported to accept their last offer of $32,843, made the year before. The GAL on Mikaila's behalf moved to enforce the settlement agreement. The court concluded the offer was properly accepted because it had not been withdrawn and it entered judgment in the amount of the first written offer.

DECISION The decision of the trial judge is reversed.

OPINION Sweeney, C. J. An offer to form a contract is open only for a reasonable time, unless the offer specifically states how long it is open for acceptance. [Citations.] "[I]n the absence of an acceptance of an offer … within a reasonable time (where no time limit is specified), there is no contract." [Citation.]

How much time is reasonable is usually a question of fact. [Citation.] But we can decide the limits of a reasonable time if the facts are undisputed. [Citation.] And here the essential facts are not disputed.

A reasonable time "is the time that a reasonable person in the exact position of the offeree would believe to be satisfactory to the offeror." [Citation.]

> The purpose of the offeror, to be attained by the making and performance of the contract, will affect the time allowed for acceptance, if it is or should be known to the offeree. In such case there is no power to accept after it is too late to attain that purpose. [Citation.]

A reasonable time for an offeree to accept an offer depends on the "nature of the contract and the character of the business in which the parties were engaged." [Citation.]

Implicit in an offer (and an acceptance) to settle a personal injury suit is the party's intent to avoid a less favorable result at the hands of a jury, a judge or, in this case, an arbitrator. The defendant runs the risk that the award might be more than the offer. The plaintiff, of course, runs the risk that the award might be less than the offer. Both want to avoid that risk. And it is those risks that settlements avoid.

* * *

* * * Here, the value of this claim was set after arbitration. It was certainly subject to appeal but nonetheless set by a fact finder.

This offer expired when the arbitrator announced the award and was not subject to being accepted.

INTERPRETATION An offer is open for a reasonable period of time.

CRITICAL THINKING QUESTION Should the courts consider the social and public policy in a case such as this? Explain.

REVOCATION

The offeror generally may cancel or *revoke* an offer (**revocation**) at any time *prior* to its acceptance. If the offeror originally promises that the offer will be open for thirty days but wishes to terminate it after five days, he may do so merely by giving the offeree notice that he is withdrawing the offer. This notice may be given by any means of communication and effectively terminates the offer when *received* by the offeree. A very few states, however, have adopted a rule that treats revocations the same as acceptances, thus making them effective upon dispatch. An offer made to the general public is revoked only by giving to the revocation publicity equivalent to that given the offer.

Notice of revocation may be communicated indirectly to the offeree through reliable information from a third person that the offeror has disposed of the property he has offered for sale or has otherwise placed himself in a position indicating an unwillingness or inability to perform the promise contained in the offer. For example, Aaron offers to sell his portable television set to Ted and tells Ted that he has ten days in which to accept. One week later, Ted observes the television set in Celia's

house and is informed that Celia purchased it from Aaron. The next day, Ted sends to Aaron an acceptance of the offer. There is no contract because Aaron's offer was effectively revoked when Ted learned of Aaron's inability to sell the television set to Ted because he had sold it to Celia.

Certain limitations, however, restrict the offeror's power to revoke the offer at any time prior to its acceptance. These limitations apply to the following five situations.

Option Contracts An option is a contract by which the offeror is bound to hold open an offer for a specified period of time. It must comply with all of the requirements of a contract, including the offeree's giving of consideration to the offeror. (**Consideration**, or the inducement to enter into a contract consisting of an act or promise that has legal value, is discussed in Chapter 12.) For example, if Ellen, in return for the payment of $500 to her by Barry, grants Barry an option, exercisable at any time within thirty days, to buy Blackacre at a price of $80,000, Ellen's offer is irrevocable. Ellen is legally bound to keep the offer open for thirty days, and any communication by Ellen to

Barry giving notice of withdrawal of the offer is ineffective. Though Barry is not bound to accept the offer, the option contract entitles him to thirty days in which to accept.

Firm Offers under the Code   The Code provides that a *merchant* is bound to keep an offer to buy or sell *goods* open for a stated period (or, if no time is stated, for a reasonable time) not exceeding three months if the merchant gives assurance in a *signed writing* that the offer will be held open. The Code, therefore, makes a merchant's **firm offer** (written promise not to revoke an offer for a stated period of time) enforceable even though no consideration is given to the offeror for that promise (i.e., an option contract does not exist). A *merchant* is defined as a person (1) who is a dealer in a given type of goods, or (2) who by his occupation holds himself out as having knowledge or skill peculiar to the goods or practices involved, or (3) who employs an agent or broker whom he holds out as having such knowledge or skill.

Statutory Irrevocability   Certain offers, such as bids made to the state, municipality, or other government body for the construction of a building or some public work, are made irrevocable by statute. Another example is preincorporation stock subscription agreements, which are irrevocable for a period of six months under many state corporation statutes.

Irrevocable Offers of Unilateral Contracts
Where the offer contemplates a *unilateral* contract—that is, a promise for an act—injustice to the offeree may result if revocation is permitted after the offeree has started to perform the act requested in the offer and has substantially but not completely accomplished it. Such an offer is not accepted and no contract is formed until the offeree has completed the requested act. By simply starting performance, the offeree does not bind himself to complete performance; historically, he did not bind the offeror to keep the offer open, either. Thus, the offeror could revoke the offer at any time before the offeree's completion of performance. For example, Jordan offers Karlene $300 if Karlene will climb to the top of the flagpole in the center of campus. Karlene starts to climb, but when she is five feet from the top, Jordan yells to her, "I revoke."

The Restatement deals with this problem by providing that where the performance of the requested act necessarily requires the offeree to expend time and effort, the offeror is obligated not to revoke the offer for a reasonable time. This obligation arises when the offeree begins performance. If, however, the offeror does not know of the offeree's performance and has no adequate means

of learning of it within a reasonable time, the offeree must exercise reasonable diligence to notify the offeror of the performance.

> **PRACTICAL ADVICE**
> When making an offer, be careful to make it irrevocable only if you so desire.

Promissory Estoppel   As discussed in the previous chapter, a noncontractual promise may be enforced when it is made under circumstances that should lead the promisor reasonably to expect that the promise will induce the promisee to take action in reliance on it. This doctrine has been used in some cases to prevent an offeror from revoking an offer prior to its acceptance.

Thus, Ramanan Plumbing Co. submits a written offer for plumbing work to be used by Resolute Building Co. as part of Resolute's bid as a general contractor. Ramanan knows that Resolute is relying on Ramanan's bid, and in fact Resolute submits Ramanan's name as the plumbing subcontractor in the bid. Ramanan's offer is irrevocable until Resolute has a reasonable opportunity to notify Ramanan that Resolute's bid has been accepted.

REJECTION

An offeree is at liberty to accept or reject the offer as he sees fit. If he decides not to accept it, he is not required to reject it formally but may simply wait until the offer terminates by lapse of time. A **rejection** of an offer is a manifestation by the offeree of his unwillingness to accept. A communicated rejection terminates the power of acceptance. From the effective moment of rejection, which is the receipt of the rejection by the offeror, the offeree may no longer accept the offer. Rejection by the offeree may consist of express language or may be implied from language or conduct.

COUNTEROFFER

A **counteroffer** is a counterproposal from the offeree to the offeror that indicates a willingness to contract but on terms or conditions different from those contained in the original offer. It is not an unequivocal acceptance of the original offer, and by indicating an unwillingness to agree to the terms of the offer, it generally operates as a rejection. It also operates as a new offer. To illustrate further, assume that Worthy writes Joanne a letter stating that he will sell to Joanne a secondhand color television set for $300. Joanne replies that she will pay Worthy

APPLYING THE LAW

Mutual Assent

Facts Taylor and Arbuckle formed a partnership for the purpose of practicing pediatric medicine together. They found new medical office space to lease and thereafter, among other things, they set about furnishing the waiting room in a way that children would find inviting. In addition to contracting with a mural painter, they decided to purchase a high-definition flat-panel television on which they could show children's programming. On a Monday, Taylor and Arbuckle visited a local retailer with a reputation for competitive pricing, called Today's Electronics. In addition to comparing the pictures on the various models on display, the doctors discussed the pros and cons of LCD (liquid crystal display) versus plasma with the store's owner, Patel.

While they were able to narrow their options down significantly, Taylor and Arbuckle nonetheless could not decide on the exact size set to purchase because they had not yet determined the configuration of the seating to be installed in the waiting room. Sensing that the doctors were considering shopping around, Patel offered them a sizeable discount: only $999 for the forty-inch LCD screen they had chosen, or the fifty-inch plasma model they favored for only $1,299. As they were leaving the store, Patel gave the doctors his business card, on which he had jotted the model numbers and discount prices, his signature, and the notation "we assure you this offer is open through Sun., April 27."

Anxious to have the waiting room completed, Taylor and Arbuckle quickly agreed on a feasible seating arrangement for the waiting room, ordered the necessary furniture, and decided that the fifty-inch television would be too big. On Friday, April 25, Taylor returned to Today's Electronics. But before she could tell Patel that they had decided on the forty-inch LCD, Patel informed her that he could not honor the discounted prices because he no longer had in stock either model the doctors were considering.

Issue Is Patel free to revoke his offer notwithstanding having agreed to hold it open through the weekend?

Rule of Law The general rule is that an offeror may revoke, or withdraw, an offer any time before it has been accepted. However there are several limitations on an offeror's power to revoke an offer before acceptance. One of these is the Uniform Commercial Code's (UCC's) "merchant's firm offer" rule. Under the UCC, a merchant's offer to buy or sell goods is irrevocable for the stated period (or, if no period is stated, for a reasonable time) not exceeding three months, when he has signed a writing assuring the offeree that the offer will be kept open for that period. The Code defines a merchant as one who trades in the types of goods in question or who holds himself out, either personally or by way of an agent, to be knowledgeable regarding the goods or practices involved in the transaction.

Application The proposed contract between the doctors and Today's Electronics is governed by Article 2 of the Code because it involves a sale of goods, in this case a television set. Both Patel and Today's Electronics are considered merchants of televisions under the Code's definition, because Patel and his store regularly sell electronics, including television sets. Patel offered to sell to Taylor and Arbuckle either the forty-inch LCD television for $999 or the fifty-inch plasma for $1,299. By reducing his offer to a signed writing, and by promising in that writing that the stated prices were assured to be open through Sun., April 27, Patel has made a firm offer that he cannot revoke during that six-day period. Whether he still has either model in stock does not affect the irrevocability of the offer.

Conclusion Patel's offer is irrevocable through Sunday, April 27. Therefore Patel's attempt to revoke it is ineffective, and Taylor may still accept it.

$250 for the set. This is a counteroffer that, on *receipt* by Worthy, terminates the original offer. Worthy may, if he wishes, accept the counteroffer and thereby create a con-

tract for $250. If, on the other hand, Joanne in her reply states that she wishes to consider the $300 offer but is willing to pay $250 at once for the set, she is making a counteroffer that does *not* terminate Worthy's original offer. In the first instance, after making the $250 counteroffer, Joanne may not accept the $300 offer. In the second instance, she may do so, because the counteroffer was stated in such a manner as not to indicate an unwillingness to accept the original offer; Joanne therefore did not terminate it. In addition, a mere inquiry about the possibility of obtaining different or new terms is not a counteroffer and does not terminate the original offer.

Another common type of counteroffer is the **conditional acceptance**, which claims to accept the offer but expressly makes the acceptance contingent on the offeror's assent to additional or different terms. Nonetheless, it is a counteroffer and generally terminates the original offer. The Code's treatment of acceptances containing terms that vary from the offer is discussed later in this chapter.

> ## PRACTICAL ADVICE
>
> Consider whether you want to make a counterproposal that terminates the original offer or whether you merely wish to discuss alternative possibilities.

GIANNETTI V. CORNILLIE

COURT OF APPEALS OF MICHIGAN, 1994
204 MICH. APP. 234, 514 N.W.2D 221

http://scholar.google.com/scholar_case?case=17128858960507849357&q=514+N.W.2d+221&hl=en&as_sdt=2,34

FACTS Defendants listed with a real estate agent a home for sale. Plaintiffs, Patrick and Anne Giannetti, offered $155,000 for the home and submitted a deposit in the amount of $2,500. The defendants countered the offer with an offer to sell the house for $160,000. The plaintiffs then inquired whether certain equipment and items of furniture could be included with the sale of the house. The defendants refused to include the questioned items in the sale. The plaintiffs then accepted the $160,000 offer, but changed the mortgage amount from $124,000 to $128,000. The agent failed to show this change to the defendants but instead told the defendants that the plaintiffs had accepted their counteroffer. Defendants then signed all papers, but before the closing sought to invalidate the agreement. The plaintiffs brought this action for specific performance to enforce the sale. The trial court granted plaintiffs' motion and the defendants appealed.

DECISION Judgment for the defendants.

OPINION Hood, J. Defendants' main argument is that the trial court clearly erred in finding that there was a contract where defendants never agreed to plaintiffs' change in the mortgage amount. We reluctantly agree.

As argued by defendants, "[a]n offer is a unilateral declaration of intention, and is not a contract. A contract is made when both parties have executed or accepted it, and not before. A counterproposition is not an acceptance." [Citations.] An acceptance must be "unambiguous and in strict conformance with an offer." [Citation.]

"[A] proposal to accept, or an acceptance, upon terms varying from those offered, is a rejection of the offer, and puts an end to the negotiation, unless the party who made the original offer renews it, or assents to the modification suggested." [Citation.] Thus, "[a]ny material departure from the terms of an offer invalidates the offer as made and results in a counter proposition, which, unless accepted, cannot be enforced." [Citation.]

Plaintiffs argue that the modification of the mortgage amount did not vitiate their purported acceptance because the mortgage amount, unlike the purchase price, was not a material term of the contract. We disagree.

* * *

In other words, before the change, plaintiffs were obligated to buy the property if they obtained a mortgage for $124,000; after the change, no obligation to buy arose unless they obtained a $128,000 mortgage. Thus, the modification had the legal effect of widening the door through which plaintiffs could escape the contract and it was therefore material. [Citation.]

INTERPRETATION A counteroffer generally operates as a rejection and thus terminates the power of acceptance.

ETHICAL QUESTION Was the defendant morally obligated to sell the property? Explain.

CRITICAL THINKING QUESTION What could the plaintiffs have done to protect themselves while at the same time seeking different terms?

DEATH OR INCOMPETENCY

The **death or incompetency** of either the offeror or the offeree ordinarily terminates an offer. On his death or incompetency, the offeror no longer has the legal capacity to enter into a contract; thus, all outstanding offers are terminated. Death or incompetency of the offeree also terminates the offer, because an ordinary offer is not assignable (transferable) and may be accepted only by the person to whom it was made. When the offeree dies or ceases to have legal capability to enter into a contract, no one else has the power to accept the offer. Therefore, the offer necessarily terminates.

The death or incompetency of the offeror or offeree, however, does *not* terminate an offer contained in an option.

DESTRUCTION OF SUBJECT MATTER

Destruction of the specific subject matter of an offer terminates the offer. Suppose that Sarah, owning a Buick, offers to sell the car to Barbara and allows Barbara five days in which to accept. Three days later the car is destroyed by fire. On the following day, Barbara, without knowledge of the destruction of the car, notifies Sarah that she accepts Sarah's offer. There is no contract. The destruction of the car terminated Sarah's offer.

SUBSEQUENT ILLEGALITY

One of the essential requirements of a contract, as we previously mentioned, is legality of purpose or subject matter. If performance of a valid contract is subsequently made illegal, the obligations of both parties under the contract are discharged. Illegality taking effect after the making of an offer but prior to acceptance has the same effect: the offer is legally terminated. For an illustration of the duration of revocable offers, see Figure 10-1.

ACCEPTANCE OF OFFER

The acceptance of an offer is essential to the formation of a contract. Once an effective acceptance has been given, the contract is formed. **Acceptance** of an offer for a bilateral contract is some overt act by the offeree that manifests his assent to the terms of the offer, such as speaking or sending a letter, a telegram, or other explicit or implicit communication to the offeror. If the offer is for a unilateral contract, acceptance is the performance of the requested act with the intention of accepting. For example, if Joy publishes an offer of a reward to anyone who returns the diamond ring that she has lost (an offer to enter into a unilateral contract) and Bob, with

Figure 10-1
Duration of Revocable Offers

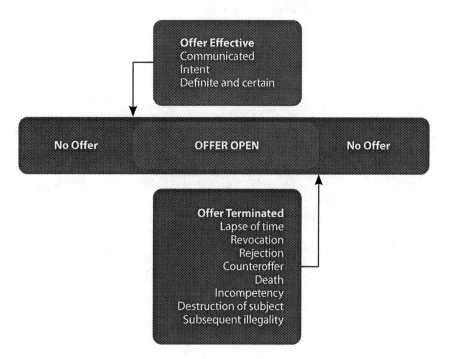

knowledge of the offer, finds and returns the ring to Joy, Bob has accepted the offer.

Communication of Acceptance

GENERAL RULE

Because acceptance is the manifestation of the offeree's assent to the offer, it must necessarily be communicated to the offeror. This is the rule as to all offers to enter into bilateral contracts. In the case of unilateral offers, however, notice of acceptance to the offeror usually is not required. If, however, the offeree in a unilateral contract has reason to know that the offeror has no adequate means of learning of the offeree's performance with reasonable promptness and certainty, then the offeree must make reasonable efforts to notify the offeror of acceptance or lose the right to enforce the contract.

SILENCE AS ACCEPTANCE

An offeree is generally under no legal duty to reply to an offer. Silence or inaction therefore does *not* indicate acceptance of the offer. By custom, usage, or course of dealing, however, the offeree's silence or inaction may operate as an acceptance. Thus, the silence or inaction of an offeree who fails to reply to an offer operates as an acceptance and causes a contract to be formed. Through previous dealings, for example, the offeree has given the offeror reason to understand that the offeree will accept all offers unless the offeree sends notice to the contrary. Another example of silence operating as an acceptance occurs when the prospective member of a mail-order club agrees that his failure to return a notification card rejecting offered goods will constitute his acceptance of the club's offer to sell the goods.

Furthermore, if an offeror sends unordered or unsolicited merchandise to a person, stating that the goods may be purchased at a specified price and that the offer will be deemed to have been accepted unless the goods are returned within a stated period of time, the offer is one for an inverted unilateral contract (i.e., an act for a promise). This practice has led to abuse, however, prompting the federal government as well as most states to enact statutes that provide that in such cases the offeree-recipient of the goods may keep them as a gift and is under no obligation either to return them or to pay for them.

EFFECTIVE MOMENT

As we discussed previously, an offer, a revocation, a rejection, and a counteroffer are effective when they are *received*. An acceptance is generally effective upon *dispatch*. This is true unless the offer specifically provides otherwise, the offeree uses an unauthorized means of communication, or the acceptance follows a prior rejection.

Stipulated Provisions in the Offer If the offer specifically stipulates the means of communication to be used by the offeree, the acceptance must conform to that specification. Thus, if an offer states that acceptance must be made by registered mail, any purported acceptance not made by registered mail would be ineffective. Moreover, the rule that an acceptance is effective when dispatched or sent does not apply in cases in which the offer provides that the acceptance must be received by the offeror. If the offeror states that a reply must be received by a certain date or that he must hear from the offeree or uses other language indicating that the acceptance must be received by him, the effective moment of the acceptance is when the offeror receives it, not when the offeree sends or dispatches it.

> ### PRACTICAL ADVICE
> Consider whether you should specify in your offers that acceptances are valid only upon receipt.

Authorized Means Historically, an authorized means of communication was either the means the offeror expressly authorized in the offer or, if none was authorized, the means the offeror used in presenting the offer. If in reply to an offer by mail, the offeree places in the mail a letter of acceptance properly stamped and addressed to the offeror, a contract is formed at the time and place that the offeree mails the letter. This assumes, of course, that the offer was open at that time and had not been terminated by any of the methods previously discussed. The reason for this rule is that the offeror, by using the mail, impliedly authorized the offeree to use the same means of communication. It is immaterial if the letter of acceptance goes astray in the mail and is never received.

The Restatement and the Code both now provide that where the language in the offer or the circumstances do not otherwise indicate, an offer to make a contract shall be construed as authorizing acceptance in any reasonable manner. Thus, an **authorized means** is usually any *reasonable* means of communication. These provisions are intended to allow flexibility of response and the ability to keep pace with new modes of communication.

See Figure 10-2 for an overview of offer and acceptance.

Figure 10-2
Mutual Assent

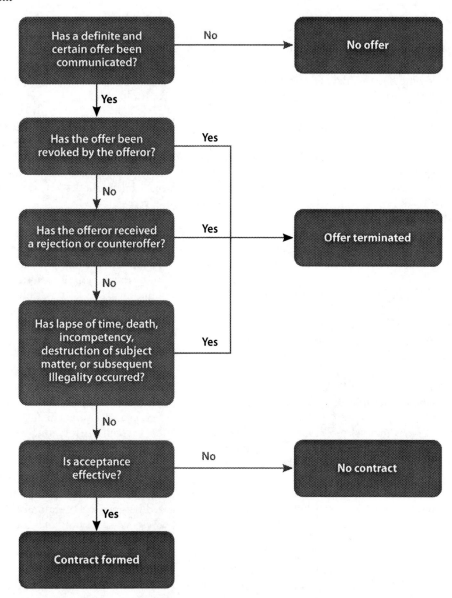

OSPREY L.L.C. v. KELLY-MOORE PAINT CO., INC.

SUPREME COURT OF OKLAHOMA 1999
1999 OK 50, 984 P.2D 194

http://scholar.google.com/scholar_case?case=15066374301719252497&q=1999+OK+50&hl=en&as_sdt=2,22

FACTS In 1977, the defendant, Kelly-Moore Paint Company, entered into a fifteen-year commercial lease with the plaintiff, Osprey, for a property in Edmond, Oklahoma. The lease contained two five-year renewal options. The lease required that the lessee give notice of its intent to renew at least six months prior to its expiration. It also provided that the renewal "may be delivered either personally or by depositing the same in United States mail, first class postage prepaid, registered or certified mail, return receipt requested." Upon expiration of the original fifteen-year lease, Kelly-Moore timely informed the lessor by certified letter of its intent to extend the lease an additional five years. The first five-year extension was due to expire on August 31, 1997. On the last day of the six-month notification deadline, Kelly-Moore faxed a letter of renewal notice to Osprey's office at 5:28 P.M. In addition, Kelly-Moore sent a copy of the faxed renewal notice letter by Federal Express that same day. Osprey denies ever receiving the fax, but it admits receiving the Federal Express copy of the notice on the following business day. Osprey rejected the notice, asserting that it was late, and it filed an action to remove the defendant from the premises. After a trial on the merits, the trial court granted judgment in favor of Kelly-Moore, finding that the faxed notice was effective. Osprey appealed. The Court of Civil Appeals reversed, determining that the plain language of the lease required that it be renewed by delivering notice either personally or by mail, and that Kelly-Moore had done neither. Kelly-Moore appealed.

DECISION The decision of the Court of Appeals is vacated and the decision of the trial court is affirmed.

OPINION Kauger, J. The precise issue of whether a faxed or facsimile delivery of a written notice to renew a commercial lease is sufficient to exercise timely the renewal option of the lease is one of first impression in Oklahoma. Neither party has cited to a case from another jurisdiction which has decided this question, or to any case which has specifically defined "personal delivery" as including facsimile delivery.

* * *

Osprey argues that (1) the lease specifically prescribed limited means of acceptance of the option, and it required that the notice of renewal be delivered either personally or sent by United States mail, registered or certified; (2) Kelly-Moore failed to follow the contractual requirements of the lease when it delivered its notice by fax; and (3) because the terms for extending the lease specified in the contract were not met, the notice was invalid and the lease expired on August 31, 1997. Kelly-Moore counters that (1) the lease by the use of the word "shall" mandates that the notice be written, but the use of the word "may" is permissive; and (2) although the notice provision of the lease permits delivery personally or by United States mail, it does not exclude other modes of delivery or transmission which would include delivery by facsimile. * * *

A lease is a contract and in construing a lease, the usual rules for the interpretation of contractual writings apply. * * *

Language in a contract is given its plain and ordinary meaning, unless some technical term is used in a manner meant to convey a specific technical concept. A contract term is ambiguous only if it can be interpreted as having two different meanings. * * * The lease does not appear to be ambiguous.

"Shall" is ordinarily construed as mandatory and "may" is ordinarily construed as permissive. The contract clearly requires that notice "shall" be in writing. The provision for delivery, either personally or by certified or registered mail, uses the permissive "may" and it does not bar other modes of transmission which are just as effective.

The purpose of providing notice by personal delivery or registered mail is to insure the delivery of the notice, and to settle any dispute which might arise between the parties concerning whether the notice was received. A substituted method of notice that performs the same function and serves the same purpose as an authorized method of notice is not defective.

Here, the contract provided that time was of the essence. Although Osprey denies that it ever received the fax, the fax activity report and telephone company records confirm that the fax was transmitted successfully, and that it was sent to Osprey's correct facsimile number on the last day of the deadline to extend the lease. The fax provided immediate written communication similar to personal delivery and, like a telegram, would be timely if it were properly transmitted before the expiration of the deadline to renew. Kelly-Moore's use of the fax served the same function and the same purpose as the two methods suggested by the lease and it was transmitted before the expiration of the deadline to renew. Under these facts, we hold that the faxed or facsimile delivery of the written notice to renew the commercial lease was sufficient to exercise timely the renewal option of the lease.

INTERPRETATION Where the language in the offer or the circumstances does not otherwise indicate, an offer to make a contract shall be construed as authorizing acceptance in any reasonable manner.

CRITICAL THINKING QUESTION Are there instances in which an offeror should require a certain mode for acceptance? When?

Unauthorized Means When the method of communication used by the offeree is unauthorized, the traditional rule is that acceptance is effective when and if received by the offeror, provided that it is received within the time during which the authorized means would have arrived. The Restatement goes further

by providing that if these conditions are met, then the effective time for the acceptance is the moment of dispatch.

Acceptance Following a Prior Rejection An acceptance sent after a prior rejection is not effective when sent by the offeree, but only when and if *received* by the offeror before he receives the rejection. Thus, when an acceptance follows a prior rejection, *the first communication* the offeror receives is the effective one. For example, Carlos in New York sends by airmail to Paula in San Francisco an offer that is expressly stated to be open for one week. On the fourth day, Paula sends to Carlos by airmail a letter of rejection, which is delivered on the morning of the sixth day. At noon on the fifth day, Paula dispatches a telegram of acceptance that Carlos receives before the close of business on that day. A contract was formed when Carlos received Paula's telegram of acceptance—it was the first communication he received.

DEFECTIVE ACCEPTANCES

A late or defective acceptance does not create a contract. After the offer has expired, it cannot be accepted. However, a late or defective acceptance does manifest a willingness on the part of the offeree to enter into a contract and therefore constitutes a new offer. To create a contract based on this offer, the original offeror must accept the new offer by manifesting his assent to it.

Variant Acceptances

A variant acceptance—one that contains terms different from or additional to those in the offer—receives distinctly different treatment under the common law and under the Code.

COMMON LAW

An acceptance must be *positive* and *unequivocal*. It may not change, add to, subtract from, or qualify in any way the provisions of the offer. In other words, it must be the **mirror image** of the offer. Any communication by the offeree that attempts to modify the offer is not an acceptance but a counteroffer, which does not create a contract.

CODE

The common law mirror image rule, by which the acceptance cannot vary or deviate from the terms of the offer, is modified by the Code. This modification is necessitated by the realities of modern business practices. A vast number of business transactions use standardized business forms. For example, a merchant

buyer sends to a merchant seller on the buyer's order form a purchase order for one thousand cotton shirts at $60 per dozen with delivery by October 1 at the buyer's place of business. On the reverse side of this standard form are twenty-five numbered paragraphs containing provisions generally favorable to the buyer. When the seller receives the buyer's order, he agrees to the buyer's quantity, price, and delivery terms and sends to the buyer on his acceptance form an unequivocal acceptance of the offer. However, on the back of his acceptance form, the seller has thirty-two numbered paragraphs generally favorable to himself and in significant conflict with the provisions on the buyer's form. Under the common law's *mirror image* rule, no contract would exist; for the seller has not accepted unequivocally all of the material terms of the buyer's offer.

The Code attempts to alleviate this **battle of the forms** by focusing on the intent of the parties. If the offeree does not expressly make her acceptance conditional upon the offeror's assent to the additional or different terms, a contract is formed. The issue then becomes whether the offeree's different or additional terms become part of the contract. If both offeror and offeree are merchants, such *additional* terms may become part of the contract provided that they do not materially alter the agreement and are not objected to either in the offer itself or within a reasonable period of time. If either of the parties is not a merchant or if the additional terms materially alter the offer, then the additional terms are merely construed as proposals to the contract. *Different* terms proposed by the offeree will not become part of the contract unless accepted by the offeror. The courts are divided over what terms to include when the terms differ or conflict. Most courts hold that the offeror's terms govern; other courts hold that the terms cancel each other out and look to the Code to provide the missing terms. Some states follow a third alternative and apply the additional terms test to different terms. (See Figure 19-1 in Chapter 19.)

Let us apply the Code to the previous example involving the seller and the buyer: because both parties are merchants and the seller's acceptance was not conditional upon assent to the seller's additional or different terms, then either (1) the contract will be formed without the seller's different terms unless the buyer specifically accepts them; (2) the contract will be formed without the seller's additional terms (unless they are specifically accepted by the buyer) because the additional terms materially alter the offer; or (3) depending upon the jurisdiction, either (a) the buyer's conflicting terms will be included in the contract, (b) the Code will

CONCEPT REVIEW 10-1

Offer and Acceptance

	Time Effective	Effect
Communications by Offeror		
• Offer	Received by offeree	Creates power to form a contract
• Revocation	Received by offeree	Terminates power
Communications by Offeree		
• Rejection	Received by offeror	Terminates offer
• Counteroffer	Received by offeror	Terminates offer
• Acceptance	Sent by offeree	Forms a contract
• Acceptance after prior rejection	Received by offeror	If received before rejection forms a contract

© Cengage Learning 2014

provide the missing terms, because the conflicting terms cancel each other out, or (c) the additional terms test is applied.

See Concept Review 10-1 explicating the effective time and effect of communications involved in offers and acceptances.

Business Law in Action

Business-to-consumer, or "B2C," transactions on the Internet allow buyers to purchase goods for delivery as quickly as overnight—everything from sports equipment and welding tools to bath towels and fresh cut flowers. And increasingly consumers can buy services in cyberspace, too, like vacation packages and movie theater tickets.

The contracting process is easy. In addition to requiring the purchaser to input data like payment details and shipping and billing addresses, Web-based providers use radio buttons or check boxes for the customer to make various selections. In some cases the customer must uncheck or deselect items, and in others, the consumer must affirmatively click on a button or series of buttons labeled "I agree," or "I accept." These cybercontracts are sometimes called "clickwrap" or "click on" agreements.

By filling in the required blanks, selecting or deselecting various options, and otherwise completing the transaction, the purchaser is indicating his or her assent to be bound by the seller's offer. Sales of goods can be relatively simple and straightforward. But services available on the Internet, particularly those that involve an ongoing relationship between the user and the provider, usually require more complex contract provisions.

Offers for video rental club memberships and software licenses, for example, frequently contain restrictions on use and such other terms as warranty disclaimers and arbitration clauses as well as privacy policy disclosures, all written primarily in legalese and taking up multiple screens of text. The reality is that many buyers simply do not read them. Nonetheless, depending on how the agreement process is set up, these terms are likely binding.

Whether a buyer's nonverbal assent to these lengthy contract provisions will pass legal muster is dependent on the online contracting process. Even if the buyer does not read the proposed terms, they will be enforced if the buyer has had the opportunity to review them, either by way of an automatic screen or a link. And, equally as important, the cyberoffer's terms will be binding when the site requires the buyer to actively select them or to click on a button or type words affirmatively indicating his or her assent.

CHAPTER SUMMARY
OFFER

Essentials of an Offer

Definition indication of willingness to enter into a contract

Communication offeree must have knowledge of the offer and the offer must be made by the offeror or her authorized agent to the offeree

Intent determined by an objective standard of what a reasonable offeree would have believed

Definiteness offer's terms must be clear enough to provide a court with a basis for giving an appropriate remedy

Duration of Offers

Lapse of Time offer remains open for the time period specified or, if no time is stated, for a reasonable period of time

Revocation generally, an offer may be terminated at any time before it is accepted, subject to the following exceptions
* *Option Contracts* contract that binds offeror to keep an offer open for a specified time
* *Firm Offer* a merchant's irrevocable offer to sell or buy goods in a signed writing that ensures that the offer will not be terminated for up to three months
* *Statutory Irrevocability* offer made irrevocable by statute
* *Irrevocable Offer of Unilateral Contracts* a unilateral offer may not be revoked for a reasonable time after performance is begun
* *Promissory Estoppel* noncontractual promise that binds the promisor because she should reasonably expect that the promise will induce the promisee (offeree) to take action in reliance on it

Rejection refusal to accept an offer terminates the power of acceptance

Counteroffer counterproposal to an offer that generally terminates the original offer

Death or Incompetency of either the offeror or the offeree terminates the offer

Destruction of Subject Matter of an offer terminates the offer

Subsequent Illegality of the purpose or subject matter of the offer terminates the offer

ACCEPTANCE OF OFFER

Requirements

Definition positive and unequivocal expression of a willingness to enter into a contract on the terms of the offer

Mirror Image Rule except as modified by the Code, an acceptance cannot deviate from the terms of the offer

Communication of Acceptance

General Rule acceptance effective upon dispatch unless the offer specifically provides otherwise or the offeree uses an unauthorized means of communication

Silence as Acceptance generally does not indicate acceptance of the offer

Effective Moment generally upon dispatch

- *Stipulated Provisions in the Offer* the communication of acceptance must conform to the specifications in the offer
- *Authorized Means* the Restatement and the Code provide that, unless the offer provides otherwise, acceptance is authorized to be in any reasonable manner
- *Unauthorized Means* acceptance effective when received, provided that it is received within the time within which the authorized means would have arrived
- *Acceptance Following a Prior Rejection* first communication received by the offeror is effective

Defective Acceptance does not create a contract but serves as a new offer

QUESTIONS

1. Ames, seeking business for his lawn maintenance firm, posted the following notice in the meeting room of the Antlers, a local lodge: "To the members of the Antlers— Special this month. I will resod your lawn for $4.00 per square foot using Fairway brand sod. This offer expires July 15."

    The notice also included Ames's name, address, and signature and specified that the acceptance was to be in writing.

    Bates, a member of the Antlers, and Cramer, the janitor, read the notice and were interested. Bates wrote a letter to Ames saying he would accept the offer if Ames would use Putting Green brand sod. Ames received this letter July 14 and wrote to Bates saying he would not use Putting Green sod. Bates received Ames's letter on July 16 and promptly wrote Ames that he would accept Fairway sod. Cramer wrote to Ames on July 10 saying he accepted Ames's offer.

    By July 15, Ames had found more profitable ventures and refused to resod either lawn at the specified price. Bates and Cramer brought an appropriate action against Ames for breach of contract. Decisions as to the respective claims of Bates and Cramer?

2. Justin owned four speedboats named *Porpoise, Priscilla, Providence,* and *Prudence.* On April 2, Justin made written offers to sell the four boats in the order named for $4,200 each to Charles, Diane, Edward, and Fran, respectively, allowing ten days for acceptance. In which, if any, of the following four situations was a contract formed?

    a. Five days later, Charles received notice from Justin that he had contracted to sell *Porpoise* to Mark. The next day, April 8, Charles notified Justin that he accepted Justin's offer.

    b. On the third day, April 5, Diane mailed a rejection to Justin that reached Justin on the morning of the fifth day. At 10:00 A.M. on the fourth day, Diane sent an acceptance by telegram to Justin, who received it at noon the same day.

    c. Edward, on April 3, replied that he was interested in buying *Providence* but declared the price appeared slightly excessive and wondered if, perhaps, Justin

would be willing to sell the boat for $3,900. Five days later, having received no reply from Justin, Edward accepted Justin's offer by letter, and enclosed a certified check for $4,200.

    d. Fran was accidentally killed in an automobile accident on April 9. The following day, the executor of her estate mailed an acceptance of Justin's offer to Justin.

3. Alpha Rolling Mill Corporation (Alpha Corporation), by letter dated June 8, offered to sell Brooklyn Railroad Company (Brooklyn Company) two thousand to five thousand tons of fifty-pound iron rails on certain specified terms and added that, if the offer was accepted, Alpha Corporation would expect to be notified prior to June 20. Brooklyn Company, on June 16, by telegram, referring to Alpha Corporation's offer of June 8, directed Alpha Corporation to enter an order for one thousand two hundred tons of fifty-pound iron rails on the terms specified. The same day, June 16, Brooklyn Company, by letter to Alpha Corporation, confirmed the telegram. On June 18, Alpha Corporation, by telegram, declined to fulfill the order. Brooklyn Company, on June 19, telegraphed Alpha Corporation: "Please enter an order for two thousand tons of rails as per your letter of the eighth. Please forward written contract. Reply." In reply to Brooklyn Company's repeated inquiries concerning whether the order for two thousand tons of rails had been entered, Alpha denied the existence of any contract between Brooklyn Company and itself. Thereafter, Brooklyn Company sued Alpha Corporation for breach of contract. Decision?

4. On April 8, Crystal received a telephone call from Akers, a truck dealer, who told Crystal that a new model truck in which Crystal was interested would arrive in one week. Although Akers initially wanted $10,500, the conversation ended after Akers agreed to sell and Crystal agreed to purchase the truck for $10,000, with a $1,000 down payment and the balance on delivery. The next day, Crystal sent Akers a check for $1,000, which Akers promptly cashed.

    One week later, when Crystal called Akers and inquired about the truck, Akers informed Crystal he had several prospects looking at the truck and would not sell for less than $10,500. The following day Akers sent

Crystal a properly executed check for $1,000 with the following notation thereon: "Return of down payment on sale of truck."

After notifying Akers that she will not cash the check, Crystal sues Akers for damages. Should Crystal prevail? Explain.

5. On November 15, Gloria, Inc., a manufacturer of crystalware, mailed to Benny Buyer a letter stating that Gloria would sell to Buyer one hundred crystal "A" goblets at $100 per goblet and that "the offer would remain open for fifteen (15) days." On November 18, Gloria, noticing the sudden rise in the price of crystal "A" goblets, decided to withdraw her offer to Buyer and so notified Buyer. Buyer chose to ignore Gloria's letter of revocation and gleefully watched as the price of crystal "A" goblets continued to skyrocket. On November 30, Buyer mailed to Gloria a letter accepting Gloria's offer to sell the goblets. The letter was received by Gloria on December 4. Buyer demands delivery of the goblets. What is the result?

6. On May 1, Melforth Realty Company offered to sell Greenacre to Dallas, Inc., for $1 million. The offer was made by telegraph and stated that the offer would expire on May 15. Dallas decided to purchase the property and sent a registered letter to Melforth on May 10 accepting the offer. As a result of unexplained delays in the postal service, the letter was not received by Melforth until May 22. Melforth wishes to sell Greenacre to another buyer who is offering $1.2 million for the tract of land. Has a contract resulted between Melforth and Dallas?

7. Rowe advertised in newspapers of wide circulation and otherwise made known that she would pay $5,000 for a complete set, consisting of ten volumes, of certain rare books. Ford, not knowing of the offer, gave Rowe all but one volume of the set of rare books as a Christmas present. Ford later learned of the offer, obtained the one remaining book, tendered it to Rowe, and demanded the $5,000. Rowe refused to pay. Is Ford entitled to the $5,000?

8. Scott, manufacturer of a carbonated beverage, entered into a contract with Otis, owner of a baseball park, whereby Otis rented to Scott a large signboard on top of the center field wall. The contract provided that Otis should letter the sign as Scott desired and would change the lettering from time to time within forty-eight hours after receipt of written request from Scott. As directed by Scott, the signboard originally stated in large letters that Scott would pay $100 to any ball player hitting a home run over the sign.

In the first game of the season, Hume, the best hitter in the league, hit one home run over the sign. Scott immediately served written notice on Otis instructing Otis to replace the offer on the signboard with an offer to pay $50 to every pitcher who pitched a no-hit game in the park. A week after receipt of Scott's letter, Otis had not changed the wording on the sign; and on that day, Perry, a pitcher for a scheduled game, pitched a no-hit game and Todd, one of his teammates, hit a home run over Scott's sign.

Scott refuses to pay any of the three players. What are the rights of Scott, Hume, Perry, and Todd?

9. Barney accepted Clark's offer to sell to him a portion of Clark's coin collection. Clark forgot at the time of the offer and acceptance that her prized $20 gold piece was included in the portion that she offered to sell to Barney. Clark did not intend to include the gold piece in the sale. Barney, at the time of inspecting the offered portion of the collection, and prior to accepting the offer, saw the gold piece. Is Barney entitled to the $20 gold piece?

10. Small, admiring Jasper's watch, asked Jasper where and at what price he had purchased it. Jasper replied, "I bought it at West Watch Shop about two years ago for around $85, but I am not certain as to that." Small then said, "Those fellows at West are good people and always sell good watches. I'll buy that watch from you." Jasper replied, "It's a deal." The next morning, Small telephoned Jasper and said he had changed his mind and did not wish to buy the watch.

Jasper sued Small for breach of contract. In defense, Small has pleaded that he made no enforceable contract with Jasper because (a) the parties did not agree on the price to be paid for the watch and (b) the parties did not agree on the place and time of delivery of the watch to Small. Are either, or both, of these defenses good?

11. Jeff says to Brenda, "I offer to sell you my PC for $900." Brenda replies, "If you do not hear otherwise from me by Thursday, I have accepted your offer." Jeff agrees and does not hear from Brenda by Thursday. Does a contract exist between Jeff and Brenda? Explain.

12. On November 19, Hoover Motor Express Company sent to Clements Paper Company a written offer to purchase certain real estate. Sometime in December, Clements authorized Williams to accept the offer. Williams, however, attempted to bargain with Hoover to obtain a better deal, specifically that Clements would retain easements on the property. In a telephone conversation on January 13 of the following year, Williams first told Hoover of his plan to obtain the easements. Hoover replied, "Well, I don't know if we are ready. We have not decided, we might not want to go through with it." On January 20, Clements sent a written acceptance of Hoover's offer. Hoover refused to buy, claiming it had revoked its offer through the January 13 phone conversation. Clements then brought suit to compel the sale or obtain damages. Did Hoover successfully revoke its offer?

13. Walker leased a small lot to Keith for ten years at $100 a month, with a right for Keith to extend the lease for another ten-year term under the same terms except as to rent. The renewal option provided:

Rental will be fixed in such amount as shall actually be agreed upon by the lessors and the lessee with the monthly rental fixed on the comparative basis of rental values as of the date of the renewal with rental values at this time reflected by the comparative business conditions of the two periods.

Keith sought to exercise the renewal right and, when the parties were unable to agree on the rent, brought suit against Walker. Who prevails? Why?

CASE PROBLEMS

14. The Brewers contracted to purchase Dower House from McAfee. Then, several weeks before the May 7 settlement date for the purchase of the house, the two parties began to negotiate for the sale of certain items of furniture in the house. On April 30, McAfee sent the Brewers a letter containing a list of the furnishings to be purchased at specific prices; a payment schedule including a $3,000 payment due on acceptance; and a clause reading: "If the above is satisfactory, please sign and return one copy with the first payment."

On June 3, the Brewers sent a letter to McAfee stating that enclosed was a $3,000 check; that the original contract had been misplaced and could another be furnished; that they planned to move into Dower House on June 12; and that they wished that the red desk also be included in the contract. McAfee then sent a letter dated June 8 to the Brewers listing the items of furniture they had purchased.

The Brewers moved into Dower House in the middle of June. Soon after they moved in, they tried to contact McAfee at his office to tell him that there had been a misunderstanding relating to their purchase of the listed items. They then refused to pay him any more money, and he brought this action to recover the outstanding balance unless the red desk was also included in the sale. Will McAfee be able to collect the additional money from the Brewers?

15. The Thoelkes were owners of real property located in Florida, which the Morrisons agreed to purchase. The Morrisons signed a contract for the sale of that property and mailed it to the Thoelkes in Texas on November 26. Subsequently, the Thoelkes executed the contract and placed it in the mail addressed to the Morrisons' attorney in Florida. After the executed contract was mailed but before it was received in Florida, the Thoelkes called the Morrisons' attorney in Florida and attempted to repudiate the contract. Does a contract exist between the Thoelkes and the Morrisons? Discuss.

16. Lucy and Zehmer met while having drinks in a restaurant. During the course of their conversation, Lucy apparently offered to buy Zehmer's 471.6-acre farm for $50,000 cash. Although Zehmer claims that he thought the offer was made in jest, he wrote the following on the back of a pad: "We hereby agree to sell to W. O. Lucy the Ferguson Farm complete for $50,000, title satisfactory to buyer." Zehmer then signed the writing and induced his wife Ida to do the same. She claims, however, that she signed only after Zehmer assured her that

it was only a joke. Finally, Zehmer claims that he was "high as a Georgia pine" at the time but admits that he was not too drunk to make a valid contract. Explain whether the contract is enforceable.

17. On July 31, Lee Calan Imports advertised a used Volvo station wagon for sale in the *Chicago Sun-Times*. As part of the information for the advertisement, Lee Calan Imports instructed the newspaper to print the price of the car as $10,795. However, due to a mistake made by the newspaper, without any fault on the part of Lee Calan Imports, the printed ad listed the price of the car as $10,095. After reading the ad and then examining the car, O'Brien told a Lee Calan Imports salesman that he wanted to purchase the car for the advertised price of $10,095. Calan Imports refuses to sell the car to O'Brien for $10,095. Is there a contract? If so, for what price?

18. On May 20, cattle rancher Oliver visited his neighbor Southworth, telling him, "I know you're interested in buying the land I'm selling." Southworth replied, "Yes, I do want to buy that land, especially because it adjoins my property." Although the two men did not discuss the price, Oliver told Southworth he would determine the value of the property and send that information to Southworth so that he would have "notice" of what Oliver "wanted for the land." On June 13, Southworth called Oliver to ask if he still planned to sell the land. Oliver answered, "Yes, and I should have the value of the land determined soon." On June 17, Oliver sent a letter to Southworth listing a price quotation of $324,000. Southworth then responded to Oliver by letter on June 21, stating that he accepted Oliver's offer. However, on June 24 Oliver wrote back to Southworth saying, "There has never been a firm offer to sell, and there is no enforceable contract between us." Oliver maintains that a price quotation alone is not an offer. Southworth claims a valid contract has been made. Who wins? Discuss.

19. On August 12, Mr. and Mrs. Mitchell, the owners of a small secondhand store, attended Alexander's Auction, where they bought a used safe for $50. The safe, part of the Sumstad estate, contained a locked inside compartment. Both the auctioneer and the Mitchells knew this fact. Soon after the auction, the Mitchells had the compartment opened by a locksmith, who discovered $32,207 inside. The Everett Police Department impounded the money. The city of Everett brought an action against the Sumstad estate and the Mitchells to determine the owner of the money. Who should receive the money? Why?

20. Irwin Schiff is a self-styled "tax rebel" who has made a career, and substantial profit, out of his tax protest activities. On February 7, Schiff appeared live on CBS News *Nightwatch*, a late-night program with a viewer participation format. During the broadcast Schiff repeated his assertion that nothing in the Internal Revenue Code stated that an individual was legally required to pay federal income tax. Schiff then challenged, "If anybody calls this show—I have the Code—and cites any section of this Code that says an individual is required to file a tax return, I will pay them $100,000." Call-in telephone numbers were periodically flashed on the screen. John Newman, an attorney, did not see Schiff's live appearance on *Nightwatch*. Newman did, however, see a two-minute videotaped segment, including Schiff's challenge, which was rebroadcast several hours later on the *CBS Morning News*. Newman researched the matter that same day, and on the following day, February 9, placed a call using directory assistance to *CBS Morning News* stating that the call was performance of the consideration requested by Mr. Schiff in exchange for his promise to pay $100,000. When Schiff refused to pay, Newman sued. Should Newman prevail? Explain.

TAKING SIDES

Cushing filed an application with the office of the Adjutant General of the State of New Hampshire for the use of the Portsmouth Armory to hold a dance on the evening of April 29. The application, made on behalf of the Portsmouth Area Clamshell Alliance, was received by the Adjutant General's office on or about March 30. On March 31 the Adjutant General mailed a signed contract after agreeing to rent the armory for the evening requested. The agreement required acceptance by the renter affixing his signature to the agreement and then returning the copy to the Adjutant General within five days after receipt. Cushing received the contract offer, signed it on behalf of the Alliance, and placed it in the outbox for mailing on April 3. At 6:30 on the evening of April 4, Cushing received a telephone call from the Adjutant General revoking the rental offer. Cushing stated during the conversation that he had already signed and mailed the contract. The Adjutant General sent a written confirmation of the withdrawal on April 5. On April 6 the Adjutant General's office received by mail from Cushing the signed contract dated April 3 and postmarked April 5.

a. What are the arguments that a binding contract exists?

b. What are the arguments that a contract does not exist or should not exist?

c. What is the proper outcome? Explain.

Chapter 11

Conduct Invalidating Assent

Fraud—A generic term embracing all multifarious means which human ingenuity can devise, and which are resorted to by one individual to get advantage over another by false suggestion or by suppression of the truth.

JOHNSON V. MCDONALD, 170 OKL. 117, 39 P.2D 150

CHAPTER OUTCOMES

After reading and studying this chapter, you should be able to:

1. Identify the types of duress and describe the legal effect of each.

2. Define undue influence and identify some of the situations giving rise to a confidential relationship.

3. Identify the types of fraud and the elements that must be shown to establish the existence of each.

4. Define the two types of nonfraudulent misrepresentation.

5. Identify and explain the situations involving voidable mistakes.

In addition to requiring offer and acceptance, the law requires that the agreement be voluntary and knowing. If these requirements are not met, then the agreement is either voidable or void. This chapter deals with situations in which the consent manifested by one of the parties to the contract is not effective because it was not knowingly and voluntarily given. We consider five such situations in this chapter: duress, undue influence, fraud, nonfraudulent misrepresentation, and mistake.

Duress

A person should not be held to an agreement he has not entered voluntarily. Accordingly, the law will not enforce any contract induced by **duress**, which in general is any wrongful or unlawful act or threat that overcomes the free will of a party.

PHYSICAL COMPULSION

Duress is of two basic types. The first type, **physical duress**, occurs when one party compels another to manifest assent to a contract through actual physical force, such as pointing a gun at a person or taking a person's hand and compelling him to sign a written contract. This type of duress, while extremely rare, renders the agreement *void*.

IMPROPER THREATS

The second and more common type of duress involves the use of **improper threats** or acts, including economic and social coercion, to compel a person to enter into a contract. Though the threat may be explicit or may be inferred from words or conduct, in either case it must leave the victim with no reasonable alternative. This type of duress makes the contract *voidable* at the option of the coerced party. For example, if Ellen, a landlord, induces Vijay, an infirm, bedridden tenant, to enter into a new lease on the same apartment at a greatly increased rent by wrongfully threatening to terminate Vijay's lease and evict him, Vijay can escape or *avoid* the new lease by reason of the duress exerted on him.

The fact that the act or threat would not affect a person of average strength and intelligence is not important if it places fear in the person actually affected and induces her to act against her will. The test is *subjective*, and the question is this: did the threat actually induce assent on the part of the person claiming to be the victim of duress?

Ordinarily, the acts or threats constituting duress are themselves crimes or torts. But this is not true in all cases. The acts need not be criminal or tortious to be *wrongful*; they merely need to be contrary to public policy or morally reprehensible. For example, if the threat involves a breach of a contractual duty of good faith and fair dealing, it is improper.

Moreover, it generally has been held that contracts induced by threats of criminal prosecution are voidable, regardless of whether the coerced party had committed an unlawful act. Similarly, threatening the criminal prosecution of a close relative is also duress. To be distinguished from such threats of prosecution are threats that resort to ordinary civil remedies to recover a debt due from another. It is not wrongful to threaten a civil suit against an individual to recover a debt. What is prohibited is threatening to bring a civil suit when bringing such a suit would be abuse of process.

PRACTICAL ADVICE

If you entered into a contract due to improper threats, consider whether you wish to void the contract. If you decide to do so, act promptly.

BERARDI v. MEADOWBROOK MALL COMPANY

SUPREME COURT OF APPEALS OF WEST VIRGINIA, 2002
212 W.VA. 377, 572 S.E.2D 900

http://scholar.google.com/scholar_case?case=16006842064576980398&hl=en&as_sdt=2&as_vis=1&oi=scholarr

FACTS Between 1985 and 1987, Jerry A. Berardi, Betty J. Berardi, and Bentley Corporation (the Berardis) leased space for three restaurants from Meadowbrook Mall Company. In 1990, the Berardis were delinquent in their rent. Meadowbrook informed Mr. Berardi that a lawsuit would be filed in Ohio requesting judgment for the total amount owed. Mr. Berardi then entered into a consent judgment with Meadowbrook granting judgment for the full amount owed. Meadowbrook in return promised that no steps to enforce the judgment would be undertaken provided the Berardis continued to operate their three restaurants.

In April 1996, Meadowbrook filed in the Circuit Court of Harrison County, West Virginia, the judgment of the Ohio lawsuits and obtained a lien on a building that was owned by the Berardis, the Goff Building. By so doing, Meadowbrook impeded the then-pending refinancing of the building by the Berardis.

In June 1997, the Berardis and Meadowbrook signed a "Settlement Agreement and Release" settling the 1990 Ohio judgments. In this document, the Berardis acknowledged the validity of the 1990 Ohio judgments and that the aggregate due under them was $814,375.97. The Berardis agreed to pay Meadowbrook $150,000 on the date the Goff Building refinancing occurred, and also to pay Meadowbrook $100,000 plus 8.5 percent interest per year on the third anniversary of the initial $150,000 payment. These payments would discharge the Berardis from all other amounts owed. The payment of the initial $150,000 would also result in Meadowbrook releasing the lien against the Goff Building.

The agreement additionally recited: "Berardis hereby release and forever discharge Meadowbrook, its employees, agents, successors, and assigns from any and all claims, demands, damages, actions, and causes of action of any kind or nature that have arisen or may arise as a result of the leases."

Nevertheless, on October 2, 2000, the Berardis filed a complaint against Meadowbrook alleging that Meadowbrook breached the October 1990 agreement by attempting to enforce the 1990 Ohio judgments and that Meadowbrook extorted by duress and coercion the 1997 agreement. Meadowbrook filed a motion to dismiss under the 1997 settlement. Meadowbrook sought summary judgment, which the circuit court granted. Berardi now appeals.

DECISION Summary judgment affirmed.

OPINION Per Curiam.

"We begin our discussion of this issue by reiterating, at the outset, that settlements are highly regarded and scrupulously enforced, so long as they are legally sound." [Citation.] "The law favors and encourages the resolution of controversies by contracts of compromise and settlement rather than by litigation; and it is the policy of the law to uphold and enforce such contracts if they are fairly made and are not in contravention of some law or public policy." [Citations.] Those who seek to avoid a settlement "face a heavy burden" [citation] and "since ... settlement agreements, when properly executed, are legal and binding, this Court will not set aside such agreements on allegations of duress ... absent clear and convincing proof of such claims." [Citation.]

The Berardis contend the 1997 settlement is invalid as it was procured by "economic duress:"

The concept of "economic or business duress" may be generally stated as follows: Where the plaintiff is forced into a transaction as a result of unlawful threats or wrongful, oppressive, or unconscionable conduct on the part of the defendant which leaves the plaintiff no reasonable alternative but to acquiesce, the plaintiff may void the transaction and recover any economic loss.

In [citation], we emphasized that there appears to be general acknowledgment that duress is not shown because one party to the contract has driven a hard bargain or that market or other conditions now make the contract more difficult to perform by one of the parties or that financial circumstances may have caused one party to make concessions.

"Duress is not readily accepted as an excuse" to avoid a contract. [Citation.] Thus, to establish economic duress, "in addition to their own statements, the plaintiffs must produce objective evidence of their duress. The defense of economic duress does not turn only upon the subjective state of mind of the plaintiffs, but it must be reasonable in light of the objective facts presented." [Citation.]

Mr. Berardi is a sophisticated businessman who has operated a number of commercial enterprises. As of 1997, the Berardis had substantial assets and a considerable net worth. While economic duress may reach large business entities as well as the "proverbial little old lady in tennis shoes," [citation], when the parties are sophisticated business entities, releases should be voided only in "extreme and extraordinary cases." [Citation.] Indeed, "where an experienced businessman takes sufficient time, seeks the advice of counsel and understands the content of what he is signing he cannot claim the execution of the release was a product of duress." [Citation.] While the presence of counsel will not per se defeat a claim of economic duress, "a court must determine if the attorneys had an opportunity for meaningful input under the circumstances." [Citation.]

* * *

No case can be found, we apprehend, where a party who, without force or intimidation and with full knowledge of all the facts of the case, accepts on account of an unlitigated and controverted demand a sum less than what he claims and believes to be due him, and agrees to accept that sum in full satisfaction, has been permitted to avoid his act on the ground that this is duress. [Citations.]

* * *

Finally, we do not believe that any relative economic inequality between the Berardis and Meadowbrook sufficiently factor into the summary judgment calculation. We have recognized that, "'in most commercial transactions it may be assumed that there is some inequality of bargaining power....'" [Citation.] Indeed, even when one sophisticated business entity enjoys "a decided economic advantage" over another such entity, economic duress is extremely circumscribed:

Because an element of economic duress is ... present when many contracts are formed or releases given, the ability of a party to disown his obligations under a contract or release on that basis is reserved for extreme and extraordinary cases. Otherwise, the stronger party to a contract or release would routinely be at risk of having its rights under the contract or release challenged long after the instrument became effective.

[Citation.]

Given the facts, the law's disfavor of economic duress, its approbation of settlements, the sophisticated nature of the parties, and the extremely high evidentiary burden the Berardis must overcome, we harbor no substantial doubt nor do we believe the circuit court abused its discretion.

INTERPRETATION Economic duress consists of unlawful threats or wrongful, oppressive, or unconscionable conduct by one party that leaves the other party no reasonable alternative but to acquiesce to the terms of a contract.

ETHICAL QUESTION Did Meadowbrook act in a proper manner? Explain.

CRITICAL THINKING QUESTION Did Berardi really have a reasonable alternative to signing the release? Explain.

Undue Influence

Undue influence is the unfair persuasion of a person by a party in a dominant position based on a *confidential relationship.* The law very carefully scrutinizes contracts between those in a relationship of trust and confidence that is likely to permit one party to take unfair advantage of the other. Examples are the relationships of guardian-ward, trustee-beneficiary, agent-principal, spouses, parent-child, attorney-client, physician-patient, and clergy-parishioner.

A transaction induced by undue influence on the part of the dominant party is *voidable.* The ultimate question in undue influence cases is whether the transaction was induced by dominating either or both the mind or emotions of a submissive party. The weakness or dependence of the person persuaded is a strong indicator of whether the persuasion may have been unfair. For example, Abigail, a person without business experience, has for years relied on Boris, who is experienced in business, for advice on business matters. Boris, without making any false representations of fact, induces Abigail to enter into a contract with Boris's confederate, Cassius. The contract, however, is disadvantageous to Abigail, as both Boris and Cassius know. The transaction is voidable on the grounds of undue influence.

PRACTICAL ADVICE

If you are in a confidential relationship with another person, when you enter into a contract with that person, make sure that (1) you fully disclose all relevant information about that transaction, (2) the contract is fair, and (3) the other party obtains independent advice about the transaction.

NEUGEBAUER V. NEUGEBAUER

SUPREME COURT OF SOUTH DAKOTA, 2011
804 N.W.2D 450, 2011 S.D. 64

http://scholar.google.com/scholar_case?case=10623090804125668458&q=804+N.W.2d+450+&hl=en&num=100&as_sdt=ffffffffffffe04&as_ylo=2010

FACTS Harold and Pearl Neugebauer owned a 159-acre farm they called the "Home Place." The farm included a house, garage, granary, machine sheds, barns, silos, and a dairy barn. During their marriage, Harold handled all of the legal and financial affairs of the farm and family. In 1980, Harold died, leaving Pearl as the sole owner of the Home Place and another farm property. Following Harold's death, Lincoln, the youngest of Harold and Pearl's seven children, began farming both properties. Lincoln also lived with his mother on the Home Place. In 1984, Lincoln and Dennis, one of Pearl's other sons, formed L & D Farms partnership to manage the farming operation on Pearl's land. L & D Farms entered into an oral ten-year lease with Pearl that included an option to purchase the Home Place for $117,000, the appraised value in 1984. In 1985, Pearl moved from the farm to a home in town. In 1989, Lincoln and Dennis dissolved L & D Farms without exercising the option to purchase the Home Place. After dissolution of the partnership, Lincoln farmed Pearl's land by himself. He paid annual rent, but Lincoln and Pearl never put their oral farm lease in writing. Pearl trusted Lincoln and left it to him to determine how much rent to pay. Pearl did, however, expect that Lincoln would be "fair." Pearl never took any steps to determine if the $6,320 annual rent Lincoln was paying was fair.

On several occasions from 2004 to 2008, Lincoln privately consulted with an attorney, Keith Goehring, about purchasing the Home Place. On December 3, 2008, Lincoln took Pearl to Goehring's office to discuss the purchase. Pearl, who had only an eighth-grade education, was almost eighty-four years old and was hard of hearing. Although Lincoln and Goehring discussed details of Lincoln's proposed purchase, Pearl said virtually nothing. She later testified that she could not keep up with the conversation and did not understand the terms discussed. A few days later, Pearl and Lincoln executed a contract for deed that had been drafted by Goehring. Goehring had been retained and his fees were paid by Lincoln. Neither Lincoln nor Goehring advised Pearl that Goehring represented only Lincoln, and neither suggested that Pearl could or should retain her own legal counsel. There is no dispute that the fair market value of the Home Place was $697,000 in 2008 when the contract for deed was executed. Under the terms of the contract, Lincoln was to pay Pearl $117,000, the farm's 1984 appraised value. The contract price was to be paid over thirty years by making annual payments of $6,902.98. After executing the contract, Lincoln told Pearl not to tell the rest of her children about the agreement. Pearl later became suspicious that something may have been wrong with the contract. In January 2009, Pearl revealed the contract to the rest of her children, and they explained the contract to her. She began to cry and wanted the contract torn up. Pearl personally and through her children asked Lincoln to tear up the contract. Lincoln refused.

Pearl then brought an action for rescission of the contract on the ground of undue influence. The trial court found that Lincoln had exerted undue influence and rescinded the contract. Lincoln appealed, claiming that the trial court erred in finding that the contract for deed was a product of undue influence.

DECISION Judgment of the trial court is affirmed.

OPINION Zinter, J. The elements [of undue influence] are: (1) a person susceptible to undue influence; (2) another's opportunity to exert undue influence on that person to effect a wrongful purpose; (3) another's disposition to do so for an improper purpose; and (4) a result clearly showing the effects of undue influence. [Citation.] The party alleging undue influence must prove these elements by a preponderance of the evidence. [Citation.]

Susceptibility to Undue Influence Lincoln argues that no evidence supported the court's finding that Pearl was susceptible to undue influence. * * * Lincoln contends that in the absence of medical evidence of mental deficits, the court erred in finding that Pearl was susceptible to undue influence.

Concededly, "'physical and mental weakness is always material upon the question of undue influence.' Obviously, an aged and infirm person with impaired mental faculties would be more susceptible to influence than a mentally alert younger person in good health." [Citations.] But this Court has not required medical evidence to prove susceptibility to undue influence. * * *

In this case, there was substantial non-medical evidence demonstrating Pearl's susceptibility to undue influence. Pearl had an eighth-grade education, and she lacked experience in business and legal transactions. When she signed the contract for deed, Pearl was almost eighty-four and hard of hearing. Pearl and Dennis testified that she had relied on her deceased husband to take care of all their business and legal matters during their marriage. This dependency continued after Harold's death. Pearl testified that, with the exception of her checking account and monthly expenses, she often asked her children for help with business and financial affairs, which she did not understand. * * * We also note that Lincoln admitted Pearl had some mental impairment. He told [Pearl's daughter] Cheryl that Pearl was "slipping," meaning that Pearl would say something and a few minutes later repeat herself because she had forgotten what she had said. * * *

Opportunity to Exert Undue Influence Lincoln contends that the court's finding of opportunity to exert undue influence was erroneous because Lincoln and Pearl had no confidential relationship and Pearl had the ability to seek independent advice between the two meetings with Goehring, but chose not to do so. * * *

In this case, Pearl testified that Lincoln was her son and someone with whom she had previously lived for

many years: someone she trusted to "do right." Lincoln conceded that on the date Pearl signed the contract, he knew Pearl trusted him and had confidence that he would treat her fairly in his business dealings with her. This type of trust and confidence by a mother in her son was sufficient to prove opportunity.

* * *

Disposition to Exert Undue Influence The court's finding that Lincoln had a disposition to exert undue influence for an improper purpose was also supported. Lincoln had substantial experience in farmland transactions and real estate appreciation. He collaborated with an attorney a number of times over four years to purchase the farm and draft the necessary documents. Yet Lincoln did not have the farm appraised as he had previously done when farming the property with his brother. Instead, Lincoln set the price at a value for which it had appraised twenty-four years earlier, a price that was one-sixth of its then current value. He also took no steps to ensure that his elderly mother understood the contract terms, including the fact that considering her age and the thirty-year amortization, she would likely never receive a substantial portion of the payments. Finally, neither Lincoln nor his attorney advised Pearl to seek legal representation. * * *

Lincoln's conduct after execution of the contract was also relevant to show disposition to exercise undue influence at the time the contract was executed. [Citation.] After this contract for deed was executed, Lincoln instructed Pearl not to tell her other children about the contract. * * *

The court finally observed that Lincoln historically took advantage of Pearl by paying her less than fair market rent under the oral lease. * * *

* * *

Result Showing Effects of Undue Influence Finally, we see no clear error in the court finding a result clearly showing the effects of undue influence. By executing the contract for deed, Pearl sold her property for $580,000 less than its value. Not only was the contract price of $117,000 substantially below the market value of $697,000, the thirty-year payment term would have required Pearl to live to 114 years-of-age to receive the payments.

INTERPRETATION Undue influence is the unfair persuasion of a person by a party in a dominant position based upon a confidential relationship.

ETHICAL QUESTION Who was harmed by Lincoln's action? Explain.

CRITICAL THINKING QUESTION Should the courts get involved in land transactions between family members? Explain.

Fraud

Another factor affecting the validity of consent given by a contracting party is fraud, which prevents assent from being knowingly given. There are two distinct types of fraud: fraud in the execution and fraud in the inducement.

FRAUD IN THE EXECUTION

Fraud in the execution, which is extremely rare, consists of a misrepresentation that deceives the defrauded person as to the very nature of the contract. Such fraud occurs when a person does not know, or does not have reasonable opportunity to know, the character or essence of a proposed contract because the other party misrepresents its character or essential terms. Fraud in the execution renders the transaction *void*.

For example, Melody delivers a package to Ray, requests that Ray sign a receipt for it, holds out a simple printed form headed "Receipt," and indicates the line on which Ray is to sign. This line, which appears to Ray to be the bottom line of the receipt, is actually the signature line of a promissory note cleverly concealed underneath the receipt. Ray signs where directed without knowing that he is signing a note. This is fraud in the execution. The note is void and of no legal effect, for, although the signature is genuine and appears to manifest Ray's assent to the terms of the note, there is no actual assent. The nature of Melody's fraud precluded consent to the signing of the note because it prevented Ray from reasonably knowing what he was signing.

FRAUD IN THE INDUCEMENT

Fraud in the inducement, generally referred to as fraud or deceit, is an intentional misrepresentation of material fact by one party to the other, who consents to enter into a contract in justifiable reliance on the misrepresentation. Fraud in the inducement renders the contract *voidable* by the defrauded party. For example, Alice, in offering to sell her dog to Bob, tells Bob that the dog won first prize in its class in the recent national dog show. In truth, the dog had not even been entered in the show. However, Alice's statement induces Bob to accept the offer and pay a high price for the dog. There is a contract, but it is voidable by Bob because Alice's fraud induced his assent.

The requisites for fraud in the inducement are as follows:

1. a false representation
2. of a fact

3. that is material and
4. made with knowledge of its falsity and the intention to deceive (scienter) and
5. which representation is justifiably relied on.

False Representation   A basic element of fraud is a false representation or a **misrepresentation** (i.e., misleading conduct or an assertion not in accord with the facts, made through a positive statement). In contrast, **concealment** is an action intended or known to be likely to keep another from learning a fact he otherwise would have learned. Active concealment can form the basis for fraud, as, for example, when a seller puts heavy oil or grease in a car engine to conceal a knock. Truth may be suppressed by concealment as much as by misrepresentation. Expressly denying knowledge of a fact that a party knows to exist is a misrepresentation if it leads the other party to believe that the fact does not exist or cannot be discovered. Moreover, a statement of misleading half-truth is considered the equivalent of a false representation.

Generally, *silence* or nondisclosure alone does not amount to fraud when the parties deal at arm's length. An *arm's-length transaction* is one in which the parties owe each other no special duties and each is acting in his or her self-interest. In most business or market transactions, the parties deal at arm's length and generally have no obligation to tell the other party everything they know about the subject of the contract. Thus, it is not fraud when a buyer possesses advantageous information about the seller's property, information of which he knows the seller to be ignorant, and does not disclose such information to the seller. A buyer is under no duty to inform the seller of the greater value or other advantages of the property for sale. Assume, for example, that Sid owns a farm that, as a farm, is worth $100,000. Brenda, who knows that there is oil under Sid's farm, also knows that Sid is ignorant of this fact. Without disclosing this information to Sid, Brenda makes an offer to Sid to buy the farm for $100,000. Sid accepts the offer, and a contract is duly made. Sid, on later learning the facts, can do nothing about the matter, either at law or in equity. As one case puts it, "a purchaser is not bound by our laws to make the man he buys from as wise as himself."

> ### PRACTICAL ADVICE
> Consider bargaining with the other party to promise to give you full disclosure.

Although nondisclosure usually does not constitute a misrepresentation, in certain situations it does. One such situation arises when (1) a person fails to disclose a fact known to him; (2) he knows that the disclosure of that fact would correct a mistake of the other party as to a basic assumption on which that party is making the contract; and (3) nondisclosure of the fact amounts to a failure to act in good faith and in accordance with reasonable standards of fair dealing. Accordingly, if the property at issue in the contract contains a substantial latent (hidden) defect, one that would not be discovered through an ordinary examination, the seller may be obliged to reveal it. Suppose, for example, that Judith owns a valuable horse, which she knows is suffering from a disease discoverable only by a competent veterinary surgeon. Judith offers to sell this horse to Curt but does not inform him about the condition of her horse. Curt makes a reasonable examination of the horse and, finding it in apparently normal condition, purchases it from Judith. Curt, on later discovering the disease in question, can have the sale set aside. Judith's silence, under the circumstances, was a misrepresentation.

> ### PRACTICAL ADVICE
> When entering into contract negotiations, first determine what duty of disclosure you owe to the other party.

In other situations, the law imposes a duty of disclosure. For example, one may have a duty of disclosure because of prior representations innocently made before entering into the contract, which are later discovered to be untrue. Another instance in which silence may constitute fraud is a transaction involving a fiduciary. A **fiduciary** is a person in a confidential relationship who owes a duty of trust, loyalty, and confidence to another. For example, an agent owes a fiduciary duty to his principal, as does a trustee to the beneficiary of the trust and a partner to her copartners. A fiduciary may not deal at arm's length, as a party in most everyday business or market transactions may, but owes a duty to disclose fully all relevant facts when entering into a transaction with the other party to the relationship.

Fact The basic element of fraud is the misrepresentation of a material fact. A **fact** is an event that actually took place or a thing that actually exists. Suppose that Dale induces Mike to purchase shares in a company unknown to Mike at a price of $100 per share by representing that she had paid $150 per share for them during the preceding year, when in fact she had paid only $50. This representation of a past event is a misrepresentation of fact.

Actionable fraud rarely can be based on what is merely a statement of **opinion**. A representation is one of opinion if it expresses only the uncertain belief of the representer as to the existence of a fact or his judgment as to quality, value, authenticity, or other matters of judgment.

The line between fact and opinion is not an easy one to draw and in close cases presents an issue for the jury. The solution often will turn on the superior knowledge of the person making the statement and the information available to the other party. Thus, if Dale said to Mike that the shares were "a good investment," she was merely stating her opinion; and normally Mike ought to regard it as no more than that. Other common examples of opinion are statements of value, such as "This is the best car for the money in town" or "This deluxe model will give you twice the wear of a cheaper model." Such exaggerations and commendations of articles offered for sale are to be expected from dealers, who are merely **puffing** their wares with "sales talk." If the representer is a professional advising a client, the courts are more likely to regard an untrue statement of opinion as actionable. Such a statement expresses the opinion of one holding himself out as having expert knowledge, and the tendency is to grant relief to those who have sustained loss by reasonable reliance on expert evaluation, as the next case shows.

Also to be distinguished from a representation of fact is a *prediction*. Predictions are similar to opinions, as no one can know with certainty what will happen in the future, and normally they are not regarded as factual statements. Likewise, promissory statements ordinarily do not constitute a basis of fraud, because a breach of promise does not necessarily indicate that the promise was fraudulently made. However, a promise that the promisor, at the time of making, had no intention of keeping is a misrepresentation of fact.

Historically, courts held that representations of *law* were not statements of fact but of opinion. The present trend is to recognize that a statement of law may have the effect of either a statement of fact or a statement of opinion. For example, a statement asserting that a particular statute has been enacted or repealed has the effect of a statement of fact. On the other hand, a statement as to the legal consequences of a particular set of facts is a statement of opinion.

MAROUN V. WYRELESS SYSTEMS, INC.

SUPREME COURT OF IDAHO, 2005
141 IDAHO 604, 114 P.3D 974

http://scholar.google.com/scholar_case?case=18286843461461582750&hl=
en&as_sdt=2&as_vis=1&oi=scholarr

FACTS Tony Y. Maroun (Maroun) was employed by Amkor when he accepted an offer to work for Wyreless, a start-up company. Wyreless promised Maroun, among other items, the following: (1) annual salary of $300,000; (2) $300,000 bonus for successful organization of Wyreless Systems, Inc.; (3) 15 percent of the issued equity in Wyreless Systems, Inc.; (4) the equity and "organization bonus" will need to be tied to agreeable milestones; (5) full medical benefits; and (6) the position of chief executive officer, president, and board member. Maroun began working for Wyreless but was terminated a few months later. Maroun then filed suit alleging he had not received 15 percent of issued equity and had not received $429,145, which represented the remainder of the $600,000. Wyreless filed a motion for summary judgment. The district court granted the motion, and Maroun appealed.

DECISION Judgment of the district court affirmed.

OPINION Trout, J. Maroun argues the district court erred in granting summary judgment in favor of Robinson on the fraud claim. Fraud requires: (1) a statement or a representation of fact; (2) its falsity; (3) its materiality; (4) the speaker's knowledge of its falsity; (5) the speaker's intent that there be reliance; (6) the hearer's ignorance of the falsity of the statement; (7) reliance by the hearer; (8) justifiable reliance; and (9) resultant injury. [Citation.] In opposition to the defendants' motion for summary judgment, Maroun filed an affidavit that stated Robinson made the following representations to Maroun:

(1) That Wyreless was to be a corporation of considerable size, with initial net revenues in excess of several hundred million dollars.

(2) That Robinson would soon acquire one and one-half million dollars in personal assets, which Robinson would make available to personally guaranty payment of my compensation from Wyreless.

(3) That he would have no difficulty in obtaining the initial investments required to capitalize Wyreless as a large,

world leading corporation with initial net revenues in excess of several hundred million dollars.

(4) That he had obtained firm commitments from several investors and that investment funds would be received in Wyreless' bank account in the near future.

"An action for fraud or misrepresentation will not lie for statements of future events." [Citation.] "[T]here is a general rule in [the] law of deceit that a representation consisting of [a] promise or a statement as to a future event will not serve as [a] basis for fraud...." [Citation.]. Statements numbered one and two both address future events. Robinson allegedly stated Wyreless "was to be" and that he "would soon acquire." "[T]he representation forming the basis of a claim for fraud must concern past or existing material facts." [Citation.] Neither of these statements constitutes a statement or a representation of past or existing fact. A "promise or statement that an act will be undertaken, however, is actionable, if it is proven that the speaker made the promise without intending to keep it." [Citation.] There is no indication in the record that Robinson did not intend to fulfill those representations to Maroun at the time he made the statements.

"Opinions or predictions about the anticipated profitability of a business are usually not actionable as fraud." [Citation.] Statement number three appears to be merely Robinson's opinion. As to statement number four, no evidence was submitted that Robinson had not received commitments at the time he made the statement to Maroun. Accordingly, the district court's grant of summary judgment against Maroun on the fraud claim is affirmed.

INTERPRETATION Fraud generally must be based on a material fact and not on predictions or a person's opinion.

ETHICAL QUESTION Did Wyreless act in an ethical manner?

CRITICAL THINKING QUESTION When should an employer be held to its "promises"?

Materiality In addition to the requirement that a misrepresentation be one of fact, it must also be material. A misrepresentation is **material** if (1) it would be likely to induce a reasonable person to manifest assent or (2) the maker knows that it would be likely to induce the recipient to do so. Thus, in the sale of a racehorse, it may not be material whether the horse was ridden in its most recent race by a certain jockey, but its running time for the race probably would be. The Restatement of Contracts provides that a contract justifiably induced by a misrepresentation is voidable if the misrepresentation is either fraudulent or material. Therefore, a fraudulent misrepresentation does not have to be material to obtain rescission, but it must be material to recover damages.

The *Reed v. King* case presents an unusual factual situation involving the duty to disclose a "material" fact.

REED V. KING

CALIFORNIA COURT OF APPEALS, 1983
145 CAL.APP.3D 261, 193 CAL. RPTR. 130

http://scholar.google.com/scholar_case?case=5758643576031100085&q=193+Cal.Rptr.+130&hl=en&as_sdt=2,34

FACTS Dorris Reed bought a house from Robert King for $76,000. King and his real estate agent knew that a woman and her four children had been murdered in the house ten years earlier and allegedly knew that the event had materially affected the market value of the house. They said nothing about the murders to Reed, and King asked a neighbor not to inform her of them. After the sale, neighbors told Reed about the murders and informed her that the house was consequently worth only $65,000. Reed brought an action against King and the real estate agent, alleging fraud and seeking rescission and damages. The complaint was dismissed, and Reed appealed.

DECISION Judgment reversed.

OPINION Blease, J. Does Reed's pleading state a cause of action? Concealed within this question is the nettlesome problem of the duty of disclosure of blemishes on real property which are not physical defects or legal impairments to use.

Reed seeks to state a cause of action sounding in contract, i.e., rescission, or in tort, i.e., deceit. In either event her allegations must reveal a fraud. [Citation.] "The elements of actual fraud, whether as the basis of the remedy in contract or tort, may be stated as follows: There must be (1) a *false representation* or concealment of a material fact (or, in some cases, an opinion) susceptible of knowledge, (2) made with *knowledge* of its falsity or without sufficient knowledge on the subject to warrant a representation, (3) with the *intent* to induce the person to whom it is made to act upon it; and such person must (4) act in *reliance* upon the representation (5) to his *damage*." ***

The trial court perceived the defect in Reed's complaint to be a failure to allege concealment of a material fact. ***

Concealment is a term of art which includes mere nondisclosure when a party has a duty to disclose. [Citation.] Rest.2d Contracts, § 161; Rest.2d Torts, § 551*** Accordingly, the critical question is: does the seller have a duty to disclose here? Resolution of this question depends on the materiality of the fact of the murders.

In general, a seller of real property has a duty to disclose: "where the seller knows of facts materially affecting the value or desirability of the property which are known or accessible only to him and also knows that such facts are not known to, or within the reach of the diligent attention and observation of the buyer, the seller is under a duty to disclose them to the buyer." [Citation.] Whether information "is of sufficient materiality to affect the value or desirability of the property *** depends on the facts of the particular case." [Citation.] Materiality "is a question of law, and is part of the concept of right to rely or justifiable reliance." [Citation.] *** Three considerations bear on this legal conclusion: the gravity of the harm inflicted by nondisclosure; the fairness of imposing a duty of discovery on the buyer as an alternative to compelling disclosure, and the impact on the stability of contracts if rescission is permitted.

Numerous cases have found nondisclosure of physical defects and legal impediments to use of real property are material. [Citation.] However, to our knowledge, no prior real estate sale case has faced an issue of nondisclosure of the kind presented here.

* * *

The murder of innocents is highly unusual in its potential for so disturbing buyers they may be unable to reside in a home where it has occurred. This fact may foreseeably deprive a buyer of the intended use of the purchase. Murder is not such a common occurrence that buyers should be charged with anticipating and discovering this disquieting possibility. Accordingly, the fact is not one for which a duty of inquiry and discovery can sensibly be imposed upon the buyer.

* * *

Whether Reed will be able to prove her allegation that the decade old multiple murder has a significant effect on market value we cannot determine. If she is able to do so by competent evidence she is entitled to a favorable ruling on the issues of materiality and duty to disclose.

INTERPRETATION A representation is material if it is likely to influence or affect a reasonable person.

ETHICAL QUESTION Should King have revealed the information to Reed? Explain.

CRITICAL THINKING QUESTION What is material information, and how should it be determined?

Knowledge of Falsity and Intention to Deceive To establish fraud, the misrepresentation must have been known by the one making it to be false and must be made with an intent to deceive. This element of fraud is known as **scienter**. Knowledge of falsity can consist of (1) actual knowledge, (2) lack of belief in the statement's truthfulness, or (3) reckless indifference as to its truthfulness.

Justifiable Reliance A person is not entitled to relief unless she has **justifiably relied** on the misrepresentation. If the complaining party's decision was in no way influenced by the misrepresentation, she must abide by the terms of the contract. She is not deceived if she does not rely on the misrepresentation. Justifiable reliance requires that the misrepresentation contribute substantially to the misled party's decision to enter into the contract. If the complaining party knew or it was obvious that the representation of the defendant was untrue, but she still entered into the contract, she has not justifiably relied on that representation. Moreover, where the misrepresentation is fraudulent, the party who relies on it is entitled to relief even though she does not investigate the statement or is contributorily negli-

gent in relying on it. Not knowing or discovering the facts before making a contract does not make a person's reliance unjustified unless her reliance amounts to a failure to act in good faith and in accordance with reasonable standards of fair dealing. Thus, most courts will not allow a person who concocts a deliberate and elaborate scheme to defraud—one that the defrauded party should readily detect—to argue that the defrauded party did not justifiably rely upon the misrepresentation.

Nonfraudulent Misrepresentation

Nonfraudulent misrepresentation is a material, false statement that induces another to rely justifiably but is made *without* scienter. Such representation may occur in one of two ways. **Negligent misrepresentation** is a false representation that is made without due care in ascertaining its truthfulness; such representation renders an agreement voidable. **Innocent misrepresentation**, which also renders a contract voidable, is a false representation made without knowledge of its falsity but with due care. To obtain relief for nonfraudulent misrepresentation, all

CONCEPT REVIEW 11-1

Misrepresentation

	Fraudulent	Negligent	Innocent
False Statement of Fact	Yes	Yes	Yes
Materiality	Yes for damages No for rescission	Yes	Yes
Fault	Scienter	Without due care (knowledge and intent)	Without due care and knowledge
Reliance	Yes	Yes	Yes
Injury	Yes for damages No for rescission	Yes for damages No for rescission	Yes for damages No for rescission
Remedies	Damages Rescission	Damages Rescission	Damages Rescission

of the other elements of fraud must be present *and* the misrepresentation must be material. The remedies that may be available for nonfraudulent misrepresentation are rescission and damages (see Chapter 18).

Mistake

A **mistake** is a belief that is not in accord with the facts. Where the mistaken facts relate to the basis of the parties' agreement, the law permits the adversely affected party to avoid or reform the contract under certain circumstances. But because permitting avoidance for mistake undermines the objective approach to mutual assent, the law has experienced considerable difficulty in specifying those circumstances that justify permitting the subjective matter of mistake to invalidate an otherwise objectively satisfactory agreement. As a result, establishing clear rules to govern the effect of mistake has proven elusive.

APPLYING THE LAW

Conduct Invalidating Assent

Facts Gillian bought a two-year-old used car from a luxury automobile dealer for $36,000. At the time of her purchase, the odometer and title documentation both indicated that the car had 21,445 miles on it. But after just a little more than a year, the engine failed, and Gillian had to take the car to a mechanic. The problem was the water pump, which needed to be replaced. Surprised that a water pump should fail in a car with so few miles on it, the mechanic more closely examined the odometer and determined that someone had cleverly tampered with it. According to the mechanic, the car probably had about sixty thousand miles on it when Gillian bought it. At the time Gillian bought the car, the retail value for the same vehicle with sixty thousand miles on it was approximately $30,000.

Gillian decided that under these conditions she no longer wanted the car. She contacted the dealership, which strenuously denied having tampered with the odometer. In fact, the dealership's records reflect that it purchased Gillian's car at auction for $34,000, after a thorough inspection that revealed no mechanical deficiencies or alteration of the car's odometer.

Issue Is Gillian's contract voidable by her?

Rule of Law Innocent misrepresentation renders a contract voidable. Innocent misrepresentation is proven when the following elements are established: (1) a false representation, (2) of fact, (3) that is material, (4) made without knowledge of its falsity but with due care, and (5) the representation is justifiably relied upon.

Application Gillian can prove all five elements of innocent misrepresentation. First, the dealership's false representation was that the mileage on the car was 21,445, when the car actually had about sixty thousand miles on it. Second, the mileage of the car at the time of sale is an actual event not an opinion or prediction. Third, as the mileage of a used car is probably the most critical determinant of its value, this misrepresentation was material to the parties' agreed sale price, inducing the formation of the contract. Indeed, while Gillian might still have purchased this car with sixty thousand miles on it, she most certainly would have done so only at a lower price. Fourth, it is highly unlikely that the dealership was aware of the incorrect odometer reading. We know this because it paid $34,000 for the car, which should have sold for something less than $30,000 in the wholesale market if the true mileage had been known. Moreover, the dealership appears to have conducted appropriate due diligence to support both its own purchase price and the price at which it offered the car to Gillian. The odometer tampering was cleverly concealed, so much so that neither the dealerships' inspection before purchase nor Gillian's mechanic's initial inspection revealed it. Fifth, Gillian's reliance on the ostensible odometer reading is justified. The car was only two years old when she bought it, and 21,445 miles is within an average range of mileage for a used car of that age. Unless the car's physical condition or something in the title paperwork should have alerted her to an inconsistency between the stated mileage and the car's actual mileage, Gillian was entitled to rely on what appeared to be a correct odometer reading.

Conclusion Because all the elements of innocent misrepresentation can be shown, Gillian's contract is voidable by Gillian.

The Restatement and modern cases treat mistakes of law in existence at the time of making the contract *no* differently than mistakes of fact. For example, Susan contracts to sell a parcel of land to James with the mutual understanding that James will build an apartment house on the land. Both Susan and James believe that such a building is lawful. Unknown to them, however, three days before they entered into their contract, the town in which the land was located had enacted an ordinance precluding such use of the land. In states that regard mistakes of law and fact in the same light, this mistake of law would be treated as a mistake of fact that would lead to the consequences discussed below.

MUTUAL MISTAKE

Mutual mistake occurs when *both* parties are mistaken as to the same set of facts. If the mistake relates to a basic assumption on which the contract is made and has a material effect on the agreed exchange, then it is *voidable* by the adversely affected party unless he bears the risk of the mistake.

Usually, market conditions and the financial situation of the parties are not considered basic assumptions. Thus, if Gail contracts to purchase Pete's automobile under the belief that she can sell it at a profit to Jesse, she is not excused from liability if she is mistaken in this belief. Nor can she rescind the agreement simply because she was mistaken as to her estimate of what the automobile was worth. These are the ordinary risks of business, and courts do not undertake to relieve against them. But suppose that the parties contract upon the assumption that the automobile is a 2013 Cadillac with fifteen thousand miles of use, when in fact the engine is that of a cheaper model and has been run in excess of fifty thousand miles. Here, a court likely would allow a rescission because of mutual mistake of a material fact. In a New Zealand case, the plaintiff purchased a "stud bull" at an auction. There were no express warranties as to "sex, condition, or otherwise." Actually, the bull was sterile. Rescission was allowed, the court observing that it was a "bull in name only."

LESHER V. STRID

COURT OF APPEALS OF OREGON, 2000
165 OR. APP. 34, 996 P.2D 988
http://caselaw.findlaw.com/scripts/getcase.pl?court=OR&vol=A99602&invol=1

FACTS In May 1995, the plaintiffs, Vernon and Janene Lesher, agreed to purchase an eighteen-acre parcel of real property from defendant with the intention of using it to raise horses. In purchasing the property, the plaintiffs relied on their impression that at least four acres of the subject property had a right to irrigation from Slate Creek. The earnest money agreement to the contract provided:

D. **Water Rights** are being conveyed to Buyer at the close of escrow…. Seller will provide Buyer with a written explanation of the operation of the irrigation system, water right certificates, and inventory of irrigation equipment included in sale.

The earnest money agreement also provided:

THE SUBJECT PROPERTY IS BEING SOLD "AS IS" subject to the Buyer's approval of the tests and conditions as stated herein. Buyer declares that Buyer is not depending on any other statement of the Seller or licensees that is not incorporated by reference in this earnest money contract [Bold in original].

Before signing the earnest money agreement, the defendants presented to the plaintiffs a 1977 Water Resources Department water rights certificate and a map purporting to show an area of the subject property to be irrigated ("area to be irrigated" map), which indicated that the property carried a four-acre water right. Both parties believed that the property carried the irrigation rights and that the plaintiffs needed such rights for their horse farm. The plaintiffs did not obtain the services of an attorney or a water rights examiner before purchasing the property.

After purchasing the property and before establishing a pasture, the plaintiffs learned that the property did not carry a four-acre water right. The plaintiffs sought rescission of the contract for sale, alleging mutual mistake of fact or innocent misrepresentation regarding the existence of water rights. The trial court ruled in favor of the plaintiffs and the defendant appeals.

DECISION Judgment of the trial court affirmed.

OPINION Wollheim, J. Grounds for rescission on the basis of a mutual mistake of fact or innocent misrepresentation must be proved by clear and convincing evidence. [Citations.] An innocent misrepresentation of fact renders a contract voidable by a party if the party's "manifestation of assent is induced by *** a material misrepresentation by the other party upon which the recipient is justified in relying[.]" [Citations.] A mutual mistake of fact renders a contract voidable by the adversely affected party, "where the parties are mistaken as to the facts existing at the time of the contract, if the mistake is so fundamental that it frustrates the purpose of the contract," [citation], and where the adversely affected party does not bear the risk of the mistake. [citation]. A mistake "is a state of mind which is not in accord with the facts." [Citation].

Even though it appears that the trial court did not apply the clear and convincing standard, ***, we find that plaintiffs' evidence meets that standard. Both defendant and plaintiffs testified that they believed that the four acres of water rights were appurtenant to the subject property. Defendant does not dispute that the 1977 water rights certificate and the "area to be irrigated" map are her representation about the water right.

* * *

Plaintiffs also established by clear and convincing evidence that the existence of the four-acre water right was material and essential to the contract. Vernon testified that the motivation for the purchase was to expand his ability to raise horses from property they already owned where they had a two-acre irrigation right and that the subject property's water right was essential to the contract. Certainly, a smaller water right would limit, not expand, plaintiffs' ability to raise horses. The mistake, therefore, goes to the very essence of the contract.

We next consider defendant's arguments that plaintiffs bore the risk of that mistake. The Restatement

(Second) of Contracts § 154 explains that a party bears the risk of a mistake, in part, if the risk is allocated to the party by agreement of the parties, or if the risk is allocated to the party "by the court on the ground that it is reasonable in the circumstances to do so." We find nothing in the contract that would allocate to plaintiffs the risk of a mistake as to the existence of a four-acre water right.

Defendant argues in the alternative that plaintiffs' mistake of fact is the result of defendant's misrepresentation, on which plaintiffs could not reasonably rely. An "innocent misrepresentation may support a claim for rescission of a real estate agreement if the party who relied on the misrepresentations of another establishes a right to have done so." [Citations.]

Defendant argues that her representations about the four-acre water right were extrinsic to the contract and that the contract's "as is" clause expressly excluded reliance on such extrinsic representations. *** The "as is" clause specifically contemplated reliance on any statements by the seller that were "incorporated by reference" in the earnest money agreement. The earnest money agreement specifically referred to the conveyance of water rights.

INTERPRETATION If both parties to a contract have a common but erroneous belief as to a basic assumption on which the contract is made, the contract is voidable.

CRITICAL THINKING QUESTION Should all contracts provide for this type of situation? If so, how? Explain.

Unilateral Mistake

Unilateral mistake occurs when only one of the parties is mistaken. Courts have been hesitant to grant relief for unilateral mistake, even though it relates to a basic assumption on which a party entered into the contract and has a material effect on the agreed exchange. Nevertheless, relief will be granted in cases in which the nonmistaken party knows, or reasonably should know, that such a mistake has been made (palpable unilateral mistake) or in cases in which the mistake was caused by the fault of the nonmistaken party. For example, suppose a building contractor makes a serious error in his computations and consequently submits a job bid that is one-half the amount it should be. If the other party knows that the contractor made such an error, or reasonably should

have known it, she cannot, as a general rule, take advantage of the other's mistake by accepting the offer. In addition, many courts and the Restatement allow rescission in cases in which the effect of unilateral mistake makes enforcement of the contract unconscionable.

Assumption of Risk of Mistake

A party who has undertaken to bear the risk of a mistake will not be able to avoid the contract, even though the mistake (which may be either mutual or unilateral) would have otherwise permitted the party to do so. This allocation of risk may occur by agreement of the parties. For instance, a ship at sea may be sold "lost or not lost." In such case the buyer is liable whether the ship was lost or not lost at the time the contract was

CONCEPT REVIEW 11-2

Conduct Invalidating Assent

Conduct	Effect
Duress by physical force	Void
Duress by improper threat	Voidable
Undue influence	Voidable
Fraud in the execution	Void
Fraud in the inducement	Voidable

made. There is no mistake; instead, there is a conscious allocation of risk.

The risk of mistake also may be allocated by conscious ignorance when the parties recognize that they have limited knowledge of the facts. For example, the Supreme Court of Wisconsin refused to set aside the sale of a stone for which the purchaser paid $1 but that was subsequently discovered to be an uncut diamond valued at $700. The parties did not know at the time of sale what the stone was and knew they did not know. Each consciously assumed the risk that the value might be more or less than the selling price.

> ### PRACTICAL ADVICE
>
> If you are unsure about the nature of a contract, consider allocating the risk of the uncertainties in your contract.

EFFECT OF FAULT UPON MISTAKE

The Restatement provides that a mistaken party's fault in not knowing or discovering a fact before making a contract does not prevent him from avoiding the contract "unless his fault amounts to a failure to act in good faith and in accordance with reasonable standards of fair dealing." This rule does not, however, apply to a failure to read a contract. As a general proposition, a party is held to what she signs. Her signature authenticates the writing, and she cannot repudiate that which she has voluntarily approved. Generally, one who assents to a writing is presumed to know its contents and cannot

escape being bound by its terms merely by contending that she did not read them; her assent is deemed to cover unknown as well as known terms.

MISTAKE IN MEANING OF TERMS

Somewhat related to mistakes of fact is the situation in which the parties misunderstand their manifestations of mutual assent. A famous case involving this problem is *Raffles v. Wichelhaus*, 2 Hurlstone & Coltman 906 (1864), popularly known as the *Peerless* case. A contract of purchase was made for 125 bales of cotton to arrive on the *Peerless* from Bombay. It happened, however, that there were two ships by the name of *Peerless* each sailing from Bombay, one in October and the other in December. The buyer had in mind the ship that sailed in October, whereas the seller reasonably believed the agreement referred to the *Peerless* sailing in December. Neither party was at fault, but both believed in good faith that a different ship was intended. The English court held that no contract existed.

The Restatement is in accord: there is no manifestation of mutual assent in cases in which the parties attach materially different meanings to their manifestations and neither party knows or has reason to know the meaning attached by the other. If blame can be ascribed to either party, however, that party will be held responsible. Thus, if the seller knew of the sailing from Bombay of two ships by the name of *Peerless*, then he would be at fault, and the contract would be for the ship sailing in October as the buyer expected. If neither party is to blame or both are to blame, there is no contract at all; that is, the agreement is void.

CHAPTER SUMMARY

Duress

Definition wrongful act or threat that overcomes the free will of a party

Physical Compulsion coercion involving physical force renders the agreement void

Improper Threats improper threats or acts, including economic and social coercion, render the contract voidable

Undue Influence

Definition taking unfair advantage of a person by reason of a dominant position based on a confidential relationship

Effect renders contract voidable

Fraud

Fraud in the Execution a misrepresentation that deceives the other party as to the nature of a document evidencing the contract; renders agreement void

Fraud in the Inducement renders the agreement voidable if the following elements are present:
* *False Representation* positive statement or conduct that misleads
* *Fact* an event that occurred or thing that exists
* *Materiality* of substantial importance
* *Knowledge of Falsity and Intention to Deceive* called scienter and includes (1) actual knowledge, (2) lack of belief in statement's truthfulness, or (3) reckless indifference to its truthfulness
* *Justifiable Reliance* a defrauded party is reasonably influenced by the misrepresentation

Nonfraudulent Misrepresentation

Negligent Misrepresentation misrepresentation made without due care in ascertaining its truthfulness; renders agreement voidable

Innocent Misrepresentation misrepresentation made without knowledge of its falsity but with due care; renders contract voidable

Mistake

Definition an understanding that is not in accord with existing fact

Mutual Mistake both parties have a common but erroneous belief forming the basis of the contract; renders the contract voidable by either party

Unilateral Mistake courts are unlikely to grant relief unless the error is known or should be known by the nonmistaken party

Assumption of Risk of Mistake a party may assume the risk of a mistake

Effect of Fault upon Mistake not a bar to avoidance unless the fault amounts to a failure to act in good faith

QUESTIONS

1. Anita and Barry were negotiating, and Anita's attorney prepared a long and carefully drawn contract that was given to Barry for examination. Five days later and prior to its execution, Barry's eyes became so infected that it was impossible for him to read. Ten days thereafter and during the continuance of the illness, Anita called Barry and urged him to sign the contract, telling him that time was running out. Barry signed the contract despite the fact he was unable to read it. In a subsequent action by Anita, Barry claimed that the contract was not binding on him because it was impossible for him to read and he did not know what it contained prior to his signing it. Should Barry be held to the contract?

2. William tells Carol that he paid $150,000 for his farm in 2008, and that he believes it is worth twice that at the present time.

   a. Relying upon these statements, Carol buys the farm from William for $225,000. William did pay $150,000 for the farm in 2008, but its value has increased only slightly, and it is presently not worth $300,000. On discovering this, Carol offers to reconvey the farm to William and sues for the return of her $225,000. Result?

   b. Modify the facts in (a) by assuming that William had paid $100,000 for the property in 2008. What is the result?

3. On September 1, Adams in Portland, Oregon, wrote a letter to Brown in New York City offering to sell to Brown one thousand tons of chromite at $48 per ton, to be shipped by *S.S. Malabar* sailing from Portland, Oregon, to New York City via the Panama Canal. Upon receiving the letter on September 5, Brown immediately mailed to Adams a letter stating that she accepted the offer. There were two ships by the name of *S.S. Malabar* sailing from Portland to New York City via the Panama Canal, one sailing in October and the other sailing in December. At the time of mailing her letter of acceptance, Brown knew of both sailings and further knew that Adams knew only of the December sailing. Is there a contract? If so, to which *S.S. Malabar* does it relate?

4. Adler owes Perreault, a police captain, $500. Adler threatens Perreault that unless Perreault gives him a discharge from the debt, Adler will disclose the fact that Perreault has on several occasions become highly intoxicated and has been seen in the company of certain disreputable persons. Perreault, induced by fear that such a disclosure would cost him his position or in any event lead to social disgrace, gives Adler a release but subsequently sues to set it aside and recover on his claim. Will Adler be able to enforce the release?

5. Harris owned a farm that was worth about $600 an acre. By false representations of fact, Harris induced Pringle to buy the farm at $1,500 an acre. Shortly after taking possession of the farm, Pringle discovered oil under the land. Harris, on learning this, sues to have the sale set aside on the ground that it was voidable because of fraud. Result?

6. On February 2, Phillips induced Mallor to purchase from her fifty shares of stock in the XYZ Corporation for $10,000, representing that the actual book value of each share was $200. A certificate for fifty shares was delivered to Mallor. On February 16, Mallor discovered that the February 2 book value was only $50 per share. Thereafter, Mallor sues Phillips. Will Mallor be successful in a lawsuit against Phillips? Why?

7. Dorothy mistakenly accused Fred's son, Steven, of negligently burning down Dorothy's barn. Fred believed that his son was guilty of the wrong and that he, Fred, was personally liable for the damage, because Steven was only fifteen years old. Upon demand made by Dorothy, Fred paid Dorothy $25,000 for the damage to Dorothy's barn. After making this payment, Fred learned that his son had not caused the burning of Dorothy's barn and was in no way responsible for its burning. Fred then sued Dorothy to recover the $25,000 that he had paid her. Will he be successful?

8. Jones, a farmer, found an odd-looking stone in his fields. He went to Smith, the town jeweler, and asked him what he thought it was. Smith said he did not know but thought it might be a ruby. Jones asked Smith what he would pay for it, and Smith said $200, whereupon Jones sold it to Smith for $200. The stone turned out to be an uncut diamond worth $3,000. Jones brought an action against Smith to recover the stone. On trial, it was proved that Smith actually did not know the stone was a diamond when he bought it, but he thought it might be a ruby. Can Jones void the sale? Explain.

9. Decedent, Joan Jones, a bedridden, lonely woman, eighty-six years old, owned outright Greenacre, her ancestral estate. Biggers, her physician and friend, visited her weekly and was held in the highest regard by Joan. Joan was extremely fearful of pain and suffering and depended on Biggers to ease her anxiety and pain. Several months before her death, Joan deeded Greenacre to Biggers for $5,000. The fair market value of Greenacre at this time was $125,000. Joan was survived by two children and six grandchildren. Joan's children challenged the validity of the deed. Should the deed be declared invalid due to Biggers' undue influence? Explain.

CASE PROBLEMS

10. In February, Gardner, a schoolteacher with no experience in running a tavern, entered into a contract to purchase for $40,000 the Punjab Tavern from Meiling. The contract was contingent upon Gardner's obtaining a five-year lease for the tavern's premises and a liquor license from the state. Prior to the formation of the contract, Meiling had made no representations to Gardner concerning the gross income of the tavern. Approximately three months after the contract was signed, Gardner and Meiling met with an inspector from the Oregon Liquor Control Commission (OLCC) to discuss transfer of the liquor license. Meiling reported to the agent, in Gardner's presence, that the tavern's gross income figures for February, March, and April were $5,710, $4,918, and $5,009 respectively. The OLCC granted the required license, the transaction was closed, and Gardner took possession on June 10. After discovering that the tavern's income was very low and that the tavern had very few female patrons, Gardner contacted Meiling's bookkeeping service and learned that the actual gross income for those three months had been approximately $1,400 to $2,000. Will a court grant Gardner rescission of the contract? Explain.

11. Dorothy and John Huffschneider listed their house and lot for sale with C. B. Property. The asking price was $165,000, and the owners told C. B. that the property contained 6.8 acres. Dean Olson, a salesman for C. B., advertised the property in local newspapers as consisting of six acres. James and Jean Holcomb signed a contract to purchase the property through Olson after first inspecting the property with Olson and being assured by Olson that the property was at least 6.6 acres. The Holcombs never asked for nor received a copy of the survey. In actuality, the lot was only 4.6 acres. Can the Holcombs rescind the contract? Explain.

12. Christine Boyd was designated as the beneficiary of a life insurance policy issued by Aetna Life Insurance Company on the life of Christine's husband, Jimmie Boyd. The policy insured against Jimmie's permanent total disability and provided for a death benefit to be paid on Jimmie's death. Several years after the policy was issued, Jimmie and Christine separated. Jimmie began to travel extensively, and, therefore, Christine was unable to keep track of his whereabouts or his state of health. Jimmie nevertheless continued to pay the premiums on the policy until Christine tried to cash in the policy to alleviate her financial distress. A loan previously had been made on the policy, however, leaving its cash surrender value, and thus the amount Christine received, at only $4.19. Shortly thereafter, Christine learned that Jimmie had been permanently and totally disabled before the surrender of the policy. Aetna also was unaware of Jimmie's condition, and Christine

requested the surrendered policy be reinstated and that the disability payments be made. Jimmie died soon thereafter, and Christine then requested that Aetna pay the death benefit. Decision?

13. Treasure Salvors and the state of Florida entered into a series of four annual contracts governing the salvage of the *Nuestra Senora de Atocha*. The *Atocha* is a Spanish galleon that sank in 1622, carrying a treasure now worth well over $250 million. Both parties had contracted under the impression that the seabed on which the *Atocha* lay was land owned by Florida. Treasure Salvors agreed to relinquish 25 percent of the items recovered in return for the right to salvage on state lands. In accordance with these contracts, Treasure Salvors delivered to Florida its share of the salvaged artifacts. Subsequently the U.S. Supreme Court held that the part of the continental shelf on which the *Atocha* was resting had *never* been owned by Florida. Treasure Salvors then brought suit to rescind the contracts and to recover the artifacts it had delivered to the state of Florida. Should Treasure Salvors prevail?

14. Jane Francois married Victor H. Francois. At the time of the marriage, Victor was a fifty-year-old bachelor living with his elderly mother, and Jane was a thirty-year-old, twice-divorced mother of two. Victor had a relatively secure financial portfolio; Jane, on the other hand, brought no money or property to the marriage.

    The marriage deteriorated quickly over the next couple of years, with disputes centered on financial matters. During this period, Jane systematically gained a joint interest and took control of most of Victor's assets. Three years after they married Jane contracted Harold Monoson, an attorney, to draw up divorce papers. Victor was unaware of Jane's decision until he was taken to Monoson's office, where Monoson presented for Victor's signature a "Property Settlement and Separation Agreement." Monoson told Victor that he would need an attorney, but Jane vetoed Victor's choice. Monoson then asked another lawyer, Gregory Ball, to come into the office. Ball read the agreement and strenuously advised Victor not to sign it because it would commit him to financial suicide. The agreement transferred most of Victor's remaining assets to Jane. Victor, however, signed it because Jane and Monoson persuaded him that it was the only way that his marriage could be saved. In October of the following year, Jane informed Victor that she had sold most of his former property and that she was leaving him permanently. Can Victor have the agreement set aside as a result of undue influence?

15. Iverson owned Iverson Motor Company, an enterprise engaged in the repair and sale of Oldsmobile, Rambler,

and International Harvester Scout automobiles. Forty percent of the business's sales volume and net earnings came from the Oldsmobile franchise. Whipp contracted to buy Iverson Motors, which Iverson said included the Oldsmobile franchise. After the sale, however, General Motors refused to transfer the franchise to Whipp. Whipp then returned the property to Iverson and brought this action seeking rescission of the contract. Should the contract be rescinded? Explain.

16. On February 10, Mrs. Sunderhaus purchased a diamond ring from Perel & Lowenstein for $6,990. She was told by the company's salesman that the ring was worth its purchase price, and she also received at that time a written guarantee from the company attesting to the diamond's value, style, and trade-in value. When Mrs. Sunderhaus went to trade the ring for another, however, she was told by two jewelers that the ring was valued at $3,000 and $3,500, respectively. Mrs. Sunderhaus knew little about the value of diamonds and claims to have relied on the oral representation of the Perel & Lowenstein's salesman and the written representation as to the ring's value. Mrs. Sunderhaus seeks rescission of the contract or damages in the amount of the sales price over the ring's value. Will she prevail? Explain.

17. Division West Chinchilla Ranch advertised on television that a five-figure income could be earned by raising chinchillas with an investment of only $3.75 per animal per year and only thirty minutes of maintenance per day. The minimum investment was $2,150 for one male and six female chinchillas. Division West represented to the plaintiffs that chinchilla ranching would be easy and that no experience was required to make ranching profitable. The plaintiffs, who had no experience raising chinchillas, each invested $2,150 or more to purchase Division's chinchillas and supplies. After three years without earning a profit, the plaintiffs sued Division West for fraud. Do these facts sustain an action for fraud in the inducement?

18. William Schmalz entered into an employment contract with Hardy Salt Company. The contract granted Schmalz six months' severance pay for involuntary termination but none for voluntary separation or termination for cause. Schmalz was asked to resign from his employment. He was informed that if he did not resign he would be fired for alleged misconduct. When Schmalz turned in his letter of resignation, he signed a release prohibiting him from suing his former employer as a consequence of his employment. Schmalz consulted an attorney before signing the release and, upon signing it, received $4,583.00 (one month's salary) in consideration. Schmalz now sues his former employer for the severance pay, claiming that he signed the release under duress. Is Schmalz correct in his assertion?

19. Glen Haumont, who owned an equipment retail business in Broken Bow, Nebraska, owed the Security State Bank more than $628,000 due to improper selling practices as well as business and inventory loans. Several times Glen tried to persuade his parents, Lee and Letha Haumont, to financially back his business debts, but each time they refused. Glen then told his parents that, according to his attorney and the bank, Glen could be prosecuted and sent to jail. Soon afterwards, David Schweitz, the president of the bank, drove out to the elder Haumonts' farm to convince them to sign as guarantors of Glen's debt. Both Schweitz and Glen stressed to the Haumonts that unless they agreed to guarantee his debt, Glen would go to jail. Letha asked that her attorney be allowed to read over the guarantee agreement, but Schweitz told her that he did not have time to wait and that she must decide right then whether Glen was to go to jail. As a result, the Haumonts signed the agreement, encumbering their previously debt-free family farm for more than $628,000. Should the guarantee agreement be set aside due to duress?

20. Conrad Schaneman was a Russian immigrant who could neither read nor write the English language. In 2011, Conrad deeded (conveyed) a farm he owned to his eldest son, Laurence, for $23,500, which was the original purchase price of the property in 1981. The value of the farm in 2011 was between $145,000 and $160,000. At the time he executed the deed, Conrad was an eighty-two-year-old invalid, severely ill, and completely dependent on others for his personal needs. He weighed between 325 and 350 pounds, had difficulty breathing, could not walk more than fifteen feet, and needed a special jackhoist to get in and out of the bathtub. Conrad enjoyed a long-standing, confidential relationship with Laurence, who was his principal adviser and handled Conrad's business affairs. Laurence also obtained a power of attorney from Conrad and made himself a joint owner of Conrad's bank account and $20,000 certificate of deposit. Conrad brought this suit to cancel the deed, claiming it was the result of Laurence's undue influence. Explain whether the deed was executed as a result of undue influence.

21. At the time of her death Olga Mestrovic was the owner of a large number of works of art created by her late husband, Ivan Mestrovic, an internationally known sculptor and artist whose works were displayed throughout Europe and the United States. By the terms of Olga's will, all the works of art created by her husband were to be sold and the proceeds distributed to members of the Mestrovic family. Also included in the estate of Olga Mestrovic was certain real property which 1st Source Bank (the Bank), as personal representative of the estate of Olga Mestrovic, agreed to sell to Terrence and Antoinette Wilkin. The agreement of purchase and sale made no mention of any works of art, although it did provide for the sale of such personal property as a dishwasher, drapes, and French doors stored in the attic. Immediately after closing on the real estate, the Wilkins complained to the Bank of the clutter left on the premises; the Bank gave the Wilkins an option of cleaning the house themselves and keeping any personal property they desired, to which the Wilkins agreed. At the time these arrangements were made, neither

the Bank nor the Wilkins suspected that any works of art remained on the premises. During cleanup, however, the Wilkins found eight drawings and a sculpture created by Ivan Mestrovic to which the Wilkins claimed ownership based upon their agreement with the Bank that, if they cleaned the real property, they could keep such personal property as they desired. Who is entitled to ownership of the works of art?

22. Frank Berryessa stole funds from his employer, the Eccles Hotel Company. His father, W. S. Berryessa (Berryessa), learned of his son's trouble and, thinking the amount involved was about $2,000, gave the hotel a promissory note for $2,186 to cover the shortage. In return, the hotel agreed not to publicize the incident or notify the bonding company. (A bonding company is an insurer that is paid a premium for agreeing to reimburse an employer for thefts by an employee.) Before this note became due, however, the hotel discovered that Frank had actually misappropriated $6,865. The hotel then notified its bonding company, Great American Indemnity Company, to collect the entire loss. W. S. Berryessa claims that the agent for Great American told him that unless he paid them $2,000 in cash and signed a note for the remaining $4,865, Frank would be prosecuted (which note would replace the initial note). Berryessa agreed, signed the note, and gave the agent a cashier's check for $1,500 and a personal check for $500. He requested that the agent not cash the personal check for about a month. Subsequently, Great American sued Berryessa on the note. He defends against the note on the grounds of duress and counterclaims for the return of the $1,500 and the cancellation of the uncashed $500 check. Who should prevail?

23. Ronald D. Johnson is a former employee of International Business Machines Corporation (IBM). As part of a downsizing effort, IBM discharged Johnson. In exchange for an enhanced severance package, Johnson signed a written release and covenant not to sue IBM. IBM's downsizing plan provided that surplus personnel were eligible to receive benefits, including outplacement assistance, career counseling, job retraining, and an enhanced separation allowance. These employees were eligible, at IBM's discretion, to receive a separation allowance of two weeks' pay. However, employees who signed a release could be eligible for an enhanced severance allowance equal to one week's pay for each six months of accumulated service with a maximum of twenty-six weeks' pay. Surplus employees could also apply for alternate, generally lower-paying, manufacturing positions. Johnson opted for the release and received the maximum twenty-six weeks' pay. He then alleged, among other claims, that IBM subjected him to economic duress when he signed the release and covenant-not-to-sue, and he sought to rescind both. What will Johnson need to show in order to prove his cause of action?

24. Etta Mae Paulson died on January 31, 2008, leaving four children: Ken, Donald, Barbara, and Larry. She had

purchased a home in Rainier in 2003, for $21,300. At that time, she had a will that she had executed in 1987, leaving all of her property to her four children in equal shares. That will was never changed. After she moved into the house in Rainier, Ken, Ken's wife, Barbara, and Don helped Etta, who suffered from arthritis in both hands, renal failure, congestive heart failure, and diabetes. As a result of these conditions, Etta had trouble getting around and, during the last part of her life, she used an electric cart. She was taking several medications, including Prozac, Prednisone, Zantac, and Procardia, and was receiving insulin daily and dialysis an average of three times a week. Although there is no evidence that she was mentally incompetent, the medications and treatments made her drowsy, tired, and depressed, and caused mood swings. It is undisputed that she was dependent on the help of others in her daily living. Larry was not in the Rainier area when his mother moved there and did not visit her. The other children and her neighbor helped her. The other children reroofed the house for her, picked fruit and stored it, and mowed the lawn; her daughter helped her with her finances and had a joint account with her, which the daughter never used. All of those children visited her frequently, and at least one of them saw her every day. Etta expressed concern about losing the house because of her medical bills and suggested that she put the house in Ken's name; he and Barbara looked into the situation and concluded that it was not necessary, and so advised their mother. At some point—it is not clear when—Larry was told by state welfare authorities, as Ken and Barbara had learned, that so long as his mother maintained her house as her primary residence and was not receiving Medicaid, she was not in danger of losing her house to the state. Some time in early 2007, Larry and his then girlfriend (later his wife) moved in with Etta and took over her care. Larry expressed his concern to his mother that the state might take her house. Not long thereafter, Larry rented a house in Longview in his name and persuaded his mother to move in with him, his girlfriend, and her child. After Etta moved to Longview, she rented her house in Rainier; the rent was used to maintain the house in Longview. At that time Etta had a savings account with approximately $2,000 in it; Larry held his mother's power of attorney. At the time of her death in January 2008, that account was exhausted, although her medical expenses were being paid by Medicare. Larry admitted that he used some of that money to buy a bicycle and a guitar. He had also used her credit card, on which there was a substantial balance after her death, which he did not pay. He said that that debt "died with his mother." On numerous occasions, Larry expressed to his mother his concern that the state would take her house if she kept it in her name. She was fearful of that, in spite of what she had been told by Ken and Barbara. Larry told her that they were wrong, and frequently urged her to make up her mind "about the deed." Etta was hospitalized three times during 2007. Finally, on September 30, 2007, Larry suggested to his mother that they go to a title company in Rainier to get a deed. Etta signed the deed and gave up all of her rights in the property. Larry then had it recorded. He did not mention it to any of his half-brothers or -sister until two months later when he boasted of it to his half-sister. Is the deed voidable? Explain.

TAKING SIDES

Mrs. Audrey E. Vokes, a widow of fifty-one years and without family, purchased fourteen separate dance courses from J. P. Davenport's Arthur Murray, Inc., School of Dance. The fourteen courses totaled in the aggregate 2,302 hours of dancing lessons at a cost to Mrs. Vokes of $31,090.45. Mrs. Vokes was induced continually to reapply for new courses by representations made by Mr. Davenport that her dancing ability was improving, that she was responding to instruction, that she had excellent potential, and that they were developing her into an accomplished dancer. In fact, she had no dancing ability or aptitude and had trouble "hearing the musical beat." Mrs. Vokes brought action to have the contracts set aside.

a. What are the arguments that the contract should be set aside?

b. What are the arguments that the contract should be enforced?

c. What is the proper outcome? Explain.

Chapter 12

CONSIDERATION

Nuda pactio obligationem non parit. (A naked agreement, that is, one without consideration, does not beget an obligation.)

LEGAL MAXIM

CHAPTER OUTCOMES

After reading and studying this chapter, you should be able to:

1. Define *consideration* and explain what is meant by legal sufficiency.

2. Describe illusory promises, output contracts, requirements contracts, exclusive dealing contracts, and conditional contracts.

3. Explain whether preexisting public and contractual obligations satisfy the legal requirement of consideration.

4. Explain the concept of bargained-for exchange and whether this element is present with past consideration and third-party beneficiaries.

5. Identify and discuss those contracts that are enforceable even though they are not supported by consideration.

Consideration is the primary—but not the only—basis for the enforcement of promises in our legal system. **Consideration** is the inducement to make a promise enforceable. The doctrine of consideration ensures that promises are enforced only in cases in which the parties have exchanged something of value in the eye of the law. **Gratuitous (gift) promises**—those made without consideration—are not legally enforceable, except under certain circumstances, which are discussed later in the chapter.

Consideration, or that which is exchanged for a promise, is present only when the parties intend an exchange. The consideration exchanged for the promise may be an act, a forbearance to act, or a promise to do either of these. Thus, there are two basic elements to

consideration: (1) legal sufficiency (something of value in the eye of the law) and (2) bargained-for exchange. Both must be present to satisfy the requirement of consideration.

Legal Sufficiency

To be **legally sufficient**, the consideration for the promise must be either a legal detriment to the promisee or a legal benefit to the promisor. In other words, in return for the promise, the promisee must give up something of legal value or the promisor must receive something of legal value.

Legal detriment means (1) the doing of (or the undertaking to do) that which the promisee was under no prior legal obligation to do or (2) the refraining from the doing of (or the undertaking to refrain from doing) that which he was previously under no legal obligation to refrain from doing. On the other hand, **legal benefit** means the obtaining by the promisor of that which he had no prior legal right to obtain. In most, if not all, cases in which there is legal detriment to the promisee, there is also a legal benefit to the promisor. However, the presence of either is sufficient.

ADEQUACY

Legal sufficiency has nothing to do with **adequacy of consideration**. The items or actions that the parties agree to exchange do not need to have the same value. Rather, the law will regard the consideration as adequate if the parties have freely agreed to the exchange. The requirement of legally sufficient consideration, therefore, is not at all concerned with whether the bargain was good or bad or whether one party received disproportionately more or less than what he gave or promised in exchange. (Such facts, however, may be relevant to the availability of certain defenses—such as fraud, duress, or undue influence—or certain remedies—such as specific performance.) The requirement of legally sufficient consideration is simply (1) that the parties have agreed to an exchange and (2) that, with respect to each party, the subject matter exchanged, or promised in exchange, either imposed a legal detriment on the promisee or conferred a legal benefit on the promisor. If the purported consideration is clearly without value, however, such that the transaction is a sham, many courts would hold that consideration is lacking.

> ### PRACTICAL ADVICE
> Be sure you are satisfied with your agreed-upon exchange, because courts will not invalidate a contract for absence of adequate consideration.

UNILATERAL CONTRACTS

In a unilateral contract, a promise is exchanged for a completed act or a forbearance to act. Because only one promise exists, only one party, the *offeror*, makes a promise, and is therefore the **promisor** while the other party, the *offeree*, is the person receiving the promise and, thus, is the **promisee**. For example, A promises to pay B $2,000 if B paints A's house. B paints A's house.

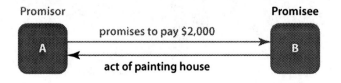

A's promise is binding only if it is supported by consideration consisting of either a legal detriment to B, the promisee (offeree), or a legal benefit to A, the promisor (offeror). B's painting the house is a legal detriment to B, the promisee, because she was under no prior legal duty to paint A's house. Also, B's painting of A's house is a legal benefit to A, the promisor, because A had no prior legal right to have his house painted by B.

A unilateral contract may also consist of a promise exchanged for a forbearance. To illustrate, A negligently injures B, for which B may recover damages in a tort action. A promises B $5,000 if B forbears from bringing suit. B accepts by not suing.

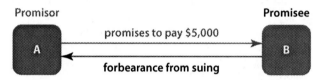

A's promise to pay B $5,000 is binding because it is supported by consideration; B, the promisee (offeree), has incurred a legal detriment by refraining from bringing suit, which he was under no prior legal obligation to refrain from doing. A, the promisor (offeror), has received a legal benefit because she had no prior legal right to B's forbearance from bringing suit.

BILATERAL CONTRACTS

In a bilateral contract there is an exchange of promises. Thus, each party is *both* a promisor and a promisee. For example, if A (the offeror) promises (offers) to purchase an automobile from B for $20,000, and B (the offeree) promises to sell the automobile to A for $20,000 (accepts the offer), the following relationship exists:

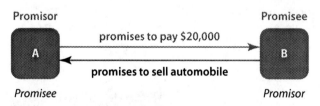

A (offeror) as promisor: A's promise (the offer) to pay B $20,000 is binding if that promise is supported by legal consideration from B (offeror), which may consist of either a legal detriment to B, the *promisee*, or a legal benefit to A, the *promisor*. B's promise to sell A the automobile is a legal detriment to B because he was under no prior legal duty to sell the automobile to A. Moreover, B's promise is also a legal benefit to A because A had no prior legal right to that automobile. Consequently, A's promise to pay $20,000 to B is supported by consideration and is enforceable.

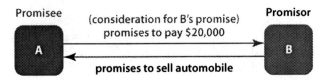

B (offeree) as promisor: *For B's promise (the acceptance)* to sell the automobile to A to be binding, it likewise must be supported by consideration from A (offeror), which may be either a legal detriment to A, the *promisee*, or a legal benefit to B, the *promisor*. A's promise to pay B $20,000 is a legal detriment to A because he was under no prior legal duty to pay $20,000 to B. At the same time, A's promise is also a legal benefit to B because B had no prior legal right to the $20,000. Thus, B's promise to sell the automobile is supported by consideration and is enforceable.

To summarize, for A's *promise* to B to be binding, it must be supported by legally sufficient consideration, which requires that the promise A receives from B in exchange either provides a legal benefit to A or constitutes a legal detriment to B. B's return promise to A must also be supported by consideration. Thus, in a bilateral contract, each promise is the consideration for the other, a relationship that has been referred to as *mutuality of obligation*. A general consequence of mutuality of obligation is that each promisor in a bilateral contract must be bound or neither is bound. See Concept Review 12-1 for an overview of consideration in both unilateral and bilateral contracts. Also see the Ethical Dilemma for a situation dealing with the disputed enforceability of a promise.

ILLUSORY PROMISES

Words of promise that make the performance of the purported promisor entirely optional do not constitute a promise at all. Consequently, they cannot serve as consideration. In this section, we will distinguish such illusory promises from promises that do impose obligations of performance upon the promisor and thus can be legally sufficient consideration.

An **illusory promise** is a statement that is in the form of a promise but imposes no obligation upon the maker of the statement. An illusory promise is not consideration for a return promise. Thus, a statement committing the promisor to purchase such quantity of goods as he may "desire" or "want" or "wish to buy" is an illusory promise because its performance is entirely optional. For example, if ExxonMobil offers to sell to Gasco as many barrels of oil as Gasco shall choose at $40 per barrel, there is no consideration. An offer containing such a promise, although accepted by the offeree, does not create a contract because the promise is illusory—Gasco's performance is entirely optional and no constraint is placed on its freedom. It is not bound to do anything, nor can ExxonMobil reasonably expect it to do anything. Thus, Gasco, by its promise, suffers no legal detriment and confers no legal benefit.

> ## PRACTICAL ADVICE
>
> Because an agreement under which one party may perform at his discretion is not a binding contract, be sure that you make a promise and receive a promise that is not optional.

CONCEPT REVIEW 12-1

Consideration in Unilateral and Bilateral Contracts

Type of Contract	Offer	Acceptance	Consideration
Unilateral	Promise by A	Performance of requested act or forbearance by B	*Promise* by A *Performance* of requested act or forbearance by B
Bilateral	Promise by A	Return promise by B to perform requested act or forbearance	*Promise* by A *Return promise* by B to perform requested act or forbearance

VANEGAS V. AMERICAN ENERGY SERVICES

SUPREME COURT OF TEXAS, 2009
302 S.W.3D 299
http://scholar.google.com/scholar_case?case=3293885797327227839&q=302+S.W.3d+299+&hl=en&as_sdt=2,34

FACTS American Energy Services (AES or employer) was formed in the summer of 1996. AES hired the employees in this case that same year. The employees allege that in an operational meeting in June 1997, they voiced concerns to John Carnett, a vice president of AES, about the continued viability of the company. The employees allege that, in an effort to provide an incentive for them to stay with the company, Carnett promised the employees, who were at-will employees and therefore free to leave the company at any time, that "in the event of sale or merger of AES, the original [eight] employees remaining with AES at that time would get 5 percent of the value of any sale or merger of AES." AES Acquisition, Inc. acquired AES in 2001. Seven of the eight original employees were still with AES at the time of the acquisition. These remaining employees demanded their proceeds, and when the company refused to pay, the employees sued, claiming AES had breached the oral agreement.

AES moved for summary judgment on the ground that the agreement was illusory. The employees argued that the promise represented a unilateral contract, and by remaining employed for the stated period, the employees performed, thereby making the promise enforceable. The trial court granted AES's motion for summary judgment, and the employees appealed. The court of appeals affirmed, holding that the alleged unilateral contract failed because it was not supported by at least one non-illusory promise.

DECISION Judgment of the court of appeals reversed, and case remanded.

OPINION Green, J. AES argues, and the court of appeals held, that our holdings in *Light* dictate the result in this case. [Citation.] In *Light*, we stated:

> Consideration for a promise, by either the employee or the employer in an at-will employment, cannot be dependent on a period of continued employment. Such a promise would be illusory because it fails to bind the promisor who always retains the option of discontinuing employment in lieu of performance. When illusory promises are all that support a purported bilateral contract, there is no contract.

* * *

Light involved an employee's challenge to a covenant not to compete. [Citation.] * * *

We revisited the issue of illusory promises in covenants not to compete in *Sheshunoff*. * * * We reaffirmed our previous holding in *Light* that covenants not to compete in bilateral contracts must be supported by "mutual non-illusory promises." [Citation.]

Citing our holdings in *Light* and *Sheshunoff*, the court of appeals [in this case] stated that "[a] unilateral contract may be formed when one of the parties makes only an illusory promise but the other party makes a non-illusory promise. The non-illusory promise can serve as the offer for a unilateral contract, which the promisor who made the illusory promise can accept by performance." [Citation.] We agree with that statement, but the court of appeals erroneously applied those holdings to the current case.

The issue turns on the distinction between bilateral and unilateral contracts. "A bilateral contract is one in which there are mutual promises between two parties to the contract, each party being both a promisor and a promisee." [Citations.] A unilateral contract, on the other hand, is "created by the promisor promising a benefit if the promisee performs. The contract becomes enforceable when the promisee performs." [Citation.] Both *Sheshunoff* and *Light* concerned *bilateral* contracts in which employers made promises in exchange for employees' promises not to compete with their companies after termination. [Citations.] The court of appeals' explanation of these cases—describing an exchange of promises where one party makes an illusory promise and the other a non-illusory promise—describes the attempted formation of a *bilateral* contract, not a unilateral contract. [Citation.] * * *

The court of appeals held that even if AES promised to pay the employees the five percent, that promise was illusory at the time it was made because the employees were at-will, and AES could have fired all of them prior to the acquisition. [Citation.] But whether the promise was illusory at the time it was made is irrelevant; what matters is whether the promise became enforceable by the time of the breach. [Citations.] Almost all unilateral contracts begin as illusory promises. Take, for instance, the classic textbook example of a unilateral contract: "I will pay you $50 if you paint my house." The offer to pay the individual to paint the house can be withdrawn at any point prior to performance. But once the individual accepts the offer by performing, the promise to pay the $50 becomes binding. The employees allege that AES made an offer to split five percent of the proceeds of the sale or merger of the company among any remaining original employees. Assuming that allegation is true, the seven remaining employees accepted this offer by remaining employed for the requested period of time. [Citation.] At that point, AES's promise became binding. AES then breached its agreement with the employees when it refused to pay the employees their five percent share.

Furthermore, the court of appeals' holding would potentially jeopardize all pension plans, vacation leave, and other forms of compensation made to at-will employees that are based on a particular term of service. * * *

The fact that the employees were at-will and were already being compensated in the form of their salaries in exchange for remaining employed also does not make the promise to pay the bonus any less enforceable.

* * *

AES allegedly promised to pay any remaining original employees five percent of the proceeds when AES was sold. Assuming AES did make such an offer, the seven remaining employees accepted the offer by staying with AES until the sale. Regardless of whether the promise was illusory at the time it was made, the promise became enforceable upon the employees' performance. The court of appeals erred in holding otherwise. * * *

INTERPRETATION An illusory promise is a statement that is in the form of a promise but imposes no obligation upon the maker of the statement.

ETHICAL QUESTION Did AES act ethically by inducing the employees to continue working in return for a promise that AES considered to be not binding? Explain.

CRITICAL THINKING QUESTION Do you agree with this decision? Explain.

Output and Requirements Contracts The agreement of a seller to sell her entire production to a particular purchaser is called an **output contract**. It gives the seller an ensured market for her product. Conversely, a purchaser's agreement to purchase from a particular seller all the materials of a particular kind that the purchaser needs is called a **requirements contract**. It ensures the buyer of a ready source of inventory or supplies. These contracts are *not* illusory. The buyer under a requirements contract does not promise to buy as much as she desires to buy, but to buy as much as she *needs*. Similarly, under an output contract, the seller promises to sell to the buyer the seller's entire production, not merely as much as the seller desires.

Furthermore, the Code imposes a good faith limitation upon the quantity to be sold or purchased under an output or requirements contract. Thus, this type of contract involves such actual output or requirements as may occur in good faith, except that no quantity unreasonably disproportionate to any stated estimate or, in the absence of a stated estimate, to any normal prior output or requirements may be tendered or demanded. Therefore, after contracting to sell to Adler, Inc., its entire output, Benevito Company cannot increase its production from one eight-hour shift per day to three eight-hour shifts per day.

> ### PRACTICAL ADVICE
>
> If you use an output or requirements contract, be sure to act in good faith and do not take unfair advantage of the situation.

Exclusive Dealing Contracts An exclusive **dealing** agreement is a contract in which a manufacturer of goods grants to a distributor an exclusive right to sell its products in a designated market. Unless otherwise agreed, an implied obligation is imposed on the manufacturer to use its best efforts to supply the goods and on the distributor to use her best efforts to promote their sale. These implied obligations are sufficient consideration to bind both parties to the exclusive dealing contract.

Conditional Promises A **conditional promise** is a promise the performance of which depends upon the happening or nonhappening of an event not certain to occur (the condition). A conditional promise is sufficient consideration *unless* the promisor knows at the time of making the promise that the condition cannot occur.

Thus, if Joanne offers to pay Barry $8,000 for Barry's automobile, provided that Joanne receives such amount as an inheritance from the estate of her deceased uncle, and Barry accepts the offer, the duty of Joanne to pay $8,000 to Barry is *conditioned* on her receiving $8,000 from her deceased uncle's estate. The consideration moving from Barry to Joanne is the transfer of title to the automobile. The consideration moving from Joanne to Barry is the promise of $8,000 subject to the condition.

PREEXISTING PUBLIC OBLIGATIONS

The law does not regard the performance of, or the promise to perform, a preexisting legal duty, public or private, as either a legal detriment or a legal benefit.

A **public duty** does not arise out of a contract; rather, it is imposed on members of society by force of the common law or by statute. Illustrations, as found in the law of torts, include the duty not to commit assault, battery, false imprisonment, or defamation. The criminal law also imposes many public duties. Thus, if Norton promises to pay Holmes, the village ruffian, $100 not to injure him, Norton's promise is unenforceable because both tort and criminal law impose a preexisting public obligation on Holmes to refrain from such abuse.

Public officials, such as the mayor of a city, members of a city council, police, and firefighters, are under a preexisting obligation to perform their duties by virtue of their public office. See *Denney v. Reppert* below.

The performance of, or the promise to perform, a **preexisting contractual duty**, a duty the terms of which are neither doubtful nor the subject of honest dispute, is also legally insufficient consideration because the doing of what one is legally bound to do is neither a detriment to a promisee nor a benefit to the promisor. For example, if Anita employs Ben for one year at a salary of $1,000 per month, and at the end of six months promises Ben that in addition to the salary she will pay Ben $3,000 if Ben remains on the job for the remainder of the period originally agreed on, Anita's promise is not binding for lack of legally sufficient consideration. However, if Ben's duties were by agreement changed in nature or amount, Anita's promise would be binding because Ben's new duties are a legal detriment to Ben and a legal benefit to Anita.

The following case deals with both preexisting public and contractual obligations.

DENNEY V. REPPERT

COURT OF APPEALS OF KENTUCKY, 1968
432 S.W.2D 647

http://scholar.google.com/scholar_case?case=14895092933351248292&q=432+S.W.2d+647&hl=en&as_sdt=2,34

FACTS In June, three armed men entered and robbed the First State Bank of Eubank, Kentucky, of $30,000. Acting on information supplied by four employees of the bank, Denney, Buis, McCollum, and Snyder, three law enforcement officials apprehended the robbers. Two of the arresting officers, Godby and Simms, were state policemen, and the third, Reppert, was a deputy sheriff in a neighboring county. All seven claimed the reward for the apprehension and conviction of the bank robbers. The trial court held that only Reppert was entitled to the reward, and Denney appealed.

DECISION Judgment affirmed.

OPINION Myre, J. The first question for determination is whether the employees of the robbed bank are eligible to receive or share in the reward. The great weight of authority answers in the negative. * * *

To the general rule that, when a reward is offered to the general public for the performance of some specified act, such reward may be claimed by any person who performs such act, is the exception of agents, employees and public officials who are acting within the scope of their employment or official duties. * * *

* * *

At the time of the robbery the claimants Murrell Denney, Joyce Buis, Rebecca McCollum, and Jewell Snyder were employees of the First State Bank of Eubank. They were under duty to protect and conserve the resources and moneys of the bank, and safeguard every interest of the institution furnishing them employment. Each of these employees exhibited great courage, and cool bravery, in a time of stress and danger. The community and the county have recompensed them in commendation, admiration and high praise, and the world looks on them as heroes. But in making known the robbery and assisting in acquainting the public and the officers with details of the crime and with identification of the robbers, they performed a duty to the bank and the public, for which they cannot claim a reward.

State Policemen Garret Godby, Johnny Simms, and [deputy sheriff] Tilford Reppert made the arrest of the bank robbers and captured the stolen money. All participated in the prosecution. At the time of the arrest, it was the duty of the state policemen to apprehend the criminals. Under the law they cannot claim or share in the reward and they are interposing no claim to it.

This leaves * * * Tilford Reppert the sole eligible claimant. The record shows that at the time of the arrest he was a deputy sheriff in Rockcastle County, but the arrest and recovery of the stolen money took place in Pulaski County. He was out of his jurisdiction, and was thus under no legal duty to make the arrest, and is thus eligible to claim and receive the award.

* * *

It is manifest from the record that Tilford Reppert is the only claimant qualified and eligible to receive the reward. Therefore, it is the judgment of the circuit court that he is entitled to receive payment of the $1,500.00 reward now deposited with the Clerk of this Court.

INTERPRETATION The law does not regard the performance of a preexisting duty as either a legal detriment or a legal benefit.

ETHICAL QUESTION Did the court treat all the parties fairly? Explain.

CRITICAL THINKING QUESTION Do you agree with the preexisting duty rule? Explain.

Modification of a Preexisting Contract A **modification of a preexisting contract** occurs when the parties to the contract mutually agree to change one or more of its terms. Under the common law, as shown in the following case, a modification of an existing contract must be supported by mutual consideration to be enforceable. In other words, the modification must be supported by some new consideration beyond that which is already owed under the original contract. Thus, there must be a separate and distinct modification contract. For example, Diane and Fred agree that Diane shall put in a gravel driveway for Fred at a cost of $2,000. Subsequently, Fred agrees to pay an additional $3,000 if Diane will blacktop the driveway. Because Diane was not bound by the original contract to provide blacktop, she would incur a legal detriment in doing so and is therefore entitled to the additional $3,000. Similarly, consideration may consist of the promisee's refraining from exercising a legal right.

The Code has modified the common law rule for contract modification by providing that the parties can effectively modify a contract for the sale of goods without new consideration, provided they both intend to modify the contract and act in good faith. Moreover, the Restatement has moved toward this position by providing that a modification of an executory contract is binding if it is fair and equitable in the light of surrounding facts that the parties had not anticipated when the contract was made. Figure 12-1 demonstrates when consideration is required to modify an existing contract.

PRACTICAL ADVICE

If you modify a contract governed by the common law, be sure to provide additional consideration to make the other party's new promise enforceable.

NEW ENGLAND ROCK SERVICES, INC. v. EMPIRE PAVING, INC.

APPELLATE COURT OF CONNECTICUT, 1999
53 CONN.APP. 771, 731 A.2D 784, CERT. DENIED, 250 CONN. 921, 738 A.2D 658
http://scholar.google.com/scholar_case?case=2815205762460431873&q=731+A.2d+784&hl=en&as_sdt=2,34

FACTS On October 26, 1995, the defendant, Empire Paving, Inc., entered into a contract with Rock Services under which Rock Services would provide drilling and blasting services as a subcontractor on the Niles Hill Road sewer project on which Empire was the general contractor and the city of New London was the owner. Rock Services was to be paid an agreed-upon price of $29 per cubic yard with an estimated amount of five thousand cubic yards, or on a time and materials basis, whichever was less. From the outset, Rock Services experienced problems on the job, the primary problem being the presence of a heavy concentration of water on the site. The water problem hindered Rock Services' ability to complete its work as anticipated. It is the responsibility of the general contractor to control the water on the work site and, on this particular job, Empire failed to control the water on the site properly. Rock Services

attempted alternative methods of dealing with the problem, but was prevented from using them by the city. Thereafter, to complete its work, Rock Services was compelled to use a more costly and time-consuming method.

In late November 1995, Rock Services advised Empire that it would be unable to complete the work as anticipated because of the conditions at the site and requested that Empire agree to amend the contract to allow Rock Services to complete the project on a time and materials basis. On December 8, Empire signed a purchase order that so modified the original agreement. Upon completion of the work, Empire refused to pay Rock Services for the remaining balance due on the time and materials agreement in the amount of $58,686.63, and Rock Services instituted this action. The trial court concluded that the modified agreement was valid and ruled in favor of Rock Services. Empire brings this appeal.

DECISION Judgment in favor of Rock Services affirmed.

OPINION Schaller, J. In concluding that the modification was valid and enforceable, the trial court determined that the later agreement was supported by sufficient consideration. * * *

"The doctrine of consideration is fundamental in the law of contracts, the general rule being that in the absence of consideration an executory promise is unenforceable." [Citation.] While mutual promises may be sufficient consideration to bind parties to a modification; [citations] a promise to do that which one is already bound by his contract to do is not sufficient consideration to support an additional promise by the other party to the contract. [Citations.]

A modification of an agreement must be supported by valid consideration and requires a party to do, or promise to do, something further than, or different from, that which he is already bound to do. [Citations.] It is an accepted principle of law in this state that when a party agrees to perform an obligation for another to whom that obligation is already owed, although for lesser remuneration, the second agreement does not constitute a valid, binding contract. [Citations.] The basis of the rule is generally made to rest upon the proposition that in such a situation he who promises the additional [work] receives nothing more than that to which he is already entitled and he to whom the promise is made gives nothing that he was not already under legal obligation to give. [Citations.]

Our Supreme Court in [citation], however, articulated an exception to the preexisting duty rule:

> [W]here a contract must be performed under burdensome conditions not anticipated, and not within the contemplation of the parties at the time when the contract was made, and the promisee measures up to the right standard of honesty and fair dealing, and agrees, in view of the changed conditions, to pay what is then reasonable, just, and fair, such new contract is not without consideration within the meaning of that term, either in law or in equity.

* * * What unforeseen difficulties and burdens will make a party's refusal to go forward with his contract equitable, so as to take the case out of the general rule and bring it within the exception, must depend upon the facts of each particular case. They must be substantial, unforeseen, and not within the contemplation of the parties when the

contract was made. [Citation.] This theory of unforeseen circumstances is applicable to the facts of this case.

Empire argues strenuously that the water conditions on the site cannot qualify as a new circumstance that was not anticipated at the time the original contract was signed. * * *

Empire's argument, however, is misplaced. Rock Services does not argue that it was unaware of the water conditions on the site but, rather, that Empire's failure to control or remove the water on the site constituted the new or changed circumstance. Rock Services argues that Empire's duty to control or remove the water on the job site arose in accordance with the custom and practice in the industry and, therefore, Empire's failure to control or remove the water on the site constituted a new circumstance that Rock Services did not anticipate at the time the original contract was signed.

* * *

In addition to finding that Empire had a duty to control or remove the water from the job site, the trial court found further that Empire's failure to control or remove the water from the site made Rock Services' working conditions sufficiently burdensome to prevent Rock Services from completing the work as anticipated, forcing Rock Services to attempt to use a different method of drilling and ultimately compelling Rock Services to use the more costly and time consuming method of casing the blasting hole. The trial court further found that Empire's failure to control or remove the water on the site constituted a new circumstance not anticipated by the parties at the time the original contract was signed. In addition, the trial court also found that Rock Services' request for the modification was not wrongful but, rather, was justified under the circumstances and did not constitute duress as a matter of law.

Upon our review of the record, we conclude that the trial court's findings of fact are supported by the record and are not clearly erroneous. * * *

INTERPRETATION The Restatement provides that a modification of an executory contract is binding if it is fair and equitable in the light of surrounding facts that the parties had not anticipated when the contract was made.

CRITICAL THINKING QUESTION Which rule for contract modification do you believe is the best: the common law, the Restatement's, or the Uniform Commercial Code's? Why?

Substituted Contracts A **substituted contract** results when the parties to a contract mutually agree to rescind their original contract and enter into a new one. This situation actually involves three separate contracts: the original contract, the contract of rescission, and the substitute contract. Substituted contracts are perfectly

valid, allowing the parties to effectively discharge the original contract and to impose obligations under the new one. The rescission is binding in that, as long as each party still had rights under the original contract, each has, by giving up those rights, provided consideration to the other.

Figure 12-1 *Modification of a Preexisting Contract*

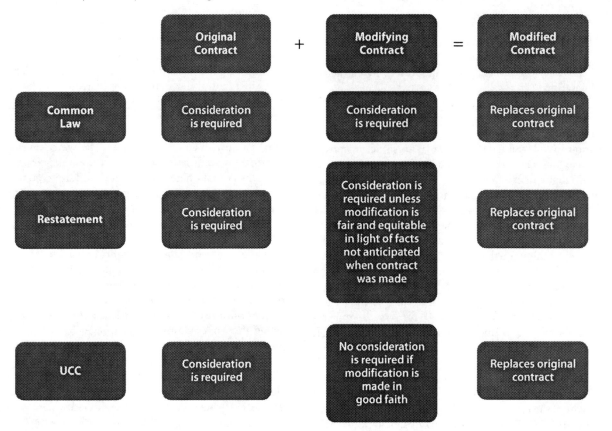

Settlement of an Undisputed Debt An **undisputed debt** is an obligation that is not contested as to its existence or its amount. Under the common law, the payment of a lesser sum of money than is owed in consideration of a promise to discharge a fully matured, undisputed debt is legally insufficient to support the promise of discharge. To illustrate, assume that Barbara owes Arnold $100, and in consideration of Barbara's paying him $50, Arnold agrees to discharge the debt. In a subsequent suit by Arnold against Barbara to recover the remaining $50, at common law Arnold is entitled to a judgment for $50 on the ground that Arnold's promise of discharge is not binding, because Barbara's payment of $50 was no legal detriment to the promisee, Barbara, because she was under a *preexisting legal obligation* to pay that much and more. Consequently, the consideration for Arnold's promise of discharge was legally insufficient, and Arnold is not bound by his promise. If, however, Arnold had accepted from Barbara any new or different consideration, such as the sum of $40 and a fountain pen worth $10 or less, or even the fountain pen with no payment of money, in full satisfaction of the $100 debt, the consideration moving from Barbara would be legally sufficient because Barbara was under no

legal obligation to give a fountain pen to Arnold. In this example, consideration would also exist if Arnold had agreed to accept $50 *before* the debt became due, in full satisfaction of the debt. Barbara was under no legal obligation to pay any of the debt before its due date. Consequently, Barbara's early payment would constitute a legal detriment to Barbara as well as a legal benefit to Arnold. The common law is not concerned with the amount of the discount, because that is simply a question of adequacy. Likewise, Barbara's payment of a lesser amount on the due date at an agreed-upon different place of payment would be legally sufficient consideration. The Restatement, however, requires that the new consideration "differ[s] from what was required by the duty in a way which reflects more than a pretense of bargain."

Settlement of a Disputed Debt A disputed debt is an obligation whose existence or amount is contested. A promise to settle a validly disputed claim in exchange for an agreed payment or other performance is supported by consideration. Where the dispute is based on contentions without merit or not made in good faith, the debtor's surrender of such contentions is not a legal detriment to the claimant. The Restatement adopts a different position by providing that the settlement of a claim that proves invalid is consideration if at the time of the settlement (1) the claimant honestly believed that the claim was valid or (2) the claim was in fact doubtful because of uncertainty as to the facts or the law.

For example, where a person has requested professional services from an accountant or a lawyer and no agreement has been made about the amount of the fee to be charged, the client has a legal obligation to pay the reasonable value of the services performed. Because no definite amount was agreed on, the client's obligation is uncertain. When the accountant or lawyer sends the client a bill for services rendered, even though the amount stated in the bill is an estimate of the reasonable value of the services, the debt does not become undisputed until and unless the client agrees to pay the amount of the bill. If the client honestly disputes the amount that is owed and offers in full settlement an amount less than the bill, acceptance of the lesser amount by the accountant or lawyer discharges the debt. Thus, if Andy sends to Bess, an accountant, a check for $120 in full payment of his debt to Bess for services rendered, which services Andy considered worthless but for which Bess billed Andy $600, Bess's acceptance (cashing) of the check releases Andy from any further liability. Andy has given up his right to dispute the billing further, and Bess has forfeited her right to further collection. Thus, there is mutuality of consideration.

> **PRACTICAL ADVICE**
>
> If your contract is validly disputed, carefully consider whether to accept any payment marked "payment in full."

Bargained-for Exchange

The central idea behind consideration is that the parties have intentionally entered into a **bargained-for exchange** with each other and have each given to the other something in a mutually agreed-upon exchange for his promise or performance. Thus, a promise to give someone a birthday present is without consideration, because the promisor received nothing in exchange for her promise of a present.

> **PRACTICAL ADVICE**
>
> Because a promise to make a gift is generally not legally enforceable, obtain delivery of something that shows your control or ownership of the item to make it an executed gift.

PAST CONSIDERATION

Consideration, as previously defined, is the inducement for a promise or performance. The element of exchange is absent where a promise is given for an act already done. Therefore, unbargained-for past events are not consideration, despite their designation as **past consideration**. A promise made on account of something that the promisee has already done is not enforceable. For example, Diana installs Tom's complex new car stereo and speakers. Tom subsequently promises to reimburse Diana for her expenses, but his promise is not binding because there is no bargained-for exchange. See *DiLorenzo v. Valve and Primer Corporation* later in this chapter.

THIRD PARTIES

Consideration to support a promise may be given to a person other than the promisor if the promisor bargains for that exchange. For example, A promises to pay B $15 if B delivers a specified book to C.

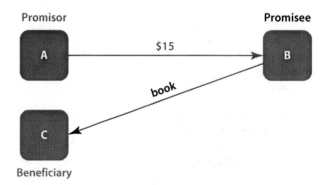

A's promise is binding because B incurred a legal detriment by delivering the book to C, because B was under no prior legal obligation to do so, and A had no prior legal right to have the book given to C. A and B have bargained for A to pay B $15 in return for B's delivering the book to C. A's promise to pay $15 is also consideration for B's promise to give C the book.

Conversely, consideration may be given by some person other than the promisee. For example, A promises to pay B $25 in return for D's promise to give a radio to A. A's promise to pay $25 to B is consideration for D's promise to give a radio to A and *vice versa*.

Contracts without Consideration

Certain transactions are enforceable even though they are not supported by consideration.

PROMISES TO PERFORM PRIOR UNENFORCEABLE OBLIGATIONS

In certain circumstances the courts will enforce new promises to perform an obligation that originally was not enforceable or that has become unenforceable by operation of law. These situations include promises to pay debts barred by the statute of limitations, debts discharged in bankruptcy, and voidable obligations. In addition, some courts will enforce promises to pay moral obligations.

Promise to Pay Debt Barred by the Statute of Limitations Every state has a statute of limitations stating that legal actions to enforce a debt must be brought within a prescribed period of time after the rights to bring the action arose. Actions not begun within the specified period—such periods vary among the states and also with the nature of the legal action—will be dismissed.

An exception to the past consideration rule extends to promises to pay all or part of a contractual or quasi-contractual debt barred by the statute of limitations. The new promise is binding according to its terms, without consideration, for a second statutory period. Any recovery under the new promise is limited to the terms contained in the new promise. Most states require that new promises falling under this rule, except those partially paid, must be in writing to be enforceable.

Promise to Pay Debt Discharged in Bankruptcy A promise to pay a debt that has been discharged in bankruptcy is also enforceable without consideration. The Bankruptcy Code, however, imposes a number of requirements that must be met before such a promise may be enforced. These requirements are discussed in Chapter 38.

Voidable Promises Another promise that is enforceable without new consideration is a new promise to perform a voidable obligation that has not previously been avoided. The power of avoidance may be based on lack of capacity, fraud, misrepresentation, duress, undue influence, or mistake. For instance, a promise to perform an antecedent obligation made by a minor upon reaching the age of majority is enforceable without new consideration. To be enforceable, the promise itself must not be voidable. For example, if the new promise is made without knowledge of the original fraud or by a minor before reaching the age of majority, then the new promise is not enforceable.

Moral Obligation Under the common law and in most states, a promise made to satisfy a preexisting moral obligation is made for past consideration and therefore is unenforceable for lack of consideration. Instances involving such moral obligations include promises to pay another for board and lodging previously furnished to one's needy relative and promises to pay debts owed by a relative.

The Restatement and a minority of states recognize moral obligations as consideration. The Restatement provides that a promise made for "a benefit previously received by the promisor from the promisee is binding to the extent necessary to prevent injustice." For instance, under the Restatement, Tim's subsequent promise to Donna to reimburse her for expenses she incurred in rendering emergency services to Tim's son is binding even though it is not supported by new consideration.

PROMISSORY ESTOPPEL

As discussed in Chapter 9, in certain circumstances in which there has been detrimental reliance, the courts enforce noncontractual promises under the doctrine of promissory estoppel. When applicable, the doctrine makes gratuitous promises enforceable to the extent necessary to avoid injustice. The doctrine applies when a promise that the promisor should reasonably expect to induce detrimental reliance does induce such action or forbearance.

Promissory estoppel does not mean that a promise given without consideration is binding simply because it is followed by a change of position on the part of the promisee. Such a change of position in justifiable reliance on the promise creates liability if injustice can be avoided only by the enforcement of the promise. For example, Ann promises Larry not to foreclose for a period of six months on a mortgage Ann owns on Larry's land. Larry then changes his position by spending $100,000 to construct a building on the land. Ann's promise not to foreclose is binding on her under the doctrine of promissory estoppel.

The most common application of the doctrine of promissory estoppel is to charitable subscriptions. Numerous churches, memorials, college buildings, stadiums, hospitals, and other structures used for religious, educational, or charitable purposes have been built with the assistance of contributions made through fulfillment of pledges or promises to contribute to particular worthwhile causes. Although the pledgor regards herself as making a gift for a charitable purpose and gift promises tend not to be enforceable, the courts have generally enforced charitable subscription promises. Although various reasons and theories have been advanced in support of liability, the one most commonly accepted is that the subscription has induced a change of position by the promisee (the church, school, or charitable organization) in reliance on the promise. The Restatement, moreover, has relaxed the reliance requirement for charitable subscriptions so that actual reliance need not be shown; the probability of reliance is sufficient.

DiLorenzo v. Valve & Primer Corporation

APPELLATE COURT OF ILLINOIS, FIRST DISTRICT, FIFTH DIVISION, 2004
807 N.E.2D 673, 283 ILL.DEC. 68

http://scholar.google.com/scholar_case?case=2583997576855586555&q=807+N.E.2d+673&hl=en&as_sdt=2,34

FACTS DiLorenzo, a forty-year employee of Valve & Primer, was also an officer, director, and shareholder of one hundred shares of stock. DiLorenzo claims that in 1987 Valve & Primer offered him a ten-year stock option that would allow DiLorenzo to purchase an additional three hundred shares at the fixed price of $250 per share. DiLorenzo claims that in reliance on that employment agreement, he stayed in his job for over nine additional years and did not follow up on any of several recruitment offers from other companies. Valve & Primer claims the 1987 employment agreement between it and DiLorenzo did not contain a stock purchase agreement. The only purported proof of the agreement is an unsigned copy of board meeting minutes of which DiLorenzo had the only copy.

In January 1996, DiLorenzo entered into a semiretirement agreement with Valve & Primer, and he attempted to tender his remaining one hundred shares pursuant to a stock redemption agreement. Shortly thereafter, Valve & Primer fired DiLorenzo. DiLorenzo argued before the trial court that, even if the purported agreement was not found to be valid, it should be enforced on promissory estoppel grounds. Valve & Primer's moved for summary judgment, which the trial court granted for lack of consideration. The trial court denied the promissory estoppel claim because of insufficient reliance. DiLorenzo appealed.

DECISION The trial court's grant of Valve & Primer's motion for summary judgment is affirmed.

OPINION Reid, J. We begin by addressing whether there was consideration for the stock options. "A stock option is the right to buy a share or shares of stock at a specified price or within a specified period." [Citation.] In order to evaluate the nature and scope of the stock options issued to DiLorenzo, we must assume, for purposes of this portion of our discussion, that DiLorenzo's corporate minutes are valid.

"A contract, to be valid, must contain offer, acceptance, and consideration; to be enforceable, the agreement must also be sufficiently definite so that its terms are reasonably certain and able to be determined." [Citation.] "A contract is sufficiently definite and certain to be enforceable if the court is able from its terms and provisions to ascertain what the parties intended, under proper rules of construction and applicable principles of equity." [Citation.] "A contract may be enforced even though some contract terms may be missing or left to be agreed upon, but if essential terms are so uncertain that there is

no basis for deciding whether the agreement has been kept or broken, there is no contract." [Citation.] A bonus promised to induce an employee to continue his employment is supported by adequate consideration if the employee is not already bound by contract to continue. [Citation.] Because we are assuming the validity of the document issuing the stock options, we now turn to whether the underlying option is supported by valid consideration so as to make it a proper contract.

"Consideration is defined as the bargained-for exchange of promises or performances and may consist of a promise, an act or a forbearance." [Citation.]

> The general principles applicable to option contracts have been long established. An option contract has two elements, an offer to do something, or to forbear, which does not become a contract until accepted; and an agreement to leave the offer open for a specified time, [citation], or for a reasonable time. [citation]. An option contract must be supported by sufficient consideration; and if not, it is merely an offer which may be withdrawn at any time prior to a tender of compliance. [Citation.] If a consideration of "one dollar" or some other consideration is stated but which has, in fact, not been paid, the document is merely an offer which may be withdrawn at any time prior to a tender of compliance. The document will amount only to a continuing offer which may be withdrawn by the offeror at any time before acceptance. [Citation.] The consideration to support an option consists of "some right, interest, profit or benefit accruing to one party, or some forbearance, detriment, loss or responsibility given, suffered or undertaken by the other' [citation]; or otherwise stated, "Any act or promise which is of benefit to one party or disadvantage to the other * * *." [Citation.]

"The preexisting duty rule provides that where a party does what it is already legally obligated to do, there is no consideration because there has been no detriment." [Citation.]

Focusing on the lack of a detriment to the employee, the trial court found no valid consideration. Based upon our view of the discussion in [citation], the trial court was correct in concluding that the option contract is merely an offer which may be withdrawn at any time prior to a tender of compliance. DiLorenzo could have exercised the option the moment it was purportedly made, then immediately quit, thereby giving nothing to the employer. Though the exercise of the option would require the transfer of money for the stock, the option itself carries with it no detriment to DiLorenzo. Therefore, there was no consideration for the option.

***

We next address DiLorenzo's claim that he is entitled to the value of the shares of stock based upon the theory of promissory estoppel. DiLorenzo argues that the trial court misapplied the law in finding that there was insufficient reliance to support a claim for promissory estoppel. He claims that, once the trial court decided there was insufficient consideration to support the option contract, promissory estoppel should have been applied by the court to enforce the agreement as a matter of equity. DiLorenzo argues that he detrimentally relied upon Valve & Primer's promise in that he worked at Valve & Primer for an additional period in excess of nine years in reliance on the stock option agreement. * * *

Valve & Primer responds that the trial court was correct in finding insufficient reliance to support the promissory estoppel claim. Valve & Primer argues that the DiLorenzo could not satisfy the detrimental reliance prong of the promissory estoppel elements. Though DiLorenzo claimed he did not act upon offers of employment he claims were made by other companies during the course of his employment with Valve & Primer, he presented to the trial court nothing but his own testimony in support of his claim. Valve & Primer argues that, since DiLorenzo essentially is claiming his stock option vested immediately, he cannot contend that he detrimentally relied upon the purported agreement in the corporate minutes by turning down those other opportunities. * * * For purposes of promissory estoppel, if DiLorenzo's allegations are taken as true, and the purported option vested immediately, it required nothing of him in order to be exercised other than the payment of $250 per share.

"Promissory estoppel arises when (1) an unambiguous promise was made, (2) the defendant relied on the promise, (3) the defendant's reliance on the promise was reasonable, and (4) the defendant suffered a detriment." [Citation.] Whether detrimental reliance has occurred is determined according to the specific facts of each case. [Citation.]

While we would accept that, under certain circumstances, it may be possible for a relinquishment of a job offer to constitute consideration sufficient to support a contract, this is not such a case. There is nothing in the language of the corporate minutes or any other source to be found in this record to suggest that Valve & Primer conditioned the alleged stock option on DiLorenzo's promise to remain in his employment. While the corporate minutes say the alleged grant of the stock option was intended to "retain and reward," it contains no mechanism making the retention mandatory. Since the corporate minutes lack a mandatory obligation on which DiLorenzo could have reasonably detrimentally relied, and he could have elected to buy the shares of stock immediately, DiLorenzo's decision to remain on the job for the additional period of over nine years must be viewed as a voluntary act. Under those circumstances, promissory estoppel would not apply. It was, therefore, not an abuse of discretion to grant Valve & Primer's motion for summary judgment on that issue.

INTERPRETATION Past consideration is not legal consideration to support a promise; promissory estoppel requires detrimental reliance.

ETHICAL QUESTION Did the parties act ethically? Explain.

CRITICAL THINKING QUESTION What would have satisfied the consideration requirement in this case?

CONTRACTS UNDER SEAL

Under the common law, when a person desired to bind himself by bond, deed, or solemn promise, he executed his promise under seal. He did not have to sign the document; rather, his delivery of a document to which he had affixed his seal was sufficient. No consideration for his promise was necessary. In some states a promise under seal is still binding without consideration.

Nevertheless, most states have abolished by statute the distinction between contracts under seal and written unsealed contracts. In these states, the seal is no longer recognized as a substitute for consideration. The Code also has adopted this position, specifically eliminating the use of seals in contracts for the sale of goods.

PROMISES MADE ENFORCEABLE BY STATUTE

Some gratuitous promises that otherwise would be unenforceable have been made binding by statute. Most significant among these are (1) contract modifications, (2) renunciations, and (3) irrevocable offers.

Contract Modifications As mentioned previously, the Uniform Commercial Code (UCC) has abandoned the common law rule requiring that a modification of an existing contract be supported by consideration to be valid. Instead, the Code provides that a contract for the sale of goods can be effectively modified without new consideration, provided the modification is made in good faith.

Renunciations   Under the Code, any claim or right arising out of an alleged breach of contract can be discharged in whole or in part without consideration by a written waiver or renunciation signed and delivered by the aggrieved party. Under the Revised UCC Article 1, a claim or right arising out of an alleged breach may be discharged in whole or in part without consideration by agreement of the aggrieved party in an authenticated record. This section is subject to the obligation of good faith and, as with all sections of Article 1, applies to a transaction to the extent that it is governed by one of the other articles of the UCC.

Firm Offers   Under the Code, a firm offer, a written offer signed by a merchant offeror to buy or sell goods, is not revocable for lack of consideration during the time within which it is stated to be open, not to exceed three months or, if no time is stated, for a reasonable time. For a summary of consideration, see Figure 12-2.

Figure 12-2
Consideration

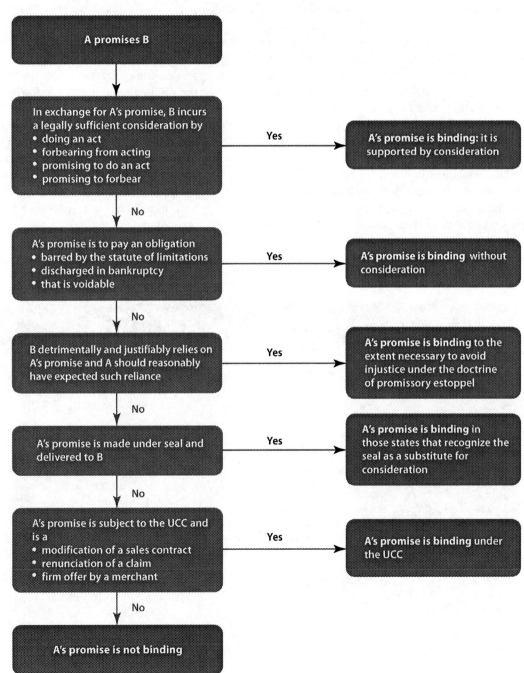

Business Law in Action

Computer Castle agreed to custom configure seventy-five personal computers and deliver them to Delber Data Corp. within ninety days. The price of each computer was $899, and Delber Data also agreed to a "Service-Pak" extended warranty plan for each unit purchased.

Computer Castle's employees worked diligently to get the order ready and had only five computers left to configure when a next-generation operating system hit the market. Prices for computers carrying the old operating system plummeted. Delber Data quickly sought to change its order, but Computer Castle had already built nearly all the computers. Delber admitted it could still use the computers with the old operating system but felt that at a minimum Computer Castle should grant a price concession.

The computers Delber Data had agreed to buy could now be sold for only $699 each at most. Not wanting to lose a possible long-term business relationship, Computer Castle agreed to lower the price of the Delber

Data computers to $799 each. Computer Castle faxed a short note to Delber confirming the new price. Thus, Delber Data has given no consideration to support the new contract price—indeed Delber is getting the very same computers for *less* than it originally agreed to pay.

Whether Computer Castle's price reduction will be enforceable depends on what law governs the parties' contract. Though Delber did purchase the warranty plan, a service, the contract is clearly one for the sale of goods—the predominant purpose of the contract is the purchase of configured personal computers. The price reduction, then, is a modification of a sales contract and is governed by the Uniform Commercial Code. Despite the lack of consideration, the Code permits enforcement of this contract modification, as the change was agreed to by both parties and sought by Delber in good faith, here based on the unanticipated emergence of newer technology.

© Cengage Learning 2014

Ethical Dilemma

Should a Spouse's Promise Be Legally Binding?

FACTS Joan Kantor is a social worker for the employees of Surf & Co., a towel manufacturer. Stan Koronetsky, a Surf employee, has confided the following problems to Kantor.

Koronetsky and his wife, Paula, have been married for ten years. Koronetsky states that three years ago his wife was unfaithful and Koronetsky began a divorce proceeding. When Paula Koronetsky promised to refrain from further infidelity and to attend marital counseling sessions, Koronetsky agreed to stop the divorce proceeding. However, although Stan dropped the divorce proceeding, his wife never attended counseling.

Koronetsky is also upset because he and his wife had agreed that she would attend medical school while he worked to support her. In exchange for his promise to put her through medical school, Paula promised that she would

support him while he obtained his MBA degree. But after Paula became a doctor, she refused to support him; consequently, Stan never got his master's degree.

Social, Policy, and Ethical Considerations

1. What should Joan Kantor do in this situation? What is the scope of her counseling responsibilities?

2. Should agreements between married parties be enforced in a court of law? If so, what types of agreements should be enforceable?

3. What are the individual interests at stake in this situation? Is it reasonable to assume that spouses make many private agreements, and that generally these agreements are made without the intention of their being legally binding?

© Cengage Learning 2014

CHAPTER SUMMARY

Consideration

Definition the inducement to enter into a contract

Elements legal sufficiency and bargained-for exchange

Legal Sufficiency of Consideration

Definition consists of either a benefit to the promisor or a detriment to the promisee
* *Legal Benefit* obtaining something to which one had no prior legal right
* *Legal Detriment* doing an act one is not legally obligated to do or not doing an act that one has a legal right to do

Adequacy of Consideration not required where the parties have freely agreed to the exchange

Illusory Promise promise that imposes no obligation on the promisor; the following promises are not illusory
* *Output Contract* agreement to sell all of one's production to a single buyer
* *Requirements Contract* agreement to buy all of one's needs from a single producer
* *Exclusive Dealing Contract* grant to a franchisee or licensee by a manufacturer of the sole right to sell goods in a defined market
* *Conditional Contract* a contract in which the obligations are contingent upon the occurrence of a stated event

Preexisting Public Obligations public duties such as those imposed by tort or criminal law are neither a legal detriment nor a legal benefit

Preexisting Contractual Obligation performance of a preexisting contractual duty is not consideration
* *Modification of a Preexisting Contract* under the common law a modification of a preexisting contract must be supported by mutual consideration; under the Code a contract can be modified without new consideration
* *Substituted Contracts* the parties agree to rescind their original contract and to enter into a new one; rescission and new contract are supported by consideration
* *Settlement of an Undisputed Debt* payment of a lesser sum of money to discharge an undisputed debt (one whose existence and amount are not contested) does not constitute legally sufficient consideration
* *Settlement of a Disputed Debt* payment of a lesser sum of money to discharge a disputed debt (one whose existence or amount is contested) is legally sufficient consideration

Bargained-for Exchange

Definition a mutually agreed-upon exchange

Past Consideration an act done before the contract is made is not consideration

Contracts without Consideration

Promises to Perform Prior Unenforceable Obligations
* *Promise to Pay Debt Barred by the Statute of Limitations* a new promise by the debtor to pay the debt renews the running of the statute of limitations for a second statutory period
* *Promise to Pay Debt Discharged in Bankruptcy* may be enforceable without consideration

- *Voidable Promises* a new promise to perform a voidable obligation that has not been previously avoided is enforceable
- *Moral Obligation* a promise made to satisfy a preexisting moral obligation is generally unenforceable for lack of consideration

Promissory Estoppel doctrine that prohibits a party from denying his promise when the promisee takes action or forbearance to his detriment reasonably based upon the promise

Contracts under Seal where still recognized, the seal acts as a substitute for consideration

Promises Made Enforceable by Statute some gratuitous promises have been made enforceable by statute; the Code makes enforceable (1) contract modifications, (2) renunciations, and (3) firm offers

QUESTIONS

1. In consideration of $1,800 paid to him by Joyce, Hill gave Joyce a written option to purchase his house for $180,000 on or before April 1. Prior to April 1, Hill verbally agreed to extend the option until July 1. On May 18, Hill, known to Joyce, sold the house to Gray, who was ignorant of the unrecorded option. On May 20 Joyce sent an acceptance to Hill who received it on May 25. Is there a contract between Joyce and Hill? Explain.

2. **a.** Ann owed $2,500 to Barry for services Barry rendered to Ann. The debt was due June 30, 2011. In March 2012, the debt was still unpaid. Barry was in urgent need of ready cash and told Ann that if she would pay $1,500 on the debt at once, Barry would release her from the balance. Ann paid $1,500 and stated to Barry that all claims had been paid in full. In August 2012, Barry demanded the unpaid balance and subsequently sued Ann for $1,000. Result?

   b. Modify the facts in (a) by assuming that Barry gave Ann a written receipt stating that all claims had been paid in full. Result?

   c. Modify the facts in (a) by assuming that Ann owed Barry the $2,500 on Ann's purchase of a motorcycle from Barry. Result?

3. **a.** Judy orally promises her daughter, Liza, that she will give her a tract of land for her home. Liza, as intended by Judy, gives up her homestead and takes possession of the land. Liza lives there for six months and starts construction of a home. Is Judy bound to convey the real estate?

   b. Ralph, knowing that his son, Ed, desires to purchase a tract of land, promises to give him the $25,000 he needs for the purchase. Ed, relying on this promise, buys an option on the tract of land. Can Ralph rescind his promise?

4. George owed Keith $800 on a personal loan. Neither the amount of the debt nor George's liability to pay the $800 was disputed. Keith had also rendered services as a carpenter to George without any agreement as to the price to be paid. When the work was completed, an honest and reasonable difference of opinion developed between George and Keith with respect to the value of Keith's services. Upon receiving Keith's bill for the carpentry services for $600, George mailed in a properly stamped and addressed envelope his check for $800 to Keith. In an accompanying letter, George stated that the enclosed check was in full settlement of both claims. Keith endorsed and cashed the check. Thereafter, Keith unsuccessfully sought to collect from George an alleged unpaid balance of $600. May Keith recover the $600 from George?

5. The Snyder Mfg. Co., being a large user of coal, entered into separate contracts with several coal companies. In each con tract, it was agreed that the coal company would supply coal during the year in such amounts as the manufacturing company might desire to order, at a price of $55 per ton. In February of that year, the Snyder Company ordered one thousand tons of coal from Union Coal Company, one of the contracting parties. Union Coal Company delivered five hundred tons of the order and then notified Snyder Company that no more deliveries would be made and that it denied any obligation under the contract. In an action by Union Coal to collect $55 per ton for the five hundred tons of coal delivered, Snyder files a counterclaim, claiming damages of $1,500 for failure to deliver the additional five hundred tons of the order and damages of $4,000 for breach of agreement to deliver coal during the balance of the year. What contract, if any, exists between Snyder and Union?

6. On February 5, Devon entered into a written agreement with Gordon whereby Gordon agreed to drill a well on Devon's property for the sum of $5,000 and to complete the well on or before April 15. Before entering into the contract, Gordon had made test borings and had satisfied himself as to the character of the subsurface. After two days of drilling, Gordon struck hard rock. On February 17, Gordon removed his equipment and advised Devon that the project had proved unprofitable and that he would not continue. On March 17, Devon went to Gordon and told Gordon that he would assume the risk of the

enterprise and would pay Gordon $100 for each day required to drill the well, as compensation for labor, the use of Gordon's equipment, and Gordon's services in supervising the work, provided Gordon would furnish certain special equipment designed to cut through hard rock. Gordon said that the proposal was satisfactory. The work was continued by Gordon and completed in an additional fifty-eight days. Upon completion of the work, Devon failed to pay, and Gordon brought an action to recover $5,800. Devon answered that he had never become obligated to pay $100 a day and filed a counterclaim for damages in the amount of $500 for the month's delay based on an alleged breach of contract by Gordon. Explain who will prevail and why.

7. Discuss and explain whether there is valid consideration for each of the following promises:

   a. A and B entered into a contract for the purchase and sale of goods. A subsequently promised to pay a higher price for the goods when B refused to deliver at the contract price.

   b. A promised in writing to pay a debt, which was due from B to C, on C's agreement to extend the time of payment for one year.

   c. A orally promised to pay $150 to her son, B, solely in consideration of past services rendered to A by B, for which there had been no agreement or request to pay.

8. Alan purchased shoes from Barbara on open account. Barbara sent Alan a bill for $10,000. Alan wrote back that two hundred pairs of the shoes were defective and offered to pay $6,000 and give Barbara his promissory note for $1,000. Barbara accepted the offer, and Alan sent his check for $6,000 and his note in accordance with the agreement. Barbara cashed the check, collected on the note, and one month later sued Alan for $3,000. Is Barbara bound by her acceptance of the offer?

9. Nancy owed Sharon $1,500, but Sharon did not initiate a lawsuit to collect the debt within the time period prescribed by the statute of limitations. Nevertheless, Nancy promises Sharon that she will pay the barred debt. Thereafter, Nancy refuses to pay. Sharon brings suit to collect on this new promise. Is Nancy's new promise binding? Explain.

10. Anthony lends money to Frank, who dies without having repaid the loan. Frank's widow, Carol, promises Anthony to repay the loan. Upon Carol's refusal to pay the loan, Anthony brings suit against Carol for payment. Is Carol bound by her promise to pay the loan?

11. The parties entered into an oral contract in June under which the plaintiff agreed to construct a building for the defendant on a time and materials basis, at a maximum cost of $56,146, plus sales tax and extras ordered by the defendant. When the building was 90 percent completed, the defendant told the plaintiff he was unhappy with the whole job as "the thing just wasn't being run right." The parties then, on October 17, signed a written agreement lowering the maximum cost to $52,000 plus sales tax. The plaintiff thereafter completed the building at a cost of $64,155. The maximum under the June oral agreement, plus extras and sales tax, totaled $61,040. Explain whether the defendant is obligated to pay only the lower maximum fixed by the October 17 agreement.

CASE PROBLEMS

12. Taylor assaulted his wife, who then took refuge in Ms. Harrington's house. The next day, Mr. Taylor entered the house and began another assault on his wife. Taylor's wife knocked him down and, while he was lying on the floor, attempted to cut his head open or decapitate him with an ax. Harrington intervened to stop the bloodshed and was hit by the ax as it was descending. The ax fell upon her hand, mutilating it badly, but sparing Taylor his life. Afterwards, Taylor orally promised to compensate Harrington for her injury. Is Taylor's promise enforceable? Explain.

13. Jonnel Enterprises, Inc., contracted to construct a student dormitory at Clarion State College. On May 6, Jonnel entered into a written agreement with Graham and Long as electrical contractors to perform the electrical work and to supply materials for the dormitory. The contract price was $70,544.66. Graham and Long claim that they believed the May 6 agreement obligated them to perform the electrical work on only one wing of the building, but that three or four days after work was started, a second wing of the building was found to be in need of wiring. At that time, Graham and Long informed Jonnel that they would not wire both wings of the building under the present contract, so the parties orally agreed upon a new contract. Under the new contract, Graham and Long were obligated to wire both wings and were to be paid only $65,000, but they were relieved of the obligations to supply entrances and a heating system. Graham and Long resumed their work, and Jonnel made seven of the eight progress payments called for. When Jonnel did not pay the final payment, Graham and Long brought this action. Jonnel claims that the May 6 contract is controlling. Is Jonnel correct in its assertion? Why?

14. Baker entered into an oral agreement with Healey, the state distributor of Ballantine & Sons' liquor products, that Ballantine would supply Baker with its products on

demand and that Baker would have the exclusive agency for Ballantine within a certain area of Connecticut. Shortly thereafter, the agreement was modified to give Baker the right to terminate at will. Eight months later, Ballantine & Sons revoked its agency. May Baker enforce the oral agreement? Explain.

15. PLM, Inc., entered into an oral agreement with Quaintance Associates, an executive "headhunter" service, for the recruitment of qualified candidates to be employed by PLM. As agreed, PLM's obligation to pay Quaintance did not depend on PLM actually hiring a qualified candidate presented by Quaintance. After several months Quaintance sent a letter to PLM, admitting that it had so far failed to produce a suitable candidate, but included a bill for $9,806.61, covering fees and expenses. PLM responded that Quaintance's services were only worth $6,060.48, and that payment of the lesser amount was the only fair way to handle the dispute. Accordingly, PLM enclosed a check for $6,060.48, writing on the back of the check "IN FULL PAYMENT OF ANY CLAIMS QUAINTANCE HAS AGAINST PLM, INC." Quaintance cashed the check and then sued PLM for the remaining $3,746.13. Decision?

16. Red Owl Stores told the Hoffman family that upon the payment of approximately $518,000 a grocery store franchise would be built for them in a new location. On the advice of Red Owl, the Hoffmans bought a small grocery store in their hometown to get management experience. After the Hoffmans operated at a profit for three months, Red Owl advised them to sell the small grocery, assuring them that Red Owl would find them a larger store elsewhere. Although selling at that point would cost them much profit, the Hoffmans followed Red Owl's directions. Additionally, to raise the required money for the deal, the Hoffmans sold their bakery business in their hometown. The Hoffmans also sold their house and moved to a new home in the city where their new store was to be located. Red Owl then informed the Hoffmans that it would take $524,100, not $518,000, to complete the deal. The family scrambled to find the additional funds. However, when told by Red Owl that it would now cost them $534,000 to get their new franchise, the Hoffmans decided to sue instead. Should Red Owl be held to its promises? Explain.

17. The plaintiff, Brenner, entered into a contract with the defendant, Little Red School House, Ltd., which stated that in return for a nonrefundable tuition of $1,080, Brenner's son could attend the defendant's school for a year. When Brenner's ex-wife refused to enroll their son, the plaintiff sought and received a verbal promise of a refund. The defendant now refuses to refund the plaintiff's money for lack of consideration. Did mutual consideration exist between the parties? Explain.

18. Tender Loving Care, Inc. (TLC), a corporation owned and operated by Virginia Bryant, eventually went out of business. The Secretary of State canceled its corporate charter, and a check drawn on TLC's account made out to the Department of Human Resources (DHR) to pay state unemployment taxes was returned for insufficient funds. Subsequently, Bryant filed individually for bankruptcy, listing the DHR as a creditor. This claim was not allowed, because Bryant was held not to be personally liable on the debts of TLC to the DHR. The DHR later called Bryant to its offices, where she was told that she needed to pay the debt owed to the DHR by TLC. Unable to contact her lawyer, Bryant was persuaded to sign a personal guarantee to cover the debt. Later, when Bryant refused to pay, the DHR filed suit. Decision?

19. Ben Collins was a full professor with tenure at Wisconsin State University in 2008. In March 2008, Parsons College, in an attempt to lure Dr. Collins from Wisconsin State, offered him a written contract promising him the rank of full professor with tenure and a salary of $65,000 for the 2008–2009 academic year. The contract further provided that the College would increase his salary by $2,000 each year for the next five years. In return, Collins was to teach two trimesters of the academic year beginning in October 2008. In addition, the contract stipulated, by reference to the College's faculty bylaws, that tenured professors could be dismissed only for just cause and after written charges were filed with the Professional Problems Committee. The two parties signed the contract, and Collins resigned his position at Wisconsin State.

In February 2010, the College tendered a different contract to Collins to cover the following year. This contract reduced his salary to $55,000 with no provision for annual increments, but left his rank of full professor intact. It also required that Collins waive any and all rights or claims existing under any previous employment contracts with the College. Collins refused to sign this new contract and Parsons College soon notified him that he would not be employed the following year. The College did not give any grounds for his dismissal; nor did it file charges with the Professional Problems Committee. As a result, Collins was forced to take a teaching position at the University of North Dakota at a substantially reduced salary. He sued to recover the difference between the salary Parsons College promised him until 2014 and the amount he earned. Will he prevail? Explain.

20. Rodney and Donna Mathis (Mathis) filed a wrongful death action against St. Alexis Hospital and several physicians, arising out of the death of their mother, Mary Mathis. Several weeks before trial, an expert consulted by Mathis notified the trial court and Mathis's counsel that, in his opinion, Mary Mathis's death was not proximately caused by the negligence of the physicians. Shortly thereafter, Mathis voluntarily dismissed the wrongful death action. Mathis and St. Alexis entered into a covenant-not-to-sue in which Mathis agreed not to pursue any claims against St. Alexis or its employees in terms of the medical care of Mary Mathis. St. Alexis,

in return, agreed not to seek sanctions, including attorney fees and costs incurred in defense of the previously dismissed wrongful death action. Subsequently, Mathis filed a second wrongful death action against St. Alexis Hospital, among others. Mathis asked the court to rescind the covenant-not-to-sue, arguing that because St. Alexis was not entitled to sanctions in connection with the first wrongful death action, there was no consideration for the covenant-not-to-sue. Is this contention correct? Explain.

21. Harold Pearsall and Joe Alexander were friends for over twenty-five years. About twice a week they would get together after work and proceed to a liquor store, where they would purchase what the two liked to refer as a "package"—a half-pint of vodka, orange juice, two cups, and two lottery tickets. Occasionally these lottery tickets would yield modest rewards of two or three dollars, which the pair would then "plow back" into the purchase of additional tickets. On December 16, Pearsall and Alexander visited the liquor store twice, buying their normal "package" on both occasions. For the first package, Pearsall went into the store alone, and when he returned to the car, he said to Alexander, in reference to the tickets, "Are you in on it?" Alexander said, "Yes." When Pearsall asked him for his half of the purchase price, though, Alexander replied that he had no money. When they went to Alexander's home, Alexander snatched the tickets from Pearsall's hand and "scratched" them, only to find that they were both worthless. Later that same evening Alexander returned to the liquor store and bought a second "package." This time, Pearsall snatched the tickets from Alexander and said that he would "scratch" them. Instead, he gave one to Alexander, and each man scratched one of the tickets. Alexander's was a $20,000 winner. Alexander cashed the ticket and refused to give Pearsall anything. Can Pearsall recover half of the proceeds from Alexander? Explain.

TAKING SIDES

Anna Feinberg began working for the Pfeiffer Company in 1965 at age seventeen. By 2003, she had attained the position of bookkeeper, office manager, and assistant treasurer. In appreciation for her skill, dedication, and long years of service, the Pfeiffer board of directors resolved to increase Feinberg's monthly salary to $4,000 and to create for her a retirement plan. The plan allowed that Feinberg would be given the privilege of retiring from active duty at any time she chose and that she would receive retirement pay of $2,000 per month for life, although the Board expressed the hope that Feinberg would continue to serve the company for many years. Feinberg, however, chose to retire two years later. The Pfeiffer Company paid Feinberg her retirement pay until 2012. The company thereafter discontinued payments.

a. What are the arguments that the company's promise to pay Feinberg $2,000 per month for life is enforceable?

b. What are the arguments that the company's promise is not enforceable?

c. What is the proper outcome? Explain.

Chapter 13

ILLEGAL BARGAINS

Pactis privatorum juri publico non derogatur. (Private contracts do not derogate from public law.)

LEGAL MAXIM

CHAPTER OUTCOMES

After reading and studying this chapter, you should be able to:

1. Identify and explain the types of contracts that may violate a statute and distinguish between the two types of licensing statutes.

2. Describe when a covenant not to compete will be enforced and identify the two situations in which these types of covenants most frequently arise.

3. Explain when exculpatory agreements, agreements involving the commitment of a tort,

and agreements involving public officials will be held to be illegal.

4. Distinguish between procedural and substantive unconscionability.

5. Explain the usual effects of illegality and the major exceptions to this rule.

A legal objective is essential for a promise or agreement to be binding. When the formation or performance of an agreement is criminal, tortious, or otherwise contrary to public policy, the agreement is illegal and *unenforceable* (as opposed to being void). The law does *not* provide a remedy for the breach of an unenforceable agreement and thus "leaves the parties where it finds them." (It is preferable to use the term *illegal bargain* or *illegal agreement* rather than *illegal contract*, because the word *contract*, by definition, denotes a legal and enforceable agreement.) The illegal bargain is made unenforceable (1) to discourage such undesirable conduct in the future and (2) to avoid the inappropriate use of the judicial process in carrying out the socially undesirable bargain.

In this chapter, we will discuss (1) agreements in violation of a statute, (2) agreements contrary to public policy, and (3) the effect of illegality on agreements.

Violations of Statutes

The courts will not enforce an agreement declared illegal by statute. For example, "wagering or gambling contracts" are specifically **declared** unenforceable in most states. Likewise, an agreement induced by criminal conduct will not be enforced. For example, if Alice enters into an agreement with Brent Co. through the bribing of Brent Co.'s purchasing agent, the agreement would be unenforceable.

LICENSING STATUTES

Every jurisdiction has laws requiring a **license** for those who engage in certain trades, professions, or businesses. Common examples are licensing statutes that apply to lawyers, doctors, dentists, accountants, brokers, plumbers, and contractors. Some licensing statutes mandate schooling and/or examination, while others require only financial responsibility and/or good moral character. Whether a person who has failed to comply with a licensing requirement may recover for services rendered depends on the terms or type of licensing statute.

The statute itself may expressly provide that an unlicensed person engaged in a business or profession for which a license is required shall not recover for services rendered. Where there is no express statutory provision, the courts commonly distinguish between regulatory statutes and those enacted merely to raise revenue through the issuance of licenses. If the statute is regulatory, a person cannot recover for professional services unless he has the required license as long as the public policy behind the regulatory purpose clearly outweighs the person's interest in being paid for his services. Some

courts balance the penalty suffered by the unlicensed party against the benefit received by the other party. In contrast, if the law is for revenue purposes only, agreements for unlicensed services are enforceable.

A **regulatory license** is a measure designed to protect the public from unqualified practitioners. Examples are licenses issued under statutes prescribing standards for those who seek to practice law or medicine or, as demonstrated by the case below, to engage in the construction business. A **revenue license**, on the other hand, does not seek to protect against incompetent or unqualified practitioners but serves simply to raise money. An example is a statute requiring a license of plumbers but not establishing standards of competence for those who practice the trade. The courts regard this as a taxing measure lacking any expression of legislative intent to prevent unlicensed plumbers from enforcing their business contracts.

PRACTICAL ADVICE

Obtain all necessary licenses before beginning to operate your business.

ALCOA CONCRETE & MASONRY V. STALKER BROS.

COURT OF SPECIAL APPEALS OF MARYLAND, 2010
993 A.2D 136, 191 MD. APP. 596

http://scholar.google.com/scholar_case?case=16829939965873776087&q=993+A.2d+136&hl=en&as_sdt=2,34

FACTS General contractor Stalker Brothers, Inc. (Stalker) hired a subcontractor Alcoa Concrete and Masonry, Inc. (Alcoa) from 2004 through 2007. Alcoa was unlicensed until March 26, 2008. In 2004, all of Alcoa's invoices were fully and timely paid. When payments in 2005 became less regular, Stalker promised to pay Alcoa when a building owned by Stalker was sold, but full payment was not made. Alcoa continued to perform subcontract work for Stalker based on an agreement that Stalker would pay Alcoa $1,500 per week against invoices for past work and new work. In November 2006, Alcoa performed the cement and masonry work for Stalker on the "Cahill" job, in which Stalker represented that there was sufficient profit to pay Alcoa for that subcontract and for the entire past due balance. In the summer of 2007, Stalker ceased paying Alcoa entirely.

Alcoa sued Stalker for $53,000 plus interest and attorneys' [leave as is] fees. Stalker was granted a summary judgment on the ground that because Alcoa was not licensed, the series of subcontracts were illegal and could not be enforced. The circuit court's decision was based on a line of Maryland cases dealing with licensing, which is illustrated in the home improvement field principally

by *Harry Berenter, Inc. v. Berman*, [citation.] If the purpose of a business licensing statute is to raise revenue, courts will enforce a contract for compensation for business activity that requires a license, even if made by an unlicensed person. But, if the purpose of the licensing requirement is to protect the public, then the Maryland cases relied upon by the court do not enforce contracts made by unlicensed persons who seek compensation for business activity for which a license is required. Alcoa argues that the rule distinguishing between revenue and regulation does not apply to the facts here, in which the agreement was between two businesses engaged in contracting. The contracts sought to be enforced were not between Alcoa and the various homeowners with whom Stalker had contracted.

DECISION The judgment of the Circuit Court is reversed, and the case remanded.

OPINION Rodowsky, J. At issue is whether a home improvement general contractor is contractually obligated to pay a subcontractor who was not licensed under the Act, either at the time of entering into the subcontract or when the subcontract was properly performed, but who was licensed when this suit was brought.

* * *

Maryland appellate decisions have applied the revenue/regulation rule in a number of contexts. All of the cases under the Act have dealt with the contractor-owner relationship. The members of the public who were protected by the regulatory licensing requirement were the owners of the home. This Court recently again has held, applying *Harry Berenter,* that a contract between the owner of the improved premises and an unlicensed contractor would not be enforced. [Citation.] * * *

* * *

Our review fails to disclose any Maryland appellate decision directly answering whether the regulatory license rule applied in *Harry Berenter,* declaring unenforceable a home improvement contract between an owner and an unlicensed contractor, applies to a subcontract between a licensed contractor and an unlicensed subcontractor. *Harry Berenter* does recognize that, pursuant to provisions of the Act * * *, the failure to comply with certain formal contractual requirements in a home improvement contract does not invalidate the contract. [Citation.]

* * *

The authors of *Corbin on Contracts,* after reviewing the revenue/regulatory rule, state:

Even when the purpose of a licensing statute is regulatory, courts do not always deny enforcement to the unlicensed party. The statute clearly may protect against fraud and incompetence. Yet, in very many cases the situation involves neither fraud nor incompetence. The unlicensed party may have rendered excellent service or delivered goods of the highest quality. The noncompliance with the statute may be nearly harmless. The real defrauder may be the defendant who will be enriched at the unlicensed party's expense by a court's refusal to enforce the contract. Although courts have yearned for a mechanically applicable rule, most have not made one in the present instance. Justice requires that the penalty should fit the crime. Justice and sound policy do not always require the enforcement of licensing statutes by large forfeitures going not to the state but to repudiating defendants.

In most cases, the statute itself does not require such forfeitures. The statute fixes its own penalties, usually a fine or imprisonment of a minor character with a degree of discretion in the court. The added penalty of unenforceability of bargains is a judicial creation. In many cases, the court may be wise to apply this additional penalty. When nonenforcement causes great and disproportionate hardship, a court must avoid nonenforcement.

* * *

After the decision in *Harry Berenter,* in which the Court relied in part on the Restatement of Contracts, the American Law Institute adopted Restatement (Second) of Contracts (1981). Section 178 states a more flexible approach to enforceability than the rigid revenue/regulatory dichotomy. Section 178 reads:

When a Term Is Unenforceable on Grounds of Public Policy

(1) A promise or other term of an agreement is unenforceable on grounds of public policy if legislation provides that it is unenforceable or the interest in its enforcement is clearly outweighed in the circumstances by a public policy against the enforcement of such terms.

(2) In weighing the interest in the enforcement of a term, account is taken of

(a) the parties' justified expectations,

(b) any forfeiture that would result if enforcement were denied, and

(c) any special public interest in the enforcement of the particular term.

(3) In weighing a public policy against enforcement of a term, account is taken of

(a) the strength of that policy as manifested by legislation or judicial decisions,

(b) the likelihood that a refusal to enforce the term will further that policy.

(c) the seriousness of any misconduct involved and the extent to which it was deliberate, and

(d) the directness of the connection between that misconduct and the term.

We find no indication in the Act or in the Maryland cases that a policy of the Act is to protect general contractors from unlicensed subcontractors. Consequently, the fact that the Act is a regulatory measure does not bar Alcoa from recovering on its subcontracts with Stalker.

INTERPRETATION A regulatory license is a measure to protect the public from unqualified practitioners; the failure to comply with such a regulation prevents the noncomplying party from recovering for services rendered if (1) the statute provides that a noncomplying agreement is unenforceable or (2) the public policy behind the regulatory purpose clearly outweighs the noncomplying party's interest in being paid for services rendered.

CRITICAL THINKING QUESTION When should the failure to obtain a license to operate a business prevent the owner or operator from receiving compensation for services?

GAMBLING STATUTES

In a **wager**, the parties stipulate that one shall win and the other lose depending on the outcome of an event in which their only "interest" is the possibility of such gain or loss. All states have legislation on gambling or wagering, and U.S. courts generally refuse to recognize the enforceability of a gambling agreement. Thus, if Smith makes a bet with Brown on the outcome of a ball game, the agreement is unenforceable by either party. Some states, however, now permit certain kinds of regulated gambling. Wagering conducted by government agencies, principally state-operated lotteries, has come to constitute an increasingly important source of public revenues.

PRACTICAL ADVICE

Make sure that your promotions that offer prizes do not fall under state gambling statutes.

USURY STATUTES

A **usury statute** is a law establishing a maximum rate of permissible interest for which a lender and borrower of money may contract. Although historically every state had a usury statute, the recent trend is to limit or relax such statutes. Maximum permitted rates vary greatly from state to state and among types of transactions. These statutes typically are general in their application, and certain types of transactions are exempted altogether. For example, many states impose no limit on the rate of interest that may be charged on loans to corporations. Furthermore, some states permit the parties to contract for any rate of interest on loans made to individual proprietorships or partnerships for the purpose of carrying on a business. Moreover, there are not many protections remaining for typical consumer transactions, including those involving credit cards. (More than half of the states have no interest rate limits on credit card transactions.)

In addition to the exceptions affecting certain designated types of borrowers, a number of states have exempted specific lenders. For example, the majority of states have enacted installment loan laws, which permit eligible lenders a higher return on installment loans than otherwise would be permitted under the applicable general interest statute. These specific lender usury statutes, which have all but eliminated general usury statutes, vary greatly but generally encompass small consumer loans, retail installment sales acts, corporate loans, loans by small lenders, real estate mortgages, and numerous other transactions.

For a transaction to be usurious, courts usually require evidence of the following factors: (1) a loan (2) of money (3) that is repayable absolutely and in all events (4) for which an interest charge is exacted in excess of the interest rate allowed by law. Nevertheless, the law does permit certain expenses or charges in addition to the maximum legal interest, such as payments made by a borrower to the lender for expenses incurred or for services rendered in good faith in making a loan or in obtaining security for its repayment. Permissible expenses commonly incurred by a lender include the costs of examining title, investigating the borrower's credit rating, drawing necessary documents, and inspecting the property. If not excessive, such expenses are not considered in determining the rate of interest under the usury statutes. As shown in the following case, however, payments made to the lender from which he derives an advantage are considered if they exceed the reasonable value of services he actually rendered.

PRACTICAL ADVICE

When calculating interest, consider all charges, including service fees, that exceed the actual reasonable expense of making the loan.

DUNNAM V. BURNS

COURT OF APPEALS OF TEXAS, EL PASO, 1995
901 S.W.2D 628
http://scholar.google.com/scholar_case?case=1178913169644146691&q=901+S.W.2d+628&hl=en&as_sdt=2,34

FACTS Defendant (Louis Dunnam) and Steve Oualline jointly borrowed $35,000 from plaintiff (Ken Burns) and agreed to repay the principal plus $5,000 six months later. After defendant defaulted on the loan, plaintiff sued to recover. Dunnam defended by claiming the loan was usurious. The trial court ruled in favor of the plaintiff, and defendant appealed.

DECISION Judgment for defendant.

OPINION Barajas, J. Appellant claims the trial court erred by refusing to submit his usury defense to the jury. Usury is interest in excess of the amount permitted by law. [Citation.] Interest is compensation for the use or forbearance of money. [Citation.] For most transactions between private persons, the maximum allowable rate of interest is 18 percent if the parties agree on a rate of interest [citation], and 6 percent if they do not, [citation]. Usurious contracts are against public policy, [citation] and persons who contract for or collect usurious interest are subject to penalties that may exceed the total value of the contract. [Citation].

We must initially determine whether the $5,000 additional sum contained in the promissory note constitutes interest. Interest need not be denominated interest. [Citation.] When money is advanced in exchange for an obligation to repay the advance plus an additional amount, the added amount is interest that may not exceed the statutory maximum. [Citations.] The foregoing principles instruct that Appellant's absolute obligation to pay $5,000 in addition to the principal renders the additional amount interest.

Appellee [Burns] does not contest that the $5,000 is interest. Neither does he claim that the amount of interest was not usurious, although we note that the promissory note effectively charges a 28.57 percent interest rate, which exceeds even the highest rate permitted by statute [citation] (permitting 28 percent interest on certain transactions). He argues, rather, that he did not "charge" such interest because the instrument was drafted by Appellant and because Appellee was actually interested in collecting only the principal amount. In so arguing, Appellee misapprehends the significance of his

intent and of the identity of the drafter of the promissory note.

A document that contains an absolute obligation to repay a loan together with interest in excess of the amount permitted by statute is usurious on its face. [Citations.] "It is not the lender's subjective intent to charge usury that makes a loan usurious, but rather his intent to make the bargain that was made." [Citations.] The specific intent of the lender is immaterial because it is presumed to be reflected in the document he signs. [Citations.] Further, "once the agreed terms have been reduced to writing in the form of a compulsory contract, the test of alleged usury is not concerned with which party might have originated the alleged[ly] usurious provisions." [Citations.]

*** The drafter of the usurious promissory note is simply irrelevant. *** The instrument embodies a usurious transaction, and Appellee, as the lender, contracted for usurious interest.

INTERPRETATION Usury statutes establish a maximum rate of interest for which a lender may charge a borrower.

CRITICAL THINKING QUESTION Should the law establish maximum rates of interest? If so, in what situations?

The legal effect of a usurious loan varies from state to state. In a few states, the lender forfeits both principal and interest. In some jurisdictions, the lender can recover the principal but forfeits all interest. In other states, only that portion of interest exceeding the permitted maximum is forfeited, whereas in still other states, the amount forfeited is a multiple (double or treble) of the interest charged. How the states deal with usurious interest already paid also varies. Some states do not allow the borrower to recover any of the usurious interest she has paid; others allow recovery of such interest or a multiple of it.

Violations of Public Policy

The reach of a statute may extend beyond its language. Sometimes the courts, by analogy, use a statute and the policy it embodies as a guide in determining a person's rights under a private contract. Conversely, the courts frequently must express the "public policy" of the state

without significant help from statutory sources. This judicially declared public policy is very broad in scope, it often being said that agreements having "a tendency to be injurious to the public or the public good" are contrary to public policy. Contracts raising questions of public policy include agreements that (1) restrain trade, (2) excuse or exculpate a party from liability for his own negligence, (3) are unconscionable, (4) involve tortious conduct, (5) tend to corrupt public officials or impair the legislative process, (6) tend to obstruct the administration of justice, or (7) impair family relationships. This section will focus on the first five of these types of agreements.

Common Law Restraint of Trade

A **restraint of trade** is any contract or agreement that eliminates or tends to eliminate competition or otherwise obstructs trade or commerce. One type of restraint of trade is a **covenant not to compete**, which is an agreement to refrain from entering into a competing trade, profession, or business.

Today, an agreement to refrain from a particular trade, profession, or business is enforceable if (1) the purpose of the restraint is to protect a property interest of the promisee and (2) the restraint is no more extensive than is reasonably necessary to protect that interest. Restraints typically arise in two situations: (1) the sale of a business and (2) employment contracts.

Sale of a Business As part of an agreement to sell a business, the seller frequently promises not to compete in that particular type of business in a defined area for a stated period of time to protect the business's goodwill (an asset that the buyer has purchased). The courts will enforce such a covenant (promise) if the restraint is within reasonable limitations. The reasonableness of the restraint depends on the geographic area the restraint covers, the period for which it is to be effective, and the hardship it imposes on the promisor and the public.

For example, the promise of a person selling a service station business in Detroit not to enter the service station business in Michigan for the next twenty-five years is unreasonable as to both area and time. The business interest would not include the entire state, so the protection of the purchaser does not require that the seller be prevented from engaging in the service station business in all of Michigan or perhaps, for that matter, in the entire city of Detroit. Limiting the area to the neighborhood in which the station is located or to a radius of a few miles probably would be adequate protection. However, in the case of a citywide business, such as a laundry or cleaning establishment with neighborhood outlets, a covenant restraining competition anywhere in the city might well be reasonable.

The same type of inquiry must be made about time limitations. In the sale of a service station, a twenty-five-year ban on competition from the seller would be unreasonable, but a one-year ban probably would not. The courts consider each case on its own facts to determine what is reasonable under the particular circumstances.

Employment Contracts Salespeople, management personnel, and other employees are frequently required to sign employment contracts prohibiting them from competing with their employers during their employment and for some additional stated period after their termination. The same is also frequently true among corporations or partnerships involving professionals such as accountants, lawyers, investment brokers, stockbrokers, or doctors. Though the courts readily enforce a covenant not to compete during the period of employment, they subject the promise not to compete after termination of employment to a test of reasonableness stricter even than that applied to noncompetition promises included in a contract for the sale of a business.

A court order enjoining (prohibiting) a former employee from competing in a described territory for a stated period of time is the usual way in which an employer seeks to enforce an employee's promise not to compete. However, before the courts will grant such injunctions, the employer must demonstrate that the restriction is necessary to protect his legitimate interests, such as trade secrets or customer lists. Because the injunction may have the practical effect of placing the employee out of work, the courts must carefully balance the public policy favoring the employer's right to protect his business interests against the public policy favoring full opportunity for individuals to gain employment. Some courts, rather than refusing to enforce an unreasonable restraint, will modify the restrictive covenant to make it reasonable under the circumstances.

Thus, one court has held unreasonable a contract covenant requiring a travel agency employee after termination of her employment to not engage in a like business in any capacity in either of two named towns or within a sixty-mile radius of those towns for two years. There was no indication that the employee had enough influence over customers to cause them to move their business to her new agency, nor was it shown that any trade secrets were involved.

Due to the rapid evolution of business practices in the Internet industry, it has been argued that noncompetition agreements for Internet company employees need their own rules. *National Business Services, Inc. v. Wright* addressed the geographic scope of an Internet noncompetition agreement, upholding a one-year time restriction and a territorial clause that prevented the employee from taking another Internet-related job anywhere in the United States. The court stated, "Transactions involving the Internet, unlike traditional 'sales territory' cases, are not limited by state boundaries."

PRACTICAL ADVICE

If you include a covenant not to compete to protect your property interests, be careful to select a reasonable duration and geographic scope.

PAYROLL ADVANCE, INC. V. YATES

MISSOURI COURT OF APPEALS, 2008
270 S.W.3D 428

http://scholar.google.com/scholar_case?case=12029870438647495616&q=270+S.W.3d+428&hl=en&as_sdt=2,22

FACTS In June of 1998, Payroll Advance, Inc. entered into an employment contract with Barbara Yates, which contained a covenant not to compete. It is customary for each of Payroll's branch offices to employ a sole employee at each branch and that sole employee is the manager of that particular branch. On November 19, 1999, as a condition of her continued employment, Payroll presented Yates with the Employment Agreement which included a provision entitled "NON-COMPETE" ("the covenant not to compete"). This provision provided:

> [Yates] agrees not to compete with [Payroll] as owner, manager, partner, stockholder, or employee in any business that is in competition with [Payroll] and within a fifty-mile radius of [Payroll's] business for a period of two (2) years after termination of employment or [Yates] quits or [Yates] leaves employment of [Payroll].

On November 8, 2007, Yates was fired for cause. Approximately thirty-two days after being terminated Yates obtained employment with Check Please, one of the Payroll's competitors. At Check Please, Yates performed basically the same duties as she had when employed with Payroll.

On February 7, 2008, Payroll filed a complaint against Yates for: (1) injunctive relief to prevent Yates from soliciting its clients for her new employer, and to stop her from using client information she purportedly obtained from her time with Payroll and (2) damages for breach of contract for violation of the covenant not to compete together with attorney fees and costs. The trial court found "[n]o evidence exists that, following [Payroll's] termination of [Yates'] ten year period of employment, [Yates] removed any customer list or other documents from [Payroll's] place of business [or] … made any personal or other contact with any previous or present customer of [Payroll's] business or intends to do so."

The trial court further determined that if the covenant not to compete were enforced as requested, Yates would be prohibited from engaging in employment with any payday loan business in at least 126 cities situated in Missouri, Arkansas, and Tennessee. Further, Yates could also be prohibited from employment at a bank, savings and loan company, credit union, pawnshop, or title-loan company within Missouri, Arkansas, and Tennessee. Accordingly, the trial court found in favor of Yates holding that the Employment Agreement's noncompete covenant signed by the parties was not valid in that it was "unreasonable under the facts and circumstances of the particular industry, agreement, and geographic location here involved." Payroll appealed.

DECISION Judgment affirmed.

OPINION Barney, J. "Generally, because covenants not to compete are considered to be restraints on trade, they are presumptively void and are enforceable only to the extent that they are demonstratively reasonable." [Citations.] "Noncompetition agreements are not favored in the law, and the party attempting to enforce a noncompetition agreement has the burden of demonstrating both the necessity to protect the claimant's legitimate interests and that the agreement is reasonable as to time and space." [Citation.]

> There are at least four valid and conflicting concerns at issue in the law of non-compete agreements. First, the employer needs to be able to engage a highly trained workforce to be competitive and profitable, without fear that the employee will use the employer's business secrets against it or steal the employer's customers after leaving employment. Second, the employee must be mobile in order to provide for his or her family and to advance his or her career in an ever-changing marketplace. This mobility is dependent upon the ability of the employee to take his or her increasing skills and put them to work from one employer to the next. Third, the law favors the freedom of parties to value their respective interests in negotiated contracts. And, fourth, contracts in restraint of trade are unlawful. [Citation.]

"Missouri courts balance these concerns by enforcing non-compete agreements in certain limited circumstances." [Citation.] "Non-compete agreements are typically enforceable so long as they are reasonable. In practical terms, a non-compete agreement is reasonable if it is no more restrictive than is necessary to protect the legitimate interests of the employer." [Citation.] Furthermore, "[n]on-compete agreements are enforceable to the extent they can be narrowly tailored geographically and temporally." [Citation.] Lastly, it is not "necessary for the employer to show that actual damage has occurred, in order to obtain an injunction. The actual damage might be very hard to determine, and this is one reason for granting equitable relief." [Citation.]

Here, viewing the evidence in a light most favorable to the trial court's holding, [citation], it is clear the trial court took umbrage with the covenant's restrictive provisions and geographical limitations on Respondent's [Yates'] ability to find employment.

* * *

The question of reasonableness of a restraint is to be determined according to the facts of the particular case and hence requires a thorough consideration of all surrounding circumstances, including the subject matter of the contract, the purpose to be served, the situation of the parties, the extent of the restraint, and the specialization of the business.

* * *

Here, the covenant not to compete grandly declares that Respondent cannot "compete with Appellant [Payroll] as owner, manager, partner, stockholder, or employee *in any business* that is in competition with [Appellant] and within a 50 mile radius of [Appellant's] business...." (Emphasis added.) There was evidence from Appellant's representative at trial that Appellant has seventeen branch offices in Missouri and still other locations in Arkansas. If this Court interprets the plain meaning of the covenant not compete as written, the covenant not to compete would prevent Respondent not only from working at a competing business within 50 miles of the branch office in Kennett, Missouri, but Respondent would also be barred from working in a competing business within 50 miles of *any* of Appellant's branch offices. Under this interpretation, Respondent would be greatly limited in the geographic area she could work.

Additionally, the covenant not to compete bars Respondent from working at "any business that is in competition with [Appellant]." Yet, it fails to set out with precision what is to be considered a competing business and certainly does not specify that it only applies to other payday loan businesses. In that Appellant is in the business of making loans, it could be inferred that in addition to barring Respondent's employment at a different payday loan establishment the covenant not to compete also bars her from being employed anywhere loans are made including banks, credit unions, savings and loan organizations, title-loan companies, pawn shops, and other financial organizations. Such a restraint on the geographic scope of Respondent's employment and upon her type of employment is unduly burdensome and unreasonable. [Citation.]

* * *

Appellant's second point relied on asserts the trial court erred in denying its petition because [t]he trial court erroneously applied the law in failing to modify the covenant not to compete to a geographic scope it found to be reasonable in that the court found the geographic scope to be unreasonable for the payday loan industry but failed to modify the covenant not to compete to reflect a geographic scope that would be reasonable and enforceable.

* * * This Court "recognize[s] that an unreasonable restriction against competition in a contract may be modified and enforced to the extent that it is reasonable, regardless of the covenant's form of wording." * * *

Having reviewed the record in this matter, it appears the record is devoid of a request by Appellant for modification of the covenant not to compete either in its pleadings, at trial, or in its motion for new trial before the trial court. It is settled law that "'appellate courts are merely courts of review for trial court errors, and there can be no review of matter which has not been presented to or expressly decided by the trial court.'" [Citation.]

INTERPRETATION Noncompete clauses in employment agreements can be enforced only to the extent necessary to protect the employer's legitimate interests and only if reasonably limited in duration and geographic scope.

CRITICAL THINKING QUESTION How should courts balance the protection of employers with the freedom of employees to change jobs? Explain.

EXCULPATORY CLAUSES

Some contracts contain an **exculpatory clause** that excuses one party from liability for her own tortious conduct. Although there is general agreement that exculpatory clauses relieving a person from tort liability for harm caused intentionally or recklessly are unenforceable as violating public policy, exculpatory clauses that excuse a party from liability for harm caused by negligent conduct undergo careful scrutiny by the courts, which often require that the clause be conspicuously placed in the contract and clearly written. Accordingly, an exculpatory clause on the reverse side of a parking lot claim check, which attempts to relieve the parking lot operator of liability for negligently damaging the customer's automobile, generally will be held unenforceable as against public policy.

Where one party's superior bargaining position has enabled him to impose an exculpatory clause upon the other party, the courts are inclined to nullify the provision. Such a situation may arise in residential leases exempting a landlord from liability for his negligence. Moreover, an exculpatory clause may be unenforceable for unconscionability.

PRACTICAL ADVICE
Because many courts do not favor exculpatory clauses, carefully limit its applicability, make sure that it is clear and understandable, put it in writing, and have it signed.

ANDERSON V. MCOSKAR ENTERPRISES, INC.

COURT OF APPEALS OF MINNESOTA, 2006
712 N.W. 2D 796

http://caselaw.lp.findlaw.com/scripts/getcase.pl?court=mn&vol=apppub\0605\opa051546-0502&invol=1

FACTS Plaintiff, Tammey J. Anderson, on April 2, 2003, joined the fitness club Curves for Women, which was owned and operated by McOskar Enterprises. As part of the registration requirements, Anderson read an "AGREEMENT AND RELEASE OF LIABILITY," initialed each of the three paragraphs in the document, and dated and signed it. The first paragraph purported to release Curves from liability for injuries Anderson might sustain in participating in club activities or using club equipment:

> In consideration of being allowed to participate in the activities and programs of Curves for Women and to use its facilities, equipment and machinery in addition to the payment of any fee or charge, I do hereby waive, release and forever discharge Curves International Inc., Curves for Women, and their officers, agents, employees, representatives, executors, and all others (Curves representatives) from any and all responsibilities or liabilities from injuries or damages arriving [sic] out of or connected with my attendance at Curves for Women, my participation in all activities, my use of equipment or machinery, or any act or omission, including negligence by Curves representatives.

The second paragraph provided for Anderson's acknowledgment that fitness activities "involve a risk of injury" and her agreement "to expressly assume and accept any and all risks of injury or death."

After completing the registration, Anderson began a workout under the supervision of a trainer. About fifteen or twenty minutes later, having used four or five machines, Anderson developed a headache in the back of her head. She contends that she told the trainer, who suggested that the problem was likely just a previous lack of use of certain muscles and that Anderson would be fine. Anderson continued her workout and developed pain in her neck, shoulder, and arm. She informed the trainer but continued to exercise until she completed the program for that session. The pain persisted when Anderson returned home. She then sought medical attention and, in June 2003, underwent a cervical diskectomy. She then filed this lawsuit for damages, alleging that Curves had been negligent in its acts or omissions during her workout at the club. Curves moved for summary judgment on the ground that Anderson had released the club from liability for negligence. The district court agreed and granted the motion. Anderson appealed.

DECISION Judgment of the district court is affirmed.

OPINION Shumaker, J. It is settled Minnesota law that, under certain circumstances, "parties to a contract may, without violation of public policy, protect themselves against liability resulting from their own negligence." [Citation.] The "public interest in freedom of contract is preserved by recognizing [release and exculpatory] clauses as valid." [Citation.]

Releases of liability are not favored by the law and are strictly construed against the benefited party. [Citation.] "If the clause is either ambiguous in scope or purports to release the benefited party from liability for intentional, willful or wanton acts, it will not be enforced." [Citation.] Furthermore, even if a release clause is unambiguous in scope and is limited only to negligence, courts must still ascertain whether its enforcement will contravene public policy. On this issue, a two-prong test is applied:

> Before enforcing an exculpatory clause, both prongs of the test are examined, to-wit: (1) whether there was a disparity of bargaining power between the parties (in terms of a compulsion to sign a contract containing an unacceptable provision and the lack of ability to negotiate elimination of the unacceptable provision) ... and (2) the types of services being offered or provided (taking into consideration whether it is a public or essential service).
> [Citation.]

The two-prong test describes what is generally known as a "contract of adhesion," more particularly explained in *Schlobohm*:

> It is a contract generally not bargained for, but which is imposed on the public for *necessary* service on a "take it or leave it" basis. Even though a contract is on a printed form and offered on a "take it or leave it" basis, those facts alone do not cause it to be an adhesion contract. There must be a showing that the parties were greatly disparate in bargaining power, that there was no opportunity for negotiation *and* that the services could not be obtained elsewhere. [Citation.]

***

*** There is nothing in the Curves release that expressly exonerates the club from liability for any intentional, willful, or wanton act. Thus, we consider whether the release is ambiguous in scope.

***

Anderson argues that the release is ambiguous because it broadly exonerates Curves from liability for "any act or omission, including negligence...." ***

***

The vice of ambiguous language is that it fails precisely and clearly to inform contracting parties of the meaning of their ostensible agreement. Because ambiguous language is susceptible of two or more reasonable meanings, each party might carry away from the agreement a different and perhaps contradictory understanding. In the context of a release in connection with an athletic, health, or fitness activity, the consumer surely is entitled to know precisely what liability is being exonerated. A release that is so vague, general, or broad as to fail to specifically designate the particular nature of the liability exonerated is not enforceable. [Citation.]

* * * It is clear from this release that Anderson agreed to exonerate Curves from liability for negligence, that being part of the express agreement that Anderson accepted and it is solely negligence of which Curves is accused.

The unmistakable intent of the parties to the Curves agreement is that Curves at least would not be held liable for acts of negligence. * * *

* * *

Even if a release is unambiguously confined to liability for negligence, it still will be unenforceable if it contravenes public policy. Anderson contends that the Curves contract is one of adhesion characterized by such a disparity in bargaining power that she was compelled to sign it without any ability to negotiate.

But her argument is unpersuasive in view of the *Schlobohm* holding that "an adhesion contract is ... forced upon an unwilling and often unknowing public for services that cannot readily be obtained elsewhere." [Citation.] It is, according to *Schlobohm,* a contract "imposed on the public for *necessary* service on a 'take it or leave

it' basis." *Schlobohm* involved a "gym or health spa" known as Spa Petite. Similar to Curves, it offered fitness services and required members to sign a contract that provided for a release of liability for negligence. The supreme court found no disparity in bargaining power between Spa Petite and the litigating member; found that there had been no showing that the spa's services were necessary or that they could not have been obtained elsewhere; and found that health and fitness clubs ordinarily are not within the public-service or public-necessity classification that make their services of great public importance and necessary for the public to obtain.

Even if there was a disparity of bargaining ability here—which has not been demonstrated—there was no showing that the services provided by Curves are necessary and unobtainable elsewhere. * * *

The Curves release did not contravene public policy, and we adopt the supreme court's conclusion in *Schlobohm:* "Here there is no special legal relationship and no overriding public interest which demand that this contract provision, voluntarily entered into by competent parties, should be rendered ineffectual." [Citation.]

INTERPRETATION An exculpatory clause is valid if it is limited in scope, not ambiguous, and not contrary to public policy.

ETHICAL QUESTION Did Curves act unethically? Explain.

CRITICAL THINKING QUESTION When should an exculpatory clause be held invalid? Explain.

Unconscionable Contracts

The Uniform Commercial Code provides that a court may scrutinize every contract for the sale of goods to determine whether in its commercial setting, purpose, and effect the contract is unconscionable, or unfair. The court may refuse to enforce an **unconscionable** contract or any part of the contract it finds to be unconscionable. The Restatement has a similar provision.

Though neither the Code nor the Restatement defines the word *unconscionable,* the term is defined in the *New Webster's Dictionary* (Deluxe Encyclopedic Edition) as "contrary to the dictates of conscience; unscrupulous or unprincipled; exceeding that which is reasonable or customary; inordinate, unjustifiable."

The doctrine of unconscionability has been justified on the basis that it permits the courts to resolve issues of

unfairness explicitly in terms of that unfairness without recourse to formalistic rules or legal fictions. In policing contracts for fairness, the courts have again demonstrated their willingness to limit freedom of contract to protect the less advantaged from overreaching by dominant contracting parties. The doctrine of unconscionability has evolved through its application by the courts to include both procedural and substantive unconscionability. **Procedural unconscionability** involves scrutiny for the presence of "bargaining naughtiness." In other words, was the negotiation process fair? Or were there procedural irregularities, such as burying important terms of the agreement in fine print or obscuring the true meaning of the contract with impenetrable legal jargon?

By comparison, in searching for **substantive unconscionability**, the courts examine the actual terms of a contract for oppressive or grossly unfair provisions such as exorbitant prices or unfair exclusions or limitations of contractual remedies. An all-too-common example of such a provision involves a buyer in pressing need who is in an unequal bargaining position with a seller who consequently obtains an exorbitant price for his product or service. In one case, a price of $749 ($920 if the purchaser wished to pay on credit over time) for a vacuum cleaner that cost the seller $140 was held unconscionable. In another case, the buyers, welfare recipients, purchased by a time payment contract a home freezer unit for $900 that, when time credit charges, credit life insurance, credit property insurance, and sales tax were added, cost $1,235. The purchase resulted from a visit to the buyers' home by a salesperson representing Your Shop At Home Service, Inc.; the maximum retail value of the freezer unit at the time of purchase was $300. The court held the contract unconscionable and reformed it by reducing the price to the total payment ($620) the buyers had managed to make. Another landmark case follows.

PRACTICAL ADVICE

When negotiating a contract, keep in mind that if your bargaining techniques or the contract terms are oppressive, a court may refuse to enforce the contract in part or in full.

SANCHEZ V. WESTERN PIZZA ENTERPRISES, INC.

COURT OF APPEALS OF CALIFORNIA, SECOND DISTRICT, DIVISION THREE, 2009
172 CAL.APP.4TH 154

http://scholar.google.com/scholar_case?case=18161264297915300969&q=172+Cal.+App.+4th+154&hl=en&as_sdt=2,34

FACTS Octavio Sanchez works as a delivery driver at a Domino's Pizza restaurant owned by Western Pizza. He drives his own car in making deliveries. His hourly wage has ranged from the legal minimum wage to approximately $0.50 above minimum wage. Western Pizza reimburses him at a fixed rate of $0.80 per delivery regardless of the number of miles driven or actual expenses incurred. Sanchez brought this class action against Western Pizza alleging that the flat rate at which drivers were reimbursed for delivery expenses violated wage and hour laws and that the drivers were paid less than the legal minimum wage.

Sanchez and Western Pizza are parties to an undated arbitration agreement. The agreement states that (1) the execution of the agreement "is not a mandatory condition of employment"; (2) any dispute that the parties are unable to resolve informally will be submitted to binding arbitration before an arbitrator "selected from the then-current Employment Arbitration panel of the Dispute Eradication Services," and that the arbitrator must be approved by both parties; (3) the parties waive the right to a jury trial; (4) the arbitration fees will be borne by Western Pizza and, except as otherwise required by law, each party will bear its own attorney fees and costs; (5) small claims may be resolved by a summary small claims procedure; and (6) the parties a waive the right to bring class arbitration. The Superior Court of Los Angeles County denied the restaurant's motion to compel arbitration, and the restaurant appealed

DECISION The denial of the motion to compel arbitration is affirmed.

OPINION Croskey, J. Western Pizza contends *** the arbitration agreement is neither procedurally nor substantively unconscionable.

***

Procedural and substantive unconscionability must both be present to justify the refusal to enforce a contract or clause based on unconscionability. [Citation.] Procedural unconscionability focuses on oppression or unfair surprise, while substantive unconscionability focuses on overly harsh or one-sided terms. [Citations.] The more procedural unconscionability is present, the less substantive unconscionability is required to justify a determination that a contract or clause is unenforceable. Conversely, the less procedural unconscionability is present, the more substantive unconscionability is required to justify such a determination. [Citation.]

[A] finding of procedural unconscionability does not mean that a contract will not be enforced, but rather that courts will scrutinize the substantive terms of the contract to ensure they are not manifestly unfair or one-sided. [Citation.] … [T]here are degrees of procedural unconscionability. At one end of the spectrum are contracts that have been freely negotiated by roughly equal parties, in which there is no procedural unconscionability. Although certain terms in these contracts may be construed strictly, courts will not find these contracts substantively unconscionable, no matter how one-sided the terms appear to be. [Citation.] Contracts of adhesion that involve surprise or other sharp practices lie on the other end of the spectrum. [Citation.] Ordinary contracts of adhesion, although they are indispensable facts of modern life that are generally enforced [citation], contain a degree of procedural unconscionability even without any notable surprises, and "bear within them the clear danger of oppression and overreaching."[Citation.]

Thus, a conclusion that a contract contains no element of procedural unconscionability is tantamount to saying that, no matter how one-sided the contract terms, a court will not disturb the contract because of its confidence that the contract was negotiated or chosen freely, that the party subject to a seemingly one-sided term is presumed to have obtained some advantage from conceding the term or that, if one party negotiated poorly, it is not the court's place to rectify these kinds of errors or asymmetries. [Citation.]

Unconscionability under California law is a generally applicable contract defense and therefore applies to arbitration agreements regardless of whether the FAA [Federal Arbitration Act] applies. [Citations.]

* * *

The Arbitration Agreement Is Procedurally Unconscionable

Procedural unconscionability focuses on oppression or unfair surprise, as we have stated. Oppression results from unequal bargaining power when a contracting party has no meaningful choice but to accept the contract terms. [Citation.] Unfair surprise results from misleading bargaining conduct or other circumstances indicating that a party's consent was not an informed choice. [Citation.]

* * *

The arbitration agreement [in this case] states that the purpose of the agreement is "to resolve any disputes that may arise between the Parties in a timely, fair and individualized manner," but otherwise does not extol the benefits of arbitration. The arbitration agreement does not limit the limitations periods, the remedies available, or the amount of punitive damages. It states, "Except as otherwise required by law, each party shall bear its own attorney fees and costs," and therefore incorporates any statutory right to recover fees rather than creating a presumption against a fee recovery. Thus, the arbitration agreement neither contains the same types of disadvantages for employees as were present in [citation] nor fails to mention such disadvantageous terms. Moreover, the arbitration agreement expressly states that the agreement "is not a mandatory condition of employment."

We conclude, however, that the record indicates a degree of procedural unconscionability in two respects. First, * * * the inequality in bargaining power between the low-wage employees and their employer makes it likely that the employees felt at least some pressure to sign the arbitration agreement. Second, the arbitration agreement suggests that there are multiple arbitrators to choose from ("the then-current Employment Arbitration panel of the Dispute Eradication Services") and fails to mention that the designated arbitration provider includes only one arbitrator. This renders the arbitrator selection process illusory and creates a significant risk that Western Pizza as

a "repeat player" before the same arbitrator will reap a significant advantage. [Citation.] These circumstances indicate that the employees' decision to enter into the arbitration agreement likely was not a free and informed decision but was marked by some degree of oppression and unfair surprise, i.e., procedural unconscionability. We therefore must scrutinize the terms of the arbitration agreement to determine whether it is so unfairly one-sided as to be substantively unconscionable.

The Arbitrator Selection Provision Is Substantively Unconscionable

"Substantively unconscionable terms may take various forms, but may generally be described as unfairly one-sided." [Citation.] "Given the lack of choice and the potential disadvantages that even a fair arbitration system can harbor for employees, we must be particularly attuned to claims that employers with superior bargaining power have imposed one-sided, substantively unconscionable terms as part of an arbitration agreement. 'Private arbitration may resolve disputes faster and cheaper than judicial proceedings. Private arbitration, however, may also become an instrument of injustice imposed on a "take it or leave it" basis. The courts must distinguish the former from the latter, to ensure that private arbitration systems resolve disputes not only with speed and economy but also with fairness.'"[Citation.]

Sanchez contends the arbitration agreement is substantively unconscionable in several respects. He cites the class arbitration waiver, the small claims provision, the absence of any provision requiring a written arbitration award, the designation of an arbitration provider consisting of a single arbitrator, and the absence of any express provision for discovery. In light of our conclusion that the trial court properly decided that the class arbitration waiver is contrary to public policy and therefore unenforceable, we need not decide whether that provision is unconscionable. [Citation.]

* * *

* * * We conclude that the absence of express provisions requiring a written arbitration award and allowing discovery does not render the arbitration agreement unconscionable. Rather, those terms are implied as a matter of law as part of the agreement. [Citation.]

* * * We conclude that the matters authorized under the small claims provision are an ordinary incident of arbitration and that the small claims provision is not substantively unconscionable.

Finally, an arbitration agreement must provide for a neutral arbitrator. * * * In our view, the designation of a "panel" of arbitrators consisting of a single arbitrator selected by Western Pizza created a false appearance of mutuality in the selection of an arbitrator. Moreover, the effective designation of a single arbitrator in what appears to be a standard arbitration agreement applicable to a large number of corporate employees gives rise to a significant risk of financial interdependence between Western Pizza and the arbitrator, and an opportunity for Western Pizza to gain an advantage through its knowledge of and experience with the arbitrator. *** We conclude that this provision is unfairly one-sided and substantively unconscionable.

THE ENTIRE ARBITRATION AGREEMENT IS UNENFORCEABLE

A trial court may either sever an unconscionable or otherwise unlawful provision from an arbitration agreement and enforce the remainder, restrict the application of the provision so as to avoid unconscionable results, or refuse to enforce the entire agreement. [Citation.] Although a court has some discretion in this regard, a court may refuse to enforce the entire agreement only if the central purpose of the agreement is tainted by illegality. [Citation.] ***

Whether a contract is severable in this regard is primarily a question of contract interpretation. "'Whether a contract is entire or separable depends upon its language and subject matter, and this question is one of construction to be determined by the court according to the intention of the parties.'" [Citation.] Questions of contract interpretation are subject to de novo review unless the interpretation turns on the credibility of extrinsic evidence. [Citation.]

***

The arbitration agreement here includes a class arbitration waiver that is contrary to public policy and an unconscionable arbitrator selection clause, as we have stated. These are important provisions that, if they were not challenged in litigation, could create substantial disadvantages for an employee seeking to arbitrate a modest claim. Although it may be true that neither of these provisions alone would justify the refusal to enforce the entire arbitration agreement [citation], we believe that these provisions considered together indicate an effort to impose on an employee a forum with distinct advantages for the employer. [Thus,] *** we conclude that the arbitration agreement is permeated by an unlawful purpose. Accordingly, the denial of the motion to compel arbitration was proper.

INTERPRETATION The doctrine of unconscionability includes both procedural and substantive unconscionability.

ETHICAL QUESTION Did Western Pizza act unethically? Explain.

CRITICAL THINKING QUESTION When should a court modify the challenged clause and when should it refuse to enforce the entire clause in question?

Some courts hold that for a contract to be unenforceable both substantive and procedural unconscionability must be present. Nevertheless, they need not exist to the same degree; the more oppressive one is, the less evidence of the other is required.

Closely akin to the concept of unconscionability is the doctrine of contracts of adhesion. An *adhesion contract,* a standard-form contract prepared by one party, generally involves the preparer offering the other party the contract on a "take-it-or-leave-it" basis. Such contracts are not automatically unenforceable but are subject to greater scrutiny for procedural or substantive unconscionability. See *Anderson v. McOsker Enterprises, Inc.* and the Ethical Dilemma at the end of this chapter.

TORTIOUS CONDUCT

An agreement that requires a person to commit a tort is an illegal agreement and thus is unenforceable. The courts will not permit contract law to violate the law of torts. Any agreement attempting to do so is considered contrary to public policy. For example, Ada and Bernard enter into an agreement under which Ada promises Bernard that in return for $5,000, she will disparage the product of Bernard's competitor, Cone, in order to provide Bernard with a competitive advantage. Ada's promise is to commit the tort of disparagement and is unenforceable as contrary to public policy.

CORRUPTING PUBLIC OFFICIALS

Agreements that may adversely affect the public interest through the corruption of public officials or the impairment of the legislative process are unenforceable. Examples include using improper means to influence legislation, to secure some official action, or to procure a government contract. Contracts to pay lobbyists for services to obtain or defeat official action by means of persuasive argument are to be distinguished from illegal influence-peddling agreements.

For example, a bargain by a candidate for public office to make a certain appointment following his election is illegal. In addition, an agreement to pay a public officer something extra for performing his official duty, such as promising a bonus to a police officer for strictly enforcing the traffic laws on her beat, is illegal. The same is true of an agreement in which a citizen promises to perform, or to refrain from performing, duties imposed

Business Law in Action

Southwestern Casualty Insurance (SCI) has issued automobile insurance policies in the southwestern United States for a number of years. Its standard-form policies historically have covered its policyholders for accidents occurring in Mexico. After reassessing the company's liabilities, SCI determined that inserting an exclusion for accidents occurring within Mexico's borders would both assist in keeping premiums in check and contribute positively to the company's bottom line. It therefore issued a new standard-form policy that was the same in all respects as its old policy, but which now contained the Mexico exclusion in a long paragraph of other policy exclusions.

Rather than simply send the new form to its customers along with a premium notice when their policies are up for renewal, SCI must take pains to make its customers aware of the change in coverage. If it does not, there is a good chance in many jurisdictions that SCI will be stopped from enforcing the exclusion, and therefore will be required to provide coverage according to its customers' reasonable expectations.

Standard-form insurance policies generally are contracts of adhesion. This is because, while some provisions regarding limits and types of coverage may be bargained for, these agreements consist largely of boilerplate provisions that are not negotiated and that often are not, nor are they expected to be, read or fully understood by the insured. Standard-form insurance contracts are useful in commerce; by narrowing the consumer's choice from a limited number of meaningful features rather than an endless combination of possible coverages, they focus the time and effort of the insurer and insured, thereby reducing costs to the benefit of all. The adhesive nature of the agreement, however, imposes an obligation of good faith on the insurer, which has been translated into a rule that insureds do not assent to standard-form terms the insurer has reason to believe that the consumer would not have accepted.

on her by citizenship. Thus, a promise by Carl to pay $50 to Rachel if she will register and vote is opposed to public policy and illegal.

Effect of Illegality

With few exceptions, illegal contracts are *unenforceable*. In most cases, neither party to an illegal agreement can sue the other for breach or recover for any performance rendered. It is often said that where parties are *in pari delicto* (in pa'·re de·lik'tow)—in equal fault—a court will leave them where it finds them. The law will provide neither with any remedy. This strict rule of unenforceability is subject to certain exceptions, however, which are discussed as follows.

PARTY WITHDRAWING BEFORE PERFORMANCE

A party to an illegal agreement may withdraw, before performance, from the transaction and recover whatever she has contributed, if the party has not engaged in serious misconduct. A common example is recovery of money left with a stakeholder for a wager before it is paid over to the winner.

PARTY PROTECTED BY STATUTE

Sometimes an agreement is illegal because it violates a statute designed to protect persons from the effects of the prohibited agreement. For example, state and federal statutes prohibiting the sale of unregistered securities are designed primarily to protect investors. In such case, even though there is an unlawful agreement, the statutes usually expressly give the purchaser a right to withdraw from the sale and recover the money paid.

PARTY NOT EQUALLY AT FAULT

Where one of the parties is less at fault than the other, he may be allowed to recover payments made or property transferred. For example, this exception would apply in cases in which one party induces the other to enter into an illegal bargain through the exercise of fraud, duress, or undue influence.

EXCUSABLE IGNORANCE

An agreement that appears to be entirely permissible on its face, nevertheless, may be illegal by reason of facts and circumstances of which one of the parties is

Ethical Dilemma

Is It Fair to Mandate an Arbitration Clause?

FACTS   Delivery drivers at Figaro's Pizza Factory drive their own car in making deliveries. Their hourly wages range from the legal minimum wage to approximately $0.50 above minimum wage. Figaro's Pizza Factory reimburses them at a fixed rate of $0.80 per delivery regardless of the number of miles driven or actual expenses incurred. All drivers are required to sign an arbitration agreement that states (1) any dispute that the parties are unable to resolve informally will be submitted to binding arbitration before an arbitrator selected from a panel of a designated arbitration service and approved by both parties; (2) the parties give up the right to a jury trial; (3) the arbitration fees will be borne by Figaro's Pizza Factory and, except as otherwise required by law, each party will bear its own attorneys' fees and costs; (4) small claims may be resolved

by a summary small claims procedure; and (5) the parties give up the right to bring class arbitration. In actuality, the arbitration provider designated by Figaro's Pizza Factory includes only one arbitrator.

Social, Policy, and Ethical Considerations

1. Is the bargaining power of the employer too great to assume that the terms of the arbitration agreement resulted from a fair negotiation process?

2. Do the terms of this agreement appear fair and reasonable to both parties?

3. What concerns are raised by the lack of real choice by the employees in selecting the arbitrator?

4. Is the compensation paid by Figaro's Pizza Factory fair?

© Cengage Learning 2014

completely unaware. For example, a man and woman make mutual promises to marry, but unknown to the woman, the man is already married. This is an agreement to commit the crime of bigamy, and the marriage, if entered into, is void. In such case, the courts permit the party who is ignorant of the illegality to maintain a lawsuit against the other party for damages.

A party may also be excused for ignorance of legislation of a minor character. For instance, Jones and Old South Building Co. enter into a contract to build a factory that contains specifications in violation of the town's building ordinance. Jones did not know of the violation and had no reason to know. Old South's promise to build would not be rendered unenforceable on grounds of public policy, and Jones consequently

would have a claim against Old South for damages for breach of contract.

PARTIAL ILLEGALITY

A contract may be partly unlawful and partly lawful. The courts view such a contract in one of two ways. First, the partial illegality may be held to taint the entire contract with illegality, so that it is wholly unenforceable. Second, the court may determine it possible to separate the illegal from the legal part, in which case the illegal part only will be held unenforceable, whereas the legal part will be enforced. For example, if a contract contains an illegal covenant not to compete, the covenant will not be enforced, though the rest of the contract may be.

CHAPTER SUMMARY

Violations of Statutes

General Rule the courts will not enforce agreements declared illegal by statute

Licensing Statutes require formal authorization to engage in certain trades, professions, or businesses
* *Regulatory License* licensing statute that is intended to protect the public against unqualified persons; an unlicensed person may not recover for services he has performed
* *Revenue License* licensing statute that seeks to raise money; an unlicensed person may recover for services he has performed

Gambling Statutes prohibit wagers, which are agreements that one party will win and the other lose depending on the outcome of an event in which their only interest is the gain or loss

Usury Statutes establish a maximum rate of interest

Violations of Public Policy

Common Law Restraint of Trade unreasonable restraints of trade are not enforceable
- *Sale of a Business* the promise by the seller of a business not to compete in that particular business in a reasonable geographic area for a reasonable period of time is enforceable
- *Employment Contracts* an employment contract prohibiting an employee from competing with his employer for a reasonable period following termination is enforceable provided the restriction is necessary to protect legitimate interests of the employer

Exculpatory Clauses the courts generally disapprove of contractual provisions excusing a party from liability for his own tortious conduct

Unconscionable Contracts unfair or unduly harsh agreements are not enforceable
- *Procedural Unconscionability* unfair or irregular bargaining
- *Substantive Unconscionability* oppressive or grossly unfair contractual terms

Tortious Conduct an agreement that requires a person to commit a tort is unenforceable

Corrupting Public Officials agreements that corrupt public officials are not enforceable

Effect of Illegality

Unenforceability neither party may recover (unenforceable) under an illegal agreement where both parties are *in pari delicto* (in equal fault)

Exceptions permit one party to recover payments
- *Party Withdrawing before Performance*
- *Party Protected by Statute*
- *Party Not Equally at Fault*
- *Excusable Ignorance*
- *Partial Illegality*

QUESTIONS

1. Johnson and Wilson were the principal shareholders in Matthew Corporation, located in the city of Jonesville, Wisconsin. This corporation was engaged in the business of manufacturing paper novelties, which were sold over a wide area in the Midwest. The corporation was also in the business of binding books. Johnson purchased Wilson's shares in Matthew Corporation and, in consideration thereof, Wilson agreed that for a period of two years he would not (a) manufacture or sell in Wisconsin any paper novelties of any kind that would compete with those sold by Matthew Corporation or (b) engage in the bookbinding business in the city of Jonesville. Discuss the validity and effect, if any, of this agreement.

2. Wilkins, a Texas resident licensed by that state as a certified public accountant (CPA), rendered service in his professional capacity in Louisiana to Coverton Cosmetics Company. He was not registered as a CPA in Louisiana. His service under his contract with the cosmetics company was not the only occasion on which he had practiced his profession in that state. The company denied liability and refused to pay him, relying on a Louisiana statute declaring it unlawful for any person to perform or offer to perform services as a CPA for compensation until he has been registered by the designated agency of the state and holds an unrevoked registration card. The statute provides that a CPA certificate may be issued without examination to any applicant who holds a valid unrevoked certificate as a CPA under the laws of any other state. The statute provides further that rendering services of the kind performed by Wilkins, without registration, is a misdemeanor punishable by a fine or imprisonment in the county jail or by both fine and imprisonment. Discuss whether Wilkins would be successful in an action against Coverton seeking to recover a fee in the amount of $1,500 as the reasonable value of his services.

3. Michael is interested in promoting the passage of a bill in the state legislature. He agrees with Christy, an attorney, to pay Christy for her services in writing the required bill, obtaining its introduction in the legislature, and making an argument for its passage before the legislative committee to which it will be referred. Christy renders these services. Subsequently, on Michael's refusal to pay Christy, Christy sues Michael for damages for breach of contract. Will Christy prevail? Explain.

4. Anthony promises to pay McCarthy $100,000 if McCarthy reveals to the public that Washington is a communist. Washington is not a communist and never has been. McCarthy successfully persuades the media to report that Washington is a communist and now seeks to recover the $100,000 from Anthony, who refuses to pay. McCarthy initiates a lawsuit against Anthony. What will be the result?

5. The Dear Corporation was engaged in the business of making and selling harvesting machines. It sold everything pertaining to its business to the HI Company, agreeing "not again to go into the manufacture of harvesting machines anywhere in the United States." The Dear Corporation, which had a national and international goodwill in its business, now begins the manufacture of such machines contrary to its agreement. Should the court stop it from doing so? Explain.

6. Charles Leigh, engaged in the industrial laundry business in Central City, employed Tim Close, previously employed in the home laundry business, as a route salesperson. Leigh rents linens and industrial uniforms to commercial customers; the soiled linens and uniforms are picked up at regular intervals by the route drivers and replaced with clean ones. Every employee is assigned a list of customers whom she services. The contract of employment stated that in consideration of being employed, on termination of his employment, Close would not "directly or indirectly engage in the linen supply business or any competitive business within Central City, Illinois, for a period of one year from the date when his employment under this contract ceases." On May 10 of the following year, Close's employment was terminated by Leigh for valid reasons. Close then accepted employment with Ajax Linen Service, a direct competitor of Leigh in Central City. He began soliciting former customers he had called on for Leigh and obtained some of them as customers for Ajax. Will Leigh be able to enforce the provisions of the contract?

7. On July 5, 2012, Bill and George entered into a bet on the outcome of the 2012 presidential election. On January 28, 2013, Bill, who bet on the winner, approached George, seeking to collect the $3,000 George had wagered. George paid Bill the wager but now seeks to recover the funds from Bill. Result?

8. Carl, a salesperson for Smith, comes to Benson's home and sells him a complete set of "gourmet cooking utensils" that are worth approximately $300. Benson, an eighty-year-old man who lives alone in a one-room efficiency apartment, signs a contract to buy the utensils for $1,450 plus a credit charge of $145 and to make payments in ten equal monthly installments. Three weeks after Carl leaves with the signed contract, Benson decides he cannot afford the cooking utensils and has no use for them. What can Benson do? Explain.

9. Consider the facts in Question 8 but assume that the price was $350. Assume further that Benson wishes to avoid the con tract based on the allegation that Carl befriended and tricked him into the purchase. Discuss.

10. Adrian rents a bicycle from Barbara. The bicycle rental contract Adrian signed provides that Barbara is not liable for any injury to the renter caused by any defect in the bicycle or the negligence of Barbara. Adrian is injured when she is involved in an accident due to Barbara's improper maintenance of the bicycle. Adrian sues Barbara for damages. Will Barbara be protected from liability by the provision in their contract?

11. Emily was a Java programmer employed with Sun Microsystems in Palo Alto, California. Upon beginning employment, Emily signed a contract which included a noncompetition clause that prevented her from taking another Java programming position with any of five companies Sun listed as "direct competitors" within three months of terminating her employment. Later that year Emily resigned and two months later accepted a position with Hewlett-Packard (HP) in Houston, Texas. HP was listed in Emily's contract as a "direct competitor," but she argues that due to the significant geographic distance between both jobs, the contract is not enforceable. Explain whether the contract is enforceable.

CASE PROBLEMS

12. Merrill Lynch employed Post and Maney as account executives. Both men elected to be paid a salary and to participate in the firm's pension and profit-sharing plans rather than take a straight commission. Thirteen years later, Merrill Lynch terminated the employment of both Post and Maney without cause. Both men began working for a competitor of Merrill Lynch. Merrill Lynch then informed them that all of their rights in the company-funded pension plan had been forfeited pursuant to a provision of the plan that permitted forfeiture in the event an employee directly or indirectly competed with the firm. Is Merrill Lynch correct in its assertion?

13. Tovar applied for the position of resident physician in Paxton Community Memorial Hospital. The hospital examined his background and licensing and assured him that he was qualified for the position. Relying upon the hospital's promise of permanent employment, Tovar resigned from his job and began work at the hospital. He was discharged two weeks later, however, because he did not hold a license to practice medicine in Illinois as required by state law. He had taken the examination but had never passed it. Tovar claims that the hospital promised him a position of permanent employment and that by discharging him, it breached their employment contract. Who is correct? Discuss.

14. Carolyn Murphy, a welfare recipient with very limited education and with four minor children, responded to an advertisement that offered the opportunity to purchase televisions without a deposit or credit history. She entered into a rent-to-own contract for a twenty-five-inch television set that required seventy-eight weekly payments of $16 (a total of $1,248, which was two and one-half times the retail value of the set). Under the contract, the renter could terminate the agreement by returning the television and forfeiting any payments already made. After Murphy had paid $436 on the television, she read a newspaper article criticizing the lease plan. She stopped payment and sued the television company. In response, the television company has attempted to take possession of the set. What will be the outcome?

15. Albert Bennett, an amateur cyclist, participated in a bicycle race conducted by the United States Cycling Federation. During the race, Bennett was hit by an automobile. He claims that employees of the Federation improperly allowed the car onto the course. The Federation claims that it cannot be held liable to Bennett because Bennett signed a release exculpating the Federation from responsibility for any personal injury resulting from his participation in the race. Is the exculpatory clause effective?

16. In February, Brady, a general contractor, signed a written contract with the Fulghums to build for them a house in North Carolina. The contract price of the house was $206,850, and construction was to begin in March of that year. Neither during the contract negotiations nor during the commencement of construction was Brady licensed as a general contractor as required by North Carolina law. In fact, Brady did not obtain his license until late October of that year, at which time he had completed more than two-thirds of the construction on the Fulghums' house. The Fulghums submitted to Brady total payments of $204,000 on the house. Brady sues for $2,850 on the original contract and $29,000 for additions and changes requested by the Fulghums during construction. Is Fulghum liable to Brady? Explain.

17. Robert McCart owned and operated an H&R Block tax preparation franchise. When Robert became a district manager for H&R Block, he was not allowed to continue operating a franchise. So, in accordance with company policy, he signed over his franchise to his wife June. June signed the new franchise agreement, which included a covenant not to compete for a two-year period within a fifty-mile radius of the franchise territory should the H&R Block franchise be terminated, transferred, or otherwise disposed of. June and Robert were both aware of the terms of this agreement, but June chose to terminate her franchise agreement anyway. Shortly thereafter, June sent out letters to H&R Block customers, criticizing H&R Block's fees and informing them that she and Robert would establish their own tax preparation services at the same address as the former franchise location. Each letter included a separate letter from Robert detailing the tax

services to be offered by the McCarts' new business. Should H&R Block be able to obtain an injunction against June? Against Robert?

18. Michelle Marvin and actor Lee Marvin began living together, holding themselves out to the general public as man and wife without actually being married. The two orally agreed that while they lived together they would share equally any and all property and earnings accumulated as a result of their individual and combined efforts. In addition, Michelle promised to render her services as "companion, homemaker, housekeeper, and cook" to Lee. Shortly thereafter, she gave up her lucrative career as an entertainer to devote her full time to being Lee's companion, homemaker, housekeeper, and cook. In return he agreed to provide for all of her financial support and needs for the rest of her life. After living together for six years, Lee compelled Michelle to leave his household but continued to provide for her support. One year later, however, he refused to provide further support. Michelle sued to recover support payments and half of their accumulated property. Lee contends that their agreement is so closely related to the supposed "immoral" character of their relationship that its enforcement would violate public policy. The trial court granted Lee's motion for judgment on the pleadings. Decision?

19. Richard Brobston was hired by Insulation Corporation of America (ICA) in 2002. Initially, he was hired as a territory sales manager but was promoted to national account manager in 2006 and to general manager in 2011. In 2013, ICA was planning to acquire computer-assisted design (CAD) technology to upgrade its product line. Prior to acquiring this technology, ICA required that Brobston and certain other employees sign employment contracts that contained restrictive covenants or be terminated and changed their employment status to "at will" employees. These restrictive covenants provided that in the event of Brobston's termination for any reason, Brobston would not reveal any of ICA's trade secrets or sales information and would not enter into direct competition with ICA within three hundred miles of Allentown, Pennsylvania, for a period of two years from the date of termination. The purported consideration for Brobston's agreement was a $2,000 increase in his base salary and proprietary information concerning the CAD system, customers, and pricing. Brobston signed the proffered employment contract. In October 2013, Brobston became vice president of special products, which included responsibility for sales of the CAD system products as well as other products. Over the course of the next year, Brobston failed in several respects to properly perform his employment duties and on August 13, 2014, ICA terminated Brobston's employment. In December 2014, Brobston was hired by a competitor of ICA who was aware of ICA's restrictive covenants. Can ICA enforce the employment agreement by enjoining Brobston from disclosing proprietary information about ICA and by restraining him from competing with ICA? If so, for what duration and over what geographic area?

20. Henrioulle, an unemployed widower with two children, received public assistance in the form of a rent subsidy. He entered into an apartment lease agreement with Marin Ventures that provided "INDEMNIFICATION: Owner shall not be liable for any damage or injury to the tenant, or any other person, or to any property, occurring on the premises, or any part thereof, and Tenant agrees to hold Owner harmless for any claims for damages no matter how caused." Henrioulle fractured his wrist when he tripped over a rock on a common stairway in the apartment building. At the time of the accident, the landlord had been having difficulty keeping the common areas of the apartment building clean. Will the exculpatory clause effectively bar Henrioulle from recovery? Explain.

21. Universal City Studios, Inc. (Universal) entered into a general contract with Turner Construction Company (Turner) for the construction of the Jurassic Park ride. Turner entered into a subcontract with Pacific Custom Pools, Inc. (PCP), for PCP to furnish and install all water treatment work for the project for the contract price of $959,131. PCP performed work on the project from April 2011 until June 2012 for which it was paid $897,719. PCP's contractor's license, however, was under suspension from October 12, 2011, to March 14, 2012. In addition, PCP's license had expired as of January 31, 2012, and it was not renewed until May 5, 2012. California Business and Professions Code Section 7031 provides that no contractor may bring an action to recover compensation for the performance of any work requiring a license unless he or she was "a duly licensed contractor at all times during the performance of that [work], regardless of the merits of the cause of action brought by the contractor." The purpose of this licensing law is to protect the public from incompetence and dishonesty in those who provide building and construction services. PCP brought suit against Universal and Turner, the defendants, for the remainder of the contract price. Explain who should prevail.

22. Between 2008 and 2013, Williams purchased a number of household items on credit from Walker-Thomas Furniture Co., a retail furniture store. Walker-Thomas retained the right in its contracts to repossess an item if Williams defaulted on an installment payment. Each contract also provided that each installment payment by Williams would be credited pro rata to all outstanding accounts or bills owed to Walker-Thomas. As a result of this provision, an unpaid balance would remain on every item purchased until the entire balance due on all items, whenever purchased, was paid in full. Williams defaulted on a monthly installment payment in 2013, and Walker-Thomas sought to repossess all the items that Williams had purchased. Discuss whether Walker-Thomas should prevail.

TAKING SIDES

EarthWeb provided online products and services to business professionals in the information technology (IT) industry. EarthWeb operated through a family of websites offering information, products, and services for IT professionals to use for facilitating tasks and solving technology problems in a business setting. EarthWeb obtained this content primarily through licensing agreements with third parties. Schlack began his employment with EarthWeb in its New York City office. His title at EarthWeb was Vice President, Worldwide Content, and he was responsible for the content of all of EarthWeb's websites. Schlack's employment contract stated that he was an employee at will and included a section titled "Limited Agreement Not To Compete." That section provided:

(c) For a period of twelve (12) months after the termination of Schlack's employment with EarthWeb, Schlack shall not, directly or indirectly:

(1) work as an employee … or in any other … capacity for any person or entity that directly competes with EarthWeb. For the purpose of this section, the term "directly competing" is defined as a person or entity or division on an entity that is

(i) an online service for Information Professionals whose primary business is to provide Information Technology Professionals with a directory of third party technology, software, and/ or developer resources; and/or an online reference library, and or

(ii) an online store, the primary purpose of which is to sell or distribute third party software or products used for Internet site or software development.

About one year later, Schlack tendered his letter of resignation to EarthWeb. Schlack revealed at this time that he had accepted a position with ITworld.com.

a. What arguments would support EarthWeb's enforcement of the covenant not to compete?

b. What arguments would support Schlack's argument that the covenant is not enforceable?

c. Which side should prevail? Explain.

Chapter 14

CONTRACTUAL CAPACITY

Youth is a blunder, manhood a struggle, old age a regret.

BENJAMIN DISRAELI (1805–1881), *CONINGSBY* (BOOK III, CH. I)

CHAPTER OUTCOMES

After reading and studying this chapter, you should be able to:

1. Explain how and when a minor may ratify a contract.

2. Describe the liability of a minor who (a) disaffirms a contract or (b) misrepresents his age.

3. Define as necessary and explain how it affects the contracts of a minor.

4. Distinguish between the legal capacity of a person under guardianship and a mentally incompetent person who is not under guardianship.

5. Explain the rule governing an intoxicated person's capacity to enter into a contract and contrast this rule with the law governing minors and incompetent persons.

A binding promise or agreement requires that the parties to the agreement have contractual capacity. Everyone is regarded as having such capacity unless the law, for public policy reasons, holds that the individual lacks such capacity. We will consider this essential ingredient of a contract by discussing those classes and conditions of persons who are legally limited in their capacity to contract: minors, incompetent persons, and intoxicated persons.

Minors

A **minor**, also called an infant, is a person who has not attained the age of legal majority. At common law, a minor was an individual who had not reached the age of twenty-one years. Today the age of majority has been changed by statute in nearly all jurisdictions, usually to age eighteen. Almost without exception a minor's contract, whether executory or executed, is *voidable* at his guardian's option. Thus, the minor is in a favored position by having the option to disaffirm the contract or to enforce it. The adult party to the contract cannot avoid her contract with a minor. Even an "emancipated" minor, one who, because of marriage or other reasons, is no longer subject to strict parental control, may nevertheless avoid contractual liability in most jurisdictions. Consequently, business people deal at their peril with minors and in situations of consequence generally require an adult to cosign or guarantee the performance of the contract. Nevertheless, most states recognize special categories of contracts that cannot be avoided (such as student loans or contracts for medical care) or that

275

have a lower age for capacity (such as bank accounts, marriage, and insurance contracts).

LIABILITY ON CONTRACTS

A minor's contract is not entirely void and of no legal effect; rather, as we have said, it is voidable at the minor's option. The exercise of this power of avoidance, called a **disaffirmance**, releases the minor from any liability on the contract. On the other hand, after the minor comes of age, he may choose to adopt or ratify the contract, in which case he surrenders his power of avoidance and becomes bound by his **ratification**.

Disaffirmance   As we stated earlier, a minor has the power to avoid liability. The minor or, in some jurisdictions, her guardian, may exercise the power to disaffirm a contract through words or conduct showing an intention not to abide by it.

A minor may disaffirm a contract at any time before reaching the age of majority. Moreover, a minor generally may disaffirm a contract within a reasonable time after coming of age as long as she has not already ratified the contract. A notable exception is that a minor cannot disaffirm a sale of land until after reaching her majority.

In most states, determining a reasonable time depends on circumstances such as the nature of the transaction, whether either party has caused the delay, and the extent to which either party has been injured by the delay. Some states, however, statutorily prescribe a time period, generally one year, in which the minor may disaffirm the contract.

Disaffirmance may be either *express* or *implied*. No particular form of language is essential, so long as it shows an intention not to be bound. This intention also may be manifested by acts or by conduct. For example, a minor agrees to sell property to Andy and then sells the property to Betty. The sale to Betty constitutes a disaffirmance of the contract with Andy.

A troublesome yet important problem in this area pertains to the minor's duty upon disaffirmance. The courts do not agree on this question. The majority hold that the minor must return any property received from the other party to the contract, provided she is in possession of it at the time of disaffirmance. Nothing more is required. If the minor disaffirms the purchase of an automobile and the vehicle has been wrecked, she need only return the wrecked vehicle. Other states require at least the payment of a reasonable amount for the use of the property or of the amount by which the property depreciated while in the hands of the minor (see *Berg v. Traylor*). A few states, however, either by statute or court ruling, recognize a duty on the part of the minor to make *restitution*—that is, to return an equivalent of what has been received so that the seller will be in approximately the same position he would have occupied had the sale not occurred.

Finally, can a minor disaffirm and recover property that he has sold to a buyer who in turn has sold it to a good-faith purchaser for value? Traditionally, the minor could avoid the contract and recover the property, even though the third person gave value for it and had no notice of the minority. Thus, in the case of the sale of real estate, a minor could take back a deed of conveyance even against a third-party good-faith purchaser of the land who did not know of the minority. The Uniform Commercial Code (UCC), however, has changed this principle in connection with sales of goods by providing that a person with voidable title (e.g., the person buying goods from a minor) has power to transfer valid title to a good-faith purchaser for value. For example, a minor sells his car to an individual who resells it to a used-car dealer, a good-faith purchaser for value. The used-car dealer would acquire legal title even though he bought the car from a seller who had only voidable title.

PRACTICAL ADVICE

In all significant contracts entered into with a minor, have an adult cosign or guarantee the written agreement.

BERG V. TRAYLOR

COURT OF APPEAL, SECOND DISTRICT, DIVISION 2, CALIFORNIA, 2007
148 CAL.APP.4TH 809, 56 CAL.RPTR.3D 140

http://scholar.google.com/scholar_case?case=1540939777753786246&q=56+Cal.Rptr.3d + 140&hl=en&as_sdt=2,22

FACTS Sharyn Berg (Berg), plaintiff, brought this action against Meshiel Cooper Traylor (Meshiel) and her minor son Craig Lamar Traylor (Craig) for unpaid commissions under a contract between Berg, Meshiel, and Craig for Berg to serve as the personal manager of Craig. On January 18, 1999, Berg entered into a two-page "Artist's

Manager's Agreement" (agreement) with Meshiel and Craig, who was then ten years old. Meshiel signed the agreement and wrote Craig's name on the signature page where he was designated "Artist." Craig did not sign the agreement. The agreement provided that Berg was to act as Craig's exclusive personal manager in exchange for a commission of 15 percent of all monies paid to him as an artist during the three-year term of the agreement. The agreement expressly provided that any action Craig "may take in the future pertaining to disaffirmance of this agreement, whether successful or not," would not affect Meshiel's liability for any commissions due Berg. The agreement also provided that any disputes concerning payment or interpretation of the agreement would be determined by arbitration in accordance with the rules of Judicial Arbitration and Mediation Services, Inc. (JAMS).

In June 2001, Craig obtained a role on the Fox Television Network show "Malcolm in the Middle" (show). On September 11, 2001, four months prior to the expiration of the agreement, Meshiel sent a certified letter to Berg stating that while she and Craig appreciated her advice and guidance, they no longer needed her management services and could no longer afford to pay Berg her 15 percent commission because they owed a "huge amount" of taxes. On September 28, 2001, Berg responded, informing appellants that they were in breach of the agreement.

The arbitration hearing was held in February 2005. The arbitrator awarded Berg commissions and interest of $154,714.15, repayment of personal loans and interest of $5,094, and attorneys' fees and costs of $13,762. He also awarded Berg $405,000 "for future earnings projected on a minimum of six years for national syndication earnings." The defendants then filed a petition with the state trial court to vacate the arbitration award. Following a hearing, the trial court trial court entered a judgment in favor of Berg against Meshiel and Craig consistent with the arbitrator's award.

DECISION The decision against Craig is reversed but the judgment against Meshiel is affirmed.

OPINION Todd, J. Simply stated, one who provides a minor with goods and services does so at her own risk. [Citation.] The agreement here expressly contemplated this risk, requiring that Meshiel remain obligated for commissions due under the agreement regardless of whether Craig disaffirmed the agreement. Thus, we have no difficulty in reaching the conclusion that Craig is permitted to and did disaffirm the agreement and any obligations stemming therefrom, while Meshiel remains liable under the agreement and resulting judgment. Where our difficulty lies is in understanding how counsel, the arbitrator, and the trial court repeatedly and systematically ignored Craig's interests in this matter. From the time Meshiel signed the agreement, her interests were not aligned with Craig's. That no one—counsel, the arbitrator, or the trial court—recognized this conflict and sought appointment of a guardian *ad litem* for Craig is nothing short of stunning. It is the court's responsibility to protect the rights of a minor who is a litigant in court. [Citation.]

* * *

"As a general proposition, parental consent is required for the provision of services to minors for the simple reason that minors may disaffirm their own contracts to acquire such services." [Citation.] According to Family Code section 6700, "a minor may make a contract in the same manner as an adult, subject to the power of disaffirmance" * * *. In turn, Family Code section 6710 states: "Except as otherwise provided by statute, a contract of a minor may be disaffirmed by the minor before majority or within a reasonable time afterwards or, in case of the minor's death within that period, by the minor's heirs or personal representative." Sound policy considerations support this provision:

> The law shields minors from their lack of judgment and experience and under certain conditions vests in them the right to disaffirm their contracts. Although in many instances such disaffirmance may be a hardship upon those who deal with an infant, the right to avoid his contracts is conferred by law upon a minor "for his protection against his own improvidence and the designs of others." It is the policy of the law to protect a minor against himself and his indiscretions and immaturity as well as against the machinations of other people and to discourage adults from contracting with an infant. Any loss occasioned by the disaffirmance of a minor's contract might have been avoided by declining to enter into the contract. [Citation.]

Berg offers two reasons why the plain language of Family Code section 6710 is inapplicable, neither of which we find persuasive. First, she argues that a minor may not disaffirm an agreement signed by a parent. * * * [This is not in accord with the law as stated in numerous cases.]

Second, Berg argues that Craig cannot disaffirm the agreement because it was for his and his family's necessities. Family Code section 6712 provides that a valid contract cannot be disaffirmed by a minor if all of the following requirements are met: the contract is to pay the reasonable value of things necessary for the support of the minor or the minor's family, the things have actually been furnished to the minor or the minor's family, and the contract is entered into by the minor when not under the care of a parent or guardian able to provide for the minor or the minor's family. These requirements are not met here. The agreement was not a contract to pay for the necessities of life for Craig or his family. While such necessities have been held to include payment for lodging [citation] and even payment of attorneys' fees [citation], we cannot conclude that a contract to secure personal management services for the purpose of advancing Craig's acting career constitutes payment for the type of necessity contemplated by Family Code section 6712. Nor is there any evidence that Meshiel was unable to provide for the family in 1999 at the time of the agreement. As such, Family Code section 6712 does not bar the minor's disaffirmance of the contract.

No specific language is required to communicate an intent to disaffirm. "A contract (or conveyance) of a minor may be avoided by any act or declaration disclosing an unequivocal intent to repudiate its binding force and effect." [Citation.] Express notice to the other party is unnecessary. [Citation.] We find that the "Notice of Disaffirmance of Arbitration Award by Minor" filed on August 8, 2005 was sufficient to constitute a disaffirmance of the agreement by Craig. * * * We find that Craig was entitled to and did disaffirm the agreement which, among other things, required him to arbitrate his disputes with Berg. On this basis alone, therefore, the judgment confirming the arbitration award must be reversed.

* * *

Appellants do not generally distinguish their arguments between mother and son, apparently assuming that if Craig disaffirms the agreement and judgment,

Meshiel would be permitted to escape liability as well. But a disaffirmance of an agreement by a minor does not operate to terminate the contractual obligations of the parent who signed the agreement. [Citation.] The agreement Meshiel signed provided that Craig's disaffirmance would not serve to void or avoid Meshiel's obligations under the agreement and that Meshiel remained liable for commissions due Berg regardless of Craig's disaffirmance. Accordingly, we find no basis for Meshiel to avoid her independent obligations under the agreement.

INTERPRETATION A minor may disaffirm his contracts during minority and for a reasonable time thereafter; nevertheless, the minor's right to disaffirm does not extend to an adult party to the agreement.

CRITICAL THINKING QUESTION Under what circumstances should minors be able to disaffirm their contracts and receive their full consideration? Explain.

Ratification A minor has the option of ratifying a contract after reaching the age of majority. Ratification makes the contract binding *ab initio* (from the beginning). That is, the result is the same as if the contract had been valid and binding from its inception. Ratification, once effected, is final and cannot be withdrawn; furthermore, it must be in total, validating the entire contract. The minor can ratify the contract only as a

Business Law in Action

Using his own money, fifteen-year-old Zach bought $160 worth of video games and DVDs at a local electronics warehouse. His parents were furious about the purchase, but initially they did nothing. Several months later Zach's father learned about the so-called infancy doctrine and insisted that Zach return the games and movies. Zach took the items back to the store and asked for a refund. But the clerk refused, pointing to the store's "Return Policy," which permitted returns on opened items like those Zach had bought only within thirty days of purchase and only for the same title when necessary to replace defects. After speaking to the manager and getting a similar result, Zach's father considered filing suit against the store in small claims court. Does a minor's right of disaffirmation void override the store's return policy in a case like this?

Generally speaking, minors may disaffirm contracts entered into during their minority. In a majority of jurisdictions this is true even if the child or teenager cannot return the consideration he or she received and even if the minor misrepresented his or her age when entering

into the transaction with the adult. However, this rule of incapacity does not excuse minors from paying the reasonable value of any necessaries for which they may have contracted. There is little question here that the purchases Zach made do not qualify as necessaries, things that supply his basic needs. Therefore, Zach is entitled to disaffirm his contract and receive a refund, although some states perhaps would subject the refund to a deduction of some amount representing depreciation of the items or the use or benefit he received.

Nonetheless, retailers need not fear or refuse transactions with minors, especially relatively insignificant ones. Most people will not go to the trouble and expense of bringing litigation to recover a small amount of money. It is also foreseeable that many courts, if given the opportunity, would not allow a minor to take unfair advantage of her minority. Moreover, teens make up a growing and lucrative segment of the retail market, with their purchases tallying in the billions of dollars each year.

whole, both as to burdens and benefits. He cannot, for example, ratify so as to retain the consideration received and escape payment or other performance on his part; nor can the minor retain part of the contract and disaffirm another part.

Note that a minor has *no* power to ratify a contract while still a minor. A ratification based on words or conduct occurring while the minor is still underage is no more effective than his original contractual promise. The ratification must take place after the individual has acquired contractual capacity by attaining his majority.

Ratification can occur in three ways: (1) through express language, (2) as implied from conduct, and (3) through failure to make a timely disaffirmance. Suppose that a minor makes a contract to buy property from an adult. The contract is voidable by the minor, and she can escape liability. But suppose that after reaching her majority she promises to go through with the purchase. The minor has *expressly* ratified the contract she entered

when she was a minor. Her promise is binding, and the adult can recover for breach if the minor fails to carry out the terms of the contract.

Ratification also may be *implied* from a person's conduct. Suppose that the minor, after attaining majority, uses the property involved in the contract, undertakes to sell it to someone else, or performs some other act showing an intention to affirm the contract. She may not thereafter disaffirm the contract but is bound by it. Perhaps the most common form of implied ratification occurs when a minor, after attaining majority, continues to use the property purchased as a minor. This use is obviously inconsistent with the nonexistence of a contract. Whether the contract is performed or still partly executory, the continued use of the property amounts to a ratification and prevents a disaffirmance by the minor. Simply keeping the goods for an unreasonable time after attaining majority has also been construed as a ratification.

In Re The Score Board, Inc.

UNITED STATES DISTRICT COURT, DISTRICT OF NEW JERSEY, 1999
238 B.R. 585

http://scholar.google.com/scholar_case?case=9690754193230293303&q=238+B.R.+585+&hl=en&as_sdt=2,34

FACTS During the spring of 1996, Kobe Bryant (Bryant), then a seventeen-year old star high school basketball player, declared his intention to forgo college and enter the 1996 National Basketball Association (NBA) lottery draft. The Score Board Inc., a company in the business of licensing, manufacturing, and distributing sports and entertainment-related memorabilia, entered into negotiations with Bryant's agent, Arn Tellem (Agent) and Bryant's father, former NBA star Joe "Jelly Bean" Bryant, to sign Bryant to a contract. In early July 1996, Score Board sent Bryant a signed written licensing agreement (agreement). The agreement granted Score Board the right to produce licensed products, such as trading cards, with Bryant's image. Bryant was obligated to make two personal appearances on behalf of Score Board and provide between a minimum of 15,000 and a maximum of 32,500 autographs. Bryant was to receive a $2 stipend for each autograph, after the first 7,500. Under the agreement, Bryant could receive a maximum of $75,000 for the autographs. In addition to being compensated for the autographs, Bryant was entitled to receive a base compensation of $10,000.

Bryant rejected this proposed agreement, and on July 11, 1996, while still a minor, made a counteroffer (counteroffer), signed it, and returned it to Score Board. The counteroffer made several changes to Score Board's

agreement, including the number of autographs. Score Board claimed that they signed the counteroffer and placed it into its files. The copy signed by Score Board was subsequently misplaced and has never been produced by Score Board during these proceedings. Rather, Score Board has produced a copy signed only by Bryant.

On August 23, 1996, Bryant turned eighteen. Three days later, Bryant deposited the check for $10,000 into his account. Bryant subsequently performed his contractual duties for about a year and a half. By late 1997, Bryant grew reluctant to sign any more autographs under the agreement and his Agent came to the conclusion that a fully executed contract did not exist. By this time, Agent became concerned with Score Board's financial condition because it failed to make certain payments to several other players. Score Board claims that the true motivation for Bryant's reluctance stems from his perception that he was becoming a "star" player, and that his autograph was "worth" more than $2.

On March 17, 1998, Score Board mistakenly sent Bryant a check for $1,130 as compensation for unpaid autographs. Bryant was actually entitled to $10,130 and the check for $1,130 was based on a miscalculation.

On March 18, 1998, Score Board filed a voluntary Chapter 11 bankruptcy petition. On March 23, 1998, Agent returned the $1,130 check. Included with the check was a letter that directed Score Board to "immediately cease and desist from any use of" Kobe Bryant's name, likeness, or other publicity rights. Subsequently, Score Board began to sell its assets, including numerous executory contracts with major athletes, including Bryant. Bryant argued that Score Board could not do this, because he believed that a contract never existed. In the alternative, if a contract had been created, Bryant contended that it was voidable because it had been entered into while he was a minor. The Bankruptcy Court ruled in favor of Score Board. Bryant appealed.

DECISION Judgment affirmed.

OPINION Irenas, J. Bryant challenges the Bankruptcy Court's finding that he ratified the agreement upon attaining majority. Contracts made during minority are voidable at the minor's election within a reasonable time after the minor attains the age of majority. [Citations]

The right to disaffirm a contract is subject to the infant's conduct which, upon reaching the age of majority, may amount to ratification. [Citation.] "Any conduct on the part of the former infant which evidences his decision that the transaction shall not be impeached is sufficient for this purpose." [Citation.]

On August 23, 1996, Bryant reached the age of majority, approximately six weeks after the execution of the agreement. On August 26, 1996, Bryant deposited

the $10,000 check sent to him from Debtor (Score Board). Bryant also performed his contractual duties by signing autographs.

The Bankruptcy Court did not presume ratification from inaction as Bryant asserts. It is clear that Bryant ratified the contract from the facts, because Bryant consciously performed his contractual duties.

Bryant asserts that he acted at the insistence of his Agent, who believed that he was obligated to perform by contract. Yet, neither Bryant nor his Agent disputed the existence of a contract until the March 23, 1998, letter by Tellem (Agent). That Bryant may have relied on his Agent is irrelevant to this Court's inquiry and is proper evidence only in a suit against the Agent. To the contrary, by admitting that he acted because he was under the belief that a contract existed, Bryant confirms the existence of the contract. Moreover, it was Bryant who deposited the check, signed the autographs, and made personal appearances.

INTERPRETATION Ratification of a contract may be implied from a person's conduct after the person attains his majority.

CRITICAL THINKING QUESTION What criteria should a court employ in determining what is a reasonable period of time for disaffirmance by a person who has attained majority?

LIABILITY FOR NECESSARIES

Contractual incapacity does not excuse a minor from an obligation to pay for **necessaries**, those things, such as food, shelter, medicine, and clothing, that suitably and reasonably supply his personal needs. Even here, however, the minor is not contractually liable for the agreed price but for the *reasonable* value of the items furnished. Recovery is based on quasi-contract. Thus, if a clothier sells a minor a suit that the minor needs, the clothier can successfully sue the minor. The clothier's recovery, however, is limited to the reasonable value of the suit only, even if this amount is much less than the agreed-upon selling price. In addition, a minor is not liable for anything on the ground that the item is a necessary, unless it has been actually furnished to him and used or consumed by him. In other words, a minor may disaffirm his executory contracts for necessaries and refuse to accept such clothing, lodging, or other items.

Defining "necessaries" is a difficult task. In general, the states regard as necessary those things that the minor

needs to maintain himself in his particular station in life. Items necessary for subsistence and health, such as food, lodging, clothing, medicine, and medical services, are included. But other less essential items, such as textbooks, school instruction, and legal advice, may be included as well. Furthermore, some states enlarge the concept of necessaries to include articles of property and services that a minor needs to earn the money required to provide the necessities of life for himself and his dependents. Nevertheless, many states limit necessaries to items that are not provided to the minor. Thus, if a minor's guardian provides her with an adequate wardrobe, a blouse the minor purchased would *not* be considered a necessary.

Ordinarily, luxury items, such as cameras, tape recorders, stereo equipment, television sets, and motorboats, do not qualify as necessaries. The question concerning whether automobiles and trucks are necessaries has caused considerable controversy, but some courts have recognized that under certain circumstances, an automobile may be a necessary where it is used by the minor for his business activities.

ZELNICK V. ADAMS

SUPREME COURT OF VIRGINIA, 2002
263 VA. 601, 561 S.E.2D 711

http://scholar.google.com/scholar_case?case=13963993610436500611&q=561+S.E.2d+711+&hl=en&as_sdt=2,34

FACTS Jonathan Ray Adams (Jonathan) was born on April 5, 1980, the son of Mildred A. Adams (Adams or mother) and Cecil D. Hylton, Jr. (Hylton or father). Jonathan's parents were never married. Nevertheless, the Florida courts did determine Hylton's paternity of Jonathan. Jonathan's grandfather, Cecil D. Hylton, Sr. (Hylton Sr.), died in 1989 and had established certain trusts under his will, which provided that the trustees had sole discretion to determine who qualified as "issue" under the will.

In 1996, Adams met with an attorney, Robert J. Zelnick (Zelnick), about protecting Jonathan's interest as a beneficiary of the trusts after she had unsuccessfully attempted to get Jonathan recognized as an heir. Adams explained that she could not afford to pay Zelnick's hourly fee and requested legal services on her son's behalf on a contingency fee basis. Zelnick subsequently informed Adams that he had examined a copy of the will and that he was willing to accept the case. Adams went to Zelnick's office the next day, where Zelnick explained that the gross amount of the estate was very large. Nevertheless, Adams signed a retainer agreement (the contract) for Zelnick's firm to represent Jonathan on a one-third contingency fee.

In May 1997, Zelnick initiated a legal action on Jonathan's behalf. A consent decree was entered on January 23, 1998, which ordered that Jonathan was "declared to be the grandchild and issue of Cecil D. Hylton" and was entitled to all benefits under the Will and Trusts of Cecil D. Hylton.

In March 1998, Jonathan's father brought suit against Adams and Zelnick, on Jonathan's behalf, to have the contract with Zelnick declared void. Upon reaching the age of majority, Jonathan filed a petition to intervene, in which he disaffirmed the contract. Jonathan filed a motion for summary judgment asserting that the contract was "void as a matter of law" because it was not a contract for necessaries. Jonathan argued that the 1997 suit was unnecessary due to the Florida paternity decree which conclusively established Hylton's paternity.

The trial court granted Jonathan's motion for summary judgment and ruled that the contingency fee agreement was not binding on Jonathan because he was "in his minority" when the contract was executed. This appeal followed.

DECISION Judgment reversed and remanded.

OPINION Lemons, J. In this appeal, we consider whether a contract for legal services entered into on behalf of a minor is voidable upon a plea of infancy or subject to enforcement as an implied contract for necessaries and, if enforceable, the basis for determining value of services rendered.

Under well- and long-established Virginia law, a contract with an infant is not void, only voidable by the infant upon attaining the age of majority. [Citation.] This oft-cited rule is subject to the relief provided by the doctrine of necessaries which received thorough analysis in the case of *Bear's Adm'x v. Bear*, [citation].

In Bear, we explained that when a court is faced with a defense of infancy, the court has the initial duty to determine, as a matter of law, whether the "things supplied" to the infant under a contract may fall within the general class of necessaries. [Citation.] The court must further decide whether there is sufficient evidence to allow the finder of fact to determine whether the "things supplied" were in fact necessary in the instant case. If either of these preliminary inquiries is answered in the negative, the party who provided the goods or services to the infant under the disaffirmed contract cannot recover. If the preliminary inquiries are answered in the affirmative, then the finder of fact must decide, under all the circumstances, whether the "things supplied" were actually necessary to the "position and condition of the infant." If so, the party who provided the goods or services to the infant is entitled to the "reasonable value" of the things furnished. In contracts for necessaries, an infant is not bound on the express contract, but rather is bound under an implied contract to pay what the goods or services furnished were reasonably worth. [Citation.]

"Things supplied," which fall into the class of necessaries, include "board, clothing and education." [Citation.] Things that are "necessary to [an infant's] subsistence and comfort, and to enable [an infant] to live according to his real position in society" are also considered part of the class of necessaries. [Citation.] * * *

Certainly, the provision of legal services may fall within the class of necessaries for which a contract by or on behalf of an infant may not be avoided or disaffirmed on the grounds of infancy. Generally, contracts for legal services related to prosecuting personal injury actions, and protecting an infant's personal liberty, security, or reputation are considered contracts for necessaries. [Citation.] "Whether attorney's services are to be considered necessaries or not depends on whether or not there is a necessity therefor. If such necessity exists, the infant may be bound.... If there is no necessity for services, there can be no recovery" for the services. [Citation.]

* * *

Other states have also broadened the definition of "necessaries" to include contracts for legal services for the protection of an infant's property rights. * * *

In determining whether the doctrine of necessaries may be applied to defeat an attempt to avoid or disaffirm a contract on the grounds of infancy, the trial court must first determine as a matter of law whether the class of "things supplied" falls within the "general classes of necessaries." We hold that a contract for legal services falls within this class. However, the inquiry does not end with this determination. The ultimate determination is an issue of fact. The trier of fact must conclude that "under all the circumstances, the things furnished were actually necessary to the position and condition of the infant ... and whether the infant was already sufficiently supplied." [Citation.] If the contract does not fall within the "general classes of necessaries," the trial court must, as a matter of law, sustain the plea of infancy and permit the avoidance of the contract. Similarly, if the contract does fall within the "general classes of necessaries," but upon consideration of all of the circumstances, the trier of fact determines that the provision of the particular services or things was not actually necessary, the plea of infancy must be sustained. Where there is a successful avoidance of the contract, the trial court may not circumvent the successful plea of infancy by affording a recovery to the claimant on the theory of *quantum meruit*. However, if the plea of infancy is not sustained, the claimant is not entitled to enforcement of the express contract. Rather, as we have previously held, "even in contracts for necessaries, the infant is not bound on the express contract but on the implied contract to pay what they are reasonably worth." [Citation.]

* * *

Upon review of the record, we hold that the * * * reason stated by the trial court for holding that the necessaries doctrine did not apply, namely that the contract "was conducted while he was in his minority and he's not bound by that," is an error of law. We hold that a contract for legal services is within the "general classes of necessaries" that may defeat a plea of infancy. * * *

* * *

The trial court's determination that the necessaries doctrine did not apply was made upon motion for summary judgment filed by Jonathan. Nowhere in Jonathan's motion for summary judgment is the issue raised that the services were unnecessary at the time rendered * * *. Although Jonathan argues that the services were not necessary at all because he alleges that the Florida litigation resolved the question of his inclusion as a beneficiary under the will of Hylton Sr., the timing of the services was not even mentioned as an issue, much less as a reason for granting summary judgment. * * *

Because the trial court erred in its determination, on this record, on summary judgment, that the doctrine of necessaries did not apply, we will reverse the judgment of the trial court and remand for further proceedings, including the taking of evidence on the issue of the factual determination of necessity "under all of the circumstances." Consistent with this opinion, should the trial court upon remand hold that the doctrine of necessaries does not apply because the evidence adduced does not support the claim, the contract is avoided and no award shall be made.

Should the trial court upon remand hold that the evidence is sufficient to defeat Jonathan's plea of infancy, the trial court shall receive evidence of the reasonable value of the services rendered. * * *

INTERPRETATION Contractual incapacity does not excuse a minor from an obligation to pay the reasonable value of a necessary.

ETHICAL QUESTION Did Jonathan act ethically? Explain.

CRITICAL THINKING QUESTION What factors should a court use in determining whether goods or services are necessary? Explain.

LIABILITY FOR MISREPRESENTATION OF AGE

The states do not agree whether a minor who fraudulently misrepresents her age when entering into a contract has the power to disaffirm. Suppose a contracting minor says that she is eighteen years of age (or twenty-one, if that is the year of attaining majority) and actually looks that old or even older. By the prevailing view in this country, despite her misrepresentation, the minor may nevertheless disaffirm the contract. Some states, however, prohibit disaffirmance if a minor misrepresented her age to an adult who, in good faith, reasonably relied on the misrepresentation. As shown in the case of *Keser v. Chagnon*, other states not following the majority rule either (1) require the minor to restore the other party to the position he occupied before making the contract or (2) allow the defrauded party to recover damages against the minor in tort.

PRACTICAL ADVICE

In all significant contracts, if you have doubts about the age of your customers, have them prove that they are of legal age.

KESER V. CHAGNON

SUPREME COURT OF COLORADO, 1966
159 COLO. 209, 410 P.2D 637

http://scholar.google.com/scholar_case?case=4555401252219612466&q=410+P.2d+637&hl=en&as_sdt=2,34

FACTS On June 11, 1964, Chagnon bought a 1959 Edsel from Keser for $995. Chagnon, who was then a twenty-year-old minor, obtained the contract by falsely advising to Keser that he was over twenty-one years old, the age of majority. On September 25, 1964, two months and four days after his twenty-first birthday, Chagnon disaffirmed the contract and, ten days later, returned the Edsel to Keser. He then brought suit to recover the money he had paid for the automobile. Keser counterclaimed that he suffered damages as the direct result of Chagnon's false representation of his age. A trial was had to the court, sitting without a jury, all of which culminated in a judgment in favor of Chagnon against Keser in the sum of $655.78. This particular sum was arrived at by the trial court in the following manner: the trial court found that Chagnon initially purchased the Edsel for the sum of $995 and that he was entitled to the return of his $995; and then, by way of setoff, the trial court subtracted from the $995 the sum of $339.22, apparently representing the difference between the purchase price paid for the vehicle and the reasonable value of the Edsel on October 5, 1964, the date when the Edsel was returned to Keser.

DECISION Judgment affirmed except as to the calculation of damages for misrepresentation.

OPINION McWilliams, J. Before considering each of these several matters, it is deemed helpful to allude briefly to some of the general principles pertaining to the long-standing policy of the law to protect a minor from at least some of his childish foibles by affording him the right, under certain circumstances, to avoid his contract, not only during his minority but also within a reasonable time after reaching his majority. In [citation] we held that when a minor elects to disaffirm and avoid his contract, the "contract" becomes invalid *ab initio* and that the parties thereto then revert to the same position as if the contract had never been made. In that case we went on to declare that when a minor thus sought to avoid his contract and had in his possession the specific property received by him in the transaction, he was in such circumstance required to return the same as a prerequisite to any avoidance.

In [citation] it is said that a minor failing to disaffirm within a "reasonable time" after reaching his majority loses the right to do so and that just what

constitutes a "reasonable time" is ordinarily a question of fact. As regards the necessity for restoration of consideration, in [citation] it is stated that the minor after disaffirming is "usually required *** to return the consideration, if he can, or the part remaining in his possession or control."

* * *

Keser's *** contention that Chagnon upon attaining his majority ratified the contract by his failure to disaffirm within a reasonable time after becoming twenty-one and by his retention and use of the Edsel prior to its return to the seller is equally untenable. In this connection it is pointed out that Chagnon did not notify Keser of his desire to disaffirm until sixty-six days after he became twenty-one and that he did not return the Edsel until ten days after his notice to disaffirm, during all of which time Chagnon had the possession and use of the vehicle in question. As already noted, when an infant attains his majority he has a reasonable time within which he may thereafter disaffirm a contract entered into during his minority. And this rule is not as strict where, as here, we are dealing with an executed contract. There is no hard and fast rule as to just what constitutes a "reasonable" time within which the infant may disaffirm. *** Suffice it to say, that under the circumstances disclosed by the record we are not prepared to hold that as a matter of law Chagnon ratified the contract either by his actions or by his alleged failure to disaffirm within a reasonable time after reaching his majority. * * *

Finally, error is predicated upon the trial court's finding in connection with Keser's setoff for the damage occasioned him by Chagnon's admitted false representation of his age. In this regard the trial court apparently found that the reasonable value of the Edsel when it was returned to Keser by Chagnon was $655.78, and accordingly went on to allow Keser a setoff in the amount of $339.22, this latter sum representing the difference between the purchase price, $995, and the value of the vehicle on the date it was returned. Finding, then, that Chagnon was entitled to the return of the $995 which he had theretofore paid Keser for the Edsel, the trial court then subtracted therefrom Keser's setoff in the amount of $339.22, and accordingly entered judgment for Chagnon against Keser in the sum of $655.78. Whether it was by accident or design we know not, but $655.78 is apparently the exact amount which Chagnon "owed" the Public Finance Corporation on his note with that company.

INTERPRETATION States vary on the rights of a minor and a defrauded party when a minor fraudulently misrepresents her age when entering into a contract.

ETHICAL QUESTION If a minor misrepresents his age, should he forfeit the right to avoid the contract? Explain.

CRITICAL THINKING QUESTION What rule would you apply in this case? Explain.

LIABILITY FOR TORT CONNECTED WITH CONTRACT

It is well settled that minors are generally liable for their torts. There is, however, a legal doctrine that if a tort and a contract are so "interwoven" that the court must enforce the contract to enforce the tort action, the minor is not liable in tort. Thus, a minor who rents an automobile from an adult enters into a contractual relationship obliging him to exercise reasonable care to protect the property from injury. By negligently damaging the automobile, he breaches that contractual undertaking. But his contractual immunity protects him from an action by the adult based on the contract. By the majority view, the adult cannot successfully sue the minor for damages on a tort theory. For, it is reasoned, a tort recovery would, in effect, be an enforcement of the contract and would defeat the protection that contract law gives the minor. Should the minor depart, however, from the terms of the agreement (e.g., by using a rental automobile for an unauthorized purpose) and in so doing negligently cause damage to the automobile, most courts would hold that the tort is independent and that the adult can collect from the minor.

Incompetent Persons

In this section, we will discuss the contract status of incompetent persons who are under court-appointed guardianship and those who are not adjudicated incompetents.

PERSON UNDER GUARDIANSHIP

If a person is under **guardianship** by *court order*, her contracts are *void* and of no legal effect. A court appoints a *guardian,* generally under the terms of a statute, to control and preserve the property of a person (the *ward* or *adjudicated incompetent*) whose impaired capacity prevents her from managing her own property. Nonetheless, a party dealing with an individual under guardianship may be able to recover the fair value of any necessaries provided to the incompetent. Moreover, the contracts of the ward may be ratified by her guardian during the period of guardianship or by the ward on termination of the guardianship.

MENTAL ILLNESS OR DEFECT

Because a contract is a consensual transaction, the parties to a valid contract must have a certain level of mental capacity. If a person lacks such capacity, or is **mentally incompetent,** the agreement is *voidable.*

Under the traditional cognitive ability test, a person is mentally incompetent if he is unable to comprehend the subject of the contract, its nature, and its probable consequences. Though he need not be proved permanently incompetent to avoid the contract, his mental defect must be something more than a weakness of intellect or a lack of average intelligence. In short, a person is competent unless he is unable to understand the nature and effect of his actions, in which case he may disaffirm the contract even if the other party did not know or had no reason to know of the incompetent's mental condition.

A second type of mental incompetence recognized by the Restatement and some states is a mental condition that impairs a person's ability to act in a reasonable manner. In other words, the person understands what he is doing but cannot control his behavior in order to act in a reasonable and rational way. If the contract he enters is entirely executory or grossly unfair, it is voidable. If, however, the contract is executed and fair and the competent party had no reason to suspect the incompetency of the other, the incompetent must restore the competent party to the *status quo* by returning the consideration he has received or its equivalent in money. If restoration to the *status quo* is impossible, avoidance will depend upon the equities of the situation.

Like minors and persons under guardianship, an incompetent person is liable on the principle of quasi-contract for *necessaries* furnished him, the amount of recovery being the reasonable value of the goods or services. Moreover, an incompetent person may *ratify* or *disaffirm* voidable contracts during a lucid period or when he becomes competent.

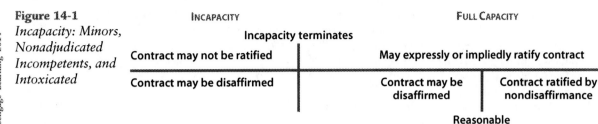

Figure 14-1
Incapacity: Minors, Nonadjudicated Incompetents, and Intoxicated

Intoxicated Persons

A person may *avoid* any contract that he enters into if the other party has reason to know that the person, because of his intoxication, is unable to understand the nature and consequences of his actions or unable to act in a reasonable manner. Such contracts, as in the case that follows, are *voidable*, although they may be ratified when the intoxicated person regains his capacity. Slight intoxication will not destroy one's contractual capacity; on the other hand, to make a contract voidable, a person need not be so drunk that he is totally without reason or understanding.

The effect that the courts allow intoxication to have on contractual capacity is similar to the effect they allow contracts that are voidable because of incompetency, although the courts are even more strict with intoxication due to its voluntary nature. Most courts, therefore,

require that, to avoid a contract, the intoxicated person on regaining his capacity must act promptly to disaffirm and generally must offer to restore the consideration he has received. Individuals who are taking prescribed medication or who are involuntarily intoxicated are treated the same as those who are incompetent under the cognitive ability test. As with incompetent persons, intoxicated persons are liable in quasi-contract for necessaries furnished during their incapacity.

PRACTICAL ADVICE

If you have doubts about the capacity of the other party to a contract, have an individual with full legal capacity cosign the contract.

Figure 14-1 summarizes the voidability of contracts made by persons with contractual incapacity.

FIRST STATE BANK OF SINAI V. HYLAND

SUPREME COURT OF SOUTH DAKOTA, 1987
399 N.W.2D 894

http://scholar.google.com/scholar_case?case=9646538788520684587&q=399+N.W.2d+894&hl=en&as_sclt=2,34

FACTS Randy Hyland, unable to pay two promissory notes due September 19, 1981, negotiated with The First State Bank of Sinai (Bank) for an extension. The Bank agreed on the condition that Randy's father, Mervin, act as cosigner. Mervin, a good customer of the Bank, had executed and paid on time over sixty promissory notes within a seven-year period. Accordingly, the Bank drafted a new promissory note with an April 20, 1982, due date, which Randy took home for Mervin to sign. On April 20, 1982, the new note was unpaid. Randy, on May 5, 1982, brought the Bank a check signed by Mervin to cover the interest owed on the unpaid note and asked for another extension. The Bank agreed to a second extension, again on the condition that Mervin act as cosigner. Mervin, however, refused to sign the last note; and

Randy subsequently declared bankruptcy. The Bank sued Mervin on December 19, 1982. Mervin responded that he was not liable since he had been incapacitated by liquor at the time he signed the note. He had been drinking heavily throughout this period, and in fact had been involuntarily committed to an alcoholism treatment hospital twice during the time of these events. In between commitments, however, Mervin had executed and paid his own promissory note with the Bank and had transacted business in connection with his farm. The trial court held that Mervin's contract as cosigner was void due to alcohol-related incapacity, and the Bank appealed.

DECISION Judgment for the Bank.

OPINION Henderson, J. Historically, the void contract concept has been applied to nullify agreements made by mental incompetents who have contracted *** after a judicial determination of incapacity had been entered. [Citations.] ***

Mervin had numerous and prolonged problems stemming from his inability to handle alcohol. However, he was not judicially declared incompetent during the note's signing.

***

Contractual obligations incurred by intoxicated persons may be voidable. [Citation.] Voidable contracts (contracts other than those entered into following a judicial determination of incapacity) *** may be rescinded by the previously disabled party. [Citation.] However, disaffirmance must be prompt, upon the recovery of the intoxicated party's mental abilities, and upon his notice of the agreement, if he had forgotten it. [Citation.] ***

A voidable contract may also be ratified by the party who had contracted while disabled. Upon ratification, the contract becomes a fully valid legal obligation. [Citation.] Ratification can either be express or implied by conduct. [Citations.] In addition, failure of a party to disaffirm a contract over a period of time may, by itself, ripen into a ratification, especially if rescission will result in prejudice to the other party. [Citations.]

Mervin received both verbal notice from Randy and written notice from Bank on or about April 27, 1982, that the note was overdue. On May 5, 1982, Mervin paid the interest owing with a check which Randy delivered to Bank. This by itself could amount to ratification through conduct. If Mervin wished to avoid the contract, he should have then exercised his right of rescission. We find it impossible to believe that Mervin paid almost $900 in interest without, in his own mind, accepting responsibility for the note. His assertion that paying interest on the note relieved his obligation is equally untenable in light of his numerous past experiences with promissory notes.

***

We conclude that Mervin's obligation to Bank was not void. *** Mervin's obligation on the note was voidable and his subsequent failure to disaffirm (lack of rescission) and his payment of interest (ratification) then transformed the voidable contract into one that is fully binding upon him.

INTERPRETATION An intoxicated party ratifies a contract by not disaffirming it when she is not intoxicated and learns of its existence and by making interest payments on it when she is not intoxicated.

CRITICAL THINKING QUESTION When should a person be allowed to invalidate an agreement because of intoxication? Explain.

Ethical Dilemma

Should a Merchant Sell to One Who Lacks Capacity?

FACTS Alice Richards is a salesclerk for an exclusive department store in Connecticut. She was working in the children's clothing department when an elderly woman, Carrie Johnson, entered the area and began to browse. Because part of her compensation is based on commissions and it had been a slow season, Richards was eager to help her. However, when Richards asked Johnson if she needed any help, Johnson replied, "No, I'm just looking for a new pocketbook." When Richards attempted to direct Johnson to the pocketbooks, Johnson did not appear to respond. Puzzled, Richards began to wonder whether the woman was mentally alert.

Johnson picked out infant's clothing and accessories worth approximately $250. At the cashier's counter she exclaimed how lovely everything was and explained that the jumpers and bath toys would go well with the other new clothes she had purchased for her son, who would soon be back from a cruise in the Bahamas.

Worried that the woman did not know what she was purchasing, Richards asked her manager for assistance. The manager said that the sale should be completed, as long as the store's credit policies were satisfied.

Social, Policy, and Ethical Considerations

1. What would you do?

2. What responsibility does a retail store have in stopping a sale where a reasonable person would assume that the customer lacks capacity? What business policies are appropriate?

3. What are the dangers in assuming a protective position? How can a retailer avoid discrimination and extend appropriate protection?

4. What alternatives does a family have when an elderly member begins to lose capacity?

CHAPTER SUMMARY

Minors

Definition person who is under the age of majority (usually eighteen years)

Liability on Contracts minor's contracts are voidable at the minor's option
* *Disaffirmance* avoidance of the contract; may be done during minority and for a reasonable time after reaching majority
* *Ratification* affirmation of the entire contract; may be done upon reaching majority

Liability for Necessaries a minor is liable for the reasonable value of necessary items (those that reasonably supply a person's needs)

Liability for Misrepresentation of Age prevailing view is that a minor may disaffirm the contract

Liability for Tort Connected with Contract if a tort and a contract are so intertwined that to enforce the tort the court must enforce the contract, the minor is not liable in tort

Incompetent and Intoxicated Persons

Person under Guardianship contracts made by a person placed under guardianship by court order are void

Mental Illness or Defect a contract entered into by a mentally incompetent person (one who is unable to understand the nature and consequences of his acts) is voidable

Intoxicated Persons a contract entered into by an intoxicated person (one who cannot understand the nature and consequence of her actions) is voidable

QUESTIONS

1. Mark, a minor, operates a one-man automobile repair shop. Rose, having heard of Mark's good work on other cars, takes her car to Mark's shop for a thorough engine overhaul. Mark, while overhauling Rose's engine, carelessly fits an unsuitable piston ring on one of the pistons, with the result that Rose's engine is seriously damaged. Mark offers to return the sum that Rose paid him for his work, but refuses to pay for the damage. Rose sues Mark in tort for the damage to her engine. Can Rose recover from Mark in tort for the damage to her engine? Why?

2. Explain the outcome of each transaction.

   a. On March 20, Andy Small became seventeen years old, but he appeared to be at least eighteen (the age of majority). On April 1, he moved into a rooming house in Chicago and orally agreed to pay the landlady $800 a month for room and board, payable at the end of each month. On April 30, he refused to pay his landlady for his room and board for the month of April.

   b. On April 4, he went to Honest Hal's Carfeteria and signed a contract to buy a used car on credit with a small down payment. He made no representation as to his age, but Honest Hal represented the car to be in top condition, which it subsequently turned out not to be. On April 25, he returned the car to Honest Hal and demanded a refund of his down payment.

   c. On April 7, Andy sold and conveyed to Adam Smith a parcel of real estate that he owned. On April 28, he demanded that Adam Smith reconvey the land although the purchase price, which Andy received in cash, had been spent in riotous living.

3. Jones, a minor, owned a 2011 automobile. She traded it to Stone for a 2012 car. Jones went on a three-week trip and found that the 2012 car was not as good as the 2011 car. She asked Stone to return the 2011 car but was told that it had been sold to Tate, who did not know that the car had been obtained by Stone from a minor. Jones thereupon sued Tate for the return of the 2011 car. Is Jones entitled to regain ownership of the 2011 car? Explain.

4. On May 7, Roy, a minor, a resident of Smithton, purchased an automobile from Royal Motors, Inc., for $12,750 in cash. On the same day, he bought a motor scooter from Marks, also a minor, for $1,750 and paid him in full. On June 5, two days before attaining his majority, Roy disaffirmed the contracts and offered to return

the car and the motor scooter to the respective sellers. Royal Motors and Marks each refused the offers. On June 16, Roy brought separate appropriate actions against Royal Motors and Marks to recover the purchase price of the car and the motor scooter. By agreement on July 30, Royal Motors accepted the automobile. Royal then filed a counterclaim against Roy for the reasonable rental value of the car between June 5 and July 30. The car was not damaged during this period. Royal knew that Roy lived twenty-five miles from his place of employment in Smithton and that he probably used the car, as he did, for transportation. What is the decision as to (a) Roy's action against Royal Motors, Inc., and its counterclaim against Roy; and (b) Roy's action against Marks?

5. On October 1, George Jones entered into a contract with Johnson Motor Company, a dealer in automobiles, to buy a car for $10,600. He paid $1,100 down and agreed to make monthly payments thereafter of $325 each. Although he made the first payment on November 1, he failed to make any more payments. Jones was seventeen years old at the time he made the contract, but he represented to the company that he was twenty-one years old because he was afraid the company would not sell the car to him if it knew his real age. His appearance was that of a man of twenty-one years of age. On December 15, the company repossessed the car under the terms provided in the contract. At that time, the car had been damaged and was in need of repairs. On December 20, George Jones became of age and at once disaffirmed the contract and demanded the return of the $1,425 paid on the contract. When the company refused to do so, Jones brought an action to recover the $1,425, and the company set up a counterclaim of $1,500 for expenses it incurred in repairing the car. Who will prevail? Why?

6. Rebecca entered into a written contract to sell certain real estate to Mary, a minor, for $80,000, payable $4,000 on the execution of the contract and $800 on the first day of each month thereafter until paid. Mary paid the $4,000 down payment and eight monthly installments before attaining her majority. Thereafter, Mary

made two additional monthly payments and caused the contract to be recorded in the county where the real estate was located. Mary was then advised by her lawyer that the contract was voidable. After being so advised, Mary immediately tendered the contract to Rebecca, together with a deed reconveying all of Mary's interest in the property to Rebecca. Also, Mary demanded that Rebecca return the money paid under the contract. Rebecca refused the tender and declined to repay any portion of the money paid to her by Mary. Can Mary cancel the contract and recover the amount paid to Rebecca? Explain.

7. Anita sold and delivered an automobile to Marvin, a minor. Marvin, during his minority, returned the automobile to Anita, saying that he disaffirmed the sale. Anita accepted the automobile and said she would return the purchase price to Marvin the next day. Later in the day, Marvin changed his mind, took the automobile without Anita's knowledge, and sold it to Chris. Anita had not returned the purchase price when Marvin took the car. On what theory, if any, can Anita recover from Marvin? Explain.

8. Ira, who in 2010 had been found not guilty of a criminal offense because of insanity, was released from a hospital for the criminally insane during the summer of 2011 and since that time has been a reputable and well-respected citizen and businessperson. On February 1, 2012, Ira and Shirley entered into a contract in which Ira would sell his farm to Shirley for $300,000. Ira now seeks to void the contract. Shirley insists that Ira is fully competent and has no right to avoid the contract. Who will prevail? Why?

9. Daniel, while under the influence of alcohol to the extent that he did not know the nature and consequences of his acts, agreed to sell his 2011 automobile to Belinda for $13,000. The next morning when Belinda went to Daniel's house with the $13,000 in cash, Daniel stated that he did not remember the transaction but that "a deal is a deal." One week after completing the sale, Daniel decides that he wishes to avoid the contract. What is the result?

CASE PROBLEMS

10. Langstraat, age seventeen, owned a motorcycle that he insured against liability with Midwest Mutual Insurance Company. He signed a notice of rejection attached to the policy indicating that he did not desire to purchase uninsured motorists' coverage from the insurance company. Later he was involved in an accident with another motorcycle owned and operated by a party who was uninsured. Langstraat now seeks to recover from the insurance company, asserting that his rejection was not valid because

he is a minor. Can Langstraat recover from Midwest? Explain.

11. G.A.S. married his wife, S.I.S., on January 19, 1995. He began to have mental health problems in 2008; that year, he was hospitalized at the Delaware State Hospital for eight weeks. Similar illnesses occurred in 2010 and in the early part of 2012, with G.A.S. suffering from symptoms such as paranoia and loss of a sense of reality. In early

2013, G.A.S. was still committed to the Delaware State Hospital, attending a regular job during the day and returning to the hospital at night. G.A.S., however, was never adjudicated to be incompetent by any court. During this time, he entered into a separation agreement prepared by his wife's attorney which was grossly unfair to G.A.S. However, G.A.S. never spoke with the attorney about the contents of the agreement; nor did he read it prior to signing. Moreover, G.A.S. was not independently represented by counsel when he executed this agreement. Can G.A.S. disaffirm the separation agreement? Explain.

12. L. D. Robertson bought a pickup truck from King and Julian, who did business as the Julian Pontiac Company. At the time of purchase, Robertson was seventeen years old, living at home with his parents, and driving his father's truck around the county to different construction jobs. According to the sales contract, he traded in a passenger car for the truck and was given $723 credit toward the truck's $1,743 purchase price, agreeing to pay the remainder in monthly installments. After he paid the first month's installment, the truck caught fire and was rendered useless. The insurance agent, upon finding that Robertson was a minor, refused to deal with him. Consequently, Robertson sued to exercise his right as a minor to rescind the contract and to recover the purchase price he had already paid ($723 credit for the car traded in plus the one month's installment). The defendants argue that Robertson, even as a minor, cannot rescind the contract because it was for a necessary item. Are they correct?

13. A fifteen-year-old minor was employed by Midway Toyota, Inc. On August 18, 2011, the minor, while engaged in lifting heavy objects, injured his lower back. In October 2011 he underwent surgery to remove a herniated disk. Midway Toyota paid him the appropriate amount of temporary total disability payments ($153.36 per week) from August 18, 2011, through November 15, 2012. In February 2013 a final settlement was reached for 150 weeks of permanent partial disability benefits totaling $18,403.40. Tom Mazurek represented Midway Toyota in the negotiations leading up to the agreement and negotiated directly with the minor and his mother, Hermoine Parrent. The final settlement agreement was signed by the minor only. Mrs. Parrent was present at the time and did not object to the signing, but neither she nor anyone else of "legal guardian status" cosigned the agreement. The minor later sought to disaffirm the agreement and reopen his workers' compensation case. The workers' compensation court denied his petition, holding that Mrs. Parrent "participated fully in consideration of the offered final settlement and … ratified and approved it on behalf of her ward … to the same legal effect as if she had actually signed [it]." The minor appealed. Decision?

14. Rose, a minor, bought a new Buick Riviera from Sheehan Buick. Seven months later, while still a minor, he attempted to disaffirm the purchase. Sheehan Buick refused to accept the return of the car or to refund the purchase price. Rose, at the time of the purchase, gave all the appearance of being of legal age. The car had been used by him to carry on his school, business, and social activities. Can Rose successfully disaffirm the contract?

15. Haydocy Pontiac sold Jennifer Lee a used automobile for $7,500, of which $6,750 was financed with a note and security agreement. At the time of the sale, Lee, age twenty, represented to Haydocy that she was twenty-one years old, the age of majority then, and capable of contracting. After receiving the car, Lee allowed John Roberts to take possession of it. Roberts took the car and has not returned. Lee has failed to make any further payments on the car. Haydocy has sued to recover on the note, but Lee disaffirms the contract, claiming that she was too young to enter into a valid contract. Can Haydocy recover the money from Lee? Explain.

16. Carol White ordered a $225 pair of contact lenses through an optometrist. White, an emancipated minor, paid $100 by check and agreed to pay the remaining $125 at a later time. The doctor ordered the lenses, incurring a debt of $110. After the lenses were ordered, White called to cancel her order and stopped payment on the $100 check. The lenses could be used by no one but White. The doctor sued White for the value of the lenses. Will the doctor be able to recover the money from White? Explain.

17. Halbman, a minor, purchased a 2008 Mercury from Lemke for $11,250. Under the terms of the contract, Halbman would pay $1,000 down and the balance in $250 weekly installments. Halbman purchased the car as a way to get around and have some fun. Upon making the down payment, Halbman received possession of the car, but Lemke retained the title until the balance was paid. After Halbman had made his first four payments, a connecting rod in the car's engine broke. Lemke denied responsibility but offered to help Halbman repair the engine if Halbman would provide the parts. Halbman, however, placed the car in a garage where the repairs cost $1,637.40. Halbman never paid the repair bill.

Hoping to avoid any liability for the vehicle, Lemke transferred title to Halbman even though Halbman never paid the balance owed. Halbman returned the title with a letter disaffirming the contract and demanded return of the money paid. Lemke refused. As the repair bill remained unpaid, the garage removed the car's engine and transmission and towed the body to Halbman's father's house. Vandalism during the period of storage rendered the car unsalvageable. Several times Halbman requested Lemke to remove the car. Lemke refused. Halbman sued Lemke for the return of his consideration, and Lemke countersued for the amount still owed on the contract. Decision?

18. On April 29, 2011, Kirsten Fletcher and John E. Marshall III jointly signed a lease to rent an apartment for the term beginning on July 1, 2011, and ending on June 30, 2012,

for a monthly rent of $525 per month. At the time the lease was signed, Marshall was not yet eighteen years of age. Marshall turned eighteen on May 30, 2011. The couple moved into the apartment. About two months later, Marshall moved out to attend college, but Fletcher remained. She paid the rent herself for the remaining ten months of the lease and then sought contribution for Marshall's share of the rent plus court costs in the amount of $2,500. Can Fletcher collect from Marshall?

19. Rogers was a nineteen-year-old (the age of majority then being twenty-one) high school graduate pursuing a civil engineering degree when he learned that his wife was expecting a child. As a result, he quit school and sought assistance from Gastonia Personnel Corporation in finding a job. Rogers signed a contract with the employment agency providing that he would pay the agency a service charge if it obtained suitable employment for him. The employment agency found him such a job, but Rogers refused to pay the service charge, asserting that he was a minor when he signed the contract. Gastonia sued to recover the agreed-upon service charge from Rogers. Should Rogers be liable under his contract? If so, for how much?

TAKING SIDES

Joseph Eugene Dodson, age sixteen, purchased a used pickup truck from Burns and Mary Shrader. The Shraders owned and operated Shrader's Auto Sales. Dodson paid $14,900 in cash for the truck. At the time of sale, the Shraders did not question Dodson's age, but thought he was eighteen or nineteen. Dodson made no misrepresentation concerning his age. Nine months after the date of purchase, the truck began to develop mechanical problems. A mechanic diagnosed the problem as a burnt valve but could not be certain. Dodson, who could not afford the repairs, continued to drive the truck until one month later, when the engine "blew up." Dodson parked the vehicle in the front yard of his parents' home and contacted the Shraders to rescind the purchase of the truck and to request a full refund.

a. What arguments would support Dodson's termination of the contract?

b. What arguments would support Shrader's position that the contract is not voidable?

c. Which side should prevail? Explain.

Chapter 15

CONTRACTS IN WRITING

To break an oral agreement which is not legally binding is morally wrong.

TALMUD

CHAPTER OUTCOMES

After reading and studying this chapter, you should be able to:

1. Identify and explain the five types of contracts covered by the general contract statute of frauds and the contracts covered by the Uniform Commercial Code (UCC) statute of frauds provision.

2. Describe the writings that are required to satisfy the general contract and the UCC statute of frauds provisions.

3. Identify and describe the other methods of complying with the general contract and the UCC statute of frauds provisions.

4. Explain the parol evidence rule and identify the situations to which the rule does not apply.

5. Discuss the rules that aid in the interpretation of a contract.

An *oral* contract, that is, one not in writing, is in every way as enforceable as a written contract *unless* otherwise provided by statute. Although most contracts do not need to be in writing to be enforceable, it is highly desirable that significant contracts be written. Written contracts avoid many problems that proving the terms of oral contracts inevitably involve. The process of setting down the contractual terms in a written document also tends to clarify the terms and bring to light problems the parties might not otherwise foresee. Moreover, the terms of a written contract do not change over time, whereas the parties' recollections of the terms might.

When the parties do reduce their agreement to a complete and final written expression, the law (under the parol evidence rule) honors this document by not allowing the parties to introduce any evidence in a lawsuit that would alter, modify, or vary the terms of the written contract. Nevertheless, the parties may differ as to the proper or intended meaning of language contained in the written agreement where such language is ambiguous or susceptible to different interpretations. To determine the proper meaning requires an interpretation, or construction, of the contract. The rules of construction permit the parties to introduce evidence to resolve ambiguity and to show the meaning of the language employed and the sense in which both parties used it.

In this chapter, we will examine (1) the types of contracts that must be in writing to be enforceable, (2) the parol evidence rule, and (3) the rules of contractual interpretation.

STATUTE OF FRAUDS

The **statute of frauds** requires that certain designated types of contracts be evidenced by a writing to be enforceable. Many more types of contracts are not subject to the statute of frauds than are subject to it. Most oral contracts, as previously indicated, are as enforceable and valid as written contracts. If, however, a given contract subject to the statute of frauds is said to be within the statute, to be enforceable it must comply with the requirements of the statute. All other types of contracts are said to be "not within" or "outside" the statute and need not comply with its requirements to be enforceable.

The statute of frauds has no relation whatever to any kind of fraud practiced in the making of contracts. The rules relating to such fraud are rules of common law and are discussed in Chapter 11. The purpose of the statute is to prevent fraud in the proof of certain oral contracts by perjured testimony in court. This purpose is accomplished by requiring certain contracts to be proved by a signed writing. On the other hand, the statute does not prevent the performance of oral contracts if the parties are willing to perform. In brief, the statute relates only to the proof or evidence of a contract. It has nothing to do with the circumstances surrounding the making of a contract or with the validity of a contract.

> ## PRACTICAL ADVICE
> Significant contracts should be memorialized in a writing signed by both parties.

Contracts within the Statute of Frauds

The following five kinds of contracts are within the statute of frauds as most states have adopted it. Compliance requires a writing signed by the party to be charged (the party against whom the contract is to be enforced).

1. Promises to answer for the duty of another

2. Promises of an executor or administrator to answer personally for a duty of the decedent whose funds he is administering

3. Agreements upon consideration of marriage

4. Agreements for the transfer of an interest in land

5. Agreements not to be performed within one year

A sixth type of contract within the original English statute of frauds applied to contracts for the sale of goods. The Uniform Commercial Code (UCC) now governs the enforceability of contracts of this kind.

The various provisions of the statute of frauds apply independently. Accordingly, a contract for the sale of an interest in land may also be a contract in consideration of marriage, a contract not to be performed in one year, *and* a contract for the sale of goods.

In addition to those contracts specified in the original statute, most states require that other contracts be evidenced by a writing as well—for example, a contract to make a will, to authorize an agent to sell real estate, or to pay a commission to a real estate broker. In addition, UCC Article 9 requires that contracts creating certain types of security interests be in writing. On the other hand, UCC Revised Article 8, which all states have adopted, provides that the statute of frauds does *not* apply to contracts for the sale of securities. Finally, Article 1 of the UCC requires that contracts for the sale of other personal property for more than $5,000 be in writing. The 2001 Revisions to Article 1, however, has deleted this requirement.

ELECTRONIC RECORDS

One significant impediment to e-commerce has been the questionable enforceability of contracts entered into through electronic means such as the Internet or e-mail because of the writing requirements under contract and sales law (statute of frauds). In response, the *Uniform Electronic Transactions Act (UETA)* was promulgated by the National Conference of Commissioners on Uniform State Laws (NCCUSL) in July 1999, and has been adopted by forty-seven states. The other three states, Illinois, New York, and Washington, have statutes pertaining to electronic transactions under consideration. UETA applies only to transactions between parties each of which has agreed to conduct transactions by electronic means. It gives full effect to electronic contracts, encouraging their widespread use, and develops a uniform legal framework for their implementation. UETA protects electronic signatures and contracts from being denied enforcement because of the statute of frauds. Section 7 of UETA accomplishes this by providing the following:

1. A record or signature may not be denied legal effect or enforceability solely because it is in electronic form.

2. A contract may not be denied legal effect or enforceability solely because an electronic record was used in its formation.

3. If a law requires a record to be in writing, an electronic record satisfies the law.

4. If a law requires a signature, an electronic signature satisfies the law.

Section 14 of UETA further validates contracts formed by machines functioning as electronic agents for parties to a transaction: "A contract may be formed by the interaction of electronic agents of the parties, even if no individual was aware of or reviewed the electronic agents' actions or the resulting terms and agreements." The Act excludes from its coverage wills, codicils, and testamentary trusts as well as all Articles of the UCC except Articles 2 and 2A.

In addition, Congress in 2000 enacted the *Electronic Signatures in Global and National Commerce (E-Sign)*. The Act, which uses language very similar to that of UETA, makes electronic records and signatures valid and enforceable across the United States for many types of transactions in or affecting interstate or foreign commerce. E-Sign does not generally preempt UETA. E-Sign does not require any person to agree to use or accept electronic records or electronic signatures. The Act defines transactions quite broadly to include the sale, lease, exchange, and licensing of personal property and services, as well as the sale, lease, exchange, or other disposition of any interest in real property. E-Sign defines an electronic record as "a contract or other re- cord created, generated, sent, communicated, received, or stored by electronic means." It defines an electronic signature as "an electronic sound, symbol, or process, attached to or logically associated with a contract or other record and executed or adopted by a person with the intent to sign the record." Like UETA, E-Sign ensures that Internet and e-mail agreements will not be unenforceable because of the statute of frauds by pro- viding that

1. a signature, contract, or other record relating to such transaction may not be denied legal effect, validity, or enforceability solely because it is in electronic form; and

2. a contract relating to such transaction may not be denied legal effect, validity, or enforceability solely because an electronic signature or electronic record was used in its formation.

To protect consumers, E-Sign provides that they must consent *electronically* to conducting transactions with electronic records after being informed of the types of hardware and software required. Prior to consent, consumers must also receive a "clear and conspicuous" statement informing consumers of their right to (1) have the record provided on paper or in nonelectronic form; (2) after consenting to electronic

records, receive paper copies of the electronic record; and (3) withdraw consent to receiving electronic records.

As defined by E-Sign, an electronic agent is a com- puter program or other automated means used inde- pendently to initiate an action or respond to electronic records or performances in whole or in part without review or action by an individual at the time of the action or response. The Act validates contracts or other records relating to a transaction in or affecting interstate or foreign commerce formed by electronic agents so long as the action of each electronic agent is legally attribut- able to the person to be bound.

E-Sign specifically excludes certain transactions, including (1) wills, codicils, and testamentary trusts; (2) adoptions, divorces, and other matters of family law; and (3) the UCC other than sales and leases of goods.

SURETYSHIP PROVISION

The **suretyship provision** applies to a contractual prom- ise by a **surety** (*promisor*) to a *creditor* (*promisee*) to perform the duties or obligations of a third person (**principal debtor**) if the principal debtor does not per- form. Thus, if a mother tells a merchant to extend $1,000 worth of credit to her son and says, "If he doesn't pay, I will," the promise is a suretyship and must be evidenced by a writing (or have a sufficient elec- tronic record) to be enforceable. The factual situation can be reduced to the simple idea that, "If X doesn't pay, I will." The promise is said to be a **collateral promise**, in that the promisor is not primarily liable. The mother does not promise to pay in any event; her promise is to pay only if the one primarily obligated, the son, defaults.

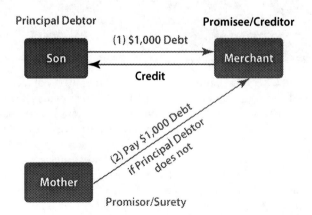

Thus, a suretyship involves three parties and two contracts. The primary contract, between the principal debtor and the creditor, creates the indebtedness. The collateral contract is made by the third person (surety) directly with the creditor, whereby the surety promises to pay the debt to the creditor in case the principal debtor fails to do so. For a complete discussion of suretyship, see Chapter 37. See *Rosewood Care Center, Inc. v. Caterpillar, Inc.* later in this chapter.

Original Promise If the promisor makes an **original promise** by undertaking to become primarily liable, then the statute of frauds does not apply. For example, a father tells a merchant to deliver certain items to his daughter and says, "I will pay $400 for them." The father is not promising to answer for the debt of another; rather, he is making the debt his own. It is to the father, and to the father alone, that the merchant extends credit; to the father alone the creditor may look for payment. The statute of frauds does not apply, and the promise may be oral.

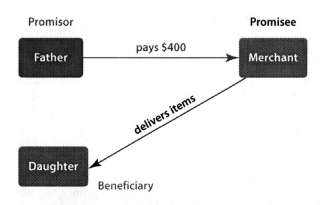

PRACTICAL ADVICE

When entering into a contract with two parties promising you that they will perform, make them both original promisors and avoid having a surety. In any event, if the contract is for a significant amount of money, have both parties sign a written agreement.

Main Purpose Doctrine The courts have developed an exception to the suretyship provision called the "main purpose doctrine" or "leading object rule." In cases in which the **main purpose** of the promisor is to obtain an economic benefit for herself that she did not previously have, then the promise comes within the exception and is *outside* the statute. The expected benefit to the surety "must be such as to justify the conclusion that his main purpose in making the promise is to advance his own interest." The fact that the surety received consideration for his promise or that he might receive a slight and indirect advantage is insufficient to bring the promise within the main purpose doctrine.

Suppose that a supply company has refused to furnish materials on the credit of a building contractor. Faced with a possible slowdown in the construction of his building, the owner of the land promises the supplier that if the supplier will extend credit to the contractor, the owner will pay if the contractor does not. Here, the purpose of the promisor was to serve an economic interest of his own, even though the performance of the promise would discharge the duty of another. The intent to benefit the contractor was at most incidental, and courts will enforce oral promises of this type.

ROSEWOOD CARE CENTER, INC., V. CATERPILLAR, INC.

SUPREME COURT OF ILLINOIS, 2007
226 ILL.2D 559, 877 N.E.2D 1091, 315 ILL.DEC. 762
http://scholar.google.com/scholar_case?case=14227814297099921037&q=877+N.E.2d+1091&hl=en&as_sdt=2,22

FACTS On January 3, 2002, Caterpillar contacted HSM Management Services (HSM), the management agent for Plaintiff, Rosewood Care Center, Inc. (Rosewood), a skilled nursing facility. Caterpillar requested that Rosewood admit Betty Jo Cook, an employee of Caterpillar, on a "managed care basis (fixed rate)." HSM advised Caterpillar that Rosewood would not admit Cook on those terms. Shortly thereafter, on January 10, Dr. Norma Just, Caterpillar's employee in charge of medical care relating to workers' compensation claims, contacted HSM. Just told HSM that Cook had sustained a work-related injury and was receiving medical care at Caterpillar's expense under the

workers' compensation laws. Just requested that Cook be admitted to Rosewood for skilled nursing care and therapy, and stated that the cost of Cook's care would be 100 percent covered and paid directly by Caterpillar to Rosewood with a zero deductible and no maximum limit. Just further advised HSM that Cook had been precertified for four weeks of care. Just asked that Rosewood send the bills for Cook's care to Caterpillar's workers' compensation division. On January 20, "Sue" from Dr. Just's office telephoned HSM and confirmed approval for Cook's transfer from the hospital to Rosewood. On January 30, Sue reconfirmed, via telephone, Caterpillar's authorization for Cook's care and treatment in accordance with the January 10 agreement, except that Sue now advised HSM that Cook was precertified for two weeks of care instead of the original four weeks. On January 30, Cook was admitted to Rosewood. Upon her admission, Cook signed a document entitled "Assignment of Insurance Benefits" as required by law. In this document, Cook assigned any insurance benefits she might receive to Rosewood and acknowledged her liability for any unpaid services. Caterpillar, through its health care management company, continued to orally "authorize" care for Cook and did so on February 8, February 25, March 11, March 21, April 8, April 18, May 16, and June 4. Cook remained at Rosewood until June 13, 2002. The total of Rosewood's charges for Cook's care amounted to $181,857. Caterpillar never objected to the bills being sent to it for Cook's care, nor did it ever advise Rosewood that treatment was not authorized. However, Caterpillar ultimately refused to pay for services rendered to Cook.

The plaintiff filed an action against Caterpillar seeking reimbursement for the services provided to Cook while she was a patient at Rosewood. In response, Caterpillar moved to dismiss the complaint, arguing that the alleged promise to pay for Cook's care was not enforceable because it was not in writing as required by the statute of frauds. The trial court granted Caterpillar's motion for summary judgment and Rosewood appealed. The appellate court reversed and remanded.

DECISION Judgment of the appellate court affirmed and remanded.

OPINION Burke, J. In general, the statute of frauds provides that a promise to pay the debt of another, *i.e.*, a suretyship agreement, is unenforceable unless it is in writing. * * *

* * *

The plain object of the statute is to require higher and more certain evidence to charge a party, where he does not receive the substantial benefit of the transaction, and where another is primarily liable to pay the debt or discharge the duty; and thereby to afford greater security against the setting up of fraudulent demands, where the party sought to be charged is another than the real debtor, and whose debt or duty, on performance of the alleged contract by such third person, would be discharged. [Citation.]* * *

II. "Main Purpose" or "Leading Object" Rule
* * * According to Rosewood, Caterpillar's promise falls outside the statute of frauds pursuant to the "main purpose" or "leading object" rule. Under this rule, when the "main purpose" or "leading object" of the promisor/surety is to subserve or advance its own pecuniary or

business interests, the promise does not fall within the statute. [Citation.] As section 11 of the Restatement (Third) of Suretyship & Guaranty states:

A contract that all or part of the duty of the principal obligor to the obligee shall be satisfied by the secondary obligor is not within the Statute of Frauds as a promise to answer for the duty of another if the consideration for the promise is in fact or apparently desired by the secondary obligor mainly for its own economic benefit, rather than the benefit of the principal obligor. [Citation.]

The reason for the "main purpose" or "leading object" rule has been explained:

Where the secondary obligor's main purpose is its own pecuniary or business advantage, the gratuitous or sentimental element often present in suretyship is eliminated, the likelihood of disproportion in the values exchanged between secondary obligor and obligee is reduced, and the commercial context commonly provides evidentiary safeguards. Thus, there is less need for cautionary or evidentiary formality than in other secondary obligations. [Citations.]

* * *

It is clear * * * that the "main purpose" or "leading object" rule, as set out in the Restatements, has been a part of Illinois law since 1873. We note that the majority of jurisdictions have adopted this rule as well. [Citations.]

Applying this rule in the case at bar, Caterpillar denies that the "main purpose" for its alleged promise to Rosewood was to promote its own interest. Caterpillar also denies that it received any benefit from the agreement. Alternatively, Caterpillar argues that we should remand this cause for further proceedings to determine the "main purpose" or "leading object" of its promise.

Whether the "main purpose" or "leading object" of the promisor is to promote a pecuniary or business advantage to it is generally a question for the trier of fact. [Citation.] * * *

Here, a decision on what was Caterpillar's "main purpose" or "leading object" in making the promise cannot be made based on the allegations in the complaint. * * * The determination must be made by the trier of fact based on evidence to be presented by the parties. * * *

III. Whether a Suretyship Was Created in This Case
* * * Rosewood argues that no suretyship was created by Caterpillar's promise. According to Rosewood, Caterpillar contracted directly with Rosewood, became liable for its own commitment, and received benefits as a result. A suretyship exists when one person undertakes an obligation of another person who is also under an obligation or duty to the creditor/obligee. [Citation.] Specifically, "[a] contract is not within the Statute of

Frauds as a contract to answer for the duty of another unless the promisee is an obligee of the other's duty, the promisor is a surety for the other, and the promisee knows or has reason to know of the suretyship relation." [Citation.] ******

The question of whether Caterpillar's promise was a suretyship or not, like the question regarding Caterpillar's "main purpose" or "leading object," cannot be determined on the basis of allegations in Rosewood's complaint. This question is a factual one to be made based on evidence to be presented by the parties.

Accordingly, this issue must also be resolved by the circuit court on remand.

INTERPRETATION When the "main purpose" or "leading object" of the surety is to advance its own pecuniary or business interests, the promise does not fall within the statute.

CRITICAL THINKING QUESTION Should the contracts of a surety have to be in writing? Explain.

Promise Made to Debtor The suretyship provision has been interpreted *not* to include promises made to a *debtor*. For example, D owes a debt to C. S promises D to pay D's debt. Because the promise of S was made to the debtor (D), not the creditor (C), the promise is enforceable even if it is oral.

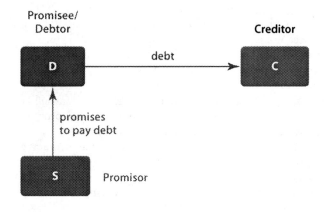

EXECUTOR-ADMINISTRATOR PROVISION

The **executor-administrator provision** applies to the promises of an executor of a decedent's will, or to those of the administrator of the estate if there is no will, to answer personally for a duty of the decedent. An **executor** or **administrator** is a person appointed by a court to carry out, subject to order of court, the administration of the estate of a deceased person. If the will of a decedent nominates a certain person as executor, the court usually appoints that person. (For a more detailed discussion of executors, administrators, and the differences between the two, see Chapter 50.) If an executor or administrator promises to answer personally for a duty of the decedent, the promise is unenforceable unless it is in writing or in proper electronic form. For example, Edgar, who is Donna's

son and executor of Donna's will, recognizes that Donna's estate will not have enough funds to pay all of the decedent's debts. He orally promises Clark, one of Donna's creditors, that he will personally pay all of his mother's debts in full. Edgar's oral promise is not enforceable. This provision does not apply, however, to promises to pay debts of the deceased out of assets of the estate.

The executor-administrator provision is thus a specific application of the suretyship provision. Accordingly, the exceptions to the suretyship provision also apply to this provision.

MARRIAGE PROVISION

The notable feature of the marriage provision is that it does not apply to mutual promises to marry. Rather, the provision applies only if a promise to marry is made in consideration for some promise other than a mutual promise to marry. Therefore, this provision covers Adams's promise to convey title to a certain farm to Barnes if Barnes accepts Adams's proposal of marriage.

LAND CONTRACT PROVISION

The land contract provision covers promises to transfer any **interest in land**, which includes any right, privilege, power, or immunity in real property. Thus, all promises to transfer, buy, or pay for an interest in land, including ownership interests, leases, mortgages, options, and easements, are within the provision.

The land contract provision does not include contracts to transfer an interest in personal property. It also does not cover short-term leases, which by statute in most states are those for one year or less; contracts to build a building on a piece of land; contracts to do work on the land; or contracts to insure a building.

An oral contract for the transfer of an interest in land may be enforced if the party seeking enforcement has so changed his position in reasonable reliance on the contract that a court can prevent injustice only by enforcing the contract. In applying this *part performance* exception, many states require that the transferee has paid a portion or all of the purchase price *and* either has taken possession of the real estate or has started to make valuable improvements on the land. Payment of part or all of the price is not sufficient in itself to make the contract enforceable under this exception. For example, Jane orally agrees to sell land to Jack for $30,000. With Jane's consent, Jack takes possession of the land, pays Jane $10,000, builds a house on the land, and occupies it Several years later, Jane repudiates the contract. The courts will enforce the contract against Jane.

An oral promise by a purchaser is also enforceable if the seller fully performs by conveying the property to the purchaser.

One-Year Provision

The statute of frauds requires that all contracts that *cannot* be fully performed within one year of the making of the contract be in writing or in proper electronic form.

The Possibility Test   To determine whether a contract falls within the one-year provision, the courts ask whether it is *possible* for the performance of the contract to be completed within a year. Under the majority rule, the **possibility test** does not ask whether the agreement is likely to be performed within one year from the date it was formed; nor does it ask whether the parties think that performance will occur within the year. The enforceability of the contract depends *not* on probabilities or on actual subsequent events but on whether the terms of the contract make it possible for performance to occur within one year. For example, an oral contract between Alice and Bill for Alice to build a bridge, which should reasonably take three years, is generally enforceable if it is possible, although extremely unlikely and difficult, for Alice to perform the contract in one year. Similarly, if Alice agrees to employ Bill for life, this contract is also not within the statute of frauds. It is possible that Bill may die within the year, in which case the contract would be completely performed. The contract is therefore one that is *fully performable* within a year. Contracts of indefinite duration are likewise excluded from the provision. On the other hand, an oral contract to employ another person for thirteen months could not possibly be performed within a year and is therefore unenforceable.

Mackay v. Four Rivers Packing Co.

Supreme Court of Idaho, 2008
179 P.3d 1064

http://scholar.google.com/scholar_case?case=3479455732652915832&q=179+P.+3d+1064+&hl=en&as_sdt=2,34

FACTS Four Rivers operates an onion packing plant near Weiser, Idaho. Randy Smith, the general manager of Four Rivers, hired Stuart Mackay as a field man during the summer of 1999 to secure onion contracts from growers in the area. Four Rivers began experiencing financial difficulties in late 1999. All employees, including Mackay, were laid off at this time because one of the owners of Four Rivers filed suit to prevent the company from conducting business. When the lawsuit was resolved, Smith rehired Mackay as a field man. According to Mackay, Four Rivers offered him a long-term employment contract in March of 2000 to continue working as a field man up to the time of his retirement. Mackay claims he accepted the long-term offer of employment and advised Four Rivers that he may not retire for approximately ten years, at around age sixty-two. Four Rivers denies extending such an offer to Mackay. In 2001, Mackay asked Four Rivers for a written contract of employment. He refused to sign the

agreement that was prepared because it gave Four Rivers the right to terminate his employment at any time. On March 7, 2003, Smith terminated Mackay's employment relationship without notice. Smith claims that Mackay's performance was not satisfactory because he was not obtaining the quantity of onions necessary to keep Four Rivers' packing plant operational on a full-time basis, resulting in the closure of the packing plant in February 2003. Four Rivers claims its employees, including Mackay, were laid off at this time as a result of the early closure. Mackay claims that Four Rivers closed due to the price of onions at the time. Mackay applied for unemployment benefits in 2003, stating in his application that he was laid off due to company financial difficulties. Smith states he offered to rehire Mackay in a different position later that year, and Mackay declined.

Mackay sued Four Rivers on August 24, 2004, claiming that Four Rivers breached his oral long-term employment contract. Four Rivers answered by alleging that a contract such as that claimed by Mackay is unenforceable under the Idaho Statute of Frauds because the agreement could not be performed within one year of its making and therefore Mackay was an "at will" employee. Four Rivers moved for summary judgment in October 2006, and the district court granted its motion. The court concluded that the alleged contract could not be performed by its terms within one year and would therefore be invalid in Idaho.

DECISION The decision of the trial court is vacated and the case is remanded.

OPINION Jones, J. The parties disagree regarding the proper application of Idaho's Statute of Frauds. According to Mackay, the longstanding rule in Idaho is that where an agreement depends upon a condition which may ripen within a year, even though it may not mature until much later, the agreement does not fall within the Statute. Since the alleged contract here contains a term that it will last until Mackay retires, and Mackay could have retired within the first year, the oral contract does not violate the Statute. * * *

Four Rivers denies entering into a long-term contract of employment, and * * * claims the contract violates [the] Idaho [Statute of Frauds] * * *

Idaho's Statute of Frauds provision * * * provides that "an agreement that by its terms is not to be performed within a year from the making thereof" is invalid, unless the same or some note or memorandum thereof, be in writing and subscribed by the party charged, or by his agent. [Citation.] * * * Under the prevailing interpretation, the enforceability of a contract under the one-year provision does not turn on the actual course of subsequent events, nor on the expectations of the parties as to the probabilities. [Citation.] Contracts of uncertain duration are simply excluded, and the provision covers only those contracts whose performance cannot possibly be completed within a year. [Citation.]

Leading treatises follow this general rule. It is well settled that the oral contracts invalidated by the Statute because they are not to be performed within a year include only those which *cannot* be performed within that period. [Citation.] A promise which is not likely to be performed within a year, and which in fact is not performed within a year, is not within the Statute, if at the time the contract is made there is a possibility in law and in fact that full performance such as the parties intended may be completed before the expiration of a year. [Citation.] The question is not what the probable, or expected, or actual, performance of the contract was, but whether the contract, according to the reasonable interpretation of its terms, required that it could not be performed within the year. [Citation.] Further, a promise which is performable at or until the happening of any specified contingency which may or may not occur within a year is not within the Statute. [Citation.]

Idaho cases are in accord. A contract which is capable of being performed and might have been fully performed and terminated within a year does not fall within the Statute. [Citation.] Where the termination of a contract is dependent upon the happening of a contingency which may occur within a year, although it may not happen until the expiration of a year, the contract is not within the Statute, since it may be performed within a year. [Citations.]

In this case, the district court applied the *Burton* decision and found that the alleged oral contract could not, by its terms, be completed within a year. In *Burton,* the plaintiff alleged there was an implied contract, which guaranteed her employment until she reached retirement, at age 65. * * * This case differs. In this case, Mackay alleges the term of the contract is until retirement. * * * Unlike the contract in *Burton,* which specified "until age 65," the alleged contract term in this case is indefinite. Thus, the district court erred when it held *Burton* applied to preclude enforcement of the contract alleged in this case.

Rather, this case falls under the general rule cited in numerous Idaho cases and in the Restatement (Second) of Contracts. For the purposes of summary judgment, we must take as true Mackay's allegation that the contract was to last "until retirement." Since Mackay could have retired within one year under the terms of the alleged contract, this contract is outside Idaho's Statute of Frauds provision. * * * Since the event at issue here—Mackay's retirement—could possibly have occurred within one year, the Statute does not bar evidence of such contract.

INTERPRETATION If it is possible to perform fully a contract within one year, the contract does not fall within the statute of frauds.

CRITICAL THINKING QUESTION Do you agree with the one-year provision? Explain.

Computation of Time   The year runs from the time the *agreement is made*, not from the time when the performance is to begin. For example, on January 1, 2012, A hires B to work for eleven months starting on May 1, 2012, under the terms of an oral contract That contract will be fully performed on March 31, 2013, which is more than one year after January 1, 2012, the date the contract was made. Consequently, the contract is *within* the statute of frauds and unenforceable because it is oral.

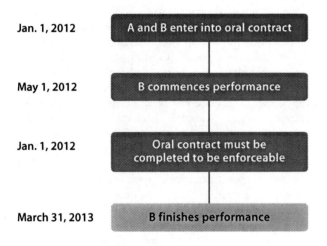

Jan. 1, 2012	A and B enter into oral contract
May 1, 2012	B commences performance
Jan. 1, 2012	Oral contract must be completed to be enforceable
March 31, 2013	B finishes performance

Similarly, a contract for a year's performance that is to begin three days after the date of the making of the contract is within the statute and, if oral, is unenforceable. If, however, the performance is to begin the day following the making or, under the terms of the agreement, *could* have begun the following day, it is not within the statute and need not be in writing.

Full Performance by One Party   Where a contract has been fully performed by one party, most courts hold that the promise of the other party is enforceable even though by its terms its performance was not possible within one year. For example, Jane borrows $4,800 from Tom. Jane orally promises to pay Tom $4,800 in three annual installments of $1,600. Jane's promise is enforceable, despite the one-year provision, because Tom has fully performed by making the loan.

SALE OF GOODS

The English statute of frauds, which applied to contracts for the sale of goods, has been used as a prototype for the UCC, Article 2, statute of frauds provision. The UCC provides that a contract for the sale of goods for the price of *$500 or more* is not enforceable unless there is some writing or record sufficient to indicate that a contract for sale has been made between the parties. The Code defines *goods* as movable personal property.

Admission   The Code permits an oral contract for the sale of goods to be enforced against a party who, in his pleading, testimony, or otherwise, admits in court that a contract was made; but the Code limits enforcement to the quantity of goods he admits. Moreover, some courts hold that, by performing over a period of time, for example, a party may implicitly admit the existence of a contract. Some courts now apply this exception to other statute of frauds provisions.

Specially Manufactured Goods   The Code permits enforcement of an oral contract for goods specially manufactured for a buyer, but only if evidence indicates that the goods were made for the buyer and the seller can show that he has made a *substantial beginning* of their manufacture before receiving any notice of repudiation. If the goods, although manufactured on special order, may be readily resold in the ordinary course of the seller's business, this exception does not apply.

KALAS V. COOK

APPELLATE COURT OF CONNECTICUT, 2002
70 CONN.APP. 477, 800 A.2D 553, 47 U.C.C. REP. SERV. 2D 1307
http://scholar.google.com/scholar_case?case=9737435026218396545&q=800+A.2d+553&hl=en&as_sdt=2,34

FACTS   The plaintiff, Barbara H. Kalas, doing business as Clinton Press of Tolland, operated a printing press and, for several decades, provided written materials, including books and pamphlets, for Adelma G. Simmons. Simmons ordered these materials for use and sale at her farm, known as Caprilands Herb Farm (Caprilands). The defendant has not suggested that these materials could have been sold on the open market. Due to limited space at Caprilands, the plaintiff and Simmons agreed that the written materials would remain stored at the plaintiff's print shop until Simmons decided that delivery was necessary. The materials were delivered either routinely or upon request by Simmons and were paid for according to the invoice from plaintiff.

In early 1997, the plaintiff decided to close her business. The plaintiff and Simmons agreed that the materials printed for Caprilands and stored at the plaintiff's print shop would be delivered and paid for upon delivery. On December 3, 1997, Simmons died. The plaintiff submitted a claim against the estate for $24,599.38 for unpaid deliveries to Caprilands. (The defendant, Edward W. Cook, is the executor of the estate of Simmons). The defendant denied these allegations and raised a defense under the statute of frauds.

The trial ruled that as a contract for the sale of goods, its enforcement was not precluded by the Uniform Commercial Code (UCC) statute of frauds provision. Accordingly, the court rendered a judgment in favor of the plaintiff in the amount of $24,599.38. The defendant appealed.

DECISION Judgment affirmed.

OPINION Peters, J. On appeal, the defendant argues that the oral contract was invalid *** because a writing was required by § 2-201. ***

Contracts for the sale of goods *** are governed by § 2-201. [Citations.]

Under § 2-201, oral agreements for the sale of goods at a price of $ 500 or more are presumptively unenforceable. [Citations.] The applicable provisions in this case, however, are other subsections of § 2-201.

Under § 2-201(3)(a), an oral contract for the sale of goods is enforceable if the goods in question are "specially manufactured." In determining whether the specially manufactured goods exception applies, courts generally apply a four part standard:

> (1) the goods must be specially made for the buyer; (2) the goods must be unsuitable for sale to others in the ordinary course of the seller's business; (3) the seller must have substantially begun to have manufactured the goods or to have a commitment for their procurement; and (4) the

manufacture or commitment must have been commenced under circumstances reasonably indicating that the goods are for the buyer and prior to the seller's receipt of notification of contractual repudiation. [Citation.]

In applying this standard, "courts have traditionally looked to the goods themselves. The term 'specially manufactured,' therefore, refers to the nature of the particular goods in question and not to whether the goods were made in an unusual, as opposed to the regular, business operation or manufacturing process of the seller." [Citations.]

Printed material, particularly that, as in this case, names the buyer, has been deemed by both state and federal courts to fall within the exception set out for specially manufactured goods. [Citations.]

It is inherent in the court's findings that the printed materials in the present case were specially manufactured goods. The materials were printed specifically for Caprilands. The materials included brochures and labels with the Caprilands name, as well as books that were written and designed by Simmons. The plaintiff testified that the books were printed, as Simmons had requested, in a rustic style with typed inserts and hand-drawn pictures. Therefore, none of these materials was suitable for sale to others. It is undisputed that, at the time of breach of the alleged contract, goods printed for Simmons already had been produced.

We conclude that, in light of the nature of the goods at issue *** this case falls within the exception for specially manufactured goods. To be enforceable, the agreement for their production was, therefore, not required to be in writing under § 2-201(3)(a).

INTERPRETATION An oral contract for the sale of goods is enforceable if the goods in question are specially manufactured.

ETHICAL QUESTION Did the executor of Simmons' estate act ethically? Explain.

CRITICAL THINKING QUESTION Do you agree with the court's decision? Explain.

Delivery or Payment and Acceptance Under the Code, delivery and acceptance of part of the goods, or payment and acceptance of part of the price, validates the contract but only for the goods that have been accepted or for which payment has been accepted. To illustrate, Liz orally agrees to buy one thousand watches from David for $15,000. David delivers three hundred watches to Liz, who receives and accepts the watches.

The oral contract is enforceable to the extent of three hundred watches ($4,500)—those received and accepted—but is unenforceable to the extent of seven hundred watches ($10,500).

A summary of the contracts within, and the exceptions to, the statute of frauds is provided in Concept Review 15-1.

CONCEPT REVIEW 15-1

The Statute of Frauds

Contracts within the Statute of Frauds	Exceptions
Suretyship—a promise to answer for the duty of another	• Main purpose rule • Original promise • Promise made to debtor
Executor–Administrator—a promise to answer personally for debt of decedent	• Main purpose rule • Original promise • Promise made to debtor
Agreements made upon consideration of marriage	• Mutual promises to marry
Agreements for the transfer of an interest in land	• Part performance plus detrimental reliance • Seller conveys property
Agreements not to be performed within one year	• Full performance by one party • Possibility of performance within one year
Sale of goods for $500 or more	• Admission • Specially manufactured goods • Delivery or payment and acceptance

© Cengage Learning 2014

MODIFICATION OR RESCISSION OF CONTRACTS WITHIN THE STATUTE OF FRAUDS

Oral contracts modifying previously existing contracts are unenforceable if the resulting contract is within the statute of frauds. The reverse is also true: an oral modification of a prior contract is enforceable if the new contract is not within the statute of frauds.

Thus, examples of unenforceable oral contracts include an oral promise to guarantee the additional duties of another, an oral agreement to substitute different land for that described in the original contract, and an oral agreement to extend an employee's contract for six months to a total of two years. On the other hand, an oral agreement to modify an employee's contract from two years to six months at a higher salary is not within the statute of frauds and is enforceable.

Under the UCC, the decisive point is the contract price after modification. If the parties enter into an oral contract to sell for $450 a motorcycle to be delivered to the buyer and later, prior to delivery, orally agree that the seller shall paint the motorcycle and install new tires and that the buyer shall pay a price of $550, the modified contract is unenforceable. Conversely, if the parties have a written contract for the sale of two hundred bushels of wheat at a price of $4 per bushel and later orally agree to decrease the quantity to one hundred bushels at the same price per bushel, the agreement as modified is for a total price of $400 and thus is enforceable.

An oral rescission is effective and discharges all unperformed duties under the original contract. For example, Jones and Brown enter into a written contract of employment for a two-year term. Later they orally agree to rescind the contract. The oral agreement is effective, and the written contract is rescinded. Where land has been transferred, however, an agreement to rescind the transaction is a contract to retransfer the land and is within the statute of frauds.

PRACTICAL ADVICE

When significantly modifying an existing common law contract, make sure that consideration is given and that the modification is in writing and signed by both parties.

Compliance with the Statute of Frauds

Even a contract within the statute of frauds will be enforced if it is contained in a *writing, memorandum,* or *record* sufficient to satisfy the statute's requirements. As long as the writing or record meets those requirements, it need not be in any specific form, nor be an attempt by the parties to enter into a binding contract, nor represent their entire agreement.

GENERAL CONTRACT PROVISIONS

The English statute of frauds and most modern statutes of frauds require that the agreement be evidenced by a writing or record to be enforceable. The statute's purpose in requiring a writing or record is to ensure that the parties have actually entered into a contract. It is, therefore, not necessary that the writing or record be in existence when the parties initiate litigation; it is sufficient to show that the memorandum existed at one time. The note, memorandum, or record, which may be formal or informal, must

1. specify the parties to the contract;
2. specify with reasonable certainty the subject matter and the essential terms of the unperformed promises; and
3. be signed by the party to be charged or by her agent.

The memorandum may be such that the parties themselves view it as having no legal significance whatever. For example, a personal letter between the parties, an interdepartmental communication, an advertisement, or the record books of a business may serve as a memorandum. The writing need not have been delivered to the party who seeks to take advantage of it, and it may even contain a repudiation of the oral agreement. For example, Sid and Gail enter into an oral agreement that Sid will sell Blackacre to Gail for $5,000. Sid subsequently receives a better offer and sends Gail a signed letter, which begins by reciting all the material terms of the oral agreement. The letter concludes: "Because my agreement to sell Blackacre to you for $5,000 was oral, I am not bound by my promise. I have since received a better offer and will accept that one." Sid's letter constitutes a sufficient memorandum for Gail to enforce Sid's promise to sell Blackacre. Because Gail did not sign the memorandum, however, the writing does not bind her. Thus, a contract may be enforceable against only one of the parties.

The "signature" may be initials or may even be typewritten or printed, as long as the party intended it to authenticate the writing or record. Furthermore, the signature need not be at the bottom of the page or at the customary place for a signature.

PRACTICAL ADVICE

To avoid becoming solely liable by signing a contract before the other party signs, include a provision to the effect that no party is bound to the contract until all parties sign the contract.

The memorandum may consist of several papers or documents, none of which would be sufficient by itself. The several memoranda, however, must together satisfy all of the requirements of a writing to comply with the statute of frauds and must clearly indicate that they relate to the same transaction. The latter requirement can be satisfied if (1) the writings are physically connected, (2) the writings refer to each other, or (3) an examination of the writings shows them to be in reference to each other.

ESTATE OF JACKSON v. DEVENYNS

SUPREME COURT OF WYOMING, 1995
892 P.2D.786

http://scholar.google.com/scholar_case?case=11233159489095516955&q=892+P.2d.786&hl=en&as_sdt=2,34

FACTS On February 9, 1993, George Jackson and his neighbors, Karen and Steve Devenyn, drafted and signed a document that purports to convey a seventy-nine-acre parcel of land owned by Jackson. By the terms of the agreement, Jackson wished to reserve a 1.3 acre portion of the parcel. Although the agreement contained a drawing and dimensions of the conveyance, it did not contain a specific description of the parcel. Jackson died on May 8, 1993, and his estate refused to honor the agreement. The Devenyns then filed a petition with the probate court to order a conveyance. Based on the parol evidence rule, the estate of Jackson objected to the admission of the witnesses' testimony that they could point out the specific area based on conversations with Jackson. However, the probate court heard the testimony and determined that, with the witnesses' testimony, a sufficient description of the parcel could be determined. Accordingly, it granted the petition. The estate appeals.

DECISION Judgment reversed.

OPINION Golden, J. A written memorandum purporting to convey real estate must sufficiently describe the property so as to comply with the requirements of the statute of frauds and permit specific performance. [Citation.] * * *

* * *

* * * This Court's decision in *Noland* [citation] concluded that a valid contract to convey land must expressly contain a description of the land, certain in itself or capable of being rendered certain by reference to an extrinsic source which the writing itself designates. [Citation.] *Noland* expressly prohibited supplying the writing's essential provisions by inferences or presumptions deduced from oral testimony. [Citation.]

* * *

The parties both recognize that the central issue is the adequacy of the property description supplied in the agreement to satisfy the statute of frauds. The estate contends the probate court improperly relied upon parol evidence in deciding the document had sufficiently described Jackson's property in satisfaction of the statute of frauds. The general rule for Wyoming is that parol evidence is admissible to identify described property, but parol evidence may not supply a portion of the description. [Citation.]

This writing insufficiently describes the property it purports to convey, to reserve, and for which it grants an option to purchase. All three of these transactions fall under the statute of frauds and each must be sufficiently definite in description to satisfy the statute of frauds or, as a matter of law, the contract is void because an essential term has been omitted. [Citation.] We also note that if the description of the property reserved out of the tract to be conveyed is indefinite and uncertain, then the general description of the land to be conveyed is indefinite and the entire conveyance must fail. [Citation.]

* * *

When a writing only states the total acreage without any description of the location of the land involved, the statute of frauds' requirement that the subject matter be reasonably certain is not satisfied and the contract is void. [Citation.] Without the prohibited supplied inference of ownership, the present description only provides the total acreage, does not provide any certainty that this particular tract was intended to be conveyed and, consequently, is too uncertain to be enforced. [Citations.]

The descriptions for the property reserved and for the option also fail to satisfy the statute of frauds. The reserved property boundaries can only be ascertained by witnesses actually directing a surveyor on-site according to the witnesses' memory of Jackson's boundary description. Parol evidence cannot supply a portion of the description. [Citation.] The option granted in the document does not provide any description at all, leaving unclear for what property an option was granted.

INTERPRETATION A writing to comply with the general contract statute of frauds must (1) specify the parties to the contract, (2) specify with reasonable certainty the subject matter and the essential terms of the promises, and (3) be signed by the party to be charged or by her agent.

CRITICAL THINKING QUESTION Should the statute of frauds provision mandate that the writing contain a reasonably certain description of the land? Explain.

SALE OF GOODS

The statute of frauds provision under Article 2 (Sales) of the UCC is more liberal. For a sale of goods, the Code requires merely a writing or record (1) sufficient to indicate that a contract has been made between the parties, (2) signed by the party against whom enforcement is sought or by her authorized agent or broker, and (3) specifying the *quantity* of goods or securities to be sold. The writing or record is sufficient even if it omits or incorrectly states an agreed-upon term; however, if the quantity term is misstated, the contract can be enforced only to the extent of the quantity stated in the writing or record.

As with general contracts, several related documents may satisfy the writing requirement. Moreover, the "signature" may be by initials or even typewritten or printed, so long as the party intended to authenticate the writing or record.

In addition, between merchants, if one party, within a reasonable time after entering into the oral contract, sends a written confirmation of the contract for a sale of goods to the other party and the written confirmation is sufficient against the sender, it is also sufficient against the recipient of the confirmation unless the recipient gives written notice of his objection within ten days after receiving the confirmation. This means that if these requirements have been met, the recipient of the writing or record is in the same position he would have assumed by signing it, and the confirmation, therefore, is enforceable against him.

For example, Brown Co. and ANM Industries enter into an oral contract that provides that ANM will deliver twelve thousand shirts to Brown at $6 per shirt. Brown sends a letter to ANM acknowledging the agreement. The letter is signed by Brown's president, contains the quantity term but not the price, and is mailed to

ANM's vice president for sales. Brown is bound by the contract once its authorized agent signs the letter, while ANM cannot raise the defense of the statute of frauds ten days after receiving the letter if it does not object within that time.

PRACTICAL ADVICE
Merchants should examine written confirmations carefully and promptly to make certain that they are accurate.

Effect of Noncompliance

Under both the statute of frauds and the Code, the basic legal effect is the same: a contracting party has a defense to an action by the other party for enforcement of an *unenforceable* oral contract—that is, an oral contract that falls within the statute and does not comply with its requirements. For example, if Kirkland, a painter, and Riggsbee, a homeowner, make an oral contract under which Riggsbee is to give Kirkland a certain tract of land in return for the painting of Riggsbee's house, the contract is unenforceable under the statute of frauds. It is a contract for the sale of an interest in land. Either party can repudiate and has a defense to an action by the other to enforce the contract.

FULL PERFORMANCE

After *all* the promises of an oral contract have been *performed* by all the parties, the statute of frauds no longer applies. Accordingly, neither party may ask the court to rescind the executed oral contract on the basis that it did not meet the statute's requirements. Thus, the statute applies to executory contracts only.

RESTITUTION

A party to a contract that is unenforceable because of the statute of frauds may have, nonetheless, acted in reliance upon the contract. In such a case, the party may recover in restitution the benefits he conferred upon the other in relying upon the unenforceable contract. Thus, if Wilton makes an oral contract to furnish services to Rochelle that are not to be performed within a year and Rochelle discharges Wilton after three months, Wilton may recover as restitution the value of the

---

Business Law in Action

When *should* a writing or record be used to memorialize a contract? The statute of frauds identifies those categories of contracts that must be evidenced by a writing or record to be enforced, but it does not prevent us from using written contracts where they are not legally called for nor does it preclude us from entering into an agreement without one.

Any time there is a doubt about the other party's ability to perform or a likelihood of future dispute over terms, the parties should have a writing—however brief or informal. For example, one should consider putting in writing service contracts that will be completed in less than a year, such as construction contracts, professional contracts, or other contracts for personal service, even though they typically do not fall within the statute of frauds.

On the other hand, there are times when insisting on a writing might actually undermine an agreement. The most common reason for disregarding the statute of frauds is business expediency. Even though goods valued at greater than $500 may be involved, the seller may not want to "bother" with the formality of a writing, and there may be a buyer who is equally motivated to consummate the transaction. Waiting for a written agreement might mean losing out on the deal. In such a case, however, both parties must understand that if the other party fails to perform, the agreement will be unenforceable.

Commerce is dynamic: depending on the type of agreement involved, it can be fast paced and fluid or it can be deliberate and painstaking. Understanding the statute of frauds is important, but one may also wish to consider other factors in deciding whether to put a contract in writing.

© Cengage Learning 2014

services he rendered during the three months. Most courts require, however, that the party seeking restitution not be in default.

PROMISSORY ESTOPPEL

A growing number of courts have used the doctrine of promissory estoppel to displace the requirement of a writing by enforcing oral contracts within the statute of frauds in cases in which the party seeking enforcement has reasonably and foreseeably relied upon a promise in such a way that the court can avoid injustice only by enforcing the promise. The remedy granted is limited, as justice requires, and depends on such factors as the availability of other remedies; the foreseeability, reasonableness, and substantiality of the reliance; and the extent to which reliance corroborates evidence of the promise. The use of promissory estoppel, however, to avoid the writing requirement of the statute of frauds has gained little acceptance in cases involving the sale of goods.

PAROL EVIDENCE RULE

A contract reduced to writing and signed by the parties is frequently the result of many conversations, conferences, proposals, counterproposals, letters, and memoranda; sometimes it is also the product of negotiations conducted, or partly conducted, by agents of the parties. At some stage in the negotiations, the parties or their agents may have reached tentative agreements that were superseded (or regarded as such by one of the parties) by subsequent negotiations. Offers may have been made and withdrawn, either expressly or by implication, or forgotten in the give-and-take of negotiations. Ultimately, though, the parties prepare and sign a final draft of the written contract, which may or may not include all of the points that they discussed and agreed on in the course of the negotiations. By signing the agreement, despite its potential omissions, the parties have declared it to be their contract, and the terms as contained in it represent the contract they have made. As a rule of substantive law, neither party is later permitted to show that the contract they made is different from the terms and provisions that appear in the written agreement. This rule, which also applies to wills and deeds, is called the "parol evidence" rule.

The Rule

When the parties express their contract in a writing that is intended to be the complete and final expression of their rights and duties, the **parol evidence rule** excludes *prior* oral or written negotiations or agreements of the parties or their *contemporaneous* oral agreements that *vary* or *change* an integrated written contract. The word *parol* literally means "speech" or "words." The term *parol evidence* refers to any evidence, whether oral or in writing, that is outside the written contract and not incorporated into it either directly or by reference.

The parol evidence rule applies only to an **integrated contract**, that is, one contained in a certain writing or writings to which the parties have assented as being the statement of the complete and exclusive agreement or contract between them. When there is such an integration of a contract, the courts will not permit parol evidence of any prior or contemporaneous agreement to vary, change, alter, or modify any of the terms or provisions of the written contract.

The reason for the rule is that the parties, by reducing their entire agreement to writing, are regarded as having intended the writing that they signed to include the whole of their agreement. The terms and provisions contained in the writing are there because the parties intended them to be in their contract. Conversely, the courts regard the parties as having omitted intentionally any provision not in the writing. The rule, by excluding evidence that would tend to change, alter, vary, or modify the terms of the written agreement, safeguards the contract as made by the parties. The rule, which applies to all integrated written contracts, deals with what terms are part of the contract. The rule differs from the statute of frauds, which governs what contracts must be evidenced by a writing to be enforceable. Does the parol evidence rule or the statute of frauds apply to the situation presented in the Ethical Dilemma at the end of this chapter?

PRACTICAL ADVICE

If your contract is intended to be the complete and final agreement, make sure that all terms are included and state your intention that the writing is complete and final. If you do not intend the writing to be complete or final, make sure that you so indicate in the writing itself.

JENKINS V. ECKERD CORPORATION

DISTRICT COURT OF APPEAL OF FLORIDA, FIRST DISTRICT, 2005
913SO.2D43

http://scholar.google.com/scholar_case?case=12402686802007965629&hl=en&as_sdt=2&as_vis=1&oi=scholarr

FACTS In January 1991, Sandhill and K & B Florida Corporation (K & B), a pharmaceutical retailer, entered into lease agreement (K & B Lease) providing for the rental of a parcel of real property located in the Gulf Breeze Shopping Center in Gulf Breeze, Florida. Shortly before the execution of the K & B Lease, Sandhill had leased space in the shopping center to Delchamps, Inc., a regional supermarket chain, as the "anchor" tenant in the shopping center. Article 2B of the K & B Lease referred to the Delchamps lease and provided:

ARTICLE 2

B. Lessor represents to Lessee that Lessor has entered into leases with the following named concerns: with Delchamps, Inc. (Delchamps) for a minimum of 45,000 square feet for supermarket grocery store and that Lessor will construct and offer for lease individual retail shops for a minimum of 21,000 square feet for various retail uses, all located and dimensioned shown on the attached Plot Plan, ... The continued leasing and payment of rent for their store in the Shopping Center by Delchamps is part of the consideration to induce Lessee to lease and pay rent for its store, ... Accordingly, should Delchamps fail or cease to lease and pay rent for its store in the Shopping Center during the Lease Term as hereinafter set out, Lessee shall have the right and privilege of: (a) canceling this Lease and of terminating all of its obligations hereunder at any time thereafter upon written notice by Lessee to Lessor, and such cancellation and termination shall be effective ninety (90) days after the mailing of such written notice; ...

The K & B Lease contained an integration clause which provided that "[t]his lease contains all of the agreements made between the parties hereto and may not be modified orally or in any manner other than by an agreement in writing." The Delchamps' lease included an assignment provision which granted Delchamps "the right, at any time after the commencement of the term hereof, to assign this lease."

In September 1997, Jitney Jungle Stores of America, Inc. (Jitney Jungle), another grocery store operator, acquired Delchamps and continued the operation of the Delchamps' grocery store in the shopping center. In 1998, Eckerd acquired the K & B drugstore. The K & B Lease was assigned to Eckerd, which began operating an Eckerd drugstore in the leased premises. In October 1999, Jitney Jungle filed for bankruptcy protection under Chapter 11 of the U.S. Bankruptcy

Code. Thereafter, an order was entered in the bankruptcy proceeding approving Delchamps' assignment of its lease in the shopping center to Bruno's Supermarkets, Inc. (Bruno's). Since the assignment, Bruno's has occupied the leased premises under the assigned Delchamps' lease and has operated a Bruno's grocery store there. Sandhill did not provide notice to, or obtain consent from, Eckerd of this assignment. On June 22, 2001, Eckerd notified Sandhill that, because Delchamps had ceased to lease and pay rent for its store in the shopping center, pursuant to the K & B Lease, Eckerd was canceling its lease effective September 20, 2001. Sandhill filed suit against Eckerd for an alleged breach of the shopping center lease. At trial, Sandhill sought to introduce testimony relating to its negotiations of the K & B Lease to explain the parties' intent in drafting the allegedly ambiguous language in article 2B. The trial court prohibited the introduction of this evidence under the parol evidence rule. The district court entered a judgment in favor of Eckerd. This appeal was filed.

DECISION Judgment affirmed.

OPINION Van Nortwick, J. It is a fundamental rule of contract interpretation that a contract which is clear, complete, and unambiguous does not require judicial construction. [Citations.]

* * *

In the case on appeal, the trial court concluded, and we agree, that article 2B of the K & B Lease clearly and unambiguously gave the lessee the option to cancel the lease if Delchamps ceased to lease and pay rent for the use of its store. As is clear from article 2B itself, the subject language was an inducement for the drugstore tenant to lease in the shopping center. * * *

* * *

Sandhill argues that the trial court erred in applying the parol evidence rule and refusing to allow the introduction of extrinsic evidence in interpreting article 2B of the K & B Lease. Sandhill correctly acknowledges that, if a contract provision is "clear and unambiguous," a court may not consider extrinsic or "parol" evidence to change the plain meaning set forth in the contract. [Citation.] Sandhill contends that parol evidence was admissible below since the lease is incomplete and contains a latent ambiguity. [Citations.] A latent ambiguity arises when a contract on its face appears clear and unambiguous, but fails to specify the rights or duties of the parties in certain situations. [Citation.] Sandhill submits that, while the reference in article 2B of the K & B Lease to the Delchamps lease may be "unambiguous" when read literally, this reference was not "clear" or "complete" with regard to the operation of the lease should the Delchamps lease be assigned. We cannot agree.

The operation of the parol evidence rule encourages parties to embody their complete agreement in a written contract and fosters reliance upon the written contract. "The parol evidence rule serves as a shield to protect a valid, complete and unambiguous written instrument from any verbal assault that would contradict, add to, or subtract from it, or affect its construction." [Citation.] The parol evidence rule presumes that the written agreement that is sought to be modified or explained is an integrated agreement; that is, it represents the complete and exclusive instrument setting forth the parties' intended agreement. [Citation.] The concept of integration is based on a presumption that the parties to a written contract intended that writing "to be the sole expositor of their agreement." [Citation.] The terms of an integrated written contract can be varied by extrinsic evidence only to the extent that the terms are ambiguous and are given meaning by the extrinsic evidence. [Citation.]

Here, *** the K & B Lease contains a so-called merger or integration clause. Although the existence of a merger clause does not *per se* establish that the integration of the agreement is total, [citation], a merger clause is a highly persuasive statement that the parties intended the agreement to be totally integrated and generally works to prevent a party from introducing parol evidence to vary or contradict the written terms. *** Here, we find that the K & B Lease is an integrated agreement complete in all essential terms.

Further, Article 2B is not in the least unclear or incomplete. It contains no latent or patent ambiguity. Although article 2B does not mention assignment by Delchamps, it unambiguously grants the lessee the right to terminate the K & B Lease if Delchamps ceases to lease and pay rent for its store in the shopping center *for any reason.* *** Accordingly, the trial court correctly ruled that it could not admit extrinsic evidence.

INTERPRETATION The parol evidence rule encourages parties to embody their complete agreement in an integrated written contract and fosters reliance upon the written contract.

CRITICAL THINKING QUESTION Do you agree with the parol evidence rule? Explain.

Situations to which the Rule Does Not Apply

The parol evidence rule, in spite of its name, is not an exclusionary rule of evidence; nor is it a rule of construction or interpretation. Rather, it is a rule of substantive law that defines the limits of a contract. Bearing this in mind, as well as the reason underlying the rule, you will readily understand that the rule does *not* apply to any of the following situations (see Figure 15-1 for an overview of the parol evidence rule):

1. A contract that is *partly* written and partly oral; that is, a contract in which the parties do not intend the writing to be their entire agreement.

2. A clerical or *typographical error* that obviously does not represent the agreement of the par ties. Where, for example, a written contract for the services of a skilled mining engineer provides that his rate of compensation is to be $8 per day, a court of equity would permit reformation (correction) of the contract to correct the mistake if both parties intended the rate to be $800 per day.

3. The lack of *contractual capacity* of one of the parties through, for instance, minority, intoxication, or mental incompetency. Such evidence would not tend to vary, change, or alter any of the terms of the written agreement but rather would show that the written agreement was voidable or void.

4. A *defense* of fraud, misrepresentation, duress, undue influence, mistake, illegality, lack of consideration, or other invalidating cause. Evidence establishing any of these defenses would not purport to vary, change, or alter any of the terms of the written agreement but rather would show such agreement to be voidable, void, or unenforceable.

5. A *condition precedent* to which the parties agreed orally at the time of the execution of the written agreement and to which the entire agreement was made subject. Such evidence does not tend to vary, alter, or change any of the terms of the agreement; rather, it shows whether the entire unchanged written agreement ever became effective.

Figure 15-1   *Parol Evidence Rule*

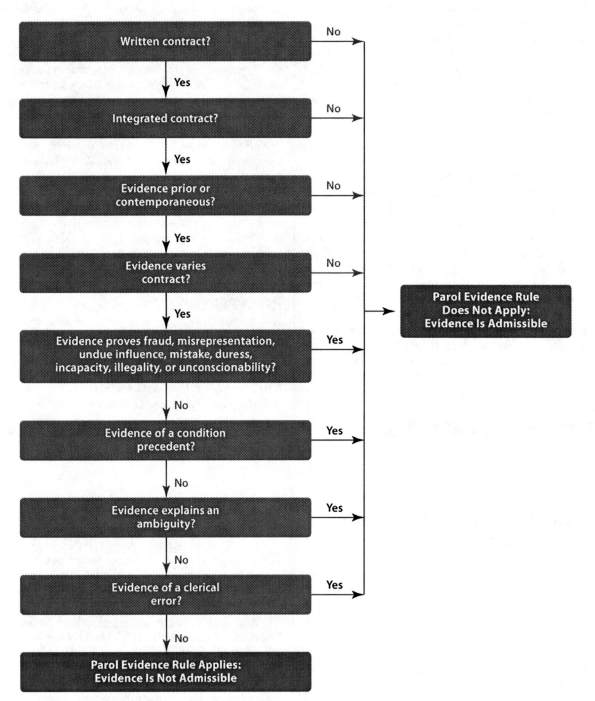

6. A *subsequent mutual rescission* or *modification* of the written contract. Parol evidence of a later agreement does not tend to show that the integrated writing did not represent the contract between the parties at the time the writing was made.

7. Parol evidence is admissible to explain *ambiguous* terms in the contract. To enforce a contract, it is

necessary to understand its intended meaning. Nevertheless, such interpretation is not to alter, change, or vary the terms of the contract.

8. A *separate contract*; the rule does not prevent a party from proving the existence of a separate, distinct contract between the same parties.

Supplemental Evidence

Although a written agreement cannot be contradicted by evidence of a prior agreement or of a contemporaneous agreement, under the Restatement and the Code, a written contract may be explained or supplemented by (1) course of dealing between the parties; (2) usage of trade; (3) course of performance; or (4) evidence of consistent additional terms, unless the writing was intended by the parties to be a complete and exclusive statement of their agreement.

A **course of dealing** is a sequence of previous conduct between the parties that a court may fairly regard as having established a common basis of understanding for interpreting their expressions and other conduct.

A **usage of trade** is a practice or method of dealing regularly observed and followed in a place, vocation, or trade.

Course of performance refers to the manner in which and the extent to which the respective parties to a contract have accepted without objection successive tenders of performance by the other party.

The Restatement and the Code permit *supplemental consistent evidence* to be introduced into a court proceeding. Such evidence, however, is admissible only if it does not contradict a term or terms of the original agreement and would probably not have been included in the original contract.

INTERPRETATION OF CONTRACTS

Although parol evidence may not change the written words or language in which the parties embodied their agreement or contract, the ascertainment (determination) of the meaning to be given to the written language is outside the scope of the parol evidence rule. Though the written words embody the terms of the contract, these words are but symbols; and, if their meaning is ambiguous, the courts may clarify this meaning by applying rules of interpretation or construction and by using extrinsic (external) evidence where necessary.

The Restatement defines **interpretation** as the ascertainment of the meaning of a promise or agreement or of a term of the promise or agreement. Where the language in a contract is unambiguous, a court will not accept extrinsic evidence tending to show a meaning different from that which the words clearly convey. To perform its function of interpreting and construing written contracts and documents, the court adopts rules of interpretation to apply a legal standard to the words contained in the agreement. These are among the rules that aid interpretation:

1. Words and other conduct are interpreted in the light of all the circumstances, and if the principal purpose of the parties is ascertainable, it is given great weight.

2. A writing is interpreted as a whole, and all writings that are part of the same transaction are interpreted together.

3. Unless the parties manifest a different intention, language that has a commonly accepted meaning is interpreted in accordance with that meaning.

4. Unless a different intention is manifested, technical terms and words of art are given their technical meanings.

5. Wherever reasonable, the parties' manifestations of intention regarding a promise or agreement are interpreted as consistent with each other and with any relevant course of performance, course of dealing, or usage of trade.

6. An interpretation that gives a reasonable, lawful, and effective meaning to all the terms is preferred over an interpretation that leaves a part unreasonable, unlawful, or of no effect.

7. Specific and exact terms are given greater weight than general language.

8. Separately negotiated or added terms are given greater weight than standardized terms or other terms not separately negotiated.

9. Express terms, course of performance, course of dealing, and usage of trade are weighted in that order.

10. Where a term or promise has several possible meanings, it will be interpreted against the party who supplied the contract or the term.

11. Where written provisions are inconsistent with typed or printed provisions, the written provision is given preference. Likewise, typed provisions are given preference to printed provisions.

12. If the amount payable is set forth in both figures and words and the amounts differ, the words control the figures.

We may observe that, through the application of the parol evidence rule (where properly applicable) and the above rules of interpretation and construction, the

Ethical Dilemma

What's (Wrong) in a Contract?

FACTS Rick Davidson was an All-American point guard on Donaldson University's varsity basketball team. He was a four-year starter and, through the cooperation of several accommodating professors, was able to graduate on time—with one small catch: he really couldn't read or write. But his classroom experiences helped convince him that he could handle any situation, and when he was drafted in the first round by a National Basketball Association (NBA) team, he decided to act as his own agent.

During the negotiations, John Stock, general manager for the team, made Rick an offer of $2.4 million to play for the team for three years. After seeing that other first-round draft choices were receiving closer to $3 million for the same three years, Rick made it known to Stock that the team's offer was unacceptable. Stock told Rick that because of the salary cap (each NBA team has a limit on the total amount of salaries it can pay its players), he would be willing to raise the offer to $2.8 million but that the extra $400,000 could not be written into the contract. This would be an oral agreement that would avoid disclosing the salary cap violation to the league. After considering the offer, Rick signed the contract for $2.4 million for three years' service, and he and Stock shook hands

on the deal for the additional $400,000 for the same three years. The contract stated that it was the complete and final agreement between the parties.

After Rick's first year, it was obvious to the team that Rick was not worth the money, and Stock decided not to pay him the first year's portion of the extra $400,000. Stock claimed that because this agreement was not in writing, it was not enforceable.

Social, Policy, and Ethical Considerations

1. What would you do?
2. Is the team legally obligated to pay the additional $400,000? Is it ethically obligated to do so?
3. What policy interests are served by the team's decision not to pay Rick the extra money? Would the fact that NBA policy makes it impossible for a player to leave a team and play for another NBA team change your answer?
4. What responsibility does the university bear in this situation?
5. What is the nature of Rick's responsibility with respect to the above facts? What should he do?

law not only enforces a contract but also, in so doing, exercises great care both that the contract being enforced is the one the parties made and that the sense and meaning of the parties' intentions are carefully ascertained and given effect.

> **PRACTICAL ADVICE**
>
> Take care to ensure that your contracts are complete and understandable, especially if you drafted the contract.

CHAPTER SUMMARY

STATUTE OF FRAUDS

Contracts within the Statute of Frauds

Rule contracts within the statute of frauds must be evidenced by a writing to be enforceable

Electronic Records full effect is given to electronic contracts and signatures

Suretyship Provision applies to promises to pay the debt of another
- *Promise Must Be Collateral* promisor must be secondarily, not primarily, liable
- *Main Purpose Doctrine* if primary object is to provide an economic benefit to the surety, then the promise is not within the statute

Executor-Administrator Provision applies to promises to answer personally for a duty of the decedent

Marriage Provision applies to promises in consideration of marriage but not to mutual promises to marry

Land Contract Provision applies to promises to transfer any right, privilege, power, or immunity in real property

One-Year Provision applies to contracts that cannot be performed within one year
* *The Possibility Test* the criterion is whether it is possible, not likely, for the agreement to be performed within one year
* *Computation of Time* the year runs from the time the agreement is made
* *Full Performance by One Party* makes the promise of the other party enforceable under majority view

Sale of Goods a contract for the sale of goods for the price of $500 or more must be evidenced by a writing or record to be enforceable
* *Admission* an admission in pleadings, testimony, or otherwise in court makes the contract enforceable for the quantity of goods admitted
* *Specially Manufactured Goods* an oral contract for specially manufactured goods is enforceable
* *Delivery or Payment and Acceptance* validates the contract only for the goods that have been accepted or for which payment has been accepted

Modification or Rescission of Contracts within the Statute of Frauds oral contracts modifying existing contracts are unenforceable if the resulting contract is within the statute of frauds

Methods of Compliance

General Contract Provisions the writing(s) or record must
* specify the parties to the contract
* specify the subject matter and essential terms
* be signed by the party to be charged or by her agent

Sale of Goods provides a general method of compliance for all parties and an additional one for merchants
* *Writing(s) or Record* must (1) be sufficient to indicate that a contract has been made between the parties, (2) be signed by the party against whom enforcement is sought or by her authorized agent, and (3) specify the quantity of goods to be sold
* *Written Confirmation* between merchants, a written confirmation that is sufficient against the sender is also sufficient against the recipient unless the recipient gives written notice of his objection within ten days

Effect of Noncompliance

Oral Contract within Statute of Frauds is unenforceable

Full Performance statute does not apply to executed contracts

Restitution is available in quasi-contract for benefits conferred in reliance on the oral contract

Promissory Estoppel oral contracts will be enforced in cases in which the party seeking enforcement has reasonably and justifiably relied on the promise and the court can avoid injustice only by enforcement

PAROL EVIDENCE RULE AND INTERPRETATION OF CONTRACTS

The Parol Evidence Rule

Statement of Rule when parties express a contract in a writing that they intend to be the final expression of their rights and duties, evidence of their prior oral or written negotiations or agreements of their contemporaneous oral agreements that vary or change the written contract are not admissible

Situations to which the Rule Does Not Apply
- a contract that is not an integrated document
- correction of a typographical error
- showing that a contract was void or voidable
- showing whether a condition has in fact occurred
- showing a subsequent mutual rescission or modification of the contract

Supplemental Evidence may be admitted
- *Course of Dealing* previous conduct between the parties
- *Usage of Trade* practice engaged in by the trade or industry
- *Course of Performance* conduct between the parties concerning performance of the particular contract
- *Supplemental Consistent Evidence*

Interpretation of Contracts

Definition the ascertainment of the meaning of a promise or agreement or a term of the promise or agreement

Rules of Interpretation include
- all the circumstances are considered and the principal purpose of the parties is given great weight
- a writing is interpreted as a whole
- commonly accepted meanings are used unless the parties manifest a different intention
- wherever possible, the intentions of the parties are interpreted as consistent with each other and with course of performance, course of dealing, or usage of trade
- technical terms are given their technical meaning
- specific terms are given greater weight than general language
- separately negotiated terms are given greater weight than standardized terms or those not separately negotiated
- the order for interpretation is express terms, course of performance, course of dealing, and usage of trade
- where a term has several possible meanings, the term will be interpreted against the party who supplied the contract or term
- written provisions are given preference over typed or printed provisions and typed provisions are given preference over printed provisions
- if an amount is set forth in both words and figures and they differ, words control the figures

QUESTIONS

1. Rafferty was the principal shareholder in Continental Corporation, and, as a result, he received the lion's share of Continental Corporation's dividends. Continental Corporation was anxious to close an important deal for iron ore products to use in its business. A written contract was on the desk of Stage Corporation for the sale of the iron ore to Continental Corporation. Stage Corporation, however, was cautious about signing the contract, and it did not sign until Rafferty called Stage Corporation on the telephone and stated that if Continental Corporation did not pay for the ore, he would pay. Business reversals struck Continental Corporation, and it failed. Stage Corporation sued Rafferty. What defense, if any, has Rafferty?

2. Green was the owner of a large department store. On Wednesday, January 26, he talked to Smith and said, "I will hire you to act as sales manager in my store for one year at a salary of $48,000. You are to begin work next Monday." Smith accepted and started work on Monday, January 31. At the end of three months, Green discharged Smith. On May 15, Smith brought an action against Green to recover the unpaid portion of the $48,000 salary. Is Smith's employment contract enforceable?

3. Rowe was admitted to the hospital suffering from a critical illness. He was given emergency treatment and later underwent surgery. On at least four occasions, Rowe's two sons discussed with the hospital the payment for services to be rendered by the hospital. The first of these four conversations took place the day after Rowe was admitted. The sons informed the treating physician that their father had no financial means but that they themselves

would pay for such services. During the other conversations, the sons authorized whatever treatment their father needed, assuring the hospital that they would pay for the services. After Rowe's discharge, the hospital brought this action against the sons to recover the unpaid bill for the services rendered to their father. Are the sons' promises to the hospital enforceable? Explain.

4. Ames, Bell, Cain, and Dole each orally ordered LCD (liquid crystal display) televisions from Marvel Electronics Company, which accepted the orders. Ames's television was to be encased in a specially designed ebony cabinet. Bell, Cain, and Dole ordered standard televisions described as "Alpha Omega Theatre." The price of Ames's television was $1,800, and the televisions ordered by Bell, Cain, and Dole were $700 each. Bell paid the company $75 to apply on his purchase; Ames, Cain, and Dole paid nothing. The next day, Marvel sent Ames, Bell, Cain, and Dole written confirmations captioned "Purchase Memorandum," numbered 12345, 12346, 12347, and 12348, respectively, containing the essential terms of the oral agreements. Each memorandum was sent in duplicate with the request that one copy be signed and returned to the company. None of the four purchasers returned a signed copy. Ames promptly called the company and repudiated the oral contract, which it received before beginning manufacture of the set for Ames or making commitments to carry out the contract. Cain sent the company a letter reading in part, "Referring to your Contract No. 12347, please be advised I have canceled this contract. Yours truly, (Signed) Cain." The four televisions were duly tendered by Marvel to Ames, Bell, Cain, and Dole, all of whom refused to accept delivery. Marvel brings four separate actions against Ames, Bell, Cain, and Dole for breach of contract. Decide each claim.

5. Moriarity and Holmes enter into an oral contract by which Moriarity promises to sell and Holmes promises to buy Blackacre for $10,000. Moriarity repudiates the contract by writing a letter to Holmes in which she states accurately the terms of the bargain, but adds "our agreement was oral. It, therefore, is not binding upon me, and I shall not carry it out." Thereafter, Holmes sues Moriarity for specific performance of the contract. Moriarity interposes the defense of the statute of frauds, arguing that the contract is within the statute and hence unenforceable. What will be the result? Discuss.

6. On March 1, Lucas called Craig on the telephone and offered to pay him $90,000 for a house and lot that Craig owned. Craig accepted the offer immediately on the telephone. Later in the same day, Lucas told Annabelle that if she would marry him, he would convey to her the property then owned by Craig that was the subject of the earlier agreement. On March 2 Lucas called Penelope and offered her $16,000 if she would work for him for the year commencing March 15, and she agreed. Lucas and Annabelle were married on June 25. By this time, Craig had refused to convey the house to Lucas. Thereafter,

Lucas renounced his promise to convey the property to Annabelle. Penelope, who had been working for Lucas, was discharged without cause on July 5; Annabelle left Lucas and instituted divorce proceedings in July.

What rights, if any, have—

a. Lucas against Craig for his failure to convey the property;

b. Annabelle against Lucas for failure to convey the house to her; and

c. Penelope against Lucas for discharging her before the end of the agreed term of employment?

7. Blair orally promises Clay to sell him five crops of potatoes to be grown on Blackacre, a farm in Idaho, and Clay promises to pay a stated price for them on delivery. Is the contract enforceable?

8. Rachel leased an apartment to Bertha for a one-year term beginning May 1, at $800 a month, "payable in advance on the first day of each and every month of said term." At the time the lease was signed, Bertha told Rachel that she received her salary on the tenth of the month, and that she would be unable to pay the rent before that date each month. Rachel replied that would be satisfactory. On June 2, Bertha not having paid the June rent, Rachel sued Bertha for the rent. At the trial, Bertha offered to prove the oral agreement as to the date of payment each month. Is the oral evidence admissible?

9. Ann bought a car from the Used Car Agency (Used) under a written contract. She purchased the car in reliance on Used's agent's oral representations that it had never been in a wreck and could be driven at least two thousand miles without adding oil. Thereafter, Ann discovered that the car had, in fact, been previously wrecked and rebuilt, that it used excessive quantities of oil, and that Used's agent was aware of these facts when the car was sold. Ann brought an action to rescind the contract and recover the purchase price. Used objected to the introduction of oral testimony concerning representations of its agent, contending that the written contract alone governed the rights of the parties. Should Ann succeed?

10. In a contract drawn up by Goldberg Company, it agreed to sell and Edwards Contracting Company agreed to buy wood shingles at $650. After the shingles were delivered and used, Goldberg Company billed Edwards Company at $650 per bunch of nine hundred shingles. Edwards Company refused to pay because it thought the contract meant $650 per thousand shingles. Goldberg Company brought action to recover on the basis of $650 per bunch. The evidence showed that there was no applicable custom or usage in the trade and that each party held its belief in good faith. Decision?

11. Amos orally agrees to hire Elizabeth for an eight-month trial period. Elizabeth performs the job magnificently, and

after several weeks Amos orally offers Elizabeth a six-month extension at a salary increase of 20 percent. Elizabeth accepts the offer. At the end of the eight-month trial period, Amos discharges Elizabeth, who brings suit against Amos for breach of contract. Is Amos liable? Why?

CASE PROBLEMS

12. Halsey, a widower, was living without family or housekeeper in his house in Howell, New York. Burns and his wife claim that Halsey invited them to give up their house and business in Andover, New York, to live in his house and care for him. In return, they allege, he promised them the house and its furniture upon his death. Acting upon this proposal, the Burnses left Andover, moved into Halsey's house, and cared for him until he died five months later. No deed, will, or memorandum exists to authenticate Halsey's promise. McCormick, the administrator of the estate, claims the oral promise is unenforceable under the statute of frauds. Explain whether McCormick is correct.

13. Ethel Greenberg acquired the ownership of the Carlyle Hotel on Miami Beach but had little experience in the hotel business. She asked Miller to participate in and counsel her operation of the hotel, which he did. He claims that, because his efforts produced a substantial profit, Ethel made an oral agreement for the continuation of his services. Miller alleges that in return for his services, Ethel promised to marry him and to share the net income resulting from the operation of the hotel. Miller maintains that he rendered his services to Ethel in reliance upon her promises and that the couple planned to wed in the fall. Ethel, due to physical illness, decided not to marry. Miller sued for damages for Ethel's breach of agreement. Is the oral contract enforceable? Discuss.

14. Dean was hired on February 12 as a sales manager of the Co-op Dairy for a minimum period of one year with the dairy agreeing to pay his moving expenses. By February 26, Dean had signed a lease, moved his family from Oklahoma to Arizona, and reported for work. After he worked for a few days, he was fired. Dean then brought this action against the dairy for his salary for the year, less what he was paid. The dairy argues that the statute of frauds bars enforcement of the oral contract because the contract was not to be performed within one year. Is the dairy correct in its assertion?

15. Yokel, a grower of soybeans, had sold soybeans to Campbell Grain and Seed Company and other grain companies in the past. Campbell entered into an oral contract with Yokel to purchase soybeans from him. Promptly after entering into the oral contract, Campbell signed and mailed to Yokel a written confirmation of the oral agreement. Yokel received the written confirmation but did not sign it or object to its content. Campbell now brings this action against Yokel for breach of contract upon Yokel's failure to deliver the soybeans. Is the agreement binding?

16. Presti claims that he reached an oral agreement with Wilson by telephone in October to buy a horse for $60,000. Presti asserts that he sent Wilson a bill of sale and a postdated check, which Wilson retained. Presti also claims that Wilson told him that for tax reasons he wished not to consummate the transaction until January 1 of the following year. The check was neither deposited nor negotiated. Wilson denies that he ever agreed to sell the horse or that he received the check and bill of sale from Presti. Presti's claim is supported by a copy of his check stub and by the affidavit of his executive assistant, who says that he monitored the telephone call and prepared and mailed both the bill of sale and the check. Wilson argues that the statute of frauds governs this transaction and that because there was no writing, the contract claim is barred. Is Wilson correct? Explain.

17. Louie E. Brown worked for the Phelps Dodge Corporation under an oral contract for approximately twenty-three years. In 2011, he was suspended from work for unauthorized possession of company property. In 2012, Phelps Dodge fired Brown after discovering that he was using company property without permission and building a trailer on company time. Brown sued Phelps Dodge for benefits under an unemployment benefit plan. According to the plan, "in order to be eligible for unemployment benefits, a laid-off employee must: (1) Have completed 2 or more years of continuous service with the company, and (2) Have been laid off from work because the company had determined that work was not available for him." The trial court held that the wording of the second condition was ambiguous and should be construed against Phelps Dodge, the party who chose the wording. A reading of the entire contract, however, indicates that the plan was not intended to apply to someone who was fired for cause. What is the correct interpretation of this contract?

18. Katz offered to purchase land from Joiner, and, after negotiating the terms, Joiner accepted. On October 13, over the telephone, both parties agreed to extend the time period for completing and mailing the written contract until October 20. Although the original paperwork deadline in the offer was October 14, Katz stated he had inserted that provision "for my purpose only." All other provisions of the contract remained unchanged. Accordingly, Joiner completed the contract and mailed it on October 20. Immediately after, however, Joiner sent Katz an overnight letter stating that "I have signed and returned contract, but have changed my mind. Do not wish to sell property." Joiner now claims an oral modification of a

contract within the statute of frauds is unenforceable. Katz counters that the modification is not material and therefore does not affect the underlying contract. Explain who is correct.

19. When Mr. McClam died, he left the family farm, heavily mortgaged, to his wife and children. To save the farm from foreclosure, Mrs. McClam planned to use insurance proceeds and her savings to pay off the debts. She was unwilling to do so, however, unless she had full ownership of the property. Mrs. McClam wrote her daughter, stating that the daughter should deed over her interest in the family farm to her mother. Mrs. McClam promised that upon her death all the children would inherit the farm from their mother equally. The letter further explained that if foreclosure occurred, each child would receive very little, but if they complied with their mother's plan, each would eventually receive a valuable property interest upon her death. Finally, the letter stated that all the other children had agreed to this plan. The daughter also agreed. Years later, Mrs. McClam tried to convey the farm to her son Donald. The daughter challenged, arguing that the mother was contractually bound to convey the land equally to all children. Donald says this was an oral agreement to sell land and is unenforceable. The daughter says the letter satisfies the statute of frauds, making the contract enforceable. Who gets the farm? Explain.

20. Butler Brothers Building Company sublet all of the work in a highway construction contract to Ganley Brothers, Inc. Soon thereafter, Ganley brought this action against Butler for fraud in the inducement of the contract. The contract, however, provided: "The contractor [Ganley] has examined the said contracts …, knows all the requirements, and is not relying upon any statement made by the company in respect thereto." Can Ganley introduce into evidence the oral representations made by Butler?

21. Alice solicited an offer from Robett Manufacturing Company to manufacture certain clothing that Alice intended to supply to the government. Alice contends that in a telephone conversation Robett made an oral offer that she immediately accepted. She then received the following letter from Robett, which, she claims, confirmed their agreement:

> Confirming our telephone conversation, we are pleased to offer the 3,500 shirts at $14.00 each and the trousers at $13.80 each with delivery approximately ninety days after receipt of order. We will try to cut this to sixty days if at all possible.
>
> This, of course, is quoted f.o.b. Atlanta and the order will not be subject to cancellation, domestic pack only. Thanking you for the opportunity to offer these garments, we are
>
> Very truly yours,
> ROBETT MANUFACTURING CO., INC.

Is the agreement enforceable against Robett?

22. Enrique Gittes was a financial consultant for NCC, an English holding company that invested capital in other businesses in return for a stake in those businesses. One of NCC's investments was a substantial holding in Simplicity Pattern Company. Gittes's consulting contract was subsequently transferred to Simplicity, and Gittes was elected to the Simplicity board of directors.

When NCC fell into serious financial straits, it became imperative that it sell its interest in Simplicity. Accordingly, a buyer was found. The buyer insisted that before closing the deal all current Simplicity directors, including Gittes, must resign. Gittes, however, refused to resign. Edward Cook, the largest shareholder of NCC and the one with the most to lose if the Simplicity sale was not completed, orally offered Gittes a five-year, $50,000-per-year consulting contract with Cook International if Gittes would resign from the Simplicity board.

Gittes and Cook never executed a formal contract. However, Cook International did issue two writings, a prospectus and a memo, that mentioned the employment of Gittes for five years at $50,000 per year. Neither writing described the nature of Gittes's job or any of his duties. In fact, Gittes was given no responsibilities, and was never paid. Gittes sued to enforce the employment contract. Cook International contended that the statute of frauds made the oral contract unenforceable. Decision?

23. Shane Quadri contacted Don Hoffman, an employee of Al J. Hoffman & Co. (Hoffman Agency), to procure car insurance. Later, Quadri's car was stolen. Quadri contacted Hoffman, who arranged with Budget Rent-a-Car for a rental car for Quadri until his car was recovered. Hoffman authorized Budget Rent-a-Car to bill the Hoffman Agency. Later, when the stolen car was recovered, Hoffman telephoned Goodyear and arranged to have four new tires put on Quadri's car to replace those damaged during the theft. Budget and Goodyear sued Hoffman for payment of the car rental and tires. Is Hoffman liable on his oral promise to pay for the car rental and the four new tires?

24. On July 5, 2003, Richard Price signed a written employment contract as a new salesman with the Mercury Supply Company. The contract was of indefinite duration and could be terminated by either party for any reason upon fifteen days' notice. Between 2003 and 2011, Price was promoted several times. In 2005, Price was made vice president of sales. In September of 2011, however, Price was told that his performance was not satisfactory and that if he did not improve he would be fired. In February of 2012, Price received notice of termination. Price claims that in 2008 he entered into a valid oral employment contract with Mercury Supply Company in which he was made vice president of sales for life or until he should retire. Is the alleged oral contract barred by the one-year provision of the statute of frauds?

25. Thomson Printing Company is a buyer and seller of used machinery. On April 10, the president of the company,

James Thomson, went to the surplus machinery department of B.F. Goodrich Company in Akron, Ohio, to examine some used equipment that was for sale. Thomson discussed the sale, including a price of $9,000, with Ingram Meyers, a Goodrich employee and agent. Four days later, on April 14, Thomson sent a purchase order to confirm the oral contract for purchase of the machinery and a partial payment of $1,000 to Goodrich in Akron. The purchase order contained Thomson Printing's name, address, and telephone number, as well as certain information about the purchase, but did not specifically mention Meyers or the surplus equipment department. Goodrich sent copies of the documents to a number of its divisions, but Meyers never learned of the confirmation until weeks later, by which time the equipment had been sold to another party. Thomson Printing brought suit against Goodrich for breach of contract. Goodrich claimed that no contract had existed and that at any rate the alleged oral contract could not be enforced because of the statute of frauds. Is the contract enforceable? Why?

26. Plaintiffs leased commercial space from the defendant to open a florist shop. After the lease was executed, the plaintiffs learned that they could not place a freestanding sign along the highway to advertise their business because the Deschutes County Code allowed only one freestanding sign on the property, and the defendant already had one in place. The plaintiffs filed this action, alleging that defendant had breached the lease by failing to provide them with space in which they could erect a freestanding sign. Paragraph 16 of the lease provides as follows: "Tenant shall not erect or install any signs ... visible from outside the leased premises with out [sic] the previous written consent of the Landlord." Explain whether this evidence is admissible.

27. Jesse Carter and Jesse Thomas had an auto accident with a driver insured by Allstate. Carter and Thomas hired an attorney, Joseph Onwuteaka, to represent them. Mr. Onwuteaka sent a demand letter for settlement of the plaintiffs' claims to Allstate's adjustor, Ms. Gracie Weatherly. Mr. Onwuteaka claims Ms. Weatherly made, and he orally accepted, settlement terms on behalf of the plaintiffs. When Allstate did not honor the agreements, Carter and Thomas filed a suit for breach of contract. Discuss the enforceability of the oral agreement.

28. Mary Iacono and Carolyn Lyons had been friends for almost thirty-five years. Mary suffers from advanced rheumatoid arthritis and is in a wheelchair. Carolyn invited Mary to join her on a trip to Las Vegas, Nevada, for which Carolyn paid. Mary contended she was invited to Las Vegas by Carolyn because Carolyn thought Mary was lucky. Sometime before the trip, Mary had a dream about winning on a Las Vegas slot machine. Mary's dream convinced her to go to Las Vegas, and she accepted Carolyn's offer to split "50–50" any gambling winnings. Carolyn provided Mary with money for gambling. Mary and Carolyn started to gamble but after losing $47, Carolyn wanted to leave to see a show. Mary begged Carolyn to stay, and Carolyn agreed on the condition that Carolyn put the coins into the machines because doing so took Mary too long. Mary agreed and led Carolyn to a dollar slot machine that looked like the machine in her dream. The machine did not pay on the first try. Mary then said, "Just one more time," and Carolyn looked at Mary and said, "This one's for you, Puddin." They hit the jackpot, winning $1,908,064 to be paid over a period of twenty years. Carolyn refused to share the winnings with Mary. Is Mary entitled to one-half of the proceeds? Explain.

TAKING SIDES

Stuart Studio, an art studio, prepared a new catalog for the National School of Heavy Equipment, a school run by Gilbert and Donald Shaw. When the artwork was virtually finished, Gilbert Shaw requested Stuart Studio to purchase and supervise the printing of twenty-five thousand catalogs. Shaw told the art studio that payment of the printing costs would be made within ten days after billing and that if the "National School would not pay the full total that he would stand good for the entire bill." Shaw was chairman of the board of directors of the school, and he owned 100 percent of its voting stock and

49 percent of its nonvoting stock. The school became bankrupt, and Stuart Studio was unable to recover the sum from the school. Stuart Studio then brought an action against Shaw on the basis of his promise to pay the bill.

a. What are the arguments that Shaw is not liable on his promise?

b. What are the arguments that Shaw is liable on his promise?

c. Is Shaw obligated to pay the debt in question? Explain.

Chapter 16

THIRD PARTIES TO CONTRACTS

The establishment of [the third-party beneficiary] doctrine ... is a victory of practical utility over theory, of equity over technical subtlety.

BRANTLY ON CONTRACTS, 2ND EDITION

CHAPTER OUTCOMES

After reading and studying this chapter, you should be able to:

1. Distinguish between an assignment of rights and a delegation of duties.

2. Identify (a) the requirements of an assignment of contract rights and (b) those rights that are not assignable.

3. Identify those situations in which a delegation of duties is not permitted.

4. Distinguish between an intended beneficiary and an incidental beneficiary.

5. Explain when the rights of an intended beneficiary vest.

In prior chapters, we considered situations that essentially involved only two parties. In this chapter, we deal with the rights and duties of third parties, namely, persons who are not parties to the contract but who have a right to or an obligation for its performance. These rights and duties arise either by (1) an assignment of the rights of a party to the contract, (2) a delegation of the duties of a party to the contract, or (3) the express terms of a contract entered into for the benefit of a third person. In an assignment or delegation, the third party's rights or duties arise after the original contract is made, whereas in the third situation, the third-party beneficiary's rights arise at the time the contract is formed. We will consider these three situations in that order.

Assignment of Rights

Every contract creates both rights and duties. A person who owes a duty under a contract is an **obligor**, while a person to whom a contractual duty is owed is an **obligee**. For instance, Ann promises to sell to Bart an automobile for which Bart promises to pay $10,000 by monthly installments over the next three years. Ann's right under the contract is to receive payment from Bart, whereas Ann's duty is to deliver the automobile. Bart's right is to receive the automobile; his duty is to pay for it.

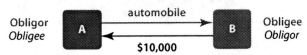

An **assignment of rights** is the voluntary transfer to a third party of the rights arising from the contract. In the above example, if Ann were to transfer her right under the contract (the installment payments due from Bart) to Clark for $8,500 in cash, this would constitute a valid assignment of rights. In this case, Ann would be the **assignor**, Clark would be the **assignee**, and Bart would be the *obligor*.

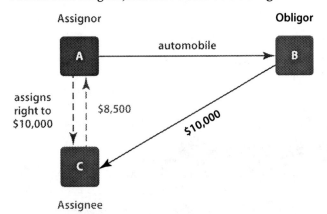

An effective assignment terminates the assignor's right to receive performance by the obligor. After an assignment, only the assignee has a right to the obligor's performance.

On the other hand, if Ann and Doris agree that Doris should deliver the automobile to Bart, this would constitute a delegation, not an assignment, of duties between Ann and Doris. A **delegation of duties** is a transfer to a third party of a contractual obligation. In this instance, Ann would be the **delegator**, Doris would be the **delegatee**, and Bart would be the *obligee*.

REQUIREMENTS OF AN ASSIGNMENT

The Restatement defines an assignment of a right as a manifestation of the assignor's intention to transfer the right so that the assignor's right to the performance of the obligor is extinguished either in whole or in part and the assignee acquires a right to such performance. No special form or particular words are necessary to create an assignment. Any words that fairly indicate an intention to make the assignee the owner of the right are sufficient.

Unless otherwise provided by statute, an assignment may be oral. The Uniform Commercial Code (UCC) imposes a writing requirement on all assignments beyond $5,000. The 2001 Revision to Article 1, however, has deleted this requirement. In addition, Article 9 requires certain assignments to be in writing.

Consideration is not required for an effective assignment. Consequently, gratuitous assignments are valid and enforceable. By giving value, or consideration, for the assignment, the assignee indicates his assent to the assignment as part of the bargained-for exchange. On the other hand, when the assignment is gratuitous, the assignee's assent is not always required. Any assignee who has not assented to an assignment, however, may disclaim the assignment within a reasonable time after learning of its existence and terms.

Revocability of Assignments When the assignee gives consideration in exchange for an assignment, a contract exists between the assignor and the assignee. Consequently, the assignor may not revoke the assignment without the assignee's assent. In contrast, a gratuitous assignment is revocable by the assignor and is terminated by the assignor's death, incapacity, or subsequent assignment of the right, unless the assignor has made an effective delivery of the assignment to the assignee, as in the case of *Speelman v. Pascal.* Such delivery can be accomplished by transferring a deed or other document evidencing the right, such as a stock certificate or savings passbook. Delivery may also consist of physically delivering a signed, written assignment of the contract right. A gratuitous assignment is also made irrevocable if, before the attempted revocation, the donee-assignee receives payment of the claim from the obligor, obtains a judgment against the obligor, or obtains a new contract with the obligor.

PRACTICAL ADVICE
Be sure to make irrevocable assignments of only those rights you wish to transfer.

SPEELMAN V. PASCAL

COURT OF APPEALS OF NEW YORK, 1961
10 N.Y.2D 313, 222 N.Y.S.2D 324, 178 N.E.2D 723

http://scholar.google.com/scholar_case?case=18121890776629170977&q=178+N.E.2d+723&hl=en&as_sdt=2,34

FACTS In 1952, the estate of George Bernard Shaw granted to Gabriel Pascal Enterprises, Limited, the exclusive rights to produce a musical play and a motion picture based on Shaw's play *Pygmalion*. The agreement contained a provision terminating the license if Gabriel Pascal Enterprises did not arrange for well-known composers, such as Lerner and Loewe, to write the musical and produce it within a specified period of time. George Pascal, owner of 98 percent of Gabriel Pascal Enterprises' stock, attempted to meet these requirements but died in July 1954 before negotiations had been completed. In February 1954, however, while the license had two years yet to run, Pascal had sent a letter to Kingman, his executive secretary, granting to her certain percentages of his share of the profits from the expected stage and screen productions of *Pygmalion*. Subsequently, Pascal's estate arranged for the writing and production of the highly successful *My Fair Lady*, based on Shaw's *Pygmalion*. Kingman then sued to enforce Pascal's gift assignment of the future royalties. The trial court entered judgment for Kingman.

DECISION Judgment for Kingman affirmed.

OPINION Desmond, C. J. The only real question is as to whether the 1954 letter *** operated to transfer to plaintiff an enforceable right to the described percentages of the royalties to accrue to Pascal on the production of a stage or film version of a musical play based on

Pygmalion. We see no reason why this letter does not have that effect. It is true that at the time of the delivery of the letter there was no musical stage or film play in existence but Pascal, who owned and was conducting negotiations to realize on the stage and film rights, could grant to another a share of the moneys to accrue from the use of those rights by others. There are many instances of courts enforcing assignments of rights to sums which were expected thereafter to become due to the assignor. *** In every such case the question must be as to whether there was a completed delivery of a kind appropriate to the subject property. *** In our present case there was nothing left for Pascal to do in order to make an irrevocable transfer to plaintiff of part of Pascal's right to receive royalties from the productions.

INTERPRETATION A gratuitous assignment becomes irrevocable upon the assignor's making an effective delivery of the assignment to the assignee.

CRITICAL THINKING QUESTION Should the law enforce assignments of contractual rights not in existence at the time of the assignment? Explain.

Partial Assignments A **partial assignment** is a transfer of a portion of the contractual rights to one or more assignees, as in *Speelman v. Pascal*. The obligor, however, may require all the parties entitled to the promised performance to litigate the matter in one action, thus ensuring that all parties are present and avoiding the undue hardship of multiple lawsuits. For example, Jack owes Richard $2,500. Richard assigns $1,000 to Mildred. Neither Richard nor Mildred can maintain an action against Jack if Jack objects, unless the other is joined in the proceeding against Jack.

RIGHTS THAT ARE ASSIGNABLE

As a general rule, most contract rights, including rights under an option contract, are assignable. The most common contractual right that may be assigned is the right to the payment of money. A contract right to other property, such as land or goods, is likewise assignable.

RIGHTS THAT ARE NOT ASSIGNABLE

To protect the obligor or the public interest, some contract rights are not assignable. These nonassignable contract rights include those that (1) materially increase the duty, risk, or burden upon the obligor; (2) transfer

highly personal contract rights; (3) are expressly prohibited by the contract; or (4) are prohibited by law.

Assignments That Materially Increase the Duty, Risk, or Burden An assignment is ineffective if performance by the obligor to the assignee would differ materially from the obligor's performance to the assignor, that is, if the assignment would significantly change the nature or extent of the obligor's duty. Thus, an automobile liability insurance policy issued to Alex is not assignable by Alex to Betty. The risk assumed by the insurance company was liability for Alex's negligent operation of the automobile. Liability for Betty's operation of the same automobile would be a risk entirely different from the one the insurance company had assumed. Similarly, Candice would not be allowed to assign to Eunice, the owner of a twenty-five-room mansion, Candice's contractual right to have David paint her small, two-bedroom house. Clearly, such an assignment would materially increase David's duty of performance. By comparison, the right to receive monthly payments under a contract may be assigned, for mailing the check to the assignee costs no more than mailing it to the assignor. Moreover, if a contract explicitly provides that it may be assigned, then rights under it are assignable even if the assignment would change the duty, risk, or burden of performance on the obligor.

Assignments of Personal Rights When the rights under a contract are highly personal, in that they are limited to the person of the obligee, such rights are not assignable. An extreme example of such a contract is an agreement of two persons to marry one another. The prospective groom obviously may not transfer the prospective bride's promise to marry to some third party.

A more typical example of contract involving personal rights would be a contract between a teacher and a school. The teacher could not assign her right to a faculty position to another teacher. Similarly, a student who is awarded a scholarship cannot assign his right to some other student. The *Reiser* case involves another example.

REISER v. DAYTON COUNTRY CLUB COMPANY

UNITED STATES COURT OF APPEALS, SIXTH CIRCUIT, 1992
972 F.2D 689

http://scholar.google.com/scholar_case?case=6023421001644754391&q=972+F.2d+689&hl=en&as_sdt=2,34

FACTS The Dayton Country Club Company (the Club) offers many social activities to its members. However, the privilege to play golf at the Club is reserved to a special membership category for which additional fees are charged. The Club chooses golfing memberships from a waiting list of members according to detailed rules, regulations, and procedures. Magness and Redman were golfing members of the Club. Upon their filing for bankruptcy, their trustee sought to assign by sale their rights under these memberships to (1) other members on the waiting list, (2) other members not on the waiting list, or (3) the general public, provided the purchaser first acquired membership in the Club. The bankruptcy court found that the Club's rules governing golf membership were essentially anti-assignment provisions and therefore the estate could not assign rights contained in the membership agreement. On appeal to the district court, the bankruptcy court's ruling was affirmed. The district court added that this case was not a lease but rather a "noncommercial dispute over the possession of a valuable membership in a recreational and social club."

DECISION Judgment affirmed.

OPINION Joiner, J. *** [T]he contracts involve complex issues and multiple parties: the members of the club, in having an orderly procedure for the selection of full golfing members; the club itself, in demonstrating to all who would become members that there is a predictable and orderly method of filling vacancies in the golfing roster; and more particularly, persons on the waiting list who have deposited substantial sums of money based on an expectation and a developed procedure that in due course they, in turn, would become full golfing members.

If the trustee is permitted to assume and assign the full golf membership, the club would be required to breach its agreement with the persons on the waiting list, each of whom has contractual rights with the club. It would require the club to accept performance from and render performance to a person other than the debtor.

***

The contracts creating the complex relationships among the parties and others are not in any way commercial. They create personal relationships among individuals who play golf, who are waiting to play golf, who eat together, swim and play together. They are personal contracts and Ohio law does not permit the assignment of personal contracts. [Citation.]

So-called personal contracts, or contracts in which the personality of one of the parties is material, are not assignable. Whether the personality of one or both parties is material depends on the intention of the parties, as shown by the language which they have used, and upon the nature of the contract.

Therefore, we believe that the trustee's motion to assign the full golf membership should be denied. We reach this conclusion because the arrangements for filling vacancies proscribe assignment, the club did not consent to the assignment and sale, and applicable law excuses the club from accepting performance from or rendering performance to a person other than the debtor.

INTERPRETATION When rights under a contract are personal, they may not be assigned.

ETHICAL QUESTION Is the court's decision fair to the creditors of Magness and Redman? Explain.

CRITICAL THINKING QUESTION Which type of contracts should not be assignable because of their personal nature? Explain.

Express Prohibition against Assignment
Though contract terms prohibiting assignment of rights under the contract are strictly construed, most courts interpret a general prohibition against assignments as a mere promise not to assign. As a consequence, the general prohibition, if violated, gives the obligor a right to damages for breach of the terms forbidding assignment but does not render the assignment ineffective.

The Restatement provides that, unless circumstances indicate the contrary, a contract term prohibiting assignment of the *contract* bars only the delegation to the assignee (delegatee) of the assignor's (delegator's) duty of performance, not the assignment of *rights*. Thus, Norman and Lucy contract for the sale of land by Lucy to Norman for $30,000 and provide in their contract that Norman may not assign the contract. Norman pays Lucy $30,000, thereby fulfilling his duty of performance under the contract. Norman then assigns his rights to George, who consequently is entitled to receive the land from Lucy (the obligor) despite the contractual prohibition of assignment.

Article 2 of the Code provides that a right to damages for breach of the whole contract or a right arising out of the assignor's due performance of his entire obligation can be assigned despite a contractual provision to the contrary. Article 2 also provides that, unless circumstances indicate the contrary, a contract term prohibiting assignment of the *contract* bars only the delegation to the assignee (delegatee) of the assignor's (delegator's) *duty* of performance, not the assignment of *rights*. Article 9 of the Code makes ineffective any term in a contract prohibiting the assignment of a security interest arising out of a sale of any right to payment for goods sold or leased or for services rendered.

> ### PRACTICAL ADVICE
> Consider including in your contract a provision prohibiting the assignment of any contractual rights without your written consent and making ineffective any such assignment.

ALDANA V. COLONIAL PALMS PLAZA, INC.

DISTRICT COURT OF APPEAL OF FLORIDA, THIRD DISTRICT, 1991
591 SO.2D 953, REHEARING DENIED

http://scholar.google.com/scholar_case?case=1977050164764776625&q=591+So.2d+953&hl=en&as_sdt=2,34

FACTS Colonial Palms Plaza, Inc. (Landlord) entered into a lease agreement with Abby's Cakes On Dixie, Inc. (Tenant). The lease included a provision in which Landlord agreed to pay Tenant a construction allowance of up to $11,250 after Tenant completed certain improvements. Prior to completion of the improvements, Tenant assigned its right to receive the first $8,000 of the construction allowance to Robert Aldana in return for a loan of $8,000 to finance the construction. Aldana sent notice of the assignment to Landlord. When Tenant completed the improvements, Landlord ignored the assignment and paid Tenant the construction allowance. Aldana sued Landlord for the money due pursuant to the assignment. Landlord relied on an anti-assignment clause in the lease to argue that the assignment was void. That clause states in part:

> TENANT agrees not to assign, mortgage, pledge, or encumber this Lease, in whole or in part, to sublet in whole or any part of the DEMISED PREMISES ... without first obtaining the prior, specific written consent of the LANDLORD at LANDLORD'S sole discretion.... Any such assignment ... without such consent shall be void.

The trial court granted Landlord summary judgment.

DECISION Summary judgment reversed and case remanded.

OPINION Per Curiam. Assignee argues * * * that under ordinary contract principles, the lease provision at issue here does not prevent the assignment of the right to receive contractual payments. We agree.

* * * [T]he lease provides that "TENANT agrees not to assign * * * this Lease, in whole or in part. * * *" Tenant did not assign the lease, but instead assigned a right to receive the construction allowance.

The law in this area is summarized in Restatement (Second) of Contracts, § 322(1), as follows:

> (1) Unless the circumstances indicate the contrary, a contract term prohibiting assignment of "the contract" bars only the delegation to an assignee of the performance by the assignor of a duty or condition.

As a rule of construction, in other words, a prohibition against assignment of the contract (or in this case, the lease) will prevent assignment of contractual duties, but does not prevent assignment of the right to receive payments due—unless the circumstances indicate the contrary. [Citations.]

Landlord was given notice of the assignment. Delivery of the notice of the assignment to the debtor fixes accountability of the debtor to the assignee. [Citation.] Therefore, Landlord was bound by the assignment. [Citation.] The trial court improperly granted final summary judgment in favor of Landlord and the judgment must be reversed.

INTERPRETATION Unless circumstances indicate the contrary, a contract term prohibiting assignment of the contract bars only delegation of the assignor's contractual duties.

ETHICAL QUESTION If the landlord had inadvertently ignored the notice of assignment, would the outcome of the case have been fair? Explain.

CRITICAL THINKING QUESTION Should the courts honor contractual prohibitions of assignments by rendering such assignments ineffective? Explain.

Assignments Prohibited by Law Various federal and state statutes, as well as public policy, prohibit or regulate the assignment of certain types of contract rights. For instance, assignments of future wages are subject to such statutes, some of which prohibit these assignments altogether, whereas others require the assignments to be in writing and subject them to certain restrictions. Moreover, an assignment that violates public policy will be unenforceable even in the absence of a prohibiting statute.

RIGHTS OF THE ASSIGNEE

Obtains Rights of Assignor The general rule is that an assignee *stands in the shoes* of the assignor. She acquires the rights of the assignor but no new or additional rights, and she takes with the assigned rights all of the defenses, defects, and infirmities to which they would be subject in an action against the obligor by the assignor. Thus, in an action brought by the assignee against the obligor, the obligor may plead fraud, duress, undue

influence, failure of consideration, breach of contract, or any other defense arising out of the original contract against the assignor. The obligor may also assert rights of setoff or counterclaim arising out of entirely separate matters that he may have against the assignor, as long as they arose before he had notice of the assignment.

The Code permits the buyer under a contract of sale to agree as part of the contract that he will not assert against an assignee any claim or defense that the buyer may have against the seller if the assignee takes the assignment for value, in good faith, and without notice of conflicting claims or of certain defenses. Such a provision in an agreement renders the seller's rights more marketable. The Federal Trade Commission, however, has invalidated such waiver of defense provisions in consumer credit transactions. This rule is discussed more fully in Chapter 25. Article 9 reflects this rule by essentially rendering waiver-of-defense clauses ineffective in consumer transactions. Most states also have statutes protecting buyers in consumer transactions by prohibiting waiver of defenses.

MOUNTAIN PEAKS FINANCIAL SERVICES, INC. v. ROTH-STEFFEN

COURT OF APPEALS OF MINNESOTA, 2010
778 N.W.2D 380

http://scholar.google.com/scholar_case?q=778+N.W.2d+380&hl=en&as_sdt=2,34&case=11662901939297878943&scilh=0

FACTS In May 1998, Catherine Roth-Steffen graduated from law school with over $100,000 in school loans from more than a dozen lenders. Of this total, Roth-Steffen received $20,350 from the Missouri Higher Education Loan Authority (MOHELA) CASH Loan program. As of November 5, 1998, Roth-Steffen had incurred interest on these loans (MOHELA loan) in the amount of $3,043.28. Roth-Steffen listed the balance of $23,401.28 in a loan consolidation application she submitted in December 1998. She requested that the MOHELA loan not be consolidated with her other loans.

In February 2003, MOHELA assigned ownership of the MOHELA loan to Guarantee National Insurance Company (GNIC), which, in turn, assigned the loan for

collection to respondent Mountain Peaks Financial Services, Inc. (Mountain Peaks). Mountain Peaks commenced a collection action claiming that it holds the MOHELA loan and that it is entitled to judgment in the amount of the outstanding balance, $23,120.52, and additional interest at the rate of 2.54% from July 19, 2007. In response, Roth-Steffen asserted that the action is barred by Minnesota's six-year statute of limitations for collection on promissory notes. The district court granted summary judgment in favor of Mountain Peaks, determining that Mountain Peaks (1) owns Roth-Steffen's loan, (2) is a valid assignee of MOHELA's right, and (3) under the federal Higher Education Act is not to be subject to any state statutes of limitation.

DECISION Summary judgment is affirmed.

OPINION Bjorkman, J. Enacted in 1965, the Higher Education Act was the first comprehensive government program designed to provide scholarships, grants, work-study funding, and loans for students to attend college. [Citations.] Pursuant to the act, the federal government makes loans and guarantees loans made by private lenders. [Citation.] In 1991, in response to rising loan defaults and an unfavorable legal ruling, Congress adopted the Higher Education Technical Amendments. [Citation.]

The amendments eliminate all statutes of limitation on actions to recover on defaulted student loans for certain classes of lenders. [Citation.] These lenders are defined in section 1091a:

* * *

(B) a guaranty agency that has an agreement with the Secretary under section 1078(c) of this title that is seeking the repayment of the amount due from a borrower on a loan made under part B of this subchapter after such guaranty agency reimburses the previous holder of the loan for its loss on account of the default of the borrower;

* * *

[Citation.] For convenience, we refer to the entities described in this statute as "named lenders."

Mountain Peaks argues that it is exempt from Minnesota's statutes of limitation because it is a valid assignee of MOHELA, a lender that has an agreement with the Secretary of Education under [section] 1091a(a)(2)(B). Roth-Steffen acknowledges that MOHELA is a named lender but argues that because Congress did not expressly identify assignees as named lenders, section 1091a does not preempt state statutes of limitation for claims asserted by assignees of named lenders.

* * *

Section 1091a does not, by its terms, extend its statutes-of-limitation exemption to assignees of named lenders. Nor does the statute expressly preclude application of the exemption to assignees. * * *

* * *

But courts interpreting federal statutes must also presume that Congress intended to preserve the common law. * * *

The common law of most states, including Minnesota, has long recognized that "[a]n assignment operates to place the assignee in the shoes of the assignor, and provides the assignee with the same legal rights as

the assignor had before assignment." [Citation]; *see generally* Restatement (Second) of Contracts § 317 (1981) (Assignment of a Right). Contractual rights and duties are generally assignable, including the rights to receive payment on debts, obtain nonmonetary performance, and recover damages. Restatement (Second) of Contracts § 316 (1981). But an assignor may not transfer rights that are personal, such as recovery for personal injuries or performance under contracts that involve personal trust or confidences. [Citation]; *see generally* Restatement (Second) of Contracts § 317 cmt. c. Under the common law, a contractual right to recover student-loan debt is assignable and does not fall within the personal-rights exclusion to the assignment rule.

* * *

We are also guided by how courts have applied other federal-loan statutes. The majority of courts hold that assignees are entitled to the benefit of the federal statute of limitations when they acquire loans made under federal programs administered by the Federal Deposit Insurance Corporation, the Federal Savings and Loan Insurance Corporation, and the Small Business Administration. * * *

* * *

* * * Because Congress legislated with a full knowledge of the common law of assignment, all contractual rights of the named lenders, including the protection from state statutes of limitations, should transfer to their assignees. This interpretation of section 1091a both preserves the common law and furthers the stated purpose of the statute. [Citation.]

We conclude that section 1091a of the Higher Education Act applies to assignees of named lenders. Mountain Peaks is an assignee of a named lender, therefore this action is not time-barred by any Minnesota statute of limitations.

INTERPRETATION An assignment places the assignee in the shoes of the assignor and provides the assignee with the same legal rights as the assignor had before the assignment.

CRITICAL THINKING QUESTION If assignees of student loans were made subject to state statutes of limitations what would be the probable effect on the availability of student loans? Explain.

Notice The obligor need not receive notice for an assignment to be valid. Giving notice of assignment is advisable, however, because an assignee will lose his rights against the obligor if the obligor, without notice

of the assignment, pays the assignor. Compelling an obligor to pay a claim a second time, when she was unaware that a new party was entitled to payment, would be unfair. For example, Donald owes Gary $1,000 due on

September 1. Gary assigns the debt to Paula on August 1, but neither Gary nor Paula informs Donald. On September 1, Donald pays Gary. Donald is fully discharged from his obligation, whereas Gary is liable for $1,000 to Paula. On the other hand, if Paula had given notice of the assignment to Donald before September 1 and Donald had paid Gary nevertheless, Paula would then have the right to recover the $1,000 from either Donald or Gary. Furthermore, notice cuts off any defenses based on subsequent agreements between the obligor and assignor and, as already indicated, subsequent setoffs and counterclaims of the obligor that may arise out of entirely separate matters.

> ## Practical Advice
>
> Upon receiving an assignment of a contractual right, promptly notify the obligor of the assignment.

Implied Warranties of Assignor

An **implied warranty** is an obligation imposed by law upon the transferor of property or contract rights. In the absence of an express intention to the contrary, an assignor who receives value makes the following implied warranties to the assignee with respect to the assigned right:

1. that he will do nothing to defeat or impair the assignment;

2. that the assigned right actually exists and is subject to no limitations or defenses other than those stated or apparent at the time of the assignment;

3. that any writing that evidences the right and that is delivered to the assignee or exhibited to him as an inducement to accept the assignment is genuine and what it purports to be; and

4. that the assignor has no knowledge of any fact that would impair the value of the assignment.

Thus, Eric has a right against Julia and assigns it for value to Gwen. Later, Eric gives Julia a release. Gwen may recover damages from Eric for breach of the first implied warranty.

Express Warranties of Assignor

An **express warranty** is an explicitly made contractual promise regarding the property or contract rights transferred. The assignor is further bound by any specific express warranties he makes to the assignee about the right assigned. Unless he explicitly states as much, however, the assignor does not guarantee that the obligor will pay the assigned debt or otherwise perform.

> ## Practical Advice
>
> Consider obtaining from the assignor an express warranty that the contractual right is assignable and guaranteeing that the obligor will perform the assigned obligation.

Successive Assignments of the Same Right

The owner of a right could conceivably make successive assignments of the same claim to different persons. Although this action is morally and legally inappropriate, it raises the question of what rights successive assignees have. Assume, for example, that B owes A $1,000. On June 1, A for value assigns the debt to C. Thereafter, on June 15, A assigns it to D, who in good faith gives value and has no knowledge of the prior assignment by A to C. If the assignment is subject to Article 9, then the article's priority rules will control, as discussed in Chapter 37. Otherwise, the priority is determined by the common law. The majority rule in the United States is that the first assignee in point of time (C) prevails over later assignees. By way of contrast, in England and in a minority of the states, the first assignee to notify the obligor prevails.

The Restatement adopts a third view. A prior assignee is entitled to the assigned right and its proceeds to the exclusion of a subsequent assignee, *except* where the prior assignment is revocable or voidable by the assignor or the subsequent assignee in good faith and without knowledge of the prior assignment gives value and obtains one of the following: (1) payment or satisfaction of the obligor's duty, (2) a judgment against the obligor, (3) a new contract with the obligor, or (4) possession of a writing of a type customarily accepted as a symbol or evidence of the right assigned.

Delegation of Duties

As we indicated, contractual *duties* are not assignable, but their performance generally may be delegated to a third person. A delegation of duties is a transfer of a contractual obligation to a third party. For example, A promises to sell B a new automobile, for which B promises to pay $10,000 by monthly installments over the next three years. If A and D agree that D should deliver the automobile to B, this would not constitute an assignment but would be a delegation of duties between A and D. In this instance, A would be the *delegator*, D would be the *delegatee*, and B would be the *obligee*. A delegation of duty does not extinguish the delegator's obligation to perform because A remains liable to B. When the delegatee accepts, or **assumes**, the delegated duty, *both* the delegator and delegatee are liable for performance of the contractual duty to the obligee.

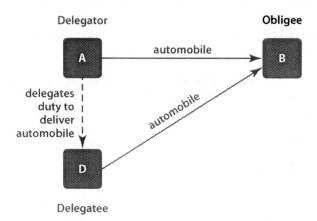

DELEGABLE DUTIES

Though contractual duties generally are delegable, a delegation will not be permitted if

1. the nature of the duties is personal in that the obligee has a substantial interest in having the delegator perform the contract;

2. the performance is expressly made nondelegable; or

3. the delegation is prohibited by statute or public policy.

The courts will examine a delegation more closely than an assignment because a delegation compels the nondelegating party to the contract (the obligee) to receive performance from a party with whom she has not dealt.

For example, a schoolteacher may not delegate her performance to another teacher, even if the substitute is equally competent, for this contract is personal in nature. On the other hand, under a contract in which performance by a party involves no special skill and in which no personal trust or confidence is involved, the party may delegate performance of his duty. For example, the duty to pay money, to deliver fungible goods such as corn, or to mow a lawn is usually delegable. The next case deals with this type of delegation.

> ### PRACTICAL ADVICE
>
> When it is important that the other party to a contract personally perform his contractual obligations, consider including a term in the contract prohibiting any delegation of duties without written consent.

PUBLIC SERVICE COMMISSION OF MARYLAND V. PANDA-BRANDYWINE, L.P.

COURT OF APPEALS OF MARYLAND, 2003
375 MD. 185, 825 A.2D 462

http://scholar.google.com/scholar_case?case=14283409950595264869&q=825+a.2d+462&hl=en&as_sdt=2,34

FACTS Potomac Electric Power Company (PEPCO) is an electric utility serving the metropolitan Washington, D.C., area. Panda-Brandywine, L.P. (Panda) is a "qualified facility" under the Public Utility Regulatory Policies Act of 1978. In August, 1991, PEPCO and Panda entered into a power purchase agreement (PPA) calling for (1) the construction by Panda of a new 230-megawatt cogenerating power plant in Prince George's County, Maryland; (2) connection of the facility to PEPCO's high-voltage transmission system by transmission facilities to be built by Panda but later transferred without cost to PEPCO; and (3) upon commencement of the commercial operation of the plant, for PEPCO to purchase the power generated by that plant for a period of twenty-five years. The plant was built at a cost of $215 million.

The PPA is 113 pages in length, single-spaced, and is both detailed and complex. It gave PEPCO substantial authority to review, influence, and, in some instances, determine important aspects of both the construction and operation of the Panda facility. Section 19.1 of the PPA provided that the agreement was not assignable and not delegable without the written consent of the other party, which consent could not be unreasonably withheld.

In 1999, Maryland enacted legislation calling for the restructuring of the electric industry in an effort to promote competition in the generation and delivery of electricity. PEPCO's proposed restructuring involved a complete divestiture of its electric generating assets and its various PPAs, to be accomplished by an auction. The sale to the winning bidder was to be accomplished by an Asset Purchase and Sale Agreement (APSA) that included the PPA to which PEPCO and Panda were parties. Under the APSA the buyer was authorized to take all actions that PEPCO could lawfully take under the PPA with Panda.

On June 7, 2000, Southern Energy, Inc. (SEI) was declared the winning bidder. On September 27, 2000, the Public Service Commission (PSC) entered an order declaring, among other things, that the provisions in the APSA did not constitute an assignment or transfer within the meaning of Section 19.1 of the Panda PPA, that PEPCO was not assigning "significant obligations and rights under the PPA," that Panda would not be harmed by the transaction, and that the APSA did not "fundamentally alter" the contract between Panda and PEPCO. The PSC thus concluded that Panda's consent to the proposed APSA was not required.

Panda disagreed and brought this lawsuit. The trial court ruled that the APSA effected an assignment of Panda's PPA and reversed the PSC order. PEPCO appealed and the appellate court concluded that, through the APSA, PEPCO effectively and improperly delegated its duties under the PPA to SEI.

DECISION Judgment affirmed.

OPINION Wilner, J. By prohibiting both non-consensual assignment and delegation, the PPA recognizes a nuance, or distinction, that is occasionally overlooked. In a bilateral contract, each party ordinarily has both rights and duties—the right to expect performance from the other party to the contract and the duty to perform what the party has agreed to perform. Although both are often the subject of transfer, the law does distinguish between them, using the term "assignment" to refer to the transfer of contractual rights and the term "delegation" to refer to the transfer of contractual duties. ***

RESTATEMENT § 317 defines the assignment of a right as "a manifestation of the assignor's intention to transfer it by virtue of which the assignor's right to performance by the obligor is extinguished in whole or in part and the assignee acquires a right to such performance." Section 317(2) permits a contractual right to be assigned unless

> (a) the substitution of a right of the assignee for the right of the assignor would materially change the duty of the obligor, or materially increase the burden or risk imposed on him by his contract, or materially impair his chance of obtaining return performance, or materially reduce its value to him,
> (b) the assignment is forbidden by statute or is inoperative on grounds of public policy, or
> (c) *assignment is validly precluded by contract.* (Emphasis added).

Section 318 speaks to the delegation of performance. Section 318(1) allows an obligor to delegate the performance of a contractual duty "unless the delegation is contrary to public policy *or the terms of his promise.*" (Emphasis added.) Section 318(2) provides that, unless otherwise agreed, a promise requires performance by a particular person "only to the extent that the obligee has a substantial interest in having that person perform or control the acts promised." Finally, § 318(3) states that, "unless the obligee agrees otherwise, neither delegation of performance nor a contract to assume the duty made with the obligor by the person delegated discharges any duty or liability of the delegating obligor."

Although using somewhat different language, we have adopted those principles. *** [W]e [have] held that "in the absence of a contrary provision ... rights and duties under an executory bilateral contract may be assigned and delegated, subject to the exception that duties under a contract to provide personal services may never be delegated, nor rights be assigned under a contract where *delectus personae* was an ingredient of the bargain."

These general statements *** regarding the extent to which rights may be assigned and duties of performance may be delegated are, as noted, subject to any valid contractual provision prohibiting assignment or delegation. Section 19.1 of the PPA very clearly prohibits both the assignment of rights and the delegation of duties of performance, absent express written consent. The issue, then, is not whether PEPCO can make such an assignment or delegation but only whether it has, in fact, done so. The answer to that lies in the effect that the [provisions of the APSA] have on the contractual relationship between PEPCO and Panda.

***

*** The APSA involves a great deal more than merely a resale of electricity purchased from Panda and even more than the effective substitution of one customer for another. Much of Panda's control over its own facility and business was subject to the approval and cooperation of PEPCO; indeed, to a large extent, the operation of the facility was, in many important respects, almost a joint venture. In agreeing to that kind of arrangement, Panda necessarily was relying on its perceptions of PEPCO's competence and managerial style. One does not ordinarily choose a business partner by auction or lottery, and there is no evidence that Panda did so in this case. Paraphrasing § 318(2) of the RESTATEMENT, Panda has "a substantial interest in having [PEPCO] perform or control the acts promised." Under [the APSA], that control has been delegated irrevocably to SEI—a stranger to Panda—with the ability of SEI to delegate it to others.

*** Virtually none of the rights and responsibilities transferred to SEI under [the APSA] are permitted under § 19.1 of the PPA. *** We hold that [the APSA] constitutes an assignment of rights and obligations under the PPA in contravention of § 19.1 of that agreement and that it is therefore invalid and unenforceable.

INTERPRETATION The extent to which contractual rights may be assigned and duties of performance delegated are subject to any valid contractual provision prohibiting assignment or delegation.

CRITICAL THINKING QUESTION If the APSA had involved only the resale of electricity purchased from Panda would the court have permitted the delegation?

DUTIES OF THE PARTIES

Even when permitted, a **delegation** of a duty to a third person leaves the delegator bound to perform. If the delegator desires to be discharged of the duty, she may enter into an agreement by which she obtains the consent of the obligee to substitute a third person (the delegatee) in her place. This is a **novation**, whereby the delegator is discharged and the third party becomes directly bound on his promise to the obligee.

Though a delegation authorizes a third party to perform a duty for the delegator, the delegatee becomes liable for performance only if he assents to perform the delegated duties. Thus, if Frank owes a duty to Grace, and Frank delegates that duty to Henry, Henry is not obligated to either Frank or Grace to perform the duty unless Henry agrees to do so. If, however, Henry promises either Frank (the delegator) or Grace (the obligee) that he will perform Frank's duty, Henry is said to have *assumed the delegated duty* and becomes liable for nonperformance to both Frank and Grace. Accordingly, when there is both a delegation of duties *and* an assumption of the delegated duties, *both* the delegator and the delegatee are liable to the obligee for proper performance of the original contractual duty. The delegatee's promise to perform creates contract rights in the obligee, who may bring an action against the delegatee as a third-party beneficiary of the contract between the delegator and the delegatee. (Third-party contracts are discussed in the next section in this chapter.)

The question of whether a party has assumed contractual duties frequently arises in the following ambiguous situation: Marty and Carol agree to an assignment of Marty's contract with Bob. The Restatement and the Code clearly resolve this ambiguity by providing that unless the language or circumstances indicate the contrary, an assignment of "the contract" or of "all my rights under the contract" or an assignment in similar general terms is an assignment of rights *and* a delegation of performance of the duties of the assignor, and its acceptance by the assignee constitutes a promise to perform those duties. For example, Cooper Oil Company has a contract to deliver oil to Halsey. Cooper makes a written assignment to Lowell Oil Company "of all Cooper's rights under the contract." Lowell is under a duty to Halsey to deliver the oil called for by the contract, and Cooper is liable to Halsey if Lowell does not perform. You should also recall that the Restatement and the Code provide that a clause prohibiting an assignment of "the contract" is to be construed as barring only the delegation to the assignee (delegatee) of the assignor's (delegator's) performance, unless the circumstances indicate the contrary.

Third-Party Beneficiary Contracts

A contract in which a party (the *promisor*) promises to render a certain performance not to the other party (the promisee) but to a third person (the beneficiary) is called a **third-party beneficiary contract**. The third person is merely a beneficiary of the contract, not a party to it. The law divides such contracts into two types: (1) intended beneficiary contracts and (2) incidental beneficiary contracts. An **intended beneficiary** is intended by the two parties to the contract (the promisor and promisee) to receive a benefit from the performance of their agreement. Accordingly, the courts generally permit intended beneficiaries to enforce third-party contracts. For example, Abbot promises Baldwin to deliver an automobile to Carson if Baldwin promises to pay $10,000. Carson is the intended beneficiary.

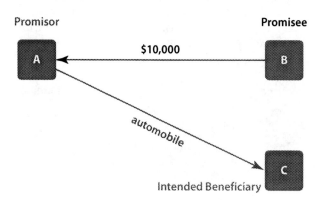

In an **incidental beneficiary** contract the third party is not intended to receive a benefit under the contract. Accordingly, courts do not enforce the third party's right to the benefits of the contract. For example, Abbot

APPLYING THE LAW

Third Parties to Contracts

FACTS Monica signed a twelve-month lease with Grandridge Apartments in Grand City. But after only two months she received a promotion that required her to move to Lakeville, three hundred miles away. Mindful of her lease obligation, she found an acquaintance, Troy, to rent the apartment for the remaining ten months. Troy promised Monica he would pay the rent directly to the landlord each month and would clean the place up before moving out at the end of the lease term.

After moving in, Troy personally delivered a check for the rent to the landlord each month until four months later when he lost his job, at which point he stopped paying rent altogether. The landlord evicted Troy and, as he was unable to find another suitable tenant, he sued Monica for the rent owed on the remainder of the lease. Monica claimed the landlord should have sued Troy.

Issue Is Monica liable for the remaining lease payments?

Rule of Law Performance of a contract obligation generally may be delegated to a third person who is willing to assume the liability. However, such a delegation by the obligor does not extinguish the obligor/delegator's duty to perform the contract. If the delegator wishes to be discharged from the contract prospectively, she should enter into a new agreement with the obligee, in which the obligee consents to the substitution of a third party (the delegatee) in the delegator's place. This is called a novation.

Application The lease is a contract obligation. Monica is the obligor, and the landlord is the obligee. Here, Monica delegated her performance under the lease to Troy. Troy assumed liability for the lease payments by agreeing to pay the rent. However, even though a valid delegation has been made, Monica is not relieved of her duty to pay the rent. Instead, both Troy and Monica are now obligated to the landlord for the remaining lease term.

Had Monica entered into a novation with the landlord, only Troy would be liable for the remaining rent. But the facts do not support finding a novation. Troy made the rent payments directly to the landlord, who ultimately evicted Troy from the apartment. Therefore, the landlord was aware that Troy had taken possession of the apartment and that Troy may have taken on some responsibility for rent payments. At most, the landlord tacitly consented to the informal assignment and delegation of the lease to Troy. However, the landlord never agreed to substitute Troy for Monica and thereby to release Monica from her legal obligations under the lease.

Conclusion In a suit by the landlord, Monica is responsible for the remaining rent payments.

promises to purchase and deliver to Baldwin an automobile for $10,000. In all probability Abbot would acquire the automobile from Davis. Davis would be an incidental beneficiary and would have no enforceable rights against either Abbot or Baldwin.

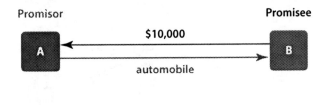

Promisor   Promisee

$10,000

A ← → B

automobile

Incidental Beneficiary   D

INTENDED BENEFICIARY

Unless otherwise agreed between the promisor and promisee, a beneficiary of a promise is an intended beneficiary if the parties intended this to be the result of their agreement. Thus, there are two types of intended beneficiaries: (1) donee beneficiaries and (2) creditor beneficiaries.

Donee Beneficiary A third party is an intended donee beneficiary if the promisee's purpose in bargaining for and obtaining the contract with the promisor was to make a gift of the promised performance to the beneficiary. The ordinary life insurance policy illustrates this type of intended beneficiary third-party contract. The insured (the promisee) makes a contract with an insurance company (the promisor), which promises, in consideration of premiums paid to it by the insured, to pay upon the death of the insured a stated sum of money to the named beneficiary (generally a relative or close friend), who is an intended donee beneficiary.

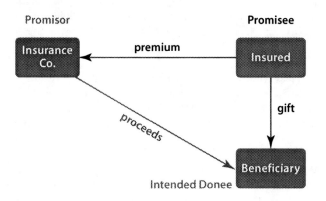

Creditor Beneficiary A third person is an intended creditor beneficiary if the promisee intends the performance of the promise to satisfy a legal duty owed to the beneficiary, who is a creditor of the promisee. The contract involves consideration moving from the promisee to the promisor in exchange for the promisor's engaging to pay a debt or to discharge an obligation the promisee owes to the third person.

To illustrate: in the contract for the sale by Wesley of his business to Susan, she promises Wesley that she will pay all of his outstanding business debts, as listed in the contract. Wesley's creditors are intended creditor beneficiaries.

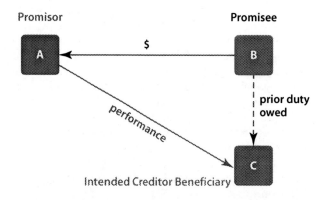

STINE V. STEWART

SUPREME COURT OF TEXAS, 2002
80 S.W.3D 586

http://caselaw.lp.findlaw.com/scripts/getcase.pl?court=tx&vol=/sc/010896&invol=1

FACTS On April 26, 1984, Mary Stine (Stine) loaned her daughter (Mary Ellen) and son-in-law William Stewart $100,000 to purchase a home. In return, the Stewarts jointly executed a promissory note for $100,000, payable on demand to Stine. The Stewarts did not give a security interest or mortgage to secure the note. The Stewarts eventually paid $50,000 on the note, leaving $50,000, plus unpaid interest, due.

The Stewarts divorced on October 2, 1992. The couple executed an Agreement Incident to Divorce, which disposed of marital property, including the home (the agreement identifies the home as the Lago Vista property). The agreement provided that if Stewart sold the home, he agreed that "any monies owing to [Stine] are to be paid in the current principal sum of $50,000.00." The agreement further states:

> The parties agree that with regard to the note to Mary Nelle Stine, after application of the proceeds of the [Lago Vista property], if there are any amounts owing to [Stine] the remaining balance owing to her will be appropriated 50% to NANCY KAREN STEWART and 50% to WILLIAM DEAN STEWART, JR. and said 50% from each party will be due and payable upon the determination that the proceeds from the sale of said residence are not sufficient to repay said $50,000.00 in full.

Stine did not sign the agreement.

On November 17, 1995, Stewart sold the Lago Vista property for $125,000, leaving $6,820.21 in net proceeds. Stewart did not pay these proceeds to Stine and did not make any further payments on the $50,000 principal. Consequently, on July 27, 1998, Stine sued Stewart for breaching the agreement.

The trial court concluded that Stine was an intended third-party beneficiary of the agreement and that Stewart breached the agreement when he refused to pay Stine. The trial court awarded Stine $28,410 in damages from Stewart. The court of appeals reversed the judgment, concluding that Stine was neither an intended third-party donee beneficiary of the agreement nor an intended third-party creditor beneficiary of the agreement.

DECISION The court of appeals' judgment is reversed and case remanded.

OPINION Per Curiam. A third party may recover on a contract made between other parties only if the parties intended to secure a benefit to that third party, and only if the contracting parties entered into the contract directly for the third party's benefit. [Citation.] A third party does not have a right to enforce the contract if she received only an incidental benefit. [Citation.] "A court will not create a third-party beneficiary contract by implication." [Citation.] Rather, an agreement must clearly and fully express an intent to confer a direct benefit to the third party. [Citation.] To determine the parties' intent, courts must examine the entire agreement when interpreting a contract and give effect to all the contract's provisions so that none are rendered meaningless. [Citation.]

To qualify as an intended third-party beneficiary, a party must show that she is either a "donee" or "creditor" beneficiary of the contract. [Citation.] An agreement benefits a "donee" beneficiary if, under the contract, "the performance promised will, when rendered, come to him as a pure donation." [Citations.] In contrast, an agreement benefits a "creditor" beneficiary if, under the agreement, "that performance will come to him in satisfaction of a legal duty owed to him by the promisee." [Citations.] This duty may be an indebtedness, contractual obligation or other legally enforceable commitment owed to the third party. [Citation.]

* * *

We agree with the court of appeals' determination that Stine was not an intended third-party donee beneficiary of the agreement. [Citation.] But, we conclude that Stine is a third-party creditor beneficiary. The agreement expressly provides that the Stewarts intended to satisfy an obligation to repay Stine the $50,000 that the Stewarts owed her. Specifically, the agreement refers to the monies owed to Stine as "the current principal sum of $50,000." Then, the agreement states that Stewart agreed to pay the property sale net proceeds "with regard to the note" to Stine.

The agreement further provides that, if the property sale net proceeds did not cover the amount owed to Stine, the remainder would be immediately due and payable from the Stewarts, with each owing one half. Thus, the agreement expressly requires the Stewarts to satisfy their existing obligation to pay Stine. [Citation.]

* * *

Furthermore, contrary to Stewart's argument, a third-party beneficiary does not have to show that the signatories executed the contract Solely to benefit her as a noncontracting party. Rather, the focus is on whether the contracting parties intended, at least in part, to discharge an obligation owed to the third party. [Citation.] Here, the entire agreement is obviously not for Stine's sole benefit. However, certain provisions in the agreement expressly state the Stewarts' intent to pay Stine the money due to her.

* * *

The agreement's language clearly shows that Stewart intended to secure a benefit to Stine as a third-party creditor beneficiary. The agreement also acknowledges the existence of a legal obligation owed to Stine and thus revives it as an enforceable obligation. Consequently, Stewart breached the agreement when he refused to pay Stine the money owed to her as the agreement requires.

INTERPRETATION An intended third-party beneficiary of a contract may enforce that contract.

CRITICAL THINKING QUESTION Why did the court conclude that Stine was not an intended third-party donee beneficiary?

Rights of Intended Beneficiary Though an intended creditor beneficiary may sue either or both parties, an intended donee beneficiary may enforce the contract against the promisor only. He cannot maintain an action against the promisee, as the promisee was under no legal obligation to him.

Vesting of Rights A contract for the benefit of an intended beneficiary confers upon that beneficiary rights that the beneficiary may enforce. Until these rights vest (take effect), however, the promisor and promisee may, by later agreement, vary or completely discharge them. There is considerable variation among the states as to when vesting occurs. Some states hold that vesting takes place immediately upon the making of the contract. In other states, vesting occurs when the

third party learns of the contract and assents to it. In another group of states, vesting requires the third party to change his position in reliance upon the promise made for his benefit. The Restatement has adopted the following position: If the contract between the promisor and promisee provides that its terms may not be varied without the consent of the beneficiary, such a provision will be upheld. If there is no such provision, the parties to the contract may rescind or vary the contract unless the intended beneficiary (1) has brought an action on the promise, (2) has changed her position in reliance on it, or (3) has assented to the promise at the request of the promisor or promisee.

On the other hand, the promisor and promisee may provide that the benefits will never vest. For example, Mildred purchases an insurance policy on her own life, naming her husband as beneficiary. The policy, as such policies commonly do, reserves to Mildred the right to change her beneficiary or even to cancel the policy entirely.

> ## PRACTICAL ADVICE
> To avoid uncertainty, consider specifying in the contract whether there are any third-party beneficiaries and, if so, who they are, what their rights are, and when their rights vest.

Defenses against Beneficiary In an action by the intended beneficiary to enforce the promise, the promisor may assert any defense that would be available to her if the action had been brought by the promisee. The rights of the third party are based upon the promisor's contract with the promisee. Thus, the promisor may assert the absence of mutual assent or consideration, lack of capacity, fraud, mistake, and the like against the intended beneficiary. Once an intended beneficiary's rights have vested, however, the promisor may not assert the defense of contractual modification or rescission entered into with the promisee.

INCIDENTAL BENEFICIARY

An incidental third-party beneficiary is a person to whom the parties to a contract did not intend a benefit but who nevertheless would derive some benefit by its performance. For instance, a contract to raze an old, unsightly building and to replace it with a costly modern house would benefit the owner of the adjoining property by increasing his property's value. He would have no rights under the contract, however, as the benefit to him would be unintended and incidental.

A third person who may benefit incidentally by the performance of a contract to which he is not a party has no rights under the contract, as neither the promisee nor the promisor intended that the third person benefit. Assume that for a stated consideration Charles promises Madeline that he will purchase and deliver to Madeline a new Sony television of the latest model. Madeline pays in advance for the television. Charles does not deliver the television to Madeline. Reiner, the local exclusive Sony dealer, has no rights under the contract, although performance by Charles would produce a sale from which Reiner would derive a benefit, for Reiner is only an incidental beneficiary.

CHAPTER SUMMARY

Assignment of Rights

Definition of Assignment voluntary transfer to a third party of the rights arising from a contract so that the assignor's right to performance is extinguished
* *Assignor* party making an assignment
* *Assignee* party to whom contract rights are assigned
* *Obligor* party owing a duty to the assignor under the original contract
* *Obligee* party to whom a duty of performance is owed under a contract

Requirements of an Assignment include intent but not consideration
* *Revocability of Assignment* when the assignee gives consideration, the assignor may not revoke the assignment without the assignee's consent
* *Partial Assignment* transfer of a portion of contractual rights to one or more assignees

Assignability most contract rights are assignable except:
* Assignments that materially increase the duty, risk, or burden upon the obligor
* Assignments of personal rights
* Assignments expressly forbidden by the contract
* Assignments prohibited by law

Rights of Assignee the assignee stands in the shoes of the assignor
* *Defenses of Obligor* may be asserted against the assignee
* *Notice* is not required but is advisable

Implied Warranties obligation imposed by law upon the assignor of a contract right

Express Warranty explicitly made contractual promise regarding contract rights transferred

Successive Assignments of the Same Right the majority rule is that the first assignee in point of time prevails over later assignees; minority rule is that the first assignee to notify the obligor prevails

Delegation of Duties

Definition of Delegation transfer to a third party of a contractual obligation
* *Delegator* party delegating his duty to a third party
* *Delegatee* third party to whom the delegator's duty is delegated
* *Obligee* party to whom a duty of performance is owed by the delegator and delegate

Delegable Duties most contract duties may be delegated except
* Duties that are personal
* Duties that are expressly nondelegable
* Duties whose delegation is prohibited by statute or public policy

Duties of the Parties
* *Delegation* delegator is still bound to perform original obligation
* *Novation Contract* a substituted contract to which the promisee is a party, which substitutes a new promisor for an existing promisor, who is consequently no longer liable on the original contract and is not liable as a delegator

Third-Party Beneficiary Contracts

Definition a third-party beneficiary contract is one in which one party promises to render a performance to a third person (the beneficiary)

Intended Beneficiaries third parties intended by the two contracting parties to receive a benefit from their contract
* *Donee Beneficiary* a third party intended to receive a benefit from the contract as a gift
* *Creditor Beneficiary* a third person intended to receive a benefit from the contract to satisfy a legal duty owed to him
* *Rights of Intended Beneficiary* an intended donee beneficiary may enforce the contract against the promisor; an intended creditor beneficiary may enforce the contract against either or both the promisor and the promisee
* *Vesting of Rights* if the beneficiary's rights vest, the promisor and promisee may not thereafter vary or discharge these vested rights

Defenses against Beneficiary in an action by the intended beneficiary to enforce the promise, the promisor may assert any defense that would be available to her if the action had been brought by the promisee

Incidental Beneficiary third party whom the two parties to the contract have no intention of benefiting by their contract and who acquires no rights under the contract

QUESTIONS

1. On December 1, Euphonia, a famous singer, contracted with Boito to sing at Boito's theater on December 31 for a fee of $45,000 to be paid immediately after the performance.

   a. Euphonia, for value received, assigns this fee to Carter.

   b. Euphonia, for value received, assigns this contract to sing to Dumont, an equally famous singer.

   c. Boito sells his theater to Edmund and assigns his contract with Euphonia to Edmund. State the effect of each of these assignments.

2. The Smooth Paving Company entered into a paving contract with the city of Chicago. The contract contained the clause "contractor shall be liable for all damages to buildings resulting from the work performed." In the process of construction, one of the bulldozers of the Smooth Paving Company struck and broke a gas main, causing an explosion and a fire that destroyed the house of John Puff. Puff brought an action for breach of the paving contract against the Smooth Paving Company to recover damages for the loss of his house. Can Puff recover under this contract? Explain.

3. Anne, who was unemployed, registered with the Speedy Employment Agency. A contract was then made under which Anne, in consideration of such position as the agency would obtain for her, agreed to pay the agency one half of her first month's salary. The contract also contained an assignment by Anne to the agency of one half of her first month's salary. Two weeks later, the agency obtained a permanent position for Anne with the Bostwick Co. at a monthly salary of $1,900. The agency also notified Bostwick Co. of the assignment by Anne. At the end of the first month, Bostwick Co. paid Anne her salary in full. Anne then quit and disappeared. The agency now sues Bostwick Co. for $950 under the assignment. Who will prevail? Explain.

4. Georgia purchased an option on Greenacre from Pamela for $10,000. The option contract contained a provision by which Georgia promised not to assign the option contract without Pamela's permission. Georgia, without Pamela's permission, assigned the contract to Michael. Michael now seeks to exercise the option, and Pamela refuses to sell Greenacre to him. Must Pamela sell the land to Michael?

5. Julia contracts to sell to Hayden, an ice cream manufacturer, the amount of ice Hayden may need in his business for the ensuing three years to the extent of not more than 250 tons a week at a stated price per ton. Hayden makes a corresponding promise to Julia to buy such an amount of ice. Hayden sells his ice cream plant to Reed and assigns to Reed all Hayden's rights under the contract with Julia. On learning of the sale, Julia refuses to furnish ice to Reed. Can Reed successfully collect damages from Julia? Explain.

6. Brown enters into a written contract with Ideal Insurance Company under which, in consideration of Brown's payment of her premiums, the insurance company promises to pay Williams College the face amount of the policy, $100,000, on Brown's death. Brown pays the premiums until her death. Thereafter, Williams College makes demand for the $100,000, which the insurance company refuses to pay on the ground that Williams College was not a party to the contract. Can Williams successfully enforce the contract?

7. Grant and Debbie enter into a contract binding Grant personally to do some delicate cabinetwork. Grant assigns his rights and delegates performance of his duties to Clarence.

   a. On being informed of this, Debbie agrees with Clarence, in consideration of Clarence's promise to do the work, that Debbie will accept Clarence's work, if properly done, instead of the performance promised by Grant. Later, without cause, Debbie refuses to allow Clarence to proceed with the work, though Clarence is ready to do so, and makes demand on Grant that Grant perform. Grant refuses. Can Clarence recover damages from Debbie? Can Debbie recover from Grant?

   b. Instead, assume that Debbie refuses to permit Clarence to do the work, employs another carpenter, and brings an action against Grant, claiming as damages the difference between the contract price and the cost to employ the other carpenter. Explain whether Debbie will prevail.

8. Rebecca owes Lewis $2,500 due on November 1. On August 15, Lewis assigns this right for value received to Julia, who gives notice on September 10 of the assignment to Rebecca. On August 25, Lewis assigns the same right to Wayne, who in good faith gives value and has no prior knowledge of the assignment by Lewis to Julia. Wayne gives Rebecca notice of the assignment on August 30. What are the rights and obligations of Rebecca, Lewis, Julia, and Wayne?

9. Lisa hired Jay in the spring, as she had for many years, to set out in beds the flowers Lisa had grown in her greenhouses during the winter. The work was to be done in Lisa's absence for $300. Jay became ill the day after Lisa departed and requested his friend, Curtis, to set out the flowers, promising to pay Curtis $250 when Jay received his payment. Curtis agreed. On completion of the planting, an agent of Lisa's, who had authority to dispense the money, paid Jay, and Jay paid Curtis. Within two days, it became obvious that the planting was a disaster. Because he did not operate Lisa's automatic watering system properly, everything set out by Curtis had died of water rot.

   May Lisa recover damages from Curtis? May Lisa recover damages from Jay, and, if so, does Jay have an action against Curtis?

10. Caleb, operator of a window-washing business, dictated a letter to his secretary addressed to Apartments, Inc., stating, "I will wash the windows of your apartment buildings at $4.10 per window to be paid on completion of the work." The secretary typed the letter, signed Caleb's name, and mailed it to Apartments, Inc. Apartments, Inc., replied, "Accept your offer."

    Caleb wrote back, "I will wash them during the week starting July 10 and direct you to pay the money you will owe me to my son, Bernie. I am giving it to him as a wedding present." Caleb sent a signed copy of the letter to Bernie.

    Caleb washed the windows during the time stated and demanded payment to him of $8,200 (two thousand windows at $4.10 each), informing Apartments, Inc., that he had changed his mind about having the money paid to Bernie.

    What are the rights of the parties?

CASE PROBLEMS

11. On April 1, members of Local 100, Transport Workers Union of America (TWU), began an eleven-day mass transit strike that paralyzed the life and commerce of the city of New York. Jackson, Lewis, Schnitzler & Krupman, a Manhattan law firm, brought a class action suit against the TWU for the direct and foreseeable damages it suffered as a result of the union's illegal strike. The law firm sought to recover as a third-party beneficiary of the collective bargaining agreement between the union and New York City. The agreement contains a no-strike clause and states that the TWU agreed to cooperate with the city to provide a safe, efficient, and dependable mass transit system. The law firm argues that its members are a part of the general public that depends on the mass transit system to go to and from work. Therefore, they are in the class of persons for whose benefit the union has promised to provide dependable transportation service. Are the members of the class action suit entitled to recover? Explain.

12. Northwest Airlines leased space in the terminal building at the Portland Airport from the Port of Portland. Crosetti entered into a contract with the Port to furnish janitorial services for the building, which required Crosetti to keep the floor clean, to indemnify the Port against loss due to claims or lawsuits based upon Crosetti's failure to perform, and to provide public liability insurance for the Port and Crosetti. A patron of the building who was injured by a fall caused by a foreign substance on the floor at Northwest's ticket counter brought suit for damages against Northwest, the Port, and Crosetti. Upon settlement of this suit, Northwest sued Crosetti to recover the amount of its contribution to the settlement and other expenses on the grounds that Northwest was a third-party beneficiary of Crosetti's contract with the Port to keep the floors clean and, therefore, within the protection of Crosetti's indemnification agreement. Will Northwest prevail? Why?

13. Tompkins-Beckwith, as the contractor on a construction project, entered into a subcontract with a division of Air Metal Industries. Air Metal procured American Fire and Casualty Company to be surety on certain bonds in connection with contracts it was performing for Tompkins-Beckwith and others. As security for these bonds, on January 3, Air Metal executed an assignment to American Fire of all accounts receivable under the Tompkins-Beckwith subcontract. On November 26 of that year, Boulevard National Bank lent money to Air Metal. To secure the loans, Air Metal purported to assign to the bank certain accounts receivable it had under its subcontract with Tompkins-Beckwith.

In June of the following year, Air Metal defaulted on various contracts bonded by American Fire. On July 1, American Fire served formal notice on Tompkins-Beckwith of Air Metal's assignment. Tompkins-Beckwith acknowledged the assignment and agreed to pay. In August, Boulevard National Bank notified Tompkins-Beckwith of its assignment. Tompkins-Beckwith refused to recognize the bank's claim and, instead, paid all remaining funds that had accrued to Air Metal to American Fire. The bank then sued to enforce its claim under Air Metal's assignment. Is the assignment effective? Why?

14. The International Association of Machinists (the union) was the bargaining agent for the employees of Powder Power Tool Corporation. On August 24, the union and the corporation executed a collective bargaining agreement providing for retroactively increased wage rates for the corporation's employees effective as of the previous April 1. Three employees who were working for Powder before and for several months after April 1, but who were not employed by the corporation when the agreement was executed on August 24, were paid to the time their employment terminated at the old wage scale. The three employees assigned their claims to Springer, who brought this action against the corporation for the extra wages. Decision?

15. In March, Adrian Saylor sold government bonds owned exclusively by him and with $6,450 of the proceeds opened a savings account in a bank in the name of "Mr. or Mrs. Adrian M. Saylor." In June of the following year, Saylor deposited the additional sum of $2,132 of his own money in the account. There were no other deposits and no withdrawals prior to the death of Saylor in May a year later. Is the balance of the account on Saylor's death payable wholly to Adrian Saylor's estate, wholly to his widow, or half to each?

16. Linda King was found liable to Charlotte Clement as the result of an automobile accident. King, who was insolvent at the time, declared bankruptcy and directed her attorney, Prestwich, to list Clement as an unsecured creditor. The attorney failed to carry out this duty, and consequently King sued him for legal malpractice. When Clement pursued her judgment against King, she received a written assignment of King's legal malpractice claim against Prestwich. Clement has attempted to bring the claim, but Prestwich alleges that a claim for legal malpractice is not assignable. Decision?

17. Rensselaer Water Company contracted with the city of Rensselaer to provide water to the city for use in homes, public buildings, industry, and fire hydrants. During the term of the contract, a building caught fire. The fire spread to a nearby warehouse and destroyed it and its contents. The water company knew of the fire but failed to supply adequate water pressure at the fire hydrant to extinguish the fire. The warehouse owner sued the water company for failure to fulfill its contract with the city. Can the owner of the warehouse enforce the contract? Explain.

18. McDonald's has an undeviating policy of retaining absolute control over who receives new franchises. McDonald's granted to Copeland a franchise in Omaha, Nebraska. In a separate letter, it also granted him a right of first refusal for future franchises to be developed in the Omaha-Council Bluffs area. Copeland then sold all rights in his six McDonald's franchises to Schupack. When McDonald's offered a new franchise in the Omaha area to someone other than Schupack, he attempted to exercise the right of first refusal. McDonald's would not recognize the right in Schupack, claiming that it was personal to Copeland and, therefore, nonassignable without its consent. Schupack brought an action for specific performance, requiring McDonald's to accord him the right of first refusal. Is Schupack correct in his contention?

19. While under contract to play professional basketball for the Philadelphia 76ers, Billy Cunningham, an outstanding player, negotiated a three-year contract with the Carolina Cougars, another professional basketball team. The contract with the Cougars was to begin at the expiration of the contract with the 76ers. In addition to a signing bonus of $125,000, Cunningham was to receive under the new contract a salary of $100,000 for the first year, $110,000 for the second, and $120,000 for the third. The contract also stated that Cunning ham "had special, exceptional and unique knowledge, skill and ability as a basketball player" and that Cunningham therefore agreed the Cougars could enjoin him from playing basketball for any other team for the term of the contract. In addition, the contract contained a clause prohibiting its assignment to another club without Cunningham's consent. In 1971, the ownership of the Cougars changed, and Cunningham's contract was assigned to Munchak Corporation, the new owners, without his consent. When Cunningham refused to play for the Cougars, Munchak Corporation sought to enjoin his playing for any other team. Cunningham asserts that his contract was not assignable. Was the contract assignable? Explain.

20. Pauline Brown was shot and seriously injured by an unknown assailant in the parking lot of National Supermarkets. Pauline and George Brown brought a negligence action against National, Sentry Security Agency, and T. G. Watkins, a security guard and Sentry employee. The Browns maintained that the defendants have a legal duty to protect National's customers, both in the store and in the parking lot, and that this duty was breached. The defendants denied this allegation. What will the Browns have to prove to prevail? Explain.

TAKING SIDES

Pizza of Gaithersburg and The Pizza Shops (Pizza Shops) contracted with Virginia Coffee Service (Virginia) to install vending machines in each of their restaurants. One year later, the Macke Company (a provider of vending machines) purchased Virginia's assets, and the vending machine contracts were assigned to Macke. Pizza Shops had dealt with Macke before but had chosen Virginia because they preferred the way it conducted its business. When Pizza Shops attempted to terminate their contracts for vending services, Macke brought suit for damages for breach of contract.

a. What arguments would support Pizza Shop's termination of the contracts?

b. What arguments would support Macke's suit for breach of contract?

c. Which side should prevail? Explain.

Chapter 17

PERFORMANCE, BREACH, AND DISCHARGE

Because contracting parties ordinarily expect that they will perform their obligations, they are usually more explicit in defining those obligations than in stating the consequences of their nonperformance.

RESTATEMENT OF CONTRACTS, INTRODUCTORY NOTE

CHAPTER OUTCOMES

After reading and studying this chapter, you should be able to:

1. Identify and distinguish among the various types of conditions.

2. Distinguish between full performance and tender of performance.

3. Explain the difference between material breach and substantial performance.

4. Distinguish among a mutual rescission, substituted contract, accord and satisfaction, and novation.

5. Identify and explain the ways discharge may be brought about by operation of law.

The subject of discharge of contracts concerns the termination of contractual duties. In earlier chapters we saw how parties may become contractually bound by their promises. It is also important to know how a person may become unbound from a contract. Although contractual promises are made for a purpose and the parties reasonably expect this purpose to be fulfilled by performance, performance of a contractual duty is only one method of discharge.

Whatever causes a binding promise to cease to be binding is a discharge of the contract. In general, there are four kinds of discharge: (1) performance by the parties, (2) material breach by one or both of the parties, (3) agreement of the parties, and (4) operation of law. Moreover, many contractual promises are not absolute promises to perform but are conditional—that is, they depend on the happening or nonhappening of a specific

event. After we discuss the subject of conditions, we will cover the four kinds of discharge.

Conditions

A **condition** is an event whose happening or nonhappening affects a duty of performance under a contract. Some conditions must be satisfied before any duty to perform arises; others terminate the duty to perform; still others either limit or modify the duty to perform. A condition is inserted in a contract to protect and benefit the promisor. The more conditions to which a promise is subject, the less content the promise has. For example, a promise to pay $8,000 provided that such sum is realized from the sale of an automobile, provided the automobile is sold within sixty days, and provided that the automobile, which has been stolen, can be found, is clearly different from, and worth considerably less than, an unconditional promise by the same promisor to pay $8,000.

A fundamental difference exists between the breach or nonperformance of a contractual promise and the failure or nonhappening of a condition. A breach of contract subjects the promisor to liability. It may or may not, depending on its materiality, excuse the nonbreaching party's nonperformance of his duty under the contract. The happening or nonhappening of a condition, on the other hand, either prevents a party from acquiring a right or deprives him of a right but subjects neither party to any liability.

Conditions may be classified by *how* they are imposed: express conditions, implied-in-fact conditions, or implied-in-law conditions (also called constructive conditions). They also may be classified by *when* they affect a duty of performance: conditions concurrent, conditions precedent, or conditions subsequent. These two ways of classifying conditions are not mutually exclusive; for example, a condition may be constructive and concurrent or express and precedent.

> ### Practical Advice
>
> Consider using conditions to place the risk of the nonoccurrence of critical, uncertain events on the other party to the contract.

Express Conditions

An **express condition** is explicitly set forth in language. No particular form of words is necessary to create an express condition, as long as the event to which the performance of the promise is made subject is clearly expressed. An express condition is usually preceded by words such as "provided that," "on condition that," "if," "subject to," "while," "after," "upon," or "as soon as."

The basic rule applied to express conditions is that they must be fully and literally performed before the conditional duty to perform arises. However, when application of the full and literal performance test would result in a forfeiture, the courts usually apply to the completed portion of the condition a substantial satisfaction test, as discussed in this chapter under "Substantial Performance."

Satisfaction of a Contracting Party   The parties to a contract may agree that performance by one of them shall be to the **satisfaction** of the other, who will not be obligated to perform unless he is satisfied. This is an express condition to the duty to perform. Assume that tailor Ken contracts to make a suit of clothes to Dick's satisfaction, and that Dick promises to pay Ken $850 for the suit if he is satisfied with it when completed. Ken completes the suit using materials ordered by Dick. The suit fits Dick beautifully, but Dick tells Ken that he is not satisfied with it and refuses to accept or pay for it. Ken is not entitled to recover $850 or any amount from Dick because the express condition did not happen. This is so if Dick's dissatisfaction is honest and in good faith, even if it is unreasonable. Where satisfaction relates to a matter of personal taste, opinion, or judgment, the law applies the **subjective satisfaction** standard, and the condition has not occurred if the promisor is in good faith dissatisfied.

If the contract does not clearly indicate that satisfaction is subjective, or if the performance contracted for relates to mechanical fitness or utility, the law assumes an **objective satisfaction** standard. For example, the objective standard of satisfaction would apply to the sale of a building or standard goods. In such cases, the question would not be whether the promisor was actually satisfied with the performance by the other party but whether, as a reasonable person, he ought to be satisfied.

> ### Practical Advice
>
> In your contracts based on satisfaction, specify which standard—subjective satisfaction or objective satisfaction—should apply to each contractual duty of performance.

Michael Silvestri v. Optus Software, Inc.

SUPREME COURT OF NEW JERSEY, 2003
175 N.J. 113, 814 A.2D 602

http://scholar.google.com/scholar_case?q=814+A.2d+602&hl=en&as_sdt=2,34&case=3846111007491599697&scilh=0

FACTS   Optus Software, Inc. (Optus), a small computer software company, hired Michael Silvestri as its director of support services at an annual salary of $70,000. Silvestri was responsible for supervising technical customer support services. More specifically, Silvestri was charged with supervision of the support services staff, responsibility for communication with resellers of the Optus computer software, and coordination of ongoing training for support staff and resellers. Silvestri's two-year employment contract began on January 4, 1999, and contained a satisfaction clause that reserved to the company the right to terminate his employment for "failure or refusal to perform faithfully, diligently or completely his duties ... to the satisfaction" of the company. Termination under that clause relieved the company of any further payment obligation to Silvestri.

During the first six months of his employment Silvestri enjoyed the full support of Joseph Avellino, the CEO of Optus. Avellino's attitude started to change during the summer months of 1999, when several clients and resellers communicated to Avellino their disappointment with the performance and attitude of the support services staff generally, and several complaints targeted Silvestri specifically. Avellino informed Silvestri of those criticisms. On September 17, 1999, Avellino terminated Silvestri under the satisfaction clause.

Silvestri filed an action for breach of contract. Silvestri did not assert that there was any reason for his termination other than Avellino's genuine dissatisfaction with his performance. Rather, Silvestri challenged the reasonableness of that dissatisfaction. He portrayed Avellino as a meddling micromanager who overreacted to any customer criticism and thus could not reasonably be satisfied.

The trial court granted summary judgment in favor of Optus, refusing to substitute its judgment for that of the president and CEO of Optus. The Appellate Division reversed, holding that an employer must meet an objective, reasonable-person test when invoking a satisfaction clause permitting termination of employment. The Supreme Court of New Jersey granted review.

DECISION The judgment of the Appellate Division is reversed, and the case remanded for entry of summary judgment in favor of Optus.

OPINION LaVecchia, J. Agreements containing a promise to perform in a manner satisfactory to another *** are a common form of enforceable contract. [Citation.] Such "satisfaction" contracts are generally divided into two categories for purposes of review: (1) contracts that involve matters of personal taste, sensibility, judgment, or convenience; and (2) contracts that contain a requirement of satisfaction as to mechanical fitness, utility, or marketability. [Citation.] The standard for evaluating satisfaction depends on the type of contract. Satisfaction contracts of the first type are interpreted on a subjective basis, with satisfaction dependent on the personal, honest evaluation of the party to be satisfied. [Citation] Absent language to the contrary, however, contracts of the second type—involving operative fitness or mechanical utility—are subject to an objective test of reasonableness, because in those

cases the extent and quality of performance can be measured by objective tests. [Citation]; Restatement (Second) of Contracts § 228; [citation].

A subjective standard typically is applied to satisfaction clauses in employment contracts because "there is greater reason and a greater tendency to interpret [the contract] as involving personal satisfaction," rather than the satisfaction of a hypothetical "reasonable" person. [Citations.]

In the case of a high-level business manager, a subjective test is particularly appropriate to the flexibility needed by the owners and higher-level officers operating a competitive enterprise. [Citation.] When a manager has been hired to share responsibility for the success of a business entity, an employer is entitled to be highly personal and idiosyncratic in judging the employee's satisfactory performance in advancing the enterprise. [Citations.]

The subjective standard obliges the employer to act "honestly in accordance with his duty of good faith and fair dealing," [citation], but genuine dissatisfaction of the employer, honestly held, is sufficient for discharge. [Citation.]

Although broadly discretionary, a satisfaction-clause employment relationship is not to be confused with an employment-at-will relationship in which an employer is entitled to terminate an employee for any reason, or no reason, unless prohibited by law or public policy. [Citation.] In a satisfaction clause employment setting, there must be honest dissatisfaction with the employee's performance. *** If *** the employer's dissatisfaction is honest and genuine, even if idiosyncratic, its reasonableness is not subject to second guessing under a reasonable-person standard. In other words, standing alone, mere dissatisfaction is sufficient so long as it does not mask any other reason for the adverse employment action.

***

We hold that a subjective test of performance governs the employer's resort to a satisfaction clause in an employment contract unless there is some language in the contract to suggest that the parties intended an objective standard. There is no such language here. ***

Turning then to application of the subjective test in this setting, *** we conclude that the entry of summary judgment in favor of defendants was appropriate. The only issue available to Silvestri is whether the dissatisfaction with his performance was genuine, and he has failed to make a *prima facie* showing that it was not.

INTERPRETATION A subjective test of performance governs an employer's use of a satisfaction clause in an employment contract unless language in the contract suggests that the parties intended an objective standard.

CRITICAL THINKING QUESTION Could an employee discharged under a satisfaction clause demonstrate that the employer was not honestly dissatisfied? Explain.

Satisfaction of a Third Party A contract may condition the duty of one contracting party to accept and pay for the performance of the other contracting party upon the approval of a third party who is not a party to the contract. For example, building contracts commonly provide that before the owner is required to pay, the builder shall furnish the architect's certificate stating that the building has been constructed according to the plans and specifications on which the builder and the owner agreed. For even though the price is being paid for the building, not for the certificate, the owner must have both the building and the certificate before she will be obliged to pay. The duty of payment was made expressly conditional on the presentation of the certificate.

IMPLIED-IN-FACT CONDITIONS

Implied-in-fact conditions are similar to express conditions in that they must fully and literally occur and in that they are understood by the parties to be part of the agreement. They differ in that they are not stated in express language; rather, they are necessarily inferred from the terms of the contract, the nature of the transaction, or the conduct of the parties. Thus, if Edna, for $1,750, contracts to paint Sy's house any color Sy desires, it is necessarily implied in fact that Sy will inform Edna of the desired color before Edna begins to paint. The notification of choice of color is an implied-in-fact condition, an operative event that must occur before Edna is subject to the duty of painting the house.

IMPLIED-IN-LAW CONDITIONS

An **implied-in-law condition**, or a constructive condition, is imposed by law to accomplish a just and fair result. It differs from an express condition and an implied-in-fact condition in two ways: (1) it is not contained in the language of the contract or necessarily inferred from the contract and (2) it need only be substantially performed. For example, Fernando contracts to sell a certain tract of land to Marie for $18,000, but the contract is silent as to the time of delivery of the deed and payment of the price. According to the law, the contract implies that payment and delivery of the deed are not independent of each other. The courts will treat the promises as mutually dependent and will therefore hold that a delivery or tender of the deed by Fernando to Marie is a condition to the duty of Marie to pay the price. Conversely, payment or tender of $18,000 by Marie to Fernando is a condition to the duty of Fernando to deliver the deed to Marie.

CONCURRENT CONDITIONS

Concurrent conditions occur when the mutual duties of performance are to take place simultaneously. As we indicated in the discussion of implied-in-law conditions, in the absence of agreement to the contrary, the law assumes that the respective performances under a contract are concurrent conditions.

CONDITION PRECEDENT

A **condition precedent** is an event that must occur before performance is due under a contract. In other words, the immediate duty of one party to perform is subject to the condition that some event must first occur. For instance, Steve is to deliver shoes to Nancy on June 1, and Nancy is to pay for the shoes on July 15. Steve's delivery of the shoes is a condition precedent to Nancy's performance. Similarly, if Rachel promises to buy Justin's land for $50,000, provided Rachel can obtain financing in the amount of $40,000 at 10 percent or less for thirty years within sixty days of signing the contract, Rachel's obtaining the specified financing is a condition precedent to her duty. If the condition is satisfied, Rachel is bound to perform; if it is not met, she is not bound to perform. Rachel, however, is under an implied-in-law duty to use her best efforts to obtain financing under these terms.

CONDITION SUBSEQUENT

A **condition subsequent** is an event that terminates an existing duty. For example, when goods are sold under terms of "sale or return," the buyer has the right to return the goods to the seller within a stated period but is under an immediate duty to pay the price unless the parties have agreed on credit. The duty to pay the price is terminated by a return of the goods, which operates as a condition subsequent. Conditions subsequent occur very infrequently in contract law; conditions precedent are quite common.

Discharge by Performance

Discharge is the termination of a contractual duty. **Performance** is the fulfillment of a contractual obligation. Discharge by performance is undoubtedly the most frequent method of discharging a contractual duty. If a promisor exactly performs his duty under the contract, the promisor is no longer subject to that duty.

Every contract imposes upon each party a duty of good faith and fair dealing in its performance and its enforcement. As discussed in Chapter 19, the Uniform Commercial Code imposes a comparable duty.

Tender is an offer by one party—who is ready, willing, and able to perform—to the other party to perform his obligation according to the terms of the contract. Under a bilateral contract, the refusal or rejection of a tender, or offer of performance, by one party may be treated as a repudiation, excusing or discharging the tendering party from further duty of performance under the contract.

Discharge by Breach

A **breach** of a contract is a wrongful failure to perform its terms. Breach of contract always gives rise to a cause of action for damages by the aggrieved (injured) party. It may, however, have a more important effect: an uncured (uncorrected) *material* breach by one party operates as an excuse for nonperformance by the other party and discharges the aggrieved party from any further duty under the contract. If, on the other hand, the breach is not material, the aggrieved party is not discharged from the contract, although she may recover money damages. Under the Code's perfect tender rule, which applies only to sales transactions, *any* deviation discharges the aggrieved party.

MATERIAL BREACH

An unjustified failure to perform *substantially* the obligations promised in a contract is a **material breach**. The key is whether the aggrieved party obtained substantially what he had bargained for, despite the breach, or whether the breach significantly impaired his rights under the contract. A material breach discharges the aggrieved party from his duty of performance. For instance, Joe orders a custom-made, tailored suit from Peggy to be made of wool, but Peggy makes the suit of cotton instead. Assuming that the labor component of this contract predominates and thus the contract is not considered a sale of goods, Peggy has materially breached the contract. Consequently, Joe is discharged from his duty to pay for the suit, and he may also recover money damages from Peggy for her breach.

Although there are no clear-cut rules as to what constitutes a material breach, several basic principles apply. First, partial performance is a material breach of a contract if it omits some essential part of the contract. Second, the courts will consider a breach material if it is quantitatively or qualitatively serious. Third, an intentional breach of contract is generally held to be material.

Fourth, a failure to perform a promise promptly is a material breach if time is of the essence; that is, if the parties have clearly indicated that a failure to perform by a stated time is material; otherwise, the aggrieved party may recover damages only for loss caused by the delay. Fifth, the parties to a contract may, within limits, specify what breaches are to be considered material.

PRACTICAL ADVICE

If the timely performance of a contractual duty is important, use a "time-is-of-the-essence" clause to make failure to perform promptly a material breach.

Prevention of Performance One party's substantial interference with, or prevention of, performance by the other generally constitutes a material breach that discharges the other party to the contract. For instance, Dale prevents an architect from giving Lucy a certificate that is a condition to Dale's liability to pay Lucy a certain sum of money. Dale may not then use Lucy's failure to produce a certificate as an excuse for nonpayment. Likewise, if Matthew has contracted to grow a certain crop for Richard and Richard plows the field and destroys the seedlings Matthew has planted, his interference with Matthew's performance discharges Matthew from his duty under the contract. It does not, however, discharge Richard from his duty under the contract.

Perfect Tender Rule The Code greatly alters the common law doctrine of material breach by adopting what is known as the **perfect tender rule**. The perfect tender rule, which we will discuss more fully in Chapter 20, essentially provides that *any* deviation from the promised performance in a sales contract under the Code constitutes a material breach of the contract and discharges the aggrieved party from his duty of performance.

SUBSTANTIAL PERFORMANCE

Substantial performance is performance that, though incomplete, does not defeat the purpose of the contract. If a party substantially, but not completely, performs her obligations under a contract, the common law generally will allow her to obtain the other party's performance, less any damages the partial performance caused. If no harm has been caused, the breaching party will obtain the other party's full contractual performance. Thus, in the specially ordered suit illustration, if Peggy, the tailor, used the correct fabric but improperly used black buttons instead of blue, she would be permitted to collect from Joe the contract

APPLYING THE LAW

Performance, Breach, and Discharge

Facts Davis manages commercial real estate. In April, Davis contracted with Bidley to acquire and plant impatiens in the flowerbeds outside fourteen office properties that Davis manages. Bidley verbally agreed to buy and plant the impatiens by May 31, for a total of $10,000. Bidley purchased the necessary plants from Ackerman, who delivered them to Bidley on May 26. Bidley completed the planting at thirteen of the office buildings by May 29, but because another job took much longer than anticipated, Bidley was unable to finish planting the flowers outside the fourteenth office building until June 1. When he received Bidley's invoice, Davis refused to pay any of the $10,000.

Issue Has Bidley's committed a material breach of the contract so as to discharge Davis's performance under the contract?

Rule of Law Breach of contract is defined as a wrongful failure to perform. An uncured material breach discharges the aggrieved party's performance, serving as an excuse for the aggrieved party's nonperformance of his obligations under the contract. A breach is material if it significantly impairs the aggrieved party's contract rights. When a breach relates to timing of performance, failure to promptly perform a contract as promised is considered a material breach only if the parties have agreed that "time is of the essence," in other words that the failure to perform on time is material. If, on the other hand, the aggrieved party does get substantially that for which he bargained, the breach is not material. In such a case the aggrieved party is not discharged from the contract but has a right to collect damages for the injury sustained as a result of the breach.

Application Bidley failed to plant all of the flowers by May 31 as he promised. Therefore, he has breached the contract. However, Bidley's breach is not material. There is no indication that the parties agreed that time was of the essence nor that there was any compelling reason the plants had to be in the ground by May 31. They simply agreed on May 31 as the date for performance.

Furthermore, Davis has gotten substantially that for which he bargained. In fact, as of May 31, Bidley had completed the planting at thirteen of the office buildings and had commenced the work at the fourteenth. One day later, the entire job was done. Given that Bidley's late performance did not significantly impair Davis's rights under the contract, the breach is not material. Therefore, Davis is entitled only to recover any damages he can prove were suffered as a result of Bidley's late performance.

Conclusion Bidley's breach is not material. Davis is not discharged from performance and must pay the $10,000 owed under the contract, less the value of any damages caused by the one-day delay in planting flowers at one office building.

price of the suit less the damage, if any, caused to Joe by the substitution of the wrongly colored buttons. The doctrine of substantial performance assumes particular importance in the construction industry in cases in which a structure is built on the aggrieved party's land. Consider the following: Adam builds a $300,000 house for Betty but deviates from the specifications, causing Betty $10,000 in damages. If the courts considered this a material breach, Betty would not have to pay for the house that is now on her land, a result that would clearly constitute an unjust forfeiture on Adam's part. Therefore, because Adam's performance has been substantial, the courts would probably not deem the breach material, and he would be able to collect $290,000 from Betty.

ANTICIPATORY REPUDIATION

A breach of contract, as discussed, is a failure to perform the terms of a contract. Although it is logically and physically impossible to fail to perform a duty before the date on which that performance is due, a party may announce before the due date that she will not perform, or she may commit an act that makes her unable to perform. Either act is a repudiation of the contract, which notifies the other party that a breach is imminent. Such repudiation before the date fixed by the contract for performance is called an **anticipatory repudiation**. The courts, as shown in the leading case that follows, view it as a breach that discharges the nonrepudiating party's duty to perform and permits her to bring suit immediately. Nonetheless, the nonbreaching party may wait until the time the performance is due, to see whether the repudiator will retract his repudiation and perform his contractual duties. To be effective, the retraction must come to the attention of the injured party before she materially changes her position in reliance on the repudiation or before she indicates to the other party that she considers the repudiation to be final. If the retraction is effective and the repudiator does perform, then there is a discharge by performance; if the repudiator does not perform, there is a material breach.

PRACTICAL ADVICE

If the other party to a contract commits an anticipatory breach, carefully consider whether it is better to sue immediately or to wait until the time performance is due.

HOCHSTER V. DE LA TOUR

QUEEN'S BENCH OF ENGLAND, 1853
2 ELLIS AND BLACKBURN REPORTS 678

FACTS On April 12, 1852, Hochster contracted with De La Tour to serve as a guide for De La Tour on his three-month trip to Europe, beginning on June 1 at an agreed-upon salary. On May 11, De La Tour notified Hochster that he would not need Hochster's services. He also refused to pay Hochster any compensation. Hochster brought this action to recover damages for breach of contract.

DECISION Judgment for Hochster.

OPINION Lord Campbell, C. J. On this motion *** the question arises, Whether, if there be an agreement between A. and B., whereby B. engages to employ A. on and from a future day for a given period of time, to travel with him into a foreign country as a [guide], and to start with him in that capacity on that day, A. being to receive a monthly salary during the continuance of such service, B. may, before the day, refuse to perform the agreement and break and renounce it, so as to entitle A. before the day to commence an action against B. to recover damages for breach of the agreement; A. having been ready and willing to perform it, till it was broken and renounced by B.

***

If the plaintiff has no remedy for breach of the contract unless he treats the contract as in force, and acts upon it down to the 1st June, 1852, it follows that, till then, he must enter into no employment which will interfere with his promise "to start with the defendant on such travels on the day and year," and that he must then be properly equipped in all respects as a [guide] for a three months' tour on the continent of Europe. But it is surely much more rational, and more for the benefit of both parties, that, after the renunciation of the agreement by the defendant, the plaintiff should be at liberty to consider himself absolved from any future performance of it, retaining his right to sue for any damage he has suffered from the breach of it. Thus, instead of remaining idle and laying out money in preparations which must be useless, he is at liberty to seek service under another employer, which would go in mitigation of the damages to which he would otherwise be entitled for a breach of the contract. It seems strange that the defendant, after renouncing the contract, and absolutely declaring that he will never act under it, should be permitted to object that faith is given to his assertion, and that an opportunity is not left to him of changing his mind.

***

The man who wrongfully renounces a contract into which he has deliberately entered cannot justly complain if he is immediately sued for a compensation in damage by the man whom he has injured: and it seems reasonable to allow an option to the injured party, either to sue immediately, or to wait till the time when the act was to be done, still holding it as prospectively binding for the exercise of the option, which may be advantageous to the innocent party, and cannot be prejudicial to the wrongdoer.

INTERPRETATION An anticipatory breach discharges the injured party and entitles her to bring suit immediately.

CRITICAL THINKING QUESTION What policy reasons support an injured party's right to bring suit immediately upon an anticipatory repudiation? Explain.

MATERIAL ALTERATION OF WRITTEN CONTRACT

An unauthorized alteration or change of any of the material terms or provisions of a written contract or document is a discharge of the entire contract. An alteration is material if it would vary any party's legal relations with the maker of the alteration or would adversely affect that party's legal relations with a third person. To constitute a discharge, the alteration must be material and fraudulent and must be the act of either a party to the contract or someone acting on his behalf. An unauthorized change in the terms of a written contract by a person who is not a party to the contract does not discharge the contract.

Discharge by Agreement of the Parties

By agreement, the parties to a contract may discharge each other from performance under the contract. They may do this by rescission, substituted contract, accord and satisfaction, or novation.

MUTUAL RESCISSION

A **mutual rescission** is an agreement between the parties to terminate their respective duties under the contract. It is, literally, a contract to end a contract; and it must contain all of the essentials of a contract. In rescinding an executory, bilateral contract, each party furnishes consideration in giving up his rights under the contract in exchange for the other party's doing the same. If one party has already fully performed, however, a mutual rescission is not binding at common law because of lack of consideration.

SUBSTITUTED CONTRACTS

A **substituted contract** is a new contract accepted by both parties in satisfaction of the parties' duties under the original contract. A substituted contract immediately discharges the original contract and imposes new obligations under its own terms.

ACCORD AND SATISFACTION

An **accord** is a contract by which an obligee promises to accept a stated performance in satisfaction of the obligor's existing contractual duty. The performance of the accord, called a **satisfaction**, discharges the original duty. Thus, if Dan owes Sara $500, and the parties agree that Dan will paint Sara's house in satisfaction of the debt, the agreement is an executory accord. When Dan performs the accord by painting Sara's house, he will by satisfaction discharge the $500 debt.

MCDOWELL WELDING & PIPEFITTING, INC. v. UNITED STATES GYPSUM CO.

SUPREME COURT OF OREGON, 2008

345 OR. 272, 193 P.3D 9

http://scholar.google.com/scholar_case?q=193+P.3d+9&hl=en&as_sdt=2,34&case=8212741394978818508&scilh=0

FACTS Defendant United States Gypsum (U.S. Gypsum) hired B E & K as general contractor on a new plant U.S. Gypsum was building in Columbia County. B E & K subcontracted with the plaintiff (McDowell Welding & Pipefitting, Inc.) to perform work on the project. During construction, the defendants asked the plaintiff to perform additional tasks, over and above the plaintiff's contractual obligations, and the defendants promised to pay the plaintiff for the additional work. After the plaintiff completed its work on the project, the parties disagreed over the amount that the defendants owed the plaintiff for the additional work.

The plaintiff filed an action against the defendants, alleging breach of contract. All of the plaintiff's claims arose out of the modification to the construction contract. B E & K's asserted an affirmative defense alleging that the plaintiff had agreed to settle its claims for a total payment of $896,000.

The trial court granted B E & K's motion to try its counterclaim before trying the plaintiff's claims against it. The plaintiff then filed a demand for a jury trial, which B E & K moved to strike, arguing that because its counterclaim was equitable, the plaintiff had no right to a jury trial on the counterclaim. The trial court granted B E & K's motion to strike the plaintiff's jury trial demand and, sitting as the trier of fact, found that the plaintiff had accepted the defendants' offer to settle its claims in return for the defendants' promise to pay the plaintiff $800,000. Although the defendants alleged that they promised to pay the plaintiff $896,000 in return for the plaintiff's promise to release its claims against them, the trial court found that the defendants had promised to pay only $800,000.

Based on its resolution of the defendants' counterclaim, the trial court entered a limited judgment directing the defendants to tender $800,000 to the court clerk and directing the plaintiff, after the defendants tendered that sum, to execute releases of its claims against the defendants. The plaintiff appealed, claiming a state constitutional right to a jury trial on the factual issues that the defendant's counterclaim had raised. A divided Court of Appeals affirmed the trial court's judgment. The Oregon Supreme Court allowed the plaintiff's petition for review.

DECISION Judgment of the Court of Appeals is affirmed in part, reversed in part, and remanded.

OPINION Kistler, J. As we discuss more fully below, a settlement agreement may take one of three forms: an executory accord, an accord and satisfaction, or a substituted contract. As we also discuss below, when the Oregon Constitution was adopted, only a court of equity would enforce an executory accord. The law courts would not enforce executory accords because they suspended the underlying obligation; they did not discharge it. By contrast, an accord and satisfaction and a substituted contract discharged the underlying obligation, albeit for different reasons, and both were enforceable in the law courts. It follows that the question whether the agreement that gave rise to defendants' counterclaim would have been cognizable in law or equity turns, at least initially, on whether it is an executory accord, an accord and satisfaction, or a substituted contract. We first describe the distinctions among those types of settlement agreements before considering which type of settlement agreement defendants alleged.

An executory accord is "an agreement for the future discharge of an existing claim by a substituted performance." [Citation.] Usually, an executory accord is a bilateral agreement; the debtor promises to pay an amount in return for the creditor's promise to release the underlying claim. When the parties enter into an executory accord, the underlying claim "is not [discharged] until the new agreement is performed. The right to enforce the original claim is merely suspended, and is revived by the debtor's breach of the new agreement." [Citation.]

Because an executory accord does not discharge the underlying claim but merely suspends it, the law courts refused to allow it to be pleaded as a bar to the underlying claim. [Citations.] Once the promised performance occurs, the accord has been executed or satisfied and the underlying claim is discharged, resulting in an accord and satisfaction. [Citation.] [Court's footnote: An accord

and satisfaction may occur in one of two ways: "The two parties may first make an accord executory, that is, a contract for the future discharge of the existing claim by a substituted performance still to be rendered. When this executory contract is fully performed as agreed, there is said to be an accord and satisfaction, and the previously existing claim is discharged. It is quite possible, however, for the parties to make an accord and satisfaction without any preliminary accord executory or any other executory contract of any kind. [For example, a] debtor may offer the substituted performance in satisfaction of his debt and the creditor may receive it, without any binding promise being made by either party." [Citation.] Because an accord and satisfaction discharges the underlying claim, that defense is legal, not equitable. [Citation.]

Finally, the parties may enter into a substituted contract; that is, the parties may agree to substitute the new agreement for the underlying obligation. [Citation.] A substituted contract differs from an executory accord in that the parties intend that entering into the new agreement will immediately discharge the underlying obligation. [Citations.] A substituted contract discharges the underlying obligation and could be asserted as a bar to an action at law. [Citation.]

With that background in mind, we turn to the question whether defendants pleaded an executory accord, an accord and satisfaction, or a substituted contract. Here, defendants alleged that they agreed to pay plaintiff $896,000 in exchange for a release of plaintiff's claims against them. Defendants did not allege that they had paid plaintiff the promised sum—an allegation necessary for an accord and satisfaction. [Citations.] Nor did they allege that, by entering into the settlement agreement, they extinguished the underlying obligation—an allegation necessary to allege a substituted contract. [Citations.] Rather, defendants alleged that plaintiff agreed to release its claims only after defendants made the promised payment. In short, defendants alleged an executory accord.

* * *

[The Oregon constitutional right to a jury trial in civil cases does not extend to the defendants' counterclaim of an executory accord. We affirm the Court of Appeals decision on the plaintiff's jury trial claim but reverse its decision on a subsidiary issue regarding prejudgment interest.]

INTERPRETATION When a debtor and a creditor enter into an executory accord, the underlying claim is not discharged until the new agreement is performed; the right to enforce the original claim is merely suspended, and is revived by the debtor's breach of the new agreement.

CRITICAL THINKING QUESTION In settling a contract dispute, what are the advantages and disadvantages of using an executory accord compared with using a substituted contract?

NOVATION

A **novation** is a substituted contract that involves an agreement among *three* parties to substitute a new promisee for the existing promisee or to replace the existing promisor with a new one. A novation discharges the old obligation by creating a new contract in which there is either a new promisee or a new promisor. Thus, if B owes A $500, and A, B, and C agree that C will pay the debt and B will be discharged, the novation is the substitution of the new promisor C for B. Alternatively, if the three parties agree that B will pay $500 to C instead of to A, the novation is the substitution of a new promisee (C for A). In each instance, the debt B owes A is discharged.

Discharge by Operation of Law

In this chapter, we have considered various ways by which contractual duties may be discharged. In all of these cases, the discharge resulted from the action of one or both of the parties to the contract. In this section, we will examine discharge brought about by the operation of law.

IMPOSSIBILITY

If a particular contracting party is unable to perform because of financial inability or lack of competence, for instance, this **subjective impossibility** does not excuse the promisor from liability for breach of contract, as the next case shows. Historically, the common law excused a party from contractual duties only for **objective impossibility**, that is, for situations in which no one could render performance. Thus, the death or illness of a person who has contracted to render personal services is a discharge of his contractual duty. Furthermore, the contract is discharged if, for example, a jockey contracts to ride a certain horse in the Kentucky Derby and the horse dies prior to the derby, for it is objectively impossible for this or any other jockey to perform the contract. Also, if Ken contracts to lease to Karlene a certain ballroom for a party on a scheduled future date, destruction of the ballroom by fire without Ken's fault before the scheduled event discharges the contract. Destruction of the subject matter or of the agreed-upon means of performance of a contract, without the fault of the promisor, is excusable impossibility.

PRACTICAL ADVICE

Use a clause in your contract specifying which events will excuse the nonperformance of the contract.

CHRISTY V. PILKINTON

SUPREME COURT OF ARKANSAS, 1954
224 ARK. 407, 273 S.W.2D 533

http://scholar.google.com/scholar_case?q=273+S.W.2d+533&hl=en&as_sdt=2,34&case=17719371089791667280&scilh=0

FACTS The Christys entered into a written contract to purchase an apartment house from Pilkinton for $30,000. Pilkinton tendered a deed to the property and demanded payment of the unpaid balance of $29,000 due on the purchase price. As a result of a decline in the Christy's used car business, the Christys did not possess and could not borrow the unpaid balance and, thus, asserted that it was impossible for them to perform their contract. This suit was brought by Pilkinton to enforce the sale of the apartment house.

DECISION Judgment for Pilkinton.

OPINION Smith, J. Proof of this kind [an inability to pay the purchase price] does not establish the type of impossibility that constitutes a defense. There is a familiar distinction between objective impossibility, which amounts to saying, "The thing cannot be done," and subjective impossibility—"I cannot do it." [Citations.] The latter, which is well illustrated by a promisor's financial inability to pay, does not discharge the contractual duty and is therefore not a bar to a [judgment in favor of the plaintiff.]

INTERPRETATION Subjective impossibility (the promisor, but not all promisors, cannot perform) does not discharge the promisor's contractual duty.

ETHICAL QUESTION Is it fair to make contracting parties strictly liable for breach of contract? Explain.

CRITICAL THINKING QUESTION What type of fact situation would have excused the Christys' duty to perform? Explain.

Subsequent Illegality If the performance of a contract that was legal when formed becomes illegal or impractical because of a subsequently enacted law, the duty of performance is discharged. For example, Linda contracts to sell and deliver to Carlos ten cases of a certain whiskey each month for one year. A subsequent prohibition law makes the manufacture, transportation, or sale of intoxicating liquor unlawful. The contractual duties that Linda has yet to perform are discharged.

Frustration of Purpose Where, after a contract is made, a party's principal purpose is substantially frustrated without his fault by the occurrence of an event whose nonoccurrence was a basic assumption on which the contract was made, his remaining duties to render performance are discharged, unless the party has assumed the risk. This rule developed from the so-called coronation cases. When, on the death of his mother, Queen Victoria, Edward VII became King of England, impressive coronation ceremonies were planned, including a procession along a designated route through London. Owners and lessees of buildings along the route made contracts to permit the use of rooms on the day scheduled for the procession. The king became ill, however, and the procession did not take place. Consequently, the rooms were not used. Numerous suits were filed, some by landowners seeking to hold the would-be viewers liable on their promises, and some by the would-be viewers seeking to recover money they had paid in advance for the rooms. Though the principle involved was novel, from these cases evolved the frustration of purpose doctrine, under which a contract is discharged if supervening circumstances make impossible the fulfillment of the purpose that both parties had in mind, unless one of the parties has contractually assumed that risk.

Commercial Impracticability The Restatement and Code have relaxed the traditional test of objective impossibility by providing that performance need not be actually or literally impossible; rather, **commercial impracticability**, or unforeseen and unjust hardship, will excuse nonperformance. This does not mean mere hardship or an unexpectedly increased cost of performance. A party will be discharged from performing her duty only when her performance is made impracticable by a supervening event not caused by her own fault. Moreover, the nonoccurrence of the subsequent event must have been a "basic assumption" made by both parties when entering into the contract, neither party having assumed the risk that the event would occur.

PRACTICAL ADVICE

Clearly state the basic assumptions of your contract and which risks are assumed by each of the parties.

NORTHERN CORPORATION V. CHUGACH ELECTRICAL ASSOCIATION

SUPREME COURT OF ALASKA, 1974
518 P.2D 76

http://scholar.google.com/scholar_case?q=518+P.2d+76&hl=en&as_sdt=2,34&case=2017068664150967540&scilh=0

FACTS Northern Corporation (Northern) entered into a contract with Chugach Electrical Association (Chugach) in August 1966 to repair and upgrade the upstream face of Cooper Lake Dam in Alaska. The contract required Northern to obtain rock from a quarry site at the opposite end of the lake and to transport the rock to the dam during the winter across the ice on the lake. In December 1966, Northern cleared a road on the ice to permit deeper freezing, but thereafter water overflowed on the ice, preventing use of the road. Northern complained of the unsafe conditions of the lake ice, but Chugach insisted on performance. In March 1967, one of Northern's loaded trucks broke through the ice and sank. Northern continued to encounter difficulties and ceased operations with the approval of Chugach. However, on January 8, 1968, Chugach notified Northern that it would be in default unless all rock was hauled by April 1. After two more trucks broke through the ice, causing the deaths of the drivers, Northern ceased operations and notified Chugach that it would make no more attempts to haul across the lake. Northern advised Chugach that it considered the contract terminated for impossibility of performance and commenced suit to recover the cost incurred in attempting to complete the contract. The trial court found for Northern.

DECISION Judgment for Northern affirmed.

OPINION Boochever, J. The focal question is whether the *** contract was impossible of performance. The September 27, 1966 directive specified that the rock was to be transported "across Cooper Lake to the dam site when such lake is frozen to a sufficient depth to permit heavy vehicle traffic thereon," and *** specified that the hauling to the dam site would be done during the winter of 1966–67. It is therefore clear that the parties contemplated that the rock would be transported across the frozen lake by truck. Northern's repeated efforts to perform the contract by this method during the winter of 1966–67 and subsequently in February 1968, culminating in the tragic loss of life, abundantly support the trial court's finding that the contract was impossible of performance by this method.

Chugach contends, however, that Northern was nevertheless bound to perform, and that it could have used means other than hauling by truck across the ice to transport the rock. The answer to Chugach's contention is that *** the parties contemplated that the rock would be hauled by truck once the ice froze to a sufficient depth to support the weight of the vehicles. The specification of this particular method of performance presupposed the existence of ice frozen to the requisite depth. Since this expectation of the parties was never fulfilled, and since the provisions relating to the means of performance were clearly material, Northern's duty to perform was discharged by reason of impossibility.

There is an additional reason for our holding that Northern's duty to perform was discharged because of impossibility. It is true that in order for a defendant to prevail under the original common law doctrine of impossibility he had to show that no one else could have performed the contract. However, this harsh rule has gradually been eroded, and the Restatement of Contracts has departed from the early common law rule by recognizing the principle of "commercial impracticability." Under this doctrine, a party is discharged from his contract obligations, even if it is technically possible to perform them, if the costs of performance would be so disproportionate to that reasonably contemplated by the

parties as to make the contract totally impractical in a commercial sense. *** Removed from the strictures of the common law, "impossibility" in its modern context has become a coat of many colors, including among its hues the point argued here—namely, impossibility predicated upon "commercial impracticability." This concept—which finds expression both in case law *** and in other authorities *** is grounded upon the assumption that in legal contemplation something is impracticable when it can only be done at an excessive and unreasonable cost.

*** The doctrine ultimately represents the ever-shifting line, drawn by courts hopefully responsive to commercial practices and mores, at which the community's interest in having contracts enforced according to their terms is out-weighed by the commercial senselessness of requiring performance. ***

In the case before us the detailed opinion of the trial court clearly indicates that the appropriate standard was followed. There is ample evidence to support its findings that "[t]he ice haul method of transporting riprap ultimately selected was within the contemplation of the parties and was part of the basis of the agreement which ultimately resulted in amendment No. 1 in October 1966," and that that method was not commercially feasible within the financial parameters of the contract. We affirm the court's conclusion that the contract was impossible of performance.

INTERPRETATION Commercial impracticability (unforeseen and unjust hardship) will excuse performance.

ETHICAL QUESTION Did Chugach act ethically in insisting on performance by Northern in face of dangerous conditions? Explain.

CRITICAL THINKING QUESTION Do you think that the court used the proper standard in this case? Explain.

BANKRUPTCY

Bankruptcy is a discharge of a contractual duty by operation of law available to a debtor who, by compliance with the requirements of the Bankruptcy Code, obtains an order of discharge by the bankruptcy court. It applies only to obligations that the Bankruptcy Code provides are dischargeable in bankruptcy. (We will treat the subject of bankruptcy in Chapter 38.)

STATUTE OF LIMITATIONS

At common law a plaintiff was not subject to any time limitation within which to bring an action. Now, however, all states have statutes providing such a limitation. The majority of courts hold that the running of the period of the statute of limitations does not operate to discharge the obligation but only to bar the creditor's right to bring an action.

For a summary of discharge of contracts, see Figure 17-1.

Figure 17-1
Discharge of
Contracts

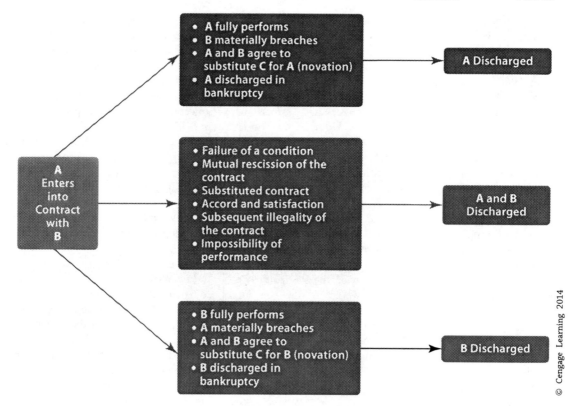

CHAPTER SUMMARY

Conditions

Definition of a Condition an event whose happening or nonhappening affects a duty of performance

Express Condition contingency explicitly set forth in language
- *Satisfaction* express condition making performance contingent on one party's approval of the other's performance
- *Subjective Satisfaction* approval based on a party's honestly held opinion
- *Objective Satisfaction* approval based on whether a reasonable person would be satisfied

Implied-in-Fact Condition contingency understood by the parties to be part of the agreement, though not expressed

Implied-in-Law Condition contingency not contained in the language of the contract but imposed by law; also called a constructive condition

Concurrent Conditions conditions that are to take place at the same time

Condition Precedent an event that must or must not occur before performance is due

Condition Subsequent an event that terminates a duty of performance

Discharge by Performance

Discharge termination of a contractual duty

Performance fulfillment of a contractual obligation resulting in a discharge

Discharge by Breach

Definition of Breach a wrongful failure to perform the terms of a contract that gives rise to a right to damages by the injured party

Material Breach nonperformance that significantly impairs the injured party's rights under the contract and discharges the injured party from any further duty under the contract
* *Prevention of Performance* one party's substantial interference with or prevention of performance by the other constitutes a material breach and discharges the other party to the contract
* *Perfect Tender Rule* standard under the Uniform Commercial Code that a seller's performance under a sales contract must strictly comply with contractual duties and that any deviation discharges the injured party

Substantial Performance performance that is incomplete but that does not defeat the purpose of the contract; does not discharge the injured party but entitles him to damages

Anticipatory Repudiation an inability or refusal to perform, before performance is due, that is treated as a breach, allowing the nonrepudiating party to bring suit immediately

Material Alteration of Written Contract a material and fraudulent alteration of a written contract by a party to the contract discharges the entire contract

Discharge by Agreement of the Parties

Mutual Rescission an agreement between the parties to terminate their respective duties under the contract

Substituted Contract a new contract accepted by both parties in satisfaction of the parties' duties under the original contract

Accord and Satisfaction substituted duty under a contract (accord) and the discharge of the prior contractual obligation by performance of the new duty (satisfaction)

Novation a substituted contract involving a new third-party promisor or promisee

Discharge by Operation of Law

Impossibility performance of contract cannot be done
* *Subjective Impossibility* the promisor—but not all promisors—cannot perform; does not discharge the promisor
* *Objective Impossibility* no promisor is able to perform; generally discharges the promisor
* *Subsequent Illegality* if performance becomes illegal or impractical as a result of a change in the law, the duty of performance is discharged
* *Frustration of Purpose* principal purpose of a contract cannot be fulfilled because of a subsequent event
* *Commercial Impracticability* where performance can be accomplished only under unforeseen and unjust hardship, the contract is discharged under the Code and the Restatement

Bankruptcy discharge available to a debtor who obtains an order of discharge by the bankruptcy court

Statute of Limitations after the statute of limitations has run, the debt is not discharged, but the creditor cannot maintain an action against the debtor

QUESTIONS

1. A-1 Roofing Co. entered into a written contract with Jaffe to put a new roof on the latter's residence for $1,800, using a specified type of roofing, and to complete the job without unreasonable delay. A-1 undertook the work within a week thereafter, and when all the roofing material was at the site and the labor 50 percent completed, the premises were totally destroyed by fire caused by lightning. A-1 submitted a bill to Jaffe for $1,200 for materials furnished and labor performed up to the time of the destruction of the premises. Jaffe refused to pay the bill, and A-1 now seeks payment from Jaffe. Should A-1 prevail? Explain.

2. By contract dated January 5, Rebecca agreed to sell to Nancy, and Nancy agreed to buy from Rebecca, a certain parcel of land then zoned commercial. The specific intent of Nancy, which was known to Rebecca, was to erect a manufacturing plant on the land; and the contract stated that the agreement was conditioned on Nancy's ability to construct such a plant on the land. The closing date for the transaction was set for April 1. On February 15, the city council rezoned the land from commercial to residential, which precluded the erection of the plant. As the closing date drew near, Nancy made it known to Rebecca that she did not intend to go through with the purchase because the land could no longer be used as intended. On April 1, Rebecca tendered the deed to Nancy, who refused to pay Rebecca the agreed purchase price. Rebecca brought an action against Nancy for breach of contract. Can Rebecca enforce the contract?

3. The Perfection Produce Company entered into a written contract with Hiram Hodges for the purchase of three hundred tons of potatoes to be grown on Hodges's farm in Maine at a stipulated price per ton. Though the land would ordinarily produce one thousand tons and although the planting and cultivation were properly done, Hodges was able to deliver only one hundred tons because an unprecedented drought caused a partial crop failure. Perfection accepted the one hundred tons but paid only 80 percent of the stipulated price per ton. Hodges sued the produce company to recover the unpaid balance of the agreed price for the one hundred tons of potatoes accepted by Perfection. Perfection counterclaimed against Hodges for his failure to deliver the additional two hundred tons. Who will prevail? Why?

4. On November 23, Sally agreed to sell to Bart her Buick automobile for $7,000, delivery and payment to be made on December 1. On November 26, Bart informed Sally that he wished to rescind the contract and would pay Sally $350 if Sally agreed. Sally agreed and took the $350 in cash. On December 1, Bart tendered to Sally $6,650 and demanded that Sally deliver the automobile. Sally refused, and Bart initiated a lawsuit. May Bart enforce the original contract?

5. Webster, Inc., dealt in automobile accessories at wholesale. Although it manufactured a few items in its own factory, among them windshield wipers, Webster purchased most of its inventory from a large number of other manufacturers. In January, Webster entered into a written contract to sell Hunter two thousand windshield wipers for $1,900, delivery to be made June 1. In April, Webster's factory burned to the ground and Webster failed to make delivery on June 1. Hunter, forced to buy windshield wipers elsewhere at a higher price, is now trying to recover damages from Webster. Will Hunter be successful in its claim?

6. Erwick Construction Company contracted to build a house for Charles. The specifications called for the use of Karlene Pipe for all plumbing. Erwick, nevertheless, got a better price on Boynton Pipe and substituted the equally good Boynton Pipe for Karlene Pipe. Charles's inspection revealed the change, and Charles now refuses to make the final payment. The contract price was for $200,000, and the final payment is $20,000. Erwick now brings suit seeking the $20,000. Will Erwick succeed in its claim?

7. Green owed White $3,500, which was due and payable on June 1. White owed Brown $3,500, which was due and payable on August 1. On May 25, White received a letter signed by Green stating, "If you will cancel my debt to you, in the amount of $3,500, I will pay, on the due date, the debt you owe Brown, in the amount of $3,500." On May 28, Green received a letter signed by White stating, "I received your letter and agree to the proposals recited therein. You may consider your debt to me canceled as of the date of this letter." On June 1, White, needing money to pay his income taxes, made a demand upon Green to pay him the $3,500 due on that date. Is Green obligated to pay the money demanded by White?

8. By written contract, Ames agreed to build a house on Bowen's lot for $145,000, commencing within ninety days of the date of the contract. Prior to the date for beginning construction, Ames informed Bowen that he was repudiating the contract and would not perform. Bowen refused to accept the repudiation and demanded fulfillment of the contract. Eighty days after the date of the contract, Bowen entered into a new contract with Curd for $142,000. The next day, without knowledge or notice of Bowen's contract with Curd, Ames began construction. Bowen ordered Ames from the premises and refused to allow him to continue. Will Ames be able to collect damages from Bowen? Explain.

9. Judy agreed in writing to work for Northern Enterprises, Inc., for three years as superintendent of Northern's manufacturing establishment and to devote herself entirely to the business, giving it her full time, attention, and skill,

for which she was to receive $72,000 per annum in monthly installments of $6,000. Judy worked and was paid for the first twelve months, when, through no fault of her own or Northern's, she was arrested and imprisoned for one month. It became imperative for Northern to employ another, and it treated the contract with Judy as breached and abandoned, refusing to permit Judy to resume work on her release from jail. What rights, if any, does Judy have under the contract?

10. The Park Plaza Hotel awarded its valet and laundry concession to Larson for a three-year term. The contract contained the following provision: "It is distinctly understood and agreed that the services to be rendered by Larson shall meet with the approval of the Park Plaza Hotel, which shall be the sole judge of the sufficiency and propriety of the services." After seven months, the hotel gave a month's notice to discontinue services based on the failure of the services to meet its approval. Larson brought an action against the hotel, alleging that its dissatisfaction was unreasonable. The hotel defended on the ground that subjective or personal satisfaction may be the sole justification for termination of the contract. Who is correct? Explain.

11. Schlosser entered into an agreement to purchase a cooperative apartment from Flynn Company. The written agreement contained the following provision: "This entire agreement is conditioned on Purchaser's being approved for occupancy by the board of directors of the Cooperative. In the event approval of the Purchaser shall be denied, this agreement shall there after be of no further force or effect." When Schlosser unilaterally revoked her "offer," Flynn sued for breach of contract. Schlosser claims the approval provision was a condition precedent to the existence of a binding contract and, thus, she was free to revoke. Decision?

12. Jacobs, owner of a farm, entered into a contract with Earl Walker in which Walker agreed to paint the buildings on the farm. As authorized by Jacobs, Walker acquired the paint from Jones with the bill to be sent to Jacobs. Before the work was completed, however, Jacobs without good cause ordered Walker to stop. Walker made offers to complete the job, but Jacobs declined to permit Walker to fulfill his contract. Jacobs refused to pay Jones for the paint Walker had acquired for the job. Explain whether Jones and Walker would be successful in an action against Jacobs for breach of contract.

CASE PROBLEMS

13. Barta entered into a written contract to buy the K&K Pharmacy, located in a local shopping center. Included in the contract was a provision stating "this Agreement shall be contingent upon Buyer's ability to obtain a new lease from Landlord for the premises presently occupied by Seller. In the event Buyer is unable to obtain a lease satisfactory to Buyer, this Agreement shall be null and void." Barta planned to sell "high-traffic" grocery items, such as bread, milk, and coffee, to attract customers to his drugstore. A grocery store in the shopping center, however, already held the exclusive right to sell grocery items. Barta, therefore, could not obtain a leasing agreement meeting his approval. Barta refused to close the sale. In a suit by K&K Pharmacy against Barta for breach of contract, who will prevail? Explain.

14. Victor Packing Co. (Victor) contracted to supply Sun Maid Raisin Growers 1,800 tons of raisins from the current year's crop. After delivering 1,190 tons of raisins by August, Victor refused to supply any more. Although Victor had until the end of the crop season to ship the remaining 610 tons of raisins, Sun Maid treated Victor's repeated refusals to ship any more raisins as a repudiation of the contract. To prevent breaching its own contracts, Sun Maid went into the market place to "cover" and bought the raisins needed. Unfortunately, between the time Victor refused delivery and Sun Maid entered the market, disastrous rains had caused the price of raisins to skyrocket. May Sun Maid recover from Victor the difference between the contract price and the market price before the end of the current crop year?

15. On August 20, Hildebrand entered into a written contract with the city of Douglasville whereby he was to serve as community development project engineer for three years at a monthly fee of $1,583.33. This salary figure could be changed without affecting the other terms of the contract. One of the provisions for termination of the contract was written notice by either party to the other at any time at least ninety days prior to the intended date of termination. The contract listed a substantial number of services and duties Hildebrand was to perform for the city; among the lesser duties were (1) keeping the community development director (Hildebrand's supervisor) informed at all times of his whereabouts and how he could be contacted and (2) attending meetings at which his presence was requested. Two years later, by which time Hildebrand's fee had risen to $1,915.83 per month, the city fired Hildebrand effective immediately, citing "certain material breaches … of the … agreement." The city specifically charged that he did not attend the necessary meetings although requested to do so and seldom if ever kept his supervisor informed of his whereabouts and how he could be contacted. Will Hildebrand prevail in a suit against the mayor and city for the amount of $5,747.49 for breach of his employment contract because of the city's failure to give him ninety days' notice prior to termination?

16. Walker & Co. contracted to provide a sign for Harrison to place above his dry cleaning business. According to the contract, Harrison would lease the sign from Walker, making monthly payments for thirty-six months. In return,

Walker agreed to maintain and service the sign at its own expense. Walker installed the sign in July, and Harrison made the first rental payment. Shortly thereafter, someone hit the sign with a tomato. Harrison also claims he discovered rust on its chrome and little spiderwebs in its corners. Harrison repeatedly called Walker for the maintenance work promised under the contract, but Walker did not respond immediately. Harrison then telegraphed Walker that, due to Walker's failure to perform the maintenance services, he held Walker in material breach of the contract. A week later, Walker sent out a crew, which did all of the requested maintenance services. Has Walker committed a material breach of contract? Explain.

17. In May, Watts was awarded a construction contract, based on its low bid, by the Cullman County Commission. The contract provided that it would not become effective until approved by the state director of the Farmers Home Administration (now part of the U.S. Department of Agriculture Rural Development Office). In September, construction still had not been authorized and Watts wrote to the County Commission requesting a 5 percent price increase to reflect seasonal and inflationary price increases. The County Commission countered with an offer of 3.5 percent. Watts then wrote the commission, insisting on a 5 percent increase and stating that if this was not agreeable, it was withdrawing its original bid. The commission obtained another company to perform the project, and on October 14, informed Watts that it had accepted the withdrawal of the bid. Watts sued for breach of contract. Explain whether Watts will prevail and why or why not.

18. K & G Construction Co. was the owner of and the general contractor for a housing subdivision project. Harris contracted with the company to do excavating and earth-moving work on the project. Certain provisions of the contract stated that (a) K & G was to make monthly progress payments to Harris; (b) no such payments were to be made until Harris obtained liability insurance; and (c) all of Harris's work on the project must be performed in a workmanlike manner. On August 9, a bulldozer operator, working for Harris, drove too close to one of K & G's houses, causing the collapse of a wall and other damage. When Harris and his insurance carrier denied liability and refused to pay for the damage, K & G refused to make the August monthly progress payment. Harris, nonetheless, continued to work on the project until mid-September, when the excavator ceased its operations due to K & G's refusal to make the progress payment. K & G had another excavator finish the job at an added cost of $450. It then sued Harris for the bulldozer damage, alleging negligence, and for the $450 damages for breach of contract. Harris claims that K & G defaulted first, having no legal right to refuse the August progress payment. Did K & G default first? Explain.

19. Mountain Restaurant Corporation (Mountain) leased commercial space in the ParkCenter Mall to operate a restaurant called Zac's Grill. The lease specified that the lessee shall "at all times have a nonexclusive and nonrevocable right, together with the other tenants and occupants of ... the shopping center, to use the parking area ... for itself, its customers and employees." Zac's Grill was to be a fast-food restaurant where tables were anticipated to "turn over" twice during lunch. Zac's operated successfully until parking close to the restaurant became restricted. Two other restaurants opened and began competing for parking spaces, and the parking lot would become full between 12:00 and 12:30 P.M. Parking, however, was always available at other areas of the mall. Business declined for Zac's, which fell behind on the rent due to ParkCenter until finally the restaurant closed. Mountain claims that it was discharged from its obligations under the lease because of material breach. Is Mountain correct? Explain.

20. In late 2009 or early 2010, the plaintiff, Lan England, agreed to sell 258,363 shares of stock to the defendant, Eugene Horbach, for $2.75 per share, resulting in a total price of $710,498.25. Although the purchase money was to be paid in the first quarter of 2010, the defendant made periodic payments on the stock at least through September 2010. The parties met in May of 2011 to finalize the transaction. At this time, the plaintiff believed that the defendant owed at least $25,000 of the original purchase price. The defendant did not dispute that amount. The parties then reached a second agreement whereby the defendant agreed to pay to the plaintiff an additional $25,000 and to hold in trust 2 percent of the stock for the plaintiff. In return, the plaintiff agreed to transfer the stock and to forgo his right to sue the defendant for breach of the original agreement.

In December 2012, the plaintiff made a demand for the 2 percent stock, but the defendant refused, contending that the 2 percent agreement was meant only to secure his payment of the additional $25,000. The plaintiff sued for breach of the 2 percent agreement. Prior to trial, the defendant discovered additional business records documenting that he had, before entering into the second agreement, actually overpaid the plaintiff for the purchase of the stock. The defendant asserts the plaintiff could not enforce the second agreement as an accord and satisfaction because (1) it was not supported by consideration and (2) it was based upon a mutual mistake that the defendant owed additional money on the original agreement. Is the defendant correct in his assertions? Explain.

21. An artist once produced a painting now called *The Plains of Meudon*. For a while, the parties in this case thought that the artist was Theodore Rousseau, a prominent member of the Barbizon school, and that the painting was quite valuable. With this idea in mind, the Kohlers consigned the painting to Leslie Hindman, Inc. (Hindman), an auction house. Among other things, the consignment agreement between the Kohlers and Hindman defined the scope of Hindman, Inc.'s authority as agent. First, Hindman was obliged to sell the painting according to the conditions of sale spelled out in the auction catalog. Those conditions

provided that neither the consignors nor Hindman made any warranties of authenticity. Second, the consignment agreement gave Hindman extensive and exclusive discretionary authority to rescind sales if in its "sole discretion" it determined that the sale subjected the company or the Kohlers to any liability under a warranty of authenticity.

Despite having some doubts about its authenticity, Thune was still interested in the painting but wanted to have it authenticated before committing to its purchase. Unable to obtain an authoritative opinion about its authenticity before the auction, Leslie Hindman and Thune made a verbal agreement that Thune could return the painting within approximately thirty days of the auction if he was the successful bidder and if an expert then determined that Rousseau had not painted it. Neither Leslie Hindman nor anyone else at Hindman told the Kohlers about the questions concerning the painting or about the side agreement between Thune and Hindman. At the auction, Thune prevailed in the bidding with a high bid of $90,000, and he took possession of the painting without paying. He then sent it to an expert in Paris who decided that it was not a Rousseau. Thune returned the painting to Hindman within the agreed-upon period. Explain whether the Kohlers would be successful in a lawsuit against either Hindman or Thune.

TAKING SIDES

Associated Builders, Inc., provided labor and materials to William M. Coggins and Benjamin W. Coggins, doing business as Ben & Bill's Chocolate Emporium, to complete a structure on Main Street in Bar Harbor, Maine. After a dispute arose regarding compensation, Associated and the Cogginses executed an agreement stating that there existed an outstanding balance of $70,000 and setting forth the following terms of repayment:

It is agreed that, two payments will be made by the Cogginses to Associated Builders as follows: Twenty Five Thousand Dollars ($25,000.00) on or before June 1, 2011, and Twenty Five Thousand Dollars ($25,000.00) on or before June 1, 2012. No interest will be charged or paid providing payments are made as agreed. If the payments are not made as agreed then interest shall accrue at 10% per annum figured from the date of default. It is further agreed that

Associated Builders will forfeit the balance of Twenty Thousand Dollars and No Cents ($20,000.00) providing the above payments are made as agreed.

The Cogginses made their first payment in accordance with the agreement. The second payment, however, was delivered three days late on June 4, 2012. Claiming a breach of the contract, Associated contended that the remainder of the original balance of $20,000, plus interest and cost, were now due.

a. What arguments would support Associated's claim for $20,000?

b. What arguments would support the claim by the Cogginses that they were not liable for $20,000?

c. For what damages, if any, are the Cogginses liable? Explain.

Chapter 18

CONTRACT REMEDIES

The traditional goal of the law of contract remedies has not been the compulsion of the promisor to perform his promise but compensation of the promisee for the loss resulting from breach.

RESTATEMENT OF CONTRACTS

CHAPTER OUTCOMES

After reading and studying this chapter, you should be able to:

1. Explain how compensatory damages and reliance damages are computed.

2. Define (a) nominal damages, (b) incidental damages, (c) consequential damages, (d) foreseeability of damages, (e) punitive damages, (f) liquidated damages, and (g) mitigation of damages.

3. Define the various types of equitable relief and explain when the courts will grant such relief.

4. Explain how restitutionary damages are computed and identify the situations in which restitution is available as a contractual remedy.

5. Identify and explain the limitations on contractual remedies.

When one party to a contract breaches the contract by failing to perform his contractual duties, the law provides a remedy for the injured party. Although the primary objective of contract remedies is to compensate the injured party for the loss resulting from the breach, it is impossible for any remedy to equal the promised performance. The relief a court can give an injured party is what it regards as an *equivalent* of the promised performance.

PRACTICAL ADVICE

Consider including in your contracts a provision for the recovery of attorneys' fees in the event of breach of contract.

In this chapter, we will examine the most common remedies available for breach of contract: (1) monetary damages, (2) the equitable remedies of specific performance and injunction, and (3) restitution. Article 2 of the Uniform Commercial Code (UCC), which provides specialized remedies that we will discuss in Chapter 23, governs the sale of goods. Contract remedies are available to protect one or more of the following interests of the injured parties:

1. their *expectation interest*, which is their interest in having the benefit of their bar gain by being put in a position as good as the one they would have been in had the contract been performed;

2. their *reliance interest*, which is their interest in being reimbursed for loss caused by reliance on the contract

by being put in a position as good as the one they would have been in had the contract not been made; or

3. their *restitution interest*, which is their interest in having restored to them any benefit that they had conferred on the other party.

The contract remedies of compensatory damages, specific performance, and injunction protect the expectation interest. The contractual remedy of reliance damages protects the reliance interest, while the contractual remedy of restitution protects the restitution interest.

PRACTICAL ADVICE

Consider including in your contracts a provision for the arbitration of contract disputes.

Monetary Damages

A judgment awarding monetary damages is the most frequently granted judicial remedy for breach of contract. Monetary damages, however, will be awarded only for losses that are foreseeable, established with reasonable certainty, and not avoidable. The equitable remedies discussed in this chapter are discretionary and are available only if monetary damages are inadequate.

COMPENSATORY DAMAGES

The right to recover compensatory damages for breach of contract is always available to the injured party. The purpose in allowing **compensatory damages** is to place the injured party in a position as good as the one he would have been in had the other party performed under the contract. This involves compensating the injured party for the dollar value of the benefits he would have received had the contract been performed less any savings he experienced by not having to perform his own obligations under the contract. These damages are intended to protect the injured party's *expectation interest,* which is the value he expected to derive from the contract. Thus, the amount of compensatory damages is the loss of value to the injured party caused by the other party's failure to perform or by the other's deficient performance *minus* the loss or cost avoided by the injured party *plus* incidental damages *plus* consequential damages.

Loss of Value   In general, **loss of value** is the *difference between the value of the promised performance* of the breaching party *and the value of the actual performance* rendered by the breaching party. If no performance is rendered at all, the loss of value is the value of the promised

performance. If defective or partial performance is rendered, the loss of value is the difference between the value that the full performance would have had and the value of the performance actually rendered. Thus, when there has been a breach of warranty, the injured party may recover the difference between the value the goods would have had, had they been as warranted, and the value of the goods in the condition in which the buyer actually received them. To illustrate, Jacob sells an automobile to Juliet, expressly warranting that it will get forty-five miles per gallon; but the automobile gets only twenty miles per gallon. The automobile would have been worth $24,000 if as warranted, but it is worth only $20,000 as delivered. Juliet would recover $4,000 in damages for loss of value.

Cost Avoided   The recovery by the injured party is reduced, however, by any cost or loss she has avoided by not having to perform. For example, Clinton agrees to build a hotel for Debra for $11 million by September 1. Clinton breaches by not completing construction until October 1. As a consequence, Debra loses revenues for one month in the amount of $400,000 but saves operating expenses of $60,000. Therefore, she may recover damages for $340,000. Similarly, in a contract in which the injured party has not fully performed, the injured party's recovery is reduced by the value to the injured party of the performance the injured party promised but did not render. For example, Victor agrees to convey land to Joan in return for Joan's promise to work for Victor for two years. Joan repudiates the contract before Victor has conveyed the land to Joan. Victor's recovery for loss from Joan is reduced by the value to Victor of the land.

Incidental Damages   **Incidental damages** are damages that arise directly out of the breach, such as costs incurred to acquire the nondelivered performance from some other source. For example, Agnes employs Benton for nine months for $40,000 to supervise construction of a factory. She then fires Benton without cause after three weeks. Benton, who spends $850 in reasonable fees attempting to find comparable employment, may recover $850 in incidental damages in addition to any other actual loss he has suffered.

Consequential Damages   **Consequential damages** are damages not arising directly out of a breach but arising as a foreseeable result of the breach. Consequential damages include lost profits and injury to person or property. Thus, if Tracy leases to Sean a defective machine that causes $40,000 in property damage and $120,000 in personal injuries, Sean may recover, in addition to damages for loss of value and incidental damages, $160,000 as consequential damages.

Business Law in Action

When contracting parties litigate over a breach, does the losing party have to pay the winner's attorneys' fees? These fees may appear to qualify as consequential damages, direct consequences of the breach of contract. However, courts in this country follow what is known as the "American Rule," which provides that each party pays its own attorneys' fees, regardless of who wins. This rule holds true unless there is an applicable statute or express contract clause to the contrary. (Some states have statutes that specifically provide for an award of reasonable attorneys' fees and costs to the prevailing party in certain suits arising out of contract.)

Even though the general rule is that attorneys' fees are not awarded in breach of contract suits, proactive contracting parties can expressly provide in their contract that the losing party will pay the reasonable attorneys'

fees of the prevailing party. Many written contracts, particularly those that are drafted by lawyers, contain so-called attorneys' fees provisions. An example of the language used follows: "In the event of any dispute arising out of the performance or breach of this agreement, the prevailing party will be entitled to an award of reasonable attorneys' fees." Then if the parties end up litigating over the contract, the judge will be able to make the nonbreaching party whole by requiring the losing party to pay the winner's reasonable attorneys' fees, in addition to any other damages or relief granted.

However, absent an attorneys' fees clause in the parties' written agreement and without an attorneys' fees statute in place, the general rule applies and attorneys' fees will not be considered part of a litigating party's damages.

© Cengage Learning 2014

PRACTICAL ADVICE

If you are the provider of goods or services, consider including a contractual provision for the limitation or exclusion of consequential damages. If you are the purchaser of goods or services, avoid such limitations.

RELIANCE DAMAGES

Instead of seeking compensatory damages, the injured party may seek reimbursement for foreseeable loss caused by her reliance on the contract. The purpose of **reliance damages** is to place the injured party in a position as good as the one she would have been in had the contract *not been made*. Reliance damages include expenses incurred in preparing to perform, in actually performing, or in forgoing opportunities to enter into other contracts. An injured party may prefer damages for reliance to compensatory damages when she is unable to establish her lost profits with reasonable certainty. For example, Donald agrees to sell his retail store to Gary, who spends $750,000 in acquiring inventory and fixtures. Donald then repudiates the contract, and Gary sells the inventory and fixtures for $735,000. Because neither party can establish with reasonable certainty what profit Gary would have made, Gary may recover from Donald as damages the loss of $15,000 he sustained on the sale of the inventory and fixtures plus any other costs he incurred in entering into the contract.

An injured party may choose reliance damages instead of compensatory damages when the agreed-upon contract would be unprofitable. In such a case, however, if the breaching party can prove with reasonable certainty the amount of the loss, it will be subtracted from the injured party's reliance damages.

NOMINAL DAMAGES

An action to recover damages for breach of contract may be maintained even though the plaintiff has not sustained or cannot prove any injury or loss resulting from the breach. In such case he will be permitted to recover **nominal damages**— a small sum fixed without regard to the amount of loss. Such a judgment may also include an award of court costs.

DAMAGES FOR MISREPRESENTATION

The basic remedy for misrepresentation is rescission (avoidance) of the contract. When appropriate, restitution will also be required. At common law, an alternative remedy to rescission is a suit for damages. The Code liberalizes the common law by not restricting a defrauded party to an election of remedies. That is, the injured party may both rescind the contract by restoring the other party to the status quo and recover damages or obtain any other remedy available under the Code. In most states, the measure of damages for misrepresentation depends on whether the misrepresentation was fraudulent or nonfraudulent.

Fraud A party who has been induced by fraud to enter into a contract may recover general damages in a tort action. A minority of states allow the injured party to recover, under the "out-of-pocket" rule, general damages equal to the difference between the value of what she has received and the value of what she has given for it. The great majority of states, however, permit the intentionally defrauded party to recover, under the "benefit-of-the-bargain" rule, general damages that are equal to the difference between the value of what she has received and the value of the fraudulent party's performance as represented. The Restatement of Torts provides the fraudulently injured party with the option of either out-of-pocket or benefit-of-the-bargain damages. To illustrate, Emily intentionally misrepresents the capabilities of a printing press and thereby induces Melissa to purchase the machine for $20,000. Though the value of the press as delivered is $14,000, the machine would be worth $24,000 if it performed as represented. Under the out-of-pocket rule, Melissa would recover $6,000, whereas under the benefit-of-the-bargain rule, she would recover $10,000. In addition to a recovery of general damages under one of the measures just discussed, consequential damages may be recovered to the extent they are proved with reasonable certainty and to the extent they do not duplicate general damages. Moreover, where the fraud is gross, oppressive, or aggravated, punitive damages are permitted. See *Merritt v. Craig* later in this chapter.

Nonfraudulent Misrepresentation When the misrepresentation is negligent, the deceived party may recover general damages (under the out-of-pocket measure) and consequential damages. Furthermore, some states permit the recovery of general damages under the benefit-of-the-bargain measure. When the misrepresentation is neither fraudulent nor negligent, however, the Restatement of Torts limits damages to the out-of-pocket measure.

PUNITIVE DAMAGES

Punitive damages are monetary damages in addition to compensatory damages awarded to a plaintiff in certain situations involving willful, wanton, or malicious conduct. Their purpose is to punish the defendant and thus discourage him, and others, from similar wrongful conduct. The purpose of allowing contract damages, on the other hand, is to compensate the plaintiff for the loss sustained because of the defendant's breach of contract. Accordingly, the Restatement provides that punitive damages are not recoverable for a breach of contract unless the conduct constituting the breach is also a tort for which the plaintiff may recover punitive damages. See *Merritt v. Craig* later in this chapter.

LIQUIDATED DAMAGES

A contract may contain a **liquidated damages** provision by which the parties agree in advance to the damages to be paid in event of a breach. Such a provision will be enforced if it amounts to a reasonable forecast of the loss that may or does result from the breach. If, however, the sum agreed on as liquidated damages bears no reasonable relationship to the amount of probable loss, it is unenforceable as a penalty. (A penalty is a contractual provision designed to deter a party from breaching her contract and to punish her for doing so.) Such equivalence is required because the objective of contract remedies is compensatory, not punitive. By examining the substance of the provision, the nature of the contract, and the extent of probable harm that a breach may reasonably be expected to cause the promisee, the courts will determine whether the agreed amount is proper as liquidated damages or unenforceable as a penalty. If a liquidated damages provision is not enforceable, the injured party nevertheless is entitled to the ordinary remedies for breach of contract.

> **PRACTICAL ADVICE**
>
> Consider including a contractual provision for reasonable liquidated damages, especially where damages will be difficult to prove.

ARROWHEAD SCHOOL DISTRICT NO. 75, PARK COUNTY, MONTANA V. KLYAP

SUPREME COURT OF MONTANA, 2003
318 MONT. 103, 79 P.3D 250
http://scholar.google.com/scholar_case?case=643756738100095281 &q=79+p.3d+250&hl=en&as_sdt=2,34

FACTS Arrowhead School District No. 75 is located in Park County, Montana, and consists of one school, Arrowhead School (School). For the 1997–98 school year, the School employed eleven full-time teachers and several part-time teachers. During that school year, the School employed James Klyap as a new teacher instructing math, language arts, and physical education for the sixth, seventh, and eighth grades. In addition, Klyap helped start a sports program and coached flag football, basketball, and volleyball. In June 1998, the School offered Klyap a contract for the 1998–99 school year, which he accepted. This contract provided for a $20,500 salary and included a liquidated damages clause. The clause calculated liquidated damages as a percentage of annual salary determined by the date of breach; a breach of contract after July 20, 1998, required payment of 20 percent of salary as damages. Klyap also signed a notice indicating he accepted responsibility for familiarizing himself with the information in the teacher's handbook which also included the liquidated damages clause. On August 12, Klyap informed the School that he would not be returning for the 1998–99 school year even though classes were scheduled to start on August 26. The School then sought to enforce the liquidated damages clause in Klyap's teaching contract for the stipulated amount of $4,100.

After Klyap resigned, the School attempted to find another teacher to take Klyap's place. Although at the time that Klyap was offered his contract the School had eighty potential applicants, only two viable applicants remained available. Right before classes started, the School was able to hire one of those applicants, a less-experienced teacher, at a salary of $19,500.

After a bench trial, the District Court determined the clause was enforceable because the damages suffered by the School were impractical and extremely difficult to fix. Specifically, the court found the School suffered damages because it had to spend additional time setting up an interview committee, conducting interviews, training the new, less-experienced teacher, and reorganizing the sports program. After concluding that the School took appropriate steps to mitigate its damages, the court awarded judgment in favor of the School in the amount of $4,100. Klyap appealed.

DECISION Judgment affirmed.

OPINION Nelson, J. The fundamental tenet of modern contract law is freedom of contract; parties are free to mutually agree to terms governing their private conduct as long as those terms do not conflict with public laws. [Citation.] This tenet presumes that parties are in the best position to make decisions in their own interest. Normally, in the course of contract interpretation by a court, the court simply gives effect to the agreement between the parties in order to enforce the private law of the contract. [Citation.] When one party breaches the contract, judicial enforcement of the contract ensures the nonbreaching party receives expectancy damages, compensation equal to what that party would receive if the contract were performed. [Citations.] By only awarding expectancy damages rather

than additional damages intended to punish the breaching party for failure to perform the contract, court enforcement of private contracts supports the theory of efficient breach. In other words, if it is more efficient for a party to breach a contract and pay expectancy damages in order to enter a superior contract, courts will not interfere by requiring the breaching party to pay more than was due under their contract. [Citation.]

Liquidated damages are, in theory, an extension of these principles. Rather than wait until the occurrence of breach, the parties to a contract are free to agree in advance on a specific damage amount to be paid upon breach. [Citation.] This amount is intended to predetermine expectancy damages. Ideally, this predetermination is intended to make the agreement between the parties more efficient. Rather than requiring a post-breach inquiry into damages between the parties, the breaching party simply pays the nonbreaching party the stipulated amount. Further, in this way, liquidated damages clauses allow parties to estimate damages that are impractical or difficult to prove, as courts cannot enforce expectancy damages without sufficient proof.

* * *

In order to determine whether a clause should be declared a penalty, courts attempt to measure the reasonableness of a liquidated damages clause. * * * [T]he threshold indicator of reasonableness is whether the situation involves damages of a type that are impractical or extremely difficult to prove. * * *

According to RESTATEMENT § 356 and other treatises, damages must be reasonable in relation to the damages the parties anticipated when the contract was executed or in relation to actual damages resulting from the breach.

* * *

* * * Liquidated damages in a personal service contract induce performance by an employee by predetermining compensation to an employer if the employee leaves. However, the employer clearly prefers performance by the specific employee because that employee was chosen for hire. * * * Further, because personal service contracts are not enforceable by specific performance, [citation], liquidated damages are an appropriate way for employers to protect their interests. * * *

* * *

After reviewing the facts of this case, we hold that while the 20% liquidated damages clause is definitely harsher than most, it is still within Klyap's reasonable expectations and is not unduly oppressive. First, as the School pointed out during testimony, at such a small school teachers are chosen in part depending on how their skills complement those of the other teachers. Therefore, finding someone who would provide services equivalent to Klyap at such a late date would be virtually impossible. This difficulty was born out when only two applicants remained available and the School hired a teacher who was less experienced than Klyap. As a teacher, especially one with experience teaching at that very School, Klyap would have to be aware of the problem finding equivalent services would pose.

Second, besides the loss of equivalent services, the School lost time for preparation for other activities in order to attempt to find equivalent services. As the District Court noted, the School had to spend additional time setting up an interview committee and conducting interviews. Further, the new teacher missed all the staff development training earlier that year so individual training was required. And finally, because Klyap was essential to the sports program, the School had to spend additional time reorganizing the sports program as one sport had to be eliminated with Klyap's loss. These activities all took away from the other school and administrative duties that had been scheduled for that time. ***

Finally, although the School testified it had an intent to secure performance and avoid the above damages by reason of the clause, ***, such an intent does not turn a liquidated damages clause into a penalty unless the amount is unreasonably large and therefore not within reasonable expectations. ***

Therefore, because as a teacher Klyap would know teachers are typically employed for an entire school year and would know how difficult it is to replace equivalent services at such a small rural school, it was within Klyap's reasonable expectations to agree to a contract with a 20% of salary liquidated damages provision for a departure so close to the start of the school year.

*** Accordingly, we hold the District Court correctly determined that the liquidated damages provision was enforceable.

INTERPRETATION A liquidated damages provision is enforceable if it is a reasonable forecast of the harm caused by the breach.

CRITICAL THINKING QUESTION What limitations, if any, should the law impose upon liquidated damages? Explain.

LIMITATIONS ON DAMAGES

To accomplish the basic purposes of contract remedies, the limitations of foreseeability, certainty, and mitigation have been imposed upon monetary damages. These limitations are intended to ensure that damages can be taken into account at the time of contracting, that they are compensatory and not speculative, and that they do not include loss that could have been avoided by reasonable efforts.

Foreseeability of Damages Contracting parties are generally expected to consider foreseeable risks at the time they enter into the contract. Therefore, compensatory or reliance damages are recoverable only for loss that the party in breach had reason to foresee as a *probable* result of a breach when the contract was made. The breaching party is not liable for loss that was not foreseeable at the time of entering into the contract. The test of **foreseeable damages** is *objective*, based on what the breaching party had reason to foresee. Loss may be deemed foreseeable as a probable result of a breach because it followed from the breach (1) in the ordinary course of events or (2) as a result of special circumstances, beyond the ordinary course of events, about which the party in breach had reason to know.

A leading case on the subject of foreseeability of damages is *Hadley v. Baxendale*, decided in England in 1854. In this case, the plaintiffs operated a flourmill at Gloucester. Their mill was compelled to cease operating because of a broken crankshaft attached to the steam engine that furnished power to the mill. It was necessary to send the broken shaft to a foundry located at Greenwich so that a new shaft could be made. The plaintiffs delivered the broken shaft to the defendants, who were common carriers, for immediate transportation from Gloucester to Greenwich, but did not inform the defendants that operation of the mill had ceased because of the nonfunctioning crankshaft. The defendants received the shaft and promised to deliver the shaft for repairs the following day. The defendants, however, did not make delivery as promised; as a result, the mill did not resume operations for several days, causing the plaintiffs to lose profitable sales. The defendants contended that the loss of profits was too remote, and therefore unforeseeable, to be recoverable. Nonetheless, the jury, in awarding damages to the plaintiffs, was permitted to take into consideration the loss of these profits. The appellate court reversed the decision and ordered a new trial on the ground that the plaintiffs had never communicated to the defendants the special circumstances that caused the loss of profits, namely, the continued stoppage of the mill while awaiting the return of the repaired crankshaft. A common carrier, the court reasoned, would not reasonably have foreseen that the plaintiffs' mill would be shut down as a result of delay in transporting the broken crankshaft. On the other hand, if the defendants in *Hadley v. Baxendale* had been informed that the shaft was necessary for the operation of the mill, or otherwise had reason to know this fact, they would be liable for the plaintiffs' loss of profit during that period of the shutdown caused by their delay. Under these circumstances, the loss would be the "foreseeable" and "natural" result of the breach.

Should a plaintiff's expected profit be extraordinarily large, the general rule is that the breaching party will be liable for such special loss only if he had reason to know of it. In any event, the plaintiff may recover for any ordinary loss resulting from the breach. Thus, if Madeline breaches a contract with Jane, causing Jane, due to special circumstances, $10,000 in damages when ordinarily such a breach would result in only $6,000 in damages, Madeline would be liable to Jane for $6,000, not $10,000, provided that Madeline was unaware of the special circumstances causing Jane the unusually large loss.

> ### PRACTICAL ADVICE
> Be sure to inform the other party to the contract of any "special circumstances" beyond the ordinary course of events that could result from a breach of contract.

Certainty of Damages Damages are not recoverable for loss beyond an amount that the injured party can establish with reasonable certainty. If the injured party cannot prove a particular element of her loss with reasonable certainty, she nevertheless will be entitled to recover the portion of her loss that she can prove with reasonable certainty. The certainty requirement creates the greatest challenge for plaintiffs seeking the recovery of consequential damages for lost profits on related transactions. Similar difficulty arises in proving lost profits caused by breach of a contract to produce a sporting event or to publish a new book, for example.

Mitigation of Damages Under the doctrine of mitigation of damages, the injured party may not recover damages for loss that he could have avoided with reasonable effort and without undue risk, burden, or humiliation. Thus, if Earl is under a contract to manufacture goods for Karl and Karl repudiates the contract after Earl has begun performance, Earl will not be allowed to recover for losses he sustains by continuing to manufacture the goods, if to do so would increase the amount of damages. The amount of loss that reasonably could have been avoided is deducted from the amount that otherwise would be recoverable as damages. On the other hand, if the goods were almost completed when Karl repudiated the contract, completing the goods might reduce the damages, because the finished goods may be resalable whereas the unfinished goods may not.

Similarly, if Harvey contracts to work for Olivia for one year for a weekly salary and after two months is wrongfully discharged by Olivia, Harvey must use reasonable efforts to mitigate his damages by seeking other employment. If, after such effort, he cannot obtain other employment of the same general character, he is entitled to recover full pay for the contract period during which he is unemployed. He is not obliged to accept a radically different type of employment or to accept work at a distant place. For example, a person employed as a schoolteacher or accountant who is wrongfully discharged is not obliged to accept employment as a chauffeur or truck driver. If Harvey does *not* seek other employment, then if Olivia proves with reasonable certainty that employment of the same general character was available, Harvey's damages are reduced by the amount he could have earned. The next case involving Shirley MacLaine turns on whether acting in a western is employment equivalent to singing and dancing in a musical.

> ### PRACTICAL ADVICE
> If the other party to the contract breaches, be sure to make reasonable efforts to avoid or mitigate damages.

PARKER V. TWENTIETH CENTURY-FOX FILM CORP.

SUPREME COURT OF CALIFORNIA, 1970
3 CAL.3D 176, 89 CAL.RPTR. 737, 474 P.2D 689

http://scholar.google.com/scholar_case?q=474+P.2d+689&hl=en&as_sdt=2,34&case=8204943341098207403&scilh=0

FACTS Shirley MacLaine Parker, a well-known actress, contracted with Twentieth Century-Fox Film Corporation (Fox) in August 1965 to play the female lead in Fox's upcoming production of *Bloomer Girl*, a motion picture musical that was to be filmed in California. The contract provided that Fox would pay Parker a minimum "guaranteed compensation" of $750,000 for fourteen weeks of Parker's services, beginning May 23, 1966. By letter dated April 4, 1966, Fox notified Parker of its intention not to produce the film and, instead, offered to employ Parker in the female lead of another film entitled *Big Country, Big Man*, a dramatic western to be filmed in Australia. The compensation offered and most of the other provisions in the substitute contract were identical to the *Bloomer Girl* provisions, except that Parker's right to approve the director and screenplay would have been eliminated or reduced under the *Big Country* contract. Parker refused to accept and brought suit against Fox to recover $750,000 for breach of the *Bloomer Girl* contract. Fox contended that it owed no money to Parker because she had deliberately failed to mitigate or reduce her damages by unreasonably refusing to accept the *Big Country* lead. The trial court granted Parker a summary judgment. (The court's opinion with respect to the rules for determining whether to grant summary judgment appears in Chapter 3.)

DECISION Judgment for Parker affirmed.

OPINION Burke, J. The general rule is that the measure of recovery by a wrongfully discharged employee is the amount of salary agreed upon for the period of service, less the amount which the employer affirmatively proves the employee has earned or with reasonable effort might have earned from other employment. [Citations.] However, before projected earnings from other employment opportunities not sought or accepted by the discharged employee can be applied in mitigation, the employer must show that the other employment was comparable, or substantially similar, to that of which the employee has been deprived; the employee's rejection of or failure to seek other available employment of a different or inferior kind may not be resorted to in order to mitigate damages. [Citations.]

***

Applying the foregoing rules to the record in the present case, with all intendments in favor of the party opposing the summary judgment motion—here, defendant—it is clear that the trial court correctly ruled that plaintiff's failure to accept defendant's tendered substitute employment could not be applied in mitigation of damages because the offer of the *Big Country* lead was of employment both different and inferior, and that no factual dispute was presented on that issue. The mere circumstance that *Bloomer Girl* was to be a musical review calling upon plaintiff's talents as a dancer as well as an actress, and was to be produced in the City of Los Angeles, whereas *Big Country* was a straight dramatic role in a "Western Type" story taking place in an opal mine in Australia, demonstrates the difference in kind between the two employments; the female lead as a dramatic actress in a western style motion picture can by no stretch of the imagination be considered the equivalent of or substantially similar to the lead in a song-and-dance production.

Additionally, the substitute *Big Country* offer proposed to eliminate or impair the director and screenplay approvals accorded to plaintiff under the original *Bloomer Girl* contract *** and thus constituted an offer of inferior employment. No expertise or judicial notice is required in order to hold that the deprivation or infringement of an employee's rights held under an original employment contract converts the available "other employment" relied upon by the employer to mitigate damages, into inferior employment which the employee need not seek or accept. [Citation.]

INTERPRETATION An injured party's damages may not be reduced by mitigation for her failure to accept or seek other employment of a different or inferior kind.

ETHICAL QUESTION Was it fair for Twentieth Century-Fox Film Corporation to expect Parker to act in the substitute film? Explain.

CRITICAL THINKING QUESTION Why should an injured party be required to mitigate damages? Explain.

Remedies in Equity

At times, damages will not adequately compensate an injured party. In these cases, equitable relief in the form of specific performance or an injunction may be available to protect the injured party's interest. Such remedies are not a matter of right but rest in the discretion of the court. Consequently, they will not be granted when there is an adequate remedy at law; when it is impossible to enforce them, as when the seller has already transferred the subject matter of the contract to an innocent third person; when the terms of the contract are unfair; when the consideration is grossly inadequate; when the contract is tainted with fraud, duress, undue influence, mistake, or unfair practices; or when the relief would cause the defendant unreasonable hardship. See *Real Estate Analytics, LLC. v. Vallas* in this chapter.

On the other hand, a court may grant specific performance or an injunction despite a provision for liquidated damages. Moreover, a court will grant specific performance or an injunction even though a term of the contract prohibits equitable relief, if denying such relief would cause the injured party unreasonable hardship.

Another equitable remedy is **reformation**, a process whereby the court "rewrites" or "corrects" a written contract to make it conform to the true agreement of the parties. The purpose of reformation is not to make a new contract for the parties but to express adequately the contract they have made for themselves. The remedy of reformation is granted when the parties agree on a contract but write it in a way that inaccurately reflects their actual agreement. For example, Acme Insurance Co. and Bell agree that for good consideration, Acme will issue an annuity paying $500 per month. Because of a clerical error, the annuity policy is issued for $50 per month. A court of equity, upon satisfactory proof of the mistake, will reform the policy to provide for the correct amount—$500 per month. In addition, as discussed in Chapter 13, when a covenant not to compete is unreasonable, some courts will reform the agreement to make it reasonable and enforceable.

SPECIFIC PERFORMANCE

Specific performance is the equitable remedy that compels the defaulting party to perform her contractual obligations. As with all equitable remedies, it is available only when there is no adequate remedy at law. Ordinarily, for instance, in a case in which a seller breaches a contract for the sale of personal property, the buyer has a sufficient remedy at law. When, however, the personal property contracted for is rare or unique, this remedy is inadequate. Examples of such property would include a famous painting or statue, an original manuscript or a rare edition of a book, a patent, a copyright, shares of stock in a closely held corporation, or an heirloom. Articles of this kind cannot be purchased elsewhere. Accordingly, on breach by the seller of the contract for the sale of any such article, money damages will not adequately compensate the buyer. Consequently, the buyer may avail herself of the equitable remedy of specific performance.

Although courts of equity will grant specific performance in connection with contracts for the sale of personal property only in exceptional circumstances, they will always grant it in case of breach of contract for the sale of real property. The reason for this is that every parcel of land is regarded as unique. Consequently, if the seller refuses to convey title to the real estate contracted for, the buyer may seek the aid of a court of equity to compel the seller to convey the title. Most courts of equity will likewise compel the buyer in a real estate contract to perform at the suit of the seller.

Courts of equity will not grant specific performance of contracts for personal services. In the first place, there is the practical difficulty, if not impossibility, of enforcing such a decree. In the second place, it is against the policy of the courts to force one person to work for or to serve another against his will, even though the person has contracted to do so. Such enforcement would closely resemble involuntary servitude. For example, if Carmen, an accomplished concert pianist, agrees to appear at a certain time and place to play a specified program for Rudolf, a court would not issue a decree of specific performance upon her refusal to appear.

REAL ESTATE ANALYTICS, LLC v. VALLAS

COURT OF APPEAL, FOURTH DISTRICT, DIVISION 1, CALIFORNIA, 2008
160 CAL.APP.4TH 463, 72 CAL.RPTR.3D 835, REVIEW DENIED 2008
http://scholar.google.com/scholar_case?case=16761955053572987435&q=72+cal.rptr.3d+835&hl=en&as_sdt=2,34

FACTS Real Estate Analytics, LLC (REA) is a limited liability company formed by Troy Shadian. In January 2004, Shadian and his business partner, Roshan Bhakta, became interested in Theodore Tee Vallas's 14.13-acre Lanikai Lane property located in Carlsbad, California, near the Pacific Coast Highway. The property contained a mobile home park with 147 individual mobile homes and numerous amenities, including a pool, playground, laundry facilities, and a long winding street. Vallas leased the property to a mobile home park operator, which managed the park and subleased the spaces to residents who owned their mobile homes. The lease began in 1951 and terminates in 2013.

REA's primary goal in purchasing the property was to make a profit for its investors and themselves. One proposed business model was to subdivide the property and sell the subdivided lots to the property's mobile home park residents. In March 2004, REA and Vallas entered into a written agreement for Vallas to sell the property to REA. Under the agreement, the sales price was $8.5 million, with REA to pay an immediate $100,000 deposit, and then pay $2.9 million at closing. In return, Vallas agreed to finance the remaining $5.5 million, with the unpaid balance to be paid over a five-year period, with the balance due on April 1, 2009. On June 14, Vallas cancelled the contract. The next day REA brought a breach of contract action seeking specific performance. The court, sitting without a jury, found Vallas breached the contract but refused to grant specific performance and instead awarded REA damages of $500,000, reflecting the difference between the contract price and the fair market value at the time of the breach. The court declined to award specific performance on the basis of its finding that damages would provide REA adequate relief.

DECISION Judgment is reversed, and the trial court is ordered to enter a new judgment granting specific performance.

OPINION Haller, J. To obtain specific performance after a breach of contract, a plaintiff must generally show: (1) the inadequacy of his legal remedy; (2) an underlying contract that is both reasonable and supported by adequate consideration; (3) the existence of a mutuality of remedies; (4) contractual terms which are sufficiently definite to enable the court to know what it is to enforce; and (5) a substantial similarity of the requested performance to that promised in the contract. [Citations.] * * *

In this case, the court refused to specifically enforce the contract based on its finding that the first element (inadequacy of legal remedy) was not satisfied because REA sought to purchase the property as an investment, and not for some particular use of the land. REA contends this finding was incorrect as a matter of law and, alternatively, unsupported by the evidence.

It is a familiar legal principle that a damage award is generally an inadequate remedy for a breach of real estate contract, and therefore courts routinely grant a plaintiff's request for specific performance. [Citation.] This rule arose in medieval England where land ownership was a primary indicator of the owner's social status and voting rights. [Citations.] * * *

Although these historical reasons no longer apply, most jurisdictions have continued the rules requiring special treatment of land sale contracts, reflecting the enduring view that: (1) each parcel of land is unique and therefore there can be no adequate replacement after a breach; and (2) monetary damages are difficult to calculate after a party refuses to complete a land sales contract, particularly expectation damages. (See Rest.2d Contracts, § 360.) * * * [L]egislatures and the courts have largely adhered to the rule that specific performance is the appropriate remedy upon a breach of a real estate contract.

In California, these principles are embodied in section 3387. Section 3387 states:

> It is to be presumed that the breach of an agreement to transfer real property cannot be adequately relieved by pecuniary compensation. In the case of a single-family dwelling which the party seeking performance intends to occupy, this presumption is conclusive. In all other cases, this presumption is a presumption affecting the burden of proof.

By imposing a conclusive presumption for certain residential transactions, the Legislature decided that monetary damages can never be satisfactory compensation for a buyer who intends to live at a single-family home, regardless of the circumstances. But by establishing a rebuttable presumption with respect to other property, the Legislature left open the possibility that damages can be an adequate remedy for a breach of a real estate contract. The rebuttable presumption shifts the burden of proof to the breaching party to prove the adequacy of the damages. By so doing, the Legislature intended that a damages remedy for a non-breaching party to a commercial real estate contract is the exception rather than the rule.

* * * [California courts] generally assume the uniqueness of land and grant specific performance after a breach of a land sale contract in both residential and commercial contexts, with little or no discussion of the adequacy of remedy issue.

* * * By imposing a rebuttable presumption on the inadequacy of remedy element for certain types of purchases, the Legislature necessarily contemplated that there may be circumstances when the presumption that damages are inadequate can be overcome. * * *

But the specific issue presented here is not whether a defendant can ever rebut the inadequacy of remedy presumption. The issue is whether Vallas did so in this case. And on this issue, we agree with REA that Vallas did not make a sufficient evidentiary showing to establish damages were adequate to compensate REA for the breach. * * * Although it did not need to do so, REA produced strong evidence to support the presumption. This evidence showed that the Lanikai Lane property is unique in terms of its size, location, and existing use—it consists of 14.13 acres near the Pacific Ocean and contains an established mobilehome community. The property has ocean views and is close to several desirable local beaches, two major vacation resorts, the Del Mar racetrack, expensive neighborhoods, and major transportation routes. REA's evidence also showed that Lanikai Lane is unique in terms of the potential profits resulting from ownership because of its existing use (mobilehome park) on a long-term lease that would terminate in 2013, and the fact that existing residents would like to obtain ownership interests in the property. REA purchased the property for investment purposes, and it intended to obtain the highest return on this investment by subdividing the property and selling it to the existing residents of the park, which could result in substantial profits.

Given the statutory presumption that damages were inadequate and the largely undisputed evidence strongly supporting this presumption, Vallas had a high threshold to satisfy his burden to show damages would be an adequate remedy. * * *

* * *

*** Thus, although REA did not necessarily intend to benefit from its personal or commercial Use of the land, the land did have a particular unique value because of the manner in which it could be used to earn profits upon a resale. *** Missing from the court's analysis was the recognition that to rebut the presumption that damages are an inadequate remedy, the defendant must come forward with evidence showing that damages will fully compensate the plaintiff for the breach. The record in this case was bereft of any such evidence.

INTERPRETATION Specific performance is an appropriate remedy when there is no adequate remedy at law.

CRITICAL THINKING QUESTION Should specific performance be available for all breaches of contract? Explain.

Injunctions

The **injunction**, as used as a contract remedy, is a formal court order enjoining (commanding) a person to refrain from doing a specific act or to cease engaging in specific conduct. A court of equity, at its discretion, may grant an injunction against breach of a contractual duty when damages for a breach would be inadequate. For example, Clint enters into a written contract to give Janice the right of first refusal on a tract of land owned by Clint. Clint, however, subsequently offers the land to Blake without first offering it to Janice. A court of equity may properly enjoin Clint from selling the land to Blake. Similarly, valid covenants not to compete may be enforced by an injunction.

An employee's promise of exclusive personal services may be enforced by an injunction against serving another employer as long as the probable result will not deprive the employee of other reasonable means of making a living. Suppose, for example, that Allan makes a contract with Marlene, a famous singer, under which Marlene agrees to sing at Allan's theater on certain dates for an agreed-upon fee. Before the date of the first performance, Marlene makes a contract with Craig to sing for Craig at his theater on the same dates. Although, as we have discussed, Allan cannot obtain specific performance of his contract by Marlene, a court of equity will, on suit by Allan against Marlene, issue an injunction against her ordering her not to sing for Craig. This is the situation in the case of *Madison Square Garden Corp., Ill. v. Carnera.*

When the services contracted for are *not* unusual or extraordinary in character, the injured party cannot obtain injunctive relief. His only remedy is an action at law for damages.

Madison Square Garden Corp., Ill. v. Carnera

UNITED STATES COURT OF APPEALS, SECOND CIRCUIT, 1931
52 F.2D 47

http://scholar.google.com/scholar_case?q=52+F.2d+47&hl=en&as_sdt=2,34&case=13332657344236100&scilh=0

FACTS Carnera (defendant) agreed with Madison Square Garden (plaintiff) to render services as a boxer in his next contest with the winner of the Schmeling-Stribling contest for the heavyweight championship title. The contract also provided that prior to the match Carnera would not engage in any major boxing contest without the permission of Madison Square Garden. Without obtaining such permission, Carnera contracted to engage in a major boxing contest with Sharkey. Madison Square Garden brought suit requesting an injunction against Carnera's performing his contract to box Sharkey. The trial court granted a preliminary injunction.

DECISION Order for Madison Square Garden affirmed.

OPINION Chase, J. The District Court has found on affidavits which adequately show it that the defendant's services are unique and extraordinary. A negative covenant in a contract for such personal services is enforceable by injunction where the damages for a breach are incapable of ascertainment. [Citations.]

The defendant points to what is claimed to be lack of consideration for his negative promise, in that the contract is inequitable and contains no agreement to employ him. It is true that there is no promise in so many words to employ the defendant to box in a contest with Stribling or Schmeling, but the agreement read as a whole binds the plaintiff to do just that, providing either Stribling or Schmeling becomes the contestant as the result of the match between them and can be induced to box the defendant. The defendant has agreed to "render services as a boxer" for the plaintiff exclusively, and the plaintiff has agreed to pay him a definite percentage of the gate receipts as his compensation for so doing. The promise to employ the defendant to enable him to earn the compensation agreed upon is implied to the same force and effect as though expressly stated. *** [Citations.]

As we have seen, the contract is valid and enforceable. It contains a restrictive covenant which may be given effect. Whether a preliminary injunction shall be issued under such circumstances rests in the sound discretion of the court. [Citations.] The District Court, in its discretion, did issue the preliminary injunction and required the plaintiff as a condition upon its issuance to secure its own performance of the contract in suit with a bond for $25,000 and to give a bond in the sum of $35,000 to pay the defendant such damages as he may sustain by reason of the injunction. Such an order is clearly not an abuse of discretion.

INTERPRETATION When damages are not adequate, an injunction may be used to enforce an agreement to perform exclusive services that are unusual and extraordinary.

CRITICAL THINKING QUESTION Should money damages have been an adequate remedy in this case? Explain.

Restitution

One of the remedies that may be available to a party to a contract is restitution. **Restitution** is the act of returning to the aggrieved party the consideration, or its value, that he gave to the other party. The purpose of restitution is to restore the injured party to the position he was in before the contract was made. Therefore, the party seeking restitution must return what has been received from the other party.

Restitution is available in several contractual situations: (1) for a party injured by breach, as an alternative remedy; (2) for a party in default; (3) for a party who may not enforce a contract because of the statute of frauds; and (4) for a party wishing to rescind (avoid) a voidable contract.

PARTY INJURED BY BREACH

A party is entitled to restitution if the other party totally breaches the contract by nonperformance or repudiation. For example, Benedict agrees to sell land to Beatrice for $60,000. After Beatrice makes a partial payment of $15,000, Benedict wrongfully refuses to transfer title. As an alternative to damages or specific performance, Beatrice may recover the $15,000 in restitution.

PARTY IN DEFAULT

Where a party, after having partly performed, commits a breach by nonperformance or repudiation that discharges the other party's duty to perform, the party in default is entitled to restitution for any benefit she has conferred in excess of the loss she has caused by the breach. For example, Nathan agrees to sell land to Milly for $60,000, and Milly makes a partial payment of $15,000. Milly then repudiates the contract. Nathan sells the land to Murray in good faith for $55,000. Milly may recover from Nathan in restitution the part payment of the $15,000 less the $5,000 damages Nathan sustained because of Milly's breach, which equals $10,000.

STATUTE OF FRAUDS

A party to a contract that is unenforceable because of the statute of frauds may, nonetheless, have acted in reliance on the contract. In such a case, that party may recover in restitution the benefits he conferred on the other in relying on the unenforceable contract. In most states the party seeking restitution must not be in default. Thus, if Wilton makes an oral contract to furnish services to Rochelle that are not to be performed within a year, and Rochelle discharges Wilton after three months, Wilton may recover as restitution the value of the services rendered during the three months.

VOIDABLE CONTRACTS

A party who has rescinded or avoided a contract for lack of capacity, duress, undue influence, fraud in the inducement, nonfraudulent misrepresentation, or mistake is entitled to restitution for any benefit he has conferred on the other. For example, Samuel fraudulently induces Edith to sell land for $60,000. Samuel pays the purchase price, and Edith conveys the land. She then discovers the fraud. Edith may disaffirm the contract and recover the land as restitution. Generally, the party seeking restitution must return any benefit that he has received under the agreement; however, as we found in our discussion of contractual capacity (Chapter 14), this is not always the case.

Figure 18-1 summarizes the remedies for breach of contract.

Figure 18-1
Contract Remedies

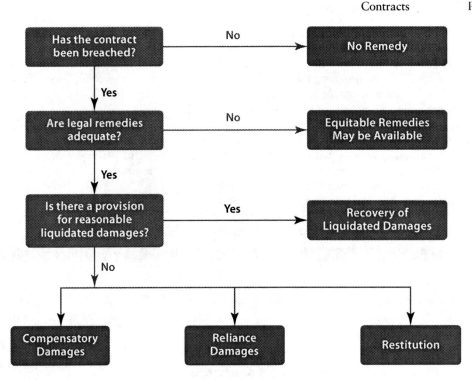

Limitations on Remedies

ELECTION OF REMEDIES

If a party injured by a breach of contract has more than one remedy available, her manifestation of a choice of one remedy, such as bringing suit, does not prevent seeking another unless the remedies are inconsistent and the other party materially changes his position in reliance on the manifestation. For example, a party who seeks specific performance, an injunction, or restitution may be entitled to incidental damages, such as those brought about by delay in performance. Damages for total breach, however, are inconsistent with the remedies of specific performance, injunction, and restitution. Likewise, the remedy of specific performance or an injunction is inconsistent with that of restitution.

With respect to contracts for the sale of goods, the Code rejects any doctrine of election of remedies. Thus, the remedies it provides, which are essentially cumulative, include all of the remedies available for breach. Under the Code, whether one remedy prevents the use of another depends on the facts of the individual case.

LOSS OF POWER OF AVOIDANCE

A party with a power of avoidance for lack of capacity, duress, undue influence, fraud, misrepresentation, or mistake may lose that power if (1) she affirms the contract, (2) she delays unreasonably in exercising the power of disaffirmance, or (3) the rights of third parties intervene.

Affirmance   A party who has the power to avoid a contract for lack of capacity, duress, undue influence, fraud in the inducement, nonfraudulent misrepresentation, or mistake will lose that power by affirming the contract. Affirmance occurs when the party, with full knowledge of the facts, either declares the intention to proceed with the contract or takes some other action from which such intention may reasonably be inferred. Thus, suppose that Pam was induced to purchase a ring from Sally through Sally's fraudulent misrepresentation. If, after learning the truth, Pam undertakes to sell the ring to Janet or does something else that is consistent only with her ownership of the ring, she may no longer rescind the transaction with Sally. In the case of incapacity, duress, or undue influence, affirmance is effective only after the circumstances that made the contract voidable cease to exist. When there has been fraudulent misrepresentation, the defrauded party may affirm only after he knows of the misrepresentation; if the misrepresentation is nonfraudulent or a mistake is involved, affirmance may occur only after the defrauded party knows or should know of the misrepresentation or mistake.

PRACTICAL ADVICE

If you have the power to avoid a contract, do not affirm the contract unless you are sure you wish to relinquish your right to rescind the contract.

MERRITT V. CRAIG

COURT OF SPECIAL APPEALS OF MARYLAND, 2000
130 MD.APP. 350, 746 A.2D 923, CERT. DENIED, 359 MD. 29, 753 A.2D 2 (2000)
http://scholar.google.com/scholar_case?case=10339288125936808164&q=746+a.2d+923&hl=en&as_sdt=2,34

FACTS In the fall of 1995, during their search for a new residence, the plaintiffs, Benjamin K. and Julie S. Merritt, advised the defendant, Virginia Craig, that they were interested in purchasing Craig's property contingent upon a satisfactory home inspection. On November 5, 1995, the plaintiffs, their inspector, and the defendant's husband Mark Craig conducted an inspection of the cistern and water supply pipes in the basement. The examination revealed that the cistern had been used to store a water supply reserve, but was not currently utilized. There were also two water lines that entered into the basement. One of the lines came from an eight-hundred-foot well that was located on the property, and the other line came from a well located on the adjacent property. The well located on the adjacent property supplied water to both the residence for sale and a guesthouse owned by Craig. The existence of the adjacent well was not disclosed to the plaintiffs.

On December 2, 1995, plaintiffs and Craig executed a contract of sale for the property, along with a "Disclosure Statement" signed by Craig and acknowledged by the plaintiffs affirming that there were no problems with the water supply to the house. Between November 5, 1995, and June 1996, Craig caused the water line from the guesthouse to the house purchased by the plaintiffs to be cut, and the cistern reactivated to store water from the existing well. On May 18, 1996, Craig's husband advised Dennis Hannibal, one of the real estate agents involved in the deal, that he had spent $4,196.79 to upgrade the water system on the property. On June 14, 1996, the plaintiffs and Craig closed the sale of the property. Later that afternoon, Craig's husband, without the plaintiffs' knowledge, excavated the inside wall of the house and installed a cap to stop a leaking condition on the water line that he had previously cut.

Upon taking possession of the house the plaintiffs noticed that the water supply in their well had depleted. The plaintiffs met with Craig to discuss a solution to the water failure problem, agreeing with Craig to conduct a flow test to the existing well and to contribute money for the construction of a new well. On October 29, 1996, the well was drilled and produced only one-half gallon of water per minute. Subsequently plaintiffs paid for the drilling of a second well on their property, but it failed to produce water. In January 1997, appellants contacted a plumber, who confirmed that the line from the guesthouse well had been cut flush with the inside surface of the basement wall and cemented closed. Plaintiffs continued to do further work on the house in an effort to cure the water problem. The plaintiffs brought suit against Craig, seeking rescission of the deed to the property and contract of sale, along with compensatory and punitive damages. The trial judge dismissed plaintiffs' claim for rescission on the ground that they had effectively waived their right to rescission. The jury returned a verdict in favor of the plaintiffs, awarding compensatory damages in the amount of $42,264.76 and punitive damages in the amount of $150,000. The plaintiffs appealed the trial court's judgment denying their right to rescind the contract. The defendant cross-appealed on the award of punitive damages.

DECISION Judgment of the trial court reversed, and the case is remanded.

OPINION Davis, J. Under Maryland law, when a party to a contract discovers that he or she has been defrauded, the party defrauded has either "a right to retain the contract and collect damages for its breach, or a right to rescind the contract and recover his or her own expenditures," not both. [Citations.] "These rights [are] inconsistent and mutually exclusive, and the discovery put[s] the purchaser to a prompt election." [Citation.] "A plaintiff seeking rescission must demonstrate that he [or she] acted promptly after discovery of the ground for rescission," otherwise the right to rescind is waived. [Citations.] * * *

In [this] case * * *, appellants [plaintiffs] claim that they were entitled to a rescission of the subject contract of sale and deed and incidental damages. Appellants also claim that they were entitled to compensatory and punitive damages arising from Craig's actions. Appellants, however, may not successfully rescind the contract while simultaneously recovering compensatory and punitive damages. Restitution is "a party's unilateral unmaking of a contract for a legally sufficient reason, such as the other party's material breach" and it in effect "restores the parties to their pre-contractual position." [Citation.] The restoration of the parties to their original position is incompatible with the circumstance when the complaining party is, at once, relieved of all obligations under the contract while simultaneously securing the windfall of compensatory and punitive damages beyond incidental expenses.

* * *

In sum, although whether appellants promptly repudiated the contract was not squarely before the court, we are not persuaded by appellees' assertion that appellants did not seek rescission in a timely fashion. We hold that, under the facts of this case, appellants must elect the form of relief, i.e., damages or rescission, * * *. * * *

* * *

We hold that * * * the appellants are entitled to be awarded punitive damages resulting from Craig's actions. A "[p]laintiff seeking to recover punitive damages must allege in detail in the complaint the facts that indicate the entertainment by defendant of evil motive or intent." [Citation.] The Court of Appeals has held that "punitive damages may only be awarded in such cases where 'the plaintiff has established that the defendant's conduct was characterized by evil motive, intent to injure, ill will or fraud * * * '". [Citation.] In cases of fraud that arise out of a contractual relationship, the plaintiff would have to establish actual malice to recover punitive damages. [Citation.] Finally, we have stated that "actual or express malice requires an intentional or willful act (or omission) * * * and 'has been characterized as the performance of an act without legal justification or excuse, but with an evil or rancorous motive influenced by hate, the purpose being to deliberately and willfully injure the plaintiff.'" [Citation.]

* * *

The jury believed that the representations made by Craig were undertaken with actual knowledge that the representations were false and with the intention to deceive appellants. The Court of Appeals, in [citation], held that a person's actual knowledge that the statement is false, coupled with his or her intent to deceive the plaintiffs by means of that statement, constitutes the actual malice required to support an award for punitive damages. [Citation.] Moreover, the record reflects that the jury could reasonably infer Craig's intention to defraud appellants by her representation in the Disclosure Statement that there were no problems with the water supply, and by subsequently making substantial changes in the water system by cutting off a water line which supplied water to appellants' residence immediately after appellants' inspector examined the system. Therefore, we hold that the circuit court was not in error in finding facts from the record sufficient to support an award of punitive damages.

Craig also challenges the punitive damages award on the basis that the amount of the award was excessive.
* * *

In the case at hand, the trial judge undertook the appropriate review of the jury's award. It is clear from the court's comments at the hearing that the court's decision not to disturb the jury's verdict was based on the evidence presented at trial and was not excessive under the criteria set forth in [citation]. Craig's conduct toward appellants was reprehensible and fully warranted punitive damages. Her conduct in willfully misrepresenting the condition of the water system in the Disclosure Statement, coupled with her actions and those of her husband in interfering and diverting the water flow subsequent to the inspection and sale of the property, constitute egregious conduct. As a result of Craig's conduct, appellants were forced to employ extreme water conservation practices due to an insufficient water supply and they attempted to ameliorate the problem by having two new wells drilled on the property which proved to be unproductive. Moreover, the lack of water supply to appellants' property clearly reduced its market value. * * *

INTERPRETATION A defrauded party may rescind a contract induced by fraud but may lose that power if he affirms the contract or delays unreasonably in exercising the power of rescission.

CRITICAL THINKING QUESTION What is the policy reason for requiring a defrauded party to elect between rescission and damages? Explain.

Delay The power of avoidance may be lost if the party who has the power to do so does not rescind within a reasonable time after the circumstances that made the contract voidable have ceased to exist. Determining a reasonable time depends on all the circumstances, including the extent to which the delay enables the party with the power of avoidance to speculate at the other party's risk. To illustrate, a defrauded purchaser of stock cannot wait unduly to see whether the market price or value of the stock appreciates sufficiently to justify retaining the stock.

> **PRACTICAL ADVICE**
>
> If you have the power to avoid a contract, be sure to rescind within a reasonable time or you will forfeit your right to do so.

Rights of Third Parties   The intervening rights of third parties further limit the power of avoidance and the accompanying right to restitution. If A transfers property to B in a transaction that is voidable by A, and B sells the property to C (a good faith purchaser for value) before A exercises the power of avoidance, A will lose the right to recover the property.

Thus, if a third party (C), who is a good faith purchaser for value, acquires an interest in the subject matter of the contract before A has elected to rescind, no rescission is permitted. Because the transaction is voidable, B acquires a voidable title to the property. Upon a sale of the property by B to C, who is a purchaser in good faith and for value, C obtains good title and is allowed to retain the property. Because both A and C are innocent, the law will not disturb the title held by C, the good faith purchaser. In this case, as in all cases in

which rescission is not available, A's only recourse is against B.

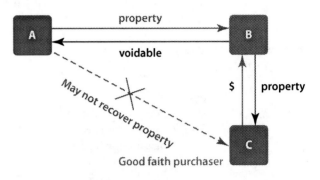

Good faith purchaser

The one notable exception to this rule is the situation involving a sale, *other than a sale of goods*, by a minor who subsequently wishes to avoid the transaction, in which the property has been retransferred to a good faith purchaser. Under this special rule, a good faith purchaser is deprived of the protection generally provided such third parties. Therefore, the third party in a transaction not involving goods, real property being the primary example, is no more protected from the minor's disaffirmance than is the person dealing directly with the minor.

CHAPTER SUMMARY

Monetary Damages

Compensatory Damages contract damages placing the injured party in a position as good as the one he would have held had the other party performed; equals loss of value minus loss avoided by injured party plus incidental damages plus consequential damages
- *Loss of Value* value of promised performance minus value of actual performance
- *Cost Avoided* loss or costs the injured party avoids by not having to perform
- *Incidental Damages* damages arising directly out of a breach of contract
- *Consequential Damages* damages not arising directly out of a breach but arising as a foreseeable result of the breach

Reliance Damages contract damages placing the injured party in as good a position as she would have been in had the contract not been made

Nominal Damages a small sum awarded when a contract has been breached but the loss is negligible or unproved

Damages for Misrepresentation
- *Out-of-Pocket Damages* difference between the value given and the value received
- *Benefit-of-the-Bargain Damages* difference between the value of the fraudulent party's performance as represented and the value the defrauded party received

Punitive Damages are generally not recoverable for breach of contract

Liquidated Damages reasonable damages agreed to in advance by the parties to a contract

Limitations on Damages
- *Foreseeability of Damages* potential loss that the party now in default had reason to know of when the contract was made

* *Certainty of Damages* damages are not recoverable beyond an amount that can be established with reasonable certainty
* *Mitigation of Damages* injured party may not recover damages for loss he could have avoided by reasonable effort

Remedies in Equity

Availability only in cases in which there is no adequate remedy at law

Types
* *Specific Performance* court decree ordering the breaching party to render promised performance
* *Injunction* court order prohibiting a party from doing a specific act
* *Reformation* court order correcting a written contract to conform with the intent of the contracting parties

Restitution

Definition of Restitution restoration of the injured party to the position she was in before the contract was made

Availability
* *Party Injured by Breach* if the other party totally breaches the contract by nonperformance or repudiation
* *Party in Default* for any benefit conferred in excess of the loss caused by the breach
* *Statute of Frauds* where a contract is unenforceable because of the statute of frauds, a party may recover the benefits conferred on the other party in reliance on the contract
* *Voidable Contracts* a party who has avoided a contract is entitled to restitution for any benefit conferred on the other party

Limitations on Remedies

Election of Remedies if remedies are not inconsistent, a party injured by a breach of contract may seek more than one remedy

Loss of Power of Avoidance a party with the power to avoid a contract may lose that power by
* Affirming the contract
* Delaying unreasonably in exercising the power of avoidance
* Being subordinated to the intervening rights of third parties

QUESTIONS

1. Edward, a candy manufacturer, contracted to buy one thousand barrels of sugar from Marcia. Marcia failed to deliver, and Edward was unable to buy any sugar in the market. As a direct consequence he was unable to make candies to fulfill unusually lucrative contracts for the Christmas trade. (a) What damages is Edward entitled to recover? (b) Would it make any difference if Marcia had been told by Edward that he wanted the sugar to make candies for the Christmas trade and that he had accepted lucrative contracts for delivery for the Christmas trade?

2. Daniel agreed to erect an apartment building for Steven for $12 million, and that Daniel would suffer a deduction of $12,000 per day for every day of delay. Daniel was twenty days late in finishing the job, losing ten days because of a strike and ten days because the material suppliers were late in furnishing him with materials. Daniel claims that he is entitled to payment in full (a) because the agreement as to $12,000 a day is a penalty and (b) because Steven has not shown that he has sustained any damage. Discuss each contention and decide.

3. Sharon contracted with Jane, a shirtmaker, for one thousand shirts for men. Jane manufactured and delivered five hundred shirts, for which Sharon paid. At the same time, Sharon notified Jane that she could not use or dispose of the other five hundred shirts and directed Jane not to manufacture any more under the contract. Nevertheless, Jane made up the other five hundred shirts and tendered them to Sharon. Sharon refused to accept the shirts. Jane then

sued for the purchase price. Is she entitled to the purchase price? If not, is she entitled to any damages? Explain.

4. Stuart contracts to act in a comedy for Charlotte and to comply with all theater regulations for four seasons. Charlotte promises to pay Stuart $1,800 for each performance and to allow Stuart one benefit performance each season. It is expressly agreed "Stuart shall not be employed in any other production for the period of the contract." Stuart and Charlotte, during the first year of the contract, have a terrible quarrel. Thereafter, Stuart signs a contract to perform in Elaine's production and ceases performing for Charlotte. Charlotte seeks (a) to prevent Stuart from performing for Elaine and (b) to require Stuart to perform his contract with Charlotte. What result?

5. Louis leased a building to Pam for five years at a rental of $1,000 per month. Pam was to deposit $10,000 as security for performance of all her promises in the lease, which was to be retained by Louis in case of any breach on Pam's part. Pam defaulted in the payment of rent for the last two months of the lease. Louis refused to return any of the deposit, claiming it as liquidated damages. Pam sued Louis to recover $8,000 (the $10,000 deposit less the amount of rent due Louis for the last two months). What amount of damages should Pam be allowed to collect from Louis? Explain.

6. In which of the following situations is specific performance available as a remedy?

   a. Mary and Anne enter into a written agreement under which Mary agrees to sell and Anne agrees to buy for $100 per share one hundred shares of the three hundred shares outstanding of the capital stock of the Infinitesimal Steel Corporation, whose shares are not listed on any exchange and are closely held. Mary refuses to deliver when tendered the $10,000.

   b. Modifying (a) above, assume that the subject matter of the agreement is stock of the U.S. Steel Corporation, which is traded on the New York Stock Exchange.

   c. Modifying (a) above, assume that the subject matter of the agreement is undeveloped farmland of little commercial value.

7. On March 1, Joseph sold to Sandra fifty acres of land in Oregon that Joseph at the time represented to be fine black loam, high, dry, and free of stumps. Sandra paid Joseph the agreed price of $140,000 and took from Joseph a deed to the land. Sandra subsequently discovered that the land was low, swampy, and not entirely free of stumps. Sandra, nevertheless, undertook to convert the greater part of the land into cranberry bogs. After one year of cranberry culture, Sandra became entirely dissatisfied, tendered the land back to Joseph, and demanded from Joseph the return of the $140,000. On Joseph's refusal to repay the money, Sandra brought an action at law against him to recover the $140,000. What judgment?

8. James contracts to make repairs to Betty's building in return for Betty's promise to pay $12,000 on completion of the repairs. After partially completing the repairs, James is unable to continue. Betty refuses to pay James and hires another builder, who completes the repairs for $5,000. The building's value to Betty has increased by $10,000 as a result of the repairs by James, but Betty has lost $500 in rents because of the delay caused by James's breach. James sues Betty. How much, if any, may James recover in restitution from Betty?

9. Linda induced Sally to enter into a purchase of a home theater receiver by intentionally misrepresenting the power output to be seventy-five watts at rated distortion, when in fact it delivered only forty watts. Sally paid $450 for the receiver. Receivers producing forty watts generally sell for $200, whereas receivers producing seventy-five watts generally sell for $550. Sally decides to keep the receiver and sue for damages. How much may Sally recover in damages from Linda?

10. Virginia induced Charles to sell Charles's boat to Virginia by misrepresentation of material fact on which Charles reasonably relied. Virginia promptly sold the boat to Donald, who paid fair value for it and knew nothing concerning the transaction between Virginia and Charles. Upon discovering the misrepresentation, Charles seeks to recover the boat. What are Charles's rights against Virginia and Donald?

CASE PROBLEMS

11. Felch was employed as a member of the faculty of Findlay College under a contract that permitted dismissal only for cause. He was dismissed by action of the President and Board of Trustees, which did not comply with a contractual provision for dismissal that requires a hearing. Felch requested the court to grant specific performance of the contract and require Findlay College to continue Felch as a member of the faculty and to pay him the salary agreed upon. Is Felch entitled to specific performance? Explain.

12. Copenhaver, the owner of a laundry business, contracted with Berryman, the owner of a large apartment complex, to allow Copenhaver to own and operate the laundry facilities within the apartment complex. Berryman terminated the five-year contract with Copenhaver with forty-seven months remaining. Within six months, Copenhaver placed the equipment into use in other locations and generated at least as much income as he would have earned at Berryman's apartment complex. He then filed suit, claiming that he was entitled to conduct the laundry operations

for an additional forty-seven months and that, through such operations, he would have earned a profit of $13,886.58, after deducting Berryman's share of the gross receipts and other operating expenses. Decision?

13. Billy Williams Builders and Developers (Williams) entered into a contract with Hillerich under which Williams agreed to sell to Hillerich a certain lot and to construct on it a house according to submitted plans and specifications. The house built by Williams was defectively constructed. Hillerich brought suit for specific performance of the contract and for damages resulting from the defective construction and delay in performance. Williams argued that Hillerich was not entitled to have both specific performance and damages for breach of the contract because the remedies were inconsistent and Hillerich had to elect one or the other. Explain whether Williams is correct in this assertion.

14. Developers under a plan approved by the city of Rye had constructed six luxury cooperative apartment buildings and were to construct six more. To obtain certificates of occupancy for the six completed buildings, the developers were required to post a bond with the city to insure completion of the remaining buildings. The developers posted a $100,000 bond upon which Public Service Mutual Insurance Company, as guarantor or surety, agreed to pay $200 for each day after the contractual deadline that the remaining buildings were not completed. After the contractual deadline, more than five hundred days passed without completion of the buildings. The city claims that its inspectors and employees will be required to devote more time to the project than anticipated because it has taken extra years to complete. It also claims that it will lose tax revenues for the years the buildings are not completed. Should the city prevail in its suit against the developers and the insurance company to recover $100,000 on the bond? Explain.

15. Kerr Steamship Company sent a telegram at a cost of $26.78 to the Philippines through the Radio Corporation of America. The telegram, which contained instructions in unintelligible code for loading cargo on one of Kerr's ships, was mislaid and never delivered. Consequently, the ship was improperly loaded and the cargo was lost. Kerr sued the Radio Corporation for the $6,675.29 in profits the company lost on the cargo because of the Radio Corporation's failure to deliver the telegram. Should Kerr be allowed to recover damages from Radio? Explain.

16. El Dorado Tire Company fired Bill Ballard, a sales executive. Ballard had a five-year contract with El Dorado but was fired after only two years of employment. Ballard sued El Dorado for breach of contract. El Dorado claimed that any damages due to breach of the contract should be mitigated because of Ballard's failure to seek other employment after he was fired. El Dorado did not provide any proof showing the availability of comparable employment. Explain whether El Dorado is correct in its contention.

17. California and Hawaiian Sugar Company (C and H) is an agricultural cooperative in the business of growing sugarcane in Hawaii and transporting the raw sugar to its refinery in California for processing. Because of the seasonal nature of the sugarcane crop, availability of ships to transport the raw sugar immediately after harvest is imperative. After losing the services of the shipping company it had previously used, C and H decided to build its own ship, a Macababoo, which had two components, a tug and a barge. C and H contracted with Halter Marine to build the tug and with Sun Ship to build the barge. In finalizing the contract for construction of the barge, both C and H and Sun Ship were represented by senior management and by legal counsel. The resulting contract called for a liquidated damages payment of $17,000 per day that delivery of the completed barge was delayed. Delivery of both the barge and the tug was significantly delayed. Sun Ship paid the $17,000 per day liquidated damages amount and then sued to recover it, claiming that without the liquidated damages provision, C and H's legal remedy for money damages would have been significantly less than that paid by Sun Ship pursuant to the liquidated damages provision. Decision?

18. Bettye Gregg offered to purchase a house from Head & Seeman, Inc. (seller). Though she represented in writing that she had between $15,000 and $20,000 in equity in another home that she would pay to the seller after she sold the other home, she knew that she did not have such equity. In reliance upon these intentionally fraudulent representations, the seller accepted Gregg's offer and the parties entered into a land contract. After taking occupancy, Gregg failed to make any of the contract payments. The seller's investigations then revealed the fraud. Head & Seeman then brought suit seeking rescission of the contract, return of the real estate, and restitution. Restitution was sought for the rental value for the five months of lost use of the property and the seller's out-of-pocket expenses made in reliance upon the bargain. Gregg contends that under the election of remedies doctrine, the seller cannot both rescind the contract and recover damages for its breach. Is Gregg correct? Explain.

19. Watson agreed to buy Ingram's house for $355,000. The contract provided that Watson deposit $15,000 as earnest money and that "in the event of default by the Buyer, earnest money shall be forfeited to Seller as liquidated damages, unless Seller elects to seek actual damages or specific performance." Because Watson did not timely comply with all of the terms of the contract, nine months after the Watson sale was to occur, Ingram sold the house to a third party for $355,000. Is Ingram entitled to Watson's $15,000 earnest money as liquidated damages? Explain.

TAKING SIDES

Sanders agreed in writing to write, direct, and produce a motion picture on the subject of lithography (a method for printing using stone or metal) for the Tamarind Lithography Workshop. After the completion of this film, *Four Stones for Kanemitsu*, litigation arose concerning the parties' rights and obligations under their agreement. Tamarind and Sanders resolved this dispute by a written settlement agreement that provided for Tamarind to give Sanders a screen credit stating: "A Film by Terry Sanders." Tamarind did not comply with this agreement and failed to include the agreed-upon screen credit for Sanders. Sanders sued Tamarind seeking damages for breach of the settlement agreement and specific performance to compel Tamarind's compliance with its obligation to provide the screen credit.

a. What arguments would support Sander's claim for specific performance in addition to damages?

b. What arguments would support Tamarind's claim that Sanders was not entitled to specific performance in addition to damages?

c. Which side's arguments are most convincing? Explain.

PART IV
SALES

Chapter 19   Introduction to Sales and Leases
Chapter 20   Performance
Chapter 21   Transfer of Title and Risk of Loss
Chapter 22   Product Liability: Warranties and Strict
              Liability
Chapter 23   Sales Remedies

INTRODUCTION TO SALES AND LEASES

The propensity to truck, barter, and exchange one thing for another ... is common to all men,
and to be found in no other race of animals.

ADAM SMITH (1723–1790), THE WEALTH OF NATIONS, 1776

CHAPTER OUTCOMES

After reading and studying this chapter, you should be able to:

1. Distinguish a sale from a lease and describe the governing law for both.

2. Identify and explain the fundamental principles of Article 2 and Article 2A of the Uniform Commercial Code (UCC).

3. Compare and contrast the manifestation of mutual assent under both the common law and under Article 2.

4. Determine how Article 2 deals with (a) the necessity of consideration to modify a contract and (b) irrevocable offers.

5. Describe the UCC's approach to requiring that certain contracts be in writing and identify the alternative methods of compliance under the Code.

Sales are the most common and important of all commercial transactions. In an exchange economy such as ours, sales are the essential means by which the various units of production exchange their outputs, thereby providing the opportunity for specialization and enhanced productivity. An advanced, complex, industrialized economy with highly coordinated manufacturing and distribution systems requires a reliable mechanism for ensuring that *future* exchanges can be entered into today and fulfilled later. Because practically everyone in our economy is a purchaser of both durable and consumable goods, the manufacture and distribution of goods involve numerous sales transactions. The critical role of the law of sales is to establish a framework in which these present and future exchanges may take place in a predictable, certain, and orderly fashion with a minimum of transaction costs. Article 2 of the Uniform Commercial Code (the Code, or UCC) governs such sales in all states except Louisiana.

Leases of personal property, also of great economic significance, exceed $100 billion annually. Leases range from a consumer's renting an automobile or a lawn mower to a Fortune 500 corporation's leasing heavy industrial machinery. Despite the frequent and widespread use of personal property leases, the law governing these transactions had been patched together from the common law of personal property, real estate leasing law, and Articles 2 and 9 of the UCC. Except for several provisions, the UCC did not directly apply to leases. Although some courts have held, nevertheless, that the UCC is applicable to leases of goods because a lease is a transaction in goods, other courts have refused to apply the Code to leases because actual title to the goods never passed. Still other courts have applied the Code to lease by analogy. Even in states in which Article 2 was extended to leases, which provisions were to be applied remained unclear. In any event, no unified or uniform statutory law governed leases of personal property for most of the twentieth century.

To fill this void, the drafters of the Code approved Article 2A—Leases in 1987 and subsequently amended the Article in 1990. An analogue of Article 2, the new article adopts many of the same rules. Article 2A is an attempt to codify in one statute all the rules governing the leasing of personal property. All states—except Louisiana—and the District of Columbia have adopted Article 2A. The UCC appears in Appendix B.

Amendments to Articles 2 and 2A were promulgated in 2003 to accommodate electronic commerce and to reflect development of business practices, changes in other law, and other practical issues. Because no states had adopted them and prospects for enactment in the near future were bleak, the 2003 amendments to UCC Articles 2 and 2A were withdrawn in 2011. However, at least forty states have adopted the 2001 Revisions to Article 1, which applies to all of the articles of the Code.

This part of the book covers both the sale of goods and the lease of goods. All chapters in this part will cover Article 2A in addition to Article 2 by stating "Article 2A" wherever Article 2A's provision is either identical to or essentially the same as the Article 2 provision. When Article 2A significantly deviates from Article 2, both rules will be discussed. In this chapter we will discuss the nature and formation of sales and lease contracts and the fundamental principles of sales and leases of goods.

NATURE OF SALES AND LEASES

The law of sales, which governs contracts involving the sale of goods, is a specialized branch of both the law of contracts (discussed in Chapters 9–18) and the law of personal property (discussed in Chapter 47). This section will cover the definition of sales and leases and the fundamental principles of Article 2 and Article 2A of the UCC.

Definitions

GOODS

Goods are essentially defined as movable, tangible, personal property. For example, the sale of a bicycle, stereo set, or this textbook is considered a sale of goods. Goods also include the unborn young of animals, growing crops, and, if removed by the seller, timber, minerals, or a building attached to real property. Under Article 2A, minerals cannot be leased prior to their extraction.

SALE

The Code defines a **sale** as the transfer of title to goods from seller to buyer for a price. The price can be money, other goods, real estate, or services.

LEASE

Article 2A defines a **lease** of goods as a "transfer of the right to possession and use of goods for a term in return for consideration, but ... retention or creation of a security interest is not a lease." A transaction within this definition of a lease is governed by Article 2A, but if the transaction is a security interest disguised as a lease, it is governed by Article 9. Categorizing a transaction as a lease has significant implications not only for the parties to the lease but for third parties as well. If the transaction is deemed to be a lease, the residual interest in the goods belongs to the lessor, who need not file publicly to protect this interest. On the other hand, if the transaction is a security interest, then the provisions of Article 9 regarding enforceability, perfection, priority, and remedies apply. UCC Section 1-201(37) and Revised Section 1-203 provide rules that govern the determination of whether a transaction in the form of a lease creates a security interest.

Consumer Leases   Article 2A affords special treatment for consumer leases. The definition of a **consumer lease** requires that (1) the transaction meet the definition of a lease under Article 2A; (2) the lessor be regularly engaged in the business of leasing *or* selling goods; (3) the lessee be an individual, not an organization; (4) the lessee take the lease interest primarily for a personal, family, or household purpose; and (5) the total payments under the lease do not exceed $25,000. Although consumer protection for lease transactions is primarily left to other state and federal law, Article 2A does contain a number of provisions that apply to consumer leases and that may *not* be varied by agreement of the parties.

Finance Leases A finance lease is a special type of lease transaction generally involving three parties instead of two. Whereas in the typical lease situation the lessor also supplies the goods, in a finance lease arrangement, the lessor and the supplier are separate parties. The lessor's primary function in a finance lease is to provide financing to the lessee for a lease of goods provided by the supplier. For example, under a finance lease arrangement, a manufacturer supplies goods pursuant to the lessee's instructions or specifications. The party functioning as the lessor will then either purchase those goods from the supplier or act as the prime lessee in leasing them from the supplier. In turn, the lessor will lease or sublease the goods to the lessee. Because the finance lessor functions merely as a source of credit, she typically will have no special expertise as to the goods. Due to the limited role the finance lessor usually plays, Article 2A treats finance leases differently from ordinary leases.

CARTER V. TOKAI FINANCIAL SERVICES, INC.

COURT OF APPEALS OF GEORGIA, 1998
231 GA.APP. 755, 500 S.E.2D 638

http://scholar.google.com/scholar_case?case=1919852511859232954&q=500+S.E.2d+638&hl=en&as_sdt=2,34

FACTS On January 3, 1996, Tokai's (now part of De Lage Landen Leasing and Trade Finance) predecessor in interest, Mitel Financial, entered into a "Master Equipment Lease Agreement" (Agreement) with Applied Radiological Control, Inc. (ARC) for the lease of certain telephone equipment valued at $42,000. Randy P. Carter of ARC personally guaranteed ARC's obligations under the Agreement. ARC made four rental payments and then defaulted on its obligations. Thereafter, Tokai repossessed the telephone equipment and sold it for $5,900. Tokai then brought this suit against Carter, and the trial court awarded Tokai $56,765.74. Carter appeals.

DECISION Judgment reversed.

OPINION Blackburn, J. 1. As an initial matter, we note that Paragraph 13 of the Agreement states that each lease contemplated therein is a finance lease as defined by Article 2A of the UCC.

> A "finance lease" involves three parties—the lessee/business, the finance lessor, and the equipment supplier. The lessee/business selects the equipment and negotiates particularized modifications with the equipment supplier. Instead of purchasing the equipment from the supplier, the lessee/business has a finance lessor purchase the selected equipment, and then leases the equipment from the finance lessor. [Citation.]

Carter contends, nonetheless, that the true intent of the parties was to enter into a security agreement.

> Whether a transaction creates a lease or security interest is determined by the facts of each case; however, a transaction creates a security interest if the consideration the lessee is to pay the lessor for the right to possession and use of the goods is an obligation for the term of the lease not subject to termination by the lessee, and (a) [t]he original term of the lease is equal to or greater than the remaining economic life of the goods, (b) [t]he lessee is bound to renew the lease for the remaining economic life of the goods or is bound to become the owner of the goods, (c) [t]he lessee has an option to renew the lease for the remaining economic life of the goods for no additional consideration or nominal additional consideration upon compliance with the lease agreement, or (d) [t]he lessee has an option to become the owner of the goods for no additional consideration or nominal additional consideration upon compliance with the lease agreement. [UCC §] 1-201(37).

Here, the Agreement's initial term was for five years, ARC was not required to renew the lease or purchase the telephone equipment at the end of the term, and ARC did not have the option to renew the lease or purchase the property at the end of the term for nominal consideration. Therefore, the Agreement does not fit within the definition of a secured transaction provided by [UCC §] 1-201(37).

Furthermore,

> it is commonly held that the "best test" for determining the intent of an agreement which provides for an option to buy is a comparison of the option price with the market value of the equipment at the time the option is to be exercised. *** If, upon compliance with the terms of the "lease," the lessee has an option to become the owner of the property for no additional or for a nominal consideration, the lease is deemed to be intended for security. [Citations.]

ARC was given the option to purchase the telephone equipment in this case at the end of the lease term for its fair market value. "Additional consideration is not nominal if *** when the option to become the owner of the goods is granted to the lessee the price is stated to be the fair market value of the goods determined at the time the option is to be performed." [UCC Section 1-201(37)(x).] Accordingly, the agreement in this case must be considered a true lease, not a secured transaction. As a result, the procedural safeguards of Article 9 of the UCC are inapplicable to the matter at hand, and Carter's claims under this enumeration must fail. [Citations.]

* * *

In Georgia, all lease contracts for "goods," including finance leases, first made or first effective on or after July 1, 1993, are governed by Article 2A of the Uniform Commercial Code. [Citations.] The Agreement was entered into by the parties on January 3, 1996; therefore, it is subject to Article 2A of the UCC.

INTERPRETATION A lease will be governed by Article 2A unless in compliance with the terms of the "lease" the lessee has the option to become the owner of the property for no additional or for a nominal consideration, in which case, the lease is deemed to be intended for security and governed by Article 9.

CRITICAL THINKING QUESTION Why might the parties attempt to disguise a security agreement as a lease?

Governing Law

Although **sales transactions** are governed by Article 2 of the Code, general contract law continues to apply in cases in which the Code has not specifically modified such law. Nevertheless, although principles of common law and equity may supplement provisions of the Code, they may not be used to supplant its provisions. Thus, the law of sales is a specialized part of the general law of contracts, and the law of contracts continues to govern unless specifically displaced by the Code.

General contract law also continues to govern all **contracts outside the scope of the Code.** Transactions not within the scope of Article 2 include employment contracts; service contracts; insurance contracts; contracts involving real property; and contracts for the sale of intangibles such as stocks, bonds, patents, and copyrights. For an illustration of the law governing contracts, see Figure 9-1. In determining whether a contract containing both a sale of goods and a service is a UCC contract or general contract, the majority of states follow the predominant purpose test. This test, as in *Pittsley v. Houser*, which follows, and in *Fox v. Mountain West Electric, Inc.* in Chapter 9 holds that if the predominant purpose of the whole transaction is a sale of goods, Article 2 applies to the entire transaction. If, on the other hand, the predominant purpose is the nongood or service portion, Article 2 does not apply. A few states apply Article 2 only to the goods part of a transaction and general contract law to the nongoods or service part of the transaction.

that have ratified the CISG. Because treaties are federal law, the CISG supersedes the UCC in any situation to which either could apply. The CISG includes provisions dealing with interpretation, trade usage, contract formation, obligations and remedies of sellers and buyers, and risk of loss. Parties to an international sales contract may, however, expressly exclude CISG governance from their contract. The CISG specifically excludes sales of (1) goods bought for personal, family, or household use; (2) stocks, shares, investment securities, negotiable instruments, or money; (3) ships or aircraft; and (4) electricity. In addition, it does not apply to contracts in which the primary obligation of the party furnishing the goods consists of supplying labor or services.

Although Article 2 governs sales, the drafters of the article have invited the courts to extend Code principles to nonsale transactions in goods. To date, a number of courts have accepted this invitation and have applied Code provisions by analogy to other transactions in goods not expressly included within the Act, most frequently to leases and bailments. The Code has also greatly influenced the revision of the Restatement, Second, Contracts, which, as previously discussed, has great effect upon all contracts.

CISG The United Nations Convention on Contracts for the International Sales of Goods (CISG), which has been ratified by the United States and more than forty other countries, governs all contracts for the international sales of goods between parties located in different nations

Practical Advice

Because it is unclear which law will govern certain contracts, be careful to specify the particulars of your agreement in your written contract.

PITTSLEY V. HOUSER

IDAHO COURT OF APPEALS, 1994
875 P.2D 232

http://scholar.google.com/scholar_case?case=12253852760654206938hl=en&as_sdt=2&as_vis=1&oi=scholarr

FACTS Jane Pittsley contracted with Donald Houser, who was doing business as Hilton Contract Co. (Hilton), to install carpet in her home. The total contract price was $4,402. From this sum, Hilton paid the installers $700 to put the carpet in Pittsley's home. Following installation, Pittsley complained to Hilton that the installation was defective in several respects. Hilton attempted to fix the installation but was unable to satisfy Pittsley. Eventually, Pittsley refused any further efforts to fix the carpet. She sued for rescission of the contract and return of the $3,500 she had previously paid on the contract plus incidental damages. Hilton counterclaimed for the balance due on the contract. The magistrate determined that the breach was not so material as to justify rescission of the contract and awarded Pittsley $250 in repair costs plus $150 in expenses. The magistrate also awarded Hilton the balance of $902 remaining on the contract. Pittsley appealed to the district court, which reversed and remanded the case to the magistrate for additional findings of fact and to apply the Uniform Commercial Code (UCC) to the transaction. Hilton appeals this ruling, asserting that application of the UCC is inappropriate because the only defects alleged were in the installation of the carpet, not in the carpet itself.

DECISION The judgment of the magistrate is vacated and the case remanded.

OPINION Swanstrom, J. The single question upon which this appeal depends is whether the UCC is applicable to the subject transaction. If the underlying transaction involved the sale of "goods," then the UCC would apply. If the transaction did not involve goods, but rather was for services, then application of the UCC would be erroneous.

Idaho Code § 2–105(l) defines "goods" as "all things (including specially manufactured goods) which are movable at the time of identification to the contract for sale. ***" Although there is little dispute that carpets are "goods," the transaction in this case also involved installation, a service. Such hybrid transactions, involving both goods and services, raise difficult questions about the applicability of the UCC. Two lines of authority have emerged to deal with such situations.

The first line of authority, and the majority position, utilizes the "predominant factor" test. The Ninth Circuit, applying the Idaho Uniform Commercial Code to the subject transaction, restated the predominant factor test as:

The test for inclusion or exclusion is not whether they are mixed, but, granting that they are mixed, whether their predominant factor, their thrust, their purpose, reasonably stated, is the rendition of service, with goods incidentally involved (e.g., contract with artist for painting) or is a transaction of sale, with labor incidentally involved (e.g., installation of a water heater in a bathroom).

[Citations.] This test essentially involves consideration of the contract in its entirety, applying the UCC to the entire contract or not at all.

The second line of authority, which Hilton urges us to adopt, allows the contract to be severed into different parts, applying the UCC to the goods involved in the contract, but not to the nongoods involved, including services as well as other nongoods assets and property. Thus, an action focusing on defects or problems with the goods themselves would be covered by the UCC, while a suit based on the service provided or some other nongoods aspect would not be covered by the UCC. ***

We believe the predominant factor test is the more prudent rule. Severing contracts into various parts, attempting to label each as goods or nongoods and applying different law to each separate part clearly contravenes the UCC's declared purpose "to simplify, clarify and modernize the law governing commercial transactions." § 1–102(2)(a). As the Supreme Court of Tennessee suggested in [citation], such a rule would, in many contexts, present "difficult and in some instances insurmountable problems of proof in segregating assets and determining their respective values at the time of the original contract and at the time of resale, in order to apply two different measures of damages."

Applying the predominant factor test to the case before us, we conclude that the UCC was applicable to the subject transaction. The record indicates that the contract between the parties called for "165 yds Masterpiece No. 2122–Installed" for a price of $4319.50. There was an additional charge for removing the existing carpet. The record indicates that Hilton paid the installers $700 for the work done in laying Pittsley's carpet. It appears that Pittsley entered into this contract for the purpose of obtaining carpet of a certain quality and color. It does not appear that the installation, either who would provide it or the nature of the work, was a factor in inducing Pittsley to choose Hilton as the carpet supplier. On these facts, we conclude that the sale of the carpet was the predominant factor in the contract, with the installation being merely incidental to the purchase. Therefore, in failing to consider the UCC, the magistrate did not apply the correct legal principles to the facts as found.

INTERPRETATION If the predominant purpose of the whole transaction is a sale of goods, then Article 2

applies to the whole transaction; if the predominant purpose is the nongood or service component, then Article 2 does not apply.

CRITICAL THINKING QUESTION Which test do you prefer? Explain.

Although **lease transactions** are governed by Article 2A of the Code, general contract law continues to apply in cases in which the Code has not specifically modified such law. In other words, the law of leases is a specialized part of the general law of contracts, and the law of contracts continues to govern unless specifically displaced by the Code.

Fundamental Principles of Article 2 and Article 2A

The purpose of Article 2 is to modernize, clarify, simplify, and make uniform the law of sales. Furthermore, the article is to be interpreted according to these principles and not according to some abstraction such as the passage of title. The Code

> is drawn to provide flexibility so that, since it is intended to be a semi-permanent piece of legislation, it will provide its own machinery for expansion of commercial practices. It is intended to make it possible for the law embodied in this Act to be developed by the courts in the light of unforeseen and new circumstances and practices. However, the proper construction of the Act requires that its interpretation and application be limited to its reason. (*General Provisions* in Comment to Section 1-102)

This open-ended drafting includes the following fundamental concepts.

The CISG governs only the formation of the contract of sales and the rights and obligations of the seller and buyer arising from such contract. It does not cover the validity of the contract or any of its provisions. In addition, one of the purposes of the CISG is to promote uniformity of the law of sales.

GOOD FAITH

All parties who enter into a contract or duty within the scope of the Code must perform their obligations in good faith. The Code defines **good faith** as "honesty

in fact in the conduct or transaction concerned." For a merchant, good faith also requires the observance of reasonable commercial standards of fair dealing in the trade. Revised UCC Section 1–201(20) provides that "good faith means honesty in fact and the observance of reasonable commercial standards of fair dealing," thus adopting the broader definition of good faith and making it applicable to both merchants and nonmerchants. For instance, if the parties agree that the seller is to set the price term, the seller must establish the price in good faith.

The CISG is also designed to promote the observation of good faith in international trade.

UNCONSCIONABILITY

The courts may scrutinize every contract of sale to determine whether in its commercial setting, purpose, and effect it is unconscionable. The reviewing court may refuse to enforce a contract (or any part of it) found to be unconscionable or may limit its application to prevent an unconscionable result. The Code does not define *unconscionable*; however, the term is defined in the *New Webster's Dictionary* (Deluxe Encyclopedic Edition) as "contrary to the dictates of conscience; unscrupulous or unprincipled; exceeding that which is reasonable or customary; inordinate, unjustifiable."

The Code denies or limits enforcement of an unconscionable contract for the sale of goods to promote fairness and decency and to correct harshness or oppression in contracts resulting from the unequal bargaining positions of the parties.

The doctrine of **unconscionability** permits the courts to resolve issues of unfairness explicitly on that basis without recourse to formalistic rules or legal fictions. In policing contracts for fairness, the courts have demonstrated their willingness to limit freedom of contract to protect the less advantaged from the overreaching of dominant contracting parties.

The doctrine of unconscionability has evolved through its application by the courts to include both procedural and substantive unconscionability. **Procedural unconscionability** involves scrutiny for the presence of "bargaining naughtiness." In other words, was the negotiation process fair? Or were there procedural irregularities such as burying important terms of the agreement in fine print or obscuring the true meaning of the contract with impenetrable legal jargon?

In the search for **substantive unconscionability**, the court examines the actual terms of the contract, seeking oppressive or grossly unfair provisions such as an exorbitant price or an unfair exclusion or limitation of contractual remedies. An all-too-common example involves a necessitous buyer in an unequal bargaining position with a seller who consequently has obtained an exorbitant price for his product or service.

PRACTICAL ADVICE

Refrain from entering into contracts with provisions that are oppressively harsh or that were negotiated under unfair circumstances.

As to *all* leases, Article 2A provides that a court faced with an unconscionable contract or clause may refuse to enforce either the entire contract or just the unconscionable clause or may limit the application of the unconscionable clause to avoid an unconscionable result. This is similar to Article 2's treatment of unconscionable clauses in sales contracts. A lessee under a consumer lease, however, is provided with additional protection against unconscionability. In the case of a consumer lease, if a court as a matter of law finds that any part of the lease contract has been induced by unconscionable conduct, the court is expressly empowered to grant appropriate relief. The same is true when unconscionable conduct occurs in the collection of a claim arising from a consumer lease contract. The explicit availability of relief for consumers subjected to unconscionable conduct (procedural unconscionability)—in addition to a provision regarding unconscionable contracts (substantive unconscionability)—represents a departure from Article 2. An additional remedy that Article 2A provides for consumers is the award of attorneys' fees. If the court finds unconscionability with respect to a consumer lease, it shall award reasonable attorneys' fees to the lessee.

The following case illustrates the application of the doctrine of unconscionability.

CONSTRUCTION ASSOCIATES, INC. v. FARGO WATER EQUIPMENT CO.

SUPREME COURT OF NORTH DAKOTA, 1989
446 N.W.2D 237

http://www.ndcourts.gov/court/opinions/10154.htm

FACTS Construction Associates (CA) was the successful bidder to construct a water supply line for the city of Breckenridge, Minnesota. CA purchased a large amount of polyvinyl chloride pipe manufactured by the Johns-Manville Sales Corporation (J-M) to construct the pipeline. CA, however, did not have any direct contact with J-M; instead, it purchased the pipe through a supply company (Fargo Water Equipment). J-M shipped the pipe directly to the work site, and included with each shipment an installation guide written for those who actually directed the installation of the pipe. On page three of the installation guide, J-M expressly warranted the pipe to be free from defects in workmanship and materials. In addition, J-M set forth a limitation of liability clause, which stated there would be no liability except for breach of the express warranty, and that J-M would be responsible only for resupplying a like quantity of nondefective pipe. J-M stated that it would not be liable for any incidental, consequential, or other damages.

Eventually the Breckenridge pipeline developed more than seventy leaks. The only way these leaks could be repaired was to remove the defective joints and replace them with stainless steel sleeves. After incurring more than $140,000 in repairs to the pipeline, CA sued J-M and Fargo. CA won a jury award of more than $140,000 in damages from J-M. J-M appealed, claiming that the limitation of liability clause should be enforced.

DECISION Judgment for CA affirmed.

OPINION Ericksted, J. [UCC § 2–719] specifically allows the parties to an agreement to limit the remedies available upon breach and to exclude consequential damages:

* * *

By its terms § 2–302 [unconscionable contract or clause] applies to any clause of the contract. Courts thus have construed §§ 2–302 and 2–719 together in holding that a general limitation of remedies clause, including those limiting liability to repair or replacement, may be subject to unconscionability analysis under the Code. [Citations.]

The determination whether a particular contractual provision is unconscionable is a question of law for the court. [Citations.] The court is to look at the contract from the perspective of the time it was entered into, without the benefit of hindsight. * * *

Courts and commentators have generally viewed the Code's unconscionability provisions within a two-pronged framework: procedural unconscionability, which encompasses factors relating to unfair surprise, oppression, and inequality of bargaining power, and substantive unconscionability, which focuses upon the harshness or one-sidedness of the contractual provision in question. [Citations.]

PROCEDURAL UNCONSCIONABILITY
We initially note that this case presents a commercial, rather than a consumer, transaction. Although courts have generally been more reluctant to find unconscionability in purely commercial settings, [citation], under appropriate circumstances a contractual provision may be found unconscionable even in a commercial setting. [Citations.]

* * *

The circumstances presented in this case demonstrate a substantial inequality in bargaining power between J-M and Construction Associates. Construction Associates is a relatively small local construction firm, while J-M is part of an enormous, highly diversified, international conglomerate. The limitation of remedies and exclusion of damages were part of a pre-printed installation guide included with all shipments of J-M Pipe. J-M has continually stressed on appeal that those limitations and exclusions are included in all of its brochures and guides. It is obvious that there is no room for bargaining or negotiation as to the warranty provisions.

We also note that the facts in this case demonstrate an actual lack of negotiation coupled with elements of unfair surprise. * * *

The limitations and exclusions clause in this case can hardly be described as "bargained for." The clauses were included on page three of a pre-printed installation guide expressly directed to the worker in the field, rather than to officers of Construction Associates. Construction Associates was not apprised at the time of contracting that their remedies under the Code were being limited or excluded. It would be within J-M's control to do so by, for example, requiring its dealers to accept orders for pipe only upon a J-M form which included the limitations and exclusions and which required the purchaser's signature. Clearly an element of procedural unconscionability is present where through a pre-printed guide which was not provided to Construction Associates (and then only to field workers) until long after the sales contract had been finalized.

SUBSTANTIVE UNCONSCIONABILITY
Substantive unconscionability focuses upon the harshness of the particular contractual terms:

* * *

The clause at issue here would limit Construction Associates' remedy for J-M's breach to a like quantity of replacement pipe, with no recovery of consequential damages. Construction Associates argues, with support in the evidence, that replacement pipe is not used when making repairs to leaking joints on a completed underground water pipeline. Because the accepted method of repair is to cut out the leaking joint and repair it with a stainless steel sleeve, Construction Associates argues, the replacement pipe would be useless in effecting repairs upon the line. The trial court determined that J-M's limited remedy "amount[ed] to nothing whatsoever." * * *

Numerous courts, in a variety of commercial and consumer contexts, have held limitations and exclusions unconscionable when they leave the non-breaching party with no effective remedy. [Citations.] This is particularly true where the defect in the product is latent, so that the buyer is unable to discover the defect until additional damages are incurred. [Citations.]. In this case, Construction Associates did not discover the defects until the pipe was assembled and placed underground.

INTERPRETATION A court can override a term of a contract if it finds that term to be unconscionable or the result of an unconscionable negotiation process.

ETHICAL QUESTION Is unconscionable conduct always unethical? Explain.

CRITICAL THINKING QUESTION How active should courts be in finding contracts or clauses to be unconscionable? Explain.

EXPANSION OF COMMERCIAL PRACTICES

An underlying policy of the Code is "to permit the continued expansion of commercial practices through custom, usage and agreement of the parties." In particular, the Code emphasizes the course of dealing and the usage of trade in interpreting agreements.

A **course of dealing** is a sequence of previous conduct between the parties that may fairly be regarded as establishing a common basis of understanding for interpreting their expressions and agreement.

A **usage of trade** is a practice or method of dealing regularly observed and followed in a place, vocation, or trade. To illustrate: Connie contracts to sell Ward one thousand feet of San Domingo mahogany. By usage of dealers in mahogany, known to Connie and Ward, good-figured mahogany of a certain density is known as San Domingo mahogany, though it does not come from San Domingo. Unless otherwise agreed, the usage is part of the contract.

CISG The parties are bound by any usage or practices that they have agreed to or established between themselves. In addition, the parties are considered, unless otherwise agreed, to be bound by any usage of international trade that is widely known and regularly observed in the particular trade.

SALES BY AND BETWEEN MERCHANTS

The Code establishes some separate rules that apply to transactions between merchants or to transactions involving a merchant as a party. A **merchant** is defined as a person (1) who is a dealer in a particular type of goods, (2) who by his occupation holds himself out as having knowledge or skill peculiar to certain goods or practices, or (3) who employs an agent or broker whom he holds out as having such knowledge or skill. (Article 2A.) These rules exact higher standards of conduct from merchants because of their knowledge of trade and commerce and because merchants as a class generally set these standards for themselves. The more significant of these merchant provisions are good faith, confirmation of oral contracts, firm offers, "battle of the forms," warranty of title, warranty of merchantability, sales on approval, retention of possession of goods by seller, entrusting of goods, risk of loss, and duties after rightful rejection.

LIBERAL ADMINISTRATION OF REMEDIES

The Code provides that its remedies shall be liberally administered in order to place the aggrieved party in a position as good as the one she would have held, had the defaulting party fully performed. The Code does make it clear, however, that remedies are limited to compensation and may not include consequential or punitive damages, unless specifically provided by the Code. According to its provisions, for cases in which the Code itself does not expressly provide a remedy for a right or obligation, the courts should provide an appropriate remedy. Remedies are discussed in Chapter 23.

FREEDOM OF CONTRACT

Most of the Code's provisions are not mandatory but permit the parties by agreement to vary or displace them altogether. However, the obligations of good faith, diligence, reasonableness, and care may not be disclaimed by agreement, although the parties may by agreement determine the standards by which to measure the performance of these obligations, as long as the standards are not obviously unreasonable.

VALIDATION AND PRESERVATION OF SALES CONTRACTS

One of the requirements of commercial law is the establishment of rules that determine when an agreement is valid. The Code approaches this requirement by reducing formal requisites to the bare minimum and by attempting to preserve agreements whenever the parties manifest an intent to enter into a contract.

FORMATION OF SALES AND LEASE CONTRACTS

As we have stated previously, the Code's basic approach to validation is to recognize contracts whenever the parties manifest such an intent. This is so whether or not the parties can identify the precise moment at which they formed the contract. (Article 2A.)

Manifestation of Mutual Assent

For a contract to exist, there must be an objective manifestation of mutual assent: an offer and an acceptance. In this section, we will examine the UCC rules that affect offers and acceptances.

DEFINITENESS OF AN OFFER

At common law, the terms of a contract were required to be definite and complete. The Code has rejected the strict approach of the common law by recognizing an agreement as valid, despite missing terms, if there is any reasonably certain basis for granting a remedy. Accordingly, the Code provides that even though a contract may omit one or more terms, the contract need not fail for indefiniteness. (Article 2A.) The Code provides standards by which the courts may ascertain and supply omitted essential terms, provided the parties intended to enter into a binding agreement. Nevertheless, the more terms the parties leave open, the less likely their intent to enter into a binding contract. Article 2A generally does not provide the same gap-filling provisions.

CISG An offer to contract is sufficiently definite if it indicates the goods and fixes or makes provision, expressly or implicitly, for determining price and quality.

Open Price The parties may enter into a contract for the sale of goods even though they have reached no agreement on the price. In such a case, the price is reasonable at the time for delivery. A contract has an open price term if the agreement (1) says nothing as to price; (2) provides that the parties shall agree later as to the price and they fail to so agree; or (3) fixes the price in terms of some agreed market or other standard, as set by a third person or agency, and the price is not so set. An agreement that the price is to be fixed by the seller or buyer means that it must be fixed in good faith.

Open Quantity: Output and Requirements Contracts As we discussed in Chapters 10 and 12, an output contract is the agreement of a buyer to purchase the entire output of a seller for a stated period, whereas a requirements contract is an agreement of a seller to supply a buyer with all her requirements for certain goods. Even though the exact quantity of goods is not specified and even though the seller may have some control over his output and the buyer over her requirements, such agreements are enforceable through the application of an objective standard based on the good faith of both parties. Moreover, the parties may not produce or request quantities disproportionate to any stated estimate of need or production or to prior output or requirements.

IRREVOCABLE OFFER

An offeror generally may withdraw an offer at any time prior to its acceptance. To be effective, the notice revoking the offer must reach the offeree before he has accepted.

An **option** is a contract by which the offeror is bound to hold open an offer for a specified time. It must comply with all of the requirements of a contract, including consideration. Option contracts apply to all types of contracts, including sales of goods.

The Code has made certain offers—called **firm offers**—irrevocable without the offeree giving any consideration for the promise to keep the offer open. The Code provides that a merchant is bound to keep an offer open for a maximum of three months if the merchant gives assurance in a signed writing that it will be held open. (Article 2A.) The Code, therefore, makes a merchant's written promise not to revoke an offer for a stated period of time enforceable even though no consideration is given the merchant-offeror for that promise.

 An offer may not be revoked if it indicates, whether by stating a fixed time for acceptance or otherwise, that it is irrevocable; it need not be in writing.

VARIANT ACCEPTANCES

The common law **mirror image** rule, by which the acceptance cannot vary or deviate from the terms of the offer, has been modified by the Code. This modification has been necessitated by the realities of modern business practices, notably by the fact that a vast number of businesses use standardized business forms. For example, a buyer sends to the seller on the buyer's order form a purchase order for 1,000 dozen cotton shirts at $60 per dozen with delivery by October 1 at the buyer's place of business. On the reverse side of this standard form are twenty-five numbered paragraphs containing provisions generally favorable to the buyer. When the seller receives the buyer's order and agrees to the buyer's quantity, price, and delivery terms, he sends to the buyer an unequivocal acceptance of the offer on his acceptance form. On the back of his acceptance form, however, the seller has thirty-two numbered paragraphs generally favorable to himself and in significant conflict with the provisions in the buyer's form. Under the common law's mirror image rule, no contract would exist, for the seller has not accepted unequivocally all of the material terms of the buyer's offer.

The Code attempts to reconcile this **battle of the forms** by focusing on the intent of the parties. If the offeree expressly makes his acceptance conditional upon assent to the additional or different terms, no contract is formed. If, however, the offeree does not expressly require such a condition, a contract is formed. The issue then becomes whether the offeree's different or **additional** terms become part of the contract. If both offeror and offeree are merchants, additional terms (terms the offeree proposed for the contract for the first time) will become part of the contract if they do not materially alter the agreement and are not objected to either in the offer itself or within a reasonable time. If either of the parties is not a merchant, or if the terms materially alter the offer, the additional terms are merely construed as proposals for addition to the contract. **Different** terms (terms that contradict or conflict with terms of the offer) proposed by the offeree generally will not become part of the contract unless specifically accepted by the offeror.

The courts are divided over what terms are included when the terms conflict. The majority of courts hold that the terms cancel each other out and look to the Code to provide the missing terms; other courts hold that the offeror's terms govern. Some states follow a third alternative and apply the additional terms test to different terms. See Figure 19-1 for a summary of the battle of the forms.

Applying Section 2–207 to the previous example: Because both parties are merchants and the seller did not

Figure 19-1
Battle of the Forms

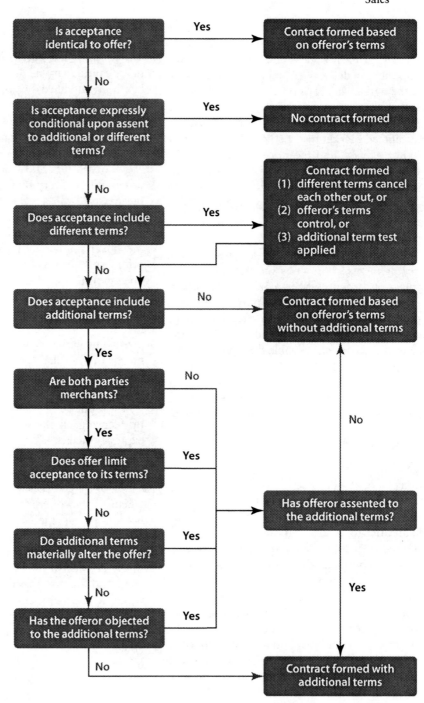

condition acceptance upon the buyer's assent to the additional or different terms, (1) the contract will be formed without the *seller's different terms* unless the buyer specifically accepts them; (2) the contract will be formed without the *seller's additional terms* unless (a) the buyer specifically accepts or (b) the additional terms do not materially alter the offer and the buyer does not object to them; and (3) depending on the jurisdiction, (a) the *conflicting terms* cancel each other out and the Code provides the missing terms, (b) the *buyer's conflicting terms* are included in the contract, or (c) the additional terms test is applied.

CISG

A reply to an offer that contains additions, limitations, or other modifications is a counteroffer that rejects the original offer. Nevertheless, a purported acceptance that contains additional or different terms acts as an acceptance if the terms do not materially alter the contract unless the offeror objects to the change. Changes in price, payment, quality, quantity, place and time of delivery, terms of delivery, liability of the parties, and settlement of a dispute are always considered to be material alterations.

Finally, subsection (3) of 2–207 deals with those situations in which the writings do not form a contract, but the conduct of the parties recognizes the existence of one. For instance, Ernest makes an offer to Gwen, who replies with a conditional acceptance. Although no contract has been formed, Gwen ships the ordered goods and Ernest accepts the goods. Subsection (3) provides that in this instance the contract consists of the written terms to which both parties agreed together with supplementary provisions of the Code.

COMMERCE & INDUSTRY INSURANCE COMPANY V. BAYER CORPORATION

SUPREME JUDICIAL COURT OF MASSACHUSETTS, 2001
433 MASS. 388, 742 N.E.2D 567, 44 U.C.C. REP. SERV. 2D 50

http://scholar.google.com/scholar_case?case=8104304470024394019&q=742+N.E.2d+567&hl=en&as_sdt=2,22

FACTS On December 11, 1995, an explosion and fire destroyed several of Malden Mills's buildings at its manufacturing facility. Malden Mills and its property insurers, the plaintiffs Commerce & Industry Insurance Company and Federal Insurance Company, brought suit in the Superior Court against numerous defendants, including Bayer Corporation. In their complaint, the plaintiffs allege that the cause of the fire was the ignition, by static electrical discharge, of nylon tow (also known as bulk nylon fiber), which was sold by Bayer to Malden Mills.

Malden Mills initiated purchases of nylon tow from Bayer either by sending its standard form purchase order to Bayer, or by placing a telephone order to Bayer, followed by a standard form purchase order. Each of Malden Mills's purchase orders contained, on the reverse side, as one of its "terms and conditions," an arbitration provision.

Another "term and condition" appearing in paragraph one on the reverse side of each purchase order provides: "This purchase order represents the entire agreement between both parties, not withstanding any Seller's order form, and this document cannot be modified except in writing and signed by an authorized representative of the buyer."

In response, Bayer transmitted Malden Mills's purchase orders to the manufacturer with instructions, in most instances, that the nylon tow was to be shipped directly to Malden Mills. Thereafter, Bayer prepared and sent Malden Mills an invoice. Each of the Bayer invoices contained the following language on its face, located at the bottom of the form in capital letters:

TERMS AND CONDITIONS: NOTWITHSTANDING ANY CONTRARY OR INCONSISTENT CONDITIONS THAT MAY BE EMBODIED IN YOUR PURCHASE ORDER, YOUR ORDER IS ACCEPTED SUBJECT TO THE PRICES, TERMS AND CONDITIONS OF THE MUTUALLY EXECUTED CONTRACT BETWEEN US, OR, IF NO SUCH CONTRACT EXISTS, YOUR ORDER IS ACCEPTED SUBJECT TO OUR REGULAR SCHEDULED PRICE AND TERMS IN EFFECT AT TIME OF SHIPMENT AND SUBJECT TO THE TERMS AND CONDITIONS PRINTED ON THE REVERSE SIDE HEREOF.

The following "condition" appears on the reverse side of each invoice: "This document is not an Expression of Acceptance or a Confirmation document as contemplated in Section 2-207 of the Uniform Commercial Code. The acceptance of any order entered by [Malden Mills] is expressly conditioned on [Malden Mills's] assent to any additional or conflicting terms contained herein."

Based on the arbitration provision in Malden Mills's purchase orders, Bayer demanded that Malden Mills arbitrate its claims against Bayer. After Malden Mills refused, Bayer moved to compel arbitration. The court ruled in favor of Malden Mills.

DECISION The order denying the motion to compel arbitration is affirmed.

OPINION Greaney, J. This case presents a dispute arising from what has been styled a typical "battle of the forms" sale, in which a buyer and a seller each attempt to consummate a commercial transaction through the exchange of self-serving preprinted forms that clash, and contradict each other, on both material and minor terms. [Citation.] Here, Malden Mills's form, a purchase order, contains an arbitration provision, and Bayer's form, a seller's invoice, is silent on how the parties will resolve any disputes. Oddly enough, the buyer, Malden Mills, the party proposing the arbitration provision, and its insurers, now seek to avoid an arbitral forum.

Section 2-207 was enacted with the expectation of creating an orderly mechanism to resolve commercial disputes resulting from a "battle of the forms." The section has been characterized as "an amphibious tank that was originally designed to fight in the swamps, but was sent to fight in the desert." [Citation.] Section 2-207 sets forth rules and principles concerning contract formation and the procedures for determining the terms of a contract. As to contract formation, under § 2-207, there are essentially three ways by which a contract may be formed. [Citation.]

First, if the parties exchange forms with divergent terms, yet the seller's invoice does not state that its acceptance is made 'expressly conditional' on the buyer's assent to any additional or different terms in the invoice, a contract is formed [under subsection (1) of § 2-207].

Second, if the seller does make its acceptance 'expressly conditional' on the buyer's assent to any additional or divergent terms in the seller's invoice, the invoice is merely a counteroffer, and a contract is formed [under subsection (1) of § 2-207] only when the buyer expresses its affirmative acceptance of the seller's counteroffer.

Third, where for any reason the exchange of forms does not result in contract formation (e.g., the buyer "expressly limits its acceptance to the terms of [its offer]" under § 2-207(2)(a), or the buyer does not accept the seller's counteroffer under the second clause of § 2-207[1]), a contract nonetheless is formed [under subsection (3) of § 2-207] if their subsequent conduct—for instance, the seller ships and the buyer accepts the goods—demonstrates that the parties believed that a binding agreement had been formed.

Bayer correctly concedes that its contract with Malden Mills resulted from the parties' conduct, and, thus, was formed pursuant to subsection (3) of § 2-207. A contract never came into being under subsection (1) of § 2-207 because (1) paragraph fourteen on the reverse side of Bayer's invoices expressly conditioned acceptance on Malden Mills's assent to "additional or different" terms, and (2) Malden Mills never expressed "affirmative acceptance" of any of Bayer's invoices. In addition, the exchange of forms between Malden Mills and Bayer did not result in a contract because Malden Mills, by means of language in paragraph one of its purchase orders, expressly limited Bayer's acceptance to the terms of Malden Mills's offers. [Citation.]

***

*** Where a contract is formed by the parties' conduct (as opposed to writings), as is the case here, the terms of the contract are determined exclusively by subsection (3) of § 2-207. [Citation.]. Under subsection (3) of § 2-207, "the terms of the particular contract consist of those terms on which the writings of the parties agree, together with any supplementary terms incorporated under any other provisions of this chapter." § 2-207 (3). In this respect, one commentator has aptly referred to subsection (3) of § 2-207 as the "fall-back" rule. [Citation.] Under this rule, the Code accepts "common terms but rejects all the rest." While this approach "serves to leave many matters uncovered," terms may be filled by "recourse to usages of trade or course of dealing under [§] 1-205 or, perhaps, the gap filling provisions of [§§] 2-300s." [Citation.]

***

Thus, the judge correctly concluded, under subsection (3) of § 2-207, that the arbitration provision in Malden Mills's purchase orders did not become a term of the parties' contract. The arbitration provision was not common to both Malden Mills's purchase orders and Bayer's invoices. Bayer properly does not argue that any of the gap-filling provisions of [the UCC] apply. Because Bayer concedes that it never previously arbitrated a dispute with Malden Mills, we reject Bayer's claim that the parties' course of dealing requires us to enforce the arbitration provision.

***

INTERPRETATION In cases in which a contract is formed by the parties' conduct (as opposed to writings), all conflicting written terms are invalid.

ETHICAL QUESTION Is it unethical for Malden Mills to try to avoid a term from its own forms? Explain.

CRITICAL THINKING QUESTION Do you agree with how the Code deals with the battle of the forms?

PRACTICAL ADVICE

In negotiating a contract, try to be the offeror and consider providing in your offer that your terms control and that any new or different terms will be made part of the contract only if you specifically agree to them in a signed writing.

MANNER OF ACCEPTANCE

As is true of contracts under common law, the offeror may specify the manner in which the offer must be accepted. If the offeror does not so specify and the circumstances do not otherwise clearly indicate, an offer to make a sales contract invites acceptance, effective upon dispatch, in any manner and in any medium reasonable in the circumstances. (Article 2A.) The Code therefore allows flexibility of response and the ability to keep pace with new modes of communication.

An offer to buy goods for prompt or current shipment may be accepted either by a prompt promise to ship or by prompt shipment. Acceptance by performance requires notice within a reasonable time, or the offer may be treated as lapsed. (Article 2A.)

AUCTIONS

The Code provides that if an auction sale is advertised or announced in explicit terms to be *without reserve*, the auctioneer may not withdraw the article put up for sale unless no bid is made within a reasonable time. Unless the sale is advertised as being without reserve, the sale is *with reserve*, and the auctioneer may withdraw the goods at any time until he announces completion of the sale. Whether with or without reserve, a bidder may retract his bid at any time prior to acceptance by the auctioneer. Such retraction, however, does not revive any previous bid.

If the auctioneer knowingly receives a bid by or on behalf of the seller, and notice has not been given that the seller reserves the right to bid at the auction sale, the bidder to whom the goods are sold can either avoid the sale or take the goods at the price of the last good faith bid.

The CISG does not apply to sales by auctions.

Consideration

In several respects, the Code has relaxed the common law requirements regarding consideration. For example, the Code provides that a contract for the sale of goods can be modified without new consideration, provided the **modification** is made in good faith. (Article 2A.) In addition, any claim of right arising out of an alleged breach of contract can be discharged in whole or in part without consideration by a written waiver or renunciation signed and delivered by the aggrieved party. Under Revised UCC Article 1, a claim or right arising out of an alleged breach may be discharged in whole or in part without consideration by agreement of the aggrieved party in an authenticated record. Moreover, a firm offer is not revocable for lack of consideration.

Consideration is not needed to modify a contract.

Form of the Contract

STATUTE OF FRAUDS

The original **statute of frauds**, which applied to contracts for the sale of goods, has been used as a prototype for the Article 2 statute of frauds provision. The Code provides that a contract for the sale of goods costing *$500 or more* is not enforceable unless there is some writing or record sufficient to evidence the existence of a contract between the parties ($1,000 or more for leases—Article 2A). As discussed in Chapter 15, forty-seven states have adopted the *Uniform Electronic Transactions Act (UETA)*, which gives full effect to contracts formed by electronic records and signatures. The Act applies to contracts governed by Articles 2 and 2A. In addition, Congress in 2000 enacted the *Electronic Signatures in Global and National Commerce (E-Sign)*. The Act, which uses language very similar to that of UETA, makes electronic records and signatures valid and enforceable across the United States for many types of transactions in or affecting interstate or foreign commerce.

A contract need not be evidenced by a writing, unless one of the parties has its place of business in a country that provides otherwise.

Modification of Contracts   An agreement modifying a contract must be in writing if the resulting contract is within the statute of frauds (Article 2A omits this provision). Conversely, if a contract that was previously within the statute of frauds is modified so as to no longer fall within it, the modification is enforceable even if it is oral. Thus, if the parties enter into an oral contract to sell for $450 a dining room table, to be delivered to the buyer, and later, prior to delivery, *orally* agree that the seller shall stain the table and that the buyer shall pay a price of $550, the modified contract is unenforceable. In contrast, if the parties have a written contract for the sale of one hundred and fifty bushels of wheat at a price of $4.50 per bushel and, later, orally agree to decrease the quantity to one hundred bushels at the same price per bushel, the agreement, as modified, is enforceable.

A signed agreement that requires modifications or rescissions of it to be in a signed writing cannot be otherwise modified or rescinded. (Article 2A.) If this requirement is on a form provided by a merchant, the other party must separately sign it unless the other party is a merchant.

Writing(s) or Record The statute of frauds compliance provisions under the Code are more liberal than the rules under general contract law. The Code requires merely some writing or record (1) sufficient to indicate that a contract has been made between the parties, (2) signed by the party against whom enforcement is sought or by her authorized agent or broker, and (3) including a term specifying the quantity of goods to be exchanged. Whereas general contract law requires that the writing include all essential terms, under the Code a writing or record may be sufficient even if it omits or incorrectly states an agreed-upon term. This is consistent with other provisions of the Code that permit contracts to be enforced even though material terms are omitted. Nevertheless, the contract is enforceable only to the extent of the quantity of goods stated. Given proof that a contract was intended and that a signed writing or record describes the goods, the quantity of goods, and the names of the parties, the court, under the Code, can supply omitted terms such as price and particulars of performance. Moreover, several related documents together may satisfy the writing or record requirement.

Between merchants, a written confirmation, if sufficient against the sender, is also sufficient against the recipient unless the recipient gives written notice of her objection within ten days after receiving the confirmation. (Article 2A does not have a comparable rule.) This means that if these requirements have been met, the recipient of the writing or record is in the same position he would have assumed by signing it; and the confirmation, therefore, is enforceable against him. For example, Brown Co. and ATM Industries enter into an oral contract providing that ATM will deliver 1,000 dozen shirts to Brown at $6 per shirt. The next day, Brown sends to ATM a letter signed by Brown's president confirming the agreement. The letter contains the quantity term but does not mention the price. Brown is bound by the contract when its authorized agent sends the letter, whereas ATM is bound by the oral contract ten days after receiving the letter, unless it objects in writing within that time. Therefore, it is essential that merchants examine their mail carefully and promptly to make certain that any written confirmations conform to their understanding of their outstanding contractual agreements. Where one or both of the parties is not a merchant, however, this rule does not apply.

Business Law in Action

Between buyers and sellers of goods, many contracts are created via preprinted forms, like pro forma invoices, purchase orders, order confirmations, and invoices. These forms typically contain legal terms not expressly negotiated by the parties. The question often arises as to whether a term appearing in only one of the two preprinted forms binds the parties.

Say Bi-Rite Systems ordered $325,000 of component parts from Kruger Corp. on account, agreeing to pay within ten days of receipt of Kruger's invoice. Bi-Rite used a standard form purchase order that accurately reflected the price, quantity, and delivery terms to which the parties had agreed but said nothing about interest on overdue balances. Kruger delivered the goods along with its standard form invoice, which stated: "Accounts not paid within 10 days from the date of billing will be subject to a finance charge of 1-1/2% per month." Bi-Rite paid Kruger's invoice twenty-five days after the date of billing. Does Bi-Rite owe the finance charge?

Code Section 2-207 provides that in contracts between merchants "additional terms" found in a form contract acceptance generally become an enforceable part of the bargain, unless (1) the offer expressly limits acceptance to the terms of the offer, (2) the additional term materially alters the offer, or (3) there is prompt objection to the proposed additional term.

Bi-Rite's purchase order is the offer and Kruger's invoice the acceptance. The invoice's finance charge provision is an "additional term." Since there is no indication that either the offer was expressly limited to its terms or that Bi-Rite made any objection to the proposed finance charge clause, the question is whether it "materially alters" the offer. Courts have routinely held that interest provisions, arbitration clauses, and even remedy limitations set out in form acceptances do *not* materially alter the terms of the offer. Therefore the finance charge clause in Kruger's preprinted form invoice is enforceable.

> **PRACTICAL ADVICE**
>
> Be aware that if you receive a signed written confirmation of a contract, you have ten business days to object if the confirmation is inaccurate.

Exceptions A contract that does not satisfy the writing requirement but is otherwise valid is enforceable in the following instances:

The Code permits an oral contract for the sale of goods to be enforced against a party who in his pleading, testimony, or otherwise in court *admits* that a contract was made; but the Code limits enforcement to the quantity of goods he admits. (Article 2A.) This provision recognizes that the policy behind the statute of frauds does not apply when the party seeking to avoid the oral contract admits under oath the existence of the contract.

The Code also permits enforcement of an oral contract for goods *specially manufactured* for the buyer. (Article 2A.) Nevertheless, if the goods are readily marketable in the ordinary course of the seller's business, even though they were manufactured on special order, the contract is not enforceable unless it is in writing.

Under the Code, delivery and acceptance of part of the goods or payment and acceptance of part of the price validates the contract, but only for the goods that have been *delivered and accepted* or for which *payment* has been *accepted*. (Article 2A.) To illustrate, Debra orally agrees to buy one thousand watches from Brian for $15,000. Brian delivers three hundred watches to Debra, who receives and accepts them. The oral contract is enforceable to the extent of three hundred watches ($4,500)—those received and accepted—but is unenforceable to the extent of seven hundred watches ($10,500).

PAROL EVIDENCE

Contractual terms that are set forth in a writing intended by the parties as a final expression of their agreement may not be contradicted by evidence of any prior agreement or of a contemporaneous oral agreement, but, under the Code, the terms may be explained or supplemented by (1) course of dealing, usage of trade, or course of performance and (2) evidence of consistent additional terms, unless the writing was intended as the complete and exclusive statement of the terms of the agreement. (Article 2A.)

CONCEPT REVIEW 19-1

Contract Law Compared with Law of Sales

Section of UCC	Contract Law	Law of Sales
Definiteness	Contract must include all material terms.	Open terms permitted if parties intend to make a contract. (Article 2, 2A)
Counteroffers	Acceptance must be a mirror image of offer. Counteroffer and conditional acceptance are rejections.	Battle of the Forms. See Figure 19-1. (Article 2)
Modification of Contract	Consideration is required.	Consideration is not required. (Article 2, 2A)
Irrevocable Offers	Options.	Options. Firm offers up to three months' binding without consideration. (Article 2, 2A)
Statute of Frauds	Writing must include all material terms.	Writing must include quantity term. Specially manufactured goods. Confirmation by merchants. Delivery or payment and acceptance. Admissions. (Article 2, Article 2A *except* merchant confirmation.)

Ethical Dilemma

What Constitutes Unconscionability in a Business?

FACTS Frank's Maintenance and Repair, Inc., orally placed with C. A. Roberts Co. an order for steel tubing to use in manufacturing front fork tubes for motorcycles. Front fork tubes bear the bulk of a motorcycle's weight, so Frank's had to use high-quality steel.

Soon, Frank's received from Roberts Co. an acknowledgment of the order. This acknowledgment included the conditions of sale, which limited consequential damages, as well as a description of restricted remedies that were available upon the contract's breach. The sale conditions required that the buyer make any claim for defective equipment promptly upon receipt of the goods. These conditions were printed on the back of the acknowledgment. On the front, a legend that read "conditions of sale on reverse side" had been stamped over in such a way that the words at first appeared to read "No conditions of sale on reverse side."

Roberts delivered the steel to Frank's in December. The steel had no visible defects. When Frank's began using the material in its manufacturing process in the summer of the following year,

however, the company discovered that the steel was hopelessly pitted and cracked. Frank's Maintenance and Repair informed Roberts Co. of the defects, revoked its acceptance of the steel, and sued for breach of the warranty of merchantability.

Social, Policy, and Ethical Considerations

1. Did Frank's Maintenance and Repair have a reasonable opportunity to understand the terms of its contract with C. A. Roberts Co.? Given the contract that Frank's received, was the company able to make a meaningful choice with regard to the terms of the agreement? Why or why not?

2. Who bears the responsibility in a situation such as this when both parties are businesspersons and thus should know enough to read all contracts carefully and thoroughly?

3. With or without the stamp, did Roberts act unconscionably in drawing up its contract? Moreover, should Roberts have the right to restrict a buyer's remedies if its steel may have a latent defect?

CHAPTER SUMMARY
NATURE OF SALES AND LEASES

Definitions

Goods movable personal property

Sale transfer of title to goods from seller to buyer for a price

Lease a transfer of right to possession and use of goods in return for consideration
- *Consumer Leases* leases by a merchant to an individual who leases for personal, family, or household purposes for no more than $25,000
- *Finance Leases* special type of lease transaction generally involving three parties: the lessor, the supplier, and the lessee

Governing Law
- *Sales Transactions* governed by Article 2 of the Code, except where general contract law has not been specifically modified by the Code, general contract law continues to apply
- *Lease Transactions* governed by Article 2A of the Code, but where general contract law has not been specifically modified by the Code, general contract law continues to apply
- *Transactions outside the Code* include employment contracts, service contracts, insurance contracts, contracts involving real property, and contracts for the sale of tangibles

Fundamental Principles of Article 2 and Article 2A

Purpose to modernize, clarify, simplify, and make uniform the law of sales and leases

Good Faith the Code requires all sales and lease contracts to be performed in good faith, which means honesty in fact in the conduct or transaction concerned; in the case of a merchant (and a nonmerchant under Revised Article 1), it also includes the observance of reasonable commercial standards of fair dealing

Unconscionability a court may refuse to enforce an unconscionable contract or any part of a contract found to be unconscionable
* *Procedural Unconscionability* unfairness of the bargaining process
* *Substantive Unconscionability* oppressive or grossly unfair contractual provisions

Expansion of Commercial Practices
* *Course of Dealing* a sequence of previous conduct between the parties establishing a common basis for interpreting their agreement
* *Usage of Trade* a practice or method of dealing regularly observed and followed in a place, vocation, or trade

Sales by and between Merchants the Code establishes separate rules that apply to transactions between merchants or involving a merchant (a dealer in goods or a person who by his occupation holds himself out as having knowledge or skill peculiar to the goods or practices involved, or who employs an agent or broker whom he holds out as having such knowledge or skill)

Liberal Administration of Remedies
* *Freedom of Contract* most provisions of the Code may be varied by agreement
* *Validation and Preservation of Sales Contracts* the Code reduces formal requisites to the bare minimum and attempts to preserve agreements whenever the parties manifest an intention to enter into a contract

FORMATION OF SALES AND LEASE CONTRACTS

Manifestation of Mutual Assent

Definiteness of an Offer the Code provides that a contract does not fail for indefiniteness even though one or more terms may have been omitted; the Code provides standards by which missing essential terms may be supplied

Irrevocable Offers
* *Option* a contract to hold open an offer
* *Firm Offer* a signed writing by a merchant to hold open an offer for the purchase or sale of goods (or lease of goods) for a maximum of three months

Variant Acceptances the inclusion of different or additional terms in an acceptance is addressed by focusing on the intent of the parties

Manner of Acceptance an acceptance can be made in any reasonable manner and is effective upon dispatch

Auction auction sales are generally with reserve, permitting the auctioneer to withdraw the goods at any time prior to sale

Consideration

Contractual Modifications the Code provides that a contract for the sale or lease of goods may be modified without new consideration if the modification is made in good faith

Firm Offers are not revocable for lack of consideration

Form of the Contract

Statute of Frauds sale of goods costing $500 or more (or lease of goods for $1,000 or more) must be evidenced by a signed writing or record to be enforceable; full effect is given to electronic contracts and signatures

- *Writing(s) or Record* the Code requires some writing(s) or record sufficient to indicate that a contract has been made between the parties, signed by the party against whom enforcement is sought or by her authorized agent or broker, and including a term specifying the quantity of goods
- *Alternative Methods of Compliance* written confirmation between merchants, admission, specially manufactured goods, and delivery or payment and acceptance

Parol Evidence contractual terms that are set forth in a writing intended by the parties as a final expression of their agreement may not be contradicted by evidence of any prior agreement or of a contemporaneous oral agreement, but such terms may be explained or supplemented by course of dealing, usage of trade, course of performance, or consistent additional evidence

QUESTIONS

1. Dickinson orders one thousand widgets at $5 per widget from International Widget to be delivered within sixty days. After the contract is consummated and signed, Dickinson orally requests that International deliver the widgets within thirty days rather than sixty days. International agrees. Is the contractual modification binding?

2. In Question 1, what effect, if any, would the following telegram have?

   International Widget:

   In accordance with our agreement of this date you will deliver the one thousand previously ordered widgets within thirty days. Thank you for your cooperation in this matter.

   (signed) Dickinson

3. Hicks, a San Francisco company, orders from U.S. Electronics, a New York company, ten thousand electronic units. Hicks's order form provides that any dispute would be resolved by an arbitration panel located in San Francisco. U.S. Electronics executes and delivers to Hicks its acknowledgment form accepting the order and containing the following provision: "All disputes will be resolved by the state courts of New York." A dispute arises concerning the workmanship of the parts, and Hicks wishes the case to be arbitrated in San Francisco. What would be the result?

4. Explain how the result in Question 3 might change if the U.S. Electronics form contained the following provisions:

   a. "The seller's acceptance of the purchase order to which this acknowledgment responds is expressly made conditional on the buyer's assent to any or different terms contained in this acknowledgment."

   b. "The seller's acceptance of the purchase order is subject to the terms and conditions on the face and reverse side hereof, which the buyer accepts by accepting the goods described herein."

   c. "The seller's terms govern this agreement—this acknowledgment merely constitutes a counteroffer."

5. Reinfort executed a written contract with Bylinski to purchase an assorted collection of shoes for $3,000. A week before the agreed shipment date, Bylinski called Reinfort and said, "We cannot deliver at $3,000; unless you agree to pay $4,000, we will cancel the order." After considerable discussion, Reinfort agreed to pay $4,000 if Bylinski would ship as agreed in the contract. After the shoes had been delivered and accepted by Reinfort, Reinfort refused to pay $4,000 and insisted on paying only $3,000. Is the contractual modification binding? Explain.

6. On November 23, Blackburn, a dress manufacturer, mailed to Conroy a written and signed offer to sell one thousand sun dresses at $50 per dress. The offer stated that it would "remain open for ten days" and that it could "not be withdrawn prior to that date."

   Two days later, Blackburn, noting a sudden increase in the price of sundresses, changed his mind. Blackburn therefore sent Conroy a letter revoking the offer. The letter was sent on November 25 and received by Conroy on November 28.

   Conroy chose to disregard the letter of November 25; instead, she happily continued to watch the price of sundresses rise. On December 1, Conroy sent a letter accepting the original offer. The letter, however, was not received by Blackburn until December 9, due to a delay in the mail.

   Conroy has demanded delivery of the goods according to the terms of the offer of November 23, but Blackburn has refused. Does a contract exist between Conroy and Blackburn? Explain.

7. Henry and Wilma, an elderly immigrant couple, agreed to purchase from Harris a refrigerator with a fair market value of $450 for twenty-five monthly installments of $60 per month. Henry and Wilma now wish to void the contract, asserting that they did not realize the exorbitant price they were paying. Result?

8. Courts Distributors needed two hundred compact refrigerators on a rush basis. It contacted Eastinghouse Corporation, a manufacturer of refrigerators. Eastinghouse said it would take some time to quote a price on an order of that size. Courts replied, "Send the refrigerators immediately

and bill us later." The refrigerators were delivered three days later, and the invoice arrived ten days after that. The invoice price was $140,000. Courts believes that the wholesale market price of the refrigerators is only $120,000. Do the parties have a contract? If so, what is the price? Explain.

CASE PROBLEMS

9. While adjusting a television antenna beside his mobile home and underneath a high-voltage electric transmission wire, Prince received an electric shock resulting in personal injury. He claims the high-voltage electric current jumped from the transmission wire to the antenna. The wire, which carried some 7,200 volts of electricity, did not serve his mobile home but ran directly above it. Prince sued the Navarro County Electric Co-Op, the owner and operator of the wire, for breach of implied warranty of merchantability under the Uniform Commercial Code (UCC). He contends that the Code's implied warranty of merchantability extends to the container of a product—in this instance, the wiring—and that the escape of the current shows that the wiring was unfit for its purpose of transporting electricity. The electric company argues that the electricity passing through the transmission wire was not being sold to Prince and that, therefore, there was no sale of goods to Prince. Is the contract covered by the UCC?

10. HMT, already in the business of marketing agricultural products, decided to try its hand at marketing potatoes for processing. Nine months before the potato harvest, HMT contracted to supply Bell Brand with one hundred thousand sacks of potatoes. At harvest time, Bell Brand would accept only sixty thousand sacks. HMT sues for breach of contract. Bell Brand argues that custom and usage in marketing processing potatoes allows buyers to give estimates in contracts, not fixed quantities, as the contracts are established so far in advance. HMT responds that the quantity term in the contract was definite and unambiguous. Can custom and trade usage be used to interpret an unambiguous contract? Discuss.

11. Schreiner, a cotton farmer, agreed over the telephone to sell 150 bales of cotton to Loeb & Co. Schreiner had sold cotton to Loeb & Co. for the past five years. Written confirmation of the date, parties, price, and conditions was mailed to Schreiner, who did not respond to the confirmation in any way. Four months later, when the price of cotton had doubled, Loeb & Co. sought to enforce the contract. Schreiner argues that he is not a merchant. Is the contract enforceable?

12. American Sand & Gravel, Inc., agreed to sell sand to Clark at a special discount if twenty to twenty-five thousand tons were ordered. The discount price was $9.45 per ton, compared with the normal price of $10.00 per ton. Two years later, Clark orders, and receives, 1,600 tons of sand from American Sand & Gravel. Clark refuses to pay more than $9.45 per ton. American Sand & Gravel sues for the remaining $0.55 per ton. Decision?

13. In September, Auburn Plastics submitted price quotations to CBS for the manufacture of eight cavity molds to be used in making parts for CBS's toys. Each quotation specified that the offer would not be binding unless accepted within fifteen days. Furthermore, CBS would be subject to an additional 30 percent charge for engineering services upon delivery of the molds. In December and January of the following year, CBS sent detailed purchase orders to Auburn Plastics for cavity molds. The purchase order forms stated that CBS reserved the right to remove the molds from Auburn Plastics without an additional or "withdrawal" charge. Auburn Plastics acknowledged the purchase order and stated that the sale would be subject to all conditions contained in the price quotation. CBS paid Auburn for the molds, and Auburn began to fabricate toy parts from the molds for CBS. Later, Auburn announced a price increase, and CBS demanded delivery of the molds. Auburn refused to deliver the molds unless CBS paid the additional charge for engineering services. CBS claimed that the contract did not provide for a withdrawal charge. Who will prevail? Why?

14. The defendant, Gray Communications, desired to have a television tower built. After a number of negotiation sessions conducted by telephone between the defendant and the plaintiff, Kline Iron, the parties allegedly reached an oral agreement under which the plaintiff would build a tower for the defendant for a total price of $1,485,368. A few days later, the plaintiff sent a written document, referred to as a proposal, for execution by the defendant. The proposal indicated that it had been prepared for immediate acceptance by the defendant and that prior to formal acceptance by the defendant it could be modified or withdrawn without notice. A few days later, without having executed the proposal, the defendant advised the plaintiff that a competitor had provided a lower bid for construction of the tower. The defendant requested that the plaintiff explain its higher bid price, which the plaintiff failed to do. The defendant then advised the plaintiff by letter that it would not be retained to construct the tower. The plaintiff then commenced suit, alleging breach of an oral contract, and asserting that the oral agreement was enforceable because the common law of contracts, not the Uniform Commercial Code (UCC), governed the transaction and that under the common law a writing is not necessary to cover this type of transaction. Even if the transaction was subject to the UCC, the plaintiff alternatively argued, the contract was within the UCC "merchant's exception." Is the contract enforceable?

15. Dorton, as a representative for The Carpet Mart, purchased carpets from Collins & Aikman that were supposedly manufactured of 100 percent Kodel polyester fiber but were, in fact, made of cheaper and inferior fibers. Dorton then brought suit for compensatory and punitive damages against Collins & Aikman for its fraud, deceit, and misrepresentation in the sale of the carpets. Collins & Aikman moved for a stay pending arbitration, claiming that Dorton was bound to an arbitration agreement printed on the reverse side of Collins & Aikman's printed sales acknowledgment form. A provision printed on the face of the acknowledgment form stated that its acceptance was "subject to all of the terms and conditions on the face and reverse side thereof, including arbitration, all of which are accepted by buyer." Holding that there existed no binding arbitration agreement between the parties, the district court denied the stay. Collins & Aikman appealed. Is the arbitration clause enforceable?

16. Emery Industries (Emery) contracted with Mechanicals, Inc. (Mechanicals), to install a pipe system to carry chemicals and fatty acids under high pressure and temperature. The system required stainless steel "stub ends" (used to connect pipe segments), which Mechanicals ordered from McJunkin Corporation (McJunkin). McJunkin in turn ordered the stub ends from the Alaskan Copper Companies, Inc. (Alaskan). McJunkin's purchase order required the seller to certify the goods and to relieve the buyer of liabilities that might arise from defective goods. After shipment of the goods to McJunkin, Alaskan sent written acknowledgment of the order, containing terms and conditions of sale different from those in McJunkin's purchase order. The acknowledgment provided a disclaimer of warranty and a requirement for inspection of the goods within ten days of receipt. The acknowledgment also contained a requirement that the buyer accept all of the seller's terms.

The stub ends were delivered to Mechanicals in several shipments over a five-month period. Each shipment included a document reciting terms the same as those on Alaskan's initial acknowledgment. Apparently, McJunkin never objected to any of the terms contained in any of Alaskan's documents.

After the stub ends were installed, they were found to be defective. Mechanicals had to remove and replace them, causing Emery to close its plant for several days. McJunkin filed a complaint alleging that Mechanicals had failed to pay $26,141.88 owed on account for the stub ends McJunkin supplied. Mechanicals filed an answer and counterclaim against McJunkin, alleging $93,586.13 in damages resulting from the replacement and repair of the defective stub ends. McJunkin filed a third-party complaint against Alaskan, alleging that Alaskan was liable for any damages Mechanicals incurred as a result of the defective stub ends. What result? Explain.

TAKING SIDES

Terminal Grain Corporation brought an action against Glen Freeman, a farmer, to recover damages for breach of an oral contract to deliver grain. According to Terminal Grain, Freeman orally agreed to two sales of wheat to Terminal Grain of four thousand bushels each at $6.21 a bushel and $6.41 a bushel, respectively. Dwayne Maher, merchandising manager of Terminal Grain, sent two written confirmations of the agreements to Freeman. Freeman never made any written objections to the confirmations. After the first transaction had occurred, the price of wheat rose to between $6.75 and $6.80 per bushel, and Freeman refused to deliver the remaining four thousand bushels at the agreed-upon price. Freeman denies entering into any agreement to sell the second four thousand bushels of wheat to Terminal Grain but admits that he received the two written confirmations sent by Maher.

a. What arguments support considering Freeman to be a merchant who is bound by the written confirmations?

b. What arguments support considering Freeman not to be a merchant seller and thus not bound by the written confirmations?

c. What is the appropriate decision?

Chapter 20

PERFORMANCE

The buyer needs a hundred eyes, the seller not one.

GEORGE HERVERT (1593–1633)

CHAPTER OUTCOMES

After reading and studying this chapter, you should be able to:

1. Explain the requirements of tender of delivery with respect to time, manner, and place of delivery.

2. Explain the perfect tender rule and the three limitations on it.

3. Explain when the buyer has the right to reject the goods and what obligations the buyer has upon rejection.

4. Explain what constitutes acceptance by the buyer and the buyer's right to revoke acceptance.

5. Identify and describe the excuses for nonperformance and the Uniform Commercial Code's provisions for protecting the parties' expectations of performance by the other party.

Performance is the process of discharging contractual obligations by carrying out those obligations according to a contract's terms. The basic obligation of the seller in a contract for the sale of goods is to transfer and deliver goods that conform to the terms of the contract. The basic obligation of the buyer is to accept and pay for conforming goods in accordance with the contract. In a lease, the basic obligation of the lessor is to transfer possession of the goods for the lease term and that of the lessee is to pay the agreed rent. A contract of sale also requires that each party not impair the other party's expectation of having the contract performed.

The obligations of the parties are determined by their contractual agreement. Thus, the contract of sale may expressly state, for example, whether the seller must deliver the goods before receiving payment of the price or whether the buyer must pay the price before receiving the goods. If the contract does not sufficiently cover the particulars of performance, these terms will be supplied by the Uniform Commercial Code (UCC), common law, course of dealings, usage of trade, and course of performance. (Article 2A provides only a few gap fillers.) In all events, both parties to the sales contract must perform their contractual obligations in good faith.

In this chapter, we will examine the performance obligations of the seller and the buyer as well as the contractual obligations that apply to both of them.

Performance by the Seller

Unless the parties have agreed otherwise, tender (offer) of performance by one party is a condition to performance by the other party. Tender of conforming goods

397

by the seller entitles him to acceptance of them by the buyer and to payment of the contractually agreed-upon price. Nonetheless, the terms of the contract may establish other rights for the parties. For example, if the seller has agreed to sell goods on sixty or ninety days' credit, he is required to perform his part of the contract by delivering the goods before the buyer performs.

Tender of delivery requires that the seller put and hold goods that conform to the contract at the buyer's disposition and that the seller give the buyer reasonable notification to enable her to take delivery. Tender must also be made at a reasonable time and be kept open for a reasonable period. For example, Jim agrees to sell Joan a home theater system composed of a speaker system (consisting of four identical speakers for the front and rear, a center channel speaker, and a subwoofer speaker), a Blu-Ray disc player, and an audio-video receiver. Each component is specified by manufacturer and model number, and delivery is to be at Jim's store. Jim obtains the ordered equipment in accordance with the contractual specifications and notifies Joan that she may pick up the system at her convenience. Jim has now tendered and thus has performed his obligations under the sales contract: he holds goods that conform to the contract, he has placed them at the buyer's disposition, and he has notified the buyer of their readiness.

> **CISG** According to the United Nations Convention on Contracts for the International Sales of Goods (CISG), the seller must deliver the goods, hand over any documents relating to them, and transfer the property in the goods, as required by the contract and the CISG.

TIME OF TENDER

Tender must be at a reasonable time, and the goods tendered must be kept available for the period reasonably necessary to enable the buyer to take possession of them. If the contract terms set no definite time for delivery, the seller is allowed a reasonable time after entering into the contract within which to tender the goods to the buyer. Likewise, the buyer has a reasonable time within which to accept delivery. What length of time is reasonable depends on the facts and circumstances of each case.

A contract may not be performed piecemeal or in installments unless the parties specifically so agree. Otherwise, all of the goods called for by a contract must be tendered in a single delivery, with payment due at the time of such tender.

> **CISG** The seller must deliver the goods: (1) if a date is fixed by or determinable from the contract, on that date; (2) if a period of time is fixed by or determinable from the contract, at any time within that period unless circumstances indicate that the buyer is to choose a date; or (3) in any other case, within a reasonable time after the conclusion of the contract.

PLACE OF TENDER

If the contract does not specify the place for delivery of the goods, the place for delivery is the seller's place of business or, if he has no place of business, his residence. If the contract is for the sale of identified goods that the parties know at the time of making the contract are not located either at the seller's place of business or residence, the location of the goods is then the place for delivery.

The parties frequently agree expressly on the place of tender, typically by using one of the various delivery terms. These terms specify whether the contract is a shipment or destination contract and determine where the seller must tender delivery of the goods.

> **CISG** If the seller is not bound to deliver the goods at any other particular place and the contract of sale does not involve carriage of the goods, his obligation to deliver consists (1) if the contract relates to specific goods, or unidentified goods to be drawn from a specific stock or to be manufactured or produced, and at the time of the conclusion of the contract the parties knew that the goods were at, or were to be manufactured or produced at, a particular place, in placing the goods at the buyer's disposal at that place and (2) in other cases, in placing the goods at the buyer's disposal at the place where the seller had his place of business at the time of the conclusion of the contract.

Shipment Contracts The delivery terms *F.O.B. (free on board) place of shipment*, *F.A.S. (free alongside ship) seller's port*, *C.I.F. (cost, insurance, and freight)*, and *C. & F. (cost and freight)* are all shipment contracts. Under a **shipment contract**, the seller is required or authorized to send the goods to the buyer, but the contract does not obligate her to deliver them at a particular destination. In these cases, the seller's tender of performance occurs at the point of shipment, provided the seller meets certain specified conditions designed to protect the interests of the absent buyer.

Under the Code, the initials **F.O.B.** and **F.A.S.** are delivery terms, even though they are used only in connection with a stated price. A contract providing that the sale is **F.O.B.** *place of shipment* or **F.A.S.** *port of shipment* is a shipment contract. Under a **C.I.F.** contract, in consideration for an agreed unit price for the goods, the seller pays all costs of transportation, insurance, and freight to the destination. Under a **C. & F.** contract, he will pay "cost and freight." A seller under a shipment contract is required to (1) deliver the goods to a carrier; (2) make a contract for their transportation that is reasonable according to the nature of the goods and other circumstances; (3) obtain and promptly deliver or tender to the buyer any document necessary to enable the buyer to obtain possession of the goods from the carrier; and (4) promptly notify the buyer of the shipment.

> **CISG** If the seller is not bound to deliver the goods at any other particular place and if the contract of sale involves carriage of the goods, his obligation to deliver consists in handing the goods over to the first carrier for delivery to the buyer.

Destination Contracts The delivery terms *F.O.B. city of buyer*, *ex-ship*, and *no arrival, no sale* are destination contracts. Because a **destination contract** requires the seller to tender delivery of conforming goods at a specified destination, the seller must place the goods at the buyer's disposition and give the buyer reasonable notice to enable him to take delivery. In addition, if the destination contract involves documents of title, the seller must tender the necessary documents.

When the contract provides that the sale is *F.O.B. place of destination*, the seller must at his own expense and risk transport the goods to that place and there tender delivery of them to the buyer. For example, if the buyer is in Boston and the seller is in Chicago, a contract providing F.O.B. Boston is a destination contract under which the seller must tender the goods at the designated place in Boston at his own expense and risk. A contract that provides for delivery **ex-ship**, or "from the ship," is also a destination contract, requiring the seller to unload the goods from the carrier at a named destination. Finally, if the contract contains the terms **no arrival, no sale**, the title and risk of loss do not pass to the buyer until the seller makes a tender of the goods after they arrive at their destination.

> ## PRACTICAL ADVICE
> In your sales contracts clearly specify by use of the correct shipment term or specific language which party pays the shipping costs and where the seller must tender delivery of the goods.

Goods Held by Bailee When goods are in the possession of a bailee and are to be delivered without being moved, in most instances the seller may either tender to the buyer a document of title or obtain an acknowledgment by the bailee of the buyer's right to possess the goods. This acknowledgment permits the buyer to obtain the goods directly from the bailee.

For a summary of performance by the seller, see Figure 20-1.

PERFECT TENDER RULE

The Code's **perfect tender rule** imposes on the seller the obligation to conform her tender of goods *exactly* to the terms of the contract. If either the tender of delivery or the goods fail in any respect to conform to the contract, the buyer may (1) reject the whole lot, (2) accept the whole lot, or (3) accept any commercial unit or units and reject the rest. (Article 2A.) A *commercial unit* means such a unit of goods that by commercial usage is a single unit and that, if divided, would be materially impaired in character or value. (Article 2A.)

Thus, a buyer may rightfully reject the delivery of 110 dozen shirts under an agreement calling for delivery of 100 dozen shirts. The size or extent of the breach does not affect the right to reject. The following case further illustrates the perfect tender rule.

MOULTON CAVITY & MOLD INC. v. LYN-FLEX IND.

SUPREME COURT OF MAINE, 1979
396 A.2D 1024

http://scholar.google.com/scholar_case?case=7850526598237666882&q=396+A.2d+1024&hl=en&as_sclt=2,34

FACTS Moulton Cavity & Mold Inc. agreed to manufacture twenty-six innersole molds to be purchased by Lyn-Flex. Moulton delivered the twenty-six molds to Lyn-Flex after Lyn-Flex allegedly approved the sample molds. However, Lyn-Flex rejected the molds, claiming that they did not satisfy the specifications exactly, and denied that it had ever approved the sample molds. Moulton then sued, contending that Lyn-Flex wrongfully rejected the molds. Lyn-Flex, arguing that the Code's perfect tender rule permitted its rejection of the imperfect molds, regardless of Moulton's substantial performance, appealed from a judgment entered by the trial court in favor of Moulton.

DECISION Judgment for Moulton reversed and a new trial ordered.

OPINION Delahanty, J. In *Smith, Fitzmaurice Co. v. Harris* [citation], a case decided under the common law, we recognized the then-settled rule that with respect to contracts for the sale of goods the buyer has the right to reject the seller's tender if in any way it fails to conform to the specifications of the contract. We held that "[t]he vendor has the duty to comply with his order in kind, quality and amount." [Citation.] Thus, in *Smith*, we ruled that a buyer who had contracted to purchase twelve dozen union suits could lawfully refuse a tender of sixteen dozen union suits. Various provisions of the Uniform Sales Act, enacted in Maine in 1923, codified the common-law approach. [Citation.] The so-called "perfect tender" rule came under considerable fire around the time the Uniform Commercial Code was drafted. No less an authority than

Karl Llewellyn, recognized as the primum mobile of the Code's tender provisions, [citations], attacked the rule principally on the ground that it allowed a dishonest buyer to avoid an unfavorable contract on the basis of an insubstantial defect in the seller's tender. [Citation.] Although Llewellyn's views are represented in many Code sections governing tender, the basic tender provision, Section 2–601, represents a rejection of Llewellyn's approach and a continuation of the perfect tender policy developed by the common law and carried forward by the draftsmen of the Uniform Sales Act. [Citations.] Thus, Section 2–601 states that, with certain exceptions not here applicable, the buyer has the right to reject "if the goods or the tender of delivery fail *in any respect* to conform to the contract * * *" (emphasis supplied). Those few courts that have considered the question agree that the perfect tender rule has survived the enactment of the Code. [Citations.] We, too, are convinced of the soundness of this position.

INTERPRETATION If the seller does not perform his contractual obligations exactly, the buyer may rightfully reject the seller's performance.

CRITICAL THINKING QUESTION Do you agree with the Code's perfect tender rule? Explain.

CISG

The CISG does not follow the perfect tender rule. The buyer may declare the contract avoided if the failure by the seller to perform any of his obligations under the contract or the CISG amounts to a **fundamental** breach of contract. A breach of contract committed by one of the parties is fundamental if it results in such detriment to the other party as substantially to deprive him of what he is entitled to expect under the contract, unless the party in breach did not foresee and a reasonable person of the same kind in the same circumstances would not have foreseen such a result.

Three basic conditions qualify the buyer's right to reject the goods upon the seller's failure to comply with the perfect tender rule: (1) agreement between the parties limiting the buyer's right to reject nonconforming goods, (2) cure by the seller, and (3) the existence of an installment contract. In addition, the perfect tender rule does not apply to a seller's breach of her obligation under a shipment contract to make a proper contract for transportation or to give proper notice of the shipment. A failure to perform either of these obligations is a ground for rejection only if material loss or delay results.

Agreement between the Parties The parties may contractually agree to limit the operation of the perfect tender rule. For example, they may agree that the seller shall have the right to repair or replace any defective parts or goods. We will discuss these contractual limitations in Chapter 23.

> **PRACTICAL ADVICE**
> If you are the seller, consider using a contractual term to limit the operation of the perfect tender rule; if you are the buyer, carefully scrutinize such a limitation.

Cure by the Seller The Code recognizes two situations in which a seller may cure, or correct, a nonconforming tender of goods. This relaxation of the seller's obligation to make a perfect tender gives the seller an opportunity either to make a second delivery or to make a substitute tender. The first opportunity for cure occurs when the time for performance under the contract has not expired. The second opportunity for cure is available after the time for performance has expired but only if the seller had reasonable grounds to believe that the nonconforming tender would be acceptable to the buyer with or without a monetary adjustment.

Figure 20-1
Tender of
Performance
by the Seller

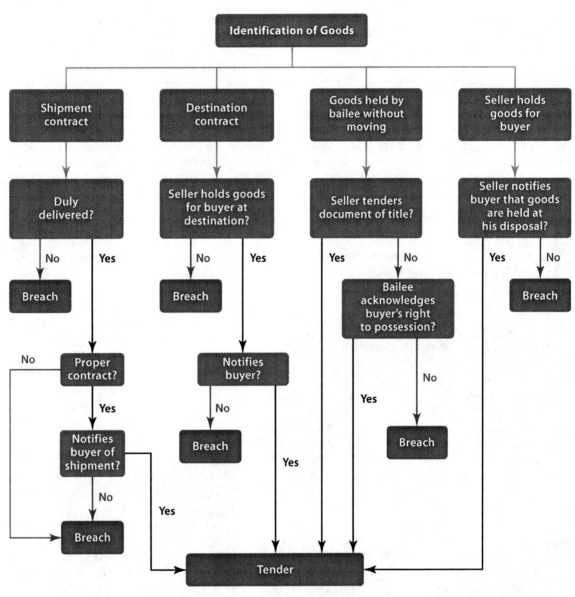

In cases in which the buyer refuses to accept a tender of goods that do not conform to the contract, the seller, by acting promptly and within the time allowed for performance, may make a proper tender or delivery of conforming goods and thereby cure the defective tender or performance. (Article 2A.) Upon notice of the buyer's rightful rejection, the seller must first give the buyer reasonable notice of her intention to cure the defect and must then make a proper tender according to the original contract. This rule gives the seller the full contractual period in which to perform but does not cause any harm to the buyer, who receives full performance within the time agreed to in the contract. For example, Neal is to deliver to Jessica twenty-five blue shirts and fifty white shirts by October 15. On October 1, Neal delivers twenty-nine blue shirts and forty-six white shirts, which Jessica rejects as not conforming to the contract. Jessica notifies Neal of her rejection and the reasons for it. Neal has until October 15 to cure the defect by making a perfect tender, provided he seasonably notifies Jessica of his intention to do so.

The Code also provides the seller an opportunity to cure a nonconforming tender that the seller had reasonable grounds to believe would be acceptable to the buyer with or without a money allowance. (Article 2A.) If, on the buyer's notice of rejection, the seller seasonably notifies the buyer of his intention to cure, the seller is permitted a reasonable time in which to substitute a conforming tender. For example, Tim orders from Noel a model 110X television to be delivered on January 20.

The 110X is unavailable, but Noel can obtain a model 110, which is last year's model of the same television and which lists for 5 percent less than the 110X. On January 20, Noel delivers to Tim the 110 at a discount price of 10 percent less than the contract price for the 110X. Tim rejects the substituted television set. Noel, who promptly notifies Tim that she will obtain and deliver a model 110X, will have a reasonable time beyond the January 20 deadline in which to deliver the 110X television set to Tim, because under these facts she had reasonable grounds to believe the model 110 would be acceptable with the money allowance in Tim's favor.

PRACTICAL ADVICE

If you want to exercise the seller's right to cure, be sure to give the buyer timely notice of your intent to cure.

CISG

If the seller has delivered goods before the date for delivery, he may, up to that date, cure any deficiency, provided that the exercise of this right does not cause the buyer unreasonable inconvenience or unreasonable expense. However, the buyer retains any right to claim damages as provided for in the CISG. If the seller does not perform on time, the buyer may fix an additional period of time of reasonable length for performance by the seller of his obligations. Unless the buyer has received notice from the seller that the seller will not perform within the period so fixed, the buyer may not, during that period, resort to any remedy for breach of contract. However, the buyer retains any right he may have to claim damages for delay in performance. If the seller does not deliver the goods within the additional period of time or declares that he will not deliver within the period so fixed, the buyer may declare the contract avoided.

The seller may, even after the date for delivery, cure a defective performance, if he can do so without unreasonable delay and without causing the buyer unreasonable inconvenience. However, the buyer retains any right to claim damages for delay in performance. If the seller requests the buyer to make known whether he will accept performance and the buyer does not comply with the request within a reasonable time, the seller may perform within the time indicated in his request.

Installment Contracts Unless the parties have otherwise agreed, the buyer does not have to pay any part of the price of the goods until the seller has delivered or tendered to her the entire quantity specified in the contract. An **installment contract** represents an instance in which the parties have otherwise agreed. It expressly provides for delivery of the goods in separate lots or installments and usually provides for payment of the price in installments. If the contract is silent about payment, the Code provides that the seller may demand the price, if it can be apportioned, for each lot.

The buyer may reject any nonconforming installment if the nonconformity substantially impairs the value of that installment and cannot be cured. However, he cannot reject if the nonconforming installment substantially impairs the value of the installment but not the value of the entire contract if the seller gives adequate assurance of the installment's cure. (Article 2A.) On the other hand, whenever the nonconformity or default of one or more of the installments substantially impairs the value of the whole contract, the buyer can treat the breach as a breach of the whole contract. (Article 2A.)

CISG

When a contract calls for delivery of goods by installments, if the seller's failure to perform any of his obligations with respect to any installment constitutes a fundamental breach of contract with respect to that installment, the buyer may declare the contract avoided with respect to that installment. A buyer who declares the contract avoided with respect to any delivery may, at the same time, declare it avoided with respect to deliveries already made or to future deliveries if, by reason of their interdependence, those deliveries could not be used for the purpose contemplated by the parties at the time of the conclusion of the contract. If the seller's failure to perform any of his obligations with respect to any installment gives the buyer good grounds to conclude that a fundamental breach of contract will occur with respect to future installments, he may declare the contract avoided for the future, provided that he does so within a reasonable time.

Performance by the Buyer

A buyer is obliged to accept conforming goods and to pay for them according to the contract terms. (Article 2A.) Payment or tender of payment by the buyer, unless otherwise agreed, is a condition of the seller's duty to tender and to complete any delivery. The buyer is not obliged to accept a tender or delivery of goods that do not conform to the contract. Upon determining that the tender or delivery is nonconforming, the buyer has three choices. He may (1) reject all of the goods, (2) accept all of the goods, or (3) accept any commercial unit or units of the goods and reject the rest. (Article 2A.) The buyer must pay the contract rate for the commercial units he accepts.

> **CISG**
>
> The buyer must pay the price for the goods and take delivery of them as required by the contract and the CISG.

INSPECTION

Unless the parties agree otherwise, the buyer has a right to inspect the goods before payment or acceptance. (Article 2A provides for the right to inspect before acceptance.) This **inspection** enables the buyer to determine whether the goods tendered or delivered conform to the contract. If the contract requires payment before acceptance (e.g., when the contract provides for shipment C.O.D., collect on delivery), payment must be made prior to inspection; however, such payment is not an acceptance of the goods and impairs neither the buyer's right to inspect nor any of her remedies.

The buyer, allowed a reasonable time to inspect the goods, may lose the right to reject or revoke acceptance of nonconforming goods by failing to inspect them within such time. Nevertheless, although the buyer must bear the expenses of inspection, she may recover them from the seller if the goods do not conform and are rightfully rejected. (Article 2A.)

> **PRACTICAL ADVICE**
>
> If you are the buyer, carefully inspect tendered goods before accepting them. If this is not feasible, inspect the goods as soon as possible.

> **CISG**
>
> The buyer is not bound to pay the price until he has had an opportunity to examine the goods, unless the parties have agreed otherwise. The buyer must examine the goods within as short a period of time as is practicable in the circumstances. The buyer loses the right to rely on a lack of conformity of the goods if he does not give notice to the seller of the nonconformity within a reasonable time after he has discovered it or ought to have discovered it.

REJECTION

Rejection is a manifestation by the buyer of her unwillingness to become the owner of the goods. It must be made within a reasonable time after the goods have been tendered or delivered and is not effective unless the buyer reasonably notifies the seller. (Article 2A.)

Rejection of the goods may be rightful or wrongful, depending on whether the goods tendered or delivered conform to the contract. The buyer's rejection of nonconforming goods or tender is rightful under the perfect tender rule.

If the buyer refuses a tender of goods or rejects it as nonconforming without disclosing to the seller the nature of the defect, she may not assert such defect as an excuse for not accepting the goods or as a breach of contract by the seller if the defect is curable. (Article 2A.)

After the buyer has rejected the goods, the Code allows her to exercise no ownership of them. (Since the lessor retains title in a lease, this does not apply to leases.) If the buyer possesses the rejected goods but has no security interest in them, she is obliged to hold them with reasonable care for a time sufficient to permit the seller to remove them. (Article 2A.) The buyer who is not a merchant is under no further obligation with regard to goods rightfully rejected. (Article 2A.)

If the seller gives no instructions within a reasonable time after notification of rejection, the buyer may (1) store the goods for the seller's account, (2) reship them to the seller, or (3) resell them for the seller's account. Such action is not an acceptance or conversion of the goods. (Article 2A.) A merchant buyer of goods who has rightfully rejected them has additional duties: she is obligated to follow reasonable instructions from the seller regarding disposal of the goods in her possession or control when the seller has no agent or business at the place of rejection. (Article 2A.) If the merchant buyer receives no instructions from the seller within a reasonable time after giving notice of the rejection, and if the rejected goods are perishable or threaten to decline in value speedily, she is obligated to make reasonable efforts to sell them for the seller's account. (Article 2A.)

When the buyer sells the rejected goods, she is entitled to reimbursement for the reasonable expenses of caring for and selling them and to a reasonable selling commission not to exceed 10 percent of the gross proceeds. (Article 2A.)

PRACTICAL ADVICE

If you have rejected nonconforming goods, be sure to notify the seller in a timely manner and do not exercise ownership of the rejected goods.

CISG

If the goods do not conform with the contract and the nonconformity constitutes a fundamental breach of contract, the buyer may require delivery of substitute goods. If the buyer has received the goods and intends to exercise any right under the contract or the CISG to reject them, he must take such steps to preserve them as are reasonable in the circumstances. He is entitled to retain them until he has been reimbursed his reasonable expenses by the seller.

FURLONG v. ALPHA CHI OMEGA SORORITY

BOWLING GREEN COUNTY MUNICIPAL COURT, 1993
73 OHIO MISC.2D 26, 657 N.E.2D 866
http://scholar.google.com/scholar_case?case=13710936984230391946&q=657+N.E.2d+866&hl=en&as_sdt=2,34

FACTS Alpha Chi Omega (AXO), a sorority, entered into an oral contract with Furlong to buy 168 "custom-designed" sweaters for the Midnight Masquerade III. The purchase price of $3,612 was to be paid as follows: $2,000 down payment and $1,612 upon delivery. During phone conversations with Furlong, Emily, the AXO social chairperson, described the design to be imprinted on the sweater. She also specified the colors to be used in the lettering (hunter green on top of maroon outlined in navy blue) and the color of the mask design (hunter green). Furlong promised to have a third party imprint the sweaters as specified. Furlong later sent to Emily a sweater with maroon letters to show her the color. He then sent her a fax illustrating the sweater design with arrows indicating where each of the three colors was to appear. On the day before delivery was due, Argento, Furlong's supplier, requested design changes, which Furlong approved without the consent of AXO. These changes included deleting the navy blue outline, reducing the number of colors from three to two, changing the maroon lettering to red, and changing the color of the masks from hunter green to red. Upon delivery, AXO gave a check for the balance of the purchase price. Later that day, Emily inspected the sweaters and was dismayed at the design changes. AXO immediately stopped payment on the check. Amy, the president of AXO, phoned Furlong, stating that the sweaters were not what AXO had ordered. She gave the specifics as to why the sweaters were not as ordered and offered to return them. Furlong refused but offered to reduce the unit price of the sweaters if AXO agreed to accept them. AXO refused this offer. Furlong then filed suit against AXO for the unpaid portion of the sweaters' purchase price ($1,612) and AXO counterclaimed for return of the down payment ($2,000).

DECISION Judgment for AXO. The court ordered Furlong to pay $2,000 plus interest and costs and AXO to return the sweaters upon such payment.

OPINION Bachman, J. Furlong and Emily created an express warranty by *** affirmation of fact (his initial phone calls); by sample (the maroon sweater); by description (the fax). This express warranty became part of the contract. Each of the three methods of showing the express warranty was not in conflict with the other two methods, and thus they are consistent and cumulative [U.C.C. § 2–317], and constitute the warranty.

The design was a "dickered" aspect of the individual bargain and went clearly to the essence of that bargain ([U.C.C. § 2–313]; Official Comment 1 to UCC 2–313). Thus, the express warranty was that the sweaters would be in accordance with the above design (including types of colors for the letters and the mask, and the number of colors for the same). Further, the express warranty became part of the contract.

***

Furlong's obligation as the seller was to transfer and deliver the goods in accordance with the contract. AXO's obligation was to accept and pay in accordance with that contract [U.C.C. § 2–301].

***

The sweaters did not conform to the contract (specifically, the express warranty in the contract). Thus (in the words of the statute), the sweaters did "fail in any respect to conform to the contract." Actually, the sweaters failed in at least five respects [U.C.C. § 2–601]. *** they were a nonconforming tender of goods [U.C.C. § 2–601].

***

AXO, as the buyer, had the right to inspect the boxes of sweaters before payment or acceptance [U.C.C. § 2–513]. AXO did so at a reasonable time and place, and in a reasonable manner, on the same day that Furlong had sent the sweaters and AXO had received them [U.C.C. § 2–513]. AXO's purpose of inspection had (in the words of the statute) "to do with the buyer's check-up on whether the seller's performance is in accordance with a contract previously made ***." (Official Comment 9 to UCC 2–513.)

* * *

According to the statute, "if the goods *** fail in any respect to conform to the contract, the buyer may: (A) reject the whole *** [.]" [U.C.C. § 2–601]. As concluded above, the sweaters were nonconforming goods. Therefore, Furlong breached the contract, and AXO had the right to reject the goods (sweaters).

* * *

As concluded above, AXO rightfully rejected the sweaters, after having paid part of the purchase price: namely $2,000. AXO is entitled to cancel the contract and to recover the partial payment of the purchase price. [Citation.]

INTERPRETATION If the goods fail in any respect to conform to the contract, the buyer may reject the whole lot.

ETHICAL QUESTION Did Furlong act in bad faith by not seeking AXO's consent to the changes? Explain.

CRITICAL THINKING QUESTION Does the court's decision remedy the situation in which the seller's breach left the sorority? Explain.

ACCEPTANCE

Acceptance of goods means a willingness by the buyer to become the owner of the goods tendered or delivered to her by the seller. Acceptance of the goods, which precludes any later rejection of them, includes overt acts or conduct that manifest such willingness. (Article 2A.) Such acts or conduct may include express words, the presumed intention of the buyer through her failure to act, or conduct of the buyer inconsistent with the seller's ownership of the goods. More specifically, acceptance occurs when the buyer, after a reasonable opportunity to inspect the goods (1) signifies to the seller that the goods conform to the contract, (2) signifies to the seller that she will take the goods or retain them in spite of their nonconformity to the contract, or (3) fails to make an effective rejection of the goods. (Article 2A.)

Acceptance of any part of a commercial unit is acceptance of the entire unit. (Article 2A.) The buyer must pay at the contract rate for any goods she accepts but may recover damages for any nonconformity of the goods, provided the buyer reasonably notifies the seller of any breach. (Article 2A, except for finance leases in some situations.) For example, Nancy agrees to deliver to Paul five hundred light bulbs, one hundred watts each, for $300 and one thousand light bulbs, sixty watts each, for $500. Nancy delivers on time, but the shipment contains only four hundred of the hundred-watt bulbs and seven hundred fifty of the sixty-watt bulbs. If Paul accepts the shipment, he must pay Nancy $240 for the hundred-watt bulbs accepted and $375 for the sixty-watt bulbs accepted, less the amount of damages Nancy's nonconforming delivery caused him.

REVOCATION OF ACCEPTANCE

A buyer might accept defective goods either because it is difficult to discover the defect by inspection or because the buyer reasonably assumes that the seller will correct the defect. In either instance, the buyer may revoke his acceptance of the goods if the uncorrected defect substantially impairs the value of the goods to him. **Revocation of acceptance** gives the buyer the same rights and duties with respect to the goods as he would have acquired by rejecting them. (Article 2A.)

More specifically, the buyer may revoke acceptance of goods that do not conform to the contract if the nonconformity *substantially* impairs the value of the goods to him, provided that his acceptance was (1) premised on the reasonable assumption that the seller would cure the nonconformity, and it was not seasonably cured or (2) made without discovery of the nonconformity, and such acceptance was reasonably induced by the difficulty of discovery before acceptance or by the seller's assurances. (Article 2A.)

Revocation of acceptance is not effective until notification is given to the seller. This must be done within a reasonable time after the buyer discovers or should have discovered the grounds for revocation and before the goods have undergone any substantial change not caused by their own defects. (Article 2A.)

PRACTICAL ADVICE

If you have cause to revoke your acceptance of goods, be sure to notify the seller within a reasonable time after discovering the grounds for revocation.

WADDELL V. L.V.R.V. INC.

SUPREME COURT OF NEVADA, 2006
125 P.3D 1160

http://caselaw.lp.findlaw.com/scripts/getcase.pl?court=nv&vol=122NevAdvOpNo3&invol=2

FACTS L.V.R.V. Inc., doing business as Wheeler's Las Vegas RV (Wheeler's) sold a 1996 Coachmen Santara motor home (the RV) to Arthur R. Waddell and Roswitha M. Waddell. Before they took possession of the RV, the Waddells requested that Wheeler's perform various repairs, including service on the RV's engine cooling system, new batteries, and alignment of the door frames. Wheeler's told Arthur Waddell that the repairs had been performed, and the Waddells took delivery of the RV on September 1, 1997.

The Waddells first noticed a problem with the RV's engine shortly after they took possession of it. They drove the RV from Las Vegas to Hemet, California. On the return trip, while climbing a moderate grade, the RV's engine overheated so much that Mr. Waddell had to pull over to the side of the road and wait for the engine to cool down. When the Waddells returned from California, they took the RV back to Wheeler's for repairs. Despite Wheeler's attempts to repair the RV, the Waddells continually experienced further episodes of engine overheating. Between September 1997 and March 1999, Wheeler's service department spent a total of seven months attempting to repair the RV.

On June 9, 2000, the Waddells filed a complaint in district court seeking both equitable relief and money damages. The district court concluded that the RV's nonconformities substantially impaired its value to the Waddells and allowed the Waddells to revoke their acceptance of the RV.

DECISION Affirmed in relevant part.

OPINION Gibbons, J. [U.C.C. § 2–608(1)] provides that a buyer may revoke his acceptance if the item suffers from a "nonconformity [that] substantially impairs its value to him" and (a) the buyer accepted the goods on the understanding that the seller would cure the nonconformity or (b) the buyer was unaware of the nonconformity and the nonconformity was concealed by the difficulty of discovery or by the seller's assurances that the good was conforming.

***

The Supreme Court of Oregon has established a two-part test to determine whether a nonconformity, under the totality of the circumstances, substantially impairs the value of the goods to the buyer. The test has both an objective and a subjective prong:

Since [the statute] provides that the buyer may revoke acceptance of goods "whose nonconformity substantially impairs its value to him," the value of conforming goods to the plaintiff must first be determined. This is a subjective question in the sense that it calls for a consideration of the needs and circumstances of the plaintiff who seeks to revoke; not the needs and circumstances of an average buyer. The second inquiry is whether the nonconformity in fact substantially impairs the value of the goods to the buyer, having in mind his particular needs. This is an objective question in the sense that it calls for evidence of something more than plaintiff's assertion that the non-conformity impaired the value to him; it requires evidence from which it can be inferred that plaintiff's needs were not met because of the nonconformity. [Citation.]

*** [W]e adopt the Supreme Court of Oregon's two-part test ***.

***

Mr. Waddell's testimony demonstrates that the RV's subjective value to the Waddells was based on their ability to spend two or three years driving the RV around the country. Thus, we must consider whether the RV's nonconformities substantially impaired the value of the RV based on the Waddells' particular needs.

Mr. Waddell testified that as a result of the RV's defects, he and his wife were unable to enjoy the RV as they had intended. Mr. Waddell further testified that the RV's engine would overheat within ten miles of embarking if the travel included any climbing. As a result of the overheating, the Waddells were forced to park on the side of the road and wait for the engine to cool down before continuing. Consequently, the RV spent a total of 213 days, or seven months and one day, at Wheeler's service department during the eighteen months immediately following the purchase. This testimony is sufficient to demonstrate an objective, substantial impairment of value.

***

Accordingly, we conclude that substantial evidence exists to support revocation of acceptance under [U.C.C. § 2–608(1)].

***

Under [U.C.C. § 2–608(2)], "revocation of acceptance must occur within a reasonable time after the buyer discovers or should have discovered the ground for it and before any substantial change in condition of the goods which is not caused by their own defects." ***

***

The seller of nonconforming goods must generally receive an opportunity to cure the nonconformity before the buyer may revoke his acceptance. * * *

Furthermore, the seller's attempts to cure do not count against the buyer regarding timely revocation. The United States District Court for the District of Nevada has held that the "time for revocation of acceptance will be tolled while the seller attempts repairs." Tolling the reasonable time for revocation of acceptance is appropriate given "the buyer's obligation to act in good faith, and to afford the seller a reasonable opportunity to cure any defect in the goods." [Citation.]

The Waddells gave Wheeler's several opportunities to repair the defects before revoking their acceptance. Because Wheeler's was unable to repair the defects after a total of seven months, the Waddells were entitled to say "that's all" and revoke their acceptance, notwithstanding Wheeler's good-faith attempts to repair the RV. Also, the reasonable time for revocation was tolled during the seven months that Wheeler's kept the RV and attempted to repair the defects. Accordingly, the district court's determination is supported by substantial evidence and is not clearly erroneous.

INTERPRETATION A buyer may revoke his acceptance if the goods suffer from a nonconformity that substantially impairs their value to him subject to the seller's right to cure the nonconformity; however, the seller's attempts to cure do not count against the buyer regarding timely revocation.

CRITICAL THINKING QUESTION Do you agree with the requirements for revocation of acceptance? Explain.

OBLIGATION OF PAYMENT

The terms of the contract may expressly state the time and place at which the buyer is obligated to pay for the goods. If so, these terms are controlling. Thus, if the buyer has agreed to pay either the seller or a carrier for the goods in advance of delivery, his duty to pay is not conditional on performance or a tender of performance by the seller. Furthermore, when the sale is on credit, the buyer is not obligated to pay for the goods when he receives them. The credit provision in the contract will control the time of payment.

In the absence of agreement, payment is due at the time and place the buyer is to receive the goods, even though the place of shipment is the place of delivery. This rule is understandable in view of the right of the buyer, in the absence of agreement to the contrary, to inspect the goods before being obliged to pay for them. Tender of payment is sufficient when made by any means or in any manner current, such as a check, in the ordinary course of business, unless the seller demands cash and allows the buyer a reasonable time within which to obtain it.

For a summary of performance by the buyer, see Figure 20-2.

CISG Unless the buyer is bound to pay the price at any other specific time, he must pay it when the seller places either the goods or documents controlling their disposition at the buyer's disposal in accordance with the contract and the CISG. The seller may make such payment a condition for handing over the goods or documents. If the buyer is not bound to pay the price at any other particular place, he must pay it to the seller (1) at the seller's place of business or (2) if the payment is to be made against the handing over of the goods or of documents, at the place where the handing over takes place.

Obligations of Both Parties

Contracts for the sale of goods necessarily involve risks concerning future events that may or may not occur. Though in some instances the parties explicitly allocate these risks, in most instances they do not. The Code contains three sections that allocate these risks when the parties fail to do so. Each provision, when applicable, relieves the parties from the obligation of full performance under the sales contract. (See also the Ethical Dilemma at the end of this chapter.)

Related to the subject of whether the Code will excuse performance is the question of whether both parties will

PRACTICAL ADVICE
Specify in your sales contract the time and other terms of payment.

Figure 20-2
Performance by the Buyer

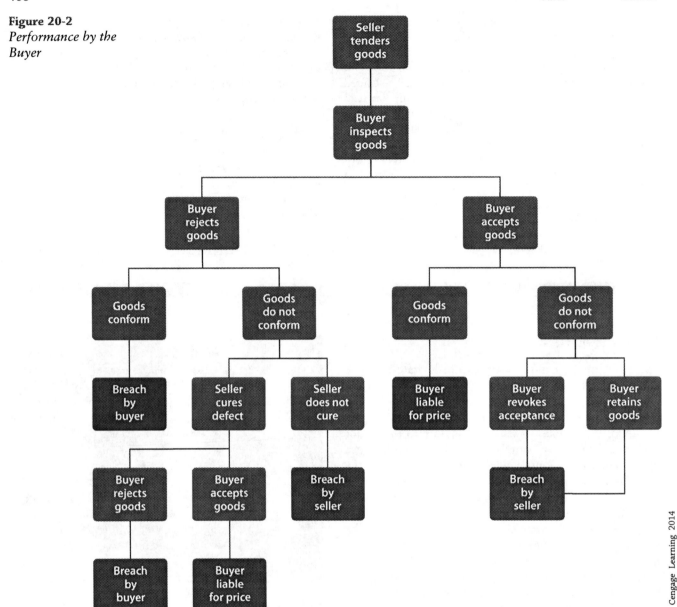

© Cengage Learning 2014

be able and willing to perform. In such instances, the Code allows the insecure party to seek reasonable assurance of the potentially defaulting party's willingness and ability to perform. In addition, if one of the parties clearly indicates an unwillingness or inability to perform, the Code protects the other party.

CASUALTY TO IDENTIFIED GOODS

If goods are destroyed before an offer to sell or to buy them is accepted, the offer is terminated by general contract law. But what if the goods are destroyed after the sales contract is formed? The rules for the passage of risk of loss, as discussed in Chapter 21, apply with one exception: the contract is for goods that are **identified** when the contract was made and the goods suffer damage without fault of either party *before* the risk of loss passes to the buyer. The outcome of this situation depends upon the degree of damage. (1) If these goods are totally lost or damaged, the contract is avoided. (Article 2A.) This means that each party is excused from his obligation to perform under the contract: the seller is no longer obligated to deliver, and the buyer need not pay the price. (2) In the case of a partial destruction or deterioration of the goods, the buyer has the option to avoid the contract or to accept the goods with due allowance or deduction from the contract price sufficient to account for the deterioration or deficiency in quantity. (Article 2A, except in a finance lease that is not a consumer lease.)

On the other hand, if the destruction or damage to the goods, whether total or partial, occurs *after* risk of loss has passed to the buyer, then the buyer has no option but must pay the entire contract price of the goods.

NONHAPPENING OF PRESUPPOSED CONDITION

Central to the Code's approach to impossibility of performance is the concept of **commercial impracticability**. Under this concept, the Code will excuse performance that, even though not actually or literally impossible, is commercially impracticable. This, however, requires more than mere hardship or increased cost of performance. For a party to be discharged, performance must be rendered impracticable as a result of an unforeseen supervening event not within the contemplation of the parties at the time of contracting. Moreover, the nonoccurrence of the event must have been a "basic assumption" that both parties made when entering into the contract. (Article 2A.) See *Northern Corporation v. Chugach Electrical Association* in Chapter 17.

Increased production cost alone does not excuse performance by the seller, nor does a collapse of the market for the goods excuse the buyer. But a party to a contract for the sale of programs for a scheduled Super Bowl that is called off, for the sale of tin horns for export that become subject to embargo, or for the production of goods at a designated factory that becomes damaged or destroyed by fire would be excused.

Although the nonhappening of presupposed conditions may relieve the seller of her contractual duty, if the contingency affects only a part of the seller's capacity to perform, the seller must, to the extent of her remaining capacity, allocate delivery and production in a fair and reasonable manner among her customers. (Article 2A.)

PRACTICAL ADVICE

Specify in your contract which events will excuse the nonperformance of the contract, the basic assumptions of your contract, and which risks are assumed by each of the parties.

CISG

A party is not liable for a failure to perform any of his obligations if he proves that the failure was due to an impediment beyond his control and that he could not reasonably be expected to have taken the impediment into account at the time of the conclusion of the contract or to have avoided or overcome it or its consequences.

SUBSTITUTED PERFORMANCE

The Code provides that when neither party is at fault and the agreed-upon manner of delivering the goods becomes commercially impracticable—because of the failure of loading or unloading facilities or the unavailability of an agreed-upon type of carrier, for example—a substituted manner of performance, if commercially reasonable, must be tendered and accepted. (Article 2A.) When a practical alternative or substitute exists, the Code excuses neither seller nor buyer on the ground that delivery in the express manner provided in the contract is impossible.

RIGHT TO ADEQUATE ASSURANCE OF PERFORMANCE

A contract of sale also requires that each party not impair the other party's expectation of having the contract performed. Therefore, when reasonable grounds for insecurity arise regarding either party's performance, the other party may demand written assurance and suspend his own performance until he receives that assurance. The failure to provide adequate assurance of performance within a reasonable time, not exceeding thirty days, constitutes a repudiation of the contract. (Article 2A.)

CISG

A party may suspend the performance of his obligations if, after the conclusion of the contract, it becomes apparent that the other party will not perform a substantial part of his obligations. A party suspending performance must immediately notify the other party of the suspension and must continue with performance if the other party provides adequate assurance of his performance.

RIGHT TO COOPERATION

When one party's cooperation is necessary to the agreed performance but is not timely forthcoming, the other party is excused with regard to any resulting delay in her own performance. The nonbreaching party either may proceed to perform in any reasonable manner or, if the time for her performance has occurred, may treat the other's failure to cooperate as a breach. In either event, the nonbreaching party has access to any other remedies the Code may provide, as discussed in Chapter 23.

ANTICIPATORY REPUDIATION

Although a repudiation in itself is a clear indication by either party to a contract that he is unwilling or unable to perform his obligations under the contract, an **anticipatory repudiation** is a repudiation made *before* the time to perform occurs. It may occur by express communication or by the repudiating party's taking an action that makes performance impossible, such as selling unique goods to a third party. It also may result from the failure of a party to give timely assurance of performance after a justifiable demand. If an anticipatory repudiation substantially impairs the value of the contract, the aggrieved party may (1) await performance for a commercially reasonable time or (2) resort to any remedy for breach. In either case, he may suspend his own performance. (Article 2A.) The repudiating party may retract his anticipatory repudiation and thereby reinstate the contract unless the aggrieved party has canceled the contract, has materially changed her position, or has otherwise indicated that she considers the anticipatory repudiation final. (Article 2A.)

 If prior to the date for performance of the contract it is clear that one of the parties will commit a fundamental breach of contract, the other party may declare the contract avoided.

HESSLER v. CRYSTAL LAKE CHRYSLER-PLYMOUTH, INC.

APPELLATE COURT OF ILLINOIS, SECOND DISTRICT, 2003
788 N.E.2D 405, 273 ILL.DEC. 96, 50 U.C.C. REP.SERV.2D 330

http://scholar.google.com/scholar_case?case=8385072036048572860&q=788+n.e.2d+405&hl=en&as_sdt=2,34

FACTS In February 1997, Chrysler Corporation introduced a new promotional vehicle called the Plymouth Prowler but did not reveal whether it would manufacture any of the vehicles. Donald Hessler (the plaintiff), aware of the vehicle and of its uncertain production, contacted several dealerships to inquire about purchasing a Prowler. On February 5, 1997, plaintiff met with Gary Rosenberg, co-owner of Crystal Lake Chrysler-Plymouth, Inc. (defendant) and signed a "Retail Order for a Motor Vehicle" (Agreement). The Agreement, which was filled out primarily by Rosenberg, stated that the order was for a 1997, V6, two-door, purple Plymouth Prowler and provided "Customer to pay $5,000 00/100 over list price by manufacturer. Money refundable if can not [deliver] by 12/30/97. Dealer to keep car 2 weeks."

The order noted that plaintiff had deposited $5,000 for the car. The Agreement contained a box labeled "TO BE DELIVERED ON OR ABOUT." Inside the box was written "ASAP," which term Rosenberg stated is used in his business "in lieu of a stock number. Just line it up in order. As soon as you can get it done, do it." Rosenberg testified that Hessler was the first person to place an order for a Prowler and that Rosenberg was "pretty sure" that plaintiff's order was the first order on which he received a deposit. On May 11, 1997, Rosenberg and Hessler agreed that the information they had received was that the manufacturer's list price would be $39,000.

On May 23, 1997, Salvatore Palandri entered into a contract with defendant to purchase a 1997 Plymouth Prowler. His contract reflected a purchase price of "50,000 + tax + lic + doc" and a $10,000 deposit. It also stated that Palandri would receive the "first one delivered to [the] dealership."

Plaintiff testified that on August 11, 1997, Rosenberg informed plaintiff that no Prowlers would be delivered to the Midwest and that he would be returning plaintiff's check. Defendant, according to the plaintiff, nevertheless, stated that should defendant receive a vehicle, it would be plaintiff's. Defendant denies having stated this.

Plaintiff testified that he attended a Chrysler customer appreciation event at Great America on September 19 and spoke to a company representative about the Prowler. Two days later, the representative sent him a fax that contained a tentative list of dealers who were to receive Prowlers. Defendant's name was on the list. Plaintiff testified that he called Rosenberg on September 22 to notify him that his dealership was on a list of dealers due to receive Prowlers. Rosenberg informed plaintiff that he would not sell plaintiff a car because plaintiff had gone behind Rosenberg's back and that contacting Chrysler would cause Rosenberg problems. Rosenberg also stated that plaintiff was not the first person with whom he contracted to sell a Prowler. Plaintiff protested, and Rosenberg informed him that he would not sell plaintiff the car.

Beginning on September 23, 1997, plaintiff contacted thirty-eight Chrysler-Plymouth dealerships to inquire about purchasing a 1997 Prowler, but did not obtain one. On October 24, 1997, plaintiff attended a Prowler coming-out party at the Hard Rock Cafe and saw a purple Prowler in the parking lot with a sign in its window that had defendant's name written on it. On October 25, plaintiff went to defendant's showroom and saw a Prowler parked there. He found Rosenberg and informed him that he was there to pick up his car. Rosenberg stated that he was not going to sell plaintiff the car and that he did not want to do business with him. Later that day, plaintiff purchased a Prowler from another dealer for $77,706. On October 27, 1997, defendant sold the only Prowler it received in that year to Palandri for a total sale price of $54,859, including his $10,000 deposit.

On April 23, 1998, plaintiff sued defendant for breach of contract. The trial court entered judgment for plaintiff and awarded him $29,853 in damages. It concluded that defendant breached the Agreement and that plaintiff properly covered by purchasing a replacement vehicle for $29,853 more than the contract price. The trial court also concluded that defendant repudiated its contract in September and October of 1997 when Rosenberg told plaintiff that he would not sell him a car. It found plaintiff "ready, willing, and able to perform the contract." The court found that the price plaintiff paid for the car at another dealership was the best price he could receive for a Prowler after Rosenberg's refusal to sell to him a car.

DECISION The judgment of the trial court is affirmed.

OPINION Callum, J. Under the UCC, certain actions by a party to a contract may constitute an anticipatory repudiation of the contract if the actions are sufficiently clear manifestations of an intent not to perform under the contract. [UCC §] 2–610; [citation.]

* * *

Comment 1 to section 2–610 provides, in relevant part:

Anticipatory repudiation centers upon an overt communication of intention or an action which renders performance impossible or demonstrates a clear determination not to continue with performance.

* * * When such a repudiation substantially impairs the value of the contract, the aggrieved party may at any time resort to his remedies for breach * * *.

[UCC §] 2–610, Comment.

Comment 2 to Section 2–610 provides, in relevant part: "It is not necessary for repudiation that performance be made literally and utterly impossible. Repudiation can result from action which reasonably indicates a rejection of the continuing obligation."

[UCC §] 2–610, Comment.

* * *

Upon learning that defendant was on a tentative list to receive a Prowler, plaintiff testified that he called Rosenberg to relate the information and that Rosenberg responded that plaintiff was not the first person to contract to purchase a Prowler. Rosenberg also stated that he would not do business with plaintiff. Further, Rosenberg's testimony about this conversation corroborated plaintiff's, in that Rosenberg stated that he told plaintiff that the vehicle was already "committed." The trial court also heard both plaintiff and Rosenberg testify that, when plaintiff went to defendant's showroom on October 25 and informed Rosenberg that he was there to pick up his car, Rosenberg told plaintiff that he did not want to do business with him.

We conclude that the trial court did not err in finding that defendant's foregoing actions reasonably indicated to plaintiff that defendant would not deliver to him a Prowler under the Agreement. As we determined above, defendant contracted to deliver a Prowler to plaintiff as soon as possible. It was not against the manifest weight of the evidence for the trial court to find that defendant repudiated the Agreement when it repeatedly informed plaintiff that it would not deliver to him the first Prowler it received. Such actions made it sufficiently clear to plaintiff that defendant would not perform under the Agreement. [Citation.]

* * * With respect to plaintiff's actions, section 2–610(b) of the UCC provides that an aggrieved party may "resort to any remedy for breach" of the contract "even though he has notified the repudiating party that he would await the latter's performance." [UCC §] 2–610(b). One such remedy is to cover. [UCC §] 2–711(1)(a) (buyer may effect cover, upon seller's repudiation, whether or not buyer cancels the contract).

Defendant next asserts that, even if there was a repudiation in September or October of 1997, plaintiff did nothing to indicate that he thought this was the case. He took no self-help measures such as: terminating the contract; seeking to enjoin the sale to Palandri; requesting a retraction; or suspending his performance obligations. Again, we disagree. The UCC does not require a party to request assurances as a condition precedent to recovery. [Citation.]

For the foregoing reasons, we conclude that the trial court's finding of repudiation was not against the manifest weight of the evidence.

Ethical Dilemma

Should a Buyer Refuse to Perform a Contract Because a Legal Product May Be Unsafe?

FACTS Carson and Olson are partners in a landscape and gardening business that operates out of three major locations and employs approximately thirty people. The business provides general lawn care predominately for residential homes; its services include grass cutting, fertilizing, and trimming of shrubbery. Carson and Olson also provide landscape design services.

One year ago, Carson and Olson entered into a two-year contract with Chem-Care, which manufactures chemical-based fertilizers effective in weed control. Because the contract was for a long term and because Carson and Olson have been excellent Chem-Care customers for the past fifteen years, they obtained an extremely favorable price of $40,000 for a two-year supply of Chem-Care fertilizers.

Chem-Care fertilizers have been approved by the government and do not violate any standards currently in place. Nevertheless, due to publicity concerning health problems associated with certain chemical lawn treatments, the majority of Carson and Olson's customers now have decided that they no longer want chemical lawn treatments. Concerned by the health hazards associated with chemical fertilizers, the customers insist upon natural fertilizers.

Carson wants to cancel the contract with Chem-Care. But Olson feels a sense of loyalty to Chem-Care and wants to honor the contract by trying to find new customers who would be willing to use the Chem-Care products.

Social, Policy, and Ethical Considerations

1. Should Carson and Olson attempt to invalidate the contract? Compare the social value of enforcing promises made with the good faith intention of being legally bound against the value of protecting the public from health or environmental threats.

2. Is it premature to characterize Chem-Care products as a threat to health or the environment?

3. Should the law excuse the performance of contracts that involve products that are under investigation for posing health or environmental problems?

4. As a practical matter, what should Carson and Olson do? Given the question as to the safety of Chem-Care products, does Olson's suggestion of getting new customers for Chem-Care products make sense from an ethical or a business standpoint?

© Cengage Learning 2014

INTERPRETATION If an anticipatory repudiation substantially impairs the value of the contract, the injured party may await performance for a commercially reasonable time or resort to any remedy for breach.

CRITICAL THINKING QUESTION At what point should a buyer have a reasonable basis for believing the seller had repudiated? Explain.

CHAPTER SUMMARY

Performance by the Seller

Tender of Delivery the seller makes available to the buyer goods conforming to the contract and so notifies the buyer
- Buyer is obligated to accept conforming goods
- Seller is entitled to receive payment of the contract price

Time of Tender tender must be made at a reasonable time and kept open for a reasonable period of time

Place of Tender if none is specified, place for delivery is the seller's place of business or, if he has no such place, his residence
- *Shipment Contracts* seller is required to tender delivery of the goods to a carrier for delivery to buyer; shipment terms include F.O.B. (free on board) place of shipment, F.A.S.

(free alongside ship) port of shipment, C.I.F. (cost, insurance, and freight), and C. & F. (cost and freight).

* *Destination Contracts* seller is required to tender delivery of the goods at a named destination; destination terms include F.O.B. place of destination, ex-ship, and no arrival, no sale
* *Goods Held by Bailee* seller must either tender to the buyer a document of title or obtain an acknowledgment from the bailee

Perfect Tender Rule the seller's tender of performance must conform exactly to the contract, subject to the following qualifications:

* *Agreement between the Parties* the parties may contractually limit the operation of the perfect tender rule
* *Cure by the Seller* when the time for performance under the contract has not expired or when the seller has shipped nonconforming goods in the belief that the nonconforming tender would be acceptable, a seller may cure or correct his nonconforming tender
* *Installment Contracts* when the contract calls for delivery of goods in separate lots, the buyer may reject a nonconforming installment if it substantially impairs the value of that installment and cannot be cured; but if nonconformity or default of one or more of the installments substantially impairs the value of the whole contract, the buyer can treat the breach as a breach of the whole contract

Performance by the Buyer

Inspection unless otherwise agreed, the buyer has a reasonable time in which to inspect the goods before payment or acceptance to determine whether they conform

Rejection buyer's manifestation of unwillingness to become the owner of the goods; must be made within a reasonable time after the goods have been tendered or delivered and gives the buyer the right to (1) reject all of the goods, (2) accept all of the goods, or (3) accept any commercial unit(s) and reject the rest

Acceptance buyer's express or implied manifestation of a willingness to become the owner of the goods

Revocation of Acceptance rescission of buyer's acceptance of the goods if nonconformity of the goods substantially impairs their value, provided that the acceptance was (1) premised on the assumption that the nonconformity would be cured by the seller and it was not, or (2) the nonconformity was an undiscovered hidden defect

Obligation of Payment in the absence of an agreement, payment is due at the time and place the buyer is to receive the goods

Obligations of Both Parties

Casualty to Identified Goods if the contract is for goods that were identified when the contract was made and those goods are *totally* lost or damaged without fault of either party and before the risk of loss has passed to the buyer, the contract is avoided

Nonhappening of Presupposed Condition the seller is excused from the duty of performance on the nonoccurrence of presupposed conditions that were a basic assumption of the contract, unless the seller has expressly assumed the risk

Substituted Performance when neither party is at fault and the agreed manner of delivery of goods becomes commercially impracticable, a substituted manner of performance must be tendered and accepted

Right to Adequate Assurance of Performance when reasonable grounds for insecurity arise regarding either party's performance, the other party may demand written assurance and suspend his own performance until he receives that assurance

Right to Cooperation if one party's required cooperation is untimely, the other party is excused from any resulting delay in her own performance

Anticipatory Repudiation if either party clearly indicates an unwillingness or inability to perform before the performance is due, the other party may await performance for a reasonable time or resort to any remedy for breach

QUESTIONS

1. Tammie contracted with Kristine to manufacture, sell, and deliver to Kristine and put in running order a certain machine. After Tammie set up the machine and put it in running order, Kristine found it unsatisfactory and notified Tammie that she rejected the machine. She continued to use it for three months but continually complained of its defective condition. At the end of the three months, she notified Tammie to come and get it. Has Kristine lost her right (a) to reject the machine? (b) to revoke acceptance of the machine?

2. Smith, having contracted to sell to Beyer thirty tons of described fertilizer, shipped to Beyer by carrier thirty tons of fertilizer that he stated conformed to the contract. Nothing was stated in the contract as to time of payment, but Smith demanded payment as a condition of handing over the fertilizer to Beyer. Beyer refused to pay unless he was given the opportunity to inspect the fertilizer. Who is correct? Explain.

3. Benny and Sheree entered into a contract for the sale of one hundred barrels of flour. No mention was made of any place of delivery. Thereafter, Sheree demanded that Benny deliver the flour at her place of business, and Benny demanded that Sheree come and take the flour from his place of business. Neither party acceded to the demand of the other. Has either one a right of action against the other?

4. Johnson, a manufacturer of air-conditioning units, made a written contract with Maxwell to sell to Maxwell forty units at a price of $200 each and to deliver them at a certain apartment building owned by Maxwell for installation by Maxwell. On the arrival of Johnson's truck for delivery at the apartment building, Maxwell examined the units on the truck, counted only thirty units, and asked the driver if that was the total delivery. The driver replied that it was as far as he knew. Maxwell told the driver that she would not accept delivery of the units. The next day, Johnson telephoned Maxwell and inquired why delivery was refused. Maxwell stated that the units on the truck were not what she ordered, that she ordered forty units, that only thirty were tendered, and that she was going to buy air-conditioning units elsewhere. In an action by Johnson against Maxwell for breach of contract, Maxwell defends on the ground that the tender of thirty units was improper, because the contract called for delivery of forty units. Is this a valid defense?

5. Edwin sells a sofa to Jack for $800. Edwin and Jack both know that the sofa is in Edwin's warehouse, located approximately ten miles from Jack's home. The contract does not specify the place of delivery, and Jack insists that the place of delivery is either his house or Edwin's store. Is Jack correct?

6. On November 4, Kim contracted to sell to Lynn five hundred sacks of flour at $4 each to be delivered to Lynn by December 12. On November 27, Kim shipped the flour. By December 5, when the shipment arrived, containing only 450 sacks, the market price of flour had fallen. Lynn refused to accept delivery or to pay. Kim shipped fifty more sacks of flour, which arrived December 10. Lynn refused delivery. Kim resold the five hundred sacks of flour for $3 per sack. What are Kim's rights against Lynn?

7. Farley and Trudy entered into a written contract whereby Farley agreed to sell and Trudy agreed to buy six thousand bushels of wheat at $10.33 per bushel, deliverable at the rate of one thousand bushels a month commencing June 1, the price for each installment being payable ten days after delivery thereof. Though Farley delivered and received payment for the June installment, he defaulted by failing to deliver the July and August installments. By August 15, the market price of wheat had increased to $12 per bushel. Trudy thereupon entered into a contract with Albert to purchase five thousand bushels of wheat at $12 per bushel deliverable over the ensuing four months. In late September, the market price of wheat started to decline and by December 1 was $9.25 per bushel. Explain whether Trudy would succeed in a legal action against Farley for breach of contract.

8. Bain ordered from Marcum a carload of lumber, which he intended to use in the construction of small boats for the U.S. Navy, pursuant to contract. The order specified that the lumber was to be free from knots, wormholes, and defects. The lumber was shipped, and immediately on receipt Bain looked into the door of the fully loaded car, ascertained that there was a full carload of lumber, and acknowledged to Marcum that the carload had been received. On the same day, Bain moved the car to his private siding and sent to Marcum full payment in accordance with the terms of the order.

   A day later, the car was moved to the work area and unloaded in the presence of the Navy inspector, who refused to allow three-fourths of it to be used because of excessive knots and wormholes in the lumber. Bain then informed Marcum that he was rejecting the order and requested refund of the payment and directions on disposi-

tion of the lumber. Marcum replied that because Bain had accepted the order and unloaded it, he was not entitled to return of the purchase price. Who is correct? Explain.

CASE PROBLEMS

9. The plaintiff, a seller of milk, had for ten years bid on contracts to supply milk to the defendant school district and had supplied milk to other school districts in the area. On June 15, the plaintiff contracted to supply the defendant's requirements of milk for the next school year, at a price of $0.0759 per half-pint. The price of raw milk delivered from the farm had for years been controlled by the U.S. Department of Agriculture. On June 15, the department's administrator for the New York/New Jersey area had mandated a price for raw milk of $8.03 per hundred-weight. By December, the mandated price had been raised to $9.31 per hundredweight, an increase of nearly 20 percent. If required to complete deliveries at the contract price, the plaintiff would lose $7,350.55 on its contract with the defendant and would face similar losses on contracts with two other school districts. Is the plaintiff correct in its assertion (a) that its performance had become impracticable through unforeseen events and (b) that it is entitled to relief from performance?

10. In April, F. W. Lang Company (Lang) purchased an ice cream freezer and refrigeration compressor unit from Fleet for $2,160. Although the parties agreed to a written installment contract providing for an $850 down payment and eighteen installment payments, Lang made only one $200 payment upon receipt of the goods. One year later, Lang moved to a new location and took the equipment along without notifying Fleet. Then, in May or June of the following year, Lang disconnected the compressor from the freezer and used it to operate an air conditioner. Lang continued to use the compressor for that purpose until the sheriff seized the equipment and returned it to Fleet pursuant to a court order. Fleet then sold the equipment for $500 in what both parties conceded was a fair sale. Lang then brought an action charging that the equipment was defective and unusable for its intended purpose and sought to recover the down payment and expenses incurred in repairing the equipment. Fleet counterclaimed for the balance due under the installment contract less the proceeds from the sale. Who will prevail? Why?

11. Deborah McCullough bought a new car from Bill Swad Chrysler, Inc. The car was protected by both a limited warranty and an extended warranty. McCullough immediately encountered problems with the automobile's brakes, transmission, and air-conditioning and discovered a number of cosmetic defects as well. She returned the car to Swad for repairs, but Swad did not fix the brakes properly or perform any of the cosmetic work. Moreover, new problems appeared with respect to the car's steering mech-

anism. McCullough returned the car twice more for repairs, but on each occasion, old problems persisted and new ones emerged. After the engine abruptly shut off on a short trip away from home and the brakes again failed on a more extensive excursion, McCullough presented Swad with a list of thirty-two of the car's defects and demanded their correction. When Swad failed to remedy more than a few of the problems, McCullough wrote a letter to Swad calling for rescission of the purchase agreement and a refund of the purchase price and offering to return the car upon receiving from Swad instructions regarding where to return it. Swad did not respond to the letter, and McCullough brought an action against Swad. She continued to operate the vehicle until the time of trial, some seventeen and one-half months (and twenty-three thousand miles) later. Can McCullough rescind the agreement?

12. On March 17, Peckham bought a new car from Larsen Chevrolet for $16,400. During the first one and one-half months after the purchase, Peckham discovered that the car's hood was dented, its gas tank contained no baffles, its emergency brake was inoperable, the car did not have a jack or a spare tire, and neither the clock nor the speedometer worked. Larsen claimed that Peckham knew of the defects at the time of the purchase. Peckham, on the other hand, claimed that he did not know the extent of the defects and that despite his repeated efforts the defects were not repaired until June 11. Then, on July 15, the car's dashboard caught fire, leaving the car's interior damaged and the car itself inoperable. Peckham then returned to Larsen Chevrolet and told Larsen that Larsen had to repair the car at its own expense or that he, Peckham, would either rescind the contract or demand a new automobile. Peckham also claimed that at the end of their conversation, he notified Larsen Chevrolet that he was electing to rescind the contract and demanded the return of the purchase price. Larsen denied having received that oral notification. On October 12, Peckham sent a written notice of revocation of acceptance to Larsen. What are the rights of the parties?

13. Joc Oil bought a cargo of fuel oil for resale. The certificate from the foreign refinery stated the sulfur content of the oil was 0.5 percent. Joc Oil entered into a written contract with Con Ed for the sale of this oil. The contract specified a sulfur content of 0.5 percent. Joc Oil knew, however, that Con Ed was authorized to buy and burn oil of up to 1 percent sulfur content and that Con Ed often bought and mixed oils of varying contents to stay within this limit. The oil under contract was delivered to Con Ed, but

independent testing revealed a sulfur content of 0.92 percent. Con Ed promptly rejected the nonconforming shipment. Joc Oil immediately offered to substitute a conforming shipment of oil, although the time for performance had expired after the first shipment of oil. Con Ed refused to accept the substituted shipment. Joc Oil sues Con Ed for breach of contract. Judgment?

14. The plaintiff, a German wine producer and exporter, contracted to ship 620 cases of wine to the defendant, a distributor in North Carolina. The contract was silent as to the shipment destination. During the next several months, the defendant called repeatedly to find out the status of the shipment. Later, without notifying the defendant, the plaintiff delivered the wine to a shipping line in Rotterdam, destined for Wilmington, North Carolina. The ship and the wine were lost at sea en route to Wilmington. When the defendant refused to pay on the contract, the plaintiff sued. Decision?

15. Can-Key Industries, Inc., manufactured a turkey-hatching unit, which it sold to Industrial Leasing Corporation (ILC), which leased it to Rose-A-Linda Turkey Farms. ILC conditioned its obligation to pay on Rose-A-Linda's acceptance of the equipment. Rose-A-Linda twice notified Can-Key that the equipment was unacceptable and asked that it be removed. Over a period of fifteen months Can-Key made several unsuccessful attempts to solve the problems with the equipment. During this time, Can-Key did not instruct Rose-A-Linda to refrain from using the equipment. Rose-A-Linda indicated its dissatisfaction with the equipment, and ILC refused to perform its obligations under the contract. Can-Key then brought suit against ILC for breach of contract. It argued that Rose-A-Linda accepted the equipment, because it used it for fifteen months. ILC countered that the equipment was unacceptable and asked that it be removed. It claimed that Can-Key refused and failed to instruct Rose-A-Linda to refrain from using the equipment. Therefore, ILC argued, Rose-A-Linda effectively rejected the turkey-hatching unit, relieving ILC of its contractual obligations. Who is correct? Explain.

16. Frederick Manufacturing Corporation ordered 500 dozen units of Import Traders' rubber pads for $2,580. The order indicated that the pads should be "as soft as possible." Import Traders delivered the rubber pads to Frederick Manufacturing on November 19. Frederick failed to inspect the goods upon delivery, even though the parties recognized that there might be a problem with the softness. Frederick finally complained about the nonconformity of the pads in April of the following year, when Import Traders requested the contract price for the goods. Can Import Traders recover the contract price from Frederick?

17. Neptune Research & Development, Inc. (the buyer), manufacturer of solar-operated valves used in scientific instruments, saw advertised in a trade journal a hole-drilling machine with a very high degree of accuracy, manufactured and sold by Teknics Industrial Systems, Inc. (the seller). Because the machine's specifications met the buyer's needs, the buyer contacted the seller in late March and ordered one of the machines to be delivered in mid-June. There was no "time-is-of-the-essence" clause in the contract.

Although the buyer made several calls to the seller throughout the month of June, the seller never delivered the machine and never gave the buyer any reasons for the nondelivery. By late August, the buyer desperately needed the machine. The buyer went to the seller's place of business to examine the machine and discovered that the still-unbuilt machine had been redesigned, omitting a particular feature that the buyer had wanted. Nonetheless, the buyer agreed to take the machine, and the seller promised that it would be ready on September 5. The seller also agreed to call the buyer on September 3 to give the buyer two days to arrange for transportation of the machine.

The seller failed to telephone the buyer on September 3 as agreed. On September 4 the buyer called the seller to find out the status of the machine and was told by the seller that "under no circumstances" could the seller have the machine ready by September 5. At this point, the buyer notified the seller that the order was canceled. One hour later, still on September 4, the seller called the buyer, retracted its earlier statement, and indicated that the machine would be ready by the agreed September 5 date. The buyer sued for the return of its $3,000 deposit. Should the buyer prevail? Explain.

18. ALPAC and Eagon are corporations that import and export raw logs. In April, Setsuo Kimura, ALPAC's president, and C. K. Ahn, Eagon's vice president, entered into a contract for ALPAC to ship about fifteen thousand cubic meters of logs between the end of July and the end of August. Eagon agreed to purchase them. Subsequently, the market for logs began to soften, making the contract less attractive to Eagon. ALPAC became concerned that Eagon would try to cancel the contract. Kimura and Ahn began a series of meetings and letters, apparently to assure ALPAC that Eagon would purchase the logs.

Eagon was troubled by the drop in timber prices and initially withheld approval of the shipment. Ahn sent numerous internal memoranda to the home office indicating that it might not wish to complete the deal, but that accepting the logs was "inevitable" under the contract.

On August 23, Eagon received a fax from ALPAC suggesting a reduction in price and volume of the contract, but Eagon did not respond. Soon after, Kimura asked Ahn whether he intended to accept the logs; Ahn admitted that he was having trouble getting approval. On August 30, Ahn informed the home office that he would attempt to avoid accepting the logs but that it would be difficult and suggested holding ALPAC responsible for shipment delay. Kimura thereafter believed that Eagon would not accept the shipment and eventually canceled the vessel reserved to ship the logs, believing that Eagon was canceling the contract. The logs were not loaded or shipped by August 31, but Ahn and Kimura continued to discuss the contract. On September 7, Ahn told Kimura that he would try to convince the firm to accept the delivery and indicated that he did not want Kimura to sell the logs to another buyer. The same day, Ahn informed Eagon that it should consider accepting the shipment in September or October.

By September 27, ALPAC had not shipped the logs and sent a final letter to Eagon stating that because it failed to take delivery of the logs, it had breached the contract. Eagon responded to the letter, stating that there was "no contract" because ALPAC's breach (not shipping by the deadline) excused Eagon's performance. Explain whether either party breached the agreement.

TAKING SIDES

On February 26, 2012, William Stem purchased a used BMW from Gary Braden for $26,600. Stem's primary purpose for buying the car was to use it to drive his child to school and various activities. Braden indicated to Stem that the car had not been wrecked and that it was in good condition. Stem thought the car had been driven only seventy thousand miles. Less than a week after the purchase, Stem discovered a disconnected plug that, when plugged in, caused the oil warning light to turn on. When Stem then took his car to a mechanic, the mechanic discovered that the front end was that of a 2002 BMW and the rear end was that of a 1998 BMW. Further investigation revealed that the front half had been driven one hundred and seventy thousand miles. On March 10, 2012, Stem sent a letter informing Braden that he refused the automobile and that he intended to rescind the sale. Braden refused. Stem then drove the automobile for seven months and nearly nine thousand miles before filing an action against Braden, seeking to revoke his acceptance and to obtain the return of the purchase price.

a. What arguments would support Stem's revocation of his acceptance and the return of the purchase price?

b. What arguments would support Braden's denial of Stem's claim?

c. Who should prevail? Explain.

Chapter 21

TRANSFER OF TITLE AND RISK OF LOSS

Aliud est possidere, aliud esse in possessione. (It is one thing to possess; it is another to be in possession.)

LEGAL MAXIM

CHAPTER OUTCOMES

After reading and studying this chapter, you should be able to:

1. Explain the relative importance of title under the common law and Article 2.

2. Explain when the seller has a right or power to transfer title and when the transfer is void or voidable.

3. Distinguish between a shipment contract and a destination contract and explain when title and risk of loss pass under each.

4. Identify and explain the rules covering (a) risk of loss in the absence of a breach and (b) risk of loss when there is a breach.

5. Explain how bulk transfers concern creditors and how the Uniform Commercial Code attempts to regulate such transfers.

Historically, the principle of title governed nearly every aspect of the rights and duties of the buyer and seller arising from a sales contract. In an attempt to add greater precision and certainty to sales contracts, the Uniform Commercial Code (UCC or the Code) has abandoned the common law's reliance on title. Instead, the Code approaches each legal issue arising from a sales contract on its own merits and provides separate and specific rules to control various transactional situations. In this chapter, we will cover the Code's approach to the transfer of title and other property rights, the passage of risk of loss, and the transfer of goods sold in bulk.

Transfer of Title

As previously stated, a sale of goods is defined as the transfer of title from the seller to the buyer for a consideration known as the price. Transfer of title is, therefore, fundamental to a sale of goods. Title, however, cannot pass under a contract for sale until existing goods have been identified as those to which the contract refers. Future goods (goods that are not both existing and identified) cannot constitute a present sale. If the buyer rejects the goods, whether justifiably or not, title reverts to the seller.

In a lease, title does not pass. Instead, the lessee obtains the right to possess and use the goods for a period of time in return for consideration.

IDENTIFICATION

Identification is the designation of specific goods as goods to which the contract of sale refers. Identification may be made by either the seller or the buyer and may be made at any time and in any manner agreed upon by the parties. To illustrate, suppose Barringer contracts to purchase a particular Buick automobile from Stevenson's car lot. Identification occurs as soon as the parties enter the contract. If, however, Barringer agreed to purchase a television set from Stevenson, who has his storeroom filled with such televisions, identification will not occur until either Barringer or Stevenson selects a particular television to fulfill the contract. (Article 2A is similar.)

If the goods are **fungible** (the equivalent of any other unit), identification of a share of undivided goods occurs when the contract is entered into. Thus, if Barringer agreed to purchase one thousand gallons of gasoline from Stevenson, who owns a five-thousand-gallon tank of gasoline, identification occurs as soon as the contract is formed.

Security Interest   The Code defines a **security interest** as an interest in personal property or fixtures that ensures payment or performance of an obligation. Any reservation by the seller of a title to goods *delivered* to the buyer is limited in effect to a reservation of a security interest. Security interests in goods are governed by Article 9 of the Code (discussed in Chapter 37).

Insurable Interest   For a contract or policy of insurance to be valid, the insured must have an **insurable interest** in the subject matter. At common law, only a person with title or a **lien** (a legal claim of a creditor on property) could insure his interest in specific goods. The Code extends an insurable interest to a buyer's interest in goods that have been identified as goods to which the contract refers. (Article 2A.) This *special property interest* of the buyer, which arises upon identification, enables her to purchase insurance protection on goods that she does not presently own but will own upon delivery by the seller. The seller also has an insurable interest in the goods, as long as he has title to them or any security interest in them. In a lease, the lessor retains an insurable interest in the goods until an option to buy, if included in the lease, has been exercised by the lessee.

PASSAGE OF TITLE

Title passes when the parties *intend* it to pass, provided the goods are in existence and have been identified.

When the parties have no explicit agreement as to transfer of title, the Code provides rules that determine when title passes to the buyer.

Physical Movement of the Goods   When delivery is to be made by moving the goods, title passes at the time and place the seller completes his performance with reference to delivery of the goods. When and where delivery occurs depends on whether the contract is a shipment contract or a destination contract.

A **shipment contract** requires or authorizes the seller to send the goods to the buyer but does not require the seller to deliver them to a particular destination. Under a shipment contract, title passes to the buyer at the time and place the seller delivers the goods to the carrier for shipment to the buyer.

A **destination contract** requires the seller to deliver the goods to a particular destination. Under a destination contract, title passes to the buyer on tender of the goods at that destination. **Tender**, as discussed in Chapter 20, requires that the seller, at a reasonable time, (1) put and hold conforming goods at the buyer's disposition, (2) give notice to the buyer that the goods are available, and (3) keep the goods available for a reasonable period of time.

No Movement of the Goods   When delivery is to be made without moving the goods, unless otherwise agreed, title passes (1) on delivery of a document of title, when the contract calls for delivery of such document (documents of title are documents that evidence a right to receive specified goods; they are discussed more fully in Chapter 47); or (2) at the time and place of contracting, if the goods at that time have been identified by either the seller or the buyer as the goods to which the contract refers and no documents are to be delivered. When the goods are not identified at the time of contracting, title passes when the goods are identified.

POWER TO TRANSFER TITLE

It is important to understand under what circumstances a seller has the right or **power to transfer title** to a buyer. If the seller is the rightful owner of goods or is authorized to sell the goods for the rightful owner, the seller has the *right* to transfer title. But when a seller possesses goods that he neither owns nor has authority to sell, the sale is not rightful. In some situations, however, unauthorized sellers may have the *power* to transfer good title to certain buyers. This section pertains to such sales by a person in possession of goods that he neither owns nor has authority to sell.

The rule of property law protecting existing ownership of goods is the starting point for any discussion of a sale of goods by a nonowner. One of the law's most basic tenets, expressly stated in the Code, is that a purchaser of goods obtains such title as his transferor had or had power to transfer. (Article 2A.) Likewise, the purchaser of a limited interest in goods acquires rights only to the extent of the interest that he purchased. By the same token, no one can transfer what he does not have. A purported sale by a thief or finder or ordinary bailee of goods does not transfer title to the purchaser.

The principal reason underlying the policy of the law in protecting existing ownership of goods is that a person should not be required to retain possession at all times of all the goods that he owns to maintain ownership of them. One valuable incident of the ownership of goods is the freedom of the owner to make a bailment of his goods as desired; the mere possession of goods by a bailee does not authorize the bailee to sell them.

Another legal policy conflicts, however, with the policy protecting existing ownership of goods; this latter protection, the protection of the good faith purchaser, is based on the importance in trade and commerce of ensuring the security of good faith transactions in goods. To encourage and make secure good faith acquisitions of goods, bona fide (good faith) purchasers for value must be protected under certain circumstances. A **good faith purchaser** is defined as one who acts honestly, gives value, and takes the goods without notice or knowledge of any defect in the title of the transferor.

PRACTICAL ADVICE

Be sure you give value and act honestly so as to obtain the protection the law grants a good faith purchaser.

Void and Voidable Title to Goods A void title is no title. A person claiming ownership of goods by an agreement that is void obtains no title to the goods. Thus, a thief or a finder of goods or a person who acquires goods from someone under physical duress or

under guardianship has no title to them and can transfer none.

A **voidable title** is one acquired under circumstances that permit the former owner to rescind the transfer and revest herself with title, as in the case of mistake, common duress, undue influence, fraud in the inducement, misrepresentation, mistake, or sale by a person without contractual capacity (other than an individual under guardianship). In these situations, the buyer has acquired legal title to the goods, which may be divested by action of the seller. If, however, the buyer were to resell the goods to a good faith purchaser for value, before the seller has rescinded the transfer of title, the right of rescission in the seller is cut off, and the good faith purchaser acquires good title. The Code defines **good faith** as "honesty in fact in the conduct or transaction concerned"; for merchants, and all parties under Revised Article 1, good faith also requires the observance of reasonable commercial standards of fair dealing. The Code defines value to include a consideration sufficient to support a simple contract.

The distinction between a void and voidable title is, therefore, extremely important in determining the rights of good faith purchasers of goods. The good faith purchaser always believes that she is buying the goods from the owner or from one with authority to sell. Otherwise, she would not be acting in good faith. In each situation, the party selling the goods appears to be the owner, whether his title is valid, void, or voidable. Given a case involving two innocent persons—the true owner who has done nothing wrong and the good faith purchaser who has done nothing wrong—the law will not disturb the legal title but will rule in favor of the one who has it. Thus, when A transfers possession of goods to B under such circumstances that B acquires no title or a void title, and B thereafter sells the goods to C, a good faith purchaser for value, B has nothing to transfer to C except possession. In a lawsuit between A and C involving the right to the goods, A will win because she has the legal title. (See Figure 21-1 for a diagram of void title.) C's only recourse is against B for breach of warranty of

Figure 21-1
Void Title

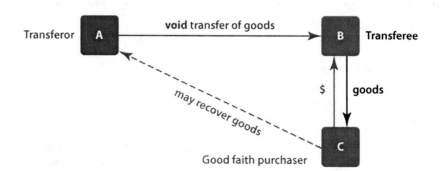

Transferor   A   void transfer of goods   B   Transferee

may recover goods

$ goods

C

Good faith purchaser

Figure 21-2
Voidable Title

title, which we will discuss in Chapter 22. If, however, B acquired a voidable title from A and resold the goods to C, in a suit between A and C over the goods, C would win. In this case, B had title, though voidable, which she transferred to the good faith purchaser. The title thus acquired by C will be protected. The voidable title in B is title until it has been avoided, and, after transfer to a good faith purchaser, it may not be avoided. (See Figure 21-2 for a diagram of voidable title.) A's only recourse is against B for restitution or damages.

ROBINSON v. DURHAM

ALABAMA COURT OF CIVIL APPEALS, 1988
537 SO.2D 966

http://scholar.google.com/scholar_case?case=15758867258525788627&hl=en&as_sdt=2&as_vis=1&oi=scholarr

FACTS Mike Durham bought a used 1968 Chevrolet Camaro from Ronald and Wyman Robinson, owners of Friendly Discount Auto Sales. Unknown to either Durham or the Robinsons, the car had been stolen. In fact, when he first bought the car, Wyman Robinson had obtained tag receipts from what turned out to be the car thief and had subsequently registered the car in his name. Durham had received all prior documentation upon purchase of the car. However, the Federal Bureau of Investigation seized the car from Durham and returned it to the original owner. Durham sued the Robinsons, alleging, among other things, breach of the warranty of title. The jury awarded Durham $5,200, the amount he had paid for the car. The Robinsons appealed.

DECISION Judgment for Durham.

OPINION Wright, J. Appellants assert that the grant of summary judgment was in error because there was "a scintilla of evidence, if not substantial evidence" from which the trial court could have concluded that appellants held good title "or at least voidable title" on the automobile, thereby conveying actual title to Durham at the time of the purchase.

Appellants' argument is without merit. It is unequivocal that "a person who has stolen goods of another cannot pass title thereto to another, whether such other knew, or did not know, that the goods were stolen."

[Citations.] A thief gets only void title and without more cannot pass any title to a subsequent purchaser, even a good faith purchaser. [Citation.] It is undisputed that the automobile had been stolen. Therefore, at the time of purchase appellants obtained no title. In other words, the title was void. Appellants could not convey good title to Durham; therefore, the subsequent sale to Durham constituted a breach of warranty of good title.

Relying on § 2–403(1), [UCC], appellants contend that they at least acquired a voidable title when they purchased the automobile. Section 2–403 recognizes that a person with voidable title has power to transfer a good title to a good faith purchaser for value. Voidable title can only arise from a voluntary transfer, and the rightful owner must assent to the transfer. "A possessor of goods does not have voidable title unless the true owner has consented to the transfer of title to him." [Citation.] In this case the rightful owner did not consent or assent to the transfer of the automobile. Appellants obtained no title.

INTERPRETATION A void title is no title.

ETHICAL QUESTION Did either of the parties act unethically? Explain.

CRITICAL THINKING QUESTION Who should bear the loss between the Robinsons and Durham? Explain.

The Code has enlarged the common law voidable title doctrine by providing that a good faith purchaser for value obtains valid title from one possessing voidable title even if that person obtained voidable title by (1) fraud as to her identity; (2) exchange for a subsequently dishonored check; (3) an agreement that the transaction was to be a cash sale, and the sales price has not been paid; or (4) criminal fraud punishable as larceny. (Article 2A is similar.)

In addition, the Code has expanded the rights of good faith purchasers with respect to sales by *minors*. Although the common law permitted a minor seller of goods to disaffirm the sale and to recover the goods from a third person who had purchased them in good faith from the party who had acquired the goods from the minor, the Code changed this rule by no longer permitting a minor seller to prevail over a good faith purchaser for value.

> ## PRACTICAL ADVICE
> A buyer should obtain a written express warranty that the seller has ownership of the property or the authority to transfer ownership.

Entrusting of Goods to a Merchant Frequently, an owner of goods entrusts (transfers possession of) goods to a bailee for resale, repair, or some other use. In some instances, the bailee violates this entrusting by selling the goods to a third party without the owner's permission or by keeping the proceeds of such a sale. Although the "true" owner has a right of recourse against the bailee for the value of the goods, what right, if any, should the true owner of the goods have against the third party? Once again, the law must balance the right of ownership against the rights of market transactions.

The Code protects buyers of goods in the ordinary course of business from merchants who deal in goods of that kind, when the owner has entrusted possession of the goods to the merchant. The Code defines a **buyer in the ordinary course of business** as a person who in good faith and without knowledge that the sale to him is in violation of the ownership rights or security interest of another buys the goods in the ordinary course of business from a person, other than a pawnbroker, in the business of selling goods of that kind. Because the merchant who deals in goods of that kind is cloaked with the appearance of ownership or apparent authority to sell, the Code seeks to protect the innocent third-party purchaser. Any such **entrusting** of possession bestows on the merchant the power to transfer all rights of the entruster to a buyer in the ordinary course of business. (Article 2A is similar.) For example, A brings his stereo for repair to B, who also sells both new and used stereo equipment. C purchases A's stereo from B in good faith and in the ordinary course of business. The Code protects the rights of C and defeats the rights of A, whose only recourse is against B.

The Code, however, does not go so far as to protect the buyer in the ordinary course of business from a merchant to whom the goods have been entrusted by a thief, a finder, or a completely unauthorized person. It merely grants the buyer in the ordinary course of business the rights of the entruster.

When a buyer of goods to whom title has passed leaves the seller in possession of the goods, the buyer has "entrusted the goods" to the seller. If that seller is a merchant and resells and delivers the goods to another buyer in the ordinary course of business, this second buyer acquires good title to the goods. Thus, Dennis sells certain goods to Sylvia, who pays the price but allows possession to remain with Dennis. Dennis thereafter sells the same goods to Karen, a buyer in the ordinary course of business. Karen takes delivery of the goods. Sylvia does not have any rights against Karen or to the goods. Sylvia's only remedy is against Dennis.

> ## PRACTICAL ADVICE
> Properly mark and identify goods you entrust to a merchant who is in the business of selling used goods of that type.

HEINRICH V. TITUS-WILL SALES, INC.

COURT OF APPEALS OF WASHINGTON, 1994
73 WASH.APP. 147, 868 P.2D 169

http://scholar.google.com/scholar_case?case=18393426036611380515&q=868+P.2d+169&hl=en&as_sdt=2,34

FACTS In 1989, Michael Heinrich retained James Wilson to purchase a new Ford pickup truck for him. Wilson had held himself out as a dealer/broker, but unbeknownst to Heinrich, Wilson had lost his vehicle dealer license. Wilson negotiated with Titus-Will Ford Sales, Inc. (Titus-Will) to purchase the truck for Heinrich. Titus-Will had dealt with Wilson as a dealer before but also did not know that he had lost his dealer license. All payments for the truck went through Wilson, and the purchase order indicated that the truck was being sold to Wilson as a dealer for resale. Wilson agreed to deliver the truck to Heinrich at Titus-Will on Saturday, October 21, 1989. Wilson delivered to a clerk at Titus-Will a postdated check for the balance of the purchase price, which the clerk accepted, and in return delivered to Wilson a packet containing the keys to the truck, the owner's manual, an odometer disclosure statement, and the warranty card. The odometer statement showed that Wilson was the transferor and Titus-Will did not fill out the warranty card as the sale appeared to be dealer to dealer. Wilson's check, however, did not clear, and Titus-Will demanded the return of the truck. On November 6, Wilson picked up the truck from Heinrich, telling him he would have Titus-Will make certain repairs under the warranty, and returned the truck to Titus-Will. On November 9, 1989, Wilson admitted to Heinrich that he did not have funds to cover his check and that Titus-Will would not release the truck without payment. Heinrich then asked Titus-Will for the truck but was refused. Heinrich sued Titus-Will and Wilson, seeking return of the truck and damages for his loss of use. By pretrial arrangement, Heinrich regained possession of, but not clear title to, the truck. Heinrich also obtained a default order against Wilson. After a bench trial, the court awarded Heinrich title to the truck and $3,050 in damages for loss of its use. Titus-Will appeals.

DECISION Judgment affirmed.

OPINION Seinfeld, J.

THE ENTRUSTMENT DOCTRINE
[UCC] 2–403(2) and (3) contain the entrustment provisions of the Uniform Commercial Code (UCC).

* * *

To prevail under this statute, Heinrich must show (1) Titus-Will "entrusted" the truck to Wilson and, thus, empowered Wilson subsequently to transfer all rights of Titus-Will in the truck to Heinrich; (2) Wilson was a merchant dealing in automobiles; and (3) Heinrich bought the truck from Wilson as a "buyer in ordinary course of business." [Citations.]

Three general policies support [§]2–403(2), the UCC provision placing the risk of loss on the entruster. First, it protects the innocent buyer who, based on his observation of goods in the possession of a merchant of those goods, believes that the merchant has legal title to the goods and can, therefore, pass title in the goods to another. [Citation.] * * *

Secondly, the entrustment clause reflects the idea that the entruster is in a better position than the innocent buyer to protect against the risk that an intermediary merchant will not pay for or not deliver the goods. [Citations.]

Thirdly, the entrustment clause facilitates the flow of commerce by allowing purchasers to rely on a merchant's apparent legal right to sell the goods. [Citations.]

Without the safeguards of the entrustment provision, a prudent buyer would have to delay the finalization of any sizeable sales transaction for the time necessary to research the merchant's ownership rights to the goods.

A. ENTRUSTING
The UCC * * * declares that "any delivery and any acquiescence in retention of possession" constitutes entrustment. 2–403(3). A person can entrust goods to a merchant by a variety of methods, such as consigning them, creating a bailment, taking a security interest in inventory, leaving them with the merchant after purchase, and delivering them for purposes of repair. [Citations.] A sale can also constitute an entrustment when some aspect of the transaction remains incomplete. [Citations.]

Titus-Will properly concedes that it entrusted the truck to Wilson. However, it argues Wilson was not a merchant and Heinrich was not a buyer in ordinary course. Further, Titus-Will contends that the timing of the entrusting deprived Wilson of the power to transfer its rights.

B. MERCHANT
Titus-Will argues that Wilson was not a merchant because he had no inventory. However, it is not necessary to possess an inventory to fit within the broad statutory definition of merchant. Article 2 of the UCC defines (in part) "merchant" as "a person who deals in goods of the kind or otherwise by his occupation holds himself out as having knowledge or skill peculiar to the practices or goods involved in the transaction." 2–104(1). Wilson was a merchant who dealt in automobiles; he held himself out as a dealer in automobiles and appeared to be a dealer in automobiles. Both parties treated him as one. Titus-Will processed all the documents as it would for a dealer and understood that Wilson was buying the truck for resale.

Titus-Will also argues that Wilson was not a merchant because he did not have a vehicle dealer license. However, the UCC does not require proper state licensing for merchant status. 2–104(1), 2–403(2). * * *

C. BUYER IN ORDINARY COURSE
There is also substantial evidence that Heinrich was a "buyer in ordinary course of business" although the trial court referred to him as a "good faith purchaser for value." A buyer in ordinary course of business is

a person who in good faith and without knowledge that the sale to him is in violation of the ownership rights or security interest of a third party in the goods buys in ordinary course from a person in the business of selling goods of that kind[.] 1–201(9). "Buying" includes receiving goods * * * under a preexisting contract for sale." 1–201(9). Good faith is "honesty in fact in the conduct or transaction concerned." 1–201(19).

The amount of the consideration is significant as evidence of good faith. [Citation.] Heinrich gave substantial value for the truck, more than Wilson agreed to pay Titus-Will. Nor did Heinrich know or have a basis to believe that Wilson's sale and delivery of the truck to him violated Titus-Will's ownership or security interest rights. There was no showing that Heinrich acted other than in good faith. *** Wilson's illegal and fraudulent activity does not taint Heinrich's status as a buyer under 2–403(2). ***

D. TIMING OF ENTRUSTMENT

Titus-Will also argues that the UCC entrustment provisions should not apply because it entrusted the truck to Wilson *after* Heinrich had completely paid Wilson. This is an issue of first impression in this jurisdiction.

Before the completion of the Wilson-Heinrich sales transaction, Titus-Will entrusted Wilson not only with the truck, but also with the signed odometer disclosure statement, the owner's manual, the warranty card, and the keys. By doing so, Titus-Will clothed Wilson with additional indicia of ownership and with the apparent authority to transfer an ownership interest in the truck. It also enabled Wilson to complete the sales transaction. 2–401(2) ("Unless otherwise explicitly agreed title passes to the buyer at the time and place at which the seller completes his performance with reference to the physical delivery of the goods"). In addition, the entrustment allowed Wilson to continue to deceive Heinrich from October 21, 1989, the date of delivery of possession, to November 9, 1989, when Wilson finally admitted the truth. We believe that under these circumstances, application of the entrustment doctrine, 2–403(2), furthers the policy of protecting the buyer who relies on the merchant's apparent legal ability to sell goods in the merchant's possession.

The second rationale for the entrustment doctrine also supports its application here. Titus-Will, in the business of selling cars, was in a better position than Heinrich to protect itself against another dealer/broker who might fail to pay for the goods. It could have insured against the loss, and it could have adopted preventive procedures. ***

The third rationale for the entrustment doctrine focuses on the flow of commerce. Here we consider the potential impact on commercial transactions of requiring purchasers to research their dealer/broker's legal title before accepting possession of the goods. Although the record contains no evidence on this issue, it seems obvious that this requirement would inevitably cause some delay. [Citation.]

Requiring the entruster to retain the burden of risk, even when the entrustment occurs after a third party purchaser gives value, supports the policies underlying the entrustment doctrine. ***

INTERPRETATION A buyer in the ordinary course of business acquires good title when buying from a merchant seller who was entrusted with possession of the goods.

CRITICAL THINKING QUESTION Should Titus-Will be held responsible in this situation? Explain.

Risk of Loss

Risk of loss, as the term is used in the law of sales, addresses the allocation of loss between seller and buyer when the goods have been damaged, destroyed, or lost without the fault of either the seller or the buyer. If the loss is placed on the buyer, he is under a duty to pay the price for the goods even though they were damaged or never received. If placed on the seller, she has no right to recover the purchase price from the buyer, although she does have a right to the return of the damaged goods.

 According to the United Nations Convention on CISG, loss of or damage to the goods after the risk of loss has passed to the buyer does not discharge the buyer from his obligation to pay the purchase price.

In determining who has the risk of loss, the Code provides definite rules for specific situations—a sharp departure from the common law concept, which essentially determined risk of loss according to who had ownership of the goods and which depended on whether title had been transferred. The Code's transactional approach is necessarily detailed and for this reason is probably more understandable and meaningful than the common law's reliance on the abstract concept of title. The Code has adopted rules for determining the risk of loss in the absence of breach separate from those that apply where a breach of the sales contract has occurred.

Except in a finance lease, risk of loss is retained by the lessor and does not pass to the lessee. In a finance lease, risk of loss passes to the lessee as discussed later.

RISK OF LOSS WHERE THERE IS A BREACH

When one party breaches the contract, the Code places the risk of loss on that party, even though this allocation differs from the passage of risk of loss in the absence of a breach. Nevertheless, when the nonbreaching party is in control of the goods, the Code places the risk of loss on him to the extent of his insurance coverage.

Breach by the Seller If the seller ships to the buyer goods that do not conform to the contract, the risk of loss remains on the seller until the buyer has accepted the goods or until the seller has remedied the defect. (Article 2A.)

When the buyer has accepted nonconforming goods but thereafter by timely notice to the seller rightfully revokes his acceptance (discussed in Chapter 20), he may treat the risk of loss as resting from the beginning on the seller, to the extent of any deficiency in the buyer's effective insurance coverage. (Article 2A.) For example, Stuart delivers to Bernard nonconforming goods, which Bernard accepts. Subsequently, Bernard discovers a hidden defect in the goods and rightfully revokes his prior acceptance. If the goods are destroyed through no fault of either party, and Bernard has insured the goods for 60 percent of their fair market value of $10,000, then the insurance company will cover $6,000 of the loss and Stuart will cover the remainder, or $4,000. Had the buyer's insurance coverage been $10,000, Stuart would not bear any of the loss.

Breach by the Buyer

When conforming goods have been identified to a contract that the buyer repudiates or breaches before risk of loss has passed to him, the seller may treat the risk of loss as resting on the buyer "for a commercially reasonable time" to the extent of any deficiency in the seller's effective insurance coverage. (Article 2A.) For example, Susan agrees to sell forty thousand pounds of plastic resin to Bella, F.O.B. (free on board) Bella's factory, delivery by March 1. On February 1, Bella wrongfully repudiates the contract by telephoning Susan and telling her that she does not want the resin. Susan immediately seeks another buyer, but before she is able to locate one, and within a commercially reasonable time, the resin is destroyed by a fire through no fault of Susan's. The fair market value of the resin is $35,000. Because Susan's insurance covers only $15,000 of the loss, Bella is liable for $20,000.

Risk of Loss in Absence of a Breach

When there is no breach, the parties may allocate the risk of loss by agreement. Where there is no breach and the parties have not otherwise agreed, the Code places the risk of loss, for the most part, on the party who is more likely to have greater control over the goods, is more likely to insure the goods, or is better able to prevent the loss of the goods.

Agreement of the Parties

The parties, by agreement, not only may shift the allocation of risk of loss but also may divide the risk between them. Such agreement is controlling. Thus, for example, the parties may agree that a seller shall retain the risk of loss even though the buyer is in possession of the goods or has title to them. Furthermore, the agreement may provide that the buyer bears 60 percent of the risk and that the seller bears 40 percent.

PRACTICAL ADVICE
Specify in your contract of sale how risk of loss should be allocated.

Trial Sales

Some sales are made with the understanding that the buyer can return the goods even though they conform to the contract. These trial sales permit the buyer to try the goods for a period of time to determine if she wishes either to keep them or to try to resell them. The Code recognizes two types of trial sales—a sale on approval and a sale or return—and provides a test for distinguishing between them: unless otherwise agreed, if the goods are delivered primarily for the buyer's use, the transaction is a sale on approval; if they are delivered primarily for resale by the buyer, it is a sale or return.

In a **sale on approval**, possession of, but not title to, the goods is transferred to the buyer for a stated period of time. If no time is stated, the buyer may use the goods for a reasonable time to determine whether she wishes to accept them. Both title and risk of loss remain with the *seller* until the buyer "approves," or accepts, the goods. Until acceptance by the buyer, the sale is a bailment with an option to purchase.

Although use of the goods consistent with the purpose of approval by the buyer is not acceptance, the buyer's failure to notify the seller within a reasonable time of her election to return the goods *is* an acceptance. The buyer also may manifest approval by exercising any dominion or control over the goods inconsistent with the seller's ownership. On approval, title and risk of loss pass to the buyer, who then becomes liable to the seller for the purchase price of the goods. If, however, the buyer then decides to return the goods and so notifies the seller, the return is at the seller's risk and expense.

In a **sale or return**, the goods are sold and delivered to the buyer with an option to return them to the seller. The risk of loss is on the *buyer*, who has title until she revests it in the seller by returning the goods. The return of the goods is at the buyer's risk and expense.

A **consignment** is a delivery of possession of personal property to an agent for sale by the agent. Under the Code, a sale on consignment is regarded as a sale or return. Therefore, the creditors of the consignee (the agent who receives the merchandise for sale) prevail over the consignor and may obtain possession of the consigned goods, provided the consignee maintains a place of business where he deals in goods of the kind involved under a name other than the name of the consignor. Nevertheless, the consignor will prevail if she (1) complies with applicable state law requiring a consignor's interest to be evidenced by a sign, (2) establishes that the consignee is generally known by his creditors to be substantially engaged in selling the goods of others, or (3) complies with the filing provisions of Article 9 (Secured Transactions).

Contracts Involving Carriers Sales contracts frequently contain terms indicating the agreement of the parties as to delivery by a carrier. These terms identify the contract as a shipment contract or as a destination contract and, by implication, indicate the time at which the risk of loss passes. If the contract does not require the seller to deliver the goods to a particular destination but merely to the common carrier (a shipment contract), risk of loss passes to the buyer when the seller delivers the goods to the carrier. If the seller is required to deliver them to a particular destination (a destination contract), risk of loss passes to the buyer at destination when the goods are tendered to the buyer. (Article 2A.)

CISG If the sales contract involves the carriage of the goods and the seller is not obligated to hand them over at a particular destination, the risk of loss passes to the buyer when the goods are handed over to the first carrier. If the contract requires the seller to deliver the goods to a carrier at a particular destination, the risk of loss passes when the goods are handed over to the carrier at that place.

PRACTICAL ADVICE
Select the shipment term that passes the risk of loss when you desire it to pass.

The following case deals with the question of when the risk of loss passes between parties whose sales contract contains no specific provision or any delivery term. The case demonstrates that if the contract is not clearly a destination contract or a shipment contract, the law assumes that it is a shipment contract.

WINDOWS, INC. V. JORDAN PANEL SYSTEMS CORP.

UNITED STATES COURT OF APPEALS, SECOND CIRCUIT, 1999
177 F.3D 114

http://laws.findlaw.com/2nd/987603.html

FACTS Jordan Panel Systems, Inc. (Jordan) ordered custom-made windows from Windows, Inc. (Windows). The purchase contract provided that the windows were to be shipped properly packaged for cross-country motor freight transit and "delivered to New York City." Windows constructed the windows according to Jordan's specifications and arranged to have them shipped to Jordan by a common carrier, Consolidated Freightways Corp. (Consolidated). Windows delivered them to Consolidated intact and properly packaged. During the course of shipment, however, the goods sustained extensive damage. Much of the glass was broken and many of the window frames were gouged and twisted. Jordan's president signed a delivery receipt noting that approximately two-thirds of the shipment was damaged due to "load shift." Jordan made a claim with Consolidated for damages it had sustained and also ordered a new shipment from Windows, which was delivered without incident. Jordan did not pay for either shipment of windows, and Windows brought suit. Jordan cross-claimed for incidental and consequential damages resulting from the damaged shipment. The parties resolved the claim by Windows, and the only issue that remains is Jordan's counterclaim. The district court granted Windows' motion for summary judgment on this matter. Jordan brings this appeal.

DECISION Judgment affirmed in favor of Windows.

OPINION Leval, J. Jordan seeks to recover incidental and consequential damages pursuant to [U.C.C.] § 2–715. Under that provision, Jordan's entitlement to recover incidental and consequential damages depends on whether those damages "result[ed] from the seller's breach." A destination contract is covered by § 2–503(3); it arises where "the seller is required to deliver at a particular destination." In contrast, a shipment contract arises where "the seller is required *** to send the goods to the buyer and the contract does not require him to deliver them at a particular destination." § 2–504. Under a shipment contract, the seller must "put the goods in the possession of such a carrier and make such a contract for their transportation as may be reasonable having regard to the nature of the goods and other circumstances of the case." § 2–504(a). ***

Where the terms of an agreement are ambiguous, there is a strong presumption under the U.C.C. favoring shipment contracts.

Unless the parties "expressly specify" that the contract requires the seller to deliver to a particular destination, the contract is generally construed as one for shipment. [Citations.]

Jordan's confirmation of its purchase order, by letter to Windows dated September 22, 1993, provided, "All windows to be shipped properly crated/packaged/boxed suitable for cross country motor freight transit and delivered to New York City." We conclude that this was a shipment contract rather than a destination contract. To overcome the presumption favoring shipment contracts, the parties must have explicitly agreed to impose on Windows the obligation to effect delivery at a particular destination. The language of this contract does not do so. Nor did Jordan use any commonly recognized industry term indicating that a seller is obligated to deliver the goods to the buyer's specified destination.

Under the terms of its contract, Windows thus satisfied its obligations to Jordan when it put the goods, properly packaged, into the possession of the carrier for shipment. Upon Windows' proper delivery to the carrier, Jordan assumed the risk of loss, and cannot recover incidental or consequential damages from the seller caused by the carrier's negligence.

This allocation of risk is confirmed by the terms of [U.C.C.] § 2–509(1)(a), entitled "Risk of Loss in the Absence of Breach." It provides that where the contract "does not require [the seller] to deliver [the goods] at a particular destination, the risk of loss passes to the buyer when the goods are duly delivered to the carrier." [U.C.C.] § 2–509(1)(a). As noted earlier, Jordan does not contest the court's finding that Windows duly delivered conforming goods to the carrier. Accordingly, as Windows had already fulfilled its contractual obligations at the time the goods were damaged and Jordan had assumed the risk of loss, there was no "seller's breach" as is required for a buyer to claim incidental and consequential damages under § 2–715.

INTERPRETATION Unless specifically designated as a destination contract, a sales contract that involves shipment by a carrier is a shipment contract.

ETHICAL QUESTION Did the court fairly decide this case? Explain.

CRITICAL THINKING QUESTION What factors should be taken into consideration in deciding whether a contract is a shipment or a destination contract? Explain.

Goods in Possession of Bailee In some sales, the goods, at the time the contract is made, are held by a bailee and are to be delivered without being moved. For instance, a seller may contract with a buyer to sell grain that is located in a grain elevator and that the buyer intends to leave in the same elevator. In such situations, the time at which the risk of loss passes to the buyer depends on the document of title involved—or, as the case may be, on whether the transaction involves such a document at all: (1) if a negotiable document of title (discussed in Chapter 48) is involved, the risk of loss passes when the buyer *receives* the document; (2) if a nonnegotiable document of title is involved, the risk passes when the document is *tendered* to the buyer; and (3) if no documents of title are employed, it passes either (a) when the seller *tenders* to the buyer written directions to the bailee to deliver the goods to the buyer or (b) when the bailee acknowledges the buyer's right to possession of the goods. (Article 2A.)

In situations 2 and 3a, if the buyer seasonably objects, the risk of loss remains upon the seller until the buyer has had a reasonable time to present the document or direction to the bailee.

CISG If the buyer is bound to take over the goods at a place other than the seller's place of business, the risk of loss passes when the buyer is aware of the fact that the goods are placed at her disposal at that location.

All Other Sales If the buyer possesses the goods when the contract is formed, risk of loss passes to the buyer at that time. (Article 2A.)

All other sales not involving breach are covered by the Code's catchall provision, which applies to those instances in which the buyer picks up the goods at the seller's place of business or those in which the seller delivers the goods using her own transportation. In these cases, risk of loss depends on whether the seller is a merchant. If the seller is a *merchant*, risk of loss passes to the buyer on the buyer's receipt of the goods. If the seller is *not a merchant*, it passes on tender of the goods from the seller to the buyer. (Article 2A.) The policy behind this rule is that so long as the merchant seller is making delivery at her place of business or with her own vehicle, she continues to control the goods and can be expected to insure them. The buyer, on the other hand, has no control over the goods and is not likely to have insurance on them.

Suppose Ted goes to Jack's furniture store, selects a particular set of dining room furniture, and pays Jack the agreed price of $800 on Jack's agreement to stain the set a darker color and to deliver it. Jack stains the furniture and notifies Ted that he will deliver it the next day. That night, the furniture is accidentally destroyed by fire. Ted can recover the $800 payment from Jack. The risk of loss is on the seller, Jack, because he is a merchant and the goods were not received by Ted but were only tendered to him.

On the other hand, suppose Debra, an accountant, having moved to a different city, contracts to sell her household furniture to Dwight for $3,000 by a written agreement signed by Dwight. Though she notifies Dwight that the furniture is available for Dwight to pick up, he delays picking it up for several days; in the interim, the furniture is stolen from Debra's residence through no fault of Debra's. Debra may recover the $3,000 purchase price from Dwight. The risk of loss is on the buyer, Dwight, because, the seller, Debra, is not a merchant and tender is sufficient to transfer the risk of loss.

CISG If the sales contract does not involve the carriage of the goods, the risk of loss passes to the buyer when he takes over the goods, or, if the buyer does not take over the goods in due time, from the time when the goods are placed at his disposal and he commits a breach of contract by failing to take delivery.

MARTIN V. MELLAND'S INC.

SUPREME COURT OF NORTH DAKOTA, 1979
283 N.W.2D 76

http://scholar.google.com/scholar_case?case=2836560129405539957&hl=en&as_sdt=2&as_vis=1&oi=scholarr

FACTS Martin entered into a written agreement with Melland's, Inc., a farm implement dealer, to purchase a truck and attached haystack mover. According to the contract, Martin was to trade in his old truck and haystack mover unit, to mail or bring the certificate of title to the old unit to Melland's within a week, and to retain the use and possession of the old unit until Melland's had the new one ready. The contract contained no provision allocating the risk of loss of the trade-in unit. After Martin mailed the certificate to Melland's, but while he still had possession of the trade-in unit itself, the unit was destroyed by fire. Martin then sued to compel Melland's to bear the loss of the trade-in, claiming that title had passed to Melland's before the destruction of the old unit. The district court dismissed the cause of action, and Martin appealed.

DECISION Judgment for Melland's Inc. affirmed.

OPINION Erickstad, C. J. Thus the concept of title under the U.C.C. is of decreased importance. * * * No longer is the question of title of any importance in determining whether a buyer or seller bears the risk of loss.

* * *

Thus, the question of this case is not answered by a determination of the location of title, but by the risk of loss provisions in [U.C.C.§ 2–509]. Before addressing the risk of loss question in conjunction with [U.C.C. § 2–509], it is necessary to determine the posture of the parties with regard to the trade-in unit, i.e., who is the buyer and the seller and how are the responsibilities allocated. It is clear that a barter or trade-in is considered a sale and is therefore subject to the Uniform Commercial Code. [Citations.] It is also clear that the party who owns the trade-in is considered the seller. [U.C.C. § 2–304], provides that the "price can be made payable in money or otherwise. If it is payable in whole or in part in goods each party is a seller of the goods which he is to transfer." [Citations.]

Martin argues that he had already sold the trade-in unit to Melland's and, although he retained possession, he did so in the capacity of a bailee (apparently pursuant to [U.C.C. § 2–509(2)]). White and Summers in their hornbook on the Uniform Commercial Code argue that the seller who retains possession should not be considered a bailee within Section 2–509.

* * *

The courts that have addressed this issue have agreed with White and Summers. [Citations.]

It is undisputed that the contract did not require or authorize shipment by carrier pursuant to Section [2–509(1)]; therefore, the residue section, subsection 3, is applicable:

"In any case not within subsection 1 or 2, the risk of loss passes to the buyer on his receipt of the goods if the seller is a merchant; otherwise the risk passes to the buyer on tender of delivery."

Martin admits that he is not a merchant; therefore, it is necessary to determine if Martin tendered delivery of the trade-in unit to Melland's.

* * *

It is clear that the trade-in unit was not tendered to Melland's in this case. The parties agreed that Martin would keep the old unit "until they had the new one ready."

* * *

We hold that Martin did not tender delivery of the trade-in truck and haystack mover to Melland's pursuant to [U.C.C. § 2–509]; consequently, Martin must bear the loss.

INTERPRETATION In a sale involving a nonmerchant seller, the risk of loss stays with the seller until the goods are tendered to the buyer.

ETHICAL QUESTION Did the court fairly decide this case? Explain.

CRITICAL THINKING QUESTION When should risk of loss pass in this type of situation? Explain.

Figure 21-3 *Passage of Risk of Loss in Absence of Breach*

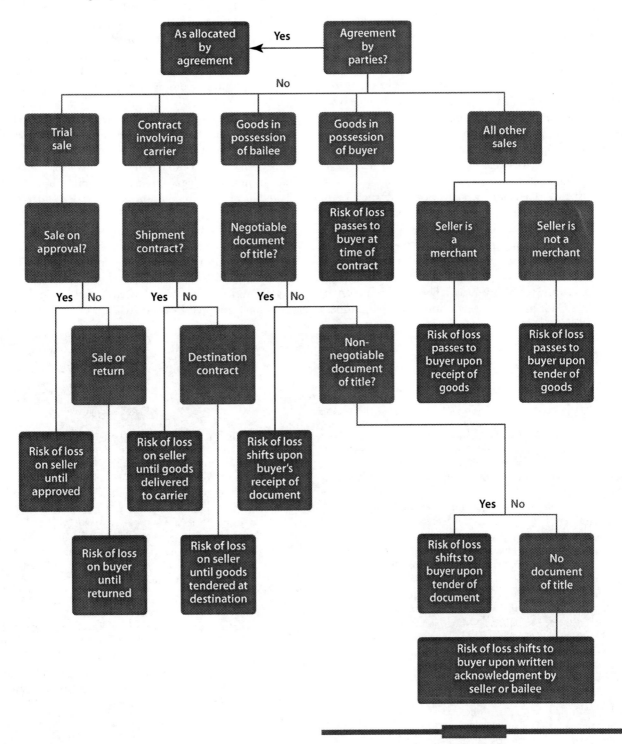

Bulk Sales

See Figure 21-3 for an illustration of risk of loss in the absence of breach. See also the Ethical Dilemma at the end of this chapter.

A sale of goods in bulk occurs when a merchant sells all or a major portion of his inventory at once. Creditors have an obvious interest in such a bulk disposal of merchandise made not in the ordinary course of business, for a debtor may secretly liquidate all or a major part of his tangible assets by a bulk sale and conceal or divert the proceeds of the sale without paying his creditors. The central purpose of bulk sales law is to deter two common forms of commercial fraud. These occur (1) when the merchant, owing debts, sells out his stock in trade to a friend for a low price, pays his creditors less than he owes them, and hopes to come back into the business "through the back door" sometime in the future; and (2) when the merchant, owing debts, sells out his stock in trade to anyone for any price, pockets the proceeds, and disappears without paying his creditors.

Article 6 of the Code, which applies to such sales, defines a **bulk transfer** as "any transfer in bulk and not in the ordinary course of the transferor's business of a major part of the materials, supplies, merchandise, or other inventory." The transfer of a substantial part of equipment is a bulk transfer only if made in connection with a bulk transfer of inventory. Those subject to Article 6 of the Code are merchants whose principal business is the sale of merchandise from stock, including those who manufacture what they sell.

The Code provides that a bulk transfer of assets is ineffective against any creditor of the transferor, unless the transfer meets certain **Article 6 requirements** designed to give the creditor notice of the bulk transfer. Should the transferor fail to comply with these requirements, the goods in the possession of the transferee continue to be subject to the claims of the transferor's unpaid creditors.

In 1988, the National Conference of Commissioners on Uniform State Laws and the American Law Institute jointly issued a recommendation stating "that changes in the business and legal contexts in which sales are conducted have made regulation of bulk sales unnecessary." They therefore recommended the repeal of Article 6 or, for those states that felt the need to continue the regulation of bulk sales, the adoption of a revised Article 6 designed to afford better protection to creditors while minimizing the obstacles to good faith transactions. Nearly every state has repealed Article 6; only a few states have adopted Revised Article 6.

Ethical Dilemma

Who Should Bear the Loss?

FACTS Stratton Corporation, a regional pharmaceutical company located in Smithville, has embarked on a policy that encourages its employees to become computer literate. Accordingly, it has made a deal with BMI, a computer manufacturer, to have computers available for purchase by Stratton's employees at considerable savings from the standard retail price. The computers, which Stratton purchases in bulk, are delivered to the home office in Smithville.

The state in which Smithville is located imposes a 7 percent sales tax on any sale that takes place in the state. For state tax purposes, the place of sale is the point of delivery. To help reduce the costs to its employees, Stratton has arranged for its personnel to pick up their purchased computers at its Somerton office, located about twenty-five miles from Smithville in a neighboring state that does not impose a sales tax.

Arthur Johnson, a Stratton employee, took advantage of the offer and purchased a computer through Stratton on December 1. The computer arrived in Smithville on December 18, and was immediately placed on a Stratton pickup truck for transfer to Somerton. Johnson, however, wanting the computer home by Christmas, suggested that he put the unit in his car and deliver it to Somerton himself, where he would immediately pick it up. Stratton, seeing a chance to save time and money, agreed to the suggestion.

On December 19, in a heavy snowfall, Johnson left Smithville with the computer bound for Somerton. As he turned onto the highway, the snowfall became a whiteout. Hearing on his car radio that blizzard conditions had already made the roads into Somerton impassable, Johnson brought the computer to his home, planning to hold it there until he could deliver it to Somerton. On the night of December 21, when snow still blocked the Somerton roads, the Johnson home and many of its furnishings were destroyed by fire. Unfortunately, Johnson had no fire insurance at the time. The computer was among the items that were destroyed. Stratton refused to accept the loss on the computer and demanded that Johnson pay for it in full. Johnson refuses.

Social, Policy, and Ethical Considerations

1. From a legal standpoint, who must bear the risk of loss for the computer? From an ethical standpoint, who should bear the loss?

2. What social responsibility did Stratton violate in setting up the computer delivery scheme? Did it have a legitimate reason for implementing the plan?

3. Do cost savings ever give a business the right to violate a social or ethical responsibility?

4. Are there any similarities between Stratton's actions in this case and a company's decision to close one of its plants?

CHAPTER SUMMARY

Transfer of Title

Identification designation of specific goods as goods to which the contract of sale refers
* *Security Interest* an interest in personal property or fixtures that ensures payment or performance of an obligation
* *Insurable Interest* buyer obtains an insurable interest and specific remedies in the goods by the identification of existing goods as goods to which the contract of sale refers

Passage of Title title passes when the parties intend it to pass; when the parties do not specifically agree, the Code provides rules to determine when title passes
* *Physical Movement of the Goods* when delivery is to be made by moving the goods, title passes at the time and place where the seller completes his performance with reference to delivery
* *No Movement of the Goods*

Power to Transfer Title the purchaser of goods obtains such title because his transferor either has or had the power to transfer; however, to encourage and make secure good faith acquisitions of goods, it is necessary to protect certain third parties under certain circumstances
* *Void Title* no title can be transferred
* *Voidable Title* the good faith purchaser acquires good title
* *Entrusting of Goods to a Merchant* buyers in the ordinary course of business acquire good title when buying from merchants

Risk of Loss

Definition allocation of loss between seller and buyer when the goods have been damaged, destroyed, or lost without the fault of either party

Risk of Loss Where There Is a Breach
* *Breach by the Seller* if the seller ships to the buyer goods that do not conform to the contract, the risk of loss remains on the seller until the buyer has accepted the goods or until the seller has remedied the defect
* *Breach by the Buyer* the seller may treat the risk of loss as resting on the buyer for a commercially reasonable time to the extent of any deficiency in the seller's effective insurance coverage

Risk of Loss in Absence of a Breach
* *Agreement of the Parties* the parties may by agreement allocate the risk of loss
* *Trial Sales* unless otherwise agreed, if the goods are delivered primarily for the buyer's use, the transaction is a sale on approval (risk of loss remains with the seller until "approval" or acceptance of the goods by the buyer); if they are delivered primarily for resale by the buyer, it is a sale or return (the risk of loss is on the buyer until she returns the goods)
* *Contracts Involving Carriers* in shipment contracts, the seller bears the risk of loss and expense until the goods are delivered to the carrier for shipment; in destination contracts, the seller bears the risk of loss and expense until tender of the goods at a particular destination
* *Goods in Possession of Bailee*
* *All Other Sales* for merchant seller, risk of loss passes to buyer on the buyer's receipt of the goods; for nonmerchant seller, risk of loss passes to buyer upon tender of goods

Bulk Sales

Definition a transfer, not in the ordinary course of the transferor's business, of a major part of inventory

Article 6 Requirements transfer is ineffective against any creditor of the transferor, unless certain requirements are met

QUESTIONS

1. Stein, a mechanic, and Beal, a life insurance agent, entered into a written contract for the sale of Stein's tractor to Beal for $6,800 cash. It was agreed that Stein would tune the motor on the tractor. Stein fulfilled this obligation and on the night of July 1 telephoned Beal that the tractor was ready to be picked up on Beal's making payment. Beal responded, "I'll be there in the morning with the money." On the next morning, however, Beal was approached by an insurance prospect and decided to get the tractor at a later date. On the night of July 2, the tractor was destroyed by fire of unknown origin. Neither Stein nor Beal had any fire insurance. Who must bear the loss?

2. Regan received a letter from Chase, the material portion of which stated, "Chase hereby places an order with you for fifty cases of Red Top Tomatoes. Ship them C.O.D." As soon as he received the letter, Regan shipped the tomatoes to Chase. While en route, the railroad car carrying the tomatoes was wrecked. When Chase refused to pay for the tomatoes, Regan started an action to recover the purchase price. Chase defended on the ground that because the shipment was C.O.D., neither title to the tomatoes nor risk of loss passed until their delivery to Chase. Who has title? Who has the risk of loss? Explain.

3. On May 10, the Adair Company, acting through Brown, entered into a contract with Clark for the installation of a milking machine at Clark's farm. Following the enumeration of the articles to be furnished, together with the price of each article, the written contract provided: "This machinery is subject to thirty days' free trial and is to be installed about June 1." Within thirty days after installation, all the purchased machinery, except for a double utility unit, was destroyed by fire through no fault of Clark's. The Adair Company sued Clark to recover the value of the articles destroyed. Explain who bears the risk of loss.

4. Brown contracted to buy sixty cases of Lovely Brand canned corn from Smith, a Toledo seller, at a contract price of $1,260. Based on the contract, Smith selected and set aside sixty cases of Lovely Brand canned corn and tagged them "For Brown." The contract required Smith to ship the corn to Brown via T Railroad, F.O.B. Toledo. Before Smith delivered the corn to the railroad, the sixty cases were stolen from Smith's warehouse.

   a. Who is liable for the loss of the sixty cases of corn, Brown or Smith?

   b. Suppose Smith had delivered the corn to the railroad in Toledo. After the corn was loaded on a freight car but before the train left the yard, the car was broken open and its contents, including the corn, were stolen. Who is liable for the loss, Brown or Smith?

   c. Would your answer in Question 4(b) be the same if this contract were F.O.B. Brown's warehouse, and all other facts remained the same?

5. Farber owned a quantity of corn that was stored in a corncrib located on Farber's farm. On March 12, Farber wrote a letter to Barber stating that he would sell to Barber all of the corn in this crib, which he estimated at between nine hundred and one thousand bushels, for $3.60 per bushel. Barber received this letter on March 13, and on the same day immediately wrote and mailed a letter to Farber stating that he would buy the corn. The corncrib and contents were accidentally destroyed by a fire that broke out about 3:00 A.M. on March 14. What are the rights and liabilities of the parties? What difference, if any, in result would there be if Farber were a merchant?

6. Franco, a New York dealer, purchased twenty-five barrels of specially graded and packed apples from a producer at Hood River, Oregon, under a contract that specified an agreed price on delivery at Franco's place of business in New York. The apples were shipped to Franco from Oregon but, through no fault of Franco, were totally destroyed before reaching New York. Does any liability rest on Franco?

7. Smith was approached by a man who introduced himself as Brown of Brown & Co. Smith, who did not know Brown, asked Dun & Bradstreet for a credit report on Brown. He thereupon sold Brown some expensive gems and billed Brown & Co. "Brown" turned out to be a clever jewel thief, who later sold the gems to Brown & Co. for valuable consideration. Brown & Co. was unaware of "Brown's" transaction with Smith. Can Smith successfully sue Brown & Co. for either the return of the gems or the price as billed to Brown & Co.?

8. Charlotte, the owner of a new Cadillac automobile, agreed to loan the car to Ellen for the month of February while she (Charlotte) went to Florida for a winter vacation. It was understood that Ellen, who was a small-town Cadillac dealer, would merely place Charlotte's car in her showroom for exhibition and sales promotion purposes. While Charlotte was away, Ellen sold the car to Bob. When Charlotte returned from Florida, she sued to recover the car from Bob. Who has title to the automobile? Explain.

9. Steven offered to sell his used automobile to Benito for $7,600 cash. Benito agreed to buy the car, gave Steven a check for $7,600, and drove away in the car. The next day, Benito sold the car for $8,000 to Jose, a good faith purchaser. The bank returned Benito's $7,600 check to Steven because of insufficient funds in Benito's account. Steven brings an action against Jose to recover the automobile. What is the judgment? Explain.

10. Justin told Jennifer he wished to buy Jennifer's collection of antique watches. He told Jennifer he wanted to take the watches to his partner for evaluation. Justin then left with the watches and never returned. Justin sold the watches in another state to Thomas and gave him a bill of sale. Can Jennifer recover the watches from Thomas? Explain.

11. On February 7, Pillsbury purchased eight thousand bushels of wheat from Landis. The wheat was being stored at the Greensville Grain Company. Pillsbury also intended to store the wheat with Greensville. On February 10, the wheat was destroyed. Landis demands payment for the wheat from Pillsbury. Who prevails? Who has title? Who has the risk of loss? Explain.

12. Johnson, who owns a hardware store, was indebted to Hutchinson, one of his suppliers. Johnson sold his business to Lockhart, one of Johnson's previous competitors. Lockhart combined the inventory from Johnson's store with his own and moved the combined inventory to a new, larger store. Hutchinson claims that Lockhart must pay Johnson's debt because the sale of the business had been made without complying with the requirements of the bulk sales law. Discuss whether Lockhart is obligated to pay Hutchinson's debt to Johnson.

13. A seller had manufactured forty thousand pounds of plastic resin pellets especially for a buyer, who agreed to accept them at the rate of one thousand pounds per day upon his issuance of shipping instructions. Despite numerous requests by the seller, the buyer issued no such instructions. On August 18, the seller, after warehousing the goods for forty days, demanded by letter that the buyer issue instructions. The buyer agreed to issue them beginning August 20, but never did. On September 22, a fire destroyed the seller's plant containing the goods, which were not covered by insurance. Who bears the risk of loss? Why?

14. McCoy, an Oklahoma cattle dealer, orally agreed with Chandler, a Texas cattle broker, to ship cattle to a New Mexico feedlot for delivery to Chandler. The agreement was for six lots of cattle valued at $119,000. After McCoy delivered the cattle, he presented invoices to Chandler that described the cattle and set forth the sales price. McCoy then demanded payment, which Chandler refused. Unknown to McCoy, Chandler had obtained a loan from First National Bank and had pledged the subject cattle as collateral. The bank had no knowledge of any interest that McCoy may have had in the cattle. McCoy sued to recover the cattle. The bank counterclaimed that it had a perfected security interest in the cattle that was superior to any interest of McCoy's. Who has title to the cattle? Explain.

CASE PROBLEMS

15. Home Indemnity, an insurance company, paid one of its insureds after the theft of his car. The car reappeared in another state and was sold to Michael Schrier for $8,300 by a used car dealer. The dealer promised to give Mr. Schrier a certificate of title. One month later, the car was seized by the police on behalf of Home Indemnity. Explain who is entitled to possession of the car.

16. Fred Lane, who sells boats, motors, and trailers, sold a boat, motor, and trailer to John Willis in exchange for a check for $6,285. The check was not honored when Lane attempted to use the funds. Willis subsequently left the boat, motor, and trailer with John Garrett, who sold the items to Jimmy Honeycutt for $2,500. Considering the boat's quality, Honeycutt was surprised at how inexpensive it was. He did not know where Garrett had obtained the boat, but he had dealt with Garrett before and described him as a "sly businessman." Garrett did not sell boats; normally; he sold fishing tackle and provisions. Honeycutt also received a forged certificate for the boat, on which he had observed Garrett forge the purported owner's signature. Can Lane compel Honeycutt to return the boat, motor, and trailer? Explain.

17. Mike Moses purchased a mobile home, including installation, from Gary Newman. Newman delivered the home to Moses's lot. Upon inspection of the home, Moses's fiancée found a broken window and water pipe. Moses also had

not received keys to the front door. Before Newman corrected these problems, a windstorm destroyed the home. Who bears the risk for the loss of the home? Why?

18. United Road Machinery Company, a dealer in heavy road equipment (including truck scales supplied by Thurman Scale Company), received a telephone call on July 21 from James Durham, an officer of Consolidated Coal Company, seeking to acquire truck scales for his coal mining operation. United and Consolidated entered into a twenty-four-month lease-purchase agreement. United then notified Thurman that Consolidated would take possession of the scales directly. United paid for the scales and Consolidated took possession of them, but the latter never signed or returned the contract papers forwarded to it by United. Consolidated also never made any of the rental payments ($608/month) due under the lease. On September 20, Consolidated, through its officer Durham, sold the scales to Kentucky Mobile Homes for $8,500. Kentucky's president, Ethard Jasper, checked the county records prior to the purchase and found no lien or encumbrance on the title; likewise, he denied knowledge of the dispute between Consolidated and United. On September 22, Kentucky sold the scales to Clyde Jasper, individually, for $8,500. His search also failed to disclose any lien on the title to the scales, and he denied knowledge of the dispute between Consolidated and United. Can United recover the scales from Jasper? Explain.

TAKING SIDES

Harrison, a men's clothing retailer located in Westport, Connecticut, ordered merchandise from Ninth Street East, Ltd., a Los Angeles–based clothing manufacturer. Ninth Street delivered the merchandise to Denver-Chicago Trucking Company (Denver) in Los Angeles and then sent four invoices to Harrison that bore the notation "F.O.B. Los Angeles." Denver subsequently transferred the merchandise to a connecting carrier, Old Colony Transportation Company, for final delivery to Harrison's Westport store. When Old Colony tried to deliver the merchandise, Harrison's wife asked the truck driver to deliver the boxes inside the store, but the driver refused. The dispute remained unresolved, and the truck departed with Old Colony still in possession of the goods. By letter, Harrison then notified Ninth Street of the nondelivery, but Ninth Street was unable to locate the shipment. Ninth Street then sought to recover the contract purchase price from Harrison. Harrison refused, contending that risk of loss remained with Ninth Street because of its refusal to deliver the merchandise to Harrison's place of business.

a. What are the arguments that the risk of loss remained with Ninth Street?

b. What are the arguments that the risk of loss passed to Harrison?

c. What is the appropriate outcome?

Chapter 22

PRODUCT LIABILITY: WARRANTIES AND STRICT LIABILITY

The explosion of [product liability] lawsuits—and the cost of insuring against them—is forcing managers to react. Some have pulled goods off the market. Other responses: raising prices, redesigning products, educating customers, and finding new ways of settling claims.

MICHAEL BRODY, IN *FORTUNE*

CHAPTER OUTCOMES

After reading and studying this chapter, you should be able to:

1. Identify and describe the types of warranties.

2. List and explain the various defenses that may be successfully raised to a warranty action.

3. Describe the elements of an action based on strict liability in tort.

4. List and explain the obstacles to an action based on strict liability in tort.

5. Compare strict liability in tort with the implied warranty of merchantability.

I n this chapter, we will consider the liability of manufacturers and sellers of goods to buyers, users, consumers, and bystanders for damages caused by defective products. The rapidly expanding development of case law has established product liability as a distinct field of law that combines and enforces rules and principles of contracts, sales, negligence, strict liability, and statutory law.

One reason for the expansion of such liability has been the modern method of distributing goods. In the twenty-first century, retailers serve principally as a conduit of goods that are prepackaged in sealed containers and that are widely advertised by the manufacturer or distributor. This has hastened the extension of product liability coverage to include manufacturers and other parties within the chain of distribution. The extension of product liability to manufacturers, however, has not noticeably lessened the liability of a seller to his immediate purchaser. Rather, it has broadened the base of liability through the development and application of new principles of law.

Products liability has attracted a great deal of public attention. According to the U.S. Consumer Product Safety Commission, deaths, injuries, and property damage from consumer product incidents cost the United States more than $800 billion annually. The resultant cost of maintaining product liability insurance has skyrocketed, causing great concern in the business community. In response to the clamor over this insurance crisis, almost all of the states have revised their tort laws to make successful tort (including product liability) lawsuits more difficult to bring. These tort reforms include legislation dealing with joint and several liability, punitive damages, noneconomic damages, and class actions. Nevertheless, repeated efforts to pass federal product liability legislation have been unsuccessful.

> ## PRACTICAL ADVICE
> Thoroughly test your products prior to releasing them into the channels of distribution to ensure that they are safe and properly designed. In addition, include all necessary warnings and instructions and be sure that they are clear and conspicuous.

The liability of manufacturers and sellers of goods for a defective product, or for its failure to perform adequately, may be based on one or more of the following: (1) negligence, (2) misrepresentation, (3) violation of statutory duty, (4) warranty, and (5) strict liability in tort. We covered the first three of these causes of actions in Chapters 8 and 11. Chapter 8 also covered traditional strict liability—where liability is imposed regardless of the defendant's negligence or intent to cause harm. In this chapter we will cover a specialized type of strict liability—strict liability in tort for products. This chapter will also explore warranty liability.

WARRANTIES

A **warranty**, under the Uniform Commercial Code (UCC or the Code), creates a duty on the part of the seller to ensure that the goods he sells will conform to certain qualities, characteristics, or conditions. A seller, however, is not required to warrant the goods; and, in general, he may, by appropriate words, disclaim (exclude) or modify a particular warranty or even all warranties.

In bringing a warranty action, the buyer must prove that (1) a warranty existed, (2) the warranty has been breached, (3) the breach of the warranty proximately caused the loss suffered, and (4) notice of the breach of warranty was given to the seller. The seller has the burden of proving defenses based on the buyer's conduct. If the seller breaches his warranty, the buyer may reject or revoke acceptance of the goods. Moreover, whether the goods have been accepted or rejected, the buyer may recover a judgment against the seller for damages. Harm for which damages are recoverable includes personal injury, damage to property, and economic loss. Economic loss most commonly involves damages for loss of bargain and consequential damages for lost profits. (Damages for breach of warranty are discussed in detail in the next chapter.) In this section, we will examine the

various types of warranties, as well as the obstacles to a cause of action for breach of warranty.

Types of Warranties

A warranty may arise out of the mere existence of a sale (a warranty of title), out of any affirmation of fact or promise made by the seller to the buyer (an express warranty), or out of the circumstances under which the sale is made (an implied warranty). In a contract for the sale of goods, it is possible to have both express and implied warranties, as well as a warranty of title. All warranties are construed as consistent with each other and cumulative, unless such construction is unreasonable. A purchaser, under Revised Article 1, means a person who takes by sale, lease, lien, security interest, gift, or any other voluntary transaction creating an interest in property. (Prior Article 1 did not include leases.)

Article 2A carries over the warranty provisions of Article 2 with relatively minor revision to reflect differences in style, leasing terminology, or leasing practices. The creation of express warranties and, except for finance leases, the imposition of the implied warranties of merchantability and fitness for a particular purpose are virtually identical to their Article 2 analogues. Article 2 and Article 2A diverge somewhat in their treatment of the warranties of title and infringement as well as in their provisions for the exclusion and modification of warranties.

WARRANTY OF TITLE

Under the UCC's **warranty of title**, the seller implicitly warrants that (1) the title conveyed is good and its transfer rightful and (2) the goods are subject to no security interest or other lien (a claim on property by another for payment of debt) of which the buyer did not know at the time of contracting. In a lease, title does not transfer to the lessee. Accordingly, Article 2A's analogous provision protects the lessee's right to possession and use of the goods from the claims of other parties arising from an act or omission of the lessor.

Let us assume that Steven acquires goods from Nancy in a transaction that is void and then sells the goods to Rachel. Nancy brings an action against Rachel and recovers the goods. Steven has breached the warranty of title because he did not have good title to the goods and, therefore, his transfer of the goods to Rachel was not rightful. Accordingly, Steven is liable to Rachel for damages.

The Code does not label the warranty of title an implied warranty, even though it arises out of the sale and not out of any particular words or conduct. Instead, the Code has a separate disclaimer provision for warranty of title; thus, the Code's general disclaimer provision for implied warranties does not apply.

EXPRESS WARRANTIES

An **express warranty** is an explicit undertaking by the seller with respect to the quality, description, condition, or performability of the goods. The undertaking may consist of an affirmation of fact or a promise that relates to the goods, a description of the goods, or a sample or model of the goods. In each of these instances, for an express warranty to be created, the undertaking must become or be made part of the basis of the bargain. It is not necessary, however, that the seller have a specific intention to make a warranty or use formal words such as "warrant" or "guarantee." Moreover, it is not necessary that, to be liable for breach of express warranty, a seller know of the falsity of a statement she makes; the seller may be acting in good faith. For example, if John mistakenly asserts to Sam that a rope will easily support two hundred pounds and Sam is injured when the rope breaks while supporting only two hundred pounds, John is liable for breach of an express warranty.

Creation A seller can create an express warranty either orally or in writing. One way in which the seller may create such a warranty is by an affirmation of fact or a promise that relates to the goods. (Article 2A.) For example, a statement made by a seller that an automobile will get forty-two miles to the gallon of gasoline or that a camera has automatic focus is an express warranty.

The Code further provides that an affirmation of the *value* of the goods or a statement purporting merely to be the seller's *opinion* or recommendation of the goods does not create a warranty. (Article 2A.) Such statements are not factual and do not deceive the ordinary buyer, who accepts them merely as opinions or *as puffery* (sales talk). A statement of value, however, may be an express warranty in cases in which the seller states the price at which the goods were purchased from a former owner, or in which she gives market figures relating to sales of similar

goods. These are affirmations of facts. They are statements of events, not mere opinions; and the seller is liable for breach of warranty if they are untrue. Also, although a statement of opinion by the seller is not ordinarily a warranty, the seller who is an expert and who gives an opinion as such may be liable for breach of warranty.

> ### PRACTICAL ADVICE
> Make only those affirmations of fact or promises about the goods being sold that you wish to stand behind. Moreover, recognize that advertising claims and the statements made by salespeople can give rise to express warranties.

A seller also can create an express warranty by the use of a *description* of the goods that becomes a part of the basis of the bargain. (Article 2A.) Under such a warranty, the seller expressly warrants that the goods shall conform to the description. Examples include statements regarding a particular brand or type of goods, technical specifications, and blueprints.

The use of a *sample* or model is another means of creating an express warranty. (Article 2A.) When a sample or model is a part of the basis of the bargain, the seller expressly warrants that the entire lot of goods sold shall conform to the sample or model. A sample is a good that is actually drawn from the bulk of goods that is the subject matter of the sale. By comparison, a model is offered for inspection when the subject matter is not at hand; it is not drawn from the bulk. See the case that follows as well as *In Re L. B. Trucking, Inc.* later in this chapter.

 According to the United Nations Convention on CISG, the seller must deliver goods that conform to the quality and description required by the contract. In addition, the goods must possess the qualities of any sample or model used by the seller.

BELDEN, INC. V. AMERICAN ELECTRONIC COMPONENTS, INC.

COURT OF APPEALS OF INDIANA, 2008
885 N.E.2D 751, 66 UCC REP.SERV.2D 399
http://scholar.google.com/scholar_case?q=885+N.E.2d+751&hl=en&as_sdt=2,34&case=6981122239976535930&scilh=0

FACTS Belden, Inc., and Belden Wire & Cable Company (Belden) manufactures wire, and American Electronic Components, Inc. (AEC) manufactures automobile sensors. Since 1989, AEC, in repeated transactions, has purchased wire from Belden to use in its sensors. In 1994, AEC indicated to its suppliers that it was adopting a quality control program to satisfy the requirements of AEC's purchasers, automobile manufacturers. Part of AEC's quality control program included an extensive production part approval process (PPAP). In 1996 and 1997, Belden sought to comply with AEC's quality control program and provided detailed information to AEC regarding the materials it used to manufacture its wire. In its assurances, Belden stated that it would use insulation from Quantum Chemical Corp. (Quantum). In 1997, AEC approved Belden's PPAP. In June 2003, however, Belden began using insulation supplied by Dow Chemical Company (Dow). The Dow insulation had different physical properties than the insulation provided by Quantum. In October 2003, Belden sold AEC wire manufactured with the Dow insulation. AEC used this wire to make its sensors, and the insulation ultimately cracked. Chrysler had installed AEC's sensors containing the faulty wire in approximately eighteen thousand vehicles. Chrysler recalled fourteen thousand vehicles and repaired the remaining four thousand prior to sale. Pursuant to an agreement with Chrysler, AEC was required to reimburse Chrysler for expenses associated with the recall. In 2004, AEC filed a complaint against Belden seeking damages for the changes in the insulation that resulted in the recall. In 2007, the trial court entered an order granting AEC's motion for partial summary judgment and denying Belden's cross-motion for summary judgment. Belden appealed on the basis that it did not create an express warranty regarding compliance with AEC's quality control program.

DECISION The trial court's granting AEC's partial motion for summary judgment and denying Belden's partial motion for summary judgment is affirmed.

OPINION Barnes, J. "Where an agreement is entirely in writing, the question of whether express warranties were made is one for the court." [Citation.] More specifically, if all of the representations upon which the parties rely were in writing, the existence of express warranties is a question of law. [Citation.] Because the alleged warranty is based on written exchanges, whether the writings are sufficient to create an express warranty is a question of law appropriate for summary judgment.

* * *

Belden claims that these 1996 and 1997 communications did not amount to an express warranty for purposes of the October 2003 contract. Section 2-313 of the UCC provides:

(1) Express warranties by the seller are created as follows:
(a) any affirmation of fact or promise made by the seller to the buyer which relates to the goods and becomes part of the basis of the bargain creates an express warranty that the goods shall conform to the affirmation or promise.

(b) any description of the goods which is made part of the basis of the bargain creates an express warranty that the goods shall conform to the description.
(c) any sample or model which is made part of the basis of the bargain creates an express warranty that the whole of the goods shall conform to the sample or model.
(2) It is not necessary to the creation of an express warranty that the seller use formal words such as "warrant" or "guarantee" or that he have a specific intention to make a warranty, but an affirmation merely of the value of the goods or a statement purporting to be merely the seller's opinion or commendation of the goods does not create a warranty.

"An express warranty requires some representation, term or statement as to how the product is warranted." [Citation.] There does not seem to be a dispute that in 1996 and 1997 Belden made express warranties regarding its wire. Instead, the issue is whether the 1996 and 1997 statements by Belden regarding certification created an express warranty that extended to the October 2003 contract.

Based on the designated evidence, we believe Belden's compliance with AEC's quality control program was essential to its contracts with AEC and was intended to extend to the parties' repeated contracts. First, Comment 7 to Section 2-313 provides in part, "The precise time when words of description or affirmation are made or samples are shown is not material. The sole question is whether the language or samples or models are fairly to be regarded as part of the contract." Thus, although Belden made its initial representations in 1996 and 1997, there is no indication that those representations were limited in time, that Belden subsequently disclaimed its compliance with AEC's quality control standards, or that AEC changed those standards. As the trial court observed, "it is illogical to believe that [AEC] intended to rely in this representation for only one (1) shipment of Wire and then to understand that Belden would follow whatever quality procedures it wanted as to future shipments."

Further, Comment 5 of Section 2-213 provides in part, "Past deliveries may set the description of quality, either expressly or impliedly by course of dealing. Of course, all descriptions by merchants must be read against the applicable trade usages with the general rules as to merchantability resolving any doubts." Belden claims that if the parties' course of dealing was insufficient to incorporate the limitation on damages into the parties' contract, then the course of dealing is also insufficient to establish an express warranty. We disagree. Irrespective of whether the course of dealing established that AEC assented to Belden's proposed limitation on damages, the parties' course of dealing established that Belden made an express warranty regarding its compliance with the quality control standards. The limitation on damages and the express warranty are unrelated issues—there is no correlation between the two.

A course of dealing is conduct "fairly to be regarded as establishing a common basis of understanding for interpreting their expressions and other conduct." § 1-205(1). It is undisputed that Belden's wire complied with the AEC's quality control requirements for the parties' more than 100 transactions, until October 2003, when Belden switched from Quantum insulation to the Dow insulation without informing AEC of the changes. *** That Belden and AEC did not repeatedly or routinely "communicate" regarding Belden's continued use of Quantum insulation does not undermine the parties' course of dealing. The very point of a course of dealing is to allow the parties' prior actions create a basis of common understanding. This is exactly what Belden's 1996 and 1997 assertions taken with its continued use of Quantum insulation did.

INTERPRETATION An express warranty is created by an affirmation of fact or promise about the goods.

CRITICAL THINKING QUESTION How long should an express warranty last between merchants who continue to do business with each other over many years?

Basis of Bargain The Code does not require that the affirmations, promises, descriptions, samples, or models the seller makes or uses be relied on by the buyer but only that they constitute a part of the **basis of the bargain**. In other words, if they are part of the buyer's assumption underlying the sale, reliance by the buyer is presumed. Some courts merely require that the buyer know of the affirmation or promise for it to be presumed to be part of the basis of the bargain, while others require some showing of reliance. See the case *In Re L. B. Trucking, Inc.*

Like statements in advertisements or catalogs, statements or promises made by the seller to the buyer prior to the sale may be express warranties, as they may form a part of the basis of the bargain. In addition, under the Code, statements or promises made by the seller subsequent to the making of the contract of sale may become express warranties even though no new consideration is given. (Article 2A.)

IMPLIED WARRANTIES

An implied warranty, unlike an express warranty, is not found in the language of the sales contract or in a specific affirmation or promise by the seller. Instead, it exists by operation of law. An **implied warranty** arises out of the circumstances under which the parties enter into their contract and depends on factors such as the type of contract or sale entered into, the seller's merchant or nonmerchant status, the conduct of the parties, and the applicability of other statutes.

Merchantability Under the Code, a *merchant seller* makes an implied warranty of the merchantability of goods that are of the kind in which he deals. The implied warranty of **merchantability** provides that the goods are reasonably fit for the *ordinary* purposes for which they are used; pass without objection in the trade under the contract description; and are of fair, average quality. (Article 2A.)

> **PRACTICAL ADVICE**
>
> Because the warranty of merchantability applies only to merchant sellers, when purchasing goods from a nonmerchant seller, attempt to obtain a written express warranty that the goods will be, at a minimum, of average quality and fit for ordinary purposes.

> **CISG** The seller must deliver goods, unless otherwise agreed, that are fit for the purposes for which goods of the same description would ordinarily be used.

Fitness for Particular Purpose Unlike the warranty of merchantability, the implied warranty of fitness for a particular purpose applies to *any* seller, whether he is a merchant or not. The implied warranty of **fitness for a particular purpose** arises if at the time of contracting the seller had reason to know the buyer's particular purpose and to know that the buyer was relying on the seller's skill and judgment to select suitable goods. (Article 2A.)

The implied warranty of fitness for a particular purpose does not require any specific statement by the seller. Rather, it requires only that the seller know that the buyer, in selecting a product for her specific purpose, is relying on the seller's expertise. The buyer need not specifically inform the seller of her particular purpose; it is sufficient if the seller has reason to know it On the other hand, the implied warranty of fitness for a particular purpose would not arise in a situation in which the buyer insists on a particular product and the seller simply conveys it to her.

In contrast to the implied warranty of merchantability, the implied warranty of fitness for a particular purpose pertains to a specific purpose for, rather than the ordinary purpose of, the goods. A particular purpose may be a specific use or may relate to a special situation in which the buyer intends to use the goods. Thus, if the seller has reason to know that the buyer is purchasing a pair of shoes for mountain climbing and that the buyer is relying on the seller's judgment to furnish suitable shoes for this purpose, a sale of shoes suitable only for ordinary walking purposes would be a breach of this implied warranty. Likewise, if a buyer indicates to a seller that she needs a stamping machine to stamp ten thousand packages in an eight-hour period and that she relies upon the seller to select an appropriate machine, the seller, by selecting a machine, impliedly warrants

that the machine selected will stamp ten thousand packages in an eight-hour period.

The seller must deliver goods, unless otherwise agreed, that are fit for any particular purpose expressly or impliedly made known to the seller by the buyer, except when the buyer did not rely on the seller's skill and judgment or when it was unreasonable for the buyer to rely on the seller.

Frequently, as in the case that follows, a seller's conduct may involve both the implied warranty of merchantability *and* the implied warranty of fitness for a particular purpose.

In Re L. B. Trucking, Inc.

UNITED STATES BANKRUPTCY COURT, 1994
163 BR 709, 23 UCC REP. SERV.2D 1093

http://scholar.google.com/scholar_case?case=6401409485061780661 &q=163+BR+709&hl=en&as_sdt=2,34

FACTS Dudley B. Durham, Jr., and his wife, Barbara Durham, owned and operated a trucking company, L. B. Trucking, Inc., and a farm, Double-D Farms, Inc. In April 1983, Dudley Durham met with Richard Thomas of Southern States Cooperative—which is in the business of supplying various agricultural supplies to farmers—about arranging for the application of herbicides to the Durhams' fields.

At a subsequent meeting in early May, Durham met with Thomas to complete credit arrangements and to arrange the application of herbicides. Durham told Thomas, "I want it done the cheapest way, the best way it can be done." Thomas responded, "Will do." Thomas then outlined with some specificity the chemicals he proposed to use on the Durhams' fields. The plan included the use of a water-based carrier that was recommended by local experts, rather than a more expensive nitrogen solution. Durham had no experience or expertise on herbicidal chemicals and relied on Thomas's briefing on the various herbicide mixtures in choosing which ones to apply.

When the herbicides were actually to be applied, Southern States herbicide applicator, Gilbert McClements, received from Mr. Thomas instructions concerning which chemicals to apply and would mix the chemicals each day prior to spraying. Apparently, though, Mr. McClements used a nitrogen solution to prepare the herbicides and did not make extensive prespraying inspections of the grass

and weeds in the fields to be sprayed. When Durham noticed a significant number of weeds and grasses had survived the herbicidal treatment, he promptly notified Southern States. Southern States attempted to remedy the problem, but the harvest was dismal and far below the county average.

In 1983, the Durhams and both their businesses filed for bankruptcy. Southern States brought a claim against the consolidated bankruptcy estate to collect payment for the herbicides as well as application and other services provided. The trustee of the estate asserted counterclaims against Southern States for negligence and breach of warranties in the application of herbicides that caused severe damage to the Durhams' 1983 crop.

DECISION Judgment for the trustee.

OPINION Balick, J.

1. Express Warranty

An express warranty may be created by a seller through: (1) any affirmation of fact or promise to the buyer relating to the goods which becomes the basis of the bargain so that the goods conform to the affirmation or promise; (2) any description of the goods which is made part of the basis of the bargain so that the whole of the goods conform to the sample of model. U.C.C. § 2–313(1)(a)–(c). The question of whether an express warranty has been made in a particular transaction is for the trier of fact. [Citation.] In the case at bar, there are no written express warranties claimed, but instead, oral statements made principally by the Middletown store manager, Thomas, to Durham which the Trustee contends were, express warranties.

The relevant testimony concerning Thomas' statements to Durham reveal several oral express warranties concerning the herbicides and their application which Southern States plainly breached. First, Thomas stated that water would be the carrier for the herbicides, especially since Durham wanted the job done inexpensively. In its application, Southern States used the nitrogen solution regardless of the University of Delaware recommendations dissuading its use and despite the fact that it is more expensive than using water as a carrier. *** In addition, Thomas' statements were more than "seller's talk" or puffing in that they were product specific and not overly broad or vague. Second, Thomas also made statements regarding the effectiveness of the herbicides in removing weeds and grass so as to promote successful no-till farming. The purchase of herbicides is characteristically the subject of express warranties because the buyer of the product cannot determine its effectiveness prior to use and evaluate its effectiveness in a given situation. Here, Thomas' statements in early May of 1983 were part of the basis of the bargain upon which Durham relied when purchasing the herbicides. Beyond this, Thomas had superior knowledge about the herbicides as opposed to Durham who had little or none. Consequently, Thomas' selection of herbicidal recipes combined with his statements as to their effectiveness amounted to an express warranty that the respective mixtures would do the job adequately. ***

2. IMPLIED WARRANTIES

There are two theories of recovery for breach of implied warranty under the Delaware UCC: breach of implied warranty of merchantability under U.C.C. § 2–314 and breach of implied warranty of fitness for a particular purpose under U.C.C. § 2–315. ***

Turning first to the implied warranty of merchantability, there are five elements which the claimant must establish: (1) that a merchant sold goods, (2) which were not merchantable at the time of sale, (3) proximately causing by the defective nature of the goods, (4) injury and damages to the claimant or his property, and (5) notice to the seller of the injury. [Citation.] As to the element requiring the seller to be a merchant, there is no doubt that Southern States was a merchant. ***

Addressing the second element concerning whether the herbicides were "merchantable," the goods must pass without objection in the trade under the contract

description *and* be fit for the ordinary purposes for which it was intended, U.C.C. 2–314(2)(a) and (c). The facts show that Southern States sprayed (and in some instances resprayed) the various Durham farm tracts with herbicidal and other chemicals in order to increase the crop yields. Nevertheless, the farms' respective crop yields did not improve, but rather fell dramatically as the result of the chemical applications. Specifically, the herbicidal recipes were unfit for the ordinary purpose for which they were intended to be used, chemical agents that would kill weeds without damaging the primary crops. [Citation.] The chemicals did not operate for their ordinary purpose which was to promote no-till farming which is why Durham purchased them in the first place.

As for proximate cause and damages, the court finds that these elements have been met. ***

Finally, the notice requirement for a breach of implied warranty of merchantability cause of action was plainly met. Durham notified Southern States as soon as he suspected that the herbicides were failing to work just a few weeks after their application. ***

Southern States also breached the implied warranty that the herbicides were fit for their particular purpose. ***

The breach of this warranty is the one most apparent on the facts. As indicated earlier, Durham relied on Thomas' skill and judgment in selecting suitable herbicides to conduct no-till farming on his farms. The chemicals were mixed by Southern States' herbicide applicator, McClements, before each job based on a formula or recipe provided by Thomas or some other Southern States official. The herbicides did not effectively do their job of keeping the fields clear of weeds and the crops died. Though thoroughly familiar with till farming, Durham had no experience with the no-till farming method and, therefore, was not a "sophisticated purchaser" who might have been able to recognize mistakes made by Southern States' personnel. As a result, the herbicides' failure to do their intended task coupled with Durham's reliance on Southern States' judgment and skill in formulating, mixing, and applying the herbicidal chemicals breached the implied warranty of fitness. [Citations.] Accordingly, Southern States is found to be liable under U.C.C. § 2–315.

INTERPRETATION In a contract for a sale of goods, it is possible to breach multiple warranties.

ETHICAL QUESTION Did any of the parties act unethically? Explain.

CRITICAL THINKING QUESTION Did the court correctly decide this case? Explain.

Obstacles to Warranty Actions

A number of technical obstacles, which vary considerably from jurisdiction to jurisdiction, limit the effectiveness of warranty as a basis for recovery. These include disclaimers of warranties, limitations or modifications of warranties, privity, notice of breach, and the conduct of the plaintiff.

DISCLAIMER OF WARRANTIES

To be effective, a **disclaimer** (negation of warranty) must be positive, explicit, unequivocal, and conspicuous. The Code calls for a reasonable construction of words or conduct to disclaim or limit warranties. (Article 2A.)

Express Exclusions In general, a seller cannot provide an **express warranty** and then disclaim it. A seller can, however, avoid making an express warranty by carefully refraining from making any promise or affirmation of fact relating to the goods, by refraining from making a description of the goods, or by refraining from using a sample or model in a sale. (Article 2A.) Oral warranties made before the execution of a written agreement containing an express disclaimer are subject to the parol evidence rule, however. Thus, as discussed in Chapter 15, if the parties intend the written contract to be the final and complete statement of the agreement between them, parol evidence of a warranty that contradicts the terms of the written contract is inadmissible.

> PRACTICAL ADVICE
>
> Recognize that once you make an express warranty, it is very difficult to disclaim the warranty.

A **warranty of title** may be excluded only by specific language or by certain circumstances, including a judicial sale or sales by sheriffs, executors, or foreclosing lienors. (Article 2A.) In the latter cases, the seller is clearly offering to sell only such right or title as he or a third person might have in the goods, because it is apparent that the goods are not the property of the person selling them.

To exclude or to modify an **implied warranty of merchantability**, the language of disclaimer or modification must mention *merchantability* and, in the case of a writing, must be *conspicuous*. Article 2A requires that a **disclaimer of an implied warranty** of merchantability mention merchantability, be in writing, and be conspicuous. For example, Bart wishes to buy a used refrigerator from Ben's Used Appliances Store for $100. Given the low purchase price, Ben is unwilling to guarantee the refrigerator's performance. Bart agrees to buy it with no warranty protection. To exclude the warranty, Ben writes conspicuously on the contract, "This refrigerator carries no warranties, including no warranty of MERCHANTABILITY." Ben has effectively disclaimed the implied warranty of merchantability. Some courts, however, do not require the disclaimer to be conspicuous where a *commercial* buyer has actual knowledge of the disclaimer. The Code's test for whether a provision is *conspicuous* is whether a reasonable person against whom the disclaimer is to operate ought to have noticed it. Revised Article 1 provides that conspicuous terms include (1) a heading in capitals equal to or greater in size than the surrounding text; or in contrasting type, font, or color to the surrounding text of the same or lesser size; and (2) language in the body of a record or display in larger type than the surrounding text; or in contrasting type, font, or color to the surrounding text of the same size; or set off from surrounding text of the same size by symbols or other marks that call attention to the language. Whether a term is conspicuous is an issue for the court.

To exclude or to modify an **implied warranty of fitness for the particular purpose** of the buyer, the disclaimer must also be in *writing* and *conspicuous*. (Article 2A.)

All implied warranties, unless the circumstances indicate otherwise, are excluded by expressions like *"as is"* or *"with all faults"* or by other language plainly calling the buyer's attention to the exclusion of warranties. (Article 2A.) Most courts require the "as is" clause to be conspicuous. Implied warranties may also be excluded by course of dealing, course of performance, or usage of trade. (Article 2A.)

> PRACTICAL ADVICE
>
> If you want to disclaim the implied warranties, be sure to use large, conspicuous type; use the appropriate language; and place the disclaimer on the first page of the agreement.

The courts will invalidate disclaimers they consider unconscionable. The Code, as discussed in Chapter 19, permits a court to limit the application of any contract or contractual provision that it finds unconscionable. (Article 2A.)

WOMCO, INC. v. NAVISTAR INTERNATIONAL CORPORATION

COURT OF APPEALS OF TEXAS, TWELFTH DISTRICT, TYLER, 2002
84 S.W.3D 272, 48 U.C.C. REP. SERV. 2D 130

http://scholar.google.com/scholar_case?case=3776672246675983367&q=84+S.W.3d+272&hl=en&as_sdt=2,22

FACTS In 1993, Womco, Inc. purchased through Price, a dealer, thirty 1993 International model 9300 tractor trucks manufactured by Navistar. Also, in 1993, C. L. Hall purchased sixteen 1994 International model 9300 tractor trucks also manufactured by Navistar through Mahaney, another dealer. Almost immediately after the trucks were put into service, Womco and Hall (plaintiffs) each had problems with their trucks' engines overheating. As the problems occurred, plaintiffs took their trucks, which were still covered under warranty, to their dealerships for service related to the overheating problem. Although repeated attempts were made, the dealerships were unable to correct the problem. Subsequently it was discovered that the trucks' radiators were unusually small and were insufficient to cool the engine.

Womco and Hall filed suit against Navistar, Price, and Mahaney (defendants). The trial court granted the defendants' motion for summary judgment based on their affirmative defenses of disclaimer of warranty. Womco and Hall appealed.

DECISION Summary judgment for defendants is reversed, and case remanded.

OPINION Griffith, J. *** [The] Appellees contend that [the] implied warranties were disclaimed. The Texas Uniform Commercial Code allows sellers to disclaim both the implied warranty of merchantability as well as the implied warranty of fitness for particular purpose. [UCC] § 2.316(b), [citation]. In order to disclaim an implied warranty of merchantability in a sales transaction, the disclaimer must mention the word "merchantability." The disclaimer may be oral or written, but if in writing, the disclaimer must be conspicuous. [Citation]; [UCC] § 2.316(b). To disclaim an implied warranty of fitness for a particular purpose, the disclaimer must be in writing and must be conspicuous. [UCC] § 2.316(b); [citation]. Whether a particular disclaimer is conspicuous is a question of law to be determined by the court. [Citation]. A term or clause is conspicuous if it is written so that a reasonable person against whom it is to operate ought to have noticed it. [UCC] § 1.201(10); [citation]. Language is "conspicuous" if it is in larger type or other contrasting font or color. [Citation]. Conspicuousness is not required

if the buyer has actual knowledge of the disclaimer. [Citation].

* * *

Further, Appellants argue that Appellees were required to offer proof of the context of the purported disclaimers, contending that in order for a disclaimer of an implied warranty to be effective, the plaintiffs must have had an opportunity to examine it prior to consummation of the contract for sale. [Citation]. *** In *Dickenson* [citation], the court held that a disclaimer of an express warranty was ineffective where the buyer was not given the opportunity to read the warranty or warranties made until after the contract is signed. Although the instant case concerns a converse situation to *Dickenson*, the rationale applied by the *Dickenson* court is helpful. One of the underlying purposes of [UCC section 2.316 is to protect a buyer from surprise by permitting the exclusion of implied warranties. [UCC] § 2.316, comment 1. We fail to see how section [UCC] 2.316 can fulfill such a purpose unless a disclaimer is required to be communicated to the buyer before the contract of sale has been completed, unless the buyer afterward agrees to the disclaimer as a modification of the contract. [Citations.]

In support of their motion for summary judgment, Appellees offered six disclaimers, all of which were deposition exhibits. None of these six disclaimers is probative as to the issue of whether the disclaimer was communicated prior to the completion of the contract of sale. ***

Accordingly, the trial court's order granting summary judgment is *reversed* as to Appellants' claims for breach of warranty filed less than four years after the delivery of the truck upon which the claim is based, and is *remanded* to the trial court for further proceedings.

INTERPRETATION A disclaimer of warranties of merchantability and fitness for a particular purpose must be communicated clearly to the buyer.

ETHICAL QUESTION Did any of the parties act unethically? Explain.

CRITICAL THINKING QUESTION Do you agree with the court's decision? Explain.

Buyer's Examination or Refusal to Examine If the buyer inspects the goods before entering into the contract, implied warranties do not apply to defects that are apparent on examination. Moreover, there is no implied warranty on defects that an examination ought to have revealed, not only when the buyer has examined the goods as fully as desired, but also when the buyer has refused to examine the goods. (Article 2A.)

> ### PRACTICAL ADVICE
>
> If you are a seller, offer the buyer an opportunity to examine the goods to avoid an implied warranty for any defects that should be detected upon inspection. If you are a buyer and are offered an opportunity to examine the goods, make sure that you make a reasonable inspection of the goods.

> **CISG**
>
> If at the time of entering into the sales contract, the buyer knew or could not have been unaware of the lack of conformity, the seller is not liable for the warranty of particular purpose, ordinary purpose, or sale by sample or model.

Federal Legislation Relating to Warranties of Consumer Goods To protect purchasers of **consumer goods** (defined as "tangible personal property normally used for personal, family or household purposes"), Congress enacted the Magnuson-Moss Warranty Act. The purpose of the Act is to prevent deception and to make sure that consumer purchasers are adequately informed about warranties. Some courts have applied the Act to leases.

The Federal Trade Commission administers and enforces the Act. The Commission's guidelines for the type of consumer product warranty information a seller must supply are aimed at providing the consumer with clear and useful information. More significantly, the Act provides that a seller who makes a written warranty cannot disclaim any implied warranty. For a complete discussion of the Act, see Chapter 44.

> ### PRACTICAL ADVICE
>
> If you are a seller of consumer goods and wish to disclaim the implied warranties, make sure that you do not provide any written express warranties.

LIMITATION OR MODIFICATION OF WARRANTIES

The Code permits a seller to *limit* or *modify* the buyer's remedies for breach of warranty. One important exception to this right is the prohibition against a seller's "unconscionable" limitations or exclusions of consequential damages. (Article 2A.) Specifically, the "[l]imitation of consequential damages for injury to the person in the case of consumer goods is prima facie unconscionable." In some cases, a seller may seek to impose time limits within which the warranty is effective. Except when such clauses result in unconscionability, the Code permits them; it does not, however, permit any attempt to shorten the time period for filing an action for personal injury to less than one year.

PRIVITY OF CONTRACT

Because of the close association between warranties and contracts, a principle of law in the nineteenth century established that a plaintiff could not recover for breach of warranty unless he was in a contractual relationship with the defendant. This relationship is known as **privity of contract.**

Under this rule, a warranty by seller Ingrid to buyer Sylvester, who resells the goods to purchaser Lyle under a similar warranty, gives Lyle no rights against Ingrid. There is no privity of contract between Ingrid and Lyle. In the event of breach of warranty, Lyle may recover only from his seller, Sylvester, who in turn may recover from Ingrid.

Horizontal privity determines who benefits from a warranty and who may therefore sue for its breach. Horizontal privity pertains to noncontracting parties who are injured by the defective goods; this group would include users, consumers, and bystanders who are not the contracting purchaser.

The Code relaxes the requirement of horizontal privity of contract by permitting recovery on a seller's warranty, at a minimum, to members of the buyer's family or household or to a guest in his home. The Code provides three alternative sections from which the states may select. Alternative A, the least comprehensive and most widely adopted alternative, provides that a seller's warranty, whether express or implied, extends to any natural person who is in the family or household of the buyer or who is a guest in his home, if it is reasonable to expect that such person may use, consume, or be affected by the goods, and who is injured in person by breach of the warranty. Alternative B extends Alternative A to "any natural person who may reasonably be expected to use, consume, or be affected by the goods." Alternative C further expands the coverage of the section to any person, not just natural persons, and to property damage as well as personal injury. (A natural person would not include artificial entities such as corporations, for example.) A seller, however, may not exclude or limit the operation of this section for injury to a person. Article 2A provides the same alternatives with slight modifications.

Nonetheless, the Code was not intended to establish outer boundaries for third-party recovery for injuries caused by defective goods. Rather, it sets a minimum standard that the states may expand through case law. Most states have judicially accepted the Code's invitation to relax the requirements of horizontal privity and, for all practical purposes, have eliminated horizontal privity in warranty cases.

Vertical privity, in determining who is liable for breach of warranty, pertains to remote sellers within the chain of distribution, such as manufacturers and wholesalers, with whom the consumer purchaser has not entered into a contract. Although the Code adopts a neutral position regarding vertical privity, the courts in most states have *eliminated* the requirement of vertical privity in warranty actions.

NOTICE OF BREACH OF WARRANTY

When a buyer has accepted a tender of goods that are not as warranted by the seller, she is required to notify the seller of any breach of warranty, express or implied, as well as any other breach, within a reasonable time after she has discovered or should have discovered it. If the buyer fails to notify the seller of any breach within a reasonable time, she is barred from any remedy against the seller. (Article 2A.) In determining whether notice was provided in a reasonable period of time, commercial standards apply to a merchant buyer while different standards apply to a retail consumer, so as not to deprive a good faith consumer of her remedy.

PLAINTIFF'S CONDUCT

Because of the development of warranty liability in the law of sales and contracts, **contributory negligence** of the buyer is no defense to an action against the seller for breach of warranty. Comparative negligence statutes do apply, however, to warranty actions in a number of states. (Comparative negligence is discussed later in this chapter.)

CONCEPT REVIEW 22-1

Warranties

Type of Warranty	How Created	What Is Warranted	How Disclaimed
Title (Article 2) Use and Possession (Article 2A)	• Seller contracts to sell goods	• Good title • Rightful transfer • Not subject to lien	• Specific language • Circumstances giving buyer reason to know that seller does not claim title
Express (Article 2 and 2A)	• Affirmation of fact • Promise • Description • Sample or model	• Conform to affirmation • Conform to promise • Conform to description • Conform to sample or model	• Specific language (extremely difficult)
Merchantability (Article 2 and 2A)	• Merchant sells goods	• Fit for ordinary purposes • Adequately contained, packaged, and labeled	• Must mention "merchantability" • If in writing must be conspicuous/in lease must be in writing and conspicuous • "As is" sale • Buyer examination • Course of dealing, course of performance, usage of trade
Fitness for a Particular Purpose (Article 2 and 2A)	• Seller knows buyer is relying upon seller to select goods suitable to buyer's particular purpose	• Fit for particular purpose	• No buzzwords necessary • Must be in writing and conspicuous • "As is" sale • Buyer examination • Course of dealing, course of performance, usage of trade

If the buyer discovers a defect in the goods that may cause injury and nevertheless proceeds to make use of them, he will not be permitted to recover damages from the seller for loss or injuries caused by such use. This is not contributory negligence but **voluntary assumption of the risk.**

STRICT LIABILITY IN TORT

The most recent and far-reaching development in the field of product liability is that of strict liability in tort. All but a very few states have now accepted the concept, which is embodied in **Section 402A** of the Restatement (Second) of Torts. A new Restatement of the Law (Third) Torts: Products Liability (the Restatement Third) was promulgated. It is far more comprehensive than the second Restatement in dealing with the liability of commercial sellers and distributors of goods for harm caused by their products. (We will discuss this revision more fully later in this chapter.)

Section 402A imposes **strict liability in tort** on merchant sellers both for personal injuries and for property damage that result from selling a product in a *defective condition, unreasonably dangerous* to the user or consumer. Section 402A applies even though "the seller has exercised all possible care in the preparation and sale of his product." Thus, negligence is not the basis of liability in strict liability cases. The essential distinction between the two doctrines is that actions in strict liability do not require the plaintiff to prove that the injury-producing defect resulted from any specific act of negligence of the seller. Strict liability actions focus on the *product*, not on the *conduct* of the manufacturer. Courts in strict liability cases are interested in the fact that a product defect arose—not in *how* it arose. Thus, even an "innocent" manufacturer—one who has not been negligent—may be liable if his product turns out to contain a defect that injures a consumer. Although liability for personal injuries caused by a defective condition that makes goods unreasonably dangerous is usually associated with sales of such goods, this type of liability also exists with respect to *leases* and *bailments* of defective goods.

Requirements of Strict Liability in Tort

Section 402A imposes strict liability in tort if (1) the defendant was engaged in the business of selling a product such as the defective one; (2) the defendant sold the product in a defective condition; (3) the defective condition made the product unreasonably dangerous to the user or consumer or to his property; (4) the defect in the product existed when it left the defendant's hands; (5) the plaintiff sustained physical harm or property damage by using or consuming the product; and (6) the defective condition was the proximate cause of the injury or damage.

This liability is imposed by law as a matter of public policy and does not depend on contract, either express or implied. Nor does it require reliance by the injured user or consumer on any statements made by the manufacturer or seller. It is not limited to persons in a buyer-seller relationship; thus, neither vertical nor horizontal privity is required. No notice of the defect is required to have been given by the injured user or consumer. The liability, furthermore, generally is not subject to disclaimer, exclusion, or modification by contractual agreement. Rather, it is solely in tort and arises out of the common law. It is not governed by the provisions of the UCC. The majority of courts considering the question, however, have held that Section 402A imposes liability only for injury to person and damage to property, not for commercial loss (such as loss of bargain or profits), which is recoverable in an action for breach of warranty.

MERCHANT SELLERS

Section 402A imposes liability only upon a person who is in the *business* of selling the product involved. It does not apply to an occasional seller, such as a person who trades in his used car or who sells his lawn mower to a neighbor. In this respect, the section is similar to the implied warranty of merchantability, which applies only to sales by a merchant of goods that are of the type in which he deals. A growing number of jurisdictions recognize the applicability of strict liability in tort even to merchant-sellers of *used* goods.

DEFECTIVE CONDITION

In an action to recover damages under the rule of strict liability in tort, though the plaintiff must prove a defective condition in the product, she is not required to prove how or why or in what manner the product became defective. The plaintiff must, however, show that at the time she was injured, the condition of the product was not substantially changed from the condition in which the manufacturer or seller sold it. In general, defects may arise through faulty manufacturing, through faulty product design, or through inadequate warnings, labeling, packaging, or instructions. Some states, however, and the Restatement Third do not impose strict liability for a design defect or a failure to provide proper warnings or instructions.

Manufacturing Defect   A **manufacturing defect** occurs when the product is not properly made; that is, it fails to meet its own manufacturing specifications. For instance, suppose a chair is manufactured with legs designed to be attached by four screws and glue. If the chair was produced without the appropriate screws, this would constitute a manufacturing defect.

Design Defect   A product contains a **design defect** when, despite its being produced as specified, the product is dangerous or hazardous because its design is inadequate. Design defects can result from a number of causes, including poor engineering, poor choice of materials, and poor packaging. An example of a design defect that received great notoriety was the fuel tank assembly of the Ford Pinto. A number of courts found the car to be inadequately designed because the fuel tank had been placed too close to its rear axle, causing the tank to rupture when the car was hit from behind.

Section 402A provides no guidance in determining which injury-producing designs should give rise to strict liability and which should not. Consequently, the courts have adopted widely varying approaches in applying 402A to defective design cases. Nevertheless, virtually none of the courts has upheld a judgment in a strict liability case in which the defendant demonstrated that the "**state of the art**" was such that the manufacturer

(1) neither knew nor could have known of a product hazard or (2) if he knew of the product hazard, could have designed a safer product given existing technology. Thus, almost all courts evaluate the design of a product on the basis of the dangers that the manufacturer could have known at the time he produced the product.

Failure to Warn   A seller is under a duty to provide adequate warning of a product's possible danger, to provide appropriate directions for its safe use, and to package the product safely. Warnings do not, however, always protect sellers from liability. A seller who could have designed or manufactured a product in a safe yet cost-effective manner, but who instead chooses to produce the product cheaply and to provide a warning of the product's hazards, cannot escape liability simply by the warning. Warnings usually will avoid liability only if no cost-effective designs or manufacturing processes are available to reduce a risk of injury.

> ## PRACTICAL ADVICE
> Warn consumers of your products of any significant danger, such as toxicity or flammability.

The duty to give a warning arises from a foreseeable danger of physical harm that could result from the normal or probable use of the product and from the likelihood that, unless warned, the user or consumer would not ordinarily be aware of such danger or hazard.

KELSO V. BAYER CORPORATION

UNITED STATES COURT OF APPEALS, SEVENTH CIRCUIT, 2005
398 F.3D 640

http://scholar.google.com/scholar_case?case=13341242500313047129&q=398+F.3d+640&hl=en&as_sdt=2,22

FACTS   Plaintiff, Ted Kelso, used Neo-Synephrine 12 HourExtra Moisturizing Spray (a product manufactured by Bayer Corporation) continuously for more than three years. After learning that his continued use of the product caused permanent nasal tissue damage requiring multiple sinus surgeries, he sued Bayer alleging that Bayer had failed to adequately warn him of the dangers associated with Neo-Synephrine. Bayer moved for summary judgment, arguing that the warning it provided, as follows, was adequate:

Do not exceed recommended dosage.
    … Stop use and ask a doctor if symptoms persist. Do not use this product for more than 3 days. Use only as directed. Frequent or prolonged use may cause nasal congestion to recur or worsen.

The district court granted Bayer summary judgment, and Kelso appealed arguing that he had presented sufficient evidence to recover in a product liability action against Bayer.

DECISION   Judgment affirmed.

OPINION   Manion, J. Kelso argues that summary judgment was inappropriate because he presented sufficient evidence to recover in a product liability action against Bayer. "To recover in a product liability action, a plaintiff must plead and prove that the injury resulted from a condition of the product, that the condition was an unreasonably dangerous one, and that the condition existed at the time the product left the manufacturer's control."

[Citation.] A product may be unreasonably dangerous because of a design defect, a manufacturing defect, "or a failure of a manufacturer to warn of a danger or instruct on the proper use of the product as to which the average consumer would not be aware." [Citation.]

Kelso claims the Neo-Synephrine was unreasonably dangerous because Bayer's warning was confusing as to whether or not the product could be used safely for more than three days, when such use was effective in relieving his congestion. *** Kelso *** interpreted the warning as meaning not to exceed three days use if the product failed to relieve the congestion; he only needed to see a physician if the product did not work to relieve the congestion. Also, because the container included much more than three days' dosage, Kelso insists that he had good reason to believe that he could safely use Neo-Synephrine for more than three days.

However, Kelso's personal reaction to the warning is not the test. Whether a warning is sufficient "is determined using an objective standard, i.e., the awareness of an ordinary person." [Citation.] Here, the plain, clear and unambiguous language of the warning states: "**Do not use this product for more than 3 days.**" Period. That the Neo-Synephrine container included doses sufficient to treat multiple users or multiple colds in no way takes away from the clear impact of the warning. Moreover, the warning clearly informs users to: "**Stop use and ask a physician if symptoms persist.**" The warning was clear. Yet Kelso continued using the product well beyond the three days. It is unreasonable to create an ambiguity that excuses extended use when the warning against such use is unequivocal.

Kelso also argues that the warning was inadequate because it did not warn users that the product could also cause permanent nasal tissue damage and also had a risk of habituation (meaning that users would become dependent on the product, causing them to use the product for more than three days). However, under Illinois law, a manufacturer need not warn of all possible consequences of failing to follow a primary warning. [Citation.] Here, the primary warning told consumers "**not [to] use this product for more than 3 days.**" That was sufficient under Illinois law. However, Bayer's warning went even further, informing consumers of the consequence of extended use, stating: "[f]requent or prolonged use may cause nasal congestion to recur or worsen." Although Kelso believes the warning should have provided him with more detailed information, Illinois law does not require more. [Citation.] Therefore, Kelso's defective warning claim fails.

INTERPRETATION The duty to give a warning arises from a foreseeable danger of physical harm that could result from the normal or probable use of the product and from the likelihood that, unless warned, the user or consumer would not ordinarily be aware of such danger or hazard.

CRITICAL THINKING QUESTION When should a warning be considered sufficient?

Unreasonably Dangerous

Section 402A liability applies only if the defective product is unreasonably dangerous to the user or consumer. An **unreasonably dangerous** product is one that contains a danger beyond that which would be contemplated by the ordinary consumer who purchases it with common knowledge of its characteristics. Thus, Comment *i* to Section 402A describes the difference between reasonable and unreasonable dangers:

> [G]ood whiskey is not unreasonably dangerous merely because it will make some people drunk, and is especially dangerous to alcoholics; but bad whiskey, containing a dangerous amount of fuel oil, is unreasonably dangerous. Good tobacco is not unreasonably dangerous merely because the effects of smoking may be harmful; but tobacco containing something like marijuana may be unreasonably dangerous. Good butter is not unreasonably dangerous merely because, if such be the case, it deposits cholesterol in the arteries and leads to heart attacks; but bad butter, contaminated with poisonous fish oil, is unreasonably dangerous.

Most courts have left the question of reasonable consumer expectations to the jury.

GREENE v. BODDIE-NOELL ENTERPRISES, INC.

UNITED STATES DISTRICT COURT, W.D. VIRGINIA, 1997
966 F.SUPP. 416
http://scholar.google.com/scholar_case?case=14855332202624539345&q=966+F.Supp.+416&hl=en&as_sdt=2,34

FACTS The plaintiff, Katherine Greene, contends that she was badly burned by hot coffee purchased from the drive-through window of a Hardees fast food restaurant, when the coffee spilled on her after it had been handed to her by the driver of the vehicle. Greene's boyfriend, Blevins, purchased the coffee and some food and handed the food and beverages to Greene. The food was on a plate, and the beverages were in cups. Greene placed the plate on her lap and held a cup in each hand. According to Greene, the Styrofoam coffee cup was comfortable to hold, and had a lid on the top, although she did not notice whether the lid was fully attached.

Blevins drove out of the restaurant parking lot, and over a "bad dip" at the point at which the lot meets the road. When the front tires of the car went slowly across the dip, the coffee "splashed out" on Greene, burning her legs through her clothes. Blevins remembers Greene exclaiming, "The lid came off." As soon as the coffee burned her, Greene threw the food and drink to the floor of the car, and in the process stepped on the coffee cup. When the cup was later retrieved from the floor of the car, the bottom of the cup was damaged, and the lid was at least partially off of the top of the cup.

After Greene was burned by the coffee, Blevins drove her to the emergency room of a local hospital, where she was treated. She missed eleven days of work and suffered permanent scarring to her thighs.

The defendant restaurant operator moved for summary judgment on the ground that the plaintiff cannot show a prima facie case of liability.

DECISION Summary judgment granted in favor of defendant.

OPINION Jones, J. Both Greene and Blevins testified that they had heard of the "McDonalds' coffee case" prior to this incident and Greene testified that while she was not a coffee drinker, she had been aware that if coffee spilled on her, it would burn her. After the accident, Greene gave a recorded statement to a representative of the defendant in which she stated, "I know the lid wasn't on there good. It came off too easy."

> [Court's footnote: On August 17, 1994, a state court jury in Albuquerque, New Mexico, awarded 81-year old Stella Liebeck $160,000 in compensatory damages and $2.7 million in punitive damages, after she was burned by coffee purchased from a drive-through window at a McDonalds restaurant. The trial judge later reduced the punitive damages to $480,000, and the parties settled the case before an appeal. According to news reports, Mrs. Liebeck contended that for taste reasons McDonalds served coffee about 20 degrees hotter than other fast food restaurants, and in spite of numerous complaints, had made a conscious decision not to warn customers of the possibility of serious burns. The jury's verdict received world-wide attention. See Andrea Gerlin, "A Matter of Degree: How a Jury Decided That One Coffee Spill Is Worth $2.9 Million," *The Wall Street Journal*]

* * *

To prove a case of liability in Virginia, a plaintiff must show that a product had a defect which rendered it unreasonably dangerous for ordinary or foreseeable use.

[Citation.] In order to meet this burden, a plaintiff must offer proof that the product violated a prevailing safety standard, whether the standard comes from business, government or reasonable consumer expectation. [Citation.]

Here the plaintiff has offered no such proof. There is no evidence that either the heat of the coffee or the security of the coffee cup lid violated any applicable standard. Do other fast food restaurants serve coffee at a lower temperature, or with lids which will prevent spills even when passing over an obstruction in the road? Do customers expect cooler coffee, which may be less tasty, or cups which may be more secure, but harder to unfasten?

In fact, the plaintiff testified that she knew, and therefore expected, that the coffee would be hot enough to burn her if it spilled. While she also expressed the opinion that the cup lid was too loose, that testimony does not substitute for evidence of a generally applicable standard or consumer expectation, since "[the plaintiff's] subjective expectations are insufficient to establish what degree of protection * * * society expects from [the product]." [Citation.]

The plaintiff argues that the mere fact that she was burned shows that the product was dangerously defective, either by being too hot or by having a lid which came off unexpectedly. But it is settled in Virginia that the happening of an accident is not sufficient proof of liability, even in products cases. [Citation.] This is not like the case of a foreign substance being found in a soft drink bottle, where a presumption of negligence arises. [Citation.]

To be merchantable, a product need not be foolproof, or perfect. As one noted treatise has expressed, "[i]t is the lawyer's challenging job to define the term 'merchantability' in [the] case in some objective way so that the court or jury can make a determination whether that standard has been breached." [Citation.]

In the present case, there has been no showing that a reasonable seller of coffee would not conclude that the beverage must be sold hot enough to be palatable to consumers, even though it is hot enough to burn other parts of the body. A reasonable seller might also conclude that patrons desire coffee lids which prevent spillage in ordinary handling, but are not tight enough to avert a spill under other circumstances, such as when driving over a bump. It was the plaintiff's obligation to demonstrate that she had proof that the defendant breached a recognizable standard, and that such proof is sufficient to justify a verdict in her favor at trial. She has not done so, and accordingly the motion for summary judgment must be granted.

INTERPRETATION Strict liability in tort only applies if the defective product is unreasonably dangerous to the user or consumer.

CRITICAL THINKING QUESTION Do you agree with the court's decision? Explain.

Obstacles to Recovery

Few of the obstacles to recovery in warranty cases present serious problems to plaintiffs in strict liability actions brought pursuant to Section 402A because this section was drafted largely to avoid such obstacles.

DISCLAIMERS AND NOTICE

Comment *m* to Section 402A provides that the basis of strict liability rests solely in tort and therefore is not subject to contractual defenses. The comment specifically states that strict product liability is not governed by the Code, that it is not affected by contractual limitations or disclaimers, and that it is not subject to any requirement that notice be given to the seller by the injured party within a reasonable time. Nevertheless, most courts have *allowed* clear and specific disclaimers of Section 402A liability in *commercial* transactions between merchants of relatively equal economic power.

PRIVITY

With respect to horizontal privity, the strict liability in tort of manufacturers and other sellers extends not only to buyers, users, and consumers, but also to injured bystanders.

In terms of vertical privity, strict liability in tort imposes liability on any seller who is engaged in the business of selling the product, including a wholesaler or distributor as well as the manufacturer and retailer. The rule of strict liability in tort also applies to the manufacturer of a defective component that is used in a larger product if the manufacturer of the finished product has made no essential change in the component.

PLAINTIFF'S CONDUCT

Many product liability defenses relate to the conduct of the plaintiff. The claim common to all of them is that the plaintiff's improper conduct so contributed to the plaintiff's injury that it would be unfair to blame the product or its seller.

Contributory Negligence Contributory negligence is conduct on the part of the plaintiff (1) that falls below the standard to which he should conform for his own protection and (2) that is the legal cause of the plaintiff's harm. Because strict liability is designed to assess liability without fault, Section 402A rejects contributory negligence as a defense. Thus, a seller cannot defend a strict liability lawsuit on the basis of a plaintiff's negligent failure to discover a defect or to guard against its possibility. But, as discussed later, contributory negligence in the form of an assumption of the risk can bar recovery under Section 402A.

Comparative Negligence Under comparative negligence, the court apportions damages between the parties in proportion to the degree of fault or negligence it finds against them. Despite Section 402A's bar of contributory negligence in strict liability cases, some courts apply comparative negligence to strict liability cases. (Some courts use the term *comparative responsibility* rather than *comparative negligence*.) There are two basic types of comparative negligence or comparative responsibility. One is pure comparative responsibility, which simply reduces the plaintiff's recovery in proportion to her fault, whatever that may be. Thus, the recovery of a plaintiff found to be 80 percent at fault in causing an accident in which she suffered a $100,000 loss would be limited to 20 percent of her damages, or $20,000. Under the other type of negligence, modified comparative responsibility, the plaintiff recovers according to the general principles of comparative responsibility *unless* she is more than 50 percent responsible for her injuries, in which case she recovers nothing. The majority of comparative negligence states follow the modified comparative responsibility approach.

Voluntary Assumption of the Risk Under the Second Restatement of Torts assumption of risk is a defense in an action based on strict liability in tort. Basically, **assumption of the risk** is the plaintiff's express or implied consent to encounter a known danger. Thus, a person who drives an automobile after realizing that the brakes are not working and an employee who attempts to remove a foreign object from a high-speed roller press without shutting off the power have assumed the risk of their own injuries.

To establish such a defense, the defendant must show that (1) the plaintiff actually knew and appreciated the particular risk or danger the defect created; (2) the plaintiff voluntarily encountered the risk while realizing the danger; and (3) the plaintiff's decision to encounter the known risk was unreasonable.

The Third Restatement of Torts: Apportionment of Liability has abandoned the doctrine of implied voluntary assumption of risk in tort actions generally; it is no longer a defense that the plaintiff was aware of a risk and voluntarily confronted it. This new Restatement limits the defense of assumption of risk to express assumption of risk, which consists of a contract between the plaintiff and another person to absolve the other person from liability for future harm.

Misuse or Abuse of the Product Closely connected to voluntary assumption of the risk is the valid defense of misuse or abuse of the product by the injured party. **Misuse or abuse** occurs when the injured party knows, or should know, that he is using the product in a manner the seller did not contemplate. The major difference between misuse or abuse and assumption of the risk is that the former includes actions that the injured party does not know to be dangerous, whereas the latter does not include such conduct. Instances of such misuse or abuse include standing on a rocking chair to change a light bulb or using a lawn mower to trim hedges. The courts, however, have significantly limited this defense by requiring that the misuse or abuse not be foreseeable by the seller. If a use is foreseeable, then the seller must take measures to guard against it.

SUBSEQUENT ALTERATION

Section 402A provides that liability exists only if the product reaches "the user or consumer without substantial change in the condition in which it is sold." Accordingly, most, but not all, courts would not hold a manufacturer liable for a faulty carburetor if a car dealer had removed the part and made significant changes in it before reinstalling it in an automobile.

STATUTE OF REPOSE

A number of lawsuits have been brought against manufacturers many years after a product was first sold. In response, many states have adopted statutes of repose. These enactments limit the period—typically between six and twelve years—for which a manufacturer is liable for

injury caused by a defective product. After the statutory time period has elapsed, a manufacturer ceases to be liable for such harm. See the Business Law in Action below and the Ethical Dilemma at the end of this chapter.

LIMITATIONS ON DAMAGES

More than half of the states have limited the punitive damages that a plaintiff can collect in a product liability lawsuit. They have done this by a number of means, including the following:

1. Placing caps on the amount of damages that can be awarded—with caps ranging from $50,000 to $20 million;

2. Providing for the state to receive all or a portion of any punitive damages awarded with the state's share ranging from 35 percent to 100 percent to reduce the plaintiff's incentive to bring products liability suits;

3. Providing for bifurcated trials—that is, separate hearings to determine liability and punitive damages;

4. Increasing the plaintiff's burden of proof for recovery of punitive damages with most states adopting the "clear and convincing" evidence standard; and

5. Requiring proportionality between compensatory and punitive damages by specifying an acceptable ratio between the two types of damages.

See Concept Review 22-2.

CONCEPT REVIEW 22-2

Product Liability

	Merchantability*	Strict Liability in Tort (Section 402A)
Condition of Goods Creating Liability	Not fit for ordinary purposes	Defective condition, unreasonably dangerous
Type of Transactions	Sales and leases; some courts apply to bailments of goods	Sales, leases, and bailments of goods
Disclaimer	Must mention "merchantability"; if in writing, must be conspicuous; must not be unconscionable (sales subject to Magnuson-Moss Act)	Not possible in consumer transactions; may be permitted in commercial transactions
Notice to Seller	Required within reasonable time	Not required
Causation	Required	Required
Who May Sue	In some states, buyer and the buyer's family or guests in home; in other states, any person who may be expected to use, consume, or be affected by goods	Any user or consumer of product; also, in most states, any bystander
Compensable Harms	Personal injury, property damage, economic loss	Personal injury, property damage
Who May Be Sued	Seller or lessor who is a merchant with respect to the goods sold	Seller who is engaged in business of selling such a product

* The warranty of fitness for a particular purpose differs from the warranty of merchantability in the following respects: (1) the condition that triggers liability is the failure of the goods to perform according to the particular purpose described in the warranty, and (2) a disclaimer need not mention "fitness for a particular purpose."

Restatement (Third) of Torts: Products Liability

The Restatement (Third) of Torts: Products Liability makes some significant changes in product liability; however, many states continue to follow Section 402A of the Second Restatement of Torts.

The new Restatement expands Section 402A into an entire treatise of its own, comprising more than twenty sections. The Restatement (Third) does not use the term strict liability but instead defines separate liability standards for each type of defect. The new Restatement continues to cover anyone engaged in the business of selling or distributing a defective product if the defect causes harm to persons or property. Its major provision (Section 2) defines a product as defective "when, at the time of sale or distribution, it contains a manufacturing defect, is defective in design, or is defective because of inadequate instructions or warnings." Thus, Section 2 explicitly recognizes the three types of product defects discussed in the next section "Defective Condition": manufacturing defects, design defects, and failure to warn. However, as discussed in the following paragraphs, strict liability is imposed only for manufacturing defects, while liability for inadequate design or warning is imposed only for foreseeable risks of harm that could have been avoided by the use of an alternative *reasonable* design, warning, or instruction.

MANUFACTURING DEFECTS

Section 2(a) provides that "A product ... contains a manufacturing defect when the product departs from its intended design even though all possible care was exercised in the preparation and marketing of the product." Therefore, sellers and distributors of products remain strictly liable for manufacturing defects, although a plaintiff may seek to recover based upon allegations and proof of negligent manufacture. In actions against the manufacturer, the plaintiff ordinarily must prove that the defect existed in the product when it left the manufacturer.

Business Law in Action

Until the 1970s, A. H. Robins of Richmond, Virginia, operated as a relatively small, essentially family-run company with a fairly wholesome image. Nearly a decade later, however, the company's name rang sourly in the public ear.

For years, the pharmaceutical firm had been headed by E. Claiborne Robins, Sr., its chairman, and his son, E. Claiborne Robins, Jr., its CEO. Both men were well respected in Richmond, and the elder Robins was known as a generous man who donated millions to education and other concerns. Initially, A. H. Robins made such popular products as Robitussin cough medicine, ChapStick lip balm, and Sergeant's flea and tick collars. Then the company decided to get into the birth-control business, and there its troubles began.

With the sexual revolution of the sixties and the advent of the birth-control pill, corporate America sensed profits to be made from any new form of birth control—potentially large profits. But the trick was to find a safe, easy-to-use, acceptable product.

At the prestigious Johns Hopkins Hospital in Baltimore in the late 1960s, Dr. Hugh J. Davis, director of the hospital's birth-control clinic, was testing a new intrauterine device (IUD), known as the Dalkon Shield. The plastic, nickel-size, crablike instrument was inserted into a woman's uterus as a way to prevent pregnancy. No one knew why or how IUDs worked.

In February 1970, Davis reported in the *American Journal of Obstetrics and Gynecology* that the pregnancy rate for his Dalkon Shield was 1.1 percent, a rate similar to or lower than that of the birth-control pill. He did not disclose, however, that he was part owner of the small Dalkon Corporation that made the new IUD.

A few months later, A. H. Robins took notice of the Dalkon Shield at a physicians' conference in Pennsylvania. By June of that year, the firm had acquired the rights to the device and had hired Davis on as a consultant. Within two weeks of the Dalkon Shield's purchase, A. H. Robins began to hear of problems. One of its own officials cited potential difficulties with the device's tail, which, unlike the tails of other IUDs, consisted of hundreds of tiny filaments enclosed in a nylon shield that was open at one end. The tail's exposed threads potentially could attract bacteria and thus cause infection.

Still, A. H. Robins rushed the Dalkon Shield into production. The company made a few design changes but conducted no more research on the device. Nor did the Food and Drug Administration (FDA) require the company to get approval for the device before introducing it, since the Dalkon Shield was classified as a medical device, not a drug.

Within six months of buying the Dalkon Shield, A. H. Robins launched a major marketing campaign. Thousands of reprints of Davis's study that included his 1.1 percent pregnancy rate were distributed across the country. Less than a year later, the Dalkon Shield had captured 60 percent of the IUD market in the United States.

Sales mounted, and the money rolled in. By February 1971, however, the company had received two reports of women developing pelvic inflammatory disease, a painful infection that can lead to sterility. Soon, more adverse evidence surfaced. New reports suggested that the pregnancy rate for the Dalkon Shield ran as high as 4.3 percent. Another study suggested that as many as one in fourteen Dalkon Shield wearers suffered from infections. But that wasn't the only danger. While some Dalkon Shield wearers were hospitalized for infection, others were admitted for perforated uteruses or, if they happened to be pregnant, for ectopic pregnancies, for septic (or infected) abortions, or for premature labor and delivery. Some became sterile. Some died. By 1973, A. H. Robins had evidence that six women wearing the Dalkon Shield had died from septic abortions—yet it did little.

Nor did the FDA respond quickly. Not until June of 1973 did the FDA write A. H. Robins to tell the company that it should stop selling the Dalkon Shield because of safety questions. Two days later, A. H. Robins voluntarily withdrew the device from the U.S. market, yet the company waited nearly another year before banning international sales of the Dalkon Shield.

By early 1974, A. H. Robins faced another threat: lawsuits from injured women. The company, however, fought back fiercely, often playing hardball with women who pressed their claims, questioning them vociferously about their sex lives and suggesting that their own behavior had led to any problems that they might be having. Until 1979, the company was able to settle many cases out of court for an average of $11,000 each.

But then things began to unravel for A. H. Robins. In 1979, a Denver jury decided against the company, awarding an injured woman more than $6.8 million, most of it in punitive damages.

By 1984, the company had paid out $314 million in some 8,300 lawsuits. It still faced three thousand eight hundred additional lawsuits, and women were filing new suits every day. Pressure was beginning to mount. Then, in February of that year, Judge Miles Lord of the U.S. District Court in Minneapolis, exasperated by the number of Dalkon Shield lawsuits that he had presided over, made national news

when he summoned three top A. H. Robins executives, including CEO E. Claiborne Robins, Jr., to his courtroom and lashed out at the officers, condemning them for their hard-heartedness and begging them to take action to protect the women who still wore the Dalkon Shield.

Obviously, the company had to do something. So, by October, A. H. Robins launched a major advertising campaign to tell women that it would pay for the removal of their Dalkon Shields. But it did not issue a recall.

Then it asked the U.S. District Court in Richmond, Virginia, to set one national trial as part of a class action suit to determine whether punitive damages should be awarded to claimants and, if so, how much. The company also moved to establish a reserve fund of $615 million to pay for pending and future claims. The fund was the biggest ever to be set aside to settle liability claims for a medical device. Unfortunately, the company underestimated the Dalkon Shield's costs.

By August 1985, A. H. Robins was in deep trouble. The company and its insurer, Aetna Life and Casualty Co., had lost $530 million in nine thousand five hundred lawsuits, and they were facing five thousand two hundred more cases. Meanwhile, four hundred new cases were being filed each month. In addition, the company had been forced to stare down a shareholders' lawsuit, which it settled for $6.9 million. With nowhere else to go, A. H. Robins filed for bankruptcy.

The Committee of the Dalkon Shield Claimants estimated their claims at between $4.2 billion and $7 billion. Robins submitted an estimate at $0.8 billion to $1.3 billion. The bankruptcy judge set a $2.5 billion cap on liability for the Dalkon Shield. In January 1988 American Home Products (AHP) won the bidding war for Robins. In July 1988 the district court approved Robins' sixth amended and restated reorganization plan (1) creating a Dalkon Shield trust fund of $2.5 billion, (2) protecting Robins executives from punitive damages, and (3) settling claims against Aetna. Robins' shareholders received $916 million in AHP stock while the Robins family received $385 million in AHP stock and other Robins executives received $280 million in that stock. In June 1989 the federal appeals court affirmed Robins' reorganization plan. In November 1989 the U.S. Supreme Court denied an appeal from the Robins reorganization.

By the time it closed on April 30, 2000, the Dalkon Shield Claimants Trust paid out nearly $3 billion to about two hundred thousand claimants.

Shortly after the sale of A. H. Robins to AHP (now Wyeth), E. Claiborne Robins, Jr., established ECR Pharmaceuticals, a privately held firm based in Richmond, Virginia.

DESIGN DEFECT

Section 2(b) states:

> A product ... is defective in design when the foreseeable risks of harm posed by the product could have been reduced or avoided by the adoption of a reasonable alternative design by the seller or other distributor, or a predecessor in the commercial chain of distribution, and the omission of the reasonable alternative design renders the product not reasonably safe.

This rule pulls back from a strict liability standard and imposes a negligence-like standard by requiring that the defect be reasonably foreseeable and that it could have been avoided by a reasonable alternative design. The Comments explain that this standard involves resolving "whether a reasonable alternative design would, at a reasonable cost, have reduced the foreseeable risk of harm posed by the product and, if so, whether the omission of the alternative design by the seller ... rendered the product not reasonably safe." The burden rests upon the plaintiff to demonstrate the existence of a reasonable alternative safer design that would have reduced the foreseeable risks of harm. However, consumer expectations do not constitute an independent standard for judging the defectiveness of product designs.

FAILURE TO WARN

Section 2(c) provides:

> A product ... is defective because of inadequate instructions or warnings when the foreseeable risks of harm posed by the product could have been reduced or avoided by the provision of reasonable instructions or warnings by the seller or other distributor, or a predecessor in the commercial chain of distribution and the omission of the instructions or warnings renders the product not reasonably safe.

Commercial product sellers must provide reasonable instructions and warnings about risks of injury associated with their products. The omission of warnings sufficient to allow informed decisions by reasonably foreseeable users or consumers renders the product not reasonably safe at time of sale. A seller, however, is under a duty to warn only if he knew or should have known of the risks involved. Moreover, warning about risks is effective only if an alternative design to avoid the risk cannot reasonably be implemented. Whenever safer products can be reasonably designed at a reasonable cost, adoption of the safer design is required rather than using a warning or instructions.

Ethical Dilemma

When Should a Company Order a Product Recall?

FACTS Walter Jones was feeding his five-month-old daughter Millie plums from a jar of Winkler baby food when she suddenly began to choke on a piece of aluminum foil that had come from the jar. Walter rushed her to the hospital, where more foil was found in her stomach. Although the amount of aluminum found was not in itself deadly, Millie was nauseous for several hours, and her parents had trouble getting her to eat for many days thereafter.

Walter sued Winkler. A number of similar incidents involving Winkler products had occurred at about the same time. Although the incidents covered a wide geographic area, their total number was not great, and the Food and Drug Administration (FDA) decided not to require a recall of the baby food. Winkler faced two choices: (1) to do nothing and settle the cases as they arose or (2) to recall all jars of the same lot to protect other children from the possibility of ingesting foreign substances.

Social, Policy, and Ethical Considerations

1. What are the social and ethical issues Winkler must consider in choosing its course of action? Should the fact that none of the incidents had been fatal affect the company's decision? What should Winkler do?

2. Would the first option be good for business? Who eventually bears the cost of the lawsuits or recalls? Who should bear the cost?

3. What actions should be taken by the baby's parents? Do they have any social responsibility in this case to seek publicity sufficient to warn others?

© Cengage Learning 2014

CHAPTER SUMMARY
WARRANTIES

Types of Warranties

Definition of Warranty an obligation of the seller to the buyer (or lessor to lessee) concerning title, quality, characteristics, or condition of goods

Warranty of Title the obligation of a seller to convey the right of ownership without any lien (in a lease the warranty protects the lessee's right to possess and use the goods)

Express Warranty an affirmation of fact or promise about the goods or a description, including a sample of the goods, which becomes part of the basis of the bargain

Implied Warranty a contractual obligation, arising out of certain circumstances of the sale or lease, imposed by operation of law and not found in the language of the sales or lease contract
- *Merchantability* warranty by a merchant seller that the goods are reasonably fit for the ordinary purpose for which they are manufactured or sold; pass without objection in the trade under the contract description; and are of fair, average quality
- *Fitness for Particular Purpose* warranty by any seller that goods are reasonably fit for a particular purpose if, at the time of contracting, the seller had reason to know the buyer's particular purpose and that the buyer was relying on the seller's skill and judgment to furnish suitable goods

Obstacles to Warranty Action

Disclaimer of Warranties a negation of a warranty
- *Express Warranty* usually not possible to disclaim
- *Warranty of Title* may be excluded or modified by specific language or by certain circumstances, including judicial sale or a sale by a sheriff, executor, or foreclosing lienor
- *Implied Warranty of Merchantability* the disclaimer must mention "merchantability" and, in the case of a writing, must be conspicuous (in a lease the disclaimer must be in writing and conspicuous)
- *Implied Warranty of Fitness for a Particular Purpose* the disclaimer must be in writing and conspicuous
- *Other Disclaimers of Implied Warranties* the implied warranties of merchantability and fitness for a particular purpose may also be disclaimed (1) by expressions like "as is," "with all faults," or other similar language; (2) by course of dealing, course of performance, or usage of trade; or (3) as to defects an examination ought to have revealed where the buyer has examined the goods or where the buyer has refused to examine the goods
- *Federal Legislation Relating to Warranties of Consumer Goods* the Magnuson-Moss Warranty Act protects purchasers of consumer goods by providing that warranty information be clear and useful and that a seller who makes a written warranty cannot disclaim any implied warranty

Limitation or Modification of Warranties permitted as long as it is not unconscionable

Privity of Contract a contractual relationship between parties that was necessary at common law to maintain a lawsuit
- *Horizontal Privity* doctrine determining who benefits from a warranty and who therefore may bring a cause of action; the Code provides three alternatives
- *Vertical Privity* doctrine determining who in the chain of distribution is liable for a breach of warranty; the Code has not adopted a position on this

Notice of Breach if the buyer fails to notify the seller of any breach within a reasonable time, she is barred from any remedy against the seller

Plaintiff's Conduct
- *Contributory Negligence* is not a defense
- *Voluntary Assumption of the Risk* is a defense

STRICT LIABILITY IN TORT

Requirements of Strict Liability in Tort

General Rule imposes tort liability on merchant sellers for both personal injuries and property damage for selling a product in a defective condition unreasonably dangerous to the user or consumer

Defective Condition
- *Manufacturing Defect* by failing to meet its own manufacturing specifications, the product is not properly made
- *Design Defect* the product, though made as designed, is dangerous because the design is inadequate
- *Failure to Warn* failure to provide adequate warning of possible danger or to provide appropriate directions for use of a product

Unreasonably Dangerous contains a danger beyond that which would be contemplated by the ordinary consumer

Obstacles to Recovery

Contractual Defenses defenses such as privity, disclaimers, and notice generally do not apply to tort liability

Plaintiff's Conduct
- *Contributory Negligence* not a defense in the majority of states
- *Comparative Negligence* most states have applied the rule of comparative negligence to strict liability in tort
- *Voluntary Assumption of the Risk* express assumption of risk is a defense to an action based upon strict liability; some states apply implied assumption of risk to strict liability cases
- *Misuse or Abuse of the Product* is a defense

Subsequent Alteration liability exists only if the product reaches the user or consumer without substantial change in the condition in which it is sold

Statute of Repose limits the time period for which a manufacturer is liable for injury caused by its product

Limitations on Damages many states have limited the punitive damages that a plaintiff can collect in a product liability lawsuit

Restatement (Third) of Torts: Products Liability

General Rule One engaged in the business of selling products who sells a defective product is subject to liability for harm to persons or property caused by the defect

Defective Conditions
- *Manufacturing Defect* a seller is held to strict liability when the product departs from its intended design
- *Design Defect* a product is defective when the foreseeable risks of harm posed by the product could have been reduced or avoided by the adoption of a reasonable alternative design
- *Failure to Warn* a product is defective because of inadequate instructions or warnings when the foreseeable risks of harm posed by the product could have been reduced or avoided by the provision of reasonable instructions or warnings

QUESTIONS

1. At the start of the social season, Aunt Lavinia purchased a hula skirt in Sadie's dress shop. The salesperson told her, "This superior garment will do things for a person." Aunt Lavinia's houseguest, her niece, Florabelle, asked and obtained her aunt's permission to wear the skirt to a masquerade ball. In the midst of the festivity, where there was much dancing, drinking, and smoking, the long skirt brushed against a glimmering cigarette butt. Unknown to Aunt Lavinia and Florabelle, its wearer, the garment was made of a fine unwoven fiber that is highly flammable. It burst into flames, and Florabelle suffered severe burns. Aunt Lavinia notified Sadie of the accident and of Florabelle's intention to recover from Sadie. Can Florabelle recover damages from Sadie, the proprietor of the dress shop, and Exotic Clothes, Inc., the manufacturer from which Sadie purchased the skirt? Explain.

2. The Talent Company, manufacturer of a widely advertised and expensive perfume, sold a quantity of this product to Young, a retail druggist. Dorothy and Bird visited the store of Young, and Dorothy, desiring to make a gift to Bird, purchased a bottle of this perfume from Young, asking for it by its trade name. Young wrapped up the bottle and handed it directly to Bird. The perfume contained a foreign chemical that upon the first use of the perfume by Bird severely burned her face and caused a permanent facial disfigurement. What are the rights of Bird, if any, against Dorothy, Young, and the Talent Company?

3. John Doe purchased a bottle of "Bleach-All," a well-known brand, from Roe's combination service station and grocery store. When John used the "Bleach-All," his clothes severely deteriorated due to an error in mixing the chemicals during the detergent's manufacture. John brings an action against Roe to recover damages. Explain whether John will be successful in his lawsuit.

4. A route salesperson for Ideal Milk Company delivered a half-gallon glass jug of milk to Allen's home. The next day, when Allen grasped the milk container by its neck to take it out of his refrigerator, it shattered in his hand and caused serious injury. Allen paid Ideal on a monthly basis for the regular delivery of milk. Ideal's milk bottles each contained the legend "Property of Ideal—to be returned," and the route salesman would pick up the empty bottles when he delivered milk. Can Allen recover damages from Ideal Milk Company? Why?

5. While Butler and his wife, Wanda, were browsing through Sloan's used car lot, Butler told Sloan that he was looking for a safe but cheap family car. Sloan said, "That old Cadillac hearse ain't hurt at all, and I'll sell it to you for $5,950." Butler said, "I'll have to take your word for it because I don't know a thing about cars." Butler asked Sloan whether he would guarantee the car, and Sloan replied, "I don't guarantee used cars." Then Sloan added,

"But I have checked that Caddy over, and it will run another ten thousand miles without needing any repairs." Butler replied, "It has to because I won't have an extra dime for any repairs." Butler made a down payment of $800 and signed a printed form contract, furnished by Sloan, that contained a provision: "Seller does not warrant the condition or performance of any used automobile."

As Butler drove the car out of Sloan's lot, the left rear wheel fell off and Butler lost control of the vehicle. It veered over an embankment, causing serious injuries to Wanda. What is Sloan's liability to Butler and Wanda?

6. John purchased for cash a Revenge automobile manufactured by Japanese Motors, Ltd., from an authorized franchised dealer in the United States. The dealer told John that the car had a "twenty-four month 24,000-mile warranty." Two days after John accepted delivery of the car, he received an eighty-page manual in fine print that stated, among other things, on page 72:

> The warranties herein are expressly in lieu of any other express or implied warranty, including any implied warranty of merchantability or fitness, and of any other obligation on the part of the company or the selling dealer.
>
> Japanese Motors, Ltd., and the selling dealer warrant to the owner each part of this vehicle to be free under use and service from defects in material and workmanship for a period of twenty-four months from the date of original retail delivery of first use or until it has been driven for 24,000 miles, whichever first occurs.

Within nine months after the purchase, John was forced to return the car for repairs to the dealer on thirty different occasions; and the car has been in the dealer's custody for more than seventy days during these nine months. The dealer has been forced to make major repairs to the engine, transmission, and steering assembly. The car is now in the custody of the dealer for further major repairs, and John has demanded that it keep the car and refund his entire purchase price. The dealer has refused on the ground that it has not breached its contract and is willing to continue repairing the car during the remainder of the "twenty-four/twenty-four" period. What are the rights and liabilities of the dealer and John?

7. Fred Lyon of New York, while on vacation in California, rented a new model Home Run automobile from Hart's Drive-A-Car. The car was manufactured by the Ange Motor Company and was purchased by Hart's from Jammer, Inc., an automobile importer. Lyon was driving the car on a street in San Jose when, due to a defect in the steering mechanism, it suddenly became impossible to steer. The speed of the car at the time was thirty miles per hour, but before Lyon could bring it to a stop, the car jumped a

low curb and struck Peter Wolf, who was standing on the sidewalk, breaking both of his legs and causing other injuries. What rights does Wolf have against (a) Hart's Drive-A-Car, (b) Ange Motor Company, (c) Jammer, Inc., and (d) Lyon?

8. The plaintiff brings this cause of action against a manufacturer for the loss of his leg below the hip. The leg was lost when caught in the gears of a screw auger machine sold and installed by the defendant. Shortly before the accident, the plaintiff's co-employees had removed a covering panel from the machine by use of sledgehammers and crowbars in order to do repair work. When finished with their repairs, they replaced the panel with a single piece of cardboard instead of restoring the equipment to its original condition. The plaintiff stepped on the cardboard in the course of his work and fell, catching his leg in the moving parts. Explain what causes of action the plaintiff may have against the defendant and what defenses the defendant could raise.

9. The plaintiff, while driving a pickup manufactured by the defendant, was struck in the rear by another motor vehicle. Upon impact, the plaintiff's head was jarred backward against the rear window of the cab, causing the plaintiff serious injury. The pickup was not equipped with a headrest, and none was required at the time. Should the plaintiff prevail on a cause of action based upon strict liability in tort? Why? Why not?

10. The plaintiff, while dining at the defendant's restaurant, ordered a chicken potpie. While she was eating, she swallowed a sliver of chicken bone, which became lodged in her throat, causing her serious injury. The plaintiff brings a cause of action. Should she prevail? Why?

11. Salem Supply Co. sells new and used gardening equipment. Ben Buyer purchased a slightly used riding lawn mower for $1,500. The price was considerably less than that of comparable used mowers. The sale was clearly indicated to be "as is." Two weeks after Ben purchased the mower, the police arrived at his house with Owen Owner, the true owner of the lawn mower, which was stolen from his yard, and reclaimed the mower. What recourse, if any, does Ben have?

12. Seigel, a seventy-three-year-old man, was injured at one of Giant Food's retail food stores when a bottle of Coca-Cola exploded as he was placing a six-pack of Coke into his shopping cart. The explosion caused him to lose his balance and fall, with injuries resulting. Has Giant breached its implied warranty of merchantability to Seigel? Why?

13. Guarino and two others (plaintiffs) died of gas asphyxiation and five others were injured when they entered a sewer tunnel without masks to answer the cries for help of their crew leader, Rooney. Rooney had left the sewer shaft and entered the tunnel to fix a water leakage problem. Having corrected the problem, Rooney was returning to the shaft when he apparently was overcome by gas because of a defect in his oxygen mask, which was manufactured by Mine Safety Appliance Company (defendant). The plaintiffs' estates brought this action against the defendant for breach of warranty, and the defendant raised the defense of the plaintiffs' voluntary assumption of the risk. Explain who will prevail.

CASE PROBLEMS

14. Green Seed Company packaged, labeled, and marketed a quality tomato seed known as "Green's Pink Shipper" for commercial sale. Brown Seed Store, a retailer, purchased the seed from Green Seed and then sold it to Guy Jones, an individual engaged in the business of growing tomato seedlings for sale to commercial tomato growers. Williams purchased the seedlings from Jones and then transplanted and raised them in accordance with accepted farming methods. The plants, however, produced not the promised "Pink Shipper" tomatoes but an inferior variety that spoiled in the field. Williams then brought an action against Green Seed for $90,000, claiming that his crop damage had been caused by Green Seed's breach of an express warranty. Green Seed argued in defense that its warranty did not extend to remote purchasers and that the company did not receive notice of the claimed breach of warranty. Who will prevail? Why?

15. Mobley purchased from Century Dodge a car described in the contract as new. The contract also contained a disclaimer of all warranties, express or implied. Subsequently,

Mobley discovered that the car had, in fact, been involved in an accident. He then sued Century Dodge to recover damages, claiming the dealer had breached its express warranty that the car was new. Century Dodge argues that it had adequately disclaimed all warranties. Decision?

16. O'Neil purchased a used diesel tractor-trailer combination from International Harvester. O'Neil claimed that International Harvester's salesman had told him that the truck had recently been overhauled and that it would be suitable for hauling logs in the mountains. The written installment contract signed by the parties provided that the truck was sold "AS IS WITHOUT WARRANTY OF ANY CHARACTER express or implied." O'Neil admitted that he had read the disclaimer clause but claimed that he understood it to mean that the tractor-trailer would be in the condition that International Harvester's salesman had promised.

O'Neil paid the $1,700 down payment, but he failed to make any of the monthly payments. He claimed that he refused to pay because his employee had many problems with the truck when he took it to the mountains. Delays resulting from those problems, O'Neil argued, had caused him to lose his permit to cut firewood and, therefore, the accompanying business. An International Harvester representative agreed to pay for one-half of the cost of certain repairs, but the several attempts made to fix the truck were unsuccessful. O'Neil then tried to return the truck and to rescind the sale, but International Harvester refused to cooperate. Decision?

17. Mrs. Embs went into Stamper's Cash Market to buy soft drinks for her children. She had removed five bottles from an upright soft drink cooler, placed them in a carton, and turned to move away from the display when a bottle of Seven-Up in a carton at her feet exploded, cutting her leg. Apparently, several other bottles had exploded that same week. Stamper's Cash Market received its entire stock of Seven-Up from Arnold Lee Vice, the area distributor. Vice in turn received his entire stock of Seven-Up from Pepsi-Cola Bottling Co. Can Mrs. Embs recover damages from (a) Stamper, (b) Vice, or (c) Pepsi-Cola Bottling? Why?

18. Catania wished to paint the exterior of his house. He went to Brown, a local paint store owner, and asked him to recommend a paint for the job. Catania told Brown that the exterior walls were stucco and in a chalky, powdery condition. Brown suggested Pierce's shingle and shake paint. Brown then instructed Catania how to mix the paint and how to use a wire brush to prepare the surface. Five months later, the paint began to peel, flake, and blister. Catania brings an action against Brown. Decision?

19. Robinson, a truck driver for a moving company, decided to buy a used truck from the company. Branch, the owner, told Robinson that the truck was being repaired and that Robinson should wait and inspect the truck before signing the contract. Robinson, who had driven the truck before, felt that inspection was unnecessary. Again, Branch suggested Robin son wait to inspect the truck, and again Robinson declined. Branch then told Robinson he was buying the truck "as is." Robinson then signed the contract. After the truck broke down four times, Robinson sued. Will Robinson be successful? What defenses can Branch raise?

20. Perfect Products manufactures balloons, which are then bought and resold by wholesale novelty distributors. Mego Corp. manufactures a doll called "Bubble Yum Baby." A balloon is inserted in the doll's mouth with a mouthpiece, and the doll's arm is pumped to inflate the balloon, simulating the blowing of a bubble. Mego Corp. used Perfect Products balloons in the dolls, bought through independent distributors. The plaintiff's infant daughter died after swallowing a balloon removed from the doll. Is Perfect Products liable to plaintiff under a theory of strict liability? Explain.

21. Patient was injured when the footrest of an adjustable X-ray table collapsed, causing Patient to fall to the floor. G.E. manufactured the X-ray table and the footrest. At trial, evidence was introduced that G.E. had manufactured for several years another footrest model complete with safety latches. However, there was no evidence that the footrest involved was manufactured defectively. The action is based on a theory of strict liability. Who wins? Why?

22. Vlases, a coal miner who had always raised small flocks of chickens, spent two years building a new two-story chicken coop large enough to house four thousand chickens. After its completion, he purchased two thousand two hundred one-day-old chicks from Montgomery Ward for the purpose of producing eggs for sale. He had selected them from Ward's catalog, which stated that these chicks, hybrid Leghorns, were noted for their excellent egg production. Vlases had equipped the coop with brand-new machinery and had taken further hygiene precautions for the chicks' health. Almost one month later, Vlases noticed that their feathers were beginning to fall off. A veterinarian's examination revealed signs of drug intoxication and hemorrhagic disease in a few of the chicks. Eight months later, it was determined that the chicks were suffering from visceral and avian leukosis, or bird cancer, which reduced their egg-bearing capacity to zero. Avian leukosis may be transmitted either genetically or by unsanitary conditions. Subsequently, the disease infected the entire flock. Vlases then brought suit against Montgomery Ward for its breach of the implied warranties of merchantability and of fitness for a particular purpose. Ward claimed that there was no way to detect the disease in the one-day-old chicks, nor was there medication available to prevent this disease from occurring. Is Montgomery Ward liable under a warranty and/or strict liability cause of action? Explain.

23. Heckman, an employee of Clark Equipment Company, severely injured his left hand when he caught it in a power press that he was operating at work. The press was manufactured by Federal Press Company and sold to Clark eight years earlier. It could be operated either by hand controls that required the use of both hands away from the point of operation or by an optional foot pedal. When the foot pedal was used without a guard, nothing remained to keep the operator's hands from the point of operation. Federal Press did not provide safety appliances unless the customer requested them, but when it delivered the press to Clark with the optional pedal, it suggested that Clark install a guard. The press had a similar warning embossed on it. Clark did, in fact, purchase a guard for $100, but it was not mounted on the machine at the time of the injury; nor was it believed to be an effective safety device.

Heckman argued that a different type of guard, if installed, would have made the press safe in 95 percent of its customary uses. Federal, in turn, argued that the furnishing of guards was not customary in the industry; that the machine's many uses made it impracticable to design and install any one guard as standard equipment; that Clark's failure to obey Federal's warning was a superseding cause of the injury; and that state regulations placed responsibility for the safe operation of presses on employers and employees. Decision?

24. For sixteen years, the late Mrs. Dorothy Mae Palmer was married to Mr. Schultz, an insulator who worked with asbestos products. Mrs. Palmer was not exposed to asbestos dust in a factory setting; rather, she was exposed when Mr. Schultz brought his work clothes home to be washed. Mrs. Palmer died of mesothelioma. This product liability suit was brought by Mrs. Palmer's daughters to recover for the alleged wrongful death of their mother. The daughters claim that Mrs. Palmer's mesothelioma was the result of exposure to asbestos-containing products manufactured by Owens-Corning. The daughters claim that the asbestos products were defective and unreasonably dangerous and that Owens-Corning was negligent in failing to warn of the dangers associated with their products. Explain whether the plaintiffs should prevail.

25. A gasoline-powered lawn mower, which had been used earlier to cut grass, was left unattended next to a water heater that had been manufactured by Sears. Expert testimony was presented to demonstrate that vapors from the mower's gas tank accumulated under the water heater and resulted in an explosion. Three-year-old Shawn Toups was injured as a result. Evidence was also presented negating any claim that Shawn had been handling the gasoline can located nearby or the lawn mower. He was not burned on the soles of his feet or the palms of his hands. Is Sears liable to the Toups in strict product liability? Explain.

26. For more than forty years, Rose Cipollone smoked between one and two packs of cigarettes a day. Upon her death from lung cancer, Rose's husband, Antonio Cipollone, filed suit against Liggett Group, Inc., Lorillard, Inc., and Philip Morris, Inc., three of the leading firms in the tobacco industry, for the wrongful death of his wife. Many theories of liability and defenses were asserted in this decidedly complex and protracted litigation.

    One theory of liability claimed by Mr. Cipollone was breach of express warranty. It is uncontested that all three manufacturers ran multimedia ad campaigns that contained affirmations, promises, or innuendos that smoking cigarettes was safe. For example, ads for Chesterfield cigarettes boasted that a medical specialist could find no adverse health effects in subjects after six months of smoking. Chesterfields were also advertised as being manufactured with "electronic miracle" technology that made them "better and safer for you." Another ad stated that Chesterfield ingredients were tested and approved by scientists from leading universities. Another brand, L&M, publicly touted the "miracle tip" filter, claiming it was "just what the doctor ordered."

    At trial, the defendant tobacco companies were not permitted to try to prove that Mrs. Cipollone disbelieved or placed no reliance on the advertisements and their safety assurances. Did the defendants breach an express warranty to the plaintiff? Explain.

27. Trans-Aire International, Inc. (TAI), converts ordinary automotive vans into recreational vehicles. TAI had been installing carpet and ceiling fabrics in the converted vans with an adhesive made by the 3M Company. Unfortunately, during the hot summer months, the 3M adhesive would often fail to hold the carpet and fabrics in place.

    TAI contacted Northern Adhesive Company (Northern), seeking a "suitable" product to replace the 3M adhesive. Northern sent samples of several adhesives, commenting that hopefully one or more "might be applicable." Northern also informed TAI that one of the samples, Adhesive 7448, was a "match" for the 3M adhesive. After testing all the samples under cool plant conditions, TAI's chief engineer determined that Adhesive 7448 was better than the 3M adhesive. When TAI's president asked if the new adhesive should be tested under summerlike conditions, TAI's chief engineer responded that it was unnecessary to do so. The president then asked if Adhesive 7448 came with any warranties. A Northern representative stated that there were no warranties, except that the orders shipped would be identical to the sample.

    After converting more than five hundred vans using Adhesive 7448, TAI became aware that high summer temperatures were causing the new adhesive to fail. Explain whether TAI should prevail against Northern in a suit claiming (a) breach of an implied warranty of fitness for a particular purpose, (b) breach of an implied warranty of merchantability, and (c) breach of express warranty.

28. Plaintiff's children purchased an Aero Cycle exercise bike for their mother to use in a weight-loss program. The Aero Cycle bike was manufactured by DP and purchased from Walmart. The second time the plaintiff, Judy Dunne, used the bike (the first time she had used it, she used it only for a few seconds), she pedaled for three or four rotations. The rear support strut failed and the bike collapsed under plaintiff. At the time of the accident, plaintiff weighed between four hundred and fifty and five hundred pounds. She fell off the bike backwards, struck her head on a nearby metal file cabinet, and was knocked unconscious. When plaintiff regained consciousness, her mouth was bleeding and her neck, left shoulder, arm, leg, knee, and ankle were injured. Plaintiff was diagnosed as having a cervical strain and multiple contusions. Plaintiff filed suit against Walmart and DP. Explain whether plaintiff should prevail.

TAKING SIDES

Brian Felley purchased a used Ford Taurus from Thomas and Cheryl Singleton for $8,800. The car had 126,000 miles on it. After test driving the car, Felley discussed the condition of the car with Thomas Singleton, who informed Felley that the only thing known to be wrong with the car was that it had a noise in the right rear and that a grommet (a connector having to do with a strut) was bad or missing. Thomas told Felley that otherwise the car was in good condition. Nevertheless, Felley soon began experiencing problems with the car. On the second day that he owned the car, Felley noticed a problem with the clutch. Over the next few days, the clutch problem worsened and Felley was unable to shift the gears. Felley presented an invoice to Thomas showing that he paid $942.76 for the removal and repair of the car's clutch. In addition, the car developed serious brake problems within the first month that Felley owned it. Felley now contends that the Singletons breached their express warranty.

a. What arguments would support Felley's contention?

b. What arguments would support the claim by the Singletons that they had not given an express warranty?

c. What is the appropriate outcome? Explain.

APPENDIX B

UNIFORM COMMERCIAL CODE (SELECTED PROVISIONS)

The Code consists of the following Articles:

1. General Provisions
2. Sales
2A. Leases
3. Commercial Paper
4. Bank Deposits and Collections
4A. Funds Transfers
5. Letters of Credit
6. Bulk Transfers
7. Warehouse Receipts, Bills of Lading and Other Documents of Title
8. Investment Securities
9. Secured Transactions: Sales of Accounts, Contract Rights and Chattel Paper
10. Effective Date and Repealer
11. Effective Date and Transition Provisions

REVISED ARTICLE 1: GENERAL PROVISIONS
PART 1—GENERAL PROVISIONS

§1-101. SHORT TITLES.
(a) This [Act] may be cited as the Uniform Commercial Code.
(b) This article may be cited as Uniform Commercial Code— General Provisions.

§1-102. SCOPE OF ARTICLE.
This article applies to a transaction to the extent that it is governed by another article of [the Uniform Commercial Code].

§1-103. CONSTRUCTION OF [UNIFORM COMMERCIAL CODE] TO PROMOTE ITS PURPOSES AND POLICIES; APPLICABILITY OF SUPPLEMENTAL PRINCIPLES OF LAW.
(a) [The Uniform Commercial Code] must be liberally construed and applied to promote its underlying purposes and policies, which are:
    (1) to simplify, clarify, and modernize the law governing commercial transactions;
    (2) to permit the continued expansion of commercial practices through custom, usage, and agreement of the parties; and
    (3) to make uniform the law among the various jurisdictions.

(b) Unless displaced by the particular provisions of [the Uniform Commercial Code], the principles of law and equity, including the law merchant and the law relative to capacity to contract, principal and agent, estoppel, fraud, misrepresentation, duress, coercion, mistake, bankruptcy, and other validating or invalidating cause supplement its provisions.

§1-104. CONSTRUCTION AGAINST IMPLIED REPEAL.
[The Uniform Commercial Code] being a general act intended as a unified coverage of its subject matter, no part of it shall be deemed to be impliedly repealed by subsequent legislation if such construction can reasonably be avoided.

§1-105. SEVERABILITY.
If any provision or clause of [the Uniform Commercial Code] or its application to any person or circumstance is held invalid, the invalidity does not affect other provisions or applications of [the Uniform Commercial Code] which can be given effect without the invalid provision or application, and to this end the provisions of [the Uniform Commercial Code] are severable.

§1-106. USE OF SINGULAR AND PLURAL; GENDER.
In [the Uniform Commercial Code], unless the statutory context otherwise requires:
    (1) words in the singular number include the plural, and those in the plural include the singular; and
    (2) words of any gender also refer to any other gender.

§1-107. SECTION CAPTIONS.
Section captions are part of [the Uniform Commercial Code].

§1-108. RELATION TO ELECTRONIC SIGNATURES IN GLOBAL AND NATIONAL COMMERCE ACT.
This article modifies, limits, and supersedes the federal Electronic Signatures in Global and National Commerce Act, 15 U.S.C. Section 7001 et seq., except that nothing in this article modifies, limits, or supersedes Section 7001(c) of that Act or authorizes electronic delivery of any of the notices described in Section 7003(b) of that Act.

PART 2—GENERAL DEFINITIONS AND PRINCIPLES OF INTERPRETATION

§1-201. GENERAL DEFINITIONS.

(a) Unless the context otherwise requires, words or phrases defined in this section, or in the additional definitions contained in other articles of [the Uniform Commercial Code] that apply to particular articles or parts thereof, have the meanings stated.

(b) Subject to definitions contained in other articles of [the Uniform Commercial Code] that apply to particular articles or parts thereof:

(1) "Action", in the sense of a judicial proceeding, includes recoupment, counterclaim, set-off, suit in equity, and any other proceeding in which rights are determined.

(2) "Aggrieved party" means a party entitled to pursue a remedy.

(3) "Agreement", as distinguished from "contract", means the bargain of the parties in fact, as found in their language or inferred from other circumstances, including course of performance, course of dealing, or usage of trade as provided in Section 1-303.

(4) "Bank" means a person engaged in the business of banking and includes a savings bank, savings and loan association, credit union, and trust company.

(5) "Bearer" means a person in possession of a negotiable instrument, document of title, or certificated security that is payable to bearer or indorsed in blank.

(6) "Bill of lading" means a document evidencing the receipt of goods for shipment issued by a person engaged in the business of transporting or forwarding goods.

(7) "Branch" includes a separately incorporated foreign branch of a bank.

(8) "Burden of establishing" a fact means the burden of persuading the trier of fact that the existence of the fact is more probable than its nonexistence.

(9) "Buyer in ordinary course of business" means a person that buys goods in good faith, without knowledge that the sale violates the rights of another person in the goods, and in the ordinary course from a person, other than a pawnbroker, in the business of selling goods of that kind. A person buys goods in the ordinary course if the sale to the person comports with the usual or customary practices in the kind of business in which the seller is engaged or with the seller's own usual or customary practices. A person that sells oil, gas, or other minerals at the wellhead or minehead is a person in the business of selling goods of that kind. A buyer in ordinary course of business may buy for cash, by exchange of other property, or on secured or unsecured credit, and may acquire goods or documents of title under a pre-existing contract for sale. Only a buyer that takes possession of the goods or has a right to recover the goods from the seller under Article 2 may be a buyer in ordinary course of business. "Buyer in ordinary course of business" does not include a person that acquires goods in a transfer in bulk or as security for or in total or partial satisfaction of a money debt.

(10) "Conspicuous", with reference to a term, means so written, displayed, or presented that a reasonable person against which it is to operate ought to have noticed it. Whether a term is "conspicuous" or not is a decision for the court. Conspicuous terms include the following:

(A) a heading in capitals equal to or greater in size than the surrounding text, or in contrasting type, font, or color to the surrounding text of the same or lesser size; and

(B) language in the body of a record or display in larger type than the surrounding text, or in contrasting type, font, or color to the surrounding text of the same size, or set off from surrounding text of the same size by symbols or other marks that call attention to the language.

(11) "Consumer" means an individual who enters into a transaction primarily for personal, family, or household purposes.

(12) "Contract", as distinguished from "agreement", means the total legal obligation that results from the parties' agreement as determined by [the Uniform Commercial Code] as supplemented by any other applicable laws.

(13) "Creditor" includes a general creditor, a secured creditor, a lien creditor, and any representative of creditors, including an assignee for the benefit of creditors, a trustee in bankruptcy, a receiver in equity, and an executor or administrator of an insolvent debtor's or assignor's estate.

(14) "Defendant" includes a person in the position of defendant in a counterclaim, cross-claim, or third-party claim.

(15) "Delivery", with respect to an instrument, document of title, or chattel paper, means voluntary transfer of possession.

(16) "Document of title" includes bill of lading, dock warrant, dock receipt, warehouse receipt or order for the delivery of goods, and also any other document which in the regular course of business or financing is treated as adequately evidencing that the person in possession of it is entitled to receive, hold, and dispose of the document and the goods it covers. To be a document of title, a document must purport to be issued by or addressed to a bailee and purport to cover goods in the bailee's possession which are either identified or are fungible portions of an identified mass.

(17) "Fault" means a default, breach, or wrongful act or omission.

(18) "Fungible goods" means:

(A) goods of which any unit, by nature or usage of trade, is the equivalent of any other like unit; or

(B) goods that by agreement are treated as equivalent.

(19) "Genuine" means free of forgery or counterfeiting.

(20) "Good faith," except as otherwise provided in Article 5, means honesty in fact and the observance of reasonable commercial standards of fair dealing.

(21) "Holder" means:

(A) the person in possession of a negotiable instrument that is payable either to bearer or to an identified person that is the person in possession; or

(B) the person in possession of a document of title if the goods are deliverable either to bearer or to the order of the person in possession.

(22) "Insolvency proceeding" includes an assignment for the benefit of creditors or other proceeding intended to liquidate or rehabilitate the estate of the person involved.

(23) "Insolvent" means:

(A) having generally ceased to pay debts in the ordinary course of business other than as a result of bona fide dispute;

(B) being unable to pay debts as they become due; or

(C) being insolvent within the meaning of federal bankruptcy law.

(24) "Money" means a medium of exchange currently authorized or adopted by a domestic or foreign government. The term includes a monetary unit of account established by an intergovernmental organization or by agreement between two or more countries.

(25) "Organization" means a person other than an individual.

(26) "Party", as distinguished from "third party", means a person that has engaged in a transaction or made an agreement subject to [the Uniform Commercial Code].

(27) "Person" means an individual, corporation, business trust, estate, trust, partnership, limited liability company, association, joint venture, government, governmental subdivision, agency, or instrumentality, public corporation, or any other legal or commercial entity.

(28) "Present value" means the amount as of a date certain of one or more sums payable in the future, discounted to the date certain by use of either an interest rate specified by the parties if that rate is not manifestly unreasonable at the time the transaction is entered into or, if an interest rate is not so specified, a commercially reasonable rate that takes into account the facts and circumstances at the time the transaction is entered into.

(29) "Purchase" means taking by sale, lease, discount, negotiation, mortgage, pledge, lien, security interest, issue or reissue, gift, or any other voluntary transaction creating an interest in property.

(30) "Purchaser" means a person that takes by purchase.

(31) "Record" means information that is inscribed on a tangible medium or that is stored in an electronic or other medium and is retrievable in perceivable form.

(32) "Remedy" means any remedial right to which an aggrieved party is entitled with or without resort to a tribunal.

(33) "Representative" means a person empowered to act for another, including an agent, an officer of a corporation or association, and a trustee, executor, or administrator of an estate.

(34) "Right" includes remedy.

(35) "Security interest" means an interest in personal property or fixtures which secures payment or performance of an obligation. "Security interest" includes any interest of a consignor and a buyer of accounts, chattel paper, a payment intangible, or a promissory note in a transaction that is subject to Article 9. "Security interest" does not include the special property interest of a buyer of goods on identification of those goods to a contract for sale under Section 2-401, but a buyer may also acquire a "security interest" by complying with Article 9. Except as otherwise provided in Section 2-505, the right of a seller or lessor of goods under Article 2 or 2A to retain or acquire possession of the goods is not a "security interest", but a seller or lessor may also acquire a "security interest" by complying with Article 9. The retention or reservation of title by a seller of goods notwithstanding shipment or delivery to the buyer under Section 2-401 is limited in effect to a reservation of a "security interest." Whether a transaction in the form of a lease creates a "security interest" is determined pursuant to Section 1-203.

(36) "Send" in connection with a writing, record, or notice means:

(A) to deposit in the mail or deliver for transmission by any other usual means of communication with postage or cost of transmission provided for and properly addressed and, in the case of an instrument, to an address specified thereon or otherwise agreed, or if there be none to any address reasonable under the circumstances; or

(B) in any other way to cause to be received any record or notice within the time it would have arrived if properly sent.

(37) "Signed" includes using any symbol executed or adopted with present intention to adopt or accept a writing.

(38) "State" means a State of the United States, the District of Columbia, Puerto Rico, the United States Virgin Islands, or any territory or insular possession subject to the jurisdiction of the United States.

(39) "Surety" includes a guarantor or other secondary obligor.

(40) "Term" means a portion of an agreement that relates to a particular matter.

(41) "Unauthorized signature" means a signature made without actual, implied, or apparent authority. The term includes a forgery.

(42) "Warehouse receipt" means a receipt issued by a person engaged in the business of storing goods for hire.

(43) "Writing" includes printing, typewriting, or any other intentional reduction to tangible form. "Written" has a corresponding meaning.

§1-202. NOTICE; KNOWLEDGE.

(a) Subject to subsection (f), a person has "notice" of a fact if the person:
  (1) has actual knowledge of it;
  (2) has received a notice or notification of it; or
  (3) from all the facts and circumstances known to the person at the time in question, has reason to know that it exists.

(b) "Knowledge" means actual knowledge. "Knows" has a corresponding meaning.

(c) "Discover", "learn", or words of similar import refer to knowledge rather than to reason to know.

(d) A person "notifies" or "gives" a notice or notification to another person by taking such steps as may be reasonably required to inform the other person in ordinary course, whether or not the other person actually comes to know of it.

(e) Subject to subsection (f), a person "receives" a notice or notification when:
  (1) it comes to that person's attention; or
  (2) it is duly delivered in a form reasonable under the circumstances at the place of business through which the contract was made or at another location held out by that person as the place for receipt of such communications.

(f) Notice, knowledge, or a notice or notification received by an organization is effective for a particular transaction from the time it is brought to the attention of the individual conducting that transaction and, in any event, from the time it would have been brought to the individual's attention if the organization had exercised due diligence. An organization exercises due diligence if it maintains reasonable routines for communicating significant information to the person conducting the transaction and there is reasonable compliance with the routines. Due diligence does not require an individual acting for the organization to communicate information unless the communication is part of the individual's regular duties or the individual has reason to know of the transaction and that the transaction would be materially affected by the information.

§1-203. LEASE DISTINGUISHED FROM SECURITY INTEREST.

(a) Whether a transaction in the form of a lease creates a lease or security interest is determined by the facts of each case.

(b) A transaction in the form of a lease creates a security interest if the consideration that the lessee is to pay the lessor for the right to possession and use of the goods is an obligation for the term of the lease and is not subject to termination by the lessee, and:

(1) the original term of the lease is equal to or greater than the remaining economic life of the goods;

(2) the lessee is bound to renew the lease for the remaining economic life of the goods or is bound to become the owner of the goods;

(3) the lessee has an option to renew the lease for the remaining economic life of the goods for no additional consideration or for nominal additional consideration upon compliance with the lease agreement; or

(4) the lessee has an option to become the owner of the goods for no additional consideration or for nominal additional consideration upon compliance with the lease agreement.

(c) A transaction in the form of a lease does not create a security interest merely because:

(1) the present value of the consideration the lessee is obligated to pay the lessor for the right to possession and use of the goods is substantially equal to or is greater than the fair market value of the goods at the time the lease is entered into;

(2) the lessee assumes risk of loss of the goods;

(3) the lessee agrees to pay, with respect to the goods, taxes, insurance, filing, recording, or registration fees, or service or maintenance costs;

(4) the lessee has an option to renew the lease or to become the owner of the goods;

(5) the lessee has an option to renew the lease for a fixed rent that is equal to or greater than the reasonably predictable fair market rent for the use of the goods for the term of the renewal at the time the option is to be performed; or

(6) the lessee has an option to become the owner of the goods for a fixed price that is equal to or greater than the reasonably predictable fair market value of the goods at the time the option is to be performed.

(d) Additional consideration is nominal if it is less than the lessee's reasonably predictable cost of performing under the lease agreement if the option is not exercised. Additional consideration is not nominal if:

(1) when the option to renew the lease is granted to the lessee, the rent is stated to be the fair market rent for the use of the goods for the term of the renewal determined at the time the option is to be performed; or

(2) when the option to become the owner of the goods is granted to the lessee, the price is stated to be the fair market value of the goods determined at the time the option is to be performed.

(e) The "remaining economic life of the goods" and "reasonably predictable" fair market rent, fair market value, or cost of performing under the lease agreement must be determined with reference to the facts and circumstances at the time the transaction is entered into.

§1-204. VALUE.

Except as otherwise provided in Articles 3, 4, [and] 5, [and 6], a person gives value for rights if the person acquires them:

(1) in return for a binding commitment to extend credit or for the extension of immediately available credit, whether or not drawn upon and whether or not a charge-back is provided for in the event of difficulties in collection;

(2) as security for, or in total or partial satisfaction of, a preexisting claim;

(3) by accepting delivery under a preexisting contract for purchase; or

(4) in return for any consideration sufficient to support a simple contract.

§1-205. REASONABLE TIME; SEASONABLENESS.

(a) Whether a time for taking an action required by [the Uniform Commercial Code] is reasonable depends on the nature, purpose, and circumstances of the action.

(b) An action is taken seasonably if it is taken at or within the time agreed or, if no time is agreed, at or within a reasonable time.

§1-206. PRESUMPTIONS.

Whenever [the Uniform Commercial Code] creates a "presumption" with respect to a fact, or provides that a fact is "presumed," the trier of fact must find the existence of the fact unless and until evidence is introduced that supports a finding of its nonexistence.

PART 3—TERRITORIAL APPLICABILITY AND GENERAL RULES

§1-301. TERRITORIAL APPLICABILITY; PARTIES' POWER TO CHOOSE APPLICABLE LAW.

(a) In this section:

(1) "Domestic transaction" means a transaction other than an international transaction.

(2) "International transaction" means a transaction that bears a reasonable relation to a country other than the United States.

(b) This section applies to a transaction to the extent that it is governed by another article of the [Uniform Commercial Code].

(c) Except as otherwise provided in this section:

(1) an agreement by parties to a domestic transaction that any or all of their rights and obligations are to be determined by the law of this State or of another State is effective, whether or not the transaction bears a relation to the State designated; and

(2) an agreement by parties to an international transaction that any or all of their rights and obligations are to be determined by the law of this State or of another State or country is effective, whether or not the transaction bears a relation to the State or country designated.

(d) In the absence of an agreement effective under subsection (c), and except as provided in subsections (e) and (g), the rights and obligations of the parties are determined by the law that would be selected by application of this State's conflict of laws principles.

(e) If one of the parties to a transaction is a consumer, the following rules apply:

(1) An agreement referred to in subsection (c) is not effective unless the transaction bears a reasonable relation to the State or country designated.

(2) Application of the law of the State or country determined pursuant to subsection (c) or (d) may not deprive the consumer of the protection of any rule of law governing a matter within the scope of this section, which both is protective of consumers and may not be varied by agreement:

(A) of the State or country in which the consumer principally resides, unless subparagraph (B) applies; or

(B) if the transaction is a sale of goods, of the State or country in which the consumer both makes the contract and takes delivery of those goods, if such State or country is not the State or country in which the consumer principally resides.

(f) An agreement otherwise effective under subsection (c) is not effective to the extent that application of the law of the State or country designated would be contrary to a fundamental policy of the State or country whose law would govern in the absence of agreement under subsection (d).

(g) To the extent that [the Uniform Commercial Code] governs a transaction, if one of the following provisions of [the Uniform Commercial Code] specifies the applicable law, that provision governs and a contrary agreement is effective only to the extent permitted by the law so specified:

(1) Section 2-402;

(2) Sections 2A-105 and 2A-106;

(3) Section 4-102;

(4) Section 4A-507;

(5) Section 5-116;

(6) Section 6-103;

(7) Section 8-110;

(8) Sections 9-301 through 9-307.

§1-302. VARIATION BY AGREEMENT.

(a) Except as otherwise provided in subsection (b) or elsewhere in [the Uniform Commercial Code], the effect of provisions of [the Uniform Commercial Code] may be varied by agreement.

(b) The obligations of good faith, diligence, reasonableness, and care prescribed by [the Uniform Commercial Code] may not be disclaimed by agreement. The parties, by agreement, may determine the standards by which the performance of those obligations is to be measured if those standards are not manifestly unreasonable. Whenever [the Uniform Commercial Code] requires an action to be taken within a reasonable time, a time that is not manifestly unreasonable may be fixed by agreement.

(c) The presence in certain provisions of [the Uniform Commercial Code] of the phrase "unless otherwise agreed", or words of similar import, does not imply that the effect of other provisions may not be varied by agreement under this section.

§1-303. COURSE OF PERFORMANCE, COURSE OF DEALING, AND USAGE OF TRADE.

(a) A "course of performance" is a sequence of conduct between the parties to a particular transaction that exists if:

(1) the agreement of the parties with respect to the transaction involves repeated occasions for performance by a party; and

(2) the other party, with knowledge of the nature of the performance and opportunity for objection to it, accepts the performance or acquiesces in it without objection.

(b) A "course of dealing" is a sequence of conduct concerning previous transactions between the parties to a particular transaction that is fairly to be regarded as establishing a common basis of understanding for interpreting their expressions and other conduct.

(c) A "usage of trade" is any practice or method of dealing having such regularity of observance in a place, vocation, or trade as to justify an expectation that it will be observed with respect to the transaction in question. The existence and scope of such a usage must be proved as facts. If it is established that such a usage is embodied in a trade code or similar record, the interpretation of the record is a question of law.

(d) A course of performance or course of dealing between the parties or usage of trade in the vocation or trade in which they are engaged or of which they are or should be aware is relevant in ascertaining the meaning of the parties' agreement, may give particular meaning to specific terms of the agreement, and may supplement or qualify the terms of the agreement. A usage of trade applicable in the place in which part of the performance under the agreement is to occur may be so utilized as to that part of the performance.

(e) Except as otherwise provided in subsection (f), the express terms of an agreement and any applicable course of performance, course of dealing, or usage of trade must be construed whenever reasonable as consistent with each other. If such a construction is unreasonable:

(1) express terms prevail over course of performance, course of dealing, and usage of trade;

(2) course of performance prevails over course of dealing and usage of trade; and

(3) course of dealing prevails over usage of trade.

(f) Subject to Section 2-209, a course of performance is relevant to show a waiver or modification of any term inconsistent with the course of performance.

(g) Evidence of a relevant usage of trade offered by one party is not admissible unless that party has given the other party notice that the court finds sufficient to prevent unfair surprise to the other party.

§1-304. OBLIGATION OF GOOD FAITH.

Every contract or duty within [the Uniform Commercial Code] imposes an obligation of good faith in its performance and enforcement.

§1-305. REMEDIES TO BE LIBERALLY ADMINISTERED.

(a) The remedies provided by [the Uniform Commercial Code] must be liberally administered to the end that the aggrieved party may be put in as good a position as if the other party had fully performed but neither consequential or special damages nor penal damages may be had except as specifically provided in [the Uniform Commercial Code] or by other rule of law.

(b) Any right or obligation declared by [the Uniform Commercial Code] is enforceable by action unless the provision declaring it specifies a different and limited effect.

§1-306. WAIVER OR RENUNCIATION OF CLAIM OR RIGHT AFTER BREACH.

A claim or right arising out of an alleged breach may be discharged in whole or in part without consideration by agreement of the aggrieved party in an authenticated record.

§1-307. PRIMA FACIE EVIDENCE BY THIRD-PARTY DOCUMENTS.

A document in due form purporting to be a bill of lading, policy or certificate of insurance, official weigher's or inspector's certificate, consular invoice, or any other document authorized or required by the contract to be issued by a third party is prima facie evidence of its own authenticity and genuineness and of the facts stated in the document by the third party.

§1-308. PERFORMANCE OR ACCEPTANCE UNDER RESERVATION OF RIGHTS.

(a) A party that with explicit reservation of rights performs or promises performance or assents to performance in a manner demanded or offered by the other party does not thereby prejudice the rights reserved. Such words as "without prejudice," "under protest," or the like are sufficient.

(b) Subsection (a) does not apply to an accord and satisfaction.

§1-309. OPTION TO ACCELERATE AT WILL.

A term providing that one party or that party's successor in interest may accelerate payment or performance or require collateral or additional collateral "at will" or when the party "deems itself insecure," or words of similar import, means that the party has power to do so only if that party in good faith believes that the prospect of payment or performance is impaired. The burden of establishing lack of good faith is on the party against which the power has been exercised.

§1-310. SUBORDINATED OBLIGATIONS.

An obligation may be issued as subordinated to performance of another obligation of the person obligated, or a creditor may subordinate its right to performance of an obligation by agreement with either the person obligated or another creditor of the person obligated. Subordination does not create a security interest as against either the common debtor or a subordinated creditor.

ARTICLE 2: SALES

PART 1—SHORT TITLE, CONSTRUCTION AND SUBJECT MATTER

§ 2-101. SHORT TITLE.

This Article shall be known and may be cited as Uniform Commercial Code—Sales.

§ 2-102. SCOPE; CERTAIN SECURITY AND OTHER TRANSACTIONS EXCLUDED FROM THIS ARTICLE.

Unless the context otherwise requires, this Article applies to transactions in goods; it does not apply to any transaction which although in the form of an unconditional contract to sell or present sale is intended to operate only as a security transaction nor does this Article impair or repeal any statute regulating sales to consumers, farmers or other specified classes of buyers.

§ 2-103. DEFINITIONS AND INDEX OF DEFINITIONS.

(1) In this Article unless the context otherwise requires

    (a) "Buyer" means a person who buys or contracts to buy goods.

    (b) "Good faith" in the case of a merchant means honesty in fact and the observance of reasonable commercial standards of fair dealing in the trade.

    (c) "Receipt" of goods means taking physical possession of them.

    (d) "Seller" means a person who sells or contracts to sell goods.

(2) Other definitions applying to this Article or to specified Parts thereof, and the sections in which they appear are:

"Acceptance". Section 2–606.
"Banker's credit". Section 2–325.
"Between merchants". Section 2–104.
"Cancellation". Section 2–106(4).
"Commercial unit". Section 2–105.
"Confirmed credit". Section 2–325.
"Conforming to contract". Section 2–106.
"Contract for sale". Section 2–106.
"Cover". Section 2–712.
"Entrusting". Section 2–403.
"Financing agency". Section 2–104.

"Future goods". Section 2–105.
"Goods". Section 2–105.
"Identification". Section 2–501.
"Installment contract". Section 2–612.
"Letter of Credit". Section 2–325.
"Lot". Section 2–105.
"Merchant". Section 2–104.
"Overseas". Section 2–323.
"Person in position of seller". Section 2–707.
"Present sale". Section 2–106.
"Sale". Section 2–106.
"Sale on approval". Section 2–326.
"Sale or return". Section 2–326.
"Termination". Section 2–106.

(3) The following definitions in other Articles apply to this Article:
"Check". Section 3–104.
"Consignee". Section 7–102.
"Consignor". Section 7–102.
"Consumer goods". Section 9–109.
"Dishonor". Section 3–507.
"Draft". Section 3–104.

(4) In addition Article 1 contains general definitions and principles of construction and interpretation applicable throughout this Article.

§ 2-104. DEFINITIONS: "MERCHANT"; "BETWEEN MERCHANTS"; "FINANCING AGENCY".

(1) "Merchant" means a person who deals in goods of the kind or otherwise by his occupation holds himself out as having knowledge or skill peculiar to the practices or goods involved in the transaction or to whom such knowledge or skill may be attributed by his employment of an agent or broker or other intermediary who by his occupation holds himself out as having such knowledge or skill.

(2) "Financing agency" means a bank, finance company or other person who in the ordinary course of business makes advances against goods or documents of title or who by arrangement with either the seller or the buyer intervenes in ordinary course to make or collect payment due or claimed under the contract for sale, as by purchasing or paying the seller's draft or making advances against it or by merely taking it for collection whether or not documents of title accompany the draft. "Financing agency" includes also a bank or other person who similarly intervenes between persons who are in the position of seller and buyer in respect to the goods (Section 2–707).

(3) "Between merchants" means in any transaction with respect to which both parties are chargeable with the knowledge or skill of merchants.

§ 2-105. DEFINITIONS: TRANSFERABILITY; "GOODS"; "FUTURE" GOODS; "LOT"; "COMMERCIAL UNIT".

(1) "Goods" means all things (including specially manufactured goods) which are movable at the time of identification to the contract for sale other than the money in which the price is to be paid, investment securities (Article 8) and things in action. "Goods" also includes the unborn young of animals and growing crops and other identified things attached to realty as described in the section on goods to be severed from realty (Section 2–107).

(2) Goods must be both existing and identified before any interest in them can pass. Goods which are not both existing and

identified are "future" goods. A purported present sale of future goods or of any interest therein operates as a contract to sell.

(3) There may be a sale of a part interest in existing identified goods.

(4) An undivided share in an identified bulk of fungible goods is sufficiently identified to be sold although the quantity of the bulk is not determined. Any agreed proportion of such a bulk or any quantity thereof agreed upon by number, weight or other measure may to the extent of the seller's interest in the bulk be sold to the buyer who then becomes an owner in common.

(5) "Lot" means a parcel or a single article which is the subject matter of a separate sale or delivery, whether or not it is sufficient to perform the contract.

(6) "Commercial unit" means such a unit of goods as by commercial usage is a single whole for purposes of sale and division of which materially impairs its character or value on the market or in use. A commercial unit may be a single article (as a machine) or a set of articles (as a suite of furniture or an assortment of sizes) or a quantity (as a bale, gross, or carload) or any other unit treated in use or in the relevant market as a single whole.

§ 2–106. Definitions: "Contract"; "Agreement"; "Contract for Sale"; "Sale"; "Present Sale"; "Conforming" to Contract; "Termination"; "Cancellation".

(1) In this Article unless the context otherwise requires "contract" and "agreement" are limited to those relating to the present or future sale of goods. "Contract for sale" includes both a present sale of goods and a contract to sell goods at a future time. A "sale" consists in the passing of title from the seller to the buyer for a price (Section 2–401). A "present sale" means a sale which is accomplished by the making of the contract.

(2) Goods or conduct including any part of a performance are "conforming" or conform to the contract when they are in accordance with the obligations under the contract.

(3) "Termination" occurs when either party pursuant to a power created by agreement or law puts an end to the contract otherwise than for its breach. On "termination" all obligations which are still executory on both sides are discharged but any right based on prior breach or performance survives.

(4) "Cancellation" occurs when either party puts an end to the contract for breach by the other and its effect is the same as that of "termination" except that the cancelling party also retains any remedy for breach of the whole contract or any unperformed balance.

§ 2–107. Goods to Be Severed From Realty: Recording.

(1) A contract for the sale of minerals or the like (including oil and gas) or a structure or its materials to be removed from realty is a contract for the sale of goods within this Article if they are to be severed by the seller but until severance a purported present sale thereof which is not effective as a transfer of an interest in land is effective only as a contract to sell.

(2) A contract for the sale apart from the land of growing crops or other things attached to realty and capable of severance without material harm thereto but not described in subsection (1) or of timber to be cut is a contract for the sale of goods within this Article whether the subject matter is to be severed by the buyer or by the seller even though it forms part of the realty at the time of contracting, and the parties can by identification effect a present sale before severance.

(3) The provisions of this section are subject to any third party rights provided by the law relating to realty records, and the contract for sale may be executed and recorded as a document transferring an interest in land and shall then constitute notice to third parties of the buyer's rights under the contract for sale.

PART 2—FORM, FORMATION AND READJUSTMENT OF CONTRACT

§ 2–201. Formal Requirements; Statute of Frauds.

(1) Except as otherwise provided in this section a contract for the sale of goods for the price of $500 or more is not enforceable by way of action or defense unless there is some writing sufficient to indicate that a contract for sale has been made between the parties and signed by the party against whom enforcement is sought or by his authorized agent or broker. A writing is not insufficient because it omits or incorrectly states a term agreed upon but the contract is not enforceable under this paragraph beyond the quantity of goods shown in such writing.

(2) Between merchants if within a reasonable time a writing in confirmation of the contract and sufficient against the sender is received and the party receiving it has reason to know its contents, it satisfies the requirements of subsection (1) against such party unless written notice of objection to its contents is given within ten days after it is received.

(3) A contract which does not satisfy the requirements of subsection (1) but which is valid in other respects is enforceable

(a) if the goods are to be specially manufactured for the buyer and are not suitable for sale to others in the ordinary course of the seller's business and the seller, before notice of repudiation is received and under circumstances which reasonably indicate that the goods are for the buyer, has made either a substantial beginning of their manufacture or commitments for their procurement; or

(b) if the party against whom enforcement is sought admits in his pleading, testimony or otherwise in court that a contract for sale was made, but the contract is not enforceable under this provision beyond the quantity of goods admitted; or

(c) with respect to goods for which payment has been made and accepted or which have been received and accepted (Sec. 2–606).

§ 2–202. Final Written Expression: Parol or Extrinsic Evidence.

Terms with respect to which the confirmatory memoranda of the parties agree or which are otherwise set forth in a writing intended by the parties as a final expression of their agreement with respect to such terms as are included therein may not be contradicted by evidence of any prior agreement or of a contemporaneous oral agreement but may be explained or supplemented

(a) by course of dealing or usage of trade (Section 1–205) or by course of performance (Section 2–208); and

(b) by evidence of consistent additional terms unless the court finds the writing to have been intended also as a complete and exclusive statement of the terms of the agreement.

§ 2–203. Seals Inoperative.

The affixing of a seal to a writing evidencing a contract for sale or an offer to buy or sell goods does not constitute the writing a sealed instrument and the law with respect to sealed instruments does not apply to such a contract or offer.

§ 2–204. FORMATION IN GENERAL.

(1) A contract for sale of goods may be made in any manner sufficient to show agreement, including conduct by both parties which recognizes the existence of such a contract.

(2) An agreement sufficient to constitute a contract for sale may be found even though the moment of its making is undetermined.

(3) Even though one or more terms are left open a contract for sale does not fail for indefiniteness if the parties have intended to make a contract and there is a reasonably certain basis for giving an appropriate remedy.

§ 2–205. FIRM OFFERS.

An offer by a merchant to buy or sell goods in a signed writing which by its terms gives assurance that it will be held open is not revocable, for lack of consideration, during the time stated or if no time is stated for reasonable time, but in no event may such period of irrevocability exceed three months; but any such term of assurance on a form supplied by the offeree must be separately signed by the offeror.

§ 2–206. OFFER AND ACCEPTANCE IN FORMATION OF CONTRACT.

(1) Unless other unambiguously indicated by the language or circumstances

(a) an offer to make a contract shall be construed as inviting acceptance in any manner and by any medium reasonable in the circumstances;

(b) an order or other offer to buy goods for prompt or current shipment shall be construed as inviting acceptance either by a prompt promise to ship or by the prompt or current shipment of conforming or non-conforming goods, but such a shipment of non-conforming goods does not constitute an acceptance if the seller seasonably notifies the buyer that the shipment is offered only as an accommodation to the buyer.

(2) Where the beginning of a requested performance is a reasonable mode of acceptance an offeror who is not notified of acceptance within a reasonable time may treat the offer as having lapsed before acceptance.

§ 2–207. ADDITIONAL TERMS IN ACCEPTANCE OR CONFIRMATION.

(1) A definite and seasonable expression of acceptance or a written confirmation which is sent within a reasonable time operates as an acceptance even though it states terms additional to or different from those offered or agreed upon, unless acceptance is expressly made conditional on assent to the additional or different terms.

(2) The additional terms are to be construed as proposals for addition to the contract. Between merchants such terms become part of the contract unless:

(a) the offer expressly limits acceptance to the terms of the offer;

(b) they materially alter it; or

(c) notification of objection to them has already been given or is given within a reasonable time after notice of them is received.

(3) Conduct by both parties which recognizes the existence of a contract is sufficient to establish a contract for sale although the writings of the parties do not otherwise establish a contract. In such case the terms of the particular contract consist of those terms on which the writings of the parties agree, together with any supplementary terms incorporated under any other provisions of this Act.

§ 2–208. COURSE OF PERFORMANCE OR PRACTICAL CONSTRUCTION.

(1) Where the contract for sale involves repeated occasions for performance by either party with knowledge of the nature of the performance and opportunity for objection to it by the other, any course of performance accepted or acquiesced in without objection shall be relevant to determine the meaning of the agreement.

(2) The express terms of the agreement and any such course of performance, as well as any course of dealing and usage of trade, shall be construed whenever reasonable as consistent with each other; but when such construction is unreasonable, express terms shall control course of performance and course of performance shall control both course of dealing and usage of trade (Section 1–205).

(3) Subject to the provisions of the next section on modification and waiver, such course of performance shall be relevant to show a waiver or modification of any term inconsistent with such course of performance.

§ 2–209. MODIFICATION, RESCISSION AND WAIVER.

(1) An agreement modifying a contract within this Article needs no consideration to be binding.

(2) A signed agreement which excludes modification or rescission except by a signed writing cannot be otherwise modified or rescinded, but except as between merchants such a requirement on a form supplied by the merchant must be separately signed by the other party.

(3) The requirements of the statute of frauds section of this Article (Section 2–201) must be satisfied if the contract as modified is within its provisions.

(4) Although an attempt at modification or rescission does not satisfy the requirements of subsection (2) or (3) it can operate as a waiver.

(5) A party who has made a waiver affecting an executory portion of the contract may retract the waiver by reasonable notification received by the other party that strict performance will be required of any term waived, unless the retraction would be unjust in view of a material change of position in reliance on the waiver.

§ 2–210. DELEGATION OF PERFORMANCE; ASSIGNMENT OF RIGHTS.

(1) A party may perform his duty through a delegate unless otherwise agreed or unless the other party has a substantial interest in having his original promisor perform or control the acts required by the contract. No delegation of performance relieves the party delegating of any duty to perform or any liability for breach.

(2) Unless otherwise agreed all rights of either seller or buyer can be assigned except where the assignment would materially change the duty of the other party, or increase materially the burden or risk imposed on him by his contract, or impair materially his chance of obtaining return performance. A right to damages for breach of the whole contract or a right arising out of the assignor's due performance of his entire obligation can be assigned despite agreement otherwise.

(3) Unless the circumstances indicate the contrary a prohibition of assignment of "the contract" is to be construed as barring only the delegation to the assignee of the assignor's performance.

(4) An assignment of "the contract" or of "all my rights under the contract" or an assignment in similar general terms is an assignment of rights and unless the language or the circumstances

(as in an assignment for security) indicate the contrary, it is a delegation of performance of the duties of the assignor and its acceptance by the assignee constitutes a promise by him to perform those duties. This promise is enforceable by either the assignor or the other party to the original contract.

(5) The other party may treat any assignment which delegates performance as creating reasonable grounds for insecurity and may without prejudice to his rights against the assignor demand assurances from the assignee (Section 2–609).

PART 3—GENERAL OBLIGATION AND CONSTRUCTION OF CONTRACT

§ 2–301. GENERAL OBLIGATIONS OF PARTIES.

The obligation of the seller is to transfer and deliver and that of the buyer is to accept and pay in accordance with the contract.

§ 2–302. UNCONSCIONABLE CONTRACT OR CLAUSE.

(1) If the court as a matter of law finds the contract or any clause of the contract to have been unconscionable at the time it was made the court may refuse to enforce the contract, or it may enforce the remainder of the contract without the unconscionable clause, or it may so limit the application of any unconscionable clause as to avoid any unconscionable result.

(2) When it is claimed or appears to the court that the contract or any clause thereof may be unconscionable the parties shall be afforded a reasonable opportunity to present evidence as to its commercial setting, purpose and effect to aid the court in making the determination.

§ 2–303. ALLOCATION OR DIVISION OF RISKS.

Where this Article allocates a risk or a burden as between the parties "unless otherwise agreed", the agreement may not only shift the allocation, but may also divide the risk or burden.

§ 2–304. PRICE PAYABLE IN MONEY, GOODS, REALTY, OR OTHERWISE.

(1) The price can be made payable in money or otherwise. If it is payable in whole or in part in goods each party is a seller of the goods which he is to transfer.

(2) Even though all or part of the price is payable in an interest in realty the transfer of the goods and the seller's obligations with reference to them are subject to this Article, but not the transfer of the interest in realty or the transferor's obligations in connection therewith.

§ 2–305. OPEN PRICE TERM.

(1) The parties if they so intend can conclude a contract for sale even though the price is not settled. In such a case the price is a reasonable price at the time for delivery if
(a) nothing is said as to price; or
(b) the price is left to be agreed by the parties and they fail to agree; or
(c) the price is to be fixed in terms of some agreed market or other standard as set or recorded by a third person or agency and it is not so set or recorded.

(2) A price to be fixed by the seller or by the buyer means a price for him to fix in good faith.

(3) When a price left to be fixed otherwise than by agreement of the parties fails to be fixed through fault of one party the other may at his option treat the contract as cancelled or himself fix a reasonable price.

(4) Where, however, the parties intend not to be bound unless the price be fixed or agreed and it is not fixed or agreed there is no

contract. In such a case the buyer must return any goods already received or if unable so to do must pay their reasonable value at the time of delivery and the seller must return any portion of the price paid on account.

§ 2–306. OUTPUT, REQUIREMENTS AND EXCLUSIVE DEALINGS.

(1) A term which measures the quantity by the output of the seller or the requirements of the buyer means such actual output or requirements as may occur in good faith, except that no quantity unreasonably disproportionate to any stated estimate or in the absence of a stated estimate to any normal or otherwise comparable prior output or requirements may be tendered or demanded.

(2) A lawful agreement by either the seller or the buyer for exclusive dealing in the kind of goods concerned imposes unless otherwise agreed an obligation by the seller to use best efforts to supply the goods and by the buyer to use best efforts to promote their sale.

§ 2–307. DELIVERY IN SINGLE LOT OR SEVERAL LOTS.

Unless otherwise agreed all goods called for by a contract for sale must be tendered in a single delivery and payment is due only on such tender but where the circumstances give either party the right to make or demand delivery in lots the price if it can be apportioned may be demanded for each lot.

§ 2–308. ABSENCE OF SPECIFIED PLACE FOR DELIVERY.

Unless otherwise agreed
(a) the place for delivery of goods is the seller's place of business or if he has none his residence; but
(b) in a contract for sale of identified goods which to the knowledge of the parties at the time of contracting are in some other place, that place is the place for their delivery; and
(c) documents of title may be delivered through customary banking channels.

§ 2–309. ABSENCE OF SPECIFIC TIME PROVISIONS; NOTICE OF TERMINATION.

(1) The time for shipment or delivery or any other action under a contract if not provided in this Article or agreed upon shall be a reasonable time.

(2) Where the contract provides for successive performances but is indefinite in duration it is valid for a reasonable time but unless otherwise agreed may be terminated at any time by either party.

(3) Termination of a contract by one party except on the happening of an agreed event requires that reasonable notification be received by the other party and an agreement dispensing with notification is invalid if its operation would be unconscionable.

§ 2–310. OPEN TIME FOR PAYMENT OR RUNNING OF CREDIT; AUTHORITY TO SHIP UNDER RESERVATION.

Unless otherwise agreed
(a) payment is due at the time and place at which the buyer is to receive the goods even though the place of shipment is the place of delivery; and
(b) if the seller is authorized to send the goods he may ship them under reservation, and may tender the documents of title, but the buyer may inspect the goods after their arrival before payment is due unless such inspection is inconsistent with the terms of the contract (Section 2–513); and
(c) if delivery is authorized and made by way of documents of title otherwise than by subsection (b) then payment is due at the

time and place at which the buyer is to receive the documents regardless of where the goods are to be received; and

(d) where the seller is required or authorized to ship the goods on credit the credit period runs from the time of shipment but post-dating the invoice or delaying its dispatch will correspondingly delay the starting of the credit period.

§ 2–311. OPTIONS AND COOPERATION RESPECTING PERFORMANCE.

(1) An agreement for sale which is otherwise sufficiently definite (subsection (3) of Section 2–204) to be a contract is not made invalid by the fact that it leaves particulars of performance to be specified by one of the parties. Any such specification must be made in good faith and within limits set by commercial reasonableness.

(2) Unless otherwise agreed specifications relating to assortment of the goods are at the buyer's option and except as otherwise provided in subsections (1)(c) and (3) of Section 2–319 specifications or arrangements relating to shipment are at the seller's option.

(3) Where such specification would materially affect the other party's performance but is not seasonably made or where one party's cooperation is necessary to the agreed performance of the other but is not seasonably forthcoming, the other party in addition to all other remedies

(a) is excused for any resulting delay in his own performance; and

(b) may also either proceed to perform in any reasonable manner or after the time for a material part of his own performance treat the failure to specify or to cooperate as a breach by failure to deliver or accept the goods.

§ 2–312. WARRANTY OF TITLE AND AGAINST INFRINGEMENT; BUYER'S OBLIGATION AGAINST INFRINGEMENT.

(1) Subject to subsection (2) there is in a contract for sale a warranty by the seller that

(a) the title conveyed shall be good, and its transfer rightful; and

(b) the goods shall be delivered free from any security interest or other lien or encumbrance of which the buyer at the time of contracting has no knowledge.

(2) A warranty under subsection (1) will be excluded or modified only by specific language or by circumstances which give the buyer reason to know that the person selling does not claim title in himself or that he is purporting to sell only such right or title as he or a third person may have.

(3) Unless otherwise agreed a seller who is a merchant regularly dealing in goods of the kind warrants that the goods shall be delivered free of the rightful claim of any third person by way of infringement or the like but a buyer who furnishes specifications to the seller must hold the seller harmless against any such claim which arises out of compliance with the specifications.

§ 2–313. EXPRESS WARRANTIES BY AFFIRMATION, PROMISE, DESCRIPTION, SAMPLE.

(1) Express warranties by the seller are created as follows:

(a) Any affirmation of fact or promise made by the seller to the buyer which relates to the goods and becomes part of the basis of the bargain creates an express warranty that the goods shall conform to the affirmation or promise.

(b) Any description of the goods which is made part of the basis of the bargain creates an express warranty that the goods shall conform to the description.

(c) Any sample or model which is made part of the basis of the bargain creates an express warranty that the whole of the goods shall conform to the sample or model.

(2) It is not necessary to the creation of an express warranty that the seller use formal words such as "warrant" or "guarantee" or that he have a specific intention to make a warranty, but an affirmation merely of the value of the goods or a statement purporting to be merely the seller's opinion or commendation of the goods does not create a warranty.

§ 2–314. IMPLIED WARRANTY: MERCHANTABILITY; USAGE OF TRADE.

(1) Unless excluded or modified (Section 2–316), a warranty that the goods shall be merchantable is implied in a contract for their sale if the seller is a merchant with respect to goods of that kind. Under this section the serving for value of food or drink to be consumed either on the premises or elsewhere is a sale.

(2) Goods to be merchantable must be at least such as

(a) pass without objection in the trade under the contract description; and

(b) in the case of fungible goods, are of fair average quality within the description; and

(c) are fit for the ordinary purpose for which such goods are used; and

(d) run, within the variations permitted by the agreement, of even kind, quality and quantity within each unit and among all units involved; and

(e) are adequately contained, packaged, and labeled as the agreement may require; and

(f) conform to the promises or affirmations of fact made on the container or label if any.

(3) Unless excluded or modified (Section 2–316) other implied warranties may arise from course of dealing or usage of trade.

§ 2–315. IMPLIED WARRANTY: FITNESS FOR PARTICULAR PURPOSE.

Where the seller at the time of contracting has reason to know any particular purpose for which the goods are required and that the buyer is relying on the seller's skill or judgment to select or furnish suitable goods, there is unless excluded or modified under the next section an implied warranty that the goods shall be fit for such purpose.

§ 2–316. EXCLUSION OR MODIFICATION OF WARRANTIES.

(1) Words or conduct relevant to the creation of an express warranty and words or conduct tending to negate or limit warranty shall be construed wherever reasonable as consistent with each other, but subject to the provisions of this Article on parol or extrinsic evidence (Section 2–202) negation or limitation is inoperative to the extent that such construction is unreasonable.

(2) Subject to subsection (3), to exclude or modify the implied warranty of merchantability or any part of it the language must mention merchantability and in case of a writing must be conspicuous, and to exclude or modify any implied warranty of fitness the exclusion must be by a writing and conspicuous. Language to exclude all implied warranties of fitness is sufficient if it states, for example, that "There are no warranties which extend beyond the description on the face hereof."

(3) Notwithstanding subsection (2)

(a) unless the circumstances indicate otherwise, all implied warranties are excluded by expressions like "as is", "with all faults" or other language which in common understanding calls the buyer's attention to the exclusion of warranties and makes plain that there is no implied warranty; and

(b) when the buyer before entering into the contract has examined the goods or the sample or model as fully as he desired or has refused to examine the goods there is no implied warranty with regard to defects which an examination ought in the circumstances to have revealed to him; and

(c) an implied warranty can also be excluded or modified by course of dealing or course of performance or usage of trade.

(4) Remedies for breach of warranty can be limited in accordance with the provisions of this Article on liquidation or limitation of damages and on contractual modification of remedy (Sections 2–718 and 2–719).

§ 2–317. Cumulation and Conflict of Warranties Express or Implied.

Warranties whether express or implied shall be construed as consistent with each other and as cumulative, but if such construction is unreasonable the intention of the parties shall determine which warranty is dominant. In ascertaining that intention the following rules apply:

(a) Exact or technical specifications displace an inconsistent sample or model or general language of description.

(b) A sample from an existing bulk displaces inconsistent general language of description.

(c) Express warranties displace inconsistent implied warranties other than an implied warranty of fitness for a particular purpose.

§ 2–318. Third Party Beneficiaries of Warranties Express or Implied.

Note: *If this Act is introduced in the Congress of the United States this section should be omitted. (States to select one alternative.)*

Alternative A A seller's warranty whether express or implied extends to any natural person who is in the family or household of his buyer or who is a guest in his home if it is reasonable to expect that such person may use, consume or be affected by the goods and who is injured in person by breach of the warranty. A seller may not exclude or limit the operation of this section.

Alternative B A seller's warranty whether express or implied extends to any natural person who may reasonably be expected to use, consume or be affected by the goods and who is injured in person by breach of the warranty. A seller may not exclude or limit the operation of this section.

Alternative C A seller's warranty whether express or implied extends to any person who may reasonably be expected to use, consume or be affected by the goods and who is injured by breach of the warranty. A seller may not exclude or limit the operation of this section with respect to injury to the person of an individual to whom the warranty extends.

§ 2–319. F.O.B. and F.A.S. Terms.

(1) Unless otherwise agreed the term F.O.B. (which means "free on board") at a named place, even though used only in connection with the stated price, is a delivery term under which

(a) when the term is F.O.B. the place of shipment, the seller must at that place ship the goods in the manner provided in this Article (Section 2–504) and bear the expense and risk of putting them into the possession of the carrier; or

(b) when the term is F.O.B. the place of destination, the seller must at his own expense and risk transport the goods to that place and there tender delivery of them in the manner provided in this Article (Section 2–503); or

(c) when under either (a) or (b) the term is also F.O.B. vessel, car or other vehicle, the seller must in addition at his own expense and risk load the goods on board. If the term is F.O.B. vessel the buyer must name the vessel and in an appropriate case the seller must comply with the provisions of this Article on the form of bill of lading (Section 2–323).

(2) Unless otherwise agreed the term F.A.S. vessel (which means "free alongside") at a named port, even though used only in connection with the stated price, is a delivery term under which the seller must

(a) at his own expense and risk deliver the goods alongside the vessel in the manner usual in that port or on a dock designated and provided by the buyer; and

(b) obtain and tender a receipt for the goods in exchange for which the carrier is under a duty to issue a bill of lading.

(3) Unless otherwise agreed in any case falling within subsection (1)(a) or (c) or subsection (2) the buyer must seasonably give any needed instructions for making delivery, including when the term is F.A.S. or F.O.B. the loading berth of the vessel and in an appropriate case its name and sailing date. The seller may treat the failure of needed instructions as a failure of cooperation under this Article (Section 2–311). He may also at his option move the goods in any reasonable manner preparatory to delivery or shipment.

(4) Under the term F.O.B. vessel or F.A.S. unless otherwise agreed the buyer must make payment against tender of the required documents and the seller may not tender nor the buyer demand delivery of the goods in substitution for the documents.

§ 2–320. C.I.F. and C. & F. Terms.

(1) The term C.I.F. means that the price includes in a lump sum the cost of the goods and the insurance and freight to the named destination. The term C. & F. or C.F. means that the price so includes cost and freight to the named destination.

(2) Unless otherwise agreed and even though used only in connection with the stated price and destination, the term C.I.F. destination or its equivalent requires the seller at his own expense and risk to

(a) put the goods into the possession of a carrier at the port for shipment and obtain a negotiable bill or bills of lading covering the entire transportation to the named destination; and

(b) load the goods and obtain a receipt from the carrier (which may be contained in the bill of lading) showing that the freight has been paid or provided for; and

(c) obtain a policy or certificate of insurance, including any war risk insurance, of a kind and on terms then current at the port of shipment in the usual amount, in the currency of the contract, shown to cover the same goods covered by the bill of lading and providing for payment of loss to the order of the buyer or for the account of whom it may concern; but the seller may add to the price the amount of premium for any such war risk insurance; and

(d) prepare an invoice of the goods and procure any other documents required to effect shipment or to comply with the contract; and

(e) forward and tender with commercial promptness all the documents in due form and with any indorsement necessary to perfect the buyer's rights.

(3) Unless otherwise agreed the term C. & F. or its equivalent has the same effect and imposes upon the seller the same obligations and risks as a C.I.F. term except the obligation as to insurance.

(4) Under the term C.I.F. or C. & F. unless otherwise agreed the buyer must make payment against tender of the required documents and the seller may not tender nor the buyer demand delivery of the goods in substitution for the documents.

§ 2–321. C.I.F. OR C. & F.: "NET LANDED WEIGHTS"; "PAYMENT ON ARRIVAL"; WARRANTY OF CONDITION ON ARRIVAL.

Under a contract containing a term C.I.F. or C. & F.

(1) Where the price is based on or is to be adjusted according to "net landed weights", "delivered weights", "out turn" quantity or quality or the like, unless otherwise agreed the seller must reasonably estimate the price. The payment due on tender of the documents called for by the contract is the amount so estimated, but after final adjustment of the price a settlement must be made with commercial promptness.

(2) An agreement described in subsection (1) or any warranty of quality or condition of the goods on arrival places upon the seller the risk of ordinary deterioration, shrinkage and the like in transportation but has no effect on the place or time of identification to the contract for sale or delivery or on the passing of the risk of loss.

(3) Unless otherwise agreed where the contract provides for payment on or after arrival of the goods the seller must before payment allow such preliminary inspection as is feasible; but if the goods are lost delivery of the documents and payment are due when the goods should have arrived.

§ 2–322. DELIVERY "EX-SHIP".

(1) Unless otherwise agreed a term for delivery of goods "ex-ship" (which means from the carrying vessel) or in equivalent language is not restricted to a particular ship and requires delivery from a ship which has reached a place at the named port of destination where goods of the kind are usually discharged.

(2) Under such a term unless otherwise agreed

(a) the seller must discharge all liens arising out of the carriage and furnish the buyer with a direction which puts the carrier under a duty to deliver the goods; and

(b) the risk of loss does not pass to the buyer until the goods leave the ship's tackle or are otherwise properly unloaded.

§ 2–323. FORM OF BILL OF LADING REQUIRED IN OVERSEAS SHIPMENT; "OVERSEAS".

(1) Where the contract contemplates overseas shipment and contains a term C.I.F. or C. & F. or F.O.B. vessel, the seller unless otherwise agreed must obtain a negotiable bill of lading stating that the goods have been loaded on board or, in the case of a term C.I.F. or C. & F., received for shipment.

(2) Where in a case within subsection (1) a bill of lading has been issued in a set of parts, unless otherwise agreed if the documents are not to be sent from abroad the buyer may demand tender of the full set; otherwise only one part of the bill of lading need be tendered. Even if the agreement expressly requires a full set

(a) due tender of a single part is acceptable within the provisions of this Article on cure of improper delivery (subsection (1) of Section 2–508); and

(b) even though the full set is demanded, if the documents are sent from abroad the person tendering an incomplete set may nevertheless require payment upon furnishing an indemnity which the buyer in good faith deems adequate.

(3) A shipment by water or by air or a contract contemplating such shipment is "overseas" insofar as by usage of trade or agreement it is subject to the commercial, financing or shipping practices characteristic of international deep water commerce.

§ 2–324. "NO ARRIVAL, NO SALE" TERM.

Under a term "no arrival, no sale" or terms of like meaning, unless otherwise agreed,

(a) the seller must properly ship conforming goods and if they arrive by any means he must tender them on arrival but he assumes no obligation that the goods will arrive unless he has caused the non-arrival; and

(b) where without fault of the seller the goods are in part lost or have so deteriorated as no longer to conform to the contract or arrive after the contract time, the buyer may proceed as if there had been casualty to identified goods (Section 2–613).

§ 2–325. "LETTER OF CREDIT" TERM; "CONFIRMED CREDIT".

(1) Failure of the buyer seasonably to furnish an agreed letter of credit is a breach of the contract for sale.

(2) The delivery to seller of a proper letter of credit suspends the buyer's obligation to pay. If the letter of credit is dishonored, the seller may on seasonable notification to the buyer require payment directly from him.

(3) Unless otherwise agreed the term "letter of credit" or "banker's credit" in a contract for sale means an irrevocable credit issued by a financing agency of good repute and, where the shipment is overseas, of good international repute. The term "confirmed credit" means that the credit must also carry the direct obligation of such an agency which does business in the seller's financial market.

§ 2–326. SALE ON APPROVAL AND SALE OR RETURN; CONSIGNMENT SALES AND RIGHTS OF CREDITORS.

(1) Unless otherwise agreed, if delivered goods may be returned by the buyer even though they conform to the contract, the transaction is

(a) a "sale on approval" if the goods are delivered primarily for use, and

(b) a "sale or return" if the goods are delivered primarily for resale.

(2) Except as provided in subsection (3), goods held on approval are not subject to the claims of the buyer's creditors until acceptance; goods held on sale or return are subject to such claims while in the buyer's possession.

(3) Where goods are delivered to a person for sale and such person maintains a place of business at which he deals in goods of the kind involved, under a name other than the name of the person making delivery, then with respect to claims of creditors of the person conducting the business the goods are deemed to be on sale or return. The provisions of this subsection are applicable even though an agreement purports to reserve title to the person making delivery until payment or resale or uses such words as "on consignment" or "on memorandum". However, this subsection is not applicable if the person making delivery

(a) complies with an applicable law providing for a consignor's interest or the like to be evidenced by a sign, or

(b) establishes that the person conducting the business is generally known by his creditors to be substantially engaged in selling the goods of others, or

(c) complies with the filing provisions of the Article on Secured Transactions (Article 9).

(4) Any "or return" term of a contract for sale is to be treated as a separate contract for sale within the statute of frauds section of this Article (Section 2–201) and as contradicting the sale aspect of the contract within the provisions of this Article on parol or extrinsic evidence (Section 2–202).

§ 2–327. SPECIAL INCIDENTS OF SALE ON APPROVAL AND SALE OR RETURN.

(1) Under a sale on approval unless otherwise agreed

(a) although the goods are identified to the contract the risk of loss and the title do not pass to the buyer until acceptance; and

(b) use of the goods consistent with the purpose of trial is not acceptance but failure seasonably to notify the seller of election to return the goods is acceptance, and if the goods conform to the contract acceptance of any part is acceptance of the whole; and

(c) after due notification of election to return, the return is at the seller's risk and expense but a merchant buyer must follow any reasonable instructions.

(2) Under a sale or return unless otherwise agreed

(a) the option to return extends to the whole or any commercial unit of the goods while in substantially their original condition, but must be exercised seasonably; and

(b) the return is at the buyer's risk and expense.

§ 2–328. SALE BY AUCTION.

(1) In a sale by auction if goods are put up in lots each lot is the subject of a separate sale.

(2) A sale by auction is complete when the auctioneer so announces by the fall of the hammer or in other customary manner. Where a bid is made while the hammer is falling in acceptance of a prior bid the auctioneer may in his discretion reopen the bidding or declare the goods sold under the bid on which the hammer was falling.

(3) Such a sale is with reserve unless the goods are in explicit terms put up without reserve. In an auction with reserve the auctioneer may withdraw the goods at any time until he announces completion of the sale. In an auction without reserve, after the auctioneer calls for bids on an article or lot, that article or lot cannot be withdrawn unless no bid is made within a reasonable time. In either case a bidder may retract his bid until the auctioneer's announcement of completion of the sale, but a bidder's retraction does not revive any previous bid.

(4) If the auctioneer knowingly receives a bid on the seller's behalf or the seller makes or procures such a bid, and notice has not been given that liberty for such bidding is reserved, the buyer may at his option avoid the sale or take the goods at the price of the last good faith bid prior to the completion of the sale. This subsection shall not apply to any bid at a forced sale.

PART 4—TITLE, CREDITORS AND GOOD FAITH PURCHASERS

§ 2–401. PASSING OF TITLE; RESERVATION FOR SECURITY; LIMITED APPLICATION OF THIS SECTION.

Each provision of this Article with regard to the rights, obligations and remedies of the seller, the buyer, purchasers or other third parties applies irrespective of title to the goods except where the provision refers to such title. Insofar as situations are not covered by the other provisions of this Article and matters concerning title became material the following rules apply:

(1) Title to goods cannot pass under a contract for sale prior to their identification to the contract (Section 2–501), and unless otherwise explicitly agreed the buyer acquires by their identification a special property as limited by this Act. Any retention or reservation by the seller of the title (property) in goods shipped or delivered to the buyer is limited in effect to a reservation of a security interest. Subject to these provisions and to the provisions of the Article on Secured Transactions (Article 9), title to goods passes from the seller to the buyer in any manner and on any conditions explicitly agreed on by the parties.

(2) Unless otherwise explicitly agreed title passes to the buyer at the time and place at which the seller completes his performance with reference to the physical delivery of the goods, despite any reservation of a security interest and even though a document of title is to be delivered at a different time or place; and in particular and despite any reservation of a security interest by the bill of lading

(a) if the contract requires or authorizes the seller to send the goods to the buyer but does not require him to deliver them at destination, title passes to the buyer at the time and place of shipment; but

(b) if the contract requires delivery at destination, title passes on tender there.

(3) Unless otherwise explicitly agreed where delivery is to be made without moving the goods,

(a) if the seller is to deliver a document of title, title passes at the time when and the place where he delivers such documents; or

(b) if the goods are at the time of contracting already identified and no documents are to be delivered, title passes at the time and place of contracting.

(4) A rejection or other refusal by the buyer to receive or retain the goods, whether or not justified, or a justified revocation of acceptance revests title to the goods in the seller. Such revesting occurs by operation of law and is not a "sale".

§ 2–402. RIGHTS OF SELLER'S CREDITORS AGAINST SOLD GOODS.

(1) Except as provided in subsections (2) and (3), rights of unsecured creditors of the seller with respect to goods which have been identified to a contract for sale are subject to the buyer's rights to recover the goods under this Article (Sections 2–502 and 2–716).

(2) A creditor of the seller may treat a sale or an identification of goods to a contract for sale as void if as against him a retention of possession by the seller is fraudulent under any rule of law of the state where the goods are situated, except that retention of possession in good faith and current course of trade by a merchant-seller for a commercially reasonable time after a sale or identification is not fraudulent.

(3) Nothing in this Article shall be deemed to impair the rights of creditors of the seller

(a) under the provisions of the Article on Secured Transactions (Article 9); or

(b) where identification to the contract or delivery is made not in current course of trade but in satisfaction of or as security for a pre-existing claim for money, security or the like and is made under circumstances which under any rule of law of the state where the goods are situated would apart from this Article constitute the transaction of a fraudulent transfer or voidable preference.

§ 2–403. POWER TO TRANSFER; GOOD FAITH PURCHASE OF GOODS; "ENTRUSTING".

(1) A purchaser of goods acquires all title which his transferor had or had power to transfer except that a purchaser of a limited interest acquires rights only to the extent of the interest purchased. A person with voidable title has power to transfer a good title to a good faith purchaser for value. When goods have been delivered under a transaction of purchase the purchaser has such power even though

(a) the transferor was deceived as to the identity of the purchaser, or

(b) the delivery was in exchange for a check which is later dishonored, or

(c) it was agreed that the transaction was to be a "cash sale", or

(d) the delivery was procured through fraud punishable as larcenous under the criminal law.

(2) Any entrusting of possession of goods to a merchant who deals in goods of that kind gives him power to transfer all rights of the entruster to a buyer in ordinary course of business.

(3) "Entrusting" includes any delivery and any acquiescence in retention of possession regardless of any condition expressed between the parties to the delivery or acquiescence and regardless of whether the procurement of the entrusting or the possessor's disposition of the goods have been such as to be larcenous under the criminal law.

(4) The rights of other purchasers of goods and of lien creditors are governed by the Articles on Secured Transactions (Article 9), Bulk Transfers (Article 6) and Documents of Title (Article 7).

PART 5—PERFORMANCE

§ 2–501. INSURABLE INTEREST IN GOODS; MANNER OF IDENTIFICATION OF GOODS.

(1) The buyer obtains a special property and an insurable interest in goods by identification of existing goods as goods to which the contract refers even though the goods so identified are nonconforming and he has an option to return or reject them. Such identification can be made at any time and in any manner explicitly agreed to by the parties. In the absence of explicit agreement identification occurs

(a) when the contract is made if it is for the sale of goods already existing and identified;

(b) if the contract is for the sale of future goods other than those described in paragraph (c), when goods are shipped, marked or otherwise designated by the seller as goods to which the contract refers;

(c) when the crops are planted or otherwise become growing crops or the young are conceived if the contract is for the sale of unborn young to be born within twelve months after contracting or for the sale of crops to be harvested within twelve months or the next normal harvest season after contracting whichever is longer.

(2) The seller retains an insurable interest in goods so long as title to or any security interest in the goods remains in him and where the identification is by the seller alone he may until default or insolvency or notification to the buyer that the identification is final substitute other goods for those identified.

(3) Nothing in this section impairs any insurable interest recognized under any other statute or rule of law.

§ 2–502. BUYER'S RIGHT TO GOODS ON SELLER'S INSOLVENCY.

(1) Subject to subsection (2) and even though the goods have not been shipped a buyer who has paid a part or all of the price of goods in which he has a special property under the provisions of the immediately preceding section may on making and keeping good a tender of any unpaid portion of their price recover them from the seller if the seller becomes insolvent within ten days after receipt of the first installment on their price.

(2) If the identification creating his special property has been made by the buyer he acquires the right to recover the goods only if they conform to the contract for sale.

§ 2–503. MANNER OF SELLER'S TENDER OF DELIVERY.

(1) Tender of delivery requires that the seller put and hold conforming goods at the buyer's disposition and give the buyer any notification reasonably necessary to enable him to take delivery. The manner, time and place for tender are determined by the agreement and this Article, and in particular

(a) tender must be at a reasonable hour, and if it is of goods they must be kept available for the period reasonably necessary to enable the buyer to take possession; but

(b) unless otherwise agreed the buyer must furnish facilities reasonably suited to the receipt of the goods.

(2) Where the case is within the next section respecting shipment tender requires that the seller comply with its provisions.

(3) Where the seller is required to deliver at a particular destination tender requires that he comply with subsection (1) and also in any appropriate case tender documents as described in subsections (4) and (5) of this section.

(4) Where goods are in the possession of a bailee and are to be delivered without being moved

(a) tender requires that the seller either tender a negotiable document of title covering such goods or procure acknowledgment by the bailee of the buyer's right to possession of the goods; but

(b) tender to the buyer of a non-negotiable document of title or of a written direction to the bailee to deliver is sufficient tender unless the buyer seasonably objects, and receipt by the bailee of notification of the buyer's rights fixes those rights as against the bailee and all third persons; but risk of loss of the goods and of any failure by the bailee to honor the non-negotiable document of title or to obey the direction remains on the seller until the buyer has had a reasonable time to present the document or direction, and a refusal by the bailee to honor the document or to obey the direction defeats the tender.

(5) Where the contract requires the seller to deliver documents

(a) he must tender all such documents in correct form, except as provided in this Article with respect to bills of lading in a set (subsection (2) of Section 2–323); and

(b) tender through customary banking channels is sufficient and dishonor of a draft accompanying the documents constitutes non-acceptance or rejection.

§ 2–504. SHIPMENT BY SELLER.

Where the seller is required or authorized to send the goods to the buyer and the contract does not require him to deliver them at a particular destination, then unless otherwise agreed he must

(a) put the goods in the possession of such a carrier and make such a contract for their transportation as may be reasonable having regard to the nature of the goods and other circumstances of the case; and

(b) obtain and promptly deliver or tender in due form any document necessary to enable the buyer to obtain possession of the goods or otherwise required by the agreement or by usage of trade; and

(c) promptly notify the buyer of the shipment. Failure to notify the buyer under paragraph (c) or to make a proper contract under paragraph (a) is a ground for rejection only if material delay or loss ensues.

§ 2–505. SELLER'S SHIPMENT UNDER RESERVATION.

(1) Where the seller has identified goods to the contract by or before shipment:

(a) his procurement of a negotiable bill of lading to his own order or otherwise reserves in him a security interest in the goods. His procurement of the bill to the order of a financing agency or of the buyer indicates in addition only the seller's expectation of transferring that interest to the person named.

(b) a non-negotiable bill of lading to himself or his nominee reserves possession of the goods as security but except in a case of conditional delivery (subsection (2) of Section 2–507) a non-negotiable bill of lading naming the buyer as consignee reserves no security interest even though the seller retains possession of the bill of lading.

(2) When shipment by the seller with reservation of a security interest is in violation of the contract for sale it constitutes an improper contract for transportation within the preceding section but impairs neither the rights given to the buyer by shipment and identification of the goods to the contract nor the seller's powers as a holder of a negotiable document.

§ 2–506. RIGHTS OF FINANCING AGENCY.

(1) A financing agency by paying or purchasing for value a draft which relates to a shipment of goods acquires to the extent of the payment or purchase and in addition to its own rights under the draft and any document of title securing it any rights of the shipper in the goods including the right to stop delivery and the shipper's right to have the draft honored by the buyer.

(2) The right to reimbursement of a financing agency which has in good faith honored or purchased the draft under commitment to or authority from the buyer is not impaired by subsequent discovery of defects with reference to any relevant document which was apparently regular on its face.

§ 2–507. EFFECT OF SELLER'S TENDER; DELIVERY ON CONDITION.

(1) Tender of delivery is a condition to the buyer's duty to accept the goods and, unless otherwise agreed, to his duty to pay for them. Tender entitles the seller to acceptance of the goods and to payment according to the contract.

(2) Where payment is due and demanded on the delivery to the buyer of goods or documents of title, his right as against the seller to retain or dispose of them is conditional upon his making the payment due.

§ 2–508. CURE BY SELLER OF IMPROPER TENDER OR DELIVERY; REPLACEMENT.

(1) Where any tender or delivery by the seller is rejected because non-conforming and the time for performance has not yet expired, the seller may seasonably notify the buyer of his intention to cure and may then within the contract time make a conforming delivery.

(2) Where the buyer rejects a non-conforming tender which the seller had reasonable grounds to believe would be acceptable with or without money allowance the seller may if he seasonably notifies the buyer have a further reasonable time to substitute a conforming tender.

§ 2–509. RISK OF LOSS IN THE ABSENCE OF BREACH.

(1) Where the contract requires or authorizes the seller to ship the goods by carrier

(a) if it does not require him to deliver them at a particular destination, the risk of loss passes to the buyer when the goods are duly delivered to the carrier even though the shipment is under reservation (Section 2–505); but

(b) if it does require him to deliver them at a particular destination and the goods are there duly tendered while in the possession of the carrier, the risk of loss passes to the buyer when the goods are there duly so tendered as to enable the buyer to take delivery.

(2) Where the goods are held by a bailee to be delivered without being moved, the risk of loss passes to the buyer

(a) on his receipt of a negotiable document of title covering the goods; or

(b) on acknowledgment by the bailee of the buyer's right to possession of the goods; or

(c) after his receipt of a non-negotiable document of title or other written direction to deliver, as provided in subsection (4)(b) of Section 2–503.

(3) In any case not within subsection (1) or (2), the risk of loss passes to the buyer on his receipt of the goods if the seller is a merchant; otherwise, the risk passes to the buyer on tender of delivery.

(4) The provisions of this section are subject to contrary agreement of the parties and to the provisions of this Article on sale on approval (Section 2–327) and on effect of breach on risk of loss (Section 2–510).

§ 2–510. EFFECT OF BREACH ON RISK OF LOSS.

(1) Where a tender or delivery of goods so fails to conform to the contract as to give a right of rejection the risk of their loss remains on the seller until cure or acceptance.

(2) Where the buyer rightfully revokes acceptance he may to the extent of any deficiency in his effective insurance coverage treat the risk of loss as having rested on the seller from the beginning.

(3) Where the buyer as to conforming goods already identified to the contract for sale repudiates or is otherwise in breach before risk of their loss has passed to him, the seller may to the extent of any deficiency in his effective insurance coverage treat the risk of loss as resting on the buyer for a commercially reasonable time.

§ 2–511. TENDER OF PAYMENT BY BUYER; PAYMENT BY CHECK.

(1) Unless otherwise agreed tender of payment is a condition to the seller's duty to tender and complete any delivery.

(2) Tender of payment is sufficient when made by any means or in any manner current in the ordinary course of business unless the seller demands payment in legal tender and gives any extension of time reasonably necessary to procure it.

(3) Subject to the provisions of this Act on the effect of an instrument on an obligation (Section 3–802), payment by check is conditional and is defeated as between the parties by dishonor of the check on due presentment.

§ 2–512. Payment by Buyer Before Inspection.

(1) Where the contract requires payment before inspection non-conformity of the goods does not excuse the buyer from so making payment unless

(a) the non-conformity appears without inspection; or

(b) despite tender of the required documents the circumstances would justify injunction against honor under the provisions of this Act (Section 5–114).

(2) Payment pursuant to subsection (1) does not constitute an acceptance of goods or impair the buyer's right to inspect or any of his remedies.

§ 2–513. Buyer's Right to Inspection of Goods.

(1) Unless otherwise agreed and subject to subsection (3), where goods are tendered or delivered or identified to the contract for sale, the buyer has a right before payment or acceptance to inspect them at any reasonable place and time and in any reasonable manner. When the seller is required or authorized to send the goods to the buyer, the inspection may be after their arrival.

(2) Expenses of inspection must be borne by the buyer but may be recovered from the seller if the goods do not conform and are rejected.

(3) Unless otherwise agreed and subject to the provisions of this Article on C.I.F. contracts (subsection (3) of Section 2–321), the buyer is not entitled to inspect the goods before payment of the price when the contract provides

(a) for delivery "C.O.D." or on other like terms; or

(b) for payment against documents of title, except where such payment is due only after the goods are to become available for inspection.

(4) A place or method of inspection fixed by the parties is presumed to be exclusive but unless otherwise expressly agreed it does not postpone identification or shift the place for delivery or for passing the risk of loss. If compliance becomes impossible, inspection shall be as provided in this section unless the place or method fixed was clearly intended as an indispensable condition failure of which avoids the contract.

§ 2–514. When Documents Deliverable on Acceptance; When on Payment.

Unless otherwise agreed documents against which a draft is drawn are to be delivered to the drawee on acceptance of the draft if it is payable more than three days after presentment; otherwise, only on payment.

§ 2–515. Preserving Evidence of Goods in Dispute.

In furtherance of the adjustment of any claim or dispute

(a) either party on reasonable notification to the other and for the purpose of ascertaining the facts and preserving evidence has the right to inspect, test and sample the goods including such of them as may be in the possession or control of the other; and

(b) the parties may agree to a third party inspection or survey to determine the conformity or condition of the goods and may agree that the findings shall be binding upon them in any subsequent litigation or adjustment.

Part 6—Breach, Repudiation and Excuse

§ 2–601. Buyer's Rights on Improper Delivery.

Subject to the provisions of this Article on breach in installment contracts (Section 2–612) and unless otherwise agreed under the sections on contractual limitations of remedy (Sections 2–718 and 2–719), if the goods or the tender of delivery fail in any respect to conform to the contract, the buyer may

(a) reject the whole; or

(b) accept the whole; or

(c) accept any commercial unit or units and reject the rest.

§ 2–602. Manner and Effect of Rightful Rejection.

(1) Rejection of goods must be within a reasonable time after their delivery or tender. It is ineffective unless the buyer seasonably notifies the seller.

(2) Subject to the provisions of the two following sections on rejected goods (Sections 2–603 and 2–604),

(a) after rejection any exercise of ownership by the buyer with respect to any commercial unit is wrongful as against the seller; and

(b) if the buyer has before rejection taken physical possession of goods in which he does not have a security interest under the provisions of this Article (subsection (3) of Section 2–711), he is under a duty after rejection to hold them with reasonable care at the seller's disposition for a time sufficient to permit the seller to remove them; but

(c) the buyer has no further obligations with regard to goods rightfully rejected.

(3) The seller's rights with respect to goods wrongfully rejected are governed by the provisions of this Article on seller's remedies in general (Section 2–703).

§ 2–603. Merchant Buyer's Duties as to Rightfully Rejected Goods.

(1) Subject to any security interest in the buyer (subsection (3) of Section 2–711), when the seller has no agent or place of business at the market of rejection a merchant buyer is under a duty after rejection of goods in his possession or control to follow any reasonable instructions received from the seller with respect to the goods and in the absence of such instructions to make reasonable efforts to sell them for the seller's account if they are perishable or threaten to decline in value speedily. Instructions are not reasonable if on demand indemnity for expenses is not forthcoming.

(2) When the buyer sells goods under subsection (1), he is entitled to reimbursement from the seller or out of the proceeds for reasonable expenses of caring for and selling them, and if the expenses include no selling commission then to such commission as is usual in the trade or if there is none to a reasonable sum not exceeding ten per cent on the gross proceeds.

(3) In complying with this section the buyer is held only to good faith and good faith conduct hereunder is neither acceptance nor conversion nor the basis of an action for damages.

§ 2–604. Buyer's Options as to Salvage of Rightfully Rejected Goods.

Subject to the provisions of the immediately preceding section on perishables if the seller gives no instructions within a reasonable time after notification of rejection the buyer may store the rejected goods for the seller's account or reship them to him or resell them for the seller's account with reimbursement as provided in the preceding section. Such action is not acceptance or conversion.

§ 2–605. Waiver of Buyer's Objections by Failure to Particularize.

(1) The buyer's failure to state in connection with rejection a particular defect which is ascertainable by reasonable inspection

precludes him from relying on the unstated defect to justify rejection or to establish breach

(a) where the seller could have cured it if stated seasonably; or

(b) between merchants when the seller has after rejection made a request in writing for a full and final written statement of all defects on which the buyer proposes to rely.

(2) Payment against documents made without reservation of rights precludes recovery of the payment for defects apparent on the face of the documents.

§ 2–606. WHAT CONSTITUTES ACCEPTANCE OF GOODS.

(1) Acceptance of goods occurs when the buyer

(a) after a reasonable opportunity to inspect the goods signifies to the seller that the goods are conforming or that he will take or retain them in spite of their nonconformity; or

(b) fails to make an effective rejection (subsection (1) of Section 2–602), but such acceptance does not occur until the buyer has had a reasonable opportunity to inspect them; or

(c) does any act inconsistent with the seller's ownership; but if such act is wrongful as against the seller it is an acceptance only if ratified by him.

(2) Acceptance of a part of any commercial unit is acceptance of that entire unit.

§ 2–607. EFFECT OF ACCEPTANCE; NOTICE OF BREACH; BURDEN OF ESTABLISHING BREACH AFTER ACCEPTANCE; NOTICE OF CLAIM OR LITIGATION TO PERSON ANSWERABLE OVER.

(1) The buyer must pay at the contract rate for any goods accepted.

(2) Acceptance of goods by the buyer precludes rejection of the goods accepted and if made with knowledge of a non-conformity cannot be revoked because of it unless the acceptance was on the reasonable assumption that the non-conformity would be seasonably cured but acceptance does not of itself impair any other remedy provided by this Article for non-conformity.

(3) Where a tender has been accepted

(a) the buyer must within a reasonable time after he discovers or should have discovered any breach notify the seller of breach or be barred from any remedy; and

(b) if the claim is one for infringement or the like (subsection (3) of Section 2–312) and the buyer is sued as a result of such a breach he must so notify the seller within a reasonable time after he receives notice of the litigation or be barred from any remedy over for liability established by the litigation.

(4) The burden is on the buyer to establish any breach with respect to the goods accepted.

(5) Where the buyer is sued for breach of a warranty or other obligation for which his seller is answerable over

(a) he may give his seller written notice of the litigation. If the notice states that the seller may come in and defend and that if the seller does not do so he will be bound in any action against him by his buyer by any determination of fact common to the two litigations, then unless the seller after seasonable receipt of the notice does come in and defend he is so bound.

(b) if the claim is one for infringement or the like (subsection (3) of Section 2–312) the original seller may demand in writing that his buyer turn over to him control of the litigation including settlement or else be barred from any remedy over and if he also agrees to bear all expense and to satisfy any adverse judgment, then unless the buyer after seasonable receipt of the demand does turn over control the buyer is so barred.

(6) The provisions of subsections (3), (4) and (5) apply to any obligation of a buyer to hold the seller harmless against infringement or the like (subsection (3) of Section 2–312).

§ 2–608. REVOCATION OF ACCEPTANCE IN WHOLE OR IN PART.

(1) The buyer may revoke his acceptance of a lot or commercial unit whose non-conformity substantially impairs its value to him if he has accepted it

(a) on the reasonable assumption that its non-conformity would be cured and it has not been seasonably cured; or

(b) without discovery of such non-conformity if his acceptance was reasonably induced either by the difficulty of discovery before acceptance or by the seller's assurances.

(2) Revocation of acceptance must occur within a reasonable time after the buyer discovers or should have discovered the ground for it and before any substantial change in condition of the goods which is not caused by their own defects. It is not effective until the buyer notifies the seller of it.

(3) A buyer who so revokes has the same rights and duties with regard to the goods involved as if he had rejected them.

§ 2–609. RIGHT TO ADEQUATE ASSURANCE OF PERFORMANCE.

(1) A contract for sale imposes an obligation on each party that the other's expectation of receiving due performance will not be impaired. When reasonable grounds for insecurity arise with respect to the performance of either party the other may in writing demand adequate assurance of due performance and until he receives such assurance may if commercially reasonable suspend any performance for which he has not already received the agreed return.

(2) Between merchants the reasonableness of grounds for insecurity and the adequacy of any assurance offered shall be determined according to commercial standards.

(3) Acceptance of any improper delivery or payment does not prejudice the aggrieved party's right to demand adequate assurance of future performance.

(4) After receipt of a justified demand failure to provide within a reasonable time not exceeding thirty days such assurance of due performance as is adequate under the circumstances of the particular case is a repudiation of the contract.

§ 2–610. ANTICIPATORY REPUDIATION.

When either party repudiates the contract with respect to a performance not yet due the loss of which will substantially impair the value of the contract to the other, the aggrieved party may

(a) for a commercially reasonable time await performance by the repudiating party; or

(b) resort to any remedy for breach (Section 2–703 or Section 2–711), even though he has notified the repudiating party that he would await the latter's performance and has urged retraction; and

(c) in either case suspend his own performance or proceed in accordance with the provisions of this Article on the seller's right to identify goods to the contract notwithstanding breach or to salvage unfinished goods (Section 2–704).

§ 2–611. RETRACTION OF ANTICIPATORY REPUDIATION.

(1) Until the repudiating party's next performance is due he can retract his repudiation unless the aggrieved party has since the repudiation cancelled or materially changed his position or otherwise indicated that he considers the repudiation final.

(2) Retraction may be by any method which clearly indicates to the aggrieved party that the repudiating party intends to perform, but must include any assurance justifiably demanded under the provisions of this Article (Section 2–609).

(3) Retraction reinstates the repudiating party's rights under the contract with due excuse and allowance to the aggrieved party for any delay occasioned by the repudiation.

§ 2–612. "Installment Contract"; Breach.

(1) An "installment contract" is one which requires or authorizes the delivery of goods in separate lots to be separately accepted, even though the contract contains a clause "each delivery is a separate contract" or its equivalent.

(2) The buyer may reject any installment which is non-conforming if the non-conformity substantially impairs the value of that installment and cannot be cured or if the non-conformity is a defect in the required documents; but if the non-conformity does not fall within subsection (3) and the seller gives adequate assurance of its cure the buyer must accept that installment.

(3) Whenever non-conformity or default with respect to one or more installments substantially impairs the value of the whole contract there is a breach of the whole. But the aggrieved party reinstates the contract if he accepts a non-conforming installment without seasonably notifying of cancellation or if he brings an action with respect only to past installments or demands performance as to future installments.

§ 2–613. Casualty to Identified Goods.

Where the contract requires for its performance goods identified when the contract is made, and the goods suffer casualty without fault of either party before the risk of loss passes to the buyer, or in a proper case under a "no arrival, no sale" term (Section 2–324) then

(a) if the loss is total the contract is avoided; and

(b) if the loss is partial or the goods have so deteriorated as no longer to conform to the contract the buyer may nevertheless demand inspection and at his option either treat the contract as avoided or accept the goods with due allowance from the contract price for the deterioration or the deficiency in quantity but without further right against the seller.

§ 2–614. Substituted Performance.

(1) Where without fault of either party the agreed berthing, loading, or unloading facilities fail or an agreed type of carrier becomes unavailable or the agreed manner of delivery otherwise becomes commercially impracticable but a commercially reasonable substitute is available, such substitute performance must be tendered and accepted.

(2) If the agreed means or manner of payment fails because of domestic or foreign governmental regulation, the seller may withhold or stop delivery unless the buyer provides a means or manner of payment which is commercially a substantial equivalent. If delivery has already been taken, payment by the means or in the manner provided by the regulation discharges the buyer's obligation unless the regulation is discriminatory, oppressive or predatory.

§ 2–615. Excuse by Failure of Presupposed Conditions.

Except so far as a seller may have assumed a greater obligation and subject to the preceding section on substituted performance:

(a) Delay in delivery or non-delivery in whole or in part by a seller who complies with paragraphs (b) and (c) is not a breach of his duty under a contract for sale if performance as agreed has been made impracticable by the occurrence of a contingency the non-occurrence of which was a basic assumption on which the contract was made or by compliance in good faith with any applicable foreign or domestic governmental regulation or order whether or not it later proves to be invalid.

(b) Where the causes mentioned in paragraph (a) affect only a part of the seller's capacity to perform, he must allocate production and deliveries among his customers but may at his option include regular customers not then under contract as well as his own requirements for further manufacture. He may so allocate in any manner which is fair and reasonable.

(c) The seller must notify the buyer seasonably that there will be delay or non-delivery and, when allocation is required under paragraph (b), of the estimated quota thus made available for the buyer.

§ 2–616. Procedure on Notice Claiming Excuse.

(1) Where the buyer receives notification of a material or indefinite delay or an allocation justified under the preceding section he may by written notification to the seller as to any delivery concerned, and where the prospective deficiency substantially impairs the value of the whole contract under the provisions of this Article relating to breach of installment contracts (Section 2–612), then also as to the whole,

(a) terminate and thereby discharge any unexecuted portion of the contract; or

(b) modify the contract by agreeing to take his available quota in substitution.

(2) If after receipt of such notification from the seller the buyer fails so to modify the contract within a reasonable time not exceeding thirty days the contract lapses with respect to any deliveries affected.

(3) The provisions of this section may not be negated by agreement except in so far as the seller has assumed a greater obligation under the preceding section.

Part 7—Remedies

§ 2–701. Remedies for Breach of Collateral Contracts Not Impaired.

Remedies for breach of any obligation or promise collateral or ancillary to a contract for sale are not impaired by the provisions of this Article.

§ 2–702. Seller's Remedies on Discovery of Buyer's Insolvency.

(1) Where the seller discovers the buyer to be insolvent he may refuse delivery except for cash including payment for all goods theretofore delivered under the contract, and stop delivery under this Article (Section 2–705).

(2) Where the seller discovers that the buyer has received goods on credit while insolvent he may reclaim the goods upon demand made within ten days after the receipt, but if misrepresentation of solvency has been made to the particular seller in writing within three months before delivery the ten day limitation does not apply. Except as provided in this subsection the seller may not base a right to reclaim goods on the buyer's fraudulent or innocent misrepresentation of solvency or of intent to pay.

(3) The seller's right to reclaim under subsection (2) is subject to the rights of a buyer in ordinary course or other good faith purchaser under this Article (Section 2–403). Successful reclamation of goods excludes all other remedies with respect to them.

§ 2–703. SELLER'S REMEDIES IN GENERAL.

Where the buyer wrongfully rejects or revokes acceptance of goods or fails to make a payment due on or before delivery or repudiates with respect to a part or the whole, then with respect to any goods directly affected and, if the breach is of the whole contract (Section 2–612), then also with respect to the whole undelivered balance, the aggrieved seller may

(a) withhold delivery of such goods;

(b) stop delivery by any bailee as hereafter provided (Section 2–705);

(c) proceed under the next section respecting goods still unidentified to the contract;

(d) resell and recover damages as hereafter provided (Section 2–706);

(e) recover damages for non-acceptance (Section 2–708) or in a proper case the price (Section 2–709);

(f) cancel.

§ 2–704. SELLER'S RIGHT TO IDENTIFY GOODS TO THE CONTRACT NOTWITHSTANDING BREACH OR TO SALVAGE UNFINISHED GOODS.

(1) An aggrieved seller under the preceding section may

(a) identify to the contract conforming goods not already identified if at the time he learned of the breach they are in his possession or control;

(b) treat as the subject of resale goods which have demonstrably been intended for the particular contract even though those goods are unfinished.

(2) Where the goods are unfinished an aggrieved seller may in the exercise of reasonable commercial judgment for the purposes of avoiding loss and of effective realization either complete the manufacture and wholly identify the goods to the contract or cease manufacture and resell for scrap or salvage value or proceed in any other reasonable manner.

§ 2–705. SELLER'S STOPPAGE OF DELIVERY IN TRANSIT OR OTHERWISE.

(1) The seller may stop delivery of goods in the possession of a carrier or other bailee when he discovers the buyer to be insolvent (Section 2–702) and may stop delivery of carload, truckload, planeload or larger shipments of express or freight when the buyer repudiates or fails to make a payment due before delivery or if for any other reason the seller has a right to withhold or reclaim the goods.

(2) As against such buyer the seller may stop delivery until

(a) receipt of the goods by the buyer; or

(b) acknowledgment to the buyer by any bailee of the goods except a carrier that the bailee holds the goods for the buyer; or

(c) such acknowledgment to the buyer by a carrier by reshipment or as warehouseman; or

(d) negotiation to the buyer of any negotiable document of title covering the goods.

(3) (a) To stop delivery the seller must so notify as to enable the bailee by reasonable diligence to prevent delivery of the goods.

(b) After such notification the bailee must hold and deliver the goods according to the directions of the seller but the seller is liable to the bailee for any ensuing charges or damages.

(c) If a negotiable document of title has been issued for goods the bailee is not obliged to obey a notification to stop until surrender of the document.

(d) A carrier who has issued a non-negotiable bill of lading is not obliged to obey a notification to stop received from a person other than the consignor.

§ 2–706. SELLER'S RESALE INCLUDING CONTRACT FOR RESALE.

(1) Under the conditions stated in Section 2–703 on seller's remedies, the seller may resell the goods concerned or the undelivered balance thereof. Where the resale is made in good faith and in a commercially reasonable manner the seller may recover the difference between the resale price and the contract price together with any incidental damages allowed under the provisions of this Article (Section 2–710), but less expenses saved in consequence of the buyer's breach.

(2) Except as otherwise provided in subsection (3) or unless otherwise agreed resale may be at public or private sale including sale by way of one or more contracts to sell or of identification to an existing contract of the seller. Sale may be as a unit or in parcels and at any time and place and on any terms but every aspect of the sale including the method, manner, time, place and terms must be commercially reasonable. The resale must be reasonably identified as referring to the broken contract, but it is not necessary that the goods be in existence or that any or all of them have been identified to the contract before the breach.

(3) Where the resale is at private sale the seller must give the buyer reasonable notification of his intention to resell.

(4) Where the resale is at public sale

(a) only identified goods can be sold except where there is a recognized market for a public sale of futures in goods of the kind; and

(b) it must be made at a usual place or market for public sale if one is reasonably available and except in the case of goods which are perishable or threaten to decline in value speedily the seller must give the buyer reasonable notice of the time and place of the resale; and

(c) if the goods are not to be within the view of those attending the sale the notification of sale must state the place where the goods are located and provide for their reasonable inspection by prospective bidders; and

(d) the seller may buy.

(5) A purchaser who buys in good faith at a resale takes the goods free of any rights of the original buyer even though the seller fails to comply with one or more of the requirements of this section.

(6) The seller is not accountable to the buyer for any profit made on any resale. A person in the position of a seller (Section 2–707) or a buyer who has rightfully rejected or justifiably revoked acceptance must account for any excess over the amount of his security interest, as hereinafter defined (subsection (3) of Section 2–711).

§ 2–707. "PERSON IN THE POSITION OF A SELLER".

(1) A "person in the position of a seller" includes as against a principal an agent who has paid or become responsible for the price of goods on behalf of his principal or anyone who otherwise holds a security interest or other right in goods similar to that of a seller.

(2) A person in the position of a seller may as provided in this Article withhold or stop delivery (Section 2–705) and resell (Section 2–706) and recover incidental damages (Section 2–710).

§ 2–708. SELLER'S DAMAGES FOR NON-ACCEPTANCE OR REPUDIATION.

(1) Subject to subsection (2) and to the provisions of this Article with respect to proof of market price (Section 2–723), the measure of damages for non-acceptance or repudiation by

the buyer is the difference between the market price at the time and place for tender and the unpaid contract price together with any incidental damages provided in this Article (Section 2–710), but less expenses saved in consequence of the buyer's breach.

(2) If the measure of damages provided in subsection (1) is inadequate to put the seller in as good a position as performance would have done then the measure of damages is the profit (including reasonable overhead) which the seller would have made from full performance by the buyer, together with any incidental damages provided in this Article (Section 2–710), due allowance for costs reasonably incurred and due credit for payments or proceeds of resale.

§ 2–709. Action for the Price.

(1) When the buyer fails to pay the price as it becomes due the seller may recover, together with any incidental damages under the next section, the price

(a) of goods accepted or of conforming goods lost or damaged within a commercially reasonable time after risk of their loss has passed to the buyer; and

(b) of goods identified to the contract if the seller is unable after reasonable effort to resell them at a reasonable price or the circumstances reasonably indicate that such effort will be unavailing.

(2) Where the seller sues for the price he must hold for the buyer any goods which have been identified to the contract and are still in his control except that if resale becomes possible he may resell them at any time prior to the collection of the judgment. The net proceeds of any such resale must be credited to the buyer and payment of the judgment entitles him to any goods not resold.

(3) After the buyer has wrongfully rejected or revoked acceptance of the goods or has failed to make a payment due or has repudiated (Section 2–610), a seller who is held not entitled to the price under this section shall nevertheless be awarded damages for non-acceptance under the preceding section.

§ 2–710. Seller's Incidental Damages.

Incidental damages to an aggrieved seller include any commercially reasonable charges, expenses or commissions incurred in stopping delivery, in the transportation, care and custody of goods after the buyer's breach, in connection with return or resale of the goods or otherwise resulting from the breach.

§ 2–711. Buyer's Remedies in General; Buyer's Security Interest in Rejected Goods.

(1) Where the seller fails to make delivery or repudiates or the buyer rightfully rejects or justifiably revokes acceptance then with respect to any goods involved, and with respect to the whole if the breach goes to the whole contract (Section 2–612), the buyer may cancel and whether or not he has done so may in addition to recovering so much of the price as has been paid

(a) "cover" and have damages under the next section as to all the goods affected whether or not they have been identified to the contract; or

(b) recover damages for non-delivery as provided in this Article (Section 2–713).

(2) Where the seller fails to deliver or repudiates the buyer may also

(a) if the goods have been identified recover them as provided in this Article (Section 2–502); or

(b) in a proper case obtain specific performance or replevy the goods as provided in this Article (Section 2–716).

(3) On rightful rejection or justifiable revocation of acceptance a buyer has a security interest in goods in his possession or control for any payments made on their price and any expenses reasonably incurred in their inspection, receipt, transportation, care and custody and may hold such goods and resell them in like manner as an aggrieved seller (Section 2–706).

§ 2–712. "Cover"; Buyer's Procurement of Substitute Goods.

(1) After a breach within the preceding section the buyer may "cover" by making in good faith and without unreasonable delay any reasonable purchase of or contract to purchase goods in substitution for those due from the seller.

(2) The buyer may recover from the seller as damages the difference between the cost of cover and the contract price together with any incidental or consequential damages as hereinafter defined (Section 2–715), but less expenses saved in consequence of the seller's breach.

(3) Failure of the buyer to effect cover within this section does not bar him from any other remedy.

§ 2–713. Buyer's Damages for Non-Delivery or Repudiation.

(1) Subject to provisions of this Article with respect to the proof of market price (Section 2–723), the measure of damages for non-delivery or repudiation by the seller is the difference between the market price at the time when the buyer learned of the breach and the contract price together with any incidental and consequential damages provided in this Article (Section 2–715), but less expenses saved in consequence of the seller's breach.

(2) Market price is to be determined as of the place for tender or, in cases of rejection after arrival or revocation of acceptance, as of the place of arrival.

§ 2–714. Buyer's Damages for Breach in Regard to Accepted Goods.

(1) Where the buyer has accepted goods and given notification (subsection (3) of Section 2–607) he may recover as damages for any non-conformity of tender the loss resulting in the ordinary course of events from the seller's breach as determined in any manner which is reasonable.

(2) The measure of damages for breach of warranty is the difference at the time and place of acceptance between the value of the goods accepted and the value they would have had if they had been as warranted, unless special circumstances show proximate damages of a different amount.

(3) In a proper case any incidental and consequential damages under the next section may be recovered.

§ 2–715. Buyer's Incidental and Consequential Damages.

(1) Incidental damages resulting from the seller's breach include expenses reasonably incurred in inspection, receipt, transportation and care and custody of goods rightfully rejected, any commercially reasonable charges, expenses or commissions in connection with effecting cover and any other reasonable expense incident to the delay or other breach.

(2) Consequential damages resulting from the seller's breach include

(a) any loss resulting from general or particular requirements and needs of which the seller at the time of contracting had reason to know and which could not reasonably be prevented by cover or otherwise; and

(b) injury to person or property proximately resulting from any breach of warranty.

§ 2–716. Buyer's Right to Specific Performance or Replevin.

(1) Specific performance may be decreed where the goods are unique or in other proper circumstances.

(2) The decree for specific performance may include such terms and conditions as to payment of the price, damages, or other relief as the court may deem just.

(3) The buyer has a right of replevin for goods identified to the contract if after reasonable effort he is unable to effect cover for such goods or the circumstances reasonably indicate that such effort will be unavailing or if the goods have been shipped under reservation and satisfaction of the security interest in them has been made or tendered.

§ 2–717. Deduction of Damages From the Price.

The buyer on notifying the seller of his intention to do so may deduct all or any part of the damages resulting from any breach of the contract from any part of the price still due under the same contract.

§ 2–718. Liquidation or Limitation of Damages; Deposits.

(1) Damages for breach by either party may be liquidated in the agreement but only at an amount which is reasonable in the light of the anticipated or actual harm caused by the breach, the difficulties of proof of loss, and the inconvenience or nonfeasibility of otherwise obtaining an adequate remedy. A term fixing unreasonably large liquidated damages is void as a penalty.

(2) Where the seller justifiably withholds delivery of goods because of the buyer's breach, the buyer is entitled to restitution of any amount by which the sum of his payments exceeds

(a) the amount to which the seller is entitled by virtue of terms liquidating the seller's damages in accordance with subsection (1), or

(b) in the absence of such terms, twenty per cent of the value of the total performance for which the buyer is obligated under the contract or $500, whichever is smaller.

(3) The buyer's right to restitution under subsection (2) is subject to offset to the extent that the seller establishes

(a) a right to recover damages under the provisions of this Article other than subsection (1), and

(b) the amount or value of any benefits received by the buyer directly or indirectly by reason of the contract.

(4) Where a seller has received payment in goods their reasonable value or the proceeds of their resale shall be treated as payments for the purposes of subsection (2); but if the seller has notice of the buyer's breach before reselling goods received in part performance, his resale is subject to the conditions laid down in this Article on resale by an aggrieved seller (Section 2–706).

§ 2–719. Contractual Modification or Limitation of Remedy.

(1) Subject to the provisions of subsection (2) and (3) of this section and of the preceding section on liquidation and limitation of damages,

(a) the agreement may provide for remedies in addition to or in substitution for those provided in this Article and may limit or alter the measure of damages recoverable under this Article, as by limiting the buyer's remedies to return of the goods and repayment of the price or to repair and replacement of non-conforming goods or parts; and

(b) resort to a remedy as provided is optional unless the remedy is expressly agreed to be exclusive, in which case it is the sole remedy.

(2) Where circumstances cause an exclusive or limited remedy to fail of its essential purpose, remedy may be had as provided in this Act.

(3) Consequential damages may be limited or excluded unless the limitation or exclusion is unconscionable. Limitation of consequential damages for injury to the person in the case of consumer goods is prima facie unconscionable but limitation of damages where the loss is commercial is not.

§ 2–720. Effect of "Cancellation" or "Rescission" on Claims for Antecedent Breach.

Unless the contrary intention clearly appears, expressions of "cancellation" or "rescission" of the contract or the like shall not be construed as a renunciation or discharge of any claim in damages for an antecedent breach.

§ 2–721. Remedies for Fraud.

Remedies for material misrepresentation or fraud include all remedies available under this Article for non-fraudulent breach. Neither rescission or a claim for rescission of the contract for sale nor rejection or return of the goods shall bar or be deemed inconsistent with a claim for damages or other remedy.

§ 2–722. Who Can Sue Third Parties for Injury to Goods.

Where a third party so deals with goods which have been identified to a contract for sale as to cause actionable injury to a party to that contract

(a) a right of action against the third party is in either party to the contract for sale who has title to or a security interest or a special property or an insurable interest in the goods; and if the goods have been destroyed or converted a right of action is also in the party who either bore the risk of loss under the contract for sale or has since the injury assumed that risk as against the other;

(b) if at the time of the injury the party plaintiff did not bear the risk of loss as against the other party to the contract for sale and there is no arrangement between them for disposition of the recovery, his suit or settlement is subject to his own interest, as a fiduciary for the other party to the contract;

(c) either party may with the consent of the other sue for the benefit of whom it may concern.

§ 2–723. Proof of Market Price: Time and Place.

(1) If an action based on anticipatory repudiation comes to trial before the time for performance with respect to some or all of the goods, any damages based on market price (Section 2–708 or Section 2–713) shall be determined according to the price of such goods prevailing at the time when the aggrieved party learned of the repudiation.

(2) If evidence of a price prevailing at the times or places described in this Article is not readily available the price prevailing within any reasonable time before or after the time described or at any other place which in commercial judgment or under usage of trade would serve as a reasonable substitute for the one described may be used, making any proper allowance for the cost of transporting the goods to or from such other place.

(3) Evidence of a relevant price prevailing at a time or place other than the one described in this Article offered by one party is not admissible unless and until he has given the other party such notice as the court finds sufficient to prevent unfair surprise.

§ 2–724. Admissibility of Market Quotations.

Whenever the prevailing price or value of any goods regularly bought and sold in any established commodity market is in issue, reports in official publications or trade journals or in newspapers or periodicals of general circulation published as the reports of such market shall be admissible in evidence. The circumstances of the preparation of such a report may be shown to affect its weight but not its admissibility.

§ 2–725. Statute of Limitations in Contracts for Sale.

(1) An action for breach of any contract for sale must be commenced within four years after the cause of action has accrued. By the original agreement the parties may reduce the period of limitation to not less than one year but may not extend it.

(2) A cause of action occurs when the breach occurs, regardless of the aggrieved party's lack of knowledge of the breach. A breach of warranty occurs when tender of delivery is made, except that where a warranty explicitly extends to future performance of the goods and discovery of the breach must await the time of such performance the cause of action accrues when the breach is or should have been discovered.

(3) Where an action commenced within the time limited by subsection (1) is so terminated as to leave available a remedy by another action for the same breach such other action may be commenced after the expiration of the time limited and within six months after the termination of the first action unless the termination resulted from voluntary discontinuance or from dismissal for failure or neglect to prosecute.

(4) This section does not alter the law on tolling of the statute of limitations nor does it apply to causes of action which have accrued before this Act becomes effective.

Article 2A: Leases

Part 1—General Provisions

§ 2A–101. Short Title.

This Article shall be known and may be cited as the Uniform Commercial Code—Leases.

§ 2A–102. Scope.

This Article applies to any transaction, regardless of form, that creates a lease.

§ 2A–103. Definitions and Index of Definitions.

(1) In this Article unless the context otherwise requires:

(a) "Buyer in ordinary course of business" means a person who in good faith and without knowledge that the sale to him [or her] is in violation of the ownership rights or security interest or leasehold interest of a third party in the goods buys in ordinary course from a person in the business of selling goods of that kind but does not include a pawnbroker. "Buying" may be for cash or by exchange of other property or on secured or unsecured credit and includes receiving goods or documents of title under a pre-existing contract for sale but does not include a transfer in bulk or as security for or in total or partial satisfaction of a money debt.

(b) "Cancellation" occurs when either party puts an end to the lease contract for default by the other party.

(c) "Commercial unit" means such a unit of goods as by commercial usage is a single whole for purposes of lease and division of which materially impairs its character or value on the market or in use. A commercial unit may be a single article, as a machine, or a set of articles, as a suite of furniture or a line of machinery, or a quantity, as a gross or carload, or any other unit treated in use or in the relevant market as a single whole.

(d) "Conforming" goods or performance under a lease contract means goods or performance that are in accordance with the obligations under the lease contract.

(e) "Consumer lease" means a lease that a lessor regularly engaged in the business of leasing or selling makes to a lessee who is an individual and who takes under the lease primarily for a personal, family, or household purpose [, if the total payments to be made under the lease contract, excluding payments for options to renew or buy, do not exceed $_____].

(f) "Fault" means wrongful act, omission, breach, or default.

(g) "Finance lease" means a lease with respect to which:

(i) the lessor does not select, manufacture, or supply the goods;

(ii) the lessor acquires the goods or the right to possession and use of the goods in connection with the lease; and

(iii) one of the following occurs:

(A) the lessee receives a copy of the contract by which the lessor acquired the goods or the right to possession and use of the goods before signing the lease contract;

(B) the lessee's approval of the contract by which the lessor acquired the goods or the right to possession and use of the goods is a condition to effectiveness of the lease contract;

(C) the lessee, before signing the lease contract, receives an accurate and complete statement designating the promises and warranties, and any disclaimers of warranties, limitations or modifications of remedies, or liquidated damages, including those of a third party, such as the manufacturer of the goods, provided to the lessor by the person supplying the goods in connection with or as part of the contract by which the lessor acquired the goods or the right to possession and use of the goods; or

(D) if the lease is not a consumer lease, the lessor, before the lessee signs the lease contract, informs the lessee in writing (a) of the identity of the person supplying the goods to the lessor, unless the lessee has selected that person and directed the lessor to acquire the goods or the right to possession and use of the goods from that person, (b) that the lessee is entitled under this Article to the promises and warranties, including those of any third party, provided to the lessor by the person supplying the goods in connection with or as part of the contract by which the lessor acquired the goods or the right to possession and use of the goods, and (c) that the lessee may communicate with the person supplying the goods to the lessor and receive an accurate and complete statement of those promises and warranties, including any disclaimers and limitations of them or of remedies.

(h) "Goods" means all things that are movable at the time of identification to the lease contract, or are fixtures (Section 2A–309), but the term does not include money, documents, instruments, accounts, chattel paper, general intangibles, or minerals or the like, including oil and gas, before extraction. The term also includes the unborn young of animals.

(i) "Installment lease contract" means a lease contract that authorizes or requires the delivery of goods in separate lots to be separately accepted, even though the lease contract contains a clause "each delivery is a separate lease" or its equivalent.

(j) "Lease" means a transfer of the right to possession and use of goods for a term in return for consideration, but a sale, including a sale on approval or a sale or return, or retention or creation of a security interest is not a lease. Unless the context clearly indicates otherwise, the term includes a sublease.

(k) "Lease agreement" means the bargain, with respect to the lease, of the lessor and the lessee in fact as found in their language or by implication from other circumstances including course of dealing or usage of trade or course of performance as provided in this Article. Unless the context clearly indicates otherwise, the term includes a sublease agreement.

(l) "Lease contract" means the total legal obligation that results from the lease agreement as affected by this Article and any other applicable rules of law. Unless the context clearly indicates otherwise, the term includes a sublease contract.

(m) "Leasehold interest" means the interest of the lessor or the lessee under a lease contract.

(n) "Lessee" means a person who acquires the right to possession and use of goods under a lease. Unless the context clearly indicates otherwise, the term includes a sublessee.

(o) "Lessee in ordinary course of business" means a person who in good faith and without knowledge that the lease to him [or her] is in violation of the ownership rights or security interest or leasehold interest of a third party in the goods, leases in ordinary course from a person in the business of selling or leasing goods of that kind but does not include a pawnbroker. "Leasing" may be for cash or by exchange of other property or on secured or unsecured credit and includes receiving goods or documents of title under a pre-existing lease contract but does not include a transfer in bulk or as security for or in total or partial satisfaction of a money debt.

(p) "Lessor" means a person who transfers the right to possession and use of goods under a lease. Unless the context clearly indicates otherwise, the term includes a sublessor.

(q) "Lessor's residual interest" means the lessor's interest in the goods after expiration, termination, or cancellation of the lease contract.

(r) "Lien" means a charge against or interest in goods to secure payment of a debt or performance of an obligation, but the term does not include a security interest.

(s) "Lot" means a parcel or a single article that is the subject matter of a separate lease or delivery, whether or not it is sufficient to perform the lease contract.

(t) "Merchant lessee" means a lessee that is a merchant with respect to goods of the kind subject to the lease.

(u) "Present value" means the amount as of a date certain of one or more sums payable in the future, discounted to the date certain. The discount is determined by the interest rate specified by the parties if the rate was not manifestly unreasonable at the time the transaction was entered into; otherwise, the discount is determined by a commercially reasonable rate that takes into account the facts and circumstances of each case at the time the transaction was entered into.

(v) "Purchase" includes taking by sale, lease, mortgage, security interest, pledge, gift, or any other voluntary transaction creating an interest in goods.

(w) "Sublease" means a lease of goods the right to possession and use of which was acquired by the lessor as a lessee under an existing lease.

(x) "Supplier" means a person from whom a lessor buys or leases goods to be leased under a finance lease.

(y) "Supply contract" means a contract under which a lessor buys or leases goods to be leased.

(z) "Termination" occurs when either party pursuant to a power created by agreement or law puts an end to the lease contract otherwise than for default.

(2) Other definitions applying to this Article and the sections in which they appear are:
"Accessions". Section 2A–310(1).
"Construction mortgage". Section 2A–309(1)(d).
"Encumbrance". Section 2A–309(1)(e).
"Fixtures". Section 2A–309(1)(a).
"Fixture filing". Section 2A–309(1)(b).
"Purchase money lease". Section 2A–309(1)(c).

(3) The following definitions in other Articles apply to this Article:
"Account". Section 9–106.
"Between merchants". Section 2–104(3).
"Buyer". Section 2–103(1)(a).
"Chattel paper". Section 9–105(1)(b).
"Consumer goods". Section 9–109(1).
"Document". Section 9–105(1)(f).
"Entrusting". Section 2–403(3).
"General intangibles". Section 9–106.
"Good faith". Section 2–103(1)(b).
"Instrument". Section 9–105(1)(i).
"Merchant". Section 2–104(1).
"Mortgage". Sect 9–105(1)(j).
"Pursuant to commitment". Section 9–105(1)(k).
"Receipt". Section 2–103(1)(c).
"Sale". Section 2–106(1).
"Sale on approval". Section 2–326.
"Sale or return". Section 2–326.
"Seller". Section 2–103(1)(d).

(4) In addition Article 1 contains general definitions and principles of construction and interpretation applicable throughout this Article.
As amended in 1990.

§ 2A–104. Leases Subject to Other Law.

(1) A lease, although subject to this Article, is also subject to any applicable:
(a) certificate of title statute of this State: (list any certificate of title statutes covering automobiles, trailers, mobile homes, boats, farm tractors, and the like);
(b) certificate of title statute of another jurisdiction (Section 2A–105); or
(c) consumer protection statute of this State, or final consumer protection decision of a court of this State existing on the effective date of this Article.

(2) In case of conflict between this Article, other than Sections 2A–105, 2A–304(3), and 2A–305(3), and a statute or decision referred to in subsection (1), the statute or decision controls.

(3) Failure to comply with an applicable law has only the effect specified therein.
As amended in 1990.

§ 2A–108. Unconscionability.

(1) If the court as a matter of law finds a lease contract or any clause of a lease contract to have been unconscionable at the time it was made the court may refuse to enforce the lease contract, or it may enforce the remainder of the lease contract

without the unconscionable clause, or it may so limit the application of any unconscionable clause as to avoid any unconscionable result.

(2) With respect to a consumer lease, if the court as a matter of law finds that a lease contract or any clause of a lease contract has been induced by unconscionable conduct or that unconscionable conduct has occurred in the collection of a claim arising from a lease contract, the court may grant appropriate relief.

(3) Before making a finding of unconscionability under subsection (1) or (2), the court, on its own motion or that of a party, shall afford the parties a reasonable opportunity to present evidence as to the setting, purpose, and effect of the lease contract or clause thereof, or of the conduct.

(4) In an action in which the lessee claims unconscionability with respect to a consumer lease:

(a) If the court finds unconscionability under subsection (1) or (2), the court shall award reasonable attorney's fees to the lessee.

(b) If the court does not find unconscionability and the lessee claiming unconscionability has brought or maintained an action he [or she] knew to be groundless, the court shall award reasonable attorney's fees to the party against whom the claim is made.

(c) In determining attorney's fees, the amount of the recovery on behalf of the claimant under subsections (1) and (2) is not controlling.

PART 2—FORMATION AND CONSTRUCTION OF LEASE CONTRACT

§ 2A–201. STATUTE OF FRAUDS.

(1) A lease contract is not enforceable by way of action or defense unless:

(a) the total payments to be made under the lease contract, excluding payments for options to renew or buy, are less than $1,000; or

(b) there is a writing, signed by the party against whom enforcement is sought or by that party's authorized agent, sufficient to indicate that a lease contract has been made between the parties and to describe the goods leased and the lease term.

(2) Any description of leased goods or of the lease term is sufficient and satisfies subsection (1)(b), whether or not it is specific, if it reasonably identifies what is described.

(3) A writing is not insufficient because it omits or incorrectly states a term agreed upon, but the lease contract is not enforceable under subsection (1)(b) beyond the lease term and the quantity of goods shown in the writing.

(4) A lease contract that does not satisfy the requirements of subsection (1), but which is valid in other respects, is enforceable:

(a) if the goods are to be specially manufactured or obtained for the lessee and are not suitable for lease or sale to others in the ordinary course of the lessor's business, and the lessor, before notice of repudiation is received and under circumstances that reasonably indicate that the goods are for the lessee, has made either a substantial beginning of their manufacture or commitments for their procurement;

(b) if the party against whom enforcement is sought admits in that party's pleading, testimony or otherwise in court that a lease contract was made, but the lease contract is not enforceable under this provision beyond the quantity of goods admitted; or

(c) with respect to goods that have been received and accepted by the lessee.

(5) The lease term under a lease contract referred to in subsection (4) is:

(a) if there is a writing signed by the party against whom enforcement is sought or by that party's authorized agent specifying the lease term, the term so specified;

(b) if the party against whom enforcement is sought admits in that party's pleading, testimony, or otherwise in court a lease term, the term so admitted; or

(c) a reasonable lease term.

§ 2A–202. FINAL WRITTEN EXPRESSION: PAROL OR EXTRINSIC EVIDENCE.

Terms with respect to which the confirmatory memoranda of the parties agree or which are otherwise set forth in a writing intended by the parties as a final expression of their agreement with respect to such terms as are included therein may not be contradicted by evidence of any prior agreement or of a contemporaneous oral agreement but may be explained or supplemented:

(a) by course of dealing or usage of trade or by course of performance; and

(b) by evidence of consistent additional terms unless the court finds the writing to have been intended also as a complete and exclusive statement of the terms of the agreement.

§ 2A–204. FORMATION IN GENERAL.

(1) A lease contract may be made in any manner sufficient to show agreement, including conduct by both parties which recognizes the existence of a lease contract.

(2) An agreement sufficient to constitute a lease contract may be found although the moment of its making is undetermined.

(3) Although one or more terms are left open, a lease contract does not fail for indefiniteness if the parties have intended to make a lease contract and there is a reasonably certain basis for giving an appropriate remedy.

§ 2A–205. FIRM OFFERS.

An offer by a merchant to lease goods to or from another person in a signed writing that by its terms gives assurance it will be held open is not revocable, for lack of consideration, during the time stated or, if no time is stated, for a reasonable time, but in no event may the period of irrevocability exceed 3 months. Any such term of assurance on a form supplied by the offeree must be separately signed by the offeror.

§ 2A–206. OFFER AND ACCEPTANCE IN FORMATION OF LEASE CONTRACT.

(1) Unless otherwise unambiguously indicated by the language or circumstances, an offer to make a lease contract must be construed as inviting acceptance in any manner and by any medium reasonable in the circumstances.

(2) If the beginning of a requested performance is a reasonable mode of acceptance, an offeror who is not notified of acceptance within a reasonable time may treat the offer as having lapsed before acceptance.

§ 2A–207. COURSE OF PERFORMANCE OR PRACTICAL CONSTRUCTION.

(1) If a lease contract involves repeated occasions for performance by either party with knowledge of the nature of the performance and opportunity for objection to it by the other, any course of performance accepted or acquiesced in without objection is relevant to determine the meaning of the lease agreement.

(2) The express terms of a lease agreement and any course of performance, as well as any course of dealing and usage of trade, must be construed whenever reasonable as consistent with each other; but if that construction is unreasonable, express terms control course of performance, course of performance controls both course of dealing and usage of trade, and course of dealing controls usage of trade.

(3) Subject to the provisions of Section 2A–208 on modification and waiver, course of performance is relevant to show a waiver or modification of any term inconsistent with the course of performance.

§ 2A–208. Modification, Rescission and Waiver.

(1) An agreement modifying a lease contract needs no consideration to be binding.

(2) A signed lease agreement that excludes modification or rescission except by a signed writing may not be otherwise modified or rescinded, but, except as between merchants, such a requirement on a form supplied by a merchant must be separately signed by the other party.

(3) Although an attempt at modification or rescission does not satisfy the requirements of subsection (2), it may operate as a waiver.

(4) A party who has made a waiver affecting an executory portion of a lease contract may retract the waiver by reasonable notification received by the other party that strict performance will be required of any term waived, unless the retraction would be unjust in view of a material change of position in reliance on the waiver.

§ 2A–209. Lessee Under Finance Lease as Beneficiary of Supply Contract.

(1) The benefit of a supplier's promises to the lessor under the supply contract and of all warranties, whether express or implied, including those of any third party provided in connection with or as part of the supply contract, extends to the lessee to the extent of the lessee's leasehold interest under a finance lease related to the supply contract, but is subject to the terms of the warranty and of the supply contract and all defenses or claims arising therefrom.

(2) The extension of the benefit of a supplier's promises and of warranties to the lessee (Section 2A–209(1)) does not: (i) modify the rights and obligations of the parties to the supply contract, whether arising therefrom or otherwise, or (ii) impose any duty or liability under the supply contract on the lessee.

(3) Any modification or rescission of the supply contract by the supplier and the lessor is effective between the supplier and the lessee unless, before the modification or rescission, the supplier has received notice that the lessee has entered into a finance lease related to the supply contract. If the modification or rescission is effective between the supplier and the lessee, the lessor is deemed to have assumed, in addition to the obligations of the lessor to the lessee under the lease contract, promises of the supplier to the lessor and warranties that were so modified or rescinded as they existed and were available to the lessee before modification or rescission.

(4) In addition to the extension of the benefit of the supplier's promises and of warranties to the lessee under subsection (1), the lessee retains all rights that the lessee may have against the supplier which arise from an agreement between the lessee and the supplier or under other law.
As amended in 1990.

§ 2A–210. Express Warranties.

(1) Express warranties by the lessor are created as follows:
(a) Any affirmation of fact or promise made by the lessor to the lessee which relates to the goods and becomes part of the basis of the bargain creates an express warranty that the goods will conform to the affirmation or promise.
(b) Any description of the goods which is made part of the basis of the bargain creates an express warranty that the goods will conform to the description.
(c) Any sample or model that is made part of the basis of the bargain creates an express warranty that the whole of the goods will conform to the sample or model.

(2) It is not necessary to the creation of an express warranty that the lessor use formal words, such as "warrant" or "guarantee," or that the lessor have a specific intention to make a warranty, but an affirmation merely of the value of the goods or a statement purporting to be merely the lessor's opinion or commendation of the goods does not create a warranty.

§ 2A–211. Warranties Against Interference and Against Infringement; Lessee's Obligation Against Infringement.

(1) There is in a lease contract a warranty that for the lease term no person holds a claim to or interest in the goods that arose from an act or omission of the lessor, other than a claim by way of infringement or the like, which will interfere with the lessee's enjoyment of its leasehold interest.

(2) Except in a finance lease there is in a lease contract by a lessor who is a merchant regularly dealing in goods of the kind a warranty that the goods are delivered free of the rightful claim of any person by way of infringement or the like.

(3) A lessee who furnishes specifications to a lessor or a supplier shall hold the lessor and the supplier harmless against any claim by way of infringement or the like that arises out of compliance with the specifications.

§ 2A–212. Implied Warranty of Merchantability.

(1) Except in a finance lease, a warranty that the goods will be merchantable is implied in a lease contract if the lessor is a merchant with respect to goods of that kind.

(2) Goods to be merchantable must be at least such as
(a) pass without objection in the trade under the description in the lease agreement;
(b) in the case of fungible goods, are of fair average quality within the description;
(c) are fit for the ordinary purposes for which goods of that type are used;
(d) run, within the variation permitted by the lease agreement, of even kind, quality, and quantity within each unit and among all units involved;
(e) are adequately contained, packaged, and labeled as the lease agreement may require; and
(f) conform to any promises or affirmations of fact made on the container or label.

(3) Other implied warranties may arise from course of dealing or usage of trade.

§ 2A–213. Implied Warranty of Fitness for Particular Purpose.

Except in a finance lease, if the lessor at the time the lease contract is made has reason to know of any particular purpose for which the goods are required and that the lessee is relying on the lessor's skill or judgment to select or furnish suitable goods, there is in the lease contract an implied warranty that the goods will be fit for that purpose.

§ 2A–214. Exclusion or Modification of Warranties.

(1) Words or conduct relevant to the creation of an express warranty and words or conduct tending to negate or limit a warranty must be construed wherever reasonable as consistent with each other; but, subject to the provisions of Section 2A–202 on parol or extrinsic evidence, negation or limitation is inoperative to the extent that the construction is unreasonable.

(2) Subject to subsection (3), to exclude or modify the implied warranty of merchantability or any part of it the language must mention "merchantability", be by a writing, and be conspicuous. Subject to subsection (3), to exclude or modify any implied warranty of fitness the exclusion must be by a writing and be conspicuous. Language to exclude all implied warranties of fitness is sufficient if it is in writing, is conspicuous and states, for example, "There is no warranty that the goods will be fit for a particular purpose".

(3) Notwithstanding subsection (2), but subject to subsection (4),

(a) unless the circumstances indicate otherwise, all implied warranties are excluded by expressions like "as is," or "with all faults," or by other language that in common understanding calls the lessee's attention to the exclusion of warranties and makes plain that there is no implied warranty, if in writing and conspicuous;

(b) if the lessee before entering into the lease contract has examined the goods or the sample or model as fully as desired or has refused to examine the goods, there is no implied warranty with regard to defects that an examination ought in the circumstances to have revealed; and

(c) an implied warranty may also be excluded or modified by course of dealing, course of performance, or usage of trade.

(4) To exclude or modify a warranty against interference or against infringement (Section 2A–211) or any part of it, the language must be specific, be by a writing, and be conspicuous, unless the circumstances, including course of performance, course of dealing, or usage of trade, give the lessee reason to know that the goods are being leased subject to a claim or interest of any person.

§ 2A–215. Cumulation and Conflict of Warranties Express or Implied.

Warranties, whether express or implied, must be construed as consistent with each other and as cumulative, but if that construction is unreasonable, the intention of the parties determines which warranty is dominant. In ascertaining that intention the following rules apply:

(a) Exact or technical specifications displace an inconsistent sample or model or general language of description.

(b) A sample from an existing bulk displaces inconsistent general language of description.

(c) Express warranties displace inconsistent implied warranties other than an implied warranty of fitness for a particular purpose.

§ 2A–216. Third-Party Beneficiaries of Express and Implied Warranties.

Alternative A A warranty to or for the benefit of a lessee under this Article, whether express or implied, extends to any natural person who is in the family or household of the lessee or who is a guest in the lessee's home if it is reasonable to expect that such person may use, consume, or be affected by the goods and who is injured in person by breach of the warranty. This section does not displace principles of law and equity that extend a warranty to or for the benefit of a lessee to other persons. The operation of this section may not be excluded, modified, or limited, but an exclusion, modification, or limitation of the warranty, including any with respect to rights and remedies, effective against the lessee is also effective against any beneficiary designated under this section.

Alternative B A warranty to or for the benefit of a lessee under this Article, whether express or implied, extends to any natural person who may reasonably be expected to use, consume, or be affected by the goods and who is injured in person by breach of the warranty. This section does not displace principles of law and equity that extend a warranty to or for the benefit of a lessee to other persons. The operation of this section may not be excluded, modified, or limited, but an exclusion, modification, or limitation of the warranty, including any with respect to rights and remedies, effective against the lessee is also effective against the beneficiary designated under this section.

Alternative C A warranty to or for the benefit of a lessee under this Article, whether express or implied, extends to any person who may reasonably be expected to use, consume, or be affected by the goods and who is injured by breach of the warranty. The operation of this section may not be excluded, modified, or limited with respect to injury to the person of an individual to whom the warranty extends, but an exclusion, modification, or limitation of the warranty, including any with respect to rights and remedies, effective against the lessee is also effective against the beneficiary designated under this section.

§ 2A–219. Risk of Loss.

(1) Except in the case of a finance lease, risk of loss is retained by the lessor and does not pass to the lessee. In the case of a finance lease, risk of loss passes to the lessee.

(2) Subject to the provisions of this Article on the effect of default on risk of loss (Section 2A–220), if risk of loss is to pass to the lessee and the time of passage is not stated, the following rules apply:

(a) If the lease contract requires or authorizes the goods to be shipped by carrier

(i) and it does not require delivery at a particular destination, the risk of loss passes to the lessee when the goods are duly delivered to the carrier; but

(ii) if it does require delivery at a particular destination and the goods are there duly tendered while in the possession of the carrier, the risk of loss passes to the lessee when the goods are there duly so tendered as to enable the lessee to take delivery.

(b) If the goods are held by a bailee to be delivered without being moved, the risk of loss passes to the lessee on acknowledgment by the bailee of the lessee's right to possession of the goods.

(c) In any case not within subsection (a) or (b), the risk of loss passes to the lessee on the lessee's receipt of the goods if the lessor, or, in the case of a finance lease, the supplier, is a merchant; otherwise the risk passes to the lessee on tender of delivery.

Part 3—Effect of Lease Contract

§ 2A–302. Title to and Possession of Goods.

Except as otherwise provided in this Article, each provision of this Article applies whether the lessor or a third party has title to the goods, and whether the lessor, the lessee, or a third party has possession of the goods, notwithstanding any statute or rule of law that possession or the absence of possession is fraudulent.

§ 2A–303. ALIENABILITY OF PARTY'S INTEREST UNDER LEASE CONTRACT OR OF LESSOR'S RESIDUAL INTEREST IN GOODS; DELEGATION OF PERFORMANCE; TRANSFER OF RIGHTS.

(1) As used in this section, "creation of a security interest" includes the sale of a lease contract that is subject to Article 9, Secured Transactions, by reason of Section 9–102(1)(b).

(2) Except as provided in subsections (3) and (4), a provision in a lease agreement which (i) prohibits the voluntary or involuntary transfer, including a transfer by sale, sublease, creation or enforcement of a security interest, or attachment, levy, or other judicial process, of an interest of a party under the lease contract or of the lessor's residual interest in the goods, or (ii) makes such a transfer an event of default, gives rise to the rights and remedies provided in subsection (5), but a transfer that is prohibited or is an event of default under the lease agreement is otherwise effective.

(3) A provision in a lease agreement which (i) prohibits the creation or enforcement of a security interest in an interest of a party under the lease contract or in the lessor's residual interest in the goods, or (ii) makes such a transfer an event of default, is not enforceable unless, and then only to the extent that, there is an actual transfer by the lessee of the lessee's right of possession or use of the goods in violation of the provision or an actual delegation of a material performance of either party to the lease contract in violation of the provision. Neither the granting nor the enforcement of a security interest in (i) the lessor's interest under the lease contract or (ii) the lessor's residual interest in the goods is a transfer that materially impairs the prospect of obtaining return performance by, materially changes the duty of, or materially increases the burden or risk imposed on, the lessee within the purview of subsection (5) unless, and then only to the extent that, there is an actual delegation of a material performance of the lessor.

(4) A provision in a lease agreement which (i) prohibits a transfer of a right to damages for default with respect to the whole lease contract or of a right to payment arising out of the transferor's due performance of the transferor's entire obligation, or (ii) makes such a transfer an event of default, is not enforceable, and such a transfer is not a transfer that materially impairs the prospect of obtaining return performance by, materially changes the duty of, or materially increases the burden or risk imposed on, the other party to the lease contract within the purview of subsection.

(5) Subject to subsections (3) and (4):

(a) if a transfer is made which is made an event of default under a lease agreement, the party to the lease contract not making the transfer, unless that party waives the default or otherwise agrees, has the rights and remedies described in Section 2A–501(2);

(b) if paragraph (a) is not applicable and if a transfer is made that (i) is prohibited under a lease agreement or (ii) materially impairs the prospect of obtaining return performance by, materially changes the duty of, or materially increases the burden or risk imposed on, the other party to the lease contract, unless the party not making the transfer agrees at any time to the transfer in the lease contract or otherwise, then, except as limited by contract, (i) the transferor is liable to the party not

making the transfer for damages caused by the transfer to the extent that the damages could not reasonably be prevented by the party not making the transfer and (ii) a court having jurisdiction may grant other appropriate relief, including cancellation of the lease contract or an injunction against the transfer.

(6) A transfer of "the lease" or of "all my rights under the lease", or a transfer in similar general terms, is a transfer of rights and, unless the language or the circumstances, as in a transfer for security, indicate the contrary, the transfer is a delegation of duties by the transferor to the transferee. Acceptance by the transferee constitutes a promise by the transferee to perform those duties. The promise is enforceable by either the transferor or the other party to the lease contract.

(7) Unless otherwise agreed by the lessor and the lessee, a delegation of performance does not relieve the transferor as against the other party of any duty to perform or of any liability for default.

(8) In a consumer lease, to prohibit the transfer of an interest of a party under the lease contract or to make a transfer an event of default, the language must be specific, by a writing, and conspicuous.
As amended in 1990.

§ 2A–304. SUBSEQUENT LEASE OF GOODS BY LESSOR.

(1) Subject to Section 2A–303, a subsequent lessee from a lessor of goods under an existing lease contract obtains, to the extent of the leasehold interest transferred, the leasehold interest in the goods that the lessor had or had power to transfer, and except as provided in subsection (2) and Section 2A–527(4), takes subject to the existing lease contract. A lessor with voidable title has power to transfer a good leasehold interest to a good faith subsequent lessee for value, but only to the extent set forth in the preceding sentence. If goods have been delivered under a transaction of purchase, the lessor has that power even though:

(a) the lessor's transferor was deceived as to the identity of the lessor;

(b) the delivery was in exchange for a check which is later dishonored;

(c) it was agreed that the transaction was to be a "cash sale"; or

(d) the delivery was procured through fraud punishable as larcenous under the criminal law.

(2) A subsequent lessee in the ordinary course of business from a lessor who is a merchant dealing in goods of that kind to whom the goods were entrusted by the existing lessee of that lessor before the interest of the subsequent lessee became enforceable against that lessor obtains, to the extent of the leasehold interest transferred, all of that lessor's and the existing lessee's rights to the goods, and takes free of the existing lease contract.

(3) A subsequent lessee from the lessor of goods that are subject to an existing lease contract and are covered by a certificate of title issued under a statute of this State or of another jurisdiction takes no greater rights than those provided both by this section and by the certificate of title statute.
As amended in 1990.

§ 2A–307. PRIORITY OF LIENS ARISING BY ATTACHMENT OR LEVY ON, SECURITY INTERESTS IN, AND OTHER CLAIMS TO GOODS.

(1) Except as otherwise provided in Section 2A–306, a creditor of a lessee takes subject to the lease contract.

(2) Except as otherwise provided in subsections (3) and (4) and in Sections 2A–306 and 2A–308, a creditor of a lessor takes subject to the lease contract unless:

(a) the creditor holds a lien that attached to the goods before the lease contract became enforceable;

(b) the creditor holds a security interest in the goods and the lessee did not give value and receive delivery of the goods without knowledge of the security interest; or

(c) the creditor holds a security interest in the goods which was perfected (Section 9–303) before the lease contract became enforceable.

(3) A lessee in the ordinary course of business takes the leasehold interest free of a security interest in the goods created by the lessor even though the security interest is perfected (Section 9–303) and the lessee knows of its existence.

(4) A lessee other than a lessee in the ordinary course of business takes the leasehold interest free of a security interest to the extent that it secures future advances made after the secured party acquires knowledge of the lease or more than 45 days after the lease contract becomes enforceable, whichever first occurs, unless the future advances are made pursuant to a commitment entered into without knowledge of the lease and before the expiration of the 45-day period.

As amended in 1990.

§ 2A–308. Special Rights of Creditors.

(1) A creditor of a lessor in possession of goods subject to a lease contract may treat the lease contract as void if as against the creditor retention of possession by the lessor is fraudulent under any statute or rule of law, but retention of possession in good faith and current course of trade by the lessor for a commercially reasonable time after the lease contract becomes enforceable is not fraudulent.

(2) Nothing in this Article impairs the rights of creditors of a lessor if the lease contract (a) becomes enforceable, not in current course of trade but in satisfaction of or as security for a pre-existing claim for money, security, or the like, and (b) is made under circumstances which under any statute or rule of law apart from this Article would constitute the transaction a fraudulent transfer or voidable preference.

(3) A creditor of a seller may treat a sale or an identification of goods to a contract for sale as void if as against the creditor retention of possession by the seller is fraudulent under any statute or rule of law, but retention of possession of the goods pursuant to a lease contract entered into by the seller as lessee and the buyer as lessor in connection with the sale or identification of the goods is not fraudulent if the buyer bought for value and in good faith.

Part 4—Performance of Lease Contract: Repudiated, Substituted and Excused

§ 2A–407. Irrevocable Promises: Finance Leases.

(1) In the case of a finance lease that is not a consumer lease the lessee's promises under the lease contract become irrevocable and independent upon the lessee's acceptance of the goods.

(2) A promise that has become irrevocable and independent under subsection (1):

(a) is effective and enforceable between the parties, and by or against third parties including assignees of the parties; and

(b) is not subject to cancellation, termination, modification, repudiation, excuse, or substitution without the consent of the party to whom the promise runs.

(3) This section does not affect the validity under any other law of a covenant in any lease contract making the lessee's promises irrevocable and independent upon the lessee's acceptance of the goods.

As amended in 1990.

Part 5—Default
A. In General

§ 2A–503. Modification or Impairment of Rights and Remedies.

(1) Except as otherwise provided in this Article, the lease agreement may include rights and remedies for default in addition to or in substitution for those provided in this Article and may limit or alter the measure of damages recoverable under this Article.

(2) Resort to a remedy provided under this Article or in the lease agreement is optional unless the remedy is expressly agreed to be exclusive. If circumstances cause an exclusive or limited remedy to fail of its essential purpose, or provision for an exclusive remedy is unconscionable, remedy may be had as provided in this Article.

(3) Consequential damages may be liquidated under Section 2A–504, or may otherwise be limited, altered, or excluded unless the limitation, alteration, or exclusion is unconscionable. Limitation, alteration, or exclusion of consequential damages for injury to the person in the case of consumer goods is prima facie unconscionable but limitation, alteration, or exclusion of damages where the loss is commercial is not prima facie unconscionable.

(4) Rights and remedies on default by the lessor or the lessee with respect to any obligation or promise collateral or ancillary to the lease contract are not impaired by this Article.

As amended in 1990.

§ 2A–504. Liquidation of Damages.

(1) Damages payable by either party for default, or any other act or omission, including indemnity for loss or diminution of anticipated tax benefits or loss or damage to lessor's residual interest, may be liquidated in the lease agreement but only at an amount or by a formula that is reasonable in light of the then anticipated harm caused by the default or other act or omission.

(2) If the lease agreement provides for liquidation of damages, and such provision does not comply with subsection (1), or such provision is an exclusive or limited remedy that circumstances cause to fail of its essential purpose, remedy may be had as provided in this Article.

(3) If the lessor justifiably withholds or stops delivery of goods because of the lessee's default or insolvency (Section 2A–525 or 2A–526), the lessee is entitled to restitution of any amount by which the sum of his [or her] payments exceeds:

(a) the amount to which the lessor is entitled by virtue of terms liquidating the lessor's damages in accordance with subsection (1); or

(b) in the absence of those terms, 20 percent of the then present value of the total rent the lessee was obligated to pay for the balance of the lease term, or, in the case of a consumer lease, the lesser of such amount or $500.

(4) A lessee's right to restitution under subsection (3) is subject to offset to the extent the lessor establishes:

(a) a right to recover damages under the provisions of this Article other than subsection (1); and

(b) the amount or value of any benefits received by the lessee directly or indirectly by reason of the lease contract.

§ 2A–507. PROOF OF MARKET RENT: TIME AND PLACE.

(1) Damages based on market rent (Section 2A–519 or 2A–528) are determined according to the rent for the use of the goods concerned for a lease term identical to the remaining lease term of the original lease agreement and prevailing at the times specified in Sections 2A–519 and 2A–528.

(2) If evidence of rent for the use of the goods concerned for a lease term identical to the remaining lease term of the original lease agreement and prevailing at the times or places described in this Article is not readily available, the rent prevailing within any reasonable time before or after the time described or at any other place or for a different lease term which in commercial judgment or under usage of trade would serve as a reasonable substitute for the one described may be used, making any proper allowance for the difference, including the cost of transporting the goods to or from the other place.

(3) Evidence of a relevant rent prevailing at a time or place or for a lease term other than the one described in this Article offered by one party is not admissible unless and until he [or she] has given the other party notice the court finds sufficient to prevent unfair surprise.

(4) If the prevailing rent or value of any goods regularly leased in any established market is in issue, reports in official publications or trade journals or in newspapers or periodicals of general circulation published as the reports of that market are admissible in evidence. The circumstances of the preparation of the report may be shown to affect its weight but not its admissibility.

As amended in 1990.

B. DEFAULT BY LESSOR

§ 2A–508. LESSEE'S REMEDIES.

(1) If a lessor fails to deliver the goods in conformity to the lease contract (Section 2A–509) or repudiates the lease contract (Section 2A–402), or a lessee rightfully rejects the goods (Section 2A–509) or justifiably revokes acceptance of the goods (Section 2A–517), then with respect to any goods involved, and with respect to all of the goods if under an installment lease contract the value of the whole lease contract is substantially impaired (Section 2A–510), the lessor is in default under the lease contract and the lessee may:

(a) cancel the lease contract (Section 2A–505(1));

(b) recover so much of the rent and security as has been paid and is just under the circumstances;

(c) cover and recover damages as to all goods affected whether or not they have been identified to the lease contract (Sections 2A–518 and 2A–520), or recover damages for nondelivery (Sections 2A–519 and 2A–520);

(d) exercise any other rights or pursue any other remedies provided in the lease contract.

(2) If a lessor fails to deliver the goods in conformity to the lease contract or repudiates the lease contract, the lessee may also:

(a) if the goods have been identified, recover them (Section 2A–522); or

(b) in a proper case, obtain specific performance or replevy the goods (Section 2A–521).

(3) If a lessor is otherwise in default under a lease contract, the lessee may exercise the rights and pursue the remedies provided in the lease contract, which may include a right to cancel the lease, and in Section 2A–519(3).

(4) If a lessor has breached a warranty, whether express or implied, the lessee may recover damages (Section 2A–519(4)).

(5) On rightful rejection or justifiable revocation of acceptance, a lessee has a security interest in goods in the lessee's possession or control for any rent and security that has been paid and any expenses reasonably incurred in their inspection, receipt, transportation, and care and custody and may hold those goods and dispose of them in good faith and in a commercially reasonable manner, subject to Section 2A–527(5).

(6) Subject to the provisions of Section 2A–407, a lessee, on notifying the lessor of the lessee's intention to do so, may deduct all or any part of the damages resulting from any default under the lease contract from any part of the rent still due under the same lease contract.

As amended in 1990.

§ 2A–509. LESSEE'S RIGHTS ON IMPROPER DELIVERY; RIGHTFUL REJECTION.

(1) Subject to the provisions of Section 2A–510 on default in installment lease contracts, if the goods or the tender or delivery fail in any respect to conform to the lease contract, the lessee may reject or accept the goods or accept any commercial unit or units and reject the rest of the goods.

(2) Rejection of goods is ineffective unless it is within a reasonable time after tender or delivery of the goods and the lessee seasonably notifies the lessor.

§ 2A–510. INSTALLMENT LEASE CONTRACTS: REJECTION AND DEFAULT.

(1) Under an installment lease contract a lessee may reject any delivery that is nonconforming if the nonconformity substantially impairs the value of that delivery and cannot be cured or the nonconformity is a defect in the required documents; but if the nonconformity does not fall within subsection (2) and the lessor or the supplier gives adequate assurance of its cure, the lessee must accept that delivery.

(2) Whenever nonconformity or default with respect to one or more deliveries substantially impairs the value of the installment lease contract as a whole there is a default with respect to the whole. But, the aggrieved party reinstates the installment lease contract as a whole if the aggrieved party accepts a nonconforming delivery without seasonably notifying of cancellation or brings an action with respect only to past deliveries or demands performance as to future deliveries.

§ 2A–511. MERCHANT LESSEE'S DUTIES AS TO RIGHTFULLY REJECTED GOODS.

(1) Subject to any security interest of a lessee (Section 2A–508(5)), if a lessor or a supplier has no agent or place of business at the market of rejection, a merchant lessee, after rejection of goods in his [or her] possession or control, shall follow any reasonable instructions received from the lessor or the supplier with respect to the goods. In the absence of those instructions, a merchant lessee shall make reasonable efforts to sell, lease, or otherwise dispose of the goods for the lessor's account if they threaten to decline in value speedily. Instructions are not reasonable if on demand indemnity for expenses is not forthcoming.

(2) If a merchant lessee (subsection (1)) or any other lessee (Section 2A–512) disposes of goods, he [or she] is entitled to reimbursement either from the lessor or the supplier or out of the proceeds for reasonable expenses of caring for and disposing of the goods and, if the expenses include no disposition commission, to such commission as is usual in the trade, or if there is none, to a reasonable sum not exceeding 10 percent of the gross proceeds.

(3) In complying with this section or Section 2A–512, the lessee is held only to good faith. Good faith conduct hereunder is neither acceptance or conversion nor the basis of an action for damages.

(4) A purchaser who purchases in good faith from a lessee pursuant to this section or Section 2A–512 takes the goods free of any rights of the lessor and the supplier even though the lessee fails to comply with one or more of the requirements of this Article.

§ 2A–512. Lessee's Duties as to Rightfully Rejected Goods.

(1) Except as otherwise provided with respect to goods that threaten to decline in value speedily (Section 2A–511) and subject to any security interest of a lessee (Section 2A–508(5)):

(a) the lessee, after rejection of goods in the lessee's possession, shall hold them with reasonable care at the lessor's or the supplier's disposition for a reasonable time after the lessee's seasonable notification of rejection;

(b) if the lessor or the supplier gives no instructions within a reasonable time after notification of rejection, the lessee may store the rejected goods for the lessor's or the supplier's account or ship them to the lessor or the supplier or dispose of them for the lessor's or the supplier's account with reimbursement in the manner provided in Section 2A–511; but

(c) the lessee has no further obligations with regard to goods rightfully rejected.

(2) Action by the lessee pursuant to subsection (1) is not acceptance or conversion.

§ 2A–513. Cure by Lessor of Improper Tender or Delivery; Replacement.

(1) If any tender or delivery by the lessor or the supplier is rejected because nonconforming and the time for performance has not yet expired, the lessor or the supplier may seasonably notify the lessee of the lessor's or the supplier's intention to cure and may then make a conforming delivery within the time provided in the lease contract.

(2) If the lessee rejects a nonconforming tender that the lessor or the supplier had reasonable grounds to believe would be acceptable with or without money allowance, the lessor or the supplier may have a further reasonable time to substitute a conforming tender if he [or she] seasonably notifies the lessee.

§ 2A–515. Acceptance of Goods.

(1) Acceptance of goods occurs after the lessee has had a reasonable opportunity to inspect the goods and

(a) the lessee signifies or acts with respect to the goods in a manner that signifies to the lessor or the supplier that the goods are conforming or that the lessee will take or retain them in spite of their nonconformity; or

(b) the lessee fails to make an effective rejection of the goods (Section 2A–509(2)).

(2) Acceptance of a part of any commercial unit is acceptance of that entire unit.

§ 2A–517. Revocation of Acceptance of Goods.

(1) A lessee may revoke acceptance of a lot or commercial unit whose nonconformity substantially impairs its value to the lessee if the lessee has accepted it:

(a) except in the case of a finance lease, on the reasonable assumption that its nonconformity would be cured and it has not been seasonably cured; or

(b) without discovery of the nonconformity if the lessee's acceptance was reasonably induced either by the lessor's assurances or, except in the case of a finance lease, by the difficulty of discovery before acceptance.

(2) Except in the case of a finance lease that is not a consumer lease, a lessee may revoke acceptance of a lot or commercial unit if the lessor defaults under the lease contract and the default substantially impairs the value of that lot or commercial unit to the lessee.

(3) If the lease agreement so provides, the lessee may revoke acceptance of a lot or commercial unit because of other defaults by the lessor.

(4) Revocation of acceptance must occur within a reasonable time after the lessee discovers or should have discovered the ground for it and before any substantial change in condition of the goods which is not caused by the nonconformity. Revocation is not effective until the lessee notifies the lessor.

(5) A lessee who so revokes has the same rights and duties with regard to the goods involved as if the lessee had rejected them.
As amended in 1990.

§ 2A–518. Cover; Substitute Goods.

(1) After a default by a lessor under the lease contract of the type described in Section 2A–508(1), or, if agreed, after other default by the lessor, the lessee may cover by making any purchase or lease of or contract to purchase or lease goods in substitution for those due from the lessor.

(2) Except as otherwise provided with respect to damages liquidated in the lease agreement (Section 2A–504) or otherwise determined pursuant to agreement of the parties (Sections 1–102(3) and 2A–503), if a lessee's cover is by a lease agreement substantially similar to the original lease agreement and the new lease agreement is made in good faith and in a commercially reasonable manner, the lessee may recover from the lessor as damages (i) the present value, as of the date of the commencement of the term of the new lease agreement, of the rent under the new lease agreement applicable to that period of the new lease term which is comparable to the then remaining term of the original lease agreement minus the present value as of the same date of the total rent for the then remaining lease term of the original lease agreement, and (ii) any incidental or consequential damages, less expenses saved in consequence of the lessor's default.

(3) If a lessee's cover is by lease agreement that for any reason does not qualify for treatment under subsection (2), or is by purchase or otherwise, the lessee may recover from the lessor as if the lessee had elected not to cover and Section 2A–519 governs.
As amended in 1990.

§ 2A–519. Lessee's Damages for Non-delivery, Repudiation, Default, and Breach of Warranty in Regard to Accepted Goods.

(1) Except as otherwise provided with respect to damages liquidated in the lease agreement (Section 2A–504) or otherwise

determined pursuant to agreement of the parties (Sections 1–102(3) and 2A–503), if a lessee elects not to cover or a lessee elects to cover and the cover is by lease agreement that for any reason does not qualify for treatment under Section 2A–518(2), or is by purchase or otherwise, the measure of damages for non-delivery or repudiation by the lessor or for rejection or revocation of acceptance by the lessee is the present value, as of the date of the default, of the then market rent minus the present value as of the same date of the original rent, computed for the remaining lease term of the original lease agreement, together with incidental and consequential damages, less expenses saved in consequence of the lessor's default.

(2) Market rent is to be determined as of the place for tender or, in cases of rejection after arrival or revocation of acceptance, as of the place of arrival.

(3) Except as otherwise agreed, if the lessee has accepted goods and given notification (Section 2A–516(3)), the measure of damages for non-conforming tender or delivery or other default by a lessor is the loss resulting in the ordinary course of events from the lessor's default as determined in any manner that is reasonable together with incidental and consequential damages, less expenses saved in consequence of the lessor's default.

(4) Except as otherwise agreed, the measure of damages for breach of warranty is the present value at the time and place of acceptance of the difference between the value of the use of the goods accepted and the value if they had been as warranted for the lease term, unless special circumstances show proximate damages of a different amount, together with incidental and consequential damages, less expenses saved in consequence of the lessor's default or breach of warranty.

As amended in 1990.

§ 2A–520. LESSEE'S INCIDENTAL AND CONSEQUENTIAL DAMAGES.

(1) Incidental damages resulting from a lessor's default include expenses reasonably incurred in inspection, receipt, transportation, and care and custody of goods rightfully rejected or goods the acceptance of which is justifiably revoked, any commercially reasonable charges, expenses or commissions in connection with effecting cover, and any other reasonable expense incident to the default.

(2) Consequential damages resulting from a lessor's default include:

(a) any loss resulting from general or particular requirements and needs of which the lessor at the time of contracting had reason to know and which could not reasonably be prevented by cover or otherwise; and

(b) injury to person or property proximately resulting from any breach of warranty.

§ 2A–521. LESSEE'S RIGHT TO SPECIFIC PERFORMANCE OR REPLEVIN.

(1) Specific performance may be decreed if the goods are unique or in other proper circumstances.

(2) A decree for specific performance may include any terms and conditions as to payment of the rent, damages, or other relief that the court deems just.

(3) A lessee has a right of replevin, detinue, sequestration, claim and delivery, or the like for goods identified to the lease contract if after reasonable effort the lessee is unable to effect cover for those goods or the circumstances reasonably indicate that the effort will be unavailing.

§ 2A–522. LESSEE'S RIGHT TO GOODS ON LESSOR'S INSOLVENCY.

(1) Subject to subsection (2) and even though the goods have not been shipped, a lessee who has paid a part or all of the rent and security for goods identified to a lease contract (Section 2A–217) on making and keeping good a tender of any unpaid portion of the rent and security due under the lease contract may recover the goods identified from the lessor if the lessor becomes insolvent within 10 days after receipt of the first installment of rent and security.

(2) A lessee acquires the right to recover goods identified to a lease contract only if they conform to the lease contract.

C. DEFAULT BY LESSEE

§ 2A–523. LESSOR'S REMEDIES.

(1) If a lessee wrongfully rejects or revokes acceptance of goods or fails to make a payment when due or repudiates with respect to a part or the whole, then, with respect to any goods involved, and with respect to all of the goods if under an installment lease contract the value of the whole lease contract is substantially impaired (Section 2A–510), the lessee is in default under the lease contract and the lessor may:

(a) cancel the lease contract (Section 2A–505(1));

(b) proceed respecting goods not identified to the lease contract (Section 2A–524);

(c) withhold delivery of the goods and take possession of goods previously delivered (Section 2A–525);

(d) stop delivery of the goods by any bailee (Section 2A–526);

(e) dispose of the goods and recover damages (Section 2A–527), or retain the goods and recover damages (Section 2A–528), or in a proper case recover rent (Section 2A–529);

(f) exercise any other rights or pursue any other remedies provided in the lease contract.

(2) If a lessor does not fully exercise a right or obtain a remedy to which the lessor is entitled under subsection (1), the lessor may recover the loss resulting in the ordinary course of events from the lessee's default as determined in any reasonable manner, together with incidental damages, less expenses saved in consequence of the lessee's default.

(3) If a lessee is otherwise in default under a lease contract, the lessor may exercise the rights and pursue the remedies provided in the lease contract, which may include a right to cancel the lease. In addition, unless otherwise provided in the lease contract:

(a) if the default substantially impairs the value of the lease contract to the lessor, the lessor may exercise the rights and pursue the remedies provided in subsections (1) or (2); or

(b) if the default does not substantially impair the value of the lease contract to the lessor, the lessor may recover as provided in subsection (2).

As amended in 1990.

§ 2A–524. LESSOR'S RIGHT TO IDENTIFY GOODS TO LEASE CONTRACT.

(1) After default by the lessee under the lease contract of the type described in Section 2A–523(1) or 2A–523(3)(a) or, if agreed, after other default by the lessee, the lessor may:

(a) identify to the lease contract conforming goods not already identified if at the time the lessor learned of the default they were in the lessor's or the supplier's possession or control; and

(b) dispose of goods (Section 2A–527(1)) that demonstrably have been intended for the particular lease contract even though those goods are unfinished.

(2) If the goods are unfinished, in the exercise of reasonable commercial judgment for the purposes of avoiding loss and of effective realization, an aggrieved lessor or the supplier may either complete manufacture and wholly identify the goods to the lease contract or cease manufacture and lease, sell, or otherwise dispose of the goods for scrap or salvage value or proceed in any other reasonable manner.

As amended in 1990.

§ 2A–525. *Lessor's Right to Possession of Goods.*

(1) If a lessor discovers the lessee to be insolvent, the lessor may refuse to deliver the goods.

(2) After a default by the lessee under the lease contract of the type described in Section 2A–523(1) or 2A–523(3)(a) or, if agreed, after other default by the lessee, the lessor has the right to take possession of the goods. If the lease contract so provides, the lessor may require the lessee to assemble the goods and make them available to the lessor at a place to be designated by the lessor which is reasonably convenient to both parties. Without removal, the lessor may render unusable any goods employed in trade or business, and may dispose of goods on the lessee's premises (Section 2A–527).

(3) The lessor may proceed under subsection (2) without judicial process if it can be done without breach of the peace or the lessor may proceed by action.

As amended in 1990.

§ 2A–526. *Lessor's Stoppage of Delivery in Transit or Otherwise.*

(1) A lessor may stop delivery of goods in the possession of a carrier or other bailee if the lessor discovers the lessee to be insolvent and may stop delivery of carload, truckload, planeload, or larger shipments of express or freight if the lessee repudiates or fails to make a payment due before delivery, whether for rent, security or otherwise under the lease contract, or for any other reason the lessor has a right to withhold or take possession of the goods.

(2) In pursuing its remedies under subsection (1), the lessor may stop delivery until

    (a) receipt of the goods by the lessee;

    (b) acknowledgment to the lessee by any bailee of the goods, except a carrier, that the bailee holds the goods for the lessee; or

    (c) such an acknowledgment to the lessee by a carrier via reshipment or as warehouseman.

(3) (a) To stop delivery, a lessor shall so notify as to enable the bailee by reasonable diligence to prevent delivery of the goods.

    (b) After notification, the bailee shall hold and deliver the goods according to the directions of the lessor, but the lessor is liable to the bailee for any ensuing charges or damages.

    (c) A carrier who has issued a nonnegotiable bill of lading is not obliged to obey a notification to stop received from a person other than the consignor.

§ 2A–527. *Lessor's Rights to Dispose of Goods.*

(1) After a default by a lessee under the lease contract of the type described in Section 2A–523(1) or 2A–523(3)(a) or after the lessor refuses to deliver or takes possession of goods (Section 2A–525 or 2A–526), or, if agreed, after other default by a lessee, the lessor may dispose of the goods concerned or the undelivered balance thereof by lease, sale, or otherwise.

(2) Except as otherwise provided with respect to damages liquidated in the lease agreement (Section 2A–504) or otherwise determined pursuant to agreement of the parties (Sections 1–102(3) and 2A–503), if the disposition is by lease agreement substantially similar to the original lease agreement and the new lease agreement is made in good faith and in a commercially reasonable manner, the lessor may recover from the lessee as damages (i) accrued and unpaid rent as of the date of the commencement of the term of the new lease agreement, (ii) the present value, as of the same date, of the total rent for the then remaining lease term of the original lease agreement minus the present value, as of the same date, of the rent under the new lease agreement applicable to that period of the new lease term which is comparable to the then remaining term of the original lease agreement, and (iii) any incidental damages allowed under Section 2A–530, less expenses saved in consequence of the lessee's default.

(3) If the lessor's disposition is by lease agreement that for any reason does not qualify for treatment under subsection (2), or is by sale or otherwise, the lessor may recover from the lessee as if the lessor had elected not to dispose of the goods and Section 2A–528 governs.

(4) A subsequent buyer or lessee who buys or leases from the lessor in good faith for value as a result of a disposition under this section takes the goods free of the original lease contract and any rights of the original lessee even though the lessor fails to comply with one or more of the requirements of this Article.

(5) The lessor is not accountable to the lessee for any profit made on any disposition. A lessee who has rightfully rejected or justifiably revoked acceptance shall account to the lessor for any excess over the amount of the lessee's security interest (Section 2A–508(5)).

As amended in 1990.

§ 2A–528. *Lessor's Damages for Non-acceptance, Failure to Pay, Repudiation, or Other Default.*

(1) Except as otherwise provided with respect to damages liquidated in the lease agreement (Section 2A–504) or otherwise determined pursuant to agreement of the parties (Sections 1–102(3) and 2A–503), if a lessor elects to retain the goods or a lessor elects to dispose of the goods and the disposition is by lease agreement that for any reason does not qualify for treatment under Section 2A–527(2), or is by sale or otherwise, the lessor may recover from the lessee as damages for a default of the type described in Section 2A–523(1) or 2A–523(3)(a), or, if agreed, for other default of the lessee, (i) accrued and unpaid rent as of the date of default if the lessee has never taken possession of the goods, or, if the lessee has taken possession of the goods, as of the date the lessor repossesses the goods or an earlier date on which the lessee makes a tender of the goods to the lessor, (ii) the present value as of the date determined under clause (i) of the total rent for the then remaining lease term of the original lease agreement minus the present value as of the same date of the market rent at the place where the goods are located computed for the same lease term, and (iii) any incidental damages allowed under Section 2A–530, less expenses saved in consequence of the lessee's default.

(2) If the measure of damages provided in subsection (1) is inadequate to put a lessor in as good a position as performance would have, the measure of damages is the present value of the

profit, including reasonable overhead, the lessor would have made from full performance by the lessee, together with any incidental damages allowed under Section 2A–530, due allowance for costs reasonably incurred and due credit for payments or proceeds of disposition.

As amended in 1990.

§ 2A–529. Lessor's Action for the Rent.

(1) After default by the lessee under the lease contract of the type described in Section 2A–523(1) or 2A–523(3)(a) or, if agreed, after other default by the lessee, if the lessor complies with subsection (2), the lessor may recover from the lessee as damages:

(a) for goods accepted by the lessee and not repossessed by or tendered to the lessor, and for conforming goods lost or damaged within a commercially reasonable time after risk of loss passes to the lessee (Section 2A–219), (i) accrued and unpaid rent as of the date of entry of judgment in favor of the lessor, (ii) the present value as of the same date of the rent for the then remaining lease term of the lease agreement, and (iii) any incidental damages allowed under Section 2A–530, less expenses saved in consequence of the lessee's default; and

(b) for goods identified to the lease contract if the lessor is unable after reasonable effort to dispose of them at a reasonable price or the circumstances reasonably indicate that effort will be unavailing, (i) accrued and unpaid rent as of the date of entry of judgment in favor of the lessor, (ii) the present value as of the same date of the rent for the then remaining lease term of the lease agreement, and (iii) any incidental damages allowed under Section 2A–530, less expenses saved in consequence of the lessee's default.

(2) Except as provided in subsection (3), the lessor shall hold for the lessee for the remaining lease term of the lease agreement any goods that have been identified to the lease contract and are in the lessor's control.

(3) The lessor may dispose of the goods at any time before collection of the judgment for damages obtained pursuant to subsection (1). If the disposition is before the end of the remaining lease term of the lease agreement, the lessor's recovery against the lessee for damages is governed by Section 2A–527 or Section 2A–528, and the lessor will cause an appropriate credit to be provided against a judgment for damages to the extent that the amount of the judgment exceeds the recovery available pursuant to Section 2A–527 or 2A–528.

(4) Payment of the judgment for damages obtained pursuant to subsection (1) entitles the lessee to the use and possession of the goods not then disposed of for the remaining lease term of and in accordance with the lease agreement.

(5) After default by the lessee under the lease contract of the type described in Section 2A–523(1) or Section 2A–523(3)(a) or, if agreed, after other default by the lessee, a lessor who is held not entitled to rent under this section must nevertheless be awarded damages for non-acceptance under Section 2A–527 or Section 2A–528.

As amended in 1990.

§ 2A–530. Lessor's Incidental Damages.

Incidental damages to an aggrieved lessor include any commercially reasonable charges, expenses, or commissions incurred in stopping delivery, in the transportation, care and custody of goods after the lessee's default, in connection with return or disposition of the goods, or otherwise resulting from the default.

Article 3: Negotiable Instruments
Part 1—General Provisions and Definitions
§ 3–101. Short Title.
This Article may be cited as Uniform Commercial Code—Negotiable Instruments.

§ 3–102. Subject Matter.

(a) This Article applies to negotiable instruments. It does not apply to money or to payment orders governed by Article 4A. A negotiable instrument that is also a certificated security under Section 8–102(1)(a) is subject to Article 8 and to this Article.

(b) In the event of conflict between the provisions of this Article and those of Article 4, Article 8, or Article 9, the provisions of Article 4, Article 8 and Article 9 prevail over those of this Article.

(c) Regulations of the Board of Governors of the Federal Reserve System and operating circulars of the Federal Reserve Banks supersede any inconsistent provision of this Article to the extent of the inconsistency.

§ 3–103. Definitions.

(a) In this Article:

(1) "Acceptor" means a drawee that has accepted a draft.

(2) "Drawee" means a person ordered in a draft to make payment.

(3) "Drawer" means a person that signs a draft as a person ordering payment.

(4) "Good faith" means honesty in fact and the observance of reasonable commercial standards of fair dealing.

(5) "Maker" means a person that signs a note as promisor of payment.

(6) "Order" means a written instruction to pay money signed by the person giving the instruction. The instruction may be addressed to any person, including the person giving the instruction, or to one or more persons jointly or in the alternative but not in succession. An authorization to pay is not an order unless the person authorized to pay is also instructed to pay.

(7) "Ordinary care" in the case of a person engaged in business means observance of reasonable commercial standards, prevailing in the area in which that person is located, with respect to the business in which that person is engaged. In the case of a bank that takes an instrument for processing for collection or payment by automated means, reasonable commercial standards do not require the bank to examine the instrument if the failure to examine does not violate the bank's prescribed procedures and the bank's procedures do not vary unreasonably from general banking usage not disapproved by this Article or Article 4.

(8) "Party" means party to an instrument.

(9) "Promise" means a written undertaking to pay money signed by the person undertaking to pay. An acknowledgment of an obligation by the obligor is not a promise unless the obligor also undertakes to pay the obligation.

(10) "Prove" with respect to a fact means to meet the burden of establishing the fact (Section 1–201(8)).

(11) "Remitter" means a person that purchases an instrument from its issuer if the instrument is payable to an identified person other than the purchaser.

(b) Other definitions applying to this Article and the sections in which they appear are:

"Acceptance" Section 3–409.

"Accommodated party" Section 3–419.

"Accommodation indorsement" Section 3–205.

"Accommodation party" Section 3–419.

"Alteration" Section 3–407.

"Blank indorsement" Section 3–205.

"Cashier's check" Section 3–104.

"Certificate of deposit" Section 3–104.

"Certified check" Section 3–409.

"Check" Section 3–104.

"Consideration" Section 3–303.

"Draft" Section 3–104.

"Fiduciary" Section 3–307.

"Guarantor" Section 3–417.

"Holder in due course" Section 3–302.

"Incomplete instrument" Section 3–115.

"Indorsement" Section 3–204.

"Indorser" Section 3–204.

"Instrument" Section 3–104.

"Issue" Section 3–105.

"Issuer" Section 3–105.

"Negotiable instrument" Section 3–104.

"Negotiation" Section 3–201.

"Note" Section 3–104.

"Payable at a definite time" Section 3–108.

"Payable on demand" Section 3–108.

"Payable to bearer" Section 3–109.

"Payable to order" Section 3–110.

"Payment" Section 3–603.

"Person entitled to enforce" Section 3–301.

"Presentment" Section 3–501.

"Reacquisition" Section 3–207.

"Represented person" Section 3–307.

"Special indorsement" Section 3–205.

"Teller's check" Section 3–104.

"Traveler's check" Section 3–104.

"Value" Section 3–303.

(c) The following definitions in other Articles apply to this Article:

"Bank" Section 4–105.

"Banking day" Section 4–104.

"Clearing house" Section 4–104.

"Collecting bank" Section 4–105.

"Customer" Section 4–104.

"Depositary bank" Section 4–105.

"Documentary draft" Section 4–104.

"Intermediary bank" Section 4–105.

"Item" Section 4–104.

"Midnight deadline" Section 4–104.

"Payor bank" Section 4–105.

"Suspends payments" Section 4–104.

(d) In addition, Article 1 contains general definitions and principles of construction and interpretation applicable throughout this Article.

§ 3–104. NEGOTIABLE INSTRUMENT.

(a) "Negotiable instrument" means an unconditional promise or order to pay a fixed amount of money, with or without interest or other charges described in the promise or order, if it:

(1) is payable to bearer or to order at the time it is issued or first comes into possession of a holder;

(2) is payable on demand or at a definite time; and

(3) does not state any other undertaking or instruction by the person promising or ordering payment to do any act in addition to the payment of money except that the promise or order may contain (i) an undertaking or power to give, maintain, or protect collateral to secure payment, (ii) an authorization or power to the holder to confess judgment or realize on or dispose of collateral, or (iii) a waiver of the benefit of any law intended for the advantage or protection of any obligor.

(b) "Instrument" means negotiable instrument.

(c) An order that meets all of the requirements of subsection (a) except subparagraph (1) and otherwise falls within the definition of "check" in subsection (f) is a negotiable instrument and a check.

(d) Notwithstanding subsection (a), a promise or order other than a check is not an instrument if, at the time it is issued or first comes into possession of a holder, it contains a conspicuous statement, however expressed, indicating that the writing is not an instrument governed by this Article.

(e) An instrument is a "note" if it is a promise, and is a "draft" if it is an order. If an instrument falls within the definition of both "note" and "draft," the person entitled to enforce the instrument may treat it as either.

(f) "Check" means (i) a draft, other than a documentary draft, payable on demand and drawn on a bank or (ii) a cashier's check or teller's check. An instrument may be a check even though it is described on its face by another term such as "money order."

(g) "Cashier's check" means a draft with respect to which the drawer and drawee are the same bank or branches of the same bank.

(h) "Teller's check" means a draft drawn by a bank (i) on another bank, or (ii) payable at or through a bank.

(i) "Traveler's check" means an instrument that (i) is payable on demand, (ii) is drawn on or payable at or through a bank, (iii) is designated by the term "traveler's check" or by a substantially similar term, and (iv) requires, as a condition to payment, a countersignature by a person whose specimen signature appears on the instrument.

(j) "Certificate of deposit" means an instrument containing an acknowledgment by a bank that a sum of money has been received by the bank, and a promise by the bank to repay the sum of money. A certificate of deposit is a note of the bank.

§ 3–105. ISSUE OF INSTRUMENT.

(a) "Issue" means the first delivery of an instrument by the maker or drawer, whether to a holder or nonholder, for the purpose of giving rights on the instrument to any person.

(b) An unissued instrument, or an unissued incomplete instrument (Section 3–115) that is completed, is binding on the maker or drawer, but nonissuance is a defense. An instrument that is conditionally issued or is issued for a special purpose is binding on the maker or drawer, but failure of the condition or special purpose to be fulfilled is a defense.

(c) "Issuer" applies to issued and unissued instruments and means any person that signs an instrument as maker or drawer.

§ 3–106. UNCONDITIONAL PROMISE OR ORDER.

(a) Except as provided in subsections (b) and (c), for the purposes of Section 3–104(a), a promise or order is unconditional unless it states (i) an express condition to payment or (ii) that the promise or order is subject to or governed by another writing, or that rights or obligations with respect to the promise or order are stated in another writing; however, a mere reference to another writing does not make the promise or order conditional.

(b) A promise or order is not made conditional (i) by a reference to another writing for a statement of rights with respect to collateral, prepayment, or acceleration, or (ii) because payment is limited to resort to a particular fund or source.

(c) If a promise or order requires, as a condition to payment, a countersignature by a person whose specimen signature appears on the promise or order, the condition does not make the promise or order conditional for the purposes of Section 3–104(a). If the person whose specimen signature appears on an instrument fails to countersign the instrument, the failure to countersign is a defense to the obligation of the issuer, but the failure does not prevent a transferee of the instrument from becoming a holder of the instrument.

(d) If a promise or order at the time it is issued or first comes into possession of a holder contains a statement, required by applicable statutory or administrative law, to the effect that the rights of a holder or transferee are subject to claims or defenses that the issuer could assert against the original payee, the promise or order is not thereby made conditional for the purposes of Section 3–104(a), but there cannot be a holder in due course of the promise or order.

§ 3–107. INSTRUMENT PAYABLE IN FOREIGN MONEY.

Unless the instrument otherwise provides, an instrument that states the amount payable in foreign money may be paid in the foreign money or in an equivalent amount in dollars calculated by using the current bank-offered spot rate at the place of payment for the purchase of dollars on the day on which the instrument is paid.

§ 3–108. PAYABLE ON DEMAND OR AT A DEFINITE TIME.

(a) A promise or order is "payable on demand" if (i) it states that it is payable on demand or at sight, or otherwise indicates that it is payable at the will of the holder, or (ii) it does not state any time of payment.

(b) A promise or order is "payable at a definite time" if it is payable on elapse of a definite period of time after sight or acceptance or at a fixed date or dates or at a time or times readily ascertainable at the time the promise or order is issued, subject to rights of (i) prepayment, (ii) acceleration, or (iii) extension at the option of the holder or (iv) extension to a further definite time at the option of the maker or acceptor or automatically upon or after a specified act or event.

(c) If an instrument, payable at a fixed date, is also payable upon demand made before the fixed date, the instrument is payable on demand until the fixed date and, if demand for payment is not made before that date, becomes payable at a definite time on the fixed date.

§ 3–109. PAYABLE TO BEARER OR TO ORDER.

(a) A promise or order is payable to bearer if it:
(1) states that it is payable to bearer or to the order of bearer or otherwise indicates that the person in possession of the promise or order is entitled to payment,
(2) does not state a payee, or
(3) states that it is payable to or to the order of cash or otherwise indicates that it is not payable to an identified person.

(b) A promise or order that is not payable to bearer is payable to order if it is payable (i) to the order of an identified person or (ii) to an identified person or order. A promise or order that is payable to order is payable to the identified person.

(c) An instrument payable to bearer may become payable to an identified person if it is specially indorsed as stated in Section 3–205(a). An instrument payable to an identified person may become payable to bearer if it is indorsed in blank as stated in Section 3–205(b).

§ 3–110. IDENTIFICATION OF PERSON TO WHOM INSTRUMENT IS PAYABLE.

(a) A person to whom an instrument is payable is determined by the intent of the person, whether or not authorized, signing as, or in the name or behalf of, the maker or drawer. The instrument is payable to the person intended by the signer even if that person is identified in the instrument by a name or other identification that is not that of the intended person. If more than one person signs in the name or behalf of the maker or drawer and all the signers do not intend the same person as payee, the instrument is payable to any person intended by one or more of the signers.

(b) If the signature of the maker or drawer of an instrument is made by automated means such as a check-writing machine, the payee of the instrument is determined by the intent of the person who supplied the name or identification of the payee, whether or not authorized to do so.

(c) A person to whom an instrument is payable may be identified in any way including by name, identifying number, office, or account number. For the purpose of determining the holder of an instrument, the following rules apply:
(1) If an instrument is payable to an account and the account is identified only by number, the instrument is payable to the person to whom the account is payable. If an instrument is payable to an account identified by number and by the name of a person, the instrument is payable to the named person, whether or not that person is the owner of the account identified by number.
(2) If an instrument is payable to:
(i) a trust, estate, or a person described as trustee or representative of a trust or estate, the instrument is payable to the trustee, the representative, or a successor of either, whether or not the beneficiary or estate is also named;
(ii) a person described as agent or similar representative of a named or identified person, the instrument is payable either to the represented person, the representative, or a successor of the representative;
(iii) a fund or organization that is not a legal entity, the instrument is payable to a representative of the members of the fund or organization; or
(iv) an office or to a person described as holding an office, the instrument is payable to the named person, the incumbent of the office, or a successor to the incumbent.

(d) If an instrument is payable to two or more persons alternatively, it is payable to any of them and may be negotiated, discharged, or enforced by any of them in possession of the instrument. If an instrument is payable to two or more persons not alternatively, it is payable to all of them and may be negotiated, discharged, or enforced only by all of them. If an instrument payable to two or more persons is ambiguous as to whether it is payable to the persons alternatively, the instrument is payable to the persons alternatively.

§ 3–111. PLACE OF PAYMENT.

Except as otherwise provided for items in Article 4, an instrument is payable at the place of payment stated in the instrument. If no place of payment is stated, an instrument is payable at the address of the drawee or maker stated in the instrument. If no address is stated, the place of payment is the place of business of the drawee or maker. If a drawee or maker has more than one place of business, the place of payment is any place of business of the drawee or maker chosen by the person entitled to enforce the instrument. If the drawee or maker has no place of business, the place of payment is the residence of the drawee or maker.

§ 3–112. INTEREST.

(a) Unless otherwise provided in the instrument, (i) an instrument is not payable with interest, and (ii) interest on an interest-bearing instrument is payable from the date of the instrument.

(b) Interest may be stated in an instrument as a fixed or variable amount of money or it may be expressed as a fixed or variable rate or rates. The amount or rate of interest may be stated or described in the instrument in any manner and may require reference to information not contained in the instrument. If an instrument provides for interest but the amount of interest payable cannot be ascertained from the description, interest is payable at the judgment rate in effect at the place of payment of the instrument and at the time interest first accrues.

§ 3–113. DATE OF INSTRUMENT.

(a) An instrument may be antedated or postdated. The date stated determines the time of payment if the instrument is payable at a fixed period after date. Except as provided in Section 4–401(3), an instrument payable on demand is not payable before the date of the instrument.

(b) If an instrument is undated, its date is the date of its issue or, in the case of an unissued instrument, the date it first comes into possession of a holder.

§ 3–114. CONTRADICTORY TERMS OF INSTRUMENT.

If an instrument contains contradictory terms, typewritten terms prevail over printed terms, handwritten terms prevail over both, and words prevail over numbers.

§ 3–115. INCOMPLETE INSTRUMENT.

(a) "Incomplete instrument" means a signed writing, whether or not issued by the signer, the contents of which show at the time of signing that it is incomplete but that the signer intended it to be completed by the addition of words or numbers.

(b) Subject to subsection (c), if an incomplete instrument is an instrument under Section 3–104, it may be enforced (i) according to its terms if it is not completed, or (ii) according to its terms as augmented by completion. If an incomplete instrument is not an instrument under Section 3–104 but, after completion, the requirements of Section 3–104 are met, the instrument may be enforced according to its terms as augmented by completion.

(c) If words or numbers are added to an incomplete instrument without authority of the signer, there is an alteration of the incomplete instrument governed by Section 3–407.

(d) The burden of establishing that words or numbers were added to an incomplete instrument without authority of the signer is on the person asserting the lack of authority.

§ 3–116. JOINT AND SEVERAL LIABILITY; CONTRIBUTION.

(a) Except as otherwise provided in the instrument, two or more persons who have the same liability on an instrument as makers, drawers, acceptors, indorsers who are indorsing joint payees, or anomalous indorsers, are jointly and severally liable in the capacity in which they sign.

(b) Except as provided in Section 3–417(e) or by agreement of the affected parties, a party with joint and several liability that pays the instrument is entitled to receive from any party with the same joint and several liability contribution in accordance with applicable law.

(c) Discharge of one party with joint and several liability by a person entitled to enforce the instrument does not affect the right under subsection (b) of a party with the same joint and several liability to receive contribution from the party discharged.

§ 3–117. OTHER AGREEMENTS AFFECTING AN INSTRUMENT.

Subject to applicable law regarding exclusion of proof of contemporaneous or prior agreements, the obligation of a party to an instrument to pay the instrument may be modified, supplemented, or nullified by a separate agreement of the obligor and a person entitled to enforce the instrument if the instrument is issued or the obligation is incurred in reliance on the agreement or as part of the same transaction giving rise to the agreement. To the extent an obligation is modified, supplemented, or nullified by an agreement under this section, the agreement is a defense to the obligation.

§ 3–118. STATUTE OF LIMITATIONS.

(a) Except as provided in subsection (e), an action to enforce the obligation of a party to pay a note payable at a definite time must be commenced within six years after the payment date or dates stated in the note or, if a payment date is accelerated, within six years after the accelerated payment date.

(b) Except as provided in subsection (d) or (e), if demand for payment is made to the maker of a note payable on demand, an action to enforce the obligation of a party to pay the note must be commenced within six years after the demand. If no demand for payment is made to the maker, an action to enforce the note is barred if neither principal nor interest on the note has been paid for a continuous period of 10 years.

(c) Except as provided in subsection (d), an action to enforce the obligation of a party to an unaccepted draft to pay the draft must be commenced within six years after dishonor of the draft or 10 years after the date of the draft, whichever period expires first.

(d) An action to enforce the obligation of the acceptor of a certified check or the issuer of a teller's check, cashier's check, or traveler's check must be commenced within six years after demand for payment is made to the acceptor or issuer, as the case may be.

(e) An action to enforce the obligation of a party to a certificate of deposit to pay the instrument must be commenced within six years after demand for payment is made to the maker, but if the instrument states a maturity date and the maker is not required to pay before that date, the six-year period begins when a demand for payment is in effect and the maturity date has passed.

(f) This subsection applies to an action to enforce the obligation of a party to pay an accepted draft, other than a certified check. If the obligation of the acceptor is payable at a definite time, the action must be commenced within six years after the payment date or dates stated in the draft or acceptance. If the obligation of the acceptor is payable on demand, the action must be commenced within six years after the date of the acceptance.

(g) Unless governed by other law regarding claims for indemnity or contribution, an action (i) for conversion of an instrument, for money had and received, or like action based on conversion, (ii) for breach of warranty, or (iii) to enforce an obligation, duty, or right arising under this Article and not governed by this section must be commenced within three years after the cause of action accrues.

§ 3–119. NOTICE OF RIGHT TO DEFEND ACTION.

In an action for breach of an obligation for which a third person is answerable over pursuant to this Article or Article 4, the defendant may give the third person written notice of the litigation, and the person notified may then give similar notice to any other person who is answerable over. If the notice states (i) that the person notified may come in and defend and (ii) that failure to do so will bind the person notified in an action later brought by the person giving the notice as to any determination of fact common to the two litigations, the person notified is so bound unless after seasonable receipt of the notice the person notified does come in and defend.

PART 2—NEGOTIATION, TRANSFER AND INDORSEMENT

§ 3–201. NEGOTIATION.

(a) "Negotiation" means a transfer of possession, whether voluntary or involuntary, of an instrument to a person who thereby becomes its holder if possession is obtained from a person other than the issuer of the instrument.

(b) Except for a negotiation by a remitter, if an instrument is payable to an identified person, negotiation requires transfer of possession of the instrument and its indorsement by the holder. If an instrument is payable to bearer, it may be negotiated by transfer of possession alone.

§ 3–202. NEGOTIATION SUBJECT TO RESCISSION.

(a) Negotiation is effective even if obtained (i) from an infant, a corporation exceeding its powers, or a person without capacity, or (ii) by fraud, duress, or mistake, or in breach of duty or as part of an illegal transaction.

(b) To the extent permitted by law, negotiation may be rescinded or may be subject to other remedies, but those remedies may not be asserted against a subsequent holder in due course or a person paying the instrument in good faith and without knowledge of facts that are a basis for rescission or other remedy.

§ 3–203. RIGHTS ACQUIRED BY TRANSFER.

(a) An instrument is transferred when it is delivered by a person other than its issuer for the purpose of giving to the person receiving delivery the right to enforce the instrument.

(b) Transfer of an instrument, regardless of whether the transfer is a negotiation, vests in the transferee any right of the transferor to enforce the instrument, including any right as a holder in due course, but the transferee cannot acquire rights of a holder in due course by a transfer, directly or indirectly, from a holder in due course if the purchaser engaged in fraud or illegality affecting the instrument.

(c) Unless otherwise agreed, if an instrument is transferred for value and the transferee does not become a holder because of lack of indorsement by the transferor, the transferee has a specifically enforceable right to the unqualified indorsement of the transferor, but negotiation of the instrument does not occur until the indorsement is made.

(d) If a transferor purports to transfer less than the entire instrument, negotiation of the instrument does not occur. The transferee obtains no rights under this Article and has only the rights of a partial assignee.

§ 3–204. INDORSEMENT.

(a) "Indorsement" means a signature, other than that of a maker, drawer, or acceptor, that alone or accompanied by other words, is made on an instrument for the purpose of (i) negotiating the instrument, (ii) restricting payment of the instrument, or (iii) incurring indorser's liability on the instrument, but regardless of the intent of the signer, a signature and its accompanying words is an indorsement unless the accompanying words, the terms of the instrument, the place of the signature, or other circumstances unambiguously indicate that the signature was made for a purpose other than indorsement. For the purpose of determining whether a signature is made on an instrument, a paper affixed to the instrument is a part of the instrument.

(b) "Indorser" means a person who makes an indorsement.

(c) For the purpose of determining whether the transferee of an instrument is a holder, an indorsement that transfers a security interest in the instrument is effective as an unqualified indorsement of the instrument.

(d) If an instrument is payable to a holder under a name that is not the name of the holder, indorsement may be made by the holder in the name stated in the instrument or in the holder's name or both, but signature in both names may be required by a person paying or taking the instrument for value or collection.

§ 3–205. SPECIAL INDORSEMENT; BLANK INDORSEMENT; ANOMALOUS INDORSEMENT.

(a) If an indorsement is made by the holder of an instrument, whether payable to an identified person or payable to bearer, and the indorsement identifies a person to whom it makes the instrument payable, it is a "special indorsement." When specially indorsed, an instrument becomes payable to the identified person and may be negotiated only by the indorsement of that person. The principles stated in Section 3–110 apply to special indorsements.

(b) If an indorsement is made by the holder of an instrument and it is not a special indorsement, it is a "blank indorsement." When indorsed in blank, an instrument becomes payable to bearer and may be negotiated by transfer of possession alone until specially indorsed.

(c) The holder may convert a blank indorsement that consists only of a signature into a special indorsement by writing, above the signature of the indorser, words identifying the person to whom the instrument is made payable.

(d) "Anomalous indorsement" means an indorsement made by a person that is not the holder of the instrument. An anomalous indorsement does not affect the manner in which the instrument may be negotiated.

§ 3–206. RESTRICTIVE INDORSEMENT.

(a) An indorsement limiting payment to a particular person or otherwise prohibiting further transfer or negotiation of the instrument is not effective to prevent further transfer or negotiation of the instrument.

(b) An indorsement stating a condition to the right of the indorsee to receive payment does not affect the right of the indorsee to enforce the instrument. A person paying the instrument or taking it for value or collection may disregard the condition, and the rights and liabilities of that person are not affected by whether the condition has been fulfilled.

(c) The following rules apply to an instrument bearing an indorsement (i) described in Section 4–201(2), or (ii) in blank or to a particular bank using the words "for deposit," "for collection," or other words indicating a purpose of having the instrument collected for the indorser or for a particular account:

(1) A person, other than a bank, that purchases the instrument when so indorsed converts the instrument unless the proceeds of the instrument are received by the indorser or are applied consistently with the indorsement.

(2) A depositary bank that purchases the instrument or takes it for collection when so indorsed converts the instrument unless the proceeds of the instrument are received by the indorser or applied consistently with the indorsement.

(3) A payor bank that is also the depositary bank or that takes the instrument for immediate payment over the counter from a person other than a collecting bank converts the instrument unless the proceeds of the instrument are received by the indorser or applied consistently with the indorsement.

(4) Except as otherwise provided in paragraph (3), a payor bank or intermediary bank may disregard the indorsement and is not liable if the proceeds of the instrument are not received by the indorser or applied consistently with the indorsement.

(d) Except for an indorsement covered by subsection (c), the following rules apply to an instrument bearing an indorsement using words to the effect that payment is to be made to the indorsee as agent, trustee, or other fiduciary for the benefit of the indorser or another person.

(1) Unless there is notice of breach of fiduciary duty as provided in Section 3–307, a person that purchases the instrument from the indorsee or takes the instrument from the indorsee for collection or payment may pay the proceeds of payment or the value given for the instrument to the indorsee without regard to whether the indorsee violates a fiduciary duty to the indorser.

(2) A later transferee of the instrument or person that pays the instrument is neither given notice nor otherwise affected by the restriction in the indorsement unless the transferee or payor knows that the fiduciary dealt with the instrument or its proceeds in breach of fiduciary duty.

(e) Purchase of an instrument bearing an indorsement to which this section applies does not prevent the purchaser from becoming a holder in due course of the instrument unless the purchaser is a converter under subsection (c).

(f) In an action to enforce the obligation of a party to pay the instrument, the obligor has a defense if payment would violate an indorsement to which this section applies and the payment is not permitted by this section.

§ 3–207. REACQUISITION.

Reacquisition of an instrument occurs if it is transferred, by negotiation or otherwise, to a former holder. A former holder that reacquires the instrument may cancel indorsements made after the reacquirer first became a holder of the instrument. If the cancellation causes the instrument to be payable to the reacquirer or to bearer, the reacquirer may negotiate the instrument. An indorser whose indorsement is canceled is discharged, and the discharge is effective against any later holder.

PART 3—ENFORCEMENT OF INSTRUMENTS

§ 3–301. PERSON ENTITLED TO ENFORCE INSTRUMENT.

"Person entitled to enforce" an instrument means (i) the holder of the instrument, (ii) a nonholder in possession of the instrument who has the rights of a holder, or (iii) a person not in possession of the instrument who is entitled to enforce the instrument pursuant to Section 3–309. A person may be a person entitled to enforce the instrument even though the person is not the owner of the instrument or is in wrongful possession of the instrument.

§ 3–302. HOLDER IN DUE COURSE.

(a) Subject to subsection (c) and Section 3–106(d), "holder in due course" means the holder of an instrument if:

(1) the instrument when issued or negotiated to the holder does not bear such apparent evidence of forgery or alteration or is not otherwise so irregular or incomplete as to call into question its authenticity, and

(2) the holder took the instrument (i) for value, (ii) in good faith, (iii) without notice that the instrument is overdue or has been dishonored or that there is an uncured default with respect to payment of another instrument issued as part of the same series, (iv) without notice that the instrument contains an unauthorized signature or has been altered, (v) without notice of any claim to the instrument stated in Section 3–306, and (vi) without notice that any party to the instrument has any defense or claim in recoupment stated in Section 3–305(a).

(b) Notice of discharge of a party to the instrument, other than discharge in an insolvency proceeding, is not notice of a defense under subsection (a), but discharge is effective against a person who became a holder in due course with notice of the discharge. Public filing or recording of a document does not of itself constitute notice of a defense, claim in recoupment, or claim to the instrument.

(c) Except to the extent a transferor or predecessor in interest has rights as a holder in due course, a person does not acquire rights of a holder in due course of an instrument taken (i) by legal process or by purchase at an execution, bankruptcy, or creditor's sale or similar proceeding, (ii) by purchase as part of a bulk transaction not in ordinary course of business of the transferor, or (iii) as the successor in interest to an estate or other organization.

(d) If, under Section 3–303(a)(1), the promise of performance that is the consideration for an instrument has been partially performed, the holder may assert rights as a holder in due course of the instrument only to the fraction of the amount payable under the instrument equal to the value of the partial performance divided by the value of the promised performance.

(e) If (i) the person entitled to enforce an instrument has only a security interest in the instrument and (ii) the person obliged to pay the instrument has a defense, claim in recoupment or claim to the instrument that may be asserted against the person who granted the security interest, the person entitled to enforce the instrument may assert rights as a holder in due course only to an amount payable under the instrument which, at the time of enforcement of the instrument, does not exceed the amount of the unpaid obligation secured.

(f) To be effective, notice must be received at such time and in such manner as to give a reasonable opportunity to act on it.

(g) This section is subject to any law limiting status as a holder in due course in particular classes of transactions.

§ 3–303. VALUE AND CONSIDERATION.

(a) An instrument is issued or transferred for value if:

(1) the instrument is issued or transferred for a promise of performance, to the extent the promise has been performed;

(2) the transferee acquires a security interest or other lien in the instrument other than a lien obtained by judicial proceedings;

(3) the instrument is issued or transferred as payment of, or as security for, an existing obligation of any person, whether or not the obligation is due;

(4) the instrument is issued or transferred in exchange for a negotiable instrument; or

(5) the instrument is issued or transferred in exchange for the incurring of an irrevocable obligation to a third party by the person taking the instrument.

(b) "Consideration" means any consideration sufficient to support a simple contract. The drawer or maker of an instrument has a defense if the instrument is issued without consideration. If an instrument is issued for a promise of performance, the drawer or maker has a defense to the extent performance of the promise is due and the promise has not been performed. If an instrument is issued for value as stated in subsection (a), the instrument is also issued for consideration.

§ 3–304. OVERDUE INSTRUMENT.

(a) An instrument payable on demand becomes overdue at the earliest of the following times:

(1) on the day after the day demand for payment is duly made;

(2) if the instrument is a check, 90 days after its date; or

(3) if the instrument is not a check, when the instrument has been outstanding for a period of time after its date which is unreasonably long under the circumstances of the particular case in light of the nature of the instrument and trade usage.

(b) With respect to an instrument payable at a definite time the following rules apply: (1) If the principal is payable in installments and a due date has not been accelerated, the instrument becomes overdue upon default under the instrument for nonpayment of an installment, and the instrument remains overdue until the default is cured. (2) If the principal is not payable in installments and the due date has not been accelerated, the instrument becomes overdue on the day after the due date. (3) If a due date with respect to principal has been accelerated, the instrument becomes overdue on the day after the accelerated due date.

(c) Unless the due date of principal has been accelerated, an instrument does not become overdue if there is default in payment of interest but no default in payment of principal.

§ 3–305. DEFENSES AND CLAIMS IN RECOUPMENT.

(a) Except as stated in subsection (b), the right to enforce the obligation of a party to pay the instrument is subject to the following:

(1) A defense of the obligor based on (i) infancy of the obligor to the extent it is a defense to a simple contract, (ii) duress, lack of legal capacity, or illegality of the transaction that nullifies the obligation of the obligor, (iii) fraud that induced the obligor to sign the instrument with neither knowledge nor reasonable opportunity to learn of its character or its essential terms, or (iv) discharge of the obligor in insolvency proceedings.

(2) A defense of the obligor stated in another section of this Article or a defense of the obligor that would be available if the person entitled to enforce the instrument were enforcing a right to payment under a simple contract.

(3) A claim in recoupment of the obligor against the original payee of the instrument if the claim arose from the transaction that gave rise to the instrument. The claim of the obligor may be asserted against a transferee of the instrument only to reduce the amount owing on the instrument at the time the action is brought.

(b) The right of a holder in due course to enforce the obligation of a party to pay the instrument is subject to defenses of the obligor stated in subsection (a)(1), but is not subject to defenses of the obligor stated in subsection (a)(2) or claims in recoupment stated in subsection (a)(3) against a person other than the holder.

(c) Except as stated in subsection (d), in an action to enforce the obligation of a party to pay the instrument, the obligor may not assert against the person entitled to enforce the instrument a defense, claim in recoupment, or claim to the instrument (Section 3–306) of another person, but the other person's claim to the instrument may be asserted by the obligor if the other person is joined in the action and personally asserts the claim against the person entitled to enforce the instrument. An obligor is not obliged to pay the instrument if the person seeking enforcement of the instrument does not have rights of a holder in due course and the obligor proves that the instrument is a lost or stolen instrument.

(d) In an action to enforce the obligation of an accommodation party to pay an instrument, the accommodation party may assert against the person entitled to enforce the instrument any defense or claim in recoupment under subsection (a) that the accommodated party could assert against the person entitled to enforce the instrument, except the defenses of discharge in insolvency proceedings, infancy, or lack of legal capacity.

§ 3–306. CLAIMS TO AN INSTRUMENT.

A person taking an instrument, other than a person having rights of a holder in due course, is subject to a claim of a property or possessory right in the instrument or its proceeds, including a claim to rescind a negotiation and to recover the instrument or its proceeds. A person having rights of a holder in due course takes free of the claim to the instrument.

§ 3–307. NOTICE OF BREACH OF FIDUCIARY DUTY.

(a) This section applies if (i) an instrument is taken from a fiduciary for payment or collection or for value, (ii) the taker has knowledge of the fiduciary status of the fiduciary, and (iii) the represented person makes a claim to the instrument or its proceeds on the basis that the transaction of the fiduciary is a breach of fiduciary duty. Notice of breach of fiduciary duty by the fiduciary is notice of the claim of the represented person. "Fiduciary" means an agent, trustee, partner, corporation officer or director, or other representative owing a fiduciary duty with respect to the instrument. "Represented person" means the principal, beneficiary, partnership, corporation, or other person to whom the duty is owed.

(b) If the instrument is payable to the fiduciary, as such, or to the represented person, the taker has notice of the breach of fiduciary duty if the instrument is (i) taken in payment of or as security for a debt known by the taker to be the personal debt of the fiduciary, (ii) taken in a transaction known by the taker to be for the personal benefit of the fiduciary, or (iii) deposited to an account other than an account of the fiduciary, as such, or an account of the represented person.

(c) If the instrument is made or drawn by the fiduciary, as such, payable to the fiduciary personally, the taker does not have notice of the breach of fiduciary duty unless the taker knows of the breach of fiduciary duty.

(d) If the instrument is made or drawn by or on behalf of the represented person to the taker as payee, the taker has notice of the breach of fiduciary duty if the instrument is (i) taken in payment of or as security for a debt known by the taker to be the personal debt of the fiduciary, (ii) taken in a transaction known by the taker to be for the personal benefit of the fiduciary, or (iii) deposited to an account other than an account of the fiduciary, as such, or an account of the represented person.

§ 3–308. PROOF OF SIGNATURES AND STATUS AS HOLDER IN DUE COURSE.

(a) In an action with respect to an instrument, the authenticity of, and authority to make, each signature on the instrument is admitted unless specifically denied in the pleadings. If the validity of a signature is denied in the pleadings, the burden of establishing validity is on the person claiming validity, but the signature is presumed to be authentic and authorized unless the action is to enforce the liability of the purported signer and the signer is dead or incompetent at the time of trial of the issue of validity of the signature. If an action to enforce the instrument is brought against a person as the undisclosed principal of a person who signed the instrument as a party to the instrument, the plaintiff has the burden of establishing that the defendant is liable on the instrument as a represented person pursuant to Section 3–402(a).

(b) If the validity of signatures is admitted or proved and there is compliance with subsection (a), a plaintiff producing the instrument is entitled to payment if the plaintiff proves entitlement to enforce the instrument under Section 3–301, unless the defendant proves a defense or claim in recoupment. If a defense or claim in recoupment is proved, the right to payment of the plaintiff is subject to the defense or claim except to the extent the plaintiff proves that the plaintiff has rights of a holder in due course which are not subject to the defense or claim.

§ 3–309. ENFORCEMENT OF LOST, DESTROYED, OR STOLEN INSTRUMENT.

(a) A person not in possession of an instrument is entitled to enforce the instrument if (i) that person was in rightful possession of the instrument and entitled to enforce it when loss of possession occurred, (ii) the loss of possession was not the result of a voluntary transfer by that person or a lawful seizure, and (iii) that person cannot reasonably obtain possession of the instrument because the instrument was destroyed, its whereabouts cannot be determined, or it is in the wrongful possession of an unknown person or a person that cannot be found or is not amenable to service of process.

(b) A person seeking enforcement of an instrument pursuant to subsection (a) must prove the terms of the instrument and the person's right to enforce the instrument. If that proof is made, Section 3–308 applies to the case as though the person seeking enforcement had produced the instrument. The court may not enter judgment in favor of the person seeking enforcement unless it finds that the person required to pay the instrument is adequately protected against loss that might occur by reason of a claim by another person to enforce the instrument. Adequate protection may be provided by any reasonable means.

§ 3–310. EFFECT OF INSTRUMENT ON OBLIGATION FOR WHICH TAKEN.

(a) Unless otherwise agreed, if a certified check, cashier's check, or teller's check is taken for an obligation, the obligation is discharged to the same extent discharge would result if an amount of money equal to the amount of the instrument were taken in payment of the obligation. Discharge of the obligation does not affect any liability that the obligor may have as an indorser of the instrument.

(b) Unless otherwise agreed and except as provided in subsection (a), if a note or an uncertified check is taken for an obligation, the obligation is suspended to the same extent the obligation would be discharged if an amount of money equal to the amount of the instrument were taken.

(1) In the case of an uncertified check, suspension of the obligation continues until dishonor of the check or until it is paid or certified. Payment or certification of the check results in discharge of the obligation to the extent of the amount of the check.

(2) In the case of a note, suspension of the obligation continues until dishonor of the note or until it is paid. Payment of the note results in discharge of the obligation to the extent of the payment.

(3) If the check or note is dishonored and the obligee of the obligation for which the instrument was taken has possession of the instrument, the obligee may enforce either the instrument or the obligation. In the case of an instrument of a third person which is negotiated to the obligee by the obligor, discharge of the obligor on the instrument also discharges the obligation.

(4) If the person entitled to enforce the instrument taken for an obligation is a person other than the obligee, the obligee may not enforce the obligation to the extent the obligation is suspended. If the obligee is the person entitled to enforce the instrument but no longer has possession of it because it was lost, stolen, or destroyed, the obligation may not be enforced to the extent of the amount payable on the instrument, and to that extent the obligee's rights against the obligor are limited to enforcement of the instrument.

(c) If an instrument other than one described in subsection (a) or (b) is taken for an obligation, the effect is (i) that stated in subsection (a) if the instrument is one on which a bank is liable as maker or acceptor, or (ii) that stated in subsection (b) in any other case.

§ 3–311. ACCORD AND SATISFACTION BY USE OF INSTRUMENT.

(a) This section applies if a person against whom a claim is asserted proves that (i) that person in good faith tendered an instrument to the claimant as full satisfaction of the claim, (ii) the amount of the claim was unliquidated or subject to a bona fide dispute, and (iii) the claimant obtained payment of the instrument.

(b) Unless subsection (c) applies, the claim is discharged if the person against whom the claim is asserted proves that the instrument or an accompanying written communication contained a conspicuous statement to the effect that the instrument was tendered as full satisfaction of the claim.

(c) Subject to subsection (d), a claim is not discharged under subsection (b) if the claimant is an organization and proves that within a reasonable time before the tender, the claimant sent a conspicuous statement to the person against whom the claim is asserted that communications concerning disputed debts, including an instrument tendered as full satisfaction of a debt, are to be sent to a designated person, office or place, and the instrument or accompanying communication was not received by that designated person, office, or place.

(d) Notwithstanding subsection (c), a claim is discharged under subsection (b) if the person against whom the claim is asserted proves that within a reasonable time before collection of the instrument was initiated, an agent of the claimant having direct responsibility with respect to the disputed obligation knew that the instrument was tendered in full satisfaction of the claim, or received the instrument and any accompanying written communication.

PART 4—LIABILITY OF PARTIES

§ 3–401. SIGNATURE.

(a) A person is not liable on an instrument unless (i) the person signed the instrument, or (ii) the person is represented by an agent or representative who signed the instrument and the signature is binding on the represented person under Section 3–402.

(b) A signature may be made (i) manually or by means of a device or machine, and (ii) by the use of any name, including any trade or assumed name, or by any word, mark, or symbol executed or adopted by a person with present intention to authenticate a writing.

§ 3–402. SIGNATURE BY REPRESENTATIVE.

(a) If a person acting, or purporting to act, as a representative signs an instrument by signing either the name of the represented person or the name of the signer, the represented person is bound by the signature to the same extent the represented person would be bound if the signature were on a simple contract. If the represented person is bound, the signature of the representative is the "authorized signature of the represented person" and the represented person is liable on the instrument, whether or not identified in the instrument.

(b) If a representative signs the name of the representative to an instrument and that signature is an authorized signature of the represented person, the following rules apply:

(1) If the form of the signature shows unambiguously that the signature is made on behalf of the represented person who is identified in the instrument, the representative is not liable on the instrument.

(2) Subject to subsection (c), if (i) the form of the signature does not show unambiguously that the signature is made in a representative capacity or (ii) the represented person is not identified in the instrument, the representative is liable on the instrument to a holder in due course that took the instrument without notice that the representative was not intended to be liable on the instrument. With respect to any other person, the representative is liable on the instrument unless the representative proves that the original parties to the instrument did not intend the representative to be liable on the instrument.

(c) If a representative signs the name of the representative as drawer of a check without indication of the representative status and the check is payable from an account of the represented person who is identified on the check, the signer is not liable on the check if the signature is an authorized signature of the represented person.

§ 3–403. UNAUTHORIZED SIGNATURE.

(a) Except as otherwise provided in this Article, an unauthorized signature is ineffective except as the signature of the unauthorized signer in favor of a person who in good faith pays the instrument or takes it for value. An unauthorized signature may be ratified for all purposes of this Article.

(b) If the signature of more than one person is required to constitute the authorized signature of an organization, the signature of the organization is unauthorized if one of the required signatures is missing.

(c) The civil or criminal liability of a person who makes an unauthorized signature is not affected by any provision of this Article that makes the unauthorized signature effective for the purposes of this Article.

§ 3–404. IMPOSTORS; FICTITIOUS PAYEES.

(a) If an impostor by use of the mails or otherwise induces the maker or drawer of an instrument to issue the instrument to the impostor, or to a person acting in concert with the impostor, by impersonating the payee of the instrument or a person authorized to act for the payee, an indorsement of the instrument by any person in the name of the payee is effective as the indorsement of the payee in favor of any person that in good faith pays the instrument or takes it for value or for collection.

(b) If (i) a person whose intent determines to whom an instrument is payable (Section 3–110(a) or (b)) does not intend the person identified as payee to have any interest in the instrument, or (ii) the person identified as payee of the instrument is a fictitious person, the following rules apply until the instrument is negotiated by special indorsement:

(1) Any person in possession of the instrument is its holder.

(2) An indorsement by any person in the name of the payee stated in the instrument is effective as the indorsement of the payee in favor of any person that in good faith pays the instrument or takes it for value or for collection.

(c) Under subsection (a) or (b) an indorsement is made in the name of a payee if (i) it is made in a name substantially similar to that of the payee or (ii) the instrument, whether or not indorsed, is deposited in a depositary bank to an account in a name substantially similar to that of the payee.

(d) With respect to an instrument to which subsection (a) or (b) applies, if a person paying the instrument or taking it for value or for collection fails to exercise ordinary care in paying or taking the instrument and that failure substantially contributes to loss resulting from payment of the instrument, the person bearing the loss may recover from the person failing to exercise ordinary care to the extent the failure to exercise ordinary care contributed to the loss.

§ 3–405. EMPLOYER RESPONSIBILITY FOR FRAUDULENT INDORSEMENT BY EMPLOYEE.

(a) This section applies to fraudulent indorsements of instruments with respect to which an employer has entrusted an employee with responsibility as part of the employee's duties. The following definitions apply to this section:

(1) "Employee" includes, in addition to an employee of an employer, an independent contractor and employee of an independent contractor retained by the employer.

(2) "Fraudulent indorsement" means (i) in the case of an instrument payable to the employer, a forged indorsement purporting to be that of the employer, or (ii) in the case of an instrument with respect to which the employer is drawer or maker, a forged indorsement purporting to be that of the person identified as payee.

(3) "Responsibility" with respect to instruments means authority (i) to sign or indorse instruments on behalf of the employer, (ii) to process instruments received by the employer for bookkeeping purposes, for deposit to an account, or for other disposition, (iii) to prepare or process instruments for issue in the name of the employer, (iv) to supply information determining the names or addresses of payees of instruments to be issued in the name of the employer, (v) to control the disposition of instruments to be issued in the name of the employer, or (vi) to otherwise act with respect to instruments in a responsible capacity. "Responsibility" does not include the assignment of duties that merely allow an employee to have access to instruments or blank or incomplete instrument forms that are being stored or transported or are part of incoming or outgoing mail, or similar access.

(b) For the purpose of determining the rights and liabilities of a person who, in good faith, pays an instrument or takes it for value or for collection, if an employee entrusted with responsibility with respect to the instrument or a person acting in concert with the employee makes a fraudulent indorsement to the instrument, the indorsement is effective as the indorsement of the person to whom the instrument is payable if it is made in the name of that person. If the person paying the instrument or taking it for value or for collection fails to exercise ordinary care in paying or taking the instrument and that failure substantially contributes to loss resulting from the fraud, the person bearing the loss may recover from the person failing to exercise ordinary care to the extent the failure to exercise ordinary care contributed to the loss.

(c) Under subsection (b) an indorsement is made in the name of the person to whom an instrument is payable if (i) it is made in a name substantially similar to the name of that person or (ii) the instrument, whether or not indorsed, is deposited in a depositary bank to an account in a name substantially similar to the name of that person.

§ 3–406. Negligence Contributing to Forged Signature or Alteration of Instrument.

(a) A person whose failure to exercise ordinary care substantially contributes to an alteration of an instrument or to the making of a forged signature on an instrument is precluded from asserting the alteration or the forgery against a person that, in good faith, pays the instrument or takes it for value.

(b) If the person asserting the preclusion fails to exercise ordinary care in paying or taking the instrument and that failure substantially contributes to loss, the loss is allocated between the person precluded and the person asserting the preclusion according to the extent to which the failure of each to exercise ordinary care contributed to the loss.

(c) Under subsection (a) the burden of proving failure to exercise ordinary care is on the person asserting the preclusion. Under subsection (d) the burden of proving failure to exercise ordinary care is on the person precluded.

§ 3–407. Alteration.

(a) "Alteration" means (i) an unauthorized change in an instrument that purports to modify in any respect the obligation of a party to the instrument, or (ii) an unauthorized addition of words or numbers or other change to an incomplete instrument relating to the obligation of any party to the instrument.

(b) Except as provided in subsection (c), an alteration fraudulently made by the holder discharges any party to whose obligation the alteration applies unless that party assents or is precluded from asserting the alteration. No other alteration discharges any party, and the instrument may be enforced according to its original terms.

(c) If an instrument that has been fraudulently altered is acquired by a person having rights of a holder in due course, it may be enforced by that person according to its original terms. If an incomplete instrument is completed and is then acquired by a person having rights of a holder in due course, it may be enforced by that person as completed, whether or not the completion is a fraudulent alteration.

§ 3–408. Drawee Not Liable on Unaccepted Draft.

A check or other draft does not of itself operate as an assignment of funds in the hands of the drawee available for its payment, and the drawee is not liable on the instrument until the drawee accepts it.

§ 3–409. Acceptance of Draft; Certified Check.

(a) "Acceptance" means the drawee's signed agreement to pay a draft as presented. It must be written on the draft and may consist of the drawee's signature alone. Acceptance may be made at any time and becomes effective when notification pursuant to instructions is given or the accepted draft is delivered for the purpose of giving rights on the acceptance to any person.

(b) A draft may be accepted although it has not been signed by the drawer, is otherwise incomplete, is overdue, or has been dishonored.

(c) If a draft is payable at a fixed period after sight and the acceptor fails to date the acceptance, the holder may complete the acceptance by supplying a date in good faith.

(d) "Certified check" means a check accepted by the bank on which it is drawn. Acceptance may be made as stated in subsection (a) or by a writing on the check which indicates that the check is certified. The drawee of a check has no obligation to certify the check, and refusal to certify is not dishonor of the check.

§ 3–410. Acceptance Varying Draft.

(a) If the terms of a drawee's acceptance vary from the terms of the draft as presented, the holder may refuse the acceptance and treat the draft as dishonored. In that case, the drawee may cancel the acceptance.

(b) The terms of a draft are not varied by an acceptance to pay at a particular bank or place in the United States, unless the acceptance states that the draft is to be paid only at that bank or place.

(c) If the holder assents to an acceptance varying the terms of a draft, the obligation of each drawer and indorser that does not expressly assent to the acceptance is discharged.

§ 3–411. Refusal to Pay Cashier's Checks, Teller's Checks, and Certified Checks.

(a) In this section, "obligated bank" means the acceptor of a certified check or the issuer of a cashier's check or teller's check bought from the issuer.

(b) If the obligated bank wrongfully (i) refuses to pay a cashier's check or certified check, (ii) stops payment of a teller's check, or (iii) refuses to pay a dishonored teller's check, the person asserting the right to enforce the check is entitled to compensation for expenses and loss of interest resulting from the nonpayment and may recover consequential damages if the obligated bank refused to pay after receiving notice of particular circumstances giving rise to the damages.

(c) Expenses or consequential damages under subsection (b) are not recoverable if the refusal of the obligated bank to pay occurs because (i) the bank suspends payments, (ii) the obligated bank is asserting a claim or defense of the bank that it has reasonable grounds to believe is available against the person entitled to enforce the instrument, (iii) the obligated bank has a reasonable doubt whether the person demanding payment is the person entitled to enforce the instrument, or (iv) payment is prohibited by law.

§ 3–412. OBLIGATION OF MAKER.

A maker of a note is obliged to pay the note (i) according to its terms at the time it was issued or, if not issued, at the time it first came into possession of a holder, or (ii) if the maker signed an incomplete instrument, according to its terms when completed as stated in Sections 3–115 and 3–407. The obligation is owed to a person entitled to enforce the note or to an indorser that paid the note pursuant to Section 3–415.

§ 3–413. OBLIGATION OF ACCEPTOR.

(a) An acceptor of a draft is obliged to pay the draft (i) according to its terms at the time it was accepted, even though the acceptance states that the draft is payable "as originally drawn" or equivalent terms, (ii) if the acceptance varies the terms of the draft, according to the terms of the draft as varied, or (iii) if the acceptance is of a draft that is an incomplete instrument, according to its terms when completed as stated in Sections 3–115 and 3–407. The obligation is owed to a person entitled to enforce the draft or to the drawer or an indorser that paid the draft pursuant to Section 3–414 or 3–415.

(b) If the certification of a check or other acceptance of a draft states the amount certified or accepted, the obligation of the acceptor is that amount. If (i) the certification or acceptance does not state an amount, (ii) the instrument is subsequently altered by raising its amount, and (iii) the instrument is then negotiated to a holder in due course, the obligation of the acceptor is the amount of the instrument at the time it was negotiated to the holder in due course.

§ 3–414. OBLIGATION OF DRAWER.

(a) If an unaccepted draft is dishonored, the drawer is obliged to pay the draft (i) according to its terms at the time it was issued or, if not issued, at the time it first came into possession of a holder, or (ii) if the drawer signed an incomplete instrument, according to its terms when completed as stated in Sections 3–115 and 3–407. The obligation is owed to a person entitled to enforce the draft or to an indorser that paid the draft pursuant to Section 3–415.

(b) If a draft is accepted by a bank and the acceptor dishonors the draft, the drawer has no obligation to pay the draft because of the dishonor, regardless of when or by whom acceptance was obtained.

(c) If a draft is accepted and the acceptor is not a bank, the obligation of the drawer to pay the draft if the draft is dishonored by the acceptor is the same as the obligation of an indorser stated in Section 3–415(a) and (c).

(d) Words in a draft indicating that the draft is drawn without recourse are effective to disclaim all liability of the drawer to

pay the draft if the draft is not a check or a teller's check, but they are not effective to disclaim the obligation stated in subsection (a) if the draft is a check or a teller's check.

(e) If (i) a check is not presented for payment or given to a depositary bank for collection within 30 days after its date, (ii) the drawee suspends payments after expiration of the 30-day period without paying the check, and (iii) because of the suspension of payments the drawer is deprived of funds maintained with the drawee to cover payment of the check, the drawer to the extent deprived of funds may discharge its obligation to pay the check by assigning to the person entitled to enforce the check the rights of the drawer against the drawee with respect to the funds.

§ 3–415. OBLIGATION OF INDORSER.

(a) Subject to subsections (b), (c) and (d) and to Section 3–419(d), if an instrument is dishonored, an indorser is obliged to pay the amount due on the instrument (i) according to the terms of the instrument at the time it was indorsed, or (ii) if the indorser indorsed an incomplete instrument, according to its terms when completed as stated in Sections 3–115 and 3–407. The obligation of the indorser is owed to a person entitled to enforce the instrument or to a subsequent indorser that paid the instrument pursuant to this section.

(b) If an indorsement states that it is made "without recourse" or otherwise disclaims liability of the indorser, the indorser is not liable under subsection (a) to pay the instrument.

(c) If notice of dishonor of an instrument is required by Section 3–503 and notice of dishonor complying with that section is not given to an indorser, the liability of the indorser under subsection (a) is discharged.

(d) If a draft is accepted by a bank after an indorsement was made and the acceptor dishonors the draft, the indorser is not liable under subsection (a) to pay the instrument.

(e) If an indorser of a check is liable under subsection (a) and the check is not presented for payment, or given to a depositary bank for collection, within 30 days after the day the indorsement was made, the liability of the indorser under subsection (a) is discharged.

§ 3–416. TRANSFER WARRANTIES.

(a) A person that transfers an instrument for consideration warrants to the transferee and, if the transfer is by indorsement, to any subsequent transferee that:

(1) the warrantor is a person entitled to enforce the instrument,

(2) all signatures on the instrument are authentic and authorized,

(3) the instrument has not been altered,

(4) the instrument is not subject to a defense or claim in recoupment stated in Section 3–305(a) of any party that can be asserted against the warrantor, and

(5) the warrantor has no knowledge of any insolvency proceeding commenced with respect to the maker or acceptor or, in the case of an unaccepted draft, the drawer.

(b) A person to whom the warranties under subsection (a) are made and who took the instrument in good faith may recover from the warrantor as damages for breach of warranty an amount equal to the loss suffered as a result of the breach, but not more than the amount of the instrument plus expenses and loss of interest incurred as a result of the breach.

(c) The warranties stated in subsection (a) cannot be disclaimed with respect to checks. Unless notice of a claim for breach of warranty is given to the warrantor within 30 days after the claimant has reason to know of the breach and the identity of the warrantor, the warrantor is discharged to the extent of any loss caused by the delay in giving notice of the claim.

(d) A cause of action for breach of warranty under this section accrues when the claimant has reason to know of the breach.

§ 3–417. PRESENTMENT WARRANTIES.

(a) If an unaccepted draft is presented to the drawee for payment or acceptance and the drawee pays or accepts the draft, (i) the person obtaining payment or acceptance, at the time of presentment, and (ii) a previous transferor of the draft, at the time of transfer, warrant to the drawee making payment or accepting the draft in good faith that:

(1) the warrantor is or was, at the time the warrantor transferred the draft, a person entitled to enforce the draft or authorized to obtain payment or acceptance of the draft on behalf of a person entitled to enforce the draft;

(2) the draft has not been altered; and

(3) the warrantor has no knowledge that the signature of the purported drawer of the draft is unauthorized.

(b) A drawee making payment may recover from any warrantor damages for breach of warranty equal to the amount paid by the drawee less the amount the drawee received or is entitled to receive from the drawer because of payment of the draft. In addition the drawee is entitled to compensation for expenses and loss of interest resulting from the breach. The right of the drawee to recover damages under this subsection is not affected by any failure of the drawee to exercise ordinary care in making payment. If the drawee accepts the draft (i) breach of warranty is a defense to the obligation of the acceptor, and (ii) if the acceptor makes payment with respect to the draft, the acceptor is entitled to recover from any warrantor for breach of warranty the amounts stated in the first two sentences of this subsection.

(c) If a drawee asserts a claim for breach of warranty under subsection (a) based on an unauthorized indorsement of the draft or an alteration of the draft, the warrantor may defend by proving that the indorsement is effective under Section 3–404 or 3–405 or the drawer is precluded under Section 3–406 or 4–406 from asserting against the drawee the unauthorized indorsement or alteration.

(d) This subsection applies if (i) a dishonored draft is presented for payment to the drawer or an indorser or (ii) any other instrument is presented for payment to a party obliged to pay the instrument, and payment is received. The person obtaining payment and a prior transferor of the instrument warrant to the person making payment in good faith that the warrantor is or was, at the time the warrantor transferred the instrument, a person entitled to enforce the instrument or authorized to obtain payment on behalf of a person entitled to enforce the instrument. The person making payment may recover from any warrantor for breach of warranty an amount equal to the amount paid plus expenses and loss of interest resulting from the breach.

(e) The warranties stated in subsections (a) and (d) cannot be disclaimed with respect to checks. Unless notice of a claim for breach of warranty is given to the warrantor within 30 days after the claimant has reason to know of the breach and the identity of the warrantor, the warrantor is discharged to the extent of any loss caused by the delay in giving notice of the claim.

(f) A cause of action for breach of warranty under this section accrues when the claimant has reason to know of the breach.

§ 3–418. PAYMENT OR ACCEPTANCE BY MISTAKE.

(a) Except as provided in subsection (c), if the drawee of a draft pays or accepts the draft and the drawee acted on the mistaken belief that (i) payment of the draft had not been stopped under Section 4–403, (ii) the signature of the purported drawer of the draft was authorized, or (iii) the balance in the drawer's account with the drawee represented available funds, the drawee may recover the amount paid from the person to whom or for whose benefit payment was made or, in the case of acceptance, may revoke the acceptance. Rights of the drawee under this subsection are not affected by failure of the drawee to exercise ordinary care in paying or accepting the draft.

(b) Except as provided in subsection (c), if an instrument has been paid or accepted by mistake and the case is not covered by subsection (a), the person paying or accepting may recover the amount paid or revoke acceptance to the extent allowed by the law governing mistake and restitution.

(c) The remedies provided by subsection (a) or (b) may not be asserted against a person who took the instrument in good faith and for value. This subsection does not limit remedies provided by Section 3–417 for breach of warranty.

§ 3–419. INSTRUMENTS SIGNED FOR ACCOMMODATION.

(a) If an instrument is issued for value given for the benefit of a party to the instrument ("accommodated party") and another party to the instrument ("accommodation party") signs the instrument for the purpose of incurring liability on the instrument without being a direct beneficiary of the value given for the instrument, the instrument is signed by the accommodation party "for accommodation."

(b) An accommodation party may sign the instrument as maker, drawer, acceptor, or indorser and, subject to subsection (d), is obliged to pay the instrument in the capacity in which the accommodation party signs. The obligation of an accommodation party may be enforced notwithstanding any statute of frauds and regardless of whether the accommodation party receives consideration for the accommodation.

(c) A person signing an instrument is presumed to be an accommodation party and there is notice that the instrument is signed for accommodation if the signature is an anomalous indorsement or is accompanied by words indicating that the signer is acting as surety or guarantor with respect to the obligation of another party to the instrument. Except as provided in Section 3–606, the obligation of an accommodation party to pay the instrument is not affected by the fact that the person enforcing the obligation had notice when the instrument was taken by that person that the accommodation party signed the instrument for accommodation.

(d) If the signature of a party to an instrument is accompanied by words indicating unambiguously that the party is guaranteeing collection rather than payment of the obligation of another party to the instrument, the signer is obliged to pay the amount due on the instrument to a person entitled to enforce the instrument only if (i) execution of judgment against the other party has been returned unsatisfied, (ii) the other party is insolvent or in an insolvency proceeding, (iii) the other party cannot be served with process, or (iv) it is otherwise apparent that payment cannot be obtained from the party whose obligation is guaranteed.

(e) An accommodation party that pays the instrument is entitled to reimbursement from the accommodated party and is entitled to enforce the instrument against the accommodated party. An accommodated party that pays the instrument has no right of recourse against, and is not entitled to contribution from, an accommodation party.

§ 3–420. CONVERSION OF INSTRUMENT.

(a) The law applicable to conversion of personal property applies to instruments. An instrument is also converted if the instrument lacks an indorsement necessary for negotiation and it is purchased or taken for collection or the drawee takes the instrument and makes payment to a person not entitled to receive payment. An action for conversion of an instrument may not be brought by (i) the maker, drawer, or acceptor of the instrument or (ii) a payee or indorsee who did not receive delivery of the instrument either directly or through delivery to an agent or a co-payee.

(b) In an action under subsection (a), the measure of liability is presumed to be the amount payable on the instrument, but recovery may not exceed the amount of the plaintiff's interest in the instrument.

(c) A representative, other than a depositary bank, that has in good faith dealt with an instrument or its proceeds on behalf of one who was not the person entitled to enforce the instrument is not liable in conversion to that person beyond the amount of any proceeds that it has not paid out.

PART 5—DISHONOR

§ 3–501. PRESENTMENT.

(a) "Presentment" means a demand (i) to pay an instrument made to the maker, drawee, or acceptor or, in the case of a note or accepted draft payable at a bank, to the bank, or (ii) to accept a draft made to the drawee, by a person entitled to enforce the instrument.

(b) Subject to Article 4, agreement of the parties, clearing house rules and the like,

(1) presentment may be made at the place of payment of the instrument and must be made at the place of payment if the instrument is payable at a bank in the United States; may be made by any commercially reasonable means, including an oral, written, or electronic communication; is effective when the demand for payment or acceptance is received by the person to whom presentment is made; is effective if made to any one of two or more makers, acceptors, drawees or other payors; and

(2) without dishonoring the instrument, the party to whom presentment is made may (i) treat presentment as occurring on the next business day after the day of presentment if the party to whom presentment is made has established a cut-off hour not earlier than 2 p.m. for the receipt and processing of instruments presented for payment or acceptance and presentment is made after the cut-off hour, (ii) require exhibition of the instrument, (iii) require reasonable identification of the person making presentment and evidence of authority to make it if made on behalf of another person, (iv) require a signed receipt on the instrument for any payment made or surrender of the instrument if full payment is made, (v) return the instrument

for lack of a necessary indorsement, or (vi) refuse payment or acceptance for failure of the presentment to comply with the terms of the instrument, an agreement of the parties, or other law or applicable rule.

§ 3–502. DISHONOR.

(a) Dishonor of a note is governed by the following rules:

(1) If the note is payable on demand, the note is dishonored if presentment is duly made and the note is not paid on the day of presentment.

(2) If the note is not payable on demand and is payable at or through a bank or the terms of the note require presentment, the note is dishonored if presentment is duly made and the note is not paid on the day it becomes payable or the day of presentment, whichever is later.

(3) If the note is not payable on demand and subparagraph (2) does not apply, the note is dishonored if it is not paid on the day it becomes payable.

(b) Dishonor of an unaccepted draft other than a documentary draft is governed by the following rules:

(1) If a check is presented for payment otherwise than for immediate payment over the counter, the check is dishonored if the payor bank makes timely return of the check or sends timely notice of dishonor or nonpayment under Section 4–301 or 4–302, or becomes accountable for the amount of the check under Section 4–302.

(2) If the draft is payable on demand and subparagraph (1) does not apply, the draft is dishonored if presentment for payment is duly made and the draft is not paid on the day of presentment.

(3) If the draft is payable on a date stated in the draft, the draft is dishonored if (i) presentment for payment is duly made and payment is not made on the day the draft becomes payable or the day of presentment, whichever is later, or (ii) presentment for acceptance is duly made before the day the draft becomes payable and the draft is not accepted on the day of presentment.

(4) If the draft is payable on elapse of a period of time after sight or acceptance, the draft is dishonored if presentment for acceptance is duly made and the draft is not accepted on the day of presentment.

(c) Dishonor of an unaccepted documentary draft occurs according to the rules stated in subparagraphs (2), (3), and (4) of subsection (b) except that payment or acceptance may be delayed without dishonor until no later than the close of the third business day of the drawee following the day on which payment or acceptance is required by those subparagraphs.

(d) Dishonor of an accepted draft is governed by the following rules:

(1) If the draft is payable on demand, the draft is dishonored if presentment for payment is duly made and the draft is not paid on the day of presentment.

(2) If the draft is not payable on demand, the draft is dishonored if presentment for payment is duly made and payment is not made on the day it becomes payable or the day of presentment, whichever is later.

(e) In any case in which presentment is otherwise required for dishonor under this section and presentment is excused under Section 3–504, dishonor occurs without presentment if the instrument is not duly accepted or paid.

(f) If a draft is dishonored because timely acceptance of the draft was not made and the person entitled to demand acceptance consents to a late acceptance, from the time of acceptance the draft is treated as never having been dishonored.

§ 3–503. NOTICE OF DISHONOR.

(a) The obligation of an indorser stated in Section 3–415(a) and the obligation of a drawer stated in Section 3–414(c) may not be enforced unless (i) the indorser or drawer is given notice of dishonor of the instrument complying with this section or (ii) notice of dishonor is excused under Section 3–504(c).

(b) Notice of dishonor may be given by any person; may be given by any commercially reasonable means including an oral, written, or electronic communication; is sufficient if it reasonably identifies the instrument and indicates that the instrument has been dishonored or has not been paid or accepted. Return of an instrument given to a bank for collection is a sufficient notice of dishonor.

(c) Subject to Section 3–504(d), with respect to an instrument taken for collection by a collecting bank, notice of dishonor must be given (i) by the bank before midnight of the next banking day following the banking day on which the bank receives notice of dishonor of the instrument, and (ii) by any other person within 30 days following the day on which the person receives notice of dishonor. With respect to any other instrument, notice of dishonor must be given within 30 days following the day on which dishonor occurs.

§ 3–504. EXCUSED PRESENTMENT AND NOTICE OF DISHONOR.

(a) Presentment for payment or acceptance of an instrument is excused if (i) the person entitled to present the instrument cannot with reasonable diligence make presentment, (ii) the maker or acceptor has repudiated an obligation to pay the instrument or is dead or in insolvency proceedings, (iii) by the terms of the instrument presentment is not necessary to enforce the obligation of indorsers or the drawer, or (iv) the drawer or indorser whose obligation is being enforced waived presentment or otherwise had no reason to expect or right to require that the instrument be paid or accepted.

(b) Presentment for payment or acceptance of a draft is also excused if the drawer instructed the drawee not to pay or accept the draft or the drawee was not obligated to the drawer to pay the draft.

(c) Notice of dishonor is excused if (i) by the terms of the instrument notice of dishonor is not necessary to enforce the obligation of a party to pay the instrument, or (ii) the party whose obligation is being enforced waived notice of dishonor. A waiver of presentment is also a waiver of notice of dishonor.

(d) Delay in giving notice of dishonor is excused if the delay was caused by circumstances beyond the control of the person giving the notice and the person giving the notice exercised reasonable diligence after the cause of the delay ceased to operate.

§ 3–505. EVIDENCE OF DISHONOR.

(a) The following are admissible as evidence and create a presumption of dishonor and of any notice of dishonor stated:

(1) a document regular in form as provided in subsection (b) which purports to be a protest;

(2) a purported stamp or writing of the drawee, payor bank, or presenting bank on or accompanying the instrument stating that acceptance or payment has been refused unless reasons for the refusal are stated and the reasons are not consistent with dishonor;

(3) a book or record of the drawee, payor bank, or collecting bank, kept in the usual course of business which shows dishonor, even if there is no evidence of who made the entry.

(b) A protest is a certificate of dishonor made by a United States consul or vice consul, or a notary public or other person authorized to administer oaths by the law of the place where dishonor occurs. It may be made upon information satisfactory to that person. The protest must identify the instrument and certify either that presentment has been made or, if not made, the reason why it was not made, and that the instrument has been dishonored by nonacceptance or nonpayment. The protest may also certify that notice of dishonor has been given to some or all parties.

PART 6—DISCHARGE AND PAYMENT

§ 3–601. DISCHARGE AND EFFECT OF DISCHARGE.

(a) The obligation of a party to pay the instrument is discharged as stated in this Article or by an act or agreement with the party which would discharge an obligation to pay money under a simple contract.

(b) Discharge of the obligation of a party is not effective against a person acquiring rights of a holder in due course of the instrument without notice of the discharge.

§ 3–602. PAYMENT.

(a) Subject to subsection (b), an instrument is paid to the extent payment is made (i) by or on behalf of a party obliged to pay the instrument, and (ii) to a person entitled to enforce the instrument. To the extent of the payment, the obligation of the party obliged to pay the instrument is discharged even though payment is made with knowledge of a claim to the instrument under Section 3–306 by another person.

(b) The obligation of a party to pay the instrument is not discharged under subsection (a) if:

(1) a claim to the instrument under Section 3–306 is enforceable against the party receiving payment and (i) payment is made with knowledge by the payor that payment is prohibited by injunction or similar process of a court of competent jurisdiction, or (ii) in the case of an instrument other than a cashier's check, teller's check, or certified check, the party making payment accepted, from the person having a claim to the instrument, indemnity against loss resulting from refusal to pay the person entitled to enforce the instrument, or

(2) the person making payment knows that the instrument is a stolen instrument and pays a person that it knows is in wrongful possession of the instrument.

§ 3–603. TENDER OF PAYMENT.

(a) If tender of payment of an obligation of a party to an instrument is made to a person entitled to enforce the obligation, the effect of tender is governed by principles of law applicable to tender of payment of an obligation under a simple contract.

(b) If tender of payment of an obligation to pay the instrument is made to a person entitled to enforce the instrument and the tender is refused, there is discharge, to the extent of the amount of the tender, of the obligation of an indorser or accommodation party having a right of recourse against the obligor making the tender.

(c) If tender of payment of an amount due on an instrument is made by or on behalf of the obligor to the person entitled to enforce the instrument, the obligation of the obligor to pay interest after the due date on the amount tendered is discharged. If presentment is required with respect to an instrument and the obligor is able and ready to pay on the due date at every place of payment stated in the instrument, the obligor is deemed to have made tender of payment on the due date to the person entitled to enforce the instrument.

§ 3–604. DISCHARGE BY CANCELLATION OR RENUNCIATION.

(a) A person entitled to enforce an instrument may, with or without consideration, discharge the obligation of a party to pay the instrument (i) by an intentional voluntary act such as surrender of the instrument to the party, destruction, mutilation, or cancellation of the instrument, cancellation or striking out of the party's signature, or the addition of words to the instrument indicating discharge, or (ii) by agreeing not to sue or otherwise renouncing rights against the party by a signed writing.

(b) Cancellation or striking out of an indorsement pursuant to subsection (a) does not affect the status and rights of a party derived from the indorsement.

§ 3–605. DISCHARGE OF INDORSERS AND ACCOMMODATION PARTIES.

(a) For the purposes of this section, the term "indorser" includes a drawer having the obligation stated in Section 3–414(c).

(b) Discharge of the obligation of a party to the instrument under Section 3–605 does not discharge the obligation of an indorser or accommodation party having a right of recourse against the discharged party.

(c) If a person entitled to enforce an instrument agrees, with or without consideration, to a material modification of the obligation of a party to the instrument, including an extension of the due date, there is discharge of the obligation of an indorser or accommodation party having a right of recourse against the person whose obligation is modified to the extent the modification causes loss to the indorser or accommodation party with respect to the right of recourse. The indorser or accommodation party is deemed to have suffered loss as a result of the modification equal to the amount of the right of recourse unless the person enforcing the instrument proves that no loss was caused by the modification or that the loss caused by the modification was less than the amount of the right of recourse.

(d) If the obligation of a party to an instrument is secured by an interest in collateral and impairment of the value of the interest is caused by a person entitled to enforce the instrument, there is discharge of the obligation of an indorser or accommodation party having a right of recourse against the obligor to the extent of the impairment. The value of an interest in collateral is impaired to the extent (i) the value of the interest is reduced to an amount less than the amount of the right of recourse of the party asserting discharge, or (ii) the reduction in value of the interest causes an increase in the amount by which the amount of the right of recourse exceeds the value of the interest. The burden of proving impairment is on the party asserting discharge.

(e) If the obligation of a party to an instrument is secured by an interest in collateral not provided by an accommodation party and the value of the interest is impaired by a person entitled to enforce the instrument, the obligation of any party who is jointly and severally liable with respect to the secured obligation is discharged to the extent the impairment causes the party asserting discharge to pay more than that party would have been obliged to pay, taking into account rights of contribution,

if impairment had not occurred. If the party asserting discharge is an accommodation party not entitled to discharge under subsection (d), the party is deemed to have a right to contribution based on joint and several liability rather than a right to reimbursement. The burden of proving impairment is on the party asserting discharge.

(f) Under subsection (d) or (e) causation of impairment includes (i) failure to obtain or maintain perfection or recordation of the interest in collateral, (ii) release of collateral without substitution of collateral of equal value, (iii) failure to perform a duty to preserve the value of collateral owed, under Article 9 or other law, to a debtor or surety or other person secondarily liable, or (iv) failure to comply with applicable law in disposing of collateral.

(g) An accommodation party is not discharged under subsection (c) or (d) unless the person agreeing to the modification or causing the impairment knows of the accommodation or has notice under Section 3–419(c) that the instrument was signed for accommodation. There is no discharge of any party under subsection (c), (d), or (e) if (i) the party asserting discharge consents to the event or conduct that is the basis of the discharge, or (ii) the instrument or a separate agreement of the party provides for waiver of discharge under this section either specifically or by general language indicating that parties to the instrument waive defenses based on suretyship or impairment of collateral.

ARTICLE 4: BANK DEPOSITS AND COLLECTIONS
PART 1—GENERAL PROVISIONS AND DEFINITIONS
§ 4–101. SHORT TITLE.

This Article shall be known and may be cited as Uniform Commercial Code—Bank Deposits and Collections.

§ 4–102. APPLICABILITY.

(1) To the extent that items within this Article are also within the scope of Articles 3 and 8, they are subject to the provisions of those Articles. In the event of conflict the provisions of this Article govern those of Article 3 but the provisions of Article 8 govern those of this Article.

(2) The liability of a bank for action or non-action with respect to any item handled by it for purposes of presentment, payment or collection is governed by the law of the place where the bank is located. In the case of action or non-action by or at a branch or separate office of a bank, its liability is governed by the law of the place where the branch or separate office is located.

§ 4–103. VARIATION BY AGREEMENT; MEASURE OF DAMAGES; CERTAIN ACTION CONSTITUTING ORDINARY CARE.

(1) The effect of the provisions of this Article may be varied by agreement except that no agreement can disclaim a bank's responsibility for its own lack of good faith or failure to exercise ordinary care or can limit the measure of damages for such lack or failure; but the parties may by agreement determine the standards by which such responsibility is to be measured if such standards are not manifestly unreasonable.

(2) Federal Reserve regulations and operating letters, clearing house rules, and the like, have the effect of agreements under subsection (1), whether or not specifically assented to by all parties interested in items handled.

(3) Action or non-action approved by this Article or pursuant to Federal Reserve regulations or operating letters constitutes the

exercise of ordinary care and, in the absence of special instructions, action or non-action consistent with clearing house rules and the like or with a general banking usage not disapproved by this Article, prima facie constitutes the exercise of ordinary care.

(4) The specification or approval of certain procedures by this Article does not constitute disapproval of other procedures which may be reasonable under the circumstances.

(5) The measure of damages for failure to exercise ordinary care in handling an item is the amount of the item reduced by an amount which could not have been realized by the use of ordinary care, and where there is bad faith it includes other damages, if any, suffered by the party as a proximate consequence.

§ 4–104. Definitions and Index of Definitions.

(1) In this Article unless the context otherwise requires

  (a) "Account" means any account with a bank and includes a checking, time, interest or savings account;

  (b) "Afternoon" means the period of a day between noon and midnight;

  (c) "Banking day" means that part of any day on which a bank is open to the public for carrying on substantially all of its banking functions;

  (d) "Clearing house" means any association of banks or other payors regularly clearing items;

  (e) "Customer" means any person having an account with a bank or for whom a bank has agreed to collect items and includes a bank carrying an account with another bank;

  (f) "Documentary draft" means any negotiable or non-negotiable draft with accompanying documents, securities or other papers to be delivered against honor of the draft;

  (g) "Item" means any instrument for the payment of money even though it is not negotiable but does not include money;

  (h) "Midnight deadline" with respect to a bank is midnight on its next banking day following the banking day on which it receives the relevant item or notice or from which the time for taking action commences to run, whichever is later;

  (i) "Properly payable" includes the availability of funds for payment at the time of decision to pay or dishonor;

  (j) "Settle" means to pay in cash, by clearing house settlement, in a charge or credit or by remittance, or otherwise as instructed. A settlement may be either provisional or final;

  (k) "Suspends payments" with respect to a bank means that it has been closed by order of the supervisory authorities, that a public officer has been appointed to take it over or that it ceases or refuses to make payments in the ordinary course of business.

(2) Other definitions applying to this Article and the sections in which they appear are:

  "Collecting bank" Section 4–105.

  "Depositary bank" Section 4–105.

  "Intermediary bank" Section 4–105.

  "Payor bank" Section 4–105.

  "Presenting bank" Section 4–105.

  "Remitting bank" Section 4–105.

(3) The following definitions in other Articles apply to this Article:

  "Acceptance" Section 3–410.

  "Certificate of deposit" Section 3–104.

  "Certification" Section 3–411.

  "Check" Section 3–104.

  "Draft" Section 3–104.

  "Holder in due course" Section 3–302.

  "Notice of dishonor" Section 3–508.

  "Presentment" Section 3–504.

  "Protest" Section 3–509.

  "Secondary party" Section 3–102.

(4) In addition Article 1 contains general definitions and principles of construction and interpretation applicable throughout this Article.

§ 4–105. "Depositary Bank"; "Intermediary Bank"; "Collecting Bank"; "Payor Bank"; "Presenting Bank"; "Remitting Bank".

In this Article unless the context otherwise requires:

  (a) "Depositary bank" means the first bank to which an item is transferred for collection even though it is also the payor bank;

  (b) "Payor bank" means a bank by which an item is payable as drawn or accepted;

  (c) "Intermediary bank" means any bank to which an item is transferred in course of collection except the depositary or payor bank;

  (d) "Collecting bank" means any bank handling the item for collection except the payor bank;

  (e) "Presenting bank" means any bank presenting an item except a payor bank;

  (f) "Remitting bank" means any payor or intermediary bank remitting for an item.

§ 4–106. Separate Office of a Bank.

A branch or separate office of a bank [maintaining its own deposit ledgers] is a separate bank for the purpose of computing the time within which and determining the place at or to which action may be taken or notices or orders shall be given under this Article and under Article 3.

  Note: *The brackets are to make it optional with the several states whether to require a branch to maintain its own deposit ledgers in order to be considered to be a separate bank for certain purposes under Article 4. In some states "maintaining its own deposit ledgers" is a satisfactory test. In others branch banking practices are such that this test would not be suitable.*

§ 4–107. Time of Receipt of Items.

(1) For the purpose of allowing time to process items, prove balances and make the necessary entries on its books to determine its position for the day, a bank may fix an afternoon hour of two p.m. or later as a cut-off hour for the handling of money and items and the making of entries on its books.

(2) Any item or deposit of money received on any day after a cut-off hour so fixed or after the close of the banking day may be treated as being received at the opening of the next banking day.

§ 4–108. Delays.

(1) Unless otherwise instructed, a collecting bank in a good faith effort to secure payment may, in the case of specific items and with or without the approval of any person involved, waive, modify or extend time limits imposed or permitted by this Act for a period not in excess of an additional banking day without discharge of secondary parties and without liability to its transferor or any prior party.

(2) Delay by a collecting bank or payor bank beyond time limits prescribed or permitted by this Act or by instructions is excused if caused by interruption of communication facilities, suspension of payments by another bank, war, emergency

conditions or other circumstances beyond the control of the bank provided it exercises such diligence as the circumstances require.

§ 4–109. PROCESS OF POSTING.

The "process of posting" means the usual procedure followed by a payor bank in determining to pay an item and in recording the payment including one or more of the following or other steps as determined by the bank:
(a) verification of any signature;
(b) ascertaining that sufficient funds are available;
(c) affixing a "paid" or other stamp;
(d) entering a charge or entry to a customer's account;
(e) correcting or reversing an entry or erroneous action with respect to the item.

PART 2—COLLECTION OF ITEMS: DEPOSITARY AND COLLECTING BANKS

§ 4–201. PRESUMPTION AND DURATION OF AGENCY STATUS OF COLLECTING BANKS AND PROVISIONAL STATUS OF CREDITS; APPLICABILITY OF ARTICLE; ITEM INDORSED "PAY ANY BANK".

(1) Unless a contrary intent clearly appears and prior to the time that a settlement given by a collecting bank for an item is or becomes final (subsection (3) of Section 4–211 and Sections 4–212 and 4–213) the bank is an agent or sub-agent of the owner of the item and any settlement given for the item is provisional. This provision applies regardless of the form of indorsement or lack of indorsement and even though credit given for the item is subject to immediate withdrawal as of right or is in fact withdrawn; but the continuance of ownership of an item by its owner and any rights of the owner to proceeds of the item are subject to rights of a collecting bank such as those resulting from outstanding advances on the item and valid rights of set-off. When an item is handled by banks for purposes of presentment, payment and collection, the relevant provisions of this Article apply even though action of parties clearly establishes that a particular bank has purchased the item and is the owner of it.
(2) After an item has been indorsed with the words "pay any bank" or the like, only a bank may acquire the rights of a holder
(a) until the item has been returned to the customer initiating collection; or
(b) until the item has been specially indorsed by a bank to a person who is not a bank.

§ 4–202. RESPONSIBILITY FOR COLLECTION; WHEN ACTION SEASONABLE.

(1) A collecting bank must use ordinary care in
(a) presenting an item or sending it for presentment; and
(b) sending notice of dishonor or non-payment or returning an item other than a documentary draft to the bank's transferor [or directly to the depositary bank under subsection (2) of Section 4–212] *(see note to Section 4–212)* after learning that the item has not been paid or accepted as the case may be; and
(c) settling for an item when the bank receives final settlement; and
(d) making or providing for any necessary protest; and
(e) notifying its transferor of any loss or delay in transit within a reasonable time after discovery thereof.
(2) A collecting bank taking proper action before its midnight deadline following receipt of an item, notice or payment acts

seasonably; taking proper action within a reasonably longer time may be seasonable but the bank has the burden of so establishing.
(3) Subject to subsection (1)(a), a bank is not liable for the insolvency, neglect, misconduct, mistake or default of another bank or person or for loss or destruction of an item in transit or in the possession of others.

§ 4–203. EFFECT OF INSTRUCTIONS.

Subject to the provisions of Article 3 concerning conversion of instruments (Section 3–419) and the provisions of both Article 3 and this Article concerning restrictive indorsements only a collecting bank's transferor can give instructions which affect the bank or constitute notice to it and a collecting bank is not liable to prior parties for any action taken pursuant to such instructions or in accordance with any agreement with its transferor.

§ 4–204. METHODS OF SENDING AND PRESENTING; SENDING DIRECT TO PAYOR BANK.

(1) A collecting bank must send items by reasonably prompt method taking into consideration any relevant instructions, the nature of the item, the number of such items on hand, and the cost of collection involved and the method generally used by it or others to present such items.
(2) A collecting bank may send
(a) any item direct to the payor bank;
(b) any item to any non-bank payor if authorized by its transferor; and
(c) any item other than documentary drafts to any non-bank payor, if authorized by Federal Reserve regulation or operating letter, clearing house rule or the like.
(3) Presentment may be made by a presenting bank at a place where the payor bank has requested that presentment be made.

§ 4–205. SUPPLYING MISSING INDORSEMENT; NO NOTICE FROM PRIOR INDORSEMENT.

(1) A depositary bank which has taken an item for collection may supply any indorsement of the customer which is necessary to title unless the item contains the words "payee's indorsement required" or the like. In the absence of such a requirement a statement placed on the item by the depositary bank to the effect that the item was deposited by a customer or credited to his account is effective as the customer's indorsement.
(2) An intermediary bank, or payor bank which is not a depositary bank, is neither given notice nor otherwise affected by a restrictive indorsement of any person except the bank's immediate transferor.

§ 4–206. TRANSFER BETWEEN BANKS.

Any agreed method which identifies the transferor bank is sufficient for the item's further transfer to another bank.

§ 4–207. WARRANTIES OF CUSTOMER AND COLLECTING BANK ON TRANSFER OR PRESENTMENT OF ITEMS; TIME FOR CLAIMS.

(1) Each customer or collecting bank who obtains payment or acceptance of an item and each prior customer and collecting bank warrants to the payor bank or other payor who in good faith pays or accepts the item that
(a) he has a good title to the item or is authorized to obtain payment or acceptance on behalf of one who has a good title; and
(b) he has no knowledge that the signature of the maker or drawer is unauthorized, except that this warranty is not given by

any customer or collecting bank that is a holder in due course and acts in good faith

> (i) to a maker with respect to the maker's own signature; or
> (ii) to a drawer with respect to the drawer's own signature, whether or not the drawer is also the drawee; or
> (iii) to an acceptor of an item if the holder in due course took the item after the acceptance or obtained the acceptance without knowledge that the drawer's signature was unauthorized; and

(c) the item has not been materially altered, except that this warranty is not given by any customer or collecting bank that is a holder in due course and acts in good faith

> (i) to the maker of a note; or
> (ii) to the drawer of a draft whether or not the drawer is also the drawee; or
> (iii) to the acceptor of an item with respect to an alteration made prior to the acceptance if the holder in due course took the item after the acceptance, even though the acceptance provided "payable as originally drawn" or equivalent terms; or
> (iv) to the acceptor of an item with respect to an alteration made after the acceptance.

(2) Each customer and collecting bank who transfers an item and receives a settlement or other consideration for it warrants to his transferee and to any subsequent collecting bank who takes the item in good faith that

(a) he has a good title to the item or is authorized to obtain payment or acceptance on behalf of one who has a good title and the transfer is otherwise rightful; and
(b) all signatures are genuine or authorized; and
(c) the item has not been materially altered; and
(d) no defense of any party is good against him; and
(e) he has no knowledge of any insolvency proceeding instituted with respect to the maker or acceptor or the drawer of an unaccepted item. In addition each customer and collecting bank so transferring an item and receiving a settlement or other consideration engages that upon dishonor and any necessary notice of dishonor and protest he will take up the item.

(3) The warranties and the engagement to honor set forth in the two preceding subsections arise notwithstanding the absence of indorsement or words of guaranty or warranty in the transfer or presentment and a collecting bank remains liable for their breach despite remittance to its transferor. Damages for breach of such warranties or engagement to honor shall not exceed the consideration received by the customer or collecting bank responsible plus finance charges and expenses related to the item, if any.

(4) Unless a claim for breach of warranty under this section is made within a reasonable time after the person claiming learns of the breach, the person liable is discharged to the extent of any loss caused by the delay in making claim.

§ 4–208. Security Interest of Collecting Bank in Items, Accompanying Documents and Proceeds.

(1) A bank has a security interest in an item and any accompanying documents or the proceeds of either

(a) in case of an item deposited in an account to the extent to which credit given for the item has been withdrawn or applied;
(b) in case of an item for which it has given credit available for withdrawal as of right, to the extent of the credit given whether or not the credit is drawn upon and whether or not there is a right of charge-back; or
(c) if it makes an advance on or against the item.

(2) When credit which has been given for several items received at one time or pursuant to a single agreement is withdrawn or applied in part the security interest remains upon all the items, any accompanying documents or the proceeds of either. For the purpose of this section, credits first given are first withdrawn.

(3) Receipt by a collecting bank of a final settlement for an item is a realization on its security interest in the item, accompanying documents and proceeds. To the extent and so long as the bank does not receive final settlement for the item or give up possession of the item or accompanying documents for purposes other than collection, the security interest continues and is subject to the provisions of Article 9 except that

(a) no security agreement is necessary to make the security interest enforceable (subsection (1)(b) of Section 9–203); and
(b) no filing is required to perfect the security interest; and
(c) the security interest has priority over conflicting perfected security interests in the item, accompanying documents or proceeds.

§ 4–209. When Bank Gives Value for Purposes of Holder in Due Course.

For purposes of determining its status as a holder in due course, the bank has given value to the extent that it has a security interest in an item provided that the bank otherwise complies with the requirements of Section 3–302 on what constitutes a holder in due course.

§ 4–210. Presentment by Notice of Item Not Payable by, Through or at a Bank; Liability of Secondary Parties.

(1) Unless otherwise instructed, a collecting bank may present an item not payable by, through or at a bank by sending to the party to accept or pay a written notice that the bank holds the item for acceptance or payment. The notice must be sent in time to be received on or before the day when presentment is due and the bank must meet any requirement of the party to accept or pay under Section 3–505 by the close of the bank's next banking day after it knows of the requirement.

(2) Where presentment is made by notice and neither honor nor request for compliance with a requirement under Section 3–505 is received by the close of business on the day after maturity or in the case of demand items by the close of business on the third banking day after notice was sent, the presenting bank may treat the item as dishonored and charge any secondary party by sending him notice of the facts.

§ 4–211. Media of Remittance; Provisional and Final Settlement in Remittance Cases.

(1) A collecting bank may take in settlement of an item

(a) a check of the remitting bank or of another bank on any bank except the remitting bank; or
(b) a cashier's check or similar primary obligation of a remitting bank which is a member of or clears through a member of the same clearing house or group as the collecting bank; or
(c) appropriate authority to charge an account of the remitting bank or of another bank with the collecting bank; or
(d) if the item is drawn upon or payable by a person other than a bank, a cashier's check, certified check or other bank check or obligation.

(2) If before its midnight deadline the collecting bank properly dishonors a remittance check or authorization to charge on itself or presents or forwards for collection a remittance instrument

of or on another bank which is of a kind approved by subsection (1) or has not been authorized by it, the collecting bank is not liable to prior parties in the event of the dishonor of such check, instrument or authorization.

(3) A settlement for an item by means of a remittance instrument or authorization to charge is or becomes a final settlement as to both the person making and the person receiving the settlement

(a) if the remittance instrument or authorization to charge is of a kind approved by subsection (1) or has not been authorized by the person receiving the settlement and in either case the person receiving the settlement acts seasonably before its midnight deadline in presenting, forwarding for collection or paying the instrument or authorization,—at the time the remittance instrument or authorization is finally paid by the payor by which it is payable;

(b) if the person receiving the settlement has authorized remittance by a non-bank check or obligation or by a cashier's check or similar primary obligation of or a check upon the payor or other remitting bank which is not of a kind approved by subsection (1)(b),—at the time of the receipt of such remittance check or obligation; or

(c) if in a case not covered by sub-paragraphs (a) or (b) the person receiving the settlement fails to seasonably present, forward for collection, pay or return a remittance instrument or authorization to it to charge before its midnight deadline,—at such midnight deadline.

§ 4–212. Right of Charge-Back or Refund.

(1) If a collecting bank has made provisional settlement with its customer for an item and itself fails by reason of dishonor, suspension of payments by a bank or otherwise to receive a settlement for the item which is or becomes final, the bank may revoke the settlement given by it, charge-back the amount of any credit given for the item to its customer's account or obtain refund from its customer whether or not it is able to return the items if by its midnight deadline or within a longer reasonable time after it learns the facts it returns the item or sends notification of the facts. These rights to revoke, charge-back and obtain refund terminate if and when a settlement for the item received by the bank is or becomes final (subsection (3) of Section 4–211 and subsections (2) and (3) of Section 4–213).

(2) [Within the time and manner prescribed by this section and Section 4–301, an intermediary or payor bank, as the case may be, may return an unpaid item directly to the depositary bank and may send for collection a draft on the depositary bank and obtain reimbursement. In such case, if the depositary bank has received provisional settlement for the item, it must reimburse the bank drawing the draft and any provisional credits for the item between banks shall become and remain final.]

Note: *Direct returns is recognized as an innovation that is not yet established bank practice, and therefore, Paragraph 2 has been bracketed. Some lawyers have doubts whether it should be included in legislation or left to development by agreement.*

(3) A depositary bank which is also the payor may charge-back the amount of an item to its customer's account or obtain refund in accordance with the section governing return of an item received by a payor bank for credit on its books (Section 4–301).

(4) The right to charge-back is not affected by

(a) prior use of the credit given for the item; or

(b) failure by any bank to exercise ordinary care with respect to the item but any bank so failing remains liable.

(5) A failure to charge-back or claim refund does not affect other rights of the bank against the customer or any other party.

(6) If credit is given in dollars as the equivalent of the value of an item payable in a foreign currency the dollar amount of any charge-back or refund shall be calculated on the basis of the buying sight rate for the foreign currency prevailing on the day when the person entitled to the charge-back or refund learns that it will not receive payment in ordinary course.

§ 4–213. Final Payment of Item by Payor Bank; When Provisional Debits and Credits Become Final; When Certain Credits Become Available for Withdrawal.

(1) An item is finally paid by a payor bank when the bank has done any of the following, whichever happens first:

(a) paid the item in cash; or

(b) settled for the item without reserving a right to revoke the settlement and without having such right under statute, clearing house rule or agreement; or

(c) completed the process of posting the item to the indicated account of the drawer, maker or other person to be charged therewith; or

(d) made a provisional settlement for the item and failed to revoke the settlement in the time and manner permitted by statute, clearing house rule or agreement. Upon a final payment under subparagraphs (b), (c), or (d) the payor bank shall be accountable for the amount of the item.

(2) If provisional settlement for an item between the presenting and payor banks is made through a clearing house or by debits or credits in an account between them, then to the extent that provisional debits or credits for the item are entered in accounts between the presenting and payor banks or between the presenting and successive prior collecting banks seriatim, they become final upon final payment of the item by the payor bank.

(3) If a collecting bank receives a settlement for an item which is or becomes final (subsection (3) of Section 4–211, subsection (2) of Section 4–213) the bank is accountable to its customer for the amount of the item and any provisional credit given for the item in an account with its customer becomes final.

(4) Subject to any right of the bank to apply the credit to an obligation of the customer, credit given by a bank for an item in an account with its customer becomes available for withdrawal as of right

(a) in any case where the bank has received a provisional settlement for the item,—when such settlement becomes final and the bank has had a reasonable time to learn that the settlement is final;

(b) in any case where the bank is both a depositary bank and a payor bank and the item is finally paid—at the opening of the bank's second banking day following receipt of the item.

(5) A deposit of money in a bank is final when made but, subject to any right of the bank to apply the deposit to an obligation of the customer, the deposit becomes available for withdrawal as of right at the opening of the bank's next banking day following receipt of the deposit.

§ 4–214. Insolvency and Preference.

(1) Any item in or coming into the possession of a payor or collecting bank which suspends payment and which item is not finally paid shall be returned by the receiver, trustee or agent

in charge of the closed bank to the presenting bank or the closed bank's customer.

(2) If a payor bank finally pays an item and suspends payments without making a settlement for the item with its customer or the presenting bank which settlement is or becomes final, the owner of the item has a preferred claim against the payor bank.

(3) If a payor bank gives or a collecting bank gives or receives a provisional settlement for an item and thereafter suspends payments, the suspension does not prevent or interfere with the settlement becoming final if such finality occurs automatically upon the lapse of certain time or the happening of certain events (subsection (3) of Section 4–211, subsections (1)(d), (2) and (3) of Section 4–213).

(4) If a collecting bank receives from subsequent parties settlement for an item which settlement is or becomes final and suspends payments without making a settlement for the item with its customer which is or becomes final, the owner of the item has a preferred claim against such collecting bank.

PART 3—COLLECTION OF ITEMS: PAYOR BANKS

§ 4–301. DEFERRED POSTING; RECOVERY OF PAYMENT BY RETURN OF ITEMS; TIME OF DISHONOR.

(1) Where an authorized settlement for a demand item (other than a documentary draft) received by a payor bank otherwise than for immediate payment over the counter has been made before midnight of the banking day of receipt the payor bank may revoke the settlement and recover any payment if before it has made final payment (subsection (1) of Section 4–213) and before its midnight deadline it

    (a) returns the item; or
    (b) sends written notice of dishonor or nonpayment if the item is held for protest or is otherwise unavailable for return.

(2) If a demand item is received by a payor bank for credit on its books it may return such item or send notice of dishonor and may revoke any credit given or recover the amount thereof withdrawn by its customer, if it acts within the time limit and in the manner specified in the preceding subsection.

(3) Unless previous notice of dishonor has been sent an item is dishonored at the time when for purposes of dishonor it is returned or notice sent in accordance with this section.

(4) An item is returned:

    (a) as to an item received through a clearing house when it is delivered to the presenting or last collecting bank or to the clearing house or is sent or delivered in accordance with its rules; or
    (b) in all other cases, when it is sent or delivered to the bank's customer or transferor or pursuant to his instructions.

§ 4–302. PAYOR BANK'S RESPONSIBILITY FOR LATE RETURN OF ITEM.

In the absence of a valid defense such as breach of a presentment warranty (subsection (1) of Section 4–207), settlement effected or the like, if an item is presented on and received by a payor bank the bank is accountable for the amount of

(a) a demand item other than a documentary draft whether properly payable or not if the bank, in any case where it is not also the depositary bank, retains the item beyond midnight of the banking day of receipt without settling for it or, regardless of whether it is also the depositary bank, does not pay or return the item or send notice of dishonor until after its midnight deadline; or

(b) any other properly payable item unless within the time allowed for acceptance or payment of that item the bank either accepts or pays the item or returns it and accompanying documents.

§ 4–303. WHEN ITEMS SUBJECT TO NOTICE, STOP-ORDER, LEGAL PROCESS OR SETOFF; ORDER IN WHICH ITEMS MAY BE CHARGED OR CERTIFIED.

(1) Any knowledge, notice or stop-order received by, legal process served upon or setoff exercised by a payor bank, whether or not effective under other rules of law to terminate, suspend or modify the bank's right or duty to pay an item or to charge its customer's account for the item, comes too late to so terminate, suspend or modify such right or duty if the knowledge, notice, stop-order or legal process is received or served and a reasonable time for the bank to act thereon expires or the setoff is exercised after the bank has done any of the following:

    (a) accepted or certified the item;
    (b) paid the item in cash;
    (c) settled for the item without reserving a right to revoke the settlement and without having such right under statute, clearing house rule or agreement;
    (d) completed the process of posting the item to the indicated account of the drawer, maker, or other person to be charged therewith or otherwise has evidenced by examination of such indicated account and by action its decision to pay the item; or
    (e) become accountable for the amount of the item under subsection (1)(d) of Section 4–213 and Section 4–302 dealing with the payor bank's responsibility for late return of items.

(2) Subject to the provisions of subsection (1) items may be accepted, paid, certified or charged to the indicated account of its customer in any order convenient to the bank.

PART 4—RELATIONSHIP BETWEEN PAYOR BANK AND ITS CUSTOMER

§ 4–401. WHEN BANK MAY CHARGE CUSTOMER'S ACCOUNT.

(1) As against its customer, a bank may charge against his account any item which is otherwise properly payable from that account even though the charge creates an overdraft.

(2) A bank which in good faith makes payment to a holder may charge the indicated account of its customer according to

    (a) the original tenor of his altered item; or
    (b) the tenor of his completed item, even though the bank knows the item has been completed unless the bank has notice that the completion was improper.

§ 4–402. BANK'S LIABILITY TO CUSTOMER FOR WRONGFUL DISHONOR.

A payor bank is liable to its customer for damages proximately caused by the wrongful dishonor of an item. When the dishonor occurs through mistake liability is limited to actual damages proved. If so proximately caused and proved damages may include damages for an arrest or prosecution of the customer or other consequential damages. Whether any consequential damages are proximately caused by the wrongful dishonor is a question of fact to be determined in each case.

§ 4–403. CUSTOMER'S RIGHT TO STOP PAYMENT; BURDEN OF PROOF OF LOSS.

(1) A customer may by order to his bank stop payment of any item payable for his account but the order must be received at such time and in such manner as to afford the bank a reasonable opportunity to act on it prior to any action by the bank with respect to the item described in Section 4–303.

(2) An oral order is binding upon the bank only for fourteen calendar days unless confirmed in writing within that period. A written order is effective for only six months unless renewed in writing.

(3) The burden of establishing the fact and amount of loss resulting from the payment of an item contrary to a binding stop payment order is on the customer.

§ 4–404. BANK NOT OBLIGATED TO PAY CHECK MORE THAN SIX MONTHS OLD.

A bank is under no obligation to a customer having a checking account to pay a check, other than a certified check, which is presented more than six months after its date, but it may charge its customer's account for a payment made thereafter in good faith.

§ 4–405. DEATH OR INCOMPETENCE OF CUSTOMER.

(1) A payor or collecting bank's authority to accept, pay or collect an item or to account for proceeds of its collection if otherwise effective is not rendered ineffective by incompetence of a customer of either bank existing at the time the item is issued or its collection is undertaken if the bank does not know of an adjudication of incompetence. Neither death nor incompetence of a customer revokes such authority to accept, pay, collect or account until the bank knows of the fact of death or of an adjudication of incompetence and has reasonable opportunity to act on it.

(2) Even with knowledge a bank may for ten days after the date of death pay or certify checks drawn on or prior to that date unless ordered to stop payment by a person claiming an interest in the account.

§ 4–406. CUSTOMER'S DUTY TO DISCOVER AND REPORT UNAUTHORIZED SIGNATURE OR ALTERATION.

(1) When a bank sends to its customer a statement of account accompanied by items paid in good faith in support of the debit entries or holds the statement and items pursuant to a request or instructions of its customer or otherwise in a reasonable manner makes the statement and items available to the customer, the customer must exercise reasonable care and promptness to examine the statement and items to discover his unauthorized signature or any alteration on an item and must notify the bank promptly after discovery thereof.

(2) If the bank establishes that the customer failed with respect to an item to comply with the duties imposed on the customer by subsection (1) the customer is precluded from asserting against the bank
   (a) his unauthorized signature or any alteration on the item if the bank also establishes that it suffered a loss by reason of such failure; and
   (b) an unauthorized signature or alteration by the same wrongdoer on any other item paid in good faith by the bank after the first item and statement was available to the customer for a reasonable period not exceeding fourteen calendar days and before the bank receives notification from the customer of any such unauthorized signature or alteration.

(3) The preclusion under subsection (2) does not apply if the customer establishes lack of ordinary care on the part of the bank in paying the item(s).

(4) Without regard to care or lack of care of either the customer or the bank a customer who does not within one year from the time the statement and items are made available to the customer (subsection (1)) discover and report his unauthorized signature or any alteration on the face or back of the item or does not within three years from that time discover and report any unauthorized indorsement is precluded from asserting against the bank such unauthorized signature or indorsement or such alteration.

(5) If under this section a payor bank has a valid defense against a claim of a customer upon or resulting from payment of an item and waives or fails upon request to assert the defense the bank may not assert against any collecting bank or other prior party presenting or transferring the item a claim based upon the unauthorized signature or alteration giving rise to the customer's claim.

§ 4–407. PAYOR BANK'S RIGHT TO SUBROGATION ON IMPROPER PAYMENT.

If a payor bank has paid an item over the stop payment order of the drawer or maker or otherwise under circumstances giving a basis for objection by the drawer or maker, to prevent unjust enrichment and only to the extent necessary to prevent loss to the bank by reason of its payment of the item, the payor bank shall be subrogated to the rights
   (a) of any holder in due course on the item against the drawer or maker; and
   (b) of the payee or any other holder of the item against the drawer or maker either on the item or under the transaction out of which the item arose; and
   (c) of the drawer or maker against the payee or any other holder of the item with respect to the transaction out of which the item arose.

PART 5—COLLECTION OF DOCUMENTARY DRAFTS

§ 4–501. HANDLING OF DOCUMENTARY DRAFTS; DUTY TO SEND FOR PRESENTMENT AND TO NOTIFY CUSTOMER OF DISHONOR.

A bank which takes a documentary draft for collection must present or send the draft and accompanying documents for presentment and upon learning that the draft has not been paid or accepted in due course must seasonably notify its customer of such fact even though it may have discounted or bought the draft or extended credit available for withdrawal as of right.

§ 4–502. PRESENTMENT OF "ON ARRIVAL" DRAFTS.

When a draft or the relevant instructions require presentment "on arrival", "when goods arrive" or the like, the collecting bank need not present until in its judgment a reasonable time for arrival of the goods has expired. Refusal to pay or accept because the goods have not arrived is not dishonor; the bank must notify its transferor of such refusal but need not present the draft again until it is instructed to do so or learns of the arrival of the goods.

§ 4–503. RESPONSIBILITY OF PRESENTING BANK FOR DOCUMENTS AND GOODS; REPORT OF REASONS FOR DISHONOR; REFEREE IN CASE OF NEED.

Unless otherwise instructed and except as provided in Article 5 a bank presenting a documentary draft
   (a) must deliver the documents to the drawee on acceptance of the draft if it is payable more than three days after presentment; otherwise, only on payment; and
   (b) upon dishonor, either in the case of presentment for acceptance or presentment for payment, may seek and follow instructions from any referee in case of need designated in the draft or if the presenting bank does not choose to utilize his services it must use diligence and good faith to ascertain the reason for dishonor, must notify its transferor of the dishonor and of the results of its effort to ascertain the reasons therefor and must request instructions.

But the presenting bank is under no obligation with respect to goods represented by the documents except to follow any reasonable instructions seasonably received; it has a right to reimbursement for any expense incurred in following instructions and to prepayment of or indemnity for such expenses.

§ 4–504. Privilege of Presenting Bank to Deal With Goods; Security Interest for Expenses.

(1) A presenting bank which, following the dishonor of a documentary draft, has seasonably requested instructions but does not receive them within a reasonable time may store, sell, or otherwise deal with the goods in any reasonable manner.

(2) For its reasonable expenses incurred by action under subsection (1) the presenting bank has a lien upon the goods or their proceeds, which may be foreclosed in the same manner as an unpaid seller's lien.

Revised Article 9: Secured Transactions

Part 1—General Provisions

§ 9–101. Short Title.

This article may be cited as Uniform Commercial Code—Secured Transactions.

§ 9–102. Definitions and Index of Definitions.

(a) [Article 9 definitions.] In this article:

(1) "Accession" means goods that are physically united with other goods in such a manner that the identity of the original goods is not lost.

(2) "Account", except as used in "account for", means a right to payment of a monetary obligation, whether or not earned by performance, (i) for property that has been or is to be sold, leased, licensed, assigned, or otherwise disposed of, (ii) for services rendered or to be rendered, (iii) for a policy of insurance issued or to be issued, (iv) for a secondary obligation incurred or to be incurred, (v) for energy provided or to be provided, (vi) for the use or hire of a vessel under a charter or other contract, (vii) arising out of the use of a credit or charge card or information contained on or for use with the card, or (viii) as winnings in a lottery or other game of chance operated or sponsored by a State, governmental unit of a State, or person licensed or authorized to operate the game by a State or governmental unit of a State. The term includes health-care-insurance receivables. The term does not include (i) rights to payment evidenced by chattel paper or an instrument, (ii) commercial tort claims, (iii) deposit accounts, (iv) investment property, (v) letter-of-credit rights or letters of credit, or (vi) rights to payment for money or funds advanced or sold, other than rights arising out of the use of a credit or charge card or information contained on or for use with the card.

(3) "Account debtor" means a person obligated on an account, chattel paper, or general intangible. The term does not include persons obligated to pay a negotiable instrument, even if the instrument constitutes part of chattel paper.

(4) "Accounting", except as used in "accounting for", means a record:

(A) authenticated by a secured party;

(B) indicating the aggregate unpaid secured obligations as of a date not more than 35 days earlier or 35 days later than the date of the record; and

(C) identifying the components of the obligations in reasonable detail.

(5) "Agricultural lien" means an interest, other than a security interest, in farm products:

(A) which secures payment or performance of an obligation for:

(i) goods or services furnished in connection with a debtor's farming operation; or

(ii) rent on real property leased by a debtor in connection with its farming operation;

(B) which is created by statute in favor of a person that:

(i) in the ordinary course of its business furnished goods or services to a debtor in connection with a debtor's farming operation; or

(ii) leased real property to a debtor in connection with the debtor's farming operation; and

(C) whose effectiveness does not depend on the person's possession of the personal property.

(6) "As-extracted collateral" means:

(A) oil, gas, or other minerals that are subject to a security interest that:

(i) is created by a debtor having an interest in the minerals before extraction; and

(ii) attaches to the minerals as extracted; or

(B) accounts arising out of the sale at the wellhead or minehead of oil, gas, or other minerals in which the debtor had an interest before extraction.

(7) "Authenticate" means:

(A) to sign; or

(B) to execute or otherwise adopt a symbol, or encrypt or similarly process a record in whole or in part, with the present intent of the authenticating person to identify the person and adopt or accept a record.

(8) "Bank" means an organization that is engaged in the business of banking. The term includes savings banks, savings and loan associations, credit unions, and trust companies.

(9) "Cash proceeds" means proceeds that are money, checks, deposit accounts, or the like.

(10) "Certificate of title" means a certificate of title with respect to which a statute provides for the security interest in question to be indicated on the certificate as a condition or result of the security interest's obtaining priority over the rights of a lien creditor with respect to the collateral.

(11) "Chattel paper" means a record or records that evidence both a monetary obligation and a security interest in specific goods, a security interest in specific goods and software used in the goods, a security interest in specific goods and license of software used in the goods, a lease of specific goods, or a lease of specific goods and license of software used in the goods. In this paragraph, "monetary obligation" means a monetary obligation secured by the goods or owed under a lease of the goods and includes a monetary obligation with respect to software used in the goods. The term does not include (i) charters or other contracts involving the use or hire of a vessel or (ii) records that evidence a right to payment arising out of the use of a credit or charge card or information contained on or for use with the card. If a transaction is evidenced by records that include an instrument or series of instruments, the group of records taken together constitutes chattel paper.

(12) "Collateral" means the property subject to a security interest or agricultural lien. The term includes:

(A) proceeds to which a security interest attaches;

(B) accounts, chattel paper, payment intangibles, and promissory notes that have been sold; and

(C) goods that are the subject of a consignment.

(13) "Commercial tort claim" means a claim arising in tort with respect to which:

(A) the claimant is an organization; or

(B) the claimant is an individual and the claim:

(i) arose in the course of the claimant's business or profession; and

(ii) does not include damages arising out of personal injury to or the death of an individual.

(14) "Commodity account" means an account maintained by a commodity intermediary in which a commodity contract is carried for a commodity customer.

(15) "Commodity contract" means a commodity futures contract, an option on a commodity futures contract, a commodity option, or another contract if the contract or option is:

(A) traded on or subject to the rules of a board of trade that has been designated as a contract market for such a contract pursuant to federal commodities laws; or

(B) traded on a foreign commodity board of trade, exchange, or market, and is carried on the books of a commodity intermediary for a commodity customer.

(16) "Commodity customer" means a person for which a commodity intermediary carries a commodity contract on its books.

(17) "Commodity intermediary" means a person that:

(A) is registered as a futures commission merchant under federal commodities law; or

(B) in the ordinary course of its business provides clearance or settlement services for a board of trade that has been designated as a contract market pursuant to federal commodities law.

(18) "Communicate" means:

(A) to send a written or other tangible record;

(B) to transmit a record by any means agreed upon by the persons sending and receiving the record; or

(C) in the case of transmission of a record to or by a filing office, to transmit a record by any means prescribed by filing-office rule.

(19) "Consignee" means a merchant to which goods are delivered in a consignment.

(20) "Consignment" means a transaction, regardless of its form, in which a person delivers goods to a merchant for the purpose of sale and:

(A) the merchant:

(i) deals in goods of that kind under a name other than the name of the person making delivery;

(ii) is not an auctioneer; and

(iii) is not generally known by its creditors to be substantially engaged in selling the goods of others;

(B) with respect to each delivery, the aggregate value of the goods is $1,000 or more at the time of delivery;

(C) the goods are not consumer goods immediately before delivery; and

(D) the transaction does not create a security interest that secures an obligation.

(21) "Consignor" means a person that delivers goods to a consignee in a consignment.

(22) "Consumer debtor" means a debtor in a consumer transaction.

(23) "Consumer goods" means goods that are used or bought for use primarily for personal, family, or household purposes.

(24) "Consumer-goods transaction" means a consumer transaction in which:

(A) an individual incurs an obligation primarily for personal, family, or household purposes; and

(B) a security interest in consumer goods secures the obligation.

(25) "Consumer obligor" means an obligor who is an individual and who incurred the obligation as part of a transaction entered into primarily for personal, family, or household purposes.

(26) "Consumer transaction" means a transaction in which (i) an individual incurs an obligation primarily for personal, family, or household purposes, (ii) a security interest secures the obligation, and (iii) the collateral is held or acquired primarily for personal, family, or household purposes. The term includes consumer-goods transactions.

(27) "Continuation statement" means an amendment of a financing statement which:

(A) identifies, by its file number, the initial financing statement to which it relates; and

(B) indicates that it is a continuation statement for, or that it is filed to continue the effectiveness of, the identified financing statement.

(28) "Debtor" means:

(A) a person having an interest, other than a security interest or other lien, in the collateral, whether or not the person is an obligor;

(B) a seller of accounts, chattel paper, payment intangibles, or promissory notes; or

(C) a consignee.

(29) "Deposit account" means a demand, time, savings, passbook, or similar account maintained with a bank. The term does not include investment property or accounts evidenced by an instrument.

(30) "Document" means a document of title or a receipt of the type described in Section 7–201(2).

(31) "Electronic chattel paper" means chattel paper evidenced by a record or records consisting of information stored in an electronic medium.

(32) "Encumbrance" means a right, other than an ownership interest, in real property. The term includes mortgages and other liens on real property.

(33) "Equipment" means goods other than inventory, farm products, or consumer goods.

(34) "Farm products" means goods, other than standing timber, with respect to which the debtor is engaged in a farming operation and which are:

(A) crops grown, growing, or to be grown, including:

(i) crops produced on trees, vines, and bushes; and

(ii) aquatic goods produced in aquacultural operations;

(B) livestock, born or unborn, including aquatic goods produced in aquacultural operations;

(C) supplies used or produced in a farming operation; or

(D) products of crops or livestock in their unmanufactured states.

(35) "Farming operation" means raising, cultivating, propagating, fattening, grazing, or any other farming, livestock, or aquacultural operation.

(36) "File number" means the number assigned to an initial financing statement pursuant to Section 9–519(a).

(37) "Filing office" means an office designated in Section 9–501 as the place to file a financing statement.

(38) "Filing–office rule" means a rule adopted pursuant to Section 9–526.

(39) "Financing statement" means a record or records composed of an initial financing statement and any filed record relating to the initial financing statement.

(40) "Fixture filing" means the filing of a financing statement covering goods that are or are to become fixtures and satisfying Section 9–502(a) and (b). The term includes the filing of a financing statement covering goods of a transmitting utility which are or are to become fixtures.

(41) "Fixtures" means goods that have become so related to particular real property that an interest in them arises under real property law.

(42) "General intangible" means any personal property, including things in action, other than accounts, chattel paper, commercial tort claims, deposit accounts, documents, goods, instruments, investment property, letter-of-credit rights, letters of credit, money, and oil, gas, or other minerals before extraction. The term includes payment intangibles and software.

(43) "Good faith" means honesty in fact and the observance of reasonable commercial standards of fair dealing.

(44) "Goods" means all things that are movable when a security interest attaches. The term includes (i) fixtures, (ii) standing timber that is to be cut and removed under a conveyance or contract for sale, (iii) the unborn young of animals, (iv) crops grown, growing, or to be grown, even if the crops are produced on trees, vines, or bushes, and (v) manufactured homes. The term also includes a computer program embedded in goods and any supporting information provided in connection with a transaction relating to the program if (i) the program is associated with the goods in such a manner that it customarily is considered part of the goods, or (ii) by becoming the owner of the goods, a person acquires a right to use the program in connection with the goods. The term does not include a computer program embedded in goods that consist solely of the medium in which the program is embedded. The term also does not include accounts, chattel paper, commercial tort claims, deposit accounts, documents, general intangibles, instruments, investment property, letter-of-credit rights, letters of credit, money, or oil, gas, or other minerals before extraction.

(45) "Governmental unit" means a subdivision, agency, department, county, parish, municipality, or other unit of the government of the United States, a State, or a foreign country. The term includes an organization having a separate corporate existence if the organization is eligible to issue debt on which interest is exempt from income taxation under the laws of the United States.

(46) "Health-care-insurance receivable" means an interest in or claim under a policy of insurance which is a right to payment of a monetary obligation for health-care goods or services provided.

(47) "Instrument" means a negotiable instrument or any other writing that evidences a right to the payment of a monetary obligation, is not itself a security agreement or lease, and is of a type that in ordinary course of business is transferred by delivery with any necessary indorsement or assignment. The term does not include (i) investment property, (ii) letters of credit, or (iii) writings that evidence a right to payment arising out of the use of a credit or charge card or information contained on or for use with the card.

(48) "Inventory" means goods, other than farm products, which:

(A) are leased by a person as lessor;

(B) are held by a person for sale or lease or to be furnished under a contract of service;

(C) are furnished by a person under a contract of service; or

(D) consist of raw materials, work in process, or materials used or consumed in a business.

(49) "Investment property" means a security, whether certificated or uncertificated, security entitlement, securities account, commodity contract, or commodity account.

(50) "Jurisdiction of organization", with respect to a registered organization, means the jurisdiction under whose law the organization is organized.

(51) "Letter-of-credit right" means a right to payment or performance under a letter of credit, whether or not the beneficiary has demanded or is at the time entitled to demand payment or performance. The term does not include the right of a beneficiary to demand payment or performance under a letter of credit.

(52) "Lien creditor" means:

(A) a creditor that has acquired a lien on the property involved by attachment, levy, or the like;

(B) an assignee for benefit of creditors from the time of assignment;

(C) a trustee in bankruptcy from the date of the filing of the petition; or

(D) a receiver in equity from the time of appointment.

(53) "Manufactured home" means a structure, transportable in one or more sections, which, in the traveling mode, is eight body feet or more in width or 40 body feet or more in length, or, when erected on site, is 320 or more square feet, and which is built on a permanent chassis and designed to be used as a dwelling with or without a permanent foundation when connected to the required utilities, and includes the plumbing, heating, air-conditioning, and electrical systems contained therein. The term includes any structure that meets all of the requirements of this paragraph except the size requirements and with respect to which the manufacturer voluntarily files a certification required by the United States Secretary of Housing and Urban Development and complies with the standards established under Title 42 of the United States Code.

(54) "Manufactured-home transaction" means a secured transaction:

(A) that creates a purchase-money security interest in a manufactured home, other than a manufactured home held as inventory; or

(B) in which a manufactured home, other than a manufactured home held as inventory, is the primary collateral.

(55) "Mortgage" means a consensual interest in real property, including fixtures, which secures payment or performance of an obligation.

(56) "New debtor" means a person that becomes bound as debtor under Section 9–203(d) by a security agreement previously entered into by another person.

(57) "New value" means (i) money, (ii) money's worth in property, services, or new credit, or (iii) release by a transferee of an interest in property previously transferred to the transferee. The term does not include an obligation substituted for another obligation.

(58) "Noncash proceeds" means proceeds other than cash proceeds.

(59) "Obligor" means a person that, with respect to an obligation secured by a security interest in or an agricultural lien on the collateral, (i) owes payment or other performance of the obligation, (ii) has provided property other than the collateral to secure payment or other performance of the obligation, or (iii) is otherwise accountable in whole or in part for payment or other performance of the obligation. The term does not include issuers or nominated persons under a letter of credit.

(60) "Original debtor", except as used in Section 9–310(c), means a person that, as debtor, entered into a security agreement to which a new debtor has become bound under Section 9–203(d).

(61) "Payment intangible" means a general intangible under which the account debtor's principal obligation is a monetary obligation.

(62) "Person related to", with respect to an individual, means:

(A) the spouse of the individual;

(B) a brother, brother-in-law, sister, or sister-in-law of the individual;

(C) an ancestor or lineal descendant of the individual or the individual's spouse; or

(D) any other relative, by blood or marriage, of the individual or the individual's spouse who shares the same home with the individual.

(63) "Person related to", with respect to an organization, means:

(A) a person directly or indirectly controlling, controlled by, or under common control with the organization;

(B) an officer or director of, or a person performing similar functions with respect to, the organization;

(C) an officer or director of, or a person performing similar functions with respect to, a person described in subparagraph (A);

(D) the spouse of an individual described in subparagraph (A), (B), or (C); or

(E) an individual who is related by blood or marriage to an individual described in subparagraph (A), (B), (C), or (D) and shares the same home with the individual.

(64) "Proceeds", except as used in Section 9–609(b), means the following property:

(A) whatever is acquired upon the sale, lease, license, exchange, or other disposition of collateral;

(B) whatever is collected on, or distributed on account of, collateral;

(C) rights arising out of collateral;

(D) to the extent of the value of collateral, claims arising out of the loss, nonconformity, or interference with the use of, defects or infringement of rights in, or damage to, the collateral; or

(E) to the extent of the value of collateral and to the extent payable to the debtor or the secured party, insurance payable by reason of the loss or nonconformity of, defects or infringement of rights in, or damage to, the collateral.

(65) "Promissory note" means an instrument that evidences a promise to pay a monetary obligation, does not evidence an order to pay, and does not contain an acknowledgment by a bank that the bank has received for deposit a sum of money or funds.

(66) "Proposal" means a record authenticated by a secured party which includes the terms on which the secured party is willing to accept collateral in full or partial satisfaction of the obligation it secures pursuant to Sections 9–620, 9–621, and 9–622.

(67) "Public-finance transaction" means a secured transaction in connection with which:

(A) debt securities are issued;

(B) all or a portion of the securities issued have an initial stated maturity of at least 20 years; and

(C) the debtor, obligor, secured party, account debtor or other person obligated on collateral, assignor or assignee of a secured obligation, or assignor or assignee of a security interest is a State or a governmental unit of a State.

(68) "Pursuant to commitment", with respect to an advance made or other value given by a secured party, means pursuant to the secured party's obligation, whether or not a subsequent event of default or other event not within the secured party's control has relieved or may relieve the secured party from its obligation.

(69) "Record", except as used in "for record", "of record", "record or legal title", and "record owner", means information that is inscribed on a tangible medium or which is stored in an electronic or other medium and is retrievable in perceivable form.

(70) "Registered organization" means an organization organized solely under the law of a single State or the United States and as to which the State or the United States must maintain a public record showing the organization to have been organized.

(71) "Secondary obligor" means an obligor to the extent that:

(A) the obligor's obligation is secondary; or

(B) the obligor has a right of recourse with respect to an obligation secured by collateral against the debtor, another obligor, or property of either.

(72) "Secured party" means:

(A) a person in whose favor a security interest is created or provided for under a security agreement, whether or not any obligation to be secured is outstanding;

(B) a person that holds an agricultural lien;

(C) a consignor;

(D) a person to which accounts, chattel paper, payment intangibles, or promissory notes have been sold;

(E) a trustee, indenture trustee, agent, collateral agent, or other representative in whose favor a security interest or agricultural lien is created or provided for; or

(F) a person that holds a security interest arising under Section 2–401, 2–505, 2–711(3), 2A–508(5), 4–210, or 5–118.

(73) "Security agreement" means an agreement that creates or provides for a security interest.

(74) "Send", in connection with a record or notification, means:

(A) to deposit in the mail, deliver for transmission, or transmit by any other usual means of communication, with postage or cost of transmission provided for, addressed to any address reasonable under the circumstances; or

(B) to cause the record or notification to be received within the time that it would have been received if properly sent under subparagraph (A).

(75) "Software" means a computer program and any supporting information provided in connection with a transaction

relating to the program. The term does not include a computer program that is included in the definition of goods.

(76) "State" means a State of the United States, the District of Columbia, Puerto Rico, the United States Virgin Islands, or any territory or insular possession subject to the jurisdiction of the United States.

(77) "Supporting obligation" means a letter-of-credit right or secondary obligation that supports the payment or performance of an account, chattel paper, a document, a general intangible, an instrument, or investment property.

(78) "Tangible chattel paper" means chattel paper evidenced by a record or records consisting of information that is inscribed on a tangible medium.

(79) "Termination statement" means an amendment of a financing statement which:

(A) identifies, by its file number, the initial financing statement to which it relates; and

(B) indicates either that it is a termination statement or that the identified financing statement is no longer effective.

(80) "Transmitting utility" means a person primarily engaged in the business of:

(A) operating a railroad, subway, street railway, or trolley bus;

(B) transmitting communications electrically, electromagnetically, or by light;

(C) transmitting goods by pipeline or sewer; or

(D) transmitting or producing and transmitting electricity, steam, gas, or water.

(b) [**Definitions in other articles.**] The following definitions in other articles apply to this article:

"Applicant" Section 5–102.
"Beneficiary" Section 5–102.
"Broker" Section 8–102.
"Certificated security" Section 8–102.
"Check" Section 3–104.
"Clearing corporation" Section 8–102.
"Contract for sale" Section 2–106.
"Customer" Section 4–104.
"Entitlement holder" Section 8–102.
"Financial asset" Section 8–102.
"Holder in due course" Section 3–302.
"Issuer" (with respect to a letter of credit or letter-of-credit right) Section 5–102.
"Issuer" (with respect to a security) Section 8–201.
"Lease" Section 2A–103.
"Lease agreement" Section 2A–103.
"Lease contract" Section 2A–103.
"Leasehold interest" Section 2A–103.
"Lessee" Section 2A–103.
"Lessee in ordinary course of business" Section 2A–103.
"Lessor" Section 2A–103.
"Lessor's residual interest" Section 2A–103.
"Letter of credit" Section 5–102.
"Merchant" Section 2–104.
"Negotiable instrument" Section 3–104.
"Nominated person" Section 5–102.
"Note" Section 3–104.
"Proceeds of a letter of credit" Section 5–114.
"Prove" Section 3–103.
"Sale" Section 2–106.

"Securities account" Section 8–501.
"Securities intermediary" Section 8–102.
"Security" Section 8–102.
"Security certificate" Section 8–102.
"Security entitlement" Section 8–102.
"Uncertificated security" Section 8–102.

(c) [**Article 1 definitions and principles.**] Article 1 contains general definitions and principles of construction and interpretation applicable throughout this article.

§ 9–103. PURCHASE-MONEY SECURITY INTEREST; APPLICATION OF PAYMENTS; BURDEN OF ESTABLISHING.

(a) [**Definitions.**] In this section:

(1) "purchase-money collateral" means goods or software that secures a purchase-money obligation incurred with respect to that collateral; and

(2) "purchase-money obligation" means an obligation of an obligor incurred as all or part of the price of the collateral or for value given to enable the debtor to acquire rights in or the use of the collateral if the value is in fact so used.

(b) [**Purchase-money security interest in goods.**] A security interest in goods is a purchase-money security interest:

(1) to the extent that the goods are purchase-money collateral with respect to that security interest;

(2) if the security interest is in inventory that is or was purchase-money collateral, also to the extent that the security interest secures a purchase-money obligation incurred with respect to other inventory in which the secured party holds or held a purchase-money security interest; and

(3) also to the extent that the security interest secures a purchase-money obligation incurred with respect to software in which the secured party holds or held a purchase-money security interest.

(c) [**Purchase-money security interest in software.**] A security interest in software is a purchase-money security interest to the extent that the security interest also secures a purchase-money obligation incurred with respect to goods in which the secured party holds or held a purchase-money security interest if:

(1) the debtor acquired its interest in the software in an integrated transaction in which it acquired an interest in the goods; and

(2) the debtor acquired its interest in the software for the principal purpose of using the software in the goods.

(d) [**Consignor's inventory purchase-money security interest.**] The security interest of a consignor in goods that are the subject of a consignment is a purchase-money security interest in inventory.

(e) [**Application of payment in non-consumer-goods transaction.**] In a transaction other than a consumer-goods transaction, if the extent to which a security interest is a purchase-money security interest depends on the application of a payment to a particular obligation, the payment must be applied:

(1) in accordance with any reasonable method of application to which the parties agree;

(2) in the absence of the parties' agreement to a reasonable method, in accordance with any intention of the obligor manifested at or before the time of payment; or

(3) in the absence of an agreement to a reasonable method and a timely manifestation of the obligor's intention, in the following order:

(A) to obligations that are not secured; and

(B) if more than one obligation is secured, to obligations secured by purchase-money security interests in the order in which those obligations were incurred.

(f) [No loss of status of purchase-money security interest in non-consumer-goods transaction.] In a transaction other than a consumer-goods transaction, a purchase-money security interest does not lose its status as such, even if:

(1) the purchase-money collateral also secures an obligation that is not a purchase-money obligation;

(2) collateral that is not purchase-money collateral also secures the purchase-money obligation; or

(3) the purchase-money obligation has been renewed, refinanced, consolidated, or restructured.

(g) [Burden of proof in non-consumer-goods transaction.] In a transaction other than a consumer-goods transaction, a secured party claiming a purchase-money security interest has the burden of establishing the extent to which the security interest is a purchase-money security interest.

(h) [Non-consumer-goods transactions; no inference.] The limitation of the rules in subsections (e), (f), and (g) to transactions other than consumer-goods transactions is intended to leave to the court the determination of the proper rules in consumer-goods transactions. The court may not infer from that limitation the nature of the proper rule in consumer-goods transactions and may continue to apply established approaches.

§ 9-104. Control of Deposit Account.

(a) [Requirements for control.] A secured party has control of a deposit account if:

(1) the secured party is the bank with which the deposit account is maintained;

(2) the debtor, secured party, and bank have agreed in an authenticated record that the bank will comply with instructions originated by the secured party directing disposition of the funds in the deposit account without further consent by the debtor; or

(3) the secured party becomes the bank's customer with respect to the deposit account.

(b) [Debtor's right to direct disposition.] A secured party that has satisfied subsection (a) has control, even if the debtor retains the right to direct the disposition of funds from the deposit account.

§ 9-105. Control of Electronic Chattel Paper.

A secured party has control of electronic chattel paper if the record or records comprising the chattel paper are created, stored, and assigned in such a manner that:

(1) a single authoritative copy of the record or records exists which is unique, identifiable and, except as otherwise provided in paragraphs (4), (5), and (6), unalterable;

(2) the authoritative copy identifies the secured party as the assignee of the record or records;

(3) the authoritative copy is communicated to and maintained by the secured party or its designated custodian;

(4) copies or revisions that add or change an identified assignee of the authoritative copy can be made only with the participation of the secured party;

(5) each copy of the authoritative copy and any copy of a copy is readily identifiable as a copy that is not the authoritative copy; and

(6) any revision of the authoritative copy is readily identifiable as an authorized or unauthorized revision.

§ 9-106. Control of Investment Property.

(a) [Control under Section 8-106.] A person has control of a certificated security, uncertificated security, or security entitlement as provided in Section 8-106.

(b) [Control of commodity contract.] A secured party has control of a commodity contract if:

(1) the secured party is the commodity intermediary with which the commodity contract is carried; or

(2) the commodity customer, secured party, and commodity intermediary have agreed that the commodity intermediary will apply any value distributed on account of the commodity contract as directed by the secured party without further consent by the commodity customer.

(c) [Effect of control of securities account or commodity account.] A secured party having control of all security entitlements or commodity contracts carried in a securities account or commodity account has control over the securities account or commodity account.

§ 9-107. Control of Letter-of-Credit Right.

A secured party has control of a letter-of-credit right to the extent of any right to payment or performance by the issuer or any nominated person if the issuer or nominated person has consented to an assignment of proceeds of the letter of credit under Section 5-114(c) or otherwise applicable law or practice.

§ 9-108. Sufficiency of Description.

(a) [Sufficiency of description.] Except as otherwise provided in subsections (c), (d), and (e), a description of personal or real property is sufficient, whether or not it is specific, if it reasonably identifies what is described.

(b) [Examples of reasonable identification.] Except as otherwise provided in subsection (d), a description of collateral reasonably identifies the collateral if it identifies the collateral by:

(1) specific listing;

(2) category;

(3) except as otherwise provided in subsection (e), a type of collateral defined in [the Uniform Commercial Code];

(4) quantity;

(5) computational or allocational formula or procedure; or

(6) except as otherwise provided in subsection (c), any other method, if the identity of the collateral is objectively determinable.

(c) [Supergeneric description not sufficient.] A description of collateral as "all the debtor's assets" or "all the debtor's personal property" or using words of similar import does not reasonably identify the collateral.

(d) [Investment property.] Except as otherwise provided in subsection (e), a description of a security entitlement, securities account, or commodity account is sufficient if it describes:

(1) the collateral by those terms or as investment property; or

(2) the underlying financial asset or commodity contract.

(e) [When description by type insufficient.] A description only by type of collateral defined in [the Uniform Commercial Code] is an insufficient description of:

(1) a commercial tort claim; or

(2) in a consumer transaction, consumer goods, a security entitlement, a securities account, or a commodity account.

§ 9–109. Scope.

(a) **[General scope of article.]** Except as otherwise provided in subsections (c) and (d), this article applies to:

(1) a transaction, regardless of its form, that creates a security interest in personal property or fixtures by contract;

(2) an agricultural lien;

(3) a sale of accounts, chattel paper, payment intangibles, or promissory notes;

(4) a consignment;

(5) a security interest arising under Section 2–401, 2–505, 2–711(3), or 2A–508(5), as provided in Section 9–110; and

(6) a security interest arising under Section 4–210 or 5–118.

(b) **[Security interest in secured obligation.]** The application of this article to a security interest in a secured obligation is not affected by the fact that the obligation is itself secured by a transaction or interest to which this article does not apply.

(c) **[Extent to which article does not apply.]** This article does not apply to the extent that:

(1) a statute, regulation, or treaty of the United States preempts this article;

(2) another statute of this State expressly governs the creation, perfection, priority, or enforcement of a security interest created by this State or a governmental unit of this State;

(3) a statute of another State, a foreign country, or a governmental unit of another State or a foreign country, other than a statute generally applicable to security interests, expressly governs creation, perfection, priority, or enforcement of a security interest created by the State, country, or governmental unit; or

(4) the rights of a transferee beneficiary or nominated person under a letter of credit are independent and superior under Section 5–114.

(d) **[Inapplicability of article.]** This article does not apply to:

(1) a landlord's lien, other than an agricultural lien;

(2) a lien, other than an agricultural lien, given by statute or other rule of law for services or materials, but Section 9–333 applies with respect to priority of the lien;

(3) an assignment of a claim for wages, salary, or other compensation of an employee;

(4) a sale of accounts, chattel paper, payment intangibles, or promissory notes as part of a sale of the business out of which they arose;

(5) an assignment of accounts, chattel paper, payment intangibles, or promissory notes which is for the purpose of collection only;

(6) an assignment of a right to payment under a contract to an assignee that is also obligated to perform under the contract;

(7) an assignment of a single account, payment intangible, or promissory note to an assignee in full or partial satisfaction of a preexisting indebtedness;

(8) a transfer of an interest in or an assignment of a claim under a policy of insurance, other than an assignment by or to a health-care provider of a health-care-insurance receivable and any subsequent assignment of the right to payment, but Sections 9–315 and 9–322 apply with respect to proceeds and priorities in proceeds;

(9) an assignment of a right represented by a judgment, other than a judgment taken on a right to payment that was collateral;

(10) a right of recoupment or set-off, but:

(A) Section 9–340 applies with respect to the effectiveness of rights of recoupment or set-off against deposit accounts; and

(B) Section 9–404 applies with respect to defenses or claims of an account debtor;

(11) the creation or transfer of an interest in or lien on real property, including a lease or rents thereunder, except to the extent that provision is made for:

(A) liens on real property in Sections 9–203 and 9–308;

(B) fixtures in Section 9–334;

(C) fixture filings in Sections 9–501, 9–502, 9–512, 9–516, and 9–519; and

(D) security agreements covering personal and real property in Section 9–604;

(12) an assignment of a claim arising in tort, other than a commercial tort claim, but Sections 9–315 and 9–322 apply with respect to proceeds and priorities in proceeds; or

(13) an assignment of a deposit account in a consumer transaction, but Sections 9–315 and 9–322 apply with respect to proceeds and priorities in proceeds.

§ 9–110. Security Interests Arising under Article 2 or 2A.

A security interest arising under Section 2–401, 2–505, 2–711(3), or 2A–508(5) is subject to this article. However, until the debtor obtains possession of the goods:

(1) the security interest is enforceable, even if Section 9–203(b)(3) has not been satisfied;

(2) filing is not required to perfect the security interest;

(3) the rights of the secured party after default by the debtor are governed by Article 2 or 2A; and

(4) the security interest has priority over a conflicting security interest created by the debtor.

PART 2—EFFECTIVENESS OF SECURITY AGREEMENT; ATTACHMENT OF SECURITY INTEREST; RIGHTS OF PARTIES TO SECURITY AGREEMENT

§ 9–201. General Effectiveness of Security Agreement.

(a) **[General effectiveness.]** Except as otherwise provided in [the Uniform Commercial Code], a security agreement is effective according to its terms between the parties, against purchasers of the collateral, and against creditors.

(b) **[Applicable consumer laws and other law.]** A transaction subject to this article is subject to any applicable rule of law which establishes a different rule for consumers and [insert reference to (i) any other statute or regulation that regulates the rates, charges, agreements, and practices for loans, credit sales, or other extensions of credit and (ii) any consumer-protection statute or regulation].

(c) **[Other applicable law controls.]** In case of conflict between this article and a rule of law, statute, or regulation described in subsection (b), the rule of law, statute, or regulation controls. Failure to comply with a statute or regulation described in subsection (b) has only the effect the statute or regulation specifies.

(d) **[Further deference to other applicable law.]** This article does not:

(1) validate any rate, charge, agreement, or practice that violates a rule of law, statute, or regulation described in subsection (b); or

(2) extend the application of the rule of law, statute, or regulation to a transaction not otherwise subject to it.

§ 9–203. Attachment and Enforceability of Security Interest; Proceeds; Supporting Obligations; Formal Requisites.

(a) **[Attachment.]** A security interest attaches to collateral when it becomes enforceable against the debtor with respect to the collateral, unless an agreement expressly postpones the time of attachment.

(b) **[Enforceability.]** Except as otherwise provided in subsections (c) through (i), a security interest is enforceable against the debtor and third parties with respect to the collateral only if:

(1) value has been given;

(2) the debtor has rights in the collateral or the power to transfer rights in the collateral to a secured party; and

(3) one of the following conditions is met:

(A) the debtor has authenticated a security agreement that provides a description of the collateral and, if the security interest covers timber to be cut, a description of the land concerned;

(B) the collateral is not a certificated security and is in the possession of the secured party under Section 9–313 pursuant to the debtor's security agreement;

(C) the collateral is a certificated security in registered form and the security certificate has been delivered to the secured party under Section 8–301 pursuant to the debtor's security agreement; or

(D) the collateral is deposit accounts, electronic chattel paper, investment property, or letter-of-credit rights, and the secured party has control under Section 9–104, 9–105, 9–106, or 9–107 pursuant to the debtor's security agreement.

(c) **[Other UCC provisions.]** Subsection (b) is subject to Section 4–210 on the security interest of a collecting bank, Section 5–118 on the security interest of a letter-of-credit issuer or nominated person, Section 9–110 on a security interest arising under Article 2 or 2A, and Section 9–206 on security interests in investment property.

(d) **[When person becomes bound by another person's security agreement.]** A person becomes bound as debtor by a security agreement entered into by another person if, by operation of law other than this article or by contract:

(1) the security agreement becomes effective to create a security interest in the person's property; or

(2) the person becomes generally obligated for the obligations of the other person, including the obligation secured under the security agreement, and acquires or succeeds to all or substantially all of the assets of the other person.

(e) **[Effect of new debtor becoming bound.]** If a new debtor becomes bound as debtor by a security agreement entered into by another person:

(1) the agreement satisfies subsection (b)(3) with respect to existing or after-acquired property of the new debtor to the extent the property is described in the agreement; and

(2) another agreement is not necessary to make a security interest in the property enforceable.

(f) **[Proceeds and supporting obligations.]** The attachment of a security interest in collateral gives the secured party the rights to proceeds provided by Section 9–315 and is also attachment of a security interest in a supporting obligation for the collateral.

(g) **[Lien securing right to payment.]** The attachment of a security interest in a right to payment or performance secured by a security interest or other lien on personal or real property is also attachment of a security interest in the security interest, mortgage, or other lien.

(h) **[Security entitlement carried in securities account.]** The attachment of a security interest in a securities account is also attachment of a security interest in the security entitlements carried in the securities account.

(i) **[Commodity contracts carried in commodity account.]** The attachment of a security interest in a commodity account is also attachment of a security interest in the commodity contracts carried in the commodity account.

§ 9–204. AFTER-ACQUIRED PROPERTY; FUTURE ADVANCES.

(a) **[After-acquired collateral.]** Except as otherwise provided in subsection (b), a security agreement may create or provide for a security interest in after-acquired collateral.

(b) **[When after-acquired property clause not effective.]** A security interest does not attach under a term constituting an after-acquired property clause to:

(1) consumer goods, other than an accession when given as additional security, unless the debtor acquires rights in them within 10 days after the secured party gives value; or

(2) a commercial tort claim.

(c) **[Future advances and other value.]** A security agreement may provide that collateral secures, or that accounts, chattel paper, payment intangibles, or promissory notes are sold in connection with, future advances or other value, whether or not the advances or value are given pursuant to commitment.

§ 9–205. USE OR DISPOSITION OF COLLATERAL PERMISSIBLE.

(a) **[When security interest not invalid or fraudulent.]** A security interest is not invalid or fraudulent against creditors solely because:

(1) the debtor has the right or ability to:

(A) use, commingle, or dispose of all or part of the collateral, including returned or repossessed goods;

(B) collect, compromise, enforce, or otherwise deal with collateral;

(C) accept the return of collateral or make repossessions; or

(D) use, commingle, or dispose of proceeds; or

(2) the secured party fails to require the debtor to account for proceeds or replace collateral.

(b) **[Requirements of possession not relaxed.]** This section does not relax the requirements of possession if attachment, perfection, or enforcement of a security interest depends upon possession of the collateral by the secured party.

PART 3—PERFECTION AND PRIORITY

§ 9–301. LAW GOVERNING PERFECTION AND PRIORITY OF SECURITY INTERESTS.

Except as otherwise provided in Sections 9–303 through 9–306, the following rules determine the law governing perfection, the effect of perfection or nonperfection, and the priority of a security interest in collateral:

(1) Except as otherwise provided in this section, while a debtor is located in a jurisdiction, the local law of that jurisdiction governs perfection, the effect of perfection or nonperfection, and the priority of a security interest in collateral.

(2) While collateral is located in a jurisdiction, the local law of that jurisdiction governs perfection, the effect of perfection or nonperfection, and the priority of a possessory security interest in that collateral.

(3) Except as otherwise provided in paragraph (4), while negotiable documents, goods, instruments, money, or tangible chattel paper is located in a jurisdiction, the local law of that jurisdiction governs:

(A) perfection of a security interest in the goods by filing a fixture filing;

(B) perfection of a security interest in timber to be cut; and

(C) the effect of perfection or nonperfection and the priority of a nonpossessory security interest in the collateral.

(4) The local law of the jurisdiction in which the wellhead or minehead is located governs perfection, the effect of perfection or nonperfection, and the priority of a security interest in as-extracted collateral.

§ 9–302. LAW GOVERNING PERFECTION AND PRIORITY OF AGRICULTURAL LIENS.

While farm products are located in a jurisdiction, the local law of that jurisdiction governs perfection, the effect of perfection or nonperfection, and the priority of an agricultural lien on the farm products.

§ 9–303. LAW GOVERNING PERFECTION AND PRIORITY OF SECURITY INTERESTS IN GOODS COVERED BY A CERTIFICATE OF TITLE.

(a) [**Applicability of section.**] This section applies to goods covered by a certificate of title, even if there is no other relationship between the jurisdiction under whose certificate of title the goods are covered and the goods or the debtor.

(b) [**When goods covered by certificate of title.**] Goods become covered by a certificate of title when a valid application for the certificate of title and the applicable fee are delivered to the appropriate authority. Goods cease to be covered by a certificate of title at the earlier of the time the certificate of title ceases to be effective under the law of the issuing jurisdiction or the time the goods become covered subsequently by a certificate of title issued by another jurisdiction.

(c) [**Applicable law.**] The local law of the jurisdiction under whose certificate of title the goods are covered governs perfection, the effect of perfection or nonperfection, and the priority of a security interest in goods covered by a certificate of title from the time the goods become covered by the certificate of title until the goods cease to be covered by the certificate of title.

§ 9–307. LOCATION OF DEBTOR.

(a) [**"Place of business."**] In this section, "place of business" means a place where a debtor conducts its affairs.

(b) [**Debtor's location: general rules.**] Except as otherwise provided in this section, the following rules determine a debtor's location:

(1) A debtor who is an individual is located at the individual's principal residence.

(2) A debtor that is an organization and has only one place of business is located at its place of business.

(3) A debtor that is an organization and has more than one place of business is located at its chief executive office.

(c) [**Limitation of applicability of subsection (b).**] Subsection (b) applies only if a debtor's residence, place of business, or chief executive office, as applicable, is located in a jurisdiction whose law generally requires information concerning the existence of a nonpossessory security interest to be made generally available in a filing, recording, or registration system as a condition or result of the security interest's obtaining priority over the rights of a lien creditor with respect to the collateral. If subsection (b) does not apply, the debtor is located in the District of Columbia.

(d) [**Continuation of location: cessation of existence, etc.**] A person that ceases to exist, have a residence, or have a place of business continues to be located in the jurisdiction specified by subsections (b) and (c).

(e) [**Location of registered organization organized under State law.**] A registered organization that is organized under the law of a State is located in that State.

(f) [**Location of registered organization organized under federal law; bank branches and agencies.**] Except as otherwise provided in subsection (i), a registered organization that is organized under the law of the United States and a branch or agency of a bank that is not organized under the law of the United States or a State are located:

(1) in the State that the law of the United States designates, if the law designates a State of location;

(2) in the State that the registered organization, branch, or agency designates, if the law of the United States authorizes the registered organization, branch, or agency to designate its State of location; or

(3) in the District of Columbia, if neither paragraph (1) nor paragraph (2) applies.

(g) [**Continuation of location: change in status of registered organization.**] A registered organization continues to be located in the jurisdiction specified by subsection (e) or (f) notwithstanding:

(1) the suspension, revocation, forfeiture, or lapse of the registered organization's status as such in its jurisdiction of organization; or

(2) the dissolution, winding up, or cancellation of the existence of the registered organization.

(h) [**Location of United States.**] The United States is located in the District of Columbia.

(i) [**Location of foreign bank branch or agency if licensed in only one state.**] A branch or agency of a bank that is not organized under the law of the United States or a State is located in the State in which the branch or agency is licensed, if all branches and agencies of the bank are licensed in only one State.

(j) [**Location of foreign air carrier.**] A foreign air carrier under the Federal Aviation Act of 1958, as amended, is located at the designated office of the agent upon which service of process may be made on behalf of the carrier.

(k) [**Section applies only to this part.**] This section applies only for purposes of this part.

§ 9–308. WHEN SECURITY INTEREST OR AGRICULTURAL LIEN IS PERFECTED; CONTINUITY OF PERFECTION.

(a) [**Perfection of security interest.**] Except as otherwise provided in this section and Section 9–309, a security interest is perfected if it has attached and all of the applicable requirements for perfection in Sections 9–310 through 9–316 have been satisfied. A security interest is perfected when it attaches if the applicable requirements are satisfied before the security interest attaches.

(b) [**Perfection of agricultural lien.**] An agricultural lien is perfected if it has become effective and all of the applicable requirements for perfection in Section 9–310 have been satisfied. An agricultural lien is perfected when it becomes effective if the applicable requirements are satisfied before the agricultural lien becomes effective.

(c) [**Continuous perfection; perfection by different methods.**] A security interest or agricultural lien is perfected continuously if it is originally perfected by one method under this article and is later perfected by another method under this article, without an intermediate period when it was unperfected.

(d) **[Supporting obligation.]** Perfection of a security interest in collateral also perfects a security interest in a supporting obligation for the collateral.

(e) **[Lien securing right to payment.]** Perfection of a security interest in a right to payment or performance also perfects a security interest in a security interest, mortgage, or other lien on personal or real property securing the right.

(f) **[Security entitlement carried in securities account.]** Perfection of a security interest in a securities account also perfects a security interest in the security entitlements carried in the securities account.

(g) **[Commodity contract carried in commodity account.]** Perfection of a security interest in a commodity account also perfects a security interest in the commodity contracts carried in the commodity account.

§ 9–309. SECURITY INTEREST PERFECTED UPON ATTACHMENT.
The following security interests are perfected when they attach:

(1) a purchase-money security interest in consumer goods, except as otherwise provided in Section 9–311(b) with respect to consumer goods that are subject to a statute or treaty described in Section 9–311(a);

(2) an assignment of accounts or payment intangibles which does not by itself or in conjunction with other assignments to the same assignee transfer a significant part of the assignor's outstanding accounts or payment intangibles;

(3) a sale of a payment intangible;

(4) a sale of a promissory note;

(5) a security interest created by the assignment of a health-care-insurance receivable to the provider of the health-care goods or services;

(6) a security interest arising under Section 2–401, 2–505, 2–711(3), or 2A–508(5), until the debtor obtains possession of the collateral;

(7) a security interest of a collecting bank arising under Section 4–210;

(8) a security interest of an issuer or nominated person arising under Section 5–118;

(9) a security interest arising in the delivery of a financial asset under Section 9–206(c);

(10) a security interest in investment property created by a broker or securities intermediary;

(11) a security interest in a commodity contract or a commodity account created by a commodity intermediary;

(12) an assignment for the benefit of all creditors of the transferor and subsequent transfers by the assignee thereunder; and

(13) a security interest created by an assignment of a beneficial interest in a decedent's estate.

§ 9–310. WHEN FILING REQUIRED TO PERFECT SECURITY INTEREST OR AGRICULTURAL LIEN; SECURITY INTERESTS AND AGRICULTURAL LIENS TO WHICH FILING PROVISIONS DO NOT APPLY.

(a) **[General rule: perfection by filing.]** Except as otherwise provided in subsection (b) and Section 9–312(b), a financing statement must be filed to perfect all security interests and agricultural liens.

(b) **[Exceptions: filing not necessary.]** The filing of a financing statement is not necessary to perfect a security interest:

(1) that is perfected under Section 9–308(d), (e), (f), or (g);

(2) that is perfected under Section 9–309 when it attaches;

(3) in property subject to a statute, regulation, or treaty described in Section 9–311(a);

(4) in goods in possession of a bailee which is perfected under Section 9–312(d)(1) or (2);

(5) in certificated securities, documents, goods, or instruments which is perfected without filing or possession under Section 9–312(e), (f), or (g);

(6) in collateral in the secured party's possession under Section 9–313;

(7) in a certificated security which is perfected by delivery of the security certificate to the secured party under Section 9–313;

(8) in deposit accounts, electronic chattel paper, investment property, or letter-of-credit rights which is perfected by control under Section 9–314;

(9) in proceeds which is perfected under Section 9–315; or

(10) that is perfected under Section 9–316.

(c) **[Assignment of perfected security interest.]** If a secured party assigns a perfected security interest or agricultural lien, a filing under this article is not required to continue the perfected status of the security interest against creditors of and transferees from the original debtor.

§ 9–311. PERFECTION OF SECURITY INTERESTS IN PROPERTY SUBJECT TO CERTAIN STATUTES, REGULATIONS, AND TREATIES.

(a) **[Security interest subject to other law.]** Except as otherwise provided in subsection (d), the filing of a financing statement is not necessary or effective to perfect a security interest in property subject to:

(1) a statute, regulation, or treaty of the United States whose requirements for a security interest's obtaining priority over the rights of a lien creditor with respect to the property pre-empt Section 9–310(a);

(2) [list any certificate-of-title statute covering automobiles, trailers, mobile homes, boats, farm tractors, or the like, which provides for a security interest to be indicated on the certificate as a condition or result of perfection, and any non-Uniform Commercial Code central filing statute]; or

(3) a certificate-of-title statute of another jurisdiction which provides for a security interest to be indicated on the certificate as a condition or result of the security interest's obtaining priority over the rights of a lien creditor with respect to the property.

(b) **[Compliance with other law.]** Compliance with the requirements of a statute, regulation, or treaty described in subsection (a) for obtaining priority over the rights of a lien creditor is equivalent to the filing of a financing statement under this article. Except as otherwise provided in subsection (d) and Sections 9–313 and 9–316(d) and (e) for goods covered by a certificate of title, a security interest in property subject to a statute, regulation, or treaty described in subsection (a) may be perfected only by compliance with those requirements, and a security interest so perfected remains perfected notwithstanding a change in the use or transfer of possession of the collateral.

(c) **[Duration and renewal of perfection.]** Except as otherwise provided in subsection (d) and Section 9–316(d) and (e), duration and renewal of perfection of a security interest perfected by compliance with the requirements prescribed by a statute, regulation, or treaty described in subsection (a) are governed by the statute, regulation, or treaty. In other respects, the security interest is subject to this article.

(d) **[Inapplicability to certain inventory.]** During any period in which collateral subject to a statute specified in subsection (a)(2) is inventory held for sale or lease by a person or leased by that person as lessor and that person is in the business of selling goods of that kind, this section does not apply to a security interest in that collateral created by that person.

§ 9–312. Perfection of Security Interests in Chattel Paper, Deposit Accounts, Documents, Goods Covered by Documents, Instruments, Investment Property, Letter-of-Credit Rights, and Money; Perfection by Permissive Filing; Temporary Perfection Without Filing or Transfer of Possession.

(a) [**Perfection by filing permitted.**] A security interest in chattel paper, negotiable documents, instruments, or investment property may be perfected by filing.

(b) [**Control or possession of certain collateral.**] Except as otherwise provided in Section 9–315(c) and (d) for proceeds:

(1) a security interest in a deposit account may be perfected only by control under Section 9–314;

(2) except as otherwise provided in Section 9–308(d), a security interest in a letter-of-credit right may be perfected only by control under Section 9–314; and

(3) a security interest in money may be perfected only by the secured party's taking possession under Section 9–313.

(c) [**Goods covered by negotiable document.**] While goods are in the possession of a bailee that has issued a negotiable document covering the goods:

(1) a security interest in the goods may be perfected by perfecting a security interest in the document; and

(2) a security interest perfected in the document has priority over any security interest that becomes perfected in the goods by another method during that time.

(d) [**Goods covered by nonnegotiable document.**] While goods are in the possession of a bailee that has issued a nonnegotiable document covering the goods, a security interest in the goods may be perfected by:

(1) issuance of a document in the name of the secured party;

(2) the bailee's receipt of notification of the secured party's interest; or

(3) filing as to the goods.

(e) [**Temporary perfection: new value.**] A security interest in certificated securities, negotiable documents, or instruments is perfected without filing or the taking of possession for a period of 20 days from the time it attaches to the extent that it arises for new value given under an authenticated security agreement.

(f) [**Temporary perfection: goods or documents made available to debtor.**] A perfected security interest in a negotiable document or goods in possession of a bailee, other than one that has issued a negotiable document for the goods, remains perfected for 20 days without filing if the secured party makes available to the debtor the goods or documents representing the goods for the purpose of:

(1) ultimate sale or exchange; or

(2) loading, unloading, storing, shipping, transshipping, manufacturing, processing, or otherwise dealing with them in a manner preliminary to their sale or exchange.

(g) [**Temporary perfection: delivery of security certificate or instrument to debtor.**] A perfected security interest in a certificated security or instrument remains perfected for 20 days without filing if the secured party delivers the security certificate or instrument to the debtor for the purpose of:

(1) ultimate sale or exchange; or

(2) presentation, collection, enforcement, renewal, or registration of transfer.

(h) [**Expiration of temporary perfection.**] After the 20-day period specified in subsection (e), (f), or (g) expires, perfection depends upon compliance with this article.

§ 9–313. When Possession by or Delivery to Secured Party Perfects Security Interest Without Filing.

(a) [**Perfection by possession or delivery.**] Except as otherwise provided in subsection (b), a secured party may perfect a security interest in negotiable documents, goods, instruments, money, or tangible chattel paper by taking possession of the collateral. A secured party may perfect a security interest in certificated securities by taking delivery of the certificated securities under Section 8–301.

(b) [**Goods covered by certificate of title.**] With respect to goods covered by a certificate of title issued by this State, a secured party may perfect a security interest in the goods by taking possession of the goods only in the circumstances described in Section 9–316(d).

(c) [**Collateral in possession of person other than debtor.**] With respect to collateral other than certificated securities and goods covered by a document, a secured party takes possession of collateral in the possession of a person other than the debtor, the secured party, or a lessee of the collateral from the debtor in the ordinary course of the debtor's business, when:

(1) the person in possession authenticates a record acknowledging that it holds possession of the collateral for the secured party's benefit; or

(2) the person takes possession of the collateral after having authenticated a record acknowledging that it will hold possession of collateral for the secured party's benefit.

(d) [**Time of perfection by possession; continuation of perfection.**] If perfection of a security interest depends upon possession of the collateral by a secured party, perfection occurs no earlier than the time the secured party takes possession and continues only while the secured party retains possession.

(e) [**Time of perfection by delivery; continuation of perfection.**] A security interest in a certificated security in registered form is perfected by delivery when delivery of the certificated security occurs under Section 8–301 and remains perfected by delivery until the debtor obtains possession of the security certificate.

(f) [**Acknowledgment not required.**] A person in possession of collateral is not required to acknowledge that it holds possession for a secured party's benefit.

(g) [**Effectiveness of acknowledgment; no duties or confirmation.**] If a person acknowledges that it holds possession for the secured party's benefit:

(1) the acknowledgment is effective under subsection (c) or Section 8–301(a), even if the acknowledgment violates the rights of a debtor; and

(2) unless the person otherwise agrees or law other than this article otherwise provides, the person does not owe any duty to the secured party and is not required to confirm the acknowledgment to another person.

(h) [**Secured party's delivery to person other than debtor.**] A secured party having possession of collateral does not relinquish possession by delivering the collateral to a person other than the debtor or a lessee of the collateral from the debtor in the ordinary course of the debtor's business if the person was instructed before the delivery or is instructed contemporaneously with the delivery:

(1) to hold possession of the collateral for the secured party's benefit; or

(2) to redeliver the collateral to the secured party.

(i) **[Effect of delivery under subsection (h); no duties or confirmation.]** A secured party does not relinquish possession, even if a delivery under subsection (h) violates the rights of a debtor. A person to which collateral is delivered under subsection (h) does not owe any duty to the secured party and is not required to confirm the delivery to another person unless the person otherwise agrees or law other than this article otherwise provides.

§ 9–314. PERFECTION BY CONTROL.

(a) **[Perfection by control.]** A security interest in investment property, deposit accounts, letter-of-credit rights, or electronic chattel paper may be perfected by control of the collateral under Section 9–104, 9–105, 9–106, or 9–107.

(b) **[Specified collateral: time of perfection by control; continuation of perfection.]** A security interest in deposit accounts, electronic chattel paper, or letter-of-credit rights is perfected by control under Section 9–104, 9–105, or 9–107 when the secured party obtains control and remains perfected by control only while the secured party retains control.

(c) **[Investment property: time of perfection by control; continuation of perfection.]** A security interest in investment property is perfected by control under Section 9–106 from the time the secured party obtains control and remains perfected by control until:

(1) the secured party does not have control; and

(2) one of the following occurs:

(A) if the collateral is a certificated security, the debtor has or acquires possession of the security certificate;

(B) if the collateral is an uncertificated security, the issuer has registered or registers the debtor as the registered owner; or

(C) if the collateral is a security entitlement, the debtor is or becomes the entitlement holder.

§ 9–315. SECURED PARTY'S RIGHTS ON DISPOSITION OF COLLATERAL AND IN PROCEEDS.

(a) **[Disposition of collateral: continuation of security interest or agricultural lien; proceeds.]** Except as otherwise provided in this article and in Section 2–403(2):

(1) a security interest or agricultural lien continues in collateral notwithstanding sale, lease, license, exchange, or other disposition thereof unless the secured party authorized the disposition free of the security interest or agricultural lien; and

(2) a security interest attaches to any identifiable proceeds of collateral.

(b) **[When commingled proceeds identifiable.]** Proceeds that are commingled with other property are identifiable proceeds:

(1) if the proceeds are goods, to the extent provided by Section 9–336; and

(2) if the proceeds are not goods, to the extent that the secured party identifies the proceeds by a method of tracing, including application of equitable principles, that is permitted under law other than this article with respect to commingled property of the type involved.

(c) **[Perfection of security interest in proceeds.]** A security interest in proceeds is a perfected security interest if the security interest in the original collateral was perfected.

(d) **[Continuation of perfection.]** A perfected security interest in proceeds becomes unperfected on the 21st day after the security interest attaches to the proceeds unless:

(1) the following conditions are satisfied:

(A) a filed financing statement covers the original collateral;

(B) the proceeds are collateral in which a security interest may be perfected by filing in the office in which the financing statement has been filed; and

(C) the proceeds are not acquired with cash proceeds;

(2) the proceeds are identifiable cash proceeds; or

(3) the security interest in the proceeds is perfected other than under subsection (c) when the security interest attaches to the proceeds or within 20 days thereafter.

(e) **[When perfected security interest in proceeds becomes unperfected.]** If a filed financing statement covers the original collateral, a security interest in proceeds which remains perfected under subsection (d)(1) becomes unperfected at the later of:

(1) when the effectiveness of the filed financing statement lapses under Section 9–515 or is terminated under Section 9–513; or

(2) the 21st day after the security interest attaches to the proceeds.

§ 9–316. CONTINUED PERFECTION OF SECURITY INTEREST FOLLOWING CHANGE IN GOVERNING LAW.

(a) **[General rule: effect on perfection of change in governing law.]** A security interest perfected pursuant to the law of the jurisdiction designated in Section 9–301(1) or 9–305(c) remains perfected until the earliest of:

(1) the time perfection would have ceased under the law of that jurisdiction;

(2) the expiration of four months after a change of the debtor's location to another jurisdiction; or

(3) the expiration of one year after a transfer of collateral to a person that thereby becomes a debtor and is located in another jurisdiction.

(b) **[Security interest perfected or unperfected under law of new jurisdiction.]** If a security interest described in subsection (a) becomes perfected under the law of the other jurisdiction before the earliest time or event described in that subsection, it remains perfected thereafter. If the security interest does not become perfected under the law of the other jurisdiction before the earliest time or event, it becomes unperfected and is deemed never to have been perfected as against a purchaser of the collateral for value.

(c) **[Possessory security interest in collateral moved to new jurisdiction.]** A possessory security interest in collateral, other than goods covered by a certificate of title and as-extracted collateral consisting of goods, remains continuously perfected if:

(1) the collateral is located in one jurisdiction and subject to a security interest perfected under the law of that jurisdiction;

(2) thereafter the collateral is brought into another jurisdiction; and

(3) upon entry into the other jurisdiction, the security interest is perfected under the law of the other jurisdiction.

(d) **[Goods covered by certificate of title from this state.]** Except as otherwise provided in subsection (e), a security interest in goods covered by a certificate of title which is perfected by any method under the law of another jurisdiction when the goods become covered by a certificate of title from this State remains perfected until the security interest would have become unperfected under the law of the other jurisdiction had the goods not become so covered.

(e) **[When subsection (d) security interest becomes unperfected against purchasers.]** A security interest described in subsection (d) becomes unperfected as against a purchaser of the goods for value and is deemed never to have been perfected as against a purchaser of the goods for value if the applicable requirements for perfection under Section 9–311(b) or 9–313 are not satisfied before the earlier of:

(1) the time the security interest would have become unperfected under the law of the other jurisdiction had the goods not become covered by a certificate of title from this State; or

(2) the expiration of four months after the goods had become so covered.

(f) **[Change in jurisdiction of bank, issuer, nominated person, securities intermediary, or commodity intermediary.]** A security interest in deposit accounts, letter-of-credit rights, or investment property which is perfected under the law of the bank's jurisdiction, the issuer's jurisdiction, a nominated person's jurisdiction, the securities intermediary's jurisdiction, or the commodity intermediary's jurisdiction, as applicable, remains perfected until the earlier of:

(1) the time the security interest would have become unperfected under the law of that jurisdiction; or

(2) the expiration of four months after a change of the applicable jurisdiction to another jurisdiction.

(g) **[Subsection (f) security interest perfected or unperfected under law of new jurisdiction.]** If a security interest described in subsection (f) becomes perfected under the law of the other jurisdiction before the earlier of the time or the end of the period described in that subsection, it remains perfected thereafter. If the security interest does not become perfected under the law of the other jurisdiction before the earlier of that time or the end of that period, it becomes unperfected and is deemed never to have been perfected as against a purchaser of the collateral for value.

§ 9–317. Interests That Take Priority over or Take Free of Security Interest or Agricultural Lien.

(a) **[Conflicting security interests and rights of lien creditors.]** A security interest or agricultural lien is subordinate to the rights of:

(1) a person entitled to priority under Section 9–322; and

(2) except as otherwise provided in subsection (e), a person that becomes a lien creditor before the earlier of the time:

(A) the security interest or agricultural lien is perfected; or

(B) one of the conditions specified in Section 9–203(b)(3) is met and a financing statement covering the collateral is filed.

(b) **[Buyers that receive delivery.]** Except as otherwise provided in subsection (e), a buyer, other than a secured party, of tangible chattel paper, documents, goods, instruments, or a security certificate takes free of a security interest or agricultural lien if the buyer gives value and receives delivery of the collateral without knowledge of the security interest or agricultural lien and before it is perfected.

(c) **[Lessees that receive delivery.]** Except as otherwise provided in subsection (e), a lessee of goods takes free of a security interest or agricultural lien if the lessee gives value and receives delivery of the collateral without knowledge of the security interest or agricultural lien and before it is perfected.

(d) **[Licensees and buyers of certain collateral.]** A licensee of a general intangible or a buyer, other than a secured party, of accounts, electronic chattel paper, general intangibles, or investment property other than a certificated security takes free of a security interest if the licensee or buyer gives value without knowledge of the security interest and before it is perfected.

(e) **[Purchase-money security interest.]** Except as otherwise provided in Sections 9–320 and 9–321, if a person files a financing statement with respect to a purchase-money security interest before or within 20 days after the debtor receives delivery of the collateral, the security interest takes priority over the rights of a buyer, lessee, or lien creditor which arise between the time the security interest attaches and the time of filing.

§ 9–320. Buyer of Goods.

(a) **[Buyer in ordinary course of business.]** Except as otherwise provided in subsection (e), a buyer in ordinary course of business, other than a person buying farm products from a person engaged in farming operations, takes free of a security interest created by the buyer's seller, even if the security interest is perfected and the buyer knows of its existence.

(b) **[Buyer of consumer goods.]** Except as otherwise provided in subsection (e), a buyer of goods from a person who used or bought the goods for use primarily for personal, family, or household purposes takes free of a security interest, even if perfected, if the buyer buys:

(1) without knowledge of the security interest;

(2) for value;

(3) primarily for the buyer's personal, family, or household purposes; and

(4) before the filing of a financing statement covering the goods.

(c) **[Effectiveness of filing for subsection (b).]** To the extent that it affects the priority of a security interest over a buyer of goods under subsection (b), the period of effectiveness of a filing made in the jurisdiction in which the seller is located is governed by Section 9–316(a) and (b).

(d) **[Buyer in ordinary course of business at wellhead or minehead.]** A buyer in ordinary course of business buying oil, gas, or other minerals at the wellhead or minehead or after extraction takes free of an interest arising out of an encumbrance.

(e) **[Possessory security interest not affected.]** Subsections (a) and (b) do not affect a security interest in goods in the possession of the secured party under Section 9–313.

§ 9–322. Priorities among Conflicting Security Interests in and Agricultural Liens on Same Collateral.

(a) **[General priority rules.]** Except as otherwise provided in this section, priority among conflicting security interests and agricultural liens in the same collateral is determined according to the following rules:

(1) Conflicting perfected security interests and agricultural liens rank according to priority in time of filing or perfection. Priority dates from the earlier of the time a filing covering the collateral is first made or the security interest or agricultural lien is first perfected, if there is no period thereafter when there is neither filing nor perfection.

(2) A perfected security interest or agricultural lien has priority over a conflicting unperfected security interest or agricultural lien.

(3) The first security interest or agricultural lien to attach or become effective has priority if conflicting security interests and agricultural liens are unperfected.

(b) **[Time of perfection: proceeds and supporting obligations.]** For the purposes of subsection (a)(1):

(1) the time of filing or perfection as to a security interest in collateral is also the time of filing or perfection as to a security interest in proceeds; and

(2) the time of filing or perfection as to a security interest in collateral supported by a supporting obligation is also the time of filing or perfection as to a security interest in the supporting obligation.

(c) **[Special priority rules: proceeds and supporting obligations.]** Except as otherwise provided in subsection (f), a security interest in collateral which qualifies for priority over a conflicting security interest under Section 9–327, 9–328, 9–329, 9–330, or 9–331 also has priority over a conflicting security interest in:

(1) any supporting obligation for the collateral; and

(2) proceeds of the collateral if:

(A) the security interest in proceeds is perfected;

(B) the proceeds are cash proceeds or of the same type as the collateral; and

(C) in the case of proceeds that are proceeds of proceeds, all intervening proceeds are cash proceeds, proceeds of the same type as the collateral, or an account relating to the collateral.

(d) **[First-to-file priority rule for certain collateral.]** Subject to subsection (e) and except as otherwise provided in subsection (f), if a security interest in chattel paper, deposit accounts, negotiable documents, instruments, investment property, or letter-of-credit rights is perfected by a method other than filing, conflicting perfected security interests in proceeds of the collateral rank according to priority in time of filing.

(e) **[Applicability of subsection (d).]** Subsection (d) applies only if the proceeds of the collateral are not cash proceeds, chattel paper, negotiable documents, instruments, investment property, or letter-of-credit rights.

(f) **[Limitations on subsections (a) through (e).]** Subsections (a) through (e) are subject to:

(1) subsection (g) and the other provisions of this part;

(2) Section 4–210 with respect to a security interest of a collecting bank;

(3) Section 5–118 with respect to a security interest of an issuer or nominated person; and

(4) Section 9–110 with respect to a security interest arising under Article 2 or 2A.

(g) **[Priority under agricultural lien statute.]** A perfected agricultural lien on collateral has priority over a conflicting security interest in or agricultural lien on the same collateral if the statute creating the agricultural lien so provides.

§ 9–323. FUTURE ADVANCES.

(a) **[When priority based on time of advance.]** Except as otherwise provided in subsection (c), for purposes of determining the priority of a perfected security interest under Section 9–322(a)(1), perfection of the security interest dates from the time an advance is made to the extent that the security interest secures an advance that:

(1) is made while the security interest is perfected only:

(A) under Section 9–309 when it attaches; or

(B) temporarily under Section 9–312(e), (f), or (g); and

(2) is not made pursuant to a commitment entered into before or while the security interest is perfected by a method other than under Section 9–309 or 9–312(e), (f), or (g).

(b) **[Lien creditor.]** Except as otherwise provided in subsection (c), a security interest is subordinate to the rights of a person that becomes a lien creditor to the extent that the security interest secures an advance made more than 45 days after the person becomes a lien creditor unless the advance is made:

(1) without knowledge of the lien; or

(2) pursuant to a commitment entered into without knowledge of the lien.

(c) **[Buyer of receivables.]** Subsections (a) and (b) do not apply to a security interest held by a secured party that is a buyer of accounts, chattel paper, payment intangibles, or promissory notes or a consignor.

(d) **[Buyer of goods.]** Except as otherwise provided in subsection (e), a buyer of goods other than a buyer in ordinary course of business takes free of a security interest to the extent that it secures advances made after the earlier of:

(1) the time the secured party acquires knowledge of the buyer's purchase; or

(2) 45 days after the purchase.

(e) **[Advances made pursuant to commitment: priority of buyer of goods.]** Subsection (d) does not apply if the advance is made pursuant to a commitment entered into without knowledge of the buyer's purchase and before the expiration of the 45-day period.

(f) **[Lessee of goods.]** Except as otherwise provided in subsection (g), a lessee of goods, other than a lessee in ordinary course of business, takes the leasehold interest free of a security interest to the extent that it secures advances made after the earlier of:

(1) the time the secured party acquires knowledge of the lease; or

(2) 45 days after the lease contract becomes enforceable.

(g) **[Advances made pursuant to commitment: priority of lessee of goods.]** Subsection (f) does not apply if the advance is made pursuant to a commitment entered into without knowledge of the lease and before the expiration of the 45-day period.

§ 9–324. PRIORITY OF PURCHASE-MONEY SECURITY INTERESTS.

(a) **[General rule: purchase-money priority.]** Except as otherwise provided in subsection (g), a perfected purchase-money security interest in goods other than inventory or livestock has priority over a conflicting security interest in the same goods, and, except as otherwise provided in Section 9–327, a perfected security interest in its identifiable proceeds also has priority, if the purchase-money security interest is perfected when the debtor receives possession of the collateral or within 20 days thereafter.

(b) **[Inventory purchase-money priority.]** Subject to subsection (c) and except as otherwise provided in subsection (g), a perfected purchase-money security interest in inventory has priority over a conflicting security interest in the same inventory, has priority over a conflicting security interest in chattel paper or an instrument constituting proceeds of the inventory and in proceeds of the chattel paper, if so provided in Section 9–330, and, except as otherwise provided in Section 9–327, also has priority in identifiable cash proceeds of the inventory to the extent the identifiable cash proceeds are received on or before the delivery of the inventory to a buyer, if:

(1) the purchase-money security interest is perfected when the debtor receives possession of the inventory;

(2) the purchase-money secured party sends an authenticated notification to the holder of the conflicting security interest;

(3) the holder of the conflicting security interest receives the notification within five years before the debtor receives possession of the inventory; and

(4) the notification states that the person sending the notification has or expects to acquire a purchase-money security interest in inventory of the debtor and describes the inventory.

(c) **[Holders of conflicting inventory security interests to be notified.]** Subsections (b)(2) through (4) apply only if the holder of the conflicting security interest had filed a financing statement covering the same types of inventory:

(1) if the purchase-money security interest is perfected by filing, before the date of the filing; or

(2) if the purchase-money security interest is temporarily perfected without filing or possession under Section 9–312(f), before the beginning of the 20–day period thereunder.

(d) **[Livestock purchase-money priority.]** Subject to subsection (e) and except as otherwise provided in subsection (g), a perfected purchase-money security interest in livestock that are farm products has priority over a conflicting security interest in the same livestock, and, except as otherwise provided in Section 9–327, a perfected security interest in their identifiable proceeds and identifiable products in their unmanufactured states also has priority, if:

(1) the purchase-money security interest is perfected when the debtor receives possession of the livestock;

(2) the purchase-money secured party sends an authenticated notification to the holder of the conflicting security interest;

(3) the holder of the conflicting security interest receives the notification within six months before the debtor receives possession of the livestock; and

(4) the notification states that the person sending the notification has or expects to acquire a purchase-money security interest in livestock of the debtor and describes the livestock.

(e) **[Holders of conflicting livestock security interests to be notified.]** Subsections (d)(2) through (4) apply only if the holder of the conflicting security interest had filed a financing statement covering the same types of livestock:

(1) if the purchase-money security interest is perfected by filing, before the date of the filing; or

(2) if the purchase-money security interest is temporarily perfected without filing or possession under Section 9–312(f), before the beginning of the 20–day period thereunder.

(f) **[Software purchase-money priority.]** Except as otherwise provided in subsection (g), a perfected purchase-money security interest in software has priority over a conflicting security interest in the same collateral, and, except as otherwise provided in Section 9–327, a perfected security interest in its identifiable proceeds also has priority, to the extent that the purchase-money security interest in the goods in which the software was acquired for use has priority in the goods and proceeds of the goods under this section.

(g) **[Conflicting purchase-money security interests.]** If more than one security interest qualifies for priority in the same collateral under subsection (a), (b), (d), or (f):

(1) a security interest securing an obligation incurred as all or part of the price of the collateral has priority over a security interest securing an obligation incurred for value given to enable the debtor to acquire rights in or the use of collateral; and

(2) in all other cases, Section 9–322(a) applies to the qualifying security interests.

§ 9–325. PRIORITY OF SECURITY INTERESTS IN TRANSFERRED COLLATERAL.

(a) **[Subordination of security interest in transferred collateral.]** Except as otherwise provided in subsection (b), a security interest created by a debtor is subordinate to a security interest in the same collateral created by another person if:

(1) the debtor acquired the collateral subject to the security interest created by the other person;

(2) the security interest created by the other person was perfected when the debtor acquired the collateral; and

(3) there is no period thereafter when the security interest is unperfected.

(b) **[Limitation of subsection (a) subordination.]** Subsection (a) subordinates a security interest only if the security interest:

(1) otherwise would have priority solely under Section 9–322(a) or 9–324; or

(2) arose solely under Section 2–711(3) or 2A–508(5).

§ 9–327. PRIORITY OF SECURITY INTERESTS IN DEPOSIT ACCOUNT.

The following rules govern priority among conflicting security interests in the same deposit account:

(1) A security interest held by a secured party having control of the deposit account under Section 9–104 has priority over a conflicting security interest held by a secured party that does not have control.

(2) Except as otherwise provided in paragraphs (3) and (4), security interests perfected by control under Section 9–314 rank according to priority in time of obtaining control.

(3) Except as otherwise provided in paragraph (4), a security interest held by the bank with which the deposit account is maintained has priority over a conflicting security interest held by another secured party.

(4) A security interest perfected by control under Section 9–104(a)(3) has priority over a security interest held by the bank with which the deposit account is maintained.

§ 9–328. PRIORITY OF SECURITY INTERESTS IN INVESTMENT PROPERTY.

The following rules govern priority among conflicting security interests in the same investment property:

(1) A security interest held by a secured party having control of investment property under Section 9–106 has priority over a security interest held by a secured party that does not have control of the investment property.

(2) Except as otherwise provided in paragraphs (3) and (4), conflicting security interests held by secured parties each of which has control under Section 9–106 rank according to priority in time of:

(A) if the collateral is a security, obtaining control;

(B) if the collateral is a security entitlement carried in a securities account and:

(i) if the secured party obtained control under Section 8–106(d)(1), the secured party's becoming the person for which the securities account is maintained;

(ii) if the secured party obtained control under Section 8–106(d)(2), the securities intermediary's agreement to comply with the secured party's entitlement orders with respect to security entitlements carried or to be carried in the securities account; or

    (iii) if the secured party obtained control through another person under Section 8–106(d)(3), the time on which priority would be based under this paragraph if the other person were the secured party; or

(C) if the collateral is a commodity contract carried with a commodity intermediary, the satisfaction of the requirement for control specified in Section 9–106(b)(2) with respect to commodity contracts carried or to be carried with the commodity intermediary.

(3) A security interest held by a securities intermediary in a security entitlement or a securities account maintained with the securities intermediary has priority over a conflicting security interest held by another secured party.

(4) A security interest held by a commodity intermediary in a commodity contract or a commodity account maintained with the commodity intermediary has priority over a conflicting security interest held by another secured party.

(5) A security interest in a certificated security in registered form which is perfected by taking delivery under Section 9–313(a) and not by control under Section 9–314 has priority over a conflicting security interest perfected by a method other than control.

(6) Conflicting security interests created by a broker, securities intermediary, or commodity intermediary which are perfected without control under Section 9–106 rank equally.

(7) In all other cases, priority among conflicting security interests in investment property is governed by Sections 9–322 and 9–323.

§ 9–329. Priority of Security Interests in Letter-of-Credit Right.

The following rules govern priority among conflicting security interests in the same letter-of-credit right:

(1) A security interest held by a secured party having control of the letter-of-credit right under Section 9–107 has priority to the extent of its control over a conflicting security interest held by a secured party that does not have control.

(2) Security interests perfected by control under Section 9–314 rank according to priority in time of obtaining control.

§ 9–330. Priority of Purchaser of Chattel Paper or Instrument.

(a) [Purchaser's priority: security interest claimed merely as proceeds.] A purchaser of chattel paper has priority over a security interest in the chattel paper which is claimed merely as proceeds of inventory subject to a security interest if:

    (1) in good faith and in the ordinary course of the purchaser's business, the purchaser gives new value and takes possession of the chattel paper or obtains control of the chattel paper under Section 9–105; and

    (2) the chattel paper does not indicate that it has been assigned to an identified assignee other than the purchaser.

(b) [Purchaser's priority: other security interests.] A purchaser of chattel paper has priority over a security interest in the chattel paper which is claimed other than merely as proceeds of inventory subject to a security interest if the purchaser gives new value and takes possession of the chattel paper or obtains control of the chattel paper under Section 9–105 in good faith, in the ordinary course of the purchaser's business, and without knowledge that the purchase violates the rights of the secured party.

(c) [Chattel paper purchaser's priority in proceeds.] Except as otherwise provided in Section 9–327, a purchaser having priority in chattel paper under subsection (a) or (b) also has priority in proceeds of the chattel paper to the extent that:

    (1) Section 9–322 provides for priority in the proceeds; or

    (2) the proceeds consist of the specific goods covered by the chattel paper or cash proceeds of the specific goods, even if the purchaser's security interest in the proceeds is unperfected.

(d) [Instrument purchaser's priority.] Except as otherwise provided in Section 9–331(a), a purchaser of an instrument has priority over a security interest in the instrument perfected by a method other than possession if the purchaser gives value and takes possession of the instrument in good faith and without knowledge that the purchase violates the rights of the secured party.

(e) [Holder of purchase-money security interest gives new value.] For purposes of subsections (a) and (b), the holder of a purchase-money security interest in inventory gives new value for chattel paper constituting proceeds of the inventory.

(f) [Indication of assignment gives knowledge.] For purposes of subsections (b) and (d), if chattel paper or an instrument indicates that it has been assigned to an identified secured party other than the purchaser, a purchaser of the chattel paper or instrument has knowledge that the purchase violates the rights of the secured party.

§ 9–331. Priority of Rights of Purchasers of Instruments, Documents, and Securities under Other Articles; Priority of Interests in Financial Assets and Security Entitlements under Article 8.

(a) [Rights under Articles 3, 7, and 8 not limited.] This article does not limit the rights of a holder in due course of a negotiable instrument, a holder to which a negotiable document of title has been duly negotiated, or a protected purchaser of a security. These holders or purchasers take priority over an earlier security interest, even if perfected, to the extent provided in Articles 3, 7, and 8.

(b) [Protection under Article 8.] This article does not limit the rights of or impose liability on a person to the extent that the person is protected against the assertion of a claim under Article 8.

(c) [Filing not notice.] Filing under this article does not constitute notice of a claim or defense to the holders, or purchasers, or persons described in subsections (a) and (b).

§ 9–332. Transfer of Money; Transfer of Funds from Deposit Account.

(a) [Transferee of money.] A transferee of money takes the money free of a security interest unless the transferee acts in collusion with the debtor in violating the rights of the secured party.

(b) [Transferee of funds from deposit account.] A transferee of funds from a deposit account takes the funds free of a security interest in the deposit account unless the transferee acts in collusion with the debtor in violating the rights of the secured party.

§ 9–333. Priority of Certain Liens Arising by Operation of Law.

(a) ["Possessory lien."] In this section, "possessory lien" means an interest, other than a security interest or an agricultural lien:

    (1) which secures payment or performance of an obligation for services or materials furnished with respect to goods by a person in the ordinary course of the person's business;

(2) which is created by statute or rule of law in favor of the person; and

(3) whose effectiveness depends on the person's possession of the goods.

(b) **[Priority of possessory lien.]** A possessory lien on goods has priority over a security interest in the goods unless the lien is created by a statute that expressly provides otherwise.

§ 9–334. PRIORITY OF SECURITY INTERESTS IN FIXTURES AND CROPS.

(a) **[Security interest in fixtures under this article.]** A security interest under this article may be created in goods that are fixtures or may continue in goods that become fixtures. A security interest does not exist under this article in ordinary building materials incorporated into an improvement on land.

(b) **[Security interest in fixtures under real-property law.]** This article does not prevent creation of an encumbrance upon fixtures under real property law.

(c) **[General rule: subordination of security interest in fixtures.]** In cases not governed by subsections (d) through (h), a security interest in fixtures is subordinate to a conflicting interest of an encumbrancer or owner of the related real property other than the debtor.

(d) **[Fixtures purchase-money priority.]** Except as otherwise provided in subsection (h), a perfected security interest in fixtures has priority over a conflicting interest of an encumbrancer or owner of the real property if the debtor has an interest of record in or is in possession of the real property and:

(1) the security interest is a purchase-money security interest;

(2) the interest of the encumbrancer or owner arises before the goods become fixtures; and

(3) the security interest is perfected by a fixture filing before the goods become fixtures or within 20 days thereafter.

(e) **[Priority of security interest in fixtures over interests in real property.]** A perfected security interest in fixtures has priority over a conflicting interest of an encumbrancer or owner of the real property if:

(1) the debtor has an interest of record in the real property or is in possession of the real property and the security interest:

(A) is perfected by a fixture filing before the interest of the encumbrancer or owner is of record; and

(B) has priority over any conflicting interest of a predecessor in title of the encumbrancer or owner;

(2) before the goods become fixtures, the security interest is perfected by any method permitted by this article and the fixtures are readily removable:

(A) factory or office machines;

(B) equipment that is not primarily used or leased for use in the operation of the real property; or

(C) replacements of domestic appliances that are consumer goods;

(3) the conflicting interest is a lien on the real property obtained by legal or equitable proceedings after the security interest was perfected by any method permitted by this article; or

(4) the security interest is:

(A) created in a manufactured home in a manufactured-home transaction; and

(B) perfected pursuant to a statute described in Section 9–311(a)(2).

(f) **[Priority based on consent, disclaimer, or right to remove.]** A security interest in fixtures, whether or not perfected, has priority over a conflicting interest of an encumbrancer or owner of the real property if:

(1) the encumbrancer or owner has, in an authenticated record, consented to the security interest or disclaimed an interest in the goods as fixtures; or

(2) the debtor has a right to remove the goods as against the encumbrancer or owner.

(g) **[Continuation of paragraph (f)(2) priority.]** The priority of the security interest under paragraph (f)(2) continues for a reasonable time if the debtor's right to remove the goods as against the encumbrancer or owner terminates.

(h) **[Priority of construction mortgage.]** A mortgage is a construction mortgage to the extent that it secures an obligation incurred for the construction of an improvement on land, including the acquisition cost of the land, if a recorded record of the mortgage so indicates. Except as otherwise provided in subsections (e) and (f), a security interest in fixtures is subordinate to a construction mortgage if a record of the mortgage is recorded before the goods become fixtures and the goods become fixtures before the completion of the construction. A mortgage has this priority to the same extent as a construction mortgage to the extent that it is given to refinance a construction mortgage.

(i) **[Priority of security interest in crops.]** A perfected security interest in crops growing on real property has priority over a conflicting interest of an encumbrancer or owner of the real property if the debtor has an interest of record in or is in possession of the real property.

(j) **[Subsection (i) prevails.]** Subsection (i) prevails over any inconsistent provisions of the following statutes.

§ 9-335. ACCESSIONS.

(a) **[Creation of security interest in accession.]** A security interest may be created in an accession and continues in collateral that becomes an accession.

(b) **[Perfection of security interest.]** If a security interest is perfected when the collateral becomes an accession, the security interest remains perfected in the collateral.

(c) **[Priority of security interest.]** Except as otherwise provided in subsection (d), the other provisions of this part determine the priority of a security interest in an accession.

(d) **[Compliance with certificate-of-title statute.]** A security interest in an accession is subordinate to a security interest in the whole which is perfected by compliance with the requirements of a certificate-of-title statute under Section 9–311(b).

(e) **[Removal of accession after default.]** After default, subject to Part 6, a secured party may remove an accession from other goods if the security interest in the accession has priority over the claims of every person having an interest in the whole.

(f) **[Reimbursement following removal.]** A secured party that removes an accession from other goods under subsection (e) shall promptly reimburse any holder of a security interest or other lien on, or owner of, the whole or of the other goods, other than the debtor, for the cost of repair of any physical injury to the whole or the other goods. The secured party need not reimburse the holder or owner for any diminution in value of the whole or the other goods caused by the absence of the accession removed or by any necessity for replacing it. A person entitled to reimbursement may refuse permission to remove until the secured party gives adequate assurance for the performance of the obligation to reimburse.

§ 9–336. COMMINGLED GOODS.

(a) [**"Commingled goods."**] In this section, "commingled goods" means goods that are physically united with other goods in such a manner that their identity is lost in a product or mass.

(b) [**No security interest in commingled goods as such.**] A security interest does not exist in commingled goods as such. However, a security interest may attach to a product or mass that results when goods become commingled goods.

(c) [**Attachment of security interest to product or mass.**] If collateral becomes commingled goods, a security interest attaches to the product or mass.

(d) [**Perfection of security interest.**] If a security interest in collateral is perfected before the collateral becomes commingled goods, the security interest that attaches to the product or mass under subsection (c) is perfected.

(e) [**Priority of security interest.**] Except as otherwise provided in subsection (f), the other provisions of this part determine the priority of a security interest that attaches to the product or mass under subsection (c).

(f) [**Conflicting security interests in product or mass.**] If more than one security interest attaches to the product or mass under subsection (c), the following rules determine priority:

(1) A security interest that is perfected under subsection (d) has priority over a security interest that is unperfected at the time the collateral becomes commingled goods.

(2) If more than one security interest is perfected under subsection (d), the security interests rank equally in proportion to the value of the collateral at the time it became commingled goods.

§ 9–337. PRIORITY OF SECURITY INTERESTS IN GOODS COVERED BY CERTIFICATE OF TITLE.

If, while a security interest in goods is perfected by any method under the law of another jurisdiction, this State issues a certificate of title that does not show that the goods are subject to the security interest or contain a statement that they may be subject to security interests not shown on the certificate:

(1) a buyer of the goods, other than a person in the business of selling goods of that kind, takes free of the security interest if the buyer gives value and receives delivery of the goods after issuance of the certificate and without knowledge of the security interest; and

(2) the security interest is subordinate to a conflicting security interest in the goods that attaches, and is perfected under Section 9–311(b), after issuance of the certificate and without the conflicting secured party's knowledge of the security interest.

PART 5—FILING

§ 9–501. FILING OFFICE.

(a) [**Filing offices.**] Except as otherwise provided in subsection (b), if the local law of this State governs perfection of a security interest or agricultural lien, the office in which to file a financing statement to perfect the security interest or agricultural lien is:

(1) the office designated for the filing or recording of a record of a mortgage on the related real property, if:

(A) the collateral is as-extracted collateral or timber to be cut; or

(B) the financing statement is filed as a fixture filing and the collateral is goods that are or are to become fixtures; or

(2) the office of [ ] [or any office duly authorized by [ ]], in all other cases, including a case in which the collateral is goods

that are or are to become fixtures and the financing statement is not filed as a fixture filing.

(b) [**Filing office for transmitting utilities.**] The office in which to file a financing statement to perfect a security interest in collateral, including fixtures, of a transmitting utility is the office of [ ]. The financing statement also constitutes a fixture filing as to the collateral indicated in the financing statement which is or is to become fixtures.

§ 9–502. CONTENTS OF FINANCING STATEMENT; RECORD OF MORTGAGE AS FINANCING STATEMENT; TIME OF FILING FINANCING STATEMENT.

(a) [**Sufficiency of financing statement.**] Subject to subsection (b), a financing statement is sufficient only if it:

(1) provides the name of the debtor;

(2) provides the name of the secured party or a representative of the secured party; and

(3) indicates the collateral covered by the financing statement.

(b) [**Real-property-related financing statements.**] Except as otherwise provided in Section 9–501(b), to be sufficient, a financing statement that covers as-extracted collateral or timber to be cut, or which is filed as a fixture filing and covers goods that are or are to become fixtures, must satisfy subsection (a) and also:

(1) indicate that it covers this type of collateral;

(2) indicate that it is to be filed [for record] in the real property records;

(3) provide a description of the real property to which the collateral is related [sufficient to give constructive notice of a mortgage under the law of this State if the description were contained in a record of the mortgage of the real property]; and

(4) if the debtor does not have an interest of record in the real property, provide the name of a record owner.

(c) [**Record of mortgage as financing statement.**] A record of a mortgage is effective, from the date of recording, as a financing statement filed as a fixture filing or as a financing statement covering as-extracted collateral or timber to be cut only if:

(1) the record indicates the goods or accounts that it covers;

(2) the goods are or are to become fixtures related to the real property described in the record or the collateral is related to the real property described in the record and is as-extracted collateral or timber to be cut;

(3) the record satisfies the requirements for a financing statement in this section other than an indication that it is to be filed in the real property records; and

(4) the record is [duly] recorded.

(d) [**Filing before security agreement or attachment.**] A financing statement may be filed before a security agreement is made or a security interest otherwise attaches.

§ 9–503. NAME OF DEBTOR AND SECURED PARTY.

(a) [**Sufficiency of debtor's name.**] A financing statement sufficiently provides the name of the debtor:

(1) if the debtor is a registered organization, only if the financing statement provides the name of the debtor indicated on the public record of the debtor's jurisdiction of organization which shows the debtor to have been organized;

(2) if the debtor is a decedent's estate, only if the financing statement provides the name of the decedent and indicates that the debtor is an estate;

(3) if the debtor is a trust or a trustee acting with respect to property held in trust, only if the financing statement:

(A) provides the name specified for the trust in its organic documents or, if no name is specified, provides the name of the settlor and additional information sufficient to distinguish the debtor from other trusts having one or more of the same settlors; and

(B) indicates, in the debtor's name or otherwise, that the debtor is a trust or is a trustee acting with respect to property held in trust; and

(4) in other cases:

(A) if the debtor has a name, only if it provides the individual or organizational name of the debtor; and

(B) if the debtor does not have a name, only if it provides the names of the partners, members, associates, or other persons comprising the debtor.

(b) [**Additional debtor-related information.**] A financing statement that provides the name of the debtor in accordance with subsection (a) is not rendered ineffective by the absence of:

(1) a trade name or other name of the debtor; or

(2) unless required under subsection (a)(4)(B), names of partners, members, associates, or other persons comprising the debtor.

(c) [**Debtor's trade name insufficient.**] A financing statement that provides only the debtor's trade name does not sufficiently provide the name of the debtor.

(d) [**Representative capacity.**] Failure to indicate the representative capacity of a secured party or representative of a secured party does not affect the sufficiency of a financing statement.

(e) [**Multiple debtors and secured parties.**] A financing statement may provide the name of more than one debtor and the name of more than one secured party.

§ 9–504. Indication of Collateral.

A financing statement sufficiently indicates the collateral that it covers if the financing statement provides:

(1) a description of the collateral pursuant to Section 9–108; or

(2) an indication that the financing statement covers all assets or all personal property.

§ 9–506. Effect of Errors or Omissions.

(a) [**Minor errors and omissions.**] A financing statement substantially satisfying the requirements of this part is effective, even if it has minor errors or omissions, unless the errors or omissions make the financing statement seriously misleading.

(b) [**Financing statement seriously misleading.**] Except as otherwise provided in subsection (c), a financing statement that fails sufficiently to provide the name of the debtor in accordance with Section 9–503(a) is seriously misleading.

(c) [**Financing statement not seriously misleading.**] If a search of the records of the filing office under the debtor's correct name, using the filing office's standard search logic, if any, would disclose a financing statement that fails sufficiently to provide the name of the debtor in accordance with Section 9–503(a), the name provided does not make the financing statement seriously misleading.

(d) [**"Debtor's correct name."**] For purposes of Section 9–508(b), the "debtor's correct name" in subsection (c) means the correct name of the new debtor.

§ 9–512. Amendment of Financing Statement.

[Alternative A]

(a) [**Amendment of information in financing statement.**] Subject to Section 9–509, a person may add or delete collateral covered by, continue or terminate the effectiveness of, or, subject to subsection (e), otherwise amend the information provided in, a financing statement by filing an amendment that:

(1) identifies, by its file number, the initial financing statement to which the amendment relates; and

(2) if the amendment relates to an initial financing statement filed [or recorded] in a filing office described in Section 9–501(a)(1), provides the information specified in Section 9–502(b).

[Alternative B]

(a) [**Amendment of information in financing statement.**] Subject to Section 9–509, a person may add or delete collateral covered by, continue or terminate the effectiveness of, or, subject to subsection (e), otherwise amend the information provided in, a financing statement by filing an amendment that:

(1) identifies, by its file number, the initial financing statement to which the amendment relates; and

(2) if the amendment relates to an initial financing statement filed [or recorded] in a filing office described in Section 9–501(a)(1), provides the date [and time] that the initial financing statement was filed [or recorded] and the information specified in Section 9–502(b).

[End of Alternatives]

(b) [**Period of effectiveness not affected.**] Except as otherwise provided in Section 9–515, the filing of an amendment does not extend the period of effectiveness of the financing statement.

(c) [**Effectiveness of amendment adding collateral.**] A financing statement that is amended by an amendment that adds collateral is effective as to the added collateral only from the date of the filing of the amendment.

(d) [**Effectiveness of amendment adding debtor.**] A financing statement that is amended by an amendment that adds a debtor is effective as to the added debtor only from the date of the filing of the amendment.

(e) [Certain amendments ineffective.] An amendment is ineffective to the extent it:

(1) purports to delete all debtors and fails to provide the name of a debtor to be covered by the financing statement; or

(2) purports to delete all secured parties of record and fails to provide the name of a new secured party of record.

§ 9–515. Duration and Effectiveness of Financing Statement; Effect of Lapsed Financing Statement.

(a) [**Five-year effectiveness.**] Except as otherwise provided in subsections (b), (e), (f), and (g), a filed financing statement is effective for a period of five years after the date of filing.

(b) [**Public-finance or manufactured-home transaction.**] Except as otherwise provided in subsections (e), (f), and (g), an initial financing statement filed in connection with a public-finance transaction or manufactured-home transaction is effective for a period of 30 years after the date of filing if it indicates that it is filed in connection with a public-finance transaction or manufactured-home transaction.

(c) [**Lapse and continuation of financing statement.**] The effectiveness of a filed financing statement lapses on the expiration of the period of its effectiveness unless before the lapse a continuation statement is filed pursuant to subsection (d). Upon lapse, a financing statement ceases to be effective and any security interest or agricultural lien that was perfected by the financing statement becomes unperfected, unless the security interest is perfected otherwise. If the security interest or agricultural lien becomes unperfected upon lapse, it is deemed never to have been perfected as against a purchaser of the collateral for value.

(d) [**When continuation statement may be filed.**] A continuation statement may be filed only within six months before the expiration of the five-year period specified in subsection (a) or the 30-year period specified in subsection (b), whichever is applicable.

(e) [**Effect of filing continuation statement.**] Except as otherwise provided in Section 9–510, upon timely filing of a continuation statement, the effectiveness of the initial financing statement continues for a period of five years commencing on the day on which the financing statement would have become ineffective in the absence of the filing. Upon the expiration of the five-year period, the financing statement lapses in the same manner as provided in subsection (c), unless, before the lapse, another continuation statement is filed pursuant to subsection (d). Succeeding continuation statements may be filed in the same manner to continue the effectiveness of the initial financing statement.

(f) [**Transmitting utility financing statement.**] If a debtor is a transmitting utility and a filed financing statement so indicates, the financing statement is effective until a termination statement is filed.

(g) [**Record of mortgage as financing statement.**] A record of a mortgage that is effective as a financing statement filed as a fixture filing under Section 9–502(c) remains effective as a financing statement filed as a fixture filing until the mortgage is released or satisfied of record or its effectiveness otherwise terminates as to the real property.

§ 9–516. WHAT CONSTITUTES FILING; EFFECTIVENESS OF FILING.

(a) [**What constitutes filing.**] Except as otherwise provided in subsection (b), communication of a record to a filing office and tender of the filing fee or acceptance of the record by the filing office constitutes filing.

(b) [**Refusal to accept record; filing does not occur.**] Filing does not occur with respect to a record that a filing office refuses to accept because:

(1) the record is not communicated by a method or medium of communication authorized by the filing office;

(2) an amount equal to or greater than the applicable filing fee is not tendered;

(3) the filing office is unable to index the record because:

(A) in the case of an initial financing statement, the record does not provide a name for the debtor;

(B) in the case of an amendment or correction statement, the record:

(i) does not identify the initial financing statement as required by Section 9–512 or 9–518, as applicable; or

(ii) identifies an initial financing statement whose effectiveness has lapsed under Section 9–515;

(C) in the case of an initial financing statement that provides the name of a debtor identified as an individual or an amendment that provides a name of a debtor identified as an individual which was not previously provided in the financing statement to which the record relates, the record does not identify the debtor's last name; or

(D) in the case of a record filed [or recorded] in the filing office described in Section 9–501(a)(1), the record does not

provide a sufficient description of the real property to which it relates;

(4) in the case of an initial financing statement or an amendment that adds a secured party of record, the record does not provide a name and mailing address for the secured party of record;

(5) in the case of an initial financing statement or an amendment that provides a name of a debtor which was not previously provided in the financing statement to which the amendment relates, the record does not:

(A) provide a mailing address for the debtor;

(B) indicate whether the debtor is an individual or an organization; or

(C) if the financing statement indicates that the debtor is an organization, provide:

(i) a type of organization for the debtor;

(ii) a jurisdiction of organization for the debtor; or

(iii) an organizational identification number for the debtor or indicate that the debtor has none;

(6) in the case of an assignment reflected in an initial financing statement under Section 9–514(a) or an amendment filed under Section 9–514(b), the record does not provide a name and mailing address for the assignee; or

(7) in the case of a continuation statement, the record is not filed within the six-month period prescribed by Section 9–515(d).

(c) [**Rules applicable to subsection (b).**] For purposes of subsection (b):

(1) a record does not provide information if the filing office is unable to read or decipher the information; and

(2) a record that does not indicate that it is an amendment or identify an initial financing statement to which it relates, as required by Section 9–512, 9–514, or 9–518, is an initial financing statement.

(d) [**Refusal to accept record; record effective as filed record.**] A record that is communicated to the filing office with tender of the filing fee, but which the filing office refuses to accept for a reason other than one set forth in subsection (b), is effective as a filed record except as against a purchaser of the collateral which gives value in reasonable reliance upon the absence of the record from the files.

§ 9–520. ACCEPTANCE AND REFUSAL TO ACCEPT RECORD.

(a) [**Mandatory refusal to accept record.**] A filing office shall refuse to accept a record for filing for a reason set forth in Section 9–516(b) and may refuse to accept a record for filing only for a reason set forth in Section 9–516(b).

(b) [**Communication concerning refusal.**] If a filing office refuses to accept a record for filing, it shall communicate to the person that presented the record the fact of and reason for the refusal and the date and time the record would have been filed had the filing office accepted it. The communication must be made at the time and in the manner prescribed by filing-office rule but [, in the case of a filing office described in Section 9–501(a)(2),] in no event more than two business days after the filing office receives the record.

(c) [**When filed financing statement effective.**] A filed financing statement satisfying Section 9–502(a) and (b) is effective, even if the filing office is required to refuse to accept it for filing under subsection (a). However, Section 9–338 applies to a filed financing statement providing information described in Section 9–516(b)(5) which is incorrect at the time the financing statement is filed.

(d) **[Separate application to multiple debtors.]** If a record communicated to a filing office provides information that relates to more than one debtor, this part applies as to each debtor separately.

PART 6—DEFAULT

§ 9–601. RIGHTS AFTER DEFAULT; JUDICIAL ENFORCEMENT; CONSIGNOR OR BUYER OF ACCOUNTS, CHATTEL PAPER, PAYMENT INTANGIBLES, OR PROMISSORY NOTES.

(a) **[Rights of secured party after default.]** After default, a secured party has the rights provided in this part and, except as otherwise provided in Section 9–602, those provided by agreement of the parties. A secured party:

(1) may reduce a claim to judgment, foreclose, or otherwise enforce the claim, security interest, or agricultural lien by any available judicial procedure; and

(2) if the collateral is documents, may proceed either as to the documents or as to the goods they cover.

(b) **[Rights and duties of secured party in possession or control.]** A secured party in possession of collateral or control of collateral under Section 9–104, 9–105, 9–106, or 9–107 has the rights and duties provided in Section 9–207.

(c) **[Rights cumulative; simultaneous exercise.]** The rights under subsections (a) and (b) are cumulative and may be exercised simultaneously.

(d) **[Rights of debtor and obligor.]** Except as otherwise provided in subsection (g) and Section 9–605, after default, a debtor and an obligor have the rights provided in this part and by agreement of the parties.

(e) **[Lien of levy after judgment.]** If a secured party has reduced its claim to judgment, the lien of any levy that may be made upon the collateral by virtue of an execution based upon the judgment relates back to the earliest of:

(1) the date of perfection of the security interest or agricultural lien in the collateral;

(2) the date of filing a financing statement covering the collateral; or

(3) any date specified in a statute under which the agricultural lien was created.

(f) **[Execution sale.]** A sale pursuant to an execution is a foreclosure of the security interest or agricultural lien by judicial procedure within the meaning of this section. A secured party may purchase at the sale and thereafter hold the collateral free of any other requirements of this article.

(g) **[Consignor or buyer of certain rights to payment.]** Except as otherwise provided in Section 9–607(c), this part imposes no duties upon a secured party that is a consignor or is a buyer of accounts, chattel paper, payment intangibles, or promissory notes.

§ 9–607. COLLECTION AND ENFORCEMENT BY SECURED PARTY.

(a) **[Collection and enforcement generally.]** If so agreed, and in any event after default, a secured party:

(1) may notify an account debtor or other person obligated on collateral to make payment or otherwise render performance to or for the benefit of the secured party;

(2) may take any proceeds to which the secured party is entitled under Section 9–315;

(3) may enforce the obligations of an account debtor or other person obligated on collateral and exercise the rights of the debtor with respect to the obligation of the account debtor or other person obligated on collateral to make payment or otherwise render performance to the debtor, and with respect to any property that secures the obligations of the account debtor or other person obligated on the collateral;

(4) if it holds a security interest in a deposit account perfected by control under Section 9–104(a)(1), may apply the balance of the deposit account to the obligation secured by the deposit account; and

(5) if it holds a security interest in a deposit account perfected by control under Section 9–104(a)(2) or (3), may instruct the bank to pay the balance of the deposit account to or for the benefit of the secured party.

(b) **[Nonjudicial enforcement of mortgage.]** If necessary to enable a secured party to exercise under subsection (a)(3) the right of a debtor to enforce a mortgage nonjudicially, the secured party may record in the office in which a record of the mortgage is recorded:

(1) a copy of the security agreement that creates or provides for a security interest in the obligation secured by the mortgage; and

(2) the secured party's sworn affidavit in recordable form stating that:

(A) a default has occurred; and

(B) the secured party is entitled to enforce the mortgage nonjudicially.

(c) **[Commercially reasonable collection and enforcement.]** A secured party shall proceed in a commercially reasonable manner if the secured party:

(1) undertakes to collect from or enforce an obligation of an account debtor or other person obligated on collateral; and

(2) is entitled to charge back uncollected collateral or otherwise to full or limited recourse against the debtor or a secondary obligor.

(d) **[Expenses of collection and enforcement.]** A secured party may deduct from the collections made pursuant to subsection (c) reasonable expenses of collection and enforcement, including reasonable attorney's fees and legal expenses incurred by the secured party.

(e) **[Duties to secured party not affected.]** This section does not determine whether an account debtor, bank, or other person obligated on collateral owes a duty to a secured party.

§ 9–608. APPLICATION OF PROCEEDS OF COLLECTION OR ENFORCEMENT; LIABILITY FOR DEFICIENCY AND RIGHT TO SURPLUS.

(a) **[Application of proceeds, surplus, and deficiency if obligation secured.]** If a security interest or agricultural lien secures payment or performance of an obligation, the following rules apply:

(1) A secured party shall apply or pay over for application the cash proceeds of collection or enforcement under Section 9–607 in the following order to:

(A) the reasonable expenses of collection and enforcement and, to the extent provided for by agreement and not prohibited by law, reasonable attorney's fees and legal expenses incurred by the secured party;

(B) the satisfaction of obligations secured by the security interest or agricultural lien under which the collection or enforcement is made; and

(C) the satisfaction of obligations secured by any subordinate security interest in or other lien on the collateral subject to the security interest or agricultural lien under which the collection or enforcement is made if the secured party receives an authenticated demand for proceeds before distribution of the proceeds is completed.

(2) If requested by a secured party, a holder of a subordinate security interest or other lien shall furnish reasonable proof of the interest or lien within a reasonable time. Unless the holder complies, the secured party need not comply with the holder's demand under paragraph (1)(C).

(3) A secured party need not apply or pay over for application noncash proceeds of collection and enforcement under Section 9–607 unless the failure to do so would be commercially unreasonable. A secured party that applies or pays over for application noncash proceeds shall do so in a commercially reasonable manner.

(4) A secured party shall account to and pay a debtor for any surplus, and the obligor is liable for any deficiency.

(b) [**No surplus or deficiency in sales of certain rights to payment.**] **If the underlying transaction is a sale of accounts, chattel paper, payment intangibles, or promissory notes, the debtor is not entitled to any surplus, and the obligor is not liable for any deficiency.**

§ 9–609. SECURED PARTY'S RIGHT TO TAKE POSSESSION AFTER DEFAULT.

(a) [**Possession; rendering equipment unusable; disposition on debtor's premises.**] After default, a secured party:

(1) may take possession of the collateral; and

(2) without removal, may render equipment unusable and dispose of collateral on a debtor's premises under Section 9–610.

(b) [**Judicial and nonjudicial process.**] A secured party may proceed under subsection (a):

(1) pursuant to judicial process; or

(2) without judicial process, if it proceeds without breach of the peace.

(c) [**Assembly of collateral.**] If so agreed, and in any event after default, a secured party may require the debtor to assemble the collateral and make it available to the secured party at a place to be designated by the secured party which is reasonably convenient to both parties.

§ 9–610. DISPOSITION OF COLLATERAL AFTER DEFAULT.

(a) [**Disposition after default.**] After default, a secured party may sell, lease, license, or otherwise dispose of any or all of the collateral in its present condition or following any commercially reasonable preparation or processing.

(b) [**Commercially reasonable disposition.**] Every aspect of a disposition of collateral, including the method, manner, time, place, and other terms, must be commercially reasonable. If commercially reasonable, a secured party may dispose of collateral by public or private proceedings, by one or more contracts, as a unit or in parcels, and at any time and place and on any terms.

(c) [**Purchase by secured party.**] A secured party may purchase collateral:

(1) at a public disposition; or

(2) at a private disposition only if the collateral is of a kind that is customarily sold on a recognized market or the subject of widely distributed standard price quotations.

(d) [**Warranties on disposition.**] A contract for sale, lease, license, or other disposition includes the warranties relating to title, possession, quiet enjoyment, and the like which by operation of law accompany a voluntary disposition of property of the kind subject to the contract.

(e) [**Disclaimer of warranties.**] A secured party may disclaim or modify warranties under subsection (d):

(1) in a manner that would be effective to disclaim or modify the warranties in a voluntary disposition of property of the kind subject to the contract of disposition; or

(2) by communicating to the purchaser a record evidencing the contract for disposition and including an express disclaimer or modification of the warranties.

(f) [**Record sufficient to disclaim warranties.**] A record is sufficient to disclaim warranties under subsection (e) if it indicates "There is no warranty relating to title, possession, quiet enjoyment, or the like in this disposition" or uses words of similar import.

§ 9–611. NOTIFICATION BEFORE DISPOSITION OF COLLATERAL.

(a) [**"Notification date."**] In this section, "notification date" means the earlier of the date on which:

(1) a secured party sends to the debtor and any secondary obligor an authenticated notification of disposition; or

(2) the debtor and any secondary obligor waive the right to notification.

(b) [**Notification of disposition required.**] Except as otherwise provided in subsection (d), a secured party that disposes of collateral under Section 9–610 shall send to the persons specified in subsection (c) a reasonable authenticated notification of disposition.

(c) [**Persons to be notified.**] To comply with subsection (b), the secured party shall send an authenticated notification of disposition to:

(1) the debtor;

(2) any secondary obligor; and

(3) if the collateral is other than consumer goods:

(A) any other person from which the secured party has received, before the notification date, an authenticated notification of a claim of an interest in the collateral;

(B) any other secured party or lienholder that, 10 days before the notification date, held a security interest in or other lien on the collateral perfected by the filing of a financing statement that:

(i) identified the collateral;

(ii) was indexed under the debtor's name as of that date; and

(iii) was filed in the office in which to file a financing statement against the debtor covering the collateral as of that date; and

(C) any other secured party that, 10 days before the notification date, held a security interest in the collateral perfected by compliance with a statute, regulation, or treaty described in Section 9–311(a).

(d) [**Subsection (b) inapplicable: perishable collateral; recognized market.**] Subsection (b) does not apply if the collateral is perishable or threatens to decline speedily in value or is of a type customarily sold on a recognized market.

(e) [**Compliance with subsection (c)(3)(b).**] A secured party complies with the requirement for notification prescribed by subsection (c)(3)(B) if:

(1) not later than 20 days or earlier than 30 days before the notification date, the secured party requests, in a commercially

reasonable manner, information concerning financing statements indexed under the debtor's name in the office indicated in subsection (c)(3)(B); and

(2) before the notification date, the secured party:

(A) did not receive a response to the request for information; or

(B) received a response to the request for information and sent an authenticated notification of disposition to each secured party or other lienholder named in that response whose financing statement covered the collateral.

§ 9–615. APPLICATION OF PROCEEDS OF DISPOSITION; LIABILITY FOR DEFICIENCY AND RIGHT TO SURPLUS.

(a) [Application of proceeds.] A secured party shall apply or pay over for application the cash proceeds of disposition under Section 9–610 in the following order to:

(1) the reasonable expenses of retaking, holding, preparing for disposition, processing, and disposing, and, to the extent provided for by agreement and not prohibited by law, reasonable attorney's fees and legal expenses incurred by the secured party;

(2) the satisfaction of obligations secured by the security interest or agricultural lien under which the disposition is made;

(3) the satisfaction of obligations secured by any subordinate security interest in or other subordinate lien on the collateral if:

(A) the secured party receives from the holder of the subordinate security interest or other lien an authenticated demand for proceeds before distribution of the proceeds is completed; and

(B) in a case in which a consignor has an interest in the collateral, the subordinate security interest or other lien is senior to the interest of the consignor; and

(4) a secured party that is a consignor of the collateral if the secured party receives from the consignor an authenticated demand for proceeds before distribution of the proceeds is completed.

(b) [Proof of subordinate interest.] If requested by a secured party, a holder of a subordinate security interest or other lien shall furnish reasonable proof of the interest or lien within a reasonable time. Unless the holder does so, the secured party need not comply with the holder's demand under subsection (a)(3).

(c) [Application of noncash proceeds.] A secured party need not apply or pay over for application noncash proceeds of disposition under Section 9–610 unless the failure to do so would be commercially unreasonable. A secured party that applies or pays over for application noncash proceeds shall do so in a commercially reasonable manner.

(d) [Surplus or deficiency if obligation secured.] If the security interest under which a disposition is made secures payment or performance of an obligation, after making the payments and applications required by subsection (a) and permitted by subsection (c):

(1) unless subsection (a)(4) requires the secured party to apply or pay over cash proceeds to a consignor, the secured party shall account to and pay a debtor for any surplus; and

(2) the obligor is liable for any deficiency.

(e) [No surplus or deficiency in sales of certain rights to payment.] If the underlying transaction is a sale of accounts, chattel paper, payment intangibles, or promissory notes:

(1) the debtor is not entitled to any surplus; and

(2) the obligor is not liable for any deficiency.

(f) [Calculation of surplus or deficiency in disposition to person related to secured party.] The surplus or deficiency following a disposition is calculated based on the amount of proceeds that would have been realized in a disposition complying with this part to a transferee other than the secured party, a person related to the secured party, or a secondary obligor if:

(1) the transferee in the disposition is the secured party, a person related to the secured party, or a secondary obligor; and

(2) the amount of proceeds of the disposition is significantly below the range of proceeds that a complying disposition to a person other than the secured party, a person related to the secured party, or a secondary obligor would have brought.

(g) [Cash proceeds received by junior secured party.] A secured party that receives cash proceeds of a disposition in good faith and without knowledge that the receipt violates the rights of the holder of a security interest or other lien that is not subordinate to the security interest or agricultural lien under which the disposition is made:

(1) takes the cash proceeds free of the security interest or other lien;

(2) is not obligated to apply the proceeds of the disposition to the satisfaction of obligations secured by the security interest or other lien; and

(3) is not obligated to account to or pay the holder of the security interest or other lien for any surplus.

§ 9–616. EXPLANATION OF CALCULATION OF SURPLUS OR DEFICIENCY.

(a) [Definitions.] In this section:

(1) "Explanation" means a writing that:

(A) states the amount of the surplus or deficiency;

(B) provides an explanation in accordance with subsection (c) of how the secured party calculated the surplus or deficiency;

(C) states, if applicable, that future debits, credits, charges, including additional credit service charges or interest, rebates, and expenses may affect the amount of the surplus or deficiency; and

(D) provides a telephone number or mailing address from which additional information concerning the transaction is available.

(2) "Request" means a record:

(A) authenticated by a debtor or consumer obligor;

(B) requesting that the recipient provide an explanation; and

(C) sent after disposition of the collateral under Section 9–610.

(b) [Explanation of calculation.] In a consumer-goods transaction in which the debtor is entitled to a surplus or a consumer obligor is liable for a deficiency under Section 9–615, the secured party shall:

(1) send an explanation to the debtor or consumer obligor, as applicable, after the disposition and:

(A) before or when the secured party accounts to the debtor and pays any surplus or first makes written demand on the consumer obligor after the disposition for payment of the deficiency; and

(B) within 14 days after receipt of a request; or

(2) in the case of a consumer obligor who is liable for a deficiency, within 14 days after receipt of a request, send to

the consumer obligor a record waiving the secured party's right to a deficiency.

(c) **[Required information.]** To comply with subsection (a)(1)(B), a writing must provide the following information in the following order:

(1) the aggregate amount of obligations secured by the security interest under which the disposition was made, and, if the amount reflects a rebate of unearned interest or credit service charge, an indication of that fact, calculated as of a specified date:

(A) if the secured party takes or receives possession of the collateral after default, not more than 35 days before the secured party takes or receives possession; or

(B) if the secured party takes or receives possession of the collateral before default or does not take possession of the collateral, not more than 35 days before the disposition;

(2) the amount of proceeds of the disposition;

(3) the aggregate amount of the obligations after deducting the amount of proceeds;

(4) the amount, in the aggregate or by type, and types of expenses, including expenses of retaking, holding, preparing for disposition, processing, and disposing of the collateral, and attorney's fees secured by the collateral which are known to the secured party and relate to the current disposition;

(5) the amount, in the aggregate or by type, and types of credits, including rebates of interest or credit service charges, to which the obligor is known to be entitled and which are not reflected in the amount in paragraph (1); and

(6) the amount of the surplus or deficiency.

(d) **[Substantial compliance.]** A particular phrasing of the explanation is not required. An explanation complying substantially with the requirements of subsection (a) is sufficient, even if it includes minor errors that are not seriously misleading.

(e) **[Charges for responses.]** A debtor or consumer obligor is entitled without charge to one response to a request under this section during any six-month period in which the secured party did not send to the debtor or consumer obligor an explanation pursuant to subsection (b)(1). The secured party may require payment of a charge not exceeding $25 for each additional response.

§ 9–617. RIGHTS OF TRANSFEREE OF COLLATERAL.

(a) **[Effects of disposition.]** A secured party's disposition of collateral after default:

(1) transfers to a transferee for value all of the debtor's rights in the collateral;

(2) discharges the security interest under which the disposition is made; and

(3) discharges any subordinate security interest or other subordinate lien [other than liens created under [cite acts or statutes providing for liens, if any, that are not to be discharged]].

(b) **[Rights of good-faith transferee.]** A transferee that acts in good faith takes free of the rights and interests described in subsection (a), even if the secured party fails to comply with this article or the requirements of any judicial proceeding.

(c) **[Rights of other transferee.]** If a transferee does not take free of the rights and interests described in subsection (a), the transferee takes the collateral subject to:

(1) the debtor's rights in the collateral;

(2) the security interest or agricultural lien under which the disposition is made; and

(3) any other security interest or other lien.

§ 9–620. ACCEPTANCE OF COLLATERAL IN FULL OR PARTIAL SATISFACTION OF OBLIGATION; COMPULSORY DISPOSITION OF COLLATERAL.

(a) **[Conditions to acceptance in satisfaction.]** Except as otherwise provided in subsection (g), a secured party may accept collateral in full or partial satisfaction of the obligation it secures only if:

(1) the debtor consents to the acceptance under subsection (c);

(2) the secured party does not receive, within the time set forth in subsection (d), a notification of objection to the proposal authenticated by:

(A) a person to which the secured party was required to send a proposal under Section 9–621; or

(B) any other person, other than the debtor, holding an interest in the collateral subordinate to the security interest that is the subject of the proposal;

(3) if the collateral is consumer goods, the collateral is not in the possession of the debtor when the debtor consents to the acceptance; and

(4) subsection (e) does not require the secured party to dispose of the collateral or the debtor waives the requirement pursuant to Section 9–624.

(b) **[Purported acceptance ineffective.]** A purported or apparent acceptance of collateral under this section is ineffective unless:

(1) the secured party consents to the acceptance in an authenticated record or sends a proposal to the debtor; and

(2) the conditions of subsection (a) are met.

(c) **[Debtor's consent.]** For purposes of this section:

(1) a debtor consents to an acceptance of collateral in partial satisfaction of the obligation it secures only if the debtor agrees to the terms of the acceptance in a record authenticated after default; and

(2) a debtor consents to an acceptance of collateral in full satisfaction of the obligation it secures only if the debtor agrees to the terms of the acceptance in a record authenticated after default or the secured party:

(A) sends to the debtor after default a proposal that is unconditional or subject only to a condition that collateral not in the possession of the secured party be preserved or maintained;

(B) in the proposal, proposes to accept collateral in full satisfaction of the obligation it secures; and

(C) does not receive a notification of objection authenticated by the debtor within 20 days after the proposal is sent.

(d) **[Effectiveness of notification.]** To be effective under subsection (a)(2), a notification of objection must be received by the secured party:

(1) in the case of a person to which the proposal was sent pursuant to Section 9–621, within 20 days after notification was sent to that person; and

(2) in other cases:

(A) within 20 days after the last notification was sent pursuant to Section 9–621; or

(B) if a notification was not sent, before the debtor consents to the acceptance under subsection (c).

(e) **[Mandatory disposition of consumer goods.]** A secured party that has taken possession of collateral shall dispose of the collateral pursuant to Section 9–610 within the time specified in subsection (f) if:

(1) 60 percent of the cash price has been paid in the case of a purchase-money security interest in consumer goods; or

(2) 60 percent of the principal amount of the obligation secured has been paid in the case of a non-purchase-money security interest in consumer goods.

(f) **[Compliance with mandatory disposition requirement.]** To comply with subsection (e), the secured party shall dispose of the collateral:

(1) within 90 days after taking possession; or

(2) within any longer period to which the debtor and all secondary obligors have agreed in an agreement to that effect entered into and authenticated after default.

(g) **[No partial satisfaction in consumer transaction.]** In a consumer transaction, a secured party may not accept collateral in partial satisfaction of the obligation it secures.

§ 9–621. Notification of Proposal to Accept Collateral.

(a) **[Persons to which proposal to be sent.]** A secured party that desires to accept collateral in full or partial satisfaction of the obligation it secures shall send its proposal to:

(1) any person from which the secured party has received, before the debtor consented to the acceptance, an authenticated notification of a claim of an interest in the collateral;

(2) any other secured party or lienholder that, 10 days before the debtor consented to the acceptance, held a security interest in or other lien on the collateral perfected by the filing of a financing statement that:

(A) identified the collateral;

(B) was indexed under the debtor's name as of that date; and

(C) was filed in the office or offices in which to file a financing statement against the debtor covering the collateral as of that date; and

(3) any other secured party that, 10 days before the debtor consented to the acceptance, held a security interest in the collateral perfected by compliance with a statute, regulation, or treaty described in Section 9–311(a).

(b) **[Proposal to be sent to secondary obligor in partial satisfaction.]** A secured party that desires to accept collateral in partial satisfaction of the obligation it secures shall send its proposal to any secondary obligor in addition to the persons described in subsection (a).

§ 9–622. Effect of Acceptance of Collateral.

(a) **[Effect of acceptance.]** A secured party's acceptance of collateral in full or partial satisfaction of the obligation it secures:

(1) discharges the obligation to the extent consented to by the debtor;

(2) transfers to the secured party all of a debtor's rights in the collateral;

(3) discharges the security interest or agricultural lien that is the subject of the debtor's consent and any subordinate security interest or other subordinate lien; and

(4) terminates any other subordinate interest.

(b) **[Discharge of subordinate interest notwithstanding noncompliance.]** A subordinate interest is discharged or terminated under subsection (a), even if the secured party fails to comply with this article.

§ 9–623. Right to Redeem Collateral.

(a) **[Persons that may redeem.]** A debtor, any secondary obligor, or any other secured party or lienholder may redeem collateral.

(b) **[Requirements for redemption.]** To redeem collateral, a person shall tender:

(1) fulfillment of all obligations secured by the collateral; and

(2) the reasonable expenses and attorney's fees described in Section 9–615(a)(1).

(c) **[When redemption may occur.]** A redemption may occur at any time before a secured party:

(1) has collected collateral under Section 9–607;

(2) has disposed of collateral or entered into a contract for its disposition under Section 9–610; or

(3) has accepted collateral in full or partial satisfaction of the obligation it secures under Section 9–622.

§ 9–624. Waiver.

(a) **[Waiver of disposition notification.]** A debtor or secondary obligor may waive the right to notification of disposition of collateral under Section 9–611 only by an agreement to that effect entered into and authenticated after default.

(b) **[Waiver of mandatory disposition.]** A debtor may waive the right to require disposition of collateral under Section 9–620(e) only by an agreement to that effect entered into and authenticated after default.

(c) **[Waiver of redemption right.]** Except in a consumer-goods transaction, a debtor or secondary obligor may waive the right to redeem collateral under Section 9–623 only by an agreement to that effect entered into and authenticated after default.

§ 9–625. Remedies for Secured Party's Failure to Comply with Article.

(a) **[Judicial orders concerning noncompliance.]** If it is established that a secured party is not proceeding in accordance with this article, a court may order or restrain collection, enforcement, or disposition of collateral on appropriate terms and conditions.

(b) **[Damages for noncompliance.]** Subject to subsections (c), (d), and (f), a person is liable for damages in the amount of any loss caused by a failure to comply with this article. Loss caused by a failure to comply may include loss resulting from the debtor's inability to obtain, or increased costs of, alternative financing.

(c) **[Persons entitled to recover damages; statutory damages in consumer-goods transaction.]** Except as otherwise provided in Section 9–628:

(1) a person that, at the time of the failure, was a debtor, was an obligor, or held a security interest in or other lien on the collateral may recover damages under subsection (b) for its loss; and

(2) if the collateral is consumer goods, a person that was a debtor or a secondary obligor at the time a secured party failed to comply with this part may recover for that failure in any event an amount not less than the credit service charge plus 10 percent of the principal amount of the obligation or the time-price differential plus 10 percent of the cash price.

(d) **[Recovery when deficiency eliminated or reduced.]** A debtor whose deficiency is eliminated under Section 9–626 may recover damages for the loss of any surplus. However, a debtor or secondary obligor whose deficiency is eliminated or reduced under Section 9–626 may not otherwise recover under subsection (b) for noncompliance with the provisions of this part relating to collection, enforcement, disposition, or acceptance.

(e) **[Statutory damages: noncompliance with specified provisions.]** In addition to any damages recoverable under subsection (b), the debtor, consumer obligor, or person named as a debtor in a filed record, as applicable, may recover $500 in each case from a person that:

(1) fails to comply with Section 9–208;

(2) fails to comply with Section 9–209;

(3) files a record that the person is not entitled to file under Section 9–509(a);

(4) fails to cause the secured party of record to file or send a termination statement as required by Section 9–513(a) or (c);

(5) fails to comply with Section 9–616(b)(1) and whose failure is part of a pattern, or consistent with a practice, of noncompliance; or

(6) fails to comply with Section 9–616(b)(2).

(f) **[Statutory damages: noncompliance with Section 9–210.]** A debtor or consumer obligor may recover damages under subsection (b) and, in addition, $500 in each case from a person that, without reasonable cause, fails to comply with a request under Section 9–210. A recipient of a request under Section 9–210 which never claimed an interest in the collateral or obligations that are the subject of a request under that section has a reasonable excuse for failure to comply with the request within the meaning of this subsection.

(g) **[Limitation of security interest: noncompliance with Section 9–210.]** If a secured party fails to comply with a request regarding a list of collateral or a statement of account under Section 9–210, the secured party may claim a security interest only as shown in the list or statement included in the request as against a person that is reasonably misled by the failure.

§ 9–626. Action in Which Deficiency or Surplus Is in Issue.

(a) **[Applicable rules if amount of deficiency or surplus in issue.]** In an action arising from a transaction, other than a consumer transaction, in which the amount of a deficiency or surplus is in issue, the following rules apply:

(1) A secured party need not prove compliance with the provisions of this part relating to collection, enforcement, disposition, or acceptance unless the debtor or a secondary obligor places the secured party's compliance in issue.

(2) If the secured party's compliance is placed in issue, the secured party has the burden of establishing that the collection, enforcement, disposition, or acceptance was conducted in accordance with this part.

(3) Except as otherwise provided in Section 9–628, if a secured party fails to prove that the collection, enforcement, disposition, or acceptance was conducted in accordance with the provisions of this part relating to collection, enforcement, disposition, or acceptance, the liability of a debtor or a secondary obligor for a deficiency is limited to an amount by which the sum of the secured obligation, expenses, and attorney's fees exceeds the greater of:

(A) the proceeds of the collection, enforcement, disposition, or acceptance; or

(B) the amount of proceeds that would have been realized had the noncomplying secured party proceeded in accordance with the provisions of this part relating to collection, enforcement, disposition, or acceptance.

(4) For purposes of paragraph (3)(B), the amount of proceeds that would have been realized is equal to the sum of the secured obligation, expenses, and attorney's fees unless the secured party proves that the amount is less than that sum.

(5) If a deficiency or surplus is calculated under Section 9–615(f), the debtor or obligor has the burden of establishing that the amount of proceeds of the disposition is significantly below the range of prices that a complying disposition to a person other than the secured party, a person related to the secured party, or a secondary obligor would have brought.

(b) **[Non-consumer transactions; no inference.]** The limitation of the rules in subsection (a) to transactions other than consumer transactions is intended to leave to the court the determination of the proper rules in consumer transactions. The court may not infer from that limitation the nature of the proper rule in consumer transactions and may continue to apply established approaches.

§ 9–627. Determination of Whether Conduct Was Commercially Reasonable.

(a) **[Greater amount obtainable under other circumstances; no preclusion of commercial reasonableness.]** The fact that a greater amount could have been obtained by a collection, enforcement, disposition, or acceptance at a different time or in a different method from that selected by the secured party is not of itself sufficient to preclude the secured party from establishing that the collection, enforcement, disposition, or acceptance was made in a commercially reasonable manner.

(b) **[Dispositions that are commercially reasonable.]** A disposition of collateral is made in a commercially reasonable manner if the disposition is made:

(1) in the usual manner on any recognized market;

(2) at the price current in any recognized market at the time of the disposition; or

(3) otherwise in conformity with reasonable commercial practices among dealers in the type of property that was the subject of the disposition.

(c) **[Approval by court or on behalf of creditors.]** A collection, enforcement, disposition, or acceptance is commercially reasonable if it has been approved:

(1) in a judicial proceeding;

(2) by a bona fide creditors' committee;

(3) by a representative of creditors; or

(4) by an assignee for the benefit of creditors.

(d) **[Approval under subsection (c) not necessary; absence of approval has no effect.]** Approval under subsection (c) need not be obtained, and lack of approval does not mean that the collection, enforcement, disposition, or acceptance is not commercially reasonable.

DICTIONARY OF LEGAL TERMS

A

abatement Reduction or elimination of gifts by category upon the reduction in value of the estate.

absolute surety Surety liable to a creditor immediately upon the default of the principal debtor.

acceptance

Commercial paper Acceptance is the drawee's signed engagement to honor the draft as presented. It becomes operative when completed by delivery or notification. UCC § 3–410.

Contracts Compliance by offeree with terms and conditions of offer.

Sale of goods UCC § 2–606 provides three ways a buyer can accept goods: (1) by signifying to the seller that the goods are conforming or that he will accept them in spite of their nonconformity, (2) by failing to make an effective rejection, and (3) by doing an act inconsistent with the seller's ownership.

acceptor Drawee who has accepted an instrument.

accession An addition to one's property by increase of the original property or by production from such property. *E.g.*, A innocently converts the wheat of B into bread. UCC § 9–315 changes the common law where a perfected security interest is involved.

accident and health insurance Provides protection from losses due to accident or sickness.

accommodation An arrangement made as a favor to another, usually involving a loan of money or commercial paper. While a party's intent may be to aid a maker of a note by lending his credit, if he seeks to accomplish thereby legitimate objects of his own and not simply to aid the maker, the act is not for accommodation.

accommodation indorser Signer not in the chain of title.

accommodation party A person who signs commercial paper in any capacity for the purpose of lending his name to another party to an instrument. UCC § 3–415.

accord and satisfaction A method of discharging a claim whereby the parties agree to accept something in settlement, the "accord" being the agreement and the "satisfaction" its execution or performance. It is a new contract that is substituted for an old contract, which is thereby discharged, or for an obligation or cause of action and that must have all of the elements of a valid contract.

account Any account with a bank, including a checking, time, interest or savings account. UCC § 4–194. Also, any right to payment, for goods or services, that is not evidenced by an instrument or chattel paper. *E.g.*, account receivable.

accounting Equitable proceeding for a complete settlement of all partnership affairs.

act of state doctrine Rule that a court should not question the validity of actions taken by a foreign government in its own country.

actual authority Power conferred upon agent by actual consent given by principal.

actual express authority Actual authority derived from written or spoken words of principal.

actual implied authority Actual authority inferred from words or conduct manifested to agent by principal.

actual notice Knowledge actually and expressly communicated.

actus reas Wrongful or overt act.

ademption The removal or extinction of a devise by act of the testator.

adequacy of consideration Not required where parties have freely agreed to the exchange.

adhesion contract Standard "form" contract, usually between a large retailer and a consumer, in which the weaker party has no realistic choice or opportunity to bargain.

adjudication The giving or pronouncing of a judgment in a case; also, the judgment given.

administrative agency Governmental entity (other than courts and legislatures) having authority to affect the rights of private parties.

administrative law Law dealing with the establishment, duties, and powers of agencies in the executive branch of government.

administrative process Entire set of activities engaged in by administrative agencies while carrying out their rulemaking, enforcement, and adjudicative functions.

---

*Many of the definitions are abridged and adapted from *Black's Law Dictionary*, 5th edition, West Publishing Company, 1979.

administrator A person appointed by the court to manage the assets and liabilities of an intestate (a person dying without a will). A person named in the will of a testator (a person dying with a will) is called the executor. Female designations are administratrix and executrix.

adversary system System in which opposing parties initiate and present their cases.

adverse possession A method of acquiring title to real property by possession for a statutory period under certain conditions. The periods of time may differ, depending on whether the adverse possessor has color of title.

affidavit A written statement of facts, made voluntarily, confirmed by oath or affirmation of the party making it, and taken before an authorized officer.

affiliate Person who controls, is controlled by, or is under common control with the issuer.

affirm Uphold the lower court's judgment.

affirmative action Active recruitment of minority applicants.

affirmative defense A response that attacks the plaintiff's legal right to bring an action as opposed to attacking the truth of the claim. *E.g.,* accord and satisfaction; assumption of risk; contributory negligence; duress; estoppel.

affirmative disclosure Requirement that an advertiser include certain information in its advertisement so that the ad is not deceptive.

after-acquired property Property the debtor may acquire at some time after the security interest attaches.

agency Relation in which one person acts for or represents another by the latter's authority.

Actual agency Exists where the agent is really employed by the principal.

Agency by estoppel One created by operation of law and established by proof of such acts of the principal as reasonably lead to the conclusion of its existence.

Implied agency One created by acts of the parties and deduced from proof of other facts.

agent Person authorized to act on another's behalf.

allegation A statement of a party setting out what he expects to prove.

allonge Piece of paper firmly affixed to the instrument.

annuity contract Agreement to pay periodic sums to insured upon reaching a designated age.

annul To annul a judgment or judicial proceeding is to deprive it of all force and operation.

answer The answer is the formal written statement made by a defendant setting forth the ground of his defense.

antecedent debt Preexisting obligation.

anticipatory breach of contract (or **anticipatory repudiation**) The unjustified assertion by a party that he will not perform an obligation that he is contractually obligated to perform at a future time. See UCC §§ 610 & 611.

apparent authority Such principal power that a reasonable person would assume an agent has in light of the principal's conduct.

appeal Resort to a superior (appellate) court to review the decision of an inferior (trial) court or administrative agency.

appeal by right Mandatory review by a higher court.

appellant A party who takes an appeal from one court to another. He may be either the plaintiff or defendant in the original court proceeding.

appellee The party in a cause against whom an appeal is taken; that is, the party who has an interest adverse to setting aside or reversing the judgment. Sometimes also called the "respondent."

appropriation Unauthorized use of another person's name or likeness for one's own benefit.

appurtenances Things appurtenant pass as incident to the principal thing. Sometimes an easement consisting of a right of way over one piece of land will pass with another piece of land as being appurtenant to it.

APR Annual percentage rate.

arbitration The reference of a dispute to an impartial (third) person chosen by the parties, who agree in advance to abide by the arbitrator's award issued after a hearing at which both parties have an opportunity to be heard.

arraignment Accused is informed of the crime against him and enters a plea.

articles of incorporation (or **certificate of incorporation**) The instrument under which a corporation is formed. The contents are prescribed in the particular state's general incorporation statute.

articles of partnership A written agreement by which parties enter into a partnership, to be governed by the terms set forth therein.

as is Disclaimer of implied warranties.

assault Unlawful attempted battery; intentional infliction of apprehension of immediate bodily harm or offensive contact.

assignee Party to whom contract rights are assigned.

assignment A transfer of the rights to real or personal property, usually intangible property such as rights in a lease, mortgage, sale agreement, or partnership.

assignment of rights Voluntary transfer to a third party of the rights arising from a contract.

assignor Party making an assignment.

assumes Delegatee agrees to perform the contractual obligation of the delegator.

assumes the mortgage Purchaser of mortgaged property becomes personally liable to pay the debt.

assumption of risk Plaintiff's express or implied consent to encounter a known danger.

attachment The process of seizing property, by virtue of a writ, summons, or other judicial order, and bringing the same into the custody of the court for the purpose of securing satisfaction of the judgment ultimately to be entered in the action. While formerly the main objective was to coerce the defendant debtor to appear in court, today the writ of attachment is used primarily to seize the debtor's property in the event a judgment is rendered.

Distinguished from execution See **execution**.

Also, the process by which a security interest becomes enforceable. Attachment may occur upon the taking of possession or upon the signing of a security agreement by the person who is pledging the property as collateral.

authority Power of an agent to change the legal status of his principal.

authorized means Any reasonable means of communication.

automatic perfection Perfection upon attachment.

award The decision of an arbitrator.

B

bad checks Issuing a check with funds insufficient to cover it.

bailee The party to whom personal property is delivered under a contract of bailment.

Extraordinary bailee Absolutely liable for the safety of the bailed property without regard to the cause of loss.

Ordinary bailee Must exercise due care.

bailment A delivery of personal property in trust for the execution of a special object in relation to such goods, beneficial either to the bailor or bailee or both, and upon a contract to either redeliver the goods to the bailor or otherwise dispose of the same in conformity with the purpose of the trust.

bailor The party who delivers goods to another in the contract of bailment.

bankrupt The state or condition of one who is unable to pay his debts as they are, or become, due.

Bankruptcy Code The Act was substantially revised in 1978 and again in 2005. Straight bankruptcy is in the nature of a liquidation proceeding and involves the collection and distribution to creditors of all the bankrupt's nonexempt property by the trustee in the manner provided by the Act. The debtor rehabilitation provisions of the Act (Chapters 11 and 13) differ from straight bankruptcy in that the debtor looks to rehabilitation and reorganization, rather than liquidation, and the creditors look to future earnings of the bankrupt, rather than to property held by the bankrupt, to satisfy their claims.

bargain Negotiated exchange.

bargained exchange Mutually agreed-upon exchange.

basis of the bargain Part of the buyer's assumption underlying the sale.

battery Unlawful touching of another; intentional infliction of harmful or offensive bodily contact.

bearer Person in possession of an instrument.

bearer paper Payable to holder of the instrument.

beneficiary One who benefits from act of another. See also **third-party beneficiary**.

Incidental A person who may derive benefit from performance on contract, though he is neither the promisee nor the one to whom performance is to be rendered. Since the incidental beneficiary is not a donee or creditor beneficiary (see **third-party beneficiary**), he has no right to enforce the contract.

Intended beneficiary Third party intended by the two contracted parties to receive a benefit from their contract.

Trust As it relates to trust beneficiaries, includes a person who has any present or future interest, vested or contingent, and also includes the owner of an interest by assignment or other transfer and, as it relates to a charitable trust, includes any person entitled to enforce the trust.

beyond a reasonable doubt Proof that is entirely convincing and satisfying to a moral certainty; criminal law standard.

bilateral contract Contract in which both parties exchange promises.

bill of lading Document evidencing receipt of goods for shipment issued by person engaged in business of transporting or forwarding goods; includes airbill. UCC § 1–201(6).

Through bill of lading A bill of lading which specifies at least one connecting carrier.

bill of sale A written agreement, formerly limited to one under seal, by which one person assigns or transfers his right to or interest in goods and personal chattels to another.

binder A written memorandum of the important terms of a contract of insurance which gives temporary protection to an insured pending investigation of risk by the insurance company or until a formal policy is issued.

blue law Prohibition of certain types of commercial activity on Sunday.

blue sky laws A popular name for state statutes providing for the regulation and supervision of securities offerings and sales, to protect citizen-investors from investing in fraudulent companies.

bona fide Latin. In good faith.

bond A certificate or evidence of a debt on which the issuing company or governmental body promises to pay the bondholders a specified amount of interest for a specified length of time and to repay the loan on the expiration date. In every case, a bond represents debt—its holder is a creditor of the corporation, not a part owner, as the shareholder is.

boycott Agreement among parties not to deal with a third party.

breach Wrongful failure to perform the terms of a contract.

Material breach Nonperformance which significantly impairs the aggrieved party's rights under the contract.

bribery Offering property to a public official to influence the official's decision.

bulk transfer Transfer not in the ordinary course of the transferor's business of a major part of his inventory.

burglary Breaking and entering the home of another at night with intent to commit a felony.

business judgment rule Protects directors from liability for honest mistakes of judgment.

business trust A trust (managed by a trustee for the benefit of a beneficiary) established to conduct a business for a profit.

but for rule Person's negligent conduct is a cause of an event if the event would not have occurred in the absence of that conduct.

buyer in ordinary course of business Person who buys in ordinary course, in good faith, and without knowledge that the sale to him is in violation of anyone's ownership rights or of a security interest.

by-laws Regulations, ordinances, rules, or laws adopted by an association or corporation for its government.

C

callable bond Bond that is subject to redemption (reacquisition) by the corporation.

cancellation One party's putting an end to a contract because of a breach by other party.

capital Accumulated goods, possessions, and assets, used for the production of profits and wealth. Owners' equity in a business. Also used to refer to the total assets of a business or to capital assets.

capital surplus Surplus other than earned surplus.

carrier Transporter of goods.

casualty insurance Covers property loss due to causes other than fire or the elements.

cause of action The ground on which an action may be sustained.

caveat emptor   Latin. Let the buyer beware. This maxim is more applicable to judicial sales, auctions, and the like than to sales of consumer goods, where strict liability, warranty, and other laws protect.

certificate of deposit   A written acknowledgment by a bank or banker of a deposit with promise to pay to depositor, to his order, or to some other person or to his order. UCC § 3–104(2)(c).

certificate of title   Official representation of ownership.

certification   Acceptance of a check by a drawee bank.

certification of incorporation   See **articles of incorporation**.

certification mark   Distinctive symbol, word, or design used with goods or services to certify specific characteristics.

certiorari   Latin. To be informed of. A writ of common law origin issued by a superior to an inferior court requiring the latter to produce a certified record of a particular case tried therein. It is most commonly used to refer to the Supreme Court of the United States, which uses the writ of certiorari as a discretionary device to choose the cases it wishes to hear.

chancery   Equity; equitable jurisdiction; a court of equity; the system of jurisprudence administered in courts of equity.

charging order   Judicial lien against a partner's interest in the partnership.

charter   An instrument emanating from the sovereign power, in the nature of a grant. A charter differs from a constitution in that the former is granted by the sovereign, while the latter is established by the people themselves.

> *Corporate law* An act of a legislature creating a corporation or creating and defining the franchise of a corporation. Also a corporation's constitution or organic law; that is to say, the articles of incorporation taken in connection with the law under which the corporation was organized.

chattel mortgage   A pre-Uniform Commercial Code security device whereby the mortgagee took a security interest in personal property of the mortgagor. Such security device has generally been superseded by other types of security agreements under UCC Article 9 (Secured Transactions).

chattel paper   Writings that evidence both a debt and a security interest.

check   A draft drawn upon a bank and payable on demand, signed by the maker or drawer, containing an unconditional promise to pay a sum certain in money to the order of the payee. UCC § 3–104(2)(b).

> *Cashier's check* A bank's own check drawn on itself and signed by the cashier or other authorized official. It is a direct obligation of the bank.

C. & F.   Cost and freight; a shipping contract.

C.I.F.   Cost, insurance, and freight; a shipping contract.

civil law   Laws concerned with civil or private rights and remedies, as contrasted with criminal laws.

The system of jurisprudence administered in the Roman empire, particularly as set forth in the compilation of Justinian and his successors, as distinguished from the common law of England and the canon law. The civil law (Civil Code) is followed by Louisiana.

claim   A right to payment.

clearinghouse   An association of banks for the purpose of settling accounts on a daily basis.

close corporation   See **corporation**.

closed-ended credit   Credit extended to debtor for a specific period of time.

closed shop   An employer who can only hire union members.

C.O.D.   Collect on delivery; generally a shipping contract.

code   A compilation of all permanent laws in force consolidated and classified according to subject matter. Many states have published official codes of all laws in force, including the common law and statutes as judicially interpreted, which have been compiled by code commissions and enacted by the legislatures.

codicil   A supplement or an addition to a will; it may explain, modify, add to, subtract from, qualify, alter, restrain, or revoke provisions in an existing will. It must be executed with the same formalities as a will.

cognovit judgment   Written authority by debtor for entry of judgment against him in the event he defaults in payment. Such provision in a debt instrument on default confers judgment against the debtor.

collateral   Secondarily liable; liable only if the party with primary liability does not perform.

collateral (security)   Personal property subject to security interest.

> *Banking* Some form of security in addition to the personal obligation of the borrower.

collateral promise   Undertaking to be secondarily liable, that is, liable if the principal debtor does not perform.

collecting bank   Any bank, except the payor bank, handling the item for collection. UCC § 4–105(d).

collective mark   Distinctive symbol used to indicate membership in an organization.

collision insurance   Protects the owner of an automobile against damage due to contact with other vehicles or objects.

commerce power   Exclusive power granted by the U.S. Constitution to the federal government to regulate commerce with foreign countries and among the states.

commercial bailment   Bailment in which parties derive a mutual benefit.

commercial impracticability   Performance can only be accomplished with unforeseen and unjust hardship.

commercial law   A phrase used to designate the whole body of substantive jurisprudence (*e.g.*, Uniform Commercial Code; Truth in Lending Act) applicable to the rights, intercourse, and relations of persons engaged in commerce, trade, or mercantile pursuits. See **Uniform Commercial Code**.

commercial paper   Bills of exchange (*i.e.*, drafts), promissory notes, bank checks, and other negotiable instruments for the payment of money, which, by their form and on their face, purport to be such instruments. UCC Article 3 is the general law governing commercial paper.

commercial reasonableness   Judgment of reasonable persons familiar with the business transaction.

commercial speech   Expression related to the economic interests of the speaker and its audience.

common carrier   Carrier open to the general public.

common law   Body of law originating in England and derived from judicial decisions. As distinguished from statutory law created by the enactment of legislatures, the common law comprises the judgments and decrees of the courts recognizing, affirming, and enforcing usages and customs of immemorial antiquity.

community property Rights of a spouse in property acquired by the other during marriage.

comparable worth Equal pay for jobs of equal value to the employer.

comparative negligence Under comparative negligence statutes or doctrines, negligence is measured in terms of percentage, and any damages allowed shall be diminished in proportion to amount of negligence attributable to the person for whose injury, damage, or death recovery is sought.

complainant One who applies to the courts for legal redress by filing a complaint (*i.e.*, plaintiff).

complaint The pleading which sets forth a claim for relief. Such complaint (whether it be the original claim, counterclaim, cross-claim, or third-party claim) shall contain (1) a short, plain statement of the grounds upon which the court's jurisdiction depends, unless the court already has jurisdiction and the claim needs no new grounds of jurisdiction to support it, (2) a short, plain statement of the claim showing that the pleader is entitled to relief, and (3) a demand for judgment for the relief to which he deems himself entitled. Fed.R. Civil P. 8(a). The complaint, together with the summons, is required to be served on the defendant. Rule 4.

composition Agreement between debtor and two or more of her creditors that each will take a portion of his claim as full payment.

compulsory arbitration Arbitration required by statute for specific types of disputes.

computer crime Crime committed against or through the use of a computer or computer/services.

concealment Fraudulent failure to disclose a material fact.

conciliation Nonbinding process in which a third party acts as an intermediary between disputing parties.

concurrent jurisdiction Authority of more than one court to hear the same case.

condition An uncertain event which affects the duty of performance.

> *Concurrent conditions* The parties are to perform simultaneously.
>
> *Express condition* Performance is contingent on the happening or non-happening of a stated event.

condition precedent An event which must occur or not occur before performance is due; event or events (presentment, dishonor, notice of dishonor) which must occur to hold a secondary party liable to commercial paper.

condition subsequent An event which terminates a duty of performance.

conditional acceptance An acceptance of an offer contingent upon the acceptance of an additional or different term.

conditional contract Obligations are contingent upon a stated event.

conditional guarantor of collection Surety liable to creditor only after creditor exhausts his legal remedies against the principal debtor.

confession of judgment Written agreement by debtor authorizing creditor to obtain a court judgment in the event debtor defaults. See also **cognovit judgment.**

confiscation Governmental taking of foreign-owned property without payment.

conflict of laws That branch of jurisprudence, arising from the diversity of the laws of different nations, states, or jurisdictions, that reconciles the inconsistencies, or decides which law is to govern in a particular case.

confusion Results when goods belonging to two or more owners become so intermixed that the property of any of them no longer can be identified except as part of a mass of like goods.

consanguinity Kinship; blood relationship; the connection or relation of persons descended from the same stock or common ancestor.

consensual arbitration Arbitration voluntarily entered into by the parties.

consent Voluntary and knowing willingness that an act should be done.

conservator Appointed by court to manage affairs of incompetent or to liquidate business.

consideration The cause, motive, price, or impelling influence which induces a contracting party to enter into a contract. Some right, interest, profit, or benefit accruing to one party or some forbearance, detriment, loss, or responsibility given, suffered, or undertaken by the other.

consignee One to whom a consignment is made. Person named in bill of lading to whom or to whose order the bill promises delivery. UCC § 7–102(b).

consignment Ordinarily implies an agency; denotes that property is committed to the consignee for care or sale.

consignor One who sends or makes a consignment; a shipper of goods. The person named in a bill of lading as the person from whom the goods have been received for shipment. UCC § 7–102(c).

consolidation In *corporate law*, the combination of two or more corporations into a newly created corporation. Thus, A Corporation and B Corporation consolidate to form C Corporation.

constitution Fundamental law of a government establishing its powers and limitations.

constructive That which is established by the mind of the law in its act of *construing* facts, conduct, circumstances, or instruments. That which has not in its essential nature the character assigned to it, but acquires such character in consequence of the way in which it is regarded by a rule or policy of law; hence, inferred, implied, or made out by legal interpretation; the word "legal" being sometimes used here in lieu of "constructive."

constructive assent An assent or consent imputed to a party from a construction or interpretation of his conduct; as distinguished from one which he actually expresses.

constructive conditions Conditions in contracts which are neither expressed nor implied but rather are imposed by law to meet the ends of justice.

constructive delivery Term comprehending all those acts which, although not truly conferring a real possession of the vendee, have been held by construction of law to be equivalent to acts of real delivery.

constructive eviction Failure by the landlord in any obligation under the lease that causes a substantial and lasting injury to the tenant's enjoyment of the premises.

constructive notice   Knowledge imputed by law.

constructive trust   Arising by operation of law to prevent unjust enrichment. See also **trustee**.

consumer goods   Goods bought or used for personal, family, or household purposes.

consumer product   Tangible personal property normally used for family, household, or personal purposes.

contingent remainder   Remainder interest, conditional upon the happening of an event in addition to the termination of the preceding estate.

contract   An agreement between two or more persons which creates an obligation to do or not to do a particular thing. Its essentials are competent parties, subject matter, a legal consideration, mutuality of agreement, and mutuality of obligation.

Destination contract Seller is required to tender delivery of the goods at a particular destination; seller bears the expense and risk of loss.

Executed contract Fully performed by all of the parties.

Executory contract Contract partially or entirely unperformed by one or more of the parties.

Express contract Agreement of parties that is expressed in words either in writing or orally.

Formal contract Agreement which is legally binding because of its particular form or mode or expression.

Implied-in-fact contract Contract where agreement of the parties is inferred from their conduct.

Informal contract All oral or written contracts other than formal contracts.

Installment contract Goods are delivered in separate lots.

Integrated contract Complete and total agreement.

Output contract A contract in which one party agrees to sell his entire output and the other agrees to buy it; it is not illusory, though it may be indefinite.

Quasi contract Obligation not based upon contract that is imposed to avoid injustice.

Requirements contract A contract in which one party agrees to purchase his total requirements from the other party; hence, such a contract is binding, not illusory.

Substituted contract An agreement between the parties to rescind their old contract and replace it with a new contract.

Unconscionable contract One which no sensible person not under delusion, duress, or in distress would make, and such as no honest and fair person would accept. A contract the terms of which are excessively unreasonable, overreaching, and one-sided.

Unenforceable contract Contract for the breach of which the law does not provide a remedy.

Unilateral and bilateral A unilateral contract is one in which one party makes an express engagement or undertakes a performance, without receiving in return any express engagement or promise of performance from the other. Bilateral (or reciprocal) contracts are those by which the parties expressly enter into mutual engagements.

contract clause   Prohibition against the states' retroactively modifying public and private contracts.

contractual liability   Obligation on a negotiable instrument, based upon signing the instrument.

contribution   Payment from cosureties of their proportionate share.

contributory negligence   An act or omission amounting to a want of ordinary care on the part of the complaining party, which, concurring with defendant's negligence, is proximate cause of injury.

The defense of contributory negligence is an absolute bar to any recovery in some states; because of this, it has been replaced by the doctrine of comparative negligence in many other states.

conversion   Unauthorized and wrongful exercise of dominion and control over another's personal property, to exclusion of or inconsistent with rights of the owner.

convertible bond   Bond that may be exchanged for other securities of the corporation.

copyright   Exclusive right granted by federal government to authors of original works including literary, musical, dramatic, pictorial, graphic, sculptural, and film works.

corporation   A legal entity ordinarily consisting of an association of numerous individuals. Such entity is regarded as having a personality and existence distinct from that of its several members and is vested with the capacity of continuous succession, irrespective of changes in its membership, either in perpetuity or for a limited term of years.

Closely held or close corporation Corporation that is owned by few shareholders and whose shares are not actively traded.

Corporation de facto One existing under color of law and in pursuance of an effort made in good faith to organize a corporation under the statute. Such a corporation is not subject to collateral attack.

Corporation de jure That which exists by reason of full compliance with requirements of an existing law permitting organization of such corporation.

Domestic corporation Corporation created under the laws of a given state.

Foreign corporation Corporation created under the laws of any other state, government, or country.

Publicly held corporation Corporation whose shares are owned by a large number of people and are widely traded.

Subchapter S corporation A small business corporation which, under certain conditions, may elect to have its undistributed taxable income taxed to its shareholders. I.R.C. § 1371 et seq. Of major significance is the fact that Subchapter S status usually avoids the corporate income tax, and corporate losses can be claimed by the shareholders.

Subsidiary and parent Subsidiary corporation is one in which another corporation (called parent corporation) owns at least a majority of the shares and over which it thus has control.

corrective advertising   Disclosure in an advertisement that previous ads were deceptive.

costs   A pecuniary allowance, made to the successful party (and recoverable from the losing party), for his expenses in prosecuting or defending an action or a distinct proceeding within an action. Generally, "costs" do not include attorneys' fees unless such fees are by a statute denominated costs or are by statute allowed to be recovered as costs in the case.

cosureties   Two or more sureties bound for the same debt of a principal debtor.

co-tenants   Persons who hold title concurrently.

counterclaim   A claim presented by a defendant in opposition to or deduction from the claim of the plaintiff.

counteroffer   A statement by the offeree which has the legal effect of rejecting the offer and of proposing a new offer to the offeror. However, the provisions of UCC § 2–207(2) modify this principle by providing that the "additional terms are to be construed as proposals for addition to the contract."

course of dealing   A sequence of previous acts and conduct between the parties to a particular transaction which is fairly to be regarded as establishing a common basis of understanding for interpreting their expressions and other conduct. UCC § 1–205(1).

course of performance   Conduct between the parties concerning performance of the particular contract.

court above—court below   In appellate practice, the "court above" is the one to which a cause is removed for review, whether by appeal, writ of error, or certiorari, while the "court below" is the one from which the case is being removed.

covenant   Used primarily with respect to promises in conveyances or other instruments dealing with real estate.

Covenants against encumbrances A stipulation against all rights to or interests in the land which may subsist in third persons to the diminution of the value of the estate granted.

Covenant appurtenant A covenant which is connected with land of the grantor, not in gross. A covenant running with the land and binding heirs, executors, and assigns of the immediate parties.

Covenant for further assurance An undertaking, in the form of a covenant, on the part of the vendor of real estate to do such further acts for the purpose of perfecting the purchaser's title as the latter may reasonably require.

Covenant for possession A covenant by which the grantee or lessee is granted possession.

Covenant for quiet enjoyment An assurance against the consequences of a defective title, and against any disturbances thereupon.

Covenants for title Covenants usually inserted in a conveyance of land, on the part of the grantor, and binding him for the completeness, security, and continuance of the title transferred to the grantee. They comprise covenants for seisin, for right to convey, against encumbrances, or quiet enjoyment, sometimes for further assurance, and almost always of warranty.

Covenant in gross Such as do not run with the land.

Covenant of right to convey An assurance by the covenantor that the grantor has sufficient capacity and title to convey the estate which he by his deed undertakes to convey.

Covenant of seisin An assurance to the purchaser that the grantor has the very estate in quantity and quality which he purports to convey.

Covenant of warranty An assurance by the grantor of an estate that the grantee shall enjoy the same without interruption by virtue of paramount title.

Covenant running with land A covenant which goes with the land, as being annexed to the estate, and which cannot be separated from the land or transferred without it. A covenant is said to run with the land when not only the original parties or their representatives, but each successive owner of the land, will be entitled to its benefit, or be liable (as the case may be) to its obligation. Such a covenant is said to be one which "touches and concerns" the land itself, so that its benefit or obligation passes with the ownership. Essentials are that the grantor and grantee must have intended that the covenant run with the land, the covenant must affect or concern the land with which it runs, and there must be privity of estate between the party claiming the benefit and the party who rests under the burden.

covenant not to compete   Agreement to refrain from entering into a competing trade, profession, or business.

cover   Buyer's purchase of goods in substitution for those not delivered by breaching seller.

credit beneficiary   See **third-party beneficiary**.

creditor   Any entity having a claim against the debtor.

crime   An act or omission in violation of a public law and punishable by the government.

criminal duress   Coercion by threat of serious bodily injury.

criminal intent   Desired or virtually certain consequences of one's conduct.

criminal law   The law that involves offenses against the entire community.

cure   The right of a seller under the UCC to correct a nonconforming delivery of goods to buyer within the contract period. § 2–508.

curtesy   Husband's estate in the real property of his wife.

cy pres   As near (as possible). Rule for the construction of instruments in equity, by which the intention of the party is carried out *as near as may be*, when it would be impossible or illegal to give it literal effect.

D

damage   Loss, injury, or deterioration caused by the negligence, design, or accident of one person, with respect to another's person or property. The word is to be distinguished from its plural, "damages," which means a compensation in money for a loss or damage.

damages   Money sought as a remedy for breach of contract or for tortious acts.

Actual damages Real, substantial, and just damages, or the amount awarded to a complainant in compensation for his actual and real loss or injury, as opposed, on the one hand, to "nominal" damages and, on the other, to "exemplary" or "punitive" damages. Synonymous with "compensatory damages" and "general damages."

Benefit-of-the-bargain damages Difference between the value received and the value of the fraudulent party's performance as represented.

Compensatory damages Compensatory damages are such as will compensate the injured party for the injury sustained, and nothing more; such as will simply make good or replace the loss caused by the wrong or injury.

Consequential damages Such damage, loss, or injury as does not flow directly and immediately from the act of the party, but only from some of the consequences or results of such act. Consequential damages resulting from a seller's breach of contract include any loss resulting from general or particular requirements and needs of which the seller at the time of contracting had reason to know and which could not reasonably be prevented by cover or otherwise, and injury to person or property proximately resulting from any breach of warranty. UCC § 2–715(2).

Exemplary or punitive damages Damages other than compensatory damages which may be awarded against a person to punish him for outrageous conduct.

Expectancy damages Calculable by subtracting the injured party's actual dollar position as a result of the breach from that party's projected dollar position had performance occurred.

Foreseeable damages Loss of which the party in breach had reason to know when the contract was made.

Incidental damages Under UCC § 2–710, such damages include any commercially reasonable charges, expenses, or commissions incurred in stopping delivery, in the transportation, care, and custody of goods after the buyer's breach, in connection with the return or resale of the goods, or otherwise resulting from the breach. Also, such damages, resulting from a seller's breach of contract, include expenses reasonably incurred in inspection, receipt, transportation, and care and custody of goods rightfully rejected, any commercially reasonable charges, expenses, or commissions in connection with effecting cover, and any other reasonable expense incident to the delay or other breach. UCC § 2–715(1).

Irreparable damages In the law pertaining to injunctions, damages for which no certain pecuniary standard exists for measurement.

Liquidated damages and penalties Damages for breach by either party may be liquidated in the agreement but only at an amount which is reasonable in the light of the anticipated or actual harm caused by the breach, the difficulties of proof of loss, and the inconvenience or nonfeasibility of otherwise obtaining an adequate remedy. A term fixing unreasonably large liquidated damages is void as a penalty. UCC § 2–718(1).

Mitigation of damages A plaintiff may not recover damages for the effects of an injury which she reasonably could have avoided or substantially ameliorated. This limitation on recovery is generally denominated as "mitigation of damages" or "avoidance of consequences."

Nominal damages A small sum awarded where a contract has been breached but the loss is negligible or unproven.

Out-of-pocket damages Difference between the value received and the value given.

Reliance damages Contract damages placing the injured party in as good a position as he would have been in had the contract not been made.

Treble damages Three times actual loss.

de facto In fact, in deed, actually. This phrase is used to characterize an officer, a government, a past action, or a state of affairs which must be accepted for all practical purposes but which is illegal or illegitimate. See also **corporation**, *corporation de facto*.

de jure Descriptive of a condition in which there has been total compliance with all requirements of law. In this sense it is the contrary of *de facto*. See also **corporation**, *corporation de jure*.

de novo Anew; afresh; a second time.

debenture Unsecured bond.

debt security Any form of corporate security reflected as debt on the books of the corporation in contrast to equity securities such as stock; *e.g.*, bonds, notes, and debentures are debt securities.

debtor Person who owes payment or performance of an obligation.

deceit A fraudulent and cheating misrepresentation, artifice, or device used to deceive and trick one who is ignorant of the true facts, to the prejudice and damage of the party imposed upon. See also **fraud; misrepresentation**.

decree Decision of a court of equity.

deed A conveyance of realty; a writing, signed by a grantor, whereby title to realty is transferred from one party to another.

deed of trust Interest in real property which is conveyed to a third person as trustee for the creditor.

defamation Injury of a person's reputation by publication of false statements.

default judgment Judgment against a defendant who fails to respond to a complaint.

defendant The party against whom legal action is sought.

definite term Lease that automatically expires at end of the term.

delectus personae Partner's right to choose who may become a member of the partnership.

delegatee Third party to whom the delegator's duty is delegated.

delegation of duties Transferring to another all or part of one's duties arising under a contract.

delegator Party delegating his duty to a third party.

delivery The physical or constructive transfer of an instrument or of goods from one person to another. See also **constructive delivery**.

demand Request for payment made by the holder of the instrument.

demand paper Payable on request.

demurrer An allegation of a defendant that even if the facts as stated in the pleading to which objection is taken be true, their legal consequences are not such as to require the demurring party to answer them or to proceed further with the cause.

The Federal Rules of Civil Procedure do not provide for the use of a demurrer, but provide an equivalent to a general demurrer in the motion to dismiss for failure to state a claim on which relief may be granted. Fed.R. Civil P. 12(b).

deposition The testimony of a witness taken upon interrogatories, not in court, but intended to be used in court. See also **discovery**.

depository bank The first bank to which an item is transferred for collection even though it may also be the payor bank. UCC § 4–105(a).

descent Succession to the ownership of an estate by inheritance or by any act of law, as distinguished from "purchase."

Descents are of two sorts, lineal and collateral. Lineal descent is descent in a direct or right line, as from father or grandfather to son or grandson. Collateral descent is descent in a collateral or oblique line, that is, up to the common ancestor and then down from him, as from brother to brother, or between cousins.

design defect Plans or specifications inadequate to ensure the product's safety.

devise A testamentary disposition of land or realty; a gift of real property by the last will and testament of the donor. When used as a noun, means a testamentary disposition of real or personal property; when used as a verb, means to dispose of real or personal property by will.

dictum Generally used as an abbreviated form of *obiter dictum*, "a remark by the way"; that is, an observation or remark made by a judge which does not embody the resolution or determination of the court and which is made without argument or full consideration of the point.

directed verdict In a case in which the party with the burden of proof has failed to present a prima facie case for jury consideration, the trial judge may order the entry of a verdict without allowing the jury to consider it because, as a matter of law, there can be only one such verdict. Fed.R. Civil P. 50(a).

disaffirmance Avoidance of a contract.

discharge Termination of certain allowed claims against a debtor.

disclaimer Negation of warranty.

discount A discount by a bank means a drawback or deduction made upon its advances or loans of money, upon negotiable paper or other evidences of debt payable at a future day, which are transferred to the bank.

discovery The pretrial devices that can be used by one party to obtain facts and information about the case from the other party in order to assist the party's preparation for trial. Under the Federal Rules of Civil Procedure, tools of discovery include depositions upon oral and written questions, written interrogatories, production of documents or things, permission to enter upon land or other property, physical and mental examinations, and requests for admission. Rules 26–37.

dishonor To refuse to accept or pay a draft or to pay a promissory note when duly presented. UCC § 3–507(1); § 4–210. See also **protest.**

disparagement Publication of false statements resulting in harm to another's monetary interests.

disputed debt Obligation whose existence or amount is contested.

dissenting shareholder One who opposes a fundamental change and has the right to receive the fair value of her shares.

dissolution The dissolution of a partnership is the change in the relation of the partners caused by any partner's ceasing to be associated with the carrying on, as distinguished from the winding up, of the business. See also **winding up.**

distribution Transfer of partnership property from the partnership to a partner; transfer of property from a corporation to any of its shareholders.

dividend The payment designated by the board of directors of a corporation to be distributed pro rata among a class or classes of the shares outstanding.

document Document of title.

document of title Instrument evidencing ownership of the document and the goods it covers.

domicile That place where a person has his true, fixed, and permanent home and principal establishment, and to which whenever he is absent he has the intention of returning.

dominant Land whose owner has rights in other land.

donee Recipient of a gift.

donee beneficiary See **third-party beneficiary.**

donor Maker of a gift.

dormant partner One who is both a silent and a secret partner.

dower A species of life-estate which a woman is, by law, entitled to claim on the death of her husband, in the lands and tenements of which he was seised in fee during the marriage, and which her issue, if any, might by possibility have inherited.

Dower has been abolished in the majority of the states and materially altered in most of the others.

draft A written order by the first party, called the drawer, instructing a second party, called the drawee (such as a bank), to pay a third party, called the payee. An order to pay a sum certain in money, signed by a drawer, payable on demand or at a definite time, and to order or bearer. UCC § 3–104.

drawee A person to whom a bill of exchange or draft is directed, and who is requested to pay the amount of money therein mentioned. The drawee of a check is the bank on which it is drawn.

When a drawee accepts, he engages that he will pay the instrument according to its tenor at the time of his engagement or as completed. UCC § 3–413(1).

drawer The person who draws a bill or draft. The drawer of a check is the person who signs it.

The drawer engages that upon dishonor of the draft and any necessary notice of dishonor or protest, he will pay the amount of the draft to the holder or to any indorser who takes it up. The drawer may disclaim this liability by drawing without recourse. UCC § 3–413(2).

due negotiation Transfer of a negotiable document in the regular course of business to a holder, who takes in good faith, without notice of any defense or claim, and for value.

duress Unlawful constraint exercised upon a person, whereby he is forced to do some act against his will.

Physical duress Coercion involving physical force or the threat of physical force.

duty Legal obligation requiring a person to perform or refrain from performing an act.

E

earned surplus Undistributed net profits, income, gains, and losses.

earnest The payment of a part of the price of goods sold, or the delivery of part of such goods, for the purpose of binding the contract.

easement A right in the owner of one parcel of land, by reason of such ownership, to use the land of another for a special purpose not inconsistent with a general property right in the owner. This right is distinguishable from a "license," which merely confers a personal privilege to do some act on the land.

Affirmative easement One where the servient estate must permit something to be done thereon, as to pass over it, or to discharge water on it.

Appurtenant easement An incorporeal right which is attached to a superior right and inheres in land to which it is attached and is in the nature of a covenant running with the land.

Easement by necessity Such arises by operation of law when land conveyed is completely shut off from access to any road by land retained by the grantor or by land of the grantor and that of a stranger.

Easement by prescription A mode of acquiring title to property by immemorial or long-continued enjoyment; refers to personal usage restricted to claimant and his ancestors or grantors.

Easement in gross An easement in gross is not appurtenant to any estate in land or does not belong to any person by virtue of ownership of an estate in other land but is a mere personal interest in or a right to use the land of another; it is purely personal and usually ends with death of grantee.

Easement of access Right of ingress and egress to and from the premises of a lot owner to a street appurtenant to the land of the lot owner.

ejectment An action to determine whether the title to certain land is in the plaintiff or is in the defendant.

electronic funds transfer A transaction with a financial institution by means of computer, telephone, or other electronic instrument.

emancipation The act by which an infant is liberated from the control of a parent or guardian and made his own master.

embezzlement The taking, in violation of a trust, of the property of one's employer.

emergency Sudden, unexpected event calling for immediate action.

eminent domain Right of the people or government to take private property for public use upon giving fair consideration.

employment discrimination Hiring, firing, compensating, promoting, or training of employees based on race, color, sex, religion, or national origin.

employment relationship One in which employer has right to control the physical conduct of employee.

endowment contract Agreement to pay insured a lump sum upon reaching a specified age or in event of death.

entirety Used to designate that which the law considers as a single whole incapable of being divided into parts.

entrapment Induced by a government official into committing a crime.

entrusting Transfer of possession of goods to a merchant who deals in goods of that kind and who may in turn transfer valid title to a buyer in the ordinary course of business.

equal pay Equivalent pay for the same work.

equal protection Requirement that similarly situated persons be treated similarly by government action.

equipment Goods used primarily in business.

equitable Just, fair, and right. Existing in equity; available or sustainable only in equity, or only upon the rules and principles of equity.

equity Justice administered according to fairness, as contrasted with the strictly formulated rules of common law. It is based on a system of rules and principles which originated in England as an alternative to the harsh rules of common law and which were based on what was fair in a particular situation.

equity of redemption The right of the mortgagor of an estate to redeem the same after it has been forfeited, at law, by a breach of the condition of the mortgage, upon paying the amount of debt, interest, and costs.

equity securities Stock or similar security, in contrast to debt securities such as bonds, notes, and debentures.

error A mistake of law, or a false or irregular application of it, such as vitiates legal proceedings and warrants reversal of the judgment.

Harmless error In appellate practice, an error committed in the progress of the trial below which was not prejudicial to the rights of the party assigning it and for which, therefore, the appellate court will not reverse the judgment.

Reversible error In appellate practice, such an error as warrants the appellate court's reversal of the judgment before it.

escrow A system of document transfer in which a deed, bond, or funds is or are delivered to a third person to hold until all conditions in a contract are fulfilled; *e.g.*, delivery of deed to escrow agent under installment land sale contract until full payment for land is made.

estate The degree, quantity, nature, and extent of interest which a person has in real and personal property. An estate in lands, tenements, and hereditaments signifies such interest as the tenant has therein.

Also, the total property of whatever kind that is owned by a decedent prior to the distribution of that property in accordance with the terms of a will or, when there is no will, by the laws of inheritance in the state of domicile of the decedent.

Future estate An estate limited to commence in possession at a future day, either without the intervention of a precedent estate or on the determination by lapse of time, or otherwise, of a precedent estate created at the same time. Examples include reversions and remainders.

estoppel A bar or impediment raised by the law which precludes a person from alleging or from denying a certain fact or state of facts, in consequence of his or her previous allegation, denial, conduct, or admission, or in consequence of a final adjudication of the matter in a court of law. See also **waiver**.

eviction Dispossession by process of law; the act of depriving a person of the possession of lands which he has held, pursuant to the judgment of a court.

evidence Any species of proof or probative matter legally presented at the trial of an issue by the act of the parties and through the medium of witnesses, records, documents, concrete objects, etc., for the purpose of inducing belief in the minds of the court or jury as to the parties' contention.

exception A formal objection to the action of the court, during the trial of a cause, in refusing a request or overruling an objection; implying that the party excepting does not acquiesce in the decision of the court but will seek to procure its reversal, and that he means to save the benefit of his request or objection in some future proceeding.

exclusionary rule Prohibition of illegally obtained evidence.

exclusive dealing Sole right to sell goods in a defined market.

exclusive jurisdiction Such jurisdiction that permits only one court (state or federal) to hear a case.

exculpatory clause Excusing oneself from fault or liability.

execution

Execution of contract includes performance of all acts necessary to render it complete as an instrument; implies that nothing more need be done to make the contract complete and effective.

Execution upon a money judgment is the legal process of enforcing the judgment, usually by seizing and selling property of the debtor.

executive order   Legislation issued by the president or a governor.

executor   A person appointed by a testator to carry out the directions and requests in his will and to dispose of the property according to his testamentary provisions after his decease. The female designation is executrix. A person appointed by the court in an intestacy situation is called the administrator(rix).

executory   That which is yet to be executed or performed; that which remains to be carried into operation or effect; incomplete; depending upon a future performance or event. The opposite of executed.

executory contract   See **contracts.**

executory promise   Unperformed obligation.

exemplary damages   See **damages.**

exoneration   Relieved of liability.

express   Manifested by direct and appropriate language, as distinguished from that which is inferred from conduct. The word is usually contrasted with "implied."

express warranty   Explicitly made contractual promise regarding property or contract rights transferred; in a sale of goods, an affirmation of fact or a promise about the goods or a description, including a sample, of goods which becomes part of the basis of the bargain.

expropriation   Governmental taking of foreign-owned property for a public purpose and with payment.

ex-ship   Risk of loss passes to buyer when the goods leave the ship. See UCC § 2–322. See also **F.A.S.**

extortion   Making threats to obtain property.

F
fact   An event that took place or a thing that exists.

false imprisonment   Intentional interference with a person's freedom of movement by unlawful confinement.

false light   Offensive publicity placing another in a false light.

false pretenses   Intentional misrepresentation of fact in order to cheat another.

farm products   Crops, livestock, or stock used or produced in farming.

F.A.S.   Free alongside. Term used in sales price quotations indicating that the price includes all costs of transportation and delivery of the goods alongside the ship. See UCC § 2–319(2).

federal preemption   First right of the federal government to regulate matters within its powers to the possible exclusion of state regulation.

federal question   Any case arising under the Constitution, statutes, or treaties of the United States.

fee simple

Absolute A fee simple absolute is an estate that is unlimited as to duration, disposition, and descendibility. It is the largest estate and most extensive interest that can be enjoyed in land.

Conditional Type of transfer in which grantor conveys fee simple on condition that something be done or not done.

Defeasible Type of fee grant which may be defeated on the happening of an event. An estate which may last forever, but which

may end upon the happening of a specified event, is a "fee simple defeasible."

Determinable Created by conveyance which contains words effective to create a fee simple and, in addition, a provision for automatic expiration of the estate on occurrence of stated event.

fee tail   An estate of inheritance, descending only to a certain class or classes of heirs; *e.g.,* an estate is conveyed or devised "to A. and the heirs of his body," or "to A. and the heirs male of his body," or "to A., and the heirs female of his body."

fellow servant rule   Common law defense relieving employer from liability to an employee for injuries caused by negligence of fellow employee.

felony   Serious crime.

fiduciary   A person or institution who manages money or property for another and who must exercise in such management activity a standard of care imposed by law or contract; *e.g.,* executor of estate; receiver in bankruptcy; trustee.

fiduciary duty   Duty of utmost loyalty and good faith, such as that owed by a fiduciary such as an agent to her principal.

field warehouse   Secured party takes possession of the goods but the debtor has access to the goods.

final credit   Payment of the instrument by the payor bank.

financing statement   Under the Uniform Commercial Code, a financing statement is used under Article 9 to reflect a public record that there is a security interest or claim to the goods in question to secure a debt. The financing statement is filed by the security holder with the secretary of state or with a similar public body; thus filed, it becomes public record. See also **secured transaction.**

fire (property) insurance   Provides protection against loss due to fire or other related perils.

firm offer   Irrevocable offer to sell or buy goods by a merchant in a signed writing which gives assurance that it will not be rescinded for up to three months.

fitness for a particular purpose   Goods are fit for a stated purpose, provided that the seller selects the product knowing the buyer's intended use and that the buyer is relying on the seller's judgment.

fixture   An article in the nature of personal property which has been so annexed to realty that it is regarded as a part of the land. Examples include a furnace affixed to a house or other building, counters permanently affixed to the floor of a store, and a sprinkler system installed in a building. UCC § 9–313(1)(a).

Trade fixtures Such chattels as merchants usually possess and annex to the premises occupied by them to enable them to store, handle, and display their goods, which generally are removable without material injury to the premises.

F.O.B.   Free on board at some location (for example, F.O.B shipping point; F.O.B destination); the invoice price includes delivery at seller's expense to that location. Title to goods usually passes from seller to buyer at the F.O.B location. UCC § 2–319(1).

foreclosure   Procedure by which mortgaged property is sold on default of mortgagor in satisfaction of mortgage debt.

forgery   Intentional falsification of a document with intent to defraud.

four unities   Time, title, interest, and possession.

franchise   A privilege granted or sold, such as to use a name or to sell products or services. The right given by a manufacturer or supplier to a retailer to use his products and name on terms and conditions mutually agreed upon.

fraud Elements include false representation; of a present or past fact; made by defendant; action in reliance thereon by plaintiff; and damage resulting to plaintiff from such misrepresentation.

fraud in the execution Misrepresentation that deceives the other party as to the nature of a document evidencing the contract.

fraud in the inducement Misrepresentation regarding the subject matter of a contract that induces the other party to enter into the contract.

fraudulent misrepresentation False statement made with knowledge of its falsity and intent to mislead.

freehold An estate for life or in fee. It must possess two qualities: (1) immobility, that is, the property must be either land or some interest issuing out of or annexed to land; and (2) indeterminate duration.

friendly fire Fire contained where it is intended to be.

frustration of purpose doctrine Excuses a promisor in certain situations when the objectives of contract have been utterly defeated by circumstances arising after formation of the agreement, and performance is excused under this rule even though there is no impediment to actual performance.

full warranty One under which warrantor will repair the product and, if unsuccessful, will replace it or refund its cost.

fungibles With respect to goods or securities, those of which any unit is, by nature or usage of trade, the equivalent of any other like unit. UCC § 1–201(17); *e.g.*, a bushel of wheat or other grain.

future estate See **estate.**

G

garnishment A statutory proceeding whereby a person's property, money, or credits in the possession or control of another are applied to payment of the former's debt to a third person.

general intangible Catchall category for collateral not otherwise covered.

general partner Member of either a general or limited partnership with unlimited liability for its debts, full management powers, and a right to share in the profits.

gift A voluntary transfer of property to another made gratuitously and without consideration. Essential requisites of "gift" are capacity of donor, intention of donor to make gift, completed delivery to or for donee, and acceptance of gift by donee.

gift causa mortis A gift in view of death is one which is made in contemplation, fear, or peril of death and with the intent that it shall take effect only in case of the death of the giver.

good faith Honesty in fact and the observance of reasonable commercial standards of fair dealing.

good faith purchaser Buyer who acts honestly, gives value, and takes the goods without notice or knowledge of any defect in the title of his transferor.

goods A term of variable content and meaning. It may include every species of personal property, or it may be given a very restricted meaning. Sometimes the meaning of "goods" is extended to include all tangible items, as in the phrase "goods and services."

All things (including specially manufactured goods) which are movable at the time of identification to a contract for sale other than the money in which the price is to be paid, investment securities, and things in action. UCC § 2–105(1).

grantee Transferee of property.

grantor A transferor of property. The creator of a trust is usually designated as the grantor of the trust.

gratuitous promise Promise made without consideration.

group insurance Covers a number of individuals.

guaranty A promise to answer for the payment of some debt, or the performance of some duty, in case of the failure of another person who, in the first instance, is liable for such payment or performance.

The terms *guaranty* and *suretyship* are sometimes used interchangeably; but they should not be confounded. The distinction between contract of suretyship and contract of guaranty is whether or not the undertaking is a joint undertaking with the principal or a separate and distinct contract; if it is the former, it is one of "suretyship," and if the latter, it is one of "guaranty." See also **surety.**

guardianship The relationship under which a person (the guardian) is appointed by a court to preserve and control the property of another (the ward).

H

heir A person who succeeds, by the rules of law, to an estate in lands, tenements, or hereditaments, upon the death of his ancestor, by descent and right of relationship.

holder Person who is in possession of a document of title or an instrument or an investment security drawn, issued, or indorsed to him or to his order, or to bearer, or in blank. UCC § 1–201(20).

holder in due course A holder who takes an instrument for value, in good faith, and without notice that it is overdue or has been dishonored or of any defense against or claim to it on the part of any person.

holograph A will or deed written entirely by the testator or grantor with his own hand and not witnessed (attested). State laws vary with respect to the validity of the holographic will.

homicide Unlawful taking of another's life.

horizontal privity Who may bring a cause of action.

horizontal restraints Agreements among competitors.

hostile fire Any fire outside its intended or usual place.

I

identified goods Designated goods as a part of a particular contract.

illegal per se Conclusively presumed unreasonable and therefore illegal.

illusory promise Promise imposing no obligation on the promisor.

implied-in-fact condition Contingencies understood but not expressed by the parties.

implied-in-law condition Contingency that arises from operation of law.

implied warranty Obligation imposed by law upon the transferor of property or contract rights; implicit in the sale arising out of certain circumstances.

implied warranty of habitability Leased premises are fit for ordinary residential purposes.

impossibility Performance that cannot be done.

in personam Against the person. Action seeking judgment against a person involving his personal rights and based on jurisdiction of his person, as distinguished from a judgment against property (*i.e.*, in rem).

in personam jurisdiction Jurisdiction based on claims against a person, in contrast to jurisdiction over his property.

in re In the affair; in the matter of; concerning; regarding. This is the usual method of entitling a judicial proceeding in which there are no adversary parties, but merely some res concerning which judicial action is to be taken, such as a bankrupt's estate, an estate in the probate court, a proposed public highway, etc.

in rem A technical term used to designate proceedings or actions instituted *against the thing*, in contradistinction to personal actions, which are said to be *in personam*.

Quasi in rem A term applied to proceedings which are not strictly and purely *in rem*, but are brought against the defendant personally, though the real object is to deal with particular property or subject property to the discharge of claims asserted; for example, foreign attachment, or proceedings to foreclose a mortgage, remove a cloud from title, or effect a partition.

in rem jurisdiction Jurisdiction based on claims against property.

incidental beneficiary Third party whom the two parties to a contract have no intention of benefiting by their contract.

income bond Bond that conditions payment of interest on corporate earnings.

incontestability clause The prohibition of an insurer to avoid an insurance policy after a specified period of time.

indemnification Duty owed by principal to agent to pay agent for losses incurred while acting as directed by principal.

indemnify To reimburse one for a loss already incurred.

indenture A written agreement under which bonds and debentures are issued, setting forth maturity date, interest rate, and other terms.

independent contractor Person who contracts with another to do a particular job and who is not subject to the control of the other.

indicia Signs; indications. Circumstances which point to the existence of a given fact as probable, but not certain.

indictment Grand jury charge that the defendant should stand trial.

indispensable paper Chattel paper, instruments, and documents.

indorsee The person to whom a negotiable instrument, promissory note, bill of lading, etc., is assigned by indorsement.

indorsement The act of a payee, drawee, accommodation indorser, or holder of a bill, note, check, or other negotiable instrument, in writing his name upon the back of the same, with or without further or qualifying words, whereby the property in the same is assigned and transferred to another. UCC § 3–202 *et seq.*

Blank indorsement No indorsee is specified.

Qualified indorsement Without recourse, limiting one's liability on the instrument.

Restrictive indorsement Limits the rights of the indorser in some manner.

Special indorsement Designates an indorsee to be paid.

infliction of emotional distress Extreme and outrageous conduct intentionally or recklessly causing severe emotional distress.

information Formal accusation of a crime brought by a prosecutor.

infringement Unauthorized use.

injunction An equitable remedy forbidding the party defendant from doing some act which he is threatening or attempting to commit, or restraining him in the continuance thereof, such act being unjust and inequitable, injurious to the plaintiff, and not such as can be adequately redressed by an action at law.

innkeeper Hotel or motel operator.

inquisitorial system System in which the judiciary initiates, conducts, and decides cases.

insider Relative or general partner of debtor, partnership in which debtor is a partner, or corporation in which debtor is an officer, director, or controlling person.

insiders Directors, officers, employees, and agents of the issuer as well as those the issuer has entrusted with information solely for corporate purposes.

insolvency Under the UCC, a person is insolvent who either has ceased to pay his debts in the ordinary course of business or cannot pay his debts as they fall due or is insolvent within the meaning of the Federal Bankruptcy Law. UCC § 1–201(23).

Insolvency (bankruptcy) Total liabilities exceed total value of assets.

Insolvency (equity) Inability to pay debts in ordinary course of business or as they become due.

inspection Examination of goods to determine whether they conform to a contract.

instrument Negotiable instruments, stocks, bonds, and other investment securities.

insurable interest Exists where insured derives pecuniary benefit or advantage by preservation and continued existence of property or would sustain pecuniary loss from its destruction.

insurance A contract whereby, for a stipulated consideration, one party undertakes to compensate the other for loss on a specified subject by specified perils. The party agreeing to make the compensation is usually called the "insurer" or "underwriter"; the other, the "insured" or "assured"; the written contract, a "policy"; the events insured against, "risks" or "perils"; and the subject, right, or interest to be protected, the "insurable interest." Insurance is a contract whereby one undertakes to indemnify another against loss, damage, or liability arising from an unknown or contingent event.

Co-insurance A form of insurance in which a person insures property for less than its full or stated value and agrees to share the risk of loss.

Life insurance Payment of a specific sum of money to a designated beneficiary upon the death of the insured.

Ordinary life Life insurance with a savings component that runs for the life of the insured.

Term life Life insurance issued for a limited number of years that does not have a savings component.

intangible property Protected interests that are not physical.

intangibles Accounts and general intangibles.

intent Desire to cause the consequences of an act or knowledge that the consequences are substantially certain to result from the act.

inter alia Among other things.

inter se or inter sese Latin. Among or between themselves; used to distinguish rights or duties between two or more parties from their rights or duties to others.

interest in land Any right, privilege, power, or immunity in real property.

interest in partnership Partner's share in the partnership's profits and surplus.

interference with contractual relations Intentionally causing one of the parties to a contract not to perform the contract.

intermediary bank Any bank, except the depositary or payor bank, to which an item is transferred in the course of collection. UCC § 4–105(c).

intermediate test Requirement that legislation have a substantial relationship to an important governmental objective.

international law Deals with the conduct and relations of nation-states and international organizations.

interpretation Construction or meaning of a contract.

interpretative rules Statements issued by an administrative agency indicating its construction of its governing statute.

intestate A person is said to die intestate when he dies without making a will. The word is also often used to signify the person himself.

>   *Compare* testator.

intrusion Unreasonable and highly offensive interference with the seclusion of another.

inventory Goods held for sale or lease or consumed in a business.

invitee A person is an "invitee" on land of another if (1) he enters by invitation, express or implied, (2) his entry is connected with the owner's business or with an activity the owner conducts or permits to be conducted on his land, and (3) there is mutual benefit or a benefit to the owner.

J

joint and several liability Liability where creditor may sue partners jointly as a group or separately as individuals.

joint liability Liability where creditor must sue all of the partners as a group.

joint stock company A general partnership with some corporate attributes.

joint tenancy See tenancy.

joint venture An association of two or more persons to carry on a single business transaction for profit.

judgment The official and authentic decision of a court of justice upon the respective rights and claims of the parties to an action or suit therein litigated and submitted to its determination.

judgment in personam A judgment against a particular person, as distinguished from a judgment against a thing or a right or *status*.

judgment in rem An adjudication pronounced upon the status of some particular thing or subject matter, by a tribunal having competent authority.

judgment n. o. v. Judgment non obstante veredicto in its broadest sense is a judgment rendered in favor of one party notwithstanding the finding of a verdict in favor of the other party.

judgment notwithstanding the verdict A final binding determination on the merits made by the judge after and contrary to the jury's verdict.

judgment on the pleadings Final binding determination on the merits made by the judge after the pleadings.

judicial lien Interest in property that is obtained by court action to secure payment of a debt.

judicial review Power of the courts to determine the constitutionality of legislative and executive acts.

jurisdiction The right and power of a court to adjudicate concerning the subject matter in a given case.

jurisdiction over the parties Power of a court to bind the parties to a suit.

jury A body of persons selected and summoned by law and sworn to try the facts of a case and to find according to the law and the evidence. In general, the province of the jury is to find the facts in a case, while the judge passes upon pure questions of law. As a matter of fact, however, the jury must often pass upon mixed questions of law and fact in determining the case, and in all such cases the instructions of the judge as to the law become very important.

justifiable reliance Reasonably influenced by a misrepresentation.

L

labor dispute Any controversy concerning terms or conditions of employment or union representation.

laches Based upon the maxim that equity aids the vigilant and not those who slumber on their rights. It is defined as neglect to assert a right or claim which, taken together with a lapse of time and other circumstances causing prejudice to the adverse party, operates as a bar in a court of equity.

landlord The owner of an estate in land, or a rental property, who has leased it to another person, called the "tenant." Also called "lessor."

larceny Trespassory taking and carrying away of the goods of another with the intent to permanently deprive.

last clear chance Final opportunity to avoid an injury.

lease Any agreement which gives rise to relationship of landlord and tenant (real property) or lessor and lessee (real or personal property).

>   The person who conveys is termed the "lessor," and the person to whom conveyed, the "lessee"; and when the lessor conveys land or tenements to a lessee, he is said to lease, demise, or let them.
>
>   *Sublease, or underlease* One executed by the lessee of an estate to a third person, conveying the same estate for a shorter term than that for which the lessee holds it.

leasehold An estate in realty held under a lease. The four principal types of leasehold estates are the estate for years, periodic tenancy, tenancy at will, and tenancy at sufferance.

leasehold estate Right to possess real property.

legacy "Legacy" is a gift or bequest by will of personal property, whereas a "devise" is a testamentary disposition of real estate.

>   *Demonstrative legacy* A bequest of a certain sum of money, with a direction that it shall be paid out of a particular fund. It differs from a specific legacy in this respect: that, if the fund out of which it is payable fails for any cause, it is nevertheless entitled to come on the estate as a general legacy. And it differs from a general legacy in this: that it does not abate in that class, but in the class of specific legacies.
>
>   *General legacy* A pecuniary legacy, payable out of the general assets of a testator.

Residuary legacy A bequest of all the testator's personal estate not otherwise effectually disposed of by his will.

Specific legacy One which operates on property particularly designated. A legacy or gift by will of a particular specified thing, as of a horse, a piece of furniture, a term of years, and the like.

legal aggregate A group of individuals not having a legal existence separate from its members.

legal benefit Obtaining something to which one had no legal right.

legal detriment Doing an act one is not legally obligated to do or not doing an act one has a legal right to do.

legal entity An organization having a legal existence separate from that of its members.

legal sufficiency Benefit to promisor or detriment to promisee.

legislative rules Substantive rules issued by an administrative agency under the authority delegated to it by the legislature.

letter of credit An engagement by a bank or other person made at the request of a customer that the issuer will honor drafts or other demands for payment upon compliance with the conditions specified in the credit.

letters of administration Formal documents issued by probate court appointing one an administrator of an estate.

letters testamentary The formal instrument of authority and appointment given to an executor by the proper court, empowering him to enter upon the discharge of his office as executor. It corresponds to letters of administration granted to an administrator.

levy To assess; raise; execute; exact; tax; collect; gather; take up; seize. Thus, to levy (assess, exact, raise, or collect) a tax; to levy an execution, *i.e.*, to levy or collect a sum of money on an execution.

liability insurance Covers liability to others by reason of damage resulting from injuries to another's person or property.

liability without fault Crime to do a specific act or cause a certain result without regard to the care exercised.

libel Defamation communicated by writing, television, radio, or the like.

liberty Ability of individuals to engage in freedom of action and choice regarding their personal lives.

license License with respect to real property is a privilege to go on premises for a certain purpose, but does not operate to confer on or vest in the licensee any title, interest, or estate in such property.

licensee Person privileged to enter or remain on land by virtue of the consent of the lawful possessor.

lien A qualified right of property which a creditor has in or over specific property of his debtor, as security for the debt or charge or for performance of some act.

lien creditor A creditor who has acquired a lien on the property by attachment.

life estate An estate whose duration is limited to the life of the party holding it or of some other person. Upon the death of the life tenant, the property will go to the holder of the remainder interest or to the grantor by reversion.

limited liability Liability limited to amount invested in a business enterprise.

limited partner Member of a limited partnership with liability for its debts only to the extent of her capital contribution.

limited partnership See **partnership**.

limited partnership association A partnership which closely resembles a corporation.

liquidated Ascertained; determined; fixed; settled; made clear or manifest. Cleared away; paid; discharged.

liquidated damages See **damages**.

liquidated debt Obligation that is certain in amount.

liquidation The settling of financial affairs of a business or individual, usually by liquidating (turning to cash) all assets for distribution to creditors, heirs, etc. To be distinguished from dissolution.

loss of value Value of promised performance minus value of actual performance.

lost property Property with which the owner has involuntarily parted and which she does not know where to find or recover, not including property which she has intentionally concealed or deposited in a secret place for safekeeping. Distinguishable from mislaid property, which has been deliberately placed somewhere and forgotten.

M

main purpose rule Where object of promisor/surety is to provide an economic benefit for herself, the promise is considered outside of the statute of frauds.

maker One who makes or executes; as the maker of a promissory note. One who signs a check; in this context, synonymous with drawer. See **draft**.

mala in se Morally wrong.

mala prohibita Wrong by law.

mandamus Latin, we command. A legal writ compelling the defendant to do an official duty.

manslaughter Unlawful taking of another's life without malice.

Involuntary manslaughter Taking the life of another by criminal negligence or during the course of a misdemeanor.

Voluntary manslaughter Intentional killing of another under extenuating circumstances.

manufacturing defect Not produced according to specifications.

mark Trade symbol.

market allocations Division of market by customers, geographic location, or products.

marketable title Free from any defects, encumbrances, or reasonable objections to one's ownership.

marshaling of assets Segregating the assets and liabilities of a partnership from the assets and liabilities of the individual partners.

master See **principal**.

material Matters to which a reasonable investor would attach importance in deciding whether to purchase a security.

material alteration Any change that changes the contract of any party to an instrument.

maturity The date at which an obligation, such as the principal of a bond or a note, becomes due.

maxim A general legal principle.

mechanic's lien A claim created by state statutes for the purpose of securing priority of payment of the price or value of work performed and materials furnished in erecting or repairing a building or other structure; as such, attaches to the land as well as buildings and improvements erected thereon.

mediation Nonbinding process in which a third party acts as an intermediary between the disputing parties and proposes solutions for them to consider.

mens rea Criminal intent.

mentally incompetent Unable to understand the nature and effect of one's acts.

mercantile law An expression substantially equivalent to commercial law. It designates the system of rules, customs, and usages generally recognized and adopted by merchants and traders that, either in its simplicity or as modified by common law or statutes, constitutes the law for the regulation of their transactions and the solution of their controversies. The Uniform Commercial Code is the general body of law governing commercial or mercantile transactions.

merchant A person who deals in goods of the kind involved in a transaction or who otherwise by his occupation holds himself out as having knowledge or skill peculiar to the practices or goods involved in the transaction or to whom such knowledge or skill may be attributed by his employment of an agent or broker or other intermediary who by his occupation holds himself out as having such knowledge or skill. UCC § 2–104(1).

merchantability Merchant seller guarantees that the goods are fit for their ordinary purpose.

merger The fusion or absorption of one thing or right into another. In corporate law, the absorption of one company by another, the latter retaining its own name and identity and acquiring the assets, liabilities, franchises, and powers of the former, which ceases to exist as a separate business entity. It differs from a consolidation, wherein all the corporations terminate their separate existences and become parties to a new one.

    Conglomerate merger An acquisition, which is not horizontal or vertical, by one company of another.

    Horizontal merger Merger between business competitors, such as manufacturers of the same type of products or distributors selling competing products in the same market area.

    Short-form merger Merger of a 90 percent subsidiary into its parent.

    Vertical merger Union with corporate customer or supplier.

midnight deadline Midnight of the next banking day after receiving an item.

mining partnership A specific type of partnership for the purpose of extracting raw minerals.

minor Under the age of legal majority (usually eighteen).

mirror image rule An acceptance cannot deviate from the terms of the offer.

misdemeanor Less serious crime.

mislaid property Property which an owner has put deliberately in a certain place that she is unable to remember, as distinguished from lost property, which the owner has left unwittingly in a location she has forgotten. See also **lost property**.

misrepresentation Any manifestation by words or other conduct by one person to another that, under the circumstances, amounts to an assertion not in accordance with the facts. A "misrepresentation" that justifies the rescission of a contract is a false statement of a substantive fact, or any conduct which leads to a belief of a substantive fact material to proper understanding of the matter in hand. See also **deceit; fraud**.

    Fraudulent misrepresentation False statement made with knowledge of its falsity and intent to mislead.

    Innocent misrepresentation Misrepresentation made without knowledge of its falsity but with due care.

    Negligent misrepresentation Misrepresentation made without due care in ascertaining its falsity.

M'Naughten Rule Right/wrong test for criminal insanity.

modify Change the lower court's judgment.

money Medium of exchange issued by a government body.

monopoly Ability to control price or exclude others from the marketplace.

mortgage A mortgage is an interest in land created by a written instrument providing security for the performance of a duty or the payment of a debt.

mortgagor Debtor who uses real estate to secure an obligation.

multinational enterprise Business that engages in transactions involving the movement of goods, information, money, people, or services across national borders.

multiple product order Order requiring an advertiser to cease and desist from deceptive statements on all products it sells.

murder Unlawful and premeditated taking of another's life.

mutual mistake Where the common but erroneous belief of both parties forms the basis of a contract.

N

necessaries Items needed to maintain a person's station in life.

negligence The omission to do something which a reasonable person, guided by those ordinary considerations which ordinarily regulate human affairs, would do, or the doing of something which a reasonable and prudent person would not do.

    Culpable negligence Greater than ordinary negligence but less than gross negligence.

negligence per se Conclusive on the issue of negligence (duty of care and breach).

negotiable Legally capable of being transferred by indorsement or delivery. Usually said of checks and notes and sometimes of stocks and bearer bonds.

negotiable instrument Signed document (such as a check or promissory note) containing an unconditional promise to pay a "sum certain" of money at a definite time to order or bearer.

negotiation Transferee becomes a holder.

net assets Total assets minus total debts.

no arrival, no sale A destination contract, but if goods do not arrive, seller is excused from liability unless such is due to the seller's fault.

no-fault insurance Compensates victims of automobile accidents regardless of fault.

nonconforming use Preexisting use not in accordance with a zoning ordinance.

nonprofit corporation One whose profits must be used exclusively for the charitable, educational, or scientific purpose for which it was formed.

nonsuit   Action in form of a judgment taken against a plaintiff who has failed to appear to prosecute his action or failed to prove his case.

note   See **promissory note.**

novation   A novation substitutes a new party and discharges one of the original parties to a contract by agreement of all three parties. A new contract is created with the same terms as the original one; only the parties have changed.

nuisance   Nuisance is that activity which arises from the unreasonable, unwarranted, or unlawful use by a person of his own property, working obstruction or injury to the right of another or to the public, and producing such material annoyance, inconvenience, and discomfort that law will presume resulting damage.

O

obiter dictum   See **dictum.**

objective fault   Gross deviation from reasonable conduct.

objective manifestation   What a reasonable person under the circumstances would believe.

objective satisfaction   Approval based upon whether a reasonable person would be satisfied.

objective standard   What a reasonable person under the circumstances would reasonably believe or do.

obligee   Party to whom a duty of performance is owed (by delegator and delegatee).

obligor   Party owing a duty (to the assignor).

offer   A manifestation of willingness to enter into a bargain, so made as to justify another person in understanding that his assent to that bargain is invited and will conclude it. Restatement, Second, Contracts, § 24.

offeree   Recipient of the offer.

offeror   Person making the offer.

open-ended credit   Credit arrangement under which debtor has rights to enter into a series of credit transactions.

opinion   Belief in the existence of a fact or a judgment as to value.

option   Contract providing that an offer will stay open for a specified period of time.

order   A final disposition made by an agency.

order paper   Payable to a named person or to anyone designated by that person.

order to pay   Direction or command to pay.

original promise   Promise to become primarily liable.

output contract   See **contracts.**

P

palpable unilateral mistake   Erroneous belief by one party that is recognized by the other.

parent corporation   Corporation which controls another corporation.

parol evidence   Literally oral evidence, but now includes prior to and contemporaneous, oral, and written evidence.

parol evidence rule   Under this rule, when parties put their agreement in writing, all previous oral agreements merge in the writing and the contract as written cannot be modified or changed by parol evidence, in the absence of a plea of mistake or fraud in the preparation of the writing. But the rule does not forbid a resort to parol evidence not inconsistent with the matters stated in the writing. Also, as regards sales of goods, such written agreement may be explained or supplemented by course of dealing, usage of trade, or course of conduct, and by evidence of consistent additional terms, unless the court finds the writing to have been intended also as a complete and exclusive statement of the terms of the agreement. UCC § 2–202.

part performance   In order to establish part performance taking an oral contract for the sale of realty out of the statute of frauds, the acts relied upon as part performance must be of such a character that they reasonably can be naturally accounted for in no other way than that they were performed in pursuance of the contract, and they must be in conformity with its provisions. See UCC § 2–201(3).

partial assignment   Transfer of a portion of contractual rights to one or more assignees.

partition   The dividing of lands held by joint tenants, copartners, or tenants in common into distinct portions, so that the parties may hold those lands in severalty.

partnership   An association of two or more persons to carry on, as co-owners, a business for profit.

Partnerships are treated as a conduit and are, therefore, not subject to taxation. The various items of partnership income (gains and losses, etc.) flow through to the individual partners and are reported on their personal income tax returns.

Limited partnership   Type of partnership comprised of one or more general partners who manage business and who are personally liable for partnership debts, and one or more limited partners who contribute capital and share in profits but who take no part in running business and incur no liability with respect to partnership obligations beyond contribution.

Partnership at will   One with no definite term or specific undertaking.

partnership capital   Total money and property contributed by partners for permanent use by the partnership.

partnership property   Sum of all of the partnership's assets.

past consideration   An act done before the contract is made.

patent   Exclusive right to an invention.

payee   The person in whose favor a bill of exchange, promissory note, or check is made or drawn.

payer *or* **payor**   One who pays or who is to make a payment, particularly the person who is to make payment of a check, bill, or note. Correlative to "payee."

payor bank   A bank by which an item is payable as drawn or accepted. UCC § 4–105(b). Correlative to "Drawee bank."

per capita   This term, derived from the civil law and much used in the law of descent and distribution, denotes that method of dividing an intestate estate by which an equal share is given to each of a number of persons, all of whom stand in equal degree to the decedent, without reference to their stocks or the right of representation. The opposite of *per stirpes.*

per stirpes   This term, derived from the civil law and much used in the law of descent and distribution, denotes that method of dividing an intestate estate where a class or group of distributees takes the share to which its deceased would have been entitled, taking thus by its right of representing such ancestor and not as so many individuals. The opposite of *per capita.*

perfect tender rule Seller's tender of delivery must conform exactly to the contract.

perfection of security interest Acts required of a secured party in the way of giving at least constructive notice so as to make his security interest effective at least against lien creditors of the debtor. See UCC §§ 9–302 through 9–306. In most cases, the secured party may obtain perfection either by filing with the secretary of state or by taking possession of the collateral.

performance Fulfillment of one's contractual obligations. See also **part performance; specific performance.**

periodic tenancy Lease with a definite term that is to be continued.

personal defenses Contractual defenses which are good against holders but not holders in due course.

personal property Any property other than an interest in land.

petty crime Misdemeanor punishable by imprisonment of six months or less.

plaintiff The party who initiates a civil suit.

pleadings The formal allegations by the parties of their respective claims and defenses.

> *Rules or codes of civil procedure* Unlike the rigid technical system of common law pleading, pleadings under federal and state rules or codes of civil procedure have a far more limited function, with determination and narrowing of facts and issues being left to discovery devices and pretrial conferences. In addition, the rules and codes permit liberal amendment and supplementation of pleadings.

> Under rules of civil procedure, the pleadings consist of a complaint, an answer, a reply to a counterclaim, an answer to a cross-claim, a third-party complaint, and a third-party answer.

pledge A bailment of goods to a creditor as security for some debt or engagement.

> Much of the law of pledges has been replaced by the provisions for secured transactions in Article 9 of the UCC.

possibility of reverter The interest which remains in a grantor or testator after the conveyance or devise of a fee simple determinable and which permits the grantor to be revested automatically of his estate on breach of the condition.

possibility test Under the statute of frauds, asks whether performance could possibly be completed within one year.

power of appointment A power of authority conferred by one person by deed or will upon another (called the "donee") to appoint, that is, to select and nominate, the person or persons who is or are to receive and enjoy an estate or an income therefrom or from a fund, after the testator's death, or the donee's death, or after the termination of an existing right or interest.

power of attorney An instrument authorizing a person to act as the agent or attorney of the person granting it.

power of termination The interest left in the grantor or testator after the conveyance or devise of a fee simple on condition subsequent or conditional fee.

precatory Expressing a wish.

precedent An adjudged case or decision of a court, considered as furnishing an example or authority for an identical or similar case afterwards arising or a similar question of law. See also **stare decisis.**

preemptive right The privilege of a stockholder to maintain a proportionate share of ownership by purchasing a proportionate share of any new stock issues.

preference The act of an insolvent debtor who, in distributing his property or in assigning it for the benefit of his creditors, pays or secures to one or more creditors the full amount of their claims or a larger amount than they would be entitled to receive on a *pro rata* distribution. The treatment of such preferential payments in bankruptcy is governed by the Bankruptcy Act, § 547.

preliminary hearing Determines whether there is probable cause.

premium The price for insurance protection for a specified period of exposure.

preponderance of the evidence Greater weight of the evidence; standard used in civil cases.

prescription Acquisition of a personal right to use a way, water, light, and air by reason of continuous usage. See also **easement.**

presenter's warranty Warranty given to any payor or acceptor of an instrument.

presentment The production of a negotiable instrument to the drawee for his acceptance, or to the drawer or acceptor for payment; or of a promissory note to the party liable, for payment of the same. UCC § 3–504(1).

presumption A presumption is a rule of law, statutory or judicial, by which a finding of a basic fact gives rise to the existence of presumed fact, until presumption is rebutted. A presumption imposes on the party against whom it is directed the burden of going forward with evidence to rebut or meet the presumption, but does not shift to such party the burden of proof in the sense of the risk of nonpersuasion, which remains throughout the trial upon the party on whom it was originally cast.

price discrimination Price differential.

price fixing Any agreement for the purpose and effect of raising, depressing, fixing, pegging, or stabilizing prices.

prima facie Latin. At first sight; on the first appearance; on the face of it; so far as can be judged from the first disclosure; presumably; a fact presumed to be true unless disproved by some evidence to the contrary.

primary liability Absolute obligation to pay a negotiable instrument.

principal

> *Disclosed principal* One whose existence and identity are known.

> *Law of agency* The term "principal" describes one who has permitted or directed another (*i.e.*, an agent or a servant) to act for his benefit and subject to his direction and control. Principal includes in its meaning the term "master" or employer, a species of principal who, in addition to other control, has a right to control the physical conduct of the species of agents known as servants or employees, as to whom special rules are applicable with reference to harm caused by their physical acts.

> *Partially disclosed principal* One whose existence is known but whose identity is not known.

> *Undisclosed principal* One whose existence and identity are not known.

principal debtor Person whose debt is being supported by a surety.

priority Precedence in order of right.

private carrier   Carrier which limits its service and is not open to the general public.

private corporation   One organized to conduct either a privately owned business enterprise for profit or a nonprofit corporation.

private law   The law involving relationships among individuals and legal entities.

privilege   Immunity from tort liability.

privity   Contractual relationship.

privity of contract   That connection or relationship which exists between two or more contracting parties. The absence of privity as a defense in actions for damages in contract and tort actions is generally no longer viable with the enactment of warranty statutes (*e.g.*, UCC § 2–318), acceptance by states of the doctrine of strict liability, and court decisions which have extended the right to sue to third-party beneficiaries and even innocent bystanders.

probable cause   Reasonable belief of the offense charged.

probate   Court procedure by which a will is proved to be valid or invalid, though in current usage this term has been expanded to include generally all matters and proceedings pertaining to administration of estates, guardianships, etc.

procedural due process   Requirement that governmental action depriving a person of life, liberty, or property be done through a fair procedure.

procedural law   Rules for enforcing substantive law.

procedural rules   Rules issued by an administrative agency establishing its organization, method of operation, and rules of conduct for practice before it.

procedural unconscionability   Unfair or irregular bargaining.

proceeds   Consideration for the sale, exchange, or other disposition of collateral.

process

Judicial process In a wide sense, this term may include all the acts of a court from the beginning to the end of its proceedings in a given cause; more specifically, it means the writ, summons, mandate, or other process which is used to inform the defendant of the institution of proceedings against him and to compel his appearance, in either civil or criminal cases.

Legal process This term is sometimes used as equivalent to "lawful process." Thus, it is said that legal process means process not merely fair on its face but valid in fact. But properly it means a summons, writ, warrant, mandate, or other process issuing from a court.

profit à prendre   Right to make some use of the soil of another, such as a right to mine metals; carries with it the right of entry and the right to remove.

profit corporation   One founded for the purpose of operating a business for profit.

promise to pay   Undertaking to pay an existing obligation.

promisee   Person to whom a promise is made.

promisor   Person making a promise.

promissory estoppel   Arises where there is a promise which promisor should reasonably expect to induce action or forbearance on part of promisee and which does induce such action or forbearance, and where injustice can be avoided only by enforcement of the promise.

promissory note   An unconditional written promise to pay a specified sum of money on demand or at a specified date. Such a note is negotiable if signed by the maker and containing an unconditional promise to pay a sum certain in money either on demand or at a definite time and payable to order or bearer. UCC § 3–104.

promoters   In the law relating to corporations, those persons who first associate themselves for the purpose of organizing a company, issuing its prospectus, procuring subscriptions to the stock, securing a charter, etc.

property   Interest that is legally protected.

Abandoned property Intentionally disposed of by the owner.

Lost property Unintentionally left by the owner.

Mislaid property Intentionally placed by the owner but unintentionally left.

prosecute   To bring a criminal proceeding.

protest   A formal declaration made by a person interested or concerned in some act about to be done, or already performed, whereby he expresses his dissent or disapproval or affirms the act against his will. The object of such a declaration usually is to preserve some right which would be lost to the protester if his assent could be implied, or to exonerate him from some responsibility which would attach to him unless he expressly negatived his assent.

Notice of protest A notice given by the holder of a bill or note to the drawer or indorser that the bill has been protested for refusal of payment or acceptance. UCC § 3–509.

provisional credit   Tentative credit for the deposit of an instrument until final credit is given.

proximate cause   Where the act or omission played a substantial part in bringing about or actually causing the injury or damage and where the injury or damage was either a direct result or a reasonably probable consequence of the act or omission.

proxy   (Contracted from "procuracy.") Written authorization given by one person to another so that the second person can act for the first, such as that given by a shareholder to someone else to represent him and vote his shares at a shareholders' meeting.

public corporation   One created to administer a unit of local civil government or one created by the United States to conduct public business.

public disclosure of private facts   Offensive publicity given to private information about another person.

public law   The law dealing with the relationship between government and individuals.

puffery   Sales talk that is considered general bragging or overstatement.

punitive damages   Damages awarded in excess of normal compensation to punish a defendant for a serious civil wrong.

purchase money security interest   Security interest retained by a seller of goods in goods purchased with the loaned money.

Q

qualified fee   Ownership subject to its being taken away upon the happening of an event.

quantum meruit   Expression "quantum meruit" means "as much as he deserves"; describes the extent of liability on a contract implied by law. Elements essential to recovery under quantum meruit are (1) valuable services rendered or materials furnished (2) for the person sought to be charged, (3) which services and materials such person accepted, used, and enjoyed, (4) under such circumstances as reasonably notified her that plaintiff, in performing such services, was expected to be paid by the person sought to be charged.

quasi Latin. As if; almost as it were; analogous to. Negates the idea of identity but points out that the conceptions are sufficiently similar to be classed as equals of one another.

quasi contract Legal fiction invented by common law courts to permit recovery by contractual remedy in cases where, in fact, there is no contract, but where circumstances are such that justice warrants a recovery as though a promise had been made.

quasi in rem See **in rem.**

quasi in rem jurisdiction Jurisdiction over property not based on claims against it.

quiet enjoyment Right of a tenant not to have his physical possession of premises interfered with by the landlord.

quitclaim deed A deed of conveyance operating by way of release; that is, intended to pass any title, interest, or claim which the grantor may have in the premises but neither professing that such title is valid nor containing any warranty or covenants for title.

quorum When a committee, board of directors, meeting of shareholders, legislature, or other body of persons cannot act unless at least a certain number of them are present.

R

rape Unlawful, nonconsensual sexual intercourse.

ratification In a broad sense, the confirmation of a previous act done either by the party himself or by another; as, for example, confirmation of a voidable act.

In the law of principal and agent, the adoption and confirmation by one person, with knowledge of all material facts, of an act or contract performed or entered into in his behalf by another who at the time assumed without authority to act as his agent.

rational relationship test Requirement that legislation bear a rational relationship to a legitimate governmental interest.

real defenses Defenses that are valid against all holders, including holders in due course.

real property Land, and generally whatever is erected or growing upon or affixed to land. Also, rights issuing out of, annexed to, and exercisable within or about land. See also **fixture.**

reasonable man standard Duty of care required to avoid being negligent; one who is careful, diligent, and prudent.

receiver A fiduciary of the court, whose appointment is incident to other proceedings wherein certain ultimate relief is prayed. He is a trustee or ministerial officer representing the court, all parties in interest in the litigation, and the property or funds entrusted to him.

recognizance Formal acknowledgment of indebtedness made in court.

redemption (a) The realization of a right to have the title of property restored free and clear of a mortgage, performance of the mortgage obligation being essential for such purpose. (b) Repurchase by corporation of its own shares.

reformation Equitable remedy used to reframe written contracts to reflect accurately real agreement between contracting parties when, either through mutual mistake or unilateral mistake coupled with actual or equitable fraud by the other party, the writing does not embody the contract as actually made.

regulatory license Requirement to protect the public interest.

reimbursement Duty owed by principal to pay back authorized payments agent has made on principal's behalf. Duty owed by a principal debtor to repay surety who pays principal debtor's obligation.

rejection The refusal to accept an offer; manifestation of an unwillingness to accept the goods (sales).

release The relinquishment, concession, or giving up of a right, claim, or privilege, by the person in whom it exists or to whom it accrues, to the person against whom it might have been demanded or enforced.

remainder An estate limited to take effect and be enjoyed after another estate is determined.

remand To send back. The sending by the appellate court of a cause back to the same court out of which it came, for the purpose of having some further action taken on it there.

remedy The means by which the violation of a right is prevented, redressed, or compensated. Though a remedy may be by the act of the party injured, by operation of law, or by agreement between the injurer and the injured, we are chiefly concerned with one kind of remedy, the judicial remedy, which is by action or suit.

rent Consideration paid for use or occupation of property. In a broader sense, it is the compensation or fee paid, usually periodically, for the use of any property, land, buildings, equipment, etc.

replevin An action whereby the owner or person entitled to repossession of goods or chattels may recover those goods or chattels from one who has wrongfully distrained or taken such goods or chattels or who wrongfully detains them.

reply Plaintiff's pleading in response to the defendant's answer.

repudiation Repudiation of a contract means refusal to perform duty or obligation owed to other party.

requirements contract See **contracts.**

res ipsa loquitur "The thing speaks for itself"; permits the jury to infer both negligent conduct and causation.

rescission An equitable action in which a party seeks to be relieved of his obligations under a contract on the grounds of mutual mistake, fraud, impossibility, etc.

residuary Pertaining to the residue; constituting the residue; giving or bequeathing the residue; receiving or entitled to the residue. See also **legacy, residuary legacy.**

respondeat superior Latin. Let the master answer. This maxim means that a master or employer is liable in certain cases for the wrongful acts of his servant or employee, and a principal for those of his agent.

respondent In equity practice, the party who makes an answer to a bill or other proceeding. In appellate practice, the party who contends against an appeal; i.e., the appellee. The party who appeals is called the "appellant."

restitution An equitable remedy under which a person who has rendered services to another seeks to be reimbursed for the costs of his acts (but not his profits) even though there was never a contract between the parties.

restraint of trade Agreement that eliminates or tends to eliminate competition.

restraint on alienation A provision in an instrument of conveyance which prohibits the grantee from selling or transferring the property which is the subject of the conveyance. Many such restraints are unenforceable as against public policy and the law's policy of free alienability of land.

restrictive covenant Private restriction on property contained in a conveyance.

revenue license Measure to raise money.

reverse An appellate court uses the term "reversed" to indicate that it annuls or avoids the judgment, or vacates the decree, of the trial court.

reverse discrimination Employment decisions taking into account race or gender in order to remedy past discrimination.

reversion The term reversion has two meanings. First, it designates the estate left in the grantor during the continuance of a particular estate; second, it denotes the residue left in grantor or his heirs after termination of a particular estate. It differs from a remainder in that it arises by an act of law, whereas a remainder arises by an act of the parties. A reversion, moreover, is the remnant left in the grantor, while a remainder is the remnant of the whole estate disposed of after a preceding part of the same has been given away.

revocation The recall of some power, authority, or thing granted, or a destroying or making void of some deed that had existence until the act of revocation made it void.

revocation of acceptance Rescission of one's acceptance of goods based upon a nonconformity of the goods which substantially impairs their value.

right Legal capacity to require another person to perform or refrain from performing an act.

right of entry The right to take or resume possession of land by entering on it in a peaceable manner.

right of redemption The right (granted by statute only) to free property from the encumbrance of a foreclosure or other judicial sale, or to recover the title passing thereby, by paying what is due, with interest, costs, etc. Not to be confounded with the "equity of redemption," which exists independently of statute but must be exercised before sale. See also **equity of redemption**.

right to work law State statute that prohibits union shop contracts.

rights in collateral Personal property the debtor owns, possesses, or is in the process of acquiring.

risk of loss Allocation of loss between seller and buyer where the goods have been damaged, destroyed, or lost.

robbery Larceny from a person by force or threat of force.

rule Agency statement of general or particular applicability designed to implement, interpret, or process law or policy.

rule against perpetuities Principle that no interest in property is good unless it must vest, if at all, not later than twenty-one years, plus period of gestation, after some life or lives in being at time of creation of interest.

rule of reason Balancing the anticompetitive effects of a restraint against its procompetitive effects.

S

sale Transfer of title to goods from seller to buyer for a price.

sale on approval Transfer of possession without title to buyer for trial period.

sale or return Sale where buyer has option to return goods to seller.

sanction Means of enforcing legal judgments.

satisfaction The discharge of an obligation by paying a party what is due to him (as on a mortgage, lien, or contract) or what has been awarded to him by the judgment of a court or otherwise. Thus, a judgment is satisfied by the payment of the amount due to the party who has recovered such judgment, or by his levying the amount. See also **accord and satisfaction**.

scienter Latin. Knowingly.

seal Symbol that authenticates a document.

secondary liability Obligation to pay is subject to the conditions of presentment, dishonor, notice of dishonor, and sometimes protest.

secret partner Partner whose membership in the partnership is not disclosed.

Section 402A Strict liability in tort.

secured bond A bond having a lien on specific property.

secured claim Claim with a lien on property of the debtor.

secured party Creditor who possesses a security interest in collateral.

secured transaction A transaction founded on a security agreement. Such agreement creates or provides for a security interest. UCC § 9–105(h).

securities Stocks, bonds, notes, convertible debentures, warrants, or other documents that represent a share in a company or a debt owed by a company.

   Certificated security Security represented by a certificate.

   Exempt security Security not subject to registration requirements of 1933 Act.

   Exempt transaction Issuance of securities not subject to the registration requirements of 1933 Act.

   Restricted securities Securities issued under an exempt transaction.

   Uncertificated security Security not represented by a certificate.

security agreement Agreement that grants a security interest.

security interest Right in personal property securing payment or performance of an obligation.

seisin Possession with an intent on the part of him who holds it to claim a freehold interest.

self-defense Force to protect oneself against attack.

separation of powers Allocation of powers among the legislative, executive, and judicial branches of government.

service mark Distinctive symbol, word, or design that is used to identify the services of a provider.

servient Land subject to an easement.

setoff A counterclaim demand which defendant holds against plaintiff, arising out of a transaction extrinsic to plaintiff's cause of action.

settlor Creator of a trust.

severance The destruction of any one of the unities of a joint tenancy. It is so called because the estate is no longer a joint tenancy, but is severed.

   Term may also refer to the cutting of crops, such as corn, wheat, etc., or to the separation of anything from realty.

share A proportionate ownership interest in a corporation.

Shelley's case, rule in Where a person takes an estate of freehold, legally or equitably, under a deed, will, or other writing, and in the same instrument there is a limitation by way of remainder of any interest of the same legal or equitable quality to his heirs, or heirs of his body, as a class of persons to take in succession from generation to generation, the limitation to the heirs entitles the ancestor to the whole estate.

The rule was adopted as a part of the common law of this country, though it has long since been abolished by most states.

shelter rule Transferee gets rights of transferor.

shipment contract Seller is authorized or required only to bear the expense of placing goods with the common carrier and bears the risk of loss only up to such point.

short-swing profits Profits made by insider through sale or other disposition of corporate stock within six months after purchase.

sight draft An instrument payable on presentment.

signature Any symbol executed with intent to validate a writing.

silent partner Partner who takes no part in the partnership business.

slander Oral defamation.

small claims courts Inferior civil courts with jurisdiction limited by dollar amount.

social security Measures by which the government provides economic assistance to disabled or retired employees and their dependents.

sole proprietorship A form of business in which one person owns all the assets of the business, in contrast to a partnership or a corporation.

sovereign immunity Foreign country's freedom from a host country's laws.

special warranty deed Seller promises that he has not impaired title.

specific performance The doctrine of specific performance is that where damages would compensate inadequately for the breach of an agreement, the contractor or vendor will be compelled to perform specifically what he has agreed to do; *e.g.*, ordered to execute a specific conveyance of land.

With respect to the sale of goods, specific performance may be decreed where the goods are unique or in other proper circumstances. The decree for specific performance may include such terms and conditions as to payment of the price, damages, or other relief as the court may deem just. UCC §§ 2–711(2)(b), 2–716.

standardized business form A preprinted contract.

stare decisis Doctrine that once a court has laid down a principle of law as applicable to a certain state of facts, it will adhere to that principle and apply it to all future cases having substantially the same facts, regardless of whether the parties and property are the same or not.

state action Actions by governments, as opposed to actions taken by private individuals.

state-of-the-art Made in accordance with the level of technology at the time the product is made.

stated capital Consideration, other than that allocated to capital surplus, received for issued stock.

statute of frauds A celebrated English statute, passed in 1677, which has been adopted, in a more or less modified form, in nearly all of the United States. Its chief characteristic is the provision that no action shall be brought on certain contracts unless there be a note or memorandum thereof in writing, signed by the party to be charged or by his authorized agent.

statute of limitation A statute prescribing limitations to the right of action on certain described causes of action; that is, declaring that no suit shall be maintained on such causes of action unless brought within a specified period after the right accrued.

statutory lien Interest in property, arising solely by statute, to secure payment of a debt.

stock "Stock" is distinguished from "bonds" and, ordinarily, from "debentures" in that it gives a right of ownership in part of the assets of a corporation and a right to interest in any surplus after the payment of debt. "Stock" in a corporation is an equity, representing an ownership interest. It is to be distinguished from obligations such as notes or bonds, which are not equities and represent no ownership interest.

Capital stock See **capital**.

Common stock Securities which represent an ownership interest in a corporation. If the company has also issued preferred stock, both common and preferred have ownership rights. Claims of both common and preferred stockholders are junior to claims of bondholders or other creditors of the company. Common stockholders assume the greater risk, but generally exercise the greater control and may gain the greater reward in the form of dividends and capital appreciation.

Convertible stock Stock which may be changed or converted into common stock.

Cumulative preferred Stock having a provision that if one or more dividends are omitted, the omitted dividends must be paid before dividends may be paid on the company's common stock.

Preferred stock A separate portion or class of the stock of a corporation that is accorded, by the charter or by-laws, a preference or priority in respect to dividends, over the remainder of the stock of the corporation, which in that case is called *common stock*.

Stock warrant A certificate entitling the owner to buy a specified amount of stock at a specified time(s) for a specified price. Differs from a stock option only in that options are granted to employees and warrants are sold to the public.

Treasury stock Shares reacquired by a corporation.

stock option Contractual right to purchase stock from a corporation.

stop payment Order for a drawee not to pay an instrument.

strict liability A concept applied by the courts in product liability cases in which a seller is liable for any and all defective or hazardous products which unduly threaten a consumer's personal safety. This concept applies to all members involved in the manufacture and sale of any facet of the product.

strict scrutiny test Requirement that legislation be necessary to promote a compelling governmental interest.

subagent Person appointed by agent to perform agent's duties.

subject matter jurisdiction Authority of a court to decide a particular kind of case.

subject to the mortgage Purchaser is not personally obligated to pay the debt, but the property remains subject to the mortgage.

subjective fault Desired or virtually certain consequences of one's conduct.

subjective satisfaction Approval based upon a party's honestly held opinion.

sublease Transfer of less than all of a tenant's interest in a leasehold.

subpoena A subpoena is a command to appear at a certain time and place to give testimony upon a certain matter. A subpoena duces tecum requires production of books, papers, and other things.

subrogation The substitution of one thing for another, or of one person into the place of another with respect to rights, claims, or securities.

Subrogation denotes the putting of a third person who has paid a debt in the place of the creditor to whom he has paid it, so that he may exercise against the debtor all the rights which the creditor, if unpaid, might have exercised.

subscribe Literally, to write underneath, as one's name. To sign at the end of a document. Also, to agree in writing to furnish money or its equivalent, or to agree to purchase some initial stock in a corporation.

subscriber Person who agrees to purchase initial stock in a corporation.

subsidiary corporation Corporation controlled by another corporation.

substantial performance Equitable doctrine protects against forfeiture for technical inadvertence, trivial variations, or omissions in performance.

substantive due process Requirement that governmental action be compatible with individual liberties.

substantive law The basic law of rights and duties (contract law, criminal law, tort law, law of wills, etc.), as opposed to procedural law (law of pleading, law of evidence, law of jurisdiction, etc.).

substantive unconscionability Oppressive or grossly unfair contractual terms.

sue To begin a lawsuit in a court.

suit "Suit" is a generic term of comprehensive signification that applies to any proceeding in a court of justice in which the plaintiff pursues, in such court, the remedy which the law affords him for the redress of an injury or the recovery of a right.

Derivative suit Suit brought by a shareholder on behalf of a corporation to enforce a right belonging to the corporation.

Direct suit Suit brought by a shareholder against a corporation based upon his ownership of shares.

summary judgment Rule of Civil Procedure 56 permits any party to a civil action to move for a summary judgment on a claim, counterclaim, or cross-claim when he believes that there is no genuine issue of material fact and that he is entitled to prevail as a matter of law.

summons Writ or process directed to the sheriff or other proper officer, requiring him to notify the person named that an action has been commenced against him in the court from which the process has issued and that he is required to appear, on a day named, and answer the complaint in such action.

superseding cause Intervening event that occurs after the defendant's negligent conduct and relieves him of liability.

supreme law Law that takes precedence over all conflicting laws.

surety One who undertakes to pay money or to do any other act in event that his principal debtor fails therein.

suretyship A guarantee of debts of another.

surplus Excess of net assets over stated capital.

T

tangible property Physical objects.

tariff Duty or tax imposed on goods moving into or out of a country.

tenancy Possession or occupancy of land or premises under lease.

Joint tenancy Joint tenants have one and the same interest, accruing by one and the same conveyance, commencing at one and the same time, and held by one and the same undivided possession. The primary incident of joint tenancy is survivorship, by which the entire tenancy on the decease of any joint tenant remains to the survivors, and at length to the last survivor.

Tenancy at sufferance Only naked possession which continues after tenant's right of possession has terminated.

Tenancy at will Possession of premises by permission of owner or landlord, but without a fixed term.

Tenancy by the entirety A tenancy which is created between a husband and wife and by which together they hold title to the whole with right of survivorship so that, upon death of either, the other takes the whole to the exclusion of the deceased's heirs. It is essentially a "joint tenancy," modified by the common law theory that husband and wife are one person.

Tenancy for a period A tenancy for years or for some fixed period.

Tenancy in common A form of ownership whereby each tenant (*i.e.*, owner) holds an undivided interest in property. Unlike the interest of a joint tenant or a tenant by the entirety, the interest of a tenant in common does not terminate upon his or her prior death (*i.e.*, there is no right of survivorship).

tenancy in partnership Type of joint ownership that determines partners' rights in specific partnership property.

tenant Possessor of a leasehold interest.

tender An offer of money; the act by which one produces and offers to a person holding a claim or demand against him the amount of money which he considers and admits to be due, in satisfaction of such claim or demand, without any stipulation or condition.

Also, there may be a tender of performance of a duty other than the payment of money.

tender of delivery Seller makes available to buyer goods conforming to the contract and so notifies the buyer.

tender offer General invitation to all shareholders to purchase their shares at a specified price.

testament Will.

testator One who makes or has made a testament or will; one who dies leaving a will.

third-party beneficiary One for whose benefit a promise is made in a contract but who is not a party to the contract.

Creditor beneficiary Where performance of a promise in a contract will benefit a person other than the promisee, that person is a creditor beneficiary if no purpose to make a gift appears from the terms of the promise, in view of the accompanying circumstances, and performance of the promise will satisfy an actual, supposed, or asserted duty of the promisee to the beneficiary.

Donee beneficiary The person who takes the benefit of the contract even though there is no privity between him and the contracting parties. A third-party beneficiary who is not a creditor beneficiary. See also **beneficiary**.

time paper   Payable at definite time.

time-price doctrine   Permits sellers to have different prices for cash sales and credit sales.

title   The means whereby the owner of lands or of personalty has the just possession of his property.

title insurance   Provides protection against defect in title to real property.

tort   A private or civil wrong or injury, other than breach of contract, for which a court will provide a remedy in the form of an action for damages.

Three elements of every tort action are the existence of a legal duty from defendant to plaintiff, breach of that duty, and damage as proximate result.

tortfeasor   One who commits a tort.

trade acceptance   A draft drawn by a seller which is presented for signature (acceptance) to the buyer at the time goods are purchased and which then becomes the equivalent of a note receivable of the seller and the note payable of the buyer.

trade name   Name used in trade or business to identify a particular business or manufacturer.

trade secrets   Private business information.

trademark   Distinctive insignia, word, or design of a good that is used to identify the manufacturer.

transferor's warranty   Warranty given by any person who transfers an instrument and receives consideration.

treaty   An agreement between or among independent nations.

treble damages   Three times actual loss.

trespass   At common law, trespass was a form of action brought to recover damages for any injury to one's person or property or relationship with another.

Trespass to chattels or personal property An unlawful and serious interference with the possessory rights of another to personal property.

Trespass to land At common law, every unauthorized and direct breach of the boundaries of another's land was an actionable trespass. The present prevailing position of the courts finds liability for trespass only in the case of intentional intrusion, or negligence, or some "abnormally dangerous activity" on the part of the defendant.

Compare **nuisance**.

trespasser   Person who enters or remains on the land of another without permission or privilege to do so.

trust   Any arrangement whereby property is transferred with the intention that it be administered by a trustee for another's benefit.

A trust, as the term is used in the Restatement, when not qualified by the word "charitable," "resulting," or "constructive," is a fiduciary relationship with respect to property, subjecting the person by whom the title to the property is held to equitable duties to deal with the property for the benefit of another person, which arises through a manifestation of an intention to create such benefit. Restatement, Second, Trusts § 2.

Charitable trust To benefit humankind.

Constructive trust Wherever the circumstances of a transaction are such that the person who takes the legal estate in property

cannot also enjoy the beneficial interest without necessarily violating some established principle of equity, the court will immediately raise a *constructive trust* and fasten it upon the conscience of the legal owner, so as to convert him into a trustee for the parties who in equity are entitled to the beneficial enjoyment.

Inter vivos trust Established during the settlor's lifetime.

Resulting trust One that arises by implication of law, where the legal estate in property is disposed of, conveyed, or transferred, but the intent appears or is inferred from the terms of the disposition, or from the accompanying facts and circumstances, that the beneficial interest is not to go or be enjoyed with the legal title.

Spendthrift trust Removal of the trust estate from the beneficiary's control.

Testamentary trust Established by a will.

Totten trust A tentative trust which is a joint bank account opened by the settlor.

Voting trust A trust which holds the voting rights to stock in a corporation. It is a useful device when a majority of the shareholders in a corporation cannot agree on corporate policy.

trustee   In a strict sense, a "trustee" is one who holds the legal title to property for the benefit of another, while, in a broad sense, the term is sometimes applied to anyone standing in a fiduciary or confidential relation to another, such as agent, attorney, bailee, etc.

trustee in bankruptcy   Representative of the estate in bankruptcy who is responsible for collecting, liquidating, and distributing the debtor's assets.

tying arrangement   Conditioning a sale of a desired product (tying product) on the buyer's purchasing a second product (tied product).

U

ultra vires   Acts beyond the scope of the powers of a corporation, as defined by its charter or by the laws of its state of incorporation. By the doctrine of ultra vires, a contract made by a corporation beyond the scope of its corporate powers is unlawful.

unconscionable   Unfair or unduly harsh.

unconscionable contract   See **contracts**.

underwriter   Any person, banker, or syndicate that guarantees to furnish a definite sum of money by a definite date to a business or government in return for an issue of bonds or stock. In insurance, the one assuming a risk in return for the payment of a premium.

undisputed debt   Obligation whose existence and amount are not contested.

undue influence   Term refers to conduct by which a person, through his power over the mind of a testator, makes the latter's desires conform to his own, thereby overmastering the volition of the testator.

unemployment compensation   Compensation awarded to workers who have lost their jobs and cannot find other employment.

unenforceable   Contract under which neither party can recover.

unfair employer practice   Conduct in which an employer is prohibited from engaging.

unfair labor practice   Conduct in which an employer or union is prohibited from engaging.

unfair union practice   Conduct in which a union is prohibited from engaging.

Uniform Commercial Code   One of the Uniform Laws, drafted by the National Conference of Commissioners on Uniform State Laws, governing commercial transactions (sales of goods, commercial paper, bank deposits and collections, letters of credit, bulk transfers, warehouse receipts, bills of lading, investment securities, and secured transactions).

unilateral mistake   Erroneous belief on the part of only one of the parties to a contract.

union shop   Employer can hire nonunion members, but such employees must then join the union.

universal life   Ordinary life divided into two components, a renewable term insurance policy and an investment portfolio.

unliquidated debt   Obligation that is uncertain or contested in amount.

unqualified indorsement   (see **indorsement**) One that imposes liability upon the indorser.

unreasonably dangerous   Danger beyond that which the ordinary consumer contemplates.

unrestrictive indorsement   (see **indorsement**) One that does not attempt to restrict the rights of the indorsee.

usage of trade   Any practice or method of dealing having such regularity of observance in a place, vocation, or trade as to justify an expectation that it will be observed with respect to the transaction in question.

usury   Collectively, the laws of a jurisdiction regulating the charging of interest rates. A usurious loan is one whose interest rates are determined to be in excess of those permitted by the usury laws.

V

value   The performance of legal consideration, the forgiveness of an antecedent debt, the giving of a negotiable instrument, or the giving of an irrevocable commitment to a third party. UCC § 1–201(44).

variance   A use differing from that provided in a zoning ordinance in order to avoid undue hardship.

vendee   A purchaser or buyer; one to whom anything is sold. See also **vendor**.

vendor   The person who transfers property by sale, particularly real estate; "seller" being more commonly used for one who sells personalty. See also **vendee**.

venue   "Jurisdiction" of the court means the inherent power to decide a case, whereas "venue" designates the particular county or city in which a court with jurisdiction may hear and determine the case.

verdict   The formal and unanimous decision or finding of a jury, impaneled and sworn for the trial of a cause, upon the matters or questions duly submitted to it upon the trial.

vertical privity   Who is liable to the plaintiff.

vertical restraints   Agreements among parties at different levels of the distribution chain.

vested   Fixed; accrued; settled; absolute. To be "vested," a right must be more than a mere expectation based on an anticipation of the continuance of an existing law; it must have become a title, legal or equitable, to the present or future enforcement of a demand, or a legal exemption from the demand of another.

vested remainder   Unconditional remainder that is a fixed present interest to be enjoyed in the future.

vicarious liability   Indirect legal responsibility; for example, the liability of an employer for the acts of an employee or that of a principal for the torts and contracts of an agent.

void   Null; ineffectual; nugatory; having no legal force or binding effect; unable, in law, to support the purpose for which it was intended.

This difference separates the words "void" and "voidable": *void* in the strict sense means that an instrument or transaction is nugatory and ineffectual, so that nothing can cure it; *voidable* exists when an imperfection or defect can be cured by the act or confirmation of the person who could take advantage of it.

Frequently, the word "void" is used and construed as having the more liberal meaning of "voidable."

voidable   Capable of being made void. See also **void**.

voir dire   Preliminary examination of potential jurors.

voluntary   Resulting from free choice. The word, especially in statutes, often implies knowledge of essential facts.

voting trust   Transfer of corporate shares' voting rights to a trustee.

W

wager (gambling)   Agreement that one party will win or lose depending upon the outcome of an event in which the only interest is the gain or loss.

waiver   Terms "estoppel" and "waiver" are not synonymous; "waiver" means the voluntary, intentional relinquishment of a known right, and "estoppel" rests upon principle that, where anyone has done an act or made a statement that would be a fraud on his part to controvert or impair, because the other party has acted upon it in belief that what was done or said was true, conscience and honest dealing require that he not be permitted to repudiate his act or gainsay his statement. See also **estoppel**.

ward   An infant or insane person placed by authority of law under the care of a guardian.

warehouse receipt   Receipt issued by a person storing goods.

warehouser   Storer of goods for compensation.

warrant, *v.* In contracts, to engage or promise that a certain fact or state of facts, in relation to the subject matter, is, or shall be, as it is represented to be.

In conveyancing, to assure the title to property sold, by an express covenant to that effect in the deed of conveyance.

warranty   A warranty is a statement or representation made by a seller of goods, contemporaneously with and as a part of a contract of sale, though collateral to express the object of the sale, having reference to the character, quality, or title of goods, and by which the seller promises or undertakes to ensure that certain facts are or shall be as he then represents them.

The general statutory law governing warranties on sales of goods is provided in UCC § 2–312 *et seq.* The three main types of warranties are (1) express warranty; (2) implied warranty of fitness; (3) implied warranty of merchantability.

warranty deed   Deed in which grantor warrants good clear title. The usual covenants of title are warranties of seisin, quiet enjoyment, right to convey, freedom from encumbrances, and defense of title as to all claims.

Special warranty deed Seller warrants that he has not impaired title.

warranty liability Applies to persons who transfer an instrument or receive payment or acceptance.

warranty of title Obligation to convey the right to ownership without any lien.

waste Any act or omission that does permanent injury to the realty or unreasonably changes its value.

white-collar crime Corporate crime.

will A written instrument executed with the formalities required by statutes, whereby a person makes a disposition of his property to take effect after his death.

winding up To settle the accounts and liquidate the assets of a partnership or corporation, for the purpose of making distribution and terminating the concern.

without reserve Auctioneer may not withdraw the goods from the auction.

workers' compensation Compensation awarded to an employee who is injured, when the injury arose out of and in the course of his employment.

writ of certiorari Discretionary review by a higher court. See also **certiorari.**

writ of execution Order served by sheriff upon debtor demanding payment of a court judgment against debtor.

Z

zoning Public control over land use.